D0073125

THE UNITED STATES
IN ASIA

THE UNITED STATES IN ASIA

A Historical Dictionary

David Shavit

Greenwood Press

New York • Westport, Connecticut • London

Library of Congress Cataloging-in-Publication Data

Shavit, David.
    The United States in Asia : a historical dictionary / David
Shavit.
        p. cm.
    Includes bibliographical references and index.
    ISBN 0–313–26788–X (lib. bdg. : alk. paper)
    1. Asia—Relations—United States—Dictionaries.   2. United
States—Relations—Asia—Dictionaries.   I. Title.
DS33.4.U6S46   1990
303.48′27305—dc20   90–36740

British Library Cataloguing in Publication Data is available.

Library of Congress Catalog Card Number: 90–36740
ISBN: 0–313–26788–X

First published in 1990

Greenwood Press, 88 Post Road West, Westport, CT   06881
An imprint of Greenwood Publishing Group, Inc.

Printed in the United States of America

The paper used in this book complies with the
Permanent Paper Standard issued by the National
Information Standards Organization (Z39.48–1984).

10 9 8 7 6 5 4 3 2 1

For Ari and Sharon

Contents

Preface

Contacts between the United States and Asia began in the seventeenth century when several Americans went to India as employees of the East India Company. They were followed by New England sea captains and merchants who began a highly profitable trade with the countries of South, Southeast, and East Asia. They were followed by missionaries, consuls and diplomats, adventurers, army and naval officers, travelers, government officials, colonial administrators, journalists, businessmen, engineers, physicians, educators, naturalists, scientists and scholars, authors and artists, and American institutions, organizations, and business firms, which established a whole gamut of relationships between the United States and Asia. This dictionary provides in alphabet format information about the persons, institutions, and events that affected the relationships between the United States and Asia; persons who actually traveled to Asia, and particularly those who left written or visual records of their stay; organizations and institutions that functioned in Asia; and events that occurred in that area.

The dictionary covers all the countries of Asia except the countries of the Middle East, which are covered in an earlier volume. The geographical names used in a specific entry are the ones used in the period covered by that entry.

The dictionary attempts to be comprehensive, including all persons, institutions, and events that brought the United States into contact with Asia. The choice of entries in a historical dictionary is always difficult. For example, of 241 chiefs of diplomatic missions who served in Asia between 1843 and 1988, only 78 appear as entries in the book. Only those who contributed to U.S.-Asian relations in some significant way are included, although this contribution may have consisted of only a book of memoirs about their service in the area. A complete list of all chiefs of American diplomatic missions in Asia is included in the appendix.[1] Specifically excluded are U.S. military and naval personnel who served in Asia during World War II, the Korean War, and the Vietnam War.[2]

Only a limited number of travelers, government agencies, and business firms are included. With regard to travelers, only those whose travel reports are of particular interest and influence are covered.[3] Although many U.S. governmental agencies, in addition to the Department of State, were involved with Asia, only a few had establishments in the area.[4] Finally, regarding business firms, only a few are covered in this dictionary. More detailed lists of firms that sold their products in Asia are available in several sources.[5]

The references at the end of each entry note whether the subject is listed in the general biographical dictionaries such as the *Dictionary of American Biography*, *National Cyclopaedia of American Biography*, *Appleton's Cyclopaedia of American Biography*, *Notable American Women*, *Who's Who in America*, *Who Was Who in America*, *Current Biography*, and *Contemporary Authors*. The references also attempt to list every book and article written about the subject, but references that appear in the *Dictionary of American Biography* and *Notable American Women* have not been duplicated. Volume and page numbers are provided only for the *National Cyclopaedia of American Biography*, because it is not arranged in alphabetical order. Asterisked entries indicate that the subject is covered separately in this volume.

Efforts have been made to include complete and accurate information, but this was not always possible because some information is no longer available and other information could not be located. Unfortunately, mistakes are also inevitable in a work of this scope. The author would appreciate receiving corrections and emendations.

Many individuals provided assistance, especially librarians, archivists, and officials of missionary societies. The dictionary would have been far less complete without their help. Special thanks are due to Rebecca Shavit and to the staff of the Interlibrary Loan Office of Northern Illinois University, DeKalb, Illinois.

NOTES

1. A complete list is available in U.S. Department of State, *Principal Officers of the Department of State and United States Chiefs of Mission 1778–1986* (Washington, D.C., 1987). A complete list of consuls who served in Asia only through 1865 is available in Walter B. Smith, II, *America's Diplomats and Consuls of 1776–1865: A Geographic and Biographic Directory of the Foreign Service from the Declaration of Independence to the End of the Civil War* (Washington, D.C., 1986).

2. See Louis L. Snyder's *Historical Guide to World War II* (Westport, Conn., 1982); Thomas Parrish, ed., *Simon and Schuster Encyclopedia of World War II* (New York, 1978); Marcel Baudot et al., eds., *The Historical Encyclopedia of World War II* (New York, 1980); and Bryan Perrett and Ian Hogg, *Encyclopedia of the Second World War* (Novato, Calif., 1989) for World War II; see Harry G. Summers, Jr., *Korean War Almanac* (New York, 1990) for the Korean War; and for the Vietnam War, James S. Olson, ed., *Dictionary of the Vietnam War* (Westport, Conn., 1988), and Harry G. Summers, Jr., *Vietnam War Almanac* (New York, 1985).

3. Harold F. Smith, *American Travels Abroad: A Bibliography of Accounts Published before 1900* (Carbondale, Ill., 1969).

4. A comprehensive list of current governmental agencies involved with Asia are available in Hong N. Kim, *Scholars' Guide to Washington, D.C., for East Asian Studies* (Washington, D.C., 1979); Enayetur Rahim, *Scholars' Guide to Washington, D.C., for South Asian Studies* (Washington, D.C., 1981); and Patrick M. Mayerchak, *Scholars' Guide to Washington, D.C., for Southeast Asian Studies* (Washington, D.C., 1983). Many nongovernmental institutions are listed in Ward Morehouse, ed., *American Institutions and Organizations Interested in Asia: A Reference Directory*, 2nd ed. (New York, 1961).

5. *Directory of American Firms Operating in Foreign Countries* (New York, 1955/ 56–). Historical information about the fifty most important American businesses in the Philippines is available in Lewis E. Gleeck, Jr., *American Business and Philippine Economic Development* (Manila, 1975).

Abbreviations

AA	*American Anthropologist*
AAAG	*Annals of the Association of American Geographers*
ACAB	*Appleton's Cyclopaedia of American Biography* (New York, 1888–1901)
ACCJ	*American Chamber of Commerce Journal*
ACWW	*American Catholic Who's Who*
Amherst	*Amherst College Biographical Record* (Amherst, Mass., 1973)
AMWS	*American Men and Women of Science*
AN	*American Neptune*
Anderson	*Imperialism and Idealism: American Diplomacy in China, 1861–1898*, David L. Anderson (Bloomington, Ind., 1985)
AndoverTS	*General Catalogue of Andover Theological Seminary* (Boston, 1908)
BAAPG	*Bulletin of the American Association of Petroleum Geologists*
BAHC	*Bulletin of the American Historical Collection*
BDABL	*Biographical Dictionary of American Business Leaders*, John H. Ingham (Westport, Conn., 1983)
BDAC	*Biographical Directory of the American Congress 1774–1971* (Washington, D.C., 1971)
BDAE	*Biographical Dictionary of American Educators*, ed. John F. Ohles (Westport, Conn., 1978)
BE	*Brethren Encyclopedia* (Philadelphia, 1983–1984)
BGSA	*Bulletin of the Geological Society of America*
BMNAS	*Biographical Memoirs of the National Academy of Science*
BRDS	*Biographical Register of the Department of State*
CA	*Contemporary Authors* (Detroit, 1962–)
CB	*Current Biography*

CCDP	*Cornejo's Commonwealth Directory of the Philippines* (Manila, 1939)
CDCWM	*Concise Dictionary of the Christian World Mission*, ed. Stephen Neill et al. (Nashville, 1971)
CE	*The Catholic Encyclopedia* (New York, 1967)
CR	*Chinese Recorder*
DAB	*Dictionary of American Biography* (New York, 1928–)
DACB	*Dictionary of American Catholic Biography*, John J. Delaney (Garden City, N.Y., 1984)
DADH	*Dictionary of American Diplomatic History*, John E. Findling (Westport, Conn., 1980)
DAMB	*Dictionary of American Medical Biography*, Howard A. Kelly (Baltimore, 1928)
DAMB 1984	*Dictionary of American Medical Biography*, ed. Martin Kaufman, Stuart Galishoff, and Todd L. Savitt (Westport, Conn., 1984)
DAMIB	*Dictionary of American Military Biography*, ed. Roger J. Spiller (Westport, Conn., 1984)
DAS	*Directory of American Scholars*
DFAF	*Directory, Foreign Area Fellows, 1952–72* (New York, 1973)
DH	*Diplomatic History*
DLB	*Dictionary of Literary Biography* (Detroit, 1978–)
DPB	*Dictionary of Philippine Biography*, E. Arsenion Manuel (Quezon City, 1955–)
DrewTS	*Alumni Record of Drew Theological Seminary, Madison, New Jersey, 1867–1925* (Madison, N.Y., 1926)
DSB	*Dictionary of Scientific Biography* (New York, 1970–1976)
DVW	*Dictionary of the Vietnam War*, ed. James S. Olson (Westport, Conn., 1988)
EAH	*Encyclopedia of Asian History* (New York, 1988)
EIHC	*Essex Institute Historical Collections*
Elarth	*The Story of the Philippines Constabulary*, Harold H. Elarth (Los Angeles, 1949)
EM	*Encyclopaedia of Missions* (New York, 1891–1904)
EMCM	*Encyclopedia of Modern Christian Missions: The Agencies*, ed. Burton L. Goddard (Camden, N.J., 1967)
EP	*Encyclopedia of the Philippines*, 3rd ed., ed. Zoila M. Garlang (Manila, 1950)
ESB	*Encyclopedia of Southern Baptists* (Nashville, Tenn., 1958–1982)
EWM	*Encyclopedia of World Methodism* (Nashville, Tenn., 1974)

Fenn	*Christian Higher Education in Changing China 1880–1950*, William P. Fenn (Grand Rapids, Mich., 1976)
FEQ	*Far Eastern Quarterly*
Foreign Pioneers	*Foreign Pioneers: A Short History of the Contribution of Foreigners to the Development of Hokkaido* (n.p., 1968)
Gleeck/Ambassadors	*Dissolving the Colonial Bond: American Ambassadors to the Philippines, 1946–1984*, Lewis E. Gleeck, Jr. (Quezon City, Philippines, 1988)
Gleeck/Frontiers	*Americans on the Philippine Frontiers*, Lewis E. Gleeck, Jr. (Manila, 1974)
Gleeck/Governors	*The American Governors-General and High Commissioners in the Philippines: Proconsuls, Nation-Builders and Politicians*, Lewis E. Gleeck, Jr. (Quezon City, Philippines, 1986)
Gleeck/Manila	*The Manila Americans (1901–1964)*, Lewis E. Gleeck, Jr. (Manila, 1977)
HDRCA	*Historical Directory of the Reformed Church in America 1628–1978*, Peter N. VandenBerge (Grand Rapids, Mich., 1978)
Hewitt	*Williams College and Foreign Missions*, John M. Hewitt (Boston, 1914)
IAB	*Indiana Authors and Their Books*, R. E. Banta and Donald R. Thompson (Bloomington, Ind., 1949–1974)
JAS	*Journal of Asian Studies*
JBEWW	*The Japan Biographical Encyclopedia and Who's Who*, 3rd ed., 1964–65 (Tokyo, 1965)
JSEAH	*Journal of South East Asian History*
JMBRAS	*Journal of the Malasyan Branch of the Royal Asiatic Society*
JSES	*Journal of Southeast Asian Studies*
KEJ	*Kodansha Encyclopedia of Japan* (Tokyo, 1983)
LC	*Lutheran Cyclopedia*, rev. ed. (St. Louis, 1975)
Lutz	*China and the Christian Colleges, 1850–1950*, Jessie G. Lutz (Ithaca, N.Y., 1971)
ME	*The Mennonite Encyclopedia* (Hillsboro, Kan., 1955)
NAW	*Notable American Women* (Cambridge, Mass., 1971–1980)
NCAB	*National Cyclopaedia of American Biography* (New York, 1898–)
NYHSD	*New York Historical Society's Dictionary of Artists in America*, George C. Groce and Davis H. Wallace (New York, 1957).
NYT	*New York Times*
OAB	*Ohio Authors and Their Books*, William Coyle, ed. (Cleveland, 1962)
PGSA	*Proceedings of the Geological Society of America*

PHR	*Pacific Historical Review*
Pier	*American Apostles to the Philippines*, Arthur S. Pier (Boston, 1950)
PolProf	*Political Profiles*, Nelson Lichtenstein, ed. (New York, 1976–1978)
PS	*Philippines Studies*
S	*Supplement*
SDAE	*Seventh-Day Adventist Encyclopedia*, rev. ed. (Washington, D.C., 1976)
Sevilla	*Justices of the Supreme Court of the Philippines: Their Lives and Outstanding Decisions: Vol. 1. 1901–1944*, Victor J. Sevilla (Quezon City, Philippines, 1984)
Tibet	*Tibet, the Sacred Realm: Photographs 1880–1950* (Philadelphia, 1983)
UnionTS	*Alumni Catalogue of the Union Theological Seminary in the City of New York 1836–1936* (New York, 1937)
USNBO	*United States Navy and Marine Corps Bases, Overseas*, ed. Paolo E. Coletta (Westport, Conn., 1985)
USNIP	*United States Naval Institute Proceedings*
Wildes	*Aliens in the East: A New History of Japan's Foreign Intercourse*, Henry E. Wildes (Philadelphia, 1937)
WWA	*Who's Who in America*
WWAW	*Who's Who among American Women*
WWE	*Who's Who in the East*
WWM	*Who's Who in the Middle West*
WWP	*Who's Who in the Philippines: A Biographical Dictionary of Notable Living Men of the Philippine Islands* (Manila, 1937–)
WWW	*Who's Who in the West*
WWWA	*Who Was Who in America*
Yale	*Alumni Directory of Yale University* (New Haven, Conn., 1929)
Yanghwajin	*Yanghwajin, Seoul Foreigners' Cemetery, Korea, An Informal History 1890–1984*, comp. and ed. Donald N. Clark (Seoul, 1984)

Place Names

Current Name	Former Name
Bangladesh	East Pakistan
Beijing	Peking/Peiping
Djakarta	Batavia
Inchon	Chemulp'o
Indonesia	Dutch East Indies
Kampuchea	Cambodia
Malaysia	Malaya/Straits Settlements
Seoul	Chosen
Sri Lanka	Ceylon
Taiwan	Formosa
Thailand	Siam
Vietnam	Annam/Cochin China/Tonkin

Chronology

1600	British East India Company received charter
1634	English began trading in Bengal
1639	Fort St. George founded in Madras
1661	East India Company gained control of Bombay
1690	Calcutta founded
1744	War between France and Britain in India
1757	Battle of Plassey destroyed French power in India
1784	Pitt's India Act; *Empress of China* arrived in Canton, opening the China trade
1786–1793	Lord Charles Cornwallis served as governor general of India
1793	Mission of James Bruce, Earl of Elgin to Peking; permanent British settlement in Bengal
1796	*Astrea* arrived in Manila and opened direct trade between the Philippines and the United States
1798	Ceylon became a British colony
1819	Britain founded Singapore
1824–1826	First Burmese War
1839–1842	Opium War; First Afghan War
1840	First American missionaries arrived in China
1842	Treaty of Nanking signed by China and Great Britain
1843	British annexed the Sind
1844	Treaty of Wanghia signed by China and the United States
1845–1846	First Sikh War
1848–1849	Second Sikh War
1849	Britain annexed the Punjab
1850–1864	Taiping Rebellion

1851–1868	Rama IV (Mongkut), king of Siam
1852–1853	Second Burmese War
1853	First railway line opened in India
1853–1855	Perry's expedition to Japan
1854	Treaty of Kangawa signed by Japan and the United States
1857–1858	Indian Mutiny
1858	Government of India Act; power transferred from the East India Company to the Crown; Treaty of Tientsin, signed by China and Great Britain, Russia, France, and the United States; Harris Treaty signed by Japan and the United States
1863	French established protectorate over Cambodia
1864	Shimonoseki bombardment
1867	The last Tokugawa shogun abdicated; Cochin China became a French colony
1868	New Imperial government established in Edo, renamed Tokyo; Burlingame Treaty signed by China and the United States
1868–1910	Rama V (Chulalongkorn), king of Siam
1868–1912	Meiji period
1871	Korean expedition
1877	Satsuma Rebellion in Japan
1882	United States-Korean Treaty signed
1883–1885	Sino-French War
1884	Annam and Tonkin became French colonies
1885	Indian National Congress founded
1885–1886	Third Anglo-Burmese War; Britain annexed Upper Burma
1887	French Indochina formed
1889	Promulgation of Meiji Constitution
1890	First session of the Imperial Diet in Japan
1892	India Councils Act
1893	Laos became French protectorate, incorporated into French Indochina
1894–1895	First Sino-Japanese War
1896	Federated Malay states created; José Protasio Rizal executed
1896–1898	Filipino revolt against Spain
1898–1905	Lord Curzon, viceroy of India
1898	Battle of Manila Bay; Philippine Islands acquired by the United States; Hundred Days of Reform
1899–1900	First Philippine Commission
1899–1902	Philippine-American War

1900	Boxer Rebellion
1900–1904	William Howard Taft, first governor of the Philippines
1902	Anglo-Japanese Alliance
1904–1905	Russo-Japanese War; Japan occupied Korea
1905	Partition of Bengal; Taft-Katsua Agreement; Treaty of Portsmouth signed by Japan and Russia
1906	Muslim League founded in India
1907	Gentlemen's Agreement signed by Japan and the United States
1908	Root-Takahira Agreement
1909	Morley-Minto reforms
1910	Japan annexed Korea
1911	Revolution in China; fall of Manchu government; first Chinese Republic established
1912	Delhi made capital of India
1915	Japan's twenty-one demands to China
1916	Jones Act
1917	Lansing-Ishii Agreement
1918–1920	U.S. intervention in Siberia
1919	May Fourth Movement; Montagu-Chelmsford Movement; Punjab riots; Amritsar Massacre
1920	Mahatma Gandhi became leader of the Indian National Congress
1920–1926	Civil War in China
1921	First Noncooperation Movement in India
1922	Gandhi arrested for civil disobedience for first time; Dutch East Indies incorporated into the Dutch Kingdom
1924	Organization of the Kuomintang in China
1925–1945	Bao Dai reigned as emperor of Vietnam
1926–1928	Northern expedition and reunification of China under the Kuomintang
1926–1989	Hirohito reigned as emperor of Japan
1927	Simon Commission in India; Nanking Incident
1930–1931	Civil disobedience movement in India
1931	Mukden Incident; Japan began conquest of Manchuria
1931–1932	Japan occupied Manchuria
1932	Stimson Doctrine; Shanghai Incident; Constitutional monarchy proclaimed in Siam
1934	Tydings-McDuffie Act
1934–1935	Chinese Communists' Long March

1935	Government of India Act; Burma is separated from India; Commonwealth established in the Philippines
1935–1942	Manuel Quezon y Molina, first president of the Philippines
1936	Abortive "February Mutiny"; Sian Incident
1937	*Panay* Incident; Marco Polo Bridge Incident; Japan invaded China
1937–1945	Second Sino-Japanese War
1938–1957	Pibul Songgram, premier and later dictator of Siam
1941	Japanese attack on Pearl Harbor
1945–1952	Allied occupation of Japan
1945–1948	U.S. military government of South Korea
1945–1949	Indonesian war for independence
1946	Philippines became independent; Vietminh forces opened hostilities in Indochina
1946–1948	Japanese war crime trials
1946–1949	Civil War in China between Nationalist and Communist governments
1946–1954	French Indochina War; Hukbalahap Insurrection in the Philippines
1947	Viscount Mountbatten, last viceroy of India; growing communal strife between Hindus and Moslems; partition of India and Pakistan; India and Pakistan became independent
1947–1964	Pandit Nehru served as first prime minister of India
1948	Burma and Ceylon became independent; outbreak of communist-led rebellions in Burma and Malaya; Mahatma Gandhi assassinated; Republic of Korea and the People's Republic of Korea established
1948–1949	India-Pakistan War over Kashmir
1948–1950	Communist insurrection in Malaya
1948–1960	Syngman Rhee, president of South Korea
1949	Chiang Kai-shek withdrew to Taiwan and established the Chinese Nationalist government; Indonesia became independent; Siam changed its name to Thailand; Chinese People's Republic was proclaimed
1949–1967	Sukarno, president of Indonesia
1950	China occupied Tibet
1950–1953	Korean War
1951	Japanese Peace Treaty signed; U.S.-Japanese security treaty
1953	Armistice in Korea; Cambodia became independent
1954	Battle of Dienbienphu; Geneva Agreements; Manila Pact; South East Asia Treaty Organization (SEATO) was formed; Laos

	became independent; Vietnam divided into North and South Vietnam
1954–1955	Quemoy and Matsu crisis
1955	South Vietnam proclaimed a republic; Bandung Conference of Asian and African States; India took over Portuguese possessions
1954–1963	Ngo Dinh Diem, president of South Vietnam
1957	Malaya became independent; military coup in Thailand
1958	"Great Leap Forward" in China; Quemoy and Matsu crisis
1958–1969	General Mohammad Ayub Khan, president of Pakistan
1959	Abortive Tibetan revolt; Dalai Lama fled to India; Chinese-Indian border incidents
1960	Protests against the U.S.-Japan security treaty
1960–1975	Vietnam War
1961	India annexed Goa; military coup in Korea
1962	Chinese-Indian border conflict; military coup in Burma
1963	Federation of Malaysia created; military coup in South Vietnam; Ngo Dinh Niem killed
1963–1965	Malaysia-Indonesia confrontation
1963–1979	General Park Chung Hee, president of Korea
1964	First China nuclear test
1965	Singapore became independent; attempted communist coup in Indonesia; Maldives became independent; India-Pakistan conflict over Kashmir
1965–1986	Ferdinand Marcos, president of the Philippines
1966	"Cultural Revolution" in China
1966–1984	Indira Gandhi, prime minister of India
1967	ASEAN (Association of Southeast Asian Nations) founded
1967–	General Suharto, president of Indonesia
1968	*Pueblo* incident
1969	Ho Chi Minh died; Nixon Doctrine
1970	Prince Norodom Sihanouk of Cambodia overthrown
1971	Civil war in East Pakistan; Bangladesh became independent
1972	Ryukyu Islands returned to Japan
1973	Last U.S. troops left Vietnam; Vietnam peace settlement
1975	India annexed Sikkum; United States evacuated South Vietnam; North Vietnam captured Saigon; war in Vietnam ended; *Mayaguez* incident; Chiang Kai-shek died; Khmer Rouge assumed control over Cambodia
1976	Mao Tse-tung died; North and South Vietnam reunified

1978	Military coup in Pakistan; Vietnam invaded Cambodia
1978–1988	General Muhammad Zia ul-Haq, president of Pakistan
1979	Park Chung Hee assassinated
1982	Military coup in Bangladesh
1983	Benigno Aquino assassinated on his return to the Philippines
1984	Brunei became independent; Indira Gandhi assassinated
1986	President Ferdinand Marcos forced to flee the Philippines
1986–	Corazon Aquino, president of the Philippines
1989	Student demonstrations in Tiananmen Square in Beijing; Emperor Hirohito died

Introduction

The United States involvement in Asia has been long and significant. It began in the seventeenth century, when several Americans went to India in the service of the East India Company. Direct U.S. contacts with Asia began in 1784, after the United States became independent. *The Empress of China* and the *United States* led the way of many trade vessels. American merchants found new opportunities in Asia and, by 1790, every major port between Salem, Massachusetts, and Norfolk, Virginia, had sent trade vessels to China, India, Sumatra, and the Philippine Islands.

The American presence in China during the first half of the nineteenth century loomed particularly large. American merchants played a major role in the China trade, including opium. The commercial and trade interests led to formal relationships and commercial treaties with Asian countries not under European colonial rule. Treaties were signed with Siam in the 1830s, with China in the 1840s, with Japan in the 1850s, and with Korea in the 1880s. The United States was granted commercial privileges in China and later also in Japan and Korea. The U.S. desire to acquire a sphere of economic influence and to support its trade interests in China led to the adoption of the Open Door policy, which it followed until World War II.

U.S.-Asian religious interactions had been established by the 1820s. Led by Adoniram Judson in Burma, thousands of American missionaries worked in Asia. (There were more than three thousand American missionaries in China in 1930.) They were involved not only in the spread of Christianity but also in the spread of Western education, medicine, technology, and culture. American missionary societies established colleges in the various countries of Asia (fourteen in China alone) and scores of schools and hospitals. American missionaries also led the way in the study of the language, religion, culture, and history of the Asian countries.

American adventurers served as leaders of the Chinese army that restored imperial authority over the Taiping rebels. Americans served in the Chinese Imperial Customs Service and other similar agencies, and as military, diplomatic, and legal advisors. More than 350 Americans served as advisors in Japan during the Meiji period. By 1899, the United States also had become a major colonial power in Asia, after acquiring the Philippine Islands, which it ruled until World War II.

The relationship between the United States and Asia during the twentieth century has been a stormy one. By 1901, U.S. armed forces had been stationed in China and remained there until 1949. The United States fought three major wars in Asia: World War II, the Korean War, and the Vietnam War. The role of the U.S. government in Asia until World War II, however, was a restricted one, except in the Philippines. Contacts were mostly nongovernmental, carried out by the individuals and institutions. Following World War II, the United States became involved in the military occupation of Japan and Korea, leading to its deep involvement in Asia. Mainland China was "lost" in 1949, the United States became embroiled in the Korean War, and U.S. forces later remained in Korea. While granting full independence to the Philippines, the United States continued its close relationship with this country because of the important military bases on the islands. On the other hand, U.S. response to Asian nationalism has been weak. In order to contain communism, the United States carried out extensive programs of economic and military assistance, continued its support of Nationalist China and the European colonial powers, created the South East Asia Treaty Organization (SEATO), and became involved in anti-communist operations in the Philippines and Indochina and eventually in Vietnam, as Southeast Asia assumed a central role in its foreign policy until its withdrawal from Vietnam.

U.S. relations with Communist China remained hostile for more than twenty years, until the beginning of the 1970s. Strategic and military considerations remained important, and the United States retained military bases in the Philippines, Japan, Korea, and the Indian Ocean; however, trade relations with Japan and several other Asian countries have become the major U.S. concern during the 1970s and 1980s.

A

ABBOTT, WILLIAM LOUIS (1860–1936). Naturalist, born February 23, 1860, in Philadelphia. Abbott graduated from the University of Pennsylvania and studied in London. After his father's death in 1886, he became heir to a considerable fortune, and, being financially independent, he devoted his time to natural history. He collected natural history specimens in Cuba and Santo Domingo in 1883, in East Africa from 1887 to 1889, and in the Seychelles Archipelago and Madagascar in 1890, 1892, and 1894. He collected in the Himalayas from 1891 to 1895 and traveled and collected in Siam, Borneo, Dutch East Indies, Malaya, and the islands of the South China Sea from 1895 to 1905. He explored the East Indies in a sailing yacht he built in Singapore, sailed around Sumatra three times, visited Borneo and the Celebes, and sent collections to the U.S. National Museum in Washington, D.C. He later explored Mauritius, Andaman and Nicobar Islands, and India. He traveled in Kashmir and crossed the Karakoram Pass into Tibet and Kashgar. He went on to travel and collect in Haiti and in Santo Domingo. Died April 2, 1936, near North East, Maryland. *References*: William Louis Abbott Papers, Smithsonian Institution Archives, Washington, D.C.; and *NCAB* 27:312.

ABEEL, DAVID (1804–1846). Missionary, born June 12, 1804, in New Brunswick, New Jersey. Abeel graduated from New Brunswick Seminary and was ordained in 1826. He was pastor from 1826 to 1828, and chaplain under the American Seamen's Friend Society in Canton, China, in 1830. He came to Bangkok, Siam, in 1831, the first American and American Board of Commissioners for Foreign Missions (ABCFM) missionary in Siam. He visited Java, Malacca, Siam, and Singapore in 1831. He left Siam in 1832 because of ill health and returned to the United States in 1833. He wrote *Journal of a Residence in China, and Neighboring Countries from 1829–1833* (New York, 1834). He was in Europe in 1833–1834 and founded the Society for Promoting Female Education in China and the East in England and in the United States during 1835–1838 to secure missionaries. He visited the Malay Archipelago in 1839, and established a mission station in Amoy, China, in 1841. Died September 4, 1846, in Albany, New York. *References*: David Abeel Papers, New Brunswick Theological Seminary Library, New Brunswick, N.J.; *ACAB*; *CDCWM*; *DAB*; *EM*; *LC*; Alvin J. Popper, "The Life and Work of David Abeel," S. T. M. thesis, Union Theological Seminary, 1959; and *WWWA*.

ABEND, HALLETT E(DWARD) (1884–1955). Journalist, born September 15, 1884, in Portland, Oregon. Abend attended Stanford University. He was a reporter for the *Spokane-Review* (Spokane, Wash.) from 1904 to 1906, a telegraph editor and general assistant editor of the *Spokane Chronicle* from 1908 to 1913, city editor of the *Honolulu Star-Bulletin* in 1915–1916, managing editor of the *Idaho Statesman* (Boise) from 1916 to 1920, city editor of the *Los Angeles Times* from 1920 to 1924, and a script and title writer in Hollywood, California, in 1924–1925. He was a freelance writer in China in 1926–1927, chief correspondent for the *New York Times* in China from 1927 to 1941, and wrote *My Life in China, 1926–1941* (New York, 1943). He was with the Washington, D.C., Bureau of the *New York Times* in 1941–1942, freelance writer and lecturer from 1942 until 1951, and associate editor of the Marshalltown (Iowa) *Times-Republican* from 1951 to 1955. He wrote *Tortured China* (New York, 1930); *Chaos in Asia* (New York, 1939); *Japan Unmasked* (New York, 1941); *Ramparts of the Pacific* (Garden City, N.Y., 1942); *Treaty Ports* (Garden City, N.Y., 1944); *The God from the West: Biography of Frederick Townsend Ward* (Garden City, N.Y., 1947); and coauthored *Can China Survive?* (New York, 1936). Died November 27, 1955, in Sonora, California. *References*: *CB* 1942; *NYT*, November 28, 1955; and *WWWA*.

ADAMS, GEORGE IRVING (1870–1932). Geologist, born August 17, 1870, in Lena, Illinois. Adams graduated from Kansas State Normal School, University of Kansas, and Princeton University, and studied at the University of Munich and Yale University. He was a field assistant to the U.S. Geological Survey from 1898 to 1904, and an assistant geologist from 1900 to 1904; he was chief hydrologist at the Cuerpo de Ingenieros de Minas del Peru from 1904 to 1906, and of mine examinations in Bolivia and Chile in 1906–1907. He was a geologist with the Division of Mines of the Bureau of Science in the Philippines from 1908 to 1910, and a professor of geology and mining at Pei Yank University in Tientsin, China, from 1911 to 1915, and at Peking University from 1915 to 1920. He was a professor of geology and mineralogy at the University of Alabama after 1920, and a geologist with the Geological Survey of Alabama after 1927. Died September 8, 1932, in Tuscaloosa, Alabama. *References*: *BAAPG* 17 (1933): 103–4; *BGSA* 44 (1933): 288–301; and *WWWA*.

ADOLPH, WILLIAM HENRY (1890–1958). Nutritionist, born September 1, 1890, in Philadelphia. Adolph graduated from the University of Pennsylvania. He was a missionary under the Board of Foreign Missions of the Presbyterian

Church in the U.S.A. in China from 1915 to 1951. He taught at Cheelo University at Tsinan from 1915 to 1926, at Yenching University in Peiping from 1926 to 1948 (and was Yenching University's acting president from 1946 to 1948), and at Peking Union Medical College from 1948 to 1951. He conducted research in nutritional chemistry and nutritional physiology as applied to the Chinese people. He was interned by the Japanese in China from 1941 until 1943. He was professor of nutrition at the American University of Beirut from 1951 to 1954. He retired in 1954, and was lecturer in nutrition and public health at Yale University after 1954. Died September 23, 1958, in New Haven, Connecticut. *References*: *NCAB* 44:290; and *NYT*, September 25, 1958.

ADVENT CHRISTIAN CHURCH. *See* AMERICAN ADVENT MISSION SOCIETY, INC.

AGNEW, ELIZA (1807–1883). Missionary, born February 2, 1807, in New York City. Agnew was a missionary under the American Board of Commissioners for Foreign Missions (ABCFM) in Ceylon from 1840 until her death. Pioneering in work for girls and women, she was stationed at Uduvil, serving as teacher and later as principal of a girls' boarding school there from 1842 until 1879. She resided at Manepay, Ceylon, after 1879. Died June 14, 1883, in Manepay. *References*: *DAB*; *EM*; *LC*; and *WWWA*.

AHERN, GEORGE P(ATRICK) (1859–1942). Army officer and forester, born December 29, 1859, in New York City. Ahern graduated from the U.S. Military Academy in 1882 and was commissioned second lieutenant in the infantry. He also graduated from Yale University. He served on frontier duty in the western United States. He was director of the Philippine Bureau of Forestry, organized the forest school in the Philippines, and was professor of forestry at the University of the Philippines from 1900 to 1914. He served in the U.S. Army during World War I. He retired in 1930 with the rank of lieutenant colonel. Died May 13, 1942, in Washington, D.C. *References*: George Patrick Ahern Papers, Manuscript Division, Library of Congress; *AMWS*; and *Yale*.

AIR AMERICA. *See* CIVIL AIR TRANSPORT

ALBATROS **EXPEDITION.** From 1907 to 1910, the U.S. Bureau of Fisheries vessel *Albatros*, under the direction of Hugh M. Smith,* made a survey of the fisheries and aquatic resources of the Philippines, its neighboring islands, and adjacent seas. *References*: Paul Bartsch, "Dr. Hugh M. Smith, Director of the Philippine Cruise of the *Albatros*," *Copeia* 1941, no. 4 (November 1941): 209–15; and Joel W. Hedgpeth, "The United States Fish Commission Steamer *Albatross*," *AN* 5 (1945): 5–26.

ALLAHABAD AGRICULTURAL INSTITUTE. Founded in 1910 by Sam Higginbottom* as the agricultural department of the Allahabad Christian College in Allahabad, India, with support from the Board of Foreign Missions of the Presbyterian Church in the U.S.A. In 1918, it became a separately financed institution with an independent board of trustees in the United States. It established a farm for experimental farming and breeding, was involved in adopting modern agricultural machinery to the special needs of Indian farming conditions, and introduced to the region contour farming, crop rotation, and other improvements. Support was broadened in 1944 to include other American churches. *Reference*: Henry C. Hart, *Campus India: An Appraisal of American College Programs in India* (East Lansing, Mich., 1961).

ALLAHABAD CHRISTIAN COLLEGE. *See* EWING CHRISTIAN COLLEGE

ALLEN, DAVID OLIVER (1799–1863). Missionary, born September 14, 1799, in Barre, Massachusetts. Allen graduated from Amherst College and Andover Theological Seminary, and was ordained in 1827. He was a missionary under the American Board of Commissioners for Foreign Missions (ABCFM) in India from 1827 to 1853, serving in Bombay. He was secretary of the Bombay Tract and Book Society and secretary of the Bombay branch of the British and Foreign Bible Society. He was editorial superintendent of the American Mission Press and was involved in the translation, revision, and publication of the Bible in Marathi. He returned to the United States in 1853. He wrote *India, Ancient and Modern, Geographical, Historical, Political, Social, and Religious, with a Particular Account of the State and Prospects of Christianity* (Boston, 1856). He held pastorates in Westford and Wenham, Massachusetts, from 1857 until 1860. Died July 19, 1863, in Lowell, Massachusetts. *References*: *Amherst*; *AndoverTS*; *DAB*; *EM*; *Hewitt*; *LC*; *NCAB* 6:56; and *WWWA*.

ALLEN, HENRY T(UREMAN) (1859–1930). Army officer, born April 13, 1859, in Sharpsburg, Kentucky. Allen attended Georgetown College (Ky.), graduated from the U.S. Military Academy in 1882, and was commissioned second lieutenant. He served in the Pacific Northwest, explored Alaska in 1885, and was military attaché in Russia from 1890 to 1895 and in Germany from 1897–1898. He served in the Spanish-American War in Cuba. He served in the Philippine-American War and was governor of the island of Leyte. He was charged with the creation of the Philippines Constabulary in 1901, and was its first chief until 1907. He later served on the Mexican border in 1916, commanded the 90th U.S. Division in France during World War I, and was commander of the American Forces in Germany and a member of the Inter-Allied Rhineland High Commission from 1919 until 1923. He retired in 1923 with the rank of lieutenant general. Died August 30, 1930, in Buena Vista Springs, Pennsylvania. *References*: Henry T. Allen Papers, Manuscript Division, Library of Congress;

ACAB; *DAB S1*; *DAMIB*; *NCAB* 44:302; *NYT*, August 31, 1930; Heath Twichell, *Allen: The Biography of an Army Officer, 1859–1930* (New Brunswick, N.J., 1974); and *WWWA*.

ALLEN, HORACE N(EWTON) (1858–1932). Medical missionary and diplomat, born April 23, 1858, in Delaware, Ohio. Allen graduated from Ohio Wesleyan University, attended Starling Medical College (Columbus, Ohio), and graduated from Miami Medical College (Cincinnati, Ohio). He was a medical missionary under the Board of Foreign Missions of the Presbyterian Church in the U.S.A. in China in 1883–1884 and in Korea from 1884 until 1905. He served as court physician in the Korean royal palace, and was unofficial advisor to the Korean king on foreign policy. He was head of the embassy sent to the United States in 1887 to assert the independence of Korea from China and to establish a legation in Washington, and was confidential advisor to the legation until 1890. He was secretary of the U.S. legation in Seoul, as well as vice- and deputy consul general. He was U.S. minister and consul general to Korea from 1897 until 1905. He returned to the United States in 1905 and retired. He wrote *Korea: Fact and Fantasy* (Seoul, 1904), and *Things Korean: A Collection of Sketches and Anecdotes, Missionary and Diplomatic* (New York, 1908). Died December 11, 1932, in Toledo, Ohio. *References*: Horace N. Allen Papers, New York Public Library; *EAH*; Fred H. Harrington, *God, Mammon, and the Japanese: Dr. Horace N. Allen and Korean-American Relations, 1884–1905* (Madison, Wis., 1944); Wi Jo Kang, "The First Protestant Missionary in Korea and Early US-Korean Relations," *Missiology* 11 (1983): 403–17; *NCAB* 28:281; Wayne Patterson, "Horace Allen and Korean Immigration to Hawaii," in *The United States and Korea: American-Korean Relations, 1866–1976*, ed. Andrew C. Nahm (Kalamazoo, Mich., 1979), pp. 137–61; and *WWWA*.

ALLEN, YOUNG J(OHN) (1836–1907). Missionary, born January 3, 1836, in Burke County, Georgia. Allen attended Emory and Henry College (Va.) and graduated from Emory College (Oxford, Ga.). He was a missionary under the Board of Missions of the Methodist Episcopal Church, South, in China from 1860 until his death. To support his family during the American Civil War, he took a position as a teacher and translator for the Chinese government. He was founder and president of the Anglo-Chinese College in Shanghai, and helped establish the Methodist Press and a school for girls. He founded and edited *Wan-kuo kung-pao* (The Globe Magazine or the Review of the Times), the first newspaper of world events printed in Chinese for the average reader. Died May 30, 1907, in Shanghai. *References*: Young J. Allen Papers, Emory University Library, Atlanta; Adrian A. Bennett, *Missionary Journalist in China: Young J. Allen and His Magazines, 1860–1883* (Athens, Ga., 1983); Adrian A. Bennett and Kwang-China Liu, "Christianity in the Chinese Idiom: Young J. Allen and the Early *Chiao-hui hsin-pao*, 1868–70," in *The Missionary Enterprise in China and America*, ed. John K. Fairbank (Cambridge, Mass., 1974), pp. 159–96;

Warren A. Candler, *Young J. Allen, the Man Who Seeded China* (Nashville, Tenn., 1931); *DAB*; *EWM*; and *NCAB* 21:483.

ALLISON, JOHN MOORE (1905–1978). Diplomat, born April 7, 1905, in Holton, Kansas. Allison graduated from the University of Nebraska. He taught school in Japan and worked for General Electric Company in Shanghai until 1930. He entered the foreign service in 1930, and served in Kobe, Tokyo, and Osaka, Japan; and in Dairen, Tsinan and Nanking, China, until 1941. He was interned by the Japanese in 1941–1942. In London he was second secretary and then first secretary from 1942 to 1946, served in the U.S. State Department from 1946 to 1951, and was assistant secretary of state for Far Eastern affairs in 1952–1953. He was U.S. ambassador to Japan from 1953 to 1957. He dealt with the Mutual Security Agency aid and its role in U.S.-Japanese defense concerns, and signed the Mutual Defence Agreement in 1954. He also negotiated a convention removing extraterritorial status from U.S. troops stationed in Japan, and handled problems relating from fallout of the U.S. atomic bomb test. He was ambassador to Indonesia in 1957–1958, and ambassador to Czechoslovakia from 1958 to 1960. He retired in 1960 and taught at the University of Hawaii. He wrote his memoirs, *Ambassador from the Prairie or Allison Wonderland* (Boston, 1973). Died October 28, 1978, in Honolulu. *References*: *CB* 1956; *DADH*; *NYT*, November 6, 1978; *PolProf: Eisenhower*; and *WWWA*.

ALLMAN, NORWOOD F(RANCIS) (1893–1987). Lawyer, born in Union Hall, Virginia. Allman graduated from the University of Virginia. He was student interpreter in the American legation in Peking in 1915, and consul in Shanghai from 1921 to 1924, when he retired from the consular service and practiced law in Shanghai. He served as editor of *Shun Pao*, a Chinese-language newspaper, and prepared the first English-language text of Chinese commercial laws. He was interned by the Japanese in 1941–1942, returned to the United States in 1942, and was director of the Asian Bureau of the Office of Strategic Services (OSS) in New York City. He returned to China after the war and practiced law until 1950. He lived in New York City from 1950 until 1981. He wrote *Shanghai Lawyer* (New York, 1943). Died February 28, 1987, in Carlisle, Pennsylvania. *Reference*: *NYT*, March 2, 1987.

AMENT, WILLIAM SCOTT (1851–1909). Missionary, born September 14, 1851, in Owosso, Michigan. Ament graduated from Oberlin College, attended Union Theological Seminary, graduated from Andover Theological Seminary, and was ordained in 1877. He was a missionary under the American Board of Commissioners for Foreign Missions (ABCFM) in China from 1877 until his death. He served at Paoting from 1877 to 1880, and in Peking from 1880 to 1885. He returned to the United States in 1885 and held a pastorate in Medina, Ohio. He went back to China in 1888 and served in Peking until his death. He edited *The North China News*, a monthly paper in Mandarin. Died January 6, 1909, in Peking. *Reference*: *DAB*.

AMERICAN ADVENT MISSION SOCIETY, INC. Founded in 1865. It began missionary work in India in 1880, in China in 1897 (closed in 1948), in Japan in 1898, in the Philippines in 1954, and in Malaya in 1959. It changed its name later to the Department of World Mission of the Advent Christian General Conference. *References*: Headquarters Archives of the Advent Christian General Conference, Charlotte, N.C.; Doris K. Colby, *Highlights of One Hundred Years* (Charlotte, N.C., 1966); and *EMCM*.

AMERICAN BAPTIST FOREIGN MISSION SOCIETY. Founded in 1814 as the American Baptist Missionary Union. It was renamed American Baptist Foreign Mission Society in 1910, and was later renamed the International Ministries of the American Baptist Church U.S.A. It began missionary work in Burma in 1813, in Siam in 1833, in India in 1840, in China in 1842, in Japan in 1872, and in the Philippines in 1900. The mission in Burma was closed down by the Burmese government in 1966. *References*: American Baptist Foreign Mission Society Archives, American Baptist Historical Society, Rochester, N.Y.; Dana M. Albaugh, *Between Two Centuries: A Study of Four Baptist Mission Fields: Assam, South India, Bengal-Orissa, and South China* (Philadelphia, 1935); David Downie, *The Lone Star. A History of the Telugu Mission of the American Baptist Foreign Mission Society* (Philadelphia, 1924); Elmer A. Fridell, *Baptists in Thailand and the Philippines* (Philadelphia, 1956); Edward N. Harris, *A Star in the East. An Account of American Baptist Missions to the Karens in Burma* (New York, 1920); Ralph L. Howard, *Baptists in Burma* (Philadelphia, 1931); Robert G. Johnson, *History of the American Baptist Chin Mission: A History of the Introduction of Christianity into the Chin Hills of Burma by Missionaries of the American Baptist Foreign Missions Society during the Years 1899 to 1966* (Valley Forge, Pa., 1988); William B. Lipphard, *The Second Century of Baptist Foreign Missions* (Philadelphia, 1926); Milton W. Meyer, "The Course of Early Baptist Missions in the Philippines," *BAHC* 15 (April–June 1987): 7–23; and (July–August 1987): 38–57; Joseph C. Robbins, *Following the Pioneers: A Story of American Baptist Mission Work in India and Burma* (Philadelphia, 1922); Victor H. Sword, *Baptists in Assam. A Century of Missionary Service, 1836–1936* (Chicago, 1935); Robert G. Torbet, *Venture of Faith: The Story of the American Baptist Foreign Mission Society and the Woman's American Baptist Foreign Mission Society, 1814–1954* (Philadelphia, 1955); and Maung Shwe Wa, *Burma Baptist Chronicle* (Rangoon, 1963).

AMERICAN BAPTIST MISSIONARY UNION. *See* AMERICAN BAPTIST FOREIGN MISSION SOCIETY

AMERICAN BIBLE SOCIETY. A nondenominational, specialized agency, founded in 1816 to translate, produce, publish, and distribute the Bible, and to prepare literacy materials for both religious and secular use. It established offices in China in 1876, in Japan in 1875, in Siam in 1890, and in the Philippines in 1899. *References*: American Bible Society Archives, New York City; Henry O. Dwight, *The Centennial History of the American Bible Society* (New York, 1916); *EMCM*; John M. Gibson, *Soldiers of the Word: The Story of the American Bible Society* (New York, 1958); and Creighton Lacy, *The Word-Carrying Giant: The Growth of the American Bible Society (1816–1966)* (Pasadena, Calif., 1977).

AMERICAN BOARD OF COMMISSIONERS FOR FOREIGN MISSIONS (ABCFM). Founded in 1810 by the Congregational Christian Church. It began missionary work in India in 1813, in Ceylon in 1816, in China in 1830, in Siam in 1831 (transferred to the American Missionary Association in 1850), in Singapore in 1834 (closed in 1843), in Japan in 1869, in Sumatra and Borneo in 1934 (closed in 1838), and in the Philippines in 1903. It was superceded in 1961 by the United Church Board for World Ministries. *References*: ABCFM Archives, Houghton Library, Harvard University, Cambridge, Mass.; *EMCM*; C. N. V. Fernando, "Christian Missionary Enterprise in the Early British Period: III. The American Missionaries, 1816–1826," *University of Ceylon Review* 8 (April 1950): 110–15; C. N. V. Fernando, "Christian Missions: Some Aspects of the Work of American Missionaries in Jaffna District, 1827–1866," *University of Ceylon Review* 9 (July 1951): 191–201; Fred F. Goodsell, *The American Board in China, 1830–1950: Review and Appraisal* (Boston, 1969); Fred F. Goodsell, *You Shall Be My Witness* (Boston, 1959); Janet E. Heiniger, "The American Board in China: The Missionaries' Experiences and Attitudes, 1911–1952." Ph.D. diss., University of Wisconsin-Madison, 1981; Joseph L. Moulton, *Faith for the Future: The American Marathi Mission, India, Susquicentennial, 1963* (New York, 1963); Clifton J. Phillips, *Protestant America and the Pagan World: The First Half Century of the American Board of Commissioners for Foreign Missions* (Cambridge, Mass., 1968); Murray A. Rubinstein, "Zion's Corner: Origins of the American Protestant Missionary Movement in China, 1827–1839," Ph.D. diss., New York University, 1976; Charlotte D. Staelin, "The Influence of Missions on Woman's Education in India: The American Marathi Mission in Ahmadnager, 1830–1930," Ph.D. diss., University of Michigan, 1977; William E. Strong, *The Story of the American Board. An Account of the First Hundred Years of the American Board of Commissioners for Foreign Missions* (Boston, 1910); and Mary A. Walker, "The Archives of the American Board of Foreign Missions," *Harvard University Bulletin* 4 (1952): 52–58.

AMERICAN BUREAU FOR MEDICAL AID TO CHINA, INC. Founded in 1937, it supported the maintenance and expansion of medical and health services and training programs in China and later in Taiwan. *Reference*: American

Bureau for Medical Aid to China Papers, Columbia University Libraries, New York City.

AMERICAN CHINA DEVELOPMENT COMPANY. Formed in 1895 to procure railway, mining, and a variety of other industrial concessions in China. In 1898 it secured a concession to build a railway from Hankow to Canton, and in 1898–1899 it sent William Barclay Parsons* to survey the proposed route. The first portion of the railway opened to traffic in 1903, but work ceased in 1904. The contract was cancelled by the Chinese in 1905 and the bonds floated by it were redeemed in 1911. *References*: William R. Braisted, "The United States and the American China Development Company," *FEQ* 11 (1952): 147–66; and *DADH*.

AMERICAN INTERNATIONAL CORPORATION. Formed in 1915 by Frank A. Vanderlip, president of the National City Bank, to create a mechanism to finance American investments abroad. It involved several major American banking houses. In 1916–1917, it entered into business contracts with the Chinese government to construct railroads and improve the Grand Canal, but construction was never started. *References*: George T. Mazuzan, "Our New Gold Goes Adventuring: The American International Corporation in China," *PHR* 43 (1974): 212–32; and Harry N. Scheiber, "World War I as Entrepreneurial Opportunity: Willard Straight and the American International Corporation," *Political Science Quarterly* 84 (1969): 486–511.

AMERICAN LUTHERAN CHURCH: DIVISION OF WORLD MISSIONS. *See* EVANGELICAL LUTHERAN CHURCH

AMERICAN MILITARY GOVERNMENT IN KOREA (AMG). *See* U.S. ARMY MILITARY GOVERNMENT IN KOREA (USAMGIK)

AMERICAN NATIONAL RED CROSS. Founded in 1881 in Washington, D.C., as the American Association of the Red Cross; became the American National Red Cross in 1893 and received a federal charter in 1900. The Red Cross was involved in various activities in East Asia, including famine relief in China and Japan, the Huai River Conservancy Project after 1914, the Red Cross China Famine Relief in 1919–1920, relief to victims of the earthquake and fire in Japan in 1923, and many activities during and after World War II. *References*: American Red Cross Archives, Washington, D.C.; and Foster R. Dulles, *The American Red Cross: A History* (New York, 1950).

AMERICAN TRADING COMPANY. The American Clock Company of Connecticut opened a branch office in Japan in 1877 to sell clocks and brass work. The name was changed to the American Clock and Brass Company in 1879 and to the American Trading Company in 1884. It opened branches in Japan, China (first branch in Shanghai in 1879), Manchuria, and Korea, and by 1920, it had branches in fifteen countries. The China trade continued until 1949.

AMERICAN TRADING COMPANY OF BORNEO. Formed in 1865 to exploit the concessions of territory in North Borneo granted by the Sultan of Brunei to Charles Lee Moses.* In 1865 the company established the colony of Ellena in Kimanis, which lasted one year. It disposed of its rights in 1878. *References*: H. G. Keith, *The United States Consul and the Yankee Raja* (Brunei, 1980); and K. G. Tregonning, "American Activity in North Borneo, 1865–1881," *PHR* 23 (1954): 357–72.

AMERICAN VOLUNTEER GROUP (AVG). A semiofficial American aviation mission in China, popularly known as the "Flying Tigers." Headed by Claire L. Chennault,* it was composed of "volunteer" aviators recruited from U.S. military service with official sanction. It flew against the Japanese in 1941–1942. *References*: Charles R. Bond, Jr., and Terry Anderson, *A Flying Tiger's Diary* (College Station, Tex., 1984); Robert B. Holtz, *With General Chennault: The Story of the Flying Tigers* (New York, 1943); Larry M. Pistole, *A Pictorial History of the Flying Tigers* (Orange, Va., 1981); Malcolm Rosholt, *Days of the Ching Pao: A Photographic Record of the Flying Tigers—14th Air Force in China in World War II* (Amherst, Wis., 1978); and Duane Schultz, *The Maverick War: Chennault and the Flying Tigers* (New York, 1987).

AMSTUTZ, HOBART B(AUMAN) (1896–1980). Missionary, born September 18, 1896, in Henrietta, Ohio. Amstutz graduated from Northwestern University and Garrett Biblical Institute (Evanston, Ill.). He was a missionary under the Board of Foreign Missions of the Methodist Episcopal Church in Malaya from 1926 until 1964, serving most of the time in Singapore. He served in the Anglo-Chinese School, was principal and founder of Trinity Theological College, professor at Union Theological Seminary, and superintendent of the Singapore and Kuala Lumpur districts. He was interned by the Japanese in Singapore during World War II. He was elected bishop of the Southeastern Central Conference of the Methodist Episcopal Church in 1956 and served until his retirement in 1964. He was recalled in 1964 and served as bishop of West Pakistan in Karachi until 1968. Died February 26, 1980. *References*: Theodore B. Doraisang, *Candles of the Lord* (Singapore, 1987), pp. 2–3; and *EWM*.

ANDERSON, DAVID LAWRENCE (1850–1911). Missionary, born February 4, 1850, in Summerhill, South Carolina. Anderson attended Washington (later Washington and Lee) College (Va.). He was a missionary under the Board of Missions of the Methodist Episcopal Church, South, in China from 1883 until his death, serving at Soochow. He was in charge of the Soochow district, opened an Anglo-Chinese school in 1894, founded Soochow University in 1899, opened the university in 1901, and was its president until his death. Died February 16, 1911, in Soochow, China. *References*: *DAB*; and *NCAB* 23:310.

ANDERSON, ROY S(COTT) (1879?–1925). Adventurer and financial agent, born to American missionary parents in Soochow, Kiangsu Province, China. Anderson took an active part in the Chinese Revolution, served as a general in the Chinese revolutionary army, and participated in the siege of Nanking in 1911. He had the confidence of various Chinese politicians and political factions, served as a trusted go-between of warlords, and was an adviser to Li Ch'un, the military governor of Kiangsu Province. He was advisor and confidant to the U.S. minister Paul S. Reinsch,* providing him with useful information and serving as an intermediary during sensitive negotiations. He was later a representative for Standard Oil Company, American International Corporation, and other companies in China. He was credited with being the best-informed foreigner concerning Chinese questions and policies in that country. His death was reported from Peking on March 12, 1925. *Reference*: *NYT*, March 13, 1925.

ANDERSON, THOMAS MCARTHUR (1836–1917). Army officer, born January 21, 1836, near Chillicothe, Ohio. Anderson graduated from Mt. St. Mary's College (Md.) and Cincinnati Law School, and was admitted to the bar. He practiced law in Cincinnati from 1858 to 1861, and served in the Union Army during the Civil War. He advanced through the ranks to brigadier general in 1899, when he retired. He was the first general commander of the U.S. Army in the Philippines, occupied Cavite in 1898, commanded the forces taking Manila, and commanded the First Division of the Eighth Army in the battles of Santana, San Pedro, Passe, and Guadelupe. Died May 8, 1917, in Portland, Oregon. *References*: Thomas McArthur Anderson Papers, Bancroft Library, University of California, Berkeley; Thomas McArthur Anderson Papers, University of Washington Library, Seattle; *ACAB*; *NCAB* 4:410; *NYT*, May 10, 1917; and *WWWA*.

ANDERSON, WILLIAM ASHLEY (1890–   ). Author, born April 13, 1890, in Red Bank, New Jersey. Anderson graduated from New York University. He was managing director of the *New Rochelle Press* (New York) and served on the editorial staff of *Literary Digest* in Asia. He was a representative of the British-American Tobacco Company in China, and described his experiences in his autobiography, *The Atrocious Crime (of Being a Young Man)* (Philadelphia, 1973). He served in the British Army and later in the U.S. Army during World War I. He was an executive in national advertising agencies from 1926 to 1941, and director of the U.S. Office of the Coordinator of Inter-American Affairs in Washington, D.C., from 1942 to 1947. He later resided in East Stroudsburg, Pennsylvania. *Reference*: *ACWW*.

ANDERSON, WILLIAM BRENNAN (1868–1940). Missionary, born December 7, 1868, in Monmouth, Illinois. Anderson graduated from Westminster College and Pittsburgh Theological Seminary, and was ordained in 1897. He was a missionary under the Board of Foreign Missions of the United Presbyterian Church of North America in India from 1897 until 1914. He was president of Gordon College in Rawalpindi from 1899 until 1903. He was associate secretary of the Board of Foreign Missions of 1909–1910 and from 1914 to 1916, and its corresponding secretary from 1916 until his retirement in 1938. He was coauthor of *Far North in India: A Survey of the Mission Field and Work of the United Presbyterian Church in the Punjab* (Philadelphia, 1909). Died January 6, 1940, in Germantown, Pennsylvania. *References*: *NYT*, January 8, 1940; and *WWWA*.

ANDERSON, WILLIAM H(ART) (1871–1954). Army officer and businessman, born May 12, 1871, in Greenville, Ohio. Anderson graduated from the U.S. Military Academy in 1892, was commissioned first lieutenant of engineers, and resigned that year. He was a civil engineer with the Baltimore and Ohio Railway Company in Cincinnati from 1893 to 1895, and a scientific engineer with the Pope Manufacturing Company in Hartford, Connecticut, from 1896 to 1898. He served in the Philippines during the Spanish-American War from 1898 to 1900. He returned to the United States but went back to the Philippines in 1901 as an assistant manager and then manager of the Pacific Oriental Trading Company from 1901 to 1904. He formed the William H. Anderson Company, importers, exporters, and commission merchants, in 1904; he was its proprietor from 1904 to 1912 and its president after 1912. He bought Erlanger and Galinger in 1915 and was its president. He was also coowner of Luzon Sugar Company. He sold out his interests to his employees in 1938 and returned to the United States. He wrote *The Philippine Problem* (New York, 1939). Died August 8, 1954, in Reno, Nevada. *References*: *Assembly* 14 (April 1955): 51–52; and *Gleeck/Manila*.

ANDREWS, ROY CHAPMAN (1884–1960). Explorer, born January 26, 1884, in Beloit, Wisconsin. Andrews graduated from Beloit College and Columbia University. He began his association with the American Museum of Natural History in 1906. He was an assistant in mammology from 1909 to 1918 and an assistant curator of the department of mammals from 1918 to 1931. He participated in explorations in British Columbia and Alaska in 1908; in the *Albatros* expedition to the Dutch East Indies, Borneo, and Celebes in 1909–1910; and studied whales off Korea and Japan in 1911–1912. He led a reconnaissance expedition to Burma and Tibet in 1916–1917, worked for U.S. Naval Intelligence in China in 1918, and was part of a survey party to northern China and Outer Mongolia in 1918–1919. He led five central Asiatic expeditions in 1922, 1923, 1925, 1928, and 1930. He was vice director of the museum from 1931 to 1934, and director from 1935 to 1942. He was coauthor of *Camps and Trails in China: A Narrative of Exploration, Adventure, And Sport in Little known China* (New

York, 1918), and wrote *Across Mongolian Plains: A Naturalist's Account of China's "Great Northwest"* (New York, 1926); *On the Trails of Ancient Man: A Narrative of the Field Work of the Central Asiatic Expedition* (New York, 1926); *Ends of the Earth* (New York, 1929); *The New Conquest of Central Asia. A Narrative of the Explorations of the Central Asiatic Expeditions in Mongolia and China, 1921/30* (New York, 1932); *This Business of Exploring* (New York, 1935); *An Explorer Comes Home: Further Adventures of Roy Chapman Andrews* (New York, 1939); and his autobiography, *Under a Lucky Star: A Lifetime of Adventure* (New York, 1943). Died March 11, 1960, in Carmel, California. *References*: Edwin H. Colbert, *Men and Dinosaurs: The Search in Field and Laboratory* (New York, 1968), pp. 1–47; *DAB S6*; *NCAB* 44:558; *NYT*, March 12, 1960; Alonzo W. Pond, *Andrews: Gobi Explorer* (New York, 1972); and *WWWA*.

ANDRUS, J(AMES) RUSSELL (1902–   ). Economist, born September 19, 1902, in Payallup, Washington. Andrus graduated from the universities of the Redlands and California. He was head of the department of economics at Judson College in Rangoon from 1928 to 1940, dean of men from 1930 to 1933, and professor of economics at the University of Rangoon from 1936 to 1941. He was a senior research analyst with the U.S. Department of Commerce in Washington, D.C., from 1942 to 1944, and served with the Office of War Information in New Delhi in 1944–1945, with the U.S. State Department from 1945 to 1947, in the U.S. embassy in Rangoon from 1947 to 1949, and in Karachi in 1949–1950. He was deputy chief of the education division of the U.S. International Cooperation Administration from 1951 to 1956, assistant program officer of the U.S. Operations mission to Korea in 1958–1959, representative of the Agency for International Development in Iraq from 1960 to 1963, assistant director for technical service at Vientiane, Laos, from 1963 to 1965, and chief of the education division of the Mission to Laos from 1965 to 1967. He was a professor of economics at Eastern College (Pa.) from 1968 until his retirement in 1972. He wrote *Burmese Economic Life* (Stanford, 1948), and coauthored *Economics of Pakistan* (Stanford, 1958) and *Trade, Finance and Development in Pakistan* (Stanford, 1966). *Reference*: *AMWS*.

ANGELL, JAMES B(URRILL) (1829–1916). Educator and diplomat, born January 7, 1829, in Scituate, Rhode Island. Angell graduated from Brown University and studied in Europe. He was a professor of modern languages and literatures at Brown University from 1853 to 1860, editor of the *Providence Journal* (Rhode Island) from 1860 to 1866, and president of the University of Vermont from 1866 to 1871 and of the University of Michigan from 1871 to 1909. He was U.S. minister to China in 1880–1881 and acted as a commissioner in negotiating a new treaty. He was a member of the Canadian Fisheries Commission in 1887, chairman of the Deep Waterways Commission in 1896, and minister to Turkey in 1897–1898. He wrote *Reminiscences* (New York, 1912).

Died April 1, 1916, in Ann Arbor, Michigan. *References*: James B. Angell Papers, Michigan Historical Collections, University of Michigan Library, Ann Arbor, Mich.; *ACAB*; *Anderson*, ch. 6; *BDAE*; Susan A. Capie, "James B. Angell, Minister to China 1880–1881: His Mission and the Chinese Desire for Equal Treaty Rights," *Bulletin of the Institute of Modern History of the Academia Sinica* [Taiwan] 11 (1982): 273–314; *DAB*; *DADH*; *NCAB* 1:25; Esson M. Gale, ed., "President James Burrill Angell's Diary as United States Treaty Commissioner and Minister to China, 1880–1881," *Michigan Alumnus Review* 49 (1942–1943): 195–208; Wilfred B. Shaw, "James B. Angell," in *Michigan and the Cleveland Era*, ed. Earl D. Babst and Lewis G. Vander Velde (Ann Arbor, Mich., 1948), pp. 43–75; Shirley W. Smith, *James Burrill Angell: An American Influence* (Ann Arbor, Mich., 1954); and *WWWA*.

ANGLIN, LESLIE M. (1882–1942). Missionary, born February 23, 1882, in Stewart County, Georgia. Anglin went into business in Albany, Georgia. He was an independent missionary in China from 1910 until his death. He organized a mission in Taian, Shantung Province, in 1912, and the Home of Onesiphorus, a home for homeless children, in Taian in 1916. Died September 1942 in Taian, China. *Reference*: Harry J. Albus, *Twentieth-Century Onesiphorus: The Story of Leslie M. Anglin and the Home of Onesiphorus* (Grand Rapids, Mich., 1951).

AOYAMA GAKUIN UNIVERSITY. A private, coeducational university in Tokyo, founded by Robert S. Maclay* of the Methodist Episcopal Church as a girls' school in 1874, and renamed the Tokyo Anglo-Japanese School in 1883. It adopted its present name in 1894 and became a college in 1904. It merged in 1927 with another school affiliated with the Methodist Episcopal Church, and which had been established in 1878. It acquired university status in 1949. *References*: Ira J. Burnstein, *The American Movement to Develop Protestant Colleges for Men in Japan, 1868–1912* (Ann Arbor, Mich., 1967); and *KEJ*.

APPENZELLER, HENRY G(ERHARD) (1858–1902). Missionary, born February 6, 1858, in Souderton, Pennsylvania. Appenzeller graduated from Franklin and Marshall College (Lancaster, Pa.) and Drew Theological Seminary (Madison, N.J.), and was ordained in 1885. He was a missionary under the Board of the Foreign Missions of the Methodist Episcopal Church in Korea from 1885 until his death. In 1886 he founded the Paichai School for Boys in Seoul; he was its first president and later principal of the theological department, and was also pastor in Seoul and superintendent of the mission until 1892. He was coeditor of *Korean Repository* and editor of the *Korean Christian Advocate*, established the first book bindery in Korea, translated portions of the New Testament into Korean, and was a librarian of the Asia Society. He was involved in establishing the Christian Hospital, which later became Severance Hospital, Medical College, and Nurses' Training School (see Yonsei University). Lost at sea, June 11, 1902, in a collision south of Chemulp'o, Korea. His daughter, **ALICE R(EBECCA)**

APPENZELLER (1885–1950), an educational missionary, was born November 9, 1885, in Seoul, the first Western child to be born in Korea. She graduated from Wellesley College and Columbia University. She was an educational missionary under the Board of Foreign Missions of the Methodist Episcopal Church in Korea from 1916 until her death. She was president of Ewha College in Seoul from 1922 until 1939. She returned to teach at Ewha College after World War II. Died February 20, 1950, in Seoul. Henry Appenzeller's son, **HENRY D(ODGE) APPENZELLER** (1889–1953), a missionary educator, was born November 6, 1889, in Seoul. He graduated from Princeton and New York universities and Drew Theological Seminary. He was a missionary under the Board of Foreign Missions of the Methodist Episcopal Church in Korea from 1917 until 1953. He was principal of Paichai Boys' High School from 1918 until World War II, and treasurer of Chosen Christian College. He was a pastor among Koreans in Hawaii until 1949, and representative of the Church World Service in Seoul from 1951 to 1953. Died December 1, 1953, in Brooklyn, New York. *References*: Henry G. Appenzeller Papers, Union Theological Seminary Library, New York City; *CDCWM*; *DAB*; Daniel M. Davies, *The Life and Thought of Henry Gerhard Appenzeller (1858–1902)* (Lewiston, N.Y., 1988); *EM*; *EWM*; J. Earnest Fisher, *Pioneers of Modern Korea* (Seoul, 1977), chs. 1–2; *NCAB* 23:290; *NYT*, February 22, 1950; and Marion W. Reininger, "Alice of Korea," *Journal of the Lancaster County Historical Society* 74 (1970): 109–23.

ARLINGTON, LEWIS CHARLES (1859– ?). Government official, born October 2, 1859, in San Francisco. Arlington went to sea as a boy. He came to Tientsin, China, in 1879; served in the Chinese Navy from 1879 to 1885; from 1886 to 1905 in the Imperial Chinese Maritime Customs in Shanghai, Chinkiang, Foochow, Swatow, Canton, Kowloon, and Soochow; and from 1906 to 1929 in the Chinese Postal Service in Tientsin, Nanking, Changsha, and Canton. He served in the Directorate General of Posts in Peking from 1919 until 1926. He retired in 1929. He wrote *Through the Dragon's Eyes: Fifty Years' Experiences of a Foreigner in the Chinese Government Service* (New York, 1931).

ARMSTRONG, JAMES F. (1817–1873). Naval officer, born November 20, 1817, in New Jersey. He was appointed midshipman in the U.S. Navy in 1832. He served in the Mediterranean and West Indies squadrons. He later served in the East India Squadron. In 1856 he commanded the force that seized and destroyed the Barrier Forts in Canton (see Barrier Forts, Battle of).* He served in the Union Navy during the Civil War. He retired in 1864, was reinstated in 1871, served on the Pacific coast, and retired again in 1872. Died April 19, 1873, in New Haven, Connecticut. *References*: *ACAB*; David F. Long, "A Case for Intervention: Armstrong, Foote, and the Destruction of the Barrier Forts, Canton, China, 1856," in *New Aspects of Naval History*, ed. Craig L. Symonds, Merrill Bartlett, et al. (Annapolis, Md., 1981), pp. 220–37; and *NCAB* 4:315.

ARNDT, E(DUARD) L(OUIS) (1864–1929). Missionary, born in Bukowin, Pomerania, and brought to the United States in 1866. Arndt graduated from Concordia Seminary (St. Louis). He was pastor in East Saginaw, Michigan, from 1885 to 1896 and was a member of the faculty of Concordia College (St. Paul, Minn.) from 1896 until 1913. He established the China mission of the Lutheran Church–Missouri Synod in 1913, and served there until his death. Died April 17, 1929, in Hankow. *References*: Eduard L. Arndt Papers, Concordia Historical Institute, St. Louis, Mo.; Edward J. Arndt, "The Search for My Father's Grave," *Concordia Historical Institute Quarterly* 55 (1982): 101–6; *LC*; and Frieda O. Thode, "The Rev. E. L. Arndt," *Concordia Historical Institute Quarterly* 47 (1974): 90–95.

ARNOLD, JULEAN (HERBERT) (1876–1946). Consul, born July 19, 1876, in Sacramento, California. Arnold graduated from the University of California. He was the first student interpreter appointed by the U.S. government to the U.S. legation in Peking in 1902. He was consul general at Hankow in 1914, and commercial attaché in China from 1914 until his retirement in 1940. He was the American delegate to the China Tariff Review Commission in Shanghai in 1918, 1922, and 1926–1927. He organized the first party to ascend Mount Morrison in Formosa in 1907. He was a field secretary of the American Red Cross in China from 1918 to 1921 and founder of the American Chamber of Commerce in Shanghai in 1916. He wrote *China: A Commercial and Industrial Handbook* (Washington, D.C., 1926). Committed suicide July 21, 1946, in Washington, D.C. *References*: Julean H. Arnold Papers, Hoover Institution on War, Revolution and Peace, Stanford, Calif.; *NYT*, July 22, 1946; and *WWWA*.

ASHMORE, WILLIAM (1824–1909). Missionary, born December 25, 1824, in Putnam, Ohio. Ashmore graduated from Granville College (later Denison University) and Western Theological Seminary. He was a pastor in Hamilton, Ohio, in 1848–1849. He was a missionary under the American Baptist Missionary Union from 1849 until 1903. He was in charge of the Chinese department of the Siam mission in Bangkok, returned to the United States in 1858 because of ill health, and went back to China in 1861. He served in the South China mission in Swatow. In 1892 he established the Biblical Training School for men (which became Ashmore Seminary in 1905). He returned to the United States in 1903. Died April 21, 1909, in Wollaston, Massachusetts. *References*: William Ashmore Family Papers, University of Oregon Library, Eugene, Ore.; *DAB*; and *NCAB* 25:76.

ASIATIC SQUADRON. Established in 1865, it replaced the East India Squadron, protecting American interests and citizens in East Asia. Elements of the squadron frequented the treaty ports in China and a river patrol was established on the Yangtze. It participated in the Spanish-American War (see Manila Bay, Battle of*). It was later renamed the Asiatic Fleet. It was defeated in 1942, under the Japanese attacks in the Philippines and Dutch East Indies. *References*: Donald M. Bishop, "Navy Blue in Old Korea: The Asiatic Squadron and the American Legation, 1882–1897," *Journal of Social Sciences and Humanities* 42 (1975): 49–63; Edwin P. Hoyt, *The Lonely Ships: The Life and Death of the U.S. Asiatic Fleet* (New York, 1976); Robert E. Johnson, *Far China Station: The U.S. Navy in Asian Waters, 1800–1898* (Annapolis, Md., 1979); James M. Merrill, "The Asiatic Squadron, 1835–1907," *AN* 29 (1969): 106–17; and Stephen S. Roberts, "The Decline of the Overseas Station Fleets: The United States Asiatic Fleet and the Shanghai Crisis, 1932," *AN* 37 (1977): 185–202.

ASSEMBLIES OF GOD, GENERAL COUNCIL OF THE: FOREIGN MISSIONS DEPARTMENT. First missionaries went to Asian countries before the Assemblies of God was officially organized in 1914. Missionaries were sent to China in 1902, to India in 1907, to Japan in 1913, and to Pakistan in 1947. *References*: Assemblies of God Archives, Springfield, Mo.; Joyce W. Booze, *Into All the World: A History of Assemblies of God Foreign Missions* (Springfield, Mo., 1980); *EMCM*; Maynard L. Ketcham, *Pentecost in the Ganges Delta: Being an Account of the Birth and Development of the Assemblies of God Mission in Bengal, India* (n.p., 1945); Gary B. McGee, *"This Gospel . . . Shall Be Preached": A History and Theology of Assemblies and God Foreign Missions to 1959* (Springfield, Mo., 1986); William W. Menzies, *Anointed to Serve: The Story of the Assemblies of God* (Springfield, Mo., 1971); and Elizabeth A. G. Wilson, *Making Many Rich* (Springfield, Mo., 1955).

ASSOCIATION OF BAPTISTS FOR WORLD EVANGELISM, INC. Independent fundamental Baptist foreign missionary society founded in 1927 as the Association of Baptists for Evangelism in the Orient. The name was changed in 1939. It began missionary work in China in 1945, in the Philippines in 1949, in India in 1949 (closed by the government), in Hong Kong in 1951, in Japan in 1953, and in Pakistan in 1956. *Reference*: *EMCM*.

ASTREA. Ship of Salem, Massachusetts, owned by Elias Hackett Derby. It arrived in Manila Bay in 1796, pioneering the direct trade between the Philippine Islands and the United States. Nathaniel Bowdich (1773–1838) served as its supercargo. It returned to the Philippines in 1800. *Reference*: Thomas R. McHale and Mary C. McHale, eds., *Early American-Philippine Trade: The Journal of Nathaniel Bowdich in Manila, 1796* (New Haven, 1962).

ATCHESON, GEORGE, JR. (1896–1947). Diplomat, born October 20, 1896, in Denver, Colorado. Atcheson graduated from the University of California at Berkeley. He entered the foreign service in 1920 and was a student interpreter in Peiping, China; vice consul in Changsha, and in North Bay, Ontario, Canada; consul in Tientsin from 1927 to 1934; second secretary in the U.S. legation at Nanking in 1934–1935 and in the U.S. embassy from 1935 to 1939, and president of the administrative commission of the diplomatic quarter in Nanking in 1938–1939. He was assistant chief of the division of Far Eastern Affairs in the State Department from 1941 to 1943, counselor of embassy and chargé d'affaires at Chungking, China, from 1942 to 1945 and political advisor to the Supreme Commander for the Allied Powers (SCAP) in Japan from 1945 until his death, holding the personal rank of ambassador after 1947. Died August 16, 1947, in a plane crash at sea near Hawaii. *References*: Jon L. Boyes, "The Political Adviser (POLAD): The Role of the Diplomatic Adviser to Selected United States and North Atlantic Alliance Military Commanders," Ph.D. diss., University of Maryland, 1971, pp. 165–82; *NCAB* 36:416; and *WWWA*.

ATENEO DE MANILA UNIVERSITY. Established by the Jesuits in 1859. In 1921, Jesuits from the New York-Maryland Province replaced the Jesuits from Barcelona, Spain, as the administrators of the university. In 1958 the management passed to the Philippine Province of the Society of Jesus. *Reference*: *CE*.

ATKINSON, FRED (WASHINGTON) (1865–1941). Educator, born May 23, 1865, in Reading, Massachusetts. Atkinson graduated from the State Normal School (Bridgewater, Mass.) and Harvard University, studied in Germany and France, and graduated from the University of Leipzig. He was principal of a high school in Springfield, Massachusetts, from 1894 to 1900. He was the first general superintendent of public instruction of the Philippines from 1900 until 1903, organizing and administering the first public school system in the Philippines. He was the superintendent of schools in Newton, Massachusetts, in 1903, and president of the Polytechnic Institute of Brooklyn from 1904 until his retirement in 1925. He wrote *The Philippine Islands* (New York, 1905). Died October 21, 1941, in Tucson, Arizona. *References*: Glen A. May, *Social Engineering in the Philippines: The Aims, Execution, and Impact of American Colonial Policy, 1900–1913* (Westport, Conn., 1980), pp. 77–96; *NCAB* 34:30; *NYT*, October 22, 1941; and *WWWA*.

AUGUSTANA LUTHERAN CHURCH: BOARD OF FOREIGN MISSIONS. Founded in 1923. Its name was changed in 1956 to the Board of World Missions, and it merged in 1962 with other Lutheran churches to form the Board of World Missions of the Lutheran Church in America. It began missionary work in India in 1870, in China in 1905, in Borneo in 1948, in Taiwan in 1951, and in Japan in 1950. *References*: *EMCM*; George F. Hall, *The Missionary Spirit in the Augustana Church* (Rock Island, Ill., 1984); and S. Hjalmar Swanson, *Foundation for Tomorrow: A Century of Progress in Augustana World Missions* (Minneapolis, 1960).

AUGUSTINE HEARD AND COMPANY. Agency house in China, formed in 1840 by Augustine Heard, Sr., and Joseph Coolidge, who broke away from Russell and Company. It was dominated by the Heard family until its demise. Branches were set up in Hong Kong, Shanghai, and Foochow during the 1850s, and in 1855 the head office was moved from Canton to Hong Kong. The business was closed down in 1874. *References*: Heard Collection, Baker Library, Harvard University, Boston, Mass.; Stephen C. Lockwood, *Augustine Heard and Company, 1858–1862: American Merchants in China* (Cambridge, Mass., 1971); and Robert W. Lovett, "The Heard Collection and Its Story," *Business History Review*, 35 (1961): 567–73.

AVERY, BENJAMIN PARKE (1828–1875). Journalist and diplomat, born November 11, 1828, in New York City. Avery had no formal education and learned the trade of bank-note engraving. He followed the gold rush to California in 1849, was a druggist and a storekeeper, and started a weekly newspaper in North San Juan, Nevada County, in 1856. In 1861 he established the *Appeal* in Marysville, the first daily newspaper in California outside San Francisco. He was elected the state printer in 1861 and served until 1863. He was the editor of the *San Francisco Bulletin* from 1863 until 1873, and editor of *Overland Monthly* in 1874. He was U.S. minister to China in 1874–1875. He played an important role in calming China and Japan, which were then on the verge of war. Died November 8, 1875, in Peking, China. *References*: Benjamin Parke Avery Papers, Bancroft Library, University of California, Berkeley, Calif.; *Anderson*, ch. 4; *DAB*; Ernest R. May, "Benjamin Parke Avery, Including a Review of the Office of State Printer, 1850–72," *California Historical Society Quarterly* 30 (1951): 125–49; and *NCAB* 1:319.

AXLING, WILLIAM (1873–1963). Missionary, born August 16, 1873, in Omaha, Nebraska, and grew up in Oakland and Gothenburg, Nebraska. Axling graduated from the University of Nebraska and Rochester Theological Seminary. He was a missionary under the American Baptist Missionary Union in Japan from 1901 until 1955. He served in Sendai from 1901 to 1904, in Morioka from 1904 to 1906, and in Tokyo after 1906. He was in charge of Misaki Tabernacle and Fukagawa Christian Center in Tokyo, and secretary of the National Christian Council. He was interned by the Japanese from 1941 to 1943, and then returned to the United States. He returned to Japan from 1946 until 1955. Died February 24, 1963, in Los Angeles. He wrote *Japan at the Midcentury: Leaves from Life* (Tokyo, 1955). *References*: Leland D. Hine, *Axling: A Christian Presence in Japan* (Valley Forge, Pa., 1969); and Leland D. Hine, "William Axling and the War Years," *Japan Christian Quarterly* 33 (Fall 1967): 267–75.

AYERS, THOMAS WILBURN (1858–1954). Medical missionary, born December 22, 1858, in Ayersville, Georgia. Ayers graduated from the College of Physicians and Surgeons (Baltimore). He was medical missionary under the

Foreign Mission Board of the Southern Baptist Convention in China from 1900 to 1926. He served in Hwanghsien, Shantung Province, and erected the first hospital built by the Southern Baptists in a foreign country. He returned to the United States in 1926 because of his wife's ill health. He wrote *Healing and Missions* (Richmond, Va., 1930) about his activities. Died January 5, 1954, in Atlanta, Georgia. *References*: Ayers Family Papers, Z. Smith Reynolds Library, Wake Forest University, Winston-Salem, N.C.; and *ESB*.

B

BACHELER, OTIS ROBINSON (1817–1901). Medical missionary, born January 17, 1817, in Antrim, New Hampshire. He was a missionary under the Free Baptist Mission Society in India from 1840 to 1851, serving in Balasore, Orissa. He returned to the United States in 1851, but returned to India in 1863, bringing with him a printing press. He was principal of a Bible school in Midnapur, West Bengal, from 1886 until his retirement in 1893. Died January 1, 1901, in New Hampton, New Hampshire. *References*: *EM*; and Thomas A. Stacy, *Rev. Otis Robinson Bacheler, M.D., D.D., Fifty-Three Years Missionary to India* (Boston, 1904).

BACHRACH, EMIL [EMMANUEL] M. (1874–1937). Businessman, born July 4, 1874, in Russia, and came to the United States in 1889. Bachrach came to the Philippines in 1901 and engaged in business. He founded the American Store and engaged in import and export. In 1907 he brought the first automobile to the Philippines, went into the business of distributing American automobiles, and established Bachrach Motor Company. He was its president and general manager. He was also the leader in organizing the Philippine Aerial Taxi Company. Died September 28, 1937, in Manila. *References*: *EP* 4:455–56; *Gleeck/ Manila*; and *NYT*, September 29, 1937.

BACON, ALICE MABEL (1858–1918). Author, born February 26, 1858, in New Haven, Connecticut. She taught at Hampton Institute from 1883 to 1888. She was in Japan in 1888–1889 and taught English at Joshi Gakushuin, a school for daughters of the Japanese nobility (later Gakushuin University) in Tokyo. She was again in Japan from 1900 to 1902, assisted in founding the advanced Girls' English Institute (later Tsuda College), and taught at the Tokyo Women's Higher Normal School (later Ochanomizu Women's University). She wrote *Japanese Girls and Women* (Boston, 1891); *A Japanese Interior* (Boston, 1893); and *In the Land of the Gods: Some Stories of Japan* (Boston, 1905). Died May 2, 1918, in New Haven, Connecticut. *References*: *DAB*; *KEJ*; *NAW*; and *WWWA*.

BADLEY, BRENTON HAMLINE (1849–1891). Missionary, born April 27, 1849, in Monmouth, Indiana. Badley graduated from Simpson College (Indianola, Ia.) and Garrett Biblical Institute (Evanston, Ill.). He was a missionary under the Board of Foreign Missions of the Methodist Episcopal Church in India from 1872 until his death. He served in Lucknow, developed a boys' school there into the Lucknow Christian College (later Reid Christian College) in 1888, and was its first principal. He was editor of the first directory of mission work in India, *Indian Missionary Directory and Memorial Volume* (Lucknow, 1876), and three subsequent editions (1881, 1885, and 1891); wrote *Tulsipur Fair: Glimpses of Life in North India* (London, n.d.), and edited the *Kaukab-i-Hind* for five years. He was the first secretary of the India Sunday School Union, which he helped found in 1876. Died November 20, 1891, in Lucknow, India. *Reference*: *EWM*.

BADLEY, BRENTON THOBURN (1876–1949). Missionary, son of Brenton Hamline Badley,* born May 29, 1876, in Gonda, United Provinces, India. Badley attended Simpson College (Ia.), and Ohio Wesleyan and Columbia universities. He was a missionary under the Board of Foreign Missions of the Methodist Episcopal Church in India from 1900 until his death. He was a professor of English literature at Lucknow Christian College from 1900 to 1910, general secretary of Epworth League for India and Burma from 1910 to 1917, associate secretary of the Board of Foreign Missions of the Methodist Episcopal Church from 1917 to 1919, executive secretary of the Centenary Movement in India from 1919 to 1923, and editor of the *Indian Witness* after 1924. He was elected bishop of the Methodist Episcopal Church in 1924, serving in the Bombay area from 1924 to 1936 and in the Delhi area after 1936. He wrote *The Making of a Christian College, in India* (Calcutta, 1916); *India, Beloved of Heaven* (New York, 1918); *New Etchings of Old India* (New York, 1918); *Hindustan's Horizons* (Calcutta, 1923); *Indian Church Problems of Today* (Madras, 1930); *The Solitary Throne: Some Religious Beliefs of Mahatma Gandhi in the Light of Christ's Teachings* (Madras, 1931); *Visions and Victories in Hindustan: The Story of the Mission Stations of the Methodist Episcopal Church in Southern India* (Madras, 1931); and a biography of Francis Wesley Warne.* Died February 1, 1949, in Mirzapore, India. *References*: *EWM*; and *WWWA*.

BAILIE, JOSEPH (1860–1935). Agriculturist, born July 11, 1860, in Ballycloughan, Randalstown, County Antrim, Ireland. Bailie attended Marlborough Street Training College (County Cork), graduated from the Royal University of Ireland, and attended Assembly College (Belfast). He came to the United States in 1889, graduated from Union Theological Seminary, and was ordained in 1890. He was a missionary under the Board of Foreign Missions of the Presbyterian Church in the U.S.A. in China from 1891 until 1898, serving in Soochow. He resigned from the mission, was a professor at Imperial University in Peking from 1899 to 1901, and sold life insurance in Shanghai until 1910. He was a professor of mathematics at the University of Nanking after 1911. He was involved in colonization schemes in China and Manchuria from 1911 to 1918, organized the Colonization Association, and established "Bailie's Colonization Scheme" in 1911 to colonize Purple Mountain, near Nanking, as a colony to enable famine refugees to earn their own living through cultivation of waste lands. He later also established colonies in Lai'an in 1913 and in Jilin, in northeast China, in 1917. He was founder of the College of Agriculture and Forestry at the University of Nanking in 1914. He was involved in flood relief work in 1917–1918, and then in placing Chinese students in engineering and other establishments in the United States for practical training. He established the Bureau of Industrial Service in China in Nanking from 1919 to 1930 and in Mukden in 1931. He was involved in flood relief in Hankow in 1931–1932 and was advisor to the magistrate of Hohsien, Anhui, in 1934–1935. Committed suicide November 15, 1935, in Berkeley, California. *References*: Victoria W. Bailie, *Bailie's Activities in China: The Account of the Life and Work of Professor Joseph Bailie in and for China, 1890–1935* (Palo Alto, Calif., 1964); Randall E. Stross, *The Stubborn Earth: American Agriculturists on Chinese Soil, 1898–1937* (Berkeley, Calif., 1986), ch. 3; and *UnionTS*.

BAIN, H(ARRY) FOSTER (1872–1948). Mining engineer, born November 2, 1872, in Seymour, India. Bain graduated from Moore's Hill (later Evansville) College and the University of Chicago, and studied at Johns Hopkins University. He was assistant state geologist of Iowa from 1895 to 1900; manager of mines in Idaho Springs and Cripple Creek, Colorado, from 1901 to 1903; geologist with the U.S. Geological Survey from 1903 to 1906; director of the Illinois Geological Survey from 1906 to 1909; editor of the *Mining and Scientific Press* in San Francisco from 1909 to 1915, and editor of *Mining Magazine* in London in 1915–1916. He conducted explorations for coal in China and tin in Malaya in 1916–1917 and 1919–1920, was assistant director of the U.S. Bureau of Mines in 1918–1919 and its director from 1921 to 1924, was a consulting engineer in Argentina and Colombia and special assistant to the U.S. Secretary of the Interior assigned to the Bureau of Mines. He was a technical advisor on mines to the president of the Philippines from 1936 to 1941. He was interned by the Japanese at Santo Tomas from 1941 to 1943. He returned to the Philippines in 1948. He wrote *Ores and Industry in the Far East* (New York, 1933). Died March 9, 1948, in Manila. *References*: *IAB*; *NCAB* 36:291; *NYT*, March 10, 1948; and *WWWA*.

BAIRD, ESTHER E. (1861–1950). Missionary, born April 19, 1861, near Mesopotamia, Ohio. Baird graduated from Lake Erie College (Plainville, Ohio) and Friends Training School (Cleveland), and became a graduate nurse. She was a missionary under the Friends Missionary Society of Ohio Yearly Meeting in Bundelkhand, India, from 1892 until 1938, and served as superintendent of the mission from 1916 until 1938. She wrote *Adventuring with God* (Mt. Pleasant, Ohio, 1932). She returned to the United States in 1938. Died August 15, 1950, in Buron, Ohio. *Reference*: E. Anna Nixon, *A Century of Planting: A History of the American Friends Mission in India* (Canton, Ohio, 1985), part 2.

BAIRD, WILLIAM M(ARTYN) (1862–1931). Missionary, born June 16, 1862, near Charlestown, Clark County, Indiana. Baird graduated from Hanover College and McCormick Theological Seminary (Chicago). He was a missionary under the Board of Foreign Missions of the Presbyterian Church in the U.S.A. in Korea from 1891 to 1931. He served in Pusan from 1891 to 1895; in Taego in 1895–1896, where he started a boys' school (later the Keisung Academy and then Keimyong University); in Seoul in 1896–1897; and in P'yongyang from 1898 until 1916. In 1898 he began classes which developed into the Sungsil Academy, and later into Sungsil College and, in 1906, Union Christian College, and was president of Union Christian College from 1906 to 1916. He was later involved in revising the Korean translation of the Bible. Died November 28, 1931, in P'yongyang. His wife, **ANNIE (LAURIE) ADAMS BAIRD** (1864–1916) was born September 15, 1864, in Decatour County, Indiana. She attended Western College for Women, and Hanover and Washburn colleges. She wrote *Fifty Helps for the Study of the Korean Language* (n.p., 1897) and *Daybreak in Korea* (New York, 1909). Died June 9, 1916, in P'yongyang. *References*: William M. and Annie Adams Papers, Presbyterian Historical Society, Philadelphia; and Richard H. Baird, *William M. Baird of Korea: A Profile* (Oakland, Calif., 1968).

BAKER, CHARLES FULLER (1872–1927). Zoologist, born March 22, 1872, in Lansing, Michigan. Baker graduated from Michigan Agricultural College and studied at Stanford University. He was assistant to the zoologist and entomologist at Colorado Agricultural College from 1892 to 1897; zoologist at the Alabama Polytechnic Institute and entomologist at the Agricultural Experiment Station from 1897 to 1899; a biology teacher in a high school in St. Louis from 1900 to 1901; assistant professor of biology at Pomona College in 1903–1904; chief of the department of botany at the Cuban Experiment Station in Santiago de las Vegas, Cuba, from 1904 to 1907; curator of the Botanical Garden and Herbarium at the Museum Goeldi in Para, Brazil, in 1907–1908; and associate professor and professor of biology at Pomona College from 1908 to 1912. He was a professor of tropical agronomy at the college of agriculture of the University of the Philippines at Los Baños from 1912 to 1927, and dean of the college from 1919 until his death. Died July 21, 1927, in Manila. *References*: Arnold Mallis, *American Entomologists* (New Brunswick, N.J., 1971), pp. 221–25; *NCAB* 21:127; and *WWWA*.

BAKER, JAMES MARION (1861–1940). Diplomat, born August 18, 1861, in Lowndesville, South Carolina. Baker attended Wofford College (Spartansburg, S.C.). He was assistant librarian of the U.S. Senate from 1893 until 1913, secretary of the U.S. Senate from 1913 to 1919, and deputy commissioner of the Internal Revenue Bureau in the U.S. Treasury Department from 1919 to 1921. He practiced law in Washington, D.C., from 1921 to 1931. He was U.S. minister to Siam from 1930 to 1937, and negotiated the revision of the 1920 treaty of commerce and friendship. He resigned because of ill health. Died November 21, 1940, in Lowndesville, South Carolina. *References*: *DADH*; *NYT*, November 22, 1940; and *WWWA*.

BAKER, JOHN EARL (1880–1957). Engineer and association official, born August 23, 1880, in Eagle, Wisconsin. Baker graduated from Whitewater (Wis.) Normal School and the University of Wisconsin, and attended the law department of George Washington University. He was a statistician with the U.S. Bureau of the Census, the Interstate Commerce Commission, the Brotherhood of Locomotive Firemen and Engineers, and the Southern Pacific Company. He served as an advisor on railway development to the Chinese Ministry of Communication from 1916 to 1926. He was director of the American Red Cross China Famine Relief in 1920–1921. He also served as the chief advisor to the Nationalist Ministry of Railways in 1930–1931. He was director of relief operations of the China International Famine Relief Committee in 1930, manager of the Chinese-American Wheat Syndicate of the Ministry of Finance from 1933 to 1935, executive secretary of the China International Relief Committee from 1937 to 1940, director of the Shanghai Relief Committee from 1937 to 1939, director of the American Red Cross in China in 1940–1941, and inspector general of the Yunnan-Burma Road during World War II. He was the chief American member of the Joint Rural Reconstruction Commission, which undertook a program of building rural irrigation and flood control facilities in Southwest China and later in Taiwan. He wrote *Explaining China* (New York, 1927). Died July 27, 1957, in Mill Valley, California. *References*: John Earl Baker, "Fighting China's Famines" (1943), Ms., University of Wisconsin Library, Madison, Wis.; Alice Baker, "The Measure of a Man: The Biography of John Earl Baker," Ms., State Historical Society of Wisconsin, Madison, Wis.; *NYT*, July 28, 1957; and *WWWA*.

BALDWIN, CHARLES FRANKLIN (1902–   ). Diplomat, born January 21, 1902, in Zanesville, Ohio. Baldwin graduated from the Georgetown University School of Foreign Service. He joined the U.S. Foreign Commerce Service in 1927, and was assistant trade commissioner and then trade commissioner in Sidney, Australia, from 1927 to 1930. He later served in the U.S. Department of Commerce and in the Department of the Navy during World War II, and entered the foreign service in 1945. He was a commercial attaché in Santiago, Chile, in 1945–1946; counselor of embassy for economic affairs in Oslo from

1946 to 1948; political advisor in Trieste in 1948–1949; counselor of embassy for economic affairs in London in 1950–1951; consul general in Singapore in 1952–1953; and deputy assistant secretary for Far Eastern economic affairs in 1954–1955. He retired in 1955. Recalled in 1961, he served as ambassador to the Federation of Malaysia from 1961 to 1964 and diplomat-in-residence in the University of Virginia from 1964 to 1970. He wrote *An Ambassador's Journey: An Exploration of People and Culture* (Lanham, Md., 1984). *Reference*: WWA.

BALDWIN, FRANK D(WIGHT) (1842–1923). Army officer, born June 26, 1842, in Manchester, Washtenaw County, Michigan. Baldwin attended Hillsdale College (Mich.). He served in the Union Army during the Civil War. He was commissioned a second lieutenant of infantry in the regular army in 1866 and served in the West. He served in the Spanish-American War in the Philippines and then in the Philippine-American War. He was commander of the Fourth Infantry regiment and later of the Twenty-Seventh Infantry and of the Lake Lanao expedition during the Moro Wars. He was involved in military operations in Mindanao, and was commander of the Department of the Visayas in 1902–1903. He returned to the United States in 1903, was commander of the Department of Colorado and then of the Southwest Division until his retirement with the rank of brigadier general in 1906. He was adjutant general of Colorado from 1917 to 1919. Died April 12, 1923, in Denver, Colorado. *References*: *NCAB* 14:340; and *NYT*, April 24, 1923.

BALDWIN, STEPHEN LIVINGSTON (1835–1902). Missionary, born January 11, 1835, in Somerville, New Jersey. He was a missionary under the Board of Foreign Missions of the Methodist Episcopal Church in Foochow, Fukien Province, China, from 1858 to 1861, when he returned to the United States because of his wife's ill health. He returned to Foochow in 1862 and served until 1882 when he resigned because of ill health. He was superintendent of the mission after 1873, founded *The Chinese Recorder* in 1869, and was its editor until 1882. He held later pastorates in several locations in New York State and was recording secretary of missions from 1888 until his death. Died July 28, 1902, in Brooklyn, New York. *References*: *EM*; and *EWM*.

BALESTIER, JOSEPH B. (fl. 1785–1852). Consul. Balestier was a temporary resident at St. Thomas, Danish West Indies, in 1822, and a consular commercial agent at Guayama, Porto Rico, in 1831. He was a consul in Rhio (Bintan), Dutch East Indies, residing in Singapore, in 1834–1835, and consul in Singapore from 1836 to 1852, when he resigned to devote his time to business. From 1849 to 1851, he was also special agent to Brunei, and in 1850 he was sent to Bangkok as a special envoy to negotiate a new commercial treaty with the government of Siam; the attempt was unsuccessful. *Reference*: Sharon Ahmat, "Joseph B. Balestier, the First American Consul in Singapore, 1833–1852," *JMBRAS* 39, pt. 2 (December 1966): 108–22.

BALL, DYER (1796–1866). Physician, born June 3, 1796, in West Boylston, Massachusetts. Ball attended Yale University, graduated from Union College, and attended Andover Theological Seminary. He graduated from Union Theological Seminary and the medical institution at Charleston, and was ordained in 1831. He was a missionary under the American Board of Commissioners for Foreign Missions (ABCFM) at Singapore from 1838 to 1841, in Macao from 1841 to 1843, in Hong Kong from 1843 to 1845, in Canton from 1845 until 1854, and again in Macao from 1857 until his death. He published a Chinese almanac for many years. Died March 27, 1866, in Canton, China. *References*: *ACAB*; *EM*; and *LC*.

BALLAGH, JAMES HAMILTON (1832–1920). Missionary, born September 7, 1832, in Hobart, New York. Ballagh graduated from Rutgers University and New Brunswick Theological Seminary, and was ordained in 1860. He served in Japan as a missionary under the Board of Foreign Missions of the Reformed Church in America from 1861 to 1920. He taught English and then founded a private school, called Ballagh School. He organized the first Protestant church in Japan in Yokohama in 1872. Died January 29, 1920, in Richmond, Virginia. *References*: *HDRCA*; and *JBEWW*.

BALLANTINE, HENRY (1813–1865). Missionary, born March 5, 1813, in Schodack, New York. Ballantine attended Ohio University, Princeton and Union (Virginia) theological seminaries, graduated from Andover Theological Seminary, and was ordained in 1835. He was a missionary under the American Board of Commissioners for Foreign Missions (ABCFM) in India after 1835. He was stationed at Ahmednagar from 1837 until his death. He translated many books into Marathi. Died November 9, 1865, off Cape St. Vincent, Portugal, on his way to the United States. *References*: *AndoverTS*; *EM*; and *LC*.

BALLANTINE, HENRY (1846–1914). Consul, born November 16, 1846, in Ahmednagar, India, to American parents. Ballantine graduated from Amherst College. He was a merchant in Bombay, India, from 1870 until 1872, and in New York City from 1872 until 1891. He was a consul in Bombay from 1891 to 1896, and later worked as a claims adjuster for an insurance company. In private business, he maintained offices in Bombay, Calcutta, and other cities in India, until his death. He wrote *On India's Frontier; or Nepal, the Gurkha's Mysterious Land* (New York, 1895). Died October 30, 1914, in Seattle, Washington. *Reference*: *Amherst*.

BANCROFT, EDGAR ADDISON (1857–1925). Lawyer and diplomat, born November 20, 1857, in Galesburg, Illinois. Bancroft graduated from Knox College and Columbia Law School. He practiced law in Galesburg from 1884 to 1892 and in Chicago after 1892; was a solicitor for the Atcheson, Topeka and Santa Fe Railroad Company from 1892 to 1895; was vice president and general solicitor for the Chicago and Western Indiana Railroad Company and the Belt Railway Company from 1894 to 1904; and was general counsel of International Harvester Company from 1907 to 1920. He was the U.S. ambassador to Japan in 1924–1925. Although anti-American sentiment was high due to the passage of the Immigration Act of 1924, which was used to bar Japanese from immigrating to the United States, he won over many Japanese citizens with his warm personality. Died July 28, 1925, in Karuizawa, Japan. *References*: Edgar Addison Bancroft Papers, Knox College Library, Galesburg, Ill.; *DAB*; *DADH*; *KEJ*; *NCAB* 14:373; *NYT*, July 29, 1925; and *WWWA*.

BANDHOLTZ, HARRY H(ILL) (1864–1925). Army officer, born December 18, 1864, in Constantine, Michigan. Bandholtz graduated from the United States Military Academy in 1890, and was commissioned second lieutenant. He served in the Spanish-American and the Philippine-American wars. He was governor of Tayabas Province in 1902–1903, assistant chief of the Philippine Constabulary from 1903 to 1907, and commanded the district of Southern Luzon and the district of Central Luzon after 1905. He was chief of the Philippine Constabulary from 1907 to 1913. He served later on the Mexican border, and was the American representative on the Interallied Military Mission to Hungary in 1915. With the U.S. Army after 1915, he served as provost marshall general with the American Expeditionary Forces in France in 1918–1919, and commanded the District of Washington after 1921. Died May 7, 1925, in Constantine, Michigan. *References*: Harry H. Bandholtz Papers, Bentley Historical Library, University of Michigan, Ann Arbor; *ACAB*; Michael Cullinane, "Quezon and Harry Bandholtz," *BAHC* 9 (January-March 1981): 79–90, 99–101; *Elarth*; *NCAB* 19:434; *NYT*, May 8, 1925; and *WWWA*.

BARBOUR, GEORGE B(ROWN) (1890–1977). Geologist and educator, born August 22, 1890, in Scotland. Barbour graduated from Edinburgh University and the University of Cambridge. He took part in several geological expeditions in China, and was associated with the discovery of the Peking Man. He was a professor of geology at the University of Cincinnati and dean of the College of Art from 1938 to 1958. He retired in 1960. He wrote *The Geology of the Kalgan Area* (Peking, 1929); *Physiographic History of the Yangtze* (Peiping, 1935); *In the Field with Teilhard de Chardin* (New York, 1965), and *In China When . . .* (Cincinnati, 1975). Died July 11, 1977, in Cincinnati, Ohio. *References*: George B. Barbour Papers, Hoover Institution on War, Revolution and Peace, Stanford, Calif.; *CA*; and *NYT*, July 13, 1977.

BARNETT, A(RTHUR) DOAK (1921–   ). Journalist, son of Eugene Epperson Barnett, born October 8, 1921, in Shanghai, China. Barnett graduated from Yale University. He served in the U.S. Marine Corps during World War II. He was a correspondent for the *Chicago Daily News* from 1947 to 1949, and 1952 to 1955; a consul and public affairs officer in Hong Kong in 1951–1952;

and associate of the American Universities Field Staff in Hong Kong from 1953 to 1955. He was a program associate of the Ford Foundation from 1959 to 1961, a professor of political science at Columbia University from 1961 to 1969, a senior fellow at Brookings Institution from 1969 to 1972, and a professor of Chinese studies at the School of Advanced International Studies of Johns Hopkins University after 1982. He wrote *Communist Economic Strategy: The Rise of Mainland China* (Washington, D.C., 1959); *Communist China and Asia: Challenge to American Policy* (New York, 1960); *Communist China in Perspective* (New York, 1962); *Communist China: The Early Years 1949–55* (New York, 1964); *Cadres, Bureaucracy and Political Power in Communist China* (New York, 1967); *China after Mao* (Princeton, N.J., 1967); *Uncertain Passage: China's Transition to the Post-Mao Era* (Washington, D.C., 1974); *China and the Major Powers in East Asia* (Washington, D.C., 1977); *China Policy, Old Problems and New Challenges* (Washington, D.C., 1977); *China and the World Food System* (Washington, D.C., 1979); *China's Economy in Global Perspective* (Washington, D.C., 1981); and *The Making of Foreign Policy in China* (Boulder, Colo., 1985). He edited *Communist Strategies in Asia: A Comparative Analysis of Governments and Parties* (New York, 1963), and *Chinese Communist Politics in Action* (Seattle, Wash., 1969), and was coeditor of *The United States and China: The Next Decade* (New York, 1970). *References*: A. Doak Barnett Papers, Columbia University Libraries, New York City; *CA*; and *WWA*.

BARNETT, EUGENE E(PPERSON) (1888–1970). Association official, born February 21, 1888, in Leesburg, Florida. Barnett graduated from Emory University and studied at Vanderbilt University. He joined the staff of the Young Men's Christian Society (YMCA) in 1908, and was a student secretary at the University of North Carolina from 1908 to 1910. He went to China in 1910, organized the YMCA in Hangchow, and was its general secretary until 1921. He served as national student secretary of the YMCA in China, with headquarters in Shanghai, until 1936. He was also the associate general secretary of the National Committee and senior secretary of the International Committee of the YMCA for China, as well as executive secretary of the International Committee of the YMCA for the United States and Canada in New York City, from 1936 until 1941. He was the general secretary of the National Council of the YMCA of the United States in New York City from 1941 until his retirement in 1953, and a member of the executive committee of the World Council of the YMCA from 1936 to 1953. Died August 7, 1970, in Arlington, Virginia. *References*: Eugene E. Barnett, *As I Look Back: Recollections of Growing Up in America's Southland and of Twenty-Six Years in Pre-Communist China, 1888–1936* (Arlington, Va., 1964); Eugene E. Barnett Papers, Columbia University Libraries, New York City; *NCAB* 55:374; and *WWWA*.

BARRETT, DAVID D(EAN) (1892–1977). Army officer, born in Central City, Colorado. Barrett graduated from the University of Colorado. He served in the U.S. Army from 1917 until 1952. He was an infantry officer in the Philippines from 1920 to 1924, and an assistant military attaché for language training in Peking from 1924 to 1928. He served with the Fifteenth Infantry Regiment in Tientsin from 1931 to 1934 as a regimental intelligence staff officer. He was an assistant military attaché in the U.S. legation in Peking in 1936–1937, in Hankow from 1937 to 1939, and in Chungking from 1939 to 1943, and was promoted to military attaché in 1942–1943. He was the commander of the first U.S. Army Observer Group to Yenan (see Dixie Mission*) in 1944. He was again an assistant military attaché in China from 1946 to 1948 and a military attaché in Taiwan from 1950 to 1952. He retired with the rank of colonel in 1952. He returned to the United States in 1954 and settled in San Francisco. He wrote *Dixie Mission: The United States Army Observer Group in Yenan, 1944* (Berkeley, Calif., 1970). Died February 3, 1977, in the Presidio of San Francisco, California. *References*: David D. Barrett Papers, Hoover Institution on War, Revolution and Peace, Stanford, Calif.; and John N. Hart, *The Making of an Army "Old China Hand": A Memoir of Colonel David D. Barrett* (Berkeley, Calif., 1985).

BARRETT, JOHN (1866–1938). Diplomat, born November 28, 1866, in Grafton, Vermont. Barrett graduated from Dartmouth College. He worked for several Pacific coast newspapers from 1889 to 1894. He was U.S. minister to Siam from 1894 to 1898, and advocated increased American commercial expansion in East Asia. He was a war correspondent in Manila during the Spanish-American War and served as an advisor to Admiral George Dewey.* He was a minister to Argentina in 1903–1904, to Panama in 1904–1905, and to Colombia in 1905–1906; he was director general of the Pan-American Union from 1907 to 1920. Died October 17, 1938, in Bellows Falls, Vermont. *References*: John Barrett Papers, Manuscript Division, Library of Congress; *DAB S2*; *DADH*; *NYT*, October 18, 1938; Salvatore Prisco III, *John Barrett, Progressive Era Diplomat: A Study of a Commercial Expansionist, 1887–1920* (University, Ala., 1973); Salvatore Prisco III, "A Vermonter in Siam: How John Barrett Began His Diplomatic Career," *Vermont History* 37 (1969): 83–93; and *WWWA*.

BARRETT, ROBERT LEMOYNE (1871–1969). Geographer, born May 28, 1871, in Chicago. Barrett graduated from Harvard University. He traveled to Russia and Siberia in 1902 and to Central Asia in 1903. With Ellsworth Huntington, he traveled in Central Asia and the Himalayas in 1905–1906. He traveled in Abyssinia in 1909, made a safari in the Himalayas in 1923–1924, and traveled in the Canary Islands in 1926 and in Patagonia in 1926–1927. He wrote *The Himalayan Letters of Gypsy Davy and Lady Ba* (Cambridge, 1927) and *Cloudtop Mosaics* (Cambridge, 1932). Died March 5, 1969, in La Crescenta, California. *Reference*: Geoffrey J. Martin, "Robert Lemoyne Barrett, 1871–1969; Last of the Founding Fathers of the Association of American Geographers," *Professional Geographer* 24 (February 1972): 29–31.

BARRIER FORTS, BATTLE OF (1856). When the USS *Portsmouth*, commanded by Commander Andrew H. Foote,* was fired upon by the barrier ports below Canton in 1856, the Americans attacked the Chinese forts in the first American use of force against China. Seven American sailors and marines were killed. *References*: E. N. McClellan, "The Capture of the Barrier Forts in the Canton River, China," *Marine Corps Gazette* 5 (September 1920): 262–76; and Julius W. Pratt, "Our First 'War' in China: The Diary of William Henry Powell, 1856," *American Historical Review* 53 (1948): 776–86.

BARROWS, DAVID PRESCOTT (1873–1954). Educator, born June 27, 1873, in Chicago. Barrows graduated from Pomona (Calif.) College and the universities of California and Chicago. He went to the Philippines in 1900, was the superintendent of city schools in Manila in 1900, the chief of the Bureau of Non-Christian Tribes from 1901 to 1903, and the general superintendent of education in the Philippines from 1903 until 1909. He wrote *A History of the Philippines* (Yonkers-on-Hudson, N.Y., 1903) and *A Decade of American Government in the Philippines* (Yonkers-on-Hudson, N.Y., 1915). He returned to the United States in 1909, was a professor of education and dean of the graduate school of the University of California from 1909 to 1911. He taught there as professor of political science from 1911 to 1913; he was dean of the faculty from 1913 until 1919, and became president of the University of California from 1919 to 1923. During World War I, he was a member of the Commission for the Relief of Belgium, and served in the U.S. Army in the Philippines and Siberia. In 1918 he assisted in the organization of the American forces to be sent to Siberia to take part in the operations designed to extricate the Czechoslovakian army in Russia, and served as the intelligence officer for those forces until 1919. Died September 5, 1954, in Lafayette, California. *References*: "Memoirs of David P. Barrows, 1873–1954" (1954), Ms., University of California Archives, Berkeley; David P. Barrows Papers, Bancroft Library, University of California, Berkeley; *ACAB*; Kenton J. Clymer, "Humanitarian Imperialism: David Prescott Barrows and the White Man's Burden in the Philippines," *PHR* 45 (1976): 495–518; *DAB S5*; Glenn A. May, *Social Engineering in the Philippines: The Aims, Execution, and Impact of American Colonial Policy, 1900–1913* (Westport, Conn., 1980), pp. 97–112; *NCAB* 52:154; Edward Norbeck, "David P. Barrows' Notes on Philippine Ethnology," *Journal of East Asiatic Studies* 5, no. 3 (July 1956): 229–54; *NYT*, September 6, 1954; and *WWWA*.

BARTLETT, HARLEY H(ARRIS) (1886–1960). Botanist, born March 9, 1886, in Anaconda, Montana. Bartlett graduated from Harvard University. He was an assistant in the Gray Herbarium at Harvard University from 1905 to 1908, a chemical biologist with the Bureau of Plant Industry of the U.S. Department of Agriculture from 1909 to 1915, and a professor of botany at the University of Michigan and director of their Botanical Garden from 1915 until his retirement in 1956. He made an expedition to Sumatra in 1918–1919 as a botanist for the United States Rubber Company, was a member of a scientific expedition to Sumatra and Formosa in 1926–1927, and served as an agent of the Office of Rubber Investigation of the U.S. Department of Agriculture in the Philippines and Haiti in 1940–1941. He also made several other scientific and professional trips to the Philippines. He wrote *The Sacred Edifices of the Batak of Sumatra* (Ann Arbor, Mich., 1934). *The Labors of the Datoe and Other Essays on the Batak of Asahan (North Sumatra)* (Ann Arbor, Mich., 1973) was published posthumously. Died February 21, 1960, in Ann Arbor, Michigan. *References*: Harley H. Bartlett Papers, Bentley Historical Library, University of Michigan, Ann Arbor, Mich.; Kenneth L. Jones, ed., *The Harley Harris Bartlett Diaries: 1926–1959* (Ann Arbor, Mich., 1975); Edward G. Voss, ''Harley Harris Bartlett,'' *Bulletin of the Torrey Botanical Club* 88 (January 1961): 47–56; and *WWWA*.

BARTLETT, MURRAY (1871–1949). Educator, born March 29, 1871, in Poughkeepsie, New York. Bartlett graduated from Harvard University and General Theological Seminary (New York City), and was ordained in 1897. He held pastorates in New York City and Rochester, New York, from 1896 until 1908. He was dean of the Protestant Episcopal Cathedral in Manila from 1908 to 1911. He was the organizer and first president of the University of the Philippines from 1911 to 1915. He served as a chaplain during World War I. He was the president of Hobart and William Smith colleges (Geneva, N.Y.) from 1919 until his retirement in 1936. Died November 13, 1949, in Canandaigua, New York. *References*: Oscar M. Alfonso, ed. *University of the Philippines: The First 75 Years (1908–1983)* (Quezon City, 1985), ch. 1; *NCAB* 38:317; *NYT*, November 14, 1949; and *WWWA*.

BARTON, FRED (1889–1967). Cowboy, born April 19, 1889, in Miles City, Montana. Barton became a cowboy at sixteen. He went to Siberia in 1911 to advise the Russians on the horse range business and to locate a place in Siberia for a horse ranch, a plan never implemented. He went to China in 1912, and in 1920, on behalf of Yen Hsi-shan, warlord of Shansi Province, he operated a horse ranch in northern China and established a model ranch covering 250,000 acres near Taiyuan. He imported horses from the United States to stock the ranch and hired a group of cowboys from Miles City. He resigned in 1921 but remained on as manager of the Shansi government Livestock Bureau, and continued to spend part of each year in China, overseeing the horse ranch and carrying on various business enterprises until 1937. After 1937, he lived in Los Angeles, and in the 1940s he owned and operated a ranch in New Mexico. Died in Los Angeles in 1967. *Reference*: Ralph Miracle, ''Asian Adventures of a Cowboy from Montana—Fred Barton,'' *Montana* 27 (1977): 44–53.

BARTON, ROY FRANKLIN (1883–1947). Anthropologist, of Pleasant Hill, Pike County, Illinois. Barton attended Rush Medical College and graduated from State Normal School (later Illinois State University, Normal, Ill.). He taught school in northern Illinois until 1906. He went to the Philippines in 1906 as a supervising teacher, serving among the Ifugao. He returned to the United States in 1916, studied dentistry at the University of California and then practiced dentistry in various places in California. He returned to the Philippines, and carried out field work among the Ifugao. He went to the Soviet Union in 1930 and was associated with the Institute of Ethnology of the Russian Academy of Science in Leningrad until 1940. He was also curator of the departments of India and Indonesia in the Museum of Anthropology and Ethnology of the academy from 1938 to 1940. He returned to the Philippines in 1940, and was interned by the Japanese, first at Baguio camp and then at Los Baños, during World War II. He returned to the United States in 1945. He wrote *Ifugao Law* (Berkeley, Calif., 1919); *Ifugao Economics* (Berkeley, Calif., 1922); *The Half-Way Sun: Life among the Head-hunters of the Philippines* (New York, 1930); *Philippine Pagans: The Autobiographies of Three Infugaos* (London, 1938); and *The Religion of the Ifugaos* (Menasha, Wis., 1946). *The Kalingas, Their Institutions and Custom Law* (Chicago, 1949) was published posthumously. Died April 19, 1947, in Chicago. *References*: *AA* 51 (1949): 91–95; *NYT*, April 28, 1947; and M. V. Staniukovich, "Neobychnaia Biografiia (Roi Franklin Barton, 1883–1947)," *Sovetskaia Etnografiia* 1979, no. 1: 76–83.

BASHFORD, JAMES W(HITFORD) (1849–1919). Missionary, born May 29, 1849, in Fayette, Wisconsin. Bashford graduated from the University of Wisconsin and the School of Theology of Boston University, and was ordained in 1878. He held pastorates in Jamaica Plain and Auburndale, Massachusetts; Portland, Maine; and Buffalo, New York, from 1878 until 1889, and was president of Ohio Wesleyan University from 1889 to 1904. He was elected bishop of the Methodist Episcopal Church in 1904, and served in China until 1915. In 1912 he urged President William Howard Taft to recognize the Chinese Republic, and persuaded the U.S. government to block Japan's Twenty-One Demands upon China in 1915 and to support China's national integrity. He returned to the United States in 1915. He wrote *The Awakening of China* (New York, 1906); *China and Methodism* (Cincinnati, 1907); and *China: An Interpretation* (New York, 1916). Died March 18, 1919, in Pasadena, California. *References*: James W. Bashford, "Diary," Ms., Union Theological Seminary Library, New York City; *CDCWM*; *DAB*; Jerry Israel, "The Missionary Catalyst: Bishop James W. Bashford and the Social Gospel in China," *Methodist History* 14 (1975): 24–43; *NCAB* 4:160; *NYT*, January 27, 1947; and *WWWA*.

BASIL, GEORGE CHESTER (1902–1954). Physician, born September 28, 1902, in Annapolis, Maryland. Basil attended St. John's College (Annapolis) and graduated from the University of Maryland School of Pharmacy and Medical

School. He was the superintendent of the Syracuse-in-China Hospital in Chung-king from 1929 to 1932. He did research work on foot and mouth disease and intestinal parasites, and wrote (with Elizabeth F. Lewis) *Test Tubes and Dragon Scales* (Shanghai, 1940). He returned to the United States in 1932 and practiced medicine in Annapolis, Maryland. Died December 5, 1954, in Annapolis. *Reference*: *NCAB* 46:105.

BATES, JOHN C(OALTER) (1842–1919). Army officer, born August 26, 1842, in St. Charles County, Missouri. Bates attended Washington University (St. Louis). He served in the Union Army during the Civil War and continued in the regular army, serving in the Northwest and along the Mexican border. He served in the Spanish-American War in Cuba. He came to the Philippines in 1899, and negotiated the so-called Bates Treaty with the Sultan of Sulu by which the sultan acknowledged the sovereignty of the United States. He was the U.S. Army chief of staff in 1906, and retired with the rank of lieutenant general the same year. Died February 4, 1919, in San Diego, California. *References*: *DAB*; *NCAB* 14:34; and *WWWA*.

BATES, M(INER) SEARLE (1897–1978). Missionary, born May 28, 1897, in Newark, Ohio. Bates graduated from Hiram College and Oxford and Yale universities. He served the International Young Men's Christian Association (YMCA) in India and Mesopotamia during World War I. He was a missionary under the United Christian Missionary Society in China from 1920 until 1950, and also a professor of history at the University of Nanking. He remained in Nanking when the university was removed to Chengtu, west China, and was in charge of maintenance of university activities and properties from 1937 to 1941. He was an organizing member of the Nanking International Safety Zone committee from 1937 to 1941, and chairman of the Nanking International Relief Committee from 1939 to 1941. He was a professor of missions at Union Theological Seminary (New York City) from 1950 to 1965. Died October 28, 1978, near Alpine, New Jersey. *References*: M. Searle Bates Papers, Divinity School Library, Yale University, New Haven, Conn.; Melville O. Williams, Cynthia McLean, and Martha L. Smalley, *Gleanings from the Manuscripts of M. Searle Bates: The Protestant Endeavor in Chinese Society, 1890–1950* (New York, 1984); *They Went to China: Biographies of Missionaries of the Disciples of Christ* (Indianapolis, 1948).

BATSON, MATTHEW A. (1867?–1917). Army officer, born in Illinois and grew up in Missouri. Batson attended Southern Illinois University. He enlisted in the U.S. Army in 1888 and was commissioned in 1891 in the Ninth Cavalry Regiment. He served in the Spanish-American War in Cuba and came to the Philippines in 1899. He organized the first companies of Filipino scouts the same year. He was wounded in 1899, returned to the United States in 1901, and retired in 1902. Died January 15, 1917. *References*: Matthew A. Batson Papers, U.S.

Army Military History Institute, Carlisle Barracks, Pa.; Edward M. Coffman, "Batson of the Philippine Scouts," *Parameters* 7, no. 3 (1977): 68–72.

BATTICOTA SEMINARY. *See* JAFFNA COLLEGE

BAWDEN, SAMUEL D(AY) (1868–1946). Missionary, born December 2, 1868, in Elyria, Ohio. Bawden graduated from the University of Illinois and attended Rochester Theological Seminary. He was the chaplain in the state industrial school in Rochester, New York, from 1895 to 1904. He was a missionary under the American Baptist Foreign Missionary Society in India from 1904 until his retirement in 1938. He was the manager of an industrial experiment station at Ongole from 1907 to 1912, and at the Erukala industrial settlement in Kavalli from 1914 to 1933; he was treasurer of the South India Mission and a pastor in Madras from 1933 to 1938. Died August 3, 1946, in Kent, Ohio. *Reference*: *WWWA*.

BEALS, ALAN ROBIN (1928–   ). Anthropologist, born January 24, 1928, in Oakland, California. Beals graduated from the universities of California at Los Angeles and Berkeley. He carried out fieldwork in India in 1953–1954 and from 1958 to 1960, and wrote *Village India: Studies in the Little Community* (Chicago, 1955); *Gopalpur, a South Indian Village* (New York, 1965); and an account of his fieldwork in "Gopalpur, 1958–1960," in *Being an Anthropologist: Fieldwork in Eleven Countries*, ed. George D. Spindler (New York, 1970). He was the coauthor of *Field Guide to India* (Washington, D.C., 1960). He was an assistant professor of anthropology at Stanford University from 1956 to 1963, associate professor there from 1963 to 1968, and professor of anthropology at the University of California at Riverside after 1968. *References*: *AMWS*; *WWA*; and *WWW*.

BEAN, ROBERT BENNETT (1874–1944). Anthropologist, born March 24, 1874, at Gala, Botetourt County, Virginia. Bean graduated from the Virginia Polytechnic Institute and Johns Hopkins Medical School. He was an instructor of anatomy at the University of Michigan from 1905 to 1907. He was an assistant professor and director of the anatomical laboratory in the Philippine Medical School in Manila from 1907 to 1910, and wrote *The Racial Anatomy of the Philippine Islanders* (New York, 1910). He was associate professor and later professor of anatomy at Tulane University from 1910 to 1916, and professor of anatomy at the University of Virginia from 1916 until his retirement in 1942. Died August 27, 1944, in Staunton, Virginia. *References*: *AA* 48 (1946): 70–74; and *NYT*, September 3, 1944.

BEARD, CHARLES A(USTIN) (1874–1948). Historian and political scientist, born November 27, 1874, near Knightstown, Indiana. Beard graduated from Depaw and Columbia universities, and studied at Oxford and Cornell universities.

He taught history, public law, and politics at Columbia University from 1904 to 1917. He resigned in 1917 and did not hold any other academic position. He was invited in 1922 by the mayor of Tokyo to conduct a study of Tokyo's municipal government, and wrote *The Administration and Politics of Tokyo* (New York, 1923). He returned to Tokyo after the earthquake of 1923 and assisted in the work of reconstruction, serving as an advisor on administration. Died September 1, 1948, in New Haven, Connecticut. *References*: *DAB S4*; *DADH*; *KEJ*; *NCAB* 34:3; Ellen Nore, *Charles A. Beard, an Intellectual Biography* (Carbondale, Ill., 1983); *NYT*, September 2, 1948; and *WWWA*.

BEARDSLEY, JAMES WALLACE (1860–1944). Engineer, born September 11, 1860, in Coventry, Chenango County, New York. Beardsley graduated from State Normal School (Cortland, N.Y.) and Cornell University. He was an assistant engineer with the Sanitary District of Chicago in charge of construction from 1892 to 1898, with the U.S. Board of Engineers on Deep Waterways in charge of St. Lawrence River surveys from 1898 to 1900, and with the U.S. Corps of Engineers in charge of harbor work from 1900 to 1902. He was a consulting engineer to the Philippine Commission in 1902–1903, chief of the Bureau of Engineering in the Philippines from 1903 to 1905, and director of public works in the Philippines from 1905 to 1908. He was a consulting engineer investigating irrigation in Java, India, and Egypt in 1908–1909, and wrote *Preliminary Report on Irrigation in Java* (Manila, 1909). He was an irrigation engineer with J. G. White and Company in New York City in 1908–1909, chief engineer of the Puerto Rico Irrigation Service from 1910 to 1916, consulting engineer from 1916 to 1918, assistant chief engineer and then chief engineer of the grand canal surveys of China in 1918–1919, chief engineer and member of the Junta Central de Caminos in Panama in 1920–1921, consulting engineer in Santo Domingo from 1926 to 1929, and in private consulting practice after 1930. Died May 15, 1944, in Auburn, New York. *References*: *NYT, May 17, 1944; and WWWA*.

BEARDSLEY, RICHARD K(ING) (1918–1978). Anthropologist, born December 16, 1918, in Cripple Creek, Colorado, and grew up in San Francisco. Beardsley graduated from the University of California in Berkeley. He served in the U.S. Navy during World War II. He carried out fieldwork in Japan in 1950 to 1953 and in 1954–1955. He was an assistant professor at the University of Michigan from 1947 to 1954, associate professor from 1954 to 1959, and professor after 1959. He served as director of the Center for Japanese Studies and the Far Eastern Studies Program after 1962. He wrote *Field Guide to Japan* (Washington, D.C., 1959), and was coauthor of *Village Japan* (Chicago, 1959) and *Japanese Sociology and Social Anthropology: A Guide to Japanese Reference and Research Materials* (Ann Arbor, 1970). He edited *Studies on Economic Life in Japan* (Ann Arbor, Mich., 1964); *Studies in Japanese Culture* (Ann Arbor, Mich., 1965); *Twelve Doors to Japan* (Ann Arbor, Mich., 1965); and *Studies* *in Japanese History and Politics* (Ann Arbor, Mich., 1967). Died June 9, 1978, in Ann Arbor, Michigan. *References*: Richard King Beardsley Papers, Bentley Historical Library, University of Michigan, Ann Arbor, Mich.; *AA* 81 (1979): 636–39; *DFAF*; and *NYT*, June 11, 1967.

BEATTIE, GEORGE WILLIAM (1859–1949). Educator, born April 10, 1859, in Kingston, Jamaica, British West Indies, to American missionary parents, and grew up in Ohio. Beattie graduated from the University of California. He taught public school in San Bernardino County from 1877 to 1887, was deputy county treasurer and county treasurer, and was elected San Bernardino County superintendent of schools from 1890 to 1895. He came to the Philippines in 1901 and was employed by the Bureau of Education as division superintendent of schools in Negros from 1901 to 1903, and superintendent of the normal school for training teachers in Manila from 1903 to 1910. He was involved in the organization of the College of Liberal Arts of the University of the Philippines, and was an associate professor of education and acting dean in 1910–1911. He retired in 1911 and returned to the United States. Died May 16, 1949, in San Bernardino, California. *Reference*: NCAB 39:267.

BEATTIE, R(OLLA) KENT (1875–1960). Botanist, born January 14, 1875, in Ashland, Ohio. Beattie graduated from Cotner University (Lincoln, Neb.) and the University of Nebraska. He was an instructor in botany at Washington State College (Pullman) from 1899 to 1903, and head of the department of botany there and botanist in the Agricultural Experiment Station in Pullman, Washington, from 1903 until 1912. He served in the Bureau of Plant Industry of the U.S. Department of Agriculture from 1912 to 1914 and the Federal Horticultural Board from 1914 to 1927, but returned to the Bureau of Plant Industry in 1927. He conducted an intensive study of blight-resistant chestnuts in Japan, Taiwan, China, and Korea from 1927 to 1930. He was later put in charge of a program aimed at controlling introduced tree diseases in the United States. He retired in 1945. Died June 2, 1960, in Bethesda, Maryland. *References*: *Journal of Forestry* 58 (1960): 670; *Phytopathology* 51 (1961): 135.

BECKER, GEORGE FERDINAND (1847–1919). Geologist, born January 5, 1847, in New York. Becker graduated from Harvard University, the University of Heidelberg, and the Royal Academy of Mines (Berlin). He was an instructor in mining and metallurgy at the University of California from 1874 to 1879, a geologist with the U.S. Geological Survey from 1879 to 1892 and after 1894, and a special agent for the U.S. Tenth Census from 1879 to 1883. He was in South Africa in 1896. He served as a geologist with the U.S. Army in the Philippines in 1898–1899, investigating the mineral resources of the islands, and wrote *Geology of the Philippine Islands* (Washington, D.C., 1901). He was also a member of a committee called by President Theodore Roosevelt to report on a plan for a scientific survey of the islands. He was later in charge of the division of chemistry and physical research of the U.S. Geological Survey, and a geophysicist at the Carnegie Institution in Washington. Died April 20, 1919, in Washington, D.C. *References*: George Ferdinand Becker papers, Manuscript Division, Library of Congress; *ACAB*; *DAB*; *DSB*; *NCAB* 20:272; *NYT*, April 22, 1919; and *WWWA*.

BEDDOE, ROBERT EARL (1882–1952). Medical missionary, born September 9, 1882, in Dallas, Texas. Beddoe graduated from Baylor Medical College (Dallas). He was a medical missionary under the Foreign Mission Board of the Southern Baptist Convention to China from 1910 to 1947. He served in Yingtak, south China, from 1910 until 1919, and in Wuchow, south China, from 1919 to 1925. He returned to the United States in 1925 and practiced medicine in Dallas until 1934, when he returned to Wuchow and served as the superintendent of the hospital there. In 1943 he moved to Kweilin, and returned to the United States in 1944. He returned again to China in 1946–1947. He retired in 1948 and served as director of hospital service administration at Oklahoma Baptist University until his death. Died January 18, 1952, in Shawnee, Oklahoma. *Reference*: Helen T. Raley, *Doctor in an Old World: The Story of Robert Earl Beddoe, Medical Missionary to China* (Waco, Tex., 1969).

BEECH, KEYES (1913–   ). Journalist, born August 13, 1913, in Pulaski, Tennessee. Beech was a copyboy at the *St. Petersburg* (Fla.) *Evening Independent* from 1931 to 1936, and a reporter in 1936–1937. He was a reporter at the *Akron Beacon Journal* from 1937 to 1942 and at the *Honolulu Star Bulletin* from 1945 to 1947. He was a combat correspondent with the U.S. Marines during World War II. He was the Far Eastern correspondent of the *Chicago Daily News* after 1947. He wrote *Tokyo and Points East* (Garden City, N.Y., 1954) and *Not Without the Americans: A Personal History* (Garden City, N.Y., 1971). *References*: *CA*; and *WWA*.

BELL, HENRY HAYWOOD (1808–1868). Naval officer, born April 13, 1808, in North Carolina. Bell was appointed midshipman in the U.S. Navy in 1823. In 1856, he commanded the USS *San Jacinto*, flagship of the East India Squadron, taking a prominent part in the capture and destruction of the barrier forts near Canton, China (see Barrier Forts, Battle of*). He served in the Union Navy during the Civil War. He was in command of the Asiatic Squadron from 1865 until 1867, and was active in subduing the pirates infesting the China Sea. Drowned January 11, 1868, near Osaka, Japan. *References*: *DAB*; *NCAB* 2:103; *NYT*, February 19, 1868; E. Mowbray Tate, "Admiral Bell and the New Asiatic Squadron, 1865–1868," *AN* 32 (1972): 123–35.

BELL, J(AMES) FRANKLIN (1856–1919). Army officer, born January 9, 1856, in Shelbyville, Kentucky. Bell graduated from the United States Military Academy in 1878, and served in the West. He was chief of the Office of Military

Information of the Philippine Expeditionary Force in 1898–1899. He served in the Philippine-American War as chief of scouts for the 2nd Division. He later commanded the Thirty-Sixth U.S. Volunteer Infantry regiment, known as the "Suicide Club," and became a specialist in guerrilla warfare. He served in the Philippines until 1903, when he returned to the United States. He headed the Command and General Staff School from 1903 to 1906, was chief of staff from 1906 to 1910, commanded the Philippine Division from 1911 to 1914, the Second Tactical Division on the Mexican frontier in 1914–1915, the Western Department from 1915 to 1917, and the Eastern Department after 1917. Died January 8, 1919, in New York City. *References*: J. Franklin Bell Papers, U.S. Army Military History Research Institute, Carlisle Barracks, Pa.; *DAB S1*; *DAMIB*; *NCAB* 22:276; and *WWWA*.

BELL, L(EMUEL) NELSON (1894–1973). Medical missionary, born July 30, 1894, in Longdale, Virginia. Bell attended Washington and Lee College and graduated from the Medical College of Virginia. He was a missionary in China under the Board of Foreign Missions of the Presbyterian Church in the United States from 1916 to 1941. He served as chief surgeon of the general hospital in Tsingkiang. He returned to the United States in 1941 and practiced medicine in Asheville, North Carolina, from 1941 to 1956. He retired from medicine in 1956, and served as executive editor of *Christianity Today* after 1955. Died August 2, 1973, in Montreat, North Carolina. *References*: *CA*; Dorothy C. Haskin, *Medical Missionaries You Would Like to Know* (Grand Rapids, Mich., 1957), pp. 14–21; John C. Pollock, *A Foreign Devil in China: The Story of Dr. L. Nelson Bell: An American Surgeon in China* (Grand Rapids, Mich., 1971); *Washington Post*, August 3, 1973; and *WWWA*.

BELL MISSION (1950). U.S. Economic Survey mission to the Philippines in 1950 to undertake a detailed survey of the Philippine economy and the government's fiscal and revenue policies, headed by Daniel W. Bell, president of the American Security and Trust Company and former undersecretary of the treasury. *Reference*: David O. D. Wurfel, "The Bell Report and After: A Study of the Political Problems of Social Reform Stimulated by Foreign Aid," Ph.D. diss., Cornell University, 1960.

BELL TRADE ACT (1946). This U.S.-Philippine Trade Agreement of 1946 granted Philippine exports preferential treatment in return for restrictions on Philippine currency management and export controls. It provided American businessmen the same rights as Philippine nationals. *References*: *EAH*; Steven R. Shalom, "Philippine Acceptance of the Bell Trade Act of 1946: A Study of Manipulatory Democracy," *PHR* 49 (1980): 499–517; and Vivian Tan, "Unequal Partners: United States Policy toward the Philippines and the Philippine Trade Act of 1946," *Philipinas* no. 8 (Spring 1987): 1–10.

BELO (TANNENBAUM), JANE (1904–1968). Anthropologist, born November 3, 1904, in Dallas, Texas, and grew up in Europe and New York City. Belo attended Bryn Mawr and Barnard colleges and the Sorbonne (Paris). She traveled in the Caribbean and taught school in Croton-on-Hudson, New York. She traveled to the Dutch East Indies with her husband, Colin McPhee,* in 1930, and lived in Bali until 1939, when she returned to the United States. She wrote *Bali: Rangda and Barong* (Seattle, Wash., 1949); *Bali: Temple Festival* (Seattle, Wash., 1953); *Trance in Bali* (New York, 1960); and edited *Traditional Balinese Culture* (New York, 1970). Died April 3, 1968. *Reference*: *AA* 70 (1968): 1168–69.

BENEDICT, LAURA WATSON (1861–1932). Anthropologist, born May 5, 1861, in Delhi, New York. Benedict attended Lewis Institute (later Illinois Institute of Technology, Chicago) and graduated from the University of Chicago and Columbia University, the first woman to earn a Ph.D. in anthropology from Columbia University. She carried out fieldwork among the Bagobo in Sta. Cruz, Davao District, Mindanao, in 1906–1907, and wrote *A Study of Bagobo Ceremonial, Magic and Myth* (Leiden, 1916). She was later a lecturer in social work at Hunter College (New York City) and Pennsylvania School of Social and Health Work (Philadelphia). Died December 13, 1932, in Philadelphia. *Reference*: Jay H. Bernstein, "The Perils of Laura Watson Benedict: A Forgotten Pioneer in Anthropology," *Philippine Quarterly of Culture and Society* 13 (1985): 171–97.

BENNETT, CEPHUS (1804–1885). Missionary and printer, born March 20, 1804, in Homer, New York. Bennett was a missionary under the American Baptist Missionary Union in Maulmain, Burma, from 1830 until 1885. He brought with him printing presses, and began to publish tracts in Burmese, and in 1832 published the Bible in Burmese. He also printed the Bible in Sgau Karen and Pwo Karen, and the New Testament in Shan. He served in Rangoon in 1834, and in Tavoy from 1837 to 1857, and was superintendent of the mission press in Burma until his death. Died November 16, 1885, in Rangoon, Burma. *References*: *EM*; and *LC*.

BENNETT, ROY COLEMAN (1889– ?). Editor, born July 2, 1889, in Centertown, Kentucky. Bennett attended the University of Kentucky and graduated from the University of Missouri School of Journalism. He was a reporter for the *Carthage Press* (Mo.) (1914 to 1916) and the *St. Petersburg* (Fla.) *Times* in 1916. He was city editor of the *Gadsden* (Ala.) *Journal* in 1917, state editor of the *New Orleans States* in 1917–1918, and managing editor of the *Lexington Herald* in 1918. He was city editor of the Manila *Cablenews-American* in 1918–1919, and associate editor of the *Manila Bulletin* from 1919 to 1922. He was traveling correspondent and political feature writer in China in 1922–1923, foreign editor of the *Philadelphia Bulletin* from 1923 to 1926, and editor and general manager of the *Manila Daily Bulletin* after 1926. *References*: *EP* 17:70–71; *Who Was Who among North American Authors, 1921–1939* (Detroit, 1976); *WWP*.

BENT, SILAS (1820–1887). Naval officer and oceanographer, born October 10, 1820, in South St. Louis. Bent was appointed midshipman in the U.S. Navy in 1836. In 1849 he served on the USS *Preble* when it sailed into Nagasaki harbor to release American sailors shipwrecked in Japanese waters and imprisoned by the Japanese. He was the flag officer aboard the USS *Mississippi*, the flag ship of Perry's expedition to Japan. He carried out hydrographic surveys in Japanese waters from 1852 to 1854, which were incorporated later in *Sailing Directions and Nautical Remarks: By Officers of the Late U.S. Naval Expedition to Japan, under the Command of Commodore M. C. Perry* (Washington, D.C., 1857). He also conducted a study of the Kuro Siwo current in the Pacific. He resigned his commission in 1860 and managed his wife's estate in St. Louis. Died August 26, 1887, in Shelter Island, Long Island. *References*: Silas Bent, "Journal of the US Naval Expedition to Japan," Ms., Rutgers University Library, New Brunswick, N.J.; and *DAB*.

BERGEN, PAUL DAVID (1860–1915). Missionary, born July 19, 1860, in Bellefontaine, Ohio. Bergen attended Park College (Mo.) and Parsons College (Ia.), and graduated from Lake Forest University (Ill.). He attended Princeton Theological Seminary and graduated from McCormick Theological Seminary (Chicago). He was a missionary under the Board of Foreign Missions of the Presbyterian Church in the U.S.A. in China from 1883 to 1913. He served at Tsinan, Shantung Province. He was president of Tengchow College in 1902, of Shantung Union College in Weihsien from 1902 and 1904, and head of the Union Arts College of Shantung Protestant University after 1904. He also established there a museum of natural history. He returned to the United States in 1913 because of ill health. Died August 8, 1915, in Hartford, Connecticut. *Reference*: *NCAB* 16:200.

BERKEY, CHARLES PETER (1867–1955). Geologist, born March 25, 1867, in Goshen, Indiana. Berkey graduated from the University of Minnesota. He was an instructor, assistant professor, and associate professor of geology at Columbia University from 1903 to 1914, and professor of geology from 1914 until his retirement in 1939. He was a geologic consultant to the Port of New York Authority from 1927 until his death, and to the U.S. Bureau of Reclamation after 1933. In 1914 he made a geologic survey of Puerto Rico. He was chief geologist of the American Museum of Natural History expeditions to the Gobi Desert in Central Asia in 1922 and 1925. Died August 22, 1955, in Palisades, New Jersey. *References*: *BMNAS* 30 (1957): 41–56; *IAB*; *NCAB* 46:489; *NYT*, August 24, 1955; *PGSA* (1965): P45–P51; and *WWWA*.

BERNARD, THEOS (1908–1947). Student of religion, born in Arizona in 1908. Bernard graduated from University of Arizona Law School and Columbia University. He went to India in 1936. He went to Sikkim and was initiated as a lama. He visited Lhasa in 1937 by invitation and was the first Westerner permitted to live within Lhasa's city limits. He described his experiences in *Penthouse of the Gods: A Pilgrimage into the Heart of Tibet and the Sacred City of Lhasa* (New York, 1939). He returned to the United States in 1938 and went on the lecture tour as "The White Lama." He wrote *Heaven Lies within Us* (New York, 1939); *Hatha Yoga: The Report of a Personal Experience* (New York, 1944); and *Hindo Philosophy* (New York, 1947). He returned to India in 1947. Killed in Kosar in 1947, on his way to the Valley of Lahut, north of the Punjab, Pakistan.

BERNSTEIN, DAVID (1915–1974). Journalist and editor, born March 6, 1915, in Hollis, New York. Bernstein began his newspaper career with *The Ithaca* (N.Y.) *Journal*. He was engaged in newspaper work in New York City from 1934 to 1936, was a staff member of the American Jewish Committee from 1936 to 1940, and was a writer for the Office of War Information in 1942. He organized, at the invitation of President Manuel L. Quezon, the Office of Special Services of the Philippine Government-in-exile. He was its director and advisor on foreign policy and information in 1942–1943. He served in the U.S. Army with the combat engineers during World War II. He was advisor to President Sergio Osmeña of the Philippines in Manila in 1945–1946, and wrote *The Philippine Story* (New York, 1947), which was based on his experiences. He was public information officer for the U.S. Federal Security Agency from 1949 to 1952. He helped found *The Middletown* (N.Y.) *Daily Record* in 1956, and was its editor until 1960. He bought *The Binghamton* (N.Y.) *Sun-Bulletin* in 1960, and was its president and editor until 1972. Died August 21, 1974, in Binghamton, New York. *References*: David Bernstein Papers, State University of New York at Binghamton Library, N.Y.; *NYT*, August 22, 1974; and *Who's Who in World Jewry: A Biographical Dictionary of Outstanding Jews*, ed. I. J. Carmin Karpman (New York, 1972).

BERREMAN, GERALD D(UANE) (1930–   ). Anthropologist, born September 2, 1930, in Portland, Oregon. Berreman graduated from the University of Oregon and Cornell University. He served in the U.S. Air Force from 1953 to 1955. He was assistant professor of anthropology at Cornell University from 1960 to 1962, associate professor of anthropology at the University of California at Berkeley from 1962 to 1965, and professor there after 1965. He carried out fieldwork in India in 1957–1958, 1968–1969, and 1981–1982; and wrote *Hindus of the Himalayas* (Berkeley, Calif., 1963); *Caste and Other Inequities: Essays on Inequality* (Meerut, India, 1979); and an account of his experiences, *Behind Many Masks: Ethnography and Impression Management in a Himalayan Village* (Ithaca, N.Y., 1962). *Reference: DFAF*.

BERRY, ARTHUR D. (1872–1941). Missionary, born August 7, 1872, in Mexico, New York. Berry graduated from Syracuse University and Drew Theological Seminary, and was ordained in 1899. He held a pastorate in Maplewood, New Jersey, from 1899 to 1902. He was a missionary under the Board of Foreign Missions of the Methodist Episcopal Church in Japan from 1902 until 1941. He was a professor at Aoyama Gakuin in Tokyo from 1905 until 1941, and dean of the theological school from 1905 to 1931. He returned to the United States in 1941. Died February 11, 1941, in Mexico, New York. *Reference*: *NYT*, February 12, 1941.

BERRY, JOHN CUTTING (1847–1936). Medical missionary, born January 16, 1847, at Small Point, Phippsburg, Maine. Berry attended the Medical School of Maine at Bowdoin College and graduated from Jefferson Medical College (Philadelphia). He was a medical missionary under the American Board of Commissioners for Foreign Missions (ABCFM) in Japan from 1873 to 1893. He was stationed in Kobe, and was director of the Kobe international hospital and head of the Hyogo prefectural hospital from 1873 until 1879. He was head of the prefectural hospital at Okayama from 1879 until 1885, and the first director of the Doshisha University's medical school hospital in Kyoto after 1885, later adding the first nurses' training school. He was an advocate of prison reform, and influenced improvements in the legal and physical treatment of prisoners. He returned to the United States in 1893 and practiced medicine in Worcester, Massachusetts. Died February 8, 1936, in Worcester. *References*: Katherine Berry, *A Pioneer Doctor in Old Japan: The Story of John C. Barry, M.D.* (New York, 1940); *KEJ*; *NCAB* 27:330; and *WWWA*.

BETTS, ARLINGTON U(LYSSES) (1868–1957). Businessman, born December 1, 1868, in Bettsville, Ohio. Betts attended Ohio State University and graduated from Northern Ohio University. He was an engineer for railways in Ohio until 1895, and operated properties in Mexico from 1895 to 1898. He served in the Spanish-American War, and came to the Philippines in 1899. He was the military governor of Albay in 1901–1902 and its civil governor from 1902 to 1905. He settled in Albay in 1905. He served with the guerrillas in the Albay Hills during the Japanese occupation. His *Recollections of the American Regime* (Manila, 1973) were published posthumously. Died in Albay in 1957. *References*: Arlington U. Betts Letters, Ohio Historical Society, Columbus, Ohio; *Gleeck/Frontiers*; and *WWP*.

BEWLEY, LUTHER B(OONE) (1876–1967). Educator, born April 28, 1876, in Mosheim, Tennessee. Bewley graduated from Maryville (Tenn.) College. He came to the Philippines in 1902 as a teacher for the Bureau of Education. He was successively supervising teacher, high school principal, division superintendent, superintendent of Manila City Schools (in 1914), second assistant and then assistant director of the Bureau of Education, and director of education of the Philippines. After the establishment of the commonwealth, he was an advisor on education to the first three presidents of the Philippines. Died December 29, 1967, in Manila. *References*: *CCDP*; *EP* 17:76; *Manila Chronicle*, December 30, 1967; *WWP*; and *WWWA*.

BEYER, H(ENRY) OTLEY (1883–1966). Anthropologist, born July 13, 1883, in Edgewood, Iowa. Beyer graduated from Cornell College (Mt. Vernon, Ia.), the University of Denver, and Harvard University. He came to the Philippines in 1905, was a supervising teacher in Banaue, Ifugao, and studied the Ifugao people of Northern Luzon from 1905 to 1908. He returned to the Mountain Province in 1909 and collected material that was later published as *Philippine Ethnographic Series*. He was an ethnologist for the Philippine Bureau of Science and head of the Philippine Museum from 1910 to 1914, instructor in anthropology and ethnology at the University of the Philippines from 1914 to 1916, assistant professor from 1916 to 1925, and professor and head of the department of anthropology and sociology from 1925 to 1954. He carried out an extensive archaeological survey of Rizal Province, Luzon, after 1928. He was interned by the Japanese during World War II. Died December 31, 1966, in Manila. *References*: *AA* 76 (1974): 361–62; *EP* 17:77–78; Juan R. Francisco, "H. Otley Beyer's Contribution to Indo-Philippine Scholarship," *BAHC* 4 (April-June 1976): 25–42; Frank Lynch, "Henry Otley Beyer, 1883–1966," *PS* 15 (January 1967): 3–8; *NYT*, January 2, 1967; Rudolf Rahmann and R. Gertrude Ang, eds., *Dr. H. Otley Beyer, Dean of Philippine Anthropology* (Cebu City, Philippines, 1968); Albert Ravenholt, "Dr. H. Otley Beyer: Pioneer Scientist on the Frontier in Asia," *American Universities Field Staff Reports, Southeast Asia Series*, 12, no. 4 (May 1964); *Scientists in the Philippines* (n.p., 1978), pp. 1–25; Wilhelm G. Solheim II, "H. Otley Beyer," *Asian Perspectives* 12 (1971): 1–18; and Mario D. Zamora, ed., *Studies in Philippine Anthropology in Honor of H. Otley Beyer* (Quezon City, 1967).

BICKEL, LUKE WASHINGTON (1866–1917). Missionary captain, born September 21, 1866, in Cincinnati, Ohio, and grew up in Germany. Bickel went to sea at eighteen on an English merchant sailing ship, and became captain at twenty-eight. He settled in London, and assumed control of the business of the London Baptist Publishing Society after 1893. He was a missionary under the American Baptist Missionary Union in Japan from 1898 until his death. He was captain of the *Fukuin Maru* from 1899 until his death, traveling among the islands of the Inland Sea of Japan, establishing and directing missions and developing missionary work and education on these islands. He became known as the "Skipper of the Gospel Ship." Died May 11, 1917, in Kobe, Japan. *References*: *DAB*; and *NYT*, June 13, 1917.

BICKMORE, ALBERT SMITH (1839–1914). Naturalist, born March 1, 1839, in Tenant's Harbor, Maine. Bickmore graduated from Dartmouth College and Lawrence Scientific School of Harvard University. He served in the Union Army during the Civil War. He studied under Louis Agassiz from 1860 to 1864 and became his assistant. From 1865 to 1868, he traveled through the Malay Archipelago, the Dutch East Indies, China, and Japan, returning via Siberia, and wrote *Travels in the East Indian Archipelago* (New York, 1869). He was a professor of natural history at Madison (now Colgate) University in 1868–1869. Involved in the founding of the American Museum of Natural History in New York City, he was superintendent of the museum from 1869 until 1884, and in charge of the museum's department of public instruction from 1884 to 1904. He traveled from 1895 to 1904, collecting data and illustrations for his lectures, which were delivered under the auspices of the state superintendent of public instruction. Died August 12, 1914, in Nonquitt, Massachusetts. *References*: Albert Smith Bickmore, "An Autobiography," Ms., American Museum of Natural History, New York City; *ACAB*; *DAB*; *NCAB* 8:268; *NYT*, August 14, 1914; D. J. Preston, "The Museum and Professor Bickmore," *Natural History* 93 (August 1984): 76–79; and *WWWA*.

BICKNELL, JOHN W(ARREN) (1886–1961). Businessman, born December 5, 1886, in Malden, Massachusetts. Bicknell graduated from Harvard University. He went to Sumatra in 1911, and was the first American businessman to reside there permanently. He opened the Singapore office of the General Rubber Company, a subsidiary of United States Rubber Company in 1912, and the Medan, Sumatra, office of the United States Rubber Plantations, Inc. (which in 1934 became a general division of United States Rubber Company) in 1914. He served as managing director of this division until 1949, when he became a consultant. He was resident general manager of Hollandsch-Amerikaansche Plantage Maatschappij (HAPM), Si Paré Paré Rubber Company, Nederland Langkat Rubber Company, and Malan American Plantation, Limited. He was consultant to the plantation division of the United States Rubber Company, New York City. During World War II, he was executive vice president of the Rubber Development Corporation, the government agency to procure natural rubber from foreign countries. He was also managing director of the plantation division of the United States Rubber Company. Died June 21, 1961, in Hopewell Junction, Dutchess County, New York. *References*: *NYT*, June 23, 1961; and *WWWA*.

BIDDLE, JAMES (1783–1848). Naval officer, born February 18, 1783, in Philadelphia. Biddle became a midshipman in the U.S. Navy in 1800. He served in the Barbary Wars and was held prisoner in Tunis from 1803 to 1805. He served during the War of 1812, was commodore of the West Indies Squadron, commander of the Philadelphia Navy Yard, commodore of the Brazilian Squadron from 1826 to 1829 and of the Mediterranean Squadron from 1829 to 1832, and governor of the Philadelphia Naval Asylum from 1838 to 1842. He was commander of the East India Squadron from 1845 until 1848. He was sent to Canton to exchange the ratifications of the Treaty of Wanghia which was signed between the United States and China. He also visited Japan in 1845–1846 and attempted unsuccessfully to initiate trade. He returned to the United States in 1848. Died October 1, 1848, in Philadelphia. *References*: Merrill L. Bartlett, "Commodore James Biddle and the First Naval Mission to Japan, 1845–1846," *AN* 41 (1981): 25–35; *DAB*; *DAMIB*; Jean G. Lee, *Philadelphians and the China Trade 1784–1844* (Philadelphia, 1984), pp. 159–160; David F. Long, *Sailor-Diplomat: A Biography of Commodore James Biddle, 1783–1848* (Boston, 1983); *NCAB* 6:55; Richard A. von Doenhoff, "Biddle, Perry, and Japan," *USNIP* 92 (November 1966): 78–87; Nicholas B. Wainwright, *Commodore James Biddle and His Sketch Book* (Philadelphia, 1966).

BIGELOW, WILLIAM STURGIS (1850–1926). Orientalist, born April 4, 1850, in Boston. Bigelow graduated from Harvard University and Harvard Medical School and studied in Vienna, Paris, and Strassburg. He set up a private bacteriological laboratory in Boston in 1879 and practiced medicine until 1882. He was in Japan from 1882 until 1888, residing in Tokyo and Nikko, and traveling widely and collecting works of art (now in the Boston Museum of Fine Art). He studied the language, philosophy, and religion of Japan. He wrote *Buddhism and Immortality* (Boston, 1908). Died October 6, 1926, in Boston. *References*: Akiko Murataka, "Selected Letters of Dr. William Sturgis Bigelow," Ph.D. diss., George Washington University, 1971; *DAB*; *KEJ*; *NCAB* 20:177; *NYT*, October 7, 1926; and *WWWA*.

BIGGERSTAFF, KNIGHT (1906–   ). Sinologist, born February 28, 1906, in Berkeley, California. Biggerstaff graduated from the University of California and Harvard University. He studied in Peking, China, from 1934 to 1936 and in Nanking in 1949. He was instructor of Oriental studies at the University of Washington from 1936 to 1938, and assistant professor to professor of Chinese history at Cornell University from 1938 until his retirement in 1972. He was a China specialist with the State Department in 1944–1945 and Chinese secretary at the U.S. embassy in Chungking in 1945–1946. He wrote *The Far East and the United States* (Ithaca, N.Y., 1943); *The Earliest Modern Government Schools in China* (Ithaca, N.Y., 1961); *Some Early Chinese Steps toward Modernization* (San Francisco, 1975); and *Nanking Letters, 1949* (Ithaca, N.Y., 1979). *Reference*: *DAS*.

BIGLER, REGINA M(ARIE) (1860–1937). Medical missionary, born March 29, 1860, in Tuscarawas County, Ohio. Bigler graduated from the medical school of the State University of Iowa. She practiced medicine in Mitchell, South Dakota. She was a medical missionary under the Women's Missionary Association of the United Brethren in Christ in South China from 1892 until her death, and was in charge of a dispensary in Canton after 1925 and also a maternity ward. Died December 15, 1937, in Canton, China. *References*: *EWM*; and *WWWA*.

BINGHAM, JOHN A(RMOUR) (1815–1900). Diplomat, born January 21, 1815, in Mercer, Pennsylvania. Bingham attended Franklin College (Pa.), studied law, and was admitted to the bar in 1840. He practiced law in Ohio, where he was district attorney of Tuscarawas County from 1846 to 1849 and a member of the U.S. House of Representatives from 1855 to 1863. He served in the Union Army during the Civil War. He served again in the U.S. House of Representatives from 1865 until 1873. He was U.S. minister to Japan from 1873 until 1885. He worked to alter the convention of 1866, a commercial treaty, which was finalized after he left Japan. He mediated a settlement between China and Japan resulting from an armed clash during the Korean revolution in 1884. Died March 19, 1900, in Cadiz, Ohio. *References*: John A. Bingham Papers, Ohio Historical Society, Columbus, Ohio; *BDAC*; Erving E. Beauregard, "John A. Bingham, First American Minister Plenipotentiary to Japan (1873–1885)," *Journal of Asian History* 22 (1988): 101–30; *DAB*; Philip N. Dare, "John A. Bingham and Treaty Revision with Japan: 1873–1885," Ph.D. diss., University of Kentucky, 1975; and *NCAB* 9:375.

BINNEY, JOSEPH G(ETCHELL) (1807–1877). Missionary, born December 1, 1807, in Boston. Binney graduated from Yale University and Newton Theological Seminary, and was ordained in 1832. He lived in Savannah, Georgia, from 1832 until 1843. He was a missionary under the American Baptist Missionary Union in Burma from 1843 until 1875, working among the Karens. He established the Karen seminary in 1845. He returned to the United States because of his wife's ill health; held pastorates in Elmira, New York, and Augusta, Georgia; and was president of Columbia College from 1854 to 1858. He returned to Burma in 1858 and resumed work among the Karens until 1875. Died November 26, 1877, on board ship in the Indian Ocean on his way to the United States. *References*: Mrs. J. G. Binney, *Twenty-Six Years in Burmah: Records of the Life and Work of Joseph G. Binney, D.D.* (Philadelphia, 1880); *LC*; and *NCAB* 3:152.

BINSTED, NORMAN S(PENCER) (1890–1961). Missionary, born October 1, 1890, in Toronto, Canada. Binsted attended St. John's College (Uniontown, Ky.), graduated from Virginia Theological Seminary, and was ordained in 1916. He was a missionary under the Domestic and Foreign Missionary Society of the Protestant Episcopal Church in the United States of America in Japan in 1917 until 1940. He served in the Holy Trinity Cathedral of Tokyo. He was consecrated as the first missionary bishop of the Tohoku Diocese in 1928 and served until 1940, when he was forced to leave Japan for the Philippines. He was a missionary bishop of the Philippines from 1940 to 1942, and bishop of the Philippines from 1942 until his retirement in 1957. He was interned by the Japanese in the

Philippines during World War II. Died February 20, 1961, in Hendersonville, North Carolina. *References*: Norman S. Binsted Papers, Archives of the Church Historical Society, Austin, Texas; and *NYT*, February 22, 1961.

BISHOP, ANCIL H(IRAM) (1891–1956). Businessman, born March 1, 1891, in Denver, Colorado. Bishop attended the University of Colorado. He came to the Philippines in 1910 as an employee of the Cooper Company, an agency for the Koppel Industrial Car and Equipment Company. He was employed in various capacities in this company until 1917, and was its manager in 1917–1918, and its president and general manager from 1918 to 1922. He was the manager of the Philippine branch of Koppel Industrial Car and Equipment Company from 1923 to 1928, and vice president of Koppel (Philippines), Inc., a subsidiary corporation, after 1928. He was interned by the Japanese during World War II. He returned to the United States in 1951 and was president of Koppel (Philippines), Inc., until his death. Died July 30, 1956, in New York City. *References*: *EP* 17:80; *NCAB* 42:530; *NYT*, July 31, 1956; and *WWP*.

BISHOP, CARL WHITING (1881–1942). Archaeologist, born July 12, 1881, in Tokyo, Japan. Bishop came to the United States in 1898, graduated from DePauw and Columbia universities, and attended Hampden-Sydney College. He was a member of the Peabody Museum expedition to Central America in 1913–1914, and assistant curator of Oriental art at the University Museum of the University of Pennsylvania from 1914 to 1918. He served in naval intelligence during World War I, and was assistant U.S. naval attaché in Shanghai from 1918 to 1920. He was associate curator and an associate in archaeology at the Freer Gallery of Art in Washington, D.C., from 1922 until his death. He conducted archaeological expeditions to China for the University Museum from 1915 to 1917, and for the Freer Gallery of Art and the Museum of Fine Arts, Boston, from 1923 to 1927 and from 1929 to 1934. He wrote *Origin of the Far Eastern Civilizations: A Brief Handbook* (Washington, D.C., 1942). Died June 16, 1942, in Alexandria, Virginia. *References*: *FEQ* 2 (1943): 204–7; *NYT*, June 17, 1942; and A. G. Wenley, "Carl Whiting Bishop (1881–1942)," *Notes on Far Eastern Studies in America* 12 (Spring 1943): 27–32.

BISSON, T(HOMAS) A(RTHUR) (1900–   ). Political scientist, born November 8, 1900, in New York City. Bisson graduated from Rutgers and Columbia universities, and studied at the School of Chinese Studies (Peking). He was an educational missionary under the Board of Foreign Missions of the Presbyterian Church in the U.S.A. in China from 1924 to 1928. He taught in a middle school at Hwaiyuen, Anhwei, and then at Yenching University. He was the Foreign Policy Association's research specialist on East Asia from 1929 to 1942, principal economist of the U.S. Board of Economic Welfare in 1942–1943, a member of the staff of the International Secretariat of the Institute of Pacific Relations from 1943 to 1945, on the staff of the U.S. Strategic Bombing Survey of the War

Department in Japan in 1945–1946, and a general assistant to the chief of the government section in the general headquarters of the Allied Expeditionary Forces in Japan in 1946–1947. He was a visiting professor of political science at the University of California from 1948 to 1953; professor of intercultural studies at Western College for Women from 1956 to 1958; professor of international studies at Denison College, University of Waterloo (Ontario, Canada), from 1969 to 1971; and director of international studies there after 1971. He wrote *Japan in China* (New York, 1938); *America's Far Eastern Policy* (New York, 1945); *Zaibatsu Dissolution in Japan* (Berkeley, Calif., 1954); and *Yenan in June 1937: Talks with the Communist Leaders* (Berkeley, Calif., 1973). *References*: *DAS*; and Howard B. Schonberger, *Aftermath of War: Americans and the Remaking of Japan, 1945–1952* (Kent, Ohio, 1989), ch. 3.

BLACK, ROBERT F(RANKLIN) (1870–1952). Missionary, born August 28, 1870, in Washington, Litchfield County, Connecticut. Black attended the University of Wisconsin, graduated from Redfield College, studied at the Chicago Theological Seminary, graduated from Union Theological Seminary, and was ordained in 1902. He was the first missionary under the American Board of Commissioners for Foreign Missions (ABCFM) in the Philippines, serving in Davao, Mindanao, from 1902 through 1917. He resigned in 1918 and returned to the United States. He held pastorates in Wisconsin from 1918 until his retirement in 1943. He later resided in Corona, California. Died October 29, 1952, in Schenectady, New York. *Reference*: *UnionTS*.

BLACKSHEAR, CHARLES COTTON (1862–1938). Chemist, born December 10, 1862, in Macon, Georgia. Blackshear graduated from Mercer University (Macon, Ga.) and Johns Hopkins University. He taught chemistry at Goucher College (Baltimore) until 1916. He visited India several times between 1904 and 1916, and visited Java in 1908. He returned to Java in 1917 and lived in Jogjakarta until his death, studying ancient history and architecture. He visited Siam in 1920 and Bali in 1921. He wrote a book on the monuments of India, Java, and Cambodia, which was never published. Died October 27, 1938, in Jogjakarta. *References*: Cotton Family Papers, Emory University Library, Atlanta; Perry L. Blackshear, *Blacksheariana: Genealogy, History, Anecdotes* (Atlanta, 1954), pp. 7–11.

BLAIR, WILLIAM MCCORMICK, JR. (1916–   ). Lawyer and diplomat, born October 24, 1916, in Chicago. Blair graduated from Stanford University and the University of Virginia. He served in the U.S. Army Air Force intelligence in the China-Burma-India theater during World War II. He practiced law in Chicago and was an administrative assistant to governor Adlai Stevenson of Illinois from 1950 to 1952. He was ambassador to Denmark from 1961 to 1964 and to the Philippines from 1964 to 1967. He negotiated an agreement giving Philippine courts more jurisdiction over American military personnel in the

Philippines. He was general director of the John F. Kennedy Center in Washington, D.C., from 1968 to 1972. *References*: *DADH*; *Gleeck/Ambassadors*, ch. 7; and *WWA*.

BLAKE, WILLIAM PHIPPS (1825–1910). Geologist and mining engineer, born June 21, 1825, in New York City. Blake graduated from Sheffield Scientific School of Yale University. He was a geologist for the U.S. Pacific Railroad survey from 1854 to 1856, investigated mineral resources in North Carolina from 1856 to 1859, and edited *Mining Magazine* in 1859–1860. He was employed as a mining engineer by the Japanese government from 1861 to 1863 to explore the island of Yezo and to teach American mining techniques. With Raphael Pumpelly,* he organized the first school of science in Japan and taught chemistry and geology there. He explored the Stickeen River region of Alaska in 1863, was a mineralogist with the California State Board of Agriculture and professor of geology and mineralogy at the College of California (later the University of California at Berkeley) from 1864 to 1867. He was a professor of geology and mining and director of the School of Mines at the University of Arizona from 1895 to 1905. Died May 22, 1910, in Berkeley, California. *References*: *DAB*; *Foreign Pioneers*; *NCAB* 25:202; *NYT*, May 23, 1910; and *WWWA*.

BLODGET, HENRY (1825–1903). Missionary, born July 25, 1825, in Bucksport, Maine. Blodget graduated from Yale University, attended New Haven and Andover theological seminaries, and was ordained in 1854. He was a missionary under the American Board of Commissioners for Foreign Missions (ABCFM) in China from 1854 until 1894. He served in Shanghai and Tientsin until 1864, and in Peking from 1864 until 1894. He was involved in the translation of the New Testament into the Mandarin colloquial dialect of Peking. He returned to the United States in 1894. Died May 23, 1903, in Bridgeport, Connecticut. *References*: *EM*; and *LC*.

BLOUNT, JAMES HENDERSON, JR. (1869–1918). Lawyer and judge, born March 3, 1869, in Clinton, Georgia. Blount graduated from the University of Georgia and Columbia University Law School, and was admitted to the bar. He practiced law in Macon, Georgia. He served in the Spanish-American War in 1898–1901, and was judge of the Court of First Instance in the Philippines from 1901 to 1905. He was forced to resign after he criticized the American occupation of the Philippines. He wrote *The American Occupation of the Philippines 1898–1912* (New York, 1912). He practiced law again in Macon until 1918, when he returned to the U.S. Army and served in the Judge Advocate's Division. Died October 7, 1918, at Hoboken, New Jersey. *References*: *Macon Daily Telegraph*, October 8, 1918; and *WWWA*.

BLUM, ROBERT FREDERICK (1857–1903). Painter, born July 9, 1857, in Cincinnati. Blum was apprenticed to a lithographic establishment in 1871, and attended the McKinnen School of Design (later the Art Academy of Cincinnati). He went to New York City in 1879, and was hired as an illustrator for *Scribner's Monthly* and *St. Nicholas* magazine. He made trips to Europe in 1880–1881 and from 1882 to 1885. In 1889, he was commissioned by Scribner's to illustrate *Japonica* by Sir Edwin Arnold, and was in Japan from 1889 to 1893. He recorded his impressions of Japan in the April 1893 issue of *Scribner's Monthly*. He later devoted his time mostly to mural decoration. Died June 8, 1903, in New York City. *References*: *DAB*; *NCAB* 10:365; *Robert F. Blum, 1857–1903: A Retrospective Exhibition* (Cincinnati, 1966); and *WWWA*.

BOARDMAN, GEORGE DANA (1801–1831). Missionary, born February 8, 1801, in Livermore, Maine. Boardman graduated from Waterville (Me.) College and Andover Theological Seminary, and was ordained in 1825. He was a missionary under the American Baptist Missionary Union in Burma from 1827 until his death. He served in Maulmain and Tavoy, and founded the Karen mission. Died February 11, 1831, on the road to Tavoy. *References*: *ACAB*; *AndoverTS*; *CDCWM*; *EM*; Alonzo King, *Memoir of George Dana Boardman* (Boston, 1875); Joseph C. Robbins, *Boardman of Burma* (Philadelphia, 1940); and *WWWA*.

BODDE, DERK (1909–   ). Sinologist, born March 9, 1909, in Brant Rock, Massachusetts. Bodde accompanied his parents to China from 1919 to 1922, and wrote articles for *St. Nicholas* magazine about China from 1923 to 1927. He graduated from Harvard University and the University of Leiden (Netherlands). He was a fellow at Harvard Yenching Institute in Peiping, China, from 1931 to 1935, and a specialist on China for the Office of Strategic Services (OSS) and the Office of War Information from 1942 to 1945. He was the first American Fulbright fellow in China in 1948–1949, and wrote *Peking Diary, a Year of Revolution* (New York, 1950). He was assistant professor and associate professor of Chinese studies at the University of Pennsylvania from 1938 to 1950, and professor there from 1950 to 1975. He was the first Dr. Sun Yat-sen Distinguished Professor of Chinese Studies at Georgetown University. *References*: *DAS*; Charles Le Blanc and Dorothy Borei, eds., *Essays on Chinese Civilization* (Princeton, N.J., 1981); and *WWA*.

BOGGS, ELI M. (fl. 1850s). Pirate. A renegade American sailor, Boggs preyed on the Pearl River traffic in Southeast China with a fleet of thirty armed junks. A reward offered for his capture by the Hong Kong government was won in 1857 by William Henry "Bully" Hayes (1927–1877), who took part in a Royal Navy raid on the pirate fleet and personally arrested its commander. In his trial, Boggs was alleged to have led his Chinese ruffians in the seizure of countless ships, murdering their crews or forcing them overboard. He was found guilty of piracy and was sentenced to transportation for life. He never went to the penal colonies; instead, he was released after three years in a Hong Kong jail because of ill health and disappeared.

BOOKWALTER, LULU G(ERTRUDE) (1884–1958). Missionary educator, born November 24, 1884, in Knoxville, Tennessee. Bookwalter attended Smith College and graduated from Otterbein College and Kansas State University. She was a missionary educator under the Women's Board of Missions and later under the American Board of Commissioners for Foreign Missions (ABCFM) in Ceylon from 1911 to 1953. She was principal of the Uduvil Girls' School at Chunnakam, Ceylon, from 1911 to 1941, and administered an interdenominational school, orphanage, and industrial center from 1943 to 1952. She retired in 1953. Died September 4, 1958, in Kensington, Maryland. *Reference*: *NYT*, September 7, 1958.

BOONE, WILLIAM JONES, JR. (1846–1891). Missionary, son of William Jones Boone, Sr.,* and born April 17, 1846, in Shanghai, China. Boone graduated from Princeton University and studied at the divinity school in Philadelphia and at the Alexandria Seminary, and was ordained in 1868. He was a missionary under the Domestic and Foreign Missionary Society of the Protestant Episcopal Church in the United States of America in China from 1869 until his death. He served at Hankow, where he was elected bishop in 1883 and consecrated in 1884, the fourth Protestant Episcopal bishop of China. Died October 5, 1891, in Shanghai, China. *References*: Muriel Boone, *The Seed of the Church in China* (Philadelphia, 1973); *NCAB* 5:16; and *NYT*, October 7, 1864.

BOONE, WILLIAM JONES, SR. (1811–1864). Missionary, born July 1, 1811, in Walterborough, South Carolina. Boone graduated from the University of South Carolina, studied law, was admitted to the bar in 1833, attended the Seminary of the Protestant Episcopal Church (Alexandria, Va.), and was ordained in 1837. He was a missionary under the Domestic and Foreign Missionary Society of the Protestant Episcopal Church in the United States of America in the Dutch East Indies and China from 1837 until his death. He served in Batavia and then in Amoy, China, and established a mission at Ku-lang Island in 1842. He was consecrated as missionary bishop to China in 1844 and was bishop of the diocese of Amoy, China, the first bishop of the Protestant Episcopal Church in China. He served in Shanghai after 1845 and was involved in the translation of the Bible. Died July 17, 1864, in Shanghai, China. *References*: Muriel Boone, *The Seed of the Church in China* (Philadelphia, 1973); *CDCWM*; *EM*; *NCAB* 5:16; and *NYT*, October 7, 1864.

BOOTH, EUGENE SAMUEL (1850–1931). Missionary, born August 16, 1850, in Trumbull, Connecticut. Booth graduated from Rutgers University and New Brunswick Theological Seminary. He was a missionary under the Board of Foreign Missions of the Reformed Church in America in Japan from 1879 until 1922. He was the principal of Ferris Seminary in Yokohama from 1882 to 1923, founded a boys' school in Nagasaki in 1880, participated in the planning of the Tokyo Women's Christian College, and was president of the Yokohama Subscription Library from 1918 to 1922. He returned to the United States in 1922. Died February 9, 1931, in New York City. His son, **FRANK S. BOOTH** (1880–1957), businessman, was born in Nagasaki. He graduated from Rutgers University. He returned to Japan in 1903 and joined Sale and Company. He was instrumental in developing Japan's can manufacturing and canning industry, and also played an important role in marketing Kamchatkan salmon abroad. He established Japan Engineering Company in 1950, and was its president. *References*: *JBEWW*; *KEJ*; and *NCAB* 23:411.

BORDEN, WILLIAM A(LANSON) (1854–1931). Librarian, born April 4, 1854, in New Bedford, Massachusetts. Borden graduated from Cornell University and studied law. He became a binder and later converted his bindery into a library supply house. He began library work in the Boston Athaneaum in 1883. He organized the Reynolds Library in Rochester, New York, in 1886–1887, and the Young Men's Institute Library in New Haven, Connecticut, from 1887 until 1910. He was a lecturer in the Columbia University Library School from 1887 to 1892. He came to India in 1910 on the invitation of the Maharaja Gaekwad of Baroda. He was the director of the state libraries of Baroda, organized the State Library Department, and planned a network of state-controlled free public libraries in the state of Baroda. He converted the palace library into a free central library, and founded a library school and a library periodical, *The Library Miscellany*. He also prepared a scheme of classification for the libraries of the Baroda State. He returned to the United States in 1913, and was a library engineer after 1915. Died November 16, 1931, in Morris Cove, New Haven, Connecticut. *References*: N. C. Divanji, "William Alanson Borden (1854–1933)," *Modern Librarian* [Lahore] 2 (1932): 130–31; Murari L. Nagar, *First American Library Pioneer in India* (Ludhiana, Punjab, 1983); and *WWWA*.

BOSWORTH, STEPHEN W(ARREN) (1939–). Diplomat, born December 4, 1939, in Grand Rapids, Michigan. Bosworth graduated from Dartmouth College. He entered the foreign service in 1961 and served in Panama, Colon, Madrid, and Paris. He was director of the Office of Fuels and Energy from 1975 to 1976, deputy assistant secretary of state from 1976 to 1979, U.S. ambassador to Tunisia from 1979 to 1981, deputy assistant secretary of state for inter-American affairs in 1981–1982, and ambassador to the Philippines from 1984 to 1987. He played an important role during the 1986 elections in the Philippines and was involved in the removal of President Ferdinand Marcos from Manila. *Reference*: *WWA*.

BOWEN, ARTHUR J(OHN) (1873–1944). Missionary educator, born January 12, 1873, in Neponset, Illinois. Bowen graduated from Northwestern and Columbia universities. He was a missionary under the Board of Foreign Missions of the Methodist Episcopal Church in China from 1897 to 1930. He was district superintendent of the Kiangsi Province and treasurer of the Central China Mission from 1901 to 1905. He was a member of the faculty of the University of Nanking from 1897 until 1930, acting president of the University in 1903–1904, and president from 1908 to 1927. He retired in 1930. Died July 28, 1944, in Altadena, Los Angeles County, California. *References*: *EWM*; *NYT*, July 30, 1944; and *WWWA*.

BOWEN, GEORGE (1816–1888). Missionary, born April 30, 1816, in Middlebury, Vermont. Bowen graduated from Union Theological Seminary. He was a missionary under the American Board of Commissioners for Foreign Missions (ABCFM) in India from 1848 until 1849, when he withdrew from the ABCFM. He resumed the relationship in 1865. He served as associate editor of the *Bombay Guardian* from 1851 to 1854, and editor from 1854 to 1888. He joined the Methodist Church in 1873. He was known as the "White Saint of India." Died February 5, 1888. *References*: *ACAB*; *DAB*; *EM*; *EWM*; *LC*; Robert E. Speer, *George Bowen of Bombay* (n.p., 1938); *UnionTS*; and *WWWA*.

BOWERS, FAUBION (1917–   ). Author, born January 29, 1917, in Miami, Oklahoma. Bowers attended the University of Oklahoma, Columbia University, the University of Poitiers, and Julliard School of Music. He went to Japan in 1940; taught at Hosei University, Tokyo, in 1940; and was a lecturer in Java in 1941. He served with military intelligence during World War II. He was a personal aide to General Douglas MacArthur in Tokyo, and civil censor of the Japanese theater during the occupation of Japan. He was later a correspondent on dance and drama. He wrote *Japanese Theatre* (New York, 1952); *Dance in India* (New York, 1954); and *Theatre in The East* (New York, 1957). *References*: *CA*; and *CB* 1959.

BOWLES, CHESTER BLISS (1901–1986). Businessman, government official, and diplomat, born April 5, 1901, in Springfield, Massachusetts. Bowles graduated from Yale University. He established an advertising agency in 1929 and worked there until 1942. He served in the U.S. Office of Price Administration in 1942–1943, was a member of the U.S. War Production Board from 1943 to 1946, and served as governor of Connecticut from 1949 to 1951. He was ambassador to India from 1951 until 1953, undersecretary of state in 1961, ambassador at large from 1961 to 1963, and again ambassador to India from 1963 to 1969. He retired in 1969. He wrote *Ambassador's Report* (New York, 1954); *A View from New Delhi* (New Delhi, 1969); his autobiography, *Promises to Keep: My Years in Public Life, 1941–1969* (New York, 1971); and *Mission to India: A Search for Alternatives in Asia* (New Delhi, 1974). Died May 23, 1986, in Essex, Connecticut. *References*: Chester B. Bowles Papers, Yale University Library, New Haven, Conn.; *CA*; *CB* 1957; Srinivas Chary, ''An Analysis of Indo-American Relations: Chester Bowles' Views,'' *Indian Journal of American Studies* 10 (1980): 3–9; *DADH*; *DVW*; *NCAB* G:348; *NYT*, May 26, 1986; and *WWWA*.

BOWLES, GILBERT (1869–1960). Missionary, born October 16, 1869, in Stuart, Guthrie County, Iowa. Bowles graduated from Pennsylvania College (Oskaloosa, Iowa). He was a missionary under the Philadelphia Yearly Meeting in Tokyo, Japan, from 1901 to 1941. He was a teacher at the Friends' Girls Higher School in Tokyo and founder of the Japan Peace Society. He was one of the promoters of the tuberculosis prevention movement in Japan, was involved in the temperance and purity movements, and worked with the blind. He returned to the United States in 1941, and lived in Honolulu until his death. He wrote *The Peace Movement in Japan* (Philadelphia, 1941). Died October 9, 1960, in Honolulu. *References*: Gilbert Bowles Papers, Records of the Philadelphia Yearly Meeting Japan Committee, Haverford College, Haverford, Pa.; Errol T. Elliott, *Quaker Profile from the American West* (Richmond, Ind., 1972), pp. 47–90; *JBEWW*; and *WWWA*.

BOWLES, GORDON T(OWNSEND) (1904–   ). Anthropologist, son of Gilbert Bowles, born June 25, 1904, in Tokyo. Bowles graduated from Earlham College and Harvard University. He carried out field work in west China and east Tibet from 1930 to 1932, and in the Himalayas and north Burma from 1935 to 1937. He was assistant professor of anthropology at the University of Hawaii from 1938 to 1942. He served with the U.S. Foreign Economic Administration in Washington, D.C., from 1942 to 1944; with the U.S. State Department from 1944 to 1947; and with the Associated Research Councils of the Conference Board in Washington, D.C., from 1947 to 1951. He was visiting professor at the University of Tokyo from 1951 to 1958, and associate managing director of the International House of Japan from 1952 to 1957. He was a professor of anthropology at Syracuse University from 1961 to 1972. He wrote *People of Asia* (New York, 1977). *References*: *AMWS*; and *CA*.

BOYD, JOHN PARKER (1764–1830). Adventurer, born December 21, 1764, in Newburyport, Massachusetts. Boyd was commissioned ensign in the U.S. Army in 1783. He came to India about 1789 in search of his fortune. He assembled a troop of some 1,800 men, and was engaged by the Nizam of Hyderabad and then by the Peshwa of Poona, and commanded an army in the Peshwa. He returned to the United States in 1808, reentered the U.S. Army, served in the War of 1812, and was later a naval officer for the port of Boston. Died October 4, 1830, in Boston. *References*: *ACAB*; *DAB*; *NCAB* 10:135; and *WWWA*.

BOYNTON, GRACE M(ORRISON) (1890–1970). Missionary educator, born August 14, 1890, in Medford, Massachusetts. Boynton graduated from Wellesley College and the University of Michigan. From 1919 to 1951 she was a missionary under the American Board of Commissioners for Foreign Missions (ABCFM) in China, and a professor of English Language and literature at Yenching University in Peking. She also taught at Nishinomiya, Japan. She wrote *The River Garden of Pure Repose* (New York, 1952). Died March 30, 1970, in Concord, New Hampshire. *Reference: WWAW.*

BRAAM HOUCKGEEST, ANDREAS EVERARDUS VAN. *See* VAN BRAAM HOUCKGEEST, ANDREAS EVERARDUS

BRADLEY, CHARLES WILLIAM (1807–1865). Consul, born June 27, 1807, in New Haven, Connecticut. Bradley graduated from General Theological Seminary (New York City). He held pastorates in Connecticut in the 1830s and 1840s, and was Connecticut's secretary of state in 1846–1847. He was a consul in Amoy, China, from 1849 to 1854; in Singapore from 1854 to 1857, and in Ningpo, China, from 1857 to 1860. He negotiated a treaty with Siam in 1857, and accompanied the Pei-ho Expedition into the interior of China in 1858. He served with the Imperial Chinese Customs Service in Hankow from 1860 to 1863. He returned to the United States in 1863. Died March 8, 1865, in New Haven, Connecticut. *References: DAB; DADH;* and *WWWA.*

BRADLEY, DAN BEACH (1804–1893). Medical missionary, born July 18, 1804, in Marcellus, New York. Bradley graduated from the New York Medical College, and was ordained in 1838. He was a medical missionary under the American Board of Commissioners for Foreign Missions (ABCFM) in Siam from 1835 until 1846, when the ABCFM decided to withdraw its mission to that country. He then became a missionary under the American Missionary Association. He introduced printing, inoculation by vaccination against smallpox, and modern obstetrics to Siam. Died June 23, 1893, in Bangkok, Siam. His son, **DAN FREEDMAN BRADLEY** (1857–1939), clergyman, born March 17, 1857, in Bangkok, wrote *Simo: A Romance of the Court of Siam* (Chicago, 1899). *References:* William L. Bradley, ed., *Siam Then: The Foreign Colony in Bangkok before and after Anna* (Pasadena, Calif., 1981); Lawrence Briggs, "Aubaret versus Bradley Case at Bangkok, 1866–1867," *FEQ* 6 (1947): 262–82; *EM*; George H. Feltus, ed., *Abstract of the Journal of Rev. Dan Beach Bradley, M.D., Medical Missionary in Siam, 1835–1873* (Cleveland, 1936); Donald C. Lord, "King and the Apostle; Mongkut, Bradley and the American Missionaries," *South Atlantic Quarterly* 66 (1967): 332–40; and Donald C. Lord, *Mo Bradley and Thailand* (Grand Rapids, Mich., 1969).

BRAYTON, DURLIN L. (1837–1900). Missionary, born October 27, 1837, in Hubbardton, Vermont. Brayton graduated from Brown University and Newton Theological Seminary. He was a missionary under the American Baptist Missionary Union in Burma from 1837 until his death. He served in the Pwo Karen mission. He was stationed at Amherst from 1838 to 1840, at Mergui from 1840 to 1845, and at Kemendine after 1855. He founded the Pwo Karen Association, and translated the Bible into the Pwo Karen dialect. Died April 23, 1900, in Rangoon, Burma. *Reference*: *EM*.

BRENT, CHARLES HENRY (1862–1929). Clergyman, born April 9, 1862, in Newcastle, Ontario, Canada. Brent graduated from Trinity College (Toronto) and was ordained in 1887. He held pastorates in Buffalo, New York, and Boston, and became a U.S. citizen. He was elected the first missionary bishop of the Protestant Episcopal Church in 1901, and was consecrated as missionary bishop of the Philippines. He built a cathedral and a hospital in Manila, and a boarding school in Baguio. He was involved in the crusade against opium, presided over the First International Opium Conference in Shanghai in 1909, and represented the United States on the League of Nations Advisory Committee on Narcotics in 1923. He left the Philippines in 1917 because of ill health. He was chief of chaplains to the American Expeditionary Force in France during World War I, and bishop of Western New York from 1919 until his death. Died March 27, 1929, in Lausanne, Switzerland. *References*: Charles Henry Brent Papers, Archives of the Church Historical Society, Austin, Texas; Charles Henry Brent Papers, Manuscript Division, Library of Congress; Frederick Ward Bates, ed., *Things that Matter: The Best of the Writings of Bishop Brent* (New York, 1949); *CDCWM*; *DAB S1*; *EP* 4:393; *Gleeck/Manila*; *LC*; *NCAB* 26:482; *NYT*, March 28, 1929; *Pier*; Emma J. Portuondo, "The Impact of Bishop Charles Henry Brent upon American Colonial and Foreign Policy, 1901–1917," Ph.D. diss., Catholic University, 1969; Michael C. Reilly, "Charles Henry Brent: Philippine Missionary and Ecumenist," *PS* 24 (1976): 303–25; *WWWA*; and Alexander C. Zabriskie, *Bishop Brent: Crusador for Christian Unity* (Philadelphia, 1948).

BRETHREN IN CHRIST FOREIGN MISSIONS. Founded in 1895, it began missionary service in India in 1914, and in Japan in 1953. The name was changed to Brethren in Christ World Missions after 1960. *References*: Archives of the Brethren in Christ Church, Messiah College, Granthan, Pa.; Doyle C. Book, "Footprints of Jesus: The Brethren in Christ in Japan 1953–1980," D.Miss. thesis, Fuller Theological Seminary, 1981; and Carlton O. Wittinger, *Quest for Piety and Obedience: The Story of the Brethren in Christ* (Nappanee, Ind., 1978).

BREWSTER, WILLIAM N(ESBITT) (1862–1916). Missionary, born December 5, 1862, in Highland, Ohio. Brewster attended Wittenberg College (Springfield, Ohio), graduated from Ohio Wesleyan University and Boston University

School of Theology, and was ordained in 1888. He was a missionary under the Board of Foreign Missions of the Methodist Episcopal Church in Singapore from 1888 to 1890, and at Hinghwa, Fukien Province, China, from 1890 until his death. He established the mission press, assisted in translating the entire Bible into the Hinghwa colloquial dialect, and wrote *The Evolution of New China* (Cincinnati, 1907) and *The Cost of Christian Conquest* (Cincinnati, 1908). Died November 22, 1916, in Chicago. *References*: CR 48 (1917): 456–60; *EWM*; and *WWWA*.

BRIDGMAN, ELIJAH C(OLEMAN) (1801–1861). Missionary, born April 22, 1801, in Belchertown, Massachusetts. Bridgman graduated from Amherst College and Andover Theological Seminary, and was ordained in 1829. He was a missionary under the American Board of Commissioners for Foreign Missions (ABCFM) in China from 1830 until his death, the first American missionary in China. He served in Canton until 1847. He was involved in organizing the Medical Missionary Society in China, was a joint secretary of the Society for the Diffusion of Useful Knowledge, and served as the editor of the North China branch of the Royal Asiatic Society. In 1833, he began publishing the *Chinese Repository*, which he edited until 1847 for the spread of information about China among English-speaking people. He wrote *Chinese Chrestomathy in the Canton Dialect* (Macao, 1841), the first practical manual of the Cantonese dialect. He moved to Shanghai in 1847 and worked on a translation of the Bible, which appeared in 1862. Died November 2, 1861, in Shanghai. *References*: Elijah C. Bridgman Papers, Belchertown Historical Association Collections, Belchertown, Mass.; *DAB*; Fred W. Drake, "Protestant Geography in China: E. C. Bridgman's Portrayal of the West," in Suzannne W. Barnett and John K. Fairbank, eds., *Christianity in China: Early Protestant Missionary Writings* (Cambridge, Mass., 1985), pp. 89–106; Frederick W. Drake, "Bridgman in China in the Early Nineteenth Century," *AN* 46 (1986): 34–42; *EM*; and Susan R. Stifler, "Elijah Coleman Bridgman, the First American Sinologist," *Notes on Far Eastern Studies in America* no. 10 (January 1942): 1–11.

BRIDGMAN, ELIZA JANE GILLET (1805–1871). Missionary educator, wife of Elijah Coleman Bridgman,* born May 6, 1805, in Derby, Connecticut. She was a missionary under the Domestic and Foreign Missionary Society of the Protestant Episcopal Church in the United States of America in China in 1845. She married Elijah Coleman Bridgman in 1845, and transferred to the American Board of Commissioners of Foreign Missions (ABCFM). She served in Canton, and after 1847, in Shanghai. In 1850 she opened the first Protestant day school for girls in Shanghai, and directed it until 1862, when she returned to the United States because of ill health. She wrote *Daughters of China: or, Sketches of Domestic Life in the Celestial Empire* (New York, 1853). She was back in China in 1864, served in the North China mission in Peking, and again opened a girls' school (which later evolved into the Woman's College of Yenching University). She went again to Shanghai in 1868 and taught in a girls' school there until her death. Died November 10, 1871, in Shanghai. *Reference*: *NAW*.

BRIGGS, CHARLES W(HITMAN) (1874–1962). Missionary, born July 17, 1874, in Deposit, New York. Briggs graduated from Colgate University and Hamilton Theological Seminary, and was ordained in 1900. He was a missionary under the American Baptist Missionary Union in Panay, Philippines, from 1900 to 1910. He established a mission in Iloilo Province, Panay Island, and founded the Jaro Industrial School for Boys (later Central Philippine University). He returned to the United States in 1911 because of ill health. He wrote *The Progressing Philippines* (Philadelphia, 1913). He held pastorates in Ballston Spa and Burnt Hills, New York, and in Bellows Falls, Vermont, from 1911 until his retirement in 1950. After 1950 he held a pastorate in Williamstown, Massachusetts. Died March 24, 1962, in North Adams, Massachusetts.

BRIGGS, GEORGE WESTON (1874–1966). Missionary, born September 21, 1874, in North Branch, Michigan. Briggs graduated from Northwestern University, studied at the University of California and Johns Hopkins University, and was ordained in 1904. He was a teacher in public schools in Michigan from 1891 to 1896. He was a missionary under the Board of Foreign Missions of the Methodist Episcopal Church in India from 1903 to 1925, and a professor of English literature at Reid Christian College in 1908–1909. He was a professor of Sanskrit language and literature at Drew University's Theological School from 1925 to 1929, and professor of the history of religions from 1929 until his retirement in 1944. He wrote *The Chamars* (Calcutta, 1920) and *Gorakhnath and the Kanphata Yogis* (Calcutta, 1937). Died April 18, 1966, in Madison, New Jersey. *References*: *NYT*, April 19, 1966; and *WWWA*.

BRILL, GEROW D(ODGE) (1864–1931). Agriculturist, born April 2, 1864, and grew up in Dutchess County, New York. Brill graduated from the College of Agriculture of Cornell University. He then returned to the family farm. He went to China in 1897, carried out an agricultural survey near Wuchang and was head of the Hupeh Agricultural College and Experimental Farm in Wuchang from 1897 until 1900. He returned to the United States in 1900 and was a scientific explorer for the Department of Public Instruction in the Philippines in 1901–1902. He was later manager of the Broadbrook Farms in Bedford Hills, New York, from 1912 to 1919 and of the Forsgate Farms in Jamesburg, New Jersey, after 1919. Died September 10, 1931, in Ithaca, New York. *References*: Gerow Brill Papers, Cornell University Library, Ithaca, N.Y.; Merle E. Curti and Kendall Birr, *Prelude to Point Four: American Technical Missions Overseas, 1838–1938* (Madison, Wis., 1954), pp. 29–35; and *NYT*, September 12, 1931.

BRITISH-AMERICAN TOBACCO COMPANY (BAT). The American Tobacco Company began exporting cigarettes to China in 1890. In 1902 it allied itself with the Imperial Tobacco Company to create the British-American Tobacco Company, which began manufacturing cigarettes in China in that year. Americans had a controlling interest in the company until 1915. *References*: Sherman Cochran, *Big Business in China: Sino-Foreign Rivalry in the Cigarette Industry, 1890–1930* (Cambridge, Mass., 1940); Sherman Cochran, "Commercial Penetration and Economic Imperialism in China: American Cigarette Company's Entrance into the Market," in *America's China Trade in Historical Perspective: The Chinese and American Performance*, ed. Ernest R. May and John K. Fairbank (Cambridge, Mass., 1986), pp. 151–203.

BRITTON, ROSWELL S(ESSOMS) (1897–1951). Educator, born July 3, 1897, in Shanghai, to American missionary parents. Britton attended Mars Hill College (N.C.) and graduated from Wake Forest College and Columbia University School of Journalism. He went to Peking in 1924, helped establish the school of journalism at Yenching University, and served as its chairman from 1924 to 1926. He became an authority on ancient Chinese writings, and was an assistant professor of Chinese and mathematics at New York University from 1930 until his death. He wrote *The Chinese Periodical Press, 1800–1912* (Shanghai, 1933) and *Yin Bone Photographs* (Shanghai, 1935). Died February 2, 1951, in New York City. *References*: *Arbitus Asia* 14 (1951): 190–91; *NYT*, February 4, 1951; *School and Society* 73 (February 10, 1951): 92–93.

BROCKMAN, FLETCHER SIMS (1867–1944). Association executive, born November 18, 1867, in Amherst County, Virginia. Brockman graduated from Vanderbilt University. He was student secretary of the International Commission of the Young Men's Christian Association (YMCA) for the Southern states from 1891 to 1897, and traveling secretary of the YMCA's International Commission in 1897–1898. He went to China in 1898 as foreign secretary of the International Committee, and established the first YMCA in Nanking. He was the first general secretary of the National Committee of YMCAs of China from 1901 to 1915, and contributed to the development of the national Chinese YMCA movement. He was associate general secretary of the National War Work Council of the YMCA during World War I, and associate general secretary of the International Committee from 1915 to 1924. He returned to East Asia in 1924 as administrative secretary of the National Council of YMCA in the Far East, with supervisory direction of YMCA work in China, Japan, Korea, Hong Kong, Indochina, the Philippine Islands, and the Straits Settlement. He retired in 1929. He wrote *I Discover the Orient* (New York, 1935). Died November 12, 1944, in Columbia, South Carolina. *References*: *NYT*, November 13, 1944; and *WWWA*.

BRONSON, MILES (1812–1883). Missionary, born July 20, 1812, in Norway, New York. Bronson graduated from the Hamilton Literary and Theological Institution (later Colgate University) and Hamilton Theological Seminary, and was ordained in 1836. He was a missionary under American Baptist Missionary Union in India from 1837 to 1880. He served in Sadiya, Assam; established a mission in Jaipur, and in the early 1840s moved to Namsang, Naga Hills. He established a mission in Nowgong in 1841, and in 1863 was the first Christian missionary to reach the Garo tribe. He moved to Dibrugarh in 1879. He compiled *A Dictionary in Assamese and English* (Sibsagar, Assam, India, 1867). He returned to the United States in 1879. Died November 9, 1883, in Eaton Rapids, Michigan. *References*: Bronson Family Papers, Andover Newton Theological School Library, Newton Center, Mass.; Harrietee B. Gunn, *In a Far Country, a Story of Christian Heroism and Achievement* (Philadelphia, 1911); and Walter S. Steward, *Later Baptist Missionaries and Pioneers* (Philadelphia, 1929), Vol. 2, pp. 177–205.

BROOKE, JOHN M(ERCER) (1826–1906). Naval officer and scientist, born December 18, 1826, in the Brooke Cantonment, Tampa, Florida. Brooke graduated from the U.S. Naval Academy in 1847. He was on duty at the Naval Observatory in Washington, D.C., from 1851 to 1853, where he invented a deep-sea sounding apparatus. He served in the North Pacific Surveying Expedition* attached to the USS *Vincennes* and with charge of the astronomical department. After he returned to the United States, he was responsible, with Commodore John Rodgers,* for preparing the charts and records of the expedition. In 1858 he was commissioned to map the topography of the sea floor of the north Pacific Ocean on the USS *Fenimore Cooper*. He made deep-sea soundings and surveys of a considerable part of the east coast of Japan, but was wrecked in 1859 during a cyclone at Giddo, Japan, and returned to the United States in 1860 in the Japanese corvette *Kanrin Maru*, which also brought the first Japanese minister to the United States and was the first Japanese ship to cross the Pacific. He served in the Confederate Navy during the Civil War, and was chief of the Confederate Bureau of Ordnance and Hydrography from 1863 to 1865. He was a professor of physics and astronomy at the Virginia Military Academy from 1866 to 1899. Died December 14, 1906, in Lexington, Virginia. *References*: George M. Brooke, Jr., ed., *Brooke Journals* (Tokyo, 1961); George M. Brooke, Jr., "A High Old Cruise: John Mercer Brooke and the American Voyage of the *Kanrin Maru*," *Virginia Cavalcade* 29 (1980): 174–83; George M. Brooke, Jr., *John M. Brooke, Naval Scientist and Educator* (Charlottesville, Va., 1980); George M. Brooke, Jr., ed., *John M. Brooke's Pacific Cruise and Japanese Adventure, 1858–1860* (Honolulu, 1986); *DAB*; *KEJ*; *NCAB* 22:29; *NYT*, December 15, 1906; and *WWWA*.

BROOKS, WILLIAM P(ENN) (1851–1938). Agriculturist, born November 19, 1851, in South Scituate, Massachusetts. Brooks graduated from Massachusetts Agricultural College and the University of Halle (Germany). He was a professor of botany at the Massachusetts Agricultural College from 1880 to 1888; acting president there from 1880 to 1883, in 1886–1887, and in 1905–1906; and a professor of agriculture there from 1889 to 1908. He taught chemistry, agriculture, and physical education at the Sapporo Agricultural College in Sapporo, Japan, from 1877 to 1880. He was an agriculturist at the Massachusetts Agricultural Experiment Station from 1889 to 1921, its director from 1906 to 1918, and a consulting agriculturist there from 1918 to 1921. Died March 8, 1938, in Springfield, Massachusetts. *References*: *Foreign Pioneers*; *NYT*, March 9, 1938; and *WWWA*.

BROWN, ELIPHALET, JR. (1816–1886). Artist, born in Newburyport, Massachusetts. Brown was working as a lithographer in New York City as early as 1839 and remained there until 1852. He was attached to Matthew C. Perry's* expedition to Japan from 1852 to 1854 as a daguerreotypist and artist, and was the first Westerner to shoot photographs in Japan. He was connected with the U.S. Navy from 1855 until his retirement in 1875. Died January 23, 1886, in New York City. *References*: *NYHSD*; *NYT*, January 24, 1886; and *WWWA*.

BROWN, GEORGE T(HOMPSON) (1921–   ). Missionary, born April 30, 1921, in Kuling, China, to American missionary parents. Brown graduated from Davidson College and Union and Princeton theological seminaries, and was ordained in 1949. He held a pastorate in Gastonia, North Carolina, from 1950 to 1952. He was a missionary under the Board of Foreign Missions of the Presbyterian Church in the United States in Korea from 1952 to 1967, and was principal of the Ho Nam Theological Seminary in Kwangju, Korea, from 1962 to 1967. He was the Asia secretary of the Board of World Missions of the Presbyterian Church in the United States in Nashville in 1967–1968; field secretary for Korea from 1968 to 1973; and staff director of the division of the international mission general executive board after 1973. He wrote *Mission to Korea* (Nashville, 1962) and *Christianity in the People's Republic of China* (Atlanta, 1983). *References*: *CA*; and *Who's Who in Religion* (Chicago, 1977).

BROWN, HENRY J(ACOB) (1879–1959). Missionary, born December 9, 1879, in Mountain Lake, Minnesota. Brown graduated from Baptist Seminary and Baptist College (St. Paul, Minn.). He was a missionary in China from 1909 to 1949. He was an independent missionary from 1909 until 1914, and was founder of the General Conference of the Mennonite Brethren Church mission in China in 1914, serving until 1941. He was interned by the Japanese from 1941 to 1943. He wrote *Chips of Experiences* (Berne, Ind., 1929); *The General Conference China Mennonite Mission* (Tamingfu, China, 1940); and *In Japanese Hands* (North Newton, Kans., 1943). He retired in 1944. Died September 23,

1959, in Freeman, South Dakota. His wife, **MARIA MILLER BROWN** (1883–1975), wrote *Praise the Lord: A Book of Personal Experiences* (Freeman, S.D., 1963). *References*: Henry J. Brown Papers, Mennonite Library and Archives, North Newton, Kans.; and *Freeman* (N.D.) *Courier*, September 24, 1959.

BROWN, NATHAN (1807–1886). Missionary, born June 22, 1807, in New Ipswich, New York. Brown graduated from Williams College and attended Newton Theological Seminary. He was editor of *The Vermont Telegraph* from 1831–1832. He was a missionary under the American Baptist Missionary Union in Burma in 1833–1834; established a mission in Sadiya, Assam, near the borders of China, in 1834; and moved in 1839 to Jaipur and in 1841 to Sibsagar. He translated portions of the New Testament into Assamese and wrote *Grammatical Notices of the Assamese Language* (Sibsagor, India, 1848). He was editor of *Orunodoi*, an illustrated Assamese monthly magazine, from 1846 to 1854. He returned to the United States in 1855 and served as editor of *American Baptist* from 1857 to 1872. He was in Yokohama, Japan, from 1873 until his death. With Jonathan Goble,* in 1876 he built the first Baptist church in Tokyo as well as a theological school there in 1884. He translated portions of the Bible into Japanese. Died January 1, 1886, in Yokohama, Japan. *References*: Elizabeth Brown, *The Whole World Kin: A Pioneer Experience among Remote Tribes and Other Labors of Nathan Brown* (Philadelphia, 1890); *EM*; *Hewitt*; and *LC*.

BROWN, ROY HOWARD (1878–1958). Missionary and educator, born May 2, 1878, in Girard, Kansas. Brown graduated from Park College (Parkville, Mo.) and McCormick Theological Seminary (Chicago), attended the University of Chicago, and was ordained in 1903. He was a missionary under the Board of Foreign Missions of the Presbyterian Church in the U.S.A. in Albay Province, the Philippines, from 1903 to 1921, and translated the Bible into Bicol. He served with the Young Men's Christian Association (YMCA) during World War I. He held pastorates in Chicago and Des Moines, Iowa, from 1922 to 1932. He returned to the Philippines in 1932, was president of Silliman University from 1932 until 1937, and professor of homiletics and pastoral theology and head of the theological department at Union Theological Seminary in Manila after 1939. He was interned by the Japanese during World War II and worked in a leper hospital. He retired in 1947. Died December 28, 1958, in Pasadena, California. *References*: *EP* 4:457; *NYT*, January 1, 1959; *WWP*; and *WWWA*.

BROWN, SAMUEL ROBBINS (1810–1880). Missionary, born June 16, 1810, in East Windsor, Connecticut, and grew up in Monson, Massachusetts. Brown graduated from Yale University, attended Columbia (S.C.) Theological Seminary and Union Theological Seminary (New York City), and was ordained in 1838. He taught at the New York Institute for the Deaf and Dumb from 1832 to 1835. He was a missionary under the American Board of Commissioners for Foreign Missions (ABCFM) in China from 1839 to 1847. He established and directed schools in Macao and Hong Kong. He returned to the United States in 1847 because of his wife's ill health. He directed a school in Rome, New York, from 1848 to 1851, and held a pastorate in Owasco Outlet, New York, from 1851 to 1859. He was again a missionary under the Board of Foreign Missions of the Reformed Mission in America in Japan from 1859 until 1879, one of the first missionaries to enter Japan. He was a teacher and missionary in Kanagawa and later in Yokohama. He was founder and president of the Asiatic Society of Japan, and from 1874 to 1879 he was chairman of the committee that translated the New Testament into Japanese. He wrote *Colloquial Japanese* (Shanghai, 1863). He returned to the United States in 1879. Died June 20, 1880, in Monson, Massachusetts. *References*: *ACAB*; *DAB*; *EM*; *KEJ*; *NCAB* 8:453; and *WWWA*.

BROWN, WILLIAM H(ENRY) (1884–1939). Botanist, born October 6, 1884, in Richmond, Virginia. Brown graduated from Richmond College and Johns Hopkins University. He made botanical investigations in Jamaica in 1910, and was a scientific assistant at the Michigan Agricultural Experiment Station and an instructor in plant physiology at the Michigan Agricultural College in 1910–1911. He was a plant physiologist at the Bureau of Science in Manila from 1911 to 1923, associate professor of botany at the University of the Philippines from 1915 to 1918, professor and head of the department there from 1919 to 1924, chief of the division of investigation of the Bureau of Forestry in Manila from 1918 to 1920, and director of the Bureau of Science in Manila from 1924 to 1933. He wrote *Vegetation of Philippine Mountains* (Manila, 1919) and *Minor Products of Philippine Forests* (Manila, 1920–1921), and was editor-in-chief of the *Philippine Journal of Science* from 1924 to 1933. He was a lecturer in botany at Johns Hopkins University after 1933. Died November 9, 1939, in Baltimore. *References*: *NCAB* 40:202; *NYT*, November 10, 1939; *Philippine Journal of Science* 72 (1940): 241–50; and *WWWA*.

BROWN, W(ILLIAM) NORMAN (1892–1975). Indologist, born June 24, 1892, in Baltimore. Brown accompanied his missionary parents to India in 1900. He returned to the United States in 1905, attended Hiram College, graduated from Johns Hopkins University, and studied at the University of Pennsylvania. He served in naval intelligence during World War I. He was in India from 1922 to 1924 as a professor of English at Prince of Wales College at Jammu and as vice principal there in 1923–1924. He was a professor of Sanskrit at the University of Pennsylvania from 1926 until his retirement in 1966. He also carried out research in India in 1928–1929, 1934–1935, and 1954–1955, and was curator of Indian art at the Philadelphia Museum of Art from 1936 to 1954. He was head of the India division in the Research and Analysis Division of the Office of Strategic Services (OSS) during World War II, and later served on the OSS planning staff. He wrote *The United States and India and Pakistan* (Cambridge, Mass., 1953). Died April 22, 1975, in West Chester, Pennsylvania. *References*: *American Oriental Society Journal* 96 (1976): 3–6; *JAS* 35 (1975): 99; *NYT*,

April 26, 1975; Rosanne Rocher, "Biographical Sketch: William Norman Brown," in *India and Indology: Selected Articles*, ed. Rosane Rocher (Delhi, 1978), pp. xvii–xxiii.

BROWNE, J(OHN) ROSS (1821–1875). Traveler, author, and diplomat, born February 11, 1821, in Dublin, Ireland. Browne came to the United States with his parents in 1821, and grew up in Louisville, Kentucky. He was a porter in the United States Senate in 1841–1842, and shipped as a sailor on a whaler from New Bedford, Massachusetts, in 1842–1843. He traveled extensively for the next twenty years; he was the official reporter to the first constitutional convention of California in 1849, and later was a confidential agent for the U.S. Treasury Department in the West. He was U.S. minister to China in 1870–1871, but was recalled after expressing opinions that were contrary to those of the U.S. government. He subsequently settled in Oakland, California. Died December 8, 1875, in Oakland. *References*: *ACAB*; *Anderson*, ch. 3; *Lina F. Browne, ed., J. Ross Browne: His Letters, Journals and Writings* (Albuquerque, N.M., 1969); Paul H. Clyde, "The China Policy of J. Ross Browne, American Minister to Peking, 1868–1869," *PHR* 1 (1932): 312–333; *DAB*; Michael Goodman, *A Western Panorama, 1849–1875: The Travels, Writings, and Influence of J. Ross Browne on the Pacific Coast, and in Texas, Nevada, Arizona, and Baja California, as the First Mining Commissioner, and Minister to China* (Glendale, Calif., 1966); *NCAB* 8:117; *NYT*, December 9, 1875; Louis Rather, *J. Ross Browne, Adventurer* (Oakland, Calif., 1978); and *WWWA*.

BROWNELL, CLARENCE LUDLOW (1864–1927). Journalist, born June 6, 1864, in Hartford, Connecticut. Brownell attended the Stevens Institute of Technology and graduated from Harvard University. He was an instructor of English and of military drill in government and public schools in Japan for five years, and also worked as a correspondent for American and English newspapers and periodicals. He wrote *Tales from Tokio* (New York, 1900), and *The Heart of Japan: Glimpses of Life and Nature Far from the Traveller's Track in the Land of the Rising Sun* (New York, 1903). He later became connected with Valparaiso University (Ind.) and made a study of educational systems, particularly in Gary, Indiana. He settled in Florida in 1922. Died February 2, 1927, in Jacksonville, Florida. *References*: *NYT*, February 3, 1927; and *WWWA*.

BRUCE, EDWARD B(RIGHT) (1879–1943). Businessman, born April 13, 1879, in Dover Plains, New York. Bruce graduated from Columbia University and Columbia Law School. He practiced law in New York from 1904 to 1907. He came to the Philippines in 1907 as an attorney for the American Philippine Railroad Company. He formed his own law firm in Manila in 1908 and was also part owner of the *Manila Times*. He was involved in various business ventures. He lived in China after 1911, and was president of the Pacific Development Company, which sought to promote Oriental trade. He made a collection of early Chinese paintings, which is now in the Fogg Museum. He returned to New York in 1919, and turned to painting in New York City, Italy, Oregon, California, and Washington, D.C. He was chief of the Section of Fine Arts of the U.S. Treasury Department after 1933. Died January 26, 1943, in Hollywood, Florida. *References*: *DAB S3*; and *WWWA*.

BRUCE, HENRY JAMES (1835–1909). Missionary, born February 5, 1835, in Hardwick, Massachusetts. Bruce graduated from Amherst College and Andover Theological Seminary, attended Bangor Seminary, and was ordained in 1862. He was a missionary under the American Board of Commissioners for Foreign Missions (ABCFM) in western India from 1862 until his death. He served in Ahmednagar from 1863 to 1872, and at Satara from 1875 until his death. While in the United States from 1872 to 1875, he learned printing. He then took a press to India and printed schoolbooks and religious books which he had translated into Marathi, as well as millions of leaflets. Died May 4, 1909, in Pauchgani, Satara, India. *Reference*: *AndoverTS*.

BRYAN, CHARLES PAGE (1856–1918). Diplomat, born October 6, 1856, in Chicago. Bryan attended the University of Virginia and Columbian Law School (Washington, D.C.) and was admitted to the bar in 1878. He practiced law in Colorado from 1879 to 1884, and was a member of the Colorado House of Representatives from 1880 until 1886 and of the Illinois House of Representatives from 1890 to 1897. He was U.S. minister to China in 1897–1898, to Brazil from 1898 to 1902, to Portugal from 1903 to 1910, and to Belgium from 1909 to 1911. He was ambassador to Japan in 1911–1912 but was recalled because of a misunderstanding with U.S. secretary of state Philander Knox. Died March 17, 1918, in Washington, D.C. *References*: *ACAB*; *NCAB* 12:452; *NYT*, March 14, 1918; and *WWWA*.

BRYAN, ROBERT THOMAS (1855–1946). Missionary, born October 14, 1855, in Duplin County, North Carolina. Bryan graduated from the University of North Carolina and Southern Baptist Theological Seminary. He was a missionary under the Foreign Mission Board of the Southern Baptist Convention in China after 1885. He served in Chinkiang, Yangchow, and Shanghai. He also founded a boys' school and a Bible class, which became the theological department of the Shanghai Baptist College and Seminary. Died April 3, 1946, in San Antonio, Texas. *References*: F. Catherine Bryan, *His Golden Cycle. The Life Story of Robert Thomas Bryan* (Richmond, 1938); and *ESB*.

BRYAN, SAMUEL M(AGILL) (1847–1903). Postal expert, born September 20, 1847, in Cadiz, Ohio. Bryan served as a drummer boy in the Union Army during the Civil War. He was a clerk in the U.S. Treasury Department from 1867 to 1869 and in the Post Office Department from 1869 to 1873, where he was chief of foreign mail. From 1873 to 1882 he assisted the Japanese government in establishing an international postal system and served as superintendent of Japan's international mail service. He negotiated a series of postal treaties with the United States, France, and Germany in 1873–1874. In 1883 he returned to the United States, where he took charge of the Chesapeake and Potomac Telephone Company. \He later became its president and was also involved in the founding of American Telephone and Telegraph. *References*: *Eminent and Representative Men of Virginia and the District of Columbia* (Madison, Wis., 1893), pp. 63–64; and Robert M. Spaulding, "The Education of Samuel M. Bryan," *Japanese Philately* 42 (1987): 195–202.

BUCK, FRANK(LIN HOWARD) (1884–1950). Animal collector, born November 17, 1884, in Gainesville, Texas, and grew up in Dallas. Buck was successively a cowboy, a carnival concessionaire, and a bellhop. He was the general manager to the owner of the Western Vaudeville Managers Association and the Western representative and correspondent of the New York *Telegraph* until 1911. He made his first bird collection expedition to Bahia, Brazil, in 1911, and then made subsequent expedition to South America. He made expeditions to Malaya, India, Borneo, and New Guinea, with headquarters in Singapore, collecting wild animals for zoos and circuses. He became a major supplier of Asian fauna. He was president of Frank Buck Enterprises, Incorporated, and Jungleland, Incorporated, and also produced several motion pictures. He was coauthor of *Bring 'Em Back Alive* (New York, 1930); *Wild Cargo* (New York, 1932); *Fang and Claw* (New York, 1935); *Tim Thompson in the Jungles* (New York, 1935); *On Jungle Trails* (New York, 1937); *Animals Are Like That!* (New York, 1939); and his autobiography (with Ferrin Fraser), *All in a Lifetime* (New York, 1941). Died March 25, 1950, in Houston, Texas. *References*: *CB* 1943; *DAB S4*; *NCAB* 40:222; *New Yorker*, 22 (September 14, 1946); *NYT*, March 26, 1950; and *WWWA*.

BUCK, J(OHN) LOSSING (1890–1975). Agricultural economist and government official, born November 27, 1890, in LaGrange Township, Dutchess County, New York. Buck graduated from Cornell University. He was an agricultural missionary under the Board of Foreign Missions of the Presbyterian Church in the U.S.A. in Nanhsuchou, Anhwei Province, China, from 1915 until 1920; established a department of agricultural economics in the College of Agriculture of the University of Nanking in 1920, and was professor and head of that department until 1934. He was also acting dean of the college from 1920 to 1922. He wrote *Chinese Farm Economy* (Shanghai, 1930) and *Land Utilization in China* (Chicago, 1937). He returned to the United States in 1934, was a monetary advisor in the U.S. Treasury Department in 1934–1935 and its representative to China from 1935 to 1939, advisor to the Ministry of Finance of the Chinese Nationalist government in Chungking in 1939–1940, professor of agricultural economics at the University of Nanking in Chengtu, China, from 1940 until 1944, and a member of the China–United States Agricultural Mission in 1945–1946. He was the first chief of the Land and Water Use Branch of the Food and Agriculture Organization (FAO) from 1946 to 1954, and director for agricultural economics of the Council on Economic and Cultural Affairs in New York City from 1954 until his retirement in 1957. Died September 27, 1975, in Poughkeepsie, New York. *References*: *CA*; *NCAB* 55:93; James Pugh, ''J. Lossing Buck, American Missionary: The Application of Scientific Agriculture in China, 1915–1944,'' Ph.D. diss., Swarthmore College, 1973; Randall E. Stross, *The Stubborn Earth: American Agriculturists on Chinese Soil, 1898–1937* (Berkeley, Calif., 1986), ch. 7; and *WWWA*.

BUCK, OSCAR MACMILLAN (1885–1941). Missionary, son of Philo Melvin Buck,* born February 9, 1885, in Cawnpore, India. buck graduated from Ohio Wesleyan University and Drew Theological Seminary, and was ordained in 1909. He was a missionary under the Board of Foreign Missions of the Methodist Episcopal Church in India from 1909 to 1913, and was a professor of Bible at the Bareilly Theological Seminary. He was a pastor in Illinois from 1913 to 1915, and professor of missions and comparative religion at Ohio Wesleyan University from 1915 to 1919 and at Drew Theological Seminary from 1920 until his death. He was the secretary of the commission of Christian higher education in India in 1930–1931. He wrote *''Our Asiatic Christ''* (New York, 1927) and *India Looks to Her Future* (New York, 1930). Died February 10, 1941, in Madison, New Jersey. *References*: *EWM*; *NYT*, February 11, 1941; and *WWWA*.

BUCK, PEARL (SYDENSTRICKER) (1892–1973). Author, born June 26, 1892, in Hillsboro, West Virginia, and grew up in China, where her parents were missionaries. Buck graduated from Randolph-Macon Woman's College (Va.). She returned to China in 1914. She married John Lossing Buck* in 1917, and moved to North China and later to Nanking. She began writing in 1922, taught at Southeastern and Chung Yang universities from 1925 until 1930, and at Nanking University from 1921 to 1931. She left China in 1934. She wrote *East Wind: West Wind* (New York, 1930); *The Good Earth* (New York, 1931); *Sons* (New York, 1932); *The Mother* (New York, 1934); *A House Divided* (New York, 1935); and biographies of her father and mother: *The Exile* (New York, 1936) and *The Fighting Angel* (New York, 1936). Her books and the motion pictures based on them probably did more to shape American views of China than the work of any other single person. In 1938 she won the Nobel Prize for literature, which was awarded for her portrayal of China and for her biographies of her parents. She later wrote *Dragon Seed* (New York, 1941); *Pavilion of Women* (New York, 1946); *Peony* (New York, 1948); *The Hidden Flower* (New York, 1952); *Imperial Woman* (New York, 1956); *Letter from Peking* (New York, 1957); and *The Living Reed* (New York, 1963). Died March 6, 1973, in Danby, Vermont. *References*: Pearl S. Buck Papers, Pearl S. Buck Birthplace Foundation, Hillsboro, West Virginia; Pearl Buck Papers, Princeton University

Library, Princeton, N.J.; *CA*; *CB* 1956; *EAS*; *NAW*; *NCAB* E:66; *NYT*, March 7, 1973; Nora Stirling, *Pearl Buck: A Woman in Conflict* (Piscataway, N.J., 1983); and *WWWA*.

BUCK, PHILO M(ELVIN) (1846–1924). Missionary, born May 15, 1846, in Corning, New York, and grew up in Kansas. Buck graduated from Drew Theological Seminary (Madison, N.J.). He was a missionary under the Board of Foreign Missions of the Methodist Episcopal Church in India from 1870 until 1922. He served at Shahjahanpur from 1871 to 1875, in the Kumaun District 1875 to 1880, at Kanpur in 1880–1881, and in Mussoorie from 1881 to 1892. He was principal of Philander Smith Institute in Mussoorie from 1881 to 1886, served at the Meerut District from 1886 until his retirement in 1922, and was superintendent of the Meerut district from 1893 to 1914. Died September 8, 1924, in Mussoorie, Uttar Pradesh, India. *References*: *DAB*; *EWM*; *NCAB* 22:22; *NYT*, September 9, 1924; and *WWWA*.

BUCKINGHAM, BENJAMIN H(ORR) (1848–1906). Naval officer, born February 11, 1848, in Canton, Ohio. Buckingham graduated from the U.S. Naval Academy in 1869. He was a naval attaché in London, Paris, Berlin, and St. Petersburg. Accompanied by George Clayton Foulk* and Walter McLean,* he traveled in 1882 from Korea across Siberia and through Russia. He coauthored *Observations upon the Korean Coast, Japanese-Korean Ports, and Siberia* (Washington, D.C., 1883). In 1898 he retired with the rank of lieutenant commander. Died January 16, 1906, in Currituck Inlet, North Carolina. *Reference*: *NCAB* 34:136.

BUKER, RAYMOND B(ATES) (1899–   ) and **BUKER, RICHARD (STEELE)** (1899–   ). Raymond B. Buker, missionary, born August 27, 1899, in Foster, Rhode Island. He graduated from Bates College and Oberlin Divinity School, and attended the University of Chicago Divinity School. He was a member of the 1924 U.S. Olympic team. He was a missionary under the American Baptist Foreign Mission Society in Burma from 1926 until 1942. He served at Lashio and later in Meng Meng, in the southern Shan States in northeastern Burma and southwestern Yunnan. He escaped to India in 1942 and then returned to the United States. He was the foreign secretary of the Conservative Baptist Foreign Mission Society (CBFMS) from 1944 to 1956, and a professor of missions at the Conservative Baptist Theological Seminary (Denver) after 1956. Richard Buker, a medical missionary, was born August 27, 1899, in Foster, Rhode Island. He graduated from Bates College, Harvard Medical School, and Harvard School of Public Health. He was a medical missionary under the American Baptist Foreign Mission Society to the Shan states of Burma from 1926 until World War II. Under the American Leprosy Missions, Incorporated, he then took charge of the McKean Memorial Hospital, a leper colony at Chiengmai, Thailand. He later practiced medicine in Eastport, Maine, and

Boca Raton, Florida. *References*: Eric S. Fife, *Against the Clock: The Story of Ray Buker, Sr., Olympic Runner and Missionary Statesman* (Grand Rapids, Mich., 1981); and Dorothy C. Haskin, *Medical Missionaries You Would Like to Know* (Grand Rapids, Mich., 1957), pp. 22–30.

BUNCE, ARTHUR C(YRIL) (1901–1953). Economist and government official, born January 11, 1901, in Manchester, England, and became naturalized U.S. citizen in 1941. Bunce graduated from the universities of Saskatchewan and Wisconsin, and studied in Denmark and India. He organized adult agricultural education for the Young Men's Christian Association (YMCA) in Korea from 1928 to 1934, and was an associate professor of economics at Iowa State College from 1937 to 1943. He served as an economist for the board of governors of the Federal Reserve System in 1944–1945, as economic advisor to Lt. Gen. John R. Hodge in Korea in 1946, and as U.S. commissioner on the Joint U.S.-U.S.S.R. Commission in Korea 1946 to 1947 with the personal rank of minister. He was chief of the U.S. Economic Cooperation Administration (ECA) special mission to Korea from 1948 to 1950, the United States special economic and technical mission to Thailand in 1950, and the Far Eastern Section of the Federal Reserve Board after 1951. Died May 27, 1953, in Washington, D.C. *References*: *NYT*, May 29, 1953; and *WWWA*.

BUNKER, ALONZO (1837–1912). Missionary, born January 30, 1837, in Atkinson, Maine. Bunker graduated from Waterville (later Colby) College and Newton Theological Institution (New Centre, Mass.) and was ordained in 1865. He was a missionary under the American Baptist Missionary Union in Burma from 1855 until 1904. He wrote *Soo Thah: A Tale of the Making of the Karen Nation* (New York, 1902) and *Sketches from the Karen Hills* (New York, 1920). Died March 8, 1912, in Groton, Massachusetts. *Reference*: *WWWA*.

BUNKER, DALZELL A(DELBERT) (1853–1932). Missionary, born August 10, 1853, in Colebrook, Ohio. Bunker attended Oberlin College, and Oberlin and Union theological seminaries, and was ordained in 1886. From 1886 to 1892, he was employed by the King of Korea to organize and teach at the Royal College in Seoul. He then was a missionary under the Board of Foreign Missions of the Methodist Episcopal Church in Korea from 1895 until 1926. He was associated with the Paichai Boys' School for many years. Died November 23, 1932, in San Diego, California. His wife, **ANNIE E(LLERS) BUNKER** (1860–1938), a missionary nurse, graduated from Rockford (Ill.) College and the Training School for Nurses of the Boston City Hospital. She was a missionary under the Board of Foreign Missions of the Presbyterian Church in the U.S.A. from 1884 to 1887, and, after her marriage in 1887, served under the Board of Foreign Missions of the Methodist Episcopal Church. She headed the nursing work at the government hospital (later Severance Hospital), and is credited with being the builder of the nursing profession in Korea. She was also the friend and confidant of the Queen of Korea, and was the queen's medical attendant until her murder in 1885. Annie Bunker died October 8, 1938, in Seoul. *References*: *UnionTS*; *Woman's Who's Who in America 1914–1915*, ed. John W. Leonard (New York, 1914); and *Yanghwajin*.

BUNKER, ELLSWORTH (1894–1984). Diplomat, born May 11, 1894, in Yonkers, New York. Bunker graduated from Yale University. He worked for the National Sugar Refining Company from 1916 until 1951, serving as president from 1940 to 1948 and chairman of the board from 1948 to 1951. He was U.S. ambassador to Argentina in 1951–1952, to Italy in 1952–1953, to India from 1956 to 1961, and to Nepal from 1956 to 1959. He negotiated a settlement to the Netherlands-Indonesia dispute over West Irian in 1962. He was U.S. representative to the Organization of American States from 1964 to 1966. He was ambassador to South Vietnam from 1967 to 1973. He worked closely with the South Vietnamese government, and supported the policy of Vietnamization and a negotiated settlement to the war. He was ambassador at large from 1973 to 1977, and negotiated the Panama Canal Treaty. Died September 27, 1984, in Brattleboro, Vermont. *References*: *CB* 1978; *DADH*; *NYT*, September 28, 1984; and *WWWA*.

BURDEN, W(ILLIAM) DOUGLAS (1898–1978). Explorer and naturalist, born September 24, 1898, in Troy, New York. Burden graduated from Harvard University. He traveled the world collecting natural history specimens for the American Museum of Natural History. In 1922 he went on an expedition to East Asia to bring back specimens for the museum, led an expedition to Komodo island in the Dutch East Indies in 1926 to capture the giant lizard known as the Komodo dragon, and wrote *The Dragon Lizards of Komodo* (New York, 1927). He established the department of animal behavior at the museum, and he founded Marineland in St. Augustine, Florida, in 1938 and was its president. During World War II, he developed a shark repellent for the U.S. Navy. He wrote *Look to the Wilderness* (Boston, 1960). Died November 14, 1978, in Charlotte, Vermont. *References*: *CA*; *NYT*, November 16, 1978; and *WWWA*.

BURGESS, EBENEZER (1805–1870). Missionary, born June 26, 1805, in Grafton, Vermont. Burgess graduated from Amherst College and Andover Theological Seminary, and was ordained in 1839. He was a missionary under the American Board of Commissioners for Foreign Missions (ABCFM) in western India from 1839 to 1854. He prepared textbooks in Marathi and revised the translation of the Bible into that language. He was an agent of the ABCFM in the United States from 1854 to 1857, and held pastorates in Centerville, Barnstable, Dracut, Lanesville, Gloucester, and South Franklin, Massachusetts, from 1857 until 1867. Died January 1, 1870, in Newton Centre, Massachusetts. *References*: *ACAB*; *Amherst*; and *AndoverTS*.

BURGESS, GEORGIA (ANNA) (BURRUS) (1866–1948). Missionary, born July 19, 1866. Burgess graduated from Healdsburg College. She taught at a Bible Training School (Oakland). She was a missionary in Calcutta, India, from 1895 until 1935–the first Seventh-Day Adventist woman foreign missionary. In 1896 she opened a girls' school in Calcutta. She returned to the United States in 1935. Died September 25, 1948, in National City, California. *References*: *SDAE*; and *Pacific Union Recorder*, October 25, 1948.

BURGESS, J(OHN) STEWART (1883–1949). Sociologist, born July 12, 1883, in Pennington, New Jersey. Burgess attended Oberlin College and Union Theological Seminary, and graduated from Princeton and Columbia universities. He taught at a commercial college in Kyoto, Japan, and served as a volunteer worker in the Young Men's Christian Association (YMCA) in Kyoto from 1905 to 1907. He was the metropolitan student secretary of the Peiping YMCA and secretary of the YMCA in China. He was head of the sociology department at Yenching University from 1919 to 1929, organized the university's College of Applied Sciences in 1929–1930, and led in the establishment of modern social work in Peiping. He was secretary of the YMCA's community service department, and was instrumental in organizing a student social service club, a federation of community councils, a prisoners' aid association, a welfare committee, and a maternity hospital. He was associate professor of sociology at Pomona College from 1930 to 1933, and chair of the department of sociology at Temple University (Philadelphia) after 1933. He wrote *The Guilds of Peking* (New York, 1928) and was coauthor of *Peking, a Social Survey . . .* (New York, 1921). Died August 16, 1949, in Claremont, California. *References*: John Stewart Burgess Papers, Princeton University Library, Princeton, N.J.; *NCAB* 39:423; and *NYT*, August 19, 1949.

BURGEVINE, HENRY ANDREA (1836–1865). Adventurer, born possibly in New Bern, North Carolina. Burgevine went adventuring as a young man and served in the Crimean War. He came to China in 1860 and was recruited by Frederick Townsend Ward* as an officer in the foreign company raised to recapture Sungkiang from the Taiping rebels. He participated in the attack on Tsingpu and became third in command of the "Ever-Victorious Army." After Ward's death in 1862 he became commander of the army, but he failed in an assignment and was dismissed. He was arrested in Fukien in 1865 on his way to join the Taiping rebels. Drowned June 26, 1865, when his boat capsized in Fukien. *References*: *DAB*; Robert H. Detrick, "Henry Andrea Burgevine in China: A Biography," Ph.D. diss., Indiana University, 1968; *NCAB* 22:8; Martin Ring, "The Burgevine Case and Extrality in China, 1863–1866," *Papers on China* 20 (1969): 134–57; Richard J. Smith, *Mercenaries and Mandarins: The Ever-Victorious Army in Nineteenth Century China* (Millwood, N.Y., 1978); and *WWWA*.

BURKE, WILLIAM B(LOUNT) (1864–1947). Missionary, born June 12, 1864, in Macon, Georgia. Burke graduated from Emory University and the theology school of Vanderbilt University. He was a missionary under the Board of Missions of the Methodist Episcopal Church, South, in China from 1887 until 1937. He was stationed in Sungkiang, was principal of the Soochow University Bible School, chairman of the Sungkiang Public Health Association, and head of the Sungkiang Orphanage. He retired in 1937 and returned to China in 1938 to do relief work. He was interned by the Japanese in 1942–1943. Died December 19, 1947, in Macon, Georgia. *References*: William B. Burke Papers, Emory University Library, Atlanta; William B. Burke Papers, University of North Carolina Library, Chapel Hill, N.C.; and James Cobb Burke, *My Father in China* (New York, 1947).

BURLING, ROBBINS (1926–   ). Anthropologist, born April 18, 1926, in Minneapolis, Minnesota. Burling graduated from Yale and Harvard universities. He served in the U.S. Navy during World War II. He carried out fieldwork in the Garo Hills, Assam, India, from 1954 to 1956, and in Burma in 1959–1960. He was assistant professor of anthropology at the University of Pennsylvania from 1959 to 1963, associate professor of anthropology at the University of Michigan from 1964 to 1967, and professor of anthropology and linguistics there after 1967. He wrote *A Garo Grammar* (Poona, India, 1961), *Rengsanggri: Family and Kinship in a Garo Village* (Philadelphia, 1963), and *Hill Farms and Padi Fields: Life in Mainland South-East Asia* (Englewood Cliffs, N.J., 1964). *References*: AMWS; CA; DAS; and WWA.

BURLINGAME, ANSON (1820–1870). Diplomat, born November 14, 1820, in New Berlin, Chenango County, New York, and grew up in Seneca County, Ohio, and Detroit. Burlingame graduated from the University of Michigan (Detroit) and Harvard Law School, and practiced law in Boston. He served in the Massachusetts Senate from 1852 to 1855, and in the U.S. Congress from 1855 to 1860. He was U.S. minister to China from 1860 to 1867. He obtained great influence among the Chinese officials. In 1868, he was head of an official Chinese delegation to foreign powers, and negotiated a treaty with the United States on behalf of China in which the former country pledged to respect Chinese sovereignty. Died February 23, 1870, in St. Petersburg, Russia. *References*: Anson Burlingame Papers, Syracuse University Library; Burlingame Family Papers, Manuscript Division, Library of Congress; *ACAB*; *Anderson*, ch. 2; David Anderson, "Anson Burlingame: American Architect of the Cooperative Policy in China, 1861–1871," *DH* 1 (1977): 239–255; David Anderson, "Anson Burlingame: Reformer and Diplomat," *Civil War History* 25 (1979): 293–308; *DAB*; Samuel S. Kim, "America's First Minister to China: Anson Burlingame and the Tsungli Yamen," *Maryland Historian* 3 (1972): 87–104; Samuel S. Kim, "Anson Burlingame: A Study in Personal Diplomacy," Ph.D. diss., Columbia University, 1966; Samuel S. Kim, "Burlingame and the Inauguration of the

Cooperative Policy," *Modern Asian Studies* 5 (1971): 337–54; *NCAB* 8:55; *NYT*, February 24, 1870; Martin Ring, "Anson Burlingame, S. Wells Williams and China, 1861–1870," Ph.D. diss., Tulane University, 1972; and *WWWA*.

BUSS, CLAUDE A(LBERT) (1903–   ). Government official and educator, born November 29, 1903, in Sunbury, Pennsylvania. Buss graduated from Washington Missionary College (Takoma Park, Md.), Susquehanna University, and the University of Pennsylvania, and studied in Paris. He was a language student in China from 1929 to 1931, vice consul in Nanking from 1931 to 1934, and professor of international relations at the University of Southern California (Los Angeles) from 1934 to 1941. He was executive assistant to the U.S. high commissioner to the Philippines from 1941 to 1944, and remained behind in Manila to meet the Japanese after the high commissioner and other officials moved to Corregidor. He was chief of the San Francisco Office of War Information from 1944 to 1946, and professor of international relations at Stanford University from 1946 until his retirement in 1969. He wrote *War and Diplomacy in Eastern Asia* (New York, 1941); *The Far East* (New York, 1955); *Southeast Asia and the World Today* (New York, 1958); *The People's Republic of China* (New York, 1962); *Contemporary Southeast Asia* (New York, 1970); *The People's Republic of China and Richard Nixon* (Stanford, Calif., 1972); *The United States and the Philippines: Background for Policy* (Washington, D.C., 1977); and *The United States and Korea: Background for Policy* (Stanford, Calif., 1982). *References*: *CA*; *DAS*; Michael P. Onorato, ed., *Claude A. Buss in Manila, 1941–1942* (Fullerton, Calif., 1986); and *WWA*.

BUTLER, ESTHER (1850–1921). Missionary, born May 10, 1850, in Damascus, Ohio. Butler taught school in Damascus, Ohio. She was a missionary under the Friends Foreign Missionary Society of the Ohio Yearly Meeting in China from 1887 until 1890, when she established the independent Friends China Mission. She served in Nanking from 1887 until her death. She founded a hospital in Nanking in 1895 and another at Luho in 1898. Died in Nanking in 1921. *Reference*: Hugh Barbour and J. William Frost, *The Quakers* (Westport, Conn., 1988), pp. 299–300.

BUTLER, SMEDLEY D(ARLINGTON) (1881–1940). Marine Corps officer, born July 30, 1881, in West Chester, Pennsylvania. Butler enlisted in the Marine Corps as a second lieutenant in 1898. He served in the Philippines in 1899–1900 and in the Boxer Rebellion in China in 1900. He served in Honduras and Panama in 1903–1904; in Olongapo, Philippines, from 1905 to 1907; commanded the Panama Mobile battalion, which was based in the Panama Canal Zone, from 1909 to 1914; served in Nicaragua in 1909–1910 and in Haiti from 1915 to 1918; and established the *Gendarmerie d'Haiti* and served as its first commandant. He commanded the major embarkation camp in Europe at Brest, France, during World War I; was commander of the marine base at Quantico from 1920 to

1924; was director of public safety in Philadelphia from 1924 to 1926; and commanded the marine expedition to China and the marine brigade in Tientsin from 1927 to 1929. He retired in 1931. Died June 21, 1940, in Philadelphia. *References*: Smedley D. Butler Papers, United States Marine Corps Historical Center, Washington, D.C.; Robert T. Cochran, "Smedley Butler, a Marine for All Seasons," *Smithsonian* 15 (June 1984): 137–56; *DAB S2*; *DAMIB*; *NCAB* 38:536; Gabrielle Neufeld and James S. Santelli, "Smedley Butler's Air Corps: First Marine Aviators in China," *USNIP* 103 (April 1977): 48–59; *NYT*, June 22, 1940; Hans Schmidt, *Maverick Marine: General Smedley D. Butler and the Contradictions of American Military History* (Lexington, Ky., 1987); and *WWWA*.

BUTLER, WILLIAM (1818–1899). Missionary, born January 30, 1818, in Dublin, Ireland, and came to the United States in 1850. Butler graduated from Hardwick Street Mission Seminary (Dublin) and Didsbury College (Manchester). He held pastorates in Williamsburg, Shelburne Falls, and Westfield, New York, and Lynn, Massachusetts. He was a founder of the India mission under the Board of Foreign Missions of the Methodist Episcopal Church in India, and served there from 1857 until 1864. He opened the mission at Bareilly, Northwestern Provinces (now United Provinces). He founded a girls' orphanage in Bareilly and a boys' orphanage in Lucknow. He returned to the United States in 1864 because of ill health. There he held pastorates in Chelsea, Melrose, and Boston, Massachusetts, was secretary of the American and Foreign Christian Union in New York City, and later was superintendent of the Methodist Church mission in Mexico City until 1879. He wrote *The Land of the Veda: Being Personal Reminiscences of India, Its People, Castes, Thugs and Fakirs* (New York, 1871), and *From Boston to Bareilly and Back* (Boston, 1885). Died August 18, 1899, in Old Orchard, Maine. *References*: *ACAB*; *DAB*; *EM*; *EWM*; *LC*; *NCAB* 12:61; and *WWWA*.

BUTTE, GEORGE C(HARLES FELIX) (1877–1940). Lawyer, government official, and colonial administrator, born May 9, 1877, in San Francisco, and grew up in Rockdale, Texas. Butte graduated from Austin (Tex.) College and the University of Texas, studied at the University of Berlin, Heidelberg University, and l'École de Droit (Paris), and was admitted to the bar in 1903. He practiced law at Muskogee, Oklahoma, from 1904 to 1911, was professor of law at the University of Texas from 1914 to 1924, and was dean there in 1923–1924. He was attorney general of Puerto Rico from 1925 to 1928 and acting governor in 1926–1927, special assistant to the attorney general of the United States from 1928 to 1930, vice governor and secretary of public instruction of the Philippines from 1930 to 1932, acting governor general in 1931 and 1932, and associate justice of the Supreme Court of the Philippines from 1932 to 1936. Died January 18, 1940, in Mexico City. *References*: George Charles Butte

Papers, University of Texas Library, Austin, Texas; *CCDP*; *NCAB* 33:79; *NYT*, January 19, 1940; *Sevilla*; and *WWWA*.

BUTTERWORTH, EMERSON MCMILLIN (1894–1961). Petroleum geologist, born August 4, 1894, in Columbus, Ohio. Butterworth graduated from the University of California. He was a field geologist with the Standard Oil Company of California from 1917 to 1925. He led an expedition to the Dutch East Indies in 1924–1925 to appraise oil prospects. He was district geologist in Los Angeles from 1925 to 1930. He was managing director of the N. V. Nederlandsche Pacific Petroleum Maatschappij (NPPM, later Caltex Pacific Oil Company) in Batavia, Java, from 1930 to 1932, and then managing director of that company in the Hague, Netherlands, from 1932 to 1936, where he negotiated an exploration concession for NPPM in Sumatra. He was assistant manager of Standard Oil of California's foreign production department from 1937 until 1942, special representative of the foreign division of the U.S. Petroleum Administration for War from 1942 to 1944, vice president of the American Overseas Petroleum Company from 1944 to 1946 and its president from 1946 to 1951, and vice president of California Texas Oil Company Limited in charge of government relations in Sumatra and New Guinea after 1951. He retired in 1959. Died December 3, 1961, in San Francisco. *References*: *BAAPG* 46 (1961): 235–37; and *NYT*, December 4, 1961.

BYRNE, PATRICK JAMES (1888–1950). Missionary, born October 26, 1888, in Washington, D.C. Byrne was educated in St. Charles College (Catonsville, Md.) and St. Mary's Seminary (Baltimore), and was ordained in 1915. He joined the Maryknoll Fathers in 1915, the first priest to join that society. He was sent to Korea in 1923, founded the Maryknoll mission there, and returned to the United States in 1929. He established the first Maryknoll mission in Kyoto, Japan, in 1935, and served there until 1946. He remained in Japan during World War II. He was named apostolic visitor to Korea in 1946 and appointed the first apostolic delegate to Korea in 1949; he was consecrated titular bishop of Gazera in 1949. He was arrested by the North Koreans when they invaded South Korea in 1950. Died November 25, 1950, at Ha Chang Ri, North Korea, on the "death march" to the Manchurian border. *References*: *CE*; *DACB*; and Raymond A. Lane, *Ambassador in Chains; the Life of Bishop Patrick James Byrne (1888–1950) Apostolic Delegate to the Republic of Korea* (New York, 1955).

C

CADBURY, WILLIAM W(ARDER) (1877–1959). Physician, born October 15, 1877, in Philadelphia. Cadbury graduated from Haverford (Pa.) College and the University of Pennsylvania Medical School, and studied in Austria and in the London School of Tropical Medicine and Hygiene. He came to China in 1909 with a medical group from the University of Pennsylvania, and remained there until 1950. He was associated with the Canton Christian College, was an internist on the staff of the Canton Hospital from 1914 to 1949, and superintendent of that hospital in 1914–1915, 1930–1931, and 1932–1935. He helped establish the medical school of Lingnan University and was a professor of internal medicine there from 1936 until his retirement in 1949. He was chairman of the International Red Cross Committee in Canton. He was interned by the Japanese from 1941 until 1943. He returned to the United States in 1950. He collected ferns in China and Australia, and was a research assistant at the Philadelphia Academy of Natural Sciences from 1950 until his death. He was coauthor of *At the Point of the Lancet: One Hundred Years of the Canton Hospital. 1835–1935* (Shanghai, 1935). Died October 15, 1959, in Philadelphia. *References*: William W. Cadbury Papers, Academy of Natural Sciences of Philadelphia Library, Philadelphia; *American Medical Association Journal* 172 (January 16, 1960): 255; *NCAB* 49:283; *NYT*, October 17, 1959; and Howard P. Wood, "William W. Cadbury, M.D., Quaker Missionary and Orchidologist in China," *Frontiers* (Philadelphia) 2 (1980): 80–85.

CADY, JOHN F(RANK) (1901–   ). Historian, born July 14, 1901, in Boonville, Indiana. Cady graduated from DePauw University and the universities of Cincinnati and Pennsylvania. He was associate professor at West Virginia State Normal School (later Marshall University) (Huntington) in 1929–1930 and professor of history and political science at Franklin College of Indiana from 1930 to 1935. He was professor of history at Judson College, Rangoon from 1935 to 1941. He was dean and professor of history at Franklin College of Indiana from 1938 to 1943, research analyst with the Office of Strategic Services (OSS) during

World War II, foreign service officer and specialist on Burma at the State Department and in Rangoon, Burma, from 1945 to 1949. He wrote an account of his experiences in *Contacts with Burma, 1935–1949: A Personal Account* (Athens, Ohio, 1983). He was professor of history at Ohio University (Athens) from 1949 to 1971. He wrote *The Development of Self-Rule and Independence in Burma, Malaya and the Philippines* (New York, 1948); *Political Institutions of Old Burma* (Ithaca, N.Y., 1954); *The Roots of French Imperialism in Eastern Asia* (Ithaca, N.Y., 1954); *A History of Modern Burma* (Ithaca, N.Y., 1958); *Southeast Asia: Its Historical Development* (New York, 1964); *Thailand, Burma, Laos and Cambodia* (Englewood Cliffs, N.J., 1966); *The History of Post-War Southeast Asia* (Athens, Ohio, 1974); *The United States and Burma* (Cambridge, Mass., 1976); and *The Southeast Asian World* (St. Louis, 1977). *References*: *CA*; *DAS*; *IAB*; and *WWA*.

CALDWELL, JOHN C(OPE) (1913–   ). Author, brother of Oliver J. Caldwell,* born November 27, 1913, in Futsing, China, to American missionary parents. Caldwell attended Earlham College and graduated from Vanderbilt University. He served with the Office of War Information in Washington, D.C., and China in 1944–1945, and with the U.S. Information Service in China and Korea from 1945 to 1950. He was a freelance writer and lecturer after 1950; he also owned a travel agency and conducted two tours each year to East Asia. He wrote *China Coast Family* (Chicago, 1953), an autobiographical account; *Still the Rice Grows Green: Asia in the Aftermath of Geneva and Panmunjom* (Chicago, 1955), *South of Tokyo* (Chicago, 1957); *South Asia Travel Guide* (New York, 1960); and *Massage Girl and other Sketches of Thailand* (New York, 1968). He also wrote (with his father) *South China Birds* (Shanghai, 1931) and was coauthor of *American Agent* (New York, 1947) and *The Korea Story* (Chicago, 1952). *Reference*: *CA*.

CALDWELL, OLIVER J(OHNSON) (1904–   ). Educator, brother of John C. Caldwell,* born November 16, 1904, in Foochow, China, to American missionary parents. Caldwell graduated from Oberlin College. He was a teacher in Hawthorne, New York, from 1929 to 1935; associate professor of English at the University of Amoy, China, in 1935–1936; and professor of English at the University of Nanking, China, from 1936 to 1938. He was public relations officer of Association of Boards of Christian Colleges in China in New York City from 1938 to 1943, served in the U.S. Army during World War II and in the State Department from 1946 to 1952, was assistant commissioner of education in the U.S. Office of Education from 1952 to 1966, and served as dean and professor at Southern Illinois University (Carbondale, Ill.) from 1966 to 1974. He wrote *A Secret War: Americans in China, 1944–1945* (Carbondale, Ill., 1972). *References*: *CA*; and *WWA*.

CALHOUN, WILLIAM JAMES (1848–1916). Lawyer and diplomat, born October 5, 1848, in Pittsburgh. Calhoun attended Union Seminary (Poland, Ohio) and was admitted to the bar in 1875. He practiced law in Danville, Illinois, from 1875 to 1898, and in Chicago after 1898. He was a counsel for the Baltimore and Ohio Railroad, and was sent by President William McKinley on a special mission to Cuba in 1897–1898 to report on the conditions there during the Civil War. He was a member of the U.S. Interstate Commerce Commission from 1898 to 1900, and a confidential agent to Venezuela in 1905. He was U.S. minister to China from 1909 to 1913 and maintained the traditional U.S. attitude of noninterference in internal Chinese affairs during the Chinese revolution. Died September 19, 1916, in Chicago. *References: DAB*; and *WWA*.

CALTEX PACIFIC INDONESIA (CPI) Standard Oil Company of California (SOCAL) formed the Nederlandsche Pacific Petroleum Maatschappij (NPPM) in 1930. In 1936 Texaco acquired a half interest in NPPM. It was granted exploring rights in Sumatra in 1936. It discovered oil in 1940 and began production in 1952. NPPM was dissolved in 1952 and was replaced by N. V. Caltex Pacific Petroleum Maatschappij. In 1963, it became PT Caltex Pacific Indonesia (CPI), an Indonesia incorporated company. *Reference: Pipeline to Progress: The Story of PT Caltex Pacific Indonesia* (Jakarta, 1983).

CANTON CHRISTIAN COLLEGE. *See* LINGNAN UNIVERSITY

CAPRON, HORACE (1804–1885). Agriculturist, born August 31, 1804, in Attleboro, Massachusetts, and grew up in Whitesboro, Oneida County, New York. He was a cotton manufacturer and superintendent of a cotton factory in Warren, Baltimore County, Maryland, from 1829 to 1836, and superintendent of a cotton factory in Laurel, Maryland, from 1836 until 1852. He also farmed, using scientific methods. He was a special agent of the Bureau of Indian Affairs in Texas in 1852–1853. He moved to Illinois in 1854, where he continued farming on a large scale and raised cattle. He served in the Union Army during the Civil War. He was U.S. Commissioner of Agriculture from 1867 to 1871. He was agricultural advisor to the Japanese government from 1871 to 1875, serving as commissioner and chief advisor to the Kaitakushi Department, which was in charge of the development and settlement of the island of Hokkaido. He introduced American methods, implements, livestock, and produce, and revolutionized agriculture there. He returned to the United States in 1875. He wrote *Reports and Official Letters to the Kaitakushi* (Tokyo, 1875). Died February 22, 1885, in Washington, D.C. *References*: "The Memoirs of Horace Capron," Ms., National Agricultural Library, Beltville, Md.; Horace Capron Papers, Manuscript Division, Library of Congress; *DAB*; *Foreign Pioneers*; Fujita Fumiko, "An Encounter between the United States and Japan: The Case of Horace C. Capron," *Journal of Tsuda College* 15 (1983): 213–42; John A. Harrison, "The Capron Mission and the Colonization of Hokkaido, 1868–1875," *Agricultural History*

25 (1951): 135–42; *KEJ*; Bogdan Mieczkowski and Seiko Mieczkowski, "Horace Capron and the Development of Hokkaido: A Reappraisal," *Journal of the Illinois State Historical Society* 67 (1974): 487–504; Donald Roden, "In Search of the Real Horace Capron: An Historical Perspective on Japanese-American Relations," *PHR* 55 (1986): 549–75; and *WWWA*.

CARAWAY, PAUL WYATT (1905–   ). Army officer, born December 23, 1905, in Jonesboro, Arkansas. Caraway graduated from the U.S. Military Academy in 1929 and also graduated from Georgetown University. He was commissioned a second lieutenant in 1929 and was admitted to the bar in 1933. He served in the Fifteenth Infantry Regiment in Tientsin, China, from 1935 to 1937; and was instructor at the U.S. Military Academy from 1938 to 1942; and served on the staff of the Strategy Section of the War Department General Staff from 1942 to 1944. He was chief of plans group and then deputy chief of staff for plans, operations, and intelligence in the China Theater in Chungking, China, in 1944–1945; commanding general of the Chungking Liaison Group in 1945–1946; chief of plans division in the Department of the Army General Staff in Washington, D.C., from 1953 to 1955; commanding general of the Seventh Infantry Division in Korea in 1955–1956; and assistant chief of staff at the headquarters of the Far Eastern Command-UN Command in Tokyo in 1956–1957. He was chief of staff headquarters of the U.S. Forces, Japan, in 1957–1958; high commissioner of the Ryukyu Islands; and commanding general of the Ryukyu Islands and Ninth Corps in Ryukyu Islands from 1961 to 1964. He resisted steps toward granting autonomy for the Ryukyu Islands. He retired with the rank of lieutenant general in 1964. He practiced law in Heber Springs, Arkansas, from 1965 to 1968, and was an instructor at Benjamin Franklin University (Washington, D.C.) after 1968. *References*: Paul Wyatt Caraway Papers, Hoover Institution on War, Revolution and Peace, Stanford, Calif.; Paul Wyatt Caraway Papers, U.S. Army Military History Institute, Carlisle Barracks, Pa.; *KEJ*; and *WWA*.

CARL, FRANCIS AUGUSTUS (1861–1930). Government official, born July 16, 1861, in Osyka, Mississippi. Carl joined the Imperial Chinese Maritime Customs in 1881, was promoted to commissioner in 1889, and served as commissioner in various treaty ports until his retirement in 1921. He was also an associate delegate for China at the International Opium Commission in Shanghai in 1909, and a delegate for China at the International Opium Conference in the Hague in 1911. Died January 5, 1930. *Reference*: *WWWA*.

CARL, KATHERINE AUGUSTA (?–1938). Painter, sister of Francis Augustus Carl,* born in Louisiana. Carl graduated from State Female College (Memphis, Tenn.) and studied art in Paris. She lived for nine months in the Forbidden City, the only Westerner ever to live as a member of the Chinese Court, and painted portraits of the Empress Dowager Tzu Hsi. She also painted

P'u-yi, Li Yuan-hung, the second president of the Republic of China, Sir Richard Dame, and Paul S. Reinsch,* among others. She wrote an account of her life in the Forbidden City in *With the Empress Dowager of China* (New York, 1906). She later painted in Europe and the United States, and established a studio in New York City. Died December 7, 1938. *Reference*: *WWWA*.

CARLIN, JAMES JOSEPH (1872–1930). Educator, born April 14, 1872, in Peabody, Massachusetts. Carlin graduated from Boston College and attended Woodstock Seminary (Md.). He joined the Society of Jesus in 1892, and was ordained in 1907. He was a professor of Latin, Greek, and English at Georgetown University from 1899 to 1904, taught theology and canon law at Woodstock College (Md.) from 1904 to 1910 and philosophy at Holy Cross College from 1910 to 1912, and served as assistant to the Maryland provincial of the Society of Jesus from 1912 to 1918. He was president of Holy Cross College from 1918 to 1925, president of Ateneo de Manila after 1925, and superior of the Jesuit mission in the Philippines after 1927. Died October 1, 1930, in Los Angeles. *References*: *DACB*; and *WWWA*.

CARLSON, AUGUSTUS B. (1846–1882). Missionary, born August 16, 1846, in Döderhult, Småland, Sweden, and came to the United States in 1862. Carlson graduated from Knox College (Galesburg, Ill.) and Evangelical Lutheran Theological Seminary (Philadelphia), and was ordained in 1878. He was a missionary under the Board of Foreign Missions of the Augustana Lutheran Church in the Telugu mission, India, from 1879 until his death, serving initially at Rajahmundry, and, after 1881, at Samulcotta. Died from sunstroke, March 29, 1882, in Madras, India. *References*: Conrad Bergendoff, *The Augustana Ministerium* (Rock Island, Ill., 1980); and S. Hjalmar Swanson, *Three Missionary Pioneers and Some Who Have Followed Them* (Rock Island, Ill., 1945), pp. 7–36.

CARLSON, EVANS F(ORDYCE) (1896–1947). Marine Corps officer, born February 26, 1896, in Sidney, New York, and grew up in Vermont and Massachusetts. Carlson enlisted in the U.S. Army in 1912, and served in Hawaii, the Philippines, and on the Mexican border. He was commissioned in 1917 and served during World War I, and with the Army of Occupation. He resigned in 1919, and was a salesman for a fruit packing company from 1919 to 1922. He enlisted as a private in the U.S. Marine Corps in 1922 and was commissioned in that year. He served in China from 1927 to 1929 and from 1933 to 1935. He was an observer with the Communist Eighth Route Army from 1937 to 1939. He resigned in 1939, and lectured and wrote from 1939 to 1941, but reentered the marine corps in 1941. He was a commander of the Second Marine Raider Battalion (Carlson's Raiders) and was wounded in action. He wrote *The Chinese Army, Its Organization and Military Efficiency* (New York, 1940) and *Twin Stars of China* (New York, 1941). He retired with the rank of brigadier general in 1946. Died May 27, 1947, in Portland, Oregon. *References*: Rewi Alley, *Six*

Americans in China (Beijing, China, 1985); *CB* 1943; *DAB S6*; *DAMIB*; *NYT*, May 28, 1947; K. E. Shewmaker, "American Liberal Dream: Evans F. Carlson and the Chinese Communists, 1937–1947," *PHR* 38 (1969): 207–16; F. Van Edgerton, "The Carlson Intelligence Mission to China," *Michigan Academician* 9 (1977): 419–32; and *WWWA*.

CARNES, JONATHAN (? –1827). Sea captain of Salem. In 1788, Carnes commanded the brig *Cadet*, the first American vessel to reach the west coast of Sumatra. In 1793, picking up information at Benkulen, Sumatra, he went to Padang, on the west coast of Sumatra, and secured a cargo of pepper, but his ship was wrecked in the West Indies. He sailed again to Sumatra in 1795–1796 on the schooner *Rajah*, and returned with a whole cargo of bulk pepper, the first to reach the United States. He returned to Sumatra in 1798–1799. The articles he brought from Sumatra in 1799 formed the nucleus of the Salem East India Marine collections. He made several other trips to Sumatra. Died December 7, 1827, in Salem. *Reference*: George G. Putnam, *Salem Vessels and Their Voyages: A History of the Pepper Trade with the Island of Sumatra* (Salem, Mass., 1924).

CAROLINE E. FOOTE. Schooner that brought the first group of American merchants and their families to Japan in 1855 and carried the first commercial cargo from Japan to the United States. *Reference*: Howard F. Van Zandt, *Pioneer American Merchants in Japan* (Tokyo, 1980).

CARPENTER, C(LARENCE) RAY (1905–1975). Psychologist and anthropologist, born November 28, 1905, in Lincoln County, Nebraska. Carpenter graduated from Duke and Stanford universities. He was assistant professor at Bard College of Columbia University from 1934 to 1938, a member of the faculty of Pennsylvania State University from 1940 to 1969, a research professor of psychology and anthropology at Pennsylvania State University, and a research professor of psychology and anthropology at the University of Georgia until 1973. He was a member of Harold J. Coolidge's Asiatic expedition, and was a leader of the Asiatic primate expedition to Siam and Sumatra in 1937, which studied gibbons in Siam. In 1939, he resettled five hundred macaques from India on Santiago Island, off the coast of Puerto Rico. He served in the U.S. Army during World War II. Died March 1, 1975, in Athens, Georgia. *References*: *American Journal of Physical Anthropology* 45 (1976): 175; *American Journal of Physical Anthropology* 56 (1981): 383–85; *CA*; *NYT*, March 4, 1975; Bruce Price, *Into the Unknown* (New York, 1968), pp. 85–116; and *WWWA*.

CARPENTER, FRANK WATSON (1871–1945). Colonial administrator, born June 16, 1871, in Corinth, New York. Carpenter studied law. He served in the U.S. Army from 1889 to 1895, was a civilian employee of the War Department from 1895 to 1898, a private secretary to General Henry W. Lawton* in 1899, a private secretary to the military governor of the Philippines from 1900 to 1902, chief clerk of the Philippine Commission from 1902 to 1904, assistant executive secretary of the commission from 1904 to 1908, and executive secretary of the commission from 1908 to 1913. He was governor of Moro Province in 1913 and governor of the Department of Mindanao and Sulu from 1914 to 1922. He retired in 1922 because of ill health. His plan to develop a farm at Novaliches, near Manila, collapsed, and he left the Philippines. He later returned to the United States. Died February 28, 1945, in Salem, Massachusetts. *References*: Frank Watson Carpenter Papers, Manuscript Division, Library of Congress; *Gleeck/Frontiers*; Peter G. Gowing, *Mandate in Moroland: The American Government of Muslim Filipinos 1899–1920* (Quezon City, 1977), ch. 9; *NYT*, March 2, 1945; *Pier*; and *WWWA*.

CARRINGTON, EDWARD (1775–1843). Merchant, born November 2, 1775, in New Haven, Connecticut. Carrington graduated from Yale University. He settled in Providence, Rhode Island, and was apprenticed to several commercial firms, becoming a partner in 1800. He sailed to Canton, China, in 1802, and traded there until 1815, representing several commercial firms. He was also vice consul in Canton in 1805–1806 and consul from 1806 to 1811. He returned to the United States in 1815 and established the firm of Edward Carrington and Company in Providence, becoming a successful merchant who built numerous ships and engaged in commercial trade in various parts of the world. After 1820, he was largely involved in the cotton manufacturing industry. He was a member of the Rhode Island General Assembly until his death, as well as major-general of militia. Died December 23, 1843, in Providence. *References*: Carrington Family Papers, Rhode Island Historical Society, Providence, R.I.; and L. E. Rogers, ed., *The Biographical Cyclopedia of Rhode Island* (Providence, R.I., 1881), pp. 81–82.

CARROLL, CHARLES J(OSEPH) (1877–1941). Railroad engineer, born September 18, 1877, in Barclay, near Towanda, Pennsylvania. Carroll graduated from Sheffield Scientific School of Yale University. He went to Mexico in 1899 where he served on the construction of the Mexican National Railway, was in charge of all engineering on that road at one time, and completed the heavy mountain work of the Lano Grande extension in 1910–1911. He came to China in 1911 as engineer in chief of the Hu-kuang Railways in central China, and was chief engineer of the Szechuan-Hankow Railway in China. He was director general of the Persian State Railways in the 1930s. He was a member of the American economic mission to China and Japan under W. Cameron Forbes* in 1935. He retired in 1936. Died July 9, 1941, in Jacksonville, Florida. *References*: *NCAB* 31:58; and *NYT*, July 10, 1941.

CARROLL, EARL (1905–   ). Businessman, born September 27, 1905, in Slocomb, Alabama. Carroll graduated from Howard College (Ala.) and Vanderbilt University. He was closely associated with the Philippine-American Life Insurance Company; he was president of that company and vice president in charge of production of the Insular Life Assurance Company. He was interned by the Japanese in Santo Tomas during World War II. *References*: Ed. C. De Jesus and Carlos Quirino, *Earl Carroll: Colossus of Philippine Insurance* (n.p., 1980); and *EP* 17:106–110.

CARSON, ADAM C(LARKE) (1869–1941). Judge, born January 14, 1869, in Enmiskillen, Ireland, and came to the United States in 1885. Carson graduated from the University of Virginia and was admitted to the bar in 1893. He served in Cuba and the Philippines during the Spanish American War from 1898 to 1901, was judge of the Court of First Instance in the Philippines from 1901 to 1904, professor at the University of the Philippines, and associate justice of the Supreme Court of the Philippines from 1904 to 1920. Died May 23, 1941, in Front Royal, Virginia. *References*: *EP* 4:396–97; *NYT*, May 25, 1941; *Sevilla*; and *WWWA*.

CARSON, ARTHUR E. (1860–1908) and **CARSON, LAURA L. HARDIN** (1858–1942). Missionaries. Arthur E. Carson was born August 6, 1860, in Columbus City, Iowa. He graduated from Shurtleff College (Upper Alton, Ill.) and Shurtleff Theological Department. He was a missionary under the American Baptist Missionary Union in Burma from 1886 until his death. He was the first missionary sent to work among the Chins. Died April 1, 1908, at Haka, Chin Hills, Burma. Laura L. Hardin Carson was born September 28, 1858, in Comint City (later Blair), Nebraska. She was a missionary under the Women's Baptist Foreign Missionary Society of the West in Burma from 1883 until 1920. She worked among the Karens at Bassein, Burma, and organized the first high school in the Sgau Karen mission. The Carsons were married in 1886 and moved to Thayetmyo in the Chin Hills to work among the Chins. They opened a station in Haka in 1899. She returned to the United States in 1920. She wrote *Pioneer Trails, Trials and Triumphs* (New York, 1927). Died July 19, 1942, in Honolulu.

CARSON, ARTHUR L(EROY) (1895–1985). Missionary and educator, born May 29, 1895, in Tionesta, Pennsylvania. Carson graduated from Pennsylvania State College and Cornell University. He was a missionary under the Board of Foreign Missions of the Presbyterian Church in the U.S.A. in China from 1921 to 1939. He was engaged in agricultural work at Weihsien, Shantung Province, from 1923 to 1926, and director of the Rural Institute of Cheeloo University, Tsinan, Shantung Province, from 1931 until 1939. He was transferred to the Philippines, where he was president of Silliman University from 1939 until 1953. During World War II, he lived in the mountain barrio of Malabo and served with the Philippine resistance forces. He was director of the Church World

Service in the Philippines in 1962–1963 and president of Trinity College in Quezon City, Philippines, from 1963 to 1967. He wrote *Silliman University, 1901–1959* (New York, 1965) and *Higher Education in the Philippines* (Washington, D.C., 1966). Died April 11, 1985, in New York City. *References*: Arthur L. Carson Papers, Presbyterian Historical Society, Philadelphia; and *NYT*, April 12, 1985.

CARTER, EDWARD CLARK (1878–1954). Association official, born June 9, 1878, in Lawrence, Massachusetts. Carter graduated from Harvard University. He was student secretary of the Young Men's Christian Association (YMCA) in India and Burma from 1902 to 1908, returned to the United States in 1908, and was national student secretary for the YMCA in the United States from 1908 to 1911. He returned to India in 1911 and was national secretary of the YMCA there from 1911 to 1919, helping to develop Indian leadership, adult education, and social welfare work. He organized the welfare services of the YMCA for the Indian Army Expeditionary Forces, and was general secretary of the YMCA for the American Expeditionary Forces during World War I. He was foreign secretary of the British YMCA from 1919 to 1923, secretary of the American council of the Institute of Pacific Relations from 1926 to 1933, and secretary general of its international institute. In 1948 he was a consultant in Asia for the United Nations Economic Commission for Asia and the Far East. He was provost of the New School for Social Research (New York City) from 1950 until his retirement in 1952. Died November 9, 1954, in New York City. *References*: *NCAB* 46:69; *NYT*, November 10, 1954; and *WWWA*.

CARY, OTIS (1851–1932). Missionary, born April 20, 1851, in Foxboro, Massachusetts. Cary graduated from Amherst College and Andover Theological Seminary, and was ordained in 1877. He was a missionary under the American Board of Commissioners for Foreign Missions (ABCFM) in Japan, serving at Kobe in 1878–1879, at Okayama from 1879 to 1889, at Osaka from 1889 to 1892, and at Kyoto from 1892 to 1918. He was a professor of homiletics and practical sociology at the Doshisha Theological Seminary from 1892 to 1918. He wrote *Japan and Its Regeneration* (New York, 1899), and *A History of Christianity in Japan* (New York, 1909). After retirement, he served as an independent missionary among Japanese migrants in Utah from 1919 to 1923. Died July 23, 1932, in Bradford, Massachusetts. His son, **FRANK CARY** (1883–1973), missionary, was born July 18, 1883, in Foxboro, Massachusetts. Frank Cary graduated from Amherst College and Oberlin Theological Seminary. He was a teacher in middle schools in Osaka from 1911 to 1913, and a missionary under the ABCFM in Japan from 1916 to 1941. He served in Tokyo from 1916 to 1918, in Sapporo from 1918 to 1920, in Otaru from 1920 to 1938, in Matsuyama from 1939 to 1941, and in Kobe College, Nishinomiya, in 1941. He then served in Davis, Philippines, from 1941 to 1943, and was interned by the Japanese in Santo Tomas, Manila, in 1944–1945. He returned to Japan in 1946, served in Nishinomiya from 1946 to 1953, in Amagasaki from 1953 to 1958, and in Kyoto in 1958–1959. He retired in 1960, and was a pastor in Plainfield, Connecticut, after 1960. He wrote *Side Excursions in History* (Kobe, 1934) and *Loose Leaves from Japanese History* (Kobe, 1935). Died December 11, 1973, in Claremont, California. His son, **OTIS CARY** (1921–   ), educator, was born October 21, 1921, in Otaro, Japan. Otis Cary returned to the United States in 1936, and graduated from Amherst College and Yale University. He served in the U.S. Navy during World War II. He served in the Civil Information and Education Section of the General Headquarters of the Supreme Commander for the Allied Powers (SCAP) in 1945–1946. He was an Amherst College representative to Doshisha University after 1947, a professor of history at Doshisha University, and the director of the Amherst House at Doshisha University, Kyoto. *References*: *Amherst*; *CA*; *DAS*; and *KEJ*.

CASE, BRAYTON C(LARKE) (1887–1944). Agricultural missionary, born August 18, 1887, to American missionary parents, in Myingyan, Burma. Case attended Brown University and Union Theological Seminary, graduated from the University of California and Columbia University, and was ordained in 1912. He was a missionary under the American Baptist Foreign Mission Society in Burma from 1913 until his death. He served at Henzada, up the Irrawaddy River, from 1913 to 1916, and in Pyinmana after 1917. He was the first agricultural missionary of the society. He founded and directed the Pyinmana Agricultural School, the first of its kind in Burma, in 1923. In 1934 he organized the first cooperatives in Burma. He was a civilian attaché of the United States Army and accompanied General Joseph W. Stilwell* on his retreat into India, and, as civilian assistant in rehabilitation, he took charge of agricultural centers in the Kachin Hills. He returned to the liberated areas in Burma in 1944. Drowned July 14, 1944, on Ludawgyi Lake, northern Burma. *References*: Robert F. Cramer, *Hunger Fighter in Burma: The Story of Brayton Case* (New York, 1968); Randolph L. Howard, ed., *Lazy-man-rest-not: The Burmah Letters of Brayton C. Case* (Philadelphia, 1946); *NYT*, August 1, 1944; and *UnionTS*.

CASWELL, JESSE (1809–1848). Missionary, born April 17, 1809, in Middletown, Vermont. Caswell graduated from Middlebury College and Lane Seminary, and attended Andover Theological Seminary; he was ordained in 1839. He was a city missionary at Cincinnati, Ohio, in 1837–1838, and agent of the American Board of Commissioners for Foreign Missions (ABCFM) in 1838. He was a missionary under the ABCFM in Siam from 1839 until his death. He was Prince Mongkut of Siam's favorite teacher. Died September 25, 1848, in Bangkok, Siam. *References*: *AndoverTS*; William L. Bradley, "Prince Mongkut and Jesse Caswell," *Journal of the Siam Society* 54, pt. 1 (1966): 29–41, and George H. Feltus, ed., *Missionary Journals of Rev. Jesse Caswell and of the Rev. and Mrs. Asa Hemenway to Siam* (Troy, N.Y., 1931).

CATHOLIC FOREIGN MISSION SOCIETY OF AMERICA. *See* MARY-KNOLL FATHERS

CATHOLIC UNIVERSITY OF PEKING. *See* FU JEN CATHOLIC UNIVERSITY

CATTELL, EVERETT LEWIS (1905–1981). Missionary, born September 16, 1905, in Kensington, Ohio. Cattell graduated from Marion College and Ohio State University, and was ordained in 1928. He held pastorates in Columbus, Springfield, and Cleveland, Ohio, from 1927 to 1936. He was a missionary under the Friends Foreign Missionary Society in India from 1936 to 1957. He served in Bundelkhand and was superintendent of the American Friends India mission. He was the promoter and first chairman of the Union Biblical Seminary at Yeotmal. He was general superintendent of the Ohio Yearly Meetings of Friends from 1957 to 1960, president of Malone College (Canton, Ohio) from 1960 to 1972, and president of the World Evangelical Fellowship from 1962 to 1968. He wrote *Christian Mission: A Matter of Life* (Richmond, Ind., 1981). Died March 2, 1981, in Columbus, Ohio. His wife, **CATHERINE D(EVOL) CATTELL,** wrote *Till Break of Day* (Grand Rapids, Mich., 1962) and *From Bamboo to Mango* (Newberg, Ohio, 1976). *References*: *CA*; Donald R. Murray, "Everett L. Cattell: Man of Wisdom and Integrity," in *Living in the Light: Some Pioneers of the 20th Century: Quakers in the U.S.A.*, ed. Leonard S. Kenworthy (Kennett Square, Pa., 1984), pp. 88–101; E. Anna Nixon, *A Century of Planting: A History of the American Friends Mission in India* (Canton, Ohio, 1985), pt. III; and *WWWA*.

CAULFIELD, GENEVIEVE (1888–   ). Educator of the blind, born May 8, 1888, in Suffolk, Virginia. Caulfield attended Trinity College (Washington, D.C.) and graduated from Columbia University Teachers College. She came to Japan in 1923 to teach Japanese children. She began working with the blind in the mid–1930s. She left Japan in 1936. She came to Bangkok, Siam, in 1937, and established the Bangkok School for the Blind. She was again in Japan from 1947 to 1952, returned to Bangkok in 1952, and organized a school for the blind and a rehabilitation center for boys in Saigon from 1956 to 1960. She wrote an autobiography, *The Kingdom Within*, ed. Ed Fitzgerald (New York, 1960). *References*: *The Ramon Magsaysay Awards 1958–1962* (Manila, 1977), pp. 283–89; and Margaret Rau, *Dawn from the West, the Story of Genevieve Caulfield* (New York, 1964).

CENTRAL PHILIPPINE UNIVERSITY. Founded in 1905 by the Southern Baptist Convention as an industrial elementary and high school for boys in Jaro. It was later transferred to Iloilo City and became a junior college and a senior college. The entire campus was destroyed during World War II. It became a university in 1953. *Reference*: Linnea A. Nelson and Elma S. Herradura, *Scientia et Fides: The Story of Central Philippine University* (Iloilo City, n.d.).

CHAFFEE, ADNA (ROMANZA) (1842–1914). Army officer, born April 14, 1842, in Orwell, Ashtabula County, Ohio. Chaffee served in the Union Army during the Civil War. He remained in the regular army after 1867, served in the Southwest until 1888, and was an instructor in the service school at Fort Leavenworth. He served in the Spanish-American War in Cuba from 1898 to 1900 and was chief of staff of the military governor of Cuba in 1900. He was commander of the American contingent of the China Relief Expedition* during the Boxer Rebellion in China, commanding the American troops in the advance on Peking, the capture of the city, and the occupation of the surrounding territory. He commanded the Philippines in 1901–1902, and was chief of staff of the army from 1904 until 1906. He retired with the rank of lieutenant general in 1906. Died November 1, 1914, in Los Angeles. *References*: *ACAB*; *DAB*; *NCAB* 30:6; *NYT*, November 4, 1914; and *WWWA*.

CHALFANT, FRANK H(ERRING) (1862–1914). Missionary, born May 29, 1862, in Mechanicsburgh, Pennsylvania. Chalfant graduated from Lafayette College (Easton, Pa.) and Western Theological Seminary, and was ordained in 1886. He was a missionary under the Board of Foreign Missions of the Presbyterian Church in the U.S.A. in China after 1888. He served in Weihsien, Shantung Province. He discovered and made the original decipherment of the inscriptions carved on the oracle bones that were first exhumed in the Honan Province in 1899. Died January 14, 1914, in Pittsburgh, Pennsylvania. *References*: Rosewell S. Britton, "Frank Herring Chalfant, 1862–1914," *Notes on Far Eastern Studies in America*, no. 11 (June 1942): 13–22; and *T'oung-Pao*, Series 2, 15 (1914): 165–66.

CHAMBERLAIN, JACOB (1835–1908). Medical missionary, born April 13, 1835, in Sharon, Connecticut. Chamberlain graduated from Western Reserve College, attended Union College, and graduated from the New Brunswick Theological Seminary, the College of Physicians and Surgeons (New York City) and Western Reserve Medical College (Cleveland). He was ordained in 1859. He was a medical missionary under the Board of Foreign Missions of Reformed Church in America at the Arcot Mission in South India from 1860 until his death. He served later in the Madras Presidency, first at Palmaner and then at Mandanapalle, from 1863 to 1901. He established a theological seminary in 1887. He did literary work in the Telugu and Tamil languages, and was chairman of the committee that revised the Bible in Telugu and prepared a Telugu Bible Dictionary. He wrote *In the Tiger Jungle* (Chicago, 1896), *The Cobra's Den* (Chicago, 1900), and *The*

Kingdom in India (Chicago, 1908). Died March 2, 1908, in Arcot, India. *References*: *ACAB*; *DAB*; *NCAB* 35:299; *OAB*; and *WWWA*.

CHAMBERLAIN, WILLIAM I(SAAC) (1862–1937). Missionary, son of Jacob Chamberlain*, born October 10, 1862, in Madras, India. Chamberlain graduated from Rutgers University, New Brunswick Theological Seminary, and Columbia University, and was ordained in 1886. He was a missionary under the Board of Foreign Missions of the Reformed Church in America in the Arcot mission in India from 1887 until 1905. He established the Vorhees College in Vellore, India, in 1898, and was its president until 1905. He returned to the United States in 1905, and was professor of logic and mental philosophy at Rutgers University from 1906 to 1909, and corresponding secretary of the Board of Foreign Missions from 1909 to 1935. He wrote *Education in India from B.C. to 1900* (New York, 1899). Died September 27, 1937, in New York City. *References*: *NYT*, September 29, 1937; and *WWWA*.

CHANDLER, JOHN HASSET (fl. 1843–1878). Businessman, born in Connecticut. Chandler came to Siam in 1843 as a Baptist lay missionary and ran a printing press. He was a teacher to Prince Chulalongkorn. By 1859, he was no longer connected with the mission. He was vice consul from 1859 to 1861, and was appointed consul in Bangkok in 1861 but the U.S. Senate failed to act on the appointment. In the 1860s he was involved in business affairs that resulted in a lawsuit that ultimately landed him in consular jail. At various times he was also a translator and broker for foreigners wishing to do business with the Siamese government, and was employed by the Siamese foreign office as translator and interpreter in 1865. He successfully built the first small steam launch during Rama IV's reign. He represented Siam at the 1876 Philadelphia Exposition. He was last heard from in 1878.

CHANDLER, JOHN SCUDDER (1849–1934). Missionary, born April 12, 1849, in Madura, South India. Chandler graduated from Yale University and Yale Divinity School, and was ordained in 1873. He was a missionary under the American Board of Commissioners for Foreign Missions (ABCFM) in India from 1873 until 1928. He served in the Battalagundu station of the Madura mission from 1873 to 1882, taught in the mission's theological seminary from 1882 to 1885, was acting principal of the Pasumalai Seminary from 1890 to 1892, and was secretary of the mission in 1893. For many years he organized annual concerts of Indian music. After 1913, he directed the revision of Miron Winslow's *Tamil and English Dictionary of High and Low Tamil*, which appeared as *Tamil Lexicon* (Madras, 1924–1936); directed the language school at Kodaikanal after 1925; and aided in the revision of the old and new Testaments in Tamil. He wrote *History of the Jesuit Mission in Madura, South India, in the Seventeenth and Eighteenth Centuries* (Madras, 1909), *Seventy-five Years in the Madura Mission* (Madras, 1912), and a biography of his father. He returned to the United States in 1928 but was back in Madura in 1932. Died June 19, 1934, in Kodaikanal, South India. *Reference*: *DAB S1*.

CHANDLER, ROBERT F(LINT), JR. (1907–   ). Agriculturist, born June 27, 1907, in Columbus, Ohio. Chandler graduated from the universities of Maine and Maryland, and studied at the University of California. He was state horticulturist in the Maine Department of Agriculture from 1929 to 1931, assistant professor of forest soils at Cornell University from 1935 to 1941, associate professor at Cornell from 1941 to 1946 and professor there in 1946–1947. He was dean of the college of agriculture at the University of New Hampshire from 1947 to 1950, and president from 1950 to 1954; he was assistant director of the division of natural sciences and agriculture of Rockefeller Foundation in New York City from 1954 to 1957, and the foundation's associate director for agricultural sciences in 1957. He was director of the International Rice Research Institute in Manila, Philippines, from 1959 to 1972, and of the Asian Vegetable Research and Development Center in Taiwan from 1972 to 1975; he was a consultant on international agriculture after 1972. He wrote *Rice in the Tropics: A Guide to the Development of Natural Programs* (Boulder, Colo., 1969) and *An Adventure in Applied Science: The Early History of the International Rice Research Institute* (Los Baños, Laguna, Philippines, 1982). *References*: *AMWS*; and *WWA*.

CHANEY, RALPH WORKS (1890–1971). Paleobotanist, born August 24, 1890, in Brainerd, near Chicago, Illinois, and grew up in Woodlawn, Illinois. Chaney graduated from the University of Chicago. He taught geology at the University of Iowa from 1917 to 1922, was a research associate of the Carnegie Institution in Washington in Berkeley, California, from 1922 to 1931, professor of paleontology at the University of California at Berkeley after 1931, and curator of its Museum of Paleontology. He was a member of the Central Asiatic Expedition of the American Museum of Natural History expedition to Mongolia and Manchuria in 1925, and investigated Shantung Province in northeastern China in 1937 and western Hupeh province in 1948. Died March 3, 1971, in Berkeley, California. *References*: *Geological Society of America Memorials* 3 (1974): 60–68; and *McGraw-Hill Modern Scientists and Engineers* (New York, 1980).

CHAPELLE, PLACIDE LOUIS (1842–1905). Clergyman, born August 28, 1842, in Runes, Lozer, France. Chapelle studied in Mende, France, and Enghien, Belgium; came to the United States in 1859; graduated from St. Mary's Seminary (Baltimore); and was ordained in 1865. He was a pastor in Baltimore and Washington, D.C., until 1891, and coadjutor to the bishop of Santa Fe from 1891 to 1893, archbishop of Santa Fe from 1894 to 1897 and to the bishop of New Orleans from 1897 until his death. He was the apostolic delegate to Cuba and Puerto Rico and an envoy extraordinary to the Philippines in 1898. He was the apostolic delegate to the Philippines from 1900 to 1902, and reorganized the Catholic church in the Philippines. Died August 9, 1905, in New Orleans. *References*: *DACB*; *DAB*; *NCAB* 7:554; *NYT* August 11, 1905; and *WWWA*.

CHAPIN, LYMAN DWIGHT (1836–1894). Missionary, born September 18, 1836, in Jewett, New York. Chapin graduated from Amherst College and Union Theological Seminary, and was ordained in 1862. He was a missionary under the American Board of Commissioners for Foreign Missions (ABCFM) in China from 1863 until 1883. He served in Tientsin from 1863 to 1867 and in Tungchow from 1867 to 1883, where he established a theological school (later Tungchow College). He returned to the United States in 1883. Died June 29, 1894, in Los Angeles. *Reference*: *Amherst*.

CHAPLIN, MAXWELL (1890–1926). Missionary, born May 9, 1890, in Morristown, New Jersey. Chaplin graduated from Princeton University and Hartford Theological Seminary. He worked for the Young Men's Christian Association (YMCA) in England during World War I. He was a missionary under the Board of Foreign Missions of the Presbyterian Church in the U.S.A. in China from 1919 until his death, serving mostly in Showchow. Died July 19, 1926, in Tsingtao, China. *Reference*: George Stewart, ed., *The Letters of Maxwell Chaplin* (New York, 1928).

CHAPLIN, WINFIELD S(COTT) (1847–1918). Educator, born August 22, 1847, in Glenburn, Maine. Chaplin graduated from the U.S. Military Academy in 1870 and was commissioned a second lieutenant that year. He was a civil engineer on the railways in 1872–1873, and a professor of mechanical engineering at Maine State College from 1873 to 1876. He was a professor of engineering at Kaisei Gakko and then at the Imperial University of Japan from 1877 to 1882. He was a professor of mathematics at Union College from 1883 to 1886, professor of engineering and dean of Lawrence Scientific School of Harvard University from 1886 to 1891, and chancellor of Washington University from 1891 until 1907. Died March 12, 1918, in St. Louis, Missouri. *References*: *NCAB* 11:211; *NYT*, March 13, 1918; and *WWWA*.

CHEELO UNIVERSITY. *See* SHANTUNG CHRISTIAN UNIVERSITY

CHENNAULT, CLAIRE LEE (1890–1958). Aviator, born September 6, 1890, in Commerce Texas, and grew up in northeast Louisiana. Chennault attended Louisiana State University and Louisiana Normal School. He entered the U.S. Army in 1917, joined the aviation section of the Signal Corps, and was discharged in 1920. He obtained a regular commission in the Air Service in 1920, was commander of the Nineteenth Pursuit Squadron in Hawaii from 1923 to 1926, and was an instructor at the Air Force Tactical School at Maxwell Field, Alabama, in the early 1930s. He retired with the rank of captain in 1937. He went to China in 1937 as an aviation advisor to the Nationalist government of Chiang Kai-shek. He helped direct Chinese air units and occasionally led them into battle during the Sino-Japanese War of 1937. He later opened a flight training school in Kunming. He assumed leadership of the American Volunteer Group (AVG)* in 1941–1942. He was then recalled to active duty, and took command of the China Air Task Force and, in 1943, the Fourteenth Air Force in China. He retired as a major general in 1945. He established the Civil Air Transport (CAT)* in 1946, which he sold to the Central Intelligence Agency in 1950. He remained active in the airline under a management contract until his retirement in 1955. He wrote *Way of a Fighter: The Memoirs of Claire Lee Chennault* (New York, 1949). Died July 27, 1958, in Washington, D.C. *References*: Claire Lee Chennault Papers, Hoover Institution on War, Revolution and Peace, Stanford, Calif.; Boyd H. Bauer, "General Claire Lee Chennault and China, 1937–1958: A Study of Chennault, His Relationship with China, and Selected Issues in Sino-American Relations," Ph.D. diss., American University, 1973; Martha Byrd, *Chennault: Giving Birds to the Tiger* (University, Ala., 1987); *DAB S6*; *DAMIB*; *NCAB* 47:10; *NYT*, July 28, 1958; Jonathan Spence, *To Change China: Western Advisers in China 1620–1960* (Boston, 1969), ch. 9; Jack Samson, *Chennault* (New York, 1987); and *WWWA*.

CHERRY, WILLIAM T(HOMAS) (1872–1941). Printer and missionary, born October 11, 1872, in Bowmanville, Canada. Cherry graduated from Union College (Schenectady, New York). He was a printing apprentice and worked as compositor. He came to Singapore in 1898, built the American Mission Press there (renamed the Methodist Publishing House in 1906), was its manager, and made it a highly profitable enterprise. He was also superintendent of the Singapore district and editor of the *Malaysia Message*. He wrote *Students' Geography of the Malay Peninsula Archipelago* (Singapore, 1915). He returned to the United States in 1924 and held pastorates in Ridley Park and Edystone, Pennsylvania. Died October 12, 1941, in Ridley Park. His son, **WILLIAM T(HOMAS) CHERRY, JR.** (fl. 1916–1930s) was associated with the press from 1916 until 1926, and was comanager of the Methodist Publishing House from 1923 to 1926. After 1926, he was the government printer for the Straits Settlement and held this position until late in the 1930s. *References*: *Malaysia Message*, November–December 1941; and Peter Hutton, *Make What I Can Sell: The Story of Jack Chia-MPH* (Singapore, 1978), ch. 2.

CHESHIRE, FLEMING DUNCAN (1849–1922). Consul, born March 4, 1849, in Brooklyn, New York. Cheshire was a merchant in China from 1869 to 1877, acting interpreter to the consulate at Foochow in 1877–1878, vice consul in Foochow in 1878–1879 and in Canton in 1879–1880, interpreter to the consulate general in Shanghai from 1880 to 1882, in charge of the Shanghai consulate from 1882 to 1884, interpreter to the U.S. legation at Peking from 1884 to 1890, consul general at Mukden from 1904 to 1906, consul general at large from 1906 to 1912, and consul general at Canton from 1912 to 1915. Died June 13, 1922, in New York City. *References*: *NYT*, June 14, 1922; and *WWWA*.

CHESNUT, ELEANOR (1868–1905). Medical missionary, born January 8, 1868, in Waterloo, Iowa, and grew up in Missouri. Chesnut attended Park College (Parkville, Mo.) and graduated from Woman's Medical College (Chicago) and Illinois Training School for Nurses (Chicago). She was a medical missionary in Samkong, northwestern Kuangtung Province, in 1894–1895, and in Lienchow after 1895, where she established a woman's hospital. Killed by a mob, October 25, 1905, in Lienchow. *Reference*: Robert E. Speer, *Servants of the King* (New York, 1909), pp. 89–113.

CHILD, JACOB T(RIPLER) (1833– ?). Editor and diplomat, born January 19, 1833, in Philadelphia and grew up in Richmond, Virginia. Child was apprenticed at the *Richmond Whig*. He went to Kansas in 1856 and to Missouri in 1857. He started the St. Joseph (Mo.) *Journal* in 1857, sold it in 1861, and founded the *Evening News*. He then purchased the *Richmond Conservator* in Richmond, Missouri, and was its editor. He served in the Union Army during the Civil War. He was a member of the Missouri General Assembly in 1875–1876 and was twice elected the mayor of Richmond. He was U.S. minister and consul general in Siam from 1886 until 1891. He wrote *The Pearl of Asia: Reminiscences of the Court of a Supreme Monarch, or Five Years in Siam* (Chicago, 1892). Died after 1892 in Richmond, Missouri.

CHINA AID ACT (1948). Title IV of the Foreign Assistance Act of 1948 intended to aid the Chinese Nationalist government. Part of a continuing policy of U.S. military and economic assistance to China after 1937, it initiated the American commitment to Taiwan. It was implemented by the U.S. Economic Cooperation Administration (ECA). *Reference*: John H. Feaver, "The China Aid Bill of 1948: Limited Assistance as a Cold War Strategy," *DH* 5 (1981): 107–20.

CHINA CLIPPER. Hydroplane, of American World Airways, Incorporated, commanded by Captain Edwin C. Music. It made the first transpacific mail flight from Alameda, California, to Manila, the Philippines, in 1935. It inaugurated the first passenger service to Manila in 1936 and to Hong Kong in 1937. *Reference*: Ronald W. Jackson, *China Clipper* (New York, 1980).

CHINA CONSORTIUMS. In 1909, American bankers were invited to join an international consortium to lend money to the Chinese government for railway building and currency reform. The support of the U.S. government was withdrawn in 1913, but in 1917 a new group of U.S. bankers joined groups from Great Britain, France, and Japan. The second consortium did not lend money to the Chinese government although it operated until 1939. *References*: *DADH*;

Frederick V. Field, *American Participation in the China Consortiums* (Chicago, 1931); John A. Moore, Jr., "The Chinese Consortiums and American China Policy, 1909–1917," Ph.D. diss., Claremont Graduate School, 1972; and Vivian L. Munson, "American Merchants of Capital in China: The Second Chinese Banking Consortium," Ph.D. diss., University of Wisconsin-Madison, 1968.

"CHINA HANDS". A group of American foreign service officers and journalists in China during and after World War II who were accused of disloyalty for reporting on events as they saw them. *References*: Ely J. Kahn, *The China Hands: America's Foreign Service Officers and What Befell Them* (New York, 1975); and Paul G. Lauren, ed., *The China Hands' Legacy: Ethics and Diplomacy* (Boulder, Colo., 1987).

CHINA INTERNATIONAL FAMINE RELIEF COMMISSION (CIFRC). Established in 1921 by eight local famine relief committees and commissions. It was designed to demonstrate and develop methods of famine relief that would be self-supporting and of permanent value, and to carry out programs and projects that would contribute to the prevention of famines in China. It developed a rural cooperative movement. It ceased to exist in 1939. *Reference*: Andrew J. Nathan, *A History of the China International Famine Relief Commission* (Cambridge, Mass., 1965).

CHINA MEDICAL BOARD. Established in 1914 as part of the Rockefeller Foundation to develop modern western medicine in China. It founded the Peking Union Medical college (PUMC). It ceased to be a division of the foundation in 1927, and the college was given to the China Medical Board of New York, Incorporated, which supported the PUMC until 1951 when it was nationalized by the Chinese Communist authorities. It continued in a program of assistance to medical institutions in East Asia. *References*: China Medical Board Archives, Rockefeller Archive Center, North Tarrytown, N.Y.; John Z. Bowers, *Western Medicine in a Chinese Palace: Peking Union Medical College, 1917–1951* (New York, 1972); and Mary E. Ferguson, *China Medical Board and Peking Union Medical College* (New York, 1970).

CHINA MEDICAL COMMISSIONS. Two commissions sent to China by the Rockefeller Foundation. The first commission, in 1914, surveyed missionary and Chinese medical schools. The second commission, in 1915, designed the China Medical Board.* *Reference*: John Bowers, *Western Medicine in a Chinese Palace, Peking Union Medical College, 1917–1951* (New York, 1972), pp. 29–66.

CHINA NATIONAL AVIATION CORPORATION (CNAC). Sino-American airline which dominated commercial aviation in China, formed in 1930 by Curtiss-Wright Corporation and the Chinese government. Service began in 1929.

The American share in CNAC was acquired by Pan American Airways in 1933 and was sold to the Chinese government in 1949. *References*: William M. Leary, Jr., *The Dragon's Wings, the China National Aviation Corporation and the Development of Commercial Aviation in China* (Athens, Ga., 1976); and *Wings over Asia: A Brief History of the China National Aviation Corporation* (n.p., 1971).

CHINA RELIEF EXPEDITION (1900). U.S. contingent commanded by General Adna R. Chaffee,* was part of the expeditionary force during the Boxer rebellion in China. It took Tientsin from the Boxers, marched overland to Peking, took Peking, and relieved the siege of the legations there. *References*: James B. Agnew, "Coalition Warfare—Relieving the Peking Legations, 1900," *Military Review* 56 (October 1976): 58–70; Aaron S. Daggett, *America in the China Relief Expedition* (Kansas City, 1903); R. Ernest Dupuy and William H. Baumer, *The Little Wars of the United States* (New York, 1968), ch. 4; and Robert D. Heinl, Jr., "Hell in China," *Marine Corps Gazette* 39 (November 1959): 55–68.

CHINA WHITE PAPER (1949). Formal title: *United States Relations with China with Special Reference to the Period 1944–1949* (Washington, D.C., 1949). Prepared and published by the U.S. State Department following the collapse of the Nationalist government in China as a record of what the U.S. government did in China and the policies it followed, and to show that the United States could have done nothing to prevent a Communist victory. It also implied that the United States should not get entangled in the events in China. *References*: *The China White Paper, August 1949*, with an introduction by Lyman P. Van Slyke (Stanford, Calif., 1967); *DADH*; and Robert P. Newman, "The Self-Inflicted Wound: The China White Paper of 1949," *Prologue* 14 (1982): 141–156.

CHINESE REPOSITORY. A monthly publication established by Elijah Coleman Bridgman* in Canton in 1832 who edited it until his move to Shanghai in 1847. It was then edited by James Granger Bridgman (1820–1850) in 1847–1848, and by Samuel Wells Williams* until 1851, when it ceased publication. *References*: Elizabeth Malcolm, *"The Chinese Repository* and Western Literature on China 1800 to 1850," *Modern Asian Studies* 7 (1973): 165–78; and Murray A. Rubinstein, "The Wars They Wanted: American Missionaries' Use of *The Chinese Repository* before the Opium War," *AN* 48 (1988): 271–82.

CHOSEN CHRISTIAN COLLEGE. Founded in Seoul, Korea, in 1915 by the Korea mission of the Presbyterian Church in the U.S.A., the Methodist Episcopal Church, and the Methodist Episcopal Church, South. It was reopened in 1945 and became Chosen Christian University, a coeducational institution, in 1948. It merged with the Severance Union Medical college in 1957 to form Yonsei University in Seoul.

CHRISTIAN AND MISSIONARY ALLIANCE. Organized in 1887 as the Evangelical Missionary Alliance and incorporated as the International Missionary Alliance in 1889. The present name was adopted after the 1897 merger with the Christian Alliance, which was incorporated in 1890. It began missionary work in India in 1887, in the Philippines in 1902, in Cambodia in 1923 (the first Protestant mission in that country), in Siam in 1929, in Laos in 1929, in Indonesia in 1929, and in Vietnam in 1929. *References*: Christian and Missionary Alliance Records, A. B. Simpson Memorial Historical Library, Nyack College, Nyack, N.Y.; Robert B. Ekvall, Harry M. Shuman, Alfred C. Sneak, et al., *After Fifty Years: A Record of God's Working through the Christian and Missionary Alliance* (Harrisburg, Pa., 1939); James H. Hunter, *Beside All Waters: The Story of Seventy-Five Years of World-Wide Ministry of the Christian and Missionary Alliance* (Harrisburg, Pa., 1964); E. F. Irwin, *With Christ in Indo-China. The Story of Alliance Missions in French Indo-China and Eastern Siam* (Harrisburg, Pa., 1937); Robert L. Niklaus, John S. Sawin, and Samuel J. Stoesz, *All for Jesus: God at Work in the Christian and Missionary Alliance over One Hundred Years* (Camp Hill, Pa., 1986); and David L. Rambo, "The Christian and Missionary Alliance in the Philippines, 1901–1970," Ph.D. diss., New York University, 1974.

CHRISTIAN CHURCH (DISCIPLES OF CHRIST) IN THE USA AND CANADA: DIVISION OF OVERSEAS MINISTRIES. *See* UNITED CHRISTIAN MISSIONARY SOCIETY (DISCIPLES OF CHRIST)

CHRISTIAN REFORMED CHURCH: BOARD OF FOREIGN MISSION. Founded in 1888. It was later renamed the Christian Reformed World Mission. It began missionary work in China in 1920 (closed in 1949), in Ceylon in 1948, in Japan in 1951, and in Taiwan in 1951. *References*: Christian Reformed Church Archives, Heritage Hall, Calvin College and Seminary, Grand Rapids, Mich.; Henry Beets, *Toiling and Trusting* (Grand Rapids, Mich., 1940); and *EMCM*.

CHRISTIE, EMERSON B(REWER) (1878–1967). Government official and ethnologist, born March 17, 1878, in Marash, Turkey, to American parents. Christie returned to the United States in 1892, graduated from Yale University, and studied at Harvard University. He was a teacher in the Philippines from 1901 to 1904, assistant in the Ethnological Survey of the Philippines from 1904 to 1907, and assistant chief of the Division of Ethnology of the Bureau of Science from 1907 until 1915. He wrote *The Subanuns of Sindangan Bay* (Manila, 1909). He returned to the United States in 1915, was special assistant in the U.S. State Department from 1918 to 1921, a drafting officer from 1921 to 1928, and chief of the Translating Bureau after 1928. Died November 29, 1967, in Great Neck, New York. *References*: Emerson B. Christie Papers, in Thomas and Carmelite Christie and Family Papers, Minnesota Historical Society, St. Paul, Minn.; and *AMWS*.

CHRISTIE, WILLIAM (1870–1955). Missionary, born April 28, 1870, in Turriff, Scotland, and came to the United States in 1888. Christie attended the Missionary Training Institute (Nyack, N.Y.). He was a missionary under the Christian and Missionary Alliance in China from 1892 to 1924. He established the Kansu-Tibetan Border Mission and tried to establish a mission in Tibet. He served at Taochow, Kansu Province (the last city near the Tibetan border) from 1895 until 1914, and at Ti Tao from 1914 to 1924. He returned to the United States in 1924, was superintendent of the northwestern district and principal for the St. Paul Bible Institute until 1926, foreign secretary after 1926, treasurer from 1930 to 1946, and vice president from 1932 to 1947. He retired in 1950. Died January 11, 1955, in New York City. *References*: Thomas Moseley, ''William Christie—the Livingstone of Northeast Tibet,'' *The Alliance Weekly*, February 16, 1955; and Howard Van Dyck, *William Christie, Apostle to Tibet* (Harrisburg, 1956).

CHURCH, JOHN ADAMS (1843–1917). Mining engineer, born April 5, 1843, in Rochester, New York. Church graduated from Columbia University School of Mines, and studied in Europe. He was the editor of *Engineering and Mining Journal* from 1872 to 1874, a member of the U.S. Geographical and Geological Survey, professor of mining and metallurgy at the State University of Ohio from 1878 to 1881, and superintendent of the Tombstone (Ariz.) Mill and Mining Company. He worked for Viceroy Li Hung Chang, opening silver mines in Mongolia and introducing American mining methods and machinery into China from 1886 to 1890. He later practiced as a mining engineer. Died February 12, 1917, in New York City. *References*: *DAB*; *Engineering and Mining Journal* 103 (March 10, 1917): 427–28; *NYT*, February 13, 1917; and *WWWA*.

CHURCH OF GOD: WORLD MISSION BOARD. Founded in 1910, it began missionary work in China in 1914 (closed down in 1927) and again in 1937 (closed down in 1941), in India in 1936, in the Philippines in 1947, in Japan in 1953, and in Indonesia in 1955 (closed down in 1957). *References*: Charles W. Conn, *Like a Mighty Army* (Cleveland, Tenn., 1955); and Charles W. Conn, *Where the Saints Have Trod: A History of Church of God Missions* (Cleveland, Tenn., 1959).

CHURCH OF JESUS CHRIST OF LATTER-DAY SAINTS. The church began missionary work in India from 1851 to 1856, in Hong Kong in 1853–1854, in Japan in 1901 (closed down in 1924 and reopened in 1948), in Korea in 1956, in the Philippines in 1961. *References*: Church of Jesus Christ of Latter-Day Saints Records, Church Library Archives, Salt Lake City; R. Lanier Britsch, ''The Closing of the Early Japan Mission,'' *Brigham Young University Studies* 15 (1975): 171–90; R. Lanier Britsch, ''The Latter-Day Saint Mission to India: 1851–1856,'' *Brigham Young University Studies* 12 (1972): 262–78; J. Christopher Conkling, ''Members without a Church: Japanese Mormons in Japan from

1924 to 1948," *Brigham Young University Studies* 15 (1975): 191–214; and Spencer J. Palmer, *The Church Encounters Asia* (Salt Lake City, Utah, 1970).

CHURCH OF THE BRETHREN: FOREIGN MISSION COMMISSION. Founded in 1908. The name was changed later to the World Ministries Commission. It began missionary service in India in 1895, in China in 1908, and in Indonesia in 1960. *References*: Church of the Brethren Archives, Brethren Historical Library and Archives, Elgin, Ill.; Anetta C. Mow et al., *Fifty Years in India, 1895–1945* (Elgin, Ill., 1945); and Elgin S. Moyer, *Missions in the Church of the Brethren: Their Development and Effect upon the Denomination* (Elgin, Ill., 1931).

CHURCH OF THE NAZARENE: DEPARTMENT OF FOREIGN MISSIONS. Organized in 1907 as an outgrowth of previous mission boards elected by the individual holiness groups which united in 1907–1908 to form the Church of the Nazarene. It began missionary work in India in 1898, in Japan in 1908, in China in 1911, and in Korea and the Philippines in 1948. The name was changed later to the World Missions Division. *References*: Church of the Nazarene Records, Nazarene Archives, Kansas City, Mo.; Edith P. Goodnow, *"Hazarded Lives"* (Kansas City, 1942); Amy N. Hinshaw, *Messengers of the Cross in India* (Kansas City, n.d.); Mendell Taylor and R. DeLong, *Fifty Years of Nazarene Missions*, vol. 2 (Kansas City, 1958); Helen Temple, *Nor Any Other Creature: The Saga of Nazarene Missions in China* (Kansas City, Mo., 1984); and Evelyn M. Witthoff, *Oh Doctor! The Story of Nazarene Missions in India* (Kansas City, 1962).

CHURCHILL, (DAVID) CARROLL (1873–1969). Mechanical engineer, born March 17, 1873, in Oberlin, Ohio. Churchill attended Oberlin College and graduated from Massachusetts Institute of Technology. He was an assistant to George Westinghouse at Westinghouse Electric Company in Pittsburgh in 1900–1901. He went to India in 1901 under the American Board of Commissioners for Foreign Missions (ABCFM) and was probably the first industrial engineer sent out by the board. He was head of an industrial school at Ahmednagar and started the American Deccan Institute. He gave his principal attention to improvements in handweaving, and established a weaving factory at Ahmednagar. He returned to the United States in 1917, where he was a consulting engineer and airplane designer at the Garford Manufacturing Company in Elyria, Ohio, from 1917 to 1921, and head of the physics department at Berea College from 1921 to 1923. In 1923 he established the Churchill Weavers, Incorporated, in Berea, Kentucky, and invented many handweaving devices. He retired in 1966. Died January 6, 1969, in Berea, Kentucky. *Reference*: NCAB 55:149.

CIVIL AIR TRANSPORT (CAT). Established in 1946 as a contract cargo carrier by Claire Lee Chennault* and Whiting Willauer.* It operated in mainland China, and during the China Civil War of 1948–1949 it frequently acted as a paramilitary adjunct of Nationalist Air Force. It was purchased in 1950 by the U.S. Central Intelligence Agency (CIA). It went out of business in 1968. *References*: William M. Leary, *Perilous Missions: Civil Air Transport and CIA Covert Operations in Asia* (University, Ala., 1984); and Peter D. Scott, *The War Conspiracy: The Secret Road to the Second Indochina War* (Indianapolis, 1972), ch. 2.

CLAPP, FREDERICK GARDNER (1879–1944). Petroleum geologist, born July 20, 1879, in Boston. Clapp graduated from Massachusetts Institute of Technology. He was a geologist with the U.S. Geological Survey from 1902 to 1908, and in 1908 he became a consulting and petroleum geologist specializing in reports on oil and gas properties. He was a managing geologist of the Associated Geological Engineers from 1912 to 1918, and later its chief geologist. He was in charge of geological explorations in China from 1913 to 1915, and made an extensive tour of northern China for the Chinese government and Standard Oil Company, investigating petroleum possibilities. He also made a survey of a large part of the Great Wall of China which he reported in the April-June 1920 issue of *Geographical Review*. He later conducted geological explorations in Australia and New Zealand, Persia, and Afghanistan. He supervised oil operations in Oklahoma from 1939 to 1943. Died February 18, 1944, in Chickasha, Oklahoma. *References*: *BAAPG* 29 (1945): 402–9; *Economic Geology* 39 (1944): 248–49; *NCAB* 32:355; *PGSA* (1944): 163–66; and *WWWA*.

CLARK, ALDEN HYDE (1878–1960). Missionary, born June 26, 1878, in Minneapolis, Minnesota. Clark graduated from Amherst College, Columbia University, and Union Theological Seminary, and was ordained in 1904. He was a missionary under the American Board of Commissioners for Foreign Missions (ABCFM) in India from 1904 to 1947. He was a district missionary at Vadala from 1904 to 1907 and principal of Union Training College at Ahmednagar from 1907 until 1918. He returned to the United States in 1918 and was acting secretary of the ABCFM from 1918 to 1923. He went back to India in 1923, founded Nagpada Neighborhood House in Bombay, was principal of Union Theological College of Ahmednagar (later the United Theological College of Western India in Poona) from 1921 to 1929, and served as regional secretary of the ABCFM from 1929 until his retirement in 1947. He wrote *India on the March* (New York, 1922). Died May 27, 1960, in Boston. *References*: *Amherst*; *NYT*, May 29, 1960; and *UnionTS*.

CLARK, EDWARD WARREN (1849–1907). Educator, born January 27, 1849, in Portsmouth, New Hampshire, and grew up in New York City. Clark graduated from Rutgers University. He was a teacher at Denshujo school in

Shizuoka, Japan, from 1871 until 1873, and was in charge of the school starting in 1873. He taught chemistry at the Kaisei Gakko (later Tokyo University) from 1873 to 1875. He returned to the United States in 1875, and held pastorates in Protestant Episcopal churches in New York State. He wrote *Life and Adventure in Japan* (New York, 1878) and *Katz Awa, Bismarck of Japan, a Story of a Noble Life* (New York, 1904). *Reference*: A. Hamish Ion, "Edward Warren Clark and Early Meiji Japan: A Case Study of Cultural Contact," *Modern Asian Studies* 11 (1977): 557–72.

CLARK, EDWARD W(INTER) (1830–1913). Missionary, born February 25, 1830, in North East, New York. Clark graduated from Brown University, attended Newton Theological Institution and Rochester Theological Seminary, and was ordained in 1859. He held a pastorate in Logansport, Indiana, and edited *The Witness* in Indianapolis. He was a missionary under the American Baptist Missionary Union in Assam, India, from 1869 until 1911. He served initially in Sibsagar, where he was in charge of the mission press. He was the first Westerner to enter Naga territory, and he established a mission among the Nagas. He served in Molung from 1876 to 1898 and in Impur from 1898 until 1911. He reduced the Ao Naga language to writing, translated portions of the Bible, and prepared a number of textbooks. He also compiled an *Ao Naga Dictionary* (Calcutta, 1911). He returned to the United States in 1911. Died May 13, 1913, in St. Augustine, Florida. His wife, **MARY (JANE) READ CLARK** (1832–1924), wrote *A Corner in India* (New York, 1907). *References*: Edward W. Clark Papers, American Baptist Missionary Union Archives, Valley Forge, Pa.; Samuel A. Perrine, "An Apostle to the Head-Hunters: An Appreciation of Edward W. Clark, D.D.," *The Examiner*, April 17, 1913; and J. Puthenpurakal, *Baptist Missions in Nagaland* (Calcutta, 1984).

CLARK, GROVER (1891–1938). Editor, born December 14, 1891, in Osaka, Japan, to American parents. Clark graduated from Oberlin College and the University of Chicago. He was engaged in teaching and magazine work in Japan from 1918 to 1920, was a member of the faculty of the National University of Peking from 1920 to 1927, and editor of the Peking *Leader*, an English newspaper, from 1921 to 1929. He was the Peking correspondent of the *Christian Science Monitor* from 1921 to 1926, editor of *The Week in China* from 1924 to 1929, a member of the executive committee of the China International Famine Relief Commission from 1928 to 1930, and its associate executive director in 1929–1930. He returned to the United States in 1930, was consultant on Far Eastern Affairs in New York City from 1930 to 1936, a lecturer at Columbia University from 1930 to 1933, an associate editor of the *American Observer* in 1936–1937, and a professor of economics at the University of Denver in 1937. He wrote *Tibet, China and Great Britain: Notes on the Present Status of the Relations between These Countries* (Peking, 1924); *Economic Rivalries in China* (New Haven, 1932); *The Great Wall Crumbles* (New York, 1935); and *A Place* *in the Sun* (New York, 1936). Died July 17, 1938, in Charlottesville, Virginia. *References*: *NYT*, July 18, 1938; and *WWWA*.

CLARK, ROBERT STERLING (1877–1956). Traveler, born June 25, 1877, in New York City. Clark graduated from Yale University Sheffield Scientific School. He led a scientific and geological expedition to Northwestern China in 1908–1909 and wrote (with Arthur de Carle Sowerby) *Through Shen-kan: An Account of the Clark Expedition to North China, 1908–9* (London, 1912). He gathered information that was later used by the U.S. War Department on a map of China. He continued to finance Sowerby's expeditions in China for the next twenty years. The natural history specimens collected in these expeditions were sent to the U.S. National Museum. He founded the Sterling and Francine Clark Art Institute in Williamstown, Massachusetts, in 1951. Died December 29, 1956, in Williamstown, Massachusetts. *Reference*: *NYT*, December 30, 1956.

CLARK, WILLIAM SMITH (1825–1886). Botanist and educator, born July 31, 1825, in Ashfield, Massachusetts. Clark graduated from Amherst College and Gottingen University. He was a faculty member at Amherst College from 1852 until 1867. He served in the Union Army during the Civil War. He was president of the Massachusetts College of Agriculture (Amherst) from 1867 until 1878. He was in Japan in 1876–1877, where he was engaged by the Japanese government to organize the Sapporo Agricultural College, and served as its first president and the director of the college farm. He also served as a technical advisor on agricultural matters to the agency responsible for the development of Hokkaido. He returned to the United States in 1877. From 1880 to 1883 he was a partner in a mining company which failed. Died March 9, 1886, in Amherst, Massachusetts. *References*: *Amherst*; *DAB*; *Foreign Pioneers*; *KEJ*; John M. Maki, "The Japan Helpers," in *Aspects of Meiji Modernization: The Japan Helpers and the Helped*, ed. Clark L. Beck and Ardath W. Burks (New Brunswick, N.J., 1983), pp. 21–39; *NCAB* 5:310; and Yuzo Ota, *Wm. Smith Clark (1826––86) & Japan: With Special Reference to His Missionary Work* (Montreal, 1978).

CLARK AIR FORCE BASE. Largest American air installation outside the United States, located thirty-five miles northeast of Subic Bay in the Philippines. It serves as the headquarters for the U.S. Thirteenth Air Force.

CLAYTON, EDWARD HYERS (1886–1946). Missionary educator, born December 10, 1886, in Asbury Park, New Jersey. Clayton graduated from Colgate and Columbia universities. He was a missionary under the American Baptist Foreign Mission Society in China from 1912 until 1942. He was stationed in Hanyang from 1912 to 1914, and in Huchow from 1917 to 1923 and was the principal of the Wayland Academy in Hangchow from 1923 to 1942. He was interned by the Japanese in 1941–1942. In 1942 he returned to the United States and was a pastor in Red Bank, New Jersey. He wrote his memoirs, entitled *Heaven Below* (New York, 1944). Died November 17, 1946, in Dayton, Ohio. *Reference*: *NYT*, November 19, 1946.

CLEMENT, ERNEST W(ILSON) (1860–1941). Educator, born February 21, 1860, in Dubuque, Iowa. Clement graduated from the University of Chicago. He went to Japan in 1887 and taught at a high school until 1891. He returned to Japan in 1894, and served as principal of the Duncan Academy in Tokyo until 1911 and at the First Higher School in Tokyo until 1927. He also edited the *Japan Evangelist*, was editor of *Christian Movement in Japan* from 1907 to 1909, and was a special correspondent for *The Chicago Daily News*. He wrote *A Handbook of Modern Japan* (Chicago, 1904). Died March 11, 1941, in Floral Park, Long Island, New York. *References*: NYT, March 12, 1941; and *WWWA*.

CLOMAN, SYDNEY AMOS (1867–1923). Army officer, born October 10, 1867, in Deavertown, Ohio. Cloman graduated from the U.S. Military Academy in 1889 and was commissioned a second lieutenant the same year. He served in the West until 1898. He came to the Philippines in 1898, one of the first American officers sent there. He participated in the Philippine-American War, was the military governor of Bongoa, served in the Sulu archipelago, and wrote of his experiences in *Myself and a Few Moros* (Garden City, N.Y., 1923). He was a military attaché in the U.S. embassy in London from 1907 to 1912. He resigned from the service in 1916 but served in the U.S. Army during World War I. Died May 12, 1923, in Burlingame, California. *References*: NCAB 21:347; and *NYT*, May 14, 1923.

CLOSE, UPTON (1894–1960). Pseudonym of Josef Washington Hall, journalist and radio commentator, born February 27, 1894, at Kelso, Washington. Close attended Washington Missionary College and graduated from George Washington University. He was head of the American legation espionage service in Shantung from 1916 to 1919, and was a correspondent in China until 1922. He also served as a correspondent in Japan and Siberia, was advisor to Chinese student revolutionaries, and served as foreign affairs chief in the regime of General Wu Pei-fu. He became an invalid and returned to the United States. He was a lecturer at the University of Washington, and after 1926, he led an annual American cultural expedition to East Asia. He was a radio broadcast commentator from 1934 until his retirement from radio in 1936. He wrote *In the Land of the Laughing Buddha: The Adventures of an American Barbarian in China* (New York, 1924); *Eminent Asians* (New York, 1927); and *Challenge: Behind the Face of Japan* (New York, 1934); and was coauthor of *Outline History of Asia* (New York, 1926) and *The Revolt of Asia* (New York, 1927). Died November 14, 1960, near Guadalajara, Mexico. *References*: *CA*; *CB* 1944; Irving E. Fang, *Those Radio Commentators!* (Ames, Ia., 1977), pp. 121–29; *NCAB* 62:291; *NYT*, November 15, 1960; and *WWWA*.

CLOUGH, JOHN E(VERETT) (1836–1910). Missionary, born July 16, 1836, near Frewsburg, New York, and grew up in Iowa. Clough attended Burlington University and graduated from Upper Iowa University. He was a U.S. deputy surveyor of the Dakota Territory from 1855 to 1859, and a field representative of the American Baptist Publication Society from 1862 to 1864. He was a missionary under the American Baptist Missionary Union in South India from 1865 until 1910. He served at Ongole, in the Telugu mission, which became known as the "Lone Star Mission." During the famines of 1876–1877, he organized thousand of Indians to work on the construction of the Buckingham Canal. In the 1890s he used the Telugu field as a laboratory for "social Christianity." He wrote (with his wife, Emma Rauschenbusch Clough) *Social Christianity in the Orient: The Story of a Man, a Mission and a Movement* (New York, 1914. Died November 24, 1910, in Rochester, New York. *References*: John E. Clough Papers, American Baptist Historical Society, Rochester, N.Y.; *ACAB*; *CDCWM*; *DAB*; H. W. Hines, *Clough: Kingdom Builder in South India* (Philadelphia, 1929); *NYT*, November 25, 1910; and Walter S. Steward, *Later Baptist Missionaries and Pioneers* (Philadelphia, 1929), 1:181–212.

CLUBB, O(LIVER) EDMUND (1901–1989). Diplomat, born February 16, 1901, in South Park, Minnesota. Clubb graduated from University of Minnesota and California College in China. He served in the U.S. Army in World War I. He entered the foreign service in 1928, was a language officer in Peking from 1929 to 1931, and served in Hankow, Tientsin, Nanking, Shanghai, Hanoi, Chungking, and Urumchi from 1931 to 1944. He was consul general in Vladivostok from 1944 to 1946, in Mukden in 1946, in Changchun in 1946–1947, and in Peking from 1947 until 1950. He was interned by the Japanese in Indochina during World War II. He was director of the Office of Chinese Affairs in the U.S. State Department from 1950 to 1952. Forced into retirement in 1952, he was later a lecturer at the East Asia Institute of Columbia University and staff editor of a Columbia University research project on men and politics in modern China from 1960 to 1966. He wrote *Twentieth Century China* (New York, 1964); *Communism in China: As Reported from Hankow in 1932* (New York, 1968); *China and Russia: The "Great Game"* (New York, 1971); and *The Witness and I* (New York, 1974). Died May 9, 1989, in New York City. *References*: *CA*; *DAS*; and *NYT*, May 11, 1989.

COCHRAN, H(ORACE) MERLE (1892–1973). Diplomat, born July 6, 1892, in Crawfordsville, Indiana. Cochran graduated from the University of Arizona. He entered the foreign service in 1914, and served in Mannheim and Nogales. He resigned in 1916 and ranched in Mexico from 1916 to 1918. He returned to the foreign service in 1918, and served as vice consul in Lugano; Kingston, Jamaica; and Montreal from 1918 to 1923; and in the State Department from 1923 to 1927. He was a consul in Paris from 1927 to 1930, and in Basel from 1930 to 1932. He was financial secretary of the U.S. embassy in Paris from 1932 to 1939, in charge of the U.S. Stabilization Fund from 1939 to 1941, and a foreign service inspector from 1942 to 1948. He was U.S. representative, and later chairman, of the United Nations Good Offices Commission for Indonesia in Java in 1948. He did much to bring the Dutch and Indonesians together, leading to a free Indonesia. At the request of the Indonesian government, he was the first U.S. ambassador to Indonesia, serving from 1949 to 1953. He was deputy managing director of the International Monetary Fund from 1953 to 1962. Died September 20, 1973, in Houston, Texas. *References*: *CB* 1950; *Washington Post*, September 23, 1973; and *WWWA*.

COHEN, THEODORE (1918–1983). Government official and businessman, born May 31, 1918, in New York City. Cohen graduated from the City College of New York and Columbia University. He served with the Office of Strategic Services (OSS) from 1941 to 1944. He was chief of the Japanese labor section in the U.S. Foreign Economic Administration in 1944–1945, chief of the labor division in the General Headquarters of the Supreme Commander for the Allied Forces (SCAP) in 1946–1947, and an economic advisor to General Douglas MacArthur from 1947 to 1950. He was vice president of M. I. Greisman and Son Limited of Canada after 1953, and managing director of Marshall Scott after 1954. He was cofounder of the Japanese Commission for Cultural Freedom, and vice president of the Jewish Community of Japan after 1962. Died December 21, 1983, in Tokyo. His memoirs of the American occupation, *Remaking Japan: The American Occupation as New Deal*, ed. Herbert Passin (New York, 1987), were published posthumously. *Reference*: *Who's Who in World Jewry* (New York, 1972).

COHN, BERNARD S(AMUEL) (1928–   ) Anthropologist, born May 13, 1928, in Brooklyn, New York. Cohn graduated from the University of Wisconsin and Cornell University. He was a research assistant at the University of Chicago from 1956 to 1960, and carried out fieldwork in India from 1957 to 1959. He was an associate professor of anthropology at the University of Rochester from 1960 to 1964, and a professor of anthropology and South Asia history at the University of Chicago after 1964. He wrote *The Development and Impact of British Administration in India* (Delhi, 1961); *India: The Social Anthropology of a Civilization* (Englewood Cliffs, N.J., 1971); and *An Anthropologist among the Historians and Other Essays* (Delhi, 1987). *References*: *AMWS*; *DAS*; and *WWA*.

COLE, FAY-COOPER (1881–1961). Anthropologist, born August 8, 1881, in Plainwell, Michigan. Cole attended the University of Southern California, graduated from Northwestern University, and studied at the University of Chicago. He was an ethnologist with the Field Museum of Natural History from 1903 to 1912, and assistant curator of Malayan ethnology and physical anthropology at the museum from 1912 to 1923. He was a special investigator for the Philippines Bureau of

Science from 1906 to 1912, and conducted an expedition to the northern Philippines in 1907–1908 and to Mindanao from 1910 to 1912. He wrote *The Wild Tribes of Davao District, Mindanao* (Chicago, 1913); *Traditions of the Tinguian: A Study in Philippine Folk-lore* (Chicago, 1915); and *The Tinguian: Social, Religious and Economic Life of a Filipino Tribe* (Chicago, 1922). He was the leader of the Field Museum expedition to the Malay Peninsula, Sumatra, Java, and Borneo in 1922–1923. He was a lecturer on anthropology at Northwestern University from 1921–1923, a lecturer at the University of Chicago in 1924, an associate professor there from 1925 to 1927, and a professor from 1929 to 1948. He wrote *The Peoples of Malaysia* (Princeton, 1945) and *The Bukidnon of Mindanao* (Chicago, 1955). He was also involved in the archaeological survey of Illinois and in training army and navy officers in the Civil Affairs Training School for the Far East during World War II. Died September 3, 1961, in Santa Barbara, California. His wife, **MABEL (COOK) COLE**, wrote *Savage Gentleman* (New York, 1929), a record of their experiences in the Philippines. *References: AA* 65 (1963): 641–48; *American Antiquity* 27 (1962): 573–75; *NYT*, September 5, 1961; *Science* 135 (February 9, 1962): 412–13; and *WWWA*.

COLLBRAN, HARRY (1852–1925). Railroad and mining engineer, born December 24, 1852, in London, England. Collbran came to the United States in 1881 and was naturalized in 1891. He was in charge of various traffic departments of the Chicago, New Orleans, and Texas Pacific Railroad from 1881 to 1888, and general manager of the Colorado Midland Railway from 1888 to 1893. He went to Korea in 1896, where he built the first steam railway, the first electric railway, and the first lighting system in Korea, as well as the first water works system in Seoul. He then operated two mining concessions in Korea and was president of the Seoul Mining Company and the Collbran-Bostwick Development Company. Died February 15, 1925, in London, England. *References: NYT*, February 16, 1925; and *WWWA*.

COLLINS, J(OSEPH) LAWTON (1896–   ). Army officer, born May 1, 1896, in New Orleans. Collins graduated from the U.S. Military Academy in 1917 and was commissioned a second lieutenant in the artillery. He served in the Twenty-Third Brigade (Philippine Scouts) and was assistant chief of staff, intelligence, in the Philippine Division from 1933 to 1936. He was assistant secretary of the War Department General Staff, chief of staff of the Sixth Corps, and commander of the Twenty-Fifth Infantry Division and the Seventh Corps during World War II. He was chief of public information of the U.S. Army from 1946 to 1948, vice chief of staff in 1948–1949, and U.S. Army chief of staff from 1949 to 1953. He was the U.S. representative to the Military Committee and Standing Group of the North Atlantic Treaty Organization (NATO) from 1954 to 1956. He was a special U.S. representative in Vietnam with the personal rank of ambassador in 1954–1955 and was assigned to assess the abilities of the South Vietnamese government to find ways for the United States to reinforce that government's stability. He made progress in the reorganization and training of the South Vietnamese armed forces. He retired with the rank of general in 1956. He was later vice chairman of Charles Pfizer and Company. He wrote *The Development and Training of the South Vietnamese Army, 1950– 1972* (Washington, D.C., 1975), and *Lightning Joe: An Autobiography* (Baton Rouge, 1979). *References*: *CB* 1949; *DAMIB*; *DVW*; *NCAB* I:342; *PolProf: Eisenhower* and *PolProf: Truman*.

COLLINS, JUDSON DWIGHT (1823–1852). Missionary, born February 12, 1823, in Rose County, New York, and grew up in Unadilla, Michigan. Collins graduated from the University of Michigan. He was a missionary under the Board of Foreign Missions of the Methodist Episcopal Church in China from 1847 until 1851, the first Methodist missionary in China. He served in Foochow, where he founded three schools, including a music school. He returned to the United States in 1851 because of ill health. Died May 13, 1852, near Unadilla, Michigan. *References*: Judson Collins, "Diary," Ms., Detroit Conference Historical Society, Adrian, Mich.; and *EWM*.

COLLINS, PERRY MCDONOUGH (1815–1900). Explorer, born in Hyde Park, Dutchess County, New York. Collins studied law in New York City. He practiced law in New York City and then worked for a steamship company in New Orleans from 1846 to 1849. He went to California in 1849, practiced law in Sonora, Tuolumne County, and was involved in real estate and other commercial ventures. In 1853, he became associated with the American-Russian Commercial Company. He was the U.S. commercial agent to the Amoor River in Siberia, explored the area between St. Petersburg and Irkutsk in 1856–1857, and wrote an account of his journey, *A Voyage down the Amoor: With a Land Journey through Siberia, and Incidental Notices of Manchuria, Kamschatka, and Japan* (New York, 1860). He was returned to Russia in 1858–1859. He was involved in the expedition to build the Russian-American extension of the Western Union Telegraphy Company from New York through Siberia to Europe, popularly known as the Collins Overland Line, in 1866–1867, when the project was canceled following the laying of the Atlantic cable. He later settled in New York City. Died January 18, 1900, in New York City. *References*: *NYT*, January 20, 1900; Vilhajlmur Stefansson, *Northwest to Fortune: The Search of Western Man for a Commercially Practical Route to the Far East* (New York, 1958), ch. 17; Charles Vevier, "The Collins Overland Line," *PHR* 28 (1959): 237– 53; Charles Vevier, "Introduction," in *Siberian Journey: Down the Amur to the Pacific, 1856–1857*, ed. Charles Vevier (Madison, Wis., 1962).

COLTMAN, ROBERT, JR. (1862–1931). Medical missionary, born August 19, 1862, in Washington, D.C. Coltman graduated from Jefferson Medical College (Philadelphia) and practiced medicine after 1881. He was a professor of anatomy at Tung Wen College in Peking from 1896 to 1898, and a professor of surgery at the

Imperial University in Peking after 1898. He was a foreign correspondent for the *Chicago Record*, *New York Tribune*, and two Shanghai newspapers during the siege of Peking. He was later a representative of Standard Oil Company of New York at Peking. He wrote *The Chinese, Medical, Political and Social* (Philadelphia, 1891), and *The Yellow Crime, or Beleaguered in Peking* (Philadelphia, 1901), an account of the siege of Peking. *References*: Robert Coltman Letterbook, Houghton Library, Harvard University, Cambridge, Mass.; and *WWWA*.

COLUMBAN FATHERS. *See* SAINT COLUMBAN'S FOREIGN MISSION SOCIETY

COMSTOCK, GROVER SMITH (1809–1844). Missionary, born March 24, 1809, in Ulysses, New York. Comstock graduated from Hamilton College, studied law, and was admitted to the bar in 1830. He then attended Hamilton Literary and Theological Institution (later Colgate University). He was a missionary under the American Baptist Missionary Union in Burma from 1834 until his death. He served at Kyouk Phyoo, Arakan. Died April 25, 1844, in Kyouk Phyoo, Burma. His "Notes on Arakan" were published in the *Journal of the American Oriental Society* in 1849. *References*: Grover S. Comstock "Journal," Baptist Historical Society, Rochester, N.Y.; and Lucius W. Smith, ed., *Heroes and Martyrs of the Modern Missionary Enterprise* (Providence, R.I., 1857), pp. 483–501.

CONANT, CHARLES A(RTHUR) (1861–1915). Economic advisor, born July 2, 1861, in Winchester, Massachusetts. Conant was a journalist at the *Boston Post* from 1889 to 1901, and was the Washington, D.C., correspondent of the *New York Journal of Commerce* and other newspapers. He wrote *The United States in the Orient: The Nature of the Economic Problem* (Boston, 1900). He went to the Philippines in 1901–1902 to investigate and report on the monetary system of the Philippines, and devised a new system of currency. The new Philippine silver pesos were long dubbed "Conants" by the Filipinos. He served as treasurer of the Morton Trust Company in New York from 1902 to 1906, and was later an economic advisor in Mexico, Nicaragua, and Cuba. Died July 4, 1915, in Cuba. *References*: *DAB*; David Healy, *United States Expansionism: The Imperialist Urge in the 1890s* (Madison, Wis., 1970), pp. 194–209; *NCAB* 14:227; *NYT*, July 7, 1915; and *WWWA*.

CONGER, EDWIN HURD (1843–1907). Diplomat, born March 7, 1843, in Galesburg, Knox County, Illinois. Conger graduated from Lombard College (Galesburg, Ill.) and Albany Law School. He served in the Union Army during the Civil War. He practiced law in Galesburg from 1866 to 1868, and was a farmer, stockman, and banker in Madison County, Iowa, after 1868. He was the state treasurer of Iowa from 1882 to 1885, a member of the U.S. Congress from 1885 to 1891, and a minister to Brazil from 1891 to 1893 and again in

1897. He was U.S. minister to China from 1898 until 1905. He was in Peking during the Boxer siege. He was head of the commission that negotiated a new commercial treaty with China in 1902, which opened Mukden and Shantung to foreign trade. He was the U.S. ambassador to Mexico in 1905. Died May 18, 1907, in Pasadena. His wife, **SARAH PIKE CONGER**, published *Letters from China, with Particular Reference to the Empress Dowager and the Women of China* (Chicago, 1909). *References*: *DAB*; *DADH*; *NCAB* 8:176; *NYT*, May 19, 1907; and *WWWA*.

CONKLIN, HAROLD C(OLYER) (1926–   ). Anthropologist, born April 27, 1926, in Easton, Pennsylvania. Conklin served in the U.S. Army during World War II, and graduated from the University of California at Berkeley and Yale University. He conducted fieldwork in the Philippines from 1945 to 1947, from 1952 to 1955, in 1957–1958, from 1961 to 1965, from 1968 to 1970, in 1973, and from 1980 to 1984. He did fieldwork in Malaya and Indonesia in 1948, 1957, and 1983. He was an assistant professor of anthropology at Columbia University from 1956 to 1960, and associate professor from 1960 to 1962. He was a professor of anthropology at Yale University and curator of anthropology at the Peabody Museum of Natural History after 1962. He was also a special consultant to the International Rice Research Institute in Los Baños, Philippines, after 1962. He wrote *Hanunoo Agriculture* (Rome, 1957) and *Ethnographic Atlas of Ifugao: A Study of Environment, Culture and Society in Northern Luzon* (New Haven, Conn., 1980). *References*: *AMWS*; *DFAF*; and *WWA*.

CONSERVATIVE BAPTIST FOREIGN MISSION SOCIETY (CBFMS). Founded in 1943. It began missionary work in India in 1945, in China in 1946 (until 1951), in Japan in 1947), in Taiwan in 1952, in Pakistan in 1954, in the Philippines in 1955, in Sri Lanka in 1955 (until 1964), in Indonesia in 1959, and in Hong Kong in 1962. *References*: *EMCM*; and *Founded on the Word, Focused on the World: The Story of the Conservative Baptist Foreign Mission Society* (Wheaton, Ill., 1978).

COOK, HERMAN H(ENRY) (1878–1916). Missionary, born September 20, 1878, in New Knoxville, Ohio. Cook graduated from Mission House (Wis.). He was a missionary under the Board of Foreign Missions of the Reformed Church in the United States in Japan from 1902 until his death. He served in Sendai from 1902 to 1908 and also taught English and German in the North Japan College. He served in Yamagata from 1908 until 1916. Died April 7, 1916, in Tokyo. *Reference*: Allen R. Bartholomew, comp., *The Apostle of Ryo-U: Herman H. Cook, Missionary in Japan* (Philadelphia, 1917).

COOKE, CHARLES M(AYNARD), JR. (1886–1970). Naval officer, born December 19, 1886, in Ft. Smith, Arkansas. Cooke graduated from the University of Arkansas and from the U.S. Naval Academy in 1910, and was commissioned an ensign in the navy in 1912. He commanded several submarines, Submarine Division 111, and the Battleship *Pennsylvania*. He was commandant of the Guantanamo Naval Station, fleet war plans officer of the U.S. Fleet from 1936 to 1938, chief staff to the commander in chief of the U.S. Fleet in the Atlantic in 1944–1945, deputy chief of naval operations in 1945, and commander of the U.S. Naval Forces in the western Pacific from 1946 to 1948. After retirement, he was head of a private military advisory group in Taiwan and a naval advisor to President Chiang Kai-shek. Died December 24, 1970, in Palo Alto, California. *References*: Charles M. Cooke Papers, Hoover Institution on War, Revolution and Peace, Stanford, Calif.: *NYT*, December 25, 1970; and *WWWA*.

COOKE, HOPE (1940–   ). Queen of Sikkim, born June 24, 1940, in San Francisco. Cooke graduated from Sarah Lawrence College. She married Palden Thondup Namgyal, crown prince of Sikkim, in 1963, and became Queen of Sikkim in 1964. She left Sikkim in 1973 and was divorced in 1980. She wrote *Time Change: An Autobiography* (New York, 1980). *References*: *CA*; F. Du Plessis Gray, "Fairy Tale that Turned into Nightmare," *NYT Book Review*, March 8, 1981; and *People*, March 9, 1981.

COOLE, ARTHUR BRADDAN (1900–   ). Missionary, born January 6, 1900, in Birmingham, Jackson County, Kansas, and grew up in Kutien, Fukien Province, China. Coole graduated from Baker University and University of Denver, and attended Iliff School of Theology. He was a missionary under the Board of Foreign Missions of the Methodist Episcopal Church in China from 1924 until 1948, where he served at Tientsin from 1924 to 1941. He was back in China in 1944 until 1948, when he returned to the United States. He retired in 1964. He wrote *A Commercial Geography of China for Middle Schools* (Tientsin, Hopeh, 1931); *Coins in China's History* (Tientsin, Hopeh, 1936); *A Bibliography on Far Eastern Numismatics and a Union Index of the Currency, Charms and Amulets of the Far East* (Peking, 1940); *An Encyclopedia of Chinese Coins* (Denver, 1967–1981); and his autobiography, *A Troubleshooter for God in China* (Mission, Kans., 1976). *Reference*: Arthur Braddan Coole Papers, University of Oregon Library, Eugene, Ore.

COOLIDGE, HAROLD J(EFFERSON) (1904–1985). Zoologist, born January 15, 1904, in Boston. Coolidge attended the University of Arizona and Cambridge University, and graduated from Harvard University. He was an assistant mammalogist with the Harvard African expedition to Liberia and the Belgian Congo in 1926–1927, and leader of the Indo-China division of the Kelley-Roosevelt Asian expedition for the Field Museum of Natural History in 1928–1929. He was also the leader of the Asiatic Primate expedition to Southeast Asia in 1937, which was sponsored by Harvard, Columbia, and Johns Hopkins universities. He wrote *The Indochinese Forest Ox or Kouprey* (Cambridge, Mass.,

1940) and was coauthor (with Theodore Roosevelt, Jr.*) of *Three Kingdoms of Indochina* (New York, 1933). He was assistant curator of mammalogy at the Museum of Comparative Zoology of Harvard University from 1929 to 1946, and an associate curator in mammalogy from 1946 to 1970. He served in the Office of Strategic Services (OSS) during World War II, devising lifesaving devices. He was the founding director and president of the International Union for the Conservation of Nature and Natural Resources, and of the World Wildlife Fund. He helped to found the International Union for the Conservation of Nature (Switzerland) and the Coolidge Center for Environmental Leadership (Cambridge, Mass.). Died February 15, 1985, in Beverly, Massachusetts. *References*: *AMWS*; *NYT*, February 16, 1985, and *WWWA*.

COOMBS, FRANK L(ESLIE) (1853–1934). Lawyer and diplomat, born December 27, 1853, in Napa, California. Coombs graduated from Columbian College (later George Washington University), and was admitted to the bar in 1876. He was a district attorney in Napa County, California, from 1879 to 1884, and a member of the California Assembly in 1887, 1889, 1891, and 1897. He was U.S. minister to Japan in 1892–1893, and was involved in negotiations toward treaty revision. He was the state librarian of California in 1898–1899, U.S. attorney for the northern district of California from 1898 to 1901, and a member of the U.S. House of Representatives from 1901 to 1903. He then practiced law in Napa. Died October 5, 1934, in Napa. *References*: *BDAC*; *DADH*; *NCAB* 13:64; and *WWWA*.

COOMBS-STRITTMATER, LUCINDA L. (1849–1919). Medical missionary, born in Cazenovia, New York. Coombs graduated from the Medical College of Pennsylvania. She was the first American medical missionary in China, serving under the Woman's Foreign Missionary Society of the Methodist Episcopal Church in China from 1873 until 1881. She served in Peking until 1877, building there the first women's hospital in China, and in Kiukiang after 1877. She later practiced medicine in Denver, Colorado. Died April 23, 1919, in Columbus, Ohio.

COOPER, JOHN SHERMAN (1901–   ). Politician and diplomat, born August 23, 1901, in Somerset, Kentucky. Cooper graduated from Yale University and Harvard Law School, and was admitted to the bar in 1928. He served in the Kentucky legislature, and was a county judge in Pulaski County, Kentucky, from 1930 until 1938. He served during World War II, and remained in Germany after the war and reorganized the Bavarian judicial system. He served in the U.S. Senate from 1946 to 1948, 1952 to 1955, and 1957 to 1973. He was attached to the U.S. delegation to the United Nations from 1949 to 1951. He was U.S. ambassador to India in 1955–1956, and succeeded in smoothing the relations between India and the United States. He retired from the U.S. Senate in 1973, and was U.S. ambassador to East Germany from 1974 to 1976. *Ref-*

erences: *BDAC*; *DADH*; Douglas A. Franklin, "The Politician as Diplomat: Kentucky's John Sherman Cooper in India, 1955–1956," *Register of the Kentucky Historical Society* 82 (1984): 28–59; *NCAB* I:376; Robert Schulman, *John Sherman Cooper: The Global Kentuckian* (Lexington, Ky., 1976); and *WWA*.

COPELAND, EDWIN BINGHAM (1873–1964). Botanist and agriculturist, born September 30, 1873, in Monroe, Wisconsin. Copeland graduated from Stanford University and the University of Halle, and studied at the universities of Wisconsin and Chicago. He was an assistant professor of botany at Indiana University in 1897–1898 and at the State Normal School (Chico, Calif.) in 1899. He was an associate professor of botany at West Virginia University in 1900–1901, and an instructor of botany at Stanford University from 1901 to 1903. He was a botanist with the Philippine government from 1903 to 1908, a superintendent of the Philippine Agriculture School in 1908–1909, and dean of the College of Agriculture and professor of plant physiology at the University of the Philippines from 1909 to 1917. He was in charge of the herbarium at the University of California from 1928 to 1932. He established the Los Baños Economic Garden in 1932, and served as its director and as a technical advisor in agriculture to the Philippine government until his retirement in 1935. He wrote *The Coco-Nut* (London, 1914) and *Fern Flora of the Philippines* (Manila, 1958). Died March 24, 1964, in Chico, California. *References*: *AMWS*; *Scientists in the Philippines* (n.p., 1978), pp. 38–48; *WWP*; and *WWWA*.

CORBETT, HUNTER (1835–1920). Missionary, born December 8, 1835, in Leatherwood, Pennsylvania. Corbett graduated from Jefferson College, attended Western Theological Seminary, and graduated from Princeton Theological Seminary. He was ordained in 1863. He was a missionary under the Board of Foreign Missions of the Presbyterian Church in the U.S.A. in Chefoo, China, from 1863 until his death. Died January 7, 1920, in Chefoo, China. *References*: Hunter Corbett Papers, Union Theological Seminary Library, New York City; James R. E. Craighead, *Hunter Corbett: Fifty-Six Years Missionary in China* (New York, 1921); Harold F. Smith, *Hunter Corbett and His Family* (Claremont, Calif., 1965); *NYT*, January 13, 1920; and *WWWA*.

CORT, EDWIN CHARLES (1879–1950). Medical missionary, born March 14, 1879, in Rochelle, Illinois. Cort graduated from Washington and Jefferson College (Washington, Pa.) and Johns Hopkins University Medical School. He was a medical missionary under the Board of Foreign Missions of the Presbyterian Church in the U.S.A. in Siam from 1908 until 1949. He served in the Lao country in northern Siam, initially at Lampang and later at Prae. He was transferred in 1914 to Chiengmai and assumed control of the hospital there, in which he served until his retirement. He founded a medical school in Chiengmai in 1916 (later discontinued) and a school for nurses in 1923. He left Thailand in 1941, and was in India from 1941 to 1944, supervising the mission hospital at

Fatehgarh. He returned to Siam in 1946 as medical director of Church World Service for that country. He retired in 1949 and returned to the United States. He worked at a veterans hospital in Fort Belvoir, Virginia. Died January 10, 1950, in Alexandria, Virginia. *References*: Edwin Charles Cort Papers, Presbyterian Historical Society, Philadelphia; *DAB S4*; *NYT*, January 12, 1950; and Chinda Singhanet, *Dr. Cort of Chieng Mai* (Bangkok, 1962).

COWEN, MYRON M(ELVIN) (1898–1965). Lawyer and diplomat, born January 25, 1898, in Logan, Iowa. Cowen attended Wofford College (Spartanburg, S.C.) and graduated from Drake University (Des Moines, Ia.). He practiced law in Des Moines from 1919 to 1926, was a commissioner for the U.S. Court of Appeals in Washington, D.C., from 1926 to 1933, and practiced law in Washington, D.C., from 1935 to 1948. He was U.S. ambassador to Australia in 1948–1949 and ambassador to the Philippines from 1949 to 1952. He promoted a less corrupt and more competent Philippine government, and proposed a covert action to oust Philippine President Elipidio Quirino. He was U.S. ambassador to Belgium in 1952–1953. He later practiced law again in Washington, D.C. Died November 1, 1965, in Washington, D.C. *References*: Myron M. Cowen Papers, Harry S. Truman Library, Independence, Mo.; *Gleeck/Ambassadors*, ch. 2; *NYT*, November 3, 1965; and *WWWA*.

COWMAN, CHARLES E. (1868–1924) and **COWMAN, LETTIE (BURD)** (1870–1960). Missionaries. Charles E. Cowman was born March 13, 1868, in Toulon, Illinois. He was a telegraph operator and chief of the Western Union division in Chicago. He graduated from the Moody Bible Training Institute. Lottie B. Cowman was born March 3, 1870, in Alton, Iowa. The Cowmans went to Japan in 1901 under the Telegraphers Mission Board, and founded the Oriental Missionary Society in Japan that same year. They established the Japanese Bible Training Institute in Tokyo and, in 1907, also in Seoul, Korea. He was editor of the *Oriental Missionary Standard*. He traveled extensively in Japan and Korea. He died September 25, 1924, in Los Angeles. She was in charge of the society from 1928 until her retirement in 1949. She died April 17, 1960, in Chicago. *References*: Lettie E. Cowman, *Charles E. Cowman, Missionary Warrior* (Los Angeles, 1928); Edward and Esther Erny, *No Guarantee but God, the Story of the Founders of the Oriental Missionary Society* (Greenwood, Ind., 1969); *NCAB* 19:295; and Benjamin H. Pearson, *The Vision Lives: A Profile of Mrs. Charles E. Cowman* (Grand Rapids, Mich., 1961).

CRAIG, AUSTIN (1872–1949). Educator and author, born February 22, 1872, in Eddytown, New York. Craig graduated from Cornell University, the University of Rochester, and Pacific University, and was admitted to the bar in 1898. He was superintendent of schools in Washington County, Oregon, from 1895 to 1898, and practiced law in Oregon from 1898 until 1904. He went to the Philippines in 1904 as a teacher under the U.S. Bureau of Education, taught in Lubang Island, at Calapan, Mindoro, and at the Philippine School of Arts and Trades in Manila, and was an instructor in history in the Philippine Normal School and the Manila High School from 1909 to 1912. He was an assistant professor, associate professor, and professor of history at the University of the Philippines from 1912 to 1922, and professor of history at the University of Manila from 1922 until 1927. He wrote *Lineage, Life and Labors of José Rizal* (Manila, 1913); *Rizal's Life and Minor Writings* (Manila, 1927); *The Background of Philippine History* (Manila, 1933); *The Filipinos' Fight for Freedom* (Manila, 1933); and *The Background of the Constitution of the Philippine Islands* (Manila, 1935–1939). He edited *The Former Philippines thru Foreign Eyes* (Manila, 1916). Died February 11, 1949, in Minneapolis. *References*: *DPB* 2; *EP* 4:458–59, 18:238–39; *WWP*; and *WWWA*.

CRAWFORD, F(RANCIS) MARION (1854–1909). Author, born August 2, 1854, in Bagni di Lucca, Tuscany, to American parents, and came to the United States in 1866. Crawford graduated from Trinity College, Cambridge, and studied at Karlsruhe and Heidelberg universities. He went to India in 1879 and edited the *Indian Herald* in Allahabad in 1879–1880. He returned to Rome, Italy, because of an illness, and lived there for the rest of his life. He wrote a novel with an Indian background, *Mr. Issacs* (New York, 1882). Died April 9, 1909, in Sorrento, Italy. *References*: *ACAB*; *DAB*; *DACB*; John C. Moran, *An F. Marion Crawford Companion* (Westport, Conn., 1981); *NCAB* 2:502; John Pilkington, Jr., *Francis Marion Crawford* (New York, 1964); and *WWWA*.

CRAWFORD, JOSEPH URY (1842–1924). Railroad engineer, born August 25, 1842, in Philadelphia. Crawford graduated from the University of Pennsylvania. He worked for several mines in Schuykill County and served in the Union Army during the Civil War. He worked as a surveying engineer and architect for several railroad lines, and supervised railroad construction until 1878. He was a consulting engineer and inspector of the Imperial Government Railways in Japan from 1878 to 1881, and supervised the construction of the first railway in the Hokkaido Province. He was later connected with various railroads in Pennsylvania and New York, and served as a consulting engineer for the Pennsylvania Railroad Company until his retirement in 1912. Died November 21, 1924, in Fox Chase, Pennsylvania. *References*: *Foreign Pioneers*; *NYT*, November 22, 1924; and *Philadelphia Inquirer*, November 22, 1924.

CRAWFORD, TARLETON PERRY (1821–1902). Missionary, born May 8, 1821, in Warren County, Kentucky. Crawford graduated from Union University (Murfreesboro, Tenn.). He was a missionary under the Foreign Mission Board of the Southern Baptist Convention in China from 1852 to 1900. He served in Shanghai from 1852 until 1863 and in Shantung from 1863 until 1900, when he returned to the United States. Died April 1902, in Dawson, Georgia. *References*: Loveless S. Foster, *Fifty Years in China: An Eventful Memoir in the*

Life of Tarleton Perry Crawford, D.D. (Nashville, 1909); and Irwin T. Hyatt, Jr., *Our Ordered Lives Confess: Three Nineteenth Century American Missionaries in East Shantung* (Cambridge, Mass., 1976), pt.1.

CRESSEY, GEORGE B(ABCOCK) (1896–1963). Geographer, born December 15, 1896, in Tiffin, Ohio. Cressey graduated from Denison University, the University of Chicago, and Clark University. He was an assistant professor at the University of Shanghai from 1923 to 1929, professor of geology and geography at Syracuse University from 1931 to 1950, and professor of geography there from 1951 until his death. He carried out fieldwork in Mongolia, Tibet, and interior China from 1923 to 1929, and in Soviet Asia in 1923, 1937, and 1944; he was known as the dean of Asian geographers. He served the U.S. Weather Bureau, the Board of Economic Warfare, the Office of the Geographer of the State Department, and the Military Intelligence Division of the War Department during World War II. He wrote *China's Geographic Foundation: A Survey of the Land and the People* (New York, 1934), and *Asia's Lands and Peoples* (New York, 1944). Died October 21, 1963, in Syracuse, New York. *References*: George B. Cressey Papers, Syracuse University Library, Ithaca, N.Y.; *AAAG* 55 (1966): 360–64; *Geographical Review* 54 (1964): 254–57; Preston E. James and Andrew D. Perejde, "George Babcock Cressey 1896–1963," *Geographers: Biobibliographical Studies* 5 (London, 1981): 21–25; *NYT*, October 22, 1963; *OAB*; and *WWWA*.

CROSBY, RALPH W(ILLIS) (1902–   ). Mining engineer and executive, born November 2, 1902, in Waverley, Nova Scotia, Canada. Crosby graduated from the Texas School of Mines. He was employed by the United Verde Copper Company in various capacities in 1924. He came to the Philippines in 1924, was an engineer and assayer for Benguet Consolidated Mining Company from 1924 to 1926, superintendent in charge of mine development for the Balatoc Mining Company from 1927 to 1930, mine superintendent for the Itogon Mining Company from 1930 to 1933, general superintendent in charge of new development and installation work for the Suyoc Consolidated Mining Company from 1933 to 1936, and assistant manager of the northern division of Marsman and Company, Incorporated, from 1936 to 1941. He was interned by the Japanese in Santo Tomas during World War II. He was a supervising engineer with the Benguet Consolidated Incorporated in Baguio from 1948 to 1962, and president of that company from 1962 to 1974. *References*: Ralph W. Crosby, "The Memoirs of Aop Crosby," *BAHC* 15 (January-March 1987): 7–21; *BAHC* 15 (April-June 1987): 31–46, (October-December 1987): 79–96; *WWA*; and *WWP*.

CROW, (HERBERT) CARL (1883–1945). Journalist and author, born September 26, 1883, in Highland, Missouri. Crow attended Carleton College and the University of Missouri. He served as a journeyman printer, and founded a weekly newspaper in 1902 which he sold in 1906. As a journalist in China and

Japan from 1911 to 1917, he was associate city editor of *The China Press* in Shanghai from 1911 to 1913 and wrote *Travelers' Handbook for China* (Shanghai, 1913). He was the business manager and acting editor of *The Japan Advertiser* in 1913–1914, and Tokyo correspondent for the United Press. He returned to the United States in 1914, bought and operated a fruit farm near San Francisco, and wrote *America and the Philippines* (Garden City, N.Y., 1913) and *Japan and America: A Contrast* (New York, 1915). He was back in China from 1916 to 1918 as the Far Eastern representative of the U.S. Committee on Public Information (Creel Committee). He founded and edited the *Shanghai Evening Post* in 1918–1919, and owned an advertising agency in Shanghai from 1919 to 1939. He also published two small magazines and directed an anticommunist campaign in China. He returned to the United States in 1938 and wrote *Four Hundred Million Customers* (New York, 1937); *I Speak for the Chinese* (New York, 1937); *The Chinese Are Like That* (New York, 1938); *Foreign Devils in the Flowery Kingdom* (New York, 1940); *China Takes Her Place* (New York, 1944); and a biography of Townsend Harris. Died June 8, 1945, in New York City. *References*: Carl Crow Papers, Western Historical Manuscripts Collection, University of Missouri at Columbus Library, Mo.; *CA*; *NCAB* 36:146; *NYT*, June 10, 1945; and *WWWA*.

CRUMPACKER, FRANKLIN HENRY (1876–1951). Missionary, born May 13, 1876, in Leeton, Missouri. Crumpacker graduated from McPherson College, and was ordained in 1907. He was a missionary under the Church of the Brethren in China from 1908 until 1941, serving at Ping-ting, Shansi Province. He directed relief efforts during the pneumonic plague epidemics of 1918 and 1928–1929. He was coauthor of *The Brethren in China* (Elgin, Ill., 1937). He returned to the United States in 1941. Died December 20, 1951. *Reference*: *BE*.

CULBERTSON, MATTHEW SIMPSON (1819–1862). Missionary, born January 18, 1819, in Chambersburg, Pennsylvania. Culbertson graduated from the U.S. Military Academy in 1839. He was an assistant professor of mathematics in the academy in 1839–1840, and served as a lieutenant of artillery during the Canadian border disturbances of 1840–1841. He resigned his commission in the army and graduated from Princeton Theological Seminary. He was a missionary under the Board of Foreign Missions of the Presbyterian Church in the U.S.A. in China from 1844 until his death. He was stationed at Ningpo from 1845 to 1851 and at Shanghai from 1851 to 1862, and was involved in the translation of the Bible into Chinese. He wrote *Darkness in the Flowery Kingdom; or, Religious Notions and Superstitions in North China* (New York, 1857). Died August 1862, in Shanghai. *References*: Matthew Simpson Culbertson Papers, Bancroft Library, University of California at Berkeley; *EM*; and *LC*.

CULIN, [ROBERT] STEWART (1858–1929). Ethnologist, born July 13, 1858, in Philadelphia. Culin attended Nazareth Hall (Pa.). He was director of the department of archaeology at the University of Pennsylvania Museum from 1892 to 1899, curator of the section on American and general ethnology at the Free Museum of Science and Arts in Philadelphia from 1899 to 1903, and curator of ethnology at the Brooklyn Museum from 1903 until his death. He made numerous scientific expeditions to Japan, Korea, China, and India. He wrote *Korean Games with Notes on the Corresponding Games of China and Japan* (Philadelphia, 1896). Died April 8, 1929, in Amityville, Long Island, New York. *References*: Stewart Culin Papers, Columbia University Libraries, New York City; Simon J. Bronner, "Stewart Culin, Museum Magician," *Pennsylvania Heritage* 11 (Summer 1985): 4–11; S. M. Lyman, "Two Neglected Pioneers of Civilization Analysis: The Cultural Perspectives of R. Stewart Culin and Frank Hamilton Cushing," *Social Research* 49 (1982): 690–729; *NCAB* 29:161; and *WWWA*.

CULPEPPER, ROBERT H(ARRELL) (1924–   ). Missionary, born December 8, 1924, in Tifton, Georgia. Culpepper graduated from Mercer University and Southern Baptist Theological Seminary, and was ordained in 1943. He held pastorates in Monroe County, Georgia, in 1943–1944, and in Franklin County, Kentucky, from 1948 to 1950. He was a missionary under the Foreign Mission Board of the Southern Baptist Convention in Japan starting in 1950. He was chairman of the Japan Baptist mission from 1966 to 1968, and professor of theology at Seinan Gakuin University in Fukuoka, Japan, after 1953. He wrote *God's Calling: A Missionary Autobiography* (Nashville, Tenn., 1981). *Reference*: *CA*.

CUNNINGHAM, EDWARD (1823–1889). Merchant. Cunningham came to China in 1845. He was a clerk with Russell and Company from 1845 to 1849, and became a partner and then managing partner from 1850 to 1857, and again from 1861 to 1863 and from 1867 to 1877. He was president of the Shanghai Steam Navigation Company in 1862–1863 and 1868–1869. He was also U.S. vice consul in Shanghai from 1850 to 1854. He made a fortune in the China trade and retired to Milton, Massachusetts. Shot on his grounds by a trespasser, he died the next day.

CUNNINGHAM, EDWIN SHEDDAN (1868–1953). Consul, born July 6, 1868, in East Tennessee. Cunningham graduated from Maryville College and the University of Michigan, and was admitted to the bar in 1893. He practiced law in Maryville, Tennessee. He was a consul in Aden; Bergen, Norway; Durban, Natal, South Africa; and Bombay from 1898 to 1912. He was consul general in Singapore from 1912 to 1914, in Hankow from 1914 to 1919, and in Shanghai from 1919 until his retirement in 1935. He was admitted to the U.S. Court for

China in 1916. Died January 20, 1953, in Maryville, Tennessee. *References*: *NYT*, January 23, 1953; and *WWWA*.

CURZON, MARY (VICTORIA LEITER) (1870–1906). Vicereine of India, born May 27, 1870, in Chicago, and grew up in Washington, D.C. She married George Nathaniel Curzon in 1895. In 1898 she became Baroness Curzon of Kedleston and Vicereine of India. Died July 18, 1906, in London. *References*: Marian Fowler, *Below the Peacock Fan: First Ladies of the Raj* (New York, 1987), ch. 4; *NAW*; Nigel Nicholson, *Mary Curzon* (London, 1977); *NYT*, July 19, 1906; and *WWWA*.

CUSHING, CALEB (1800–1879). Politician, government official, and diplomat, born January 17, 1800, in Salisbury, Massachusetts, and grew up in Newburyport, Massachusetts. Cushing graduated from Harvard University and attended Harvard Law School, and was admitted to the bar in 1821. He practiced law in Newburyport, Massachusetts. He served in the Massachusetts state legislature from 1824 to 1835, and was a member of the U.S. House of Representatives from 1835 until 1843. He was U.S. minister and Commissioner to China in 1843–1844. He negotiated the Treaty of Wanghia with China in 1844, which opened five Chinese ports to American merchants, provided commercial advantages for Americans, and established the principle of extraterritoriality. He served again in the Massachusetts legislature in 1845–1846, served in the Mexican War, was judge of the supreme court of Massachusetts from 1852 to 1855, was attorney general of the United States from 1855 to 1857, and served again in the Massachusetts legislature after 1857. He was a minister to Spain from 1874 to 1877. Died January 2, 1879, in Newburyport, Massachusetts. *References*: Margaret C. S. Christman, *Adventurous Pursuits: Americans and the China Trade 1784–1844* (Washington, D.C., 1984), pp. 147–61; *DAB*; William J. Donohue, "The Caleb Cushing Mission," *Modern Asian Studies* 16 (1982): 193–216; P. C. Kuo, "Caleb Cushing and the Treaty of Wanghia, 1844," *Journal of Modern History* 5 (1933): 34–54; *NCAB* 4:151; *NYT*, January 3, 1879; Richard E. Welch, Jr., "Caleb Cushing's Chinese Mission and the Treaty of Wanghia: A Review," *Oregon Historical Quarterly* 58 (1957): 328–57; and *WWWA*.

CUSHING, JOHN PERKINS (1787–1862). Merchant, born April 22, 1787, in Boston. Cushing became a clerk in the mercantile firm of Perkins and Company in Boston at an early age. He went to Canton, China in 1803, and became the firm's resident agent in China. He then became a partner, amassed a large fortune, and became the most highly respected foreign merchant in Canton. He returned to the United States in 1830, and became involved in various philanthropies. Died April 22, 1862, in Watertown, Massachusetts. *References*: John Perkins Cushing Papers, Baker Library, Harvard University, Boston; John Perkins Cushing "Diary," Ms., Boston Athaneum, Boston; *BDABL*; *DAB*; Henrietta M. Larson, "A China Trader Turns Investor—A Biographical Chapter in American Business History," *Harvard Business Review* 12 (1934): 345–58; and *WWWA*.

CUSHING, JOSIAH NELSON (1840–1905). Missionary, born May 4, 1840, in North Attleboro, Massachusetts. Cushing graduated from Brown University and Newton Theological Institution, and was ordained in 1865. He was a missionary under the American Baptist Missionary Union in Burma from 1867 until his death. He was stationed at Toungoo from 1867 to 1874, at Bhamo, near the Chinese border, from 1876 to 1880, and in Rangoon from 1880 to 1885. He translated the Bible into Shan. He was principal of Baptist College in Rangoon in 1887–1888, and pastor in Rangoon from 1888 to 1890. He established a college (later Judson College), and ran it from 1892 to 1905. He wrote *Christ and Buddha* (Philadelphia, 1907). Died May 17, 1905, in Rangoon. *References*: *DAB*; and *NCAB* 12:384.

CUTTING C(HARLES) SUYDAM (1889–1972). Naturalist, born January 17, 1889, in New York City. Cutting graduated from Harvard University. He was in engineering sales with the M. W. Kellog Company, and, after 1919, was involved in the management of his father's estate. He served in the U.S. Army during World War I. In 1925 he accompanied Theodore Roosevelt, Jr.,* and Kermit Roosevelt on an expedition to Ladakh and Turkestan, and traveled also in Burma, Assam, Szechuan, and Yunnan in China. Reputedly the first American ever to visit the forbidden city of Lhasa in Tibet, he made three trips to Tibet and twice visited Lhasa. He traveled in 1930 to Gyantse and Kampa Dzong, and, in 1935, following five years of negotiations with the Dalai Lama, he was permitted to visit Lahasa. He returned to Lahasa again in 1937 with his wife, **HELEN MCMAHON CUTTING**, who became the first American woman to visit the home of the Dalai Lama. He served in the U.S. Army during World War II. He wrote *The Fire Ox and Other Years* (New York, 1947). Died August 24, 1972, in Chappaquidick Island, Edgartown, Massachusetts. *References*: *NCAB* 57:696; *NYT*, August 25, 1972; *Tibet*; and *WWWA*.

CUZNER, HAROLD (1878–1956). Forester, born March 19, 1878, in Beckington, Somerset, England, and came with his parents to the United States. Cuzner graduated from the University of Minnesota. He was an assistant inspector in the Bureau of Forestry in the Philippines in 1905, superintendent of the Lamao Experiment Station, and agricultural explorer and horticulturist from 1905 to 1909. He was successively farm superintendent, assistant professor of agronomy and farm superintendent, associate professor and professor of agricultural engineering in the College of Agriculture from 1909 until 1921. He was professor of dendrology at the College of Forestry, and later professor of silviculture and forest physiography at the School of Forestry from 1921 to 1928 and forester-in-charge of the school. He was interned by the Japanese during World War II. He served as acting dean of the School of Forestry after the liberation. Died September 25, 1956. *Reference*: *DPB* 2.

D

DALL, CHARLES HENRY APPLETON (1816–1886). Clergyman and missionary, born February 12, 1816, in Baltimore. Dall graduated from Harvard University and Harvard Divinity School, and was ordained in 1841. He became the first foreign missionary of the Unitarian Church in America, and was a missionary in India from 1855 until his death, serving in Calcutta. There he established a girls' school and a school for homeless children. He published notes of his travels in various periodicals. Died July 18, 1886, in Calcutta, India. *References*: Charles Henry Dall Papers, Andover-Harvard Theological Library, Harvard University Divinity School, Cambridge, Mass.; Dall Family Correspondence, Brown University Library, Providence, R.I.; *ACAB*; Spencer Lavan, *Unitarians and India: A Study in Encounter and Response* (Boston, 1977), ch. 8; and Pamela G. Price, "Reform and Patriotism in mid-Century Bengal: Charles Dall and the Brahimo Somaj, 1855–1856," M.A. thesis, University of Wisconsin, 1971.

DANKER, W(ILLIAM) JOHN (1914–   ). Missionary, born June 9, 1914, in Willow Creek, Minnesota. Danker attended Concordia College, graduated from Concordia Seminary (St. Louis) and Wheaton College, studied at the University of Chicago, and was ordained in 1937. He was a pastor in Harvard, Illinois and West Chicago, Illinois, from 1937 to 1948. He was a missionary under the Missionary Board of the Lutheran Church—Missouri Synod in Japan from 1948 to 1956. He was founder and chairman of the Japan Mission. He was the director of the missionary training program and professor of missions at Concordia Seminary after 1956. *References*: *CA*; Wi Jo Kang, "William Danker's Presence in Japan: Introduction," in *Christian Presence in Japan*, ed. W. Kang (Tokyo, 1981), pp. 9–20; and *Who's Who in Religion* (Chicago, 1977).

DAVIDSON, JAMES WHEELER (1872–1933). Consul and financial agent, born June 14, 1872, in Austin, Minnesota. Davidson graduated from Northwestern Military Academy (Highland Park, Ill.). He was a member of the Peary

Arctic expedition to North Greenland in 1893–1894; a war correspondent with the Chinese Army in 1895 and with the Japanese Army in 1895–1896; a member of the Botel Tobago exploring party in 1896; a special correspondent in Formosa in 1897; a consular agent in Tamsui, Formosa, in 1897; consul for Formosa and the Ryukyu Islands in 1898; a commercial attaché in Shanghai in 1904; consul in Nanking in 1904 and in Antung, Manchuria, in 1904–1905; special agent in charge of the consulate general at Shanghai in 1904–1905; vice president and managing director of Staples and Company, Limited, from 1905 to 1907; president and managing director of Crown Lumber Company, Limited, from 1908 to 1914; and vice president and general manager of Beiseker and Davidson, Limited, in 1917. He was vice president of Rotary International, and its general commissioner from 1928 to 1931, organizing rotary clubs in India, Burma, Ceylon, the Straits Settlements, the Federated Malay States, Java, Sumatra, Siam, and China. He wrote *The Island of Formosa Past and Present: Historical View from 1430 to 1900. History, People, Resources, and Commercial Prospects* (London, 1903). Died July 18, 1933, in Calgary, Alberta, Canada. *Reference*: *WWWA*.

DAVIES, JOHN PATON, JR. (1908–   ). Diplomat, born April 6, 1908, in Kiating, China, to American missionary parents. Davies attended the University of Wisconsin and Yenching University (Peking), and graduated from Columbia University. He entered the foreign service in 1931; served as consul in Kunming, Peking, Mukden, Hankow, and Chungking; and was first secretary in Moscow in 1947. He was a member of the policy planning staff of the State Department from 1947 to 1950, director of political affairs in the U.S. mission to Germany from 1951 to 1953, and counselor to Peru in 1953–1954. He was dismissed by Secretary of State John Foster Dulles in 1954 after an attack on him by Senator Joseph McCarthy. His name was cleared in 1968. He was in furniture business in Lima, Peru from 1953 until 1964. He wrote *Foreign and Other Affairs* (New York, 1964), and *Dragon by the Tail: American, British, Japanese and Russian Encounters with China and One Another* (New York, 1972). *References*: *CA*; James A. Fetzer, "The Case of John Paton Davies, Jr.," *Foreign Service Journal* 54 (November 1977): 15–22, 31–32; *PolProf: Eisenhower*; and *PolProf: Truman*.

DAVIS, DWIGHT F(ILLEY) (1879–1945). Government official and colonial administrator, born July 5, 1879, in St. Louis, Missouri. Davis graduated from Harvard University and Washington University Law School. He became involved in local civic affairs, and was a city park commissioner from 1911 to 1915. He served in the U.S. Army during World War I. He was assistant secretary of war from 1923 to 1925, and secretary of war from 1925 until 1929. He was governor general of the Philippines from 1929 until 1932, where he worked to improve economic conditions. He was director general of the Army Specialist Corps during World War II. Died November 28, 1945, in Washington, D.C. *Refer-*

ences: *ACAB*; Melchor P. Aquino, "Dwight F. Davis," *BAHC* 2 (April-June 1974): 7–11; *DAB S3*; *EP* 4:372–73; *Gleeck/Governors*, ch. 10; *NCAB* 40:50; *NYT*, November 29, 1945; and *WWWA*.

DAVIS, GEORGE WHITEFIELD (1839–1918). Army officer and engineer, born July 26, 1839, in Thompson, Windham County, Connecticut. Davis served in the Union Army during the Civil War. He was commissioned a captain in the United States Army in 1867, served as engineer in the Southwest, was assistant engineer on the construction of the Washington Monument, and vice president and general manager of the Nicaraguan Canal Company from 1890 to 1893. He served in the Spanish-American War in Cuba and was governor of Puerto Rico in 1899–1900. He came to the Philippines in 1901, and was commander of the Department of Mindanao and Sulu in 1901–1902, and commanding general of the Philippine Division in 1902–1903. He retired with the rank of brigadier general in 1903. He was later a member of the Isthmian Canal Commission. Died July 12, 1918, in Washington, D.C. *References*: *ACAB*; *DAB*; *NCAB* 13:368; and *WWWA*.

DAVIS, HASSOLDT (1907–1959). Explorer and author, born July 3, 1907, in Boston. Davis attended Harvard University. He traveled to the South Pacific islands in 1929–1930, and later helped Andre Roosevelt to make *Goona Goona*, a film of Bali. He was a writer and photographer with the Denis-Roosevelt Asiatic expedition of 1939, driving up Burma Road into China. He later visited Nepal and made a collection of ethnological data and photographs of Nepal. He served with the Free French Forces during World War II, and led expeditions to French Guiana in 1947–1948 and to the Ivory Coast in 1949–1950. He wrote *Islands under the Winds* (London, 1933); *Land of the Eye: A Narrative of the Labors, Adventures, Alarums and Excursions of the Denis-Roosevelt Asiatic Expedition to Burma, China, India and the Lost Kingdom of Nepal* (New York, 1940); and *World without a Roof, an Autobiography* (New York, 1957). Died September 9, 1959, in Boston. *References*: *NYT*, September 12, 1959; and *WWWA*.

DAVIS, JEROME DEAN (1838–1910). Missionary, born January 17, 1838, in Groton, Tompkins County, New York. Davis attended Lawrence University (Appleton, Wis.) and graduated from Beloit College and Chicago Theological Seminary. He served in the Union Army during the Civil War. He was a missionary under the American Board of Commissioners for Foreign Missions (ABCFM) in Japan from 1871 until his death, serving in Kobe. He taught in and formed the nucleus of what became Kobe College. He later helped found and shape Doshisha University in Tokyo. He wrote *A Maker of New Japan: Rev. Joseph Hardy Neesima* (New York, 1890). Died November 4, 1910, in Oberlin, Ohio. His son, **JOHN MERLE DAVIS** (1875–1960), an association official, was born in Kyoto, Japan; graduated from Oberlin College and Hartford

Theological Seminary; and studied in Germany. He was the Young Men's Christian Association (YMCA) secretary in Japan from 1905 to 1922, first in Nagasaki and later in Tokyo. He wrote a biography of his father and *An Autobiography* (Tokyo, 1960). *References*: *CDCWM*; *DAB*; and *NYT*, November 6, 1910.

DAVIS, MORGAN J(ONES) (1898–1979). Petroleum geologist, born November 18, 1898, in Anson, Jones County, Texas. Davis attended Texas Christian University and graduated from the University of Texas. He was employed by Humble Oil and Refining Company (later Exxon) from 1925 to 1929. He left for the Nederlandsche Koloniale Petroelum Maatschappij (NKPM) and was in charge of geologic exploration in Java and Sumatra from 1929 to 1934. He returned to Humble Oil in 1934, where he was chief geologist from 1941 to 1948, director and vice president from 1948 to 1957, president from 1957 to 1961, and chairman and chief executive from 1961 until his retirement in 1963. Died December 31, 1979, in Houston, Texas. *References*: *BAAPG* 65 (1981): 1650–52; and *WWWA*.

DAWLEY, WILLIAM SANBORN (1856–1927). Railroad engineer, born November 27, 1856, in Stevens Point, Portage County, Wisconsin. Dawley graduated from the University of Minnesota. He worked on various railroad and construction projects for several railroad companies from 1879 until 1888, was special assistant engineer to the vice president of the Chicago and Eastern Illinois Railway Company from 1888 to 1890, principal assistant engineer from 1890 to 1894, and chief engineer of maintenance of way from 1894 to 1906. He was chief engineer of the Missouri and North Arkansas Railway Company from 1906 to 1909. He was chief engineer of the newly formed Yunnan, Szechuan, and Teng Yueh Railway Company in China from 1909 to 1913, and carried out explorations and reconnaissance surveys in the mountainous district of southwestern China. The railroad was never constructed. He returned to the United States in 1913 and practiced as a private consulting engineer. Died May 18, 1927, in St. Louis. *Reference*: *NCAB* 26:418.

DEAN, WILLIAM (1807–1895). Missionary, born June 21, 1807, in Morrisville, New York. Dean graduated from the Hamilton Literary and Theological Institution (later Colgate University), and was ordained in 1833. He was a missionary under the American Baptist Missionary Union in Siam from 1835 to 1842. He was engaged in missionary work among the Chinese in Bangkok. He was transferred to Hong Kong in 1842 and served there until 1865, when he returned to Bangkok. He was the tutor of King Mongkut of Siam. He wrote *The China Mission. Embracing a History of the Various Missions of All Denominations among the Chinese* (New York, 1859). He returned to the United States in 1884. Died August 13, 1895, in San Diego, California. *References*: William Dean Papers, American Baptist Historical Society, Rochester, N.Y.; *ACAB*; and Francis W. Goddard, *Called to Cathay* (New York, 1948).

DEARING, JOHN LINCOLN (1858–1916). Missionary, born December 10, 1858, in Webster, Maine. Dearing graduated from Colby College and Newton Theological Institution, and was ordained in 1889. He was a missionary under the American Baptist Missionary Union in Japan from 1889 until his death, serving in Yokohama. He was president of the Yokohama Baptist Theological Seminary and professor of theology and ethics there from 1894 to 1908. He was the general missionary superintendent of the American Baptist Missionary Union for Japan, China, and the Philippines from 1908 to 1911, and later was secretary of the Federated Missions in Japan and editor of *The Christian Movement in the Japanese Empire* until his death. Died December 20, 1916, in Clifton Springs, New York. *References*: *DAB*; and *WWWA*.

DEFOREST, CHARLOTTE B(URGIS) (1879–1971). Missionary educator, daughter of John Hyde DeForest,* born February 23, 1879, in Osaka, Japan, and grew up in Sendai, Japan. DeForest graduated from Smith College, attended Chicago Theological Seminary, Oxford University, and Kennedy School of Missions. She was a missionary under the American Board of Commissioners for Foreign Missions (ABCFM) from 1903 until 1950. She taught English and the Bible at Kobe College in Nishinomiya, Japan, from 1903 to 1915, and was president of Kobe College from 1915 to 1940. She served as a social worker for the Japanese detainees in Boston in 1942–1943 and then in Manzanar, California, in 1944–1945. She returned to Kobe College in 1947 and taught there until 1950. She wrote *The History of Kobe College* (Nishinomiya, Japan, 1950), and a biography of her father. *References*: Charlotte B. DeForest Papers, Hoover Institution on War, Revolution and Peace, Stanford, Calif.; and *CA*.

DEFOREST, JOHN (KINNE) H(YDE) (1844–1911). Missionary, born June 25, 1844, in Westbrook, Connecticut, and grew up in Greenwich, Connecticut. DeForest served during the Civil War and then graduated from Yale University and Yale Divinity School, and was ordained in 1871. He was a missionary under the American Board of Commissioners for Foreign Missions (ABCFM) in Japan from 1874 until his death. He served in Osaka from 1874 to 1886 and in Sendai after 1886. He opened a boys' school in Sendai in 1887 (closed in 1892). He traveled to Manchuria, China, and Korea. He wrote *Sketch of the Japan Mission of the A.B.C.F.M., 1869–1904* (Boston, n.d.), and *Sunrise in the Sunrise Kingdom* (New York, 1904). Died May 8, 1911, in Tokyo. *References*: *DAB*; and *NYT*, May 9, 1911.

DE FOREST, LOCKWOOD (1850–1932). Artist, born June 23, 1850, in New York City. De Forest studied in Rome. He traveled though Egypt, Syria, and Greece from 1875 to 1878, and resided in India in 1881–1882. He founded workshops for the revival of wood carving at Ahmedabad in 1881, and exhibited his works by special request at the First Indian Exhibition at Lahore in 1882. He wrote *Indian Domestic Architecture* (Boston, 1885) and *Indian Architecture* *and Ornament* (Boston, 1887), and also published a portfolio of design illustrations based on indian motifs. He collected Tibetan handicrafts and oriental art, which he contributed to the Metropolitan Museum of Art. He and his wife, Meta K. De Forest, wrote an account of their visit to Nepal in the May 1901 issue of *Century Magazine*. Died April 3, 1932, in Santa Barbara, California. *References*: Anne S. Lewis, *Lockwood de Forest, Painter, Importer, Decorator* (Huntington, N.Y., 1976); *NYT*, April 5, 1932; and *WWWA*.

DEIGNAN, HERBERT G(IRTON) (1906–   ). Ornithologist, born December 5, 1906, in East Orange, New Jersey. Deignan graduated from Princeton University. He was master of the Prince Royal's College at Chiangmai, Siam, from 1928 to 1932, and again from 1935 to 1937. He was a field associate of the U.S. National Museum in Siam from 1935 to 1937. He traveled extensively in Siam, explored the highest peaks in northern Siam, and collected zoological specimens. He was assistant curator in the division of birds of the U.S. National Museum from 1940 to 1942, associate curator there from 1942 to 1959, and curator from 1959 to 1962. He served with the Office of Strategic Services (OSS) during World War II. He was a member of the Asiatic Primate expedition to North Borneo in 1937, the Arnhem Land expedition to North Australia in 1948, and the Smithsonian expedition to Madagascar in 1962. He wrote *The Birds of Northern Thailand* (Washington, D.C., 1945) and *Checklist of the Birds of Thailand* (Washington, D.C., 1963). *Reference*: AMWS.

DELANO, WARREN, JR. (1809–1898). Merchant, born July 13, 1809, in Fairhaven, Massachusetts. Delano was employed by a firm of merchant bankers and shipowners in Boston, and later by a mercantile firm in New York City. He was a partner of Russell and Company in Canton from 1840 until 1846. He was engaged in mercantile operations in New York City from 1846 until 1861, returned to Canton in 1861, and was again a partner of Russell and Company until 1866. Later he lived in semiretirement. Died January 17, 1898, in Newburgh, New York. *References*: Daniel W. Delano, Jr., *Franklin Roosevelt and the Delano Influence* (Pittsburgh, Pa., 1946), ch. 9; and *NCAB* 34:55.

DE LONG, CHARLES E. (1832–1876). Lawyer and diplomat, born August 13, 1832, in Beekmanville, Dutchess County, New York. De Long went to California in 1850 and worked mining claims. He was the deputy sheriff and bailiff of Yuba County in 1856, and he studied law and was admitted to the bar in 1857. He was a member of the state assembly from 1857 to 1859 and a member of the state senate from 1859 to 1863. He practiced law in Virginia City, Nevada, from 1863 until 1869. He was U.S. minister to Japan from 1869 to 1873. He recognized Japan's claims to the Ryukyu Islands, and supported Japan's military expeditions to Korea and Formosa. He also acted as the representative for the Kingdom of Hawaii in Japan. He returned to the United States in 1873 and practiced law in Virginia City until his death. Died October 26,

1876, in Virginia City. *References*: De Long Family Papers, Bancroft Library, University of California at Berkeley, Calif.; *DADH*; *KEJ*; and Robert M. Spaulding, Jr., "A Mining Town Lawyer as American Minister in Japan, 1869–1873," in *Selected Faculty Papers of the Southwest Cultural Heritage Festival 1982* (Stillwater, Okla., 1982), 2:31–34.

DENBY, CHARLES (1830–1904). Lawyer and diplomat, born June 16, 1830, in Mount Joy, Botetourt County, Virginia. Denby attended Georgetown University and the College Royal (Marseilles, France), and graduated from Virginia Military Institute (Lexington). He studied law in Evansville, Indiana, and was admitted to the bar in 1855. He practiced law in Evansville, Indiana, after 1856. He served in the Union Army during the Civil War, and returned to law practice in 1863. He was U.S. minister to China from 1885 to 1898. He represented Japan's interests in China during the Sino-Japanese War, and was involved in peace negotiations between the two countries. He was a member of the committee to investigate the conduct of the war with Spain in 1898, and a member of the Philippines Commission in 1899. Died January 13, 1904, in Jamestown, New York. His work *China and Her People* (Boston, 1906), with reproductions of the photographs he collected in China, was published posthumously. *References*: *Anderson*, ch. 7; John W. Cassey, "The Mission of Charles Denby and International Rivalries in the Far East, 1885–1898," Ph.D. diss., University of Southern California, 1959; *DAB*; *DADH*; Britten Dean, "The United States and China in the Nineteenth Century: An Incident in the Career of Minister Charles Denby," *Bulletin of the Institute of Modern History of the Academia Sinica* (Taiwan) 7 (1978): 611–25; David Healy, *US Expansionism: The Imperial Urge in the 1890s* (Madison, Wis., 1970), ch. 10; *NCAB* 8:276; *NYT*, January 14, 1904; David M. Silver, ed., "Charles Denby and the Sino-Japanese War, 1894–1895," *Indiana Magazine of History* 52 (1956): 285–88; and *WWWA*.

DENBY, CHARLES, JR. (1861–1938). Consul, son of Charles Denby,* born November 14, 1861, in Evansville, Indiana. Denby graduated from Princeton University and studied law in Evansville. He was second secretary in the U.S. legation in Peking from 1885 to 1894, and first secretary from 1894 to 1897. He was engaged in business in Tientsin from 1897 to 1900, was secretary general of the provisional government established by the allied powers for the district of Tientsin from 1900 to 1902, and foreign advisor to the viceroy of the Province of Chihli in north China from 1902 to 1905. He was chief clerk in the State Department in Washington, D.C., from 1905 to 1907, and consul general in Shanghai from 1907 to 1909, and in Vienna from 1909 to 1914. He resigned in 1914, and was vice president of Hupp Motor Car Corporation in Detroit from 1915 to 1917, director of the Bureau of Foreign Agents of the War Trade Board in 1917–1918, special representative of the State Department in Japan and China in 1918, and special representative of the U.S. Shipping Board in China and

Japan in 1922–1923. Died February 4, 1938, in Washington, D.C. *References*: *DADH*; *NCAB* 39:50; *NYT*, February 15, 1938; and *WWWA*.

DENISON, HENRY W(ILLARD) (1846–1914). Legal advisor, born May 11, 1846, in Guildhall, Vermont. Denison attended Columbia (later George Washington) University. He was a consular clerk in Yokohama, Japan, from 1868 to 1870, and practiced law in Yokohama until 1880. He was a legal advisor to the Japanese Ministry of Foreign Affairs from 1880 until his death, serving as an aide to the Japanese foreign ministers. He helped to guide the negotiations that led to the Anglo-Japanese commercial treaty of 1894; represented Japan in drafting the peace treaty with Russia at Portsmouth, New Hampshire, in 1905; and was involved in the planning of the Anglo-Japanese treaty of 1902 and its revisions in 1905 and 1911. He was one of Japan's representatives to the Permanent Court of Arbitration in the Hague, and technical delegate for Japan to the second Peace Conference at the Hague. Died July 3, 1914, in Tokyo, Japan. *References*: Deborah C. Church, "The Role of the American Diplomatic Advisers to the Japanese Foreign Ministry, 1872–1887," Ph.D. diss., University of Hawaii, 1978, ch. 4; *KEJ*; *NYT*, July 4, 1914; Noboru Umetani, *The Role of the Foreign Employees in the Meiji Era of Japan* (Tokyo, 1971), ch. 6; and *WWWA*.

DENNY, OWEN N(ICKERSON) (1838–1900). Legal advisor, born September 4, 1838, in Morgan County, Ohio, and grew up in Oregon Territory. Denny graduated from Willamette College (Salem, Ore.), studied law, and was admitted to the bar in 1862. He was the judge of Wasco County until 1868; police court judge in Portland, Oregon, from 1870 to 1874; and collector of revenue for Oregon and Alaska from 1874 to 1877. He was consul in Tientsin, China, from 1877 to 1880, and consul general in Shanghai from 1880 to 1883. He was an advisor to King Kojong of Korea from 1886 to 1890. He was vice president of the Home Ministry and director of foreign affairs, and played a crucial role in negotiating the Franco-Korean treaty of 1886 and the Russo-Korean trade treaty of 1888. He wrote *China and Korea* (Shanghai, 1888). He returned to the United States in 1891, where he was a receiver at the Portland Savings Bank and state senator from 1892 to 1896. Died in Portland, Oregon. *References*: Owen N. Denny Letterbook, University of Oregon Library, Eugene, Ore.; Gertrude Hall Denny "Diary," Ms., Oregon Historical Society, Portland, Ore.; Robert R. Swartout, Jr., ed., *An American Adviser in Late Yi Korea: The Letters of Owen Nickerson Denny* (University, Ala., 1984); Robert R. Swartout, Jr., *Mandarins, Gunboats, and Power Politics: Owen Nickerson Denny and the International Rivalries in Korea* (Honolulu, 1980); and Robert R. Swartout, Jr., ed., "Journey to Old Korea: The 1886 Diary of Gertrude Hall Denny," *Transactions of the Royal Asiatic Society Korea Branch* 61 (1986): 35–68.

DENTAN, ROBERT K(NOX) (1936–   ). Anthropologist, born August 28, 1936, in New Haven, Connecticut. Dentan graduated from Yale University. He carried out fieldwork in Malaya from 1961 to 1963, and wrote *The Semai: A Non-Violent People of Malaya* (New York, 1968). He was an assistant and associate professor at Ohio State University from 1964 to 1969, associate professor of anthropology and American studies at the State University of New York at Buffalo from 1969 to 1974, and a member of the faculty of Millard Fillmore College after 1974. *References*: *AMWS*; and *DFAF*.

DENTON, MARY FLORENCE (1857–1947). Missionary educator, born July 4, 1857, in a mining camp in Nevada County, California. Denton graduated from Poston Collegiate School (Oakland) and then taught in Pasadena, California. She was a missionary under the American Board of Commissioners for Foreign Missions (ABCFM) in Japan from 1888 until 1928. She was associated with Doshisha University in Kyoto from 1888 until 1941, with the exception of the years 1897 to 1900, when a dispute between Doshisha University and ABCFM made it necessary for her to withdraw, and she taught at a girls' school in Tokyo. She taught English, Bible, and Western-style cooking in Doshisha University, the nurses' training school, the high school for boys and girls, and the women's junior college. She retired in 1928 but remained in Japan, continuing to teach until 1941. She lived in Japan during World War II. Died December 24, 1947, in Kyoto. *Reference*: *NAW*.

DENYES, JOHN R(USSELL) (1869–1936). Missionary, born January 24, 1869, in Brookfield Missouri. Denyes graduated from Northwestern University and Garrett Bible Institute, and was ordained in 1897. He was a missionary under the Board of Foreign Missions of the Methodist Episcopal Church in Sumatra from 1897; founded Methodist missions in Java, Sumatra, and Borneo from 1907 to 1912; studied educational work and the revolutionary movement in China in 1911; and was the director of education for the Methodist Episcopal Church in Malaysia from 1913 to 1916. He was a lecturer for the Board of Foreign Missions from 1917 to 1919, professor of missions at the Drew Theological Seminary in 1919–1920, financial agent of the Wesley Foundation of Madison, Wisconsin, from 1921 to 1923, and professor of religion and missions at Lawrence College (Wis.) after 1923. He wrote *Malaysia* (Columbus, Ohio, 1919) and *The Malaysia Mission of the Methodist Episcopal Church* (New York, 1905?). Died January 22, 1936, in Appleton, Wisconsin. *Reference*: *WWWA*.

DEPPERMANN, CHARLES E(DWARD) (1889–1957). Scientist, born March 28, 1889, in New York City. Deppermann graduated from St. Andrews on the Hudson (Poughkeepsie, N.Y.), Woodstock College, and Johns Hopkins University, and studied at the University of California and Lick Observatory. He entered the novitiate of the Society of Jesus in 1910 and was ordained in 1920. He came to the Philippines in 1926, where he was chief of the astronomical division of the Weather Bureau from 1926 to 1928, chief of the meteorological division from 1928 to 1932, and assistant director of the Weather Bureau from 1932 until 1941. He was interned by the Japanese at Los Baños during World War II. He returned to the Philippines in 1948 and was director of the Manila Observatory at Mirador, Baguio City, from 1948 until his death. Died May 8, 1957, in Baguio City, Philippines. *References*: *DPB* 3; James J. Hennessey, "Charles Deppermann, S.J., Philippine Scientist," *PS* 5 (1957): 311–35; *NYT*, May 10, 1957; and *WWP*.

DERBYSHIRE, CHARLES E. (1880–1933). Educator, born January 17, 1880, in Huntington, West Virginia. Derbyshire graduated from Marshall College (Huntington) and West Virginia University. He taught Spanish at Marshall College from 1898 to 1901. He came to the Philippines as a teacher in 1901 on the transport *Thomas*, and taught until 1910. He was a translator in the Philippine Executive Bureau in 1910–1911 and in the Philippine supreme court from 1911 to 1916. He translated José Rizal's novels and poems into English. The *Social Cancer* and *Reign of Greed*, translations of *Noli Me Tangere* and *El Filibusterismo*, respectively, were published in Manila in 1912. Died April 10, 1933, in Chillicotte, Ohio. *Reference*: *DPB* 3.

DEVALOIS, JOHN J(AMES) ("JACK") (1892–1988). Agricultural missionary, born November 3, 1892, in Boyden, Iowa. DeValois graduated from Iowa State University, Central University of Iowa, and Moody Bible Institute. He was an agricultural missionary under the Board of Foreign Mission of the Reformed Church of America in India from 1920 to 1960, and was the founder and principal of the Katpadi Agricultural Institute of the Arcot mission in South India. He wrote *Poultry in India* (Madras, 1944); *Vegetables in India* (Madras, 1946); *Milk Goats in India* (Madras, 1949); and *Autobiography of John James DeValois: Agricultural Missionary, Church of South India* (n.p., 1978). He was later a pastor in Holland, Michigan. Died October 14, 1988, in Holland, Michigan. *Reference*: *Who's Who in Religion* (Chicago, 1977).

DEWEY, GEORGE (1837–1917). Naval officer, born December 26, 1837, in Montpelier, Vermont. Dewey attended Norwich University and graduated from the U.S. Naval Academy in 1858. He served in the Union Navy during the Civil War. He later served as executive officer and commanded a number of ships. He was chief of the Navy's Bureau of Equipment and Recruiting from 1889 to 1895, and president of the Board of Inspection and Survey from 1895 to 1898. He was commander of the Asiatic Squadron from 1897 to 1900, and commanded the U.S. forces in the Battle of Manila Bay (see Manila Bay, Battle of*). He was a member of the first Philippine Commission. He was president of the general board of the U.S. Navy Department from 1900 until his death. He wrote *Autobiography of George Dewey, Admiral of the Navy* (New York, 1913). Died January 16, 1917, in Washington, D.C. *References*: *ACAB*; *DAB*; *DADH*;

DAMIB; *NCAB* 9:3; *Pier*; Nathan Sargent, *Admiral Dewey and the Manila Campaign* (Washington, D.C., 1947); Ronald Spector, *Admiral of the New Empire: The Life and Career of George Dewey* (Baton Rouge, La., 1974); and *WWWA*.

DEWEY, JOHN (1859–1952). Educator, born October 20, 1859, in Burlington, Vermont. Dewey graduated from the University of Vermont and Johns Hopkins University. He taught philosophy at the universities of Minnesota and Michigan, and was head of the department of philosophy, psychology, and pedagogy at the University of Chicago from 1894 to 1904. He established the laboratory school there in 1896 and was its director until 1904. He was professor of philosophy at Columbia University from 1904 until his retirement in 1930. He went to Japan in 1919 and gave lectures at the Imperial University of Tokyo. He then was in China from 1919 until 1921, traveling widely, lecturing, and exerting an important influence on Chinese education. He wrote *Impressions of Soviet Russia and the Revolutionary World: Mexico-China-Turkey* (New York, 1929). Died June 1, 1952, in New York City. *References*: John Dewey with Alice C. Dewey, *Letters from China and Japan,* ed. Evelyn Dewey (New York, 1920); Thomas Berry, "Dewey's Influence in China," in *John Dewey: His Thought and Influence*, ed. John Blewell (New York, 1960), pp. 199–230; Robert W. Clopton and Tsuin-chen Ou, eds., *John Dewey: Lectures in China, 1919–1920* (Honolulu, 1973); *DAB*; Cecile B. Dockser, "John Dewey and the May Fourth Movement in China: Dewey's Social and Political Philosophy in Relation to His Encounter with China (1919–1921)," Ed.D. diss., Harvard University, 1983; George Dykhuizen, *The Life and Mind of John Dewey* (Carbondale, Ill., 1973); Lewis S. Feuer, "John Dewey's Sojourn in Japan," *Teachers College Record* 71 (September 1969): 123–45; Barry Keenan, *The Dewey Experiment in China: Educational Reform and Political Power in the Early Republic* (Cambridge, Mass., 1977); Victor N. Kobayashi, *John Dewey in Japanese Educational Thought* (Ann Arbor, 1964); *NCAB* 40:1; *NYT*, June 2, 1952; Hu Shih, "John Dewey in China," in *Philosophy and Culture: East and West*, ed. Charles A. Moore (Honolulu, 1962), pp. 762–69; and *WWWA*.

DEWITT, CLYDE A(LTON) (1879–1956). Lawyer, born May 16, 1879, in Port Hope, Michigan. DeWitt graduated from Michigan State Normal School. He served in the U.S. Army during the Spanish-American War. He came to the Philippines as a teacher in 1901, resigned in 1905, returned to the United States, graduated from the College of Law of the University of Michigan, returned to the Philippines in 1908, and practiced law in Manila. He served in the U.S. Army during World War I. He was the Philippine public utility commissioner from 1916 to 1920, and later was a legal advisor to the Philippine high commissioners. He was interned by the Japanese in Santo Tomas during World War II. He returned to the United States in 1947. Died November 3, 1956, in New York City. *References*: *ACCJ* 32 (1956): 514; *EP* 18:243–245; *NYT*, November 5, 1956; and *WWP*.

DIAMOND, NORMA (JOYCE) (1933–   ). Anthropologist, born February 12, 1933, in New York City. Diamond attended Queens College and graduated from the University of Wisconsin and Cornell University. She carried out field-work in Taiwan from 1959 to 1962 and in 1969–1970; and wrote *K'un Shen: A Taiwan Village* (New York, 1969). She described her experiences in "Fieldwork in a Complex Society: Taiwan," in *Being an Anthropologist: Fieldwork in Eleven Cultures*, ed. George D. Spindler (New York, 1970). She was assistant professor of anthropology at the University of Michigan after 1963, and professor after 1975. *References*: *AMWS*; *CA*; *WWA*; and *WWAW*.

DICK, R(OBERT) MCCULLOUGH (1873–1960). Journalist, born January 22, 1873, in Edinburgh, Scotland, and came to the United States in 1892. Dick graduated from Park College (Mo.). He was a reporter for the *New Rochelle* (N.Y.) *Paragraph* in 1899–1900. He came to the Philippines in 1900; and was a reporter for the *Cablenews-American* from 1900 to 1902; and was a reporter, city editor, and then editor of the *Manila Times* from 1902 to 1908. He was the proprietor, editor, and publisher of the *Philippine Free Press* after 1908. He was interned by the Japanese during World War II. He resumed publishing in 1946. Died September 14, 1960, in Manila. *References*: Peggy Durdin, "One-Man Point Four Project," *New York Times Magazine*, August 28, 1955; *EP* 17:157; *NYT*, September 17, 1960; *The Ramon Magsayay Awards 1958–1962* (Manila, 1977), pp 59–67; and *WWP*.

DICKSON, LILLIAN (RUTH LEVESCONTE) (1901–1983). Missionary, born January 29, 1901, in Prior Lake, Minnesota. Dickson graduated from Macalester College (St. Paul, Minn.) and attended Biblical Seminary and National Bible Institute (New York City). She was a missionary under the Board of Missions of the Presbyterian Church in Canada in Taiwan from 1927. She was stationed in Taipe from 1927 to 1929 and in Tamsui from 1929 until 1940, when she returned to the United States. She served in British Guiana from 1941 to 1945, and returned to Taiwan in 1945. She founded Mustard Seed, Inc., an interdenominational faith ministry in Taiwan in 1954. She wrote *These My People: Serving Christ among the Mountain People of Formosa* (London, 1966), and *Chuckles behind the Door: Lillian Dickson's Personal Letter*, ed. Marilyn D. Tank (n.p., 1977?). Died January 14, 1983, in Taipei, Taiwan. *References*: H. C. Hall, "Littlest Lady with the Biggest Heart," *Reader's Digest* 40 (July 1962): 159–64; and Kenneth L. Wilson, *Angel at Her Shoulder: Lillian Dickson and Her Taiwan Mission* (New York, 1964).

DIEGO GARCIA NAVAL BASE. An atoll, one of the islands making up the Chagos Archipelago, part of the British Indian Ocean Territory, and created in 1965. It is a joint military/naval facility leased to the United States since 1966. It serves as a U.S. naval support facility in the Indian Ocean. *References*: Jack Fuller, "Dateline Diego Garcia: Paved-Over Paradise," *Foreign Policy*, no. 28

(Fall 1977): 175–86; K. S. Jawatkar, *Diego Garcia in International Diplomacy* (Bombay, 1983); Jooneed Khan, "Diego Garcia: The Militarization of an Indian Ocean Island," in *African Islands and Enclaves*, ed. Robin Cohen (Beverly Hills, Calif., 1983), pp. 175–93; Joel Larus, "Diego Garcia: The Military and Legal Limitations of America's Pivotal Base in the Indian Ocean," in *The Indian Ocean: Perspectives on a Strategic Arena*, ed. William L. Dowdy and Russell B. Trood (Durham, N.C., 1985), pp. 435–51; Paul B. Ryan, "Diego Garcia," *USNIP* 110 (September 1984): 132–36; and *USNBO*.

DINSMORE, HUGH ANDERSON (1850–1930). Lawyer and diplomat, born December 24, 1850, in Cave Springs, Benton County, Arkansas. Dinsmore studied law and was admitted to the bar in 1874. He practiced law in Fayetteville, Arkansas, after 1875, and was the prosecuting attorney of the fourth judicial district from 1878 to 1884. He was U.S. minister and consul general to Korea from 1887 until 1890. He later resumed his practice of law, farmed, and was a member of the U.S. House of Representatives from 1893 to 1905. Died May 2, 1930, in St. Louis, Missouri. *References*: *BDAC*; Yur-Bok Lee, *Diplomatic Relations between the United States and Korea, 1866–1887* (New York, 1970), pp. 163–86; and *NCAB* 5:264.

DISCIPLES OF CHRIST. *See* UNITED CHRISTIAN MISSIONARY SOCIETY (DISCIPLES OF CHRIST)

DIVINE WORD, SOCIETY OF THE. Founded in 1875 in Steyl, Holland. The American chapter was established in 1897 in Shermanville (later Northbrook), Illinois. It began missionary work in China in 1879, in the Dutch East Indies and in Japan in 1907, in the Philippines in 1908, and in India in 1932. Fu Jen University in Peking was entrusted to the society in 1933. *References*: *CE*; *The Word in the World: Divine Word Missionaries, 1875–1975* (Techny, Ill., 1973).

DIXIE MISSION (1944–1945). The U.S. Army Observer Group to Yenan, led initially by Colonel David D. Barrett,* was a mission of observers to the Chinese Communists' headquarters in Yenan, China. *References*: David D. Barrett, *Dixie Mission: The United States Army Observer Group in Yenan, 1944* (Berkeley, Calif., 1970); and Michael Schaller, *The U.S. Crusade in China, 1938–1945* (New York, 1979), pp. 181–85, 228–30.

DODD, WILLIAM CLIFTON (1857–1919). Missionary, born October 15, 1857, in Marion, Iowa. Dodd graduated from Parsons College (Fairfield, Ia.) and McCormick Theological Seminary (Chicago), and was ordained in 1886. He was a missionary under the Board of Foreign Missions of the Presbyterian Church in the U.S.A. in Siam from 1886 until his death. He was treasurer of the Laos mission from 1887 to 1890, and later founded a theological seminary in connection with the mission. He made extensive missionary tours in Siam, Burma, and China. He was a leader in establishing the mission among the Tai people in southern China and Indo-China. Died October 18, 1919, at Chiengrung, Siam. His work, *The Thai Race—the Elder Brothers of the Chinese* (Cedar Rapids, 1923) was published posthumously. *Reference*: *WWWA*.

DODGE LINE. A series of financial measures designed by Joseph Morrell Dodge, Michigan banker, to control the inflation that gripped Japan during the years immediately following World War II. The ultimate goal of the Dodge line was to promote Japanese economic recovery. *References*: Joseph M. Dodge Papers, Detroit Public Library; *KEJ*; Dick K. Nanto, "The Dodge Line: A Reevaluation," in *The Occupation of Japan: Economic Policy and Reform*, ed. Lawrence H. Redford (Norfolk, Va., 1980); and Howard B. Schonberger, *Aftermath of War: Americans and the Remaking of Japan, 1945–1952* (Kent, Ohio, 1989), ch. 7.

DOLAN, BROOKE, II (1908–1945). Explorer and naturalist, born October 12, 1908, in Philadelphia. Dolan attended Princeton and Harvard universities. He organized and led two expeditions for the Philadelphia Academy of Natural Sciences to Szechuan Province in China and to northeastern Tibet in 1931–1932, and again to northeastern Tibet in 1934. He served in the U.S. Army Air Force Intelligence in the China-Burma theatre during World War II, and was a member (with Ilia Tolstoy*) of the Office of Strategic Services (OSS) mission to Tibet in 1942–1943. He undertook a second mission for the OSS in 1945. Killed August 19, 1945, while attempting the rescue of an Allied bomber downed behind enemy lines in Chungking, China. *References*: Brooke Doland II "Journals," 1942, Ms., Philadelphia Academy of Sciences; *NYT*, August 24, 1945; and *Tibet*.

DOLBEARE, FREDERICK R(USSELL) (1885–1962). Legal advisor, born October 8, 1885, in Oshkosh, Wisconsin. Dolbeare graduated from Yale University and Columbia Law School, and studied at the University of Munich. He served as secretary of embassy or legation in Vienna, Berne, Paris, Warsaw, Berlin, London, Ottawa, and Istanbul from 1915 to 1928. He then joined the J. Henry Schroder banking firm and served as its representative in London and New York. He was a foreign affairs advisor to the Ministry of Foreign Affairs of Thailand from 1935 to 1940 and was instrumental in redrafting and negotiating the American-Thai treaty of 1937. He was in the service of the U.S. government during World War II. Died July 17, 1962, in Bar Harbor, Maine. *Reference*: *NYT*, July 18, 1962.

DOLTZ, PAUL (1875–1943). Missionary, born September 23, 1875, in Young America, Minnesota. Doltz graduated from Princeton Theological Seminary. He was a missionary under the Board of Foreign Missions of the Presbyterian Church in the U.S.A. in the Philippines from 1902 to 1936. He served at Iloilo, was vice president of Silliman University from 1916 to 1926, and was pastor of the student church until his retirement in 1936. Died February 6, 1943, in Portland, Oregon. *References*: Paul Doltz Papers, Presbyterian Historical Society, Philadelphia; and *NYT*, February 7, 1943.

DOMINO THEORY. Announced by President Dwight D. Eisenhower in 1954, it argued that if Vietnam fell to communist guerrillas, the rest of Southeast Asia would follow. The theory was used to justify the commitment of American resources to South Vietnam in the 1960s. *References*: *DADH*; and *DVW*.

DOOLEY, THOMAS A(NTHONY) (1927–1961). Physician, born January 17, 1927, in St. Louis. Dooley graduated from Notre Dame and St. Louis universities. He served as medical corpsman in the U.S. Navy during World War II. He was commissioned a medical officer in the Navy in 1953, was sent to Japan, and assisted North Vietnamese refugees at a refugee camp he established in Haiphong. He founded a hospital and started a nursing home in northern Laos. He resigned from the Navy in 1956. He founded (with Peter Commanduras) the Medical International Corporation (MEDICO) to provide health services in underdeveloped areas throughout the world. He spent much time in Laos giving medical aid to the natives. He later oversaw the establishment of seven hospitals in four Asian countries. He wrote of his experiences in *Deliver Us from Evil* (New York, 1956); *The Edge of Tomorrow* (New York, 1958); and *The Night They Burned the Mountain* (New York, 1960). Died January 18, 1961, in New York City. *References*: Tom Dooley Papers, University of Missouri-St. Louis Library; *DAB S7*; *DACB*; Teresa Gallagher, *Give Joy to My Youth, a Memoir of Dr. Tom Dooley, 1927–1961* (New York, 1965); *NYT*, January 19, 1961; and *WWWA*.

DOOLITTLE, JUSTUS (1823–1880). Missionary, born June 23, 1823, in Rutland, New York. Doolittle graduated from Hamilton College and Auburn Theological Seminary, and was ordained in 1849. He was a missionary under the American Board of Commissioners for Foreign Missions (ABCFM) from 1850 to 1869, and under the Board of Foreign Missions of the Presbyterian Church in the U.S.A. from 1869 to 1872. He served in Foochow, China, from 1850 to 1872 (except for the period 1866 to 1868, when he served in Tientsin). He was involved in writing, editing, publishing, and distributing missionary literature. He wrote *Social Life of the Chinese: With Some Account of Their Religious, Governmental, Educational, and Business Customs and Opinions* (New York, 1865) and *A Vocabulary and Hand-Book of the Chinese Language* (New York, 1872). He returned to the United States in 1873. Died June 15, 1880, in Clinton, New York. *References*: *Auburn Theological Seminary: General Biographical Catalogue, 1818–1918* (Auburn, 1918); Suzanne W. Barnett, "Justus Doolittle at Foochow: Christian Values in the Treaty Ports," in *Christianity in China: Early Protestant Missionary Writings*, ed. Suzanne W. Barnett and John K. Fairbank (Cambridge, Mass., 1985), pp. 107–19; Marilyn Blatt, "Problems of a China Missionary—Justus Doolittle,'' *Papers on China* 12 (1958): 28–46; and *CR* 12 (1881): 59–63.

DOOMAN, EUGENE H(OFFMAN) (1890–1969). Diplomat, born March 25, 1890, in Osaka, Japan, to American missionary parents. Dooman came to the United States in 1903 and graduated from Trinity College (Hartford, Conn.). He entered the American consular service in 1912; and was vice consul in Kobe, Japan, from 1912 until 1920; consul in Taihoku in 1920–1921; assistant Japanese secretary at the embassy in Tokyo from 1921 to 1925; second secretary and Japanese secretary from 1926 to 1930; and first secretary in the embassy in London from 1931 to 1933. He held the Japanese desk of the State Department in Washington, D.C., from 1933 to 1937, and was counselor of embassy in Tokyo from 1937 until 1941. He was interned by the Japanese in 1941–1942, was chargé d'affaires and later minister-counselor in the embassy in Moscow in 1942–1943, and chairman of the subcommittee for the Far East of the U.S. State, War and Navy Coordinating Committee from 1943 until his retirement in 1945. Died February 2, 1969, in Litchfield, Connecticut. *References*: Eugene H. Dooman Papers, Hoover Institution on War, Revolution and Peace, Stanford, Calif.; and *NCAB* 55:373.

DORN, FRANK (1901–1981). Army officer, born June 25, 1901, in San Francisco. Dorn attended the San Francisco Institute of Art, graduated from the U.S. Military Academy in 1923, and studied at the College of Chinese Studies (Peking). He was commissioned in the U.S. Army in 1923. He served in the Philippines and was assistant military attaché in Peking. He was an aide to General Joseph W. Stilwell* during World War II and retreated with him to India. He was later appointed an honorary general in the Chinese army. He returned to the United States in 1946, worked at the Army Information School at Carlisle Barracks, Pennsylvania, and was deputy chief of information in the Department of the Army until his retirement, with the rank of brigadier general, in 1953. He was president of General Logging Company, Santa Rosa, California, from 1954 to 1957. A painter, he had several one-man shows. He wrote *Forest Twilight* (London, 1935), a novel of the Philippines; *The Forbidden City: The Biography of a Palace* (New York, 1970); *Walkout: With Stilwell in Burma* (New York, 1971); and *The Sino-Japanese War, 1937–41: From Marco Polo Bridge to Pearl Harbor* (New York, 1974). Died July 26, 1981, in Washington, D.C. *References*: *CA*; and *Washington Post*, July 28, 1981.

DORR, SULLIVAN (1778–1858). Merchant, born October 12, 1778, in Boston. Dorr came to Canton, China, in 1799, and represented his father's firm and others until 1803, when he returned to the United States. He also served as U.S. vice consul in Canton. He settled in Providence, Rhode Island, in 1805, and was president of the Washington Insurance Company. Died March 3, 1858, in Providence. *References*: Howard Corning, ''Sullivan Dorr, an Early China Merchant: Extracts from a Notebook Kept by Him in Canton, 1801," *EIHC* 78 (1942): 158–75; and Howard Corning, "Sullivan Dorr, China Trader," *Rhode Island History* 3 (1944): 75–90.

DORSETT, P(ALEMON) H(OWARD) (1862–1943). Plant explorer, born April 21, 1862, in Carlinville, Illinois. Dorsett graduated from the University of Missouri. He served in the U.S. Department of Agriculture after 1891, was special agent of the Bureau of Plant Industry from 1901 to 1904, and assistant in charge of plant exploration and plant introduction field stations from 1904 to 1924, building up six plant introduction gardens. He was leader of plant exploring expeditions to Brazil in 1913–1914 and to China from 1924 to 1927 and from 1927 to 1929, and coleader of an expedition to Japan, Korea, Manchuria, and northern China from 1929 to 1931 to seek soybean cultivars. Died April 1, 1943, in Washington, D.C. *References*: *AMWS*; *Science* 97 (April 9, 1943): 322; and *WWWA*.

DOSHISHA UNIVERSITY. Founded in 1875 in Kyoto, Japan, by Joseph Hardy Neesima (1843–1890), alumnus of Amherst College and Andover Theological Seminary, with the assistance of John Cutting Berry,* Marquis Lafayette Gordon,* and Jerome Dean Davis,* as the Doshisha English school. It became a college in 1912, and was reorganized as a university in 1920. *References*: Paul F. Boller, Jr., "The American Board and the Doshisha, 1875–1900," Ph.D. diss., Yale University, 1947; Martin Bronfenbrenner, *Academic Encounter, the American University in Japan and Korea* (New York, 1961); Paul V. Griesy, "The Doshisha, 1875–1919: The Indignization of an Institution," Ed.D. diss., Columbia University Teachers College, 1973; and *KEJ*.

DOSSER, WILLIAM EARL (1882– ?). Army officer, born December 5, 1882, in Jonesboro, Tennessee. Dosser joined the U.S. Army in 1900, served in China during the Boxer Rebellion, and came to the Philippines in 1901. He joined the Philippine Constabulary in 1907 as a third lieutenant, and served in the Mountain Province after 1908. He was lieutenant governor of Ifugao from 1916 to 1924, governor of the Mountain Province from 1929 to 1936, district commander of northern Luzon in 1936, and inspector general of the Philippine Army after 1936. His memoirs, "The Dosser Story," were serialized in *The Mountaineer* (Baguio City), February 15, 1958 to September 20, 1959. *References*: *CCDP*; Frank L. Jenista, *The White Apos: American Governors on the Cordillera Central* (Quezon City, 1987); and *WWP*.

DOTY, ELIHU (1809–1864). Missionary, born September 20, 1809, in Berne, Albany County, New York. Doty graduated from Rutgers College and Rutgers Theological Seminary (New Brunswick, N.J.), and was ordained in 1836. He was a missionary under the American Board of Commissioners for Foreign Missions (ABCFM) in Batavia, Java, and Singapore from 1836 to 1839, and in

Borneo from 1839 to 1844 (when the mission failed), working among the Chinese-speaking population there. He joined the Amoy mission in China in 1844 (after 1858, serving under the Board of Foreign Missions of the Reformed Church in America). He was in charge of the first Chinese day school in the province and later involved in literary work. He wrote *Some Thoughts on the Proper Term of God in the Chinese* (Shanghai, 1850), and *Manual of the Amoy Dialect* (Canton, 1855). Died November 30, 1864, in Amoy, China. *Reference*: Doty-Dubois Family Papers, New York Public Library; *DAB*; and *EM*.

DOUGHERTY, DENNIS J(OSEPH) (1865–1951). Clergyman, born August 16, 1865, in Ashland, Pennsylvania. Dougherty attended Ste. Marie College (Montreal) and St. Charles Borromeo Seminary (Philadelphia), graduated from the North American College (Rome), and was ordained in 1890. He taught at St. Charles Borromeo Seminary from 1900 to 1903. He was consecrated the first American bishop in the Philippines in 1903 as bishop of Nueva Segovia (Vigan). He was transferred in 1908 to Jaro. He returned to the United States in 1915 as bishop of Buffalo, New York; was archbishop of Philadelphia in 1918; and became a cardinal in 1921. Died May 31, 1951, in Philadelphia. *References*: *DAB S5*; *DACB*; *NCAB* 16:90; *NYT*, June 1, 1951; Francis B. Thornton, *Our American Princes* (New York, 1963), pp. 100–118; and *WWWA*.

DOWNES, JOHN (1784–1854). Naval officer, born December 23, 1784, in Canton, Massachusetts. Downes was appointed acting midshipman in the U.S. Navy in 1800, and midshipman in 1802. He served in the Mediterranean during the Barbary Wars and the War of 1812. He was in command of the frigate USS *Potomac* in East Asia from 1830 until 1834. He led the attack against Quallah Battoo* in 1832, the first official American armed intervention in Asia. He was later commandant of the Boston Navy Yard and the port captain in Boston. Died August 11, 1854, in Charlestown, Massachusetts. *References*: *ACAB*; *DAB*; *NCAB* 11:76; and *WWWA*.

DOZIER, CHARLES KELSEY (1879–1933). Missionary, born January 1, 1879, in La Grange, Georgia. Dozier graduated from Mercer University and Southern Baptist Theological Seminary (Louisville, Ky.), and was ordained in 1904. He was a missionary under the Foreign Mission Board of the Southern Baptist Convention in Japan from 1906 until his death. He was professor in the theological seminary, principal of the night school, and founder of Seinan Gakuin the Southern Baptist School in Fukuoka. He became its dean and later its president. Died May 31, 1933, in Kokura, Japan. *References*: Maude B. Dozier, *Charles Kelsey Dozier of Japan: A Builder of Schools* (Nashville, Tenn., 1953); and *ESB*.

DOZIER, EDWARD P. (1916–1971). Anthropologist, born April 23, 1916, in Santa Clara Pueblo, New Mexico. Dozier graduated from the universities of New Mexico and California at Los Angeles. He served in the U.S. Army Air Force during World War II. He was associate professor of anthropology at Northwestern University until 1958, carried out fieldwork in the Philippines in 1959–1960, and was professor of anthropology and linguistics at the University of Arizona after 1960. He wrote *The Kalinga of Northern Luzon, Philippines* (New York, 1967). Died May 2, 1971, in Tucson, Arizona. *References*; *CA*; *Newsweek*, March 24, 1952; and *NYT*, May 4, 1971.

DOZIER, EDWIN BURKE (1908–1969). Missionary, son of Charles Kelsey Dozier,* born April 16, 1908, in Nagasaki, Japan, and grew up in Fukuoka, Japan. Dozier graduated from Wake Forest College (N.C.) and Southern Baptist Theological Seminary (Louisville, Ky.), and was ordained in 1929. He was a missionary under the Foreign Mission Board of the Southern Baptist Convention in Japan from 1932 until 1941. He served in Hawaii from 1941 to 1945, working with Japanese-speaking people, and returned to Japan in 1946. He was professor and later president of Seinan Gakuin in Fukuoka, Japan. He wrote *A Golden Milestone in Japan* (Nashville, Tenn., 1939), and *Japan's New Day* (Nashville, Tenn., 1949). Died May 10, 1969, in Fukuoka, Japan. *Reference*: Lois Whaley, *Edwin Dozier of Japan: Man of the Way* (Birmingham, Ala., 1983).

DRAKE, NOAH FIELDS (1864–1945). Geologist, born January 30, 1864, in Summers, Washington County, Arkansas. Drake graduated from the University of Arkansas and Stanford University. He did geologic work at the Arkansas Geological Survey in 1887, the Texas Geological Survey from 1889 to 1893, and the U.S. Geological Survey in 1897. He was professor of geology and mining at Pei-yang University in Tientsin, China, from 1898 to 1900 and from 1905 to 1911, engineer in the Public Works Department of Tientsin in 1900–1901, consulting geologist for the American China Development Company from 1902 to 1904, and chairman of the board of the Tientsin Land and Development Company Limited from 1904 to 1911. He was an associate professor of economic geology at Stanford University in 1911–1912, professor of geology and mining at the University of Arkansas from 1912 to 1920, and a consulting geologist after 1920. Died May 4, 1945, in Fayetteville, Arkansas. *References*: Noah Fields Drake Papers, University of Arkansas Libraries, Fayetteville, Ark.; and *WWWA*.

DRAPER MISSION (1948). An economic mission to Japan composed of fifteen members and headed by William Henry Draper, Jr., under secretary of the army, which was sent by the secretary of the army to evaluate political and economic conditions in Japan. It recommended various measures to accelerate Japan's economic recovery. *References*: *KEJ*; Howard B. Schonberger, *Aftermath of*

War: Americans and the Remaking of Japan, 1945–1952 (Kent, Ohio, 1989), ch. 6.

DREW, E(DWARD) B(ANGS) (1843–1924). Government official, born August 24, 1843, in Orleans, Massachusetts, and grew up in Newton, Massachusetts. Drew graduated from Harvard University and studied law. He served in the Imperial Chinese Maritime Customs from 1865 until 1908. He was deputy commissioner of customs and Chinese secretary to the Inspector General of Customs in 1867–1868, and commissioner in Kiukiang from 1868 to 1871. In 1871, he accompanied the Korean Expedition as acting secretary of the U.S. legation and interpreter. He was commissioner of customs in Chefoo in 1874–1875, in Foochow from 1875 to 1877, and in Ningpo from 1877 to 1880. He was statistical secretary on staff of the inspector general in Shanghai from 1882 to 1887, chief secretary in Peking from 1889 to 1893, and commissioner in Canton from 1893 to 1899, in Tientsin in 1899–1900, and in Foochow from 1902 to 1906. He resigned in 1906 and returned to the United States. Died August 16, 1924, in Cotuit, Cape Cod, Massachusetts. *Reference*: *NYT*, August 18, 1924.

DUANE, WILLIAM (1760–1835). Journalist, born May 17, 1760, near Lake Champlain, New York. He was taken by his mother to Ireland in 1765. Duane learned the printer's trade. He went to India in 1787 and lived there until 1794. He established the *Indian World* in Calcutta, which brought him both prestige and fortune. Because of his denunciations of the methods of the East India Company and his espousal of the grievances of an army officer, he was arrested without a charge, deported without a trial, and his property was confiscated. He returned to London, served as parliamentary reporter for the *General Advertiser*, and tried to obtain restitution for his property. He returned to the United States and was editor of the *Aurora* in Philadelphia from 1798 until 1822. He served as adjutant general during the War of 1812 and was prothonotary for the supreme court of Pennsylvania until his death. Died November 24, 1835, in Philadelphia. *References*: *ACAB*; *DAB*; Jonathan Daniels, *They Will Be Heard* (New York, 1965), pp. 41–57; *NCAB* 8:180; and *WWWA*.

DU BOIS, COERT (1881–1960). Diplomat, born November 10, 1881, in Hudson, New York. Du Bois attended Biltmore Forest School (Asheville, N.C.). He served in the U.S. Forest Service from 1900 to 1917, and was district forester of the California district from 1911 to 1917. He served with the U.S. Army engineers during World War I. He entered the foreign service in 1919; was consul in Paris, Nantes, and Port Said from 1919 to 1924; was in charge of the Visa Office in the State Department from 1924 to 1927; consul general in Batavia, Java, from 1927 to 1930; foreign service inspector in India in 1930; consul general in Genoa and Naples, Italy, and Havana, Cuba, from 1931 to 1941; and in charge of the Caribbean Office at the State Department from 1941 to 1944.

In 1948, with a rank of minister, he was the U.S. delegate to the United Nations Security Council's Good Offices Committee to try to obtain a cease-fire between the forces of The Netherlands and the Republic of Indonesia and a political settlement in Java, Dutch East Indies. He retired in 1950. He wrote his memoirs, *Trail Blazers* (Stonington, Conn., 1957). Died March 6, 1960, in Westerley, Rhode Island. *References*: *NYT*, March 7, 1960; and *WWWA*.

DU BOIS, CORA (1903–   ). Anthropologist, born October 26, 1903, in Brooklyn, New York. Du Bois graduated from Barnard College, Columbia University, and the University of California at Berkeley. She was a research associate in anthropology at the University of California from 1932 to 1935, and a teacher at Hunter College in 1936–1937 and at Sarah Lawrence College from 1939 to 1942. She carried out fieldwork in Alor, Dutch East Indies, from 1937 to 1939. She was chief of the Indonesia Section of the Research and Analysis Branch of the Office of Strategic Services (OSS) in 1942–1943, and chief of the South East Asian Branch of the Division of Research for the Far East in the Office of Intelligence of the U.S. State Department from 1943 to 1950. She was a social science consultant to the World Health Organization in 1950–1951, director of research to the Institute of International Education from 1951 to 1954, and professor of anthropology at Harvard University and Radcliffe College from 1954 until her retirement in 1969. She wrote *The People of Alor: A Social-Psychologist Study of an East Indian Island* (New York, 1944), and *Social Forces in Southeast Asia* (Minneapolis, 1949). She initiated and carried out an interdisciplinary study of sociocultural change in Bhubaneswar, Orissa, India, from 1961 to 1972. She described her experiences in "The Form and Substance of Status: A Javanese-American Relationship," in *In the Company of Man: Twenty Portraits of Anthropologists*, ed. Joseph B. Casagrande (New York, 1960), and "Studied in an Indian Town," in *Women in the Field: Anthropological Experiences*, ed. Peggy Golde (Chicago, 1970). *References*: *AMWS*; Susan Seymor, "Cora Du Bois (1903–   )," in *Women Anthropologists: A Biographical Dictionary*, ed. Ute Gacs et al. (Westport, Conn., 1988), pp. 72–79; and *WWA*.

DUBOSE, H(AMPDEN) C(OIT) (1845–1910). Missionary, born September 30, 1845, in Darlington, South Carolina. DuBose graduated from the University of South Carolina and Columbia Theological Seminary, and was ordained in 1871. He was a missionary under the Board of Foreign Missions of the Presbyterian Church in the United States in China from 1872 until his death, serving at Soochow. He was involved in the work of the Anti-Opium League in China. He wrote *The Dragon, Image and Demon: or, The Three Religions of China, Confucianism, Buddhism and Taoism* (London, 1886). Died March 22, 1910, in Soochow. *References*: *CR* 41 (1910): 353–56; and Nattie D. Junkin, comp., *For the Glory of God: Memoirs of Dr. and Mrs. H. C. DuBose of Soochow, China* (Lewisburg, W.Va., 1915?).

DUBS, C(HARLES) NEWTON (1862–1936). Missionary, born August 1862 in Plainfield, Illinois. Dubs graduated from Oberlin College and studied in Tubingen and Bonn, Germany. He was editor of the *Evangelische Zeitschrift* in Harrisburg, Pennsylvania, from 1890 to 1900. He was the first missionary for the United Evangelical Church in China from 1900 until his death. He established the mission in Changsha, Hunan Province, and was superintendent of the mission until 1927. He returned to the United States in 1927 because of ill health but was back in China in 1931. Died July 9, 1936, in Changsha, Hunan, China. *Reference*: *EWM*.

DUCKWORTH-FORD, ROBERT GEOFFREY ALEXANDER (1877–1949). Army officer, born July 4, 1877, in Colombo, Ceylon. Duckworth-Ford attended King's College (London, England) and the University of Aberdeen (Scotland). He served with the British Mounted Police in Rhodesia in 1896–1897. He came to the Philippines in 1901 with the U.S. Army, and served in the Philippine Constabulary from 1903 to 1914. He served with British Army and later with the U.S. Army during World War I. He rejoined the Philippines Constabulary in 1922, was inspector general in 1927, and superintendent of the Philippine Constabulary Academy from 1928 until his retirement, with the rank of colonel, in 1932. He wrote *The Bamboo Brigade, and Other Verses* (Baguio, Philippines, 1929). Died April 19, 1949, in San Diego. *References*: *Elarth*; James J. Halsema, "How Colonel Duckworth-Ford Lost His Job," *BAHC* 10 (April-June 1982): 16–24; and *WWP*.

DUN, EDWIN (1848–1931). Agriculturist and diplomat, born July 19, 1848, in Springfield, Ohio. Dun attended Miami College (Ohio). He was a dairy farmer in Springfield from 1871 to 1873. He went to Japan in 1873, accompanying a shipment of cattle from the United States. He was manager of a government farm in Aoyama and introduced advanced techniques of the dairy business in Japan. He served as agricultural advisor to the Hokkaido Colonization Bureau in Sapporo, Hokkaido, Japan, from 1876 until 1882, and set up dairy farms in Hokkaido. He returned to the United States in 1882 but was back in Japan in 1884. He was second secretary and later first secretary of the U.S. legation from 1884 until 1893, and U.S. minister to Japan from 1893 until 1897. He was manager of the International Oil Company at Naoetsu, Niigata Prefecture, from 1900 to 1907, and was involved later in other business enterprises. Died May 16, 1931, in Tokyo. *References*: Edwin Dun, "Reminiscences of Nearly Half a Century in Japan," Ms., National Agricultural Library, Beltsville, Md.; *DADH*; *Foreign Pioneers*; *NCAB* 12:121; and *WWWA*.

DUNCAN, MARION H(ERBERT) (1896–   ). Missionary, born January 17, 1896, in Celina, Mercer County, Ohio. Duncan graduated from Hiram College. He was a missionary under the United Christian Missionary Society in Western China from 1921 to 1932. He served in Batang, on the Tibetan border.

He wrote *The Mountain of Silver Snow* (Cincinnati, 1929); *The Yangtze and the Yak: Adventurous Trails In and Out of Tibet* (Alexandria, Va., 1952); *Harvest Festival Dramas of Tibet* (Hong Kong, 1955); and *Customs and Superstitions of Tibetans* (London, 1964). He was a member of the second Brooke Dolan* expedition to eastern Tibet from 1934 to 1936. He later resided in Alexandria, Virginia, and served on various governmental agencies as a Tibetan language teacher and translator. He was also stationed in Japan from 1947 to 1951 and in 1955. *Reference*: Marion Herbert Duncan Papers, Academy of Natural Science of Philadelphia Library; and *OAB*.

DUNN, NATHAN (1782–1844). Merchant, born November 11, 1782, near Woodstown, Salem County, New Jersey. Dunn was engaged in trade in Philadelphia after 1802. He was in Canton, China, from 1818 until 1831. He returned to the United States in 1831. He may be said to have been the first American to inform Americans—by actual examples and artifacts—of daily life in China. He established a museum in Philadelphia and produced a widely distributed catalogue, *"Ten Thousand Chinese Things." A Descriptive Catalogue of the Chinese Collection. With Miscellaneous Remarks upon the Manners, Customs, and Government of the Celestial Empire (Philadelphia, 1839)*. He transferred the museum to London in 1842. Died September 19, 1844, in Vevey, Switzerland. *References*: Nathan Dunn Letterbook, G. W. Blunt White Library, Mystic Seaport, Mystic, Conn.; and Arthur W. Hummel, "Nathan Dunn," *Quaker History* 59 (1970): 34–39.

DURBROW, ELBRIDGE (1903–   ). Diplomat, born September 21, 1903, in San Francisco. Durbrow graduated from Yale University and studied at Stanford, Dijon, and the Hague. He entered the foreign service in 1930 and served in Warsaw, Bucharest, Moscow, Naples, Rome, and Lisbon. He was a counselor in Moscow from 1946 to 1948, instructor in the National War College from 1948 to 1950, chief of the Division of Foreign Service Personnel from 1950 to 1952, and minister-counselor and deputy chief of mission in Rome from 1952 to 1957. He was U.S. ambassador to Vietnam from 1957 to 1961. He openly criticized Ngo Dinh Diem and became isolated from him. He was alternate permanent representative to the North Atlantic Council from 1961 to 1965, and advisor to the commander of Air University (Maxwell Air Force Base) from 1965 until his retirement in 1968. *References*: *DADH*; *DVW*; and *WWA*.

DURDIN, (FRANK) TILLMAN (1907–   ). Journalist, born March 30, 1907, in Elkhart, Texas. Durdin attended Texas Christian University. He was a reporter with the *San Antonio Express* in 1928–1929, the *Los Angeles Times* in 1929–1930, and the *Shanghai Evening Post* from 1930 to 1932, and managing editor of *China Press* from 1932 to 1974. He was a member of the staff of *The New York Times* from 1937 to 1961. He was a foreign correspondent in the Far East, Africa, and Europe from 1937 to 1961, member of the editorial board from 1961 to 1964, foreign correspondent in Australia and Southwest Pacific from 1964 to 1967, and chief of the bureau in Hong Kong from 1967 until his retirement in 1974, becoming the ''dean'' of American reporters on China from the 1950s through 1972. He wrote *China and the World* (New York, 1953) and *Southeast Asia* (New York, 1965), and was coauthor of *The New York Times Report from Red China* (New York, 1971). *Reference*: *WWA*.

DUTCH REFORMED CHURCH IN AMERICA. *See* REFORMED CHURCH IN AMERICA: BOARD OF FOREIGN MISSIONS

DYE, WILLIAM MCENTYRE (1831–1899). Military officer, born February 1831 in Pennsylvania. Dye graduated from the U.S. Military Academy in 1853 and served in the Union Army during the Civil War. He resigned from the army in 1870 and went into farming. He joined the Egyptian general staff in 1873 as an assistant to General Charles Pomeroy Stone, participated in the battle of Gura during the Egyptian Abyssinian War of 1875–1876, and was wounded. He returned to the United States in 1878 and served as chief of police in Washington, D.C. He was chief military advisor to the King of Korea from 1888 to 1895, personal bodyguard of the king in 1895–1896, and supervisor of the governmental experimental farm from 1896 until 1899. He returned to the United States in 1899. Died November 13, 1899, in Muskegon, Michigan. *References*: Donald M. Bishop, ''Shared Failure: American Military Advisors in Korea, 1888–1896,'' *Transactions of the Royal Asiatic Society Korea Branch* 58 (1983): 53–76; *DAB*; Herman M. Katz, *KMAG's Heritage: The Story of Brigadier General William McEntire [sic] Dye* (Seoul, n.d.); and Richard P. Weinert, ''The Original KMAG,'' *Military Review* 45 (June 1965): 93–99.

DYHRENFURTH, NORMAN GUNTER (1918–   ). Mountain climber, May 7, 1918, in Breslau, Germany, and grew up in Zurich, Switzerland. Dyhrenfurth came to the United States in 1938 and was naturalized in 1944. He was a certified ski instructor, director of Willard Pictures in New York City from 1939 to 1944, and associate professor and head of the motion picture division at the University of California at Los Angeles from 1948 to 1953. He produced and directed films for the U.S. Department of Interior, and the army, navy and air force. He was chief of the motion picture department of Convair-Aeronautics Company from 1957 to 1960. He was cameraman and director of the Swiss Mount Everest Expedition in 1952, leader of the International Himalayan expedition in 1955, deputy leader of the Slick-Johnson Snowman expedition in 1958, cameraman and director of the Swiss Himalayas expedition to Dhaulgari in 1960, organizer and leader of the American Mount Everest expedition in 1963, and organizer and leader of the Inter-Himalayan expedition to Mount Everest in 1971. *References*: H. P. S. Ahluwalia, *Faces of Everest* (New Delhi, 1978), pp. 73–82; *CB* 1965; Thomas F. Hornbein, *Everest, the West Ridge* (San Francisco, 1965); and *WWA*.

DYSON, VERNE (1879–1971). Author, born January 25, 1879, in Rolla, Missouri. Dyson graduated from Central College (Fayette, Mo.). He was a reporter with the *Kansas City Star* from 1906 to 1911, and with the *Los Angeles Times* from 1912 to 1918. He was a teacher and writer in China from 1920 to 1928; dean of Williams College, Shanghai, in 1921; traveling lecturer in China and Japan in 1924–1925; professor of English at Kwang Hua University in Shanghai in 1926–1927; and literary editor of *China Courier* and *Orient Magazine* in 1927. He was a lecturer on Far Eastern affairs and politics, and an assistant professor of English at the University of the Philippines from 1928 to 1933. He was also dramatic critic of the *Manila Daily Bulletin* and contributing editor of the *Philippine Social Science Review*. He wrote *Forgotten Tales of Ancient China* (Shanghai, 1927), and *Land of the Yellow Spring* (New York, 1937). He was director of the Institute of Chinese Studies in New York City from 1933 to 1945; occupational director and manager of the printing plant at the Pilgrim State Hospital in Brentwood, Long Island, from 1945 to 1950; editor of the *Brentwood Bulletin* from 1951 to 1961; and editor of *Deer Park-Wyandanch News* from 1952 to 1961. Died in Los Angeles. *References*: *WWP*; and *WWWA*.

E

EAKIN, JOHN ANDERSON (1854–1929). Educator, born February 28, 1854, in Rosepoint, Pennsylvania. Eakin graduated from Washington and Jefferson College (Washington, Pa.) and Western Theological Seminary (Pittsburgh), and was ordained in 1888. He was a teacher in the king's school in Bangkok, Siam, from 1880 to 1884. He was a missionary in Siam from 1888 until 1925, founded a Christian high school in Bangkok in 1888 and directed it until 1907, and served in Petchaburi from 1907 until his retirement in 1925. He introduced telegraphic equipment into Siam. Died January 21, 1929, in Bangkok. *Reference*: Paul A. Eakin, *The Eakin Family in Thailand* (Bangkok, 1955).

EAST INDIA SQUADRON. Created in 1835 by the U.S. Navy Department to protect American lives and property and to promote American commercial and strategic interests on the China coast. It was recalled in 1861 to participate in the Civil War. *References*: Curtis T. Henson, Jr., *Commissioners and Commodores: The East India Squadron and American Diplomacy in China* (University, Ala., 1982); Robert E. Johnson, *Far China Station: The U.S. Navy in Asian Waters 1800–1898* (Annapolis, Md., 1979); Sarah Larson, "East India Squadron Letters: A Passage of Arms," *Prologue* 13 (1981): 39–48; and James B. Wood, "The American Response to China, 1784–1844: Consensus Policy and the Origin of the East India Squadron," Ph.D. diss., Duke University, 1968.

EASTLAKE, F(REDERICK) WARRINGTON (1858–1905). Educator and editor, born in Germany and studied at the University of Berlin. Eastlake came to the United States and became a U.S. citizen. He went to Japan in 1884, and began and edited the *Tokyo Independent*, the first English-language weekly magazine to be published in Japan. He founded an English school in 1890 and published textbooks for studying English. He compiled *An Anglo-Japanese Compendium of Conversation for Study and Reference* (Tokyo, 1902), and was coauthor of *Heroic Japan: A History of the War between China and Japan* (London, 1897). *Reference*: JBEWW.

ECKARD, JAMES READ (1805–1887). Missionary, born November 22, 1805, in Philadelphia. Eckard graduated from the University of Pennsylvania and Princeton Theological Seminary, and was ordained in 1833. He studied and practiced law from 1826 to 1830. He was a missionary under the American Board of Commissioners for Foreign Missions (ABCFM) in Ceylon from 1833 until 1843. He wrote *A Personal Narrative of Residence as a Missionary in Ceylon and Southern Hindoostan* (Philadelphia, 1844). He was principal of an academy in Savannah, Georgia; a pastor in Washington, D.C.; and a professor of rhetoric at Lafayette College from 1858 until 1871. Died March 12, 1887, in Abington, Pennsylvania. *References*: *ACAB*; *LC*; *NCAB* 11:245; *WWWA*.

ECKEL, WILLIAM A. (1892–1976). Missionary, born June 10, 1892, in Charleroi, Pennsylvania. Eckel graduated from Olivet College and was ordained in 1912. He was a missionary under the Church of the Nazarene to the Japanese in Los Angeles from 1914 to 1916, and in Japan from 1916 to 1976. He served in Kyoto from 1916 to 1918, in Yokohama in 1918–1919, and again in Kyoto until 1936. He also taught English and Japanese history in a military academy in Kyoto from 1929 to 1934. He established a mission in Tokyo in 1936 and served until 1940, when he returned to the United States and became district superintendent of the Rocky Mountain District of the Church of the Nazarene in Billings, Montana, from 1941 to 1945. He returned to Japan in 1947 and was district superintendent of the Church in Japan from 1948 until his retirement in 1976. Died December 26, 1976, in Camarillo, California. *Reference*: Juliaette Tyner and Catherine Eckel, *God's Samurai: The Life and Work of Dr. William A. Eckel* (Kansas City, Mo., 1979).

EDDY, (GEORGE) SHERWOOD (1871–1963). Missionary and publicist, born January 19, 1871, in Leavenworth, Kansas. Eddy graduated from Yale University and attended Union and Princeton theological seminaries. He was the national secretary of the Young Men's Christian Association (YMCA) among students in India from 1896 to 1911, and secretary for Asia for the YMCA International Committee from 1910 until 1931. He was the YMCA secretary for the British Army and later for the U.S. Army during World War I. After the war, in 1936, joined the Socialist Party and started a cooperative farm in Mississippi. He wrote *India Awakening* (New York, 1911); *The New Era in Asia* (New York, 1913); *The Students of Asia* (New York, 1915), *The World's Danger Zone: Manchuria* (New York 1932); *I Have Seen God Work in China: Personal Impressions from Three Decades with the Chinese (New York, 1944); and Eighty Adventurous Years; An Autobiography* (New York, 1955). Died March 3, 1963, in Jacksonville, Illinois. *References*: Sherwood Eddy Papers, Divinity School Library, Yale University, New Haven, Conn.; *Christian Century* 80 (April 1, 1963): 421; Deane W. Ferm, "Sherwood Eddy: Evangelist and YMCA Secretary;" Ph.D. diss., Yale University, 1954, *NYT*, March 5, 1963; and *Twentieth Century Authors*, ed. Stanley J. Kunitz and Howard Haycraft (New York, 1942).

EDMUNDS, CHARLES K(EYSER) (1876–1949). Educator, born September 21, 1876, in Baltimore. Edmunds graduated from Johns Hopkins University. He served as a magnetic observer with the U.S. Coast and Geodetic Survey in 1899–1900, and was a fellow in physics at Johns Hopkins University in 1901–1902. He was a professor of physics and electrical engineering at Canton Christian College (Later Lingnan University) from 1903 to 1907, vice president in 1907, and president from 1908 until 1924. He was also a magnetic observer in China for the Carnegie Institution of Washington from 1906 to 1917. He returned to the United States in 1924, and was provost of Johns Hopkins University from 1924 to 1927, and president of Pomona College from 1928 until 1941. Died January 8, 1949, in Claremont, California. *References*: Charles K. Edmunds Papers, Claremont Colleges Library, Claremont, Calif.; *NCAB* 37:533; *NYT*, January 10, 1949; and *WWWA*.

EDWARDS, HARRY T(AYLOR) (1877–1949). Agriculturist, born October 28, 1877, in Chesterfield, Massachusetts. Edwards graduated from Massachusetts Agricultural College (later the University of Massachusetts). He was a clerk with Houghton, Mifflin and Company, Boston publishers, and with the Boston Book Company from 1896 until 1901. He went to the Philippines in 1901, was an instructor in English and history, and secretary of the Philippine Nautical School in Manila in 1901–1902; fiber expert for the Philippine Bureau of Agriculture from 1902 to 1907, assistant to the director of the bureau from 1907 to 1914; assistant director in 1914; and director of the Bureau of Agriculture from 1914 to 1916. He was also associate editor of *The Philippine Agricultural Review* from 1908 to 1916, and editor of *The Philippine Farmer* from 1914 to 1916. He was a fiber specialist in the U.S. Department of Agriculture from 1917 until 1925, a technologist from 1925 to 1936, and a senior technologist from 1936 until his retirement in 1945. In 1925, he supervised the collection, packing, and shipment of growing abacá plants from the Philippines to Panama, and pioneered in introducing manila hemp plantations in tropical America. He wrote *The Introduction of Abacá (Manila Hemp) into the Western Hemisphere* (Washington, D.C., 1945). Died May 6, 1949, in Washington, D.C. *References*: *AMWS*; *NCAB* 39:258; and *NYT*, May 10, 1949.

EDWINS, AUGUST W(ILLIAM) (1871–1942). Missionary, born August 12, 1871, near Swede Valley, Iowa. Edwins graduated from Augustana College and Augustana Seminary, and was ordained in 1902. He held a pastorate in Stillwater, Minnesota, from 1902 to 1905. He was the first missionary under the Board of Foreign Missions of the Augustana Lutheran Church in China from 1905 until his death. He served at Hsunchang and Kikungshan, Honan Province, and was a professor at the Union Theological Seminary in Shekow, near Hankow, from 1922 to 1942. Died July 2, 1942, at sea, on his way to the United States. *References*: Conrad Bergendoff, *The Augustana Ministerium* (Rock Island, Ill.,

1980); and S. Hjalmar Swenson, *Three Missionary Pioneers and Some Who Have Followed Them* (Rock Island, Ill., 1945), pp. 51–86.

EGAN, MARTIN (1872–1938. Journalist and publicist, born June 18, 1872, in Martinez, California. Egan studied law and was admitted to the bar in 1898, but did not practice. He was a reporter for the *San Francisco Chronicle* and a war correspondent in the Philippines during the Spanish-American War. He joined the Associated Press and covered the Boxer Rebellion, the China Relief Expedition, the Philippine-American War, and the Russo-Japanese War. He was in charge of the Associated Press bureau in Tokyo from 1905 to 1907, was Associated Press representative in Manila in 1908, and also was the publisher and editor of the *Manila Times* form 1908 to 1913. He was associated with J. P. Morgan and Company in New York after 1913, serving as a liaison officer between the firm, the press, and the public, and accompanied Thomas W. Lamont to Japan and China in 1920 when the China Consortium was arranged. Died December 7, 1938, in New York City. *References*: *EP* 4:405; *NYT*, December 8, 1938; and *WWWA*.

EGBERT, NELLY YOUNG (1843–1913). Librarian, born in Washington, D.C. Egbert came to the Philippines in 1899 with her husband, an army officer, who was killed that year. She became president of the Manila Aid Society, which provided services to disabled soldiers. She was the first librarian of the American Circulating Library (later the Philippine Library and Museum) in Manila from 1900 to 1909, and its superintendent and librarian until her retirement in 1911. She returned to the United States in 1911. Died June 2, 1913. *Reference*: *DPB* 2.

EGGAN, FRED(ERICK) R(USSELL) (1906–   ). Anthropologist, born September 12, 1906, in Seattle, and grew up in Chicago. Eggan graduated from the University of Chicago. He carried out fieldwork on culture change in the northern Philippines in 1934–1935. He was an instructor in anthropology at the University of Chicago from 1935 to 1940, assistant professor there from 1940 to 1942, associate professor from 1942 to 1948, and professor from 1948 to his retirement in 1974. He was a consultant to the U.S. Board of Economic Warfare in 1942, and chief of research for the Philippine government-in-exile in 1943. He organized and directed the Civil Affairs Training School for the Far East in Chicago from 1943 to 1945. He founded and directed the Philippine Studies program at the University of Chicago after 1953. He resumed fieldwork in the Mountain Province in the Philippines from 1948 to 1950. *References*: *AMWS*; *International Encyclopedia of the Social Sciences* (New York, 1979) 189:163–66; *WWA*; and Mario D. Zamora, "Fred Eggan: His Career and Contributions to Philippine Anthropology," *Journal of Northern Luzon* 12 (July 1981–January 1982): 61–72.

EICHELBERGER, ROBERT LAWRENCE (1886–1961). Army officer, born March 9, 1886, in Urbana, Ohio. Eichelberger attended Ohio State University, graduated from the U.S. Military Academy in 1909, and was commissioned a second lieutenant in the infantry. He was assistant chief of staff and subsequently chief intelligence officer for General William S. Graves,* commander of the American Expeditionary Force in Siberia, from 1918 to 1920; instructor at the General Staff School at Fort Leavenworth, Kansas, from 1926 to 1929; adjutant general of the U.S. Military Academy at West Point from 1931 to 1934; secretary to the General Staff from 1935 to 1937; and superintendent of the U.S. Military Academy in 1940–1941. He was a senior field commander in the southwestern Pacific during World War II, and commanded the forces in Buna in 1942–1943 and the Eighth Army in the Philippine campaign in 1944–1945. He was commander of the army of occupation and second-ranking officer in the occupation forces in Japan from 1945 to 1948. He retired with the rank of general in 1948. He wrote *Our Jungle Road to Tokyo* (New York, 1950). Died September 26, 1961; in Asheville, North Carolina. *References*: Robert Lawrence Eichelberger Papers and Diaries, Duke University Library, Durham, N.C.; *DAB S7*; *DAMIB*; *KEJ*; *NACB* F:386; *NYT*, September 27, 1961; John F. Shortal, *Forged by Fire: General Robert L. Eichelberger and the Pacific War* (Columbia, S.C., 1987); and *WWWA*.

EKVALL, ROBERT BRAINERD (1898–   ). Missionary, born February 18, 1898, in Minhsien, Kansu, China, to American missionary parents. Ekvall graduated from Wheaton College (Ill.) and studied at the Missionary Training Institute and the University of Chicago. He was a missionary under the Christian and Missionary Alliance as teacher and school administrator in China and Tibet from 1923 to 1941. He was interned by the Japanese in Indochina from 1941 to 1943. He served in the U.S. Army in Burma and China from 1944 to 1951, and was a research associate in the department of Anthropology of the University of Chicago from 1951 to 1953. Recalled to the army in 1953, he served as an interpreter at the truce negotiations in Korea, with the Military Armistice Commission, and at the conference in Geneva. He was a research fellow and chairman of the Inner Asia Research project at the University of Washington (Seattle) from 1958 to 1960, research instructor and fellow at their Far East Department from 1960 to 1964, curator of Asian ethnology at the Thomas Burke Memorial Museum from 1965 to 1969, and research associate from 1969 to 1973. He wrote *Gateway to Tibet* (Harrisburg, Pa., 1938); *Cultural Relations on the Kansu-Tibetan Border* (Chicago, 1939); *Tibetan Voices* (New York, 1946); *Tibetan Sky Lines* (New York, 1952); *Tents against the Sky a Novel of Tibet* (New York, 1954); *Religious Observances in Tibet: Patterns and Function* (Chicago, 1964); *Fields on the Hoof: Nexus of Tibetan Pastoralism* (New York, 1968); and *The Lama Knows: A Tibetan Legend Is Born* (New Delhi, 1979); and was coauthor of *A Tibetan Principality: The Political System of Saskya* (Ithaca, N.Y., 1969). *References*: *AMWS*; and *CA*.

ELIZA. Merchantman of New York, Captain William Robert Stewart, chartered by the Dutch East India Company and sailed under Dutch colors to Nagasaki, Japan, in 1797, the first known voyage of an American vessel to Japan. *Reference*: Madora Kanai, "Salem and Nagasaki: Their Encounter, 1797–1807," *Contemporary Japan* 29 (1968): 82–89.

ELLIOTT, CHARLES B(URKE) (1861–1935). Lawyer and colonial administrator, born January 6, 1861, in Morgan County, Ohio. Elliott attended Marietta College, graduated from the State University of Iowa Law School and the University of Minnesota, and was admitted to the bar in 1882. He practiced law in Aberdeen, South Dakota, and then in Minneapolis; was professor of corporate and international law at the University of Minnesota from 1890 to 1899; judge of the municipal court of Minneapolis from 1890 to 1893; judge of the fourth judicial district of Minnesota from 1893 to 1904; and associate judge of the Minnesota Supreme Court from 1904 to 1909. He was an associate justice of the Philippine Supreme Court in 1909–1910, a member of the Philippine Commission from 1910 to 1912, and the secretary of commerce and police. He was fired in 1912 after intriguing against Governor-General W. Cameron Forbes.* He wrote *The Philippines to the End of the Military Regime* (Indianapolis, 1916), and *Philippines to the End of Commission Government: A Study in Tropical Democracy* (Indianapolis, 1917). He again practiced law in Minneapolis from 1913 until his death. Died September 18, 1935, in Minneapolis. *References*: *DAB*: *NCAB* 15:103; *Sevilla*; *WWWA*; and *WWP*.

ELMER, A(DOLPH) D(ANIEL) E(DWARD) (1870–1942). Botanist and plant collector, born June 14, 1870, in Vandyne, Wisconsin. Elmer graduated from Washington State College and Stanford University. He came to the Philippines in 1903, and was a collector of plants for the Bureau of Government Laboratories (later the Bureau of Science) from 1903 until 1905. After 1905, he was a private collector and student of Philippine plants. He made extensive travels in the Philippines and assembled the largest single collection of Philippine plants made by any one individual. He edited and published *Leaflets of Philippine Botany* (Manila, 1906–1939). Died April 17, 1942, in Manila. *References*: *AMWS*; and Edwin B. Copeland, "A. D. E. Elmer: Leaflets of Philippine Botany," *Philippine Journal of Science* 78 (1949): 1–4.

EMBREE, JOHN FEE (1908–1950). Anthropologist, born August 26, 1908, in New Haven, Connecticut. Embree graduated from the universities of Hawaii, Toronto, and Chicago. He conducted fieldwork in the village of Sue, Kuma District, Kumamoto Prefecture, from 1935 to 1936, and wrote *Suye Mura: A Japanese Village* (Chicago, 1939). He was assistant professor of anthropology at the University of Hawaii from 1937 until 1941; studied the Japanese of the Kona Valley, Hawaii; and wrote *Acculturation among the Japanese of Kona, Hawaii* (Menasha, Wis., 1941). He aided in the preparation of pocket guides for the Office of Strategic Services (OSS), and was principal community analyst for the War Relocation Authority, associate professor of anthropology, and head of the Japanese area studies of the Civil Affairs Training School for the Far East for the War Department in Chicago from 1943 to 1945. He was a cultural attaché in Bangkok in 1947 and in Saigon in 1948. He was associate professor of sociology at Yale University after 1948, and director of Southeast Asia studies there in 1950. He wrote *The Japanese* (Washington, D.C., 1943); *Japanese Peasant Songs* (Philadelphia, 1943); and *The Japanese Nation: A Social Survey* (New York, 1945); and was coauthor of *Bibliography of Peoples and Cultures of Mainland Southeast Asia* (New Haven, Conn., 1950), and *Ethnic Groups of Northern Southeast Asia* (New Haven, Conn., 1950). Killed by an automobile, December 22, 1950, in Hamden, Connecticut. *References*: *AA* 53 (1951): 376–32; *American Sociological Review* 9 (1950): 116–17; *FEQ* 11 (1952): 219–25; *Human Organization* 9 (1950): 33–34; *KEJ*; and *NYT*, December 23, 1950.

EMMERSON, JOHN K(ENNETH) (1908–1984). Diplomat, born March 17, 1908, in Canon City, Colorado. Emmerson graduated from Colorado College and New York University, and studied at the Sorbonne (Paris) and Georgetown University. He entered the foreign service in 1936, was a language student in Tokyo from 1936 to 1938, vice consul in Taiwan from 1938 to 1940, and third secretary in Tokyo from 1940 to 1942. He was political advisor to the U.S. military in China from 1943 to 1945, assistant chairman of the Division of Japanese Affairs at the State Department in 1946–1947, first secretary in Moscow in 1947–1948, planning advisor to the Bureau of Far Eastern Affairs from 1950 to 1952, counselor and deputy chief of mission in Pakistan from 1952 to 1955 and in Lebanon from 1955 to 1957, political counselor in France in 1957, consul general in Lagos, Nigeria, from 1958 to 1960, and in Salisbury, Federation of Rhodesia and Nyasaland, from 1960 to 1962, and consul general (with a rank of minister) in Tokyo from 1962 to 1967. He was a diplomat in residence at Stanford University in 1967, and a senior research fellow at the Hoover Institution on War, Revolution and Peace after 1968. He wrote *Arms, Yen and Power: The Japanese Dilemma* (New York, 1971), and *The Japanese Thread: A Life in the U.S. Foreign Service* (New York, 1978), and was coauthor of *Will Japan Rearm? A Study in Attitudes* (Washington, D.C., 1973). Died March 24, 1984, in Stanford, California. *References*: *CA*; *NYT*, March 27, 1984; and *WWA*.

EMPRESS OF CHINA. The first American ship to enter Chinese waters. It was fitted out by merchants of Philadelphia and New York. Under the command of Captain John Green, it came to China in 1784, loaded with ginseng and other commodities from the United States. It returned to the United States in 1785, bringing back tea. *References*: Philip C. F. Smith, *The Empress of China* (Philadelphia, 1984); Philip C. F. Smith, *"The Empress of China's* Voyage, 1784–1785,"* AN* 46 (1986): 25–33; Clarence L. Van Steeg, "Financing and Outfitting the First United States Ship to China," *PHR* 22 (1953): 1–12; and Samuel W.

Woodhouse, Jr., "The Voyage of the *Empress of China*," *Pennsylvania Magazine of History and Biography* 63 (1939): 24–30.

ENDICOTT, CHARLES MOSES (1793–1863). Sea captain, born December 6, 1793, in Danvers, Massachusetts. Endicott was employed in a mercantile firm in Boston until 1812. He was supercargo in 1812 in a voyage to East Asia, and traded along the Sumatra coast, being engaged chiefly in the pepper trade for the next fifteen years. He made a careful and reliable survey of the coast, prepared a chart of the coast, and wrote *Sailing Directions for the Pepper Ports on the West Coast of Sumatra, from Pulo Riah to Sinkel* (Salem, Mass., 1833). He was master of *Friendship* in 1830–1831, which was attacked by Malays at Quallah Battoo.* Many of his sailors were massacred and his ship was looted. He succeeded in escaping and later recaptured his ship. He left the sea in 1835, settled in Salem, and was cashier of the Salem Bank. His own story appeared in volume 1 (1859) of *Essex Institute Historical Collections*. Died December 14, 1863, in Salem, Massachusetts. *Reference*: DAB.

ENGBRING, FRANCIS XAVIER (1857–1895). Clergyman, born June 20, 1857, in Cincinnati, Ohio, and grew up in Effingham, Illinois. Engbring entered the Franciscan novitiate (Teutopolis, Ill.) in 1874, attended the Franciscan friaries in Quincy, Illinois, and St. Louis, and was ordained in 1880. He was professor of philosophy in the friary in Quincy, Illinois, from 1880 to 1882, and professor of theology in the friary in St. Louis from 1882 to 1888. He went to China in 1888, the first native-born American Catholic priest in China. He was rector of a seminary in Tsaitung, Hunan, in 1889–1890, and in Wuchang, Hupeh, in 1891–1892; dean of Church in Northeastern Hupeh in 1893–1894, and procurator apostolic in Hankow, Hupeh, in 1895. Died July 31, 1895, in Hankow. *Reference*: Marion A. Habig, *Pioneering in China: The Story of the Rev. Francis Xavier Engbring. O.F.M., First Native American Priest in China, 1857–1895, with Sketches of His Missionary Comrades* (Chicago, 1930).

ENSMINGER, DOUGLAS (1910–   ). Agriculturist, born in Stover, Missouri. Ensminger graduated from the University of Missouri and Cornell University. He served in the U.S. Department of Agriculture in 1939 until 1951, where he was in charge of community research and extension evaluation. He went to India in 1951 as the Ford Foundation's representative, and headed the foundation's India Program, its first program outside the United States, until 1970. The program covered all phases of India's national development. He was a professor of rural sociology at the University of Missouri after 1970. He was coauthor of *Conquest of World Hunger and Poverty* (Ames, Iowa, 1980). *Reference*: *Agronomy Journal* 73 (1981): 197–98.

ERSKINE, W(ILLIAM) H(UGH) (1879–1954). Missionary, born in Pittsburgh. Erskine graduated from Bethany College and studied at the University of Chicago. He was assistant professor of mathematics at Bethany College from 1902 to 1904, and then held a pastorate in Pittsburgh. He was a missionary under the United Christian Missionary Society in Japan from 1904 to 1933, serving at the Akita district and then in Osaka. He wrote *Japanese Customs, Their Origins and Value* (Tokyo, 1925), and *Japanese Festival and Calendar Lore* (Tokyo, 1933). He returned to the United States in 1933; held a pastorate in Uhrichville, Ohio, from 1933 to 1941; and served as a translator with the Federal Bureau of Investigation (FBI) during World War II, and later with the National Institute of Health. Died February 17, 1954. *Reference: They Went to Japan: Biographies of Missionaries of the Disciples of Christ* (Indianapolis, 1948).

EVANGELICAL ALLIANCE MISSION, THE (TEAM). Founded in 1890 as the Scandinavian Alliance Mission of North America. The name was changed in 1949. Missionary work began in China and Japan in 1891, in India in 1892, in Mongolia in 1895, in Pakistan in 1946, on the Tibetan frontier in 1947, in Taiwan in 1951, and in Korea in 1953. TEAM also worked in Ceylon. *References*: Thomas J. Bach, *Pioneer Missionaries for Christ and His Church* (Wheaton, Ill., 1955); *EMCM*; Dorothy R. Pape, *A Branch of God's Planting: The Story of TEAM's Seventy Years in Japan* (Chicago, 1962); and J. W. Swanson, comp. and ed., *Three Score Years . . . and Then: Sixty Years of Worldwide Missionary Advance* (Chicago, 1951?)

EVANGELICAL COVENANT CHURCH OF AMERICA: BOARD OF MISSIONS. Founded in 1885 as the Evangelical Mission Covenant Church of America. The name was later changed to the Department of World Missions. It began missionary work in China in 1890 (terminated in 1951), in Japan in 1949, in Taiwan in 1952, in Indonesia in 1958, and in Korea in 1963. *References*: Evangelical Covenant Church of America Archives, Covenant Archives and Historical Library, North Park College and Theological Seminary, Chicago; *EMCM*; and P. Matson., E. B. Larsson, and W. D. Thornblood, eds., *Half a Century of Covenant Foreign Missions*, (Chicago, 1940).

EVANGELICAL FREE CHURCH OF AMERICA: BOARD OF OVERSEAS MISSION. Founded in 1888. The name was later changed to the Department of Overseas Mission. It began missionary work in China in 1888, in Hong Kong and Japan in 1949, in the Philippines in 1951, and in Malaysia in 1957. *References*: Evangelical Free Church of America Archives, Trinity Divinity School Library, Deerfield, Ill.; and *EMCM*.

EVANGELICAL LUTHERAN CHURCH. Formed in 1917 and known until 1946 as the Norwegian Lutheran Church of America. In 1960 it merged with the American Lutheran Church and the United Evangelical Lutheran Church to become the American Lutheran Church, Division of World Missions. It began missionary work in China in 1890, in Japan in 1949, and in Taiwan in 1952. *References*: Archives of the American Lutheran Church, Luther Northwestern Seminary Library, St. Paul, Minn.; George Drach, *The Telugu Mission of the General Council of the Evangelical Lutheran Church* (Philadelphia, 1914); and Roger K. Ose, "A History of the Evangelical Lutheran Church of America's Mission Policy in China, 1890–1940," Ph.D. diss., New York University, 1970.

EVANGELICAL SYNOD OF NORTH AMERICA: BOARD OF FOREIGN MISSIONS. In 1884, it took over the mission founded in India by the German Evangelical Missionary Society. It merged with the Board of Foreign Mission of the Reformed Church in the United States in 1934, which then merged with the Congregational Christian Churches in 1957 to form the United Church of Christ. *References*: Eden Archives and Library of the Historical Society of the Evangelical and Reformed Church, Eden Theological Seminary, Webster Groves, Mo.; David Dunn et al., *A History of the Evangelical Reformed Church* (Philadelphia, 1961); Edith M. Melick, *The Evangelical Synod in India* (St. Louis, 1930); and Theodore C. Seybold, *God's Guiding Hand: A History of the Central India Mission 1868–1967* (Harrisburg, Pa., 1967).

EVANS, RICHARD T(AYLOR) (1885–1940). Lawyer, born April 27, 1885, in Indianapolis. Evans graduated from Harvard University and Harvard Law School. He was professor of common, Roman, international, and admiralty law at the University of Peiyang in Tientsin, China, until 1920. He then established a law practice in Tientsin until 1938, and served as special justice of the United States Court for China from 1938 until his death. He was also engaged in banking and real estate operations in Tientsin, organized and was president of the China Securities Company, Incorporated, and was contributor to, and, for a time, editor of, the *North China Star*. Died December 23, 1940, in Tientsin. *References*: *NCAB* 30:461; and *NYT*, December 26, 1940.

EVANS-WENTZ, W(ALTER) Y(EELING) (1878–1965). Student of religion, born February 2, 1878, in Trenton, New Jersey, and grew up in La Mesa, California. Evans-Wentz graduated from Stanford and Oxford universities and the University of Rennes (France). He traveled in India in 1917 to study mysticism and religion, and spent five years traveling from Ceylon to the Himalayas. He lived three years with a Buddhist monk, from 1919 until 1922. He edited *The Tibetan Book of the Dead, or, The After-death Experiences on the Baroda Plane* (London, 1927); *Tibet's Great Yogei, Milarepa* (London, 1928); *Tibetan Yoga and Secret Doctrines; or, Seven Books of Wisdom of the Great Path* (London, 1935); and *The Tibetan Book of the Great Liberation; or, The Method* *of Realizing Nirvana through Knowing the Mind* (London, 1954). He visited the ashram of Sri Ramana Maharshi at Tiruvanamalai, South India. Died July 17, 1965, in San Diego. *References*: W. Y. Evans-Wentz Papers, Stanford University Libraries, Stanford, Calif.; Richard M. Dorson, "American Folklorists in Britain," *Journal of the Folklore Institute* 7 (1970): 187–219; Leslie Shepard, "Introduction," in W. Y. Evans-Wentz, *Fairy-Faith in Celtic Countries* (New Hyde Park, N.Y., 1966).

EWHA WOMANS UNIVERSITY. Korea's first university for women, founded in 1886 in Seoul, Korea, as Ewha ('Pear blossom'), the first girls' school in Korea, by Mary F. Scranton under the Methodist Episcopal Church, South. A high school department was added in 1904 (and became a separate institution in 1924). Ewha became a college in 1910 (Korea's first college for women), and a university in 1945. *References*: Marion L. Conrow, *Our Ewha: A Historical Sketch of Ewha Womans University, 1886–1956* (Seoul, 1956); and *EWM*.

EWING, ARTHUR HENRY (1864–1912). Missionary, brother of James C. R. Ewing,* born October 18, 1864, in Saltsburg, Pennsylvania. Ewing graduated from Washington and Jefferson College, Western Theological Seminary (Pa.), and Johns Hopkins University, and was ordained in 1890. He was a missionary under the Board of Foreign Missions of the Presbyterian Church in the U.S.A. from 1890 until his death. He was principal of a Christian boys' boarding school in Ludhiana, Punjab, India, from 1891 to 1898, and principal of the Allahabad Christian College from 1901 until his death. (It was later renamed after him.) He was also treasurer of the North India mission after 1902. Died September 13, 1912, in Allahabad, India. *Reference*: *WWWA*.

EWING, JAMES CARUTHERS RHEA (1854–1925). Missionary, brother of Arthur H. Ewing,* born June 23, 1854, in Rural Valley, Armstrong County, Pennsylvania. Ewing graduated from Washington and Jefferson College and Western Theological Seminary, and was ordained in 1879. He was a missionary under the Board of Foreign Missions of the Presbyterian Church in the U.S.A. in India after 1879. He served in the United Provinces, first at Mainpuri and then at Fatehgarh, and, after 1888, in the Ludhiana mission. He was principal of the Jumma High School, Allahabad, from 1882 to 1884; professor in the theological seminary for the North India Presbyterian mission from 1884 to 1888; president of Forman Christian College in Lahore from 1888 to 1918; and dean of the faculty of arts of the University of Punjab from 1890 to 1907. He was secretary of the India Council of the Presbyterian Church in the U.S.A. from 1918 to 1922. Died August 20, 1925, in Princeton, New Jersey. *References*: *DAB*; *NYT*, August 22, 1925; and *WWWA*.

EWING CHRISTIAN COLLEGE. Established by the North India Mission of the Presbyterian Church in the U.S.A. as the Allahabad Christian College in Allahabad, India, in 1902. It began as a school in 1849 and was later also a high school. It was renamed after Arthur H. Ewing.* It became a unit of Allahabad University in 1933.

F

FAGEN, DAVID (1875–1901?). Guerilla officer, born in Tampa, Florida. Fagen was employed by a phosphate processor. He served in the U.S. Army in 1898–1899, reenlisted in 1899, and came to the Philippines. He fought in the Philippine-American War in central Luzon. He defected to the Filipinos and served as an officer with the Filipino revolutionaries. Allegedly killed December 1, 1901. *References*: Rayford W. Logan and Michael P. Winston, eds., *Dictionary of American Negro Biography* (New York, 1982); and Michael C. Robinson and Frank N. Schubert, "David Fagen: An Afro-American Rebel in the Philippines, 1899–1901," *PHR* 44 (1975): 68–83.

FAIRBANK, JOHN K(ING) (1907–). Sinologist, born May 24, 1907, in Huron, South Dakota. Fairbank attended the University of Wisconsin, graduated from Harvard and Oxford universities, and studied at the College of Chinese Studies in Peking. He was a lecturer at Tsing Hua University in Peking in 1933–34, and studied in China from 1934 to 1936. He was a member of faculty of Harvard University after 1936 and professor of history there from 1946 to 1977. He was the director of the East Asian Research Center from 1955 to 1973. He served with the Office of Strategic Services (OSS) in 1941–1942; was special assistant to the U.S. ambassador in Chungking, China, in 1942–1943; acting deputy director in charge of Far Eastern operations in the Office of War Information in Washington, D.C., in 1944–1945; and director of the U.S. Information Service in China in 1945–1946. He wrote *The United States and China* (Cambridge, Mass., 1948); *Trade and Diplomacy on the China Coast: The Opening of the Treaty Ports 1842–1854* (Cambridge, Mass., 1953); *China: The People's Middle Kingdom and U.S.A.* (Cambridge, Mass., 1967); *China Perceived: Images and Policies in Chinese-American Relations* (New York, 1974); *Chinese-American Interactions: A Historical Summary* (New Brunswick, N.J., 1975); *The Great Chinese Revolution, 1800–1985)* (New York, 1986); and *China Watch* (Cambridge, Mass., 1987). He was coauthor of *A Documentary History of Chinese Communism* (Cambridge, Mass., 1952); *China's Response to the West:*

A Documentary Survey 1839–1923 (Cambridge, Mass., 1954–1959); and *East Asia: The Modern Transformation* (Boston, 1965). He was editor of *Chinese Thought and Institutions* (Chicago, 1957); *The Chinese World Order: Traditional China's Foreign Relations* (Cambridge, Mass., 1968); and *The Missionary Enterprise in China and America* (Cambridge, Mass., 1974); and coeditor of *America's Trade in Historical Perspective: The Chinese and American Performance* (Cambridge, Mass., 1986). He was general editor of *The Cambridge History of China* (New York, 1978–   ). He also wrote *Chinabound: A Fifty-year Memoir* (New York, 1982). *References: CA; CB* 1966; *DAS;* Percy M. Evans, *John Fairbank and the American Understanding of Modern China* (New York, 1988); Percy M. Evans, "The Long Way Home: John Fairbank and American China Policy, 1941–42," *International Journal* 37 (1982): 584–605; *PolProf: Johnson; Polprof: Truman;* and *WWA.*

FAIRBANK, SAMUEL BACON (1822–1898). Missionary, born December 14, 1822, in Stamford, Connecticut. Fairbank graduated from Illinois College and Andover Theological Seminary. He was a missionary under the American Board of Commissioners for Foreign Missions (ABCFM) in India from 1846 until 1869. He served at Ahmednagar from 1846 to 1850; then he was transferred to Bombay and took charge of the mission press. He served in Vadala, Bombay Presidency, from 1857 until 1869. He remained in India and devoted his time to translation and literary work. Died May 31, 1898. His son, **HENRY S. FAIRBANK** (1862–1926), missionary was born January 30, 1862, in Wadale, Bombay Presidency, India. Fairbank graduated from Amherst College, attended Andover Theological Seminary, graduated from Yale Divinity School, and was ordained in 1886. He was a missionary under the ABCFM in Wadale, India, from 1886 to 1898 and at Ahmednagar from 1899 to 1926. He was principal of the divinity college and of the Union Training School at Ahmednagar after 1919. He wrote *Birds of Mahableshwar* (Ahmednagar, 1921). Died September 19, 1926, in Ahmednagar, India. *References: Amherst; AndoverTS;* and *EM.*

FAIRCHILD, DAVID GRANDISON (1869–1954). Plant explorer, born April 7, 1869, in Lansing, Michigan. Fairchild graduated from Kansas State College of Agriculture. Between 1895 and 1903, he went on expeditions to the Dutch East Indies, India, Ceylon, the Straits Settlements, Siam, and other parts of the world in search of plants for introduction to the United States. He organized the Plant Introduction Section of the U.S. Department of Agriculture, serving as its first chief from 1906 to 1928. He directed the Allison V. Armour expeditions to the Dutch East Indies from 1925 to 1927 and in 1932–1933, and was later in charge of the scientific work of the Fairchild Garden expedition to the Philippines and the Dutch East Indies. He introduced a large number of plants from Asia into the United States. He established the Fairchild Tropical Garden near Miami in 1938. He wrote *Exploring for Plants: From Notes of the Allison Vincent*

Armour Expeditions for the United States Department of Agriculture, 1925, 1926 and 1927 (New York, 1930); *The World Was My Garden: Travels of a Plant Explorer* (New York, 1938); and *Garden Islands of the Great East* (New York, 1945). Died August 2, 1954, in Coconut Grove, Florida. *References*: *AMWS*; *CB* 1953; *DAB S5*; Marjory S. Douglas, *Adventures in a Green World: The Story of David Fairchild and Barbour Lathrop* (Coconut Grove, Fla., 1973); *NCAB* C:253; *NYT*, August 7, 1954; Beryl Williams and Samuel Epstein, *Plant Explorer: David Fairchild* (New York, 1961); and *WWWA*.

FAIRFIELD, WYNN C(OWAN) (1886–1961). Missionary, born October 27, 1886, in Tabor, Iowa. Fairfield graduated from Oberlin College and Oberlin Graduate School of Theology. He was a missionary under the American Board of Commissioners for Foreign Missions (ABCFM) in China from 1910; served in Taiku, Shansi, from 1910 to 1917; and was treasurer, dean, and vice president of Oberlin Shansi Memorial Academy from 1918 to 1928. He was the acting associate secretary for China and Japan of the ABCFM in 1929–1930, associate secretary from 1930 to 1934, secretary from 1934 to 1945, secretary for general administration of the Foreign Missions Conference of North America from 1945 to 1950, and executive director of the Church World Service of the National Council of Churches of Christ in the U.S.A. from 1950 to 1954. Died October 14, 1961, in Claremont, California. *References*: *NYT*, October 18, 1961; and *WWWA*.

FANSLER, DEAN SPRUILL (1885–1945). Educator and folklorist, born September 21, 1885, in Alton, Illinois. Fansler graduated from Northwestern and Columbia universities. He was an instructor of English at the Philippine Normal School from 1908 to 1910, assistant professor of English at the University of the Philippines from 1910 to 1912, and associate professor there from 1910 to 1912. He was a lecturer and then associate professor at Columbia University from 1914 to 1921. He returned to the Philippines in 1921, and was professor and department head of the University of the Philippines from 1921 until 1924. He then returned to the United States and was a professor at Brown University from 1927 to 1931. Back in the Philippines, he was a professor at Far Eastern University in 1937–1938 and at the University of the Philippines from 1938 to 1941. He was interned by the Japanese in Manila during World War II. He wrote *Filipino Popular Tales* (Lancaster, Pa., 1921). Died July 12, 1945, in San Francisco. *References*: Fred Eggan, "Foreword," in Dean Spruill Fansler, *Filipino Popular Tales* (Hatboro, Pa., 1965); E. Asenio Manuel, "The Contributions of Dean S. Fansler to Philippinesian Folk Literature," *Philippine Social Sciences and Humanities Review* 46 (January–June 1982): 99–113; and *WWP*.

FAR EAST BROADCASTING COMPANY, INC. Noncommercial, interdenominational Christian broadcasting organization, founded in 1945. It first went on the air in 1948 in Manila. *References*: *EMCM*; and Gleasons H. Ledyard,

Sky Waves: The Incredible Far East Broadcasting Company Story (Chicago, 1968).

FARMER, (MARTHA) ADA BEESON (1871–1911). Missionary, born December 30, 1871, in Etowah County, Alabama. Farmer attended the Arcadia (La.) Female College, graduated from Marengo Female Institute (Demopolis, Ala.), and studied at the Nyack (N.Y.) Missionary Training School. She taught at Paradise and Chico, Texas. She was a missionary under the Christian and Missionary Alliance in China from 1902 until her death, serving at Wucheo, P'ingloh, and Liuchow, Kwangsi Province. She established a girls' training school at Liuchow. Died March 14, 1911, at Liuchow, Kuangsi, China. *Reference*: Wilmoth A. Farmer, *Ada Beeson Farmer, a Missionary Heroine in Kuang Si, South China* (Atlanta, 1912).

FARMER, HARRY (1872–1932). Missionary, born April 18, 1872, in West Bend, Wisconsin. Farmer graduated from George Washington University and Garrett Bible Institute, and was ordained in 1905. He held a pastorate at Center Point, Iowa, from 1902 to 1904. He was a missionary under the Board of Foreign Missions of the Methodist Episcopal Church in the Philippines from 1904 until 1916. He served at Pangasinan from 1904 to 1907 and in Manila from 1907 to 1916, and was a founder of the Union Theological Seminary in Manila. He was associate secretary of the Board of Foreign Missions from 1916 to 1924, lecturer on missions in Roman Catholic countries at the Drew Theological Seminary after 1920, and general secretary of the American Mission to Lepers after 1924. He held a pastorate in Lake Worth, Florida, in 1931–1932. He wrote *The Philippine Mission of the Methodist Episcopal Church* (New York, 1910). Died September 27, 1932, in Lake Worth, Florida. *References*: "Private Journal of Harry Farmer: Beginnings of Methodism in the Agno Valley Area, the Philippines, 1904–1907," Ms., United Methodist Headquarters, Manila; *DrewTS*; and *WWWA*.

FARRAR, CYNTHIA (1795–1862). Missionary, born April 20, 1795, in Marlborough, New Hampshire. Farrar studied at Union Academy (Plainfield, N.H.), and was a teacher in New Hampshire and Boston. She was a missionary under the American Board of Commissioners for Foreign Missions (ABCFM) from 1827 until her death, the first single American woman missionary sent overseas. She served in the Marathi mission in Bombay and established schools there. She was transferred in 1939 to Ahmednagar, where she organized schools for girls and directed them. Died January 25, 1862, in Ahmednagar, India. *References*: Cynthia Farrar Letters, in Farrar Family Papers, Michigan Historical Collections, University of Michigan, Ann Arbor, Mich.; and *NAW*.

FAUST, ALLEN KLEIN (1869–1953). Educator, born August 20, 1869, in Bernville, Pennsylvania. Faust graduated from Keystone State Normal School, Franklin and Marshall College (Lancaster, Pa.), Lancaster Theological Seminary, and the University of Pennsylvania. He was a missionary under the Board of Foreign Missions of the Reformed Church in the United States in Japan from 1900 to 1930. He was a teacher of history and sociology at the North Japan College from 1900 to 1913, and president of Miyagi College in Sendai from 1913 to 1930. He founded the Anti-Tuberculosis Association of Japan in 1910, and was engaged in famine relief. He was a professor of social science and dean of men at Catawba College from 1930 to 1944. He wrote *Christianity as a Social Factor in Modern Japan* (Lancaster, Pa., 1909), and *The New Japanese Womanhood* (New York, 1926). Died September 13, 1953, in Allentown, Pennsylvania. *References*: *NYT*, September 14, 1953; and *WWWA*.

FAY, LYDIA MARY (ca. 1802–1878). Missionary, born in Essex County, Virginia. She was a missionary under the Domestic and Foreign Missionary Society of the Protestant Episcopal Church in the United States of America in China from 1851 until her death. She was the first single woman sent from the United States to China by a missionary society. She developed a school in Shanghai and was a teacher there. Died October 5, 1878, in Chefoo. *Reference*: Annie Gracey, *Eminent Missionary Women* (New York, 1898), pp. 66–70.

FEARN, ANNE WALTER (1865–1939). Physician, born May 21, 1865, in Hilly Springs, Mississippi. Fearn attended Charlotte (N.C.) Female Institute and Cooper Medical School (San Francisco), and graduated from Woman's Medical College of Pennsylvania (Philadelphia). She was employed by the Woman's Board of Missions of the Methodist Episcopal Church, South, in charge of a woman's hospital in Soochow, China, from 1893 until 1907. She started a pioneer coeducational medical school for Chinese students in 1895. She also began a private practice in Soochow in 1896, practiced medicine in Shanghai from 1908 to 1930, and operated the Fearn Sanatorium, her own hospital for private patients, from 1916 to 1926. She worked for the National Child Welfare Association of China after 1932. She returned to the United States in 1938 and wrote her autobiography, *My Days of Strength: An American Woman Doctor's Forty Years in China* (New York, 1939). Died April 28, 1939, in Berkeley, California. *References*: *NAW*; *NCAB* 31:381; and *NYT*, April 30, 1939.

FEE [MACFEE], WILLIAM T(HOMAS) (1854–1919). Consul, born May 6, 1854, in Niles, Ohio. Fee graduated from Lafayette College, studied law, and was admitted to the bar in 1879. He later graduated from Western Reserve University Medical School and studied at the University of Gottingen. He practiced law in Warren, Ohio, in 1879; and was city solicitor of Niles in 1879–1880 and mayor of Warren for two terms. He was a consul at Cienfuegos, Cuba, in 1898–1899 and a consul in Bombay from 1899 to 1906. He was chairman of the American-Indian Relief Commission in 1899–1900, and was instrumental in shipping mango grafts to the United States. He was a consul in Bremen, Germany, from 1906 until 1917. Died April 1, 1919, in Warren, Ohio. *Reference*: *WWWA*.

FENN, COURTENAY H(UGHES) (1866–1953). Missionary, born in Clyde, New York. Fenn graduated from Hamilton College and Auburn Theological Seminary. He was a missionary under the Board of Foreign Missions of the Presbyterian Church in the U.S.A. in China from 1893 until 1925. He was principal of the North China Union Theological College from 1905 to 1915, and headed the Union Bible Institute in Peiping from 1915 to 1925. He was China secretary of the Board of Foreign Missions from 1928 to 1936. He compiled *The Concordance of the Old and New Testaments in the Revised Union Mandarin Version* (Shanghai, 1923); *The Five Thousand Dictionary* (Shanghai, 1926); and *Fenn's Chinese-English Pocket-Dictionary* (Cambridge, Mass., 1942). Died September 17, 1953, in Princeton, New Jersey. *Reference*: *NYT*, September 18, 1953.

FENOLLOSA, ERNEST (FRANCISCO) (1853–1908). Student of Oriental Art, born February 18, 1853, in Salem, Massachusetts. Fenollosa graduated from Harvard University and attended Harvard Divinity School and the school of the Boston Museum of Fine Arts. He went to Japan in 1878, was a professor of political economy and philosophy at Tokyo University from 1878 to 1880, and a professor of philosophy and logic from 1880 to 1886. He studied Japanese art, literature, and culture, and became a practicing Buddhist. He was the imperial fine arts commissioner to the Japanese government in 1886–1887, and then professor of aesthetics, manager of the Tokyo Fine Arts Academy, and manager of the art department in the Imperial Museum in Tokyo from 1888 to 1890. He returned to the United States in 1890, and was curator of the department of Oriental art in the Boston Museum of Fine Arts from 1890 to 1897. He returned to Japan in 1897 and was a professor of English literature in the Imperial Normal School in Tokyo from 1897 to 1900. He returned to the United States in 1900 to write and lecture on Oriental art. He wrote *The Masters of Ukioye* (New York, 1896) and *Epochs of Chinese and Japanese Arts* (New York, 1911), and was coauthor of *'Noh' or, Accomplishment, a Study of the Classical Stage of Japan* (London, 1916). Died September 21, 1908, in London. His wife, **MARY MCNEILL FENOLLOSA** (1865?–1954), author, was born in Mobile, Alabama. She traveled in Europe and Japan, and resided in Japan for eight years. She wrote several novels about Japan under the nom de plume of Sidney McCall. Died January 11, 1954, in Montrose, Alabama. *References*: Ernest Fenollosa Papers, Houghton Library, Harvard University, Cambridge, Mass.; Mary McNeil Fenollosa Papers, Museum of the City of Mobile, Ala.; Van Wyck Brooks, *Fenollosa and His Circle; with Essays in Biography* (New York, 1962); Lawrence W. Chisolm, *Fenollosa: The Far East and American Culture* (New Haven, Conn,

1963); *DAB*; *KEJ*; *NYT*, January 13, 1954; Noboru Umetani, *The Role of Foreign Employees in the Meiji Era in Japan* (Tokyo, 1971), ch. 13; and *WWWA*..

FERGUSON, JOHN C(ALVIN) (1866–1945). Missionary educator, government official, adventurer, and student of Oriental art, born March 1, 1866, in Belleville, Ontario, Canada. Ferguson attended Albert College (Belleville), graduated from Boston University, and was ordained in 1886. He was a missionary under the Board of Foreign Missions of the Methodist Episcopal Church in China from 1887 until 1897. He founded Nanking University in 1887, and was its first president from 1887 until 1897. He left the mission field in 1897 to establish Nanyang College (later Chiaotung University) in Shanghai, and was its first president from 1897 until 1902. He was owner and publisher of the Chinese-language daily newspaper in Shanghai from 1899 to 1929, and of the *Shanghai Times* from 1907 to 1911. He carried out various small commissions for Chinese officials, thus enabling him to advertise himself as advisor to the viceroy of Nanking from 1898 to 1911 and to the viceroy of Wuchang from 1900 until 1910. He was secretary to the Chinese Ministry of Commerce in 1902–1903, chief secretary of the Imperial Chinese Railway Administration from 1903 to 1905, and foreign secretary to the Ministry of Posts and Communication from 1911 until 1915. He was chairman of the Central China Famine Relief Commission during the famine of 1910–1911. Between 1901 and 1919, he was sent by the Chinese government on several missions to the United States. He returned to the United States in 1914 but was back in China in 1915 at the request of the Chinese government, and served as a political advisor until World War II. He was a member of the Chinese delegation to the Washington Conference of 1921. He collected Chinese paintings, bronzes, porcelains, and other art objects, which he presented to Nanking University in 1935. He wrote *Outlines of Chinese Art* (Chicago, 1919); *Chinese Painting* (Chicago, 1927); *Chinese Mythology* (Boston, 1928); and *Survey of Chinese Art* (Shanghai, 1939). He was interned by the Japanese in Peiping from 1941 to 1943. Died August 3, 1945, in Clifton Springs, New York. *References*: *ACAB*; *DAB S3*; *EWM*; Feng Han-yi and John K. Shryock, "Chinese Mythology and Dr. Ferguson," *Journal of the American Oriental Society* 53 (1933): 58–65; *NCAB* 34:208; *NYT*, August 4, 1945; and *WWWA*.

FERGUSSON, ARTHUR WALSH ("ART") (1859–1908). Colonial administrator, born December 4, 1859, in Benicia, California, and spent his early childhood in Mexico. Fergusson graduated from St. Augustine College (Calif.) and Georgetown University Law School. He owned and edited *The Benicia* (Calif.) *New Era*, a weekly newspaper, from 1879 to 1882; practiced law in Washington, D.C., from 1886 to 1891; and was official interpreter to various international commissions and chief translator to the Bureau of American Republics from 1897 to 1900. He was Spanish secretary to the U.S. Philippine Commission in 1900, chief secretary in 1900–1901, and executive secretary for the Philippines from 1901 until his death. Died January 30, 1908, in Manila. *References*: *DPB* 2; *Gleeck/Manila*; *NYT*, January 31, 1908; and *WWWA*.

FIELDE, ADELE M(ARION) (1839–1916). Missionary, born March 30, 1839, in East Rodman, New York. Fielde graduated from Albany Normal School. She was a missionary under the American Baptist Missionary Union in Siam from 1865 to 1872, and in South China from 1872 to 1890. She prepared *A Pronouncing and Defining Dictionary of the Swatow Dialect, Arranged According to Syllables and Tones* (Shanghai, 1883). She was a lecturer at the League for Political Education in New York from 1894 to 1907, and traveled after 1907. She wrote *Pagoda Shadows: Studies from Life in China* (Boston, 1884); *Chinese Nights' Entertainment: Forty Stories Told by Almond-Eyed Folk Actors in the Romance of the Strayed Arrow* (New York, 1893); *A Corner of Cathay: Studies from Life among the Chinese* (Boston, 1894); and *Chinese Fairy Tales* (New York, 1912). Died February 3, 1916. *References*: Adele Marion Fielde Papers, Academy of Natural Sciences of Philadelphia Library; Frederick B. Hoyt, " 'When a Field Was Found Too Difficult for a Man, a Woman Should Be Sent': Adele M. Fielde in Asia, 1865–1890," *Historian* 44 (1982): 314–34; Helen N. Stevens, *Memorial Biography of Adele M. Fielde: Humanitarian* (New York, 1918); and *WWWA*.

FISCHER, ARTHUR F(REDERICK) (1888–1962). Forester, born February 6, 1888, in Chicago. Fischer graduated from Ohio Northern University and Yale School of Forestry. He was employed by the Tennessee Coal, Iron and Railroad Company in Ensley, Alabama, from 1906 to 1910. He was a forester with the Bureau of Forestry in the Philippines from 1911 to 1916, acting director of the bureau in 1916–1917, and director from 1916 until 1936. He was assistant professor of forest engineering at the University of the Philippines from 1912 to 1917, and professor of tropical forestry and dean of the School of Forestry from 1917 to 1936. He was an advisor on natural resources in the Commonwealth of the Philippines after 1937. He served in the U.S. Army during World War II, and was director of the San Diego Museum of Natural History from 1946 to 1956. Died October 31, 1962, in San Diego, California. *References*: *CCDP*; *DPB* 3; *Journal of Forestry* 61 (1963): 70; *WWP*; and *WWWA*.

FISCHER, EMIL S(IGMUND) (1865–1945). Banker and traveler, born in Vienna. Fischer was a banker in Vienna, Paris, Buenos Aires, and Rio de Janiero until 1892, when he settled in New York City. He came to China in 1894 and was a banker in Shanghai until 1898. He returned to the United States in 1899 and lived in New York City until 1906. He returned to China in 1906 and settled in Tientsin. He was also involved as an importer and exporter. He wrote *Guide to Peking and Its Environs* (Tientsin, 1909) and *Travels in China, 1894–1940*

(Tientsin, 1941). He was made a U.S. citizen by an act of Congress. He was held prisoner by the Japanese from 1941 until his death. Died February 21, 1945, in Tientsin. *Reference*: *NYT*, March 2, 1945.

FISHER, FREDERICK BOHN (1882–1938). Clergyman, born February 14, 1882, in Greencastle, Pennsylvania, and grew up in Muncie, Indiana. Fisher graduated from Asbury College and Boston University School of Theology, and was ordained in 1905. He was a missionary under the Board of Foreign Missions of the Methodist Episcopal Church in India in 1905–1906. He returned to the United States in 1906 and held pastorates in North Cohasset and Boston, Massachusetts. He then served as field secretary and associate secretary of the Board of Foreign Missions, secretary and associate general secretary of the Laymen's Missionary Movement, and secretary of the India Mass Movement Commission. He was elected bishop in 1920 and was resident bishop in Calcutta, India, from 1920 to 1930. He resigned his bishopric in 1930 and held pastorates in Ann Arbor and Detroit, Michigan, until his death. He was coauthor of *India's Silent Revolution* (New York, 1919) and *That Strange Little Brown Man, Gandhi* (New York, 1932), which was suppressed by the British authorities. Died April 15, 1938, in Detroit. *References*: Frederick Bohn Fisher Papers, Theological School Library, Boston University; *DAB S2*; *NCAB* 28:149; *NYT*, April 16, 1938; and *WWWA*.

FISHER, GALEN MERRIAM (1873–1955). Association official, born April 12, 1873, in Oakland, California. Fisher graduated from the University of California and Harvard University. He was student secretary of the Boston Young Men's Christian Association (YMCA) in 1896–1897, secretary of the Japan International Committee of the YMCA from 1897 to 1900, and senior secretary from 1900 to 1919. He was associate executive secretary of the Rockefeller Institute of Social and Religious Research in 1921–1922 and executive secretary for the institute from 1923 to 1934; he was general director of research in India, China, and Japan for the Laymen's Foreign Mission Inquiry in 1930–1931. He was a champion of the Japanese-Americans who were interned in concentration camps in the United States during World War II. He wrote *Creative Forces in Japan* (New York, 1923). Died January 2, 1955, in Berkeley, California. *References*: *NYT*, January 3, 1955; and *WWWA*.

FISHER, WELTHY (BLAKESLEE) HONSINGER (1879–1980). Missionary educator, wife of Frederick Bohn Fisher,* born September 18, 1879, in Rome, New York. Fisher graduated from Syracuse University. She was a missionary under the Board of Foreign Missions of the Methodist Episcopal Church at Nanchang, Kiangsi Province, China, from 1906 to 1911, and was headmistress of the Baldwin mission school. She returned to the United States in 1917 and worked with the Young Women's Christian Association (YWCA) in France from 1918 to 1920. She lived in India from 1924 until 1938, returned to India in 1951 as a consultant to the government-sponsored program for training teachers in

Allahabad, established Literacy House in Allahabad in 1952, and moved it to Lucknow in 1956. She wrote *Beyond the Moon Gate, Being a Diary of Ten Years in the Interior of the Middle Kingdom* (New York, 1924); *A String of Chinese Pearls: Ten Tales of Chinese Girls Ancient and Modern* (New York, 1924); *The Top of the World* (New York, 1926); *Freedom: A Story of Young India* (New York, 1930); *To Light a Candle* (New York, 1962); and a biography of her husband. Died December 16, 1980, in Southbury, Connecticut. *References: CB* 1969; Colleen A. Kelly, "The Educational Philosophy and Work of Welthy Honsinger Fisher in China and India: 1906–1980," Ph.D. diss., University of Connecticut, 1983; *NYT*, December 17, 1980; *The Ramon Magsaysay Awards 1963–1965* (Manila, 1980), pp. 211–28; and John Spencer, *Workers for Humanity* (London, 1962), pp. 51–61.

FITCH, GEORGE A(SHMORE) (1883–1979). Association official, born January 23, 1883, in Soochow, China. Fitch graduated from the University of Wooster and Union Theological Seminary, and attended Columbia University. He held a pastorate in Poughkeepsie, New York, in 1906–1907. He was the secretary of the International Committee of the Young Men's Christian Association (YMCA) in China from 1909 to 1946. He served in Shanghai from 1909 to 1936, in Nanking from 1936 to 1938, in Chungking from 1938 to 1944, in northwest China in 1944–1945, and in Lanchow in 1945. He was an advisor to the War Area Service Corps in Nanking in 1936–1937, director of the Nanking Safety Zone during its siege and occupation by Japanese in 1937–1938, executive advisor to the Chinese Industrial Cooperatives from 1941 to 1943, deputy director of United Nations Relief and Rehabilitation Administration (UNRRA) in Kaifeng, Honan, in 1946, and secretary of the National Council of YMCA in Korea from 1947 to 1949. He later served as publicist for Nationalist Chinese interests in the United States. He wrote *My 80 Years in China* (Taipei, Taiwan, 1967). Died January 21, 1979, in Pomona, California. *References: CA; NYT*, January 23, 1979; and *WWWA*.

FLEISHER, B(ENJAMIN) W(ILFRID) (1870–1946) and **FLEISHER, WILFRID** (1897–1976). Publishers and editors. Benjamin W. Fleisher was born January 5, 1870, in Philadelphia. He graduated from the University of Pennsylvania and worked for Fleisher Yarn Company, his family's firm. After the loss of a considerable part of his personal fortune in stock market speculation and a nervous breakdown, in 1907 he went on a round-the-world trip, and stopped at Yokohama, Japan. He went to work for *The Japan Advertiser* as a reporter and then business manager, and acquired the newspaper in 1908. He moved it to Tokyo in 1913 and built it into the most influential English-language daily newspaper in East Asia. He served as Far Eastern correspondent for the United Press Association of America, the *New York World*, the *New York Times* and the *Philadelphia Public Ledger*. He also published *Trans-Pacific*, a monthly (and later a weekly magazine) after 1919, and a yearbook of finance, industry, and commerce after 1927. He imported the first linotype machines used in Japan. In 1940 he was forced to sell the paper to the

Japanese and returned to the United States. Died April 29, 1946, in Rochester, Minnesota. His son, Wilfrid Fleisher, was born November 19, 1897, in Philadelphia. He attended Columbia University. He was a correspondent with the American Expeditionary Force in Siberia. He was managing editor of *The Japan Advertiser* from 1929 to 1940, and a newspaper correspondent in Japan for the *New York World*, *New York Times* and *New York Herald Tribune* from 1923 to 1925 and from 1931 to 1940. He was a newspaper correspondent in Washington, D.C., from 1926 to 1928 and from 1940 to 1942, and a radio commentator with ABC Radio from 1942 to 1946. He wrote *Volcanic Island* (Garden City, N.Y., 1941), *Our Enemy Japan* (Philadelphia, 1942), and *What to Do with Japan* (Garden City, N.Y., 1945). He was press secretary at the U.S. embassy in Stockholm, Sweden, after 1949, and later a reporter for *Newsweek* and the *Washington Post* in Sweden. Died July 13, 1976, in Stockholm, Sweden. *References*: *CA*; *DAB S4*; *NYT*, April 30, 1946; *Washington Post*, July 21, 1976; and *WWWA*.

FLEMING, BETHEL (HARRIS) (1901–   ) and **FLEMING, ROBERT L(ELAND)** (1905–   ). Bethel Fleming, medical missionary born December 13, 1901, in Elysburg, Pennsylvania. She graduated from Wilson College (Chambersburg, Pa.) and Woman's Medical College of Pennsylvania. Robert L. Fleming, ornithologist and missionary, born March 22, 1905, in Ludington, Michigan. He graduated from Albion College, Drew University, and the University of Chicago. She was a medical missionary at Pategarh, India, from 1932 to 1936, and at Mussoorie, India, from 1936 to 1954. He was a missionary in Mussoorie, India, teaching science and serving as superintendent of the high school. He also collected birds in India after 1938 and made several collecting trips to Nepal after 1949. He wrote *India: Past and Present* (Mysore, 1949); *Notes on Birds from Nepal* (Chicago, 1961); *Further Notes on Birds from Nepal* (Chicago, 1964); and *The General Ecology, Flora and Fauna of Midland Nepal* (Kathmandu, 1973). He was coauthor of *Birds from Nepal* (Chicago, 1957), and *Birds of Nepal: With Reference to Kashmir and Sikkim* (Kathmandu, 1976). In 1954 Bethel and Robert founded the United Christian Medical Mission in Kathmandu, Nepal, the first medical ministry and modern hospital in Nepal. She was the chief physician and he was the administrator of the hospital. *References*: *AMWS*; *EWM*; and Grace N. Fletcher, *The Fabulous Flemings of Kathmandu: The Story of Two Doctors in Nepal* (New York, 1964).

FLEMING, DANIEL JOHNSON (1877–1969). Missionary educator, born January 30, 1877, in Xenia, Ohio. Fleming graduated from Wooster College, Columbia University, and the University of Chicago. He was a missionary under the Board of Foreign Missions of the Presbyterian Church in the U.S.A. in India from 1898 to 1912. He taught mathematics and physics at Forman Christian College in Lahore from 1898 to 1901 and again from 1904 to 1914, and served as vice president from 1910 to 1912 and as acting president in 1912. He returned to the United States in 1912, was director of the department of foreign service at the Union Theological Seminary from 1915 to 1944 and professor of missions there from 1918 until his retirement in 1944. He wrote *Schools with a Message in India* (London, 1921), and *Building with India* (New York, 1922). Died April 19, 1969, in Fairmont, California. *References*: *NCAB* 55:500; *NYT*, April 21, 1969; *OAB*; and *WWWA*.

FLYING TIGERS. *See* AMERICAN VOLUNTEER GROUP (AVG)

FOOTE, ANDREW HULL (1806–1863). Naval officer, born September 12, 1806, in New Haven, Connecticut, and grew up in Cheshire, Connecticut. He was appointed acting midshipman in the U.S. Navy in 1822. He served in the Mediterranean and in a cruise around the world, and was commander of a ship in the African Squadron from 1849 to 1851. He served in the East Asia Squadron from 1856 to 1858, and was the senior officer present in Canton during the hostilities between England and China. He commanded a party of American seamen that stormed and demolished the four barrier forts below Canton (see Barrier Forts, Battle of*). He was later in charge of the Brooklyn Navy Yard, and served in the Union Navy during the Civil War. Died June 26, 1863, in New York City. *References*: Andrew Hull Foote Papers, Manuscript Division, Library of Congress; *ACAB*; *DAB*; *DAMIB*; David F. Long, "A Case for Intervention: Armstrong, Foote, and the Destruction of the Barrier Forts, Canton, China, 1856," in *New Aspects of Naval History*, ed. Craig L. Symonds and Merril Bartlett et al. (Annapolis, Md., 1981), pp. 220–37; Allan Keller, *Andrew Hull Foote, Gunboat Commodore (1806–1863)* (Hartford, Conn., 1864); John D. Milligan, "Andrew Foote: Zealous Reformer, Administrator, Warrior," in *Captains of the Old Steam Navy: Makers of the American Naval Tradition, 1840–1880*, ed. James C. Bradford (Annapolis, Md., 1986), pp. 115–41; *NCAB* 5:10; and *WWWA*.

FOOTE, ARTHUR B(URLING) (1877–1964). Mining engineer, born April 29, 1877, in New Almaden, Santa Clara County, California. Foote graduated from Massachusetts Institute of Technology. He was employed by the North Star Mines Company in Grass Valley, California, in 1900–1901. He was a surveyor and later an assistant superintendent for Oriental Consolidated Mining Company in Wonsan (later Genzan), Korea, from 1901 to 1904. He rejoined the North Star Mines Company in 1904 as an assistant superintendent, and became superintendent and general manager from 1913 until 1929. He practiced privately as consulting mining engineer in Grass Valley, California, from 1929 until his retirement in 1941. Died July 1, 1964, in Grass Valley. *Reference*: *NCAB* 51:204.

FOOTE, LUCIUS H(ARWOOD) (1826–1913). Diplomat, born April 10, 1826, in Winfield, New York. Foote attended Knox College and Western Reserve University. He moved to California in 1853, studied law, and was admitted to the bar in 1856. He was a municipal judge in Sacramento from 1856 to 1860, collector of the Port of Sacramento from 1861 to 1865, adjutant general of California from 1872 to 1876, and consul in Valparaiso, Chile, from 1878 to 1882. He was sent on a special consular mission to Aspinwall, Colombia, in 1883. He was the U.S. minister to Korea from 1882 until 1885, the first minister from a Western power accredited to Korea. He was later secretary and treasurer of the California Academy of Science from 1891 until his death. Died June 4, 1913, in San Francisco. *References: DAB*; Soon C. Hong, "The Active Diplomatic Role Taken by American Minister Foote During the Post-Kapsin Coup Period: December 4, 1884–January 9, 1885," *Journal of Korean Studies* 1, no. 2 (1971): 85–95; Soon C. Hong, "The Kapsin Coup and Foote: The Role of an American Diplomat," *Koreana Quarterly* 15 (Fall-Winter 1973); 60–70; Mary V. T. Lawrence, *A Diplomat's Helpmate: How Rose F. Foote, Wife of the First U.S. Minister and Envoy Extraordinary to Korea, Served Her Country in the Far East* (San Francisco, 1918); *NCAB* 7:267; *NYT*, June 5, 1913; and *WWWA*.

FORBES, ROBERT B(ENNET) (1804–1889). Sea captain and merchant, born September 18, 1904, in Jamaica Plain, near Boston, Massachusetts. Forbes entered the employ of his uncles, merchants in Boston. He went to sea at thirteen and received command of a ship at twenty. He was employed by Russell and Company in China from 1830 to 1834 and again after 1837, and became head of the firm in 1839–1840. He was again head of Russell and Company in China from 1849 to 1851, and also served as U.S. and French vice-consul. He wrote *Remarks on China and the China Trade* (Boston, 1844), and *Personal Reminiscences* (Boston, 1876). Died November 23, 1889, in Boston. *References*: Margaret C. S. Christman, *Adventurous Pursuits: Americans and the China Trade 1784–1844* (Washington, D.C., 1984), pp. 111–23; James B. Connoly, *Canton Captain* (Garden City, N.Y., 1942); *DAB*; and *WWWA*.

FORBES, W(ILLIAM) CAMERON (1870–1959). Colonial administrator, born May 21, 1870, in Milton, Massachusetts. Forbes graduated from Harvard University. He was involved in investment banking after 1899. He was a member of the Philippine Commission and secretary of commerce and police in the Philippines from 1904 to 1908, vice-governor in 1908–1909, and governor-general of the Philippines from 1909 until 1913. He concentrated on economic growth and on developing and improving transportation in the Philippines, but opposed Philippine independence. He was again involved in business affairs, was a member of the Wood-Forbes Mission* to the Philippines in 1921. He wrote *The Philippine Islands* (Boston, 1928). He was an unsuccessful ambassador to Japan from 1930 until 1932. Died December 24, 1959, in Boston. *References* "Journal of W. Cameron Forbes," Manuscript Division, Library of Congress; W. Cameron Forbes Papers, Houghton Library, Harvard University; *DAB S6*; *EAH*; *EP* 4:362–63; *Gleeck/Governors*, ch. 6; Lewis E. Gleeck, Jr., "W. Cameron Forbes and the Abortive 'Valhalla' Project of 1956," *BAHC* 4 (July–September 1976): 68–103; Camillus Gott, "William Cameron Forbes and the Philippines, 1904–1946," Ph.D. diss., Indiana

University, 1974; *NYT*, December 26, 1959; Gary Ross, "W. Cameron Forbes: The Diplomacy of a Darwinist," in *Diplomats in Crisis: United States–Chinese–Japanese Relations, 1919–1941*, ed. Richard D. Burns and Edward M. Bennett (Santa Barbara, Calif., 1974), pp. 49–64; Robert Spector, "W. Cameron Forbes in the Philippines: A Study in Proconsular Power," *JSEAH* 7 (1966): 74–92; Pater W. Stanley, "William Cameron Forbes: Proconsul in the Philippines," *PHR* 35 (1966): 285–301; and *WWWA*.

FORD, FRANCIS XAVIER (1892–1952). Missionary, born January 11, 1892, in Brooklyn, New York. Ford attended Cathedral College (N.Y.) and Maryknoll Seminary, and was ordained in 1917. He went to China in 1918 as one of the first four Maryknoll missionaries to China. He served in Yeongkong, Southern China, and opened the first Maryknoll seminary in China in 1921. He was named prefect apostolic of a new mission in Northern Kwangtung at Kaying in 1925, and appointed titular bishop of Etenne and vicar apostolic of Kaying in 1935. He was chairman of the Chinese Catholic Welfare Conference for Southern China. He was arrested by the Communists in 1950, and was tried and tortured. Died February 21, 1952, in prison in Canton. *References*: Eva K. Betz, *To Far Places: The Story of Francis X. Ford* (New York, 1962); John F. Donovan, *The Pagoda and the Cross: The Life of Bishop Ford of Maryknoll* (New York, 1967); Raynold A. Lane, ed., *Stone in the King's Highway: Selections from the Writings of Bishop Francis Xavier Ford (1892–1952)* (New York, 1953); and *NYT*, September 4, 1952.

FORD MISSION (1913). Henry Jones Ford, close friend and former academic associate of President Woodrow Wilson, served in 1913 as the president's personal representative to report on conditions in the Philippines. *References*: Charles M. Farkas, "Relieving the White's Man Burden," *BAHC* 6 (January–March 1978): 71–85; Charles M. Farkas, "Wilsonian Progressives in the Philippines: Henry Jones Ford and Francis Burton Harrison," *Kabar Sebarang* no. 3 (1978): 11–18; and Henry J. Ford, "The Ford Report on the Situation in the Philippines," *Historical Bulletin of the Philippine Historical Association* 17 (1973): 353–431.

FOREIGN CHRISTIAN MISSIONARY SOCIETY. *See* UNITED CHRISTIAN MISSIONARY SOCIETY (DISCIPLES OF CHRIST).

FORMAN, CHARLES W(ILLIAM) (1821–1894). Missionary, born in Kentucky. Forman graduated from Princeton Theological Seminary. He was a missionary under Board of Foreign Missions of the Presbyterian Church in the U.S.A. in India from 1848 until his death. He served in the Punjab, and in 1849 went to Lahore and began a school there. In 1864 he opened a college section in connection with the school, but it was closed in 1866. It was reopened as a separate institution in 1886, and he served as its principal until 1888. (The college was later renamed Forman Christian College.) Died August 27, 1894, in Kassauli, India. *References*: *CDCWM*; *EM*; and *LC*.

FORMAN, HARRISON (1904–1978). Explorer and journalist, born June 15, 1904, in Milwaukee. Forman attended Chicago Academy of Fine Arts and Layton School of Art (Milwaukee), and graduated from the University of Wisconsin. He was instructor of navigation and meteorology in San Francisco in 1930, and went to China in the early 1930s to sell American aircrafts and train pilots. He was a cameraman for the *March of Time* newsreel service in China in the late 1930s, and served as technical advisor for the film *Lost Horizons* (1937). He was a war correspondent in China from 1937 to 1949, and made an expedition to Tibet in 1937–1938. He was later president of Harrison Forman World Photos in New York City. He wrote *Through Forbidden Tibet, an Adventure into the Unknown* (New York, 1935); *Horizon Hunter, the Adventures of a Modern Marco Polo* (New York, 1940); *Report from Red China* (New York, 1945); *Changing China* (New York, 1948); and *Blunder in Asia* (New York, 1950). Died February 1, 1978, in New York City. *References*: *CA*; *NYT*, February 2, 1978; and *WWWA*.

FORMAN CHRISTIAN COLLEGE. Founded in 1864 by Charles W. Forman* in Lahore, India, the oldest Christian college in India. It began as a school founded by the mission of the Presbyterian Church in the U.S.A. in Lahore in 1847. The college was closed down in 1869 but was reopened in 1886 and became the Lahore Christian College. It was renamed Forman Christian College in 1894 and became affiliated with Punjab University. In 1930, the mission of the Methodist Episcopal Church joined the support of the college. *References*: S. K. Datta, *History of Forman Christian College* (Lahore, 1939); and S. K. Datta, ed., *Selections from the Records of Forman Christian College, 1869–1936* (Lahore, 1939).

FOULK, GEORGE CLAYTON (1856–1893). Naval officer and diplomat, born October 30, 1856, in Marietta, Pennsylvania. Foulk graduated from the U.S. Naval Academy in 1876. He served in the Asiatic Squadron. In 1882, with Benjamin H. Buckingham* and Walter McLean, he crossed Siberia into Russia and prepared a report, *Observations upon the Korean Coast, Japanese Korean Ports, and Siberia* (Washington, D.C., 1883). He served in the naval library from 1877 to 1883. He was a naval attaché to the American legation in Korea from 1883 until 1885 and chargé d'affaires from 1885 until 1887. He was withdrawn despite the protests of the Korean king, to whom he had become a personal advisor. He resigned his commission in 1887 and went to Japan. He was employed by the American Trading Company from 1888 until 1890, and professor of mathematics at Doshisha University from 1890 until his death. Died August 6, 1893, in Kyoto. *References*: George C. Foulk Papers, Bancroft Library, University of California, Berkeley, Calif.; George C. Foulk Papers, Manuscript Division, Library of Congress; George C. Foulk Papers, Manuscript

Division, New York Public Library; Donald M. Bishop, "Policy and Personality in Early Korean-American Relations: The Case of George Clayton Foulk," in *The United States and Korea: American-Korean Relations, 1866–1976*, ed. Andrew C. Nahm (Kalamazoo, Mich., 1979), pp. 27–63; *DAB*; Tyler Dennett, "Early American Policy in Korea, 1883–87: The Services of Lieutenant George C. Foulk," *Political Science Quarterly* 38 (1923): 82–103; and Robert E. Reordan, "The Role of George Clayton Foulk in United States–Korean Relations, 1884–1887," Ph.D. diss., Fordham University, 1955.

FOX, ROBERT B(RADFORD) (1918–1985). Anthropologist and archaeologist, born May 11, 1918, in Galveston, Texas. Fox graduated from the universities of Southern California, Texas, and Chicago. He served in the U.S. Navy during World War II, and arrived in the Philippines in 1946. He was administrative director of the Philippine Institute for the Armed Forces in Manila in 1946–1947, anthropologist at the National Museum of the Philippines from 1947 to 1951, and chief anthropologist there after 1955. He was also a professional lecturer in the Department of Anthropology of the University of the Philippines after 1965, and a presidential advisor on anthropology. He carried out fieldwork among the Pinatubo Negritos in 1948–1949, and with the Tagbanuwa and the Batak in Palawan Island in 1952. He discovered and excavated the Tabon Caves in Palawan Islands from 1962 to 1965. Died May 25, 1985, in Baguio City, Philippines. *References*: Harold C. Conklin, "A Bibliography of the Works of Robert B. Fox," *Philipinas*, no. 7 (Fall 1986); 75–85; *JAS* 45 (1986): 667; Jesus T. Perlta, "Robert Bradford Fox: Anthropologist," *Archipelago* 6 (April 1979): 8–12; and Mario D. Zamora, "Robert Bradford Fox: A Pioneer in Philippine Archaeology (1918–1985)," *Kabar Seberang* no. 16 (1985): 181–82.

FOXWORTHY, FRED WILLIAM (1877–1950). Forester, born July 7, 1877, in Goodland, Indiana. Foxworthy graduated from DePauw and Cornell universities. He came to the Philippines in 1904 as a teacher. He was a botanist in the Bureau of Science in Manila after 1906, and gradually became a forester. He was a wood technologist in the bureau, associate professor of dendrology at the University of the Philippines in Manila, and cofounder of the School of Forestry in the university's College of Agriculture. He was a forest research officer under the government of the Federated Malay States from 1918 until 1932, the only non-British subject in the British Civil Service. He built a museum of forest products and a forest herbarium. He retired in 1932 and returned to the United States. Died February 4, 1950, in Berkeley, California. *References*: *AMWS*; and *Nature* 165 (May 6, 1950): 710–11.

FRAME, ALICE SEYMOUR BROWNE (1878–1941). Missionary educator, born October 29, 1878, in Harpoot, Turkey, to American missionary parents. Frame graduated from Mount Holyoke College and Hartford Theological Seminary. She was the secretary of young people's work of the Woman's Board of

Missions of the Congregational Church from 1903 to 1905. She was a missionary under the American Board of Commissioners for Foreign Missions (ABCFM) in China from 1905 until 1940. She served in Tungchow from 1905 to 1919, and was principal of a girls' school in Tungchow from 1906 to 1910, in charge of the Women's College in Peking in 1918–1919, and dean of the Women's College (which became affiliated with Yenching University) from 1922 to 1931. She was secretary of religious education of the North China Congregational Church in Peking from 1931 until 1933, when she returned to the United States, and was back in Tungchow from 1934 to 1940. Died August 16, 1941, in Newton, Massachusetts. *References*: Alice Seymour Browne Frame Papers, Archives of the United Church Board of World Ministries, Boston; *DAB*; *NAW*; *NYT*, August 18, 1941; and *WWWA*.

FRANCK, HARRY A(LVERSON) (1881–1962). Traveler and author, born June 29, 1881, in Munger, Michigan. Franck graduated from the University of Michigan and studied at Harvard and Columbia universities. He taught modern languages at Bellefonte Academy (Pa.) in 1905–1906 and at Browning School (New York City) from 1906 to 1908, and was head of the modern language department at the Technical High School (Springfield, Mass.) from 1908 to 1911. He traveled around the world from 1911 to 1942, writing about his experiences as a vagabond and his problems living off the land. He wrote *Wandering in Northern China* (New York, 1923); *Glimpses of Japan and Formosa* (New York, 1924); *Roving through Southern China* (New York, 1925); and *East of Siam, Ramblings in the Five Divisions of French Indo-China* (New York, 1926). He served in the U.S. Army during World War I and in the U.S. Army Air Force during World War II. Died April 17, 1962, in Langhorne, Pennsylvania. *References*: *CA*; *NCAB* 52:404; *NYT*, April 19, 1962; and *WWWA*.

FRANKLIN. Merchantman of Boston under Captain James Devereux. The first American ship to bring a cargo directly from Japan to the United States. *References*: *Franklin* "Journal," Ms., Peabody Museum of Salem, Salem, Mass.; and Peter J. Petchko, "Salem Trading Voyages to Japan during the Early Nineteenth Century," *AN* 46 (1986): 50–54.

FRAZAR, EVERETT (1834–1901). Merchant, born in Duxbury, Massachusetts. Frazar sailed for Shanghai in 1858, and established the firm of Frazar and Company, an import-export business. He opened branches in Nagasaki and Yokohama, Japan, and in Hong Kong. He moved the main office to New York City in 1872. It was later engaged in introducing electric lighting in Japan and China. He wrote *Korea and Her Relations to China, Japan and the United States* (Orange, N.J., 1884). He was later a consul general of Korea in the United States. Died January 3, 1901, in Orange, New Jersey. *Reference*: *NYT*, January 4, 1901.

FRAZAR, EVERETT W(ELLES) (1867–1951). Merchant, son of Everett Frazar,* born August 17, 1867, in Shanghai, China. Frazar attended Columbia University and graduated from Stevens Institute of Technology (Hoboken, N.J.). He was employed by the Edison Phonograph Company in West Orange, New Jersey, and by the Thomas A. Edison Laboratory from 1890 until 1896, when he joined his father's firm, Frazar and Company, and went to Japan in charge of its engineering department. He took over the business in 1900. In 1903, he consolidated it with a British firm to create Sale and Frazar Limited, which became one of the largest foreign engineering and trading companies in Japan. He was also a representative in East Asia of many American manufacturers, and set up assembly plants in China for several of them. He opened an office in Peking in 1915, in Tientsin in 1916, and later in other Chinese cities. In 1926 he incorporated the firm as Frazar Federal Incorporated, U.S.A., which acted as distributor of many American manufacturers in North China. He was assistant commissioner of the American Red Cross in Vladivostok, Siberia, during World War I. He dissolved Sale and Frazer in 1928, and established Frazer and Company, taking over the company's engineering connections in Japan. The company's property was frozen during World War II, and he established Frazar International (Japan), Limited, in 1950. The business in China was also closed during World War II, but was reopened in 1946 and sold in 1947. Died October 14, 1951, in Daytona Beach, Florida. *References*: *NCAB* 40:393; *NYT*, October 15, 1951; and *WWWA*.

FREE METHODIST CHURCH OF NORTH AMERICA: GENERAL MISSIONARY BOARD. Founded in 1882, it began missionary work in India in 1881, in Japan in 1895, in China in 1905 (terminated in 1951), in the Philippines in 1949, and Hong Kong in 1951. *References*: Free Methodist Church of North America Collections, Marston Memorial Historical Center, Winona Lake, Ind.; Carrie T. Burritt, *The Story of Fifty Years* (Winona Lake, Inc., n.d.); *EMCM*; Byron S. Lamson, *Lights in the World: Free Methodist Missions at Work* (Winona Lake, Ind., 1951); and *Venture: The Frontiers of Free Methodist* (Winona Lake, Ind., 1960).

FREEMAN, JOHN EDGAR (1809–1857). Missionary, born December 27, 1809, in New York City. Freeman graduated from Princeton University and Princeton Theological Seminary, and was ordained in 1838. He was a missionary under the Board of Foreign Missions of the Presbyterian Church in the U.S.A. in India from 1838 until his death. He was stationed in Allahabad from 1838 to 1851, in Mainpuri from 1851 to 1856, and in Fatehgrah after 1856. He was taken prisoner by the Sepoys during the Sepoy Rebellion, and was killed, June 13, 1857, at Cawnpur. *Reference*: *EM*.

FREEMAN, JOHN RIPLEY (1855–1932). Engineer, born July 27, 1855, in West Bridgton, Maine. Freeman graduated from the Massachusetts Institute of Technology. He was an assistant engineer for the Essex Power Company from 1876 to 1886; chief of the corps of factory inspectors for the Associated Factory Mutual Fire Insurance Companies of Boston from 1886 to 1896; president and treasurer of the Manufacturers' Rhode Island and Mechanics Mutual Fire Insurance Companies in Providence, Rhode Island, from 1896 to 1903; and president and treasurer of the State, Enterprise and American Fire Insurance Companies (later Manufacturer Mutual Fire Insurance Company) after 1903. He came to China in 1919, and was employed by the Chinese government as a consultant on the rebuilding of the Grand Canal and the control of floods in the Yellow River and Hwai River valleys. He drew up plans for deepening and narrowing the channels of the Yangtze and Yellow rivers. Died October 6, 1932, in Providence, Rhode Island. *References*: *BMNAS* 17 (1937): 171–87; *DAB S1*; *NCAB* 36:11; and *WWWA*.

FREER, PAUL CASPAR (1862–1912). Chemist, born March 27, 1862, in Chicago. Freer graduated from Rush Medical College (Chicago) and the University of Munich (Germany). He was an instructor at Tufts College from 1887 to 1889, a lecturer in 1889–1890, and professor of general chemistry at the University of Michigan from 1890 until 1901. He was superintendent of the Bureau of Government Laboratories in Manila, Philippines, from 1901 until 1905; director of the Bureau of Science, Manila, after 1905; and dean of the Philippine Islands Medical School (now College of Medicine and Surgery) after 1906. He was also a professor of chemistry at the University of Philippines, and founder and editor of the *Philippine Journal of Science*. Died April 17, 1912, in Baguio, Philippines. *References*: *EP* 4:408; "In Memoriam: Paul Caspar Freer," *Philippines Journal of Science* 7 (July 1912); *NCAB* 19:423; *Scientists in the Philippines* (n.p., 1975), pp. 75–94; and *WWWA*.

FRIENDS FOREIGN MISSIONARY SOCIETY OF OHIO YEARLY MEETING. Founded in 1884, it began missionary work in China in 1887 and in India in 1892. It established the American Friends India Mission in Bundelkhand, India, in 1896. *References*: *EMCM*; E. Anna Nixon, *A Century of Planting: A History of the American Friends Mission in India* (Canton, Ohio, 1985); and Walter R. Williams, *These Fifty Years with Ohio Friends in China; An Intimate Story of Missionary Work in China, under the Direction of Ohio Yearly Meeting of the Friends Church, 1890–1940* (Damascus, Ohio, 1940).

FRILLMANN, PAUL W(ILLIAM) (1911–1972). Missionary, born December 12, 1911, in Melrose Park, Illinois. Frillmann graduated from Concordia Seminary (St. Louis). He was a missionary in the Evangelical Lutheran Mission in Hankow, China, from 1936 until 1941. He was a chaplain with the American Volunteer Group in China in 1941–1942, served in the U.S. Army Air Forces in China, and later with the Office of Strategic Services (OSS), and was chief of the OSS in China in 1945. He was an information officer with the U.S. Information Service (USIS) in Mukden, China, in 1946–1947 and in Shanghai from 1947 until 1949; and head of the USIS office in the Hong Kong Consulate from 1950 to 1953. He resigned from the State Department in 1953 and returned to the United States. He was an account executive and vice president of H. L. Oram, Incorporated, of New York City, a public relations and fund-raising organization, from 1953 to 1963, and president of Oram International Corporation from 1964 until his death. He co-wrote (with Graham Peck) *China: The Remembered Life* (Boston, 1968). Died August 19, 1972, in Scituate, Massachusetts. *References*: *CA*; *NCAB* 57:186; and *NYT*.

FRITZ, CHESTER (1892–1983). Banker, born March 25, 1892, near Buxton, North Dakota, and grew up in Fargo and Lidgerwood, North Dakota. Fritz attended the University of North Dakota, graduated from the University of Washington, and attended its law school. He became an employee of Fisher Flour Mills Company in Seattle in 1915, and went to Hong Kong in 1915 as its representative in Asia. In 1917, he made a journey to the interior of China and its border with Tibet. His journal of this journey was published later as *China Journey: A Diary of Six Months in Western Inland China 1917* (Seattle, Wash., 1981). He then became involved in mining tungstan, was a representative of the American Metal Company in Asia after 1922, and later manager of its Shanghai office until 1928. In 1929, he founded Swan, Culbertson and Fritz, an international investment and private banking firm, which by the mid 1930s had become the largest investment firm in East Asia and the leading foreign account on the New York Stock Exchange. It was closed in 1941 and he was interned by the Japanese until 1943. He returned to Asia after World War II and reestablished the firm, but left China in 1951 and settled in Europe. He was coauthor (with Dan Rylance) of *Ever Westward to the Far East: The Story of Chester Fritz* (Grand Forks, N.D., 1982). Died July 28, 1983, in Lausanne, Switzerland. *References*: Chester Fritz Papers, University of North Dakota Library, Grand Forks, N.D.; *Grand Forks Herald*, July 29, 1983; and Kenneth B. Pyle, "Chester Fritz: A Biographical Note," in Chester Fritz, *China Journey: A Diary of Six Months in Western Inland China 1917* (Seattle, Wash., 1981).

FU JEN CATHOLIC UNIVERSITY. Founded in Peking in 1925 under the sponsorship of the Benedictine Archabbey of St. Vincent, USA; administrative responsibility was transferred to the Society of the Divine Word in 1933. The university was closed down in 1950 but was reestablished in Taipei, Taiwan, in 1963, and was administered jointly by Chinese local clergy and members of the Society of the Divine Word and the Society of Jesus.

FUKIEN CHRISTIAN UNIVERSITY. Fukien Union College was founded in 1916 by the mission of the American Board of Commissioners for Foreign Missions (ABCFM), the Methodist Episcopal Church, the Reformed Church in America, and three British missions in Foochow, Province of Fukien. It was the result of a merger of Foochow College (founded in 1853), the Foochow Anglo-Chinese College (founded in 1885), and St. Mark's Anglo-Chinese College (founded in 1906). It became the Fukien Christian University in 1918, and obtained a charter from the University of the State of New York. It became coeducational in the 1930s and was united with Hwa Nan College in 1951. It was nationalized in 1952. *References*: *Fenn*; *Lutz*; and Roderick Scott, *Fukien Christian University: A Historical Sketch* (New York, 1954).

FULTON, MARY HANNAH (1854–1927). Medical missionary, born May 31, 1854, in Ashland, Ohio. Mary Fulton attended Lawrence University (Appleton, Wis.) and graduated from Hillsdale (Mich.) College and the Woman's Medical College of Pennsylvania. She was a medical missionary under the Board of Foreign Missions of the Presbyterian Church in the U.S.A. in the South China mission from 1884 to 1918. She served in Kwai Ping, Kwangsi Province, in 1885–1886, and in Canton after 1886. She established two dispensaries in Canton in 1887 and another at Fati in 1891. She taught pediatrics and was in charge of women patients in Canton Hospital. She built a hospital for women and children, a training school for nurses, and a medical college for women in Canton in 1902. She moved to Shanghai in 1915 for health reasons, retired in 1918, and returned to the United States. She wrote a memoir, *"Inasmuch": Extracts from Letters, Journals, Papers, etc.* (West Medford, Mass., 1915?). Died January 7, 1927, in Pasadena, California. Her brother, **ALBERT A(NDREW) FULTON**, (1849–1934), a missionary, was born June 4, 1849, in Ashland, Ohio. Albert Fulton graduated from Princeton University and Union Theological Seminary, and was ordained in 1880. He was a missionary under the Board of Foreign Missions of the Presbyterian Church in the U.S.A. in Canton, China, from 1880 until 1922. Died December 9, 1934, in Pasadena, California. *References*: Fulton Family Papers, United Presbyterian Mission Library, New York City; *CR* 66 (1935): 57; *NAW*; and *UnionTS*.

FUNSTON, FREDERICK (1865–1917). Army officer, born November 9, 1865, in New Carlisle, Ohio, and grew up in Iola, Kansas. Funston attended Kansas State University (Lawrence). He was a botanical explorer for the U.S. Department of Agriculture from 1891 to 1895 in the Dakotas; Death Valley, California; and Alaska. He volunteered for service in the Cuban insurrection from 1896 to 1898, and served as an artillery commander with the Cuban revolutionary forces. He then served in the Spanish-American War in the Philippines in 1898–1899. In 1899, he commanded the Fourth District of the Department of Northern Luzon. In 1901, with a small raiding party, he succeeded in capturing Emilio Aguinaldo, the Philippine leader. He was commissioned a brigadier general in the regular army in

1901, and returned to the United States. He commanded the departments of the Colorado, the Columbia, and the Lakes, the Southwestern Division, and the Department of California. He was commander of the Department of Luzon in the Philippines from 1911 to 1913, and of the Hawaiian Department in 1913–1914. He commanded the army troops in the expedition to Veracruz, Mexico, in 1914, and was commander of the Southern Department in 1915. He wrote *Memories of Two Wars: Cuban and Philippines Experiences* (New York, 1911). Died February 19, 1917, in San Antonio, Texas. *References*: Frederick Funston Papers, Kansas State Historical Society, Topeka, Kan.; *ACAB*; David H. Bain, *Sitting in Darkness: Americans in the Philippines* (Boston, 1984); Thomas W. Crouch, "The Making of a Soldier: The Career of Frederick Funston, 1865–1902," Ph.D. diss., University of Texas at Austin, 1969; *DAB*; *DAMIB*; Brian M. Linn, "Guerilla Fighter: Frederick Funston in the Philippines, 1900–1901," *Kansas History* 10 (Spring 1987): 2–16; *NCAB* 11:40; *NYT*, February 24, 1917; John B. B. Trussell, Jr., "Frederick Funston: The Man Destiny Just Missed." *Military Review* 53 (June 1973): 59–73; and *WWWA*.

FURLONG, LEONARD (1877–1911). Army officer, born November 3, 1877, in Philadelphia. Furlong served in the U.S. Army during the Spanish-American War in Cuba and in the Philippines. He returned to the United States in 1901, and was a civil engineer with the Metropolitan Public Works of New York City from 1901 to 1903. He was back in the Philippines in 1903, and was commissioned third lieutenant in the Philippines Constabulary in 1903. He served in Misamis, Cotabato, Sulu, Basilan, and Davao from 1903 to 1910, and in Pangasinan in 1910–1911. Committed suicide July 9, 1911, in Manila. *References*: Leonard Furlong Papers, University of Oregon Library, Eugene, Ore.; Russell Roth, "Behind the Furlong Legend; the Hero as Enigma," in *Muddy Glory: America's 'Indian Wars' in the Philippines 1899–1935* (W. Hanover, Mass., 1981), ch. 8; and Victor Hurley, "Unpublished Biography," University of Oregon Library, Eugene, Ore.

FURNESS, WILLIAM HENRY, 3RD (1866–1920). Traveler, born August 18, 1866, in Wallingford, Pennsylvania. Furness graduated from Harvard University and studied medicine at the University of Pennsylvania, but practiced little. From 1895 to 1901, with Alfred C. Harrison* and Hiram M. Hiller,* he began an extended voyage to East, South, and Southeast Asia. He also made several trips to study the Ainu in Hokkaido, Japan. He was secretary and curator of the University Museum of the University of Pennsylvania after 1904. He spent several years attempting to educate apes. He wrote *Home Life of Borneo Head Hunters, Its Festival and Folklore* (Philadelphia, 1902). Died September 9, 1920, in Wallingford, Pennsylvania. *Reference*: *WWWA*.

G

GACHES, SAMUEL FRANCIS (1878–1946). Businessman, born September 30, 1878, in La Conner, Washington. Gaches graduated from Stanford University. He came to the Philippines with the United States Postal Service in 1900, was superintendent of the money order division of the Bureau of Posts from 1901 to 1905, chief agent of the Internal Revenue Bureau from 1905 to 1910, treasurer and assistant general manager of H. E. Heacock Company from 1910 to 1914, and president and general manager after 1914. Died January 6, 1946. His wife, **ELSIE MCCLOSKEY GACHES** (1882–1966), a nurse, was born in Brattleboro, Vermont. She graduated from the University of Pennsylvania and studied at the Municipal Hospital of Contagious Diseases in Philadelphia. She worked at the Henry Street Settlement in New York City, and organized and administered the Vanderbilt School of Nursing for Colored Women in North Carolina. She was chief nurse of the Philippine General Hospital in Manila, and head of the Philippine General Hospital School of Nursing from 1910 until 1916. She prepared a cookbook, *Good Cooking and Health in the Tropics* (Manila, 1922), which was republished as *Culinary Art in the Tropics, circa 1922*, ed. Carlos Quirino, with an introduction by Nora V. Daza (Manila, 1978). Died March 9, 1966, in Forbes Park, Philippines. *References*: *ACCJ* 42 (1966): 160–62; *EP* 4:462–64; and *WWP*.

GAGE, BROWNELL (1874–1945). Educator, born April 14, 1874, in Astoria, Long Island, New York. Gage attended the College of the City of New York, and graduated from Yale University and Union Theological Seminary. He was one of the founders of Yale-in-China in Changsha, China, in 1904. He served as its dean and later as provost and chairman of the governing board until 1923. He served with the Young Men's Christian Association (YMCA) in France during World War I. He was the headmaster of Suffield Academy (Conn.) from 1924 until 1939, and a pastor in Bolton, Connecticut, after 1940. Died February 3, 1945, in Bolton, Connecticut. *References*: *NYT*, February 5, 1945; *UnionTS*; *WWWA*.

GAILEY, ROBERT R(EED) (1869–1950). Association official, born November 26, 1869, in Pylesville, Maryland. Gailey graduated from Lafayette College and McCormick and Princeton theological seminaries, and was ordained in 1897. He was the Young Men's Christian Association (YMCA) secretary in Tientsin, China, from 1898 until 1905; and secretary of "Princeton Work in Peking" and teacher from 1907 until his retirement in 1930. He remained in Peiping, collecting ancient Chinese books and scrolls, until 1941, when he returned to the United States and settled in Los Angeles. Died January 18, 1950, in Pasadena, California. *References*: D. Arthur Hatch, ed., *Biographical Record of the Men of Lafayette 1832–1948* (Easton, Pa., 1948); and *NYT*, January 21, 1950.

GAINES, NANNIE B(ETT) [ANN ELIZABETH] (1860–1932). Missionary, born April 23, 1860, in Franklin Kentucky. Gaines graduated from Franklin Female College. She taught in public schools in Union County and Leesburg, Florida, and then in the Florida Conference College (Leesburg). She was a missionary under the Board of Missions of the Methodist Episcopal Church, South, in Hiroshima, Japan, from 1887 until her death, serving in the Mission of the Inland Sea. She was the principal of the Hiroshima Girls' School from 1889 until her retirement in 1920. She also started a kindergarten in 1891 and a kindergarten normal training program in 1895. Died February 26, 1932, in Hiroshima, Japan. *References*: Nannie B. Gaines Papers, Archives and History Center, United Methodist Church, Madison, N.J.; Samuel M. Hilburn, *Gaines Sensei: Missionary to Hiroshima* (Kobe, 1936); Dorothy Robins-Mowry, "Not a Foreigner, but a *Sensei*—a Teacher: Nannie B. Gaines of Hiroshima," in *Women's Work for Women: Missionaries and Social Change in Asia*, ed. Leslie A. Flemming (Boulder, Colo., 1989), pp. 87–115.

GALBRAITH, JOHN KENNETH (1908–   ). Economist and diplomat, born October 15, 1908, near Iona Station, Ontario, Canada. Galbraith graduated from the universities of Toronto and California at Berkeley, and attended Cambridge University. He was an assistant professor of economics at Princeton University from 1939 to 1941; served in the U.S. Office of Price Administration in Washington, D.C., from 1941 to 1943; and was a member of the board of editors of *Fortune* from 1943 to 1948; lecturer in economics at Harvard University in 1948–1949; and professor in economics from 1949 until his retirement in 1975. He was John F. Kennedy's floor manager in the Democratic National Convention of 1960. He was U.S. ambassador to India from 1961 to 1963. He sought an increase in American military and economic aid for India, acted as an informal advisor on economic development, and assisted in the Indian government during the Chinese border war in 1962. He wrote *Ambassador's Journal: A Personal Account of the Kennedy Years* (Boston, 1969), and *A Life in Our Times: Memoirs* (Boston, 1981). *References*: John Kenneth Galbraith Papers, John F. Kennedy Library, Waltham, Mass.; *CA*; *CB* 1975; *DADH*; *DVW*; John S. Gambs, *John Kenneth Galbraith* (New York, 1975); and *WWA*.

GALE, ESSON M(CDOWELL) (1884–1964). Government official, born December 8, 1884, in Bad Axe, Michigan. Gale graduated from the University of Michigan. He was appointed a student interpreter in the American legation in Peking in 1908. He was a deputy consul general, interpreter, and acting Mixed Court assessor in Shanghai from 1911 to 1914. He was an associate commissioner of the Chinese Salt Revenue Administration for the Chinese Ministry of Finance in the central China provinces from 1914 to 1922 and from 1924 to 1927, and in northern Manchuria from 1922 to 1924. He returned to the United States in 1927, and was a lecturer in Oriental languages at the University of California from 1928 to 1932. He returned to China in 1932 and was the English secretary of the Chief Inspectorate of the Chinese Salt Revenue Administration in Shanghai from 1932 to 1937, and acting associate director general of the Salt Administration from 1937 to 1939. He was a special representative of the Office of the Co-ordinator of Information in the Far East and special assistant to Clarence E. Gauss* in 1942; and counselor to foreign students, director of the International center, and lecturer in political science at the University of Michigan from 1943 until his retirement in 1955. He wrote *Basics of the Chinese Civilization* (Shanghai, 1934), and *Salt for the Dragon, a Personal History of China, 1908–1945* (East Lansing, Mich., 1953). Died May 15, 1964, in Bay City, Michigan. *References*: Esson M. Gale Papers, Michigan Historical Collections, University of Michigan Library, Ann Arbor, Mich.; *NCAB* 51:675; *NYT*, May 16, 1964; and *WWWA*.

GALLIN, BERNARD (1929–   ). Anthropologist, born February 9, 1929, in Brooklyn, New York. Gallin graduated from the City College of New York and Cornell University. He carried out fieldwork in Taiwan in 1957–1958, in 1965–1966, and in 1969–1970. He was an assistant professor of anthropology at Wayne State University in 1960–1961, and at Harpur College of the State University of New York in 1961–1962; he was assistant professor of anthropology at Michigan State University from 1962 to 1965, an associate professor there from 1965 to 1968, and a professor after 1968. He wrote *Hsin Hsing, Taiwan: A Chinese Village in Change* (Berkeley, Calif., 1966). With Rita Schlesinger Gallin, he described his experiences in "The Rural-to-Urban Migration of an Anthropologist in Taiwan," in *Anthropologists in Cities*, ed. George M. Foster and Robert V. Kemper (Boston, 1974). *References*: *DFAF*; and *WWA*.

GALLMAN, JEFFERSON D(AVIS) ("JEFF") (1876–1945). Army officer, born in Gallman, Mississippi, and grew up in Holland, Texas. Gallman served in the U.S. Army during the Spanish-American War and in the Philippines after 1901. He was commissioned a third lieutenant in the Philippine Constabulary in 1905 and resigned in 1913. He was lieutenant governor of Ifuago from 1908 to 1913. Died in Sawtelle, Los Angeles. *References*: *Elarth*; and Frank L. Jenista, *The White Apos: American Governors on the Cordillera Central* (Quezon City, 1987), pp. 50–82.

GALT, HOWARD SPILMAN (1872–1948). Missionary, born September 15, 1872, in Shenandoah, Iowa. Galt graduated from Tabor College (Ia.), the University of Chicago, and Hartford Theological Seminary, and was ordained in 1899. He was a missionary under the American Board of Commissioners for Foreign Missions (ABCFM) in north China from 1899 until 1935. He was a teacher at the North China Union College from 1902 to 1910, president from 1911 to 1917, professor of education at Yenching University at Peiping, China after 1918, head of the department of education there from 1918 to 1935, and chairman of the graduate division from 1931 to 1934. He wrote *The Development of Chinese Educational Theory: The Historical Development of the Theory of Education in China to the Close of the Han Dynasty, A.D. 220* (Shanghai, 1929). Died November 7, 1948, in Claremont, California. *Reference*: *WWWA*.

GALVIN, EDWARD J. (1882–1956). Missionary, born November 23, 1882, in Crookstown, County Cork, Ireland. Galvin attended St. Patrick's College (Maynooth), and was ordained in 1909. He was a curate in Brooklyn, New York, from 1909 to 1912. He worked with the French Vincentians in Shanghai from 1912. He founded the Saint Columban's Foreign Mission Society in 1916, and recruits from the United States soon joined him. He established a mission in Hanyang, Hupeh Province, in 1920. He became prefect apostolic in Hanyang in 1924, vicar apostolic in 1927, and head of the see in 1946. He was held under house arrest by the Communists from 1949 to 1952, and was expelled from China in 1952. Died February 23, 1956, in Nava, Ireland. *References*: William E. Barrett, *The Red Lacquered Gate: The Story of Bishop Galvin, Co-Founder of the Columban Fathers* (New York, 1967); *CE*; and *NYT*, February 25, 1956.

GAMBLE, SIDNEY D(AVID) (1890–1968). Missionary, born July 12, 1890, in Cincinnati, Ohio. Gamble graduated from Princeton University and the University of California. He was secretary of the International Committee of the Young Men's Christian Association (YMCA) in China in 1918–1919 and from 1924 to 1927, and recording secretary after 1944. He was treasurer of the Church World Service from 1948 to 1953, vice chairman from 1953 to 1960, and chairman from 1960 to 1964. He wrote *Peking: A Social Survey* (New York, 1921); *How Chinese Families Live in Peiping* (New York, 1933); *Ting Hsien: A North China Rural Community* (New York, 1954); and *North China Villages: Social, Political, and Economic Activities before 1933* (Berkeley, Calif., 1963). Died March 29, 1968, in New York City. *References*: *CA*; James P. Eyster II, "A Princetonian in Asia: Sidney Gamble's Social Surveys in China, 1918–1934," *Princeton University Library Chronicle* 48 (1987): 239–52; *NYT*, March 30, 1968; *OAB*; and *WWWA*.

GAMEWELL, FRANK [FRANCIS] D(UNLAP) (1857–1950). Missionary, born August 31, 1857, in Camden, South Carolina. Gamewell attended Rensselaer Polytechnic Institute and Cornell University, and graduated from Dickinson College. He was a missionary under the Board of Foreign Missions of the Methodist Episcopal Church in China from 1881 until 1901. He was principal of a boys' school in Peking, superintendent of the West China mission from 1884 to 1887, and professor of chemistry and physics at Peking University in 1889–1890. He was chief of staff, in charge of the fortifications in the British legation, during the Siege of Peking in 1900. He was field secretary and associate secretary of the Board of Foreign Missions in New York City from 1901 to 1908, secretary of education for China (later China Christian Educational Association) of the Methodist Episcopal Church from 1912 to 1925, and associate secretary for eastern Asia, China, Japan, and Korea of the Board of Foreign Missions in New York City from 1924 to 1929. He retired in 1930. Died August 7, 1950, in Clifton Springs, New York. His second wife, **MARY LOUISE (NINDE) GAMEWELL** (1858–1947), wrote *The Gateway to China: Pictures of Shanghai* (New York, 1916); *New Life Currents in China* (New York, 1919); and *King-kwong, "City of the Morning Light"* (West Medford, Mass., 1924). *References*: Francis Dunlap Gamewell Papers, Manuscript Division, Library of Congress; *EWM*; and *WWWA*.

GARDNER, CORNELIUS (1849–1921). Army officer, born September 4, 1849, in the Netherlands, and came to the United States in 1852. Gardner attended Hope College and graduated from the U.S. Military Academy in 1873. He was commissioned a second lieutenant in the Nineteenth U.S. Infantry in 1873, and served in the Indian Wars from 1874 to 1880; on the Rio Grande from 1881 to 1890; at Fort Wayne, Detroit, from 1891 to 1896; and in the Spanish-American War in Cuba and the Philippines. He was civil governor of the province of Tayabas, Luzon, in 1901–1902. He returned to the Philippines from 1904 to 1907. He retired in 1913. Died January 2, 1921, in Claremont, California. *References*: Cornelius Gardner, "A View of the American Campaign Against 'Filipino Insurgents': 1900," ed. Melvin G. Holli, *PS* 17 (1969): 97–111; *NCAB* 19:339; and *WWWA*.

GARST, CHARLES E(LIAS) (1853–1898). Missionary, born August 23, 1853, in Dayton, Ohio. Garst attended Agricultural College (Ames, Ia.), graduated from the U.S. Military Academy in 1870, was commissioned, and served in the Southwest. He resigned from the army in 1883 and was a missionary under the Foreign Christian Missionary Society in Japan from 1883 until his death. He served in Yokohama in 1883–1884, in Akita from 1884 to 1888, in Tsurugaoka from 1888 to 1892, and in Tokyo from 1893 until his death. Died December 28, 1898, in Tokyo. His wife **LAURA DELANY GARST** (1861–1925), wrote *In the Shadow of the Drum Tower* (Cincinnati, 1911), and his biography, *A West-Pointer in the Land of the Mikado* (New York, 1913). *Ref-*

erences: *OAB*; and *They Went to Japan: Biographies of Missionaries of the Disciples of Christ* (Indianapolis, 1949).

GARVAN, JOHN M. (1875– ?). Ethnologist, born November 19, 1875, in Ireland. Garvan came to the United States in 1895 and became a U.S. citizen in 1902. He attended a college in Louisiana, and was a teacher in various colleges for five years. He came to the Philippines in 1903 as a teacher and served until 1907. He was later a shopkeeper in the interior of the islands and lived among the Manobo for many years. He studied the Manobos of Mindanao, and wrote *The Manobos of Mindano* (Washington, D.C., 1929). He also visited and studied the Negritos of Northern Luzon, Zambalaes, Camarines, Tayabas, Negros, and Mindanao. His study, *The Negritos of the Philippines*, ed. Hermann Hochegger (Horn-Vienna, 1965), was published posthumously. He returned to the United States in 1925 and lived in Berkeley, California. Died sometime between 1938 and 1941. *Reference*: Fritz Bornemann, "J. M. Garvans Materialien über die Negritos der Philippinen and P. W. Schmidt's Notizen dazu," *Anthropos* 50 (1955): 899–930.

GAUSS, CLARENCE E(DWARD) (1887–1960). Diplomat, born January 12, 1887, in Washington, D.C. Gauss was a clerk in a law office from 1903 to 1906, clerk in the State Department in 1906–1907, and deputy consul general in Shanghai from 1907 to 1909. He entered the foreign service in 1912, served in Shanghai, was a consul in Tientsin in 1916, and in Amoy from 1916 to 1919. He was consul general in Mukden in 1923–1924, in Tientsin from 1924 to 1926 and from 1927 to 1931, and in Shanghai in 1926–1927. He served in the State Department from 1931 to 1933, and was counselor of legation in Peiping from 1933 to 1935, consul general in Shanghai, and counselor of embassy from 1935 to 1940. He was president of the Court of Consuls and leader of Shanghai's international settlement. He was the first U.S. minister to Australia in 1940–1941. He was U.S. ambassador to China from 1941 until his resignation in 1944. He tried, unsuccessfully, to unite the Nationalists and Communists in the fight against Japan, and criticized the Nationalist government's corruption and mis-managment, causing enmity between himself and Generalissimo Chiang Kai-shek. He retired in 1945 and was a member of the board of the Export-Import Bank from 1945 to 1952. Died April 8, 1960, in Los Angeles. *References*: *CB* 1941; *DAB S6*; *DADH*; *NCAB F*:365; *NYT*, April 9, 1960; and *WWWA*.

GAY, W(INCKWORTH) ALLAN (1821–1910). Painter, born August 18, 1821, in West Hingham, Massachusetts. Gay studied art at West Point, New York, and in Europe from 1847 to 1851, working mostly in Paris. He opened a studio in Boston in 1851. He toured Europe from 1873 to 1875 and toured Egypt in 1874. He was in Japan from 1877 until 1881, and spent one winter in China. He was in Ceylon and India in 1881–1882, and was again in Paris from 1882 to 1884. He continued to paint until 1890. Died February 23, 1910, in

West Hingham, Massachusetts. *References*: W. Allan Gay Papers, Columbia University Libraries, New York City; *ACAB*; Wayne Craven, "Winckworth Allan Gay, Boston Painter of the White Mountain, Paris, the Nile, and Mount Fujiyama," *Magazine Antiques* 120 (November 1981): 1222–32; *DAB*; *NCAB* 11:296; *NYT*, February 23, 1910; and *WWWA*.

GEE, NATHANIEL GIST (1876–1937). Biologist, born April 20, 1876, in Union, South Carolina. Gee graduated from Wofford College (Spartanburg, N.C.). He was principal of Jordan Academy (S.C.) from 1896 to 1898, and professor of natural science at Columbia College (S.C.) from 1898 to 1901. He was a professor of natural science at Soochow University in Soochow from 1901 to 1915, and professor and head of the department of biology there from 1915 to 1920. He organized the first department of biology in any Chinese college. He returned to the United States in 1920, and was superintendent of public schools at Summerton, South Carolina, in 1920–1921. He was back in China in 1921, where he was a representative of Spencer Lens Company in East Asia in 1921–1922, an advisor on premedical education to the China Medical Board of the Rockefeller Foundation in Peiping from 1922 to 1925, resident director of the China Medical Board from 1926 to 1928, field director of the division of medical education of the Rockefeller Foundation in 1927–1928, and an advisor for China in natural sciences from 1928 to 1932. He was vice president in charge of the American office of Yenching University from 1932 to 1935, and head of the biology department at Lander College (Greenwood, S.C.) from 1935 until his death. Died December 18, 1937, in Greenwood, South Carolina. *References*: *NCAB* 28:366; *NYT*, December 19, 1937; and *WWWA*.

GEERTZ, CLIFFORD (JAMES) (1926–   ). Anthropologist, born August 23, 1926, in San Francisco. Geertz graduated from Antioch College and Harvard University. He was assistant professor of anthropology at the University of California at Berkeley in 1959–1960 and at the University of Chicago in 1960–1961, associate professor there from 1961 to 1964 and professor of anthropology from 1964 to 1970, and professor of social science at the Institute for Advanced Study (Princeton, N.J.) after 1970. He carried out fieldwork in East Java, Indonesia, from 1952 to 1954, and in South Bali, Indonesia, in 1957–1958. He wrote *The Development of the Javanese Economy: A Sociocultural Approach* (Cambridge, Mass, 1956); *The Social Context of Economic Change: An Indonesian Case Study* (Cambridge, Mass., 1956); *Modjokuto: Religion in Java* (Cambridge, Mass., 1958); *The Religion of Java* (New York, 1960); *Agricultural Involution: The Process of Ecological Change in Indonesia* (Berkeley, 1963); *Peddlers and Princes: Social Change and Economic Modernization in Two Indonesian Towns* (Chicago, 1963); *The Social History of an Indonesian Town* (Cambridge, Mass., 1965); *Person, Time and Conduct in Bali: An Essay in Cultural Analysis* (New Haven, 1966); *Islam Observed: Religious Development in Morocco and Indonesia* (New Haven, Conn., 1968); *Negara: The Theatre*

State in Nineteenth Century Bali (Princeton, 1980); and *Works and Lives: The Anthropologist as Author* (Stanford, Calif., 1988); and was coauthor of *Kinship in Bali* (Chicago, 1975). *References*: *AMWS*; *CA*; and *WWA*.

GEERTZ, HILDRED (STOREY) (1927–   ). Anthropologist, wife of Clifford Geertz,* born February 12, 1927, in New York City. Geertz graduated from Antioch College and Radcliffe College. She carried out research in Java, Indonesia, from 1952 to 1954, and in Bali, Indonesia, in 1957–1958. She wrote *The Javanese Family: A Study of Kinship and Socialization* (Glencoe, Ill., 1961), and was coauthor of *Kinship in Bali* (Chicago, 1975). She was assistant professor of social science at the University of Chicago in 1969–1970, associate professor of anthropology at Princeton University from 1971 to 1975, and a professor there after 1975. *References*: *AMWS*; *CA*; *WWA*; and *WWAW*.

GEIL, WILLIAM EDGAR (1865–1925). Explorer and author, born near Doylestown, Pennsylvania. Geil graduated from Lafayette College (Easton, Pa.). He made a four-year trip around the world. He was best known for his exploration of the Great Wall of China. He wrote *A Yankee on the Yangtze: Being a Narrative of a Journey from Shanghai through the Central Kingdom to Burma* (New York, 1904); *The Great Wall of China* (New York, 1909); and *Eighteen Capitals of China* (Philadelphia, 1911). He lectured all over the United States, and later became an evangelist. Died April 12, 1925, in Venice, Italy, on his way back from Jerusalem. *References*: *ACAB*; *NYT*, April 14, 1925; and *WWWA*.

GENERAL SHERMAN INCIDENT. Merchant schooner seeking trade with Korea which dropped anchor off P'yongyang, Korea, in 1866. It went aground because of a fall in the water level, and the Koreans burned it. The members of the crew were drowned or beheaded by the Koreans. *Reference*: Ching Youngchoe, *The Rule of the Taewon'gun 1864–1873: Restoration in Yi Korea* (Cambridge, Mass., 1972), pp. 110–12.

GEORGESON, C(HARLES) C(HRISTIAN) (1851–1931). Agriculturist, born June 26, 1851, on the Island of Langleland, Denmark, and came to the United States in 1873. Georgeson graduated from Michigan State College of Agriculture. He was assistant editor of the *Rural New Yorker* from 1878 to 1880, and professor of agriculture and horticulture at Texas State Agricultural and Mechanical College from 1880 to 1883. He was professor of agriculture at the College of Agriculture of the Imperial University of Tokyo from 1885 to 1889. He brought soybean seeds from Japan to the United States and experimented with their cultivation in Kansas. He was a professor of agriculture at Kansas State Agricultural College from 1890 to 1897, went to Alaska during the gold rush to establish an agricultural station for the federal government, was the agronomist in charge of the Alaska Experiment Station from 1915 to 1928, and its director from 1923 until his retirement in 1928. Died April 1, 1931. *References*: *AMWS*; and *WWWA*.

GIBSON, WALTER MURRAY (1823–1888). Adventurer, born at sea between England and the United States. Gibson grew up in New York and New Jersey. He then visited Central America. In 1852, he came to Sumatra where a native revolt against the Dutch promised a market for a schooner he had bought. He was arrested by the Dutch on a charge of treason and spent sixteen months in prison in Batavia. He was tried and sentenced to exposure in the pillory and twelve years of forced labor, but he escaped in 1853, returned to the United States, and recounted his adventures in *The Prison of Weltevreden and a Glance at the East Indian Archipelago* (New York, 1856). He went to Utah, embraced Mormonism, and went to Hawaii in 1861. He was premier of Hawaii from 1882 until 1887. He was then forced to leave Hawaii and returned to San Francisco. Died January 21, 1888, in San Francisco. *References*: *ACAB*; Jacob Adler and Robert M. Kamins, *The Fantastic Life of Walter Murray Gibson, Hawaii's Minister of Everything* (Honolulu, 1986); Paul Bailey, *Hawaii's Royal Prime Minister: The Life and Times of Walter Murray Gibson* (New York, 1980); *DAB*; James W. Gould, "The Filibuster of Walter Murray Gibson," *Hawaiian Historical Society Annual Report for 1959* (Honolulu, 1960), pp. 7–32; *NCAB* 23:287; and *WWWA*.

GIFFORD, DANIEL L(YMAN) (1861–1900). Missionary, born January 9, 1861, in Elgin, Illinois. Gifford graduated from Amherst College and McCormick Theological Seminary, and was ordained in 1888. He was a missionary under the Board of Foreign Missions of the Presbyterian Church in the U.S.A. in Korea from 1890 until his death. He wrote *Every-Day Life in Korea: A Collection of Studies and Stories* (Chicago, 1898). Died April 10, 1900, in Chang Won, near Seoul. *Reference*: *Amherst*.

GILBERT, NEWTON WHITNEY (1862–1939). Lawyer, born May 24, 1862, in Worthington, Ohio. Gilbert attended Ohio State University, and was admitted to the bar in 1885. He practiced law at Angola, Indiana, and was a member of the Indiana Senate from 1896 to 1900, lieutenant governor of Indiana from 1900 to 1904, and a member of the U.S. House of Representatives from 1905 to 1907. He was a member of the Philippine Commission in 1908–1909, judge of the court of first instance in Manila from 1906 to 1908, secretary of public instruction of the Philippines in 1909, vice-governor from 1909 to 1913, acting governor general in 1912–1913, and president of the board of regents of the University of the Philippines from 1908 to 1913. He practiced law in New York City after 1916. Died July 5, 1939, in Santa Ana, California. *References*: *BDAC*; *EP* 4:364; *NYT*, July 6, 1939; and *WWWA*.

GILBERT, RODNEY (YONKERS) (1889–1968). Journalist, born in Lancaster, Pennsylvania. Gilbert graduated from Franklin and Marshall College and studied at Harvard University. He went to China in 1912 and remained until 1929, first as a medicine salesman and then as a correspondent for *The North*

China Daily News of Shanghai. He was an editorial writer for the *Chicago Tribune* from 1929 to 1944. He conducted several investigative trips to west China on behalf of the U.S. government, was dean of the Graduate School of Journalism at Chungking from 1944 to 1946, and columnist for the *New York Herald Tribune* from 1946 to 1949. After 1950, he worked for the *Far Eastern Review* in Taiwan and became its editor. He wrote *What's Wrong with China?* (New York, 1926); *The Unequal Treaties: China and the Foreigner* (London, 1929); and a novel, *The Indiscretions of Lin Mang* (London, 1929). Died January 11, 1968, in Morristown, New Jersey. *References*: *National Review* 20 (January 30, 1968): 70–71; and *NYT*, January 12, 1968.

GILHOUSER, HENRY (1881–1964). Army officer, born in Essen, Germany, and came to the United States with his family in the late 1880s. Gilhouser enlisted in the U.S. Army in 1898, served in the Spanish-American War in Cuba and Puerto Rico. He was appointed third lieutenant in the Philippine Constabulary in 1903, and was governor of Davao from 1910 to 1912 and provincial governor of Lanao from 1912 until his retirement in 1917 with the rank of lieutenant colonel. He was later an executive and branch manager of the Standard Vacuum Oil Company until 1937. He was appointed by Philippine President Manuel Quezon in 1941 as fuel and transportation administrator in the Civilian Emergency Administration. He was interned by the Japanese in Santo Tomas during World War II. After the liberation, he was in charge of the Emergency Control Commission and a member of the United States–Philippine War Damage Commission after 1947. Died in Manila. *References*: *BAHC* 1 (May 1973): 44–45; and *Gleeck/Frontiers*.

GILMAN, ALFRED A(LONZO) (1878–1966). Missionary, born August 23, 1878, in North Platte, Nebraska. Gilman graduated from the University of Nebraska and Philadelphia Divinity School, and was ordained in 1902. He was a missionary under the Domestic and Foreign Missionary Society of the Protestant Episcopal Church in the United States of America in Wyoming and Colorado in 1901–1902, and in China from 1902 to 1948. He served in Hankow from 1902 to 1907 and in Changsha from 1907 to 1913. He was editor of *Chinese Churchman* from 1913 to 1916, a teacher at Boone University in 1916–1917 and its president from 1917 to 1924, and president of Central China University (later Huachung University) from 1924 to 1929. He was suffragan bishop of Hankow from 1925 to 1937 and bishop of Hankow from 1937 until his retirement in 1948. He played a major role in emergency relief to refugees in the Hankow area. The Chinese government placed the city in his charge when it was evacuated before the oncoming Japanese. He was interned by the Japanese. Died September 13, 1966, in Pompton Lakes, New Jersey. *References*: *NYT*, September 15, 1966; and *WWWA*.

GILMORE, EUGENE ALLEN (1871–1953). Lawyer and colonial administrator, born July 4, 1871, in Brownville, Nebraska. Gilmore graduated from
DePauw and Harvard universities, and was admitted to the bar in 1895. He
practiced law in Boston from 1899 until 1902, and taught law at the University
of Wisconsin from 1902 to 1922. He was vice-governor-general of the Philippine
Islands from 1922 to 1927, and acting governor-general in 1927–1928 and 1929.
He was also secretary of the Department of Public Instruction. He extended the
public school system and improved the public health service. He was dean of
the College of Law of the University of Iowa from 1930 until 1934, president
of the State University of Iowa from 1934 until 1940, dean of the law school
at the University of Pittsburgh from 1940 to 1942, and professor of law at the
State University of Iowa from 1942 until his retirement in 1950. Died November
4, 1953, in Iowa City, Iowa. *References*: *NCAB* 44:56; *NYT*, November 5, 1953;
and *WWWA*.

GILMORE, GEORGE W(ILLIAM) (1858–1933). Educator, born May 12,
1858, in London, England. Gilmore graduated from Princeton University and
Union Theological Seminary, and was ordained in 1886. He went to Korea in
1886 in response to the request of the King of Korea, and was a teacher at the
Royal College (Yugyong Kongwon) in Seoul from 1886 to 1889. He wrote
Korea from Its Capital: With a Chapter on Mission (Philadelphia, 1892). He
was engaged in literary work and teaching at the Brooklyn Polytechnic Institute
from 1889 to 1892, and was an instructor and then professor at the Bangor
Technological Seminary from 1893 to 1899; a professor at Meadville (Pa.)
Theological School from 1899 to 1906; a bibliographer, associate editor, indexer,
and writer for the *New Schaff-Herzog Encyclopedia of Religious Knowledge* from
1905 to 1914; associate editor of *Homiletic Review* from 1911 to 1924; and
editor of that publication from 1924 until his death. Died August 22, 1933, in
Mere Point, Maine. *References*: *UnionTS*; and *WWWA*.

GILMORE, JOHN W(ASHINGTON) (1872–1942). Agriculturist, born May
9, 1872, in White County, Arkansas. Gilmore graduated from Cornell University.
He went to Wuchang, China, in 1898, and established there the first western
agricultural school and the first courses in western agriculture in China. He was
a teacher of science and nature study at the Honolulu Normal and Training
School in Hawaii Territory in 1900–1901. He was a fiber expert in the Department
of Agriculture in the Philippines in 1901–1902, and assisted in the establishment
of agricultural schools in the Philippines. He was also an agricultural advisor to
the commissioner of agriculture in India. He returned to the United States in
1902, was assistant professor of agriculture at Cornell University from 1902 to
1907, professor of agronomy at the Pennsylvania State College in 1907–1908,
organizer and president of the College of Hawaii (later University of Hawaii)
from 1908 to 1913, and professor of agronomy at the University of California
from 1913 until his death. He also served as agricultural expert to Chile, the

Dominican Republic, and Mexico. Died June 25, 1942, in Woodland, California. *References*: *NCAB* 40:462; *NYT*, June 26, 1942; and *WWWA*.

GINGLING COLLEGE. College for women founded in Nanking, China, in 1913 by the missions of the American Baptist Foreign Mission Society; the United Christian Missionary Society; the Methodist Episcopal Church; the Methodist Episcopal Church, South; and the Presbyterian Church in the U.S.A.; and opened in 1915. It moved in 1938 to Chengtu and returned to Nanking in 1946. It came under Communist control in 1949, and was merged into the National Gingling University in 1951. *References*: *Fenn*; *Lutz*; and Matilda S. Thurston and Ruth M. Chester, *Gingling College* (New York, 1955).

GLEECK, LEWIS E(DWARD), JR. (1912–   ). Diplomat and historian, born November 2, 1912, in Lyon, Mississippi. Gleeck graduated from Pomona College and studied at the University of Chicago. He entered the foreign service in 1940, and served in Canada, Finland, Sweden, Austria, Iceland, and Norway from 1940 until 1949. He worked in the office of Eastern European Affairs at the State Department in 1950–1951 and with the International Broadcasting Service from 1951 to 1953. He was the first secretary of embassy in Japan from 1953 to 1955; consul in charge of commercial and economic affairs at Osaka, Japan, from 1955 to 1957; officer in charge of economic affairs in the Office of North East Asian Affairs as special assistant of SEATO (Southeast Asia Treaty Organization) affairs in Washington, D.C., from 1958 to 1961; counselor in Pakistan in 1961–1962; and consul general in Manila from 1962 to 1968. He wrote *Americans on the Philippine Frontiers* (Manila, 1974); *American Business and Philippine Economic Development* (Manila, 1975); *American Institutions in the Philippines (1898–1941)* (Manila, 1976); *The Manila Americans: 1901–1964* (Manila, 1977); *Laguna in American Times* (Manila, 1981); *Nueva Ecija in American Times* (Manila, 1981); *The American Half-Century, 1898–1946* (Manila, 1984); *The American Governors-General and High Commissioners in the Philippines* (Quezon City, 1986); and *Dissolving the Colonial Bond: American Ambassadors in the Philippines, 1946–1984* (Manila, 1988). *References*: Lewis E. Gleeck, Jr., "The Philippines, 1962–1969: A Personal Memoir," *BAHC* 15 (January-March 1987) to (October-December 1987); Lewis E. Gleeck, Jr., "USAID: Philippine Land Reform and Rural Development (1966–1976)," *BAHC* 16 (January-February 1988) to (April-June 1988); and *WWA*.

GLEYSTEEN, WILLIAM H(ENRY) (1876–1948). Missionary educator, born July 17, 1876, in Alton, Iowa. Gleysteen graduated from the University of Michigan, Columbia University, and Union Theological Seminary, and was ordained in 1905. He was a missionary under the Board of Foreign Missions of the Presbyterian Church in the U.S.A. He served in the North China Mission in Shanghai, was principal of a boys' school from 1907 to 1927, helped coordinate educational work in North China, and was executive secretary of Yenching

University in 1918–1919. He did active relief work in 1905, 1918, and 1920–
1921. He was interned by the Japanese from 1941 to 1943. He returned to the
United States in 1943 and retired in 1947. Died January 17, 1948, in Jenkintown,
Pennsylvania. *References*: *NCAB* 35:520; *NYT*, January 19, 1948; and *UnionTS*.

GLOVER, ROBERT H(ALL) (1871–1947). Missionary, born October 17,
1871, in Leeds, Quebec, Canada. Glover attended the University of Toronto,
graduated from the New York Missionary Training College and New York
Medical College, and was ordained in 1896. He was a missionary under the
Christian and Missionary Alliance in China from 1894 until 1913. He helped
establish the mission in Kwangtung Province and founded the Bible Training
School at Wuchow and the Bible Institute in Wuchang. He was foreign secretary
of the Christian and Missionary Alliance after 1913, director of the missionary
course in the Moody Bible Institute (Chicago) from 1921 to 1926, assistant
home-director of the China Inland Mission in Philadelphia from 1926 to 1929
and its director from 1929 to 1943. He wrote *Ebenezer—A Record of Divine
Deliverance in China* (New York, 1905). Died March 23, 1947, in Philadelphia.
References: *NCAB* 37:311; *NYT*, March 25, 1947; and *WWWA*.

GLYNN, JAMES (1801–1871). Naval officer, born June 28, 1801, in Philadelphia. Glynn was appointed midshipman in the U.S. Navy in 1815. He served
in the Mexican War. He commanded the USS *Preble* in the East India Squadron
after 1848. He rescued a number of American seamen held captive in Nagasaki,
Japan, in 1849, including Ranald MacDonald.* His reports helped pave the way
for Matthew C. Perry's expedition. He served in the Union Navy during the
Civil War. Died May 13, 1871, in New Haven, Connecticut. *References*: *ACAB*;
DAB; and *WWWA*.

GOBLE, JONATHAN (1827–1896). Missionary, born March 4, 1827, in
Keuka, Steuben County, New York. Goble enlisted in the U.S. Marines in 1851,
and served as a marine on the USS *Mississippi* in Perry's expedition from 1853
to 1855. He graduated from Hamilton Institution (later Colgate University) and
Hamilton Theological Seminary, and was ordained in 1859. He was a missionary
under the American Baptist Free Mission Society in Japan from 1860 to 1872,
and under the American Baptist Missionary Union from 1872 until 1883. He
served in Yokohama but had to work for Yamanouchi, Lord of Tosa, at Nagasaki
in 1867–1868. He later returned to Yokohama. He translated the Gospel of
Matthew into Japanese and worked as an interpreter and translator. He invented
the first *jinrikisha*, a small two-wheeled carriage drawn by one or two men, in
Japan. He returned to the United States in 1883. Died May 1, 1896, in St. Louis.
References: Jonathan Goble "Journal," Ms., William Jewell College Library,
Liberty, Mo.; Earnest W. Clement, "Jonathan Goble and His Japanese Protege,"
Japan Evangelist, April 1913; *JBEWW*; F. Calvin Parker, "Jonathan Goble,

Missionary Extraordinary," Ms., American Baptist Historical Society, Rochester, N.Y.

GODDARD, JOSIAH (1813–1854). Missionary, born October 17, 1813, in Wendell, Massachusetts. Goddard attended Brown University, graduated from Newton Theological Institution (Newton Center, Mass.), and was ordained in 1838. He was a missionary under the American Baptist Missionary Union in Singapore in 1839–1840, and in Bangkok, Siam, from 1840 until 1847, serving among the Chinese. He moved to Ningpo, China in 1848 and served in Ningpo from 1849 until his death. He wrote *A Chinese and English Vocabulary, in the Tie Chiu Dialect* (Bangkok, 1847). Died September 4, 1854, in Ningpo, China. *References*: *ACAB*; and Francis W. Goddard, *Called to Cathay* (New York, 1948).

GOETTE, REMY (1856–1920), **GOETTE, ATHANASIUS** (1857–1908), and **GOETTE, JOHN CAPISTRAN** (1859–1919). Missionaries. Remy Goette was born April 27, 1856, in Paderborn, Germany. He entered the Franciscan order in 1873. His brother, Athanasius Goette, was born April 11, 1857, in Paderborn, Germany, and entered the Franciscan order in 1874. John Capistran Goette was born March 2, 1859, in Paderborn, Germany, and entered the Franciscan order in 1874. They came to the United States in 1875, and studied at St. Joseph's College (Teutopolis, Ill.). Remy was ordained in 1881. He was a missionary in China from 1881 until his death. The first Catholic priest to go to China from the United States, he served in Eastern Hupeh Province until 1888 and later in Northern Hupeh Province until his death, July 31, 1920, in Hankow, China. Athanasius was ordained in 1881. He was a missionary in China from 1881 until his death, and served in Sian, Shensi Province, from 1883 until 1905. He was appointed vicar apostolic of northern Shensi in 1905, and consecrated bishop in 1905, the first American bishop in China. Died March 29, 1908, in Tung-yuenfang. John Capistran was ordained in 1882. He was a missionary in China from 1884 until his death, and served in Hengchow, Hunan Province. Died August 1, 1919, in Siasniu, Shensi Province. *Reference*: Marion A. Habig, *Pioneering in China: The Story of the Rev. Francis Xavier Engbring, O.F.M., First Native American Priest in China, 1857–1895, with Sketches of His Missionary Comrades* (Chicago, 1930).

GOHEEN, JOHN (LAWRENCE) (1883–1948). Missionary, born December 10, 1883, in Kolhapur, Bombay Residency, India, to American missionary parents, and returned to the United States in 1890. Goheen graduated from Wooster College (Ohio) and the University of California. He was director of physical education at Occidental and Franklin colleges, and athletic director in a high school in Cleveland. He was a missionary under the Board of Foreign Missions of the Presbyterian Church in the U.S.A. in India. He was principal of an industrial and agricultural school at Sangli, near Bombay, after 1911;

executive director of the Presbyterian West India mission; and administrator in the Indian state of Ichalkaranji from 1930 to 1934. He was principal of the Allahabad Agricultural Institute from 1944 until his death. Died February 3, 1948, in New York City. *Reference*: *NYT*, February 4, 1948

GOODNOW, FRANK J(OHNSON) (1859–1939). Political scientist, born January 18, 1859, in Brooklyn, New York. Goodnow graduated from Amherst College and Columbia University, and studied at the École Libre des Sciences Politiques (Paris) and the University of Berlin. He was an instructor in history and a lecturer on administrative law at Columbia University from 1883 to 1887, adjunct professor there from 1887 to 1891, professor of administrative law from 1891 to 1903, and professor of administrative law and municipal science from 1903 to 1914. He was a legal advisor to the Chinese government in 1913–1914, and prepared a draft of a constitution for China. He wrote *China, an Analysis* (Baltimore, 1926). He was president of Johns Hopkins University from 1914 until his retirement in 1929. Died November 15, 1939, in Baltimore. *References*: Frank J. Goodnow Papers, Johns Hopkins University Library, Baltimore; *DAB S2*; *NCAB* 29:276; *NYT*, November 16, 1939; Noel Pugach, "Embarrassed Monarchist: Frank J. Goodnow and Constitutional Development in China, 1913–1915," *PHR* 42 (1973): 499–517; and *WWWA*.

GOODRICH, CHAUNCEY (1836–1925). Missionary, born June 4, 1836, in Hinsdale, Berkshire County, Massachusetts. Goodrich graduated from Williams College and Andover Theological Seminary, attended Union Theological Seminary, and was ordained in 1864. He was a missionary under the American Board of Commissioners for Foreign Missions (ABCFM) in China from 1865 until his death. He served in T'ungchou, near Peking. He was professor of astronomy and Christian evidences in the North China College (later North China Union College), and dean of the Gordon Missionary Theological Seminary from 1873 to 1911. He translated portions of the Gospels into Mongol, was involved in translating the Bible into Mandarin, and wrote *A Pocket Dictionary (Chinese–English and Pekinese Syllabary* (Peking, 1891), and *A Character Study in Mandarin Colloquial* (Peking, 1898). Died September 25, 1925, in Tungchou. *References*: *DAB*; *Hewitt*; and *WWWA*.

GOODRICH, JOSEPH KING (1850–1921). Author, born January 13, 1850, in Philadelphia. Goodrich organized the department of ethnology at the U.S. National Museum in Washington, D.C., from 1881 to 1884, and was assistant editor of the Smithsonian Institution from 1884 to 1886. He was a professor of English at the Imperial Government College in Osaka, Japan, and later at Kyoto, Japan, from 1886 to 1910. He wrote *The Coming China* (Chicago, 1911), and *Our Neighbors: The Japanese* (Chicago, 1913). Died August 13, 1921, in Brooklyn, New York. *Reference*: *WWWA*.

GOODYEAR TIRE AND RUBBER COMPANY. The company conducted initial surveys of rubber-growing land in Sumatra in 1916, 1927, and 1931, and in the Philippines in 1931. The plantations were appropriated in 1965 by the Indonesian government but were returned to Goodyear's control in 1967. *References*: Hugh Allen, *The House of Goodyear* (Cleveland, 1949); and Maurice O'Reilly, *The Goodyear Story* (Elmsford, N.Y., 1983).

GORDON, ANDREW (1828–1887). Missionary, born September 17, 1828, in Putnam, Washington County, New York. Gordon graduated from Franklin College (New Athens, Oh.) and the theological seminary at Canonsburg, Pennsylvania, and was ordained in 1854. He was a missionary under the Board of Foreign Missions of the Associate Presbyterian Synod (after 1858, the United Presbyterian Church of North America) in Sialkot, the Punjab, India, from 1855 until 1865 and from 1875 until 1885. He returned to the United States in 1865 because of ill health, but was back in India in 1875 and was stationed at Gurdaspur, Northern India. He wrote *Our India Mission: A Thirty Year History of the India Mission of the United Presbyterian Church* (Philadelphia, 1886). Died August 13, 1887, in Philadelphia. *References*: DAB; *EM*; *LC*; and *WWWA*.

GORDON, MARQUIS LAFAYETTE (1843–1900). Missionary, born July 18, 1843, in Waynesburg, Pennsylvania. Gordon graduated from Waynesburg College, Andover Theological Seminary, Long Island College Hospital (Brooklyn, N.Y.), and the College of Physicians and Surgeons (New York City). He served in the Union Army during the Civil War. He was a missionary under the American Board of Commissioners for Foreign Missions (ABCFM) in Japan from 1872 until his death. He was stationed first at Osaka and later was involved with the work of Doshisha University in Kyoto. He wrote *An American Missionary in Japan* (Boston, 1892), and his *Thirty Eventful Years: The Story of the American Board Mission in Japan, 1869–1899* (Boston, 1901) was published posthumously. Died November 4, 1900, in Kyoto, Japan. *Reference*: *EM*.

GORMAN, CHESTER ("CHET") (1938–1981). Archaeologist, born March 11, 1938. Gorman graduated from the University of Hawaii. He was associate professor of anthropology at the University of Pennsylvania, and associate curator in charge of the South and Southeast Asia section of the University Museum of Philadelphia after 1974. In 1965 he discovered Spirit Cave near the Burmese border in northern Thailand, and in 1973 he uncovered a Bronze Age grave at Ban Chiang, a village near the Laotian border, and was later codirector of the Ban Chiang project. He produced evidence of one of the world's earliest agricultural and Bronze Age societies. Died June 7, 1981, in Sacrament, California. *References*: *Asian Perspectives* 25 (1982–1983): 1–12; *NYT*, June 10, 1981; and *The* (London) *Times*, June 24, 1981.

GOULD, RANDALL C(HASE) (1898–1979). Journalist, born June 22, 1898, in Excelsior, Minnesota. Gould attended the University of Wisconsin. He was the news editor of the *Japan Times* in Tokyo in 1923–1924, news editor of the *Peking Daily News* in Peking, and bureau manager of the United Press in Peking, Shanghai, and Manila from 1925 to 1931. He was editor of the *Shanghai Evening Post and Mercury*, the only American-owned newspaper in Shanghai, from 1931 to 1941, and its editor and publisher from 1945 to 1949. He was in the United States from 1941 to 1945. He was forced to leave China again in 1949 after a dispute with Chinese Communist members of his staff. He worked for the *Denver Post* from 1949 to 1959, and for the *San Rafael Independent-Journal* from 1959 until his retirement in 1963. He wrote *Chungking Today* (Shanghai, 1941), and *China in the Sun* (New York, 1946). Committed suicide, October 23, 1979, in Mill Valley, California. *References*: Randall C. Gould Papers, Hoover Institution on War, Revolution and Peace, Stanford, Calif.; *CA*; and *NYT*, October 26, 1979.

GOURLEY, LOUIS HILL (1889–1950). Diplomat, born October 17, 1889, in Springfield, Illinois. Gourley graduated from the University of Illinois and George Washington University, and studied at Columbia University. He was vice-consul at Veracruz, Mexico, and Warsaw, Poland, from 1916 to 1921, and then consul in Warsaw, Lourenço Marques, Mozambique, Port Elizabeth, South Africa, and São Paolo, Brazil. He was consul in Medan, Sumatra, from 1931 to 1933; Hong Kong from 1933 to 1936; Shanghai from 1936 to 1938; Tsingtao in 1938; Kobe, Japan, from 1938 to 1940; Dairen, Manchuria, in 1940; and Harbin, Manchuria, in 1940–1941. He was interned by the Japanese in 1941–1942. Died March 28, 1950, in Detroit. *References*: *NYT*, March 30, 1950; and *WWWA*.

GOWDY, JOHN (1869–1963). Missionary, born December 7, 1869, in Glasgow, Scotland, and came to the United States as a youth. Gowdy graduated from Wesleyan University and Drew Theological Seminary. He was a missionary under the Board of Foreign Missions of the Methodist Episcopal Church in China from 1902 until 1940. He taught in the Anglo-Chinese College in Foochow from 1902 to 1904, and again from 1928 to 1930. He was president of the college from 1904 to 1923, and president of Fukien Christian University in Foochow from 1923 to 1927. He was elected bishop in 1930, and served as bishop of the Eastern Asia Central Conference of the Methodist Episcopal Church from 1930 until his retirement in 1940. Died September 9, 1963, in Winter Park, Florida. *Reference*: *EWM*.

GOWING, PETER G(ORDON) (1930–1983). Historian, born May 9, 1930, in Norwood, Massachusetts. Gowing attended Oberlin College; graduated from the University of Maine, Bangor Theological Seminary, and Boston University; and was ordained in 1954. He held a pastorate in North Berwick, Maine, from

1957 to 1960. He was assistant professor of history at Silliman University in Dumaguete City, Philippines, from 1960 to 1963; associate professor there from 1963 to 1967; and a professor from 1967 to 1971. He was the founder and first director of the Southeast Asian Studies program from 1968 to 1971; regional professor at the South East Asia Graduate School of Theology, Singapore, from 1971 to 1974, and director of the Dansalan Research Center in Marawi City, Philippines, from 1974 until his death. He wrote *Mosque and Moro: A Study of Muslims in the Philippines* (Manila, 1964); *Islands under the Cross: The Story of the Church in the Philippines* (Manila, 1967); *The Muslim Filipinos* (Manila, 1975); *Mandate in Moroland: The American Government of Muslim Filipinos, 1899–1920* (Quezon City, 1977); and *Muslim Filipinos—Heritage and Horizon* (Quezon City, 1979). He was coauthor of *Islam and Muslims: Some Basic Information* (Quezon City, 1981) and coeditor of *Acculturation in the Philippines: Essays on Changing Societies* (Quezon City, 1971). Died July 10, 1983, in the Islamic City of Marawi, Philippines. *References*: *CA*; *DAS*; Moctar I. Matuan, "Dr. Peter Gordon Gowing," *Mindanao Journal* 10 (July–September 1983): 4–9; and "Special Issue in Honor of Two American Scholars: Donn V. Hart and Peter G. Gowing," *Kinaadman: A Journal of the Southern Philippines* 7 (1985), entire issue.

GRABAU, AMADEUS WILLIAM (1870–1946). Geologist and paleontologist, born January 9, 1870, in Cedarburgh, Pennsylvania. Grabau graduated from Massachusetts Institute of Technology and Harvard University. He was a professor of geology at Rensselaer Polytechnic Institute in 1900–1901, a lecturer in paleontology at Columbia University in 1901–1902, adjunct professor there from 1902 to 1905, and professor after 1905. His pro-German views forced him to leave Columbia University in 1919, and he immigrated to China. He was a professor of paleontology at the National University of Peking after 1920, and chief paleontologist of the National Geological Survey of China and manager of its paleontological laboratory. He wrote *Stratigraphy of China* (Peking, 1923). He was interned by the Japanese during World War II. Died March 20, 1946, in Peking. *References: DAB S4*; *DSB*; *NCAB* 34:89; *NYT*, March 27, 1946; and *Science* 103 (June 7, 1946): 690.

GRAHAM, DAVID CROCKETT (1884–1961). Animal collector, born March 21, 1884, in Green Forest, Arkansas. Graham graduated from Whitman College, Rochester Theological Seminary, and the University of Chicago, and was ordained in 1911. He was a missionary under the American Baptist Foreign Mission Society in China from 1911 to 1948. He served in Suifu, Szechwan Province, from 1911 to 1931, and in Chengtu from 1931 to 1948. He was involved in work for the blind, and was instrumental in reopening the Chengtu orphanage for the blind. He undertook a number of journeys to west China as a missionary and collector of natural history specimens for the Smithsonian Institution. His studies were concentrated in Szechwan Province from 1911 to 1948, and he

spent twenty years in the city of Suifu. Between 1919 and 1939, he headed
fourteen summer expeditions to Szechwan and the China-Tibetan border. In 1929
he collected the first giant panda skin in the Smithsonian Institution. He was an
associate in biology at the Smithsonian from 1931 until his death. He wrote
Religion in Szechuan Province, China (Washington, 1928); *Song and Stories of
the Ch'uan Miao* (Washington, D.C., 1954); *The Customs and Religion of the
Ch'iang* (Washington, D.C., 1958); and *Folk Religion in Southwest China*
(Washington, D.C., 1961). Died September 15, 1961, in Englewood, Colorado.
References: David Crocket Graham Papers, Smithsonian Institution Archives,
Washington, D.C.; Photographs Collection, National Anthropological Archives,
Washington, D.C.; and *The Watchman-Examiner*, October 19, 1961.

GRAHAM, FRANK P(ORTER) (1886–1972). Educator and government official, born October 14, 1886, in Fayetteville, North Carolina. Graham graduated
from the University of North Carolina and Columbia University, and studied at
the University of Chicago and the London School of Economics. He was a
teacher at Raleigh High School, served during World War I. He was a professor
of history at the University of North Carolina from 1914 to 1927, dean of students
there in 1919–1920, and president of the University of North Carolina from 1930
until 1949. He was appointed a U.S. senator in 1949–1950 but was defeated in
the 1950 election. He was a member of the Good Offices Committee between
The Netherlands and Indonesia on the USS *Renville*.* As UN Representative
for India and Pakistan in their dispute over Kashmir from 1951 to 1967, he
sought in vain to resolve the dispute between the two nations. Died February
16, 1972, in Raleigh, North Carolina. *References*: Frank P. Graham Papers,
Southern Historical Collection, University of North Carolina Library, Chapel
Hill, N.C.; Warren Ashby, *Frank Porter Graham, a Southern Liberal* (Winston-
Salem, N.C., 1980); *BDAC*; *BDAE*; *CB 1951; NCAB D*:409; *NYT*, February 17,
1972; and *WWWA*.

GRANGER, WALTER (WILLIS) (1872–1941). Paleontologist, born November 7, 1872, in Middletown Springs, Vermont. Granger was employed by the
American Museum of Natural History after 1890, serving successively as an
assistant in taxidermy and a field collector in zoology. He was transferred to the
department of vertebrate paleontology in 1909, was assistant curator of fossil
mammals from 1909 to 1911, associate curator from 1911 to 1927, and curator
after 1927. He participated in nineteen collecting expeditions to the western
United States between 1896 and 1918, and in an expedition to Fayum, Egypt,
in 1907. He was paleontologist and second in command in the museum's Central
Asiatic expeditions from 1921 to 1931, and spent five summers in the Gobi
Desert of Mongolia. During three winters, he visited a remote region of Szechwan. Died September 6, 1941, in Lusk, Wyoming. *References*: *DAB S3*; *DSB*;
NCAB 35:405; *NYT*, September 8, 1941; and *WWWA*.

GRANT, JOHN B(LACK) (1890–1962). Physician, born August 31, 1890, in Ningpo, China, to Canadian missionary parents. Grant graduated from Acadia University (Wolfville, Nova Scotia, Canada), the University of Michigan Medical School, and the School of Hygiene and Public Health of Johns Hopkins University. He served on the staff of the international health division of the Rockefeller Foundation from 1918 until 1960, was professor of public health at Peking Union Medical College from 1922 to 1933, and was head of its department of hygiene and public health. He was a representative of the international health division at the Rockefeller Foundation in the Far East from 1937 to 1939. He was director of the All India Institute of Hygiene and Public Health in Calcutta from 1939 to 1945; director of the European region of the international health division of the Rockefeller Foundation in Paris, France, from 1948 to 1952; and consultant in public health to the U.S. Economic Cooperation Administration in Southeast Asia in 1950. He was associate director of their division of medicine and public health from 1951 to 1956, and consultant in the Department of Health of Puerto Rico after 1956. Died October 16, 1962, in Hato Rey, Puerto Rico. *References*: Mary M. Butler, *An American Transplant: The Rockefeller Foundation and Peking Union Medical College* (Berkeley, Calif., 1980), ch. 6; *NYT*, October 18, 1962; Conrad Seipp, ed., *Health Care for the Community: Selected Papers of Dr. John B. Grant* (Baltimore, 1963); and *WWWA*.

GRAVES, FREDERICK R(OGERS) (1858–1940). Missionary, born October 24, 1858, in Auburn, New York, and grew up in Geneva, New York. Graves graduated from Hobart College and General Theological Seminary, and was ordained in 1882. He was a missionary under the Domestic and Foreign Missionary Society of the Protestant Episcopal Church in United States of America in China from 1881 until his retirement. He served at Wuchang from 1881 to 1893, and was professor at the theological school of St. John's College in Shanghai from 1885 to 1887. He was consecrated missionary bishop of Shanghai and the Yangtze Valley in 1893 and served until 1901, and then served as bishop of Shanghai only, in charge of the Kiangsu Province, from 1901 until his retirement in 1937. Died May 17, 1940, in Shanghai, China. *References*: Frederick Rogers Graves Papers, Church Historical Society Library and Archives, Austin, Texas; *DAB S2*; *NYT*, May 18, 1940; an *WWWA*.

GRAVES, ROSEWELL H(OBART) (1833–1912). Medical missionary, born May 29, 1833, in Baltimore, Maryland. Graves graduated from St. Mary's College and studied medicine. He was a medical missionary under the Foreign Mission Board of the Southern Baptist Convention in China from 1856 until his death. He served n the Kwangtung and Kwangsi provinces of South China. He founded Graves Theological Seminary. He wrote *Forty Years in China, or, China in Transition* (Baltimore, 1895). Died June 3, 1912, in Canton, China. *References*: *DAB*; and *ESB*.

GRAVES, WILLIAM SIDNEY (1865–1940). Army officer, born March 27, 1865, in Mount Calm, Texas. Graves graduated from the U.S. Military Academy in 1899 and was commissioned in the infantry. He served in the Philippine-American War from 1899 to 1902, and was a member of the General Staff from 1909 until 1918. He was the commander of the American Expeditionary Force in Siberia from 1918 until 1920. He was the commanding general successively of the First Infantry Brigade, the First Division, the Sixth Army Corps Area, the Panama Canal Division, and the Panama Canal Department. He retired in 1928. He wrote *America's Siberian Adventure* (New York, 1931). Died February 27, 1940, in Shrewbury, New Jersey. *References*: *DAB S2*; *DAMIB*; *NYT*, February 28, 1940; and *WWWA*.

GREATHOUSE, CLARENCE R(IDGLEY) (1846–1899). Legal advisor, born September 17, 1846, in Woodford County, Kentucky, and grew up in California. Greathouse practiced law in San Francisco after 1870, and was general manager of the *San Francisco Examiner*. He was consul general in Kanagawa (Yokohama), Japan, from 1886 to 1889, and was legal advisor to the Korean government and vice president of the Home Office after 1890. He was also head of the Korean Post Office Department and counselor to the Korean Minister of Foreign Affairs from 1893 to 1898. In addition, he was confidential advisor to the King of Korea on foreign affairs. Died October 21, 1899, in Seoul, Korea. *References*: *DAB*; and *WWWA*.

GREEN, JOHN C(LEVE) (1800–1875). Merchant, born April 4, 1800, in Maidenhead (later Lawrenceville), New Jersey. Green entered the employment of a New York merchants' firm and was supercargo of its ships from 1823 to 1835. He joined Russell and Company in Canton in 1833, and became head of the firm in 1834. He retired in 1839 and returned to the United States. He was later involved in railroads and philanthropy. Died April 29, 1875, in New York City. *References*: *ACAB*; *BDABL*; *DAB*; *DADH*; NCAB 11:336; and *WWWA*.

GREEN, SAMUEL FISK (1822–1884). Medical missionary, born October 10, 1822, in Green Hill, Worcester, Massachusetts. Green graduated from the College of Physicians and Surgeons (New York City). He practiced medicine in Worcester. He was a medical missionary under the American Board of Commissioners for Foreign Missions (ABCFM) in Ceylon from 1847 until 1873. He served in Jaffna, Batticota, and Manepay. In 1848 he began training Tamil men as physicians, and prepared medical textbooks in the Tamil language. He returned to the United States in 1873 because of ill health, and settled in Green Hill. Died May 28, 1884, in Green Hill, Worcester, Massachusetts. *References*: Ebenezer Coulter, comp., *Life and Letters of Samuel Fisk Green, M.D., of Green Hill* (New York, 1891); and *EM*.

GREENE, DANIEL CROSBY (1843–1913). Missionary, born February 11, 1843, in Roxbury, Massachusetts. Greene graduated from Dartmouth College, attended Chicago Theological Seminary, and graduated from Andover Theological Seminary. He was a missionary under the American Board of Commissioners for Foreign Missions (ABCFM) in Japan from 1869 until his death. He served in Kobe until 1874, when he was transferred to Yokohama and was involved in the translation of the New Testament into Japanese. He served in Kyoto from 1881 to 1890, helping to develop Doshisha University, and in Tokyo after 1903. Died September 15, 1913, in Tokyo. *References*: *DAB*; *NCAB* 23:324; *NYT*, September 16, 1913; and *WWWA*.

GREENE, PHILLIPS FOSTER (1892–1967). Medical missionary, born May 30, 1892, in Van, Turkey, to American missionary parents. Greene graduated from Amherst College and Harvard Medical School. He was a professor of anatomy at Constantinople College (Turkey) from 1921 to 1923, assistant professor of general surgery at the University of Wisconsin from 1927 to 1931, professor of surgery at the Hsiang-ya Medical College in Changsha, China, from 1931 until 1941, acting dean there from 1931 to 1936, and director of the American Red Cross China relief unit in 1941–1942. He returned to the United States in 1943, was associate dean of the Long Island College of Medicine from 1943 to 1950, and senior surgeon of the U.S. Public Health Service, serving in the Department of Surgery of the University of Rangoon and Rangoon General Hospital in Rangoon, Burma, from 1951 to 1958. He returned to the United Sates in 1958 and was in medical practice after 1959. Died April 11, 1967, in New Richmond, Ohio. His wife **RUTH ALTMAN GREENE** (1896–   ), wrote *Hsiang-Ya Journal* (Hamden, Conn., 1977). *References*: Phillips Foster Greene Papers, Yale-China Association Collection, Yale University Library, New Haven, Conn.; and *Amherst*.

GREENE, ROGER S(HERMAN) (1881–1947). Association official, son of Daniel Crosby Greene,* born May 29, 1881, in Westborough, Massachusetts. Greene graduated from Harvard University. He served in the consular service from 1911 to 1914 in Brazil, Japan, Siberia, Manchuria, and China, and was consul general in Hankow from 1911 to 1914. He joined the Rockefeller Foundation in 1914 as a member of the foundation's commission that surveyed the medical and public health needs of China, and resident director in China of the China Medical Board until 1935. He was vice president of the Rockefeller Foundation in the Far East from 1927 to 1929, and acting director of the Peking Union Medical College in 1927. He resigned from the China Medical Board in 1934 and from the Peking Union Medical College in 1935. He was chairman of the American Committee for Non-Participation in Japanese Aggression from 1938 to 1941, and associate director of William Allen White's Committee to Defend America by Aiding the Allies in 1940–1941. Died March 27, 1947, in West Palm Beach, Florida. *References*: Roger S. Greene Papers, Houghton

Library, Harvard University; Mary B. Bullock, *An American Transplant: The Rockefeller Foundation and Peking Union Medical College* (Berkeley, Calif., 1980), ch. 3; Warren I. Cohen, *The Chinese Connection: Roger S. Greene, Thomas W. Lamont, George E. Sokolosky and American-East Asian Relations* (New York, 1978), ch. 3; *DAB S4*; *NYT*, March 29, 1947; and *WWWA*.

GREENE, WARWICK (1879–1929). Colonial administrator, born December 18, 1879, in Washington, D.C. Greene graduated from Harvard University and Harvard Law School. He served during the Spanish-American War. He was secretary to W. Cameron Forbes* in the Philippines from 1905 to 1910, and director of the Bureau of Public Works in the Philippines from 1910 to 1915. He returned to the United States in 1916. He was director of War Relief Commission of the Rockefeller Foundation in 1916, and a member of the American Red Cross Commission in France and Belgium in 1917. He served in the air service during World War I, was attached to the American Commission to Negotiate Peace in 1919, was chief of the U.S. mission to Finland, Estonia, Latvia, and Lithuania. He was later vice president of the Petroleum Heat and Power Company of Boston, and president of the New England Oil Refining Company. Died November 18, 1929, in Boston. *References*: Richard W. Hale, ed., *The Letters of Warwick Greene, 1915–1928* (Boston, 1931); *Pier*; *NCAB* 24:191; and *WWWA*.

GREGG, RICHARD BARTLETT (1885–). Author, born February 14, 1885, in Colorado Springs, Colorado. Gregg graduated from Harvard University and Harvard Law School. He practiced law from 1911 to 1913, and accompanied his brother-in-law on a business trip to India in 1913. He then became involved in industrial labor relations work, and served in the U.S. Shipping Board during World War I. He was back in India from 1925 to 1928, taught village school in Simla, and studied social, economic, and political conditions there. He lived for seven months in Gandhi's ashram on the Sabarmati, and became a personal friend of Gandhi. He visited Java, Ceylon, and India in 1930. He became a force in the American nonviolence movement. He wrote *Economics of Khaddar* (Triplicane, Madras, 1928); *The Psychology and Strategy of Gandhi's Non-Violent Resistance* (Madras, 1929); *Gandhÿi's Satyagraha: Or Nonviolent Resistance* (Triplicane, Madras, 1930); *Gandhism Versus Socialism* (New York, 1932); and *The Power of Non-Violence* (Philadelphia, 1934). He became involved in the biodynamic method of farming and gardening after 1941. He returned to India from 1956 to 1958, and taught Gandhian economics in Gandhigram, Madura State. *Reference*: Harvard University, *Harvard Class of 1907 Fiftieth Anniversary Report* (Cambridge, 1957), pp. 270–75.

GREW, JOSEPH CLARK (1880–1965). Diplomat, born May 27, 1880, in Boston. Grew graduated from Harvard University. He traveled in East Asia, and wrote *Sport and Travel in the Far East* (Boston, 1910). He entered the foreign service in 1904, and served in Cairo, Mexico City, and Moscow. He was second secretary in Berlin from 1908 to 1911, first secretary in Vienna in 1911–1912 and again in Berlin from 1912 to 1918, and chief of the Division of Western European Affairs in the State Department from 1918 to 1920. He was the U.S. minister to Denmark in 1920–1921, U.S. representative to the Lausanne Conference on Near Eastern Affairs in 1922–1923, undersecretary of state from 1924 to 1927, and ambassador to Turkey from 1927 to 1932. He was ambassador to Japan from 1932 until 1941. Struggling to hold back the growing conflict between the United States and Japan, he tried to avert a war. He was special assistant to the secretary of state from 1942 to 1944, director of the Far Eastern Affairs Division in 1944, and undersecretary of state in 1944–1945. He retired in 1945. He wrote *Ten Years in Japan* (New York, 1944), and *Turbulant Era: A Diplomatic Record of Forty Years, 1904-1945*, ed. Walter Johnson (Boston, 1952). Died May 25, 1965, at Manchester-by-the-Sea, Massachusetts. *References*: Joseph C. Grew Papers, Houghton Library, Harvard University; *DAB S8*; *DADH*; K. Martin Friedrich, "In Search of a Far Eastern Policy: Joseph Grew, Stanley Hornbeck, and American-Japanese Relations, 1937–1941," Ph.D. diss., Washington State University, 1974; *KEJ*; *NCAB* 55:163; *NYT*, May 27, 1965; and *WWWA*.

GRIFFIN, LAWRENCE EDMONDS (1874–1949). Zoologist, born September 10, 1874, in Dalton, New York. Griffin graduated from Hamline and Johns Hopkins universities, and studied at the University of Minnesota. He was a professor of biology at Missouri Valley College (Marshall, Mo.) from 1902 to 1908, and a research assistant at the Carnegie Institute in 1904–1905. He came to the Philippines in 1908, was assistant professor of zoology at the government medical school in Manila, and then associate professor at the University of the Philippines from 1908 to 1913 and dean of the College of Liberal Arts from 1910 to 1913. He developed the field of herpetology in the Philippines. He returned to the United States in 1913, and was a professor of zoology at the University of Pittsburgh from 1914 to 1920, and a professor of biology at Reed College (Portland, Ore.) after 1920. Died September 12, 1949, in Portland, Oregon. *References*: *NCAB* 37:262; *NYT*, September 13, 1949; and *WWWA*.

GRIFFIN, SUSAN ELIZABETH CILLEY (1851–1926). Missionary, born February 28, 1851, in Boston. Griffin graduated from Hillsdale College, attended New York Medical College, and was ordained in 1893. She was a Free Baptist missionary to India. She served at Midnapore from 1873 to 1876, at Balasore from 1883 to 1893, and at Santipore from 1904 to 1909. She was later a co-pastor in Elmira Heights, New York, from 1893 to 1904, and in Keuka Park, New York, from 1909 to 1914. She wrote *The Life of a Hindu Woman* (Keuka Park, N.Y., 1927). *Reference*: Zebina F. Griffin, *The Biography of Libbie Cilley Griffin* (Keuka Park, N.Y., 1927).

GRIFFIN MISSION (1950). United States economic survey mission to Southeast Asia in 1950, which visited Indochina, Malaya, Singapore, Burma, Thailand, and Indonesia, and recommended the initiation of U.S. technical and economic assistance to those countries. The mission was headed by R. Allen Griffin, editor-publisher of the Monterey (Calif.) *Peninsular Herald* and deputy chief of the China mission of the Economic Cooperation Administration in 1948–1949. *Reference*: Samuel P. Hayes, ed., *The Beginning of American Aid to Southeast Asia: The Griffin Mission of 1950* (Lexington, Mass., 1971).

GRIFFING, JOHN B. (1885–1962). Agriculturist, born December 4, 1885, in Tecumseh, Kansas. Griffing graduated from Kansas Agricultural College and Columbia University, and attended Drake University and Union Theological Seminary. He was a professor at the Normal School in Tempe, Arizona, from 1913 to 1919. He was a professor of agricultural science at the University of Nanking, China, from 1919 until 1927, and director of the extension there from 1922 to 1927. From 1920 to 1922, he directed a cotton improvement program and tried later to implement it. He was an instructor in social science at San Bernardino (Calif.) Junior College from 1927 to 1929, and its president from 1929 to 1933. He was director of education for the Civil Conservation Corps (CCC) in San Francisco from 1933 to 1936; director of the agricultural college at Vicosa, Minas Geraes, Brazil, from 1936 to 1939; director of the American International Association at São Paolo, Brazil, from 1945 to 1953; and consultant for Nelson Rockefeller's Latin American Projects after 1953. Died November 12, 1962, in Columbia, South Carolina. *References*: Randall E. Stross, *The Stubborn Earth: American Agriculturists on Chinese Soil, 1898–1937* (Berkeley, Calif., 1986), pp. 123–33; and *UnionTS*.

GRIFFIS, WILLIAM ELLIOT (1843–1928). Educator and author, born September 17, 1843, in Philadelphia. Griffis graduated from Rutgers University. He came to Japan in 1870, taught science at Fukui in Echizen (now Fukui Prefecture) in 1871–1872, and organized the first chemical laboratory in Japan. He then taught chemistry and physics at one of the schools that was later to form part of Tokyo University from 1882 to 1884. He returned to the United States in 1874. He wrote *The Mikado's Empire* (New York, 1876), which had gone through twelve editions by 1912; *Corea—The Hermit Nation* (New York, 1882); *Japan—In History, Folk-lore, and Art* (New York, 1892); *The Religions of Japan from the Dawn of History to the Era of Meiji* (New York, 1895); *American in the East* (New York, 1899); *The Japanese Nation in Evolution* (New York, 1907); and *The Mikado—Institution and Person* (New York, 1915); as well as biographies of Guido H. F. Verbeck,* James C. Hepburn,* Samuel Robbins Brown,* Henry G. Appenzeller,* and Townsend Harris.* He held pastorates in Schenectady and Ithaca, New York, and in Boston. Died February 5, 1928, in Winter Park, Florida. *References*: William Elliot Griffis Papers, Rutgers University Libraries, New Brunswick, N.J.; *BDAE*; Edward R. Beauchamp, *An American Teacher in Early Meiji Japan* (Honolulu, 1976); Ardath Burks, "William Elliot Griffis, Class of 1869," *Journal of the Rutgers University Library* 29 (1966); 91–100; Ardath W. Burks and Jerome Cooperman, "The William Elliot Griffis Collection," *JAS* 28 (1960): 61–68; *DAB*; Hazel T. Jones, "The Griffis Thesis and Meiji Policy towards Hired Foreigners," in *The Modernizers: Overseas Students, Foreign Employees, and Meiji Japan*, ed. Ardath Burks (Boulder, Colo., 1985), pp. 219–52; *KEJ: NCAB* 21:118; Umetenai Noboru, "William Elliot Griffis' Studies in Japanese History and Their Significance," in *The Modernizers: Overseas Students, Foreign Employees, and Meiji Japan*, ed. Ardath Burks (Boulder, 1985). pp. 393–407; *NYT*, February 6, 1928; Robert A. Rosenstone, *Mirror in the Shrine: American Encounters with Meiji Japan* (Cambridge, Mass., 1988); *WWWA*; Shoji Yamamoto, "William Elliot Griffis as an Interpreter of the Meiji Society: The First American Envoy to New Japan," Ph.D. diss., State University of New York at Buffalo, 1987; and Motoyama Yukohiko, "The Education Policy of Fukui and William Elliot Griffis," in *The Modernizers: Overseas Students, Foreign Employees, and Meiji Japan*, ed. Ardath Burks (Boulder, 1985), pp. 265–300.

GRINNAN, R(ANDOLPH) BRYAN (1860–1942). Missionary, born April 21, 1860, in Brampton, Madison County, Virginia. Grinnan attended Hampden-Sidney College, the University of Virginia, and Union Theological Seminary (Va.), and was ordained in 1885. He was a missionary under the Board of Foreign Missions of the Presbyterian Church in the United States in Japan from 1885 until 1898, teaching in schools at Kochi, Province of Tosa, Island of Shikoku. He returned to the United States n 1898, and held pastorates at Louisville, Kentucky; Henderson, North Carolina; Columbia, South Carolina; and Norfolk, Virginia; until his retirement in 1936. Died July 1942, in Norfolk, Virginia. *References*: R. Bryan Grinnan Papers, University of Virginia Library, Charlottesville, Va.; and Robert L. Hilldrup, *An American Missionary in Meiji Japan* (Norfolk, Va., 1970).

GRINNELL, HENRY WALTON (1843–1920). Naval officer, born November 19, 1843, in New York City. Grinnell attended the New York Free Academy (later the College of the City of New York). He entered the U.S. Navy in 1861 and served in the Civil War. He was discharged in 1868. In 1868 he accepted a commission as captain in the Imperial Japanese Navy and trained seamen at the Heigo Naval School. He also served as inspector general with the rank of rear admiral from 1868 to 1870. He saw active service at the Battle of the Yalu River during the Sino-Japanese War, and was discharged as a vice admiral at the end of the war. He returned to the United States and served later during the Spanish-American War. He was also a naval advisor to the Republic of Ecuador in 1872–1873. He made several trips into little-known parts of Asia, and described a trip to Eastern Manchuria and Korea in the *Journal of the American*

Geographical Society of 1873. Died September 2, 1920. *References*: *DAB*; and *NCAB* 22:380.

GRISWOLD, HERVEY DEWITT (1860–1945). Missionary, born May 24, 1860, in Dryden, New York. Griswold graduated from Union College (Schenectady, N.Y.) and Union Theological Seminary, studied at the universities of Oxford and Berlin, and was ordained in 1910. He was a missionary under the Board of Foreign Missions of the Presbyterian Church in the U.S.A. in India from 1890 to 1926, first as district missionary from 1890 to 1894, and then as a professor of philosophy at Forman Christian College in Lahore from 1894 to 1914. He was secretary of the Council of American Presbyterian Missions in India from 1914 to 1919 and from 1923 to 1926. He retired in 1928. He wrote *Brahman, a Study in the History of Indian Philosophy* (New York, 1900); *The Religion of the Rigveda* (New York, 1923); and *Insights into Modern Hinduism* (New York, 1934). Died May 15, 1945, in Stratford, Connecticut. *References: NYT*, May 19, 1945; and *WWWA*.

GROFF, G(EORGE) WEIDMAN ("DADDY") (1884–1954). Agricultural missionary, born March 29, 1884, in Annville, Pennsylvania. Groff graduated from Pennsylvania State University. He was a professor of horticulture at Lingnan University in Canton after 1907. He organized the College of Agriculture of Lingnan University and was its dean from 1921 to 1924. He made various agricultural explorations in South China, Indochina, Siam, and Malaya from 1911 to 1940, and led the National Geographical Society–Lingnan expedition into Northwestern Kwangsi, China, in 1937. He wrote *Agricultural Reciprocity between America and China* (New York, 1911); *The Lychee and Lungan* (New York, 1921); and *Plants of Lungt'aushan and Vicinities, North River Area, Kwangtung Province, China* (Canton, 1930). Died December 4, 1954, in Laurel, Florida. *References*: G. Weidman Groff Papers, Pennsylvania State University Libraries, University Park, Pa.; *NYT*, December 7, 1954; and *WWWA*.

GRUEN, OLIVE DOROTHY [GRÜN, OLIVA DOROTHEA] (1883–1963). Missionary, born June 20, 1883, in St. Louis, Missouri. Gruen graduated from Valparaiso University and attended Moody Bible Institute (Chicago). She taught in St. Louis until 1921. She was a missionary under the Missionary Board of the Lutheran Church–Missouri Synod in China from 1921 until 1960. She taught in a school for girls and women in Hankow from 1922 to 1926, was supervisor of the girls' department of the orphanage at Enshih, and taught in high school at Wanhsien. She returned to China in 1945 and served until 1949. Denied reentry in 1950, she served in Taiwan from 1951 until 1960. She returned to the United States in 1960. Died May 11, 1963. *Reference: LC*.

GULICK, JOHN THOMAS (1832–1923). Missionary, born March 13, 1832, in Waimea, Kauai, Hawaii Islands. Gulick graduated from Williams College and studied at Union Theological Seminary. He was a missionary under the American Board of Commissioners for Foreign Missions (ACBFM) at Kanagawa, Japan, from 1862 to 1864; in Peking, China, in 1864–1865; in Kalgan, China, from 1865 to 1875; in Kobe, Japan, from 1875 to 1882; and in Osaka, Japan, from 1882 to 1899. He returned to the United States in 1899, resided in Oberlin, Ohio, from 1900 to 1905, and went to Hawaii in 1906. He made original contributions to the theory of evolution and had some impact on the acceptance of the Darwinian theory in Japan. Died April 16, 1923, in Honolulu, Hawaii. *References*: *DAB*; Addison Gulick, *Evolutionist and Missionary: John Thomas Gulick, Portrayed through Documents and Discussions* (Chicago, 1932); *Hewitt*; Watanabee Masao, "John Thomas Gulick: American Evolutionist and Missionary in Japan," *Japanese Studies in the History of Science* no. 5 (1966): 140–49; and *NCAB* 11:463.

GULICK, LUTHER HALSEY (1828–1891). Missionary, brother of Orramel Hinkcley Gulick,* born June 10, 1828, in Honolulu, Hawaii. Gulick graduated from the Medical College of the University of the City of New York, and was ordained in 1850. He was a medical missionary under the American Board of Commissioners for Foreign Missions (ABCFM) at Ponape and Ebon in the Caroline Islands from 1852 to 1863, and secretary of the Hawaiian Evangelical Association from 1863 to 1870. He inaugurated ABCFM missions in Spain and Italy from 1871 to 1874. He was the agent for East Asia for the American Bible Society; founded Bible House in Yokohama, Japan; and worked in China. He edited *Chinese Record and Missionary Journal* from 1885 to 1889, and founded the *Medical Missionary Journal*. Died April 8, 1891, in Springfield, Massachusetts. *References*: *DAB*; and *NCAB* 26:370.

GULICK, ORRAMEL H(INCKLEY) (1830–1923). Missionary, brother of Luther Halsey Gulick,* born October 7, 1830, in Honolulu to American missionary parents. Gulick studied at Punahou School (later Oahu College), and was ordained in 1862. He was a missionary under the American Board of Commissioners for Foreign Missions (ABCFM) in Hawaii from 1862 until 1874. He was transferred to the Japan mission in 1871 and served until 1894. He was stationed at Kobe and later at Osaka and Niigata. In 1875, he began publishing *Weekly Miscellany*, a Christian newspaper. He was reassigned to Hawaii in 1893, and served until his death. Died September 23, 1923, in Honolulu. *Reference*: *CDCWM*.

GULICK, SIDNEY L(EWIS) (1860–1945). Missionary, son of Luther Halsey Gulick,* born April 10, 1860, in Ebon in the Marshall Islands and grew up in Hawaii, Europe, and California. Gulick graduated from Dartmouth College, attended Union Theological Seminary, and was ordained in 1886. He was a missionary under the American Board of Commissioners for Foreign Missions (ABCFM) in Japan from 1887 until 1913. He worked in Kumamoto and Matsuyama in southern Japan for more than ten years. He wrote *Evolution of the Japanese, Social and Psychic* (New York, 1903). He was a professor of theology at Doshisha University in Kyoto from 1906 until 1913. He was also a lecturer on comparative religion at the Kyoto Imperial University, and became associated with some of Japan's most progressive political leaders. He was the organizer and vice president of the American Peace of Society of Japan. He returned to the United States in 1913, wrote *The American Japanese Problem: A Study of the Racial Relations of the East and the West* (New York, 1914). He was secretary of the Commission on Relations with Japan of the Federal Council of the Churches of Christ in America from 1914 to 1934, secretary of the National Committee on American-Japanese Relations from 1921 to 1934, and secretary of the National Committee for Constructive Immigration Legislation from 1919 to 1934. He wrote *The Winning of the Far East: A Study of the Christian Movement in China, Korea and Japan* (New York, 1923). He retired in 1934. Died December 20, 1945, in Boise, Idaho. *References*: *DAB S3*; *DADH*; *NYT*, December 24, 1945; Sandra C. Taylor, *Advocate of Understanding: Sidney Gulick and the Search for Peace with Japan* (Kent, Ohio, 1984); and Sandra C. Taylor, ''Japan's Missionary to the Americans: Sidney L. Gulick and America's Interwar Relations with Japan,'' *DH* 4 (1980): 387–407.

GUTHRIE, GEORGE W(ILKINS) (1848–1917). Lawyer and diplomat, born September 5, 1848, in Pittsburgh, Pennsylvania. Guthrie graduated from the Western University of Pennsylvania (later the University of Pittsburgh) and Columbian College (later George Washington University), and was admitted to the bar in 1869. He practiced law in Pittsburgh after 1869, and was mayor of Pittsburgh from 1906 to 1909. He took an active part in Democratic Party politics, and was chairman of the Pennsylvania State Democratic Committee in 1912. He was U.S. ambassador to Japan from 1913 until his death. He tried to ease tensions between Japan and the United States, and handled German affairs in Japan after the outbreak of World War I. Died March 8, 1917, in Tokyo, Japan. *References*: *DAB*; *DADH*; *NCAB* 18:19; *NYT*, March 9, 1917; and *WWWA*.

H

HABERSHAM, ALEXANDER WYLLY (1826–1883). Naval officer, born March 24, 1826, in New York City. Habersham graduated from the U.S. Naval Academy in 1848. He served with the Pacific Squadron in 1851–1852, and was a member of the North Pacific Surveying Expedition* from 1853 to 1856. He wrote an account of the expedition in *My Last Cruise, or Where We Went and What We Saw: Being an Account of Visits to the Malay and Loo-Choo Islands, the Coasts of China, Formosa, Japan, Kamtschatka, Siberia and the Mouth of the Amoor River* (Philadelphia, 1857). He resigned from the navy in 1860 and engaged in business in Japan in 1860–1861. He was responsible for one of the first shipments of Japanese tea ever imported into the United States. He returned to the United States in 1861, was a partner in an importing business in Baltimore from 1866 to 1870, and was a coffee merchant after 1871. Died March 26, 1883, in Annapolis, Maryland. *References: ACAB; DAB; NCAB* 22:95; and *WWWA*.

HAGENSTEIN, AUGUST (1858–1921). Missionary, born August 11, 1858, in Kienitz on the Oder, Prussia. Hagenstein was apprenticed to a gardener and florist in Gutzow, and later in Minden, West Westphalia. He studied at the theological seminary at St. Chrischona (Basel, Switzerland). He came to the United States in 1881, graduated from Lutheran College (Mendota, Ill.), and was ordained in 1888. He held a pastorate in New Baden, Texas, from 1887 to 1890. He was a missionary under the Board of Foreign Missions of the Evangelical Synod of North America in India from 1890 to 1921. He served in the Chattisgarhi division, Central Provinces, and later in the Bisrampur mission in the Raipur division. In 1894 he established a mission at Parsabhader, near Baloda Bazar, and served also as the village headman. Died May 30, 1921, in Parsabhader. *Reference*: Martin P. Davis, *Sadhu Hagenstein: A White Man among the Brown: A Record of a Man of God* (St. Louis, 1930).

HAGERTY INCIDENT (1960). A demonstration that took place in 1960, when James C. Hagerty, press secretary to President Dwight D. Eisenhower, arrived in Tokyo to make final preparations for the president's visit. The demonstration was a manifestation of public opposition to government policy as reflected in the United States–Japan Security Treaty of 1960. *References: KEJ*; and George R. Packard III, *Protest in Tokyo: The Security Treaty Crisis of 1960* (Princeton, N.J., 1966).

HAHN, EMILY (1905–   ). Author, born January 14, 1905, in St. Louis, Missouri. Hahn graduated from the University of Wisconsin's College of Engineering, and studied at Columbia and Oxford universities. She was a mining engineer in St. Louis; a tourist guide in Santa Fe, New Mexico; an instructor in geology at Hunter College; and worked with the Red Cross in the Belgian Congo until 1931. She published her first story in 1929 and her first book in 1930. She went to China in 1935, was China coast correspondent of *The New Yorker*, and an instructor in English at the Customs College in Shanghai from 1935 until 1938, in Chungking in 1940, and in Hong Kong in 1941. She was a freelance writer after 1938. She was interned by the Japanese from 1941 to 1943. She resided in England after 1946. She wrote *The Soong Sisters* (New York, 1941); *Raffles of Singapore: A Biography* (Garden City, N.Y., 1946); *Miss Jill* (Garden City, N.Y., 1947) (reprinted as *House in Shanghai* (Greenwich, Conn., 1958)); *James Brooke of Sarawak* (London, 1953); *Chiang Kai-shek: An Unauthorized Biography* (Garden City, N.Y., 1955); *The Tiger House Party: The Last Days of the Maharajas* (Garden City, N.Y., 1959); *China Only Yesterday, 1850–1950: A Century of Change* (Garden City, N.Y., 1963); and several autobiographies, including *China to Me, a Partial Autobiography* (Garden City, N.Y., 1944); and *Hong Kong Holiday* (Garden City, N.Y., 1946). *References*: Emily Hahn Papers, Indiana University Libraries, Bloomington, Ind.; *CA: NCAB* H:173; Patricia L. Neils, "Emily Hahn," *American Women Writers*, ed. Lina Mainiero and Langdon C. Foust (New York, 1980), 2:204–6; N. Robertson, "Emily Hahn: 73, Still Feisty," *NYT*, June 23, 1978; *WWA*; and *WWAW*.

HALDERMAN, JOHN A(COMING) (1833–1908). Diplomat, born April 15, 1833, in Fayette County, Kentucky. Halderman read law and was admitted to the bar. He was private secretary to the first governor of Kansas in 1854, and judge of the probate court of Leavenworth County, Kansas. He served in the Union Army during the Civil War. He was mayor of Leavenworth, and served in both houses of the Kentucky legislature. He was a consul in Bangkok, Siam, in 1880–1881; consul general in 1881–1882; and the first U.S. minister and consul general in Siam from 1882 to 1885. He succeeded in introducing postal and telegraphic systems in Siam. Died September 21, 1908, in Atlantic City, New Jersey. *References: ACAB; DAB;* and *NYT*, September 23, 1908.

HALE, WALTER FRANKLIN ("SAPAO") (1874–1952). Colonial administrator, born July 27, 1874, in Plattsmouth, Nebraska. Hale graduated from Cotner University (Lincoln, Nebr.). He served in the Spanish-American War, and came to the Philippines, in 1898. He went to La Trinidad, Benguet, in 1900, prospecting for gold. He was lieutenant governor of Amburayan from 1903 to 1907, stationed at Alilem; and lieutenant governor of Kalinga from 1907 to 1915, stationed at Tabuk. He resigned from government service in 1915. He was involved in rice growing at Balbalan; was later manager of a cattle ranch in Bukindon, Midanao; and then joined the Johnson-Pickett Rope Company in Manila. He was employed by Benguet Consolidated Mining Company in Baguio after 1926. He was interned by the Japanese in Baguio during World War II. Died July 28, 1952, at Baguio. *References: Gleeck/Frontiers*; and Laurence L. Wilson, "Sapao: Walter Franklin Hale. In Memoriam," *Journal of East Asiatic Studies* 5 (April 1956): 1–38.

HALL, FITZEDWARD (1825–1901). Indologist, born March 21, 1825, in Troy, New York. Hall graduated from Harvard University. He was sent by his father to India in 1846 to find a brother who had run away to sea. He was wrecked in the Hugli River and remained in Calcutta until 1849 and in Ghazipur in 1849–1850. He was an instructor in the government college in Benares from 1850 to 1853, professor of Sanskrit in the college from 1853 to 1855, inspector of public instruction for Ajmer-Merwara in 1855, and inspector of public instruction to the Central Provinces at Saugor in 1856–1857. He was in Europe and the United States from 1857 to 1860, was back in India from 1860 to 1862, was a professor of Sanskrit, Hindustani, and Indian jurisprudence at King's College (London) after 1862 as well as librarian to the India Office, and was examiner for the British civil service commissioners. He retired in 1869. He prepared thirty volumes of translations, texts, and commentaries of Sanskrit scripts, and was the first American to edit a Sanskrit text. He wrote *Hindi Grammer* (Hartford, 1870). Died February 1, 1901, in Marlesford, near London, England. *References: ACAB; DAB; NCAB* 11:448; and *WWWA.*

HALL, GEORGE ROGERS (1820–1899). Merchant and plant collector, born March 1820, in Bristol, Rhode Island. Hall graduated from Trinity College (Hartford) and Harvard Medical School. He went to China in 1846 and practiced medicine in the foreign settlement of Shanghai. He gave up his medical practice and became involved in trade, along with Edward Cunningham and David Oakes Clark, in 1854. He made a voyage to Japan in 1855 and again in 1875. He sent specimens of plants from China to the United States, some of which now bear his name, and was the first person to send Japanese plants direct to the United States. He returned to the United States in 1861 or 1862, settled in Bristol, Rhode Island, and Jacksonville and Fort George Island, Florida. Died December 24, 1899, in Milton, Massachusetts. *References*: James M. Howe, Jr., "George Rogers Hall, Lover of Plants," *Journal of the Arnold Arboretum* 4 (April 1923): 91–98; and Richardson L. Wright, *Gardener's Tribute* (Philadelphia, 1949), pp. 119–42.

HALL, GORDON (1784–1826). Missionary, born April 8, 1784, in Tolland, Connecticut. Hall graduated from Williams College and Andover Theological Seminary, and was ordained in 1812. He was a missionary under the American Board of Commissioners for Foreign Missions (ABCFM) in Bombay, India, from 1813 until his death. He translated portions of the New Testament into Marathi. Died March 20, 1826, at Dorlee Dhapoor, near Nasseek, on the way to Bombay. *References: AndoverTS*; H. Bardwell, *Memoir of Rev. Gordon Hall, Missionary to India* (Andover, Mass., 1834); Gordon Hall, *Anecdotes of the Bombay Mission for the Conversion of the Hindoos, Extracted from the Letters and Journals of the Rev. Gordon Hall* (London, 1836); *Hewitt; LC*; and *NCAB* 10:246.

HALL, JOSEF WASHINGTON *See* CLOSE, UPTON

HALL, ROBERT B(URNETT) (1896–1975). Geographer, born July 18, 1896, in Espanola, New Mexico. Hall graduated from the University of Michigan. He was associate professor of geography at the University of Michigan from 1935 to 1938, and professor from 1938 until his retirement in 1965. He directed geographic expeditions to Japan in 1928, 1929, 1931, 1933, and 1935–1936. He was director of the Institute of Far Eastern Studies at the University of Michigan from 1937 to 1939. He was director of the Pacific Coast unit of the Office of Strategic Services (OSS) in 1942–1943, and in China and Burma in 1943–1944. He founded the Center for Japanese Studies at the University of Michigan in 1947, and served as its director until 1957. After World War II, he organized the University of Michigan's first research station at Okayama Prefecture in Japan, the first U.S. field station to operate in Japan during the postwar years. Died April 4, 1975, in Ann Arbor, Michigan. *References: NCAB* 62:291; and *WWWA*.

HALL, ROSETTA SHERWOOD (1865–1951). Medical missionary, born September 19, 1865, in Liberty, New York. Hall graduated from Oswego State Normal School and Woman's Medical College of Pennsylvania (Philadelphia). She was a medical missionary under the Woman's Foreign Missionary Society of the Methodist Episcopal Church in Korea from 1890 until 1933. She founded a dispensary in Seoul, which later became a hospital. In 1894 she moved to P'yongyang, but returned to the United States in 1895, after the death of her husband. She was back in Seoul in 1897 and in P'yongyang in 1898. She returned to Seoul in 1917. She was one of the founders of the Women's Medical Training Institute in Seoul in 1928, and head of the Institute for the Blind and the Deaf in P'yongyang. She devised a braille-like system of embossed printing for the Korean alphabet. She returned to the United States in 1933 and retired in 1943. She edited a biography of her husband **WILLIAM JAMES HALL** (1860–1894), a medical missionary in Korea from 1891 until his death there. Died April 5, 1951, in Ocean Grove, New Jersey. Her son, **SHERWOOD HALL** (1893–   ), a medical missionary, was born November 10, 1893, in Seoul. Sherwood Hall returned to the United States in 1910, and graduated from Mount Union College (Alliance, Oh.) and the University of Toronto. He served as a medical missionary under the Board of Foreign Missions of the Methodist Episcopal Church in Korea from 1926 until 1940, and in India from 1940 until 1963. He was best known for the introduction of Christmas seals in Korea in 1933 to raise money for the treatment of lung disease. He wrote an autobiography, *With Stethoscope in Asia: Korea* (McLean, Va., 1978). *References: NAW;* and *NYT*, April 7, 1951.

HALLOCK, HENRY GALLOWAY COMINGO (1870–1951). Missionary, born March 31, 1870, in Holliday's Cove, Hanock County, West Virginia. Hallock graduated from Princeton University, Princeton Theological Seminary, and Richmond (Ohio) College, and was ordained in 1896. He was a missionary under the Board of Foreign Missions of the Presbyterian Church in the U.S.A. in China from 1896 until 1951. He became a self-supporting missionary in 1905; was professor of homiletics and dean of the theological school of the University of China at Chenju, near Shanghai, from 1925 to 1927; acting National Christian Endeavor general secretary for China in 1907–1908; honorary secretary of the International Bible Reading Association for the Empire of China from 1906 to 1914; founder, secretary, and treasurer of the National Tract Society for China; founder and secretary of the Anti-Cigarette Society of China; and pastor of the Endeavorers' Church in Shanghai. He was interned by the Japanese in Shanghai. Died January 24, 1951, in Shanghai. *References: NYT*, January 19, 1951; and *WWWA*.

HALSEMA, EUSEBIUS JULIUS (1882–1945). Engineer, born December 12, 1882, in New Bremen, Ohio. Halsema graduated from Ohio State University. he formed the firm of Kistler and Halsema in Los Angeles in 1907. He came to the Philippines in 1908 as an engineer for the Bureau of Public Works. He held various positions with the bureau, was assistant engineer in charge of waterworks construction in Cebu in 1911–1912, served in the U.S. Army during World War I, and was district manager and district engineer of the National Coal Company in Malangas, Zamboanga, in 1919. He was mayor of Baguio and district engineer of Benguet from 1920 until his retirement in 1936. Died April 29, 1945, in Baguio. *References: CCDP; DPB* 2: *EP* 17:153–55; *Gleeck/Frontiers*; and James J. Halsema, "E. J. Halsema—Colonel Engineer," *BAHC* 11 (April-June 1983) to 16 (October-December 1988).

HAMILTON, CHARLES R(OBERT) (1872–1954). Missionary and educator, born June 18, 1872, in Lebanon, Indiana. Hamilton attended the College of Emporio (Kans.) and graduated from Hanover College (Hanover, Ind.) and McCormick Theological Seminary (Chicago). He held pastorates in Manchester, Iowa, and Buffalo, New York, from 1896 to 1907. He was a missionary under the Board of Foreign Missions of the Presbyterian Church in the U.S.A. in the Philippines, stationed at Pagsanjan, Santa Cruz, and Los Baños, Laguna Province, from 1907 until 1929. He was editor of the *Philippine Presbyterian* from 1915 to 1926, acting president of Silliman Institute (later Silliman University) from 1929 to 1932, and president of the Union Theological Seminary in Manila from 1932 until 1941. Died April 4, 1954, in Wooster, Ohio. *References: CCDP; EP* 17:255–256; *NYT*, April 6, 1954; and *WWWA*.

HANGCHOW UNIVERSITY. Hangchow Christian College was founded in 1897 by the missions of the Presbyterian Church in the U.S.A. and the Presbyterian Church in the United States as the Hangchow Presbyterian College in Hangchow. It started as a boys' school in Ningpo in 1846, which was moved to Hangchow in 1866, and became a junior college in 1893. It became Hangchow Christian University in 1914, and was chartered by the District of Columbia in 1920. It became a coeducational institution in 1929. It moved to Shanghai from 1938 to 1942, and to Shaowu, northwestern Fukien, in 1942. It was reopened in Hangchow in 1946 and was recognized as Hangchow University in 1948. It came under Communist control in 1949 and was dissolved in 1951. *References*: Clarence B. Day, *Hangchow University: A Brief History* (New York, 1955); *Fenn*; and *Lutz*.

HANKS, JANE RICHARDSON (1908–   ). Anthropologist, wife of Lucien Mason Hanks*, born August 2, 1908, in Berkeley, California. Hanks graduated from the University of California at Berkeley and from Columbia University. She carried out fieldwork in Thailand from 1951 to 1953, in 1963–1964, and in 1968–1969. She was a research associate of the Cornell Research Center in Bangkok from 1953 to 1955, and of the Southeast Asia Program at Cornell University after 1955. She wrote *Maternity and Its Rituals among the Bang Chan* (Ithaca, N.Y., 1963), and was coauthor of *Food Habits and Nutrient Intakes in a Siamese Rice Village: Studies in Bang Chan* (Ithaca, N.Y., 1958); *A Report on Tribal Peoples in Chiengrai Province, North of the Mai Kok River* (Bangkok, 1964); and *Ethnological Notes on Northeastern Thailand* (Ithaca, N.Y., 1965), *References: AMWS*; May Ebihara, "Jane Richardson Hanks (1908–   )," in *Women Anthropologists: A Biographical Dictionary*, ed. Ute Gacs et al. (Westport, Conn., 1988), pp. 140–47; and *WWAW*.

HANKS, LUCIEN M(ASON) (1910–   ). Anthropologist, born March 25, 1910, in Madison, Wisconsin. Hanks graduated from the University of Wisconsin and Columbia University. He was an instructor in psychology at the University of Illinois from 1937 to 1942, and assistant professor of psychology and anthropology and later professor at Bennington College (Vt.) from 1942 to 1969. He was a psychologist for the Office of Strategic Services (OSS) from 1943 to 1945, and was affiliated with the Southeast Asia Program of Cornell University from 1952 to 1957. He carried out fieldwork in Thailand in 1953–1954; was coeditor of *Ethnographic Notes on Northern Thailand* (Ithaca, N.Y., 1965); wrote *Rice and Man: Agricultural Ecology in Southeast Asia* (Chicago, 1972); and was coauthor of *Bang Chan: Social History of a Rural Community in Thailand* (Ithaca, N.Y., 1978); and *A Report on Tribal Peoples in Chiengrai Province, North of the Mai Kok River* (Bangkok, 1964). *Reference: CA.*

HANSON, OLA (1864–1929). Missionary, born in Åhus, Skåne, Sweden, came to the United States in 1881 and grew up in Oakland, Nebraska. Hanson attended Swedish Baptist (later Bethel) Seminary (St. Paul, Minn.), graduated from Madison Theological Seminary (Hamilton, N.Y.), and was ordained in 1890. He was a missionary under the American Baptist Foreign Mission Society in Burma among the Kachins from 1890 until 1928, serving at Bhamo. He established a mission in Namkham in the Hsenwi district in 1910. He reduced the Kachin language to writing; translated the Bible into Kachin; compiled *A Grammer of the Kachin Language* (Rangoon, 1896), and *A Dictionary of the Kachin Language* (Rangoon, 1906); and wrote *The Kachins, Their Customs and Traditions* (Rangoon, 1913) and *Missionary Pioneers among the Kachins* (New York, 1922). Died October 17, 1929, in St. Paul, Minnesota. *Reference*: Gustaf A. Sword, *Light in the Jungle: Life Story of Dr. Ola Hanson of Burma* (Chicago, 1954).

HAPPER, ANDREW P(ATTON) (1818–1894). Medical missionary, born October 20, 1818, near Monongahela City, Washington County, Pennsylvania. Happer graduated from Jefferson College, Western Theological Seminary, and the University of Pennsylvania Medical School, and was ordained in 1844. He was a medical missionary under the Board of Foreign Missions of the Presbyterian Church in the U.S.A. from 1844 to 1884. He served in Macao from 1844 to 1847 and in Canton after 1847. He edited the *Chinese Recorder* from 1880 to 1884, and assisted in translating the Bible into the Canton colloquial dialect. He returned to the United States in 1884, but was back in China in 1888. He founded the Canton Christian College and was in charge of the college until 1891, when he retired because of ill health. Died October 27, 1894, in Wooster, Ohio. *References*: Loren W. Crabtree, "Andrew P. Happer and Presbyterian Missions in China, 1844–1891," *Journal of Presbyterian History* 62 (1984): 19–34; and *DAB*.

HARE-HAWES-CUTTING ACT (1933). A law that accorded independence to the Filipinos after ten years, during which time they would govern themselves as a commonwealth. American business was to be favored during this period, and Philippine goods would enter the United States under generous quotas. It also reserved to the United States the rights to military and naval bases. It was rejected by the Philippines legislature on the ground that its real aim was to exclude Philippine products and labor from the United State. *References*: Theodore Friend, "American Interest and Philippine Independence, 1929–1933," *PS* 11 (1963): 505–23; Theodore Friend, "Philippine Independence and the Last

Lame-Duck Congress,'' *PS* 12 (1964): 260–76; Theodore Friend, "Philippine Interest and the Mission for Independence, 1929–1932,'' *PS* 12 (1964): 63–82; and Theodore Friend, "Veto and Repassage of the Hare-Hawes-Cutting Act: A Catalogue of Motives,'' *PS* 12 (1964): 666–80.

HARING, DOUGLAS GILBERT (1894–1970). Anthropologist, born August 6, 1894, in Watkins Glen, New York. Haring graduated from Colgate and Columbia universities and Rochester Theological Seminary, and studied at the School of Japanese Language and Culture (Tokyo). He was a missionary under American Baptist Foreign Mission Society in Japan from 1917 to 1922 and from 1924 to 1926, and professor of history in Tokyo Gakuin in 1925–1926. He was a lecturer in sociology at Columbia University in 1926–1927, member of the faculty of Syracuse University from 1926 to 1946, and professor of anthropology from 1946 to 1970. He carried out fieldwork in the Ryukyu Islands and Japan in 1951–1952, and wrote *The Land of Gods and Earthquakes* (New York, 1929); *Blood on the Rising Sun* (Philadelphia, 1943); *The Island of Amami Oshima in the Northern Ryukyus* (Washington, D.C., 1952); and *Okinawan Customs: Yesterday and Today* (Rutland, Vt., 1969). He was editor of *Japan's Prospect* (Cambridge, Mass., 1946). Died August 24, 1970, in Syracuse, New York. *Reference*: WWWA.

HARKNESS, RUTH (1901–1947). Animal collector. Originally a dress designer, Ruth Harkness became a zoological collector when her husband, William H. Harkness, Jr., a field zoologist, died in Shanghai in 1935 on the eve of a panda hunt in Tibet. She resolved to carry out his intentions, and organized an expedition in 1936 to the Tibetan border of China to capture a live giant panda. She captured a baby panda and brought it to the United States. She captured a second specimen in 1938 and brought it to the United States. She wrote *The Lady and the Panda, an Adventure* (New York, 1938). She later conducted an expedition to the Peruvian Andes. Died July 20, 1947, in Pittsburgh. *References*: Erika Brady, "First U.S. Panda, Shanghaied in China, Stirred Up a Ruckus," *Smithsonian* 14 (December 1983): 145–64; Ramona Morris and Desmond Morris, *Men and Pandas* (New York, 1966), ch. 4; and *NYT*, July 21, 1947.

HARLAN, JOSIAH (1799–1871). Adventurer, born June 12, 1799, in Newlin Township, Chester County, Pennsylvania. Harlan came to India in 1823, entered the employ of the East India Company as an assistant surgeon, and served as a medical officer in the Bengal Artillery during the first Burmese war. He resigned in 1826, went to north India, and attached himself to Shah Shoja-ul-Mulk, ex-king of Kabul, who was then living in exile in Ludhiana, the Punjab, and who in 1828 appointed Harlan as a secret agent with a commission to revolutionize Afghanistan. He traveled to Kabul disguised as a dervish, but his mission was unsuccessful and he returned to India and entered the service of Maharajah Ranjit Singh, sovereign of the Punjab in Lahore, serving him for seven years. He was governor of the province of Gujarat and was later sent by Ranjit to prevent the invasion of the Afghan army in 1835. He then went to Kabul, joined the forces of Dost Mohammad Khan as an aide-de-camp and general of regular troops, and trained the Afghan infantry in Western military tactics. He commanded a division of the Afghan army which was sent to Balkh. He returned to the United States in 1841 and wrote *A Memoir of India and Afghanistan with Observations on the Present Exciting And Critical State and Future Prospects of Those Countries* (Philadelphia, 1842). He served in the Union Army during the Civil War. He later practiced medicine in San Francisco. Died October 1871 in San Francisco. *References: DAB*; Frank E. Ross, ed., *Central Asia: Personal Narrative of General Josiah Harlan, 1823–1841* (London, 1931); and *WWWA*.

HARPSTER, JOHN HENRY (1844–1911). Missionary, born April 27, 1844, in Center Hall, Pennsylvania. Harpster, served in the Civil War, attended Missionary Institute (Selinsgrove, Pa.) and the Gettysburg (Pa.) Theological Seminary, and was ordained in 1871. he was a missionary under the Board of Foreign Missions of the General Synod of the Lutheran Church in the Telugu mission at Guntur, India, from 1872 to 1876. He returned to the United States in 1876 because of ill health, and held pastorates in Ellsworth and Hayes City, Kansas; Trenton, New Jersey; and Canton, Ohio; from 1879 until 1893. He went back to the Guntur mission in India in 1893 and served until 1901. He directed the mission at Rajahmundry from 1901 to 1909, when he returned to the United States. Died February 1, 1911, in Mount Airy, Philadelphia. *References: DAB; LC; NCAB* 15:153; and *WWWA*.

HARRINGTON, CHARLES KENDALL (1858–1920). Missionary, born March 14, 1858, in Sydney, Cape Breton, Nova Scotia, Canada. Harrington graduated from Acadia College and Morgan Park Theological Seminary (Chicago), and attended Newton Theological Institution (Mass.). He was a missionary under the American Baptist Missionary Union in Japan from 1886 until 1920. He was a member of the teaching staff of the Baptist Theological Seminary in Yokohama, and a member of the revising committee of the Japanese New Testament from 1910 to 1916. He wrote a biography of Luke Washington Bickel.* Died May 13, 1920, in Albany, New York. *References*: Watson Kirk Connell, ed., *The Acadia Record 1838–1953* (Wolfville, Nova Scotia, 1953); and *WWWA*.

HARRIS, EDWARD NORMAN (1860–1947). Missionary, born April 27, 1860, in Rangoon, Burma, to American missionary parents. Harris graduated from Madison (later Colgate) University and Crozer Theological Seminary. He was a missionary under the American Baptist Foreign Mission Society in Burma from 1893 until 1932, serving the Karens. He was stationed at Shwegyin from 1893 until 1918, and at Toungoo from 1918 to 1928. He did literary work at Kalaw from 1928 until his retirement in 1932. He was involved in revising the

Karen Bible and Karen dictionary. He wrote *A Star in the East: An Account of American Baptist Missions to the Karens of Burma* (New York, 1920), and *'Way Away Tales, from Away-Off-from-anywhere Land* (Philadelphia, 1940), a collection of Burmese tales. Died August 9, 1947, in Redlands, California.

HARRIS, MERRIMAN COLBERT (1846–1921). Missionary, born July 9, 1846, in Beallsville, Monroe County, Ohio. Harris attended theological schools in Harlem Springs, Washington, and Scio, Ohio, and graduated from Allegheny College (Meadville, Pa.). He served in the Union Army during the Civil War; taught school at Fairview, Ohio, from 1867 to 1869 and was pastor at Urichsville, Ohio, from 1869 to 1871. He was a missionary under the Board of Foreign Missions of the Methodist Episcopal Church in Northern Japan from 1873 until 1886 and from 1904 until his death. The first Protestant missionary in Hokkaido, he established a mission in Hakodate in 1874. He was a vice-consul in Hakodate from 1875 to 1877 and a consular agent from 1877 to 1879. He served in Tokyo from 1879 until 1886, when he returned to the United States. He was superintendent of the Japanese mission in San Francisco from 1886 to 1904 and organized the Pacific Japanese mission. He was the Methodist bishop of Japan and Korea from 1904 until his retirement in 1916. He wrote *Christianity in Japan* (Cincinnati, 1907). Died May 8, 1921, in Aoyama, Japan. *References: DAB; EWM; KEJ: NCAB* 14:122; *NYT*, May 9, 1921; and *OAB*.

HARRIS, THOMAS BRADLEY (1826–1866). Merchant, born October 29, 1826, in New York City. Harris was a partner in a firm of grocers in New York City. He was sent to Hong Kong in 1862 and was there as a commission agent and ship broker until 1866. He was a partner in the American Trading Company of Borneo after 1865, and served as chief secretary of the Colony of Ambong and Marudu. Died May 22, 1866, in Kimanis, North Borneo. *Reference*: H. G. Keith, *The United States Consul and the Yankee Raja* (Brunei, 1980).

HARRIS, TOWNSEND (1804–1878). Diplomat, born October 3, 1804, in Sandy Hill, Washington County, New York. Harris was involved in the business of importing china and earthware. He served as president of the New York Board of Education, and helped found the Free Academy (later the City College of New York). The business was dissolved in 1848, and he purchased an interest in a trading vessel and went to California. He then embarked on trading voyages in the Pacific and India oceans, and lived in or visited several of the Chinese treaty ports and coastal cities of Southeast Asia from 1849 to 1855. On the way to his position in Japan, he negotiated a commercial treaty with Siam in 1856. He was the first U.S. consul general in Shimoda, Japan, from 1856 until 1859. He negotiated and signed the Japanese-American treaty of Amity and Commerce (Harris Treaty) in Edo (later Tokyo) in 1858. He was U.S. minister resident in Japan from 1859 until 1862. He returned to the United States in 1862. Died February 25, 1878, in New York City. *References*: Townsend Harris Papers, Archives of the City College in the City University of New York; William A. Borst, "The American Merchant and the Genesis of Japanese-American Commercial Relations, 1790–1858," Ph.D. diss., St. Louis University, 1972, chs. 10–11; Mario E. Cosinga, ed., *The Complete Journals of Townsend Harris* (New York, 1930); Carl Crow, *He Opened the Door of Japan: Townsend Harris and the Story of His Amazing Adventures in Establishing American Relations with the Far East* (New York, 1939); *DAB; DADH; EAH; Israel E. Levine, Behind the Silken Curtain: The Story of Townsend Harris* (New York, 1961); *KEJ*; John McMaster, "Alcock and Harris, Foreign Diplomacy in Bakumatsu Japan," *Monumenta Nipponica* 22 (1967): 305–67; John W. Moon, "The United States Relations with Thailand: The Mission of Townsend Harris," *Asian Profile* 1 (October 1973): 355–63; *NCAB* 5:493; Oliver Statler, *Shimoda Story* (New York, 1969); and *WWWA*.

HARRISON, ALFRED C(RAVEN), JR. (1876–1925). Explorer, born in Philadelphia. Harrison graduated from the University of Pennsylvania. With William Henry Furness* and Hiram M. Hiller*, he made several extended voyages to east, south, and Southeast Asia from 1895 to 1901. He spent several years among the peoples living in Sarawak and Kalimantan in Borneo. He also conducted expeditions to the Gobi Desert, Mongolia, and Siberia. He owned a sugar plantation in Cuba after 1903. Died July 7, 1925, in London. *References*: Alfred C. Harrison Photographs Collection, University Museum, University of Pennsylvania, Philadelphia; and *NYT*, July 10, 1925.

HARRISON, FRANCIS BURTON (1873–1957). Colonial administrator, born December 18, 1873, in New York City. Harrison graduated from Yale and New York Law School, and was admitted to the bar in 1898. He never practiced law, and instead served during the Spanish-American War and was a member of the U.S. House of Representatives from 1902 to 1904 and from 1906 to 1913. He was governor-general of the Philippines from 1913 to 1921. He pursued policies designed to bring about the "Filipinization" of the government, bureaucracy, and economy of the islands, and filled many of the positions with Filipinos. He wrote *The Cornerstone of the Philippine Independence: A Narrative of Seven Years* (New York, 1922). He settled in Teaninich Alness, Scotland, in 1921. He returned to the Philippines in 1935. He was a presidential advisor to President Manuel Quezon, and was made a citizen of the Philippines in 1936 by a special act of the Philippine legislature. He later moved to Charlottesville, Virginia, and resumed his post as advisor to Quezon's government-in-exile in Washington, D.C. He was U.S. commissioner of civil claims in the Philippines in 1946–1947, and then served as a special advisor to the first three presidents of the Philippine Republic. Died November 21, 1957, in Flemington, New Jersey. *References*: Francis B. Harrison Papers, in the Harrison Family Collection, Manuscript Division, Library of Congress; *ACAB; DAB S6; EAH; EP* 4:365–66; Charles Farkas, "Wilsonian Progressives in the Philippines: Henry Jones Ford and Francis Burton Harrison," *Kabar Sebarano*, no. 3 (1978): 11–18;

Gleeck/Governors, ch. 7; Eugene H. Masse, "Francis Burton Harrison, Governor-General of the Philippine Islands, 1913–1921," Ph.D. diss., the Catholic University of America, 1971; *NYT*, November 22, 1957; Michael P. Onorato, "Francis Burton Harrison, Liberal Proconsul," *BAHC* 4 (January-March 1976): 7–23; "Governor General Francis Burton Harrison and Filipinization," *BAHC* 3 (July-September 1975); 7–11; and Michael P. Onorato, ed., *Origins of the Philippines Republic: Extracts from the Diaries and Records of Francis Burton Harrison* (Ithaca, N.Y., 1974).

HART, DONN V(ORHIS) (1918–1983). Anthropologist, born February 15, 1918, in Anaheim, California. Hart graduated from the University of California, Harvard, and Syracuse University. He was assistant professor at the University of Denver from 1951 to 1954, and professor of anthropology at Syracuse University from 1958 to 1971 and at Northern Illinois University (DeKalb, Ill.) from 1971 until his death and director of the Center for Southeast Asian studies from 1971 to 1981. He carried out fieldwork in Visayas, Philippines, in 1950–1951, 1955–1956, and 1964–1965. Died July 10, 1983, in DeKalb, Illinois. *References: AMWS*; "In Honor of Two American Filipinist Scholars: Donn V. Hart, 1918–1983, and Peter G. Gowing, 1930–1983," *Kinaadman: A Journal of the Southern Philippines* 7 (1985), entire issue; and *WWA*.

HART, VIRGIL CHITTENDEN (1840–1904). Missionary, born January 2, 1840, in Lorraine, New York. Hart graduated from Northwestern University and Garrett Biblical Institute, and was ordained in 1865. He was a missionary under the Board of Foreign Missions of the Methodist Episcopal Church in China from 1866 until 1900. he opened a mission in central China in 1867 and established mission stations in Kiukiang, Chinkiang, Wuhu, Nanking, and Nanchang. He also opened a mission in Szechuan, West China, in 1887–1888, and established mission stations in Chungking and Chengtu. He resigned because of ill health, but returned to Szechuan in 1892, under the Canadian Methodist Church. He opened the West China mission, and established mission stations in Chengtu and Chungking from 1892 until 1900. He wrote *Western China; a Journey to the Great Buddhist Centre of Mount Omei* (Boston, 1888). Died February 24, 1904, in Burlington, Ontario, Canada. *References: DAB;* and *EWM.*

HARTENDORP, A(BRAM) V(AN) H(EYNINGEN) (1893–   ). Editor, publisher, and author, born September 3, 1893, in Haarlem, the Netherlands. As a boy, Hartendorp came to the United States with his parents. He attended the University of Colorado. He came to the Philippine Islands in 1917 as a teacher, and was a high school teacher in Cuyo, Palawan, in 1917–1918; supervising teacher in Borongan district, Samar, in 1918–1919; and supervising teacher in Sibuguey Bay in Zamboanga in 1919–1920. He was associate editor, and later editor, of the *Manila Times*, for 1920–1923. He was editor and later manager of the *Philippine Magazine* from 1925 to 1933, and its proprietor after 1933.

He was editor of *The American Chamber of Commerce Journal*. He wrote *History of Industry and Trade in the Philippines* (Manila, 1958); *The Santo Tomas Story* (New York, 1964); and *The Japanese Occupation of the Philippines* (Manila, 1967). *References: CA; EP* 17:257; *Gleeck/Manila*; Frederic S. Maruardt and Angus L. Campbell, "Two Tributes to Hartendorp: A. V. H. Hartendorp—A Great Editor," *BAHC* 4 (April-June 1976): 7–13; and Albert Ravenhold, "A. V. H. Hartendorp; Manila's Doughty Seventy-One-Year-Old American Editor," *American Universities Field Staff Reports, Southeast Asia Series* 12, no. 13 (December 1964).

HARTMAN, WARD (1882–1967). Missionary, born October 6, 1882, in Alpha, near Dayton, Ohio. Hartman graduated from Heidelberg College (Tiffin, Ohio) and its theological seminary (later Central Theological Seminary, Dayton, Ohio), and was ordained in 1911. He was a missionary under the Board of Foreign Missions of the Reformed Church in the United States from 1911 until 1952, serving at Shenchow until 1922. He pioneered missionary work among the Miao tribe at Yungsui from 1922 to 1931. He returned to the United States in 1932 and was a pastor in Columbus, Ohio, from 1932 to 1936. He was back in Yungsui, Hunan, from 1936 to 1944. He returned to the United States in 1944, and was back again in Yungsui from 1946 until 1952. He returned to the United States in 1952 and retired in 1954. Died January 21, 1967, in Columbus, Ohio. *References*: Ward Hartman Papers, Evangelical and Reformed Historical Society, Lancaster Central Archives and Library, Lancaster, Pa.; and George R. Snyder, *Ward Hartman: Pioneer midst Change* (Piqua, Ohio, 1967?).

HARTWELL, JESSE BOARDMAN, JR. (1835–1912). Missionary, born October 17, 1835, in Darlington, South Carolina. Hartwell graduated from Furman University (Greenville, S.C.). He was a professor of mathematics at Mt. Lebanon University. He was a missionary under the Foreign Missionary Board of the Southern Baptist Convention in China from 1859 until 1875. He served in Chefoo and later in Tungchow. He returned to the United States in 1875, where he was a missionary to the Chinese community in San Francisco and superintendent of Chinese missions on the Pacific coast under the American Baptist Home Mission Society from 1879 to 1893. He was back in China in 1893 and served until his death. He was president of Bush Theological Seminary in Hwanghein. Died January 3, 1912, in Hwanghein, China. *References*: Hartwell Family Papers, Divinity School Library, Yale University, New Haven, Conn.; and *Minutes of the South Carolina Baptist Convention* (1912), pp. 109–11.

HARTY, JEREMIAH J(AMES) (1853–1927). Clergyman, born November 7, 1853, in St. Louis. Harty studied at the University of St. Louis and St. Vincent's Seminary (Cape Girardeau, Mo.), and was ordained in 1878. He was engaged in parish work in St. Louis. In 1903, he was appointed the first American archbishop in Manila, Philippines. He convoked the first provincial council of the Philippine Islands in 1907. He returned to the United States in 1916 because of ill health. He was later archbishop of Omaha, Nebraska. Died October 29, 1927, in Los Angeles. *References: DACB; Gleeck/Manila; NCAB* 15:45; *NYT*, October 30, 1927; and *WWWA*.

HASCALL, WILLIAM HOSMER SHAILER (1850–1927). Missionary, born December 30, 1850, in Pittsford, Vermont. Hascall learned the printing trade. He was a printer for the mission founded by Adoniram Judson* in Rangoon, Burma, from 1872 to 1875, when he discontinued this work because of eye strain. He was ordained in 1877, and was a missionary in Maulmain from 1875 until 1880. He returned to the United States in 1880 because of his wife's ill health, studied at the Newton Theological seminary, and was a pastor in Farmington, Maine. He was back in Burma in 1883 and was stationed at Henzada until 1888, and at Sagaing in 1888–1889. He then returned to the United States. He held pastorates in Fall River, Massachusetts; Dover, New Hampshire; and New York City. He went back to Burma in 1903. He served at Thonze until 1907, later in Bassein, and then in the delta of the Irrawaddy River from 1912 until 1917, when he returned to the United States. Died March 24, 1927, in Baldwin, New York. *References: NCAB* 21:245; and *NYT*, March 26, 1927.

HASTINGS, EUROTAS PARMELEE (1821–1890). Missionary, born April 1821, in Clinton, New York. Hastings graduated from Union College and Union Theological Seminary, and was ordained in 1846. He was a missionary under the American Board of Commissioners for Foreign Missions (ABCFM) in Ceylon from 1847 until his death. He was an instructor in the Batticota Seminary until it was closed in 1855. He was later stationed at Chavakachcheri and at Manepay. He was president of the Jaffna College from 1872 until his retirement in 1889. He then took charge of the Manepay station. Died July 31, 1890, in Manepay, Ceylon, *References*: *EM*; and *LC*.

HATCH, D(UANE) SPENCER (1888–1963). Association official, born September 3, 1888, in Greenwich, Washington County, New York. Hatch graduated from Cornell University. He was the foreign secretary of the Young Men's Christian Association (YMCA) in India from 1922 to 1940. He organized a demonstration experiment in Martandam, Travancore, and set up rural reconstruction centers in Baroda and Hyderabad. In 1940 he returned to the United States and later directed the Camohmila YMCA center of Mexico. He returned to India in 1950 as UNESCO (United Nations Educational, Scientific, and Cultural Organization) advisor. He wrote *Up from Poverty in Rural India* (Bombay, 1933), *Further Upward in Rural India* (London, 1938), and *Toward Freedom from Want from India to Mexico* (Bombay, 1949). Died July 15, 1963, in Cooperstown, New York. *Reference: Time*, March 26, 1951.

HATEM, (SHAFIK) GEORGE [MA HAIDE] (1910–1988). Physician, born September 26, 1910, in Buffalo, New York, and grew up in Greenville, North Carolina. Hatem graduated from the University of North Carolina, studied at the American University of Beirut, and graduated from the University of Geneva. He came to China in 1933 and served in hospitals in Shanghai from 1933 to 1936. In 1936, he went to Pao'an and held various positions in the International Peace Hospital and the military medical department of the Eighth Route Army in Yenan. He was also advisor to the medical service of the army. He was medical advisor to the Chinese Liberated Areas Relief Administration, dealing with the United Nations Relief and Rehabilitation Administration (UNRRA) and the American Red Cross in Peking from 1946 to 1949. He was a consultant and helped to organize the Ministry of Public Health after 1949. He helped organize the Chinese Institute of Dermatology and Venereology after 1953, and was its chief of staff and consultant. He played an important part in the campaign to eradicate venereal disease during the early 1950s. He was senior advisor to the ministry of public health in Beijing after 1977. Died October 2, 1988 in Beijing. *References:* Rewi Alley, *Six Americans in China* (Beijing, China, 1985); *EAH; NYT,* October 6, 1988; and Judie Talfer, "George Hatem: American Doctor in China," *Beijing Review* 31 (October 31, 1988): 32–34.

HAUSSERMANN, JOHN W(ILLIAM) (1867–1965). Lawyer and mining executive, born December 14, 1867, in Pierce Township, Claremont County, Ohio. Haussermann graduated from the University of Cincinnati. He practiced law and was city attorney in Leavenworth, Kansas, from 1889 until 1898. He came to the Philippines in 1898 with the U.S. Army, and was a judge advocate during the last months of the Philippine-American War, city attorney of Manila in 1900, and assistant attorney general of the Philippines in 1902. He practiced law in Manila after 1902. He was president and general manager of Benguet Consolidated Mining Company, Incorporated, and Balatoc Mining Company, Incorporated, and was called "the gold king of the Philippines." He left the Philippines during World War II, but returned in 1948. He retired in 1962. Died July 11, 1965, in Cincinnati, Ohio. *References: EP* 17:258–260; *Gleeck/Manila; NCAB* 52:218; *NYT,* July 12, 1965; "Untame Capitalist of Luzon," *Fortune* 37 (May 1978): 117–19; and *WWWA.*

HAYDEN, JOSEPH R(ALSTON) (1887–1945). Colonial administrator, born September 24, 1887, in Quincy, Illinois, Hayden graduated from Knox College (Galesburg, Ill.) and the University of Michigan. He served in the U.S. Navy during World War I. He was a member of the faculty of political science of the University of Michigan after 1921, and professor of political science from 1924 to 1933 and after 1937. He was vice-governor-general of the Philippines from 1933 to 1935, and secretary of public instruction. He was a civilian advisor and consultant on Philippine civil affairs for the War Department from 1943 to 1945, and a civil affairs advisor in the Philippines in 1945. He wrote *The Philippines:*

A Study in National Development (New York, 1942) and edited a new edition of Dean C. Worcester's *The Philippines Past and Present* (New York, 1930). Died May 19, 1945, in Washington, D.C. *References*: Joseph Ralston Hayden Papers, Bentley Historical Library, University of Michigan, Ann Arbor; Ronald K. Edgerton, "Joseph Ralston Hayden: The Education of a Colonialist," in *Compadre Colonialism: Studies on the Philippines under American Rule*, ed. Norman G. Owen (Ann Arbor, Mich., 1971), pp. 195–226; *EP* 17:260–61; Edward W. Mill, "Joseph Ralston Hayden: Scholar in Government," *Michigan Alumnus Quarterly Review* 46 (1946): 509–12; *NYT*, May 22, 1945; and *WWWA*.

HAYES, JAMES T. G. (1889–1980). Clergyman, born February 11, 1889, in New York City. Hayes graduated from St. Francis Xavier College (New York City) and Woodstock College (Maryland), and studied at Tronchiennes, Belgium. He entered the Society of Jesus in 1907 and was ordained in 1921. He taught at Regis High School in Boston, was an instructor in the Classics at Boston College in 1918–1919, and was dean of discipline at Fordham University from 1923 to 1925. He was a missionary in the Philippines from 1926 to 1972. He was superior of the Jesuits in Mindanao from 1927 to 1930, and superior of the Jesuits in the Philippines from 1930 to 1933. He was consecrated the first Catholic bishop of Cagayan in 1933, and its first archbishop in 1951. He was placed under house arrest during the Japanese occupation of the Philippines. He retired in 1972. Died March 28, 1980, in Cagayan de Oro, Philippines, *References*: Miguel A. Bernard, "Archbishop James T. Hayes, S. J., 1889–1980," *Kinaadman: A Journal of the Southern Philippines* 3 (1981): 243–73; *DACB; EP* 17:261; *NYT*, April 3, 1980; and *WWWA*.

HAYES, WATSON M(ACMILLAN) (1857–1944). Missionary, born November 23, 1857, near Greenfield, Mercer County, Pennsylvania. Hayes graduated from Westminster College (Pa.) and Western Theological Seminary (Pittsburgh), and was ordained in 1882. He was a missionary under the Board of Foreign Missions of the Presbyterian Church in the U.S.A. He was a professor at Tengchow College from 1893 to 1895 and its president from 1896 to 1901. He was founder and president of the Provincial University of Shantung from 1901 to 1903; professor at Union Theological Seminary in Tsinan, Shantung Province, from 1904 to 1919; president of North China Theological Seminary from 1919 to 1937; and founder of the North China Women's Bible Seminary in 1924. He was the editor and publisher of *Shantung Times*. He refused to return to the United States, and instead was interned by the Japanese during World War II. Died August 2, 1944, in a concentration camp at Weihsien, Shantung, China. *References: NYT*, September 29, 1944; and *WWWA*.

HAYES, W(ILLIAM) BREWSTER (1900–1957). Agricultural missionary, from California. Hayes graduated from Oregon State University (Corvallis, Ore.). He was a member of the faculty of Allahabad Agricultural Institute in

Allahabad, India, from 1921 until his death. One of the pioneers in the study of horticulture in India, he wrote the first textbook on the subject, *Fruit Growing in India* (Allahabad, 1945). Died August 20, 1957 in Allahabad, India.

HAYGOOD, LAURA A(SKEW) (1845–1900). Missionary, born October 14, 1845, in Watkinsville, Georgia, and grew up in Atlanta. Haygood graduated from Wesleyan Female College (Macon, Ga.). She taught at Oxford, Georgia, and at Atlanta, where she opened a private school for girls that she directed until 1872. She was instructor and then principal of a girls' high school in Atlanta until 1884. She was a missionary under the Woman's Board of Missions of the Methodist Episcopal Church, South, in China from 1884 until her death. She established a normal school in Shanghai, and developed a comprehensive school system. She was director of the woman's board of the church in China from 1896 until 1899. Died April 29, 1900, in Shanghai. *References*: Laura Askew Haygood Papers, in Atticus Greene Haygood Papers, Emory University Library, Atlanta; *DAB*; *EWM*; and Linda M. Papageorge, " 'The Hand that Rocks the Cradle Rules the World': Laura Askew Haygood and Methodist Education in China, 1884–1899," *Proceedings and Papers of the Georgia Association of Historians* 1982: 123–32.

HAZEN, HERVEY CROSBY (1841–1914). Missionary, born June 26, 1841, in Ithaca, New York. Hazen graduated from Amherst College, studied at Auburn Theological Seminary, and was ordained in 1867. He was a missionary under the American Board of Commissioners for Foreign Missions (ABCFM) in India from 1868 to 1870, serving in Madura, South India. He returned to the United States in 1870, and held pastorates in Liverpool, Manlius, Spencer, and Holley, New York, from 1870 until 1883. He was back in India in 1883 and served at Manamadura, South India, until his death. Died July 20, 1914, in Manamadura. *References*: Hervey Crosby Hazen Papers, Cornell University Libraries, Ithaca, N.Y.: *Amherst*; and *NYT*, July 29, 1914.

HEADLAND, ISAAC TAYLOR (1859–1942). Missionary, born August 16, 1859, in Freedom, Pennsylvania. Headland graduated from Mount Union College and Boston University School of Theology, and was ordained in 1890. He was a missionary under the Board of Foreign Missions of the Methodist Episcopal Church in China from 1890 until 1914. He was a professor of science at Peking University from 1890 to 1907, and president of the Anglo-Chinese College in Foochow from 1901 to 1914. He was a member of the faculty of Mount Union College from 1914 to 1937, teaching comparative religion. He wrote *The Chinese Boy and Girls* (New York, 1901); *Chinese Heroes: Being a Record of Persecutions Endured by Native Christians in the Boxer Uprising* (New York, 1902); *Court Life in China: The Capital, Its Officials and People* (New York, 1909); *China's New Day. A Study of Events that Have Led to Its Coming* (West Medford, Mass., 1912); *Some By-Products of Missions* (Cincinnati, 1912); and *Home Life* *in China* (New York, 1914). Died August 2, 1942, in Alliance, Ohio. *References: OAB; NYT*, August 3, 1942; and *WWWA*.

HEARD, AUGUSTINE (1785–1868). Sea captain and merchant, born March 30, 1785, in Ipswich, Massachusetts. He was in the employ of Ebenezer Francis, one of the principal merchants of Boston, in 1803. He sailed to India in 1805 as supercargo, became a master in 1812, and was a sea captain until 1829. He was a partner in the firm of Samuel Russell and Company in Canton from 1830 until 1834, when he returned to the United States because of ill health and settled in Boston. He established the firm of Augustine Heard and Company in 1840. He was back in China in 1841 to assume charge of the business there as head of the trading, banking, and shipping firm of Augustine Heard and Company, one of the largest firms operating in China. In 1844 he returned to the United States. Died September 14, 1868, in Ipswich, Massachusetts. *References: DAB*; and *WWWA*.

HEARD, AUGUSTINE (1827–1905). Merchant and diplomat, nephew of Augustine Heard (1785–1868),* born December 7, 1827, in Ipswich, Massachusetts. Heard graduated from Harvard University. He went to China in 1847 and engaged in mercantile activities. He was employed in Canton and Hong Kong as an agent of Augustine Heard and Company. He was said to have been the first Western businessman permitted to trade in Siam. He returned to the United States in 1857, and later resided many years in Europe, representing his firm's interests in England, France, and Russia. He was U.S. minister and consul general in Korea from 1890 to 1893. He resigned because of ill health. Died December 12, 1905, at sea off Gibraltar. *References: NCAB* 28:327; and *WWWA*.

HEARN, LAFCADIO (1850–1904). Author, born June 27, 1850, on Leukas in the Ionian Islands of Greece, and grew up in Dublin, Ireland. He came to the United States in 1869 and lived in New York City and Cincinnati. He was a reporter for several Cincinnati newspapers, an associate editor on the New Orleans *Item* from 1877 to 1881, and a reporter on the *New Orleans Times-Democrat* from 1881 to 1887. He was in Martinique, French West Indies, from 1887 to 1889. He came to Japan in 1890, and taught English at a middle school in Matsue, Shimane Prefecture, in 1890–1891, and at the government college at Kumamoto from 1891 to 1894. He married a Japanese woman and became a Japanese citizen in 1895. He was the editor of the *Kobe Chronicle* in 1894–1895, and a lecturer on English literature at Tokyo University from 1896 until 1903. He wrote *Glimpses of an Unfamiliar Japan* (Boston, 1894); *Out of the East* (Boston, 1895); *Kokoro* (Boston, 1896); *In Ghostly Japan* (Boston, 1899); *Shadowings* (Boston, 1900); *A Japanese Miscellany* (Boston, 1901); and *Japan: An Attempt at Interpretation* (New York, 1904); and *Kwaidan* (Boston, 1904). Died September 26, 1904, in Okubo (now part of Tokyo), Japan. *References:* Lafcadio Hearn Collection, University of Virginia Library: Lafcadio Hearn Papers, Houghton Library, Harvard University; *CA; DAB; DLB; EAH;* Orcutt W. Frost, *Young Hearn* (Tokyo, 1958); Sanki Ichiwaka, ed., *Some New Letters and Writings of Lafcadio Hearn* (Tokyo, 1925); Koizumi Kazuo, *Father and I: Memories of Lafcadio Hearn* (Boston, 1935); *KEJ*: Arthur E. Kunst, *Lafcadio Hearn* (New York, 1969); Vera S. McWilliams, *Lafcadio Hearn* (New York, 1946); *NCAB* 1:409; *NYT*, September 29, 1904; D. Stempel, "Lafcadio Hearn: Interpreter of Japan," *American Literature* 20 (1948): 1–19; Elizabeth Stevenson, *Lafcadio Hearn* (New York, 1961); *WWWA*; and Beongcheon Yu, *An Ape of the Gods: The Art and Thought of Lafcadio Hearn* (Detroit, 1964).

HEATH, DONALD READ (1894–   ). Diplomat, born August 12, 1894, in Topeka, Kansas. Heath graduated from Washburn College and studied at the University of Montpellier (France). He served during World War I. He entered the foreign service in 1920 and served in Bucharest, Warsaw, Bern, and Port-au-Prince. He was assistant chief of the division of Latin American Affairs from 1933 to 1937, first secretary in Germany from 1938 to 1941, and counselor in Chile from 1941 to 1944. He was attached to the Office of Military Government in Germany from 1944 to 1947, and was the U.S. minister to Bulgaria from 1947 to 1950. He was the first U.S. minister to the Associated States of Indochina—Vietnam, Cambodia, and Laos—from 1950 to 1952, following a pro-French policy, and he also served as ambassador in Vietnam and Cambodia from 1952 to 1955. In 1954, he negotiated military aid to South Vietnam. He was an ambassador to Lebanon from 1955 to 1957 and to Saudi Arabia from 1957 until his retirement in 1961. He was vice president and then president of the Foreign Bondholders Protective Council from 1961 until 1971. *References: DADH; PolProf: Truman;* and *WWA.*

HEDGES, FRANK HINCKLEY (1895–1940). Journalist, born April 19, 1895, in Springfield, Missouri. Hedges graduated from Drury College (Springfield, Mo.) and the University of Missouri. He was, successively, news editor in Miami, Oklahoma, and Corpus Christie, Texas, and feature writer in the *Washington* (D.C.) *Herald.* He served in the U.S. Army during World War I. He was on the staff of the *Japan Advertiser* in Peking and Tokyo, and was managing editor in Tokyo from 1923 to 1927, chief of the Far Eastern Bureau of the *Christian Science Monitor* in Tokyo from 1927 to 1932, staff correspondent of *The* (London) *Times* in 1930–1931, and executive secretary of the Press Congress of the World after 1934. He was also Far Eastern representative of the North American Newspaper Alliance; Japan correspondence of the *Washington Post,* London *Daily Telegraph,* London *Morning Post,* and *North-China Daily News;* and contributing editor of *The Japan Times and Mail* after 1935. He wrote *In Far Japan: Glimpses and Sketches* (Tokyo, 1935). Died April 10, 1940, in Tokyo. *Reference: NYT,* April 13, 1940; and *WWWA.*

HEFLIN, CLYDE E(VERETTE) (1888–1958). Missionary educator, born July 12, 1888, in Monmouth, Illinois. Heflin graduated from the Normal Department of Valparaiso University, William and Vashti College (Aledo, Ill.), McCormick Theological Seminary (Chicago), and Columbia University. He served during World War I as an army chaplain. He was a member of the faculty of Silliman University in Dumaguete, Philippines, after 1919. He was the librarian, head of the department of education, dean of its colleges of Liberal Arts and Education, and professor of education and sociology after 1935; later he was dean of the graduate school. He was interned by the Japanese during World War II in Manila. He returned to Silliman university after the war to aid in its post war rehabilitation. He retired in 1957. Died July 6, 1958, in Wooster, Ohio. *Reference: NYT*, July 9, 1958.

HEINE, PETER BERNARD WILHELM (1827–1885). Artist, born January 30, 1827, in Dresden, Germany. Heine studied at the Dresden Academy. He came to the United States in 1849 and became a U.S. citizen in 1855. He served as the principal artist with Perry's Expedition to Japan from 1852 to 1854. He published illustrated accounts of the expedition in English and German. In 1856, he exhibited a panorama of China and Japan in New York City. He lived in New York City until 1859, when he returned to Europe. In 1860–1861, he accompanied the Prussian expedition to East Asia. He returned to the United States with the outbreak of the Civil War and served in the Union Army. He was a consular clerk in Paris, Florence, and Liverpool from 1866 to 1871. Died October 5, 1885, in Loessnitz, near Dresden, Germany. *Reference: NYHSD*; and *WWWA*.

HEINRICHS, JACOB (1860–1947). Missionary, born March 2, 1860, in Alenstein, Germany, and came to the United States in 1881. Heinrichs attended the University of Rochester, graduated from Rochester Theological Seminary, and was ordained in 1889. He was a missionary under the American Baptist Missionary Union in India from 1889 to 1917. He served in Nellore, Ongole, and Vinukonda, and was president of the Baptist Mission Theological Seminary at Ramapatnam, South India, from 1895 to 1917. He was dean and professor of systematic theology at the Northern Baptist Theological Seminary (Chicago), from 1918 to 1933. Died August 30, 1947, in Middlebury, Vermont.

HEISER, VICTOR GEORGE (1873–1972). Public health physician, born February 5, 1873, in Johnstown, Pennsylvania. Heiser graduated from Jefferson Medical College (Philadelphia). He entered the U.S. Marine Health Service (later the U.S. Public Health Service) in 1898, was chief quarantine officer in the Philippines from 1903 to 1915, and served as director of health in the Philippines from 1905 until 1915. He organized sanitation systems and preventive medicine in the islands, and was involved in building the Philippine General Hospital, the College of Medicine and Surgery in Manila, and many hospitals throughout the Philippines. He was also professor of hygiene at the College of Medicine. He was associate director of the international health division of the Rockefeller Foundation from 1914 until 1934. He retired in 1934. He wrote *An American Doctor's Odyssey* (New York, 1936). Died February 27, 1972, in New York City. *References*: Victor George Heiser Papers, American Philosophical Society Library, Philadelphia; *CA; CB* 1942; *NYT*, February 28, 1972; and *WWWA*.

HEMENWAY, ASA (1810–1892). Missionary, born July 6, 1810, in Shoreham, Vermont, Hemenway graduated from Middlebury College and Andover Theological Seminary, and was ordained in 1839. He was a missionary under the American Board of Commissioners for Foreign Missions (ABCFM) in Siam from 1839 to 1850. He was later a pastor in Cornwall, Mooers, and West Hartford, Vermont; and Ripton, Keeseville, and East Chazy, New York. He wrote a geography and history in Siamese. Died February 26, 1892, in Manchester, Vermont. *References: AndoverTS:* and George H. Feltus, ed., *Missionary Journals of Rev. Jesse Caswell and of the Rev. and Mrs. Asa Hemenway* (Troy, N.Y., 1931).

HEMENWAY, RUTH V. (1894–1974). Medical missionary, born in Williamsburg, Massachusetts. Hemenway graduated from Tufts Medical School. She was a medical missionary under the Women's Board of Foreign Missions of the Methodist Episcopal Church in China from 1924 to 1941. She was superintendent of the hospital for women at Mintsing, Fukien Province, from 1924 to 1936, and later served in Nanchang, Kiangsi Province, Chungking, and Tzechow. She returned to the United States in 1941 and practiced medicine in Sharon, Pennsylvania, and later in Williamsburg, Massachusetts. Died July 9, 1974, in Williamsburg. *A Memoir of Revolutionary China 1924–1941*, ed. with an introd. by Fred Drake (Amherst, Mass., 1977) was published posthumously. *References*: Ruth V. Hemenway Diaries, Smith College Library, Northampton, Mass.; *Hampshire Gazette*, July 9, 1974.

HENDERSON, ALBERT HALEY (1866–1937). Medical missionary, born February 27, 1866, in St. James, Jamaica, and came to the United States in 1889. Henderson studied in the medical school of the International Medical Missionary Society in New York City. He was a missionary under the American Baptist Foreign Mission Society in Burma from 1893 until his retirement in 1943. He served in Mongnai and later at Taunggyi, Shan States. He retired in 1934, and continued to live in Burma. Died February 21, 1937, in Taunggyi, Burma. *Reference*: Katherine L. Read with Robert O. Ballou, *Bamboo Hospital, The Story of a Missionary Family in Burma* (Philadelphia, 1961).

HENDERSON, LOY W(ESLEY) (1892–). Diplomat, born June 28, 1892, near Rogers, Arkansas. Henderson graduated from Northwestern University and attended Denver University Law School. He served with the Red Cross in France during World War I and until 1921. He entered the diplomatic service in 1922, and served in Dublin, Queenstown, Ireland, Riga, Kaunas, and Tallinn. He was a second secretary of embassy at Moscow from 1935 to 1936, first secretary from 1936 to 1938, assistant chief of the division of East European Affairs from 1938 to 1942, counselor of embassy at Moscow in 1942–1943, minister to Iraq from 1943 to 1945, and chief of the division of Near Eastern and African Affairs from 1945 to 1948. He was U.S. ambassador to India and minister to Nepal from 1948 to 1951. He was ambassador to Iran from 1951 to 1955, assistant secretary of state in 1955, and deputy undersecretary of state from 1955 until his retirement in 1961. *References*: Loy W. Henderson Papers, Manuscript Division, Library of Congress; *CB* 1948; *DADH*; Surandra K. Gupta, ''Loy Henderson as Truman's Ambassador in India,'' *Asian Profile* (Hong Kong) 14 (1986): 335–42; and *WWA*.

HENDRICK, THOMAS A(UGUSTINE) (1849–1909). Clergyman, born October 29, 1849, in Penn Yan, New York. Hendrick graduated from Seton Hall College (S. Orange, N.J.) and St. Joseph's Theological Seminary (Troy, N.Y.), and was ordained in 1873. He held pastorates in Rochester, Charlotte, and Union Springs, New York, from 1873 to 1903. He was consecrated the first American Roman Catholic bishop of Cebu, Philippines, in 1903, and served there from 1904 until his death. Died November 29, 1909, in Manila. *References*: Thomas A. Hendrick Papers, Nazareth College Archives, Rochester, N.Y.; John J. Delaney and James E. Tobin, *Dictionary of Catholic Biography* (Garden City, N.Y., 1961); Charles L. Higgins, ''The Hendrick Papers,'' *PS* 28 (1980): 420–50; *NYT*, December 1, 1909; and *WWWA*.

HENKE, FREDERICK G(OODRICH) (1876–1963). Educator, born August 2, 1876, in Alden, Iowa. Henke graduated from Morningside College, Northwestern University, and the University of Chicago, and was ordained in 1900. He was a missionary under the Boards of Foreign Missions of the Methodist Episcopal Church in Kiukiang, China, from 1901 to 1904, district superintendent of Kiukiang and vice president and professor of homiletics at William Nast College in Kiukiang from 1904 to 1907; and professor of philosophy and psychology at the University of Nanking, China, from 1910 to 1913. In 1910 he established the first psychological laboratory in China. He was a professor of philosophy and education at Willamette (Ore.) University in 1913–1914, and professor of philosophy and education at Allegheny College (Meadville, Pa.) from 1914 until his retirement in 1942. Died October 27, 1963, in Charles City, Iowa. *Reference: WWWA*.

HENRY, HAROLD (1909–1976). Missionary, born July 11, 1909, in Northfield, Minnesota. Henry studied at St. Senan's College (County Clare, Ireland) and St. Columban's Seminary (Omaha, Neb.), and was ordained in 1932. He was a missionary under the St. Columban's Foreign Mission Society in Korea from 1933 until his death. He served in the province of Cholla Namdo, Southwest Korea, in 1934–1935, and was pastor of the parish of Naju from 1935 until 1941. He was interned by the Japanese in 1941–1942, and served as a military chaplain during World War II. He returned to Korea in 1947, and served at Mokpo. He was pro-prefect apostolic of the prefecture of Kwangju until 1954, and prefect apostolic of Kwangu from 1954 until 1971. He was consecrated bishop in 1957 and archbishop in 1962. He was prefect apostolic of Cheju, Korea, from 1971 until his death. Died March 1, 1976, in Cheju. *Reference*: Edward Fischer, *Light in the Far East: Archbishop Harold Henry's Forty-Two Years in Korea* (New York, 1976).

HENRY, JAMES MCCLURE (1880–1958). Missionary educator, born December 2, 1880, in Canton, China, to American parents. Henry graduated from the University of Wooster and Union Theological Seminary. He was a missionary under the Board of Foreign Missions of the Presbyterian Church in the U.S.A. in China from 1909 to 1948. He served in Canton from 1909 to 1919 and with Lingnan University after 1919. He was president of Lingnan University in 1924 and its provost from 1927 to 1948. He was chairman of the Canton Refugee Areas Relief Commission from 1938 to 1941. He was interned by the Japanese from 1941 to 1943. He was attached to the Fourteenth U.S. Air Force in Northern Kwangtung in 1944–1945, was deputy director of the United Nations Relief and Rehabilitation Agency (UNRRA) in the Kwangtung regional office from 1945 to 1947, advisor to the Kwangtung provincial government in 1948, and chief of the Overseas Chinese section of the Committee for Free Asia in 1951–1952. Died December 18, 1958, in Nokomis, Florida. *References: NYT*, December 29, 1958; and *WWWA*.

HENRY, PHILIP WALTER (1864–1947). Engineer, born March 24, 1864, in Scranton, Pennsylvania. Henry graduated from Rensselaer Polytechnic Institute. He was vice president of the American International Corporation from 1916 to 1923, in charge of its engineering investigations. As vice president of Siems-Carey Railway and Canal Company from 1923 to 1927, he was responsible for the engineering organization that made the Chinese government a survey for a railroad to connect Chengtu with Hankow for the purpose of opening up the province of Szechwan, as well as surveys to rehabilitate the Grand Canal between the Yangtze River and Tientsin, together with an extensive reclamation project. Died November 7, 1947, in New York City. *References: NCAB* 36:247; *NYT*, November 9, 1947; and *WWWA*.

HEPBURN, J(AMES) C(URTIS) (1815–1911). Medical missionary, born March 13, 1815, in Milton, Pennsylvania. Hepburn graduated from Princeton University and the University of Pennsylvania Medical School. He was a medical missionary under the Board of Foreign Missions of the Presbyterian Church in the U.S.A. in Singapore from 1841 to 1843 and in Amoy, China, from 1843 to 1845. He returned to the United States in 1845 and practiced medicine in New York City until 1859, when he went to Japan. He operated a dispensary in Kanagawa (now part of Yokohama). He was one of the founders of Meiji Gakuin University, and served as its first president. He also taught physiology and hygiene there. He prepared *A Japanese and English Dictionary* (Shanghai, 1867), the first for these particular languages. He adopted a system of romanization of Japanese, and was the popularizer of the so-called Hepburn system of romanizing Japanese. He also played a major role in translating the Bible into Japanese. He returned to the United States in 1892. Died September 21, 1911, in East Orange, New Jersey. *References; CDCWM; DAB; EAH; KEJ;* Elizabeth G. Mitchell, "Dr. James Curtis Hepburn in Old Yokohama," *Japan Christian Quarterly* 25 (1959): 26–33; *NYT*, September 22, 1911, and Michio Takaya, ed., *The Letters of Dr. J. C. Hepburn* (Tokyo, 1955).

HERON, JOHN W(ILLIAM) (1856–1890). Medical missionary, born June 15, 1856, in England. Heron came to the United States in 1870 and grew up in Knoxville, Tennessee. He graduated from Maryville College (Tenn.) and the medical department of the University of Tennessee, and studied at the medical department of the University of New York. He was a medical missionary under the Board of Foreign Missions of the Presbyterian Church in the U.S.A. in Korea from 1885 until his death. He was in charge of a government hospital in Seoul (later Severance Hospital), and was court physician to the Korean royal family after 1887. Died July 26, 1890, in Seoul. *References: CR* 21 (1890); 412–16; and Daniel L. Gifford, "John W. Heron, M.D.," *Korean Repository* 4 (1897): 441–43.

HERRE, ALBERT W(ILLIAM) C(HRISTIAN) T(HEODORE) (1868– 1962). Naturalist, born September 16, 1868, in Toledo, Ohio. Herre graduated from Stanford University. He was assistant superintendent of schools in Springfield, Illinois, from 1890 to 1900, and a teacher of biology there from 1895 to 1900. He was an assistant with the U.S. Bureau of Fisheries in 1903–1904, a teacher of biology in San Jose, California, from 1904 to 1910, and vice principal of a high school from 1910 to 1912. He was professor of geography at Washington State Normal School (Bellingham, Wash.) from 1912 to 1917, and professor of biology there from 1917 to 1919. He was chief of the department of fisheries of the Bureau of Science in the Philippines from 1920 to 1928. He was curator of the Zoological Museum at Stanford University from 1928 until his retirement in 1948. He subsequently was an ichthyologist for the Philippine fishery project of the U.S. Fish and Wildlife Service in 1947–1948, and a professor at the

University of Washington School of Fisheries from 1948 until 1959. He served as a consultant to the governments of the Philippines, China, and India, was a member of the Crane Pacific expedition in 1928–1929, and led the Herre Philippine expedition in 1931. He also led expeditions to the Philippines, China, Malaya, and Ceylon in 1933–1934; to China, the Philippines, Borneo, Malaya, Burma, and India in 1940–1941. He wrote *The Gobies of the Philippines and the China Sea* (Manila, 1927); *Philippine Fish Tales* (Manila, 1935); *Stories of Philippine Fishes* (n.p., 1938); and *Check List of Philippine Fishes* (Washington, D.C., 1953). Died January 16, 1962, in Santa Cruz, California. *References: NCAB* 52:596; and *WWWA*.

HERRICK, JAMES (1814–1891). Missionary, born March 19, 1814, in Broome, Canada. Herrick graduated from Williams College and Andover Theological Seminary, and was ordained in 1845. He was a missionary under the American Board of Commissioners for Foreign Missions (ABCFM) in the Madura Mission, India, from 1846 until 1883, serving at Tirumangalam, with the exception of four years at Pasumalai. He returned to the United States in 1883. Died November 30, 1891, in West Brattleboro, Vermont. His son, **DAVID SCUDDER HERRICK** (1863–1954), missionary, was born March 29, 1863, in Tirumangalam, India, and graduated from Williams College and Union Theological Seminary. He studied at Oxford University, and was ordained in 1894. He was a missionary under the ABCFM in India after 1885. He taught at Pasumalai College, at the mission high school in Madura, and served at Batalagundu. Later he taught at the American College (successor of Pasumalai College) and was a professor at the United Theological College in Bangalore. Died January 22, 1954, in West Haven, Massachusetts. *Reference: Hewitt.*

HERVEY, HARRY (CLAY) (1900–1951). Author, explorer, and screen writer, born November 5, 1900, in Beaumont, Texas. Hervey sold his first story when he was sixteen years old. He traveled in Asia, Africa, and the islands of the Pacific. In 1925 he led an expedition to upper Indochina, where he discovered additional Khmer ruins. He wrote *Where Strange Gods Call: Pages Out of the East* (New York, 1924) and *King Cobra: An Autobiography of Travel in French Indo-China* (New York, 1927). Died August 12, 1951, in New York City. *References: NYT*, August 13, 1951; and *WWWA*.

HESTER, E(VETT) D(ORELL) (1893–1984). Financial advisor and diplomat, born May 25, 1893, in Capron, Illinois. Hester graduated from Northwestern University and studied at Georgetown University and the University of Madrid. He came to the Philippines in 1916 and was a high school teacher from 1916 to 1919, and a professor of economics at University of the Philippines from 1919 to 1925. He entered the Bureau of Foreign and Domestic Commerce of the U.S. Department of Commerce in 1925 and was assistant commercial attaché from 1926 to 1929 and trade commissioner from 1929 to 1935. He was executive officer of the Philippine Sugar Administration from 1934 to 1937, assistant financial expert in the Office of the Governor General from 1935 to 1939, and economic advisor in the U.S. Department of the Interior from 1940 to 1946. He entered the foreign service in 1946, was an economic advisor in 1946–1947, an attaché in 1947–1948, and a counselor for economic affairs in Manila from 1948 to 1950. Died July 27, 1984, in Banawe, Philippines. *References*: E. D. Hester Papers, Manuscript Division, Library of Congress; and *BAHC* 12 (October–December 1984): 95–98.

HEUSKEN, HENRY (1832–1861). Diplomat, born January 20, 1832, in Amsterdam, the Netherlands. Heusken came to the United States in 1853. He was a secretary to Townsend Harris,* the first U.S. consul general to Japan, from 1855 until his death. Murdered January 16, 1861, in Edo, Japan. *References*: Henry Heusken, *Japan Journal, 1855–1861*, trans. and ed. Jeanette C. van der Corput and Robert A. Wilson (New Brunswick, N.J., 1964); and *KEJ*.

HEWES, LAWRENCE I(LSLEY) (1902–   ). Economist and government official, born April 17, 1902, in Kingston, Rhode Islands. Hewes graduated from Dartmouth College and George Washington and Harvard universities. He was an investment banker in San Francisco from 1925 to 1933, associated with the State Relief Administration in San Francisco from 1933 to 1935, assistant to the undersecretary of agriculture in 1935, assistant to the administrator of the Farm Security Administration in Washington, D.C., from 1935 to 1939, and its regional director in San Francisco from 1939 to 1944. He was West Coast director of the American Council on Race Relations in San Francisco from 1944 to 1947. He was a land reform advisor in the General Headquarters of the Supreme Commander for the Allied Powers (SCAP) in Tokyo from 1947 to 1949. He was the chief land settlement and agricultural economist for the Bureau of Land Reclamation in Denver, Colorado, from 1950 to 1959; chief of forecasts and economics of the U.S. Outdoor Recreation Resources Review Commission from 1959 to 1962; assistant to the administrator of the Office of Rural Areas Development in 1962–1963; rural development advisor to mission to India of the Agency for International Development in New Delhi from 1962 to 1965; chief of natural resources conservation for the Rural Community Development Service from 1965 to 1968; and senior consultant to the United Nations Food and Agriculture Organization development programs from 1968 to 1973. He wrote *Japanese Land Reform Program* (Tokyo, 1950); *Japan: Land and Men: An Account of the Japanese Land Reform Program, 1945–51* (Ames, Ia., 1955); and an autobiography, *Boxcar in the Sand* (New York, 1957). *References: AMWS; CA;* and *WWA.*

HEYER, JOHN [JOHANN] CHRISTIAN FREDERICK (1793–1873). Missionary, born July 10, 1793, in Heimstedt, Duchy of Brunswick, Germany. Heyer studied at Göttingen University. Afterward, in 1807, he came to the United

States and settled in Philadelphia. He was ordained in 1820, and held pastorates in Somerset and Carlisle, Pennsylvania, until 1832. He was a missionary under the Pennsylvania Ministerium and later under the Foreign Missionary Society of the General Synod of the Evangelical Lutheran Church in India from 1842 to 1857 and again from 1869 to 1872. He served in Guntur and Gurjal, Madras Residency, until 1855, and later in Rajahmundry. Died November 7, 1873, in Philadelphia. *References*: Johann Christian Frederick Heyer Papers, Lutheran Theological Seminary Library, Philadelphia; *ACAB*; E. Theodore Bachman, *They Called Him Father: The Life Story of John Christian Frederick Heyer* (Philadelphia, 1942); *DAB*; George Drach, *Kingdom Pathfinders: Biographical Sketches of Foreign Missionaries* (Philadelphia, 1942), pp. 1–24; and *LC*.

HIBBARD, DAVID S(UTHERLAND) (1868–1967). Missionary and educator, born October 31, 1868, in Hamden, Vinton County, Ohio. Hibbard graduated from the College of Emporia, Princeton University, and Princeton Theological Seminary, and was ordained in 1896. He was a pastor in Lyndon, Kansas, from 1896 to 1899. He was a missionary under the Board of Foreign Missions of the Presbyterian Church in the U.S.A. in the Philippines from 1899 until 1938. He served in Manila in 1899–1900 and in Iloilo in 1900–1901. He opened a school at Dumaguete, Negros Oriental (later Silliman University*) in 1901, and was its president until 1929. He wrote *The First Quarter: A Brief History of Silliman Institute during the First Twenty-five Years of Its Existence* (Manila, 1926), and *Making a Nation: The Changing Philippines* (New York, 1926). He was a professor of philosophy at Union Theological Seminary, Manila, from 1931 until 1938. Died January 1967, in Pasadena, California. *References: EP* 17:27–271; *OAB*; and *WWWA*.

HIGDON, ELMER KELSO (1887–1961). Missionary, born October 14, 1887, in Clarence, Illinois. Higdon attended Eureka College and graduated from Yale University. He was a missionary under the Christian Churches (Disciples of Christ) in the Philippines from 1917 until 1937. He was principal of the Bible Training School at Vigan, Ilocos Sur, from 1917 to 1919; professor, vice president, and acting president of Union Theological Seminary in Manila; and a pastor in Manila. He was executive secretary of the National Christian Council of the Philippine Islands from 1930 to 1936, and editor of the *National Christian Council Bulletin*. He returned to the United States in 1937, where he was executive secretary of the Foreign Missions Conference of North America from 1937 to 1939, executive secretary of the Department of Oriental Missions of the United Christian Missionary Society from 1939 to 1949, and executive secretary of the department of missionary selection and training from 1949 until his retirement in 1955. He wrote (with I. W. Higdon) *From Carabao to Clipper* (New York, 1941). Died April 15, 1961, in Manila. *References: EP* 17:271–72; and *NYT*, April 21, 1961.

HIGGINBOTTOM, SAM (1874–1958). Agricultural missionary, born October 27, 1874, in Manchester, England, and came to the United States in 1903. Higginbottom attended Amherst College and graduated from Princeton and Ohio State universities. He was a missionary under the Board of Foreign Missions of the Presbyterian Church in the United States in India from 1903 to 1945. He was a teacher of economics, biology, English, and Bible at the Allahabad Christian College (later the Ewing Christian College) from 1903 to 1909, and was teacher of economics and Bible and president of the college from 1933 to 1945. He began a campaign to improve the living standards of the Indian country people, and in 1911 founded a school farm (which was to become the Allahabad Agricultural Institute) of which he was the president. He was credited with introducing to the region contour farming, crop rotation, and many other agricultural improvements. He devised India's unique and most successful agricultural education curriculum, which placed emphasis on practical training, and organized the first large-scale development program. He was director of agriculture in the state of Gwailor from 1916 to 1919, and agricultural advisor to several Indian states. He wrote *The Gospel and the Plow, or, the Old Gospel and Modern Farming in Ancient India* (New York, 1921). He retired from India in 1945. He wrote *Sam Higginbottom, Farmer: An Autobiography* (New York, 1949). Died June 11, 1958, in Port Washington, Long Island, New York. *References*: Sam Higginbottom Papers, University of Virginia Library, Charlottesville, Va.; *Amherst*; Gary R. Hess, *Sam Higginbottom of Allahabad: Pioneer of Point Four to India* (Charlottesville, Va., 1967); *NCAB* 44:481; *NYT*, June 12, 1958; and *WWWA*.

HIGGINS, JON B. (1939–1984). Ethnomusicologist, born September 18, 1939, in Cambridge, Massachusetts. Higgins attended the University of Denver and graduated from Wesleyan University. He was in India from 1964 to 1967, where he studied Carnatic music. He became the first Westerner to master the art of Carnatic music of southern India. He was a member of the faculty of York University from 1971 to 1978, and a professor of music at Wesleyan University and director of the Wesleyan's Center for the Arts after 1978. Killed December 7, 1984, by a hit-and-run driver, in Middletown, Connecticut. *References: DFAF*; and *NYT*, December 10, 1984.

HIGGINSON, NATHANIEL (1652–1708). Merchant, born October 11, 1652, in Guilford, Connecticut, and grew up in Salem, Massachusetts. Higginson graduated from Harvard University. He left for England in 1674, was a tutor for the children of Lord Wharton from 1674 to 1681, was employed in the mint of the Tower of London from 1681 to 1683, entered the service of the English East India Company in 1683, and went to India in 1684. He was stationed at Fort Saint George, Madras, from 1684 to 1692. He was governor of Fort Saint George from 1692 until 1698, and mayor of Madras in 1688–1689. He returned to England in 1700. Died October 31, 1708, in Soper Lane, Pancreas Parish, London. *References: DAB; and WWWA.*

HILL, PERCY A. (?   –1937). Farmer. Hill served in the Philippine Constabulary from 1901 until 1904, and was later a rice farmer, pioneering rice farming in northern Nueva Ecija in Central Luzon. For many years he wrote the monthly column on rice for the *Journal of the American Chamber of Commerce.* He also wrote *Romance and Adventure in Old Manila* (Manila, 1928). He was murdered in 1937. *References: Elarth; and Gleeck/Frontiers.*

HILLER, HIRAM M(ILLIKEN) (1867–1921). Physician and traveler, born March 8, 1867, in Kahokaa, Missouri. Hiller graduated from Parsons College (Ia.) and the University of Pennsylvania, and studied at the universities of Berlin, Vienna, and Paris. He practiced medicine in Chester, Pennsylvania, after 1891. With William Furness* and Alfred C. Harrison,* he made a series of extended scientific voyages to east, south, and Southeast Asia between 1895 and 1901. He spent several years among the people living in Sarawak and Kalimantan, Borneo; studied hill people in western India, Naga Hills, and in Ceylon; and made several trips to study the Ainu in Japan. He gave his collections to the University Museum of the University of Pennsylvania and to the Philadelphia Academy of Natural Science. Died August 7, 1921, in Swarthmore, Pennsylvania. *References*: Hiram M. Hiller Journals and Correspondence, University Museum Archives, University of Pennsylvania, Philadelphia; and *WWWA.*

HINTON, WILLIAM H(OWARD) (1919–   ). Agriculturist, born February 2, 1919, in Chicago. Hinton attended Harvard University and graduated from Cornell University. He was a propaganda analyst in China for the Office of War Information in 1945–1946. He was a tractor technician in China for the United Nations Relief and Rehabilitation Administration (UNRRA) in 1947, for North China People's Government in Shansi Province from 1947 to 1949, and for the People's Republic of China in Peking from 1949 to 1953. He lived in the farming village of Chang Chuang (Long Bow) in southwestern Shansi Province in 1948, and returned in 1971. He was a truck mechanic in Philadelphia from 1956 to 1963, and a grain farmer in Fleetwood, Pennsylvania, from 1963 to 1979. He was consultant to the Chinese Ministry of Agriculture in Beijing in 1978 and 1985, and to the United Nations Grassland Project in Inner Mongolia from 1980 to 1983. He wrote *Fanshen: A Documentary of Revolution in a Chinese Village* (New York, 1966); *Iron Oxen: A Documentary of Revolution in Chinese Farming* (New York, 1970); *Hundred Day War: The Cultural Revolution at Tsinghua University* (New York, 1972); *Turning Point in China: An Essay on the Cultural Revolution* (New York, 1972); and *Shenfan, the Continuing Revolution in a Chinese Village* (New York, 1983). *Reference: CA.*

HIPPS, JOHN BURDER (1884–1967). Missionary, born February 12, 1884, in Madison County, North Carolina. Hipps graduated from Wake Forest College, Southern Baptist, and Union theological seminaries, and from Columbia University. He was a teacher in Spring Creek, North Carolina, from 1902 to 1905, and principal of a school in Pennington Gap, Virginia, from 1907 to 1910. He was a missionary under the Foreign Mission Board of the Southern Baptist Convention in China from 1913 until 1949. He served at the University of Shanghai as instructor, professor, dean of the theological seminary from 1923 to 1935, and chairman of the Division of Religious Studies. He left China in 1941, but was back in 1944 and aided in the rehabilitation of the university. He returned to the United States in 1949 and was a professor of missions at Southeastern Baptist Theological Seminary (Wake Forest, N.C.) from 1951 until his retirement in 1957. He wrote *History of the University of Shanghai* (Richmond, Va., 1964), and *Forty Years in Christian Missions: An Autobiography* (Raleigh, N.C., 1966). Died December 30, 1967, in Wake Forest, North Carolina. *References*: John Burder Hipps Papers, North Carolina Baptist Historical Collection, Wake Forest University Library, Winston-Salem, N.C.; and *ESB S3*.

HIRST, JESSE WATSON (1864-1952). Medical missionary, born March 30, 1864, in Fall River, Massachusetts. Hirst graduated from Princeton University and Jefferson Medical College, and studied at Johns Hopkins University. He practiced medicine in Philadelphia from 1898 to 1904. He was a medical missionary under the Board of Foreign Missions of the Presbyterian Church in the U.S.A. in Korea from 1904 until his retirement in 1934. He served in Seoul after 1904; and founded the Union Medical College (later Severance Union Medical College) in 1904. He also served as a physician to the emperor of Korea. Died April 28, 1952, in Saint Petersburg, Florida. *Reference: NCAB* 42:127; and *NYT*, April 30, 1952.

HITCHCOCK, JOHN T(HAYER) (1917–   ). Anthropologist, born June 29, 1917, in Springfield, Massachusetts. Hitchcock graduated from Amherst College, the University of Chicago, and Cornell University, and studied at the University of Copenhagen. He served in the U.S. Navy during World War II. He was an assistant professor of anthropology at the University of California at Los Angeles from 1958 to 1963, associate professor there from 1963 to 1966, and professor of anthropology and South Asian studies at the University of Wisconsin after 1966. He carried out fieldwork in India from 1953 to 1955, and in Nepal from 1960 to 1962 and from 1966 to 1968. He was coauthor of *The Magars of Banyan Hill* (New York, 1966); *The Rajputs of Khalpur, India* (New York, 1966); and *Sickle and Khukri* (Madison, Wis., 1971); and produced several ethnographic movies. He described his experiences in "Fieldwork in Gurkha Country," in *Being an Anthropologist: Fieldwork in Eleven Countries*, ed. George D. Spindler (New York, 1970). *References: Amherst; AMWS; DFAF;* and *WWA*.

HITCHCOCK, ROMYN (1851–1923). Scientist, born December 1, 1851, in St. Louis. Hitchcock attended Cornell University and graduated from Columbia School of Mines. He was assistant professor of chemistry at Lehigh University from 1872 to 1874; engaged in the test of heavy guns at the government arsenal in Springfield, Massachusetts, from 1874 to 1876; professor of chemistry and toxicology in the Chicago Homeopathic Medical College in 1876–1877; editor of the *American Quarterly Microscopical Journal* and the *American Microscopical Journal* from 1878 to 1886; and curator of the National Museum in Washington, D.C., from 1883 to 1886. He was professor of English at the Koto Chu Gakko in Osaka, Japan, from 1886 to 1889, was in charge of the photographic work of the United States eclipse expedition to Japan in 1887, and served as U.S. commissioner to China for the World Columbian Exposition from 1887 to 1889. He later conducted botanical research. Died November 30, 1923, in Baltimore, Maryland. *References*: Romyn Hitchcock Papers, Cornell University Library, Ithaca, N.Y.: *NCAB* 19:42; and *WWWA*.

HOBART, ALICE TISDALE (NOURSE) (1882–1967). Author, born January 28, 1882, in Lockport, New York, and grew up near Chicago. Hobart attended Northwestern University and the University of Chicago. She came to China in 1908 to visit her sister, and taught in Hangchow until 1914, when she married Earle Tisdale Hobart, a Standard Oil representative in China. She remained in China until 1927, living in frontier villages in Manchuria, Mongolia, and various cities. When her home in Nanking was attacked in 1927, she returned to the United States. She wrote several books based on her experiences in China: *Pioneering When the World Is Old: Leaves from a Manchurian Diary* (New York, 1917); *By the City of the Long Sand, a Tale of New China* (New York, 1926); *Within the Walls of Nanking* (New York, 1928); *Pidgin Cargo* (New York, 1929); *Oil for the Lamps of China* (Indianapolis, 1933); *Yang and Yin: A Novel of an American Doctor in China* (Indianapolis, 1936); an autobiography, *Gusty's Child* (New York, 1959); and *The Innocent Dreamers* (Indianapolis, 1963). Died March 14, 1967, in Oakland, California. *References: CA; DAB S8*; Mary J. DeMarr, *American Women Writers* (New York, 1980), 2:304–6; *NYT*, March 15, 1967; and *WWWA*.

HOBBS, CECIL (CARLTON) (1907–   ). Librarian, born April 22, 1907, in Martins Ferry, Ohio. Hobbs graduated from University of Illinois and Colgate Rochester Divinity School. He was a missionary under the American Board of Commissioners for Foreign Missions (ABCFM) as a field administrator in Burma from 1935 to 1940 as well as a professor at the Pierce Divinity College and Burman Theological Seminary in Insein, Burma. He was head of the South Asia section of the Library of Congress, specialist on Southeast Asia from 1943 to 1972, and a consultant after 1972. He made several acquisition trips to Southeast Asia after 1958. He wrote *The Burmese Family: An Inquiry into Its History, Customs, and Traditions* (Washington, D.C., 1952). *References; CA;* and DAS.

HOBERECHT, EARNEST (1918–   ). Journalist, born January 1, 1918, in Watonga, Oklahoma. Hoberecht graduated from the University of Oklahoma. He was a reporter for the *Memphis* (Tenn.) *Press Scimitar* in 1941–1942, editor of the *Pearl Harbor Bulletin* in 1944–1945, United Press International (UPI) war correspondent in 1945, correspondent in Japan from 1946 to 1948, UPI bureau manager in Tokyo from 1948 to 1951, and general manager for Asia from 1951 to 1966. He was vice president of UPI from 1953 to 1966, and president of American Suppliers, Incorporated, after 1966. He wrote *Tokyo Romance* (New York, 1947), a novel, and *Asia Is My Beat* (Tokyo, 1961). *References: CA; JBEWW;* and *WWA*.

HODGE, JOHN R(EED) (1893–1963). Army officer, born June 12, 1893, in Golconda, Illinois. Hodge attended Southern Illinois University, the University of Illinois, and Army Officers Training School (Fort Sheridan, Ill.), and was commissioned a second lieutenant in 1917. He served in France during World War I, and then served in various infantry units. He was assistant division commander of the Twenty-Fifth Division in 1942–1943, commanding general of the American Division in 1943–1944, and commander of the Twenty-Fourth Corps from 1945 to 1948. After the surrender of Japan, he moved his corps to Korea and commanded the U.S. Forces in the American Zone of Occupation until 1948. His command established a government for South Korea. Friction with Syngman Rhee, the president of Korea, led to his recall to Washington, D.C. He was commander of the Third Army from 1950 to 1952, and chief of the Army Field Forces from 1952 until his retirement with the rank of general in 1953. Died November 12, 1963, in Washington, D.C. *References*: Soon-Sung Cho, "Hodge's Dilemma: Failure of Korean Trusteeship," *Korean Affairs* 4 (May 1965): 58–74; J. Earnest Fisher, *Pioneers of Modern Korea* (Seoul, 1977), pp. 125–35; Han Mu Kang, "The United States Military Government in Korea, 1945–1948; An Analysis and Evaluation of Its Policy," Ph.D. diss., University of Cincinnati, 1970; Richard E. Lauterbach, "Hodge's Korea," *Virginia Quarterly Review* 23 (1947): 349–68; *NCAB* 51:693; and *NYT*, November 13, 1963.

HODOUS, LEWIS (1872–1949). Educator, born December 31, 1872, in Bohemia, and came to the United States in 1882. Hodous graduated from Western Reserve University and Hartford Theological Seminary, studied at the University of Halle, and was ordained in 1901. He was a missionary under the American Board of Commissioners for Foreign Missions (ABCFM) in China from 1901 to 1917. He served in Ponasang from 1901 to 1904, teaching at the mission's theological seminary, and was president of Foochow Theological Seminary from 1902 to 1912 and of the Foochow Union Theological Seminary from 1914 to 1917. He was professor of Chinese culture at the Kennedy School of Missions of Hartford Seminary Foundation from 1917 to 1945, and professor of history and philosophy of religion at the seminary from 1928 to 1941. He wrote *Buddhism* *and Buddhists in China* (New York, 1924), and *Folkways in China* (London, 1929). He edited *Careers for Students of Chinese Language and Civilization* (Chicago, 1933), and was coauthor of *A Dictionary of Chinese Buddhist Terms* (London, 1937). Died August 9, 1949, in Northfield, Massachusetts. *References*: Lewis Hodous Papers, Hartford Seminary Foundation Library, Hartford, Conn.; *FEQ* 10 (1950–1951): 63–68; *NYT*, August 10, 1949; and *WWWA*.

HOISINGTON, HENRY R(ICHARD) (1801–1858). Missionary, born August 23, 1801, in Vergennes, Vermont. Hoisington graduated from Williams College and Auburn Theological Seminary, and was ordained in 1831. He was a missionary under the American Board of Commissioners for Foreign Misions (ABCFM) in Ceylon from 1833 until 1854. He served in Manepay in 1834, opened the mission in Madura, India, in 1834–1835, and returned to Ceylon in 1835. He was an instructor in English in Batticota Seminary in 1835–1836, and its principal from 1836 until 1841. He returned to the United States in 1841 because of ill health, but was back in Ceylon in 1844 and resumed the principalship until 1849, when he returned again to the United States. He was an agent of the ABCFM until 1854, and later held pastorates in Williamstown, Massachusetts, and Centerbrook, Connecticut. He translated *The Oriental Astronomer: Being a Complete System of Hindu Astronomy* (Jaffna, Ceylon, 1848). Died May 16, 1858, in Centerbrook, Connecticut. *References*: *DAB*; *EM*; *Hewitt*; *NCAB* 24:244; and *WWWA*.

HOKKAIDO UNIVERSITY. *See* SAPPORO AGRICULTURAL COLLEGE

HOLCOMBE, CHESTER (1844–1912). Missionary and diplomat, born October 16, 1844, in Winfield, New York. Holcombe graduated from Union College. He taught in schools in Troy, New York; Hartford and Norwich, Connecticut; and Brooklyn, New York; and was a missionary of the American Sunday School Union in Georgia in 1868–1869. He was a missionary under the American Board of Commissioners for Foreign Missions (ABCFM) in China from 1869 until 1876, serving in Peking and conducting a school for boys. He was also an interpreter for the U.S. legation in Peking from 1871 until 1876. He retired in 1876 from the ABCFM, and became secretary of the legation until 1885. He assisted in the drafting of the American-Chinese treaty of 1880, and negotiated the first American treaty with Korea in 1882. After returning to the United States in 1885, he was involved in dealing in Chinese curios, and in lecturing and writing on Chinese subjects. He wrote *The Real Chinaman* (New York, 1895), and *The Real Chinese Question* (New York, 1900). Died April 25, 1912, in Rochester, New York. *References: DAB*; *DADH*; and *NCAB* 3:311.

HOLTOM, DANIEL CLARENCE (1884–1962). Missionary and ethnologist, born July 7, 1884, in Jackson, Michigan. Holtom graduated from Kalamazoo (Mich.) College, Newton Theological Institution, and the University of Chicago, and was ordained in 1910. He was a missionary under the American Baptist Foreign Mission Society in Japan from 1914 until 1940. He was a professor of modern languages at Tokyo Gakuin in 1914–1915, professor of church history at Japan Baptist Theological Seminary from 1915 to 1925, professor of the history of religion and church history at Kanto Gakuin from 1926 to 1936, and dean of theology there in 1935–1936. He was also a professor of theology at Aoyama Gakuin from 1936 to 1940. He became the foremost American student of Shinto. He wrote *Political Philosophy of Modern Shinto: A Study of the State Religion of Japan* (Tokyo, 1922); *The Japanese Enthronement Ceremonies* (Tokyo, 1928); *The National Faith of Japan* (New York, 1938); and *Modern Japan and Shinto Nationalism: A Study of Present-Day Trends in Japanese Religion* (Chicago, 1943). Died August 17, 1962, in San Gabriel, California. *References: AA* 65 (1963): 892–93; and *WWWA*.

HOMMEL, RUDOLPH [RUDOLF] P. (1887–1950). Antiquarian, born in Munich, Germany, and came to the United States in 1908. Hommel studied at a theological seminary in Neuen Dettelsau, and at Harvard and Lehigh universities. He was employed in various industrial enterprises. He was commissioned by Henry Chapman Mercer (1856–1930) to conduct fieldwork in China for a study of Chinese implements of daily life. He was in China from 1921 to 1926 and from 1928 to 1930, and wrote *China at Work, an Illustrated Record of the Primitive Industries of China's Masses, Whose Life is Toil, and Thus an Account of Chinese Civilization* (New York, 1937). He was later also curator and librarian of the Montgomery County Historical Society in Norristown, Pennsylvania. He later operated an antique shop in Richlandtown, Bucks County, Pennsylvania. Died March 18, 1950, in West Chester, Pennsylvania, from injuries suffered in an automobile accident. *References*: G. S. Dunbar, "Rudolf Hommel and Chinese Technology," *The China Geographer*, no. 2 (Fall 1975): 49–55; *Hobbies* 55 (May 1950): 55; and *NYT*, March 19, 1950.

HOOVER, HERBERT CLARK (1874–1964). Mining engineer, born August 10, 1874, in West Branch, Iowa. Hoover graduated from Stanford University. He was engaged in mining operations in Australia from 1897 to 1899, came to China in 1899 as chief engineer for the Chinese Engineering and Mining Company, and discovered rich coal deposits in Chihli Province. During the Boxer Rebellion, he helped organize relief activities in the foreign settlement in Tientsin. He was later involved in the development of the Bawdwin lead and silver mines in Burma. He was a consulting engineer after 1908, served as chairman of the Commission for Relief in Belgium (CRB) and the U.S. food administrator during World War I. He was secretary of commerce from 1921 to 1928, and president of the United States from 1929 to 1933. His *Memoirs of Herbert Hoover. Volume I, Years of Adventure* (New York, 1951) deals with his activities in Asia. Died October 20, 1964, in New York City. *References*: Herbert Hoover Papers, Herbert Hoover Presidential Library, West Branch, Iowa; *DAB S7*; Hugh

Deane, "Herbert Hoover and the Kailan Mines Swindle," *Eastern Horizon* (Hong Kong) 20, no. 5 (1981): 34–38; George H. Nash, *The Life of Herbert Hoover: The Engineer 1874–1914* (New York, 1983); *NCAB* 56:295; *NYT*, October 21, 1964; George B. Rea, "Hoover in China: The Story of the Kaiping Mining Deal," *Far Eastern Quarterly* 24 (1928): 482–491; Tom Walsh, "Herbert Hoover and the Boxer Rebellion," *Prologue* 19 (1987): 34–40; and *WWWA*.

HOOVER, JAMES MATTHEWS (1872–1935). Missionary, born August 26, 1872, in Greenvillage, Franklin County, Pennsylvania. Hoover graduated from State Normal College (Shippensburg, Pa.), and taught in the Franklin County schools. He was a missionary under the Board of Foreign Missions of the Methodist Episcopal Church in Penang, Malaya, from 1901 to 1903. He was transferred to Sibu in Sarawak, Borneo, in 1903, serving Chinese Methodists who had settled there. He established more than forty churches and schools in Borneo. He brought to Sarawak the bicycle, the motor launch, ice-making machinery, mechanical rice mills, electric lighting for churches and hospitals, new medical techniques and equipment, export-import procedures, improved agricultural facilities, and the radio. Died February 11, 1935, in Kuching, Sarawak. *References: CDCWM; DAB S1; EWM; NYT*, February 11, 1935; and *WWWA*.

HOPPER, RICHARD H(UTCHINSON) ("DICK") (1914–   ). Petroleum geologist, born May 13, 1914, in Los Angeles. Hopper graduated from the University of California and California Institute of Technology. He was reconnaissance geologist with the Nederlandsche Pacific Petroleum Maatschappij (NPPM) of the Standard Oil Company of California in the Dutch East Indies from 1939 to 1942, a geologist from 1946 to 1949, manager of explorations of Caltex Pacific Petroleum Company from 1949 to 1959, and vice president of American Overseas Petroleum Limited after 1959. *References; AMWS*.

HORNBECK, STANLEY K(UHL) (1883–1966). Government official, born May 4, 1883, in Franklin, Massachusetts. Hornbeck attended the University of Colorado and graduated from the University of Denver, Christ Church College, Oxford University, and the University of Wisconsin. He was in China from 1909 to 1913, and taught political science and history at the Chekiang Provincial College in Hangchow and the Fengtien Law College in Mukden, Manchuria. He was a technical expert on the Far East for the American Commission to Negotiate Peace in 1918–1919. He was associated with the Institute of Politics of Williams College from 1922 to 1924, and was lecturer at Harvard University from 1924 to 1927. He was the chief of the Far Eastern Affairs Division in the U.S. State Department from 1928 to 1937, special advisor on political affairs to the secretary of state from 1938 until 1944, and the director of the Office of Far Eastern Affairs in 1944. He was U.S. ambassador to the Netherlands from 1944 until his retirement in 1947. He wrote *Contemporary Politics in the Far East* (New York, 1916); *China Today: Political* (Boston, 1927); and *The*

United States and the Far East: Certain Fundamentals of Policy (Boston, 1942). Died December 10, 1966, in Washington, D.C. *References*: Stanley K. Hornbeck Papers, Hoover Institution on War, Revolution and Peace, Stanford, Calif.; Richard D. Burns, "Stanley K. Hornbeck: The Diplomacy of the Open Door," in *Diplomats in Crisis: United States-Chinese-Japanese Relations, 1919–1941*, ed. Richard D. Burns and Edward M. Bennett (Santa Barbara, Calif., 1974), pp. 91–117; Russell H. Buhite, "The Open Door in Perspective: Stanley K. Hornbeck and American Far Eastern Policy," in *Makers of American Diplomacy*, ed. Frank J. Merli and Theodore A. Wilson (New York, 1974), 2: 127–53; *DADH*; Justus D. Doenecke, comp., *The Diplomacy of Frustration: The Manchurian Crisis of 1931–1933 as Revealed in the Papers of Stanley K. Hornbeck* (Stanford, Calif., 1981); Kenneth G. McCarthy, "Stanley K. Hornbeck and the Far East, 1931–1941," Ph.D. diss., Duke University, 1970; Kenneth G. McCarthy, "Stanley K. Hornbeck and the Manchurian Crisis," *Southern Quarterly* 10 (1972): 305–24; *NCAB* 60:133; *NYT*, December 12, 1966; and *WWWA*.

HORSFIELD, THOMAS (1773–1859). Explorer and naturalist, born May 12, 1773, near Bethlehem, Pennsylvania. Horsfield graduated from the University of Pennsylvania Medical School. He made a trip to Java in 1799–1800 as ship surgeon on a merchant ship, and published an account of his voyage in the *Philadelphia Medical Museum* of 1805. He returned to Java in 1801 as a surgeon in the Dutch colonial army and remained there until 1819. He was employed after 1811 by the East India Company. He collected and described the island's flora. He returned to London in 1819, and was curator of East India Company Museum from 1820 until his death. He wrote *An Essay on the Copas or Poison Tree of Java* (Batavia, 1813); *Essay on the Geography, Mineralogy and Botany of the Western Portion of the Territory of the Native Princes of Java* (Batavia, 1816); *On the Mineralogy of Java* (Batavia, 1816); *Short Account of the Medicinal Plants of Java* (Batavia, 1816); and *Zoological Researches in Java, and the Neighboring Islands* (London, 1824); and was coauthor of *Annulose Javanica* (London, 1825); *Plantae Javanicae Rariores* (London, 1838–1852), and several catalogs of lepidoptera, insects, mammals, and birds. Died July 24, 1859, in London, England. *References: ACAB; EAH;* and *WWWA*.

HOSKINS, COLIN MACRAE (1890–1967). Realtor, born July 31, 1890, in San Jose, California. Hoskins came to the Philippines in 1909, and was a clerk in the Bureau of Agriculture in 1909–1910. He transferred to the Bureau of Internal Revenue in 1910, and successively was an agent, chief of administrative law division, chief of the income tax division, chief of the tobacco industry division, and special deputy collector of internal revenue. He assisted in the organization of the Bureau of Commerce in 1918. He served in the U.S. Army during World War I. He was employed by the Pacific Commmercial Company in 1919–1920, and was manager of the Manila department of the Lawyers Cooperative Publishing Company from 1920 to 1922. He established his own real estate brokerage in 1923, organizing C. M. Hoskins and Company, and later, in 1937, also Realty Investments, Incorporated, and Bay Boulevard Subdivision, Incorporated. He organized the Manila Realty Board in 1937. He was interned by the Japanese in Santo Tomas and Los Baños internment camps during World War II. He was later a technical consultant to the War Damage Commission. In 1960 he gave his business to his employees. Died January 28, 1967, in San Francisco. *References; CCDP; Gleeck/Manila*; and A. V. H. Hartendorp, "Colin MacRoe Hoskins," *BAHC* 1 (March 1973): 39–45.

HOTCHKISS, H(ENRY) STUART (1878–1947). Engineer, born in New Haven, Connecticut. Hotchkiss graduated from Yale University. In 1901 he entered the employ of L. Candee and Company, a subsidiary of the United States Rubber Company, of which he later became vice president. In 1907 he went to Southeast Asia to survey rubber possibilities. He became board chairman of the United States Rubber Plantations, Inc., and its subsidiaries, and spent much time in the development of rubber plantations in Sumatra and the Malay Peninsula. He served in the U.S. Air Service during World War I, and was senior military attaché in the U.S. embassy in London. He was chairman of the board of the General Rubber Company, General Latex and Chemical Corporation, and Cambridge Rubber Company. Died September 16, 1947, in East River, Connecticut. *Reference*: *NYT*, September 17, 1947.

HOUGHTON, HENRY SPENCER (1880–1975). Physician and educator, born March 27, 1880, in Toledo, Ohio. Houghton graduated from Ohio State and Johns Hopkins universities. He was physician in the Wuhu General Hospital in Wuhu, China, from 1906 to 1911, and dean of Harvard Medical School of China in Shanghai from 1912 to 1917, also teaching tropical medicine and parasitology. He served with the China Medical Board in New York City 1917 to 1928, and represented the board in planning and constructing a new teaching hospital. He was acting director of the Peking Union Medical College from 1918 to 1921, and its director from 1921 to 1928. He returned to the United States in 1928, was dean and director of clinical services of the Medical College of the University of Iowa from 1928 to 1934, director of university clinics and associate dean of the division of biological sciences of the University of Chicago in 1933–1934, special representative of the China Medical Board from 1934 to 1937, and director of the Peking Union Medical College from 1937 to 1944. He was held as a political prisoner by the Japanese Army from 1941 to 1945. He retired in 1946. Died March 21, 1975, in Nashville, Tennessee. *References; NYT* March 24, 1975; and *WWWA*.

HOUGHTON, WILLIAM ADDISON (1852–1917). Educator, born March 10, 1852, in Holliston, Massachusetts. Houghton graduated from Yale University and studied at the University of Berlin. He was principal of the preparatory department of Olivert (Mich.) College from 1873 to 1875, professor of English literature at the Imperial University at Tokyo from 1877 to 1882, associate professor of English literature and later also of Latin at New York University from 1884 to 1892, and professor of Latin language and literature at Bowdoin College from 1892 to 1907. Died October 24, 1917. *References; WWWA*; and *Yale*.

HOUSE, EDWARD HOWARD (1836–1901). Journalist and publicist, born September 5, 1836, in Boston. House was the music and drama critic for the *Boston Courier* from 1854 to 1858 and for the *New York Tribune* after 1858. He was a correspondent during the Civil War, theatrical manager in New York and London from 1865 to 1868, with the *New York Tribune* from 1868 to 1870, and with *The New York Times* in 1870–1871. He was professor of English language and literature at Kaisei Gakko Tokyo (later Imperial University) from 1871 to 1873, and a counselor and war correspondent with the Japanese Army's expedition to Formosa in 1873. He established *Tokyo Times* in 1875, a weekly English-language newspaper which subsidized by the Japanese government until 1877, and edited it until 1880. He returned to the United States in 1880, but then moved to London in 1881 and became involved in theatrical management there. He came back to Japan in 1883, trained the Imperial Band, and helped found the Meiji Musical Society (which developed into the Imperial Conservatory of Music). As Japan's first official foreign publicist, he played an important role in shaping American opinion about Japan and the Japanese. He wrote *The Japanese Expedition to Formosa* (Tokyo, 1875); *Japanese Episodes* (Boston, 1881); and a novel, *Yone Santom a Child of Japan* (Chicago, 1889). Died December 17, 1901, in Tokyo. *References: DAB; DADH*; James L. Huffman, "Edward Howard House: In the Service of Meiji Japan," *PHR* 56 (1987): 231–56; *KEJ*; and *NCAB* 13:458.

HOUSE, SAMUEL REYNOLDS (1817–1899). Medical missionary, born October 16, 1817, in Waterford, New York. House attended Rensselaer Polytechnic Institute (Troy, N.Y.) and Dartmouth College, graduated from Union College (Schenectady, N.Y.), attended the University of Pennsylvania and Albany Medical College, graduated from the College of Physicians and Surgeons (New York City), and was ordained in 1856. House was the first medical missionary under the Board of Foreign Missions of the Presbyterian Church in the U.S.A. He served in Bangkok, Siam, from 1847 until 1876, conducted a dispensary in a floating house on the Menam from 1847 to 1851; and became one of the counselors of King Mongkut in 1851. He abandoned medicine and took charge of a boys' school after 1852 (later the Bangkok Christian College) which popularized Western education in Siam. He retired in 1876 and returned to the United States. Died August 13, 1899, in Waterford, New York. *References*: Samuel Reynolds House Papers, Presbyterian Historical Society, Philadelphia; *DAB*; and *WWWA*.

HOUSTON, CHARLES SNEAD (1913–   ). Physician and mountain climber, born August 24, 1913, in New York City. Houston graduated from Harvard and Columbia universities. He served in the U.S. Navy during World War II. He practiced medicine in Exeter, New Hampshire, from 1947 to 1956; in Aspen, Colorado, from 1957 to 1962; was director for India for the Peace Corps from 1962 to 1964; was special assistant to the director in charge of medical program development in Washington, D.C., in 1965–1966; and served as a professor in the department of epidemiology and environmental medicine, College of Medicine in the University of Vermont (Burlington, Vt.), after 1966. He was coleader of the British-American Himalayan expedition in 1936, which climbed to the summit of Nanda Devi. He was leader of the first and third American expeditions which conducted reconnaissance of K2, the highest peak in the Karakoram range in the Himalayas, in 1938 and 1953 and leader of the first American reconnaissance of Mount Everest, which reconnoitered Khumbu Glacier in 1950. He was director of Mt. Logan High Altitude Physiology Project after 1968. He was coauthor of *Five Miles High: The Story of an Attack on the Second Highest Mountain of the World* (London, 1939), and *K–2, The Savage Mountain* (New York, 1954). *References: AMWS*; and *WWA*.

HOWARD, HARVEY JAMES (1880–1956). Physician, born January 30, 1880, in Churchville, New York. Howard graduated from the University of Pennsylvania Department of Medicine. He went to China in 1910, he was head of the department of ophthalmology at the University Medical College in Canton from 1910 to 1913, ophthalmologist at the Canton Christian College from 1912 to 1915, ophthalmic surgeon at the Canton Hospital from 1912 to 1915, and fellow of the China Medical Board of the Rockefeller Foundation at Harvard from 1916 to 1918 and at Vienna in 1923–1924. He was professor and head of the department of ophthalmology at the Peking Union Medical College and medical advisor to the department of aeronautics of the Chinese government from 1920 to 1923. He was professor and head of the department of ophthalmology at the Washington University School of Medicine (St. Louis) and chief of ophthalmic service at several hospitals in St. Louis. He was a captive of Chinese bandits in Heilungchiang Province in 1925 and wrote *Ten Weeks with Chinese Bandits* (New York, 1926). Died November 6, 1956, in Clearwater, Florida. *References: American Medical Association Journal* 163 (January 12, 1957): 138; *NYT*, November 7, 1956; and *WWWA*.

HOWLAND, WILLIAM WARE (1817–1892). Missionary, born February 25, 1817, in West Brookfield, Massachusetts. Howland graduated from Amherst College and Union Theological Seminary, and was ordained in 1845. He was a missionary under American Board of Commissioners for Foreign Missions (ABCFM) in Jaffna, Ceylon, from 1846 until his death. He was a teacher at Batticota Seminary until 1868, when he moved to Tellipally. In 1873 he became the senior missionary of the ABCFM mission in Ceylon, and was stationed at

Uduville until his death. Died August 26, 1892, in Jaffna. *References: Amherst*; and *EM*.

HOY, WILLIAM E(DWIN) (1858–1927). Missionary, born June 4, 1858, near Mifflinburg, Pennsylvania. Hoy graduated from Franklin and Marshall College and Lancaster Theological Seminary, and was ordained in 1885. He was a missionary under the Foreign Mission Board of the Reformed Church in the United States in Japan from 1885 until 1901. He was stationed in Sendai, where he was involved in the establishment of a boys' school and the Sendai Theological Training School (later Tohoku Gakuin), and edited *The Japan Evangelist*. He then served in Yochow, Hunan Province, China, from 1901 until 1927. Died March 3, 1927, at sea. *Reference*: William Edwin Hoy Papers, Evangelical and Reformed Historical Society, Lancaster Central Archives and Library, Lancaster, Pa.; C. William Mensendiek, *Not without Struggle: The Story of William E. Hoy and the Beginnings of Tohoku Gakuin* (Sendai, Japan, 1986).

HSIANG-YA MEDICAL COLLEGE Established in 1913 in an agreement between Yale-in-China and the Hunan provincial government, and opened in Changsha in 1916. Yale-in-China built the hospital and recruited medical staff and teachers. A nursing school was opened in 1913. It was nationalized by the Chinese Communist authorities in 1951. *References*: William Reeves, Jr., "Sino-American Cooperation in Medicine: The Origins of Hsiang-ya (1902–1914)," in *American Missionaries in China: Papers from the Harvard Seminars*, ed. Kwang-ching Liu (Cambridge, Mass., 1970), pp. 129–82.

HUACHUNG UNIVERSITY. Central China University was established in Huachang in 1924. It originated in the Boone School which was established in Wuchanng in 1871 (and became Boone University in 1909), in Wesley College (founded in 1885), and in Griffith John College (founded in Hankow in 1899). It merged with Huping College in Yochow and Yale-in-China in Changsha to become Huachang College in 1929. It moved to the Burma border from 1937 until 1946, when it was reopened in Huachung. It became Huachung University in 1946. It came under Communist control in 1949 and became a government normal school in 1951. *References*: John L. Coe, *Huachung University* (New York, 1962); *Fenn*; and *Lutz*.

HUBBARD, HUGH W(ELLS) (1887–1975). Missionary, ornithologist, and stamp authority, born March 19, 1887, in Sivas, Turkey, to American missionary parents. Hubbard graduated from Amherst and Oberlin colleges, and attended Columbia and Union theological seminaries. He was a missionary under the American Board of Commissioners for Foreign Missions (ABCFM) in China from 1908 until 1952. He served in Paoting, north China, and was also student secretary of the Young Men's Christian Association (YMCA) from 1913 to 1933 and secretary of the National Christian Council of China in 1930–1931. He initiated the Fan Village experiment from 1934 to 1938. He was general secretary of the North China Congregational Churches from 1941 to 1943 and in 1945–1946. With George D. Wilder, he conducted bird studies, collected birds, and wrote *Birds of Northeastern China: A Practical Guide Based on Studies Made Chiefly in Hopei Province* (Peking, 1938). He was under house arrest by the Japanese from 1941 to 1943, and then was interned from 1943 to 1945. He was the United Nations Educational, Scientific, and Cultural Organization (UNESCO) China consultant in fundamental education from 1948 to 1952, head of the UNESCO China audiovisual project in 1949, and executive director of the Audio Visual Commission of the Philippine Federation of Christian Churches from 1954 to 1959. He retired in 1960. He also wrote *Handbook of Early Chinese Communist Stamps, 1928–1938* (n.p., 1969). Died March 9, 1975, in Washington, D.C. *References: Amherst*; and *NYT*, March 11, 1975.

HUBBARD, RICHARD B(ENNETT) (1832–1901). Lawyer and diplomat, born November 1, 1832, in Walton County, Georgia. Hubbard graduated from Mercer University, studied law at the University of Virginia, and was admitted to the bar. He practiced law in Tyler, Texas, after 1853; was U.S. district attorney for the Western district of Texas from 1857 to 1859; and served as a member of the Texas legislature from 1859 to 1862. He served in the Confederate Army during the Civil War. He was lieutenant governor of Texas from 1873 to 1877, and governor of Texas from 1877 to 1879. He was U.S. minister to Japan from 1885 to 1889, and wrote *The United States in the Far East; or Modern Japan and the Orient* (Richmond, Va., 1899). Died July 12, 1901, in Tyler, Texas. *References: DAB; DADH*; Jean S. Duncan, "Richard Bennett Hubbard: Texas Politician and Diplomat," Ph.D. diss., Texas A&M University, 1972; *NCAB* 9:72; and *WWWA*.

HUFFNAGLE, CHARLES (1808–1860). Consul. Huffnagle came to Calcutta in 1826 and practiced medicine. He later gave up medicine and became a partner in the banking house of Smith, Huffnagle and Company, acting as an agent of the East India Company. He was U.S. consul in Calcutta from 1847 to 1855, and the first U.S. consul to British India from 1855 until his death. He imported the first sacred cow to the United States, and exhibited the first collection of Indica in his mansion in New Hope, Bucks County, Pennsylvania. He wrote *Fragment of a Journal of a Holyday Trip from Bengal to the United States by the Way of the Holy Land, in 1847* (Calcutta, 1848). Died December 8, 1860, in London, England, while en route to India from a sick leave in the United States. *Reference*: Charles Huffnagle Papers, Bucks County Historical Society, Doylestown, Pa.

HUIZENGA, LEE S(JOERDS) (1881–1945). Medical missionary, born June 28, 1881, in Lioessens, Friesland, the Netherlands. Huizenga came to the United States in 1883 and grew up in Grand Rapids, Michigan. He graduated from

Calvin College and Seminary (Grand Rapids, Mich.) and Homeophatic Medical College (New York City), and studied at the New York Ophthalmic College. He was ordained in 1909. He was a pastor in Englewood, New Jersey, and a missionary to the Navaho Indians in New Mexico. He was a medical missionary under the Foreign Missionary Board of Christian Reformed Church in America in China from 1920 until his death. He served at Jukao from 1924 until 1937 and later served in Shanghai. He was interned by the Japanese from 1943 until 1945. He wrote *Passing Out: An Autobiographical Sketch* (Grand Rapids, Mich., 1946). Died July 25, 1945, in Shanghai, China. *References*: Lee Sjoerds Huizenga Papers, Calvin College and Seminary Archives, Grand Rapids, Mich.; *AMWS*; Lambertus J. Lamberts, *The Life Story of Dr. Lee S. Huizenga: an Adventure in Faith* (Grand Rapids, Mich., 1950); *NYT*, August 8, 1945; and *WWWA*.

HUIZINGA, HENRY (1873–1945). Missionary, born January 8, 1873, in New Groningen, Michigan. Huizenga graduated from Hope College (Holland, Mich.), Western Theological Seminary, and the University of Michigan, and was ordained in 1896. He was a missionary under the American Baptist Foreign Mission Society in India from 1896 to 1917. He was principal of schools in Vellore, Ongole, and Kurnool, and president of Ongole College. He was professor of English and head of the English department of the Shanghai Baptist College (later University of Shanghai) from 1917 to 1937. He wrote *Missionary Education in India* (Cuttack, Orissa, India, 1909). Died December 3, 1945, in Kalamazoo, Michigan. *Reference: NYT*, December 12, 1945; and *WWWA*.

HULBERT, HOMER B(EZALEEL) (1863–1949). Educator and Koreanologist, born January 26, 1863, in New Haven, Vermont. Hulbert graduated from Dartmouth College and attended Union Theological Seminary. At the king of Korea's request for three Americans to teach English to young nobles, he came to Korea in 1884. He was an instructor in the Royal College in Chosen from 1886 to 1891 and principal of the Imperial Normal School for training teachers in Seoul from 1897 to 1905. He was manager of the Trilingual Press of the Methodist mission in Seoul from 1893 to 1897, and editor of the *Korean Review* from 1900 to 1906. He went on a diplomatic mission to Washington, D.C., for the Korean government in 1905–1906, and was special envoy to the Hague Tribunal in 1907. He returned to the United States in 1908. He wrote *History of Korea* (Seoul, 1905); *Comparative Grammer of Korean Language and the Dravidian Languages* (Seoul, 1906); *The Passing of Korea* (New York, 1906); and *Omjee the Wizard: Korean Folk Stories* (Springfield, Mass., 1925). He was back in Korea in 1949. Died August 5, 1949, in Seoul, Korea. *References: NYT*, August 6, 1949; Clarence N. Weems, "Profile of Homer Bezaleel Hulbert, in *Hulbert's History of Korea* (New York, 1962), pp. ED23-ED62; *UnionTS*; and *WWWA*.

HULL, JOHN A(DLEY) (1874–1944). Army officer and colonial administrator, born August 7, 1874, in Bloomfield, Iowa. Hull graduated from the State University of Iowa, and was admitted to the bar in 1896. He practiced law in Des Moines, Iowa. He served in the Iowa National Guard and in the Philippines during the Spanish-American War, and was chairman of the liquidation commission that carried out the provisions of the Treaty of Paris. He returned to the United States in 1900, joined the U.S. Army in 1901, was back in the Philippines in 1904, served as judge advocate until 1915, and was legal advisor on international affairs to the governor general of the Philippines in 1914–1915. He returned to the United States in 1915, and was a judge advocate general from 1924 until he retired with rank of major general in 1928. He was again legal advisor to the governor general of the Philippines from 1930 to 1932, and served as associate justice of the Supreme Court of the Philippines from 1932 to 1936. Died April 17, 1944, in Washington, D.C. *References: CCDP; EP* 17:277–78; *NYT*, April 18, 1944; *Sevilla*; and *WWWA*.

HUME, EDWARD H(ICKS) (1876–1957). Physician and educator, grandson of Robert Wilson Hume,* born May 13, 1876, in Ahmednagar, India, to American missionary parents. Hume graduated from Yale University and Johns Hopkins University Medical School, and studied at the University of Liverpool. He was acting assistant surgeon with the U.S. Public Health Service in Bombay, India, from 1903 to 1905, and carried out research on the bubonic plague. He joined Yale-in-China in Changsha, China, in 1905, assisted in founding the Yale mission hospital in 1906, and served as senior physician in the hospital from 1906 until 1923. He organized Hsiang-ya Medical College in Changsha in 1914, and was its dean from 1914 to 1927, professor of medicine there from 1916 to 1923, professor of clinical medicine from 1923 to 1925, and president of the Yale-in-China colleges from 1923 to 1927. He was also editor of the *China Medical Journal* from 1910 to 1919. He returned to the United States in 1927, was director of the New York Post-Graduate Medical School and Hospital of Columbia University from 1931 to 1933, made a survey of medical facilities for the Chinese National Health Administration from 1934 to 1937 and a similar survey in India in 1938, and was founder of Christian Medical Council for Overseas Work in New York City as well as its secretary from 1938 to 1946. He wrote *The Chinese Way in Medicine* (Baltimore, 1940); *Doctors Courageous* (New York, 1950); an autobiography, *Doctors East, Doctors West: An American Physician's Life in China* (New York, 1946); and a biography of William Winston Pettus.* Died February 9, 1957, in Wallingford, Connecticut. *References*: Edward H. Hume Papers, Missionary Research Library, New York City; Edward H. Hume Papers, Yale-China Association Collection, Yale University Library, New Haven, Conn.; Lotte C. Hume, *Drama at Doctor's Gate: The Story of Doctor Edward Hume of Yale-in-China* (New Haven, 1961); *NCAB* 42:686; *NYT*, February 10, 1957; Jonathan Spence, *To Change China: Western Advisers in China 1620–1960* (Boston, 1969), ch. 6; and *WWWA*.

HUME, ROBERT ALLEN (1847–1929). Missionary, son of Robert Wilson Hume,* born March 8, 1847, in Byculla, Bombay, India, and grew up in Springfield, Massachusetts. Hume graduated from Yale University, Yale Divinity School, and Andover Theological Seminary, and was ordained in 1874. He was a missionary under the American Board of Commissioners for Foreign Missions (ABCFM) in India from 1874, and served at Ahmednagar. In 1878 he founded a theological seminary (later United Divinity College) and was its head until 1926. He was also superintendent of the Parner district, west of Ahmednagar; principal of Ahmednagar high school and girls' school; editor of *Dnyanodaya*, and Anglo-Marathi periodical; and a member of the Ahmednagar municipality. He was prominent in famine work in 1900. He wrote *Missions from the Modern View* (New York, 1905), and *The Interpretation of India's Religious History* (New York, 1911). His autobiography appeared in the *Congregationalist* (Boston) in 1921. He retired in 1926 and returned to the United States. Died June 24, 1929, in Brookline, Massachusetts. *References*: Robert Allen Hume Papers, Hartford Seminary Foundation Library, Hartford, Conn.; *ACAB; AndoverTS; NCAB* 26–358; and *WWWA*.

HUME, ROBERT ERNEST (1877–1948). Missionary, son of Robert Allan Hume,* born March 20, 1877, in Ahmednagar, Bombay Presidency, India. Hume graduated from Yale University and Union Theological Seminary, studied at the University of Göttingen, and was ordained in 1905. He was a missionary under the American Board of Commissioners for Foreign Missions (ABCFM) in India from 1907 until 1914. He served on the faculty of Ahmednagar Theological Seminary from 1907 to 1909, and was editor of the bilingual weekly *Dhyanodaya* in Bombay from 1909 to 1914. He also taught at Williams College in Bombay and helped organize the Social Service League of Bombay. He returned to the United States in 1914 and was professor of the history of religions at Union Theological Seminary from 1914 to 1943. He also lectured at various universities in India. Died January 4, 1948, in New York City. *References*: *NCAB* 36:156; *NYT*, January 5, 1948; *UnionTS*; and *WWWA*.

HUME, ROBERT WILSON (1809–1854). Missionary, born November 8, 1809, in Stamford, New York. Hume graduated from Union College, attended Princeton Theological Seminary, graduated from Andover Theological Seminary, and was ordained in 1839. He was a missionary under the American Board of Commissioners for Foreign Missions (ABCFM) in the Marathi mission in Bombay, India, from 1839 until his death. He was secretary of the Bombay Temperence Society and the Bombay Tract and Book Society, and edited *Dnyanodaya*, a monthly magazine in Marathi, from 1844 until 1854. Died November 26, 1854, off the Cape of Good Hope, on his way to the United States. *References: AndoverTs; EM*; and *LC*.

HUMMEL, ARTHUR W(ILLIAM) (1884–1975). Missionary educator and librarian, born March 6, 1884, in Warrenton, Missouri, and grew up in Nashville, Illinois. Hummel graduated from the University of Chicago. He was an instructor of English in the Kobe Higher Commercial School (later Kobe University of Commerce) in Kobe, Japan, from 1912 to 1914 and was a missionary under the American Board of Commissioners for Foreign Missions (ABCFM) in China from 1913 until 1927. He served in Fenchow, Sansi Province, from 1915 until 1924. He also collected old Chinese coins and maps. He lectured on Chinese history and civilization in the Yenching School of Chinese Studies (later known as the College of Chinese Studies) in Peking from 1924 to 1927. He was chief of the Division of Chinese Literature in the Library of Congress from 1928 until his retirement in 1954. He translated *The Autobiography of a Chinese Historian* (Leyden, 1931) and edited *Eminent Chinese of the Ch'ing Period (1644–1912)* (Washington, D.C., 1943–1944). Died March 10, 1975, in Sandy Springs, Maryland. *References: JAS* 35 (1976): 265–66; *NYT*, March 11, 1975; and *WWWA*.

HUNT, LEIGH S. J. (1855–1933). Businessman, born August 11, 1855, in Larwill, Indiana. Hunt was a teacher in the Indiana schools, school superintendent of Des Moines, Iowa, and president of the State Agricultural College of Iowa (Ames) in 1884–1885. He began a business career in Seattle, Washington, in 1886, and was owner and editor of the Seattle *Post-Intelligencer*. He went to Japan and China in 1893, and was associated with the American Trading Company. He examined gold mines in northern Korea, bought the concession for gold mining in Korea in Unasan in 1897, established the Oriental Consolidated Mining Company, and developed his properties on an extensive scale. He also obtained a concession for a railroad from Chemulp'o to Seoul from the king of Korea, and took an active interest in the Yalu timber concession. He went to Egypt in 1903 and demonstrated the possibility of growing cotton commercially in the Anglo-Egyptian Sudan. He returned to the United States in 1910 and settled in Las Vegas, Nevada, in 1924. Died October 5, 1933, Las Vegas. *References: NCAB* 24:13; and *WWWA*.

HUNT, PHINEAS R. (1816–1878). Missionary, born January 30, 1816, in Arlington, Vermont. He was a missionary under the American Board of Commissioners for Foreign Missions (ABCFM) in Madras, India, from 1839 until 1868. He was in charge of the mission press and improved the style of Tamil printing. He was also treasurer of the mission. He went to Peking, China, in 1868, and established the first printing office in Peking in which the foreign press and metallic moveable type were used. Died May 29, 1878. *References: EM*; and *LC*.

HUNTER, DARD (1883–1966). Papermaker and printer, born November 29, 1883, in Steubenville, Ohio. Hunter attended Ohio State University, graduated from Graphische Lehr und Versuchs-Anstalt (Vienna), and studied at Kunstgewerbe Schule (Vienna) and the Royal Technical College (London). He was art director of the Roycroft Shop in East Aurora, New York, from 1903 to 1910. He settled on a farm in New York State in 1913, and then moved to Chillicothe, Ohio, in 1919. He made the paper for limited editions of books that he issued himself; designed, cast, and set the type; and printed them on a hand press. He also tried to revive the craft of papermaking by hand in the United States. In the 1930s, he visited paper mills, and papermakers in Japan, Korea, China, Siam, Indochina, and India, and established a school of papermaking in Rajahmundry, India, in 1937. He established the Dard Hunter Paper Museum in the Massachusetts Institute of Technology in 1939 (moved to the Institute of Paper Technology, Appleton, Wisconsin, in 1954). He wrote *Old Papermaking in China and Japan* (Chillicothe, Ohio, 1932); *Papermaking in Southern Siam* (New York, 1936); *A Papermaking Pilgrimage to Japan, Korea and China* (New York, 1936); *Papermaking by Hand in India* (New York, 1939); *Papermaking in Indo-China* (Chillicothe, Oh., 1947); and *My Life with Paper, an Autobiography* (New York, 1958). Died February 20, 1966, in Chillicothe, Ohio. *References: American Antiquarian Society Proceedings* 76, no. 1 (1966): 12–15; *CA; CB* 1960; *NYT*, February 22, 1966; *OAB*; and *WWWA*.

HUNTER, WILLIAM C. (1812–1891). Merchant and author, born in Kentucky. Hunter was apprenticed to the Canton, China, agency of Thomas H. Smith and Sons of New York City from 1825 to 1829, and was employed as a clerk with Russell and Company from 1829 until 1842, when he became a partner in that company. He studied at the Anglo-Chinese College in Malacca, and was probably the first American to devote himself to the systematic study of the spoken and written Chinese language. He lived in Macao after 1842, and was part owner of *Midas*, the first American steamship to ply the Chinese waters. He wrote *Bits of Old China* (London, 1855) and *The "Fan Kwae" of Canton before Treaty Days, 1825–1844* (London, 1882). Died June 25, 1891, in Nice, France. *References: DAB;* Philip de Vargas, "Hunter's Books on the Old Canton Factories," *Yenching Journal of Social Studies* 2 (July 1939): 91–117; and Arthur W. Hummel and Philip de Vargas, "Correspondence Concerning William C. Hunter," *Yenching Journal of Social Studies* 2 (1940): 294–96.

HUNTINGTON, DANIEL TRUMBULL (1868–1950). Missionary, born August 4, 1868, in Norwich, Connecticut. Hungtington graduated from Yale University, attended General Theological Seminary, and graduated from Berkeley Divinity School. He was ordained in 1890. He was a missionary under the Board of Foreign Missions of the Protestant Episcopal Church in the United States of America in China from 1895 until 1940. He served in Hankow from 1896 to 1900 and in Ichang from 1900 to 1911. He was elected bishop of Wuhu (later the District of Anking) in 1911, consecrated the first bishop of the diocese in 1912, and served until his retirement in 1940. He wrote *The Diocese of Anking* (Hartford, Conn., 1943). Died May 1, 1950, in Wellesley, Massachusetts. *References: NCAB* 40:189; *NYT*, May 4, 1950; and *WWWA*.

HUNTINGTON, ELLSWORTH (1876–1947). Geographer, born September 16, 1876, in Galesburg, Illinois, and grew up in Gotham, Maine, and Milton, Massachusetts. Huntington graduated from Beloit College and Harvard and Yale universities. He was assistant to the president of Euphrates College in Harpoot, Turkey, from 1897 to 1901. He was a member of the Pumpelly expedition to Central Asia in 1903–1904, and with Robert L. Barrett,* he made a journey through the Himalayas into the basin of inner Asia in 1905–1906. He wrote *Pulse of Asia: A Journey in Central Asia Illustrating the Geographic Basis of History* (Boston, 1907). He was an assistant professor at Yale University from 1910 to 1915 and a research associate there with professorial rank from 1919 until his death. Died October 17, 1947, in New Haven, Connecticut. *References*: Ellsworth Huntington Papers, Yale University Library, New Haven, Conn.; *DAB S4*; Geoffrey Martin, "The Ellsworth Huntington Papers," *Yale University Library Gazette* 45 (1971): 185–95; *NCAB* 37:43; *NYT*, October 18, 1947; and *WWWA*.

HURLEY, G. VIC(TOR) (1898–1978). Author, born October 6, 1898, in Springfield, Missouri, and grew up in the Northwest. Hurley attended the University of Washington. He served in the U.S. Army during World War I. He later came to the Philippines, and lived in Zamboanga, Mindanao, as a coconut planter and a Goodyear Rubber plantation executive. He served in the U.S. Navy during World War II. He wrote *Southeast of Zamboanga* (New York, 1935); *Men in Sun Helmets* (New York, 1936); *Swish of the Kris: The Story of the Moros* (New York, 1936); and *Jungle Patrol* (New York, 1938). Died June 1978, in Lacey, Washington. *References*: Vic Hurley Papers, University of Oregon Library, Eugene, Ore.; Vic Hurley Photographs, Washington State Museum, University of Washington, Seattle; and *CA*.

HURLEY, JOHN F. (1892–1967). Clergyman, born in New York City. Hurley was employed by a stock brokerage firm on Wall Street from 1912 to 1915. He joined the Society of Jesus in 1915 and was ordained 1927. He was a member of the faculty of the Ateneo de Manila from 1927 to 1936, and superior of Jesuit missions in the Philippines from 1936 to 1945. During World War II he became widely known as "Father Mercy" for his work in conveying medicines, food, and money to American and other allied prisoners of war, and to civilians interned by the Japanese. After the war, he organized the operated the Catholic Welfare Organization in the Philippines. Died December 5, 1967, in New York City. *References: NYT*, December 7, 1967; and Harrison F. Wilkins, "Father Hurley and the 'Holy War,' " *BAHC* 3 (January–March 1973): 33–43.

HURLEY, PATRICK JAY (1883–1963). Government official and lawyer, born January 8, 1883, in Indian Territory (later Oklahoma). Hurley attended Baptist Indian University (later Bacone Junior College) and graduated from National University (Washington, D.C.) and George Washington University. He practiced law in Tulsa, Oklahoma, from 1912 to 1929. He served with the U.S. Army in France during World War I. He was assistant secretary of war and then secretary of war from 1929 to 1933, and later practiced law in Washington, D.C. He was a U.S. minister to New Zealand in 1942–1943 and then special representative of the president to the Middle East. He was the president's personal representative to China in 1944, and was sent to Chungking to persuade the Nationalists and Communists to settle their differences and fight the Japanese and to harmonize the relationships between the Chinese and American military establishments. He was U.S. ambassador to China in 1944–1945. He then moved to New Mexico and was three times an unsuccessful candidate for the U.S. Senate. Died July 30, 1963, in Santa Fe, New Mexico. *References*: Patrick J. Hurley Papers, University of Oklahoma Library, Norman, Okla.; Russel D. Buhite, *Patrick J. Hurley and American Foreign Policy* (Ithaca, N.Y., 1973); Russel D. Buhite, "Patrick J. Hurley and American Policy toward China," *Chronicles of Oklahoma* 45 (1967–1968): 376–92; *CB* 1944; *DADH; EAH;* Ching-tung Liang, "Patrick Hurley: The China Mediator," *Bulletin of the Institute of Modern History of the Academia Sinica* (Taiwan) 6 (1977): 329–53; Don Lohbeck, *Patrick J. Hurley* (Chicago, 1956); *NYT*, July 31, 1963; *NCAB* 53:21; *PolProf: Truman*; and *WWWA*.

HURTH, PETER JOSEPH (1857–1935). Clergyman, born March 30, 1857, in Nittel-on-Moselle, Rhine province, Germany, and came to the United States in 1874. Hurth graduated from Notre Dame University (Ind.), and was ordained in 1880. He held pastorates in Cincinnati, Ohio, and Austin, Texas, from 1881 until 1894. He was appointed bishop of Dacca, India, in 1894, was consecrated in that year, and served until 1910, when he left India because of ill health. He was bishop of Nueva Segovia, Philippines, from 1913 until 1926. He became the titular archbishop of Bostra in 1926. Died August 1, 1935, in Manila. *References: WWP*; and *WWWA*.

HUTCHISON, JAMES LAFAYETTE (1890?–1937). Businessman, born in Charlotte, North Carolina. Hutchison graduated from Duke University. He went to China in 1911 as a representative of the British-American Tobacco Company (BATC). He returned to the United States in 1917 but went back to China in 1929 as an advertising advisor for the BATC. He was a member of the Cable Censorship Bureau during World War I. He was later an executive of the J. Walter Thomson Advertising Agency of New York, and of Blackett, Sample and Hummert Company in Chicago, and advertising manager of the United Drug Company in Boston. He wrote *China Hand* (Boston, 1936). Died March 20, 1937, in Cambridge, Massachusetts. *References: NYT*, March 21, 1937.

HWA NAN COLLEGE. It began as the Foochow College Preparatory of Foochow Woman's College in Foochow by the Woman's Foreign Missionary Society of the Methodist Episcopal Church in 1908. It became the Woman's College of South China in 1914 and Hwa Nan College in 1917. It moved to Nanping in 1938 and returned to Foochow in 1946. In 1951, it merged into the National Fukein University. *Reference: Fenn; Lutz*; and L. Ethel Wallace, *Hwa Nan College* (New York, 1956).

HYDE, HELEN (1868–1919). Artist, born April 6, 1868, in Lima, New York, and grew up in San Francisco. Hyde studied at the Art Students' League (New York City), in Berlin, Paris, Holland, and England. She went to Japan and stayed in Tokyo until 1912, when she returned to the United States. She became proficient in woodblock painting, cutting, and printing. She wrote *Jingles from Japan* (San Francisco, 1901). She settled in Chicago. Died May 13, 1919, in Chicago. *References: DAB*; and *WWWA*.

HYDE, JOHN NELSON (1865–1912). Missionary, born November 9, 1865, at Carrollton, Illinois. Hyde graduated from Carthage College (Ill.) and McCormick Theological Seminary. He was a missionary under the Board of Foreign Missions of the United Presbyterian Church in North America in India from 1892 until 1911. He served in the Ferozepore district in the Punjab and later also in Lahore. He formed the Punjab Prayer Union in 1904. He returned to the United States in 1911 because of ill health. Died February 17, 1912, in Clifton Springs, New York. *References*: Victor R. Edman, *They Found the Secret* (Grand Rapids, Mich., 1960), pp. 78–81; and Basil Miller, *Praying Hyde: A Man of Prayer* (Grand Rapids, Mich., 1943).

I

IDE, HENRY CLAY (1844–1921). Lawyer and colonial administrator, born September 18, 1844, in Barnet, Vermont. Ide graduated from Dartmouth College. He was Vermont state attorney from 1876 to 1878, a member of the Vermont Senate from 1882 to 1885, the U.S. commissioner to Samoa in 1891, and chief justice of Samoa, under joint appointment of England, Germany, and the United States, from 1893 to 1897. He was a member of the Philippine Commission in 1900, secretary of finance and justice for the Philippines from 1901 to 1904, vice-governor of the Philippines in 1904–1905, acting governor in 1905–1906, and governor-general in 1906. He was U.S. minister to Spain from 1909 to 1913. Died June 13, 1921, in St. Johnsbury, Vermont. *References: ACAB; DAB; DADH; EP* 4:358–359; *Gleeck/Governors*, ch. 4; *NCAB* 23:29; *NYT*, June 14, 1921; Arthur F. Stone, *The Life of Henry Clay Ide* (Binghamton, N.Y., 1935); and *WWWA*.

IGLEHART, EDWIN T(AYLOR) (1878–1964). Missionary, born in Greencastle, Indiana. Iglehart graduated from Columbia College and Drew Theological Seminary, and was ordained in 1904. He held pastorates in Washington, New York and Carmel, New York, from 1899 to 1904. He was a missionary under the Board of Foreign Missions of the Methodist Episcopal Church in Japan from 1904 to 1948. He was a teacher at Aoyama Gakuin in Tokyo from 1904 to 1909, served in Hirosaki from 1910 to 1912, was manager of the Methodist Publishing House in Tokyo, and served as associate dean of the Aoyama Gakuin in Tokyo after 1914. He served on the committee for the relief of Japanese residents on the Eastern Seabord during World War II. He returned to Japan in 1946 to help with the reconstruction of Aoyama Gakuin, and remained there until his retirement in 1948. Died January 31, 1964, in Mount Kisco, New York. *References: DrewTS; NYT*, February 2, 1964.

INGALLS, MARILLA BAKER (1828–1902). Missionary, born November 25, 1828, in Greenefield Centre, New York. Ingalls was a missionary under the American Baptist Missionary Union in Burma from 1851 until her death. She served with her husband, Lovell Ingalls, at Akyab, Arakan, Lower Burma, until his death in 1856. She returned to the United States in 1856 but was back in Burma in 1858 and established the mission at Thonze, a remote village in Lower Burma. She also established reading rooms and libraries for the British employees of the railroad. Died December 17, 1902, in Thongze, Burma. *References: DAB;* and *WWWA.*

INGERSOLL, FRANK B(ASSETT) (1866–1944). Lawyer, born November 29, 1866, in Greenville, Tennessee. Ingersoll graduated from the University of Tennessee, and was admitted to the bar. He practiced law in Seattle, Washington, until 1896, when he was elected judge. He came to the Philippines during the early part of the occupation, was prosecuting attorney of the city of Manila, and later served as judge of the municipal court. He resigned from government service and practiced law in Manila. He returned to the United States in 1940. Died April 25, 1944, in California. His wife, **JOSHENA M. INGERSOLL**, wrote her memoirs, *Golden Years in the Philippines* (Palo Alto, Calif., 1971). *Reference: CCDP.*

INGERSOLL, ROBERT STEPHEN, JR. (1914–   ). Businessman and diplomat, born January 28, 1914, in Galesburg, Illinois. Ingersoll graduated from Yale University. He was employed by Armco Steel Corporation and the Ingersoll Steel and Disc division of the Borg-Warner Corporation from 1937 to 1945, president of Ingersoll Products division from 1945 to 1954, administrative vice president of Borg-Warner Corporation from 1953 to 1956, president from 1956 to 1961, and chairman from 1961 to 1972. He was U.S. ambassador to Japan from 1972 to 1974, and was concerned mainly with trade matters. He was assistant secretary for East Asian affairs in 1974, and deputy secretary of state from 1974 to 1976. *References: DADH* and *WWWA.*

INGLE, JAMES ADDISON (1867–1903). Missionary, born March 11, 1867, in Frederick, Maryland. Ingle graduated from the University of Virginia, and studied at the Virginia Theological Seminary (Alexandria). He was a missionary under the Domestic and Foreign Missionary Society of the Protestant Episcopal Church in the United States of America in China from 1891 until his death. He wrote *Hankow Syllabary* (Hankow, 1890), a dictionary of the Hankow dialect. He was consecrated the first Protestant Episcopal bishop of Hankow in 1902. Died December 7, 1903, in Hankow, China. *References*: William H. Jeffreys, *James Addison Ingle (Yin Teh-sen): First Bishop of the Missionary District of Hankow, China* (New York, 1913); *NCAB* 5:185; *NYT*, December 8, 1903; and *WWWA.*

IRELAND, ALLEYNE (1871–1951). Author, born January 19, 1871, in Manchester, England. Ireland traveled extensively as an able seaman from 1887 to 1897. He lectured at Cornell University, the University of Chicago and

Lowell Institute (Boston) from 1899 to 1902 and was correspondent for *The Times* (London) in East Asia from 1902 to 1904. He served in the Philippine-American War, and was a private secretary to Joseph Pulitzer in 1911 and a member of the editorial staff of the *New York World* from 1912 to 1915. He wrote *Tropical Colonization: Introduction to the Study of the Subject* (New York, 1899); *China and the Powers: Chapters in the History of Chinese Intercourse with Western Nations* (Boston, 1902); *The Far Eastern Tropics: Studies in the Administration of Tropical Dependencies* (Boston, 1905); *The Province of Burma* (Boston, 1907); and *The New Korea* (New York, 1927). Died December 23, 1951, in Poughkeepsie, New York. *References: NYT*, December 24, 1951; and *WWWA*.

IRWIN, ROBERT W(ALKER) (1844–1925). Businessman, born January 7, 1844, in Philadelphia. Irwin went to Japan in 1866, was a clerk with Walsh, Hall and Company in Yokohama, and later was a partner of that firm and an agent of the Pacific Mail Company. He took part in the foundation of the Mitsui-Bussaan Company of Japan in 1876, and was later a foreign manager of Kyodo Unyu Company. He was vice-consul of Hawaii in Yokohama from 1867 to 1881, the first consul general of the Kingdom of Hawaii in Japan from 1881 to 1884, and minister resident and special of agent the Bureau of Immigration for the Hawaiian government in 1884. He played a major role in the negotiation of an immigration treaty between the Hawaiian and the Japanese governments, and was involved in the recruitment and transportation of government contract laborers from Japan to Hawaii after 1885. In 1900 he established the Formosa Sugar Manufacturing Company, a sugar refinery, in Formosa. He later became a naturalized Japanese citizen. Died February 1925, in Tokyo. His daughter, **SOPHIA A. IRWIN** (1884–1957), an educator, known also as Bella Irwin, was born in Tokyo. She graduated from Columbia University Teachers College. She returned to Japan in 1916 and in 1917 established in Tokyo the Gyokusei Training School for Kindergarten teachers and an adjoining kindergarten. She became a naturalized Japanese citizen in 1942. She expanded her school in 1947 (it later became the Irwin Gakuen Foundation). Died June 1957 in Tokyo. *References: KEJ*; and Tatsumaro Tezuka, ''Japanese Emigration to Hawaii Marks the 75th Anniversary; Notes on Robert Walker Irwin,'' *Tokyo Municipal News*, July 1960.

ISAACS, HAROLD R(OBERT) (1910–   ). Journalist, born September 13, 1910, in New York City. Isaacs graduated from Columbia University. He was a reporter with the *New York Times* from 1928 to 1930 and with the *Honolulu Advertiser* in 1930; a reporter and editor for the *China Press* in Shanghai and Peking, China, from 1930 to 1935; news editor for the Havas News Agency in Shanghai and New York City from 1935 to 1940; writer and editor for Columbia Broadcasting Systems (CBS) in New York City and Washington, D.C., from 1940 to 1943; and associate editor and correspondent for *Newsweek* in Washington, D.C., China, India, Southeast Asia, and New York City from 1943 to

1950. He wrote *The Tragedy of the Chinese Revolution* (London, 1938) and *No Peace for Asia* (New York, 1947), and edited *New Cycle in Asia: Selected Documents on Major International Developments in the Far East, 1943–1947* (New York, 1947). He was a research associate at the Center for International Studies of the Massachusetts Institute of Technology from 1953 to 1965, and professor of political science there from 1965 until his retirement in 1976. He wrote *Scratches on Our Mind: American Images of China and India* (New York, 1958), *India's Ex-Untouchables* (New York, 1965), and *Re-Encounters in China* (Armonk, N.Y., 1985), and edited *Straw Sandals: Chinese Short Stories 1918–1933* (Cambridge, Mass., 1974). *References: AMWS; CA;* and *WWA.*

ISABELLA THOBURN COLLEGE Founded as a girls' school in Lucknow, India, in 1870 by Isabella Thoburn.* It became a college in 1886, the first Christian college for women in Asia. It was named after its founder after her death in 1901. In 1921 it became the Woman's College of Lucknow University. *References*: Marjorie A. Dimmitt, *Isabella Thoburn College: A Record from Its Beginning to Its Diamond Jubilee* (n.p., n.d.) and *EWM.*

J

JACOBS, JOSEPH E(ARLE) (1893–1971). Diplomat, born October 31, 1893, in Johnston, South Carolina. Jacobs graduated from the College of Charleston. He was a student interpreter in Peking, China, from 1915 to 1918, vice consul in Foochow in 1917–1918; vice consul and interpreter in Shanghai in 1918; assessor of the International Mixed Court in Shanghai from 1918 to 1925; judge of the consular court for the district of Shanghai in 1919–1920; and consul in Yunnan, China, from 1926 to 1928 and in Shanghai from 1928 to 1930. He served in the Far Eastern Division of the State Department from 1930 to 1934, was foreign service inspector in 1935–1936, chief of the Office of Philippine Affairs in the State Department from 1936 to 1940, counselor of legation in Cairo from 1940 to 1945, and representative to Albania in 1945–1946. He was a political advisor to the commanding general in Korea in 1947–1948. He was later ambassador to Czechoslovakia in 1948–1949, special assistant for Mutual Defense Assistance program (with rank of minister) in Rome from 1949 to 1955, and ambassador to Poland from 1955 to 1957. Died January 5, 1971, in Washington, D.C. *References*: Joseph E. Jacobs Papers, Hoover Institution on War, Revolution and Peace, Stanford, Calif.; Jon L. Boyes, "The Political Adviser (POLAD): The Role of the Diplomatic Adviser to Selected United States and North Atlantic Alliance Military Commanders," Ph.D. diss., University of Maryland, 1971, pp. 182–91; *NYT*, January 7, 1971; and *WWWA*.

JACOCKS, WILLIAM P(ICARD) (1877–1965). Public health physician, born December 9, 1877, in Windsor, North Carolina. Jacocks graduated from the University of North Carolina and Johns Hopkins University. He worked for the North Carolina State Board of health from 1912 to 1915. He joined the Rockefeller Sanitary Commission in North Carolina in 1913 for the Rockefeller Foundation in Texas, Arkansas, and Tennessee, and also served on its International Health Commission in the West Indies until 1917. He served in the Army Medical Corps during World War I. He went to Ceylon in 1917 for the International Health Division of the Rockefeller Foundation and established the basis for public health operations there. In 1929, he undertook a public health program in Travancore, India. He was the division's regional director for India and Ceylon until his retirement in 1942. He returned to the United States in 1942 and worked again for the North Carolina State Board of Health until 1948. Died February 17, 1965, in Windsor, North Carolina. *References*: William P. Jacocks Papers, Southern Historical Collection, University of North Carolina Library, Chapel Hill, N.C.; William P. Jacocks Photographs, Rockefeller Archive Center, North Tarrytown, N.Y.; *Nature* 206 (May 8, 1965): 559; and William S. Powell, ed., *Dictionary of North Carolina Biography* (Chapel Hill, N.C., 1988), 3:266–67.

JAFFNA COLLEGE. Successor to the Batticota Seminary which was established in Vadducoddi, Ceylon, in 1823 as the first institution of higher education in Ceylon, and closed down in 1855. It was reopened in 1872 and was a secondary school much of the time. It developed later into a junior college, and since 1947 has been a senior college. *Reference*: J. V. Chelliah, *A Century of English Education. The Story of Batticota Seminary and Jaffna College* (Tellippali, Ceylon, 1922).

JAMES, ELDON R(EVARE) (1875–1949). Lawyer and diplomatic advisor, born November 21, 1875, in Newport, Kentucky. James graduated from the University of Cincinnati and Harvard University, and was admitted to the bar in 1899. He practiced law in Cincinnati from 1899 until 1911. He was an instructor and later a professor of law at the University of Cincinnati Law School from 1900 to 1912, professor of law at the University of Wisconsin in 1912–1913 and at the University of Minnesota in 1913–1914, and dean of the University of Missouri Law School from 1914 to 1918. He was an advisor on foreign affairs to the Siamese government from 1918 until 1923. He served as an advisor to the Siamese delegation at the Paris Peace Conference in 1919, represented Siam at the International Court of Arbitration in the Hague, the Netherlands, from 1918 to 1935, and was also a judge of the Supreme Court of Siam. He was appointed member of the parliament in Siam, and was made a minister plenipotentiary in 1925. In 1920 he negotiated a new treaty of commerce and friendship with the United States. He was a professor of law and librarian at the Harvard Law School from 1923 until his retirement in 1942, special assistant to the U.S. attorney general in 1942, attorney in the legal division of the Transportation Corps in the War Department in 1942–1943, a law librarian of Congress from 1943 to 1946, and a law school consultant for the Lawyers Cooperative Publishing Company (Rochester, N.Y.) from 1946 until his death. Died January 2, 1949, in Gloucester, Massachusetts. *References*: Eldon R. James Papers, Harvard Law School Library, Cambridge, Mass.; *NCAB* 42:149; *NYT*, January 3, 1949; and *WWWA*.

JAMES, MARY LATIMER (1883–1963). Medical missionary, born February 3, 1883, in Gambier, Ohio. James graduated from Bryn Mawr College and the Woman's Medical College of Pennsylvania, and studied at the University of Pennsylvania. She was a medical missionary to the Ute Indians in Utah from 1909 to 1911, and practiced medicine in Cedar City, Utah, in 1911–1912. In 1912, on assignment from the Chinese Republican government, she became a staff physician of Pei-Yang Woman's Hospital, Tientsin, China. She was a medical missionary under the Domestic and Foreign Missionary Society of the Protestant Episcopal Church in the United States of America in Hankow from 1914 until 1937. She served as superintendent of the woman's department in the Church General Hospital in Wuchang, and was later superintendent of the entire hospital until 1937. She expanded the hospital and its outpatient clinics, and developed training schools for Chinese nurses and midwives. She returned to the United States in 1937, and practiced in North Haven, Connecticut, from 1946 until her retirement in 1957. Died September 4, 1963, in North Haven, Connecticut. *Reference: NCAB* 51:322.

JAMESON, C(HARLES) D(AVIS) (1855–1927). Engineer, born July 2, 1855, in Bangor, Maine. Jameson traveled widely, working as an engineer in New Brunswick, Canada; Memphis, Tennessee; Charleston, South Carolina; Mexico; and the Isthmus of Panama. He taught at the Massachusetts Institute of Technology and the Iowa State University. He was in China from 1895 to 1918 as chief consulting engineer and architect for the Imperial Chinese Government, and later as chief engineer for the American Red Cross in connection with the Huai River Conservancy Project. He wrote *River, Lake and Land Conservancy in Portions of the Provinces of Anhui and Kiangsu North of the Yangtze River* (Shanghai, 1913). Died February 13, 1927, in Sarasota, Florida. *Reference*: C. D. Jameson Papers, Brown University Library, Providence, R.I.

JANES, L(EROY) L(ANSING) (1837–1909). Educator, born March 27, 1837, in New Philadelphia, Ohio. Janes graduated from the U.S. Military Academy in 1861 and served in the Union Army during the Civil War. He resigned his commission in 1867. He accepted an invitation in 1871 to teach at the Kumamoto School for Western Studies in Kumamoto, Japan, was its headmaster, and taught mathematics, history, and natural sciences from 1871 until 1877. He also served as an agricultural advisor. Later, he taught briefly at the Osaka Eigo Gakko. He returned to the United States in 1877, but was back in Japan in 1893 and taught at the Third College in Kyoto from 1893 to 1895. Died March 12, 1909, in San Jose, California. *References*: L. L. Janes Papers, Princeton University Library; *CDCWM; JBEWW; KEJ*; F. G. Notehelfer, *American Samurai: Captain L. L. Janes and Japan* (Princeton, N.J., 1985); and F. G. Notehelfer, "L. L. Janes in Japan: Carrier of American Culture and Christianity," *Journal of Presbyterian History* 53 (1975): 313–38.

JANVIER, LEVI (1816–1864). Missionary, born April 25, 1816, in Pittsgrove, New Jersey. Janvier graduated from Princeton University and Princeton Theological Seminary. He was a missionary under the Board of Foreign Missions of the Presbyterian Church in the U.S.A. in India from 1841 until his death. He was stationed at Fatehgarh, Ludhiana, Ambala, and Sabathu. He helped prepare *A Dictionary of the Panjabi Language* (Lodiana, India, 1854). Killed by a Sikh, March 24, 1864, at Anandpur, India. *References*: Janvier Family Papers, Presbyterian Historical Society, Philadelphia; *ACAB*; and *EM*.

JAYNE, HORACE H(OWARD) F(URNESS) (1898–1975). Archaeologist, born June 9, 1898, in Cape May, New Jersey. Jayne graduated from Harvard University and the University of Pennsylvania. He was an assistant at the University Museum of the University of Pennsylvania from 1921 to 1923, curator of Oriental art from 1923 to 1926, chief of the Eastern Division and curator of sculpture after 1926, and director of the museum from 1928 to 1940. He was vice director of the Metropolitan Museum of Art in New York City from 1941 to 1949; with the international broadcasting division of the U.S. State Department from 1949 to 1953 and chief of its Chinese desk from 1950 to 1954; vice director of the Philadelphia Museum of Art from 1955 to 1965; with the Museum of Fine Arts, St. Petersburg, Florida, after 1965; and then curator of Oriental art at the Norton Gallery of Art in West Palm Beach, Florida. He was a member of the first China expedition of the Fogg Museum of Harvard in 1923–1924 as well as participating in the second expedition and acting as a field agent in Asia for Harvard in 1924–1925. Died August 1, 1975, in West Palm Beach. Florida. *References: NCAB* 13:299; *NYT*, August 2, 1975; and *WWWA*.

JENKS, ALBERT E(RNEST) (1869–1953). Anthropologist, born November 28, 1869, in Ionia, Michigan. Jenks graduated from Kalamazoo College and the universities of Chicago and Wisconsin. He was an assistant ethnologist and then ethnologist with the Bureau of American Ethnology in Washington, D.C., in 1901–1902, assistant chief of the Bureau of Non-Christian Tribes in the Philippines in 1902–1903 and chief of the Ethnological Survey of the Philippines from 1903 to 1905. He was chief of the ethnological department of the Philippine exhibition of the St. Louis Exhibition in 1904, assistant professor of sociology at the University of Minnesota in 1906–1907, and professor of anthropology there from 1907 until his retirement in 1938. He later investigated tribes of the North African desert, the Ojibwa Indians, the Mimbres culture of New Mexico, and the prehistory of Minnesota and the Dakotas. He wrote *Ba-long-long, the Igorot Boy* (Chicago, 1907), and *The Bontoc Igorot* (Manila, 1905). Died June 6, 1953, in Lake Minnetonka, Minnesota. The letters of his wife, **MAUD HUNTLEY JENKS** (1874–1950) were published in *Death Stalks the Philippine Wilds: Letters of Maud Huntley Jenks*, selected and edited by Carmen N. Richards (Minneapolis, 1951). *References: NYT* June 9, 1953; and *WWWA*.

JENKS, JEREMIAH WHIPPLE (1856–1929). Economist, born September 2, 1856, in St. Claire, Michigan. Jenks graduated from the universities of Michigan and Halle (Germany), and was admitted to the bar in 1881. He taught at Knox College from 1886 to 1889, and was professor of economics and social science at Indiana University from 1889 to 1891, professor of political economy of Cornell University from 1891 to 1912, and professor of government at New York University after 1912. He visited British and Dutch colonies in Asia on behalf of the War Department in 1901 to study currencies, taxation, and police systems, and wrote *Certain Economic Questions in the English and Dutch Colonies in the Orient* (Washington, D.C., 1902). He was in China in 1903 as a representative of the Commission on International Exchange. He returned to China again in 1928. Died August 24, 1929, in New York City. *References: ACAB; DAB; NCAB* 14:64; *NYT*, August 25, 1929; and *WWWA*.

JERNIGAN, THOMAS R(OBERTS) (1847–1920). Consul, born February 24, 1847, at Barfield, Hertford County, North Carolina. Jernigan served in the Confederate Army during the Civil War and graduated from the University of North Carolina. He studied law and then practiced it in Hertford County, and was state senator from 1874 to 1876. He was U.S. consul in Kobe, Japan, from 1885 to 1889; newspaper proprietor and editor in Raleigh from 1889 to 1893; and consul general in Shanghai from 1893 to 1897. He remained in Shanghai, where he practiced law and was an attorney for Standard Oil Company in China. He was chairman of the international settlement of Shanghai for several years. He wrote *China's Business Methods and Policy* (Shanghai, 1904); *China in Law and Commerce* (New York, 1905); and *Shooting in China* (Shanghai, 1908). Died November 1, 1920, in Nanking, China. *Reference*: William S. Powell, ed. *Dictionary of North Carolina Biography* (Chapel Hill, N.C., 1988), 3:280–81.

JESUITS. Several provinces of the Society of Jesus in the United States have carried out missionary work in Asia. The American Jesuits in India of the Chicago and Detroit Provinces was founded in 1921. The Jesuit Seminary and Mission Bureau of the New York Province was founded in the Philippines in 1926. American Jesuits in China of the California Province began missionary work in 1928. The Jesuit Ceylon Mission of the New Orleans Province was founded in 1945. The Jesuit Mission Bureau of the Maryland Province began missionary work in India in 1947 and in Burma in 1958. The Jesuit Mission Service of the Wisconsin Province began missionary work in Korea in 1955. *Reference*: Peter J. Fleming, ''Chosen for China: The California Province Jesuits in China, 1928–1957: A Case Study in Mission and Culture.'' Ph.D. diss., Graduate Theological Union, 1987.

JESUP NORTH PACIFIC EXPEDITION. A scientific expedition to the North Pacific in 1897 to study migrations between Asia and North America and to investigate the relationship between the peoples of Northeastern Asia and Northwestern North America, sponsored by the American Museum of Natural History and financed by Morris Ketchum Jesup (1830–1908), president of the museum. *References*: William W. Fitzhugh and Aron Crowell, *Crossroads of Continents* (Washington, D.C. 1988), pp. 97–103; Stanley A. Freed, Ruth S. Freed, and Laila Williamson, "Capitalist Philanthropy and Russian Revolutionaries: The Jesup North Pacific Expedition (1897–1902)," *AA* 90 (1988): 7–25; and Stanley A. Freed, Ruth S. Freed, and Laila Williamson, "Scholars amid Squalor," *Natural History* 97 (March 1988): 60–68.

JOHNSON, ELIAS FINLEY (1861–1933). Lawyer and judge, born June 24, 1861, in Van Wert, Ohio. Johnson graduated from National University (Lebanon, Oh.) and the University of Michigan. He was a member of the Ohio House of Representatives from 1883 to 1887, assistant instructor and later instructor in law at the University of Michigan from 1890 to 1894, associate professor there from 1894 to 1895, and professor of law from 1895 to 1901. He came to the Philippines in 1901, was judge of the Court of First Instance of Pangasinan from 1901 to 1903, and associate justice of the Supreme Court of the Philippines from 1903 to 1933. He was several times acting chief justice of the Supreme Court. He resigned because of ill health. Died August 1, 1933, in Palo Alto, California. *References: CCDP; Sevilla; WWP;* and *WWWA*.

JOHNSON, HERBERT BUELL (1858–1925). Missionary educator, born April 30, 1858, near Fairfield, New York. Johnson graduated from Drew Theological Seminary and Illinois Wesleyan University. He was a missionary under the Board of Foreign Missions of the Methodist Episcopal Church in Japan from 1883 until 1904. He was principal of the Chinzei Seminary at Nagasaki from 1887 to 1894, dean of the Anglo-Japanese College in Tokyo, principal of the preparatory department of Aoyama Gakuin from 1894 to 1896, treasurer of the Japan mission in 1897–1898, and superintendent of the South Japanese mission from 1898 to 1904. He was superintendent of the Pacific Japanese mission on the west coast of the United States from 1904 until his death. Died November 24, 1925, in Berkeley, California. *References: DrewTS*; and *EWM*.

JOHNSON, LOUIS A(RTHUR) (1891–1966). Lawyer and government official, born January 10, 1981, in Roanoke, Virginia. Johnson graduated from the University of Virginia and was admitted to the bar in 1913. He practiced law in Clarksburg, West Virginia, from 1912 until his death. He was a member of the West Virginia House of Delegates in 1916–1917, and served in the U.S. Army during World War I and in the Army of Occupation in Germany. He was assistant secretary of war from 1937 until 1940. He was President Franklin D. Roosevelt's personal representative to India, and chairman of the United States Advisory Mission to that country in 1942. He played an active role in the negotiations between Sir Stafford Cripps and Indian nationalists. He was secretary of defense in 1949–1950. Died April 24, 1966, in Washington, D.C.

References: Louis Johnson Papers, University of Virginia Library, Charlottesville, Va.; *CB* 1949; Kenton J. Clymer, "Franklin D. Roosevelt, Louis Johnson, India, and Anticolonialism: Another Look," *PHR* 57 (1988): 261–84; *DAB S8; NCAB* 51:213; *NYT*, April 25, 1966; and *PolProf: Truman*.

JOHNSON, NELSON TRUSLER (1887–1954). Diplomat, born April 3, 1887, in Washington, D.C. Johnson attended George Washington University. He was a student interpreter in China from 1907 to 1909, vice-consul and then deputy consul general and interpreter in Mukden, Manchuria, Harbin, Hankow, and Shanghai from 1909 to 1914, and consul in Changsha and Shanghai from 1914 to 1918. He served in the Division of Far Eastern Affairs in the State Department from 1919 to 1925, was chief of the division from 1925 to 1927, and assistant secretary of state from 1927 to 1929. He was U.S. minister to China from 1929 to 1935, and ambassador to China from 1935 to 1941. Serving during the Manchurian crisis of 1931, he assisted in the negotiations that resolved the Sino-Japanese conflict. During the Sino-Japanese War, which began in 1937, he moved with the Nationalist government to Hankow and later to Chungking. He was ambassador to Australia from 1941 to 1946, and secretary general of the Far Eastern Commission from 1946 to 1952. Died December 3, 1954, in Washington, D.C. *References*: Nelson Trusler Johnson Papers, Manuscript Division, Library of Congress; Russell D. Buhite, *Nelson T. Johnson and American Policy toward China 1925–1941* (East Lansing, Mich., 1968); *DADH; NCAB* 43:241; *NYT*, December 4, 1954; Herbert J. Wood, "Nelson Trusler Johnson: The Diplomacy of Benevolent Pragmatism," in *Diplomats in Crisis: United States-Chinese-Japanese Relations, 1919–1941*, ed. Richard D. Burns and Edward M. Bennett (Santa Barbara, Calif., 1974), pp. 7–26; and *WWWA*.

JOINT U.S. MILITARY ADVISORY GROUP (JUSMAG). Established by the United States to advise the armed forces of the Republic of the Philippines. It played an important part in helping the Philippines military defeat the Huks in the early 1950s.

JONES, E(LI) STANLEY (1884–1973). Missionary, born January 3, 1884, in Baltimore. Jones graduated from Asbury College, and was ordained in 1908. He was a missionary under the Board of Foreign Missions of the Methodist Episcopal Church in India from 1907 until 1954. He served in Lucknow from 1907 to 1910 and at Sitapur after 1910. He was elected bishop in 1928 but declined to be consecrated. In 1951 he helped found the Nur Manzil Psychiatric Center in Lucknow. He retired in 1954. He wrote *The Christ of the Indian Road* (New York, 1925); *Along the Indian Road* (New York, 1939); and a spiritual autobiography, *Song of Ascents* (Nashville, Tenn., 1968). Died January 25, 1973, in Bareilly, India. *References*: Martin R. Johnson, "The Christian Vision of E. Stanley Jones: Missionary Evangelist, Prophet, and Statesman," Ph.D. diss., Florida State University, 1978; *EWM; LC; NCAB* 58:147; *NYT*, January

26, 1973; Violet Paranjoti, *An Evangelist on the Indian Scene, Dr. E. Stanley Jones* (Bombay, 1970); C. Chacko Thomas, "The Work and Thought of Eli Stanley Jones with Special Reference to India," Ph.D. diss., Iowa State University, 1955; Richard W. Taylor, ed., *The Contribution of E. Stanley Jones* (Madras, 1973); and *WWWA*.

JONES, GEORGE HEBER (1867–1919). Missionary, born August 14, 1867, in Mohawk, New York. Jones was a missionary under the Board of Foreign missions of the Methodist Episcopal Church in Korea from 1887 until 1909. He taught in the Paichai high school and college in Seoul from 1887 to 1893, and was its principal in 1892–1893. He served in Chemulp'o from 1893 to 1902. He was superintendent of the Methodist Episcopal Church throughout Korea from 1897 to 1899 and from 1907 to 1909, and editor of the *Korean Repository* from 1895 to 1898. he was departmental secretary of the Board of Foreign Missions in New York City from 1903 to 1906. He organized the Methodist Union Theological Seminary in 1907 and headed it until 1909. He was a member of the board of translators of the Bible into Korean from 1902 and 1905, and also organized the Korean emigration movement to the Hawaiian Islands between 1903 and 1905. He returned to the United States in 1909, and was editorial secretary and associate secretary of the Board of Foreign Missions from 1913 to 1919. He wrote *Korea: The Land, People and Customs* (Cincinnati, 1907). Died May 11, 1919, in Miami, Florida. *References; DAB; EWM*; and *NCAB* 18:263.

JONES, HOWARD P(ALFREY) (1899–1973). Editor and diplomat, born January 2, 1899, in Chicago. Jones attended the University of Wisconsin and graduated from Columbia University. He was employed in the New York bureau of The United Press, was managing editor of *The Evansville* (Ind.) *Press*, and later was editor-in-chief and a partner in a chain of nine small newspapers in Michigan. He was public relations secretary with the National Municipal League from 1929 to 1933, and executive director of the league and editor of its publications from 1933 to 1939. After World War II, he was in charge of public finance in Germany and director of the Berlin element of the United States High Commission for Germany. He was a counselor in Taiwan from 1951 to 1954, chief of the U.S. Operations mission to Indonesia in 1954–1955, and deputy assistant secretary of state for Far Eastern economic affairs from 1955 to 1958. He was U.S. ambassador to Indonesia from 1958 to 1965. In 1961, he averted a war between Indonesia and the Netherlands, instead persuading the countries to negotiate the issue. He wrote *Indonesia: The Possible Dream* (New York, 1971). He resigned in 1965 and was chancellor of the East-West Center at the University of Hawaii. Died September 18, 1973 in Stanford California. *References; CA; CB* 1963; *NYT*, September 20, 1973; *PolProf: Eisenhower*; and *WWWA*.

JONES, J(AMES) WELDON (1896–1982). Financial advisor, born February 28, 1896, in Copeville, Texas. Jones graduated from Baylor University and the University of Texas and studied at Ohio State University. He served in the U.S. Army during World War I. He worked as a certified public accountant in Houston from 1922 to 1929, and was assistant professor at the Ohio State University from 1929 to 1933. He was auditor general of the Philippines from 1933 until 1935, and financial advisor to the U.S. high commissioner from 1935 to 1940. He was acting high commissioner in 1936–1937 and 1939. He wrote *Philippine Commonwealth Handbook* (Manila, 1936). He was assistant director in charge of the fiscal division of the U.S. Bureau of the Budget from 1940 to 1952, economic advisor to the bureau from 1952 to 1955, and a member of the U.S. Tariff Commission from 1955 until his retirement in 1961. He was also sent as a special envoy to the Philippines in 1945 to survey the war damage. Died November 24, 1982, in Houston, Texas. *References*: J. Weldon Jones Papers, Harry S. Truman Presidential Library, Independence, Mo.; *CCDP; Gleeck/Governors*, ch. 13; and *WWP*.

JONES, JOHN PETER (1847–1916). Missionary, born September 4, 1847, in Wrexham, Denbighshire, Wales, and came to the United States in 1866. Jones graduated from Western Reserve College (Hudson, Ohio) and Andover Theological Seminary, and was ordained in 1878. He was a missionary under the American Board of Commissioners for Foreign Missions (ABCFM) in the Madura District of India from 1878 until 1914. He was stationed at Manamadura, state of Sivaganga, from 1879 to 1883, and was in charge of the theological seminary and associated school at Pasumalai in 1883–1884. He was secretary-treasurer of the mission in Madura from 1884 to 1892 and in 1884 opened the first Christian high school in Madura. He was principal of the theological school at Pasumalai from 1892 to 1914, and he managed the mission press and edited the mission periodical *Satyavartamani*. He wrote *India's Problem, Krishna or Christ* (New York, 1903), and *India, Its Life and Thought* (Cincinnati, 1908). He was a professor at the Kennedy School of Missions from 1914 to 1916. Died October 3, 1916, in Hartford, Connecticut. *References*: John Peter Jones Papers, Hartford Seminary Foundation Library, Hartford, Conn.; *AndoverTS; DAB; OAB*; and *NCAB* 23:137.

JONES, JOHN TAYLOR (1802–1851). Missionary, born July 16, 1802, in New Ipswich, New Hampshire. Jones attended Brown University, graduated from Amherst College and Andover Theological seminary, and was ordained in 1830. He was a missionary under the American Baptist Missionary Union in Maulmain, Burma, from 1830 to 1833, and in Bangkok, Siam, from 1833 until his death. He was the first American missionary in Siam and the first American to master the Siamese language. He wrote *Brief Grammatical Notices of the Siamese Language* (Bangkok, 1842), prepared a vocabulary, and translated the

New Testament into Siamese. Died September 13, 1851, in Bangkok. *References: ACAB; Amherst; AndoverTS; DAB; LC;* and *WWWA*.

JONES, THOMAS E(LSA) (1888–1973). Educator, born March 22, 1888, in Fairmount, Indiana. Jones graduated from Earlham College, Hartford Theological Seminary, and Columbia University. He was national secretary of the Young Friends Movement from 1914 to 1917, worked in the Society of Friends mission in Japan from 1917 to 1920, and taught economics and political science at Keio University in Tokyo from 1920 to 1924. He wrote *Mountain Folk of Japan: A Study in Method* (New York, 1926). He was Young Friends representative to the Young Men's Christian Association (YMCA) in Vladivostok, Siberia, in 1918–1919. He returned to the United States in 1924, and was president of Fisk University from 1926 to 1946 and president of Earlham College from 1946 until his retirement in 1958. He wrote an autobiography, *Light on the Horizon; The Quaker Pilgrimage of Tom Jones* (Richmond, Va., 1973). Died August 5, 1973, in Richmond, Indiana. *References: IAB* 1917; Paul A. Lacey, "Thomas E. Jones: The Dreamer and the Builder," in *Living in the Light: Some Quaker Pioneers of the 20th Century, Vol. I: In the U.S.A.*, ed. Leonard S. Kenworthy (Kennett Square, Pa., 1984), pp. 131–45; *NCAB* 60:57; and *WWWA*.

JONES, WILLIAM (1871–1909). Ethnologist, born March 28, 1871, on the Sauk and Fox Indian Reservation in Indian Territory (now Oklahoma). Jones came to the Philippines in 1906, investigated the language and customs of the tribes of the Philippines from 1906 to 1909, and lived many months among the Ilongots. Killed in an attack by the Ilongots, March 29, 1909, in Dumabatu, Isabela Province, Luzon, Philippines. *References: DAB*; and *NCAB* 24:283.

JONES, WILLIAM PATTERSON (1831–1886). Consul, born April 23, 1831, in Philadelphia, and grew up in St. Louis and Alton, Illinois. Jones graduated from Allegheny College (Meadville, Pa.). He established the Northwestern Female College in Evanston, Illinois, in 1855 (later absorbed in Northwestern University). He was consul in Macao and later in Amoy, and in Canton from 1862 to 1868. He returned to the United States in 1868 and lectured throughout the country about the conditions in China. Died August 3, 1886, in Fullerton, Nebraska. *References: DAB*; Barbara B. Kehoe, "William Patterson Jones, American Consul to China, 1862–1868," *Journal of the Illinois State Historical Society* 73 (1980): 45–52; *NCAB* 11:368; and *WWWA*.

JONES ACT (1916). Passed by the U.S. Congress, it reaffirmed the U.S. intention to withdraw its sovereignty over the Philippines and to recognize that country's independence as soon as a stable government was established. It provided for a bill of rights, male suffrage, and an elective senate, and vested the executive power in a governor to be appointed by the president. It also provided for free trade between the Philippines and the United States. *References*: Wong

Kwok Chu, "The Jones Bills, 1912–16: A Reappraisal of Filipino Views on Independence," *JSES* 13 (1982): 252–69; Roy W. Curry, *Woodrow Wilson and Far Eastern Policy, 1913–1921* (New York, 1957), pp. 82–96; Michael Onorato, "The Jones Act and Filipino Participation in Government," in *A Brief Review of American Interest in Philippine Development and Other Essays* (Manila, 1972), pp. 13–28, and Michael Onorato, "The Jones Act and the Establishment of a Filipino Government, 1916–1921," *PS* 14 (1966): 448–59.

JOUETT, JOHN H(AMILTON) (1892–1968). Aviation executive, born May 14, 1892, in San Francisco. Jouett graduated from the U.S. Military Academy in 1914, and was commissioned a second lieutenant in the U.S. Army Air Corps. He resigned from the army in 1930, and was an aviation executive with Standard Oil of New Jersey from 1930 to 1932 and in 1935–1936. He was an aviation advisor to the Republic of China from 1932 to 1935. He was later president of Fairchild Aircraft Corporation from 1936 to 1938, president of Aeronautical Chamber of Commerce and Aeronautical Exposition Corporation from 1939 to 1942, executive vice president of Higgins Aircraft, Incorporated, after 1942, and president of Caribbean Corporation after 1945, and president of the Jouett Insurance Agency after 1948. Died October 18, 1968, at sea. *References*: William M. Leary, Jr., "Wings for China: The Jouett Mission, 1932–1935," *PHR* 38 (1969): 447–62; *NYT*, October 22, 1968; and *WWWA*.

JOY, BENJAMIN (1758–1830). Merchant, born December 9, 1758, in Salisbury, Massachusetts. Joy was the first U.S. consul in Calcutta from 1794 to 1796. The East India Company did not acknowledge his consular status, but did allow him to remain as a commercial agent. Died March 21, 1830, in Salisbury, Massachusetts. *References*: Benjamin Joy Papers, Massachusetts Historical Society, Boston; and Holden Furber, "The Letters of Benjamin Joy, First American Consul in India," *Indian Archives* 4 (1950): 219–27.

JOY, CHARLES TURNER (1895–1956). Army officer, born February 17, 1895, in St. Louis, Missouri. Joy graduated from the U.S. Naval Academy in 1916, and was commissioned an ensign in the U.S. Navy. He served on the staff of the commander of the Yangtze Patrol from 1923 to 1925, and later served at sea as executive officer of a destroyer, and as assistant gunnery officer on a battleship and on the staff of the commander of destroyers. He was commander of a destroyer from 1933 to 1935. He was operations officer for the commander of the Scouting Force, commanded the cruiser USS *Louisville*, headed the Pacific Plans Division of the Navy in Washington, D.C., and was commander of Cruiser Division Six during World War II. He later commanded Amphibious Group Two, and Task Forces Seventy-Three and Seventy-Four. He was commander of the Naval Proving Ground in Dahlgren, Virginia; commander of the U.S. Naval Force, Far East, in 1949–1950; and allied naval commander in the Korean War. He served as senior UN delegate at the Korean Armistice Conference held at

Kaesong and later Panmunjon in 1951–1952. He wrote *How Communists Negotiate* (New York, 1955). His diaries of the armistice talks were edited by Allan E. Goodman as *Negotiating while Fighting: The Diary of Admiral C. Turner Joy at the Korean Armistice Conference* (Stanford, Calif., 1978). He was superintendent of the U.S. Naval Academy from 1952 to 1954. He retired with the rank of admiral in 1954. Died June 6, 1956, in San Diego, California. *References*: Charles Turner Joy Papers, Hoover Institution on War, Revolution and Peace, Stanford, Calif.; *DAB S6; NCAB* 45:54; *NYT*, June 7, 1956; and *WWWA*.

JUDSON, ADONIRAM (1788–1850). Missionary, born August 9, 1788, in Malden, Massachusetts. Judson graduated from Brown University and Andover Theological Seminary. He was sent as a missionary under the American Board of Commissioners for Foreign Missons (ABCFM) in 1812 to Burma, but in 1814 he transferred to the American Baptist Missionary Union. He served in Rangoon and translated the Bible into Burmese. After 1823 he served in Ava. He was arrested and held in prison in 1824–1825. He was then released and served as an interpreter between the Burmese and the British. He moved to Amherst but accompanied the British embassy to Ava in 1826. He then served in Maulmain. He complied *A Dictionary of the Burman Language* (Calcutta, 1826); *Dictionary, English and Burmese* (Maulmain, 1849); and *A Dictionary, Burmese and English* (Maulmain, 1852). Died April 12, 1850, at sea, during a sea voyage taken to recover his health. *References*: Adoniram Judson Papers, American Baptist Historical Society, Rochester, N.Y.; Adoniram Judson Papers, Andover Newton Theological School Library, Newton Centre, Mass.; Courtney Anderson, *To the Golden Shore* (Boston, 1956); Joan J. Brumberg, *Mission for Life: The Story of the Family of Adoniram Judson, the Dramatic Events of the First American Foreign Mission, and the Course of Evangelical Religion in the Nineteenth Century* (New York, 1980); *CDCWM; DAB*; and *NCAB* 3:92.

JUDSON, ANN HASSELTINE (1789–1826). Missionary, first wife of Adoniram Judson,* born December 22, 1789, in Bradford, Massachusetts. Ann Hasseltine Judson accompanied her husband to Burma in 1814, and served in Rangoon, Ava, and Amherst until her death. She wrote *An Account of the American Baptist Mission to the Burman Empire* (London, 1823). Died October 24, 1826, in Amherst, Burma. *References*: Joan J. Brumberg, "The Case of Ann Hasseltine Judson," in *Women in New Worlds*, ed. Rosemary S. Keller, Louise L. Queen, and Hilah F. Thomas (Nashville, Tenn., 1982), pp. 234–48; *DAB; EM*; Gordon L. Hall, *Golden Boats from Burma* (Philadelphia, 1961); *NAW*; and *NCAB* 3:93.

JUDSON, EMILY CHUBBUCK (1817–1854). Missionary, third wife of Adoniram Judson,* born August 22, 1817, in Eaton, near Hamilton, New York. Emily Chubbuck Judson graduated from Utica Female Seminary and was a teacher of English at the seminary from 1841 until 1845. She married Adoniram

Judson in 1846 and came with him to Burma. She lived in Maulmain. She returned to the United States in 1851 and settled in Hamilton, New York. She wrote *The Kathayan Slave, and Other Papers Connected with Missionary Life* (Boston, 1853); *My Two Sisters: A Sketch from Missouri* (Boston, 1854); and a memoir of Sarah Hall Boardman Judson.* Died June 1, 1854, in Hamilton, New York. *References: DAB; EM; LC; NAW*; and *NCAB* 3:93.

JUDSON, SARAH HALL BOARDMAN (1803–1845). Missionary, second wife of Adoniram Judson,* born November 4, 1803, in Alstead, New Hampshire, and grew up in Salem, Massachusetts. Sarah Hall Boardman Judson married George Dana Boardman* in 1825 and came with him to Burma in 1827. They served in Maulmain and later in Tavoy. She remained in Burma after her husband's death in 1831, married Adoniram Judson in 1834, and moved to Maulmain. Died September 1, 1845, in St. Helena, while on her way to the United States to attempt to remedy her ill health. *References: DAB; EM; NAW*; and *NCAB* 3:93.

JUDSON COLLEGE. Founded as Cushing High School by the Baptist mission in Rangoon, Burma, in 1872. It became Baptist College in 1894 and was renamed Judson College in 1918. It was an integral part of the University of Rangoon from 1920 until 1942, when it closed down. It ceased to function in 1948 when the government of Burma created a unitary university and appropriated most of the Judson College buildings. *Reference*: Daw Hnin Mya Kyi, *Development of Higher Education in Burma* (Rangoon, 1975).

K

KADES, CHARLES LOUIS (1906–   ). Lawyer and government official, born March 2, 1906, in Newburgh, New York. Kades graduated from Cornell University and Harvard Law School, and was admitted to the bar in 1931. He was assistant general counsel of the Federal Emergency Administration from 1933 to 1937 and of the Treasury Department from 1938 to 1942. He served with the general staff of the War Department from 1943 to 1945, and in the U.S. Army in 1944–1945. He was deputy chief of the government section in the general headquarters of the Supreme Commander for the Allied Powers (SCAP) in Japan from 1945 to 1949. He practiced law in New York City from 1949 to 1979. *References*: Justin Williams, *Japan's Political Revolution under MacArthur: A Participant's Account* (Tokyo, 1979), ch. 3; and *WWA*.

KANE, SAMUEL E. (? –1933). Colonial administrator and businessman, Kane served in the Spanish-American War in the Philippines and in the Philippine-American War. He was discharged from the army but remained in the Philippines, searching for gold. He settled in the Bontoc Province, and was its governor from 1902 to 1918. He resigned because of ill health but remained there and supervised his various business interests until 1931, when he returned to the United States. He wrote *Baguio, Gateway to Wonderland* (Manila, 1931), and *Life and Death in Luzon: Thirty Years of Adventure with the Philippine Highlanders* (Indianapolis, 1933). Died May 31, 1933, in New York City. *Reference*: *NYT*, June 1, 1933.

KANSEI GAKUIN UNIVERSITY. Founded in Kobe in 1899 by Walter R. Lambuth of the Methodist Episcopal Church, South. In 1910, Japanese, American, and Canadian Methodist churches became joint sponsors. The campus moved to Nishinomiya, Hyogo Prefecture, in 1920. University status was granted in 1932. *References*: *KEJ*; and *Sixty Years of Kansai Gakuin* (Nichinomiya, Japan, 1949).

KAPLAN, GABRIEL L(OUIS) (1901–1968). Government official, born September 14, 1901, in New York City. Kaplan attended Swarthmore College and Columbia University, and graduated from New York University. He was admitted to the bar in 1926. He practiced law in New York City from 1926 until 1952. He served in the U.S. Army Air Force during World War II. He came to the Philippines in 1951 and served as the Central Intelligence Agency (CIA) agent in Manila under the cover of the Catherwood Foundation of Philadelphia, the Committee for Free Asia (later the Asia Foundation), and as resident director of the Committee for Philippine Action in Development, Reconstruction and Education (COMPADRE) from 1954 to 1958. He also formed the National Committee for Free Elections in the Philippines. He returned to the United States in 1958 and founded the Community Development Counseling Service (CDCS) in Arlington, Virginia, in 1959, and was its president from 1959 until 1966. Died September 17, 1968, in Bethesda, Maryland. *References*: Gabriel Louis Kaplan Papers, Cornell University Library, Ithaca, N.Y.; *NCAB* 54:15; and *NYT*, September 18, 1968.

KAUFFMAN, JAMES (LEE) (1886–1968). Lawyer and educator, born January 18, 1886, in Columbia, Pennsylvania. Kauffman graduated from Princeton University and Harvard Law School, and was admitted to the bar in 1911. He practiced law in Lancaster, Pennsylvania, from 1911 to 1913. He was a professor of English and American law at the Imperial University of Tokyo from 1913 to 1919. He was then president of the Japanese subsidiary of the Fuller Construction Company. He returned to the United States in 1926 and practiced law in New York City until 1951. He went back to Japan in 1951 and practiced law in Tokyo until his death. Died June 5, 1968, in Tokyo. *References*: *KEJ*; *NYT*, June 7, 1968; and *WWWA*.

KAUFMAN, HOWARD K(EVA) (1922–   ). Anthropologist, born November 5, 1922, in New York City. Kaufman graduated from the University of California at Berkeley, Oberlin College, and Indiana University. He served in the U.S. Army during World War II. He carried out fieldwork in Thailand in 1953–1954. He was community development advisor for the Agency for International Development (AID) in Laos from 1955 to 1957, in Korea from 1958 to 1960, and in Nepal from 1960 to 1962. He was socioeconomic advisor to the Ministry of Agriculture of Vietnam from 1962 to 1964, senior anthropologist in the Special Operations Research Office of American University from 1964 to 1966, anthropologist and consultant at Cornell Aeronautical Laboratories from 1967 to 1970, and associate professor of anthropology at Ripon College (Wis.) after 1970. He wrote *Bangkhuad: A Community Study in Thailand* (Locust Valley, N.Y., 1960), and *Culao: A Fishing Village Cooperative in South Vietnam* (Ithaca, N.Y., 1973). *Reference*: *AMWS*.

KEARNY, LAWRENCE (1789–1868). Naval officer, born November 30, 1789, in Perth Amboy, New Jersey. Kearny was appointed mishipman in the U.S. Navy in 1807. He served in the War of 1812 and later in the Caribbean and the Mediterranean. He was commander of the East India Squadron from 1840 until 1846. Instructed to protect American interests in China, he promoted friendly feelings with the Chinese authorities and pressured them for the right to trade in the five open ports. He was later president of the board to examine midshipmen, commandant of the Norfolk Navy Yard, general superintendent of ocean mail steamships in New York, and commandant of the New York Navy Yard. He retired in 1861 with the rank of commodore. Died November 29, 1868, in Perth Amboy, New Jersey. *References*: Carroll S. Alden, *Lawrence Kearny, Sailor Diplomat* (Princeton, N.J., 1936); *DAB*; *DADH*; and *NCAB* 21:335.

KEENAN, JOHN L(AWRENCE) (1889–1944). Engineer, born in Boston. Keenan graduated from Yale University. He joined the Wharton Steel Company in New Jersey and then became an expert blast furnace operator with the Gary Steel Company of Gary, Indiana. He went to India in 1913 and helped develop the Tata firm into a vast organization, which made Jamshedpur, Bihar, the tenth greatest steel center in the world. He started there as a blast furnace expert, and became general manager of the Tata Steel and Iron Company of Bombay and Jamshedpur, India, in 1930. He returned to the United States in 1938. He wrote (with Lerone Sorsby) *A Steel Man in India* (New York, 1943). He went to China in 1943 on a confidential mission for the State Department. Died January 7, 1944, in Kunming, China. *Reference*: NYT, January 8, 1944.

KEENE, DONALD (LAWRENCE) (1922–). Japanologist, born June 18, 1922, in Brooklyn, New York. Keene graduated from Columbia University. He served in the U.S. Navy during World War II. He was a lecturer in Japanese at Cambridge University (England) from 1949 to 1954, and professor of Japanese at Columbia University after 1955. He wrote *The Japanese Discovery of Europe, 1720–1830* (London, 1952); *Japanese Literature: An Introduction for Western Readers* (New York, 1955); *Living Japan* (Garden City, N.Y., 1959); *Modern Japanese Novels and the West* (Charlottesville, Va., 1961); *Bunraku: The Art of the Japanese Theatre* (Tokyo, 1965); *No: The Classical Theatre of Japan* (Tokyo, 1967); *Landscape and Portraits* (Tokyo, 1971); *World within Walls* (New York, 1976); *Meeting with Japan* (Tokyo, 1979); and *The Pleasures of Japanese Literature* (New York, 1988). He also edited several anthologies of Japanese and Chinese literature, and translated Japanese plays. *References*: CA; DAS; DFAF; and WWA.

KEESING, FELIX M(AXWELL) (1902–1961). Anthropologist, born January 5, 1902, in Taiping, British Malaya. Keesing graduated from the University of New Zealand, and studied at Yale University and the University of Chicago.

He then returned to New Zealand and studied the Maori. He was director of an international research project on the dependencies and native peoples of the Pacific for the Institute of Pacific Relations from 1930 to 1933. This project took him to American Samoa, China, and the Philippines. He wrote (with Marie Keesing) *Taming Philippine Headhunters: A Study of Government and of Cultural Change in Northern Luzon* (Stanford, 1934), and *The Philippines—A Nation in the Making* (Shanghai, 1937). He was chair of the Department of Anthropology and Sociology at the University of Hawaii (Honolulu) from 1934 until 1942, and served in the Office of Strategic Services (OSS) during World War II. He became a U.S. citizen in 1945. He was head of the Department of Anthropology and Sociology at Stanford University from 1948 to 1956, and of the Department of Anthropology after 1956. He also served as a technical consultant to the United Nations Mission to Western Samoa, and senior commissioner for the United States on the South Pacific Commission. Died April 22, 1961, in Palo Alto, California. *References*: *AA* (1962): 351–55; *NYT*, April 23, 1961; and *WWWA*.

KEITH, AGNES (NEWTON) (1901–   ). Author, born July 6, 1901, in Oak Park, Illinois, and grew up in California. Keith graduated from the University of California. She was a reporter for the *San Francisco Examiner*. She lived in Sandakan, North Borneo, from 1934 until 1942 with her husband, who was director of agriculture in North Borneo. She was interned in Japanese prison camps from 1942 to 1945. She returned to Borneo in 1947, and accompanied her husband to the Philippines in 1952 and to Libya from 1955 to 1964. She wrote *Land below the Wind* (Boston, 1939); *Three Came Home* (Boston, 1947) on her experiences in a Japanese internment camp during World War II; *White Man Return* (Boston, 1951); *Bare Feet in the Palace* (Boston, 1955), about her experiences in the Philippines and *Beloved Exiles* (Boston, 1972), an autobiographical novel. *References*: Mary J. DeMarr, "Agnes Newton Keith", in *American Women Writers*, ed. Lina Mainiero and Langdon L. Faust (New York, 1980), 2:432–34; *CA*; and *WWAW*.

KELLOGG, SAMUEL HENRY (1839–1899). Missionary, born September 6, 1839, in Quogue, Long Island, New York. Kellogg attended Williams College, graduated from Princeton University and Princeton Theological Seminary, and was ordained in 1864. He was a missionary under the Board of Foreign Missions of the Presbyterian Church in the U.S.A. in India from 1865 until 1873, serving at the Farukhabad mission in Barhpur, near Fatehgarh, North India. He returned to the United States in 1871 because of ill health, but was back in India in 1873 and began to teach at the Theological School in Allahabad. He wrote *Grammer of the Hindi Language* (Allahabad, 1876). He returned again to the United States in 1876, was a pastor in Pittsburgh, professor of systematic theology at the Allegheny (Pa.) Theological Seminary from 1877 until 1885, and pastor in Toronto, Canada, until 1892. He was recalled to India in 1892 to help revise the Hindi Old Testament. Died May 3, 1899, in Landour, a station in the Himalayas. *References*: *ACAB*; *DAB*; *EM*; *Hewitt*; and *WWWA*.

KENDRICK, JOHN (ca. 1740–1794). Sea captain, born in Harwich, Cape Cod, Massachusetts. Kendrick went to sea early, served in the French and Indian War, and commanded privateers during the Revolutionary War. He was a pioneer in the maritime fur trade with the Pacific Northwest in 1787–1788, and explored Nootka Sound. He sailed to China in 1789 on the sloop *Washington*, and opened the trade in sandalwood with that country. He returned to the Northwest Coast in 1791, visiting Japan on the way. His vessel was the first to fly the American flag in Japan. He sailed again to China in 1793 and 1794. Killed in an accident, December 12, 1794, in Honolulu Harbour, Hawaii. *References*: *DAB*; *Wildes*, ch. 8; *WWWA*.

KENNALLY, VINCENT IGNATIUS (1895–1977). Clergyman, born June 11, 1895, in Boston. Kennally attended Boston College, graduated from Woodstock College (Md.), joined the Society of Jesus in 1915, and was ordained in 1928. He was a teacher at the Ateneo de Manila in the Philippines from 1922 to 1925, professor of philosophy at Boston College in 1929–1930, and assistant editor of *Jesuit Missions* in 1930–1931. He was superior of the mission at Cagayan de Oro in the Philippines from 1933 to 1939, and rector and master of novices at Novaliches in the Philippines from 1940 to 1945. He was apostolic administrator and religious superior of the Caroline and Marshall Islands from 1946 to 1951, vice-provincial of the Jesuit vice-province of the Philippines from 1952 to 1956, and bishop of the Caroline and Marshall Islands from 1956 until his retirement in 1971. Died April 12, 1977, on Truk, the Caroline Islands. *References*: *DACB*; and *WWWA*.

KENNAN, GEORGE (1845–1924). Explorer and journalist, born February 16, 1845, in Norwalk, Ohio. Kennan became an expert telegrapher and served as military telegrapher in Cincinnati during the Civil War. In 1865 he became a member of the Siberian expedition of the Western Union Telegraph Company for the purpose of surveying a possible route for the extension of the telegraph system from America to Europe by way of Alaska and the Bering Strait and across Siberia, and lived in Northeastern Siberia from 1865 to 1867. He then made a journey by dog sled to St. Petersburg. He wrote of his experiences in *Tent Life in Siberia* (New York, 1870). He traveled in Russian Caucasus in 1870–1871. He was in business in Medine, New York, and New York City until 1877, and was assistant manager of the Associated Press in Washington, D.C., from 1877 to 1885. He went again to Siberia in 1885–1886 for Century Company, and wrote *Siberia and the Exile System* (New York, 1891). He became a Russian scholar and was also a correspondent during the Spanish-American and Russo-Japanese wars. Died May 10, 1924, in Elberton, New Jersey. *References*: George Kennan Papers, Manuscript Division, Library of Congress; George Kennan Papers, New York Public Library; *DAB*; *NYT*, May 11, 1924; T. Stults, "George Kennan: Russian Specialist of the 1890s," *Russian Review* 29 (1970): 275–85; Frederick F. Travis, "George Kennan and the Philippines," *PS* 27 (1979): 527–36; and *WWWA*.

KENNEDY, RAYMOND (1906–1950). Sociologist, born December 11, 1906, in Holyoke, Massachusetts. Kennedy graduated from Yale University. He was an instructor at the Brent School in Baguio, Philippines, in 1928–1929; field representative for General Motors Corporation in Java and Sumatra, Dutch East Indies, from 1929 to 1932; instructor of sociology at Yale University from 1935 to 1940; assistant professor there from 1940 to 1943; associate professor from 1943 to 1947; and professor from 1947 until his death. He was a consultant on Southeastern affairs to the State Department and the Office of Strategic Services (OSS) during World War II. He wrote *The Ageless Indies* (New York, 1942); *Islands and Peoples of the Indies* (Washington, D.C., 1943); and *Bibliography of Indonesian Peoples and Cultures* (New Haven, Conn., 1945). He was again in Indonesia from 1948 to 1950 studying the effect of Western civilization on Indonesia natives. Killed April 27, 1950, in Central Java, on route from Bandung to Jogjakarta. *References*: *American Sociological Review* 15 (1950): 440–41; *FEQ* 10 (1951): 170–72; *NYT*, April 29, 1950; and *WWWA*.

KERN, EDWARD M(EYER) (1823–1863). Artist, born October 26, 1823, in Philadelphia. Kern served as a topographer with John Charles Fremont's third expedition to the Southwest from 1845 to 1847, in California during the Mexican War, with Fremont's fourth expedition to the Colorado Rockies in 1848–1849, and a topographer with Simpson's expedition into Navajo country in 1849. He was official artist to North Pacific Surveying Expedition from 1853 to 1856. He joined the U.S. Navy expedition to survey the route from California to China from 1858 to 1860. He served during the Civil War. Died November 25, 1863, in Philadelphia. *References*: Robert V. Hine, *Edward Kern and American Expansion* (New Haven, Conn., 1962); *NYHSD*; and *WWWA*.

KERR, JOHN G(LASGOW) (1824–1901). Medical missionary, born November 30, 1824, near Duncansville, Adams County, Ohio, and grew up in Lexington, Virginia. Kerr attended Denison and Transylvania universities, and graduated from Jefferson Medical College (Philadelphia). He practiced medicine in Brown and Adams counties, Ohio, until 1854. He was a medical missionary under the Board of Foreign Missions of the Presbyterian Church in the U.S.A. in Canton, China, from 1854 until his death. He was in charge of the hospital of the Medical Missionary Society in China in Canton from 1855 to 1898. He began a medical education program in connection with his hospital in 1869, and was the first president of the Medical Missionary Association in China in 1886. In Canton he founded the first hospital in China for the treatment of the insane in 1892, and was in charge of it from 1898 until his death. He took a leading part in introducing Western medicine to China. Died August 10, 1901, in Canton, China. *References*: *DAB*; *DAMB 1984*; and *EM*.

KERR, JOHN STUART (fl. 1796–1815). Merchant and consul. A native of Philadelphia, Kerr was among the first Americans to try their luck in Manila, seeking cargoes of hemp, indigo, pepper, and sugar, and was the first-known permanent American resident in the Philippines. He was also the first U.S. consul in Manila, holding the office from 1801 until 1815.

KERSHNER, BRUCE (LESHER) (1871–1949). Educator and missionary. Kershner held pastorates in western Pennsylvania from 1893 to 1903, was professor of Greek language and literature at Bethany College (W.Va.) from 1903 to 1905, and professor of Latin language and literature at Kee Mar College (Hagerstown, Md.) in 1905–1906. He was a missionary under the Disciplines of Christ in the Philippines from 1905 to 1917, serving as president of Manila College of the Bible. He wrote *The Head Hunter and Other Stories of the Philippines* (Cincinnati, 1921). He was later professor of Biblical history and literature at Lynchburg College (Va.) from 1918 to 1925, and professor of New Testament language and literature at Butler University (Indianapolis) from 1925 until his retirement. Died July 12, 1949. *References*: Bruce Kershner Papers, Disciplines of Christ Historical Society, Nashville, Tenn.; Bruce Lesher Kershner Papers, Christian Theological Seminary Library, Indianapolis; and *School and Society* 70 (July 30, 1949): 77.

KEYES, CHARLES F(ENTON) (1937–   ). Anthropologist, born October 3, 1937, in Hyannis, Nebraska. Keyes graduated from the University of Nebraska and Cornell University. He was assistant and associate professor of psychology at the University of Washington (Seattle) from 1965 to 1973, and associate professor of anthropology after 1973. He carried out fieldwork in Thailand from 1966 to 1968, and wrote *Isan: Regionalism in Northeast Thailand* (Ithaca, N.Y., 1967). He edited *Ethnic Adaptation and Identity: The Karen on the Thai Frontier with Burma* (Philadelphia, 1979), and *The Golden Peninsula: Culture and Adaptation in Mainland Southeast Asia* (New York, 1977). *Reference*: AMWS.

KIDDER, MARY E. (1834–1910). Missionary, born January 31, 1834, in Wardsboro, Vermont. She was a missionary under the Board of Foreign Missions of the Reformed Church in America in Japan from 1869 until 1910, the first single missionary woman in Japan. In 1875 she started Ferris Seminary in Yokohama, the first school of higher education for girls in Japan. Died June 25, 1910, in Tokyo. *Reference*: HDRCA.

KILBOURNE, ERNEST (ALBERT) (1865–1928). Missionary, born March 13, 1865, in Niagra Falls, Ontario, Canada, and grew up in Conestoga and Winterburn, Ontario. Kilbourne became a telegraph operator, came to the United

States, and worked for Western Union in San Francisco and Virginia City, Nevada. He was then a divisional chief for Western Union in Chicago. He attended Moody Bible Institute. He was a missionary under the Oriental Missionary Society in Japan from 1902 to 1907. He wrote *The Story of a Mission in Japan* (Tokyo, 1907). He came to Korea in 1907 and moved to China in 1925. Died April 13, 1928. *Reference*: Edward and Esther Erny, *No Guarantee but God: The Story of the Founders of The Oriental Missionary Society* (Greenwood, Ind., 1969).

KINCAID, EUGENIO (1798–1883). Missionary, born in Wethersfield, Connecticut. Kincaid graduated from Hamilton Literary and Theological Institution. He was a missionary under the American Baptist Missionary Union in Burma from 1830 until 1863. He served initially in Maulmain, and went to Ava in 1833. In 1839 he tried to reach Assam by crossing the mountains between Burma and Assam, but was forced to turn back. He left Burma because of ill health, but returned in 1850. He served later at Prome until 1863. In 1857 he conducted the first Burmese diplomatic mission to the United States. Died April 3, 1883, in Girard, Kansas. *References*: *ACAB*; Alfred S. Patton, *The Hero Missionary, or A History of the Labors of the Rev. Eugenio Kincaid* (New York, 1858); and Willis S. Webb, *Incidents and Trials in the Life of Rev. Eugenio Kincaid, D. D., the "Hero" Missionary to Burma, 1830–1865* (Fort Scott, Kans., 1890).

KING, CHARLES WILLIAM (ca. 1809–1845). Merchant. King attended Brown University. He went to China in 1826 as an employee of Talbot, Olyphant and Company. For many years he was a partner in the firm of Olyphant and Company. In 1837 he attempted to open Japan to American trade. He led an expedition on the ship *Morrison* (see *Morrison* Incident*) but was refused permission to land and returned to China. King then argued for U.S. action to open Japan. He left China in 1845. Died September 27, 1845, at sea not far from Aden. *References*: William A. Borst, "The American Merchant and the Genesis of Japanese-American Commercial Relations, 1790–1858," Ph.D. diss., St. Louis University, 1972, chs. v–vi; and *DAB*.

KING, HAMILTON (1852–1912). Educator and diplomat, born in St. John's, Newfoundland, Canada. King graduated from Oliver College (Mich.) and studied at the College Theological Seminary, the University of Leipzig, and the American School at Athens. He was principal of the preparatory department of Oliver College from 1879 until 1898. He was minister and consul general in Siam from 1898 to 1912. Died September 1, 1912, in Bangkok. *References*: *NCAB* 12:122; *NYT*, September 3, 1912; and *WWWA*.

KINGDOM OF HUMANITY/REPUBLIC OF MORAC-SONGHRATI-MEADS. A group of private Americans who claimed to have established a number of settlements in the Spratly Islands in the South China Sea and to form, after 1914, their own nation-state called the "Kingdom of Humanity" or the "Republic of Morac-Songhrati-Meads" or both, which they developed and occupied until World War II and again after 1946. The end of the Kingdom came in 1972 when all its members were drowned during a typhoon. *References*: Marwyn S. Samuels, *Contest for the South China Sea* (New York, 1982), pp. 168–72, and Hsiao Shi-ching, "The Nanshas (Spratleys) Dispute," *The Annals of Philippines Chinese Historical Association* 6 (1976): 63–67.

KINSMAN, NATHANIEL (1798–1847). Sea captain and merchant, born in Salem, Massachusetts. Kinsman went to sea in 1818 and sailed several times to Batavia. He came to Canton in 1839 as master of the ship *Zenobia*. He returned to Canton in 1843 with his wife **REBECCA CHASE KINSMAN** and his family. He was a partner with Wetmore and Company in Canton. Died May 1, 1847, in Macao. *References*: Kinsman Family Papers, Essex Institute, Salem, Mass.; "Journal of Rebecca Chase Kinsman Kept on Her Voyage to China in 1843," *EIHC* 90 (1954): 289–308, 389–409; "Life in Macao in the 1840s; Letters of Rebecca Chase Kinsman to Her Family in Salem," *EIHC* 86 (1950): 15–40, 106–42, 257–84, 311–30; *EIHC* 87 (1951): 114–49, 269–305, 388–409; *EIHC* 88 (1952): 18–99; and Mary K. Monroe, "Nathaniel Kinsman, Merchant of Salem, in the China Trade, from the Kinsman Family Manuscripts," *EIHC* 85 (1949): 9–40, 101–42.

KLAUS, ARMIN VINCENT (1887–1965). Missionary, born December 14, 1887, in La Crosse, Wisconsin. Klaus graduated from Charles City College, Garrett Biblical Institute, and Northwestern University. He was a missionary under the Board of Foreign Missions of the Methodist Episcopal Church in Java from 1913 until 1928, when the mission was closed. He was in charge of the Methodist Book Room in Batavia, and served as district superintendent and mission treasurer. He was transferred to Sumatra in 1928, where he was principal of boys schools in Medan and Palembang, district superintendent, mission treasurer, and mission superintendent. He was principal of the Sipoholon Theological Seminary in 1941–1942. He was interned by the Japanese from 1942 to 1945. He returned to the United States in 1945 but was back in Sumatra in 1947. He was superintendent of the Chinese district and mission treasurer until his retirement in 1955. Died April 27, 1965, in Long Beach, California. *Reference*: EWM.

KLEIN, FREDERICK C. (1857–1926). Missionary, born May 17, 1857, in Washington, D.C. Klein graduated from Western Maryland College, and was ordained in 1880. He was the first foreign missionary under the Board of Foreign Missions of the Methodist Protestant Church in Japan from 1883 to 1892. He served in Yokohama and Nagoya, established Nagoya College, and was its first president. He returned to the United States in 1908 because of ill health and held pastorates in various states. He was corresponding secretary and treasurer of the Board of Foreign Missions until 1916. Died December 27, 1926, in Berwyn, Maryland. *References*: *EWM*, and *WWWA*.

KNAPP, ARTHUR MAY (1841–1921). Missionary and editor, born May 29, 1841, in Charlestown, Massachusetts. Knapp graduated from Harvard University and Harvard Divinity School, and was ordained in 1868. He served in the Union Army during the Civil War. He held pastorates in Providence, Rhode Island; Bangor, Maine; and Watertown, Massachusetts; until 1887. He was sent by the American Unitarian Association to Japan in 1888 to examine religious conditions. He returned to Japan in 1889 and established a mission in Tokyo. He also established a magazine in Japanese. He returned to the United States in 1894 and held a pastorate in Fall River, Massachusetts, until 1900. He was back in Japan in 1900, and was proprietor and editor of the *Japan Advertiser* in Yokohama from 1900 to 1909. He wrote *Feudal and Modern Japan* (Boston, 1897). He returned to the United States in 1910. Died January 29, 1921, in West Newton, Massachusetts. *References*: Samuel A. Eliot, ed., *Heralds of a Liberal Faith, IV: The Pilots* (Boston, 1952), pp. 177–80; and *WWWA*.

KNOX, GEORGE W(ILLIAM) (1853–1912). Author and educator, born August 11, 1853, in Rome, New York. Knox graduated from Hamilton College and Auburn Theological Seminary, and was ordained in 1877. He was a missionary under the Board of Foreign Missions of the Presbyterian Church in the U.S.A. in Japan from 1877 until 1893. He taught homiletics at Union Theological Seminary in Tokyo from 1881 until 1893, and was professor of philosophy and ethics at the Tokyo Imperial University from 1886 until 1893. He returned to the United States in 1893; held a pastorate in Rye, New York; was lecturer on apologetics at Union Theological Seminary from 1896 until 1899; and was a professor of philosophy and the history of religions from 1899 until his death. He wrote *A Japanese Philosopher and Other Papers upon the Chinese Philosophy in Japan* (Yokohama, 1892); *Japanese Life in Town and Country* (New York, 1904); *Imperial Japan: The Country and Its People* (London, 1905); *The Spirit of the Orient* (New York, 1906); and *The Development of Religion in Japan* (New York, 1907). He went on a lecture tour of East Asia in 1911. Died April 25, 1912, in Seoul, Korea. *References*: *DAB*; *NCAB* 23:245; *NYT*, April 27, 1912; and *WWWA*.

KNOX, THOMAS WALLACE (1835–1896). Author and traveler, born June 26, 1835, in Pembroke, New Hampshire. Knox was a teacher and principal of an academy that he established at Kingston, New Hampshire. He went to Colorado during the gold rush of 1860; was special reporter and then city editor of the Denver *Daily News*; served in the Union Army during the Civil War; and was a war correspondent for the *New York Herald*. As a correspondent for the

New York Herald, he traveled across Siberia in 1866 with the American company engaged in laying a telegraph line for the Russian government, and wrote *Overland through Asia: Pictures of Siberian, Chinese, and Tartar Life* (Hartford, Conn., 1870). He traveled in East Asia in 1877, and secured material for his series of books *The Boy Travellers in the Far East* (New York, 1881). He later settled in New York City in 1879, and was engaged in writing until his death. Died January 6, 1896, in New York City. *References*: *DAB*; and *NYT*, January 7, 1896.

KOBE COLLEGE. Founded in 1875 as a home school for girls under the auspices of the Woman's Board of Missions of the Interior in Kobe, Japan. It became a college in 1894 and a nonsectarian Christian college in 1940. *Reference*: Charlotte B. DeForest, *The History of Kobe College* (Nishinomiya, Japan, 1950).

KOKE, ROBERT A. (1910–   ). Hotel keeper and government official, born October 13, 1910, in Los Angeles, and grew up in Santa Barbara. Koke attended Santa Barbara State University and the University of California at Los Angeles. He was a professional tennis player, and was employed in the art department of Metro-Goldwyn-Mayer in Hollywood until 1936. He came to Bali in 1936, established Kuta Beach Hotel at Bali, and founded surfing in that country. He returned to the United States in 1941 and wrote of his experiences in the May 1942 issue of *Fortune* magazine. He served with the Coordinator of War Information and later with the Office of Strategic Services (OSS). He was stationed in Ceylon and served with the occupation forces in Singapore. He was chief of the OSS station in Batavia, Dutch East Indies, and later served in Shanghai until 1946. He was then employed by the Central Intelligence Agency (CIA) until his retirement in 1970. His wife, **LOUISE G(ARRETT) KOKE**, wrote *Our Hotel in Bali: How Two Young Americans Made a Dream Come True—A Story of the 1930s* (Wellington, New Zealand, 1987). *Reference*: Hugh Mabbett, *In Praise of Kuta: From Slave Port to Fishing Village to the Most Popular Resort in Bali* (Wellington, New Zealand, 1987).

KOREAN EXPEDITION (1871). Five-vessel squadron, under the command of Rear Admiral John Rodgers,* sent to Korea with the intention of negotiating a diplomatic and commercial treaty. Frederick F. Low,* U.S. minister to China, was in charge of the diplomatic talks. The squadron proceeded up the Salee River without official authorization, and after the Korean fort fired on a surveying party, a military confrontation between the American and Korean forces arose. The Americans destroyed five forts and killed or wounded 350 Koreans. Three Americans were killed. *References*: Jack Bauer, "The Korean Expedition of 1871," *USNIP* 74 (February 1948): 197–204; Albert Castle and Andrew C. Nahm, "Our Little War with the Heathen," *American Heritage* 19 (April 1968): 19–23, 72–75; H. A. Gosnell, "The Navy in Korea," *AN* 7 (1947): 107–14; Robert Swartout, Jr., "Cultural Conflict and Gunboat Diplomacy: The Development of the 1871 Korean-American Incident," *Journal of Social Sciences and Humanities* (Seoul) no. 43 (1976): 117–69; and Carolyn A. Tyson, *Marine Amphibious Landing in Korea, 1871* (Washington, D.C., 1966).

KUDER, EDWARD M. ("ED") (1896–1970). Educator, born May 15, 1896, in Salem, Virginia, and grew up in India. Kuder graduated from Roanoke College (Salem, Va.). He served in the U.S. Army during World War I. He was teacher in the Philippines from 1922 until 1941. He was superintendent of schools in Pangasinan in 1922, in Pampanga in 1923, in Ilocos Sur in 1924–1925, and in Cotabato from 1926 to 1932. He was division superintendent of Lanao from 1932 to 1934, of Sulu from 1934 to 1941, and of Lanao in 1941. He was civil affairs officer for Lanao under the guerrilla forces in 1942–1943, and was evacuated in 1943. He returned to the Philippines after World War II, served with the U.S. Veterans Administration, and was later an advisor to the Philippine government on matters relating to non-Christian groups until his death. *References*: *CCDP*; *Gleeck/Frontiers*; and Victor G. Van Vactor, "Four Decades of American Educators in Mindanao and Sulu," *Dansalan Quarterly* 3 (1981): 38–43.

KUGLER, ANNA SARAH (1856–1930). Medical missionary, born April 19, 1856, in Ardmore, Pennsylvania. Kugler graduated from the Woman's Medical College of Pennsylvania. She was assistant physician at the State Hospital for the Insane in Norristown, Pennsylvania, from 1880 to 1883. She was a medical missionary under the Women's Missionary Society of the Evangelical Lutheran Church India from 1883 until her death. She opened the first dispensary for women in Telugu Country in Guntur in 1886, and founded a hospital there in 1898. She helped Ida Scudder* to establish the Vellore Medical College for Women. She wrote *Guntur Mission Hospital, Guntur, India* (Philadelphia, 1928). Died July 26, 1930, in Guntur. *References*: Anna Sarah Kugler Papers, Archives of the Lutheran Church of America, Lutheran School of Theology, Chicago; George Drach, *Kingdom Pathfinders: Biographical Sketches of Foreign Missionaries* (Philadelphia, 1942), pp. 49–66; *LC*; *NAW*; and Ellen J. Smith, "Medical Missionaries," in *"Send Us a Lady Physician": Women Doctors in America, 1835–1920*, ed. Ruth J. Abram (New York, 1985), pp. 199–204.

KWANSEI GAKUIN UNIVERSITY. Founded in 1889 by Walter R. Lambuth,* president of the Japan Mission of the Methodist Episcopal Church, South in Kobe. It came under joint sponsorship of the Methodist churches of Japan, the United States, and Canada. It developed a theological seminary in 1908, became a college in 1921, moved to Nishinomiya in 1929, and became a university in 1931.

L

LACY, GEORGE CARLETON (1888–1951). Missionary, son of William Henry Lacy,* born December 28, 1888, in Foochow, China. Lacy graduated from Ohio Wesleyan University, Garrett Bible Institute, and Northwestern University; studied at Nanking University; and was ordained in 1914. He was a missionary under the Board of Foreign Missions of the Methodist Episcopal Church in China from 1914 until his death. He was district superintendent in Kiangsi Province in 1916–1917 and 1919–1920, president of William Nast College in Kiukiang in 1918–1919, agency secretary of the American Bible Society in China from 1921 to 1941, secretary of the China Bible House from 1933 to 1941 and bishop of the Methodist Church in Foochow after 1941. He was coauthor of *The Great Migration and the Church in West China* (Shanghai, 1941). Died December 11, 1951, in Foochow. *References*: *EWM*; *NYT*, December 20, 1951; and *WWWA*.

LACY, WILLIAM HENRY (1858–1925). Missionary, born January 8, 1858, in Milwaukee, Wisconsin. Lacy graduated from Northwestern University and Garrett Bible Institute, and was ordained in 1883. He was a missionary under the Board of Foreign Missions of the Methodist Episcopal Church in China from 1887 until his death. He served in Foochow, and was professor at the Anglo-Chinese College in Foochow from 1887 to 1894, superintendent of the Anglo-Chinese Book Concern in Foochow from 1891 to 1902, senior manager from 1902 to 1906, and manager of the Methodist Publishing House in China in Foochow and Shanghai after 1907. Died September 3, 1925, in Shanghai. *References*: *EWM*; and *WWWA*.

LADD, GEORGE TRUMBULL (1842–1921). Psychologist, born January 19, 1842, in Plainesville, Ohio. Ladd graduated from Western Reserve College (later Case Western Reserve University) and Andover Theological Seminary. He held pastorates in Edinburg, Ohio, and Milwaukee from 1869 to 1879; and was professor of philosophy at Bowdoin College from 1879 to 1881, and professor of moral philosophy and metaphysics at Yale University from 1881 until his retirement in 1906. He visited Japan in 1892, 1899, and 1906, lecturing at Kyoto, Tokyo, and Kobe. In 1899 he also made an extended journey to India, and lectured in Bombay, Calcutta, Madras, and Benares. He wrote *In Korea with Marquis Ito* (New York, 1908), *Rare Days in Japan* (New York, 1910), and *Intimate Glimpses of Life in India* (Boston, 1919). Died August 8, 1921, in New Haven, Connecticut. *References*: *ACAB*; *DAB*; Eugene S. Mills, *George Trumbull Ladd: Pioneer American Psychologist* (Cleveland, 1969); *NCAB* 33:561; *NYT*, August 9, 1921; *OAB*; and *WWWA*.

LADEJINSKY, WOLF (ISAAC) (1901–1975). Agricultural economist, born March 15, 1901, in Ekaterinopol, Russian Ukraine, and came to the United States in 1922. Ladejinsky graduated from Columbia University. He was employed by the Office of Foreign Agricultural Relations of the U.S. Department of Agriculture from 1935 until 1945, specializing in Asian problems. He served in Japan from 1945 to 1954, and played a major role in developing and introducing a land reform program in Japan during the occupation. He was an agricultural attaché in the U.S. embassy in Tokyo in 1954 in charge of American programs in the Far East. He was also an advisor on land reform to President Chiang Kai-shek's government, first in mainland China and then on Taiwan. He was a member of the U.S. Aid mission to South Vietnam in 1955–1956, and a personal advisor on land reform to President Ngo Dinh Diem of South Vietnam from 1956 to 1961, working on land reform and refugee resettlement. He was a roving regional consultant for the Ford Foundation from 1961 to 1964, advising the foundation's work in Nepal, India, Indonesia, and the Philippines. He was employed by the World Bank from 1964 to 1975, and was a member of the bank's permanent resident mission in India. He played a key role in agrarian reforms in Asia. He was also a collector of Asian art. Died July 3, 1975, in Washington, D.C. *References*: *JAS* 36 (1977): 327–28; Mary S. McAuliffe, "Dwight D. Eisenhower and Wolf Ladejinsky: The Politics of the Declining Red Scare, 1954–55," Prologue 14 (1982): 109–27; Helen Mears, "Ladejinksy's Real Role: Footnote to an Incident," *Nation* 180 (February 19, 1955): 157–59; *NYT*, July 4, 1975; *PolProf: Eisenhower*; and Louis J. Walinsky, ed., *Reform as Unfinished Business: The Selected Papers of Wolf Ladejinsky* (Washington, D.C., 1977).

LADY WASHINGTON, THE. Brigantine, commanded by Captain John Kendrick,* which entered Japanese waters off the coast of Kashinoura (now Wakayama Prefecture) in 1791, the first known American ship to enter Japan.

LA FARGE, JOHN (1835–1910). Painter, born March 31, 1835, in New York City. La Farge attended St. John's College (later part of Fordham University), and graduated from Mount St. Mary's College (Emmitsburg, Md.). He studied law briefly, and went to Paris in 1856 and studied painting. He returned to the

United States in 1858. He began painting murals in 1876, and later became involved in creating stained glass. With Henry Adams (1838–1918), he went to Japan in 1886 and to Tahiti in 1890. He wrote *An Artist's Letters from Japan* (New York, 1897). Died November 14, 1910, in Providence, Rhode Island. *References*: La Farge Family Papers, Manuscripts and Archives Division, Yale University Library; Henry Adams, "John La Farge and Japan," *Apollo* 119 (February 1984): 120–29; Henry Adams, "John La Farge, 1835–1910: From Amateur to Artist," Ph.D. diss., Yale University, 1980; Henry Adams et al., *John La Farge* (Pittsburgh, 1987); Patricia J. Lefor, "John La Farge and Japan: An Instance of Oriental Influence in American Art," Ph.D. diss., Northwestern University, 1978; *NCAB* 9:59; *WWWA*; and James L. Yarnell, "John La Farge and Henry Adams in Japan," *American Art Journal* 21, no. 1 (1989): 41–77.

LAMBUTH, JAMES WILLIAM (1830–1892). Missionary, born March 2, 1830, in Greene County, Alabama, and grew up in Mississippi. Lambuth graduated from the University of Mississippi. He was a missionary under the Board of Foreign Missions of the Methodist Episcopal Church, South, in China from 1854 until 1885, serving in Shanghai. In 1885, he and his son, Walter Russell Lambuth,* accepted the commission to lay the foundation of Southern Methodist missions in Japan. James served in the territory around the Inland Sea, which centered on Kobe and Osaka, and established the Inland Sea mission. Died April 28, 1892, in Kobe, Japan. *References*: *DAB*; and *WWWA*.

LAMBUTH, WALTER RUSSELL (1854–1921). Medical missionary, son of James William Lambuth,* born November 10, 1854, in Shanghai, China, and grew up in Tennessee, Mississippi, and Cambridge, New York. Lambuth attended Emory and Henry College (Washington County, Va.), Vanderbilt University, and Bellevue Hospital Medical College. He was a medical missionary under the Board of Missions of the Methodist Episcopal Church, South, in China, serving in Shanghai and the adjacent villages of Nanziang. In 1885–1886, he inaugurated, along with his father, mission work in Japan, and was superintendent of the mission with headquarters in Kobe. He founded the college and theological school known as Kwansei Gakuin, as well as a girls' school. He returned to the United States in 1891, and was general secretary of the Board of Foreign Missions from 1894 until 1910. He was elected bishop of the Methodist Episcopal Church, South, in 1910. Died September 26, 1921, in Yokohama. *References*: *DAB*; *NCAB* 19:294; *NYT*, September 28, 1921; and *WWWA*.

LAMSON-SCRIBNER, FRANK (1851–1938). Botanist, born April 19, 1851, in Cambridgeport, Massachusetts, and grew up in Manchester, Maine. Lamson-Scribner graduated from Maine State Agricultural and Mechanical College (later the University of Maine). He was a prefect at Girard College (Philadelphia) from 1876 to 1885, special agent in charge of the mycological section of the Botany Division in the U.S. Department of Agriculture in 1885–1886, and chief of the department's section of vegetable pathology in 1887–1888. He was professor of botany at the University of Tennessee from 1888 to 1894, director of the Tennessee Agricultural Experiment Station from 1889 to 1894, and chief of the division of agrostology at the Department of Agriculture from 1895 to 1900. He was chief of the Bureau of Agriculture in the Philippines from 1901 to 1904. He was a special agent and expert on exhibits for the U.S. Department of Agriculture in Washington, D.C., from 1904 until his retirement in 1922. Died February 22, 1938, in Washington, D.C. *References*: Frank Lamson-Scribner Papers, Manuscript Division, Library of Congress; *NCAB* 40:395; *NYT*, February 23, 1938; and *WWWA*.

LANDIS, ELI BARR (1865–1898). Medical missionary and Koreanologist, born December 18, 1865, in Landis Valley, Lancaster, Pennsylvania. Landis attended State Normal School (Millersville, Pa.), and graduated from the medical department of the University of Pennsylvania. He practiced medicine from 1888 until 1890. He was a medical missionary under the Church of England mission in Korea from 1890 until his death. He served in Chemulp'o and Seoul, was in charge of Seoul hospitals, and established an orphanage. He was also a medical officer of the Korean Customs Service after 1893. A scholar of Korean, he translated Buddhist writings into English. Died April 16, 1898, in Chemulp'o, Korea. *Reference*: Richard Rutt, "An Early Koreanologist: Eli Barr Landis, 1865–1898," *Transactions of the Korea Branch of the Royal Asiatic Society* 36 (1960): 101–28.

LANDON, KENNETH PERRY (1903–   ) and **LANDON, MARGARET (DOROTHEA MORTENSON)** (1903–   ). Kenneth Perry Landon, missionary and government official, was born March 27, 1903, in Meadville, Pennsylvania. Landon graduated from Wheaton College, Princeton Theological Seminary, and the University of Chicago, and was ordained in 1927. He was a missionary under the Board of Foreign Missions of the Presbyterian Church in the U.S.A. in Siam from 1927 to 1937; he was stationed at Nakon Srithamarat in 1927–1928 and at Trang from 1928 to 1937. He was assistant professor of philosophy at Earlham College from 1939 to 1941, social science analyst at the office of U.S. Coordinator of Information in 1941–1942, economic analyst in the U.S. Board of Economic Warfare in 1942–1943, international relations officer on Southeast Asian affairs at the State Department from 1943 to 1945, senior area specialist for south and Southeast Asia countries in the National Security Council from 1955 to 1961, professor of Southeast Asia studies at American University after 1965, and director of the Center for South and Southeast Asian Studies there from 1965 to 1970. He wrote *Siam in Transition* (New York, 1939); *Chinese in Thailand* (London, 1941); and *Southeast Asia: Crossroads of Religions* (Chicago, 1949). Margaret Landon, author, was born September 7, 1903, in Somers, Wisconsin. She graduated from Wheaton College (Ill.) and studied at Northwestern University. She accompanied her husband to Siam in 1927, and was principal of a high school there. She wrote the novel *Anna and* *the King of Siam* (New York, 1944) (adapted as the musical "The King and I" in 1951 and filmed in 1956); and *Never Dies the Dream* (Garden City, N.Y., 1949), a novel about a missionary in Thailand. *References*: Dorothy H. Brown, "Margaret Dorothea Mortenson Landon," in *American Women Writers*, ed. Lina Mainiero and Langdon L. Faust (New York, 1980), 2:496–97; *CA*; *CB* 1945; *DAS*; *WWA*; and *WWAW*.

LANE, ORTHA MAY (1894–   ). Missionary, born April 18, 1894, in Lone Tree, Iowa. Lane graduated from Cornell University, Chicago Training School for Home and Foreign Missions, Boston University, and the State University of Iowa. She was a missionary under the Board of Foreign Missions of the Methodist Episcopal Church in north China from 1919 until 1941 and again from 1946 to 1948. She was principal of the Peiping Union Bible Training School for Women in 1929–1930, and secretary of religious work for women and children in north China. She was stationed in Tientsin from 1935 to 1941 and from 1946 to 1948. She was director of the department of home and family life of the Philippine Federation of Christian Churches in Manila from 1950 to 1955, and director of family life work of the Taiwan district of the Methodist Church in Tianan, Taiwan, after 1956. She wrote *Under Marching Orders in North China* (Tyler, Tex., 1971). *Reference*: *WWAW*.

LANGDON, WILLIAM RUSSELL (1891–1963). Diplomat, born July 31, 1891, in Smyrna, Turkey, to American parents. Langdon graduated from Trinity College (Hartford, Conn.). He entered the foreign service in 1911, and was a language student in Japan from 1914 to 1917, assistant Japanese secretary in Tokyo from 1918 to 1921, and vice-consul in Yokohama in 1920–1921. He was consul in Antung, Tsinan, Mukden, Dairen, Seoul, and again in Mukden from 1922 to 1941. He served in the Department of State from 1941 to 1943, and was the department's representative on the Swedish ship *Gripsholm*, supervising the exchange of Japanese and American internees. He was consul general in Kunking from 1943 to 1945, political advisor to John R. Hodge* in 1945–1946, and consul general in Seoul from 1946 to 1948 and in Singapore from 1948 to 1951. He later lectured at the Fletcher School of Law and Diplomacy of Tufts University. Died July 18, 1963, in Wellesley, Massachusetts. *References*: *BRDS*; and *NYT*, July 20, 1963.

LANSDALE, EDWARD G(EARY) (1908–1987). Government official, born February 6, 1908, in Detroit, Michigan. Lansdale graduated from the University of California at Los Angeles. He worked for an advertising agency in San Francisco. He served with the Office of Strategic Services (OSS) and then as an intelligence officer in the U.S. Army during World War II. He joined the U.S. Air Force in 1947. He served as an advisor to Ramon Magsaysay, Philippine defense minister and later president, in the early 1950s in his campaign against the Huk rebels. He counseled him in counterinsurgency techniques and psychological warfare, for which he was financed by the Central Intelligence Agency (CIA), an effort that had proven successful by 1953. He was sent to Vietnam in 1954 to plan, coordinate, and implement a psychological warfare campaign, and acted as a personal advisor to Ngo Dinh Diem, premier of South Vietnam, from 1954 to 1956. He was special assistant to the U.S. ambassador in South Vietnam from 1965 to 1968. He wrote *In the Midst of Wars: An American's Mission to Southeast Asia* (New York, 1972). He was depicted in *The Ugly American* by William J. Lederer and Eugene Burdick (New York, 1958) and in *The Quiet American* by Graham Greene (New York, 1955). Died February 23, 1987, in McLean, Virginia. *References*: Edward G. Lansdale Papers, Hoover Institution on War, Revolution and Peace, Stanford, Calif.; *BAHC* 15 (April-June 1987): 97–99; Cecil B. Currey, *Edward Lansdale: The Unquiet American* (Boston, 1989); Richard Drinnon, *Facing West: The Metaphysics of Indian-Hating and Empire-Building* (Minneapolis, 1980), chs. 25–26; *NYT*, February 24, 1987; *PolProf: Eisenhower*; *PolProf: Kennedy*; and *WWA*.

LANSING-ISHII AGREEMENT (1917). The name commonly given to the diplomatic notes exchanged on November 2, 1917, between U.S. Secretary of State Robert Lansing and Ishii Kikujiro, Japanese diplomat, in which the United States and Japan enunciated the principles that were to guide their conduct in dealing with China. It affirmed the principle of the Open Door, and agreed to respect China's independence and territorial and administrative integrity. *References*: Burton F. Beers, *Vain Endeavor: Robert F. Lansing's Attempts to End the American-Japanese Rivalry* (Durham, N.C., 1962); Roy W. Curry, *Woodrow Wilson and Far Eastern Policy, 1913–1921* (New York, 1957); *DADH*; *EAH*; *KEJ*; Francis C. Prescott, "The Lansing-Ishii Agreement," Ph.D. diss., Yale University, 1949; and John C. Vinson, "The Annulment of the Lansing-Ishii Agreement," *PHR* 27 (1958): 57–69.

LAPP, GEORGE JAY (1879–1951). Missionary, born May 26, 1879, in Juniata, Nebraska. Lapp attended Elkhart Institute and Northwestern University, and was ordained in 1905. He was a missionary under the Mennonite Church in India from 1905 until 1945, serving in the Central Provinces. He was the founder of the Mennonite Bible School and its director from 1910 until 1931. He was ordained as bishop of India in 1928. He wrote *The Christian Church and Rural India* (Calcutta, 1938). Died January 25, 1951, at Goshen, Indiana. *References*: George Jay Lapp Papers, Archives of the Mennonite Church, Goshen College, Goshen, Ind.; George Jay Lapp, "Memoirs of an Indian Missionary," Ms., Archives of the Mennonite Church; and *ME*.

LAPP, MAHLON CASSIUS (1872–1923). Missionary, born February 4, 1872, in Line Lexington, Bucks County, Pennsylvania, and grew up in Roseland, Nebraska. He was a city missionary in Chicago from 1899 to 1901, and a missionary under the Mennonite Church in India from 1901 until his death. He served at

Dhamtari, Central Provinces. He was co-bishop of India from 1901 until 1908, and bishop of India until his death. He was superintendent of the mission from 1908 until 1920. Died May 30, 1923, in Calcutta, India. *Reference: ME.*

LARUE, CARL (DOWNEY) (1885–1955). Botanist, born April 22, 1888, in Williamsville, Illinois. LaRue graduated from Valparaiso University and the University of Michigan. He was a botanist at the Hollandsch-Amerikaansche Plantage Maatschappij (HAPM) in Sumatra from 1917 to 1920. He was instructor, assistant professor, and associate professor of botany at the University of Michigan from 1920 to 1944, and professor after 1944; he was a member of the Michigan Biological Station staff from 1925 to 1950. He developed the method for breeding commercial rubber trees, was in charge of the South American rubber expedition for the U.S. Department of Agriculture in 1923–1924, and codirected the Ford Motor Amazon-Tapajos expedition in 1926–1927 and the rubber investigation expedition to Bolivia, Nicaragua, and Mexico for the U.S. Department of Agriculture in 1940–1941. Died August 19, 1955, in Ann Arbor. *References*: "The Reminiscences of Carl D. LaRue," (1955), Henry Ford Museum and Archives, Dearborn, Mich.; *NYT*, August 21, 1955; and *WWWA*.

LA SALETTE, MISSIONARIES OF OUR LADY OF. Founded in 1852 in Grenoble, France. The American province was founded in 1895 in Hartford, Connecticut. It began missionary work in Burma in 1937 and in the Philippines in 1948. *Reference: CE.*

LATIMER, JOHN R(ICHARDSON) (1793–1865). Merchant, born December 10, 1793. Latimer went to Philadelphia before 1816 and worked in the counting house of his uncle George Latimer. He was a commission merchant in Canton, China, from 1816 to 1821, and again from 1824 to 1834, when he retired. Died January 1865, near Wilmington, Delaware. *References*: John R. Latimer Papers, University of Delaware Library, Newark, Del.; and Charles Hummel, "John Richardson Latimer Comments on the American Scene," *Delaware History* 66 (1955): 267–87.

LATTIMORE, OWEN (1900–1989). Sinologist, born July 29, 1900, in Washington, D.C., and grew up in China, and later in Lausanne, Switzerland, and Cumberland, England. He returned to China in 1919, was in business in Tientsin and Shanghai, and worked as a journalist with the Peking and Tientsin *Times*. From 1922 until 1925, he was employed by a company that exported produce from China's western frontier. He traveled in Mongolia and Sinkiang in 1926–1927, and carried out anthropological research in Peking from 1930 to 1933. He was editor of *Pacific Affairs* from 1934 to 1941, a lecturer at Johns Hopkins University in 1938–1939, and director of its School of International Relations after 1939. He was a personal advisor to Generalissimo Chiang Kai-shek in 1941–1942, and deputy director of Pacific operations for the U.S. Office of War

Information from 1942 to 1944. He was a principal target of Senator Joseph R. McCarthy in the 1950s, and was indicted by a federal grand jury in 1952 for perjury but was eventually vindicated. He resigned from his position as director of the School of International Relations at Johns Hopkins University in 1953, and was head of the department of Chinese studies at Leeds University in England from 1963 until his retirement in 1975. He wrote *The Desert Road to Turkestan* (Boston, 1929); *High Tartary* (Boston, 1930); *Manchuria, Cradle of Conflict* (New York, 1932); *The Mongols of Manchuria* (London, 1935); *Inner Asian Frontiers of China* (London, 1940); *Mongol Journeys* (New York, 1941); *Solution in Asia* (Boston, 1945); *The Situation in Asia* (Boston, 1949); *Ordeal by Slander* (Boston, 1950); *The Pivot of Asia* (Boston, 1950); *Nationalism and Revolution in Mongolia* (New York, 1955); *Nomads and Commissars: Mongolia Revisited* (New York, 1962); and *Studies in Frontier History: Collected Papers, 1928–1958* (London, 1963). Died May 31, 1989, in Providence, Rhode Island. His wife **ELEANOR (HOLGATE) LATTIMORE** (1895–1970) wrote *Turkestan Revolution* (New York, 1934). *References*: *CB* 1964; James Cotton, *Asian Frontier Nationalism: Owen Lattimore and the American Policy Debate* (Manchester, 1989); James Cotton, "Owen Lattimore and China: The Development of a Frontier Perspective," in *China and Europe in the Twentieth Century*, ed. Yu-ming Shaw (Taipe, Taiwan, 1986), pp. 240–61; *JAS* 48 (1989): 945–46; *NYT*, June 1, 1989; *PolProf: Truman*; and *WWA*.

LAUBACH, FRANK C(HARLES) (1884–1970). Missionary, born September 2, 1884, in Benton, Pennsylvania. Laubach graduated from Princeton and Columbia universities and Union Theological Seminary. He was a missionary under the American Board of Commissioners for Foreign Missions (ABCFM) in the Philippines from 1915 to 1920, serving in Cagayan and Misamis provinces. He was dean of Union College in Manila and dean of the College of Education of Manila University from 1922 to 1926. He was founder and head of the Lanao Folk School in Dansalan, Lanao Province, from 1930 to 1941, conducting literacy campaigns in Lanao and later in southern Asia. He was a traveling representative of the World Literacy and Christian Literature Committee of the Federal Council of Churches of America from 1941 to 1954. He was founder and executive director of the Laubach Literacy Fund (later Laubach Literacy, Inc.) in Syracuse, New York, from 1955 to 1963, and its president and world representative from 1964 to 1970. He wrote *The People of the Philippines: Their Religious Progress and Preparation for Spiritual Leadership in the Far East* (New York, 1925); *Seven Thousand Emeralds* (New York, 1929); *Rizal, Man and Martyr* (Manila, 1936); *India Shall Be Literate* (Jubbulpore, C. P., India, 1940); *The Silent Billion Speak* (New York, 1943); *Thirty Years with the Silent Billion: Adventuring in Literacy* (Westwood, N.J., 1959); and *Forty Years with the Silent Billion* (Old Tappan, N.J., 1970). Died June 11, 1970, in Syracuse, New York. *References*: Frank C. Laubach Papers, Syracuse University Library, Syracuse, N.Y.; *BDAE*; *CA*; *CB* 1950; *EP* 17:319–320; Deborah R. Chmaj and Menbere Wolde, comps.,

The Laubach Collection: Personal Papers of Frank C. Laubach, Documents of Laubach Literacy Inc. (Syracuse, N.Y., 1974); Peter G. Gowing, "The Legacy of Frank Charles Laubach," *Dansalan Quarterly* 4 (1983): 191–204; Frank C. Laubach, *Open Windows, Swinging Doors: Personal Diary of Dr. Frank C. Laubach* (Glendale, Calif., 1955); David E. Mason, *Frank C. Laubach, Teacher of Millions* (Minneapolis, 1967); Marjorie Medardy, *Each One Teach One; Frank Laubach, Friend to Millions* (New York, 1954); *NYT*, June 12, 1970; Helen M. Roberts, *Champion of the Silent Billion: The Story of Frank C. Laubach, Apostle of Literacy* (St. Paul, Minn., 1961); and *WWWA*.

LAUFER, BERTHOLD (1874–1934). Orientalist, born October 11, 1874, in Cologne, Germany. Laufer attended the University of Berlin and the Seminar for Oriental Languages (Berlin), and graduated from the University of Leipzig. He came to the United States in 1898. He was leader of the Jesup North Pacific expedition to Sakhalin Island and the Amur region of eastern Siberia in 1898–1899, the Jacob H. Schiff expedition to China from 1901 to 1904, the Blackstone expedition to Tibet and China from 1908 to 1910, and the Marshall Field expedition to China in 1923. He was an assistant in ethnography at the American Museum of Natural History from 1904 to 1906, a lecturer in anthropology and East Asiatic languages at Columbia University from 1905 to 1907, assistant curator of Asiatic ethnology at the Field Museum of Natural History from 1908 to 1911, associate curator there from 1911 to 1915, and curator of anthropology after 1915. He wrote *Chinese Pottery of the Han Dynasty* (Leiden, 1909); *Jade: A Study in Chinese Archaeology and Religion* (Chicago, 1912); *The Beginnings of Porcelain in China* (Chicago, 1917); *Oriental Theatricals* (Chicago, 1923); and *Ivory in China* (Chicago, 1925). Died September 13, 1934, in Chicago. *References*: *AA* (1952): 163–64; *DAB S1*; *Journal of the American Oriental Society* 54 (1934): 352–62; and *WWWA*.

LAUREL-LANGLEY TRADE AGREEMENT (1955). Trade agreement between the Philippines and the United States, revising the Bell Trade Act.* It was in effect until 1974. *References*: Aurelio B. Calderon, *The Laurel-Langley Agreement: A Critically Annotated and Selected Bibliography* (Manila, 1979); and *EAH*.

LAWNEY, JOSEPHINE C. (1881–1962). Medical missionary, born April 29, 1881. Lawney graduated from the Woman's Medical College of Pennsylvania. She was a medical missionary under the Woman's American Baptist Foreign Mission Society in China from 1919 to 1949. She visited many hospitals in east and west China, and conducted a survey of tuberculosis from 1919 to 1921. She was chief of medicine at the Margaret Williamson Hospital and the Women's Christian Medical College in Shanghai, and dean and professor of medicine at the Women's Christian Medical College in Shanghai from 1921 to 1943. She studied nutrition and did research on beriberi and anemia. She was interned by the Japanese from 1941 to 1943. She returned to China in 1946 to establish a medical service, but was forced out in 1949. She was staff physician of the Associated Missions Medical Office in New York City from 1949 until her retirement in 1955. Died February 27, 1962, in New York City. *Reference*: *NYT*, March 1, 1962.

LAWRENCE, FRED T(ULUS) (1877–1940). Educator, born February 17, 1877, in Hartford, Kansas. Lawrence attended the State University of Washington. He served in the Spanish-American War, and came to the Philippines in 1901. He was a teacher of English in the Philippine Bureau of Education's schools until 1918, and organized and operated a private school in San Miguel, Bulacan, after 1925. Died January 18, 1940, in San Miguel, the Philippines. *References*: *CCDP*; *Gleeck/Frontiers*; *NYT*, January 18, 1940; and *WWP*.

LAWTON, HENRY ·W(ARE) (1843–1899). Army officer, born March 17, 1843, in Manhattan, near Toledo, Ohio, and grew up in Fort Wayne, Indiana. Lawton served in the Union Army during the Civil War. He was commissioned a second lieutenant in the regular army in 1866. He served in the Indian wars and in the Geronimo campaign of 1886, and later in the Inspector General's Department. He served in the Spanish-American War in Cuba, and was military governor of the Santiago district. He came to the Philippines in 1898, and commanded the First Division of the Eighth Army Corps in Luzon. He organized the first native municipal governments in Cavite Province. Shot, December 19, 1899, during an attack on the city of San Mateo. *References*: Henry W. Lawton Papers, Manuscript Division, Library of Congress; *ACAB*; *DAMIB*; *Major General Henry Lawton of Fort Wayne, Indiana* (Fort Wayne, Ind., 1954); *NCAB* 10:290; and *WWWA*.

LAWTON, WESLEY WILLINGHAM (1869–1943). Missionary, born October 31, 1869, in Allendale, South Carolina. Lawton graduated from Furman University and Southern Baptist Theological Seminary. He was a missionary under the Foreign Mission Board of the Southern Baptist Convention in China from 1894 to 1939, working in Chinkiang, Kiangsu Province, and in Kaifeng, Honan Province. With W. Eugene Sallee,* he pioneered in opening the Southern Baptists' Interior China mission. Died March 3, 1943, in Asheville, North Carolina. *Reference*: *ESB*.

LEA, HOMER (1876–1912). Adventurer, born November 17, 1876, in Denver, Colorado. Lea attended Occidental College and Stanford University. He went to China in 1899. Supporting the reforms of K'ang Yu-wei, he participated in an abortive uprising in south China. He returned to the United States in 1901, and became involved in recruiting and training Chinese-Americans to fight against the Manchus in China. He wrote *The Valor of Ignorance* (New York, 1909). He was back in China in 1911–1912 as a military advisor to Sun Yat-

sen. Died November 1, 1912, at Ocean Park, near Los Angeles. *References*:
Joshua B. Powers Collection, Hoover Institution on War, Revolution and Peace,
Stanford, Calif.; *ACAB*; Eugene Anschel, *Homer Lea, Sun Yat-sen and the
Chinese Revolution* (New York, 1984); *DAB*; *DADH*; *DAMIB*; *NCAB* 2:501;
NYT, November 2, 1912; and *WWWA*.

LEDNICKY, VICTOR (1888–1970). Mining engineer, born October 25, 1888,
in Everest, Kansas. Lednicky attended Notre Dame University and graduated
from the University of Kansas. He came to the Philippines in 1914, was chief
of the Division of Mines and Mining of the Bureau of Science in the Philippines,
and aided in drafting the mining law of the Philippines. He was involved with
E. N. Nell Company, a mining firm, from 1925 until his retirement in 1956,
becoming president and general manager. He was then chairman of the board
and president of Lepanto Mining Company. At the outbreak of World War II,
he was General Douglas MacArthur's civilian liaison agent in the evacuation of
Manila. Died February 9, 1970, in Manila.

LEE, EDWIN F(ERDINAND) (1884–1948). Missionary, born July 10, 1884,
in Eldorado, Iowa. Lee attended Upper Iowa and Chicago universities, graduated
from Northwestern University, and was ordained in 1908. He was a pastor in
New Hampton, Iowa, from 1908 to 1910; a missionary under the Board of
Foreign Missions of the Methodist Episcopal Church in Batavia, Java; and pastor
in Kuala Lumpur, Malaya, from 1910 to 1912, and in Manila, Philippines, from
1912 to 1915. He was a pastor in Rockford, Illinois, from 1915 to 1917, and
chaplain in the U.S. Army during World War I. He was associate secretary of
the Board of Foreign Missions in New York City from 1919 to 1924, a pastor
in Singapore, and superintendent of the Singapore District from 1924 to 1928.
He served as missionary bishop of Malaya and the Philippines from 1928 until
his retirement in 1948. He was evacuated in 1942, but returned after the war
and reestablished churches and schools. Died September 14, 1948, in Rochester,
Minnesota. *References*: *CCDP*; *EWM*; *NYT*, September 16, 1948; *WWP*; and
WWWA.

LEECH, JOHN S(YLVANUS) (1868–1948). Printer and government official,
born July 2, 1868, in Bloomington, Illinois. Leech learned the printing trade in
Bloomington and was employed by the Government Printing Office in Washington, D.C., from 1889 to 1901. He came to the Philippines in 1901, organized
the government printing office of the Philippines, and was director of the Bureau
of Printing in Manila from 1901 to 1908. He returned to the United States in
1908 and was public printer of the United States. He then returned to the Philippines and resumed direction of the Philippines Bureau of Printing. He left
government service in 1917 and joined the public relations staff of J. P. Morgan
and Company until his retirement in 1931. Died January 29, 1948, in New York
City. *References*: *NYT*, January 30, 1948; and *Pier*.

LEGENDRE, CHARLES W(ILLIAM) (1830–1899). Adventurer and diplomatic advisor, born August 26, 1830, in Ouillins, France. LeGendre studied at the University of Paris. He came to the United States after 1854 and became a naturalized U.S. citizen. He served in the Union Army during the Civil War. He was consul at Amoy, China, from 1866 to 1872. He led an expedition across Formosa and established relations with various tribes on the island. He came to Japan in 1872, and was advisor to the Japanese Ministry of Foreign Affairs from 1872 to 1875. He played an important role in organizing the Japanese punitive expedition to Formosa in 1874. He remained in Japan until 1890, working in a private capacity for Okuma Ahigenobu, a political party leader. He was vice president of the Korean Home Office in 1890, and an advisor to the household department of the king of Korea from 1890 until his own death. He wrote *How to Deal with China* (Amoy, 1871), and *Progressive Japan: A Study of the Political and Social Needs of the Empire* (New York, 1878). Died September 1, 1899, in Seoul, Korea. *References*: Emily H. Atkins, "General Charles LeGendre and the Japanese Expedition to Formosa, 1874," Ph.D. diss., University of Florida, 1953; Sandra C. T. Caruthers, "Anodyne for Expansion: Meiji Japan, the Mormons and Charles LeGendre," *PHR* 38 (1969): 129–40; Sandra C. T. Caruthers, "Charles LeGendre, American Diplomacy, and Expansion in Meiji Japan, 1868–1893," Ph.D. diss., University of Colorado, 1966; *DAB*; *DADH*; Leonard Gordon, "Charles W. LeGendre, A Heroic Civil War Colonel Turned Adventurer in Taiwan," *Smithsonian Journal of History* 3 (Winter 1968–1969): 63–76; *KEJ*; *NCAB* 25:79; Ernest L. Presseisen, "Root of Japanese Imperialism: A Memorandum of Gen. LeGendre," *Journal of Modern History* 29 (1957): 108–11; and Sandra C. Thomson, "Filibustering to Formosa: General Charles LeGendre and the Japanese," *PHR* 40 (1971): 442–56.

LEGENDRE, SIDNEY J(ENNINGS) (1903–1948). Businessman and explorer, born November 1, 1903, in London, England, and grew up in New Orleans. Legendre attended Tulane University and graduated from Princeton University. He was president of Trinkomet Company of Charleston, South Carolina. He made a trip to Indochina for the American Museum of Natural History, collected specimens of mammals and birds, and wrote *Land of the White Parasol and the Million Elephants: A Journey through the Jungles of Indochina* (New York, 1936). Died March 8, 1948, at Midway Plantation, Berkeley County, South Carolina. *Reference*: *NYT*, March 9, 1948.

LEHMAN, FREDERICK K(RIS) (1924–   ). Anthropologist, born February 5, 1924. Lehman graduated from New York and Columbia universities and studied at the University of Pennsylvania. He was assistant professor of anthropology and linguistics at the University of Illinois from 1963 to 1965, associate professor there from 1965 to 1968, and professor after 1968. He carried out fieldwork in Burma in 1957–1958 and in 1961–1962, and wrote *The Structure of Chin Society. A Tribal People of Burma Adopted to a Non-Western Civilization*

(Urbana, Ill., 1963). He also edited *Burma under Military Rule. A Kaleidoscope of Views* (Singapore, 1981). *References*: *AMWS*; and *WWA*.

LELAND, GEORGE ADAMS (1850–1924). Physician, born September 7, 1850, in Boston. Leland graduated from Amherst College and Harvard Medical School. He went to Japan in 1878, recommended the introduction of a system of physical education into the schools of Japan, was in charge of physical culture in the National Education Department and of training physical education teachers until 1881, when he returned to the United States. He later studied laryngology and otology in Vienna, served as an otologist to the City Hospital of Boston, and was professor of laryngology at Dartmouth Medical School from 1893 to 1914. Died March 17, 1924, in Boston. *References*: *DAB*; and Paul C. Phillias, "The Amherst Illustrious: George A. Leland," *Amherst Graduates' Quarterly* 4 (1924–1925): 29–33.

LEONARD, CHARLES ALEXANDER (1882–1973). Missionary, born June 26, 1882, in Statesville, Iredell County, South Carolina. Leonard graduated from Wake Forest College and Southern Baptist Theological Seminary (Louisville, Ky.). He held a pastorate in Lexington, Kentucky, from 1908 to 1910. He was a missionary under the Foreign Mission Board of the Southern Baptist Convention in China from 1910 to 1924, and served as principal of a boys' school in Laichow, Shantung Province, and in Harbin, Manchuria, from 1924 to 1940. He was secretary of the International Committee of the Young Men's Christian Association (YMCA) during World War I, working with Chinese laborers in France. He began Southern Baptist missionary work in Honolulu, Hawaii, in 1940, and was involved in relief work in unoccupied China from 1942 to 1944. He retired in 1949, and was later an associate missionary of the Wilmington (N.C.) Association, and a pastor in Havelock, North Carolina. He wrote his memoirs, *Repaid a Hundredfold* (Grand Rapids, Mich., 1969). Died April 20, 1973, in Deming, New Mexico. *Reference*: Charles Alexander Leonard Papers, Wake Forest University Library, Winston-Salem, N.C.

LEROY, JAMES A(LFRED) (1875–1909). Colonial administrator, born December 9, 1875, in Pontiac, Michigan. Leroy graduated from the University of Michigan. He was principal of the Pontiac High School in 1896–1897, political reporter for the Detroit *Free Press* and *Evening News*, and later Sunday editor of the *Baltimore Herald*. He was secretary to Dean C. Worcester* from 1901 until 1903. He was a consul in Durango, Mexico, from 1905 to 1908. He wrote *Philippine Life in Town and Country* (New York, 1905) and *The Americans in the Philippines* (Boston, 1914), which was published posthumously. Died in Fort Bayard, New Mexico. *References*: James A. Leroy Papers, Bentley Historical Library, University of Michigan, Ann Arbor; Harry Coleman, "James Alfred Leroy," in James A. Leroy, *The Americans in the Philippines* (Boston, 1914); and *EP* 4:311–312.

LERRIGO, P(ETER) H(UGH) J(AMES) (1875–1958). Medical missionary, born October 6, 1875, in Birmingham, England, and came to the United States in 1886. Lerrigo graduated from New York Homeopathic Medical College and Hospital, and the Medico-Chirurgical College (Philadelphia), and studied at the Post-Graduate School of Medicine (New York City). He was a medical missionary under the American Baptist Foreign Mission Society in the Philippines from 1902 to 1913, and established the mission in Capiz in 1903. He was candidate secretary of the Foreign Mission Society in 1919–1920; home secretary, medical director, and secretary for Africa of the Foreign Mission Society from 1921 to 1940; and executive secretary of the World Relief Committee of the North Baptist Committee in 1940–1941. He retired in 1941, but reentered active service in 1943. He was an executive secretary of the Foreign Missions Conference of North America from 1943 to 1945, and president of Central Philippine College in Iloilo after 1950. He wrote *Anita: A Tale of the Philippines* (Philadelphia, 1925). Died March 24, 1958, in Claremont, California. *Reference*: *WWWA*.

LEWIS, CHARLES (1865–1932). Medical missionary, born November 3, 1865, in Perry Township, Jefferson County, Pennsylvania. Lewis graduated from Washington and Jefferson College and the University of Pennsylvania Medical School. He was a medical missionary under the Board of Foreign Missions of the Presbyterian Church in the U.S.A. in China from 1896 until 1932. He served in the East Shantung mission, first at Tengchow, then at Tsinan, and, after 1902, in Paoting. He served with the American Red Cross in Siberia in 1915 and 1918. Died July 4, 1932, in Grove City, Pennsylvania. *Reference*: Robert E. Speer, *"Lu Taifu," Charles Lewis, M.D., a Pioneer Surgeon in China* (New York, 1934).

LIGHT, S(OL) F(ELTY) (1886–1947). Entomologist, born Mary 5, 1886, in Elm Mills, Kansas. Light graduated from Park College (Parkville, Mo.), Princeton University, and the University of California at Berkeley. He was an instructor at the University of the Philippines from 1912 to 1914, and later professor of zoology and chairman of the Department of Zoology from 1916 until 1922. He taught at the University of Amoy in China, and was chairman of the zoology department there from 1922 to 1924. He was on the faculty of the University of California at Berkeley after 1924, and a professor there after 1929. Drowned June 21, 1947, in Clear Lake, California. *References*: *AMWS*; E. O. Essig, "Sol Felty Light," *Pan-Pacific Entomology* 24 (1948): 49–55; Arnold Mallis, *American Entomologists* (New Brunswick, N.J., 1971), pp. 473–74; and *Science* 106 (November 21, 1947): 483–84.

LINEBARGER, PAUL M(YRON) A(NTHONY) (1913–1966). Political scientist, son of Paul Myron Wentworth Linebarger,* born July 11, 1913, in Milwaukee, Wisconsin. Linebarger attended the University of Nanking and North

China Union Language School, graduated from George Washington and Johns Hopkins universities, and studied at the University of Michigan. He was an instructor and later an associate professor at Duke University (Durham, N.C.) from 1937 to 1946, and professor of Asiatic politics at the School of Advanced International Studies of Johns Hopkins University from 1946 to 1956. He was a member of the Operations, Planning and Intelligence Board during World War II, serving in Washington, D.C., and Chungking, China. He organized the U.S. Army's psychological warfare section, and was consultant to British land forces in Malaya in 1950 and to the Eighth Army in Korea from 1950 to 1952. He wrote *The Political Doctrines of Sun Yat-sen* (Baltimore, 1937); *Government in Republican China* (New York, 1938); and *The China of Chiang Kai-shek* (Boston, 1941); and was coauthor of *Far Eastern Governments and Politics* (New York, 1954). Died August 6, 1966, in Baltimore. *References*: *CA*; James J. Halsema, "Remember Judge Paul Linebarger," *BAHC* 10 (April-June 1982): 72–75; *NYT*, August 7, 1966; and *WWWA*.

LINEBARGER, PAUL M(YRON) W(ENTWORTH) (1871–1939). Lawyer and author, born June 15, 1871, in Warren, Illinois. Linebarger attended Naperville College and Lake Forest University, studied in Paris and Madrid and at the University of Heidelberg, and was admitted to the bar in 1893. He practiced law in Chicago from 1896 to 1898, and was the attorney for the town of Jefferson from 1898 to 1901. He served in the Spanish-American War, and was judge of the Seventh District in the Philippines from 1901 to 1907. In 1907 he became an advisor to Sun Yat-sen, and served until Sun's death in 1925. He was also a financial agent for Sun. He left China in 1926 but returned in 1930, and was legal advisor to the Chinese Nationalist government from 1930 until his retirement in 1937. He wrote *Sun Yat Sen and the Chinese Republic* (New York, 1925); *The Gospel of Chung Shan According to Paul Linebarger* (Paris, 1932); and *The Ocean Men: An Allegory of the Sun Yat-sen Revolution* (Washington, D.C., 1934). He was founder in 1936 and editor of *Chinese Nationalist* until 1938. Died February 20, 1939, in Washington, D.C. *References*: *NCAB* 38:276; and *WWWA*.

LINGNAN UNIVERSITY. The Christian College in China was founded by Andrew P. Happer* in 1888 in Canton under the China mission of the Presbyterian Church in the U.S.A. It was closed in 1890, was chartered by the Regents of the State of New York in 1893, and was reopened in 1894 as Canton Christian College. It became Lingnan University in 1926. It moved to KuKong during World War II, and was reopened in Canton in 1945. It was taken over in 1952 by the Communist government, and became the college of arts of Sun Yat-sen University. *References*: Charles H. Corbett, *Lingnan University* (New York, 1963); Frederick B. Hoyt, "The Lesson of Confrontation: Two Christian Colleges Face the Chinese Revolution, 1925–1927," *Asian Forum* 8 (Summer 1976): 45–62; and Edward J. M. Rhoads, "Lingnan's Response to the Rise of

Chinese Nationalism: The Shakee Incident (1925)," in *American Missionaries in China: Papers from Harvard Seminars*, ed. Liu Kwang-ching (Cambridge, Mass., 1966), pp. 183–214.

LINN, HUGH H. (1878–1948). Medical missionary, born September 28, 1878, in Shelby, Iowa. Linn graduated from Simpson College (Indianola, Ia.) and Northwestern Medical School. He was a medical missionary under the Board of Foreign Missions of the Methodist Episcopal Church in India from 1909 until his death. He served in Bidar, Hyderabad State, from 1909 to 1917; in Vikarabad from 1917 to 1929; and in Bowringpet after 1929. In 1929 he established the All India Mission Tablet Industry in Bowringpet to produce pills. He wrote *Diagnosis and Treatment of Common Diseases for Village Workers* (Madras, 1928), which was translated into six Indian languages. Died September 15, 1948, in Kolar, India. *Reference*: Minnie V. Linn, *Dr. Hugh H. Linn: Medical Missionary* (Mangalore, India, 1950).

LITTLE, L(ESTER) K(NOX) (1892–1981). Government official, born March 20, 1892, in Pawtucket, Rhode Island. Little graduated from Dartmouth College and Brown University. He joined the Chinese Maritime Customs Service in 1914, and served until 1950. He was interned by the Japanese in 1941–1942. He returned to China in 1943, and was the last foreign inspector general of the Chinese Maritime Customers Service from 1943 until 1950, the only American to head this service. He served as advisor to the Nationalist Chinese Ministry of Finance in Taiwan from 1950 until 1954, was assistant director of personnel of the U.S. Information Agency from 1955 to 1960, and served as a consultant until his retirement in 1963. Died October 27, 1981, in Windsor, Vermont. *References*: *Manchester* (N.H.) *Union Leader*, October 28, 1981; and *NYT*, October 31, 1981.

LOBENSTINE, EDWIN C(ARLYLE) (1872–1958). Missionary, born January 18, 1872, in Leavenworth, Kansas. Lobenstine graduated from Yale University, attended Union and Auburn theological seminaries, and was ordained in 1898. He was a missionary under the Board of Foreign Missions of the Presbyterian Church in the U.S.A.* in China from 1898 until 1937. He served in Anhwei Province from 1898 to 1911, superintendent of famine relief at Anhwei Province in 1910–1911, secretary of the Continuation Committee of the National Christian Conference in Shanghai from 1913 to 1922, secretary of the National Christian Council of China from 1922 to 1935, secretary of the China Christian Educational Association from 1924 to 1935, and member of the China International Famine Relief Commission from 1932 to 1935. He was chairman of the China Medical Board in New York City from 1936 to 1945, and president of Yale-in-China Association from 1935 to 1944. He was an unofficial advisor to American Committee for Non-Participation in Japanese Aggression. Died July 1958, in New York City. *Reference*: *WWWA*.

LOBINGIER, CHARLES SUMNER (1866–1956). Lawyer and judge, born April 30, 1866, in Lanark, Illinois. Lobingier graduated from the University of Nebraska and studied law. He practiced law at Omaha, Nebraska, from 1892 to 1902, and was a member of the Nebraska Supreme Court Commission in 1902–1903. He was judge of the Court of First Instance in the Philippines from 1905 to 1914, and judge of the U.S. Court of China from 1914 to 1924. He organized the Far East American Bar Association, and was its president from 1914 to 1922. He promulgated a code to govern the procedure of the American courts in China, and assisted in organizing the law department of Soochow University in 1915. He returned to the United States in 1924, was special assistant to the attorney general of the United States from 1925 to 1934, a Securities and Exchange Commission officer from 1934 to 1946, and chief advisor on codification and a member of the Property Claims Commission of the U.S. Military Government in Korea from 1946 to 1949. Died April 28, 1956, in Washington, D.C. *Reference*: *NCAB* 43:35.

LOCKE, ROBERT D. (1850–1943). Oil driller, born in Lancaster, New Hampshire, and grew up in Tittusville, Pennsylvania. Locke became involved with the oil industry at the age of twelve, was a full-fledged machinist at the age of fifteen, and later had a varied experience in many aspects of drilling for oil. With A. Port Karens, in 1877–1878 he drilled China's first oil well on Formosa, on contract with the Chinese government. He returned to the United States in 1878, established a foundry and machine shop from 1878 to 1898, and engaged in oil production after 1896. Died February 1943, in Tittusville, Pennsylvania. *References*: Paul H. Giddes, ed., ''China's First Oil Well: Recollections of Robert D. Locke, Tittusville Oil Pioneer,'' *Pennsylvania History* 47 (1980): 29–37; and Sampson Hsian-chang Kuo, ''Drilling Oil in Taiwan: A Case Study of Two American Technicians' Contribution to Modernization in Late Nineteenth-Century China,'' Ph.D. diss., Georgetown University, 1983.

LOCKHART, FRANK P. (1881–1949). Diplomat, born April 8, 1881, in Pittsburg, Texas. Lockhart graduated from Grayson College (Whitewright, Tex.). He was associate editor of the *Pittsburg* (Tex.) *Gazette* from 1900 to 1902, and secretary to Representative and later Senator Morris Sheppard of Texas from 1902 to 1914. He was assistant chief of the Division of Far Eastern Affairs from 1914 to 1925, chief of the division in 1925, and technical delegate to the Conference on Limitation of Arms in Washington, D.C., in 1921–1922. He was consul general in Hankow 1925 to 1931 and in Tientsin from 1931 to 1935, counselor of legation in Peiping in 1935, counselor of embassy there from 1935 to 1940, and consul general in Shanghai in 1940–1941. He was interned by the Japanese in 1941–1942. He was chief of the Office of Philippine Affairs in the State Department from 1942 to 1946. Died August 25, 1949, in Washington, D.C. *References*: *NYT*, August 26, 1949; and *WWWA*.

LODGE, HENRY CABOT, JR. (1902–1985). Politician and diplomat, born July 5, 1902, in Nahant, Massachusetts. Lodge graduated from Harvard University. He was a journalist with the Boston *Evening Transcript* and then the *New York Herald Tribune*. He was a member of the Massachusetts legislature from 1932 to 1936, member of the U.S. Senate from 1936 until 1953, ambassador to the United Nations from 1953 until 1960, and the Republican vice presidential candidate in the elections of 1960. He was ambassador to Vietnam in 1963–1964 and again from 1965 to 1967. He was involved in the generals' coup that overthrew the government of Ngo Dinh Diem in 1963. He later tried to stabilize the South Vietnam government, and in 1966, he was involved in an abortive peace effort. He was ambassador at large and ambassador to West Germany from 1967 to 1969. He was head of the U.S. delegation to the Paris peace talks with North Vietnam in 1969–1970. He was special envoy to the Vatican from 1970 to 1975. He wrote *The Storm Has Many Eyes, a Personal Narrative* (New York 1973), and *As It Was: An Inside View of Politics and Power in the '50s and '60s* (New York, 1976). Died February 27, 1985, in Beverly, Massachusetts. *References*: *BDAC*; *CA*; *CB* 1954; *DADH*; *DVW*; *NYT*, February 28, 1985; *Polprof: Eisenhower*; *Polprof: Johnson*; and *WWWA*.

LOEB, EDWIN MEYER (1894–1966). Anthropologist, born March 15, 1894, in New York City. Loeb graduated from Yale University, and studied in Vienna, Austria, and Leyden, the Netherlands. He was a lecturer on anthropology and geography at the University of California at Berkeley from 1922 until 1961. He carried out fieldwork in New Zealand and the Island of Niue in 1923, and in Indonesia in 1926–1927. He wrote *Sumatra: Its History and People* (Vienna, 1935). He was a specialist in Southeast Asia for the Office of Strategic Services (OSS) during World War II. He was a member of the University of California Africa expedition in 1946–1947, and again carried out fieldwork in Indonesia in 1955. Died August 16, 1966, in Santa Monica, California. *References*: *AA* 69 (1967): 200–203; and *NCAB* J:168.

LOEWENTHAL, ISIDOR (ca. 1827–1864). Missionary, born in Posen, Prussia, and came to the United States in 1846. Loewenthal graduated from Lafayette College (Wilmington, Del.) and Princeton Theological Seminary, and was ordained in 1855. He was a missionary under the Board of Foreign Missions of the Presbyterian Church in the U.S.A. in India from 1855 until his death, working in Peshawar, particularly among the Afghans. He also made a tour of Kashmir. He translated the New Testament into Pashtu. Died April 27, 1864, in Peshawar, India. *References*: *DAB*; *EM*; *LC*; and *WWWA*.

LOHR, OSCAR (1824–1907). Missionary, born March 28, 1824, in Loehm, Silesia, Germany. Lohr was a missionary under the Gossner Mission Society to the Kols in Bengal, India, until 1857, when he left because of the Indian Mutiny, and came to the United States. He served as a pastor in several communities.

He returned to India as a missionary under the German Evangelical Mission Society in the United States in 1868 (and after 1884, under the Evangelical Synod of North America). He established a mission station at Bisrampur, Chatigarh district, United Provinces, among the Chamars, and served there until 1905. Died May 31, 1907, in Bisrampur. *Reference*: John W. Flucke, *Evangelical Pioneers*, 2nd ed. (St. Louis, 1931), ch. 12.

LOVE, HARRY H(OUSER) (1880–1966). Agriculturist, born March 19, 1880, in Taylorsville, Illinois. Love graduated from Illinois Wesleyan University and Cornell University, attended the University of Illinois, and studied in Europe. He was an assistant professor at Cornell University from 1909 to 1911, professor after 1911, and head of the plant-breeding department there after 1944. He was a special consultant on plant breeding in the University of Nanking in 1925 and 1929, and an advisor on agriculture and crop improvement to the Ministry of Industries of the National government of China and the provincial departments of Kiangsu and Chekiang from 1931 to 1933. He was an advisor on agricultural research in Hawaii in 1929, and in Puerto Rico in 1939–1940. He was in Thailand from 1950 to 1956, researching local rice seed breeds and carrying out a rice production improvement program. Died April 20, 1966, in Ithaca, New York. *References*: Harry H. Love Papers, Cornell University Libraries, Ithaca, N.Y.; *NYT*, April 22, 1966; and *WWWA*.

LOVING, WALTER H(OWARD) (1872–1945). Military bandmaster, born December 17, 1872, in Lovingston, Nelson County, Virginia. Loving attended the Boston Conservatory of Music. He enlisted in the U.S. Army in 1893, and served as musician and later chief musician and bandmaster until 1901. He organized the Philippine Constabulary Band in 1901, and was its first director from 1902 to 1916 and again from 1919 to 1923. He was an advisor to President Manuel Quezon. Killed February 1945, during a Japanese attack in Manila. *References*: Walter H. Loving Letters, Chicago Historical Society, Chicago; Julia Davis, ''Walter Howard Loving: Military Band Conductor,'' *Negro History Bulletin* 33 (1970): 127; *EP* 4:419–20; and Eileen Southern, *Biographical Dictionary of Afro-American and African Musicians* (Westport, Conn., 1982).

LOW, ABIEL ABBOTT (1811–1893). Merchant, born February 7, 1811, in Salem, Massachusetts. Low was employed by his father as an importer of drugs and Indian wares in Brooklyn, New York, from 1829 to 1833. He went to China in 1833 where he was a clerk with Russell and Company and a partner in the firm from 1837 until 1840. He then engaged in a joint enterprise with a Chinese merchant. He established A. A. Low and Brothers in New York City, a firm involved in trade in Chinese tea and Japanese silk, and was later involved in other business interests, including the Atlantic cable and railroads. Died January 7, 1893, in Brooklyn, New York. His sister, **HARRIET LOW** (1809–1877) accompanied her uncle, William H. Low (1795–1834), and his wife to China in

1829. She resided in Macao until 1834, keeping a journal of her travels and her sejourn in Canton and Macao. *References*: Harriet Low Journals, Low-Mills Family Papers, Manuscript Division, Library of Congress; *BDABL*; Margaret C. S. Christman, *Adventurous Pursuits: Americans and the China Trade 1784–1844* (Washington, D.C., 1984), pp. 96–105; *DAB*; Arthur W. Hummel, "The Journal of Harriet Low," *Library of Congress Quarterly Journal of Acquisitions* 2 (January-June 1945): 45–60; Elma Loines, ed., *The China Trade Post-Bag of the Seth Low Family of Salem and New York, 1829–1873* (Manchester, Me., 1953); *NCAB* 1:500; and *WWWA*.

LOW, FREDERICK F(ERDINAND) (1828–1894). Politician and diplomat, born June 30, 1828, in Frankfort (later Winterport), Maine. At fifteen he was apprenticed to the East India firm of Russell, Sturgis and Company in Boston. He went to California in 1849, and became a merchant and banker in San Francisco and later in Marysville, California. He was a member of the U.S. House of Representatives in 1862–1863, and governor of California from 1863 to 1867. He was minister to China from 1870 to 1874. He tried, unsuccessfully, to negotiate a treaty with Korea in 1871 (see Korean Expedition*). He returned to the United States in 1874, and was joint manager of the Anglo-California Bank from 1874 to 1891. Died July 21, 1894, in San Francisco. *References*: *ACAB*; *Anderson*, ch. 4; David L. Anderson, "Between Two Cultures: Frederick F. Low in China," *California History* 59 (1980): 240–54; Paul H. Clyde, "Frederick F. Low and the Tientsin Massacre," *PHR* 2 (1933): 100–108; *DAB*; *NCAB* 4:109; and *WWWA*.

LOW-RODGERS EXPEDITION. *See* KOREAN EXPEDITION.

LOWDERMILK, WALTER C(LAY) (1888–1974). Irrigation engineer and soil scientist, born July 1, 1888, in Liberty, North Carolina. Lowdermilk graduated from Park College (Md.) and the universities of Arizona and California, and studied at Oxford University. He served in the Lumberjack division of the Corps of Engineers during World War I. He was employed by the U.S. Forest Service from 1915 to 1917 and from 1919 to 1922. He was a research professor of forestry at the University of Nanking from 1922 to 1927. He was a project leader for the U.S. Forest Service's California Forest and Range Experiment Station from 1927 to 1933, and was associate chief, chief of research, and assistant chief of the Soil Conservation Service of the U.S. Department of Agriculture from 1933 to 1947. He made a survey of North Africa and the Middle East in 1938–1939. He worked for the Chinese government in Chungking from 1942 to 1944. He was later a consultant for the Food and Agricultural Administration. He wrote a memoir, *Soil, Forest, and Water Conservation Reclamation in China, Israel, Africa, United States* (Berkeley, Calif., 1969). Died May 6, 1974, in Berkeley, California. *References*: Walter C. Lowdermilk Papers, American Heritage Center, University of Wyoming; Walter C. Lowdermilk Papers,

Bancroft Library, University of California, Berkeley, Calif.; Walter C. Low-dermilk Papers, Hoover Institution on War, Revolution and Peace, Stanford, Calif.; J. Douglas Helms, "Walter Lowdermilk's Journey: Forester to Land Conservationist," *Environmental Review* 8 (1984): 132–45; *NCAB* 63:295; and *NYT*, May 9, 1974.

LOWELL, PERCIVAL (1855–1916). Astronomer and author, born March 13, 1855, in Boston. Lowell graduated from Harvard University. He entered business in 1877. He traveled and lived in East Asia, mostly in Japan, from 1883 to 1893. He served as a counselor and foreign secretary to the special mission from Korea to the United States, and later went to Korea as a guest of the government. He related his travels and experiences in *Chosen—The Land of the Morning Calm: A Sketch of Korea* (Boston, 1886); *The Soul of the Far East* (Boston, 1888); *Noto* (Boston, 1891); and *Occult Japan, or The Way of the Gods* (Boston, 1895). He later developed an interest in astronomy; founded the Lowell Observatory in Flagstaff, Arizona, in 1894; and began observations of the planets, especially Mars. He was a nonresident professor of astronomy at the Massachusetts Institute of Technology after 1902. Died November 13, 1916, in Flagstaff, Arizona. *References*: *DAB*; Robert S. Ellwood, "Percival Lowell's Journey to the East," *Sewanee Review* 78 (1970): 285–309; Ferris Greenslet, *The Lowells and Their Seven Worlds* (Boston, 1946); *KEJ*; A. Lawrence Lowell, *Biography of Percival Lowell* (New York, 1935); *NCAB* 8:309; and *WWWA*.

LOWRIE, JOHN C(AMERON) (1808–1900). Missionary, born December 16, 1808, in Butler, Pennsylvania. Lowrie graduated from Jefferson College (Pa.), attended Western and Princeton theological seminaries, and was ordained in 1833. He was a missionary under the Board of Foreign Missions of the Presbyterian Church in the U.S.A. in the Punjab, India, from 1833 to 1836. He wrote *Two Years in Upper India* (New York, 1850). He returned to the United States in 1836 because of ill health. He was a pastor in New York City from 1845 to 1850, and secretary of the Board of Foreign Missions from 1850 until 1891. Died May 31, 1900, in East Orange, New Jersey. His brother, **REUBEN POST LOWRIE** (1827–1860), missionary, was born November 24, 1827, in Butler, Pennsylvania. Reuben Post Lowrie graduated from the University of New York and Princeton Theological Seminary, attended Union Theological Seminary, and was ordained in 1853. He was a missionary under the Board of Foreign Missions of the Presbyterian Church in the U.S.A. in China from 1854 until his death, serving in Shanghai. Died April 26, 1860, in Shanghai. His other brother, **WALTER M(ACON) LOWRIE** (1819–1847), missionary, was born February 18, 1819, in Butler, Pennsylvania. Walter M. Lowrie graduated from Jefferson College and Princeton Theological Seminary, and was ordained in 1841. He was a missionary under the Board of Foreign Missions of the Presbyterian Church in the U.S.A. in China from 1842 until his death. Killed August 19, 1847, by pirates, while on a boat from Shanghai to Ningpo, China. Reuben Post Lowrie's son, **JAMES WALTER LOWRIE** (1856–1930), missionary, was born September 16, 1856, in Shanghai. James Walter Lowrie returned to the United States in 1860 and grew up in Lawrenceville, New Jersey. He graduated from Princeton University and Princeton Theological Seminary, and was ordained in 1883. He was a missionary under the Board of Foreign Missions of the Presbyterian Church in the U.S.A. in China from 1883 until his death. He served in Peking from 1883 until 1892, founded a mission in Paoting in 1893, and served there until 1910. He was first chairman of the China Council, the executive body of the seven China missions of the Presbyterian Church in the U.S.A. in Shanghai, from 1910 to 1925. Died January 26, 1930, in Paoting. *References*: *ACAB*; *DAB*; *EM*; *Memoirs of the Rev. Walter M. Lowrie, Missionary to China*, ed. by his father (New York, 1850); *NCAB* 12:382; *NYT*, January 29, 1930; and *WWWA*.

LOWRY, GENTRY E(DWARD) (1884–1942). Missionary, born June 3, 1884, in Springville, Tennessee. Lowry graduated from Southern Training School (Graysville, Tenn.). He was a missionary under the Seventh-Day Adventist Church in India from 1909 until his death. He worked among the Tamil-speaking peoples in south India until 1912, was principal of South India Training School from 1914 to 1917, superintendent of mission work in South India from 1917 to 1926, and superintendent of Northeast India Union from 1926 to 1934. He supervised the Northwest India Union Mission as well from 1934 to 1936. He returned to India in 1937 to supervise the South India Union Mission, and was acting president and later president of the Southern India Division after 1941. He wrote *Korada, a Child Widow of India* (Nashville, Tenn., 1931). Died May 4, 1942, in Mahableshwar, India. *References*: *Advent Review and Sabbath Herald*, July 30, 1942; and *SDAE*.

LOWRY, HIRAM HARRISON (1843–1924). Missionary, born May 29, 1843, near Zanesville, Ohio. Lowry served in the Union Army during the Civil War, graduated from Ohio Wesleyan University, and was ordained in 1867. He was a missionary under the Board of Foreign Missions of the Methodist Episcopal Church in China from 1867. He served in Foochow from 1867 to 1869 and in Peking after 1869, founding there the Methodist mission in north China, of which he was superintendent from 1873 to 1893. He was head of a school for the training of Chinese preachers (later the Wiley College of Theology at Peking University), acting president of Peking University (later Yenching University) in 1893–1894, and president of the university from 1894 to 1918. He retired in 1922. Died January 13, 1924, in Peking. *References*: *DAB*; *EWM*; and *WWWA*.

LUCE, HENRY WINTERS (1868–1941). Missionary, born September 24, 1868, in Scranton, Pennsylvania. Luce graduated from Yale University and Princeton Theological Seminary, and attended Union Theological Seminary. He was a missionary under the Board of Foreign Missions of the Presbyterian Church in the U.S.A. from 1897 until 1928. He served in the Shantung Province, and was a member of the faculty of Tengchow College in Tengchow. He was secretary of the China Christian Education Association from 1917 to 1919, and vice president of Yenching University from 1919 to 1928, representing it in the United States. He resigned in 1928 from active missionary service, was professor in the Chinese department of Kennedy School of Missions of the Hartford Seminary Foundation from 1928 to 1935, and was later involved in the organization and promotion of the Interpreters Institute and the Pacific Area Seminar at Silver Bay, New York. Died December 8, 1941, in Haverford, Pennsylvania. *References*: Henry W. Luce Papers, Hartford Seminary Foundation Library, Hartford, Conn.; *DAB S3*; Bettis A. Garside, *One Increasing Purpose: The Life of Henry Winters Luce* (New York, 1948); *NCAB* 34:36; and *UnionTS*.

LUCKNOW CHRISTIAN COLLEGE. Founded as a school in Lucknow, India, in 1877, it became a high school in 1882 and a college in 1888, which was affiliated with Calcutta University. It was an intermediate college from 1920 to 1946, but degree classes were restored in 1946. *Reference*: *EWM*.

LUCKNOW WOMEN'S COLLEGE. *See* ISABELLA THOBURN COLLEGE

LUTHERAN BRETHREN IN AMERICA, CHURCH OF THE: BOARD OF FOREIGN MISSIONS. Founded in 1900, it began missionary work in China in 1902, in Japan in 1949, and in Taiwan in 1952. *References*: *EMCM*; *Fiftieth Anniversary of the China Mission* (Fergus Falls, Minn., 1953); and Juline Klein, *Forty Years in China* (Fergus Falls, Minn., 1952).

LUTHERAN CHURCH IN AMERICA: BOARD OF WORLD MISSIONS. *See* AUGUSTANA LUTHERAN CHURCH: BOARD OF FOREIGN MISSIONS and UNITED LUTHERAN CHURCH IN AMERICA: BOARD OF FOREIGN MISSIONS

LUTHERAN CHURCH—MISSOURI SYNOD: MISSIONARY BOARD. Organized in 1847, it initiated a foreign program only in 1893. It was succeeded by the Board for Mission Services and later the Board of World Missions. It began missionary work in India in 1894, in China in 1913 (terminated in 1951), in the Philippines in 1946, in Japan in 1948, in Hong Kong in 1950, in Taiwan in 1951, and in Korea in 1957. *References*: Archives of the Missionary Board, Concordia Historical Institute Collections, St. Louis; Karl J. R. Arndt, "The Birth of Our China Missions (1912–62)," *Concordia Historical Institute Quarterly* 35 (1963): 113–271; William J. Danker, *Two Worlds or None: Rediscovering Missions* (St. Louis, 1964); F. Dean Lueking, *Missions in the Making: The Missionary Enterprise among Missouri Synod Lutherans, 1846–1963* (St. Louis, 1964); and Roy A. Suelflow, "The Mission Enterprise of the Lutheran Church—Missouri Synod in Mainland China, 1913–1952," Ph.D. diss., University of Wisconsin, 1971.

LYMAN, BENJAMIN SMITH (1835–1920). Geologist and mining engineer, born December 11, 1835, in Northampton, Massachusetts. Lyman graduated from Harvard University and the Imperial School of Mines (Paris), and studied at the Royal Academy of Mines (Freiberg, Germany). He was a consulting mining engineer, and practiced in Philadelphia after 1862. He was employed as a mining engineer by the Public Works Department of India to survey oil fields in the Punjab in 1870–1871. He was a geologist and mining engineer for the Japanese government from 1873 until 1887, and made the first geological survey of Japan. He discovered and surveyed valuable coal and mineral deposits, and assisted in developing several of these deposits. He was assistant geologist for the State of Pennsylvania from 1887 until 1895, and was later engaged in geological research in the United States, Europe, India, China, and the Philippines. He wrote *General Report on the Punjab Oil Lands* (Lahore, India, 1870); *Geological Survey of Japan* (Tokei, 1875–1879); and *Geological Survey of Hokkaido* (Tokei, Japan, 1876). Died August 30, 1920, in Philadelphia, Pennsylvania. *References*: Benjamin Smith Lyman Papers, American Philosophical Society Library, Philadelphia; *ACAB*; *DAB*; *DSB*; *Foreign Pioneers*; Fumiko Fujita, "Understanding of a Different Culture: The Case of Benjamin Smith Lyman," in *Aspects of Meiji Modernization: The Japan Helpers and the Helped*, ed. Clark L. Beck and Ardath W. Burks (New Brunswick, N.J., 1983), pp. 40–48; Gonpei Kuwada, *Biography of Benjamin Smith Lyman* (Tokyo, 1937); *NCAB* 9:217; *NYT*, August 31, 1920; and *WWWA*.

LYMAN, HENRY (1809–1834). Missionary, born November 23, 1809, in Northampton, Massachusetts. Lyman graduated from Amherst College and Andover Theological Seminary, studied at Harvard University and Bowdoin College, and was ordained in 1832. He was a missionary under the American Board of Commissioners for Foreign Missions (ABCFM) in Sumatra (with Samuel Munson*) from 1833 until his death. Murdered June 28, 1834, in Sacca, Sumatra. *References*: *ACAB*; *AndoverTS*; *EM*; *LC*; Hannah Lyman, *The Martyr of Sumatra* (New York, 1856); and William Thompson, *Memories of the Rev. Samuel Munson and the Rev. Henry Lyman* (New York, 1843).

LYMAN, RICHARD SHERMAN (1891–1959). Physician, born January 29, 1891, in Hartford, Connecticut. Lyman graduated from Yale and Johns Hopkins University, and studied at the Massachusetts Institute of Technology and in England and Leningrad. He served with the American Red Cross typhus unit in Serbia in 1916, and with the Aviation Section of the U.S. Army Signal Corps during World War I. He was associate professor of medicine at the medical school of the University of Rochester (N.Y.) from 1926 to 1930. He was associate professor at the first national medical school in Shanghai and at the Red Cross Hospital in Shanghai in 1931–1932, and was associate professor of neurology at the Peking Union Medical College from 1932 to 1937, where he organized the first modern psychiatric hospital under the auspices of the college and developed the first tests for aphasia in Chinese. He edited *Social and Psychological Studies in Neuropsychiatry in China* (Peking, 1939). He was professor of neuropsychiatry at Duke University School of Medicine (Durham, N.C.) from 1940 to 1951, and visiting professor of neuropsychiatry at Meharry Medical College (Nashville, Tenn.) from 1951 until 1955. Died June 13, 1959, in Montclair, New Jersey. *Reference*: *NCAB* 48:183.

LYNCH, DENIS (1859–1934). Missionary, born February 1859, in County Clare, Ireland. Lynch joined the Society of Jesus in the Maryland Province. He was a missionary in Jamaica, and then came to the Philippines in 1905. He was assigned to Cagayan de Misamis, northern Mindanao, from 1905 to 1908, and to Davao, southern Mindanao, from 1908 to 1910. He served in India from 1910 to 1917, and then returned to the Philippines and joined the Jesuit community at the Ateneo de Manila. Died November 13, 1934, in Manila. *Reference*: Arthur A. Weiss, ''American Jesuit Pioneers in the Philippines,'' *Woodstock Letters* 71 (1942): 181–87.

LYNCH, FRANK [FRANCIS XAVIER] (1921–1978). Sociologist, born April 2, 1921, in Orange, New Jersey, and grew up in New York City. Lynch attended Fordham University and Weston College, and graduated from Woodstock College and the universities of the Philippines and Chicago. He entered the Society of Jesus in 1940. He came to the Philippines in 1946, and taught at Ateneo de Naga from 1946 to 1948 and at Ateneo de Manila in 1948–1949. He was codirector of the area handbook of the Philippines for the Human Relations Area Files from 1954 to 1956. He carried out fieldwork in Bicol, Philippines, in 1957–1958. He established the department of sociology and anthropology at Ateneo de Manila in 1959 and was its chairman; he established the Institute of Philippine Culture in 1960 and was its director. He became a Philippine citizen in 1976. He wrote *A Bittersweet Taste of Sugar, a Preliminary Report on the Sugar Industry in Negros Occidental* (Quezon City, 1970); was coauthor of *Brain Drain in the Philippines* (Manila, 1969); and *The Filipino Family, Community and Nation: The Same Yesterday, Today and Tomorrow?* (Quezon City, 1978). He edited *View from the Paddy: Empirical Studies of Philippine Rice Farming and Tenancy* (Manila, 1972). Died September 28, 1978, in Manila. *References*: Aram H. Yengoyan and Perla Q. Makil, ed., *Philippine Society and the Individual, Selected Essays of Frank Lynch, 1949–1976* (Ann Arbor, 1984).

LYON, DAVID WILLARD (1870–1949). Association official, born Mary 13, 1870, in Ningpo, China, to American missionary parents. Lyon graduated from the College of Wooster (Ohio), attended McCormick Theological Seminary (Chicago), and was ordained in 1895. He was educational secretary of the Student Volunteer Movement, and edited their publication, *Student Volunteer*, in 1894–1895. He was a Young Men's Christian Association (YMCA) worker and administrator in China after 1895, initially at Tsinan. During the Boxer Rebellion in 1901, he sought refuge in Korea and started the Korean YMCA. The first official YMCA secretary in China, he was general secretary and then associate secretary of the National Committee of the Chinese YMCA from 1901 until his retirement in 1930. He remained in East Asia until 1934 recruiting workers for YMCA. Died March 16, 1949, in Claremont, California. *References*: David Willard Lyon Papers, Union Theological Seminary Library, New York City; *DAB S4*; and *NYT*, March 18, 1949.

M

MACARTHUR, ARTHUR (1845–1912). Army officer, born June 2, 1845, in Springfield, Massachusetts, and grew up in Milwaukee, Wisconsin. MacArthur served in the Union Army during the Civil War. He was commissioned a second lieutenant in the U.S. Army in 1866, and served on troop duty in the Western states. He went to the Philippines in 1898, and participated in the Spanish-American War and later in the Philippine-American War as commanding officer of the Second Division and the Department of Northern Luzon. He was commanding general of the Division of the Philippines, and military governor of the Philippines in 1900–1901. He returned to the United States in 1901, and commanded the departments of Colorado, the Lakes, and the East, and the Division of the Pacific. He was an observer of the Russo-Japanese War in Manchuria in 1905, and a military attaché in Tokyo. He surveyed the armies and operations of the countries of Southeast and east Asia in 1905–1906. He retired with the rank of lieutenant general in 1906. Died September 5, 1912, in Milwaukee. *References*: Rowland T. Berthoff, "Taft and MacArthur, 1900–1901: A Study in Civil-Military Relations," *World Politics* 5 (1953): 166–213; *DAB S1*; *DAMIB*; Ralph E. Minger, "Taft, MacArthur, and the Establishment of Civil Government in the Philippines," *Ohio Historical Quarterly* 70 (1961): 308–31; *NCAB* 14:151; *NYT*, September 8, 1912; Carol M. Petillo, *Douglas MacArthur: The Philippine Years* (Bloomington, Ind., 1981), ch. 2; and *WWWA*.

MACARTHUR, DOUGLAS (1880–1964). Army officer, son of Arthur,* born January 26, 1880, in Little Rock, Arkansas. MacArthur graduated from the U.S. Military Academy in 1903, and was commissioned a second lieutenant of engineers. He served in the Philippines in 1903–1904 and in Japan in 1905–1906. He was an aide-de-camp to President Theodore Roosevelt in 1906–1907, chief of staff of the Forty-Second Division and later its commanding general during World War I, and superintendent of the U.S. Military Academy. He was commander of the Manila District in the Philippines from 1922 to 1925, and commander of the Philippines Department from 1928 to 1930. He was chief of staff of the U.S. Army from 1930 to 1935. He returned to the Philippines in 1935 as a military advisor to the Philippine Commonwealth and director of the commonwealth's organization of national defense. He was field marshal in the Philippine Army in 1936–1937. He retired from the U.S. Army in 1937, but was recalled to service in 1941. He was commander of the U.S. Army Forces in the Far East and later of the Southwest Pacific Theater during World War II. He was commanding general of the U.S. Army Forces in the Pacific after 1945, and Supreme Commander for the Allied Forces (SCAP) in Japan from 1945 until 1951, directing the Occupation of Japan.* He was head of the Far East Command after 1947, and commander in chief of the United Nations in Korea in 1950–1951 until he was relieved of his command in 1951. He wrote his *Reminiscences* (New York, 1964). Died April 5, 1964, in Washington, D.C. *References*: Douglas MacArthur Papers, MacArthur Memorial Archives and Library, Norfolk, Va.; *DAB S7*; *DADH*; *DAMIB*; *EAH*; D. Clayton James, *The Years of MacArthur* (Boston, 1970–1985); William Manchester, *American Caesar* (Boston, 1978); *NYT*, April 6, 1964; Carol M. Petillo, "Douglas MacArthur and Manuel Quezon: A Note on an Imperial Bond," *PHR* 48 (1979): 107–17; Carol M. Petillo, *Douglas MacArthur: The Philippine Years* (Bloomington, Ind., 1981); Michael Schaller, *Douglas MacArthur: The Far Eastern General* (New York, 1989); Howard B. Schonberger, *Aftermath of War: Americans and the Remaking of Japan, 1945–1952* (Kent, Ohio, 1989), ch. 2; Robert Smith, *MacArthur in Korea: The Naked Emperor* (New York, 1982); *WWP*; and *WWWA*.

MCCARTEE, DIVIE BETHUNE (1820–1900). Medical missionary and diplomat, born January 13, 1820, in Philadelphia, and grew up in New York City. McCartee attended Columbia University and graduated from the University of Pennsylvania Medical School. He became a medical missionary under the Board of Foreign Missions of the Presbyterian Church in the U.S.A. in China in 1844 and served at Ningpo, where he founded a hospital. He served in Chefoo from 1861 to 1865, and was also vice-consul there from 1862 to 1865. He was again in Ningpo from 1865 to 1872, transferred to Shanghai in 1872, and joined the consular staff in Shanghai as interpreter and assessor in the mixed court. He accompanied a Chinese embassy to Japan, and remained there as professor of law and science in the Imperial University of Tokyo from 1872 until 1877. He was secretary to the permanent Chinese legation in Tokyo from 1877 to 1880. He returned to the United States in 1880, and was secretary to the Japanese legation in Washington, D.C., in 1885. He was again a missionary under the Board of Foreign Missions in Tokyo from 1887 until 1900. Died July 17, 1900, in San Francisco. *References*: McCartee Family Papers, Presbyterian Historical Society, Philadelphia; *DAB*; *DADH*; *NCAB* 24:159; and Robert E. Speer, ed., *A Missionary in the Far East: A Memorial of Divie Bethune McCartee*.

MCCASKEY, H(IRAM) D(WYER) (1871–1936). Mining engineer, born April 10, 1871, in Fort Totten, Dakota Territory. McCaskey graduated from Lehigh University (Bethlehem, Pa.). He was a chemist and assayer with a company in Montana; an instructor in mathematics and later headmaster and instructor in English in Mississippi, and an instructor in mathematics and English in California until 1900. He was a mining engineer in the Mining Bureau of the Philippines in Manila from 1900 to 1903, and chief of the Mining Bureau from 1903 to 1906. He was assistant geologist in the U.S. Geological Survey from 1907 to 1910, geologist after 1911, chief of the metals section from 1912 to 1919, and also chief of the mineral resources division from 1915 to 1919. Died April 26, 1936, in Bora Da, Oregon. *References*: *PGSA* 1937, pp. 183–89; and *WWWA*.

MACCAULEY, CLAY (1843–1925). Clergyman and missionary, born May 8, 1843, in Chambersburg, Pennsylvania. MacCauley graduated from Princeton University and Presbyterian Theological Seminary of the Northwest (Chicago), and studied at the universities of Heidelberg and Leipzig (Germany). He was ordained in 1868. He served in the Union Army during the Civil War. He was a pastor in Waltham, Massachusetts, and Washington, D.C., from 1869 to 1881, and was commissioned by the Bureau of American Ethnology to study Indian tribes east of the Mississippi River. He was a missionary under the American Unitarian Association in Japan, director of the Unitarian mission there from 1890 to 1920, and president and professor of philosophic and historic theology at the College for Advanced Learning in Tokyo from 1891 to 1899. He wrote *An Introductory Course in Japanese* (Yokohama, 1896); *A Day in "The Very Noble City," Manila* (Yokohama, 1899); and an autobiography, *Memories and Memorials: Gatherings from an Eventful Life* (Tokyo, 1914). He edited the Japanese Unitarian magazine, and was Japan correspondent of the *Boston Transcript* from 1890 to 1900. Died November 15, 1925, in Berkeley, California. *References*: *DAB*; Samuel A. Eliot, ed., *Heralds of a Liberal Faith, IV: The Pilots* (Boston, 1952), pp. 180–83; and *WWWA*.

MCCLOSKEY, JAMES P(AUL) (1870–1945). Clergyman, born December 1870, in Philadelphia. McCloskey attended La Salle College (Philadelphia) and St. Charles Seminary (Philadelphia), and was ordained in 1898. He was assistant rector in Philadelphia from 1898 to 1903; secretary to the Roman Catholic bishop of Vigan and professor and vice-rector of Vigan Seminary in the Philippines from 1903 to 1905; rector in West Conshohocken, Pennsylvania, from 1905 to 1909; secretary to the vicar-general of Jaro Diocese in the Philippines from 1909 to 1916; and rector of Media, Pennsylvania, in 1916–1917. He was consecrated bishop in 1917, and served as bishop of the Zamboanga Diocese from 1917 to 1920, and as bishop of the Jaro Diocese from 1920 until 1941. Died April 9, 1945, in Philadelphia. *References*: *EP* 17:372; *NYT* April 15, 1945; *WWP*; and *WWWA*.

MCCLURE, FLOYD A(LONZO) (1897–1970). Botanist, born August 14, 1897, near Sidney, Shelby County, Ohio. McClure graduated from Ohio State University. He taught horticulture at Canton Christian College (later Lingnan University) from 1919 until 1927, and was professor of botany there from 1928 to 1932, and professor and curator of economic botany from 1936 until 1940. He led four Lingnan University expeditions to the Island of Hainan in 1921, 1922, 1929, and 1932, and was botanist to the National Geographic Society-Lingnan University expedition to Kwangsi in 1937. He was an agricultural explorer in China after 1924, developed a bamboo herbarium, and became one of the world's leading authorities on bamboo. He returned to the United States in 1941, was employed by the Smithsonian Institution from 1941 to 1944, and was a consultant on bamboos to the Office of Foreign Agricultural Relations of the U.S. Department of Agriculture from 1944 to 1954. He wrote *The Bamboos—A Fresh Perspective* (Cambridge, Mass., 1966). Died April 15, 1970, in Bethesda, Maryland. *References*: *AMWS*; *Economic Botany* 26 (1972): 1–12; and *NYT*, April 17, 1970.

MCCOLLUM, J(OHN) W(ILLIAM) (1864–1910). Missionary, born June 5, 1864, in Dallas County, Alabama. McCollum graduated from Howard College and Southern Baptist Theological Seminary. He was a missionary under the Foreign Mission Board of the Southern Baptist Convention in Japan from 1889 until 1909. He was stationed in Osaka from 1891 to 1893, in Moji from 1893 to 1895, and at Fukuoka after 1895. He was a teacher in the theological seminary in Fukuoka from 1907 until 1909, when he returned to the United States because of ill health. Died January 23, 1910, in Seattle, Washington. *References*: W. Thorburn Clark, *Outriders for the King* (Nashville, 1931), pp. 99–123; and *ESB*.

MCCONAUGHY, DAVID (1860–1846). Association official, born December 21, 1860, in Gettysburg, Pennsylvania. McConaughy graduated from Pennsylvania College (later Gettysburg College). He was general secretary of the Young Men's Christian Association (YMCA) in Harrisburg, Pennsylvania; in the Harlem branch of New York City; and in Philadelphia from 1880 until 1888. He was the founder and first secretary of the YMCA in Madras, India, from 1889 until 1902. He wrote *Pioneering with Christ among the Young Men of India and the Churches of America: Leaves from the Life-History of David McConaughy, Telling of His Role in the Introduction of the Young Men's Christian Association to India* (New York, 1941). He was later in charge of Every Member Canvass for Foreign Missions of the Presbyterian Church, and chairman of the World Stewardship Council from 1937 until his death. Died August 19, 1946, in Winter Park, Florida. *Reference*: *NYT*, August 21, 1946.

MCCONAUGHY, WALTER PATRICK, JR. (1908–   ). Diplomat, born September 11, 1908, in Montevallo, Alabama. McConaughy graduated from Birmingham Southern College and studied at Duke University. He entered the foreign service in 1930, and served in Tampico, Kobe, Osaka, and Peking. He was interned by the Japanese in Peking in 1941–1942. He then served in La Paz and Rio de Janiero, and in Shanghai in 1948. He was the last U.S. Foreign Service officer to leave mainland China after the Communist victory in the civil war. He was consul general in Hong Kong from 1950 to 1952, director of the Office of Chinese Affairs in the State Department from 1952 to 1957, U.S. ambassador to Burma from 1957 to 1959 and to Korea from 1959 to 1961, assistant secretary of state for Far Eastern Affairs in 1961–1962, and ambassador to Pakistan from 1962 to 1966 and to the Republic of China (Taiwan) from 1966 until his retirement in 1974. *References*: *DADH*; and *WWA*.

MCCORMICK, FREDERICK (1870–1951). Journalist, born in Brookfield, Missouri. McCormick was a newspaper correspondent in East Asia from 1900 to 1922. He covered the Boxer War for *Harper's Weekly*, and the Russo-Japanese War and East Asia for the Associated Press until 1922. He was later a radio commentator specializing in Pacific affairs, and a contributor to popular magazines. He wrote *The Flowery Republic* (New York, 1913), and *The Menace of Japan* (Boston, 1917). Died August 8, 1951, in Pauma Valley, California. *References*: Frederick McCormick Letters, in Howard McCormick Collection, Cornell University Library, Ithaca, N.Y.; and *WWWA*.

MCCORMICK, J. SCOTT (1894–1941). Educator, born January 13, 1894, in Hartford, Connecticut. McCormick came to the Philippines in 1916. He was a teacher and later acting division superintendent in Cavite from 1920 to 1922, superintendent of the Philippine Normal School from 1922 until 1925, chief of the academic division of the Bureau of Education from 1925 until 1936, division superintendent for Lanao from 1936 to 1941, and division superintendent for Jolo in 1941. Killed December 25, 1941, by a Japanese soldier, in Jolo, Philippines. *References*: Dalmacio Martin, *J. Scott McCormick: Apostle of Education in the Philippines* (Manila, 1948); and Lloyd G. Van Vactor, "Four Decades of American Educators in Mindanao and Sulu," *Dansalan Quarterly* 3 (1981): 29–54.

MCCOY, FRANK R(OSS) (1874–1954). Army officer and diplomat, born October 29, 1874, in Lewistown, Pennsylvania. McCoy graduated from the United States Military Academy in 1897, and was commissioned a second lieutenant in the cavalry. He served in the Spanish-American War in Cuba and in the Philippine-American war, and was aide-de-camp to Major General Leonard Wood,* President Theodore Roosevelt, and Secretary of War William Howard Taft. He served again in the Philippines from 1903 to 1906. He served on the Mexican border and during World War I. He was an assistant to Leonard Wood, governor-general of the Philippines, from 1921 to 1925, and in charge of American relief activities in Japan after the earthquakes of 1923. He headed the settlement commission in the Chaco dispute in 1929, and was a member of the

League of Nations' international commission inquiring into the situation in Manchuria that had arisen from the Japanese occupation in 1932. He retired in 1938. He served in various positions during World War II, and was chairman of the Far Eastern Commission from 1945 to 1949. Died June 4, 1954, in Washington, D.C. *References*: Frank R. McCoy Papers, Manuscript Division, Library of Congress; A. J. Bacevich, *Diplomat in Khaki: Major General Frank Ross McCoy and American Foreign Policy, 1898–1949* (Lawrence, Kans., 1989); Susan Bradshaw, "The United States and East Asia: Frank Ross McCoy and the Lytton Commission, 1931–1933," Ph.D. diss., Georgetown University, 1974; Thomas Carter, "The Real McCoy in Moroland," in *Then and Now (The Mechanics of Integration)* (Manila, 1983), pp. 41–52; *NCAB* 44:578; *NYT*, June 5, 1954; and *WWWA*.

MCCUNE, GEORGE (MCAFEE) (1908–1948). Educator, brother of Shannon McCune,* born June 16, 1908, in P'yongyang, Korea, to American missionary parents. McCune attended Huron College and Rutgers University, and graduated from Occidental College and the University of California. He returned to Korea in 1930, taught at Union Christian College in P'yongyang, and managed a successful import and export business there until 1932. He carried out research in Korea in 1937–1938, and was a member of the faculty of Occidental College after 1939. He served in the Office of Strategic Services (OSS), the Board of Economic Warfare, and the State Department during World War II. He was an associate professor of Oriental history at the University of California from 1947 until his death. He wrote *Korea Today* (Cambridge, Mass., 1950). Died November 5, 1948, in Berkeley, California. *References*: *American Historical Review* 54 (1951): 987; *FEQ* 9 (1950): 185–91; and *NYT*, November 7, 1948.

MCCUNE, SHANNON (BOYD-BAILEY) (1913–   ). Geographer, brother of George McAfee McCune,* born April 6, 1913, in Sonch'on, P'yong-an Pukdo, Korea, to American missionary parents. McCune graduated from the College of Wooster, and Syracuse and Clark universities. He was a member of the department of geography at Ohio State University from 1939 to 1947, and at Colgate University from 1947 to 1955. He served with the U.S. Board of Economic Warfare and Economic Administration in Washington, D.C., India, Ceylon, and China from 1942 to 1945, and was deputy director of the Far East Program Division for the U.S. Economic Cooperation Administration in 1950–1951. He was provost of the University of Massachusetts-Amherst from 1955 to 1961. He was civil administrator of the U.S. Civil Administration of the Ryukyu Islands from 1962 to 1964, director of the department of education at UNESCO (United Nations Educational, Scientific, and Cultural Organization) in Paris in 1961–1962, president of the University of Vermont in 1965–1966, director of the American Geographical Society from 1967 to 1969, and professor of geography at the University of Florida (Gainesville) from 1969 to 1979. He wrote *Korea's Heritage, a Regional and Social Geography* (Tokyo, 1956);

Korea: Land of Broken Calm (Princeton, N.J., 1956); *Geographical Aspects of Agricultural Changes in the Ryukyu Islands* (Gainesville, Fla., 1975); *The Ryukyu Islands* (Newton Abbot, Eng., 1975); *Views of the Geography of Korea 1935–1960* (Seoul, 1980); and *Islands in Conflict in East Asian Waters* (Hong Kong, 1984). *References*: *AMWS*; *CA*; *Geographical Review* 57 (1967): 461–62; and *WWA*.

MACDONALD, ALEXANDER (1908–   ). Publisher and editor, born in Lynn, Massachusetts. Macdonald worked for *The Boston American* and other newspapers in Bridgeport, Connecticut; Honolulu; and Tokyo. He served in the U.S. Navy during World War II, and was attached to the Office of Strategic Services (OSS) in Thailand. He founded the *Bangkok Post*, an English-language daily newspaper, in Bangkok, in 1946, and was its editor and publisher. He wrote *Bangkok Editor* (New York, 1949). *References*: *Newsweek* 28 (October 7, 1946): 68–69; and *Newsweek* 34 (November 28, 1949): 52.

MACDONALD, RANALD (1824–1894). Adventurer, born in Astoria, Oregon. MacDonald was an apprentice clerk at a bank in St. Thomas, Ontario, and then a seaman. In 1847 he left the Hawaiian Islands in a whaler bound for the Sea of Japan. He jumped ship in 1848 off the western coast of Hokkaido, and made his way by boat to the islands of Yagishiri and Rishiri. He was arrested and sent to Nagasaki, where he was held captive in a temple until 1849. He taught English to several official interpreters, and is regarded as the first instructor of English in Japan. He left Japan in 1849 on board the USS *Preble*, which had come to Nagasaki to pick up Western castaways. He then went to Australia to join the gold rush, returned to British Columbia in 1853, and engaged in various occupations until 1885, when he settled in Fort Colville, Washington. He prepared his memoir, *Ranald MacDonald, the Narrative of His Early Life on the Columbia under the Hudson Bay Company's Regime; of His Experience in the Pacific Whale Fishery; and of His Great Adventure to Japan; with a Sketch of His Later Life on the Western Frontier, 1824–1894*, ed. William S. Lewis and Naojiro Murakami (Spokane, Wash., 1923). *References*: *DAB*; *KEJ*; *Wildes*, ch. 22; and *WWWA*.

MCDOUGAL, DAVID STOCKTON (1809–1882). Naval officer, born September 27, 1809, in Ohio. McDougal entered the U.S. Navy in 1828. He served in the West India Squadron and in the Mexican War. He was in command of the USS *Wyoming* from 1861 to 1864 in east Asia, searching Confederate commerce raiders. In 1863, he attacked the Japanese force in Shimonoseki Straits (see Shimonoseki Bombardment*) in retaliation for its firing on the American steamer *Pembroke*. He was later in charge of Mare Island Navy Yard, and commander of the South Pacific Squadron. He retired with the rank of rear admiral in 1873. Died August 7, 1882, near San Francisco. *References*: *DAB*;

Benjamin F. Gilbert, "Lincoln's Far Eastern Navy," *Journal of the West* 8 (1969): 356–63; and *NCAB* 13:130.

MCFARLAND, GEORGE B(RADLEY) (1866–1942). Physician and linguist, son of Samuel Gamble McFarland,* born December 1, 1866, in Bangkok, Siam. McFarland attended Washington and Jefferson College and graduated from Western Pennsylvania Medical School. He returned to Bangkok in 1891, took charge of the government hospital, and conducted a newly organized medical school (after 1903, the Royal Medical College). He also practiced dentistry. After the death of his brother **EDWIN HUNTER MCFARLAND** (1866–1895), who invented the first Thai typewriter, he took over the sales agency for the typewriter. He later modified and perfected this device, and built a company for the sale and repair of typewriters and other business machines in Siam. He was a professor in the medical school from 1902 until his retirement in 1926. He published *An English-Siamese Pronouncing Handbook* (Bangkok, 1900), and a revised edition of his father's *An English-Siamese Dictionary* (Bangkok, 1903). He was affiliated with the Siam mission of the Board of Foreign Missions of the Presbyterian Church in the U.S.A. after 1926. He edited *Historical Sketch of Protestant Missions in Siam, 1828–1928* (Bangkok, 1928), and prepared a *Thai-English Dictionary* (Bangkok, 1941). He wrote *Reminiscences of Twelve Decades of Service to Siam, 1860–1936* (Bangkok, 1936). Died May 3, 1942, in Bangkok. *Reference*: *DAB S3*.

MCFARLAND, SAMUEL GAMBLE (1830–1897). Missionary, born December 11, 1830, in Washington County, Pennsylvania. McFarland graduated from Washington College (later Washington and Jefferson College) and Western Theological Seminary, and was ordained in 1860. He was a missionary under the Board of Foreign Missions of the Presbyterian Church in the U.S.A. in Siam from 1860 until 1878, and served at Petchaburi, outside Bangkok. He resigned in 1878 to become principal of the royal school for princes and sons of nobles. He helped in the educational department of the Siamese government, and laid the foundation for the system of universal compulsory education that was eventually established in Siam. He resigned in 1896 because of ill health. He compiled *An English-Siamese Dictionary* (Bangkok, 1865). Died April 25, 1897, in Canonsburg, Pennsylvania. *References*: Samuel McFarland Papers, Presbyterian Historical Society, Philadelphia; *DAB*; *WWWA*; David K. Wyatt, "Samuel McFarland and Early Educational Modernization in Thailand 1877–1895," in *Felicitation Volumes of Southeast-Asian Studies Presented to His Highness Prince Dhaninivat* (Bangkok, 1965), 1:1–16.

MCGAVRAN, DONALD (ANDERSON) (1897–   ). Missionary, born December 15, 1897, in Damoh, India, to American missionary parents. McGavran graduated from Butler University, Yale Divinity School, and Columbia University. He served in the U.S. Army during World War I. He was a missionary under the United Christian Missionary Society in India from 1923 until 1957. He was professor of missions at the College of Missions (Indianapolis) from 1957 to 1960, director of the Institute of Church Growth at Northwest Christian College (Eugene, Ore.) from 1961 to 1965, dean of the School of World Mission at Fuller Theological Seminary (Pasadena, Calif.) from 1965 to 1971, and professor of missions there after 1971. He founded the Church Growth movement. He wrote *Multiplying Churches in the Philippines* (Manila, 1957). *References*: Donald McGavran Papers, Billy Graham Center Archives, Wheaton College; *CA*; and T. Stafford, "The Father of Church Growth," *Christianity Today* 30 (February 21, 1986): 19–23.

MCGIFFIN, PHILO NORTON (1860–1897). Naval officer, born December 13, 1860, in Washington, Pennsylvania. McGiffin graduated from the U.S. Naval Academy in 1882. He served in the Pacific Squadron until 1885, when he was discharged because no commissions were available in the U.S. Navy. He was given a commission in the Chinese Navy in 1885, and was professor of seamanship and gunnery at the Naval College in Tienttsin. He was sent to England to supervise the construction of ironclads for the Chinese navy. He served in the Sino-Japanese War, and was executive and second in command on board the battleship *Chen Yuen*. He participated in the Battle of Yalu in 1894, and was wounded and burned. He resigned and returned to the United States. He published his personal account of the battle in the August 1895 issue of *Century Magazine*. Committed suicide February 11, 1897, in New York City. *References*: "Notes on Life of Phil. Norton McGiffin, 1860–1897," compiled by Richard Harding Davis, University of Virginia Library, Charlottesville, Va.; Richard E. Bradford, "That Prodigal Son: Philo McGiffin and the Chinese Navy," *AN* 38 (1978): 157–69; *DAB*; Earle R. Forest, "Captain Philo McGiffin at the Battle of the Yalu," *AN* 8 (1948): 267–78; Lee McGiffin, *Yankee of the Yalu: Philo Norton McGiffin, American Captain in the Chinese Navy (1885–1895)* (New York, 1968); *NCAB* 25:285; *NYT*, February 12, 1897; R. O. Patterson, "Commander for China," *USNIP* 80 (December 1954): 1366–75; and *WWWA*.

MCGILVARY, DANIEL (1828–1911). Missionary, born May 16, 1828, in Moore County, South Carolina. McGilvary graduated from Princeton Theological Seminary, and was ordained in 1857. He was a missionary under the Board of Foreign Missions of the Presbyterian Church in the U.S.A. in Siam from 1858 until his death. He initially established a mission station at Petchaburi, and then made an exploratory trip into the Lao States. He established a station at Chiengmai in 1867, and founded the mission to the Lao, becoming known as "the Apostle to the Lao." He was instrumental in obtaining from the king of Siam an edict of religious toleration. He made several elephant tours through the provinces, and investigated the aboriginal tribes of the mountains. Died August 22, 1911, in Chiengmai, Siam. His autobiography, *A Half Century*

Among the Siamese and the Lao: An Autobiography (New York, 1912) was published posthumously. *Reference*: *DAB*.

MCGOVERN, WILLIAM MONTGOMERY (1897–1964). Political scientist, born September 28, 1897, in New York City. McGovern graduated from Oxford University and studied at the Sorbonne (Paris) and the University of Berlin. He was a lecturer at the School of Oriental Studies of London University from 1919 to 1924, and assistant curator in the anthropology department of the Field Museum of Natural History in Chicago in 1927–1928. He allegedly made an expedition through Tibet disguised as a coolie in 1922–1923, and he wrote *To Lhasa in Disguise, an Account of a Secret Expedition through Mysterious Tibet* (London, 1924). He was associate professor of political science at Northwestern University from 1929 to 1936, and professor from 1936 until his death. He wrote *Colloquial Japanese (London, 1920); Modern Japan* (London, 1920); *An Introduction to Mahayana Buddhism* (London, 1922); and *A Manual of Buddhist Philosophy* (London, 1923). Died December 12, 1964, in Evanston, Illinois. *References*: *National Review* 17 (January 12, 1965): 14; *NYT*, December 14, 1964; and *WWWA*.

MCGREGOR, RICHARD CRITTENDEN (1871–1936). Ornithologist, born February 24, 1871, in Sydney, Australia. McGregor graduated from Stanford University. He was a deck officer and recorder in the U.S. Coast and Geodetic Survey in Washington, D.C., and served in the Spanish-American War. He served with the Bureau of Education in the Philippines after 1909, and was chief of publications of the Philippine Department of Agriculture and Natural Resources from 1933 to 1936. He made extensive ornithological studies in the Philippines, and wrote *A Handlist of the Birds of the Philippine Islands* (Manila, 1906), and *Philippine Birds for Boys and Girls* (Manila, 1922). *An Introduction to Philippine Birds* (Manila, 1940) was published posthumously. Died December 30, 1936. *References*: Charles P. Alexander, "Richard Crittenden McGregor," *Philippine Journal of Science* 63 (1937): 359–61; and *Scientists in the Philippines* (n.p., 1975), pp. 115–37.

MCHUGH, JAMES MARSHALL (1899–1966). Marine Corps officer, born December 27, 1899, in Nevada, Missouri. McHugh graduated from the U.S. Naval Academy in 1922. He went to China in 1923 as a language student. He wrote *Introductory Mandarin Lessons* (Shanghai, 1931), which was used as a textbook by the British and American embassies and the armed forces in China. He served as an intelligence officer for the Fourth Marines and U.S. Asiatic Fleet in Shanghai from 1933 to 1935. He was a special assistant naval attaché in the U.S. embassy in Nanking, Hankow, and Chungking from 1935 to 1940; naval attaché and naval attaché for air from 1940 to 1943; and special representative of Secretary of the Navy Frank Knox to Generalissimo Chiang Kai-shek. He was officer in charge of the Far East Secret Intelligence, and served on the staff of the Fifth Amphibious Corps, but was recalled in 1943 because of ill health. He served in the Navy Department until his retirement in 1946. He later served as an economic consultant for several corporations with interests in East Asia. Died November 7, 1966, in Needwood Forest near Knoxville, Maryland. *References*: James Marshall McHugh Papers, Cornell University Library, Ithaca, N.Y.; and William M. Leary, "Portrait of an Intelligence Officer: James McHugh in China, 1937–42," in *Naval History: The Seventh Symposium of the U.S. Naval Academy*, ed. William B. Congres (Wilmington, Del., 1988), pp. 249–63.

MCKEAN, JAMES W(ILLIAM) (1860–1949). Medical missionary and leprologist, born March 10, 1860, in Scotch Grove, Jones County, Iowa. McKean attended Lenox College (Ia.), and graduated from Bellevue Hospital Medical School (New York City). He practiced medicine in Omaha, Nebraska. He was a medical missionary under the Board of Foreign Missions of the Presbyterian Church in the U.S.A. in Siam from 1889 until 1931. He was assigned to Chiengmai, northern Siam, and established there a dispensary and then a hospital. He manufactured smallpox vaccine, trained vaccinators, and eliminated smallpox through north Siam. He then imported and manufactured quinine and other drugs, and supplied medicine for the population. In 1908, he created a Chiangmai leprosarium on an island in the Menam River (later renamed McKean Leprosy Hospital). He retired in 1931. Died February 9, 1949, in Long Beach, California. *References*: *DAB S4*; Calman de Panty, *James W. McKean 1860–1949* (Bangkok, 1968); Edward M. Dodd, "Doctor and Friend: James W. McKean," in *Answering Distant Calls*, ed. Mabel H. Erdman (New York, 1942), pp. 89–96; *NCAB* 37:441; and *NYT*, February 11, 1949.

MACKENZIE, RODERICK D(EMPSTER) (1865–1941). Artist, born April 30, 1865, in London, England; brought to the United States in 1872 and grew up in Mobile, Alabama. MacKenzie studied at the School of Art of the Boston Museum of Fine Arts, and in Academie Julian and l'École des Beaux Arts in Paris. He maintained a studio in Mobile from 1885 to 1889. He went to India in 1893 and worked as painter there until 1906, painting in the Northwest Frontier and the Khyber Pass from 1897 to 1899. He lived in Paris from 1906 to 1908, and in London from 1908 to 1913. He returned to Mobile in 1913. Died January 17, 1941, in Mobile, Alabama. *References*: Roderick D. MacKenzie Papers, Museum of the City of Mobile, Ala.; Anil B. Ganguly, *Roderick MacKenzie: Life Sketch* (Delhi, 1985); Donald B. Kuspit et al., *Painting in the South, 1564–1980* (Richmond, Va., 1983); and *WWWA*.

MCKIM, JOHN (1852–1936). Missionary, born July 17, 1852, in Pittsfield, Massachusetts. McKim attended Griswold College (Davenport, Ia.), graduated from Nashotah Theological Seminary (Wis.), and was ordained in 1879. He was a missionary under the Domestic and Foreign Missionary Society of the Protestant Episcopal Church in the United States of America in Japan from 1880 to 1893. He was elected and consecrated bishop of Tokyo in 1893, and served until 1935. Died April 4, 1936, in Honolulu. *References*: *NCAB* 13:280; *NYT*, April 5, 1936; and *WWWA*.

MCKINNON, WILLIAM DANIEL (1858–1902). Clergyman, born August 1, 1858, in Melrose, Prince Edward Island, Canada, and came to the United States in 1875. McKinnon graduated from Santa Clara College and studied at Mission San Jose (Calif.) and St. Mary's Seminary (Baltimore). He was ordained in 1887. He was a chaplain during the Spanish-American War in the Philippines. He later helped establish schools, directed relief work, and ministered to the victims of typhus and smallpox epidemics. Died September 25, 1902, in Manila. *References*: *CE*; *DACB*; and Lewis E. Gleeck, Jr., "A Forgotten Hero," *BAHC* 5 (October-December 1977): 68–73.

MCLANE, ROBERT MILLIGAN (1815–1898). Politician and diplomat, born June 23, 1815, in Wilmington, Delaware. McLane graduated from the U.S. Military Academy in 1837. He fought in the Seminola War, studied law, and was admitted to the bar in 1840. He served in the Maryland legislature from 1845 to 1847, and in the U.S. House of Representatives from 1847 to 1851. He was U.S. commissioner to China in 1853–1854. He was unsuccessful in his attempts to get the commercial treaty between China and the United States renewed. He was minister to Mexico in 1859–1860, served again in the U.S. House of Representatives from 1879 to 1883, was governor of Maryland from 1883 to 1885, and served as minister to France from 1885 to 1889. Died April 16, 1898, in Paris. *References*: Robert Milligan McLane Letters in Louis McLane Papers, Manuscript Division, Library of Congress; *BDAC*; *DAB*; and *DADH*.

MACLAY, ARTHUR COLLINS (1853–1930). Lawyer, son of Robert Samuel Maclay,* born August 14, 1853, in Hong Kong. Maclay graduated from Wesleyan University and Columbia University Law School. He taught in a government school in Hirosaki, Japan, in 1872–1873, and in the Imperial College in Tokyo from 1874 to 1876. He returned to the United States in 1876, and practiced law in New York City from 1880 until his retirement in 1898. He was later a lecturer on East Asian topics and wrote *A Budget of Letters from Japan: Reminiscences of Work and Travel in Japan* (New York, 1886), and a novel, *Mito Tashiki, a Tale of Old Japan* (New York, 1889). Died November 12, 1930, in Plainfield, New Jersey. *Reference*: *NCAB* 25:230.

MACLAY, ROBERT SAMUEL (1824–1907). Missionary, born February 7, 1824, in Concord, Pennsylvania. Maclay graduated from Dickinson College, and was ordained in 1847. He was a missionary under the Board of Foreign Missions of the Methodist Episcopal Church in China from 1847 until 1883, and in Japan from 1883 until 1888. He was secretary and treasurer of the mission in Foochow from 1852 until 1872. He assisted in translating the New Testament into the local dialect, wrote *Life among the Chinese* (New York, 1861), and was coauthor of *An Alphabetical Dictionary of the Chinese Language in the Foochow Dialect* (Foochow, 1870). He organized the Anglo-Chinese College in Foochow in 1881. He was superintendent of the mission in Japan from 1883 until 1888, opened the Anglo-Japanese College in Tokyo in 1883, and served as its president until 1887. He also established the Philander Smith Biblical Institute in Tokyo in 1884, and was its dean until 1887. He helped to translate the New Testament into Japanese. He returned to the United States in 1888, and was dean of the Maclay College of Theology (San Fernando, Calif.) from 1888 until his retirement in 1893. Died August 18, 1907, in San Fernando, California. *References*: Charles E. Cole, "Robert S. Maclay (1824–1907)," in *Something More than Human*, ed. Charles E. Cole (Nashville, Tenn., 1986), pp. 121–39; *DAB*; *DADH*; *EWM*; and *WWWA*.

MCLEAN, FRANKLIN C(HAMBERS) (1888–1968). Physician and educator, born February 29, 1888, in Maroa, Illinois. Mclean graduated from the University of Chicago and Rush Medical College (Chicago), and studied at the University of Graz (Austria). He was a professor of pharmacology and materia medica at the University of Oregon from 1911 to 1914, and a member of the hospital staff of the Rockefeller Institute for Medical Research in New York City from 1914 to 1916. He was involved in the planning of the medical school built by the China Medical Board in China, director of the Peking Union Medical College from 1916 until 1920, and professor of medicine there from 1916 to 1923. He returned to the United States in 1923, and was professor of medicine at the University of Chicago from 1923 until 1932 and professor of pathologic physiology from 1932 until his retirement in 1953. He served in the U.S. Army Medical Corps during World War I and again during World War II. Died September 10, 1968, in Chicago. *References*: Franklin C. Mclean Papers, University of Chicago Library, Chicago; *NCAB* 54:367; and *NYT*, September 11, 1968.

MCLEAN, WALTER (1855–1930). Naval officer, born July 30, 1855, in Elizabeth, New Jersey. McLean graduated from the U.S. Naval Academy in 1876 and was commissioned an ensign in the U.S. Navy. He served on the Asiatic Station from 1878 to 1882. With Benjamin H. Buckingham* and George C. Foulk,* he made a trip across Siberia and Russia from Nagasaki, Japan, to Moscow in 1882, and was coauthor of *Observation upon the Korea Coast, Japanese-Korean Ports and Siberia* (Washington, D.C., 1883). He was a senior aide to Commodore George Dewey in 1898. He commanded the Fourth Atlantic Fleet in 1914–1915, and was commandant of the Navy Yard and Station, Norfolk, Virginia, and the Fifth Naval District in 1915. He retired with the rank of rear admiral. Died March 20, 1930, in Lutherville, Maryland. *Reference*: *WWWA*.

MACMURRAY, JOHN V(AN) A(NTWERP) (1881–1960). Diplomat, born October 6, 1881, in Schenectady, New York. MacMurray graduated from Princeton University. He was third secretary of the U.S. legation in Siam; second secretary in Russia; assistant chief of information in the State Department in Washington, D.C., from 1908 to 1911; assistant chief and then chief of the Division of Near Eastern Affairs from 1911 to 1913; secretary of legation in Peking from 1913 to 1917; counselor of the embassy in Japan from 1917 to 1919; chief of the Far Eastern Affairs Division from 1919 to 1924; and assistant secretary of state in 1924–1925. He was U.S. minister to China from 1925 to 1928. He edited *Treaties and Agreements with and Concerning China, 1894–1919* (New York, 1921). He was minister to Estonia, Latvia, and Lithuania from 1933 to 1936; ambassador to Turkey from 1936 to 1941; and special assistant to the secretary of state from 1942 until his retirement in 1944. Died September 25, 1960, in Norfolk, Connecticut. *References*: John V. A. MacMurray Papers, Princeton University Library, Princeton, N.J.; Thomas Buckley, "John Van Antwerp MacMurray: The Diplomacy of an American Mandarin," in *Diplomats in Crisis: United States–Chinese–Japanese Relations, 1919–1941*, ed. Richard D. Burns and Edward M. Bennett (Santa Barbara, Calif., 1974), pp. 27–48; *NYT*, September 26, 1960; and *WWWA*.

MACNAIR, HARLEY F(ARNSWORTH) (1891–1947). Historian, born July 22, 1891, in Greenfield, Erie County, Pennsylvania, and grew up in California. MacNair graduated from the University of the Redlands, Columbia University, and the University of California at Berkeley. He was an instructor in history at St. John's University in Shanghai from 1912 until 1927. He became professor of history and government in 1916, and head of the department in 1919. He wrote *Modern Chinese History* (Shanghai, 1923); *China's New Nationalism and Other Essays* (Shanghai, 1925); *China's International Relations and Other Essays* (Shanghai, 1926); and *Far Eastern International Relations* (Shanghai, 1928). He returned to the United States in 1927 and was professor of Far Eastern history and institutions at the University of Chicago from 1928 until his death. He frequently returned to China, and in 1932 aided in refugee work in north China and Manchuria. He wrote *The Real Conflict between China and Japan* (Chicago, 1937). He served as a consultant to the Office of Strategic Services (OSS) during World War II. Died June 22, 1947, in Chicago. His wife, **FLOR-ENCE (WHEELOCK) AYSCOUGH MACNAIR** (1878–1942), sinologist, born January 20, 1878, in Shanghai, came to the United States in 1889, and grew up in Boston. She returned to Shanghai in the late 1890s and was librarian of the North China branch of the Royal Asiatic Society in Shanghai after 1907. She wrote *A Chinese Mirror: Being Reflections of the Reality behind Appearance* (Boston, 1925); *Tu Fu, the Autobiography of a Chinese Poet*, A.D. 712–770, 2 vols. (London, 1929, 1934); and *Chinese Women Yesterday and Today* (Boston, 1937). Died April 24, 1942, in Chicago. *References*: Harley Farnsworth MacNair Collection, University of the Redlands Library, Redlands, Calif.; *DAB S4*; Harley F. MacNair, ed., *The Incomparable Lady: Tributes and Other Memorabilia Pertaining to Florence Wheelock Ayscough MacNair* (Chicago, 1946); *NCAB*

42:177; *Notes on Far Eastern Studies in America*, no. 12 (Spring 1943): 23–27; *NYT*, June 24, 1947; and *WWWA*.

MCNUTT, PAUL V(ORIES) (1891–1955). Lawyer and colonial administrator, born July 19, 1891, in Franklin, Indiana. McNutt graduated from Indiana University and Harvard Law School. He served in the U.S. Army during World War I. He was a professor in the law school of Indiana University from 1917 and its dean after 1925. He was governor of Indiana from 1932 to 1937. He was high commissioner to the Philippines from 1937 to 1939, administrator of the Federal Security Agency from 1939 to 1945, and chairman of the War Manpower Commission during World War II. He returned to the Philippines as the first U.S. ambassador in 1945–1946. Died March 24, 1955, in New York City. *References*: Paul V. McNutt Papers, Indiana University Library, Bloomington, Ind.; *CB* 1940; *DAB S5*; *Gleeck/Ambassadors*, ch. 1; *Gleeck/Governors*, ch. 14; *IAB*; *NYT*, March 25, 1955; *Polprof: Truman*; and *WWWA*.

MCPHEE, COLIN (CARHART) (1900–1964). Composer and ethnomusicologist, born March 15, 1900, in Montreal, Canada. McPhee graduated from the Peabody Conservatory and studied in Paris. He lived in New York City from 1926 until 1934. He was in Bali from 1936 until 1938. He was the first Westerner to study Balinese music with native teachers, and he played different instruments in Balinese gamelan orchestras. He immersed himself in the music, drama, and ceremonial aspects, and compiled the most complete record of Indonesian music. He was music consultant to the Office of War Information during World War II. He was composer-in-residence at the Huntington Hartford Foundation in Los Angeles, and a lecturer in harmony, composition, orchestration, Indonesian music, and Balinese compositional technique at the University of California at Los Angeles. He wrote *A House in Bali* (New York, 1944), a children's book titled *A Club of Small Men* (New York, 1948), and *Music in Bali* (New Haven, 1966). Died January 7, 1964, in Los Angeles. *References*: *NYT*, January 8, 1964; and Card J. Oja, "Colin McPhee (1900–1964): A Composer in Two Worlds," Ph.D. diss., City University of New York, 1985; and Stanley Sadie, ed., *The New Grove Dictionary of Music and Musicians* (New York, 1980).

MCSHANE, DANIEL L(EO) (1888–1927). Missionary, born September 13, 1888, in Columbus, Indiana. McShane studied at St. Joseph's and St. Mary's seminaries (Baltimore), and at Maryknoll Seminary. He was ordained in 1914, the first priest to be ordained in the Maryknoll Order. He went to China in 1919, worked in Kwangtung Province, and opened an orphanage in Loting. Died June 4, 1927, in Loting, Kwangtung Province. *References*: John J. Delaney and James E. Tobin, *Dictionary of Catholic Biography* (Garden City, N.J., 1961); and James E. Walsh, *Father McShane of Maryknoll* (Maryknoll, N.Y., 1932, reprinted as *The Man on Joss Stick Alley: Missioner in South China* [New York, 1947]).

MACVEAGH, CHARLES (1860–1931). Lawyer and diplomat, born June 6, 1860, in West Chester, Pennsylvania. MacVeagh graduated from Harvard and Columbia universities. He practiced law in New York City after 1883. He was general solicitor and assistant general counsel to the U.S. Steel Corporation from 1901 to 1925. He was U.S. ambassador to Japan from 1925 to 1929. He succeeded in winning the confidence of the Japanese government and improving relations between Japan and the United States, aided the Red Cross following the Tokyo earthquake and fire of 1927, and influenced Japan to sign the Kellogg-Briand Treaty. Died December 4, 1931, in Santa Barbara, California. *References*: *DAB*; *DADH*; *NCAB* 23:17; and *WWWA*.

MAGRUDER, JOHN (1887–1958). Army officer, born June 3, 1887, in Woodstock, Virginia. Magruder graduated from Virginia Military Institute, and was commissioned a second lieutenant in the U.S. Army in 1910. He served in the Philippines from 1913 to 1915, and in France during World War I. He was assistant military attaché in Peking, China, from 1920 to 1924; assistant military attaché in Paris, France, from 1926 to 1930; commandant of the Virginia Military Institute from 1932 to 1935; military attaché in Berne, Switzerland, from 1935 to 1938; and chief of the intelligence branch of the War Department General Staff from 1938 to 1941. He was chief of the American Military Mission to China (AMMISCA) in 1941–1942. He returned to the United States after a dispute with Generalissimo Chiang Kai-shek, was deputy director of the Office of Strategic Services (OSS) from 1943 to 1945, and served as director of the strategic services unit in the War Department in 1945–1946. He retired with the rank of brigadier general. Died April 29, 1958, in Washington, D.C. *References*: *NYT*, May 1, 1958; and *WWWA*.

MALCOLM, GEORGE ARTHUR (1881–1961). Colonial administrator and judge, born November 5, 1881, in Concord, Michigan. Malcolm graduated from the University of Michigan and its law school. He came to the Philippines in 1906, where he was executive bureau clerk in the Bureau of Justice, assistant attorney, and then acting attorney general for the Philippines. He established the first English-language law school in the Philippines in 1911 (later the College of Law of the University of the Philippines), and was its first dean until 1917. He was associate justice of the Supreme Court of the Philippines from 1917 until 1936, and legal advisor to the U.S. high commissioners from 1936 to 1939. He was attorney general of Puerto Rico from 1939 until 1942. He wrote *The Government of the Philippine Islands* (Rochester, N.Y., 1916); *The Constitutional Law of the Philippine Islands* (Rochester, N.Y., 1920); *The Commonwealth of the Philippines* (New York, 1936); *The First Malayan Republic: The Story of the Philippines* (Boston, 1951); and his autobiography, *American Coloniel Careerist: Half a Century of Official Life and Personal Experience in the Philippines and Puerto Rico* (Boston, 1957). Died May 16, 1961, in Los Angeles. *References*: George A. Malcolm Papers, Bentley Historical Library, University of

Michigan, Ann Arbor; *CB* 1954; *EP* 17:360–361; *NCAB* 49:456; *NYT*, May 18, 1961; *Sevilla*; and *WWP*.

MALCOLM, HOWARD (1799–1879). Missionary, born January 19, 1799, in Philadelphia. Malcolm attended Dickinson College and Princeton Theological Seminary. He held pastorates in Hudson, New York, and Boston from 1820 to 1835; and was agent of the General Missionary Convention from 1835 to 1838, president of Georgetown (Ky.) College from 1840 to 1849, pastor in Philadelphia from 1849 to 1851, president of Lewisburg (Pa.) University from 1851 to 1857, and president of the American Baptist Historical Society from 1860 to 1876. He traveled in South, Southeast, and East Asia from 1835 to 1838, and wrote *Travels in South-Eastern Asia, Embracing Hindustan, Malaya, Siam and China* (Boston, 1839). Died March 25, 1879, in Philadelphia. *References*: Howard Malcolm Papers, American Baptist Historical Society, Rochester, N.Y.; *DAB*; and *NCAB* 12:300.

MALLORY, WALTER H(AMPTON) (1892–1980). Association official, born July 27, 1892, in Newburgh, New York. Mallory attended Harvard University. He was a leader of the Columbia Relief Commission to Serbia in 1915; executive officer of the Near East Relief in 1915–1916; and special assistant to the U.S. ambassador in Petrograd, Russia, in 1916–1917. He served in the U.S. Army during World War I, and was foreign representative of the U.S. Shipping Board in 1919. He worked with the International Famine Relief Committee from 1920 to 1926, and was executive secretary of the China International Famine Relief Commission in Peking from 1922 to 1926. He wrote *China: Land of Famine* (New York, 1926). He was executive director of the Council on Foreign Relations in New York City from 1927 to 1959, director after 1959, and editor of the annual *Political Handbook of the World*. He was also president and treasurer of the China Institute of America. Died June 17, 1980, in Dunkirk, New York. *References*: *CA*; *NYT*, June 18, 1980; and *WWWA*.

MANDELBAUM, DAVID G(OODMAN) (1911–1987). Anthropologist, born August 22, 1911, in Chicago. Mandelbaum graduated from Northwestern and Yale universities. He was an instructor at the University of Minnesota and at Cambridge University, and a professor of anthropology at the University of California at Berkeley after 1948. He carried out fieldwork in south India at various times between 1937 and 1976, and in north India in 1963–1964. He wrote *Society in India* (Berkeley, Calif., 1970), and *Human Fertility in India: Social Components and Policy Perspectives* (Berkeley, Calif., 1974). Died April 19, 1987, in Berkeley, California. *References*: *AMWS*; *CA*; Paul Hockings, ed., *Dimensions of Social Life: Essays in Honor of David G. Mandelbaum* (Berlin, 1987); *JAS* 46 (1987): 951; *NYT*, April 23, 1987; and *WWA*.

MANILA AMERICAN CEMETERY AND MEMORIAL. Located southeast of the city of Manila, Philippines, it contains 17,206 military dead of World War II and includes a memorial for 36,280 missing. *Reference*: American Battle Monument Commission, *Manila American Cemetery and Memorial* (Washington, D.C., 1961).

MANILA BAY, BATTLE OF (1898). During the Spanish-American War, a battle between the U.S. Asiatic Squadron, commanded by Commodore George Dewey, and the Spanish squadron that took place in Manila Bay, Philippines, in 1898. The Manila shore batteries were silenced and all Spanish ships were destroyed or disabled, with no loss of life to the Americans. The U.S. forces then blocked the city of Manila, which surrendered. *Reference*: Nathan Sargent, *Admiral Dewey and the Manila Campaign* (Washington, D.C., 1947).

MANILA PACT (1954). Formally the Southeast Asia Collective Defense Treaty, negotiated and signed at the Manila Conference in 1954. It provided for the defense of the South Pacific Area and called for joint action to counteract further communist advances into the area. It also provided for economic and social cooperation. It established the Southeast Asia Treaty Organization (SEATO)* to administer the pact. *References*: Ralph J. D. Braibanti, *International Implications of the Manila Pact* (New York, 1957); and *DADH*.

MANSELL, WILLIAM ALBERT (1864–1913). Missionary, born March 30, 1864, in Moradabad, India, to American missionary parents, returned to the United States in 1871 and grew up in Newark, Ohio. Mansell graduated from Ohio Wesleyan University and Boston University School of Theology, and was ordained in 1890. He was a missionary under the Board of Foreign Missions of the Methodist Episcopal Church in India from 1889 until his death. He was a teacher of philosophy and English literature at Lucknow (later Reid) Christian College, vice principal there from 1890 to 1893, and principal from 1893 until 1898. He also edited *India's Young Folks*. In 1896, he was one of the organizers of the Student Volunteer Movement in India. He was superintendent of the Oudh district from 1897 to 1900, and superintendent of the Bijanor district from 1901 to 1904. He was secretary of the India Epworth League, and editor of *Kaukab-i-Hind*. He was principal of the church's theological seminary at Bareilly from 1904 until his death. Died March 4, 1913, at Bareilly, India. *Reference*: *DAB*.

MANSFIELD, MICHAEL JOSEPH ("MIKE") (1903–   ). Politician and diplomat, born March 16, 1903, in New York City. Mansfield served in the U.S. Navy in 1918–1919, U.S. Army in 1919–1920, and U.S. Marine Corps from 1920 to 1922. He graduated from the University of Montana and attended the University of California. He taught history at the University of Montana from 1933 to 1942. He served in the U.S. House of Representatives from 1942 to 1953, and in the U.S. Senate from 1953 to 1976. He went on a confidential mission to China in 1944 to provide President Franklin D. Roosevelt an independent assessment of the political and military situation there. He was U.S. ambassador to Japan from 1977 to 1988, the longest serving ambassador to that country, and was involved in trying to resolve the trade clashes between Japan and the United States and to improve relations between the countries. *References*: Louis Baldwin, *Hon. Politician: Mike Mansfield of Montana* (Missoula, Mont., 1979); *BDAC*; *CB* 1978; Charles Hood, " 'China Mike' Mansfield," Ph.D. diss., Washington State University, 1980; *NYT*, April 5, 1988; *PolProf: Eisenhower*; *PolProf: Johnson*; *PolProf: Kennedy*; and *PolProf: Nixon/Ford*.

MARINES IN NORTH CHINA (1945–1946). Fifty thousand U.S. Marines, commanded by Major General Keller E. Rockey, were stationed in north China in 1945–1946 to disarm and repatriate Japanese troops and civilians and help Nationalist forces reoccupy North China. All marines were withdrawn by early 1947. *References*: Charles M. Dobbs, "American Marines in North China, 1945–1946," *South Atlantic Quarterly* 76 (1977): 318–31; Benis N. Frank and Henry I. Shaw, Jr., *Victory and Occupation: History of U.S. Marine Corps Operations in World War II* (Washington, D.C., 1968); Henry I. Shaw, Jr., *The United States Marines in North China, 1945–1949* (Washington, D.C., 1968); and David Wilson, "Leathernecks in North China, 1945," *Bulletin of Concerned Asian Scholars* 4 (Summer 1972): 33–37.

MARQUARDT, FREDERICK S(YLVESTER) (1905–   ). Journalist and editor, son of Walter William Marquardt,* born December 10, 1905, in Manila, Philippines. Marquardt graduated from Hamilton College. He was a reporter with the *Utica* (N.Y.) *Daily Press* in 1927–1928, on the staff of the *Philippine Free Press* from 1928 to 1935, a member of the editorial staff of the *Canton* (Ohio) *Repository* in 1936–1937, and associate editor of the *Philippines Free Press* from 1936 to 1941. He was also Manila correspondent of the International News Service from 1929 to 1936 and from 1937 to 1941, for Reuters from 1933 to 1936, and for the *Detroit News* from 1928 to 1931. He was assistant foreign editor and Far Eastern expert of the *Chicago Sun* from 1941 to 1943, and foreign news editor from 1945 to 1948. He was chief of the Office of War Information in the South Pacific during World War II. He wrote *Before Bataan and After: Personalized History of Our Philippine Experiment* (Indianapolis, 1943). He was editorial page editor of the *Phoenix Gazette* from 1950 to 1954, and of the *Arizona Republic* (Phoenix) from 1954 to 1970; he was the latter paper's editor after 1956. *References*: Frederick S. Marquardt Papers, Bentley Historical Library, University of Michigan, Ann Arbor; Michael P. Onorato, ed., *Frederick S. Marquardt: Philippine Memories* (Fullerton, Calif., 1986); *WWA*; and *WWP*.

MARQUARDT, WALTER WILLIAM (1878–1962). Educator, government official, and business executive, born September 8, 1878, in Dayton, Ohio. Marquardt graduated from Ohio Wesleyan University. He came to the Philippines in 1901, was successively a teacher at Tanauan, Leyte; division supervisor at Leyte; superintendent of the Philippine School of Arts and Trades in Manila; second assistant director of education for the Philippines from 1901 to 1916; and director of education from 1916 to 1919. He was a Philippine educational agent in the United States from 1919 to 1923, and an American Book Company representative in the Philippines from 1923 until 1941, when he returned to the United States. Died June 18, 1962, in Ossining, New York. *Reference*: *NYT*, June 19, 1962.

MARQUAT, WILLIAM F(REDERIC) (1894–1960). Army officer, born March 17, 1894, in St. Louis, Missouri. Marquat was a reporter from 1913 to 1917, served in the Coast Artillery during World War I, and was automobile editor of *The Seattle Times* in 1919–1920. He was commissioned a captain in the U.S. Army in 1920. He became a member of General Douglas MacArthur's military mission to the Philippines in 1939, helped to train the Philippine Army, and served in World War II with General MacArthur in the Pacific. He was chief of the Economic and Scientific Section of General Headquarters of the Supreme Commander for the Allied Powers (SCAP) from 1945 to 1952, and directed the economic rehabilitation of Japan. He was chief of the Office of Civil Affairs and Military Government of the U.S. Army Staff from 1952 to 1955. He retired with the rank of major general in 1955. Died May 29, 1960, in Washington, D.C. *References*: *KEJ*; *NYT*, May 30, 1960; and *WWWA*.

MARRIOTT, MCKIM (1924–   ). Anthropologist, born February 1, 1924, in St. Louis. Marriott attended Harvard and Stanford universities, graduated from the University of Chicago, and studied at the University of Pennsylvania. He served in the U.S. Army Signal Corps during World War II. He was research anthropologist at the Institute of East Asiatic Studies of the University of California at Berkeley, assistant professor of anthropology and social sciences at the University of Chicago from 1957 to 1960, associate professor there from 1960 to 1964, and professor after 1964. He carried out fieldwork in Uttar Pradesh, India, from 1950 to 1952 and in 1968–1969. He wrote *Caste Ranking and Community Structure in Five Regions of India and Pakistan* (Poona, India, 1960), and *Kishan Garhi Village—A Generation of Change* (New York, 1972), and edited *Village India* (Chicago, 1955). He described his experiences in "The Feast of Love," in *Encounter and Experience: Personal Accounts of Fieldwork*, ed. Andre Beteille and T. N. Madan (Honolulu, 1975). *References*: *AMWS*; *DFAF*; and *WWA*.

MARSHALL, HARRY I(GNATIUS) (1878–1952). Missionary and ethnologist, born January 24, 1878, in Nashua, New Hampshire. Marshall graduated from Dartmouth College, Ohio State University, and Newton Theological Institute. He was a missionary under the American Baptist Foreign Mission Society in Burma in 1903 until 1942. He served among the Karen people, and was president of the Karen Theological Seminary at Insein, Burma, from 1921 to 1935. He wrote *The Karen People of Burma: A Study in Anthropology and Ethnology* (Columbus, Ohio, 1922); *The Karens of Burma* (London, 1945); *Flashes along the Road* (New York, 1946); and *Naw Su. A Story of Burma* (Portland, Me., 1947), a historical novel. With his wife, Emma W. Marshall, he wrote *On the Threshold of the Century: An Historical Sketch of the Karen Mission 1828–1928 and the Burma Annual for 1928* (Rangoon, 1929) and a biography of Daniel Appleton White Smith.* Died March 19, 1952, in Coral Gables, Florida.

MARSHALL, HUMPHREY (1812–1872). Politician and diplomat, born January 13, 1812, in Frankfort, Kentucky. Marshall graduated from the U.S. Military Academy in 1832, and was commissioned a lieutenant in the Mounted Rangers. He resigned from the army in 1833 and studied law. He practiced law in Frankfort in 1833–1834 and in Louisville from 1834 to 1846. He served in the state militia from 1836 to 1846, and also in the War with Mexico. He served in the U.S. House of Representatives from 1849 to 1853. He was U.S. minister to China in 1853–1854, and dealt with American shipping in Chinese ports. He served again in the House of Representatives from 1855 to 1859. He served in the Confederate Army during the Civil War, and was a member of the Second Confederate Congress. He practiced law in Louisville from 1866 until his death. Died March 28, 1872, in Louisville, Kentucky. *References*: Chester A. Bain, "Commodore Matthew Perry, Humphrey Marshall, and the Taiping Rebellion," *FEQ* 10 (1951): 258–70; *BDAC*; *DAB*; Laurence A. Schneider, "Humphrey Marshall, Commissioner to China, 1853–1854," *Register of the Kentucky Historical Society* 63 (1965): 97–120.

MARSHALL, RAY(MOND) GIFFORD (1881–1946). Journalist, born February 18, 1881, in Yankton, South Dakota. Marshall attended the University of Minnesota. He began newspaperwork in 1903, and was city editor of the *Minneapolis Journal* in 1918–1919. He was director of publicity for the International Famine Relief Commission in China in 1920–1921. At the request of the Chinese Foreign Office, he investigated the foreign occupation of Manchuria and Shantung, compiled a report for the Conference on Disarmament in Washington, D.C. in 1921, and served as a member of the Chinese delegation to the conference. He joined the United Press in 1921, was correspondent and business representative of its Peiping, China, branch from 1921 to 1925, and in 1923 established first American daily cable news service in China for Chinese- and English-language newspapers. He was the Pacific cable editor for the United Press in San Francisco from 1926 to 1932, in charge of the Shanghai bureau of the United Press and its Far Eastern news reports in 1932–1933, and manager of its Japan bureau from 1933 to 1939. He was Pacific foreign editor of the United Press in San Francisco from 1939 until his retirement in 1941. Died

February 22, 1946, in Redwood City, California. *References*: *NYT*, February 23, 1946; and *WWWA*.

MARSHALL MISSION (1945–1947). United States mission to China, headed by George C. Marshall, the aims of which were to end the north China hostilities, to repatriate all Japanese in China, to end the U.S. Marines's mission, to arrange a political conference, and to obtain agreement on a compromise Chinese government in an attempt to mediate the civil war in China. *References*: China Mission Papers, George C. Marshall Research Foundation, Virginia Military Institute, Lexington, Va.; *Marshall's Mission to China, December 1945–January 1947: The Report and Appended Documents*, introd. Lyman P. Van Slyke (Arlington, Va., 1976); John R. Beal, *Marshall in China* (Garden City, N.Y., 1970); Steven I. Levine, "A New Look at American Mediation in the Chinese Civil War: The Marshall Mission and Manchuria," *DH* 3 (1979): 349–75; John F. Melby, "The Marshall Mission in Retrospect: A Review Article," *Pacific Affairs* 50 (1977): 272–77; John R. Miller, "George C. Marshall Mission to China, 1945–1947," Ph.D. diss., University of Georgia, 1975; and Harry C. Shallcross, "The Marshall Mission to China, December 1945–January 1947: A Study of US Foreign Policy Decisions," Ph.D. diss., Florida State University, 1984.

MARSMAN, JAN HENDRICK (1892–1956). Mining executive, born July 29, 1892, in Amsterdam, Holland. Marsman graduated from the College of Technology (Amsterdam). He was employed as a chemical engineer, and traveled around the world selling franchises for the manufacture of sugar solutions. He came to the Philippines in 1919, where he was an engineer and sugar technologist. He sold the franchise to the Malabon Sugar Refining Company, and was vice president and general manager of the company from 1920 to 1925. He moved to Baguio in 1925, began developing the Itogon gold mine, and established the Itogon Mining Company. In 1929 he established Marsman and Company, and later founded several other companies. He also operated mines in the Dutch East Indies and in Kowloon, China. He became a Philippine citizen in 1934. He was in Hong Kong in 1941 but escaped the Japanese in 1942, wrote *I Escaped from Hong Kong* (New York, 1942), and served as financial and economic advisor to President Manuel Quezon in Washington, D.C. He returned to the Philippines after World War II. Died May 5, 1956, in Manila, Philippines. *References*: *ACCJ* 32 (1956): 206–8; and *NCAB* H:39.

MARTIN, GRAHAM ANDERSON (1912–1990). Diplomat, born September 12, 1912, in Mars Hill, North Carolina. Martin graduated from Wake Forest University. He worked for various governmental agencies after 1933, and served in the U.S. Army Air Corps during World War II. He entered the foreign service in 1947, served in Paris until 1955, and was special assistant to the U.S. undersecretary of state from 1957 to 1959. He was U.S. ambassador to Thailand from 1963 to

1967, ambassador to Italy from 1969 to 1973, and ambassador to South Vietnam from 1973 until 1975, the last person to hold this post. He was later special assistant to the secretary of state, and ambassador-at-large for the Pacific. Died March 13, 1990, in Winston-Salem, North Carolina. *References: DADH*; *DVW*; *NYT*, March 15, 1990; *PolProf: Johnson*; *PolProf: Nixon/Ford*; and *WWA*.

MARTIN, W(ILLIAM) A(LEXANDER) P(ARSONS) ("WAP") (1827–1916). Missionary, born April 10, 1827, in Livonia, Indiana. Martin graduated from Indiana University and attended the Presbyterian Seminary (New Albany, Ind.). He was a missionary under the Board of Foreign Missions of the Presbyterian Church in the U.S.A.* in Ningpo, China, from 1850 to 1860. He acted as interpreter for U.S. minister William B. Reed* in negotiating the treaty with China in 1858. He was a missionary at Peking from 1863 to 1868, president and professor of international law at Tung Wen College in Peking from 1868 to 1894, and the first president of the Imperial University of China from 1898 to 1900. He was in Peking during the siege of the legations in 1900. He was an advisor to the Chinese authorities on matters of international law in several international disputes with European powers. He wrote *Chinese Legends and other Poems* (Shanghai, 1894); *A Cycle of Cathay or China South and North with Personal Reminiscences* (New York, 1900); *Siege in Peking* (New York, 1900); *The Awakening of China* (New York, 1907); *Chinese Legends and Lyrics* (Shanghai, 1912); and *The Lore of Cathay or The Intellect of China* (New York, 1912). Died December 18, 1916, in Peking. *References: CDCWM*; Ralph R. Covell, *W.A.P. Martin, Pioneer of Progress in China* (Washington, D.C., 1978); *DAB*; Peter Duus, "Science and Salvation in China: The Life and Work of W.A.P. Martin (1827–1916)," in *American Missionnaries in China: Papers from Harvard Seminars,* ed. Kwang-ching Liu (Cambridge, Mass., 1966), pp. 11–41; *EAH*; *NCAB 15:20*; Jonathan Spence, *To Change China: Western Advisers in China 1620–1960* (Boston, 1969), ch. 5; and *WWWA*.

MARVIN, GEORGE (1873–1955). Journalist and editor, born July 31, 1873, in Brewster, New York. Marvin graduated from Harvard University and attended Harvard Law School. He taught English and history at Groton School from 1899 until 1907. He was vice-consul at Mukden under Willard Straight* in 1907–1908, and was then employed as the first public relations officer of the Imperial government of China from 1908 to 1910. He was private secretary to the U.S. ambassador in Paris from 1908 to 1910, correspondent for *Collier's Weekly* during the Balkan War of 1912–1913, and served in the U.S. Army during World War I. He served as secretary to the American syndicate of New York banks organized for the first China Consortium in 1909, was editorial writer for the *New York Press* from 1911 to 1913, Washington editor for *World's Work*, and editor-in-chief of the Spanish-language version of *World's Work*. He was a member of the writers' project of the Works Progress Administration from 1935 to 1941, and served in the Navy's department of public information during World

War II. Died December 21, 1955, in Washington, D.C. *References*: *NYT*, December 24, 1955; and *WWWA*.

MARYKNOLL FATHERS. Founded in 1911 under the legal title of the Catholic Foreign Mission Society of America. It began missionary work in China in 1918 (terminated in 1950), in Korea in 1922 (terminated in 1941), in the Philippines in 1926, in Manchuria in 1932 (terminated in 1941), in Japan in 1935, in Taiwan in 1950, in Hong Kong in 1950, and in South Korea in 1956. *References*: Maryknoll Fathers and Brothers Archives, Maryknoll, N.Y.; *CE*; James Keller and Meyer Berger, *Men of Maryknoll* (New York, 1944); Glenn D. Kittler, *The Maryknoll Fathers* (Cleveland, 1961); James Smith, *Maryknoll Hong Kong Chronicle, 1918–1975* (Maryknoll, N.Y., 1978); and Jean-Paul Wiest, *Maryknoll in China. A History, 1918–1955* (Armonk, N.Y., 1988).

MARYKNOLL SISTERS. Formal name is Congregation of the Foreign Mission Sisters of St. Dominic. Founded in 1912, it began missionary work in China in 1921, in Korea in 1924, in the Philippines in 1926, in Japan in 1937, in Manchuria in 1930, and in Ceylon in 1949. *References*: Maryknoll Sisters Archives Maryknoll, N.Y.; *CE*; Mary D. Cogan, *Sisters of Maryknoll: Through Troubled Waters* (New York, 1947); Gabriella Mulherin, *Brief History of the Maryknoll Sisters in Korea, 1924–1950* (New York, 1959); and Mary Ann Schintz, "An Investigation of the Modernizing Role of the Maryknoll Sisters in China," Ph.D. diss., University of Wisconsin, 1978.

MASON, FRANCIS (1799–1874). Missionary, born April 2, 1799, in York, England; grew up in Hull and Leeds; and came to the United States in 1818. He worked as a shoemaker. He graduated from Newton Theological Seminary, and was ordained in 1830. He was a missionary under the American Baptist Missionary Union in Burma from 1830 until his death. He served in Tavoy, working among the Karens. He translated the Bible into Karen. He wrote *Synopsis of the Grammar of the Karen Language* (Tavoy, 1846); *The Natural Productions of Burmah; or, Notes on the Fauna, Flora, and Minerals of the Tenasserim Provinces and the Burman Empire* (Maulmain, 1850); and *The Karen Apostle, or Memoir of Ko Thah-Byu, the First Karen Convert* (Boston, 1861). He later established a mission station in Toungoo. He wrote an autobiography, *The Story of a Working Man's Life* (New York, 1870). Died March 3, 1874, in Toungoo, Burma. *References*: *ACAB*; *DAB*; *EM*; and *WWWA*.

MASON, LUTHER WHITING (1828–1896). Music educator, born April 3, 1828, in Turner, Maine. Mason was self-taught in music. He was a supervisor of music in the public schools in Louisville, Kentucky, and Cincinnati, Ohio, from 1853 to 1861; and served as a drum major in the Union Army during the Civil War. He invented a successful and popular teaching method. He was supervisor of music in the public schools of Boston from 1865 to 1880 and after

1883. He supervised music instruction in schools in Japan and introduced Western music to Japanese schools. He was an advisor to the Ministry of Education of Japan from 1880 to 1883, and laid the foundation for a national music school (later part of Tokyo University of Fine Arts and Music). Died July 14, 1896, in Buckfield, Maine. *References*: *BDAE*; *DAB*; Kenneth R. Hartley, "The Life and Works of Luther Whiting Mason," Ed.D. diss., Florida State University, 1959; *KEJ*; and *WWWA*.

MASTERSON, WILLIAM FRANCIS (1910–   ). Clergyman, born December 17, 1910, in Brooklyn, New York. Masterson graduated from Woodstock College (Md.) and Georgetown University, and was ordained in 1939. He was a member of the Society of Jesus. He came to the Philippines in 1933, was a teacher of English at the Ateneo de Manila, and special national field commissioner for Catholic scouting until 1936, when he returned to the United States. He was the business editor of *Jesuit Missions* from 1941 to 1943. He was director of the Jesuit Philippines Bureau from 1943 to 1947. He was released by the Jesuit order to set up a relief program for children from 1945 to 1947. He was rector of Ateneo de Manila from 1947 to 1950, and counselor and professor of English, sociology and social philosophy at Ateneo de Cagayan (later Xavier University) in northern Mindanao after 1950. He founded the College of Agriculture in 1953 and was its director. He established an extension service in 1961 and a Cooperative Credit Union Promotion Division. *Reference*: *The Ramon Magsaysay Awards 1973–1975* (Manila, 1982), pp. 191–201.

MATEER, CALVIN WILSON (1836–1908). Missionary, born January 9, 1836, near Harrisburg, Cumberland County, Pennsylvania. Mateer graduated from Jefferson College (later Washington and Jefferson College) and the Allegheny Theological Seminary. He was a missionary under the Board of Foreign Missions of the Presbyterian Church in the U.S.A. in China from 1863 until his death. He served at Tengchow, Shantung Province, where he established a boys' school which became a college (later Shantung Christian University) and was its president until 1905. He wrote *A Course of Mandarin Lessons, Based on Idioms* (Shanghai, 1892), the standard text for Protestant missionaries for many years, and *A Short Course of Primary Lessons in Mandarin* (Shanghai, 1901). Died September 28, 1908, Tsingtao, China. *References*: *CDCWM*; Charles H. Corbett, "Calvin W. Mateer's Mandarin Lessons," *Notes on Far Eastern Studies in America* 12 (Spring 1943): 9–15; *DAB*; Irwin T. Hyatt, Jr., "The Missionary as Entrepreneur: Calvin Mateer in Shantung," *Journal of Presbyterian History* 49 (1971): 303–27; Irwin T. Hyatt, Jr., *Our Ordered Lives Confess: Three Nineteenth-Century American Missionaries in East Shantung* (Cambridge, Mass., 1976), pt. 3; and *WWWA*.

MATSON, PETER (1868–1943). Missionary, born March 27, 1868, in Dal-älven, Nås County, Sweden; came to the United States in 1879; grew up in Alexandria, Minnesota; and was naturalized in 1890. Matson graduated from Chicago Theological Seminary, and was ordained in 1890. He was the first missionary under the Evangelical Covenant Church of America in China from 1890 until 1940. He served in Fancheng from 1892 to 1901 and at Siangyang from 1901 until 1940. He returned to the United States in 1941. He wrote *Our China Mission: A Story of the Mission Covenant Work in China* (Chicago, 1934). Died May 30, 1943, in Chicago. *References*: Peter Matson Papers, Evangelical Covenant Church of America Archives, Chicago; Edla C. Matson, *Peter Matson: Covenant Pathfinder in China* (Chicago, 1951); and *NYT*, June 1, 1943.

MATTOON, STEPHEN (1816–1889). Missionary, born May 5, 1816, in Champion, Jefferson County, New York, and grew up in Geneva, New York. Mattoon graduated from Union College and Princeton Theological Seminary, and was ordained in 1846. He was a missionary under the Board of Foreign Missions of the Presbyterian Church in the U.S.A. in Siam from 1847 until 1865. He served in Bangkok and was pastor of the first Presbyterian church in Bangkok from 1860 to 1866. He made a new translation of the New Testament into Siamese (published in 1865). He served as unofficial interpreter to the king of Siam in his treaty negotiations with British in 1855, and as official interpreter to Townsend Harris's* embassy to negotiate a treaty revision in 1856. He was the first U.S. consul in Bangkok from 1856 to 1859. He resigned from the mission in 1865 and returned to the United States in 1866. He was a pastor in Ballston Spa, New York, president of Biddle Institute (later J. C. Johnson University, in Charlotte, N.C.) from 1870 to 1885, and later professor in the institute's theological department until his death. Died August 15, 1889, in Marion, Ohio. *References*: *ACAB*; *DAB*; *EM*; and *WWWA*.

MAYAGUEZ **INCIDENT** (1975). The American merchant ship *Mayaguez* was captured by a Cambodian gunship, and the ship and its crew were taken to the Cambodian island of Poulo Wai. U.S. marine, navy and air force units made a successful attack that restored the vessel to American control. The crew was released by the Cambodian authorities. *References*: *DVW*; Christopher J. Lamb, *Belief System and Decision Making in the Mayaguez Crisis* (Gainesville, Fla., 1989); J. A. Messegee et al., " 'Mayday' for the *Mayaguez*," *USNIP* 102 (November 1976): 93–112; David R. Metz, *Land-Based Air Power in Third World Crises* (Maxwell AFB, Ala., 1986), ch. 3; and Roy Rowan, *Four Days of Mayaguez* (New York, 1975).

MAYER, ALBERT (1897–1981). Architect, born December 29, 1897, in New York City. Mayer attended Columbia University and graduated from the Massachusetts Institute of Technology. He practiced architecture in New York after 1935, and served as a U.S. Army engineer during World War II, where he met

Jawaharlal Nehru. In 1946, he began work on a pilot development project for rural villages in the district of Etawah, India. This was eventually adapted for three hundred villages throughout the country. He designed the original scheme for Chandigarh in 1949–1950. He was coauthor of *Pilot Project, India: The Story of Rural Development at Etawah, Uttar Pradesh* (Berkeley, Calif., 1958). He later planned several new towns, notably that of Kitimat, British Columbia. He retired in 1961. Died October 14, 1981, in New York City. *References*: Albert Mayer Papers, University of Chicago Library; *CA*; Robert C. Emmett, *Guide to the Albert Mayer Papers on India in the University of Chicago Library* (Chicago, 1977); *NYT*, October 16, 1981; and Alice Thorner, "Nehru, Albert Mayer, and Origins of Community Projects," *Economic and Political Weekly* (Bombay) 16 (January 24, 1981): 117–20.

MAYO, KATHERINE (1867–1940). Author, born January 24, 1867, in Ridgway, Pennsylvania, and grew up in Cambridge, Massachusetts, and Atlantic Heights, New Jersey. Mayo lived in Surinam (Dutch Guiana) from 1899 to 1907, and settled in Bedford Hill, New York, after 1911. She began writing in 1892, and traveled extensively. She visited the Philippines and wrote *The Isles of Fear: The Truth about the Philippines* (New York, 1925). She also visited India and wrote *Mother India* (New York, 1927), which raised much controversy. She wrote *The Slaves of God* (New York, 1931), *Volume Two* (New York, 1931), and *The Face of Mother India* (New York, 1935) which was banned in India because of her handling of Hindu-Muslim problems. Died October 9, 1940, in Bedford Hill, New York. *References*: Katherine Mayo Papers, Yale University Library, New Haven, Conn.; Howard B. Gotlieb, "Miss Mayo Recalled," *Yale University Library Gazette* 33 (1959): 119–25; Manoranjan Jha, *Katherine Mayo and India* (New Delhi, 1971); *NAW*; *NCAB* 30:30; *NYT*, October 10, 1940; and *WWWA*.

MEIJI GAKUIN UNIVERSITY. The Union Theological School was founded in 1877 in Tokyo by Samuel R. Brown.* Union College was the descendent of various schools established by the missions of the Presbyterian Church in the U.S.A. and the Reformed Church in America. The two institutions merged in 1886 and adopted the current name. It was recognized as a university in 1949. *References*: Ira J. Burnstein, *The American Movement to Develop Protestant Colleges for Men in Japan, 1868–1912* (Ann Arbor, Mich., 1967); Willis Lamott, *Meiji Gakuin, the Story of a Christian School* (Tokyo, 1937); Gordon Van Wyk, *Meiji Gakuin 1877–1957, Eighty Years of Concern* (Tokyo, 1957); and Teisaburo Washiyama, *Fifty Years of Meiji Gakuin* (Tokyo, 1927).

MELBY, JOHN F(REMONT) (1913–   ). Diplomat, born July 1, 1913. Melby graduated from Illinois Wesleyan University and the University of Chicago. He entered in the foreign service in 1937 and served in Ciudad Juárez; Tampico; Caracas, Venezuela; and Moscow until 1944. He was second secretary and vice-consul in Chungking in 1944–1945 and at Nanking in 1946–1947; second secretary and consul in Nanking in 1947–1948; assistant chief of the Division of Philippine Affairs in the State Department in 1949; officer in charge of Philippine Affairs in 1949–1950; and assistant to the assistant secretary of state for Far Eastern Affairs from 1950 to 1953. He compiled the China White Paper.* He wrote *The Mandate of Heaven: Record of a Civil War, 1945–49* (Toronto, 1968). He was later executive vice chairman of the National Council on Asian Affairs from 1955 to 1959, director of foreign students and lecturer on political studies at the University of Pennsylvania from 1959 to 1964, and professor of political studies at the University of Guelph (Guelph, Ontario, Canada) after 1966. *References*: John F. Melby Papers, Harry S. Truman Library, Independence, Mo.; *AMWS*; and Robert P. Newman, *The Cold War Romance of Lillian Helman and John Melby* (Chapel Hill, N.C., 1989).

MELBY-ERSKINE MISSION (1950). Joint State–Defense–Mutual Defense Assistance Program survey mission to Southeast Asia in 1950 under the direction of John F. Melby* of the State Department, Major General Graves B. Erskine of the Department of Defense, and Glen Craig of the Economic Cooperation Administration, to report on means by which military assistance could be used to prevent communist advances into Southeast Asia. *Reference*: John Melby, "Vietnam—1950," *DH* 6 (1982): 97–109.

MENDELSON, RALPH WALDO (1888–1968). Physician, born December 22, 1888, in Lakota, North Dakota. Mendelson attended the University of Colorado and graduated from Northwestern University. He studied at Drake and Harvard universities and the Massachusetts Institute of Technology. He was a member of the American Red Cross Sanitary Commission to the Balkans in 1915, and served in the U.S. Army Medical Corps during World War I. He was principal civil medical officer of health to the Royal Siamese government, with headquarters in Bangkok, from 1916 to 1927. He taught at the University Medical School and was involved in establishing a new medical school. He was an assistant professor of tropical diseases at Tulane University in 1927–1928, and then practiced medicine in Albuquerque, New Mexico, until his death. He served again in the Army Medical Corps during World War II. *I Lost a King* (New York, 1964) recounted his experiences in Siam. Died April 5, 1968, in Albuquerque, New Mexico. *Reference*: *NCAB* 54:400.

MENDENHALL, THOMAS CORWIN (1841–1924). Physicist, born October 4, 1841, near Hanoverton, Ohio. Mendenhall graduated from Southwest Normal School (Lebanon, Ohio). He taught mathematics and science in various high schools in Ohio until 1873. He was professor of physics and mechanics at Ohio Agricultural and Mechanical College (later Ohio State University, Columbus) from 1873 until 1884. He was professor of physics at the Imperial University in Tokyo, Japan, from 1878 to 1881. He taught the first systematic course in physics at Tokyo University, built the first physics laboratory and meteorological observatory, and began regular meteorological observations. He promoted the study of earthquakes and helped found the Japan Seismological Society. He returned to the United States in 1881 and helped direct the Ohio Weather Bureau until 1884. He was professor of electrical science in the U.S. Signal Corps in Washington, D.C., from 1884 to 1886; president of Rose Polytechnic Institute in Terre Haute, Indiana, from 1886 to 1889; superintendent of the U.S. Coast and Geodetic Survey from 1889 to 1894; and president of Worcester Polytechnic Institute from 1894 until 1901, when he resigned because of ill health. Died March 22, 1924, in Ravenna, Ohio. *References*: Thomas C. Mendenhall Papers, American Institute of Physics, Center for History and Philosophy of Physics Collections, New York City; Richard Rubinger, ed., *An American Scientist in Early Meiji Japan: The Autobiographical Notes of Thomas C. Mendenhall* (Honolulu, 1989); *DAB*; *KEJ*; *NCAB* 10:117; and *WWWA*.

MENNONITE BRETHREN CHURCH, THE GENERAL CONFERENCE OF THE: BOARD OF MISSION. Founded in 1874, it began missionary work in India in 1899, in China in 1911, and in Japan in 1948. *References*: *Foreign Missions, India. The American Mennonite Brethren Mission in India, 1898–1948* (Hillsboro, Kans., 1948); A. E. Janzen, *Survey of Mennonite Brethren Missions* (Hillsboro, Kans., 1950); and G. W. Peters, *The Growth of Mennonite Brethren Foreign Missions* (Hillsboro, Kans., 1952).

MENNONITE CHURCH: MENNONITE BOARD OF MISSIONS AND CHARITIES. Founded in 1906, it began missionary work in India in 1899, and in China in 1911. *References*: Records of the Mennonite Board of Missions and Charities, Archives of the Mennonite Church, Goshen College, Goshen, Ind.; *EMCM*; and John A. Lapp, *The Mennonite Church in India 1897–1962* (Scotsdale, Pa., 1972).

MENNONITE CHURCH, THE GENERAL CONFERENCE: FOREIGN MISSION BOARD. Established in 1872. The name was changed later to the Commission on Overseas Mission. It began missionary work in India in 1900. *References*: Records of the General Conference Mennonite Church, Mennonite Library and Archives, Bethel College, North Newton, Kans.; James C. Juhnke, *A People of Mission: A History of General Conference Mennonite Overseas Missions* (Newton, Kans., 1979); Samuel F. Pannabecker, *Open Doors: The History of the General Conference Mennonite Church* (Newton, Kans., 1975); and R. Ratzlaff, *Fellowship in the Gospel in India 1900–1950* (Newton, Kans., 1950).

MERRELL, GEORGE R(OBERT) (1898–1962). Diplomat, born July 13, 1898, in St. Louis, Missouri. Merrell graduated from Cornell University. He served in the U.S. Army Air Corps during World War I. He entered the foreign service in 1922, served in the Hague; Port au Prince, Haiti; Paris; Tegucigalpa, Honduras; Panama; and the Latin American division in the State Department until 1935. He was first secretary of embassy in Peiping from 1935 to 1937, and in charge of the consulate general in Harbin from 1937 to 1940. He was consul general in Calcutta, India, in 1941–1942; secretary to the personal representative of President of the United States in New Delhi from 1942 to 1945; and commissioner of the United States to India from 1942 to 1947 with the personal rank of minister. He was U.S. minister to Ethiopia from 1947 to 1949, and ambassador to Afghanistan in 1951–1952. Died December 16, 1962, in London. *References*: *NCAB G*:125; *NYT*, December 18, 1962; and *WWWA*.

MERRILL, ELMER D(REW) (1876–1956). Botanist, born October 15, 1876, in East Auburn, Maine. Merrill graduated from the University of Maine and attended George Washington University. He was an assistant agrostologist at the U.S. Department of Agriculture in Washington, D.C., from 1899 to 1902. He went to the Philippines in 1902. He was a botanist in the Bureau of Agriculture in Manila in 1902, in the bureaus of Agriculture and Forestry in 1902–1903, in the Bureau of Government Laboratories from 1903 to 1905, and in the Bureau of Science after 1906. He was director of the Bureau of Science in the Philippines from 1919 to 1923. He established a herbarium in the Philippines and an extensive research library, and was editor of the *Philippine Journal of Science*. He was associate professor of botany at the University of the Philippines from 1912 to 1919 and professor from 1916 to 1919. He wrote *A Dictionary of the Planet Names of the Philippine Islands* (Manila, 1903); *Flora of Manila* (Manila, 1912); and *Enumeration of Philippine Flowering Plants* (Manila, 1922–1926). He was dean of the College of Agriculture and director of the Agricultural Experiment Station at the University of California from 1923 to 1929; director of the California Botanical Garden, Los Angeles, from 1926 to 1928; professor of botany at Columbia University and director of the New York Botanical Garden from 1930 to 1935; professor of botany, director of the Arnold Arboretum, and administrator of the botanical collections at Harvard University from 1935 to 1946; and professor of botany at Harvard University from 1946 until his retirement in 1948. He served as a special consultant to the secretary of war during World War II. He was coauthor of *Bibliography of Eastern Asiatic Botany* (Jamaica Plains, Mass., 1938). Died February 25, 1956, in Forrest Hills, Massachusetts. *References*: Harley H. Bartlett and Roger McVaugh, eds., "Autobiographical: Early Years, the Philippines, California," *Asa Gray Bulletin* 2 (1953): 335–70; *DAB S6*; *DSB S1*; Harry B. Humphrey, *Makers of North American Biography* (New York, 1961), pp. 169–74; Elmer D. Merrill, *Merrilleana: A Selection from the General Writings of Elmer Drew Merrill* (Waltham, Mass., 1946); *NCAB* 45:220; *NYT*, February 26, 1956; *Philippine Journal of Science* 85 (1956): 181–88; *Scientists in the Philippines* (n.p., 1975), pp. 138–72; and *WWWA*.

MERRILL, HENRY F(ERDINAND) (1853–1935). Government official, born June 15, 1853, in White River, Vermont. Merrill graduated from Harvard University. He served in the Imperial Chinese Maritime Customs after 1874; was acting commissioner in Takow, Formosa, in 1884; served during the Franco-Chinese War; was chief commissioner of customs in Korea from 1885 to 1900; and organized the customs service there. He was commissioner of customs in China from 1892 and 1897, and assisted in establishing imperial post offices in various parts of China from 1899 to 1904. He was commissioner of customs in Tientsin from 1906 to 1908, commissioner of customs and director of the Conservancy Board at Shanghai from 1909 to 1913, and commissioner of customs in Canton in 1915–1916. He retired and returned to the United States. Died July 10, 1935, in East Newton, Massachusetts. *References*: Henry F. Merrill Papers, Houghton Library, Harvard University, Cambridge, Mass.; Philip M. Woo, "The Historical Development of Korean Tariff and Customs Administration, 1875–1958," Ph.D. diss., New York University, 1963, pp. 55–68; and *WWWA*.

MERRITT, WESLEY (1836–1910). Army officer, born June 16, 1836, in New York. Merritt graduated from the U.S. Military Academy in 1860 and was commissioned a brevet lieutenant in the Second Dragoons. He served in the Union Army during the Civil War. He was superintendent of the U.S. Military Academy from 1882 to 1887. He was military commander in charge of the first detachment of U.S. troops which landed on the Philippines, and the land operations against Manila were conducted under his command. Died December 3, 1910, at Natural Bridge, Virginia. *References*: *ACAB*; *DAMIB*; *EP* 4:349–350; *NCAB* 9:28; *NYT*, December 5, 1910; and *WWWA*.

METHODIST EPISCOPAL CHURCH: BOARD OF FOREIGN MISSIONS. Founded in 1819. It began missionary work in China in 1848, in India in 1857, in Japan in 1873, in Burma in 1880, in Korea in 1884, in Singapore in 1885, in Malaya in 1893, in the Philippines in 1900, in Sarawak in 1903, and in Dutch East Indies in 1905. It merged in 1939 with the Methodist Protestant Church and the Methodist Episcopal Church, South, to form the Methodist Church, which merged in 1968 with the Evangelical United Brethren Church to form the United Methodist Church and its Board of Global Ministries. *References*: General Commission on Archives and History of the United Methodist Church, Madison, N.J.; Dionisio D. Alejandro, *From Darkness to Light: A Brief Chronicle of the Beginnings and Spread of Methodism in the Philippines* (n.p., 1974); Brenton T. Badley, ed., *Visions and Victories in Hindustan. A Story of the Mission Stations of the Methodist Episcopal Church in Southern India* (Madras, 1931); Wade C. Barclay, *History of Methodist Missions* (New York, 1949, 1973); Richard L. Deats, *The Story of Methodism in the Philippines* (Manila, 1964); Theodore T. Doraisamy, *March of Methodism in Singapore and Malaysia from 1880–1980* (Singapore, 1982); Walter N. Lacy, *A Hundred Years of China*

Methodism (New York, 1948); and Charles A. Sauer, *Methodists in Korea, 1930–1960* (Seoul, 1973).

METHODIST EPISCOPAL CHURCH, SOUTH: BOARD OF MISSIONS. Founded in 1844 when it broke off from the Methodist Episcopal Church, it began missionary work in China in 1848, in Japan in 1886, in Korea in 1894, and in Siberia in 1921. It merged in 1939 with the Methodist Episcopal Church and the Methodist Protestant Church to form the Methodist Church, which merged in 1968 with the Evangelical United Brethren Church to form the United Methodist Church and its Board of Global Ministries. *References*: General Commission on Archives and History of the United Methodist Church, Drew University, Madison, N.J.; James Cannon III, *History of Southern Methodist Missions* (Nashville, 1926); Walter N. Lacy, *A Hundred Years of China Methodism* (New York, 1948); J. S. Ryang, ed., *Southern Methodists in Korea* (Seoul, 1927); and Noreen D. Tatum, *A Crown of Service: A Story of Woman's Work in the Methodist Episcopal Church, South, from 1878–1940* (Nashville, Tenn., 1960).

METHODIST PROTESTANT CHURCH: BOARD OF FOREIGN MISSIONS. Founded in 1834, it began missionary work in Japan in 1880, in China in 1910, and in India in 1921. It merged in 1939 with the Methodist Episcopal Church and the Methodist Episcopal Church, South, to form the Methodist Church, which merged in 1968 with the Evangelical United Brethren Church to form the United Methodist Church and its Board of Global Ministries.

MEYER, ARMIN HENRY (1914–   ). Diplomat, born January 19, 1914, in Fort Wayne, Indiana. Meyer attended Lincoln College (Ill.) and graduated from Capitol University (Ohio) and Ohio State University. He served with the Office of War Information in Iraq and Egypt during World War II, and was a U.S. public affairs officer in Baghdad in 1947–1948. He entered the foreign service in 1948, and served in Beirut and Kabul until 1961. He was U.S. ambassador to Lebanon from 1961 to 1965, and ambassador to Iran from 1965 to 1969. He was ambassador to Japan from 1969 to 1972, and dealt with the return of the Ryukyu Islands to Japan. He wrote an account of his experiences in *Assignment Tokyo: An Ambassador Journal* (Indianapolis, 1974). He taught at American University in 1974–1975, and at Georgetown University after 1975. *References*: *DADH*; and *WWA*.

MEYER, BERNARD F(RANCIS) (1891–1975). Missionary, born February 16, 1891, in Brooklyn, Iowa, and grew up in Stuart, Guthrie County, Iowa. Meyer graduated from St. Ambrose College (Davenport, Ia.), and attended St. Mary's Seminary (Baltimore) and Catholic Foreign Mission Seminary (Maryknoll, N.Y.). He entered the Maryknoll Society in 1914 and was ordained in 1916. He was a missionary in China from 1918 to 1949, one of the first group of Maryknoll Fathers assigned to missionary work in China. He served in the Kongmoon mission, Kwangtung Province, from 1918 to 1925. He was the first superior of the Maryknoll Missionaries in Kwangsi from 1925 to 1931, superior of the Wuchu independent mission from 1931 to 1934, and prefect apostolic of Wuchu, Kwangsi Province, from 1934 until 1940. He was interned by the Japanese in Hong Kong during World War II. He remained in China, serving in Canton, until 1950, when he was expelled from China by the Communist authorities. He was coauthor of *The Student's Cantonese-English Dictionary* (St. Louis, 1947). Died May 8, 1975, in North Terrytown, New York. *References*: *ACWW*; *CA*; John F. Donovan, *A Priest Named Horse* (Huntington, Ind., 1977); and *NYT*, May 10, 1975.

MEYER, CLARENCE EARLE (1891–1965). Businessman, born August 14, 1891, in East Ashford, Cattaraugus County, New York. Meyer graduated from Syracuse University. He was employed by the Standard Oil Company of New York as a marketer of petroleum products in East Asia. His first assignment was in Kongmoon, Kwangtung Province, and he was later affiliated with the Hong Kong office. He served in the interests of the Socony-Vacuum Oil Corporation (after 1933, Standard-Vacuum Oil Company) in Hong Kong from 1932 to 1934, and was general manager of Standard-Vacuum Oil Company in Japan from 1934 to 1941. He was interned in Japan in 1941–1942. He was petroleum attaché at the U.S. embassy in London during World War II. He was vice president of Standard-Vacuum Oil Company in China and Japan from 1946 until his retirement in 1950. He later served on various missions to East Asia for the Mutual Security Agency, and later for the International Cooperation Administration. He also was director of economic aid and chief of economic affairs at the U.S. embassy in Tokyo from 1955 to 1957. Died March 15, 1965, in Washington, D.C. *References*: NCAB 51:736; and *NYT*, March 17, 1965.

MEYER, FRANK N(ICHOLAS) (1875–1918). Plant explorer, born November 29, 1875, in Amsterdam, the Netherlands. Meyer was a gardener at the botanic gardens of Amsterdam. He came to the United States in 1901, and was employed as a gardener in the greenhouse of the U.S. Department of Agriculture in Washington, D.C., and in the plant improvement garden in Santa Ana, California. He was an agricultural explorer for the U.S. Department of Agriculture from 1905 until his death. He explored in China in 1905–1906, 1907–1908, and 1913 to 1918; in Manchuria in 1906–1907 and 1913; in Korea in 1906; in Eastern Siberia in 1906–1907; in Russian Turkestan in 1910; in Chinese Turkestan in 1910–1911; and in Mongolia in 1911. He wrote *Agricultural Explorations in the Fruit and Orchards of China* (Washington, D.C., 1911) and *Chinese Plant Names* (New York, 1911). Disappeared June 1, 1918, from a riverboat on the Yangtze River, on his way from Hankow to Nanking. *References*: Isabel S. Cunningham, *Frank N. Meyer: Plant Hunter in Asia* (Ames, Iowa, 1984); *NCAB*, 20:306; and *NYT*, June 19, 1918.

MICHAEL, WILLIAM HENRY (1845–1916). Consul, born July 14, 1845, in Marysville, Ohio. Michael attended the University of Iowa. He served in the Union Army and then in the Union Navy during the Civil War. He was city editor of the *Sioux City* (Iowa) *Journal* in 1873, and editor and owner of Nebraska newspapers from 1875 to 1881. He was admitted to the bar in 1880 and practiced law until 1887. He was the Washington, D.C., correspondent for three newspapers from 1887 to 1890, clerk of the U.S. Senate, compiler of the *Congressional Directory*, and editor of the messages and documents of Congress from 1887 to 1896. He was chief clerk at the State Department from 1897 to 1905, and consul general in Calcutta, India, from 1905 to 1912. Died May 17, 1916, in Washington, D.C. *References*: *NYT*, May 18, 1916; and *WWWA*.

MILES, MILTON E(DWARD) ("MARY") (1900–1961). Naval officer, born April 6, 1900, in Jerome, Arizona. Miles enlisted in the U.S. Navy in 1917, graduated from the U.S. Naval Academy in 1922, and was commissioned an ensign in the U.S. Navy. He was joint commander of the Sino-American Cooperative Organization (SACO)* in China during World War II. He was later commander of Cruiser Divisions Four and Six of the Atlantic Fleet, commandant of the Naval Department in the Panama Canal Zone, and commandant of the Third Naval District in New York City from 1956 until his retirement. He retired with the rank of vice admiral in 1958. Died March 25, 1961, in Bethesda, Maryland. *A Different Kind of War: The Little-Known Story of the Combined Guerilla Forces Created by the U.S. Navy and the Chinese during World War II* (Garden City, N.Y., 1967) was prepared by Hawthorne Daniel and published posthumously. *References*: Milton E. Miles Papers, Center for Naval History, Washington, D.C.; Milton E. Miles Papers, Hoover Institution on War, Revolution and Peace, Stanford, Calif.; *NYT*, March 26, 1961; and *WWWA*.

MILITARY ASSISTANCE AND ADVISORY GROUP (MAAG), INDO-CHINA. Created by the U.S. Government in 1950 to process, monitor, and evaluate American military aid to the French forces fighting in Indochina. In 1955 it became MAAG, Vietnam, and took over from the French the training and organizing of the Vietnamese National Army. It was replaced in 1962 with the Military Assistance Command, Vietnam. *References*: *DVW*; and Ronald H. Spector, *United States Army in Vietnam: Advise and Support: The Early Years, 1941–1960* (Washington, D.C., 1983).

MILLARD, THOMAS F(RANKLIN FAIRFAX) (1868–1942). Journalist and publisher, born July 8, 1868, in Phelps County, Ohio. Millard attended the Missouri School of Mines and Metallurgy, and graduated from the University of Missouri. He began his newspaper career in 1895 in St. Louis, worked for the *New York Herald* after 1898, and was a war correspondent for various American newspapers in various parts of the world before going to China, where he founded and became editor of *The China Press* in Shanghai from 1910 to

1917. In 1917 he founded *Millard's Review* (the name was later changed to *China Weekly Review*), also in Shanghai. He was considered the dean of American newspaper men in East Asia. He was an advisor to the Chinese Nationalist government after 1920, and served as an unofficial advisor to the Chinese delegation to the Versailles Peace Conference in 1919. He had close connections with the Kuomintang, and was said to have received a subsidy from them and to have served as an advisor to the Kuomintang government from 1929 to 1935. He wrote *The New Far East* (New York, 1906); *America and the Far Eastern Question* (New York, 1909); *Our Eastern Question* (New York, 1916); *Democracy and the Eastern Question* (New York, 1919); *Conflict of Policies in Asia* (New York, 1924); *China, Where It Is Today and Why* (New York, 1928); and *The End of Extraterritoriality in China* (Shanghai, 1931). He returned to the United States in 1941. Died September 8, 1942, in Seattle, Washington. *References*: John M. Hamilton, "The Missouri News Monopoly and American Altruism in China: Thomas F. F. Millard, J. B. Powell, and Edgar Snow," *PHR* 55 (1986): 27–48; *NYT*, September 9, 1942; and *WWWA*.

MILLER, EDGAR R(AYMOND) (1899–   ) and **MILLER, ELIZABETH (JANE) (BUCKE)** (1901–   ). Medical missionaries. Edgar R. Miller was born April 19, 1899, in New Freedom, Pennsylvania. He graduated from Dickinson College and the University of Maryland Medical School. Elizabeth Miller was born April 21, 1901, in Oldwich, New Jersey. She graduated from Dickinson College and Woman's Medical College of Pennsylvania. They practiced medicine in Wilmington, Delaware, from 1928 to 1956. They were medical missionaries under the United Mission to Nepal in Kathmandu from 1956 to 1965. References: *Biographical Directory of the American College of Physicians 1979* (New York, 1979); Eleanor P. Clarkson, *Medics in the Mountains. The Story of Edgar and Elizabeth Miller* (New York, 1968); and *WWAW*.

MILLER, HARRY WILLIS (1879–1977). Medical missionary, born July 1, 1879, in Ludlow Falls, Ohio. Miller graduated from Mount Vernon (Ohio) College and the American Medical Missionary College (Battle Creek, Mich.). He was a medical missionary under the Foreign Mission Board of the Seventh-Day Adventist Church in China after 1903. He served in Shangtsai from 1904 until 1908, and in Shanghai from 1908 until 1910. In 1910, he established a medical unit near Hangchow and a school at Chouchiakou. He returned to the United States in 1911 because of ill health. He became a medical secretary to the church's General Conference in Washington, D.C., and medical director of the Washington Sanitarium in Takoma Park, Maryland. He returned to China in 1925 and supervised the building of Shanghai Sanitarium. He moved in 1937 to Hankow, but was forced to leave China in 1939. He returned again to China in 1949 for a short time. He organized a hospital in Taiwan in 1953 and in Hong Kong in 1959. A pioneer in the field of nutrition, he developed the process of making soybean milk to feed poorly nourished Chinese children in areas where cow's milk was unavailable. He also served as a physician to Chou En-lai, General and Madame Chiang Kai-shek, Madame Sun Yat-sen, and Marshall Chang Hsueh-liang. Died January 1, 1977, in Riverside, California. *References*: *CB* 1962; Raymond S. Moore, *China Doctor, the Life Story of Harry Willis Miller* (New York, 1961); and *NYT*, January 9, 1977.

MILLER, HENRY B. (1854–1921). Consul, born April 11, 1854, in Sidney, Ohio. Miller was a bridge engineer, contractor, and in the lumber business in Oregon from 1879 to 1895. He was president of Oregon Agricultural College (Corvallis) in 1897–1898, and president of the State Board of Agriculture in 1899–1900. He was consul at Chungking, China, in 1900; and consul general at Newchwang, China, from 1901 to 1904, and at Yokohama, Japan, from 1905 to 1909. He served as president of the Chinese Refugee and Aid Society in Manchuria during the Russo-Japanese War. Died November 28, 1921, in Portland, Oregon. *References*: Henry B. Miller Papers, University of Oregon Library, Eugene, Ore.; and *WWWA*.

MILLER, WARREN HASTINGS (1876–1960). Author, born August 21, 1876, in Honesdale, Pennsylvania. Miller graduated from Stevens Institute of Technology. He served in the Spanish-American War. He was a construction engineer with various companies from 1900 to 1908. He studied music in Paris from 1908 to 1910, and was editor of *Field and Stream* magazine and vice president of its publishing company from 1910 to 1918. He served with the U.S. Navy during World War I. He traveled to New Guinea, Java, Borneo, and Sumatra in 1921 to gather material for adventure novels for Harper and Brothers. He wrote *The Castways of Banda Sea* (New York, 1921); *Medicine Gold* (New York, 1924); and the "Boy Explorers" series, including *The Boy Explorers in Darkest New Guinea* (New York, 1921); *The Boy Explorers in Borneo* (New York, 1922); *The Boy Explorers and the Ape-man of Sumatra* (New York, 1923); *The Boy Explorers on Tiger Trails in Burma* (New York, 1925); and *The Boy Explorers in the Pirate Archipelago* (New York, 1926). He also wrote *Tiger Bridge: A Story of Railroad Building in Indo-China* (Boston, 1937). Died July 14, 1960, in Melbourne, Florida. *References*: *NCAB* 48:105; *NYT*, July 15, 1960; and *WWWA*.

MINER, (SARAH) LUELLA (1861–1935). Missionary educator, born October 30, 1861, in Oberlin, Ohio. Miner graduated from Oberlin College. She was a missionary under the Women's Board of Missions of the Interior and the American Board of Commissioners for Foreign Missions (ABCFM) in China from 1887 until her death. She served at Paoting in 1887–1888 and at Tungchow from 1888 to 1901. She was a teacher at a boys' high school, at the North China College, and at its theological seminary, and wrote the first textbook on geology in Chinese. She was principal of a girls' school in Peking from 1903 to 1913, organized the first college for women in China in 1905, and served as president of North China Union Woman's College until 1920. After that school became affiliated with Yenching University in 1920, she was dean there until 1922. She served at Cheeloo University in Tsinan as teacher, acting dean of the women's medical unit, and dean of women from 1923 until her death. She edited *Two Heroes of Cathay, an Autobiography and a Sketch* (New York, 1903), and wrote *China's Books of Martyrs, a Record of Heroic Martyrdom and Marvelous Deliverances of Chinese Christians during the Summer of 1900* (Cincinnati, 1903). Died December 2, 1935, in Tsinan. *References*: Luella Miner Papers, University of Washington Libraries, Seattle, Wash.; *NAW*; *OAB*; and *WWWA*.

MIYAGI GAKUIN WOMEN'S COLLEGE. Founded as a girls' school in 1886 in Sendai, Japan, by the Reformed Church in the United States. It adopted its current name in 1949. *Reference*: C. William Mensendiek, *A Dream Incarnate: The Beginnings of Miyagi Gakuin for Women* (Senadi, Japan, 1986).

MOFFETT, SAMUEL AUSTIN (1864–1939). Missionary, born January 25, 1864, in Madison, Indiana. Moffett graduated from Hanover (Ind.) College and McCormick Theological Seminary, and was ordained in 1888. He was a missionary under the Board of Foreign Missions of the Presbyterian Church in the U.S.A. in Korea from 1890 until 1936. He was a pastor in P'yongyang from 1893 until 1925. In 1901, he founded the Presbyterian Theological Seminary of Korea, was a member of its faculty from 1902 until 1935, and its president from 1902 to 1924. He was president of Soongsil College from 1918 until 1928. He was forced to leave Korea in 1936 for opposing compulsory attendance at Shinto shrines. Died October 24, 1939, in Monrovia, California. *References*: Samuel Austin Moffett, *First Letters from Korea (1890–1891)* (Seoul, 1975); William N. Blair, *Precious Memories of Dr. Samuel A. Moffett* (Duarte, Calif., n.d.); *CDCWM*; Jony Hyeong Lee, "Samuel Austin Moffett: His Life and Work in the Development of the Presbyterian Church of Korea 1890–1936," Ph.D. diss., Union Theological Seminary, Virginia, 1983; *NYT*, October 26, 1939; and *WWWA*.

MOLE, ROBERT L. (1923–   ). Clergyman, born August 10, 1923, in Kissimmee, Florida. Mole graduated from Madison College (Tenn.), Seventh-Day Adventist Theological Seminary (Washington, D.C.), and Lutheran School of Theology (Maywood, Ill.). He was a missionary under the Seventh-Day Adventist Church in Lebanon and Cyprus from 1946 to 1952, serving also as associate professor of religion and history at Middle East College in Beirut, Lebanon. He served as a chaplain in the U.S. Navy from 1953 to 1976, including assignments on mainland Southeast Asia. He wrote *The Religions of South Vietnam in Faith and Fact* (Washington, D.C., 1967); *The Montagnards of South Vietnam: A Study of Nine Tribes* (Rutland, Vt., 1970); and *Thai Values and Behavior Patterns* (Rutland, Vt., 1971). He later served with the U.S.

Veterans Administration in Martinez and Loma Linda, California. *Reference*: *CA*.

MONAHAN, JOHN J. (1875–1926). Missionary, born August 12, 1875, in Curralee, County Roscommon, Ireland, and came to the United States in 1891. He studied dentistry and graduated from the Woodstock Seminary. He entered the Society of Jesus in 1906. He taught in high schools in Washington, D.C., Boston, and Buffalo, New York. He was a missionary in the Philippines from 1923 until his death, serving at Vigan, Ilocos Sur, from 1923 to 1925; at Zamboanga in 1925; and in Cagayan de Misamis in 1926. Died May 8, 1926, in Manila. *References*: Miguel A. Bernard, "Early American Jesuit Missionaries in Mindanao: The Pioneer Period: 1905–1926," *Kinaadman: A Journal of the Southern Philippines* 3 (1981): 105–19; Thomas F. Feeney, *The Padre of the Press: Recollections of Father John J. Monahan* (New York, 1931); and Joseph P. Merrick, "Father John J. Monahan," *Woodstock Letters* 56 (1927): 304–18.

MOON, (CHARLOTTE) LOTTIE DIGGES (1840–1912). Missionary, born December 12, 1840, near Scottsville, Albermale County, Virginia. Moon graduated from Valley Union Seminary (later Hollins College) and Albermale Institute (Charlottesville, Va.). She then organized a girls' school in Cartersville, Georgia. She was a missionary under the Foreign Mission Board of the Southern Baptist Convention in China from 1873 until her death. She served at Tengchow and Pingtu, Shantung Province. Died December 24, 1912, aboard a ship in the harbor of Kobe, Japan. *References*: Lottie Moon Papers, Virginia Baptist Historical Society, Richmond, Va.; Catherine B. Allen, *The New Lottie Moon Story* (Nashville, 1980); *ESB*; Irwin T. Hyatt, Jr., *Our Ordered Lives Confess: Three Nineteenth-Century American Missionaries in East Shantung* (Cambridge, Mass., 1976), pt. 2; *NAW*; and Jester Summers, *Lottie Moon of China* (Nashville, 1971).

MOORE, FREDERICK (1877–1956). Journalist, born November 17, 1877, in New Orleans. Moore was a correspondent for various American and British newspapers in Washington, D.C., London, the Balkan States, Morocco, and Turkey from 1900 until 1909. He was an Associated Press correspondent in China from 1910 to 1915, and managing editor of *Asia* magazine in New York City in 1917–1918. He served as an advisor to the Japanese Ministry of Foreign Affairs from 1921 until 1926, was correspondent for the *New York Times* in China and Japan in 1927, and was again an advisor to Japanese government from 1929 until 1941. He wrote *With Japan's Leaders: An Intimate Record of Fourteen Years as Counsellor to the Japanese Government* (New York, 1942). *Reference*: *WWWA*.

MORDEN, WILLIAM J(AMES) (1886–1958). Explorer, born January 3, 1886, in Chicago. Morden graduated from Sheffield Scientific School of Yale University. He was an engineer and manufacturer at the Union Bag and Paper Corporation from 1908 to 1922, and an explorer and field collector after 1922. He was a member of the scientific staff of the American Museum of Natural History from 1926 to 1940. He was leader of the Morden-Clark Asiatic expedition to Chinese Turkestan in 1926–1927, of the Morden-Graves North Asiatic expedition in 1929–1930, and of the Morden African expedition in 1947. He served in U.S. Army during World War I and World War II. He wrote *Across Asia's Snows and Deserts* (New York, 1927). Died January 23, 1958, in Chappaqua, New York. *References*: *NYT*, January 24, 1958; and *WWWA*.

MORO WARS (1899–1913). Conflict between the Muslim Filipinos, who inhabit the southern islands of Mindanao and Palawan, and the Sulu Archipelago and the U.S. Army, which carried out several pacification campaigns in this area between 1899 and 1913, when it finally broke the main resistance. *References*: George W. Jornacion, "The Time of the Eagles: United States Army Officers and the Pacification of the Philippine Moros, 1899–1913," Ph.D. diss., University of Maine, 1973; and Richard K. Kolb, "Campaign in Moroland: A War the World Forgot," *Army* 33 (September 1983): 50–59.

MORRIS, JAMES HENRY (1871–1942). Businessman, born June 26, 1871, near Barrie, Ontario. Morris came to San Francisco in 1888 and became a U.S. citizen. He was employed by the Market Street Railway Company. He went to Seoul, Korea, in 1899 with a group of engineers contracted to construct the first streetcar system and the first public water system in Seoul. He remained in Korea, developed an importing business, and was an agent for steamship lines and several insurance companies; automobile, motorcycle, and film distribution agencies; and owned an auto maintenance and repair garage. He returned to the United States. Died February 16, 1942, in Millbrae, near San Francisco. *Reference*: J. Earnest Fisher, *Pioneers of Modern Korea* (Seoul, 1977), pp. 159–70.

MORRIS, ROLAND SLETOR (1874–1945). Lawyer and diplomat, born March 11, 1874, in Olympia, Washington. Morris graduated from Princeton University and the University of Pennsylvania. He practiced law in Philadelphia from 1899 until his death. He was active in Democratic politics. He was U.S. ambassador to Japan from 1917 to 1920, and succeeded in lessening the friction between Japan and the United States. He was sent in 1919 on a special mission to the anti-Bolshevik government of Aleksander Kolchak in Omsk, Siberia. Died November 23, 1945, in Philadelphia. *References*: Roland Sletor Morris Papers, Manuscript Division, Library of Congress; *DADH*; *NCAB* 43:458; *NYT*, November 24, 1945; and *WWWA*.

MORRISON INCIDENT. In 1837, the American merchant ship *Morrison*, owned by the firm of Olyphant and Company, tried to repatriate seven ship-wrecked Japanese sailors and sought to initiate trade with Japan. It was bombarded and forced to retreat out of Japanese territorial waters. *References*: William A. Borst, "The American Merchant and the Genesis of Japanese Relations, 1790–1858," Ph.D. diss., St. Louis University, 1972, ch. v.; *KEJ*; and *Wildes*, ch. 18.

MORROW, JAMES (1820–1865). Scientist, born August 7, 1820, in Willington, McCormick County, South Carolina. Morrow attended the University of Georgia (Athens) and the University of Pennsylvania Medical School, and studied at the Medical College of the State of South Carolina. He practiced medicine in Charleston, South Carolina, and developed an interest in agriculture and taxidermy. He served as an agriculturist with the Perry Expedition to Japan from 1853 to 1855, collecting plants, seeds, and natural history specimens. He served in the Confederate Army during the Civil War. Died December 11, 1865, in Willington, South Carolina. *References*: Allan B. Cole, ed., *A Scientist with Perry in Japan: The Journal of Dr. James Morrow* (Chapel Hill, N.C., 1947); A. Hunter Dupree, "Science vs. the Military: Dr. James Morrow and the Perry Expedition," *PHR* 22 (1953): 29–37.

MORSE, EDWARD S(YLVESTER) (1838–1925). Zoologist, born June 18, 1838, in Portland, Maine. Morse was one of the special students of Louis Agassiz at Lawrence Scientific School of Harvard University. He was at the Essex Institute until 1867, was curator of Radiata and Mollusca at the Peabody Academy of Science (later Peabody Museum) from 1867 to 1871, and professor of zoology at Bowdoin College from 1871 to 1874. He was professor of zoology at Tokyo University from 1877 to 1879. He was instrumental in establishing the Japanese Imperial Museum, helped introduce modern scientific methods to the study of zoology and biology in Japan, and introduced and popularized Darwinian theories. He worked at the Omori shell mounds (now part of Tokyo). He returned to Japan in 1882–1883, and assembled a collection of pottery (now in the Boston Museum of Fine Arts). He also collected Japanese artifacts. He was director of the Peabody Museum in Salem until his retirement in 1916. He wrote *Japanese Homes and Their Surroundings* (Boston, 1885), and *Japan Day by Day* (Boston, 1917). Died December 20, 1925, in Salem, Massachusetts. *References*: Edward Sylvester Morse Papers, Phillips Library, Peabody Museum of Salem, Salem, Mass.; *DAB*; *DSB*; Money Hickman and Peter Fetchko, *Japan Day by Day: An Exhibition Honoring Edward Sylvester Morse and Commemorating the Hundredth Anniversary of His Arrival in Japan in 1877* (Salem, Mass., 1977); *KEJ*; *NYT*, December 21, 1925; Robert A. Rosenstone, *Mirror in the Shrine: American Encounters with Meiji Japan* (Cambridge, Mass., 1988); John E. Thayer, "Morse in Japan and His Impact There," *AN* 46 (1986): 55–65; Noboru Umetani, *The Role of Foreign Employees in the Meiji Era in Japan* (Tokyo, 1971), ch.

12; Dorothy G. Wayman, *Edward Sylvester Morse: A Biography* (Cambridge, Mass., 1942); and *WWWA*.

MORSE, HOSEA BALLOU (1855–1934). Government official, born July 18, 1855, in Brookfield, Nova Scotia, and grew up in Medford, Massachusetts. Morse graduated from Harvard University. He was an assistant in the Imperial Chinese Maritime Customs from 1874 to 1887, deputy commissioner from 1887 to 1896, and commissioner after 1896. He was statistical secretary to the inspector general of customs, and chief of the Department of Statistics, Printing and Supplies from 1903 to 1907. He helped negotiate the peace agreement terminating the Franco-Chinese War of 1885, and negotiated the opening of Hunan Province to foreign trade in 1899. He retired in 1909. He wrote *Currency of China* (Shanghai, 1906); *The Trade and Administration of the Chinese Empire* (Shanghai, 1908); *The Gilds of China* (London, 1909); *International Relations of the Chinese Empire* (London, 1910, 1918); *The Chronicles of the East India Company, Trading to China, 1635–1834* (Oxford, 1926, 1929); and *In the Days of the Taipings* (Salem, Mass., 1927); and was coauthor of *Far Eastern International Relations* (Shanghai, 1931). Died February 13, 1934, in Camberley, Kent, England. *References*: Hosea B. Morse Letterbooks, Houghton Library, Harvard University, Cambridge, Mass.; *The* [London] *Times*, February 20, 1934; and *WWWA*.

MORSE, JAMES R(OLLAND) (1848–1921). Businessman. Morse went to Japan in 1875 and was one of the American pioneer traders there. He established a branch of the American Clock Company in Yokohama in 1877, which became the American Clock and Brass Company in 1879 and the American Trading Company in 1884. He was manager of the company in Yokohama until 1889 and again from 1898 until 1902. He was also vice president and later president of the company in New York City from 1889 until his death. Died December 23, 1921, in New York City. *Reference*: *NYT*, December 24, 1921.

MORSE, WILLIAM REGINALD (1874–1939). Physician, born August 30, 1874, in Lawrencetown, Annapolis County, Nova Scotia, Canada. Morse graduated from Acadia and McGill universities. He practiced medicine in Westport and South Ohio, Nova Scotia, and then in Providence, Rhode Island, until 1909. He was a medical missionary under the American Baptist Foreign Mission Society in China from 1909 until 1938. He worked in Suifu, Szechwan Province, from 1909 to 1914, and was professor of anatomy and surgery at the West China Union University at Chengtu from 1914 until 1938; dean of the medical school in 1919, and director of the college of medicine and dentistry in 1935. He wrote *Three Crosses in the Purple Mists, an Adventure in Medical Education under the Eaves of the Roof of the World* (Shanghai, 1928); *Chinese Medicine* (New York, 1934); and *Schedule of Physical Anthropology Measurements and Ob-*

servations on the Ethnic Groups of Szechwan Province, West China (Chengtu, China, 1937). Died November 11, 1939, in Boston. *References*: *NCAB* 39:433; and *NYT*, November 12, 1939.

MOSES, BERNARD (1846–1930). Educator and colonial administrator, born August 27, 1846, in Burlington, Connecticut. Moses graduated from the universities of Michigan and Heidelberg (Germany). He was professor of history at Albion (Mich.) College in 1875–1876, professor of history and political economy at the University of California from 1876 to 1903, and professor of history and political science from 1903 until his retirement in 1911. He was a member of the Philippine Commission from 1900 to 1902, served as secretary of education, and organized the Philippine system of public education. Died March 4, 1930, in Walnut Creek, Contra Costa County, California. His wife, **EDITH MOSES**, wrote *Unofficial Letters of an Official's Wife* (New York, 1908). *References*: Bernard Moses Papers, Bancroft Library, University of California, Berkeley, Calif.; *DAB*; *NCAB* 26:120; *NYT*, September 24, 1920; J. E. Watson, "Bernard Moses: Pioneer in Latin American Scholarship," *Hispanic American Historical Review* 42 (1962): 212–16; and *WWWA*.

MOSES, CHARLES LEE (1824–1868). Merchant and consul, born May 24, 1824, in Charleston, North Carolina. Moses went to sea at an early age, and was engaged in the Southeast Asian commerce and in local shipping in Bangkok, Siam, by 1857. He served in the U.S. Navy during the Civil War. He was consul in Brunei from 1864 to 1867. In 1865 he secured from the sultan of Brunei a grant of territory in north Borneo. He was a partner in the American Trading Company of Borneo,* and was involved in establishing the colony of Ellena in Kimanis, north Borneo, in 1865–1867. He left Brunei in 1867 and returned to Bangkok. Lost at sea on his way to the United States. *Reference*: H. G. Keith, *The United States Consul and the Yankee Raja* (Brunei, 1980).

MOSHER, ARTHUR T(HEODORE) (1910–   ). Agriculturist, born October 4, 1910, in Ames, Iowa. Mosher graduated from the universities of Illinois and Chicago. He was an instructor in agricultural engineering at Allahabad Agricultural Institute in Allahabad, India, from 1933 to 1940, head of the extension department from 1946 to 1950, and principal of the institute from 1948 to 1953. He was visiting professor of economics and cultural change at the University of Chicago from 1953 to 1955, president of the Agricultural Development Council in New York City from 1957 to 1963, and its associate in Sri Lanka from 1974 to 1976, and writer after 1976. *References*: *AMWS*; *CA*; and *WWE*.

MOSHER, GOUVERNEUR FRANK (1871–1941). Missionary, born October 28, 1871, in Stapleton, Staten Island, New York. Mosher graduated from State Normal School (Albany, N.Y.), Union College (Schenectady, N.Y.), and Berkeley Divinity School (Middleton, Conn.), and was ordained in 1898. He was a missionary under the Domestic and Foreign Missionary Society of the Protestant Episcopal Church in the United States of America in China from 1896 until 1920. He initially worked in the rescue mission in Shanghai, and opened a mission in Wusih in 1902. He was a missionary bishop of the Protestant Episcopal Church in the Philippines from 1920 to 1940. He extended the work of the church among the Igorots in the mountains of Luzon and among the Tiruri people of southern Mindanao, establishing schools and hospitals from 1920 to 1940. Died July 19, 1941, in New York City. *References*: Gouverneur Frank Mosher Papers, Archives of the Church Historical Society, Austin, Tex.; *EP* 17:388–89; *NYT*, July 20, 1941; *WWP*; and *WWWA*.

MOSS, CLAUDE R(USSELL) (1875–1958). Educator and folklorist, born September 29, 1875, in Tusquittee, North Carolina. Moss graduated from Young Harris College. He came to the Philippines in 1904 as a teacher with the Bureau of Education, taught in the Mountain Province, and was division superintendent of schools in Bontoc, Mountain Province, and later in Kabayan. He retired from government service in 1917, returned to the United States, and graduated from the University of California at Berkeley. He wrote *Nabaloi Songs* (Berkeley, Calif., 1919); *Kankanay Ceremonies* (Berkeley, Calif., 1920); *Nabaloi Law and Ritual* (Berkeley, Calif., 1920); and *Nabaloi Tales* (Berkeley, Calif., 1924). Died December 21, 1958. *Reference*: *DPB* 3.

MOYER, SAMUEL T(YSON) (1893–1972). Missionary, born April 10, 1893, in Lansdale, Pennsylvania. Moyer graduated from Pennsylvania State College and Witmarsum Seminary, and attended Biblical Seminary (New York) and New York University. He was a pastor in Pulaski, Iowa, in 1919–1920; and a missionary under the Board of Mission of the General Conference of the Mennonite Brethren Church in India from 1920 to 1956. He served in the Basna mission station from 1924 to 1927, established the Jagdispur Station, and was principal of the school there. He returned to the United States in 1956 and was a pastor in Pekin, Illinois, from 1956 to 1967. He wrote *With Christ on the Edge of the Jungles* (Hillsboro, Kans., 1941), and *They Heard the Call* (Newton, Kans., 1970), which includes his autobiography. *References*: Samuel T. Moyer Papers, Mennonite Library and Archives, North Newton, Kans.

MUCCIO, JOHN J(OSEPH) (1900–1989). Diplomat, born in Valle Agricole, Italy, and grew up in Providence, Rhode Island. Muccio graduated from Brown and George Washington universities. He entered the foreign service in 1921, served in Hamburg, Germany; Hong Kong; Shanghai; La Paz, Bolivia; Panama; and Havana. He was the first U.S. ambassador to South Korea from 1949 to 1952. He served in Seoul at the time of the North Korean invasion in 1950, and was in charge of the evacuation of Seoul and other critical matters during the height of the crisis. He was a minister to Iceland in 1954, ambassador there from 1954 until 1959, and ambassador to Guatemala from 1959 to 1961. Died

May 19, 1989, in Washington, D.C. *References*: *CB* 1952; *NCAB H*:155; *NYT*, May 22, 1989; and *PolProf: Truman*.

MUDGE, JAMES (1844–1918). Missionary, born April 5, 1844, in West Springfield, Massachusetts. Mudge graduated from Wesleyan University (Middletown, Conn.) and Boston University School of Theology, and was ordained in 1868. He was a pastor in Wilbraham, Massachusetts, from 1870 to 1873. He was a missionary under the Board of Foreign Missions of the Methodist Episcopal Church in India from 1873 to 1883. He was stationed in Lucknow, was editor of the *Lucknow Witness* from 1873 to 1882, and was pastor from 1878 to 1882. He served in Shahjahanpur in 1882–1883. He returned to the United States in 1883, held several pastorates in Massachusetts, and was a lecturer on missions in the Boston School of Theology from 1888 to 1904. Died May 7, 1918, in Malden, Massachusetts. *References*: *DAB*; *EWM*; and *WWWA*.

MUNGER, HENRY WESTON (1876–1962). Missionary, born November 30, 1876, in New Britain, Pennsylvania. Munger graduated from the University of Chicago and Crozer Theological Seminary (Chester, Pa.), and was ordained in 1904. He was a missionary under the American Baptist Foreign Mission Society in the Philippines from 1904 until 1945. He was mission president and treasurer, founder and principal of the Jaro Industrial School, and superintendent of the Philippine Mission Press. He was interned by the Japanese in Los Baños during World War II. He wrote *Christ and the Filipino Soul: A History of the Philippine Baptists* (n.p., 1967). Died October 19, 1962, in Bowling Green, Missouri. *Reference*: Henry Weston Munger Papers, American Baptist Historical Society, Rochester, N.Y.

MUNROE, HENRY S(MITH) (1850–1933). Mining engineer, born March 25, 1850, in Brooklyn, New York. Munroe graduated from Columbia University. He was an assistant geologist with the Ohio State Geological Survey in 1870–1871, and assistant chemist with the U.S. Department of Agriculture from 1870 to 1872. He was an assistant geologist and mining engineer with the Geological Survey of Yeso, Japan, from 1872 to 1875, conducted a geological survey of the coal deposits at the island of Hokkaido and wrote *Yeso Coals* (Tokyo, 1874). He was a professor of geology and mining at the University of Tokyo in 1875–1876. He was adjunct professor of surveying and practical mining at Columbia University from 1877 to 1891, and professor of mining from 1891 to 1915. Died May 4, 1933, in Litchfield, Connecticut. *References*: Henry S. Munroe Papers, Connecticut Historical Society, Hartford, Conn.; and *WWWA*.

MUNSON, SAMUEL (1804–1834). Missionary, born March 23, 1804, in New Sharon, Maine. Munson graduated from Bowdoin College and Andover Theological Seminary. He was missionary under the American Board of Commissioners for Foreign Missions (ABCFM)* with Henry Lyman* in Sumatra from

1833 until his death. Murdered June 28, 1834, in Sacca, Sumatra. *References*: *AndoverTS*; *LC*; and William Thompson, *Memoir of the Rev. Samuel Munson and the Rev. Henry Lyman, Late Missionaries to the Indian Archipelago, with a Journal of Their Exploring Tour* (New York, 1839).

MURPHY, FRANK (1890–1949). Government official and colonial administrator, born April 13, 1890, in Sand Beach (later Harbor Beach), Huron County, Michigan. Murphy graduated from the University of Michigan. He practiced law in Detroit from 1914 to 1917, and served in the U.S. Army during World War I. He was first assistant U.S. attorney for the Eastern District of Michigan from 1919 until 1922, practiced law again in Detroit, served as a judge on Detroit's Recorder's Court from 1924 to 1930, and was mayor of Detroit from 1930 until 1933. He was governor-general of the Philippines from 1933 to 1935, and high commissioner of the Philippines in 1935–1936. He provided the islands with a fiscally sound government that was committed to the protection of civil liberties. He secured the adoption of female suffrage and significant reforms in the administration of justice. He was governor of Michigan from 1936 to 1938, attorney general of the United States in 1939–1940, and justice of the Supreme Court from 1940 until his death. Died July 19, 1949, in Detroit. *References*: Frank Murphy Papers, Bentley Historical Library, University of Michigan, Ann Arbor; Melchor P. Acquino, "Frank Murphy," *BAHC* 1 (July-September 1973): 11–17; *CB* 1940; *DAB S4*; *EP* 4:376–379; *Gleeck/Governors*, ch. 12; *NCAB* 37:22; *NYT*, July 20, 1949; and *WWWA*.

MURRAY, DAVID (1830–1905). Educator, born October 15, 1830, in Bovina, Delaware County, New York. Murray graduated from Union College (N.Y.). He was teacher and principal of Albany Academy (N.Y.) until 1863, and professor of mathematics and astronomy at Rutgers University from 1863 to 1873. He was superintendent of educational affairs and a top-ranking advisor to the Japanese Ministry of Education from 1873 to 1879. He contributed to the establishment of a modern universal educational system in Japan, particularly women's education, and directed the implementation of the Education Order of 1872. He urged the establishment of a girls' normal school, set up Japan's first kindergarten, and recommended the establishment of Japan Academy and the National Museum. He was secretary of the board of regents of the University of the State of New York from 1880 until his retirement in 1889. Died March 6, 1905, in New Brunswick, New Jersey. *References*: David Murray Papers, Manuscript Division, Library of Congress; William I. Chamberlain, ed., *In Memoriam, David Murray, Ph.D., LL.D., Superintendent of Educational Affairs in the Empire of Japan, and Adviser to the Japanese Imperial Minister of Education, 1873–1879* (New York, 1915); *DAB*; *KEJ*; Keno Tadashi, "Contributions of David Murray to Modernization of School Administration in Japan," in *The Modernizers: Overseas Students, Foreign Employees, and Meiji Japan*, ed. Ardath W. Burks (Boulder, Colo., 1985), pp. 301–21; Noboru Umetani,

The Role of Foreign Employees in the Meiji Era in Japan (Tokyo, 1971), ch. 11; and *WWWA*.

MUSTARD, ROBERT WEST (1839–1900). Merchant, born in Lewes, Delaware. Mustard was employed as a merchant in Lewes from 1860 until 1864, and in St. Louis, Missouri, in 1864–1865. He came to Shanghai in 1865, was employed by Augustine Heard and Company from 1865 to 1868, and then established a commission business, Mustard and Company. His company served as the agent for the American Tobacco Company in China. Died July 18, 1900, in Shanghai. *References*: Mustard Collection, Historical Society of Delaware, Wilmington, Del.; and Paula S. Holloway, "Robert West Mustard: An American Merchant in Shanghai, 1865–1900," *Delaware History* 22 (1986): 63–98.

N

NANKING, UNIVERSITY OF. Union Christian College was established in Nanking in 1906 as a merger of Nanking University, Nanking Christian College, and Presbyterian Academy, which were founded in Nanking in the 1980s. It became the University of Nanking in 1910, and was chartered by the Regents of the State of New York in 1911. It was removed to Chengtu in 1938 and was reopened in Nanking in 1946. In 1951, it was merged by the Communist authorities with Gingling College to form National Gingling University. *References: Fenn*; and *Lutz*.

NASH, MANNING (1924–   ). Anthropologist, born May 4, 1924, in Philadelphia. Nash graduated from Temple University and the University of Chicago. He served in the U.S. Army during World War II. He was assistant professor of anthropology at the University of Washington (Seattle) in 1956–1957, associate professor of anthropology at the University of Chicago from 1957 to 1962, and professor there after 1962. He carried out fieldwork in Upper Burma in 1960–1961, and in Malaya in 1964, 1966, and 1968. He wrote *The Golden Road to Modernity. Village Life in Contemporary Burma* (New York, 1965); *Primitive and Peasant Economic Systems* (San Francisco, 1966); and *Peasant Citizens: Politics, Religion, and Modernization in Kelantan, Malaysia* (Athens, 1974); and was coauthor of *Anthropological Studies in Theravada Buddhism* (New Haven, Conn., 1974). *References: AMWS; CA*; and *WWA*.

NATHORST, CHARLES E. (1862–1945). Army officer, born June 20, 1862, in Dagsholm, Sweden. Nathorst graduated from Malmo University and Alnarps Landtbruks Institute, and did agricultural research in Edinburgh, Scotland. He came to the United States and was naturalized in 1892. He worked for the Northern Pacific, Chicago, and Great Western railroads from 1883 until 1898. He enlisted in the U.S. Army in 1898, and came to the Philippines that year. He was employed in rebuilding the Manila-Dagupan Railroad by the military government in 1899–1900. In 1901 he was appointed lieutenant in the Philippine

Constabulary and commanded the first Igorot Constabulary from 1901 to 1903. He was governor of Bontoc from 1904 to 1906 and of Lepanto-Bontoc in 1906–1907. In 1927 he became chief of the Philippine Constabulary with the rank of brigadier-general. He retired in 1932. He was a prisoner of war during World War II. Burned to death in Manila, during the week it was liberated. *Reference: CCDP*; and *Elarth*.

NATIONAL CHRISTIAN COUNCIL OF CHINA. Created in 1922 to act on behalf of the cooperating churches and missions in China on matters that concerned their common interest, including public and moral questions, and to provide an effective voice to Christians in China. It ceased functioning in 1950. *References*: National Christian Council of China Archives, Union Theological Seminary Library, New York City; and Paul E. Callahan, "Christianity and Revolution as Seen in the National Christian Council of China," *Papers on China* 5 (1950): 75–106.

NELSON, DANIEL (1853–1926). Missionary, born April 10, 1853, in Sveen, Søndhordland, Norway. Nelson went to the sea as a boy and came to the United States in 1882. He attended Augsburg Seminary (Minneapolis) and Valparaiso University, and was ordained in 1890. He was a missionary under the Norwegian American Lutheran Church, and after 1903, under the Evangelical Lutheran Church, in China from 1890 until his death. He served in Hankow from 1890 to 1900, at Sinyangchow from 1902 to 1919, and at Sinyang from 1921 until his death. Killed by a sniper's bullet, February 8, 1926, in Sinyang. His son, **BERT N. NELSON** (1888–1932), missionary, was born April 9, 1888, in Eagle Grove, Iowa. Bert N. Nelson attended Waldorf College and graduated from St. Olaf College and United Lutheran Seminary (St. Paul, Minn.). He was a missionary under the Board of Foreign Missions of the Norwegian Lutheran Church of America in China from 1917 until his death, serving in Loshan from 1917 to 1928, and at Kwangshui after 1930. He was captured by Chinese bandits in Honan in October 1930. Ransom was paid but he was killed nonetheless in October 1932. *References: CR* 68 (1932): 711; Lowell L. Hesterman, *Missionary Pioneers of the American Lutheran Church* (Minneapolis, 1967), pp. 27–31; Daniel Nelson, *The Apostle to the Chinese Communists* (Minneapolis, 1935); Mary Lee Nelson, *Daniel Nelson* (Shanghai, n.d.); and *Who's Who among Pastors in All the Norwegian Lutheran Synods of American 1843–1927* (Minneapolis, 1928).

NELSON, RICHARD N(EWMAN) (1897–1964). Petroleum geologist, born August 27, 1897, in Forest City, Iowa. Nelson graduated from the University of California at Berkeley. He was a field geologist with the Standard Oil Company of California after 1923. He participated in the expedition to the Dutch East Indies in 1924–1925. He returned to the Dutch East Indies from 1930 to 1938, represented Nederlandsche Pacific Petroleum Maatschappij (NPPM) in Holland in 1940, and returned to Java the same year to take charge of land negotiations and the administration of geological work in the other islands. He left Java in 1942 after having shut down the activities of NPPM and destroying its equipment in advance of the Japanese invasion. He returned to Java after World War II to reorganize NPPM's activities. He headed the geological division of California-Texas Overseas Organizations in New York City from 1952 until his retirement in 1962. Died August 3, 1964, in Bronxville, New York. *Reference: BAAPG* 48 (1964): 1952–55.

NEVILLE, EDWIN LOWE (1884–1944). Diplomat, born November 16, 1884, in Cleveland, Ohio. Neville graduated from the University of Michigan. He entered the foreign service in 1907. He was a student interpreter in Japan; and consul in Antung, China, in 1913–1914; in Taihoku, Formosa, from 1914 to 1916; and in Nagaksaki, Japan, from 1916 to 1920. He held the Japanese desk in the division of Foreign Affairs of the State Department from 1920 to 1925, and was secretary of embassy in Tokyo in 1925, consul general in Tokyo from 1925 to 1935, and counselor of embassy in Tokyo from 1928 until 1937. He was U.S. minister to Siam from 1937 until his retirement in 1940. Died April 7, 1944, in Pasadena, California. *References: NYT*, April 9, 1944; and *WWWA*.

NEVIUS, JOHN LIVINGSTON (1829–1893). Missionary, born March 4, 1829, in Ovid, Seneca County, New York. Nevius graduated from Union Academy and Princeton Theological Seminary, and was ordained in 1853. He was a missionary under the Board of Foreign Missions of the Presbyterian Church in the U.S.A. in China from 1853 until his death. He served at Ningpo, and established mission stations in Hangchow in 1859 and later in Shantung Province. He wrote *China and the Chinese* (New York, 1868); *San-Poh; or, The North of the Hills. A Narrative of Missionary Work in an Out-Station in China* (Philadelphia, 1869); and *Demon Possession and Allied Themes* (Chicago, 1894), which was published posthumously. He experimented in acclimatizing Western fruits and vegetables to China. He also developed the "Nevius Method" of preparing missionaries. Died October 19, 1893, in Chefoo, China. His wife, **HELEN SANFORD COAN NEVIUS** (1833–1910) wrote *Our Life in China* (New York, 1869) and her husband's biography. *References: DAB*; and *LC*.

NEWELL, SAMUEL (1785–1821). Missionary, born July 25 (or 24), 1785, in Durham, Maine. Newell graduated from Harvard University and Andover Theological Seminary, and was ordained in 1812. He went to India the same year. Forbidden to disembark at Calcutta, India, he went to the Isle of France (Mauritius) and then to Ceylon. He returned to India in 1817 and was a missionary under the American Board of Commissioners for Foreign Missions (ABCFM) in Bombay until his death. Died March 30, 1821, in Bombay, India. *References: ACAB; AndoverTS; EM*; and *LC*.

NEWMAN, THOMAS A. (1903–1978). Missionary, born November 3, 1903, in Waterbury, Connecticut. Newman joined the La Salette Fathers. He graduated from La Salette Seminary (Ipswich, Mass.) and the Gregorian University (Rome), and was ordained in 1929. He was a missionary under the Missionaries of Our Lady of La Salette in Burma for forty years, and was consecrated the first bishop of Prome, Burma, in 1961. Died March 9, 1978, in Hartford, Connecticut. *References: DACB*; and *ACWW*.

NEWTON, JOHN (1810–1891). Missionary. Newton was a missionary under the Board of Foreign Missions of the Presbyterian Church in the U.S.A. in Ludhiana, India, from 1835 until his death. He was one of the founders of the modern Punjabi language and literature. He established a printing press, laid the foundation for a publishing establishment, and translated the New Testament into Punjabi (published in 1868). He prepared the first comprehensive *Grammar of the Punjuabi Language* (Ludhiana, 1851). He began the translation of the Old Testament into Punjabi (with Levi Janvier) and prepared the first *Dictionary of the Punjabi Language* (Ludhiana, 1854). Died July 21, 1891, in Muree, India. *References: EM*; and James Massey, "Presbyterian Missionaries and the Development of Punjabi Language and Literature, 1834–1984," *Journal of Presbyterian History* 62 (1984): 258–61.

NEWTON, JOHN CALDWELL CALHOUN (1848–1931). Missionary, born May 25, 1848, in Anderson County, South Carolina. Newton attended Kentucky Wesleyan College, graduated from Kentucky Military Institute and Johns Hopkins University, and was ordained in 1874. He held pastorates in Kentucky from 1874 to 1880, taught at Millersburg (Ky.) Female College, and was a pastor in Warrenton, Virginia, from 1886 to 1888. He was a missionary under the Board of Missions of the Methodist Episcopal Church, South, in Japan from 1888 until 1923; taught at Aoyama Gakuin in 1888–1889; and organized the theological department of Kwansei Gakuin in Kobe from 1889 until 1897. He returned to the United States in 1897 because of ill health, and was a pastor in Virginia, but returned to Japan in 1903, continuing at Kwansei Gakuin. He was president of the school from 1914 to 1921, making it the largest Methodist college in east Asia. He continued as a lecturer in the divinity school until 1923, when he returned to the United States. He wrote *Japan, the Country, Court and People* (New York, 1900). Died November 10, 1931, in Atlanta, Georgia. *Reference: NCAB* 23:271.

NICHOLS, FLORENCE (1865–1958). Missionary educator, born October 27, 1865, in Lynn, Massachusetts. Nichols graduated from Boston University and attended Deaconess Training School (Boston). She was a missionary educator under the Board of Foreign Missions of the Methodist Episcopal Church in Lucknow, India, from 1894 until 1925. She was principal of the Isabella Thoburn College of Lucknow from 1901 to 1908. She returned to the United States in

1908 because of ill health. She was back in India in 1921, and was again principal of the Isabella Thoburn College from 1921 to 1925, when the college became an integral but semiindependent part of the University of Lucknow. She returned to the United States in 1925. Died February 4, 1958, in Lynn, Massachusetts. *Reference: EWM.*

NICHOLS, FRANCIS H(ENRY) (1868–1904). Newspaper correspondent and author, born October 31, 1868, in Brooklyn. Nichols was a correspondent for New York newspapers in Cuba, Puerto Rico, Haiti, and Jamaica during the Spanish-American War, and a correspondent of the *Christian Herald* in China in 1901. In 1901, he visited the western part of China in connection with famine relief, and in 1903, he attempted to make a journey to Lhasa disguised as a Chinese, but was forced to turn back when within the borders of Tibet. He tried again to enter Tibet from Burma. He rode from Peking to Sian in Shensi Province, and then by canoe on the Han River to Hankow. He wrote *Through Hidden Shensi* (New York, 1902). Died December 19, 1904, at Gyangtse. *References: NYT*, February 3, 1905; and *WWWA.*

NIXON DOCTRINE Announced in 1969 by President Richard M. Nixon. While maintaining the protection of Southeast Asia and Japan by means of the "nuclear umbrella," the United States insisted that Asian soldiers, rather than American troops, would have to carry the burden of land warfare in the future. *References*: Cecil V. Crabb, Jr., *The Doctrines of American Foreign Policy: Their Meaning, Role, and Future* (Baton Rouge, La., 1982), pp. 278–324; *DADH; DVW*; and Edward A. Olsen, "The Nixon Doctrine in East Asian Perspective," *Asian Forum* 5 (1973): 17–28.

NOBLE, HAROLD JOYCE (1903–1953). Historian and government official, son of William Arthur Noble,* born January 10, 1903, in P'yongyang, Korea. Noble graduated from Ohio Wesleyan and Ohio State universities and the University of California at Berkeley. He taught at Ehwa College in Seoul from 1926 to 1928. He was assistant professor of Far Eastern History at the University of Oregon from 1931 to 1934, associate professor there from 1934 to 1945, and professor after 1945. He was a combat intelligence and Japanese language officer with the U.S. Marine Corps during World War II, a correspondent for the *Saturday Evening Post* in 1946–1947, chief of the Publications Branch of the Civil Intelligence section of the General Headquarters of the Far East Command in 1947–1948, and chief of the political liaison office in the Headquarters of the U.S. Army Forces in Korea and political advisor to Lieutenant General John R. Hodge* in 1948–1949. He was first secretary at the U.S. embassy in Korea from 1949 to 1951, and the embassy's chief liaison officer to Korean President Syngman Rhee. He served with the Committee for a Free Asia from 1951 to 1953. Died December 22, 1953, on a plane en route from Tokyo to Honolulu. His memoir, *Embassy at War*, edited and with an introduction by Frank Baldwin

(Seattle, Wash., 1975) was published posthumously. *References*: Frank Baldwin, "Introduction," in *Embassy at War*, ed. Frank Baldwin (Seattle, Wash., 1975); and *NYT*, December 24, 1953.

NOBLE, WILLIAM ALEXANDER (MAY) (1895–1978). Medical missionary, born November 27, 1895, in Fraserburgh, Scotland; came to the United States in 1901; and grew up in Worcester, Massachusetts, and Sorrento and Eustis, Florida. Noble graduated from the Ohio Institute of Pharmacy (Columbus) and the Atlanta School of Medicine (later the medical department of Emory University). He served in the U.S. Army Medical Corps during World War I. He was a medical missionary under the Salvation Army in India from 1920 until his retirement in 1965, serving in Moradabad, Uttar Pradesh, in 1920–1921, and in Bagercoil, Travancore, after 1921. He established satellite dispensaries and branch hospitals, and oversaw the establishment of Cochin State Leper Hospital in Koratty, Travancore Kochin. He returned to the United States in 1965, and served as a medical consultant to the American National Red Cross and a medical officer to the Salvation Army school for officers' training in Atlanta. Died August 4, 1978, in Atlanta. *Reference*: Lillian E. Hansen, *The Double Yoke, the Story of William Alexander Noble, M.D., Fellow of the American College of Surgeons, Fellow of the International College of Surgeons, Doctor of Humanities, Medical Missionary Extraordinary in India, His Adopted Land* (New York, 1968).

NOBLE, WILLIAM ARTHUR (1866–1945). Missionary, born September 13, 1866, in Springdale, Pennsylvania. Noble attended the Wyoming Seminary and graduated from Drew Theological Seminary. He was a missionary under the Board of Foreign Missions of the Methodist Episcopal Church in Korea from 1892 until 1933. He taught in Paichai College in Seoul from 1892 to 1895, and served in the P'yongyang from 1895 to 1910 and in Seoul from 1910 until his retirement in 1933. He wrote a novel, *Ewa, A Tale of Korea* (New York, 1906). He returned to the United States in 1934. Died January 6, 1945, in Stockton, California. *Reference: EWM*.

NOLTING, FREDERICK E(RNEST) (1911–1989). Diplomat, born August 24, 1911, in Richmond, Virginia. Nolting graduated from the University of Virginia and Harvard University. He served in the U.S. Navy during World War II. He entered the foreign service in 1945. He was a member of the North Atlantic Treaty Organization (NATO) delegation from 1955 to 1957, and an alternate permanent representative to NATO from 1957 to 1961. He was U.S. ambassador to South Vietnam from 1961 to 1963. He developed a close and supportive relationship with President Ngo Dinh Diem of South Vietnam, and worked to get him American military and economic support. He was replaced because of disagreements with President John F. Kennedy. He resigned from the State Department in 1963, and was a member of Morgan Guaranty Trust Company from 1963 to 1970, and a member of the faculty and director of the

White Burkett Miller Center for Public Affairs in the University of Virginia after 1970. He wrote *From Trust to Tragedy: The Political Memoirs of Frederick Nolting, Kennedy's Ambassador to Diem's Vietnam* (New York, 1988). Died December 14, 1989, in Charlottesville, Virginia. *References: DADH; DVW; NYT*, December 16, 1989; *PolProf: Kennedy*; and *WWA*.

NORBECK, EDWARD (1915–   ). Anthropologist, born March 18, 1915, in Prince Albert, Saskatchewan, Canada. Norbeck graduated from the University of Michigan. He served in the U.S. Army military intelligence during World War II. He was an instructor and assistant professor of anthropology at the University of Utah (Salt Lake City) from 1952 to 1954, assistant professor of anthropology at the University of California at Berkeley from 1954 to 1960, associate professor of anthropology at Rice University (Houston, Tex.) from 1960 to 1962, and professor there after 1962. He carried out research in Japan in 1950–1951, 1958–1959, 1964–1965, 1966, and 1974; and in Hawaii in 1956; and wrote *Takashima: A Fishing Community of Japan* (Salt Lake City, 1954); *Changing Japan* (New York, 1965); *Religion and Society in Modern Japan: Continuity and Change* (Houston, 1970); *The Study of Japan in the Behavioral Sciences* (Houston, Tex., 1970); and *Country to City: The Urbanization of a Japanese Hamlet* (Salt Lake City, 1978). He wrote an account of his experiences in "Changing Japan: Field Research," in *Being an Anthropologist: Fieldwork in Eleven Cultures*, ed. George D. Spindler (New York, 1970). *References: AMWS; CA*; and *WWA*.

NORDLUND, VICTOR LEONARD (1869–1937). Missionary, born January 19, 1869, in Gronön, Axmar, Helsingland, Sweden, and came to the United States in 1889. Nordlund attended the Bible Institute in Chicago. He was a missionary under the Scandinavian Alliance Mission and later the Evangelical Mission Covenant Church of America from 1891 to 1926, serving in Taiyuan in 1891–1892, in Kuwuh from 1892 to 1894, in Fanchang from 1912 until 1920, in Nanchang from 1920 to 1922, and in Icheng from 1922 to 1926. He returned to the United States in 1926, and was a missionary in Alaska from 1927 to 1929. Died April 10, 1937, in Chicago. *Reference*: Esther Nordlund, comp., *The Life and Work of Victor Leonard Nordlund 1869–1937: Thirty-five Years in China under the Scandinavian Alliance Mission and the Evangelical Mission Covenant Church of America* (San Fernando, La Union, Philippines, 1940).

NORTH CHINA UNION COLLEGE. *See* YENCHING UNIVERSITY

NORTH JAPAN COLLEGE. *See* TOHOKU GAKUIN UNIVERSITY

NORTH PACIFIC SURVEYING EXPEDITION (1853–1856). A scientific and hydrographic expedition to Japan, the China Sea, and the North Pacific, commanded by Lieutenant Cadwalader Ringgold,* with Lieutenant John Rodgers* as second-in-command. *References*: Allan B. Cole, "The Ringgold-Rodgers-Brooke Expedition to Japan and the North Pacific, 1853–59," *PHR* 16 (1947): 152–62; Allan B. Cole, ed., *Yankee Surveyers in the Shogun's Seas: Records of the U.S. Surveying Expedition to the North Pacific Ocean, 1853–1856* (Princeton, N.J., 1947); John D. Kazar, "The United States Navy and Scientific Exploration, 1837–1860," Ph.D. diss., University of Massachusetts, 1973; Vincent Ponko, Jr., *Ships, Seas, and Scientists: U. S. Naval Exploration and Discovery in the Nineteenth Century* (Annapolis, Md., 1974).

NOTT, SAMUEL (1788–1869). Missionary, born September 11, 1788, in Franklin, Connecticut. Nott graduated from Union College and Andover Theological Seminary, and was ordained in 1812. He was a missionary under the American Board of Commissioners for Foreign Missions (ABCFM) in India from 1812 to 1816. He returned to the United States because of ill health. He was a teacher in New York City from 1816 to 1823, and a pastor in Galway, New York, from 1823 to 1829, and Wareham, Massachusetts, from 1829 to 1849. He established a private academy in Wareham in 1849. Died June 1, 1869, in Hartford, Connecticut. *References: ACAB*; and *AndoverTS*.

NURGE, ETHEL (1920–   ). Anthropologist, born August 21, 1920, in Brooklyn, New York. Nurge graduated from the universities of New Mexico and Chicago and Cornell University. She served in the U.S. Navy Waves during World War II. She carried out fieldwork in the Philippines in 1955–1956 and wrote *Life in a Leyte Village* (Seattle, 1965). She was professor of anthropology at South Dakota University (Brookings) from 1963 to 1965, research associate at the Frobenius Institute (Frankfurt, Germany) in 1965–1966, associate professor at McMaster University (Hamilton, Ont.) from 1966 to 1968, and associate professor in the Department of Community Health of the University of Kansas Medical Center (Kansas City) after 1968. *References: AMWS*; and *CA*.

NYE, GIDEON, JR. (1808–1888). Merchant, born in Achushnet, Massachusetts. Nye came to China in 1833 and was engaged as a tea trader in Canton. He established the trading firm of Nye, Parkins and Company in 1843, which became Nye Brothers and Company in 1853. The firm collapsed in 1856. He then moved to Macao and did commission work. He proposed in 1857 that the United States seize and annex the island of Formosa. He was deputy consul and later vice-consul in Macao from 1858 until 1863. He wrote *The Morning of My Life in China* (Canton, 1873); and *Peking the Goal,—the Sole Hope of Peace. Comprising an Inquiry into the Origin of the Pretension of Universal Supremacy by China and into the Cause of the First War* (Canton, 1873). Died in Canton. *References*: Harold D. Langley, "Gideon Nye and the Formosa Annexation Scheme," *PHR* 34 (1965): 397–420; and *NYT*, March 4, 1888.

O

OBERLIN-IN-CHINA. Founded as Oberlin Shansi Mission Association in 1907, it supported a middle school and a college at Taiku, Shansi Province from 1907 to 1937, and at Chengtu, Szechuan Province, from 1947 to 1951. It was later involved with educational institutions in India and Taiwan. *References*: Oberlin-in-China Records, Oberlin College Library, Oberlin, Ohio; Mary T. Campfield, "Oberlin-in-China, 1881–1951," Ph.D. diss., University of Virginia, 1974; and Ellsworth C. Carlson, *Oberlin in Asia: The First Hundred Years, 1882–1982* (Oberlin, Ohio, 1982).

O'BRIEN, FREDERICK (1869–1932). Journalist, born June 16, 1869, in Baltimore. O'Brien attended Loyola College and studied law. He was a sailor, hobo, and casual worker from 1887 to 1894. After 1894, he worked for various newspapers in Marion, Ohio; New York City; San Francisco; and Honolulu. He was editor and publisher of the Manila *Cablenews* from 1902 to 1909, and was a correspondent of the *New York Herald* in the Philippines from 1903 to 1909. He was manager of the Riverside (Calif.) *Enterprise* and the Oxnard *Courier* from 1910 to 1913. He then disappeared among the islands of the South Pacific until World War I. He was later connected with the California Railroad Commission and the U. S. Food Administration, and was editor of the *Manila Times* in 1918–1919. Died January 9, 1932, in Sausalito, California. *References: DAB; NYT*, January 10, 1932; *OAB*; and *WWWA*.

O'BRIEN, THOMAS JAMES (1842–1933). Lawyer and diplomat, born July 30, 1842, in Jackson, Michigan. O'Brien graduated from the University of Michigan, and was admitted to the bar in 1865. He practiced law in Marshall, Michigan, from 1865 to 1871 and at Grand Rapids after 1871, and was assistant and general counsel of the Grand Rapids and Indiana Railway from 1871 to 1905. He was minister to Denmark from 1905 to 1907 and ambassador to Japan from 1907 to 1911. He was involved in negotiating the "gentlemen's agreement" of 1907 which ended most Japanese immigration to the United States, and he also negotiated a new commercial treaty. He was ambassador to Italy from 1911 to 1913. He returned to the United States in 1917 and continued his law practice in Grand Rapids. Died May 19, 1933, in Grand Rapids, Michigan. *References*: Thomas James O'Brien Papers, Michigan Historical Collection, University of Michigan Library, Ann Arbor; *DAB S1; DADH; NCAB* 25:420; *NYT*, May 20, 1933; and *WWWA*.

OCCUPATION OF JAPAN. Japan was occupied by the United States from 1945 until 1952. The occupation was administered by the General Headquarters of the Supreme Commander for the Allied Powers (SCAP).* The main objectives of the occupation were to eliminate Japan's militaristic order and to demilitarize the country, and to democratize its political system, including constitutional reform, encouragement of political parties, establishment of human rights, granting of political and legal rights to women, land reform, and reform of governmental machinery. In 1948, the policy shifted from political and social reforms to economic stability and rehabilitation. The occupation was terminated in 1952 after the implementation of the peace treaty with Japan. *References*: Theodore Cohen, *Remaking Japan: The American Occupation as New Deal*, ed. Herbert Passin (New York, 1987); *EAH*; Kazuo Kawai, *Japan's American Interlude* (Chicago, 1960); John C. Perry, *Beneath the Eagle's Wings: Americans in Occupied Japan* (New York, 1980); Michael Schaller, *The American Occupation of Japan: The Origins of the Cold War in Asia* (New York, 1985); Howard B. Schonberger, *Aftermath of War: Americans and the Remaking of Japan, 1945– 1952* (Kent, Ohio, 1989); and Robert E. Ward and Sakamoto Yoshikazu, eds., *Democratizing Japan: The Allied Occupation* (Honolulu, 1987).

OCCUPATION OF KOREA. *See* U.S. ARMY MILITARY GOVERNMENT IN KOREA (USAMGIK)

OCHTERLONY, SIR DAVID (1758–1825). Army officer, born February 12, 1758, in Boston. Ochterlony graduated from Dummer Academy (N.H.). A loyalist, he entered the Bengal Army of the East India Company as a cadet in 1776 and came to India in 1777. He was promoted to lieutenant in 1778, and then rose to major general. He served in the campaign against the Jats in 1803, and was instrumental in conquering Nepal in 1814–1815 and in the campaign against the Marathas in 1817–1818. He was deputy adjutant general at the battle of Delhi. He was representative of the East India Company at the court in Delhi and later in Rajputana. He was dismissed by the governor-general of India, and was knighted in 1815. Died July 15, 1825, in Meerut, India. *References: ACAB*; H. Bullock, "Sir David Ochterlony," *American Mercury* 76 (May 1953): 107– 10; and *EAH*.

O'DANIEL, JOHN W(ILSON) ("IRON MIKE") (1894–1975). Army officer, born February 15, 1894, in Newark, Delaware. O'Daniel graduated from the University of Delaware. He was commissioned a second lieutenant in the U.S. Army in 1917. He served in France during World War I and later in various infantry units. He was a military attaché in Moscow from 1948 to 1950, commander of the I Corps in Korea in 1951–1952, and commander of the U.S. Forces, Pacific, in Hawaii from 1952 to 1954. He was chief of the Military Assistance Advisory Group (MAAG) for Indochina from 1953 until 1956. He wrote *The Nation That Refused to Starve: The Challenge of the New Vietnam* (New York, 1960), and *Vietnam Today: The Challenge of a Divided Nation* (New York, 1966). He retired with the rank of lieutenant general in 1956. Died March 28, 1975, in San Diego, California. *References: DVW; NCAB* 62:57; *NYT*, March 29, 1975; and *WWWA*.

OHLINGER, FRANKLIN (1845–1919). Missionary, born November 29, 1845, in Mud Creek, near Fremont, Ohio. Ohlinger attended the German-Wallace College (Berea). He was a missionary under the Board of Foreign Missions of the Methodist Episcopal Church in Foochow, China, from 1870 until 1887, and in Korea from 1887 until 1893. He founded the first printing press in Korea in 1890, which was known as the Trilingual Press. He was an independent missionary in China after 1895, and later founded an orphanage for the blind in Antau. He was dean of the theological school in Foochow from 1901 to 1905, and served in Shanghai from 1905 to 1908. After 1909, he was in the service of the Chinese government as a teacher of language in the newly founded provincial university. He returned to the United States in 1911. Died January 6, 1919. *Reference*: Ohlinger Family Collection, Rutherford B. Hayes Presidential Center Library, Fremont, Ohio.

OLCOTT, HENRY STEEL (1832–1907). Theosophist, born August 2, 1832, in Orange, New Jersey. Olcott attended the University of the City of New York. He engaged in farming in northern Ohio from 1848 to 1853. He returned to New York in 1853 and started the Westchester Farm School in Mount Vernon, New York. He was associate agricultural editor of the *New York Tribune* from 1858 to 1860. He served in the Union Army during the Civil War. He then studied law, was admitted to the bar, and practiced law in New York City. In 1874 he met Helena Petrovna Hahn Blavatsky; he became involved in the study of occultism and was the first president of the Theosophical Society after 1875. He went with Madame Blavatsky to India in 1878. They settled first in Bombay and later in Adyar, a suburb of Madras. He made a trip to Ceylon in 1881. He developed the Theosophical Society and edited *The Theosophist* until his death. He wrote *Old Diary Leaves: The True Story of the Theosophical Society* (New York, 1895, 1910). He also opened in India four free schools for pariahs. Died February 17, 1907, in Adyar, India. *References: DAB*; Ananda Gutruge, *Return to Righteousness* (Colombo, 1965); Howard Murphet, *Hammer on the Mountain:*

Life of Henry Steel Olcott (1832–1907) (Wheaton, Ill., 1972); *NCAB* 8:464; *NYT*, February 18, 1907; and *WWWA*.

OLDHAM, WILLIAM F(ITZJAMES) (1854–1937). Missionary, born December 15, 1854, in Bangalore, India. Oldham was educated at Madras Christian College and served as a government engineer and surveyor. He came to the United States, studied at Allegheny College (Meadville, Pa.), graduated from Boston University, and was ordained in 1885. He was a missionary under the Board of Foreign Missions of the Methodist Episcopal Church in Singapore from 1885 to 1890, organizing and superintending the mission there. He returned to the United States, was a pastor in Pittsburg, a professor of missions and comparative religions at Ohio Wesleyan University from 1895 to 1900, and assistant corresponding secretary of the Missionary Society of the Methodist Episcopal Church in Chicago from 1900 to 1904. He was elected missionary bishop of the Methodist Episcopal Church in Southern Asia in 1904, and served in Singapore from 1904 to 1912. He was corresponding secretary of the Board of Foreign Missions in New York City from 1912 to 1916, and general superintendent of the South American mission from 1916 until his retirement in 1928. He wrote *Malaysia—Nature's Wonderland* (New York, 1907); *India, Malaya, and the Philippines. A Practical Study in Missions* (New York, 1914); and a biography of James Mills Thoburn.* Died March 27, 1937, in Glendale, California. *References: CDCWM; DAB S2; EWM*; Theodore R. Doraisamy, *Oldham: Called of God* (Singapore, 1979); *NCAB* 14:336; *NYT*, March 30, 1937; "Rescuing the Oldham Legend," *Methodist History* 18 (October 1979): 61–65; and *WWWA*.

OLIVER, ROBERT T(ARBELL) (1909–   ). Educator, born July 7, 1909, in Sweet Home, Oregon. Oliver graduated from Pacific University and the universities of Oregon and Wisconsin. He was dean of Clark Junior College (Vancouver, Wash.) from 1933 to 1935, a member of the faculty of Bucknell University (Lewisburg, Pa.) from 1937 to 1942, administrative head of the food conservation program of the War Foods Administration in 1943–1944, associate professor and head of the division of rhetoric and public address at Syracuse University from 1944 to 1947, professor and head of the department of speech at Pennsylvania State University (University Park) from 1949 to 1965, and research professor of international speech there after 1965. He served as an advisor to President Syngman Rhee and the Republic of South Korea from 1947 to 1960, and made thirteen trips to East Asia. He was advisor to the Korean delegation to the United Nations from 1945 to 1960, and manager of the Korean Research and Information Office in Washington, D.C., from 1947 to 1960. He wrote *Korea: Forgotten Nation* (Washington, D.C., 1944); *Why War Came in Korea* (New York, 1950); *The Truth behind Korea* (London, 1951); *Verdict in Korea* (State College, Pa., 1952); *Syngman Rhee: The Man Behind the Myth* (New York, 1955); *Leadership in Twentieth Century Asia: The Rhetoric, Principles and Practice of the Leaders of China, Korea, and India from Sun Yat-*

sen to Jawaharlal Nehru (State College, Pa., 1966); *Syngman Rhee and American Involvement in Korea, 1942–1960: A Personal Narrative* (Seoul, 1978); and *Leadership in Asia: Persuasive Communication in the Making of Nations, 1850–1950* (Newark, Del., 1989). He edited *Korean Survey* from 1951 to 1960. *References: CA*; and *WWA*.

OLSEN, VIGGO B(RANDT) (1926–   ). Medical missionary, born August 24, 1926, in Omaha, Nebraska. Olsen attended Tulane University, graduated from the University of Nebraska and its college of medicine, and studied at the Liverpool School of Tropical Medicine. He was a medical missionary under the Association of Baptists for World Evangelism, Inc., in East Pakistan (later in Bangladesh) after 1962. He served in Chittagong and founded the Memorial Christian Hospital there. He was also the first acting director of Medical Assistance Programs, Inc. (MAP). He wrote, with Jeanette Lockerbie, *A Muslim Bengali-English Dictionary* (Chittagong, 1967); *Daktar/Diplomat in Bangladesh* (Chicago, 1975); and *Daktar II* (Chicago, 1990).

OLSEN, WALTER S(EVERIN) (1914–1972). Missionary, born May 19, 1914, in Chicago. Olsen graduated from Moody Bible Institute (Chicago). He was a missionary under the Scandinavian Alliance Mission (later the Evangelical Alliance Mission, or TEAM) in the Ozark Mountains from 1936 to 1939; in Amalner, East Khandesh, India, from 1939 to 1952; and in Ootacamund, South India, from 1952 to 1954. He was TEAM's representative-at-large in the Ozarks from 1954 until 1959. Died in Tulsa, Oklahoma. *Reference*: Nolan F. Balman, *God's Viking: The Biography of Walter S. Olsen* (Wheaton, Ill., 1973).

OLYPHANT, DAVID WASHINGTON CINCINNATUS (1789–1851). Merchant, born March 7, 1789, in Newport, Rhode Island. He went to New York in 1806 and was employed by King and Talbot, a firm engaged in trade with China. He moved to Baltimore from 1812 to 1817, but was back in New York from 1817 to 1820. He was an agent of Thomas H. Smith in Canton from 1820 to 1823 and again in 1826–1827. He then formed the firm of Olyphant and Company in Canton. He returned to China from 1834 to 1837, and again in 1850–1851. He provided free passage to China for American missionaries and free quarters in Canton for the mission, and underwrote the publication of the *Chinese Repository*. Died June 10, 1851, in Cairo, Egypt, on his way to the United States. *Reference: DAB*.

OLYPHANT, ROBERT MORRISON (1824–1918). Merchant, son of David W. C. Olyphant,* born September 9, 1824, in New York City. Olyphant graduated from Columbia University. He entered his father's firm in 1842, and went to China in 1844–1845. He reorganized his father's firm in Canton from 1858 to 1862, and then directed the business from New York until his retirement from the China trade in 1873. He was later involved in the affairs of the Delaware and Hudson Canal Company (later Delaware and Hudson Company), and served as its president from 1884 until 1903. Died May 3, 1918, in New York City. *References: DAB*; and *NYT*, May 4, 1918.

OLYPHANT AND COMPANY. A company formed in Canton, China, by David W. C. Olyphant* and C. N. Talbot, and involved in the China trade. It was reorganized by Robert Morrison Olyphant* in 1858. It was engaged in a general importing, shipping, commission, and mercantile business with East Asia. It closed its business in 1878.

OPEN DOOR POLICY. The principle of the Open Door originated in the concept of equality of commercial opportunity for nations trading with China. The United States first espoused this principle in 1899. It also championed the preservation of China's political and territorial integrity. It had become the publicly established policy of the United States toward China by the 1920s. *References: Anderson*, ch. 8; Charles S. Campbell, Jr., *Special Business Interests and the Open Door Policy* (New Haven, Conn., 1951); Cecil V. Crabb, Jr., *The Doctrines of American Foreign Policy: Their Meaning, Role, and Future* (Baton Rouge, La., 1982), pp. 56–106; *DADH*; Ian J. Dickerton, "John Hay's Open Door Policy: A Re-Examination," *Australian Journal of Politics and History* 23 (1977): 54–66; Raymond A. Esthus, "The Changing Concept of the Open Door," *Mississippi Valley Historical Review* 46 (1959): 435–54; Raymond A. Esthus, "The Open Door and the Integrity of China, 1899–1922—Hazy Principles for Changing Policy," in *Aspects of Sino-American Relations since 1784*, ed. Thomas E. Etzold (New York, 1984), pp. 48–74; Jerry Israel, " 'For God, for China, and for Yale'—The Open Door in Action," *American Historical Review* 75 (1970): 796–807; *KEJ*; John A. Moore, Jr., "From Reaction to Multicultural Agreement: The Expansion of America's Open Door Policy in China, 1899–1922," *Prologue* 15 (1983): 23–36; and Charles Vevier, "The Open Door: An Idea in Action," *PHR* 24 (1955): 49–62.

OPENING OF JAPAN. *See* PERRY EXPEDITION

OPPLER, ALFRED C. (1893–1982). Jurist and government official, born in Alsace-Lorraine, Germany. Oppler studied law in the universities of Munich, Freiburg, Berlin, and Strassburg. He served in the German Army during World War I, and was associate justice of the Prussian Supreme Administrative Court and vice president of the Supreme Disciplinary Court in Berlin from 1918 until 1933. He came to the United States in 1939, was a researcher and instructor at Harvard University until 1944, and worked with the Foreign Economic Administration in Washington, D.C., in 1944–1945, and with the War Department in 1945–1946. He served in the General Headquarters of the Supreme Commander for the Allied Powers (SCAP) in Tokyo after 1946 as chief of the courts and the law division in the government section, and later headed the legislative and justice division of the legal section. He was the principal architect of the legal and judicial reforms during the occupation of Japan. After the occupation, he was chief of the political and legal unit of the G–5 (later J–5) section of the Far East Command until 1957, and was an international relations officer in the headquarters of the United States Forces, Japan, from 1957 until his retirement in 1959. He wrote an account of his activities, *Legal Reform in Occupied Japan: A Participant Looks Back* (Princeton, N.J., 1976). Died April 24, 1982, in Hightstown, New Jersey. *References: KEJ*; and *NYT*, April 27, 1982.

ORIENTAL BOAT MISSION. Founded in 1909 as the South China Boat Mission, popularly known as the Gospel Navy, it conducted a program of mission work and education in a boat colony near Canton, China, and later among the boat people of the Pearl River. After the Communist victory in Mainland China, it shifted operations to boat colonies and fishing communities in Japan, Hong Kong, and Thailand. It was merged into International Missions, Inc., in 1966. *Reference: EMCM.*

ORIENTAL CONSOLIDATED MINING COMPANY. Organized in Korea in 1900, it became the most lucrative producer of gold in Asia. The Americans sold out their interest to the Japanese in 1939. *Reference*: Spencer J. Palmer, "American Gold Mining in Korea's Unsan District," *PHR* 31 (1962): 379–91.

ORIENTAL EDUCATIONAL COMMISSION (1908–1909). Funded by John D. Rockefeller, Sr., and led by Ernest DeWitt Burton (1856–1925) of the University of Chicago, it surveyed the educational scene in China in 1909. *References*: Ernest D. Burton Papers, University of Chicago Library, Chicago; and David L. Lindberg, "The Oriental Educational Commission's Recommendations for Mission Strategy in Higher Education," Ph.D. diss., University of Chicago, 1972.

ORIENTAL MISSIONARY SOCIETY. Founded in 1901, it began missionary work in Japan in 1901, in Korea in 1907, in China in 1925, in India in 1940, in Taiwan in 1950, and in Hong Kong in 1954. *References*: Oriental Missionary Society (OMS) International Collection, Asbury Theological Seminary Library, Wilmore, Ky.; *EMCM*; Edward Erny and Esther Erny, *No Guarantee but God, the Story of the Oriental Missionary Society* (Greenwood, Ind., 1969); and John J. Merwin, "The Oriental Missionary Society Holiness Church in Japan, 1901–1983," D. Miss. thesis, Fuller Theological Seminary, 1983.

OSBORN, LOIS STEWART (1875–1935). Educator, born in Kewanee, Illinois. Osborn graduated from Oregon State College and Columbia University. She was a teacher and principal in schools in Baker, Oregon, and Juneau, Alaska. She came to the Philippines in 1905 and taught at Nueva Ecija and Pampanga. She was head of the English department of the Philippine Normal School from

1914 to 1920, assistant professor of education at the University of the Philippines from 1920 until 1926, and professor of English and library science there from 1926 until her retirement in 1935. She organized the Children's Library in Manila in 1923. Died August 10, 1935. *Reference: DPB* 3.

OSGOOD, CORNELIUS (1905–1985). Anthropologist, born March 20, 1905, in Winchester, Massachusetts. Osgood graduated from the University of Chicago. He was an ethnologist with the National Museum of Canada in Ottawa in 1928–1929, assistant curator of anthropology at the Peabody Museum of Natural History at Yale University from 1930 to 1934, and curator from 1934 to 1973. He was an instructor in anthropology at Yale University from 1930 to 1934, assistant professor there from 1934 to 1940, associate professor from 1940 to 1944, and professor from 1944 until 1973. He carried out fieldwork in China, Korea, and Hong Kong, and wrote *The Koreans and Their Culture* (New York, 1951); *Blue-and-White Chinese Procelain: A Study of Form* (New York, 1956); *Village Life in Old China: A Community Study of Kao Yao, Yunan* (New York, 1963); and *The Chinese: A Study of a Hong Kong Community* (Tucson, Ariz., 1975). Died January 4, 1985, in New Haven, Connecticut. *References: AMWS; Anthropology Newsletter* 26 (April 1985): 3–4; William E. Biernatzki, "Cornelius Osgood, an Anthropological Appreciation," *Journal of Social Sciences and Humanities* no. 62 (December 1985): 37–42; *CA; NYT*, January 7, 1985; and *WWA*.

OSGOOD, ELLIOTT I(RVING) (1871–1940). Medical missionary, born March 11, 1871, in Allgena, Michigan. Osgood graduated from Hiram College and Cleveland Homeopathic College. He was a missionary under the United Christian Missionary Society (UCMS) in China from 1898 to 1927. He served in Chuchow, where he opened a dispensary and later built a hospital. He wrote *Breaking Down Chinese Walls: From a Doctor's Viewpoint* (New York, 1908); *China's Crossroads* (Cincinnati, 1922); and *Shi, the Story-teller* (Cincinnati, 1926). He was a field representative of the UCMS after 1927, and a pastor in Chardon, Ohio, until his retirement in 1936. Died April 13, 1940, in Hiram, Ohio. *References*: Elliott I. Osgood Papers, Disciples of Christ Historical Society, Nashville, Tenn.; *They Went to China: Biographies of Missionaries of the Disciples of Christ* (Indianapolis, 1948).

O'SHEA, JOHN A. (1887–1969). Missionary, born in Deep River, Connecticut. O'Shea graduated from Niagara University, studied in the Novitiate of the Vincentian Fathers of the Eastern Province in Germantown, Pennsylvania, and was ordained in 1914. He led the first nine American Vincentian missionaries to Kanchow, Kiangsi Province, China, in 1921. He was consecrated coadjutor bishop of the vicariate of Kanchow in 1928, and was named vicar apostolic in 1931 (the vicariate became a diocese in 1947). He took refuge in the mountains of western China during the Japanese invasion. He was held captive by the

Chinese Communists and expelled from China in 1952. Died October 6, 1969, in Washington, D.C. *Reference: NYT*, October 8, 1969.

OSTRAND, JAMES ADOLPH (1871–1937). Lawyer and judge, born January 20, 1871, in Tromsø, Norway, and immigrated to the United States in 1891. Grew up in Bock, Minnesota. Ostrand graduated from the University of Minnesota. He served in the Spanish-American War, joined the U.S. Quartermaster Corps in 1900, and served in the Philippines from 1900 to 1903. He practiced law in Manila, Lingayen, and Pangasinan from 1903 to 1909, and was associate judge of the court of land registration from 1909 to 1911, and chief judge from 1911 to 1914. He was judge of the fourth branch of the Court of First Instance in Manila from 1914 to 1920. He organized the land court in the Dominican Republic, was chief justice of the Santo Domingo Appelate Land Court in 1920–1921, and was associate justice of the supreme court of the Philippines from 1921 to 1933. Died April 15, 1937, in Livermore, California. *References: NCAB* 29:245; *NYT*, April 17, 1937; *Sevilla*; and *WWWA*.

OTIS, ELWELL S(TEPHEN) (1838–1909). Army officer, born March 25, 1838, in Frederick, Maryland. Otis graduated from the University of Rochester and Harvard Law School. He practiced law in New York City. He served in the Union Army during the Civil War. He remained in the regular army and served in the Northwest and in various Indian campaigns. He established the Fort Leavenworth army school in 1881, and was its commander until 1885. He served in the Spanish-American War, came to the Philippines in 1898, and was in command of the Eighth Army Corps and then commander of the Department of the Pacific and military governor of the Philippines until 1900. He commanded the Department of the Lakes until his retirement in 1902 with the rank of major general. Died October 21, 1909, in Rochester, New York. *References*: Elwell S. Otis Papers, University of Rochester Library, Rochester, N.Y.; *DAB; EP* 4:351–52; *NCAB* 33:188; *NYT*, October 23, 1909; and *WWWA*.

O'TOOLE, GEORGE BARRY (1886–1944). Educator, born December 11, 1886, in Toledo, Ohio. O'Toole graduated from St. John's University (Toledo) and Urban University (Rome), and was ordained in 1911. He was secretary to the bishop of Toledo from 1912 to 1915; pastor in Bowling Green, Ohio, from 1915 to 1917; and professor of philosophy at St. Vincent Seminary (Latrobe, Pa.) in 1917–1918. He served as a chaplain during World War I, and was again professor of philosophy and dogmatic theology at St. Vincent Seminary and professor of animal biology at Seton Hall College (Greenburg, Pa.) in 1919–1920 and 1923–1924. He visited China in 1920–1921 to help establish the Catholic University of Peking, and served as its rector from 1925 to 1933. He was professor of philosophy at Duquesne University (Pittsburgh) from 1934 to 1937, and at Catholic University from 1937 until his death. He was editor of the *China Monthly* from 1939 to 1944. Died March 26, 1944, in Washington, D.C. *References: CE; DACB; NYT*, March 27, 1944; and *OAB*.

P

PACIFIC MAIL STEAMSHIP COMPANY. Chartered in 1848, it inaugurated the first regular and the only lasting steamship service across the Pacific Ocean to East Asia in 1867, opening a line of monthly steamers from San Francisco to Yokohama and Hong Kong. It also established branch service from Yokohama to Kobe, Nagasaki, and Shanghai. It began making regular calls to Manila in 1914, and to Singapore, Calcutta, and Colombo in 1917, but the lines to Manila and India were dropped in 1922, and the company withdrew from the transpacific trade in 1925. *References*: Pacific Mail Steamship Company Records, Huntington Library, San Marino, Calif.; *DADH*; and John H. Kemble, "A Hundred Years of the Pacific Mail," *AN* 10 (1950): 123–43.

PACK, WILLIAM F. (1860?–1944). Army officer, from Michigan. Pack was commissioned a second lieutenant in the U.S. Army in 1898, and served in the Spanish-American War in Cuba. He then served in the Philippine-American War. He was governor of the Benguet Province in the Philippines from 1901 to 1909, and of the Mountain Province from 1909 to 1913. He was credited with taming the head-hunting Igorots. He resigned in 1913 because of ill health and returned to the United States. He settled in Miami Beach, Florida, in 1934. Died September 3, 1944, in Miami Beach. *References: The Miami Herald*, September 4, 1944; and *NYT*, September 4, 1944.

PACKARD, HARRY (1914–   ). Art collector, born September 3, 1914, in Salt Lake City, and grew up in Seattle and California. Packard studied at the University of California. He served in the U.S. Navy during World War II as a Japanese language officer. He was in charge of the camp for Japanese repatriates in Nagasaki, and began collecting Japanese art. He attended Waseda University (Tokyo), worked for a news agency, and, after 1960, was employed by a Tokyo engineering consulting firm. He sold his extensive collection of Japanese art to the Metropolitan Museum of Art in 1975. *References*: Richard Halloran, "Packard-san, the Persistent Collector," *NYT*, September 4, 1975; and J. L.

Hess and P. Pringle, "Inscrutable Met, the Mysterious East, and the Big Spender," *New York* 12 (February 19, 1979): 40–44.

PADDOCK, PAUL E(ZEKIEL), JR. (1907–1975). Diplomat, born October 31, 1907, in Des Moines, Iowa. Paddock attended the University of Minnesota, and graduated from Princeton University. He entered the foreign service in 1937; was vice consul in Mexico City, Batavia, Dutch East Indies, Melbourne, Australia, and Auckland, New Zealand, Casablanca, Morocco, and Moscow; and was second secretary in the Soviet Union and Afghanistan. He was vice-consul and then consul in Dairen, China, from 1947 to 1950. His account of his experiences there, *China Diary: Critical Diplomacy in Dairen* (Ames, Iowa, 1977) was published posthumously. He served in Korea in 1951–1952, in Malta in 1953–1954, in Laos in 1954–1955, and in the Philippines in 1955–1956. He retired in 1956. Died August 29, 1975, in Palm Beach, Florida. *References: CA*; and *NYT*, August 30, 1975.

PAGE, HERBERT C(LAIBORNE) (1877–1949). Army officer, born September 17, 1877, in Petersburg, Virginia. Page attended Roanoke College (Va.). He was employed in clerical positions in Wall Street houses from 1896 to 1904. He came to the Philippines in 1904, and served with the U.S. Army from 1904 to 1907. He was commissioned a third lieutenant in the Philippine Constabulary in 1907, and retired with the rank of major about 1937. He was deputy provincial governor of various stations in Sulu; acting deputy governor in Lanao; deputy provincial governor in Cotabato; deputy provincial treasurer in Sulu; special inspector for the Bureau of prisons in Puerto Princesa, Palawan; assistant district commander of the district of Southern Mindanao; and inspector of the department of Southern Luzon. He then had a plantation in Glan Cotabato. He was a guerilla leader during the Japanese occupation of the Philippines. Died April 17, 1949, in Manila. *References: Elarth*; and *WWP*.

PALMER, JOHN W(ILLIAMSON) (1825–1906). Physician, born April 4, 1825, in Baltimore. Palmer graduated from the University of Maryland. He was the first city physician in San Francisco, practicing in 1849–1850. He traveled to Hawaii in 1850 and then to South and East Asia from 1850 to 1853. He served as surgeon of a war steamer in the service of the East India Company during the second Burmese war in 1851–1852. He then traveled in India and China. He returned to the United States in 1853, gave up medicine, took up writing, and settled in New York City. He wrote *The Golden Dragon; or, Up and Down the Irrawaddi. Being Passages of Adventure in the Burman Empire "by an American"* (New York, 1856) and *The New and the Old; or, California and India in Romantic Aspects* (New York, 1859). He was a correspondent for *The New York Times* during the Civil War, and later served in the Confederate Army. He then resumed literary work in New York City. Died February 26, 1906, in Baltimore. *References: ACAB; DAB; NCAB* 8:222; and *WWWA*.

PALMER, MARION BOYD (1877–1952). Missionary educator, born January 14, 1877, in Philadelphia, Missouri. Palmer graduated from Park College (Parkville, Mo.) and Auburn Theological Seminary, and was ordained in 1906. He taught at the Institute Ingles in Santiago, Chile, from 1899 to 1904. He was a missionary under the Board of Foreign Missions of the Presbyterian Church in the U.S.A. in Siam from 1906 until 1948. He was teacher in Chiengmai, Laos, from 1906 to 1910, principal of both a boys' school at Muang Nan, Siam, from 1910 until 1920, and president of the Bangkok Christian College from 1920 until 1939. Died October 8, 1952, in Birmingham, Alabama. *References: General Biographical Catalogue of Auburn Theological Seminary, 1818–1918* (Auburn, N.Y., 1918); *NYT*, October 10, 1952; and *School and Society* 76 (October 18, 1952): 255.

PANAY INCIDENT (1937). Diplomatic incident surrounding an attack, in 1937, by Japanese naval planes on the gunboat USS *Panay* and other American vessels on the Yangtze River in China. The Japanese later apologized to the American government and paid an indemnity. *References: DADH; KEJ*; Manny T. Koginos, *The Panay Incident: Prelude to War* (Lafayette, Ind., 1967); Hamilton D. Perry, *The Panay Incident: Prelude to Pearl Harbor* (New York, 1969); and H. J. Swanson, "The *Panay* Incident: Prelude to Pearl Harbor," *USNIP* 93 (December 1967): 26–37.

PARDY, JAMES V. (1898–1983). Clergyman, born March 9, 1898, in Brooklyn, New York. Pardy joined Maryknoll Fathers in 1925, graduated from St. Francis College (Brooklyn, N.Y.) and Catholic University, and was ordained in 1930. He taught at Maryknoll Junior College (Pa.) from 1930 to 1932, and was a missionary to Korea after 1932. He was superior of Maryknoll missions in Korea after 1939. He was a chaplain in the U.S. Army during World War II, rector of Maryknoll Junior Seminary (Mass.) from 1945 to 1948, and director of the Maryknoll candidates' program from 1948 to 1951. He returned to Korea in 1951, and was again superior of Maryknoll missions in Korea in 1953, and vicar general of Maryknoll in 1956. He was appointed the first vicar apostolic of Cheong-Ju, Korea, in 1958, and the first bishop of the newly established diocese of Cheong-Ju in 1962. He resigned from the bishopric in 1969. Died February 16, 1983, in Mountain View, California. *References: DACB; NYT* February 19, 1983; and *WWAC*.

PARKER, ALVIN PIERSON (1850–1924). Missionary, born August 7, 1850, near Austin, Texas, and grew up in Missouri. He was a missionary under the Board of Missions of the Methodist Episcopal Church, South, in China from 1875 until 1906. He was stationed in Soochow, established Buffington School (later part of Soochow University), and served as its head. He served in Shanghai from 1896 until his death, and was president of the Anglo-Chinese College until 1906. He assisted in translating the Bible into the Soochow and Shanghai dialects.

He was editor of the *Chinese Christian Advocate*. He wrote *Southern Methodism in China* (Dallas, Tex., 1924). Died September 10, 1924, in Oakland, California. *Reference: DAB*.

PARKER, EDWARD C(ARY) (1881–1939). Agriculturist, born August 4, 1881, in St. Paul, Minnesota. Parker graduated from the University of Minnesota. He was an assistant agriculturist in the Minnesota Agricultural Experiment Station from 1905 to 1908, and an agricultural advisor to the Manchurian government from 1908 to 1912. He was involved in ranching and land development in Montana from 1913 to 1923, and was secretary of the Montana Ranches Company from 1915 to 1919, president and treasurer of the State Ranches Company from 1919 to 1923, marketing specialist at the U.S. Department of Agriculture from 1923 to 1933, and in charge of federal grain supervision in the U.S. Bureau of Agricultural Economics after 1933. Died July 21, 1939, in Chevy Chase, Maryland. *References*: Randall E. Stross, *The Stubborn Earth: American Agriculturists on Chinese Soil, 1898–1937* (Berkeley, Calif., 1986), pp. 51–60; and *WWWA*.

PARKER, EDWIN WALLACE (1833–1901). Missionary, born January 21, 1833, in St. Johnsbury, Vermont. Parker attended Methodist Biblical Institute (Concord, N.H.), and was ordained in 1859. He was a missionary under the Board of Foreign Missions of the Methodist Episcopal Church in India from 1859 until his death, serving much of the time at Moradabad, northern India. He was elected missionary bishop for southern Asia in 1900. Died June 4, 1901, in Naini Tal, India. *References: DAB; EWM; NCAB* 5:514; and *WWWA*.

PARKER, PETER 1804–1888). Medical missionary and diplomat, born June 18, 1804, in Framingham, Massachusetts. Parker attended Amherst College, graduated from Yale University, and was ordained in 1834. The first Protestant medical missionary to China, he served under the American Board of Commissioners for Foreign Missions (ABCFM) in Canton from 1834 until 1857. He practiced medicine in Canton, specializing in eye diseases, and opened a hospital there. He also gave instruction in medicine to the Chinese. He accompanied the *Morrison* expedition to Japan in 1837 (see *Morrison* Incident*), organized the Medical Missionary Society in China in 1838, and opened a hospital in Macao, also in 1838. He returned to the United States in 1840 because of the war between Great Britain and China, but was back in China in 1842 and again practiced medicine in Canton. He served as one of the secretaries to Caleb Cushing* in the negotiations for the first treaty between the United States and China, was secretary of the U.S. legation in 1845, and was American commissioner and minister to China from 1855 until 1857. He returned to the United States in 1857. Died January 10, 1888, in Washington, D.C. *References*: Peter Parker Journals, Yale School of Medicine Library, New Haven, Conn.; C. J. Bartlett, "Peter Parker, the Founder of Modern Medical Missions, a Unique Collection of Paintings," *Journal of the American Medical Association* 67 (1916): 407–11; *CDCWM*; Margaret C. S.

Christman, *Adventurous Pursuits: Americans and the China Trade 1784–1844* (Washington, D.C., 1984), pp. 127–40; *DAB; DADH; EM*; Edward V. Gulick, *Peter Parker and the Opening of China* (Cambridge, Mass., 1973); Samuel C. Harvey, "Peter Parker: Initiator of Modern Medicine in China," *Yale Journal of Biology and Medicine* 8 (1936): 225–41; Edward H. Hume, "Peter Parker and the Introduction of Anesthesia into China," *Journal of the History of Medicine* 1 (1946): 670–74; Jonathan Spence, *To Change China: Western Advisers in China 1620–1960* (Boston, 1969), ch. 2; and *WWWA*.

PARRISH, EDWARD J(AMES) (1846–1920). Tobacco merchant, born October 20, 1846, in Orange (later Durham) County, North Carolina. Parrish attended Trinity College (later Duke University). He was a mailing clerk and a salesman in a drygoods store in Raleigh, and then held a government position until 1870. He was an auctioneer in the first tobacco warehouse to be opened in Durham in 1871, and established a tobacco business in 1876. He represented the American Tobacco Company in Japan from 1899 to 1904 (and after 1902, the British-American Tobacco Company), and was vice president of the Murai Brothers Company, Limited, which was bought by the American Tobacco Company. He also collected Japanese art. Died October 22, 1920, in Durham, North Carolina. *References*: Edward J. Parrish Papers, Duke University Library, Durham, N.C.; Samuel Ashe, Stephen B. Weeks, and Charles L. Van Noppen, eds., *Biographical History of North Carolina: From Colonial Times to the Present* (Greensboro, N.C.; 1905, 1917), 8:403–8; Robert F. Durden, "Tar Heel Tobacconist in Tokyo, 1899–1904," *North Carolina Historical Review* 53 (1976): 347–63; and *NCAB* 38:408.

PARRISH, (SARAH) REBECCA (1869–1952). Medical missionary, born November 1, 1869, in Bowers, Montgomery County, Indiana. Parrish graduated from the State Medical School (Indianapolis). She was a medical missionary under the Woman's Foreign Missionary Society of the Methodist Episcopal Church in the Philippines from 1906 to 1933. She founded a hospital and a school of nursing in the Tondo district of Manila in 1908, and was its director until her retirement in 1936. She wrote her memoirs, *Orient Seas and Lands Afar* (New York, 1936). Died August 22, 1952, in Indianapolis. *References: CDCWM; DPB* 3; *IAB*; and *NYT*, August 24, 1952.

PARSONS, WILLIAM BARCLAY (1859–1932). Engineer, born April 15, 1859, in New York City. Parsons graduated from Columbia University and its Engineering School and School of Mines. He was a consulting engineer in New York City from 1885 to 1891, and deputy chief engineer and then chief engineer of the Rapid Transit Commission of New York City from 1891 to 1904. He conducted a survey of Chinese railways in 1898–1899, and wrote *An American Engineer in China* (New York, 1900). He served as chief of engineers in the Spanish-American War, and was chief engineer of the Cape Cod Canal from

1905 to 1914, and chairman of the Chicago Transit Committee after 1916. He served in the U.S. Army during World War I. Died May 9, 1932, in New York City. *References: DAB; NCAB* 14:217; and *NYT*, May 10, 1932.

PARSONS, WILLIAM E(DWARD) (1872–1939). Architect, born June 19, 1872, in Akron, Ohio. Parsons graduated from Yale and Columbia universities, and studied at the Ecole des Beaux Arts (Paris). He was a draftsman in an architectural office in New York City from 1901 to 1905. He was a consulting architect for the U.S. government in the Philippines from 1905 to 1914, and directed the execution of Daniel Burnham's plans for Manila and Baguio. He designed many buildings, including the Philippine General Hospital, the University of the Philippines, and the Manila Hotel, and planned the restoration of the old city walls and moats of Manila as public parks. He returned to the United States in 1914 and practiced architecture in Chicago until 1938. He was an associate professor of architecture in Yale University in 1938–1939. Died December 17, 1939, in New Haven, Connecticut. *References: NYT*, December 18, 1939; A. N. Rebori, "The Work of William E. Parsons in the Philippine Islands," *Architectural Record* 41 (1917): 305–24, 423–34; Henry F. Whitey, *Biographical Dictionary of American Architects, Deceased* (Los Angeles, 1956); and *WWWA*.

PARTRIDGE, FREDERICK WILLIAM (1824–1899). Consul, born August 19, 1824, in Norwich, Vermont. Partridge attended Dartmouth College and studied law in Concord, New Hampshire. He was in charge of the Harrisburg Military Academy (Pa.) from 1845 to 1847; served in the Mexican War; farmed in Kendall County, Illinois, from 1847 to 1855; continued the study of law in Chicago; and practiced in Sandwich, Illinois, from 1857 to 1861. He served in the Union Army during the Civil War, and again practiced law in Sandwich and Chicago. He was consul general in Bangkok, Siam, from 1869 to 1876. He saved the life of the son of the king of Siam and promoted the safety of missionaries. He returned to the United States in 1876, and was an examiner of pensions in Rushville, Indiana, and Tifin, Ohio, from 1882 to 1889. Died January 22, 1899, in Sycamore, Illinois.

PARTRIDGE, SIDNEY C(ATLIN) (1857–1930). Missionary, born September 1, 1857, in New York City. Partridge graduated from Yale University and Berkeley Divinity School, and was ordained in 1885. He was a missionary under the Domestic and Foreign Missionary Society of the Protestant Episcopal Church in the United States of America in Shanghai, China, from 1885 until his death. He taught and was a chaplain at St. John's College from 1884 to 1887, and was a rector of Boone School and a missionary at Wuchang from 1887 to 1890. He was consecrated the missionary bishop of Kyoto, Japan, in 1900 and served there until 1911. He was the bishop of West Missouri after 1911. Died June 22, 1930, in Kansas City, Missouri. *References: WWWA*; and *Yale*.

PASSIN, HERBERT (1916–   ). Sociologist, born December 16, 1916, in Chicago. Passin attended the University of Illinois and graduated from the University of Chicago. He was a social science researcher in the Division of Program Surveys of the U.S. Department of Agriculture in Washington, D.C., in 1942–1943, and in the Bureau of Opinion Research of the Office of War Information in 1943. He was a relocation officer at the War Relocation Office in Detroit in 1943–1944. He was a Japanese language officer in the U.S. Army from 1944 to 1947, deputy chief and later chief of the Public Opinion and Sociological Research Division of the General Headquarters of the Supreme Commander for the Allied Powers (SCAP) in Japan from 1946 to 1951, a researcher for the Social Science Research Council in Japan in 1952–1953, and Far Eastern representative of *Encounter* magazine in Tokyo from 1954 to 1957. He was director of the international seminar program of the Congress for Cultural Freedom in Paris, France, from 1957 to 1959; professor of sociology at Columbia University after 1962; and executive director of the United States–Japan parliamentary exchange program for the School of International Affairs after 1967. He wrote *China's Cultural Diplomacy* (New York, 1963); *Society and Education in Japan* (New York, 1965); *Japanese and the Japanese* (Tokyo, 1977); *The Outlook of Intellectuals in Japan* (New York, 1980); and *Encounter with Japan* (Tokyo, 1982). *References: AMWS; CA*; and *WWA*.

PASSIONISTS. Established in the United States in 1852. St. Paul of the Cross ("Eastern") Province began missionary work in Hunan, China, in 1921 and continued until 1955, when its missionaries were expelled by the Communist authorities. It also began missionary work in the Philippines in 1957. Holy Cross ("Western") Province began missionary work in Japan in 1953 and in Korea in 1964. *References*: Robert Carbonneau, "The Passionists in China, 1921–1929: An Essay in Mission Experience," *Catholic Historical Quarterly* 66 (1980): 392–416; and *CE*.

PATTI, ARCHIMEDES L(EONIDA) A(TTILIO) (1913–   ). Army officer, born July 21, 1913, in New York City. Patti graduated from the University of Maryland. He served in the U.S. Army from 1936 until 1957. He headed an Office of Strategic Services (OSS) special mission to French Indochina in 1944–1945, and wrote an account of his experiences in *Why Viet Nam? Prelude to America's Albatross* (Berkeley, Calif., 1980). He was a special advisor to the Turkish high command in Ankara in 1951–1952, and assistant chief of staff for intelligence from 1952 to 1957. He retired with the rank of lieutenant colonel in 1957. He was a political analyst in the Executive Office of the President from 1959 to 1971, and a consultant on national security affairs from 1971 to 1975. *Reference: CA*.

PAUL, HENRY MARTYN (1851–1931). Astronomer, born June 25, 1851, in Dedham, Massachusetts. Paul graduated from Dartmouth College and its Thayer School of Engineering. He was a junior assistant at the U.S. Naval Observatory in Washington, D.C., from 1875 until 1880. He was the first professor of astronomy at Tokyo University from 1880 to 1883. He returned to the Naval Observatory in 1883 and served until 1897. He was a professor of mathematics in the U.S. Navy from 1897 to 1899, an engineer with the Bureau of Yards and Docks from 1899 to 1905, and a teacher of mathematics at the Naval Academy from 1905 until 1912. He retired from the navy in 1913. Died March 15, 1931, in Washington, D.C. *References: ACAB; DAB; NCAB* 10:403; and *WWWA*.

PAULEY MISSION (1945). U.S. reparations mission to Japan in 1945, headed by Edwin Wendel Pauley, which recommended the removal of all equipment from Japanese war industries and a drastic reduction of capacity in defense-related industries. The recommendations were never carried out. *References: CB* 1945; and *KEJ*.

PAWLEY, WILLIAM DOUGLAS (1896–1977). Aviation executive, born September 7, 1896, in Florence, South Carolina. He was engaged in various business enterprises in Venezuela, Colombia, Cuba, and Haiti from 1914 to 1922. He was active in aviation in Cuba from 1928 to 1932, and was executive vice president and later president of Intercontinental Corporation in New York City after 1932. In 1933 he undertook to operate China National Aviation Corporation in Shanghai, China's first commercial airline, and was its president in 1933–1934, until it was sold to Pan American Airways. He then developed with the Chinese Nationalist government a plan to build China's first airplane factory, which was in production by mid–1934. In 1940 he organized the American Volunteer Group.* He went to India in 1940 to build an aircraft factory, and was president of the Hindustan Aircraft Manufacturing Company in Bangalore, which became the principal maintenance and overhaul base for the U.S. Army Air Force in the China-Burma-India theater. He returned to the United States in 1945. He was U.S. ambassador to Peru in 1945–1946 and to Brazil from 1946 to 1948. He went to Cuba in 1949 and organized a bus company there. He was owner, president, and general manager of the Miami Beach Railway Company and the Miami Transit Company from 1954 to 1962; president of several mining companies in the Dominican Republic; and president of Talisman Sugar Corporation in Belle Glade, Florida, from 1964 until his retirement in 1972. Died June 7, 1977, in Miami Beach, Florida. *References: NCAB* 60:215; *NYT*, January 9, 1977; and *WWWA*.

PAXTON, J(OHN) HALL (1899–1952). Diplomat, born July 28, 1899, in Galesburg, Illinois. Paxton graduated from Yale University and studied at Magdalene College, Cambridge University, and L'Ecole Libre des Sciences Politiques (Paris). He served in the U.S. Army during World War I. He entered the foreign service in 1925, served in Nanking, was consul in Canton from 1932 to 1934 and at Chefoo from 1934 to 1936, was second secretary at the embassy in Nanking in 1936–1937, and served as consul in Shanghai from 1938 to 1941. He was interned by the Japanese in 1941–1942. He was a representative on the Middle East Supply Center in Teheran in 1943, secretary in Nanking in 1945–1946, consul in Urumchi in 1946, and consul in Tihwa, Sinkiang Province, China, from 1946 to 1949. He led an escape party of women and children over the Himalaya Mountains to India in 1950, and described his experiences in the April 19, 1950, issue of the *Saturday Evening Post.* He was chief of the South and Southeast Asia section of the International Broadcasting Division (Voice of America) in New York City in 1950–1951, and consul in Isfahan, Iran, in 1951–1952. Died June 23, 1952, in Isfahan. *References*: J. Hall Paxton Papers, Yale University Library, New Haven, Conn.; *NYT*, June 25, 1952; and *WWWA*.

PEACE CORPS. United States government agency, created in 1961, which sent volunteers to many countries, several thousands of whom went to the countries of Asia. Volunteers have served in India (1962–1976), Indonesia (1963–1965), Malaysia (1962–   ), Nepal (1962–   ), Pakistan (1961–1967), Philippines (1961–   ), South Korea (1966–1981), Sri Lanka (1962–1964 and 1967–1970), and Thailand (1962–1967, 1968–   ). *References*: Kevin Lowther and C. Payne Lucas, *Keeping Kennedy's Promise: The Peace Corps* (Boulder, Colo., 1978); Gerard T. Rice, *Twenty Years of Peace Corps* (Washington, D.C., 1981); and Robert B. Textor, ed., *Cultural Frontiers of the Peace Corps* (Cambridge, Mass., 1966).

PEACOCK, JAMES LOWE, III (1937–   ). Anthropologist, born October 31, 1937, in Montgomery, Alabama. Peacock graduated from Duke and Harvard universities. He was assistant professor of anthropology at Princeton University from 1965 to 1967 and at the University of North Carolina (Chapel Hill) from 1967 to 1969, associate professor there from 1970 to 1972, and professor after 1973. He carried out fieldwork in Indonesia in 1962–1963 and in 1969–1970. He wrote *Rites of Modernization. Symbolic and Social Aspects of Indonesian Proletarian Drama* (Chicago, 1968); *Indonesia: An Anthropological Perspective* (Pacific Palisades, Calif., 1973); *Muslim Puritans: Reformist Psychology in Southeast Asian Islam* (Berkeley, Calif., 1978); and *Purifying the Faith: The Muhammadijah Movement in Indonesian Islam* (Menlo Park, Calif., 1978). *References: AMWS*; and *WWA*.

PECK, GRAHAM (1914–1968). Author, born April 6, 1914, in Derby, Connecticut. Peck graduated from Yale University. He traveled for two years in China, and wrote and illustrated *Through China's Wall* (Boston, 1940). He served in the Office of War Information in China during World War II, and wrote *Two Kinds of Time* (Boston, 1950). He also wrote (with Paul Frillmann) *China: The*

Remembered Life (Boston, 1968). Died July 3, 1968, in Rutland, Vermont. *Reference: NYT*, July 23, 1968.

PECK, WILLYS R(UGGLES) (1882–1952). Diplomat, born October 24, 1882, in Tientsin, China, to American parents. Peck graduated from the University of California. He was a student interpreter in China in 1906; assistant Chinese secretary in the U.S. legation in Peking from 1908 to 1913; Chinese secretary in 1913–1914; consul in Tsingtao, Hankaw, Shanghai, and Tientsin from 1914 to 1919; acting Chinese secretary to the U.S. legation in Peking from 1919 to 1921; and Chinese secretary from 1921 to 1926. He served in the State Department from 1926 to 1928, and was the assistant chief of the Division of Far Eastern Affairs from 1928 to 1930. He was consul general in Nanking 1931 to 1935, counselor of embassy from 1935 to 1940, and minister to Thailand in 1941. He was interned in Bangkok in 1941–1942. He was a special assistant in the division of cultural relations in charge of the China section of the State Department from 1942 to 1944; and assistant chief of the division of cultural relations in charge of the Far Eastern Branch in 1944–1945. He retired in 1945. Died September 2, 1952, in Belmont, San Francisco. *References*: Willys R. Peck Papers, Hoover Institution on War, Revolution and Peace, Stanford, Calif.; *NYT*, September 3, 1952; and *WWWA*.

PEELE, HUBBELL AND COMPANY Trading company, established in Manila in 1822 by George William Hubbell (1796–1831) of Bridgeport, Connecticut. It was involved in exporting sugar and later in the abacá trade. J. W. Peele of Salem became a partner in 1832. The firm went into bankruptcy in 1887. *References*: Benito Legarda, Jr., "American Entrepreneurs in the 19th Century Philippines," *Explorations in Entrepreneurial History* 9 (1957): 142–59; and Norman G. Owen, "Americans in the Abacá Trade: Peele, Hubbell & Co., 1856–1875," in *Reappraising an Empire: New Perspectives on Philippine-American Relations*, ed. Peter W. Stanley (Cambridge, Mass., 1984), pp. 201–30.

PEERS, WILLIAM R(AYMOND) (1914–1984). Army officer, born June 14, 1914, in Stuart, Iowa, and grew up in California. Peers attended the University of California. He was commissioned a second lieutenant in the U.S. Army in 1938. He was commanding officer of the Office of Strategic Services (OSS) in northern Burma, and (with Dean Brelis) wrote about his experiences in *Behind the Burma Road: The Story of America's Most Successful Guerilla Force* (Boston, 1963). He was then commanding officer of the OSS in China, and sent American spy teams to Japanese prison camps in China and Korea. He also led a Chinese parachute assault on Nanking to occupy that city. He was the U.S. Army's Chief of Staff's Special Assistant for Special Warfare Activities; head of Central Intelligence Agency (CIA) clandestine training in 1949; and head of Western Enterprises, Inc., in Taiwan, from 1951 to 1953, a cover for the CIA that trained and equipped the launching of Chinese Nationalist commando raids on mainland

China from Quemoy and Matsu islands. He was a special assistant to the Joint Chiefs of Staff in 1965–1966, commander of the Fourth Infantry Division and First Field Force in Vietnam, and then chief of army reserves in Washington. In 1969–1970, he headed the inquiry into the army's handling of the 1968 My Lai massacre in Vietnam, and wrote *My Lai Inquiry* (New York, 1979). He was deputy commander of the Eighth Army in Korea from 1971 to 1973. He retired with the rank of lieutenant general in 1973. Died April 6, 1984, in San Francisco. *References: CA; NYT*, April 9, 1984; and *WWWA*.

PEERY, RUFUS BENTON (1868–1934). Clergyman, born April 9, 1868, in Burkes Garden, Virginia. Peery graduated from Roanoke College (Salem, Va.) and Theological Seminary (Gettysburg, Pa.), and was ordained in 1892. He was a professor of theology in Japan from 1892 to 1903, a lecturer on Oriental and missionary subjects from 1903 to 1905, a pastor in Denver from 1905 to 1912, president of Midland College (Atchison, Kans.) from 1912 to 1919, professor of philosophy at Lenoir College (Hickory, N.C.) from 1920 to 1924, and a pastor in Wooster, Ohio, from 1924 to 1931, and in Raleigh, North Carolina, after 1931. He wrote *The Gist of Japan: The Islands, Their People and Missions* (New York, 1897), and *Lutherans in Japan* (Newberry, S.C., 1900). Died October 25, 1934, in Raleigh, North Carolina. *References: OAB*; and *WWWA*.

PEET, LYMAN BERT (1809–1878). Missionary, born March 1, 1809, in Cornwall, Vermont. Peet graduated from Middlebury College and Andover Theological Seminary, and was ordained in 1837. He was a missionary under the American Board of Commissioners for Foreign Missions (ABCFM) in Siam from 1839 to 1846, and in the Foochow mission in China from 1846 to 1871. He was a pastor in West Haven, Connecticut, from 1871 until his death. Died January 11, 1878, in West Haven, Connecticut. His son, **L(YMAN) P(LIMPTON) PEET** (1860–1945), missionary, was born October 24, 1860, in Foochow, China. L. P. Peet graduated from Yale University and Yale Theological Seminary, and was ordained in 1888. He was a missionary under the ABCFM in Foochow, China, from 1888 until 1917. He was president of Foochow College from 1890 to 1913, president of North Fukien Religious Tract Society from 1907 to 1915, director of the language school of new missionaries to north Fukien from 1915 to 1920, and secretary to the U.S. consulate in Foochow after 1921. He wrote a revised and enlarged *An English-Chinese Dictionary* (Shanghai, 1922); and *A Handy Vocabulary of the Foochow Dialect* (Foochow City, 1928). Died July 30, 1945, in Santa Barbara, California. *References: AndoverTS*; and *WWWA*.

PEFFER, NATHANIEL (1890–1964). Author and educator, born June 30, 1890, in New York City. Peffer graduated from the University of Chicago. He was a Far Eastern correspondent for the *New York Herald* from 1911 to 1937. He served as a fellow of the Guggenheim Memorial Foundation for Research in

China from 1927 to 1929. He returned to the United States in 1937, was a lecturer at Columbia University from 1937 to 1939, an associate professor of international relations there from 1939 to 1943, and a professor from 1943 until his retirement in 1958. He wrote *The White Man's Dilemma: Climax of the Age of Imperialism* (New York 1927); *China: The Collapse of a Civilization* (New York, 1930); *Must We Fight in Asia?* (New York, 1935); *Basis for Peace in the Far East* (New York, 1942); and *The Far East: A Modern History* (Ann Arbor, Mich., 1958). Died April 12, 1964, in White Plains, New York. *References: NYT*, April 14, 1964; *Political Science Quarterly* 79 (1964): 484–86; and *WWWA*.

PEKING UNION MEDICAL COLLEGE (PUMC). A medical school in Peking, China, founded in 1917. Buildings were erected by the China Medical Board, and faculty were drawn mostly from the United States. It became the leading medical center and medical school in China, also conducting extensive research programs, especially in public health. It was seized by the Japanese in 1941 and was closed until 1947, when it was reopened. It was nationalized by the Communist Chinese government. *References*: John Z. Bowers, *Western Medicine in a Chinese Palace: Peking Union Medical College, 1917–1951* (Philadelphia, 1972); Mary B. Bullock, *An American Transplant: The Rockefeller Foundation and Peking Union Medical College* (Berkeley, Calif., 1980); and Mary Ferguson, *China Medical Board and Peking Union Medical College; a Chronology of Fruitful Collaboration* (New York, 1970).

PEKING UNIVERSITY. *See* YENCHING UNIVERSITY

PELZER, DOROTHY (WEST) (1915–1972). Architect, born May 6, 1915, in New Jersey. Pelzer attended Cornell University, graduated from Principia College (Elsah, Ill.), studied at the Institute of Design in Chicago, and graduated from the Massachusetts Institute of Technology. She taught dance and sculpture at Principia College from 1941 to 1943, was an architectural designer at the Container Corporation of America in Chicago from 1943 to 1947, and practiced architecture until 1958. She made a study tour of Asia in 1958–1959, and traveled extensively in Southeast Asia from 1962 until 1970, documenting the traditional architecture of that region. In 1967, she established herself in Tanah Rata, Cameron Highlands, Malaysia. The impressions of her travel in Indonesia in 1965 were published posthumously as *Trek across Indonesia* (Singapore, 1982). Died April 28, 1972, in Boston. *Reference*: "People in Houses: A Tribute to Dorothy Pelzer," in *Southeast Asian Cultural Heritage: Images of Traditional Communities*, comp. Ong Choo Suat (Singapore, 1986), pp. 13–18.

PELZER, K(ARL) J(OSEF) (1909–1980). Geographer, born February 23, 1909, in Oberpleis, Germany. Pelzer graduated from the University of Bonn, came to the United States in 1935 and was naturalized in 1940. He conducted research in 1936–1937; and was a research associate at Johns Hopkins University from 1939 to 1941; an associate in geography there from 1942 to 1944; a senior regional specialist at the Office of War Information in 1944–1945; an agricultural economist at the Office of Foreign Agricultural Relations, U.S. Department of Agriculture, from 1945 to 1947; an associate professor of geography at Yale University from 1947 to 1952; a professor there from 1952–1977; and also director of the Southeast Asian Studies Program from 1958 to 1977. He carried out fieldwork in the Philippines in 1950, in Indonesia in 1955–1956, and in Malaya in 1968, and wrote *Pioneer Settlement in the Asiatic Tropics. Studies in Land Utilization and Agricultural Colonization in Southeastern Asia* (New York, 1945). Died November 9, 1980, in New Haven, Connecticut. *Reference: WWWA.*

PENDLETON, ROBERT L(ARIMORE) ("POPSIE") (1890–1957). Soil scientist, born June 25, 1890, in Minneapolis, and grew up in California. Pendleton graduated from the University of California at Berkeley. He was an instructor in soils at Ewing Christian College in 1917–1918, assistant director of the Department of Agriculture at Gwalior State, India, from 1918 to 1920, and director there from 1920 to 1923. He was a professor of soil technology at the College of Agriculture of the University of the Philippines in Los Baños, Laguna, from 1923 to 1925; head of the department of soils from 1930 to 1935; chief soil technologist of the National Geological Survey of China from 1931 to 1933; and a soil scientist and agriculturist in the Royal Department of Agriculture and Fisheries of the Siamese government in Bangkok from 1935 to 1942. He was interned in Siam in 1942, and then returned to the United States. He was a soil scientist in the Office of Foreign Agricultural Relations of the U.S. Department of Agriculture from 1945 to 1952, professor of tropical soils and agriculture at Johns Hopkins University from 1946 to 1955, agricultural advisor to the Food and Agriculture Organization mission to Thailand in 1947–1948, and soil scientist with the Mutual Security Agency's Special Technical and Economic Mission (STEM) to Thailand in 1952–1953, soil technologist to the Ministry of Agriculture of Thailand after 1956, and editor of the *Natural History Bulletin of the Siam Society.* Died June 23, 1957, in Bangkok, Thailand. *References: Geographical Review* 48 (1958): 124–26; and *WWWA.*

PENHALLOW, DAVID P(EARCE) (1854–1910). Botanist, born May 25, 1854, in Kittery Point, Maine. Penhallow graduated from Massachusetts State Agricultural College. He was in Japan from 1876 to 1880, was involved in founding the Sapporo Agricultural College, and served as a professor of botany and chemistry there. He laid the foundation for the study of botany in north Japan. He lived for many months among the Ainus, and is credited with being the first Westerner to have been accorded that privilege. He was a professor of botany at McGill University from 1883 until his death. Died October 20, 1910, aboard a ship bound for Liverpool, England. *References: Foreign Pioneers; NCAB* 20:216; *NYT*, October 27, 1910; and *WWWA*.

PENNER, PETER A. (1871–1949). Missionary, born April 2, 1871, in Belo Sirko, south Russia; came to the United States in 1875; and grew up in Mountain Lake, Minnesota. Penner attended Minnesota State Normal School (Mankato), Bethel Academy (Newton, Kans.), and Missionary Training Institute (Brooklyn, N.Y.). He was a missionary under the Board of Foreign Mission of the Central Conference Mennonite Church in India from 1900 until 1941. He served in Chapma, Central Provinces (later Madhya Pradesh) and established there a le-prosarium, the Bethesda Leper Home. He returned to the United States in 1941. Died October 3, 1949, in Newton, Kansas. *References: ME*; Samuel T. Moyer, *They Heard the Call* (Newton, Kans., 1970), pp. 12–28.

PENNER, PETER WILLIAM (1876–1953). Missionary, born February 12, 1876, in Prangenau, Molotschna, south Russia; came to the United States in 1878; and grew up in Hilsboro, Kansas. Penner attended Bethel College and Mennonite Educational Institute (Gretna, Kans.), and graduated from the German (later Baldwin) Wallace College (Berea, Ohio) and its seminary. He was a missionary under the Board of Foreign Mission of the Central Conference Mennonite Church in India from 1908 until 1949. He served at Janjgir, Central Provinces (later Madhya Pradesh), and was secretary-treasurer of the mission. He retired in 1949. Died February 2, 1953, in Hillsboro, Kansas. *References: ME*; and Samuel T. Moyer, *They Heard the Call* (Newton, Kans., 1970), pp. 63–72.

PENTECOSTAL HOLINESS CHURCH: DEPARTMENT OF FOREIGN MISSION. Founded in 1904, it began missionary work in China in 1922, and in India in 1910. The name was changed later to World Missions Department of the International Pentecostal Holiness Church. *References*: Pentecostal Holiness Church Archives, Church Headquarters, Oklahoma City, Okla.; Joseph E. Campbell, *The Pentecostal Holiness Church 1898–1948: Its Background and History* (Franklin Springs, Ga., 1951); and *EMCM*.

PERCIVAL, JOHN ("MAD JACK") (1779–1862). Naval officer, born April 3, 1779, in West Barnstable, Massachusetts. Percival went to sea in 1793, was impressed into the British Navy in 1797, and escaped in 1799. He entered the U.S. Navy in 1799, and was commissioned a midshipman in 1800. He was discharged in 1801, served on merchant ships, and reentered the navy in 1809. He served in the War of 1812, in the West Indies, and in the Pacific. He commanded the USS *Dolphin* in 1825–1826 in the Pacific, and served in the Brazil Squadron from 1833 to 1835. He commanded the USS *Constitution* on its voyage around the world from 1844 to 1846. He was in Tourane (later Da Nang), Annam, in 1845, and was involved in the first hostile action by the United

States against Indochina. He retired in 1855. Died September 7, 1862, in Dorchester, Massachusetts. *References: ACAB; DAB*; David Long, " 'Mad Jack' Percival in Vietnam: First American Hostilities, May 1845," *AN* 47 (1987): 169–73; *NCAB* 20:437; Allan Westcott, "Captain 'Mad Jack' Percival," *USNIP* 61 (March 1935): 313–19; and *WWWA*.

PEREZ, GILBERT S(OMERS) (1885–1959). Educator, born February 8, 1885, in Pensacola, Florida. Perez graduated from Bucknell University and the University of Chicago. He came to the Philippines in 1909, and was employed by the Bureau of Education as a teacher and principal of schools in Baliuag, San Miguel, Hagonoy, Bulacan, Jagna, Bohol, and Tayabas, from 1909 until 1917. He was acting superintendent of schools in Tayabas Province from 1917 to 1926, acting superintendent of the Philippine School of Arts and Trades from 1926 to 1928, chief of the vocational division in 1926–1927, and chief of the industrial division from 1927 to 1929, and again chief of the vocational division from 1929 until 1941. He was interned by the Japanese in Santo Tomas, Manila, during World War II. He retired in 1946, and was later a technical advisor in the Department of Education. He wrote a biography of José Rizal, and *From the Transport Thomas to Sto. Tomas: The History of the American Teachers in the Philippines* (Manila, 1949). Died November 22, 1959, in Manila. *References: DPB* 3; *NYT*, November 24, 1959; and *WWP*.

PERIN, CHARLES PAGE (1861–1937). Engineer, born August 23, 1861, in West Point, New York. Perin graduated from Harvard University and studied at École des Mines (Paris). He served in various capacities with Carnegie Steel Company, and was general manager and president of blast furnaces collieries in Virginia and Kentucky. He made a study of fuel supply for the Trans-Siberian Railway for the Russian government. He conducted surveys for iron and coal across India, and developed iron resources in that country, resulting in the Tata Iron and Steel Company and Mysore Iron Works. He was a consulting engineer for the Lung Yen Mining Corporation in China, and chief of an engineering appraisal commission attached to the Peace Commission in 1919. He was later a member of the firm Perin and Marshall in New York City. Died February 6, 1937, in New York City. *Reference: WWWA*.

PERKINS, EUGENE ARTHUR (1887–1956). Lawyer and consul, born May 6, 1887, in Bangkok, Siam, to American parents. Perkins graduated from St. Lawrence University (N.Y.), and Brookline Law School, and was admitted to the bar. He came to the Philippines in 1908, and worked in the attorney general's office from 1908 until 1912 as a prosecuting attorney and as attorney for the Bureau of Lands. He practiced law in Manila after 1912. He was consul for Siam in the Philippines from 1931 to 1938, and consul general after 1938. He also built an important collection of Filipiniana. Died April 28, 1956, in Manila,

Philippines. *References: ACCJ* 32 (1956): 206; *EP* 18:313–14; and *Gleeck/Manila*.

PERKINS AND COMPANY. The Canton branch office of J. & T. H. Perkins of Boston was established in 1803, the first American *branch house* in Canton. It closed down in the winter of 1827–1828, and handed over its commission business to Russell and Company. *References*: Perkins and Company Records, Baker Library, Harvard University, Boston, Mass.; Carl Seaburg and Stanley Paterson, *Merchant Prince of Boston: Colonel T. H. Perkins 1764–1854* (Cambridge, Mass., 1971).

PERRY, LILLA CABOT (1848–1933). Painter, born January 13, 1848, in Boston. Perry studied art in Boston and Paris and lived in Paris until 1889, when she returned to Boston. She lived in Japan from 1898 until 1901 with her husband Thomas Sargeant Perry (1845–1928), who was professor of English literature at Keiogijiku College in Tokyo, and painted more than eighty pictures of Japanese life and landscapes. Died February 28, 1933, in Hancock, New Hampshire. *References*: Stuart P. Feld, *Lilla Cabot Perry: A Retrospective Exhibition* (New York, 1969); and Virginia Harlow, *Thomas Sargeant Perry: A Biography* (Durham, N.C., 1950).

PERRY, MATTHEW C(ALBRAITH) (1794–1858). Naval officer, born April 10, 1794, in South Kingstown, Rhode Island. Perry entered the U.S. Navy in 1809 as a midshipman, took part in the War of 1812, and was commissioned a lieutenant in 1813. He served on the African coast from 1820 to 1822, and helped to establish the colony at Cape Mesurado (later Monrovia, Liberia). He was commander of the African Squadron from 1843 to 1845, and served in the Mexican War. He commanded the expedition to Japan (see Perry Expedition*) from 1853 to 1855. He wrote *Narrative of the Expedition of an American Squadron to the China Seas and Japan* (Washington, D.C., 1856). Died March 4, 1858, in New York City. *References*: Matthew C. Perry Papers, Manuscript Division, Library of Congress; Chester A. Bain, "Commodore Matthew Perry, Humphrey Marshall, and the Taiping Rebellion," *FEQ* 10 (1951): 258–70; *DADH; DAMIB; EAH; KEJ*; Samuel E. Morison, *"Old Bruin": Commodore Matthew C. Perry, 1794–1858, the American Naval Officer Who Helped Found Liberia* (Boston, 1967); *NCAB* 4:42; Roger Pineau, ed., *The Japan Expedition, 1852–54: The Personal Journal of Commodore Matthew C. Perry* (Washington, D.C., 1968); John H. Schroeder, "Matthew Calbraith Perry: Antebellum Precursor of the Steam Navy," in *Captains of the Old Navy: Makers of the American Naval Tradition 1840–1880*, ed. James C. Bradford (Annapolis, Md., 1986), pp. 3–25; Richard A. von Doenhoff, "Biddle, Perry, and Japan," *USNIP* 92 (November 1966): 78–87; and *WWWA*.

PERRY EXPEDITION (1853–1855). A naval squadron, under the command of Commodore Matthew C. Perry,* which arrived at the Bay of Yedo (Tokyo) in Japan in 1853 with a demand to the Japanese authorities from the American president to open Japan's ports for trade. Perry returned with his squadron to Yokohama, Japan, in 1854. Negotiations were carried out with the shogunate that were concluded in the Kanagawa Treaty, opening the ports of Shimoda and Hakodate to American ships. *References*: Allan B. Cole, ed., *With Perry in Japan*: *The Diary of Edward York McCauley* (Princeton, N.J., 1942); Henry F. Graff, ed., *Blue Jackets with Perry in Japan: A Day-to-day Account Kept by Master's Mate John R. C. Lewis and Cabin Boy William B. Allen* (New York, 1952); William L. Neumann, "Religion, Morality, and Freedom: The Ideological Background of the Perry Expedition," *PHR* 23 (1954): 247–57; Roger Pineau, ed., *The Japan Expedition, 1853–1854. The Personal Journal of Commodore Matthew C. Perry* (Washington, D.C., 1968); George H. Prebble, *The Opening of Japan: A Diary of Discovery in the Far East, 1852–1856*, ed. Boleslaw Szczesniak (Norman, Okla., 1962); and Arthur Walworth, *Black Ships off Japan: The Story of Commodore Perry's Expedition* (New York, 1946).

PERSHING, JOHN J(OSEPH) (1860–1948). Army officer, born September 13, 1860, in Laclede, Missouri. Pershing graduated from Kirksville (Mo.) Normal School and from the U.S. Military Academy in 1886. He served in the Sixth Cavalry in the West, was an instructor in military science at the University of Nebraska from 1891 to 1895, and served in the Spanish-American War in Cuba. He came to the Philippines in 1899, was adjutant general of Mindanao Department, and served in the Moro Wars until 1903. He was a U.S. military attaché in Japan in 1905–1906, served again in the Philippines in 1907–1908, and was governor of the Moro Province from 1909 to 1913. He served on the Mexican border from 1914 to 1916, commanded the Mexican Punitive Expedition in 1916–1917, and was commander of the American Expeditionary Forces during World War I. He was made general of the armies in 1919, was army chief of staff from 1921 to 1924, and remained on active duty until his death. Died July 15, 1948, in Washington, D.C. *References: ACAB; DAB S4; DAMIB*; Thomas J. Fleming, "Pershing's Island War," *American Heritage* 19 (August 1968); 32–35, 101–4; Peter G. Gowing, *Mandate in Moroland: The American Government of Muslim Filipinos 1899–1920* (Diliman, Quezon, 1977), ch. 8; *NCAB* 35:1; *Pier*; Donald Smythe, *Guerilla Warrior: The Early Life of John J. Pershing* (New York, 1973); Wayne W. Thompson, "Governors of the Moro Province: Wood, Bliss and Pershing in the Southern Philippines, 1903–1913," Ph.D. diss., University of California at San Diego, 1975; and *WWWA*.

PETHICK, WILLIAM N. (? - 1901). Adventurer. Pethick served in the Union Army during the Civil War. He went to China shortly after the Civil War and engaged in commercial activities in Tientsin. He became associated with Viceroy Li Hung-chang, was tutor to his children, and served as his private secretary and diplomatic advisor until a short time before Li's death. He assisted in negotiations with foreign banks and promoters and with foreign governments. He obtained for Li the services of American engineers, mineralogists, and railroad experts, and assisted him in developing an adequate library in these fields. He drew up the anti-opium convention of 1876. He also served many years as a member of the American consular corps in Tientsin until 1894. Died December 20, 1901, in Peking. *Reference: NYT*, December 21, 1901.

PETTUS, WILLIAM BACON (1880–1959). Missionary, born August 28, 1880, in Mobile, Alabama. Pettus attended the University of Missouri and graduated from Columbia University. He also studied at the universities of Nanking and Hamburg, and the Oriental Seminary of Berlin University. He was president of the College of Chinese Studies in Peking from 1916 to 1945. He was secretary of the International Committee of the Young Men's Christian Association (YMCA) of North America from 1906 to 1942, and of the National Committee of YMCA of China also from 1906 to 1942. Died December 8, 1959, in Oakland, California. His son, **(WILLIAM) WINSTON PETTUS** (1912–1945), medical missionary, was born February 25, 1912, in Shanghai. Winston Pettus graduated from Yale University and Yale Medical School. He was a medical missionary under Yale-in-China in China from 1939 until 1942, serving in Changsha, Kweiyang, and Chungking. He returned to the United States in 1942 because of ill health, but was back in Chungking, China, in 1944. Killed in airplane accident, November 18, 1945, at Huangping, Kweichow, China. *References*: William B. Pettus Papers, Claremont College Library, Claremont, Calif.; Winston Pettus Papers, Yale-China Association Collection, Yale University Library, New Haven, Conn.; Edward H. Hume, *Dauntless Adventures, the Story of Dr. Winston Pettus* (New Haven, Conn., 1952): *NYT*, December 9, 1959; and *WWWA*.

PHILIPPINE-AMERICAN WAR (1899–1902). Known often as the Philippines Insurrection. Military hostilities between the U.S. Army and Filipino revolutionaries began after Spain ceded the Philippines to the United States in 1899, and continued until 1902. *References: EAH*; John M. Gates, *Schoolbooks and Krags: The United States Army in the Philippines, 1899–1902* (Westport, Conn., 1975); Brian M. Linn, *The U.S. Army and Counterinsurgency in the Philippine War, 1899–1902* (Chapel Hill, N.C., 1989); Stuart C. Miller, *"Benevolent Assimilation": The American Conquest of the Philippines, 1899–1903* (New Haven, Conn., 1983); Russell Roth, *Muddy Glory: America's 'Indian Wars' in the Philippines* (West Hanover, Mass., 1981); John R. M. Taylor, *History of the Philippine Insurrection against the United States, 1898–1903: A Compilation of Documents and Introduction* (Pasay City, Philippines, 1971); Richard E. Welch, *Response to Imperialism: The United States and the Philippine-American War, 1899–1902* (Chapel Hill, N.C., 1978); and Leon Wolff, *Little Brown Brother: How the United States Purchased and Pacified the Philippine Islands at the Century's Turn* (Garden City, N.Y., 1961).

PHILIPPINE COMMISSIONS. The first, the Schurman Commission, headed by Jacob G. Schurman,* was appointed in 1899 by President William McKinley to gather information about the Philippines, to study the situation there, and to recommend policies. The commission's final report urged the United States to replace the military rule by a civilian government, to assure individual liberties, and to promote local self-government with continuation of U.S. rule for an indefinite period. The second, the Taft Commission, was appointed in 1900. It became the civil government in 1901, and exercised both legislative and executive powers from 1900 to 1916. It served as the bicameral legislature from 1900 to 1907, and the upper house of the legislature from 1907 to 1916. The president of the commission served as governor-general. The Philippine Commission was eliminated in 1916. *References: EAH*; and Winfred L. Thompson, *The Introduction of American Law in the Philippines and Puerto Rico, 1898–1905* (Fayetteville, Ark., 1989).

PHILIPPINE CONSTABULARY. Semimilitary national police force in the Philippines, under the control of the civil government, established in 1901 by the Philippine Commission. Composed of Filipinos led by American Army officers (and later also Filipino officers), it was the mainstay of law and order in the Philippines. *References*: George Y. Coats, "The Philippine Constabulary: 1901–1917," Ph.D. diss., Ohio State University, 1968; Harold H. Elarth, *The Story of the Philippine Constabulary* (Los Angeles, 1949); Vic Hurley, *Jungle Patrol: The Story of the Philippine Constabulary* (New York, 1938); and Richard W. Smith, "Philippine Constabulary," *Military Review* 48 (May 1968): 73–80.

PHILIPPINE INSURRECTION. *See* PHILIPPINE-AMERICAN WAR

PHILIPPINE SCOUTS. An official branch of the U.S. Army, it was a Filipino contingent under the direct supervision of the officer commanding the Philippine Division. By 1922, it had become the backbone of the American garrison in the Philippines. *References*: Charles W. Franklin, *A History of the Philippine Scouts, 1898–1936* (Fort Humphreys, D.C., 1935); Clayton D. Laurie, "The Philippine Scouts: America's Colonial Army, 1899–1913," *PS* 37 (1989): 174–91; Antonio Tabaniag, "The Pre-War Philippine Scouts," *Journal of East Asiatic Studies* (Manila) 9 (October 1960): 7–26; and James R. Woodland, "The Philippine Scouts: The Development of America's Colonial Army," Ph.D. diss., Ohio State University, 1975.

PHILLIPS, JEREMIAH (1812–1879). Missionary, born January 5, 1812, in Plainfield, New Jersey. Phillips graduated from Hamilton Literary and Theological Institute (later Colgate University), and was ordained in 1835. He was a missionary under the Free Baptist Missionary Society in India from 1836 until 1878. He was stationed at Majurbhanj, Orissa, and served as a missionary to the Santals. He reduced their language to writing, and is credited with opening the first educational facility for the Santals at Jellasore in 1845. He established a farming colony of Christian Santals in 1852. He returned to the United States in 1855 because of ill health, and settled on a farm in the Midwest, but was back in India in 1865. He opened a teachers' training school in 1866, and was involved in famine relief in that year. He published *An Introduction to the Santal Language* (Calcutta, 1852), and translated parts of the Bible into that language. He returned to the United States in 1879. Died December 9, 1879, in Hillsdale, Michigan. *References: EM*; and Johan Nyhagen, "Jeremiah Phillips: Pioneer Missionary among the Santals," *Foundations* 21 (1978): 150–66.

PHILLIPS, WILLIAM (1878–1968). Diplomat, born May 30, 1878, in Beverly, Massachusetts. Phillips graduated from Harvard University and Harvard Law School. He entered the foreign service in 1905, and was second secretary in Peking from 1905 to 1907, assistant to the third assistant secretary of state for Far Eastern Affairs in 1907–1908, chief of the Division of Far Eastern Affairs in 1908, third assistant secretary of state in 1908–1909, first secretary in the U.S. embassy in London from 1909 to 1912, again third secretary of state from 1914 to 1917, and assistant secretary of state from 1917 to 1920. He was U.S. minister to the Netherlands and Luxembourg from 1920 to 1922, undersecretary of state from 1922 to 1924, ambassador to Belgium and minister to Luxembourg from 1924 to 1927, first minister to Canada from 1927 to 1929, undersecretary of state from 1933 to 1936, and ambassador to Italy from 1936 until 1941. He was director of the Office of Strategic Services (OSS) Office in London in 1942, and a personal representative of President Franklin D. Roosevelt in India with the rank of ambassador in 1942–1943. He recommended that the United States support the Indian nationalists. He was a political advisor to General Dwight D. Eisenhower in 1943–1944, served on the Anglo-American Committee on Palestine in 1946, and headed an international commission to adjust a boundary dispute between Siam and French Indochina in 1947. He wrote his memoirs, *Ventures in Diplomacy* (Boston, 1952). Died February 23, 1968, in Sarasota, Florida. *References*: Kenton J. Clymer, "The Education of William Phillips: Self Determination and American Policy toward India, 1942–1945," *DH* 8 (1984): 13–35; *DADH*; M. A. Khair, "William Phillips' Mission to India, 1942–1943," *Journal of the Asiatic Society of Pakistan* 9 (December 1964): 65–72; *NYT*, February 24, 1968; and *WWWA*.

PIERSON, GEORGE PECK (1861–1939). Missionary, born January 14, 1861, in Elizabeth, New Jersey. Pierson graduated from Princeton Theological Seminary, and was ordained in 1888. He was a missionary under the Board of Foreign Missions of the Presbyterian Church in the U.S.A. in Japan from 1888 until 1928. He served in Tokyo from 1888 until 1894, and then in Sapporo, Hokkaido, from 1894 until his retirement in 1928. He wrote (with Ida G. Pierson) *Forty Happy Years in Japan, 1888–1928* (New York, 1936). Died August 1, 1939, in Philadelphia. *References: Foreign Pioneers*; and *NYT*, August 1, 1939.

PITKIN, WOLCOTT H(OMER) (1881–1952). Lawyer and diplomatic advisor, born December 6, 1881, in Albany, New York. Pitkin graduated from Harvard University and Harvard Law School. He practiced law in New York City, and was assistant U.S. attorney for the southern district of New York from 1909 to 1912, and attorney general of Puerto Rico from 1912 to 1914. He was acting general advisor and advisor on foreign affairs to the government of Siam from 1915 to 1917. He wrote *Siam's Case for Revision of Obsolete Treaty Obligations, Admittedly Inapplicable to Present Conditions* (New York, 1919). He was in private law practice until 1925, when he joined the legal department of International Telegraph and Telephone Corporation and was its vice president and general counsel. Died August 18, 1952, in Ho-Ho-Kus, New Jersey. *References: NYT*, August 19, 1952; and *WWWA*.

PITMAN, NORMAN HINSDALE (1876–1925). Educator and author, born June 12, 1876, in Lamont, Michigan. Pitman graduated from the University of Tennessee. He was a teacher at Chihli Province College in China from 1909 to 1912, and a professor of English at Peking Teachers College from 1912 to 1921, and at Peiyang University in Tientsin after 1922. He wrote *Chinese Fairy Stories* (New York, 1910); *Chinese Playmates: or, The Boy Gleaners* (Boston, 1911); *The Lady Elect: A Chinese Romance* (New York, 1913); *A Chinese Christmas Tree* (New York, 1914); *A Chinese Wonder Book* (New York, 1919); and *Dragon Lure, a Romance of Peking in the Days of Yuan Shih Kai* (Shanghai, 1925). Died March 6, 1925. *Reference: WWWA*.

PLUMER, JAMES MARSHALL (1899–1960). Government official and educator, born July 10, 1899, in Newton Centre, Massachusetts. Plumer graduated from Harvard University. He worked as an able seaman in commercial steamships from 1921 to 1923, and was administrative officer in the Chinese Maritime Customs Service from 1923 to 1937. He made archaeological investigations in several locations in China. He was a lecturer on Far Eastern art at the University of Michigan from 1935 to 1941, associate professor there from 1941 to 1959, and professor after 1959. He was an organizer and administrator of the China unit of the Army Map Service of the U.S. Corps of Engineers in 1943–1944, consultant on the Far East to the American Commission for the Protection and Salvage of Artistic and Historic Monuments in War Areas in 1944, and fine arts advisor with the civilian information and education section for the General Headquarters of the Supreme Commander for the Allied Powers (SCAP) in Tokyo in 1948–1949. Died June 15, 1960, in Concord, New Hampshire. *References*: James Marshall Plumer Papers, Bentley Historical Library, University of Michigan, Ann Arbor; University of Michigan Museum of Art, *James Marshall Plumer Memorial Collection* (Ann Arbor, Mich., 1977); and *NCAB* 49:82.

POLK, MAY (1864–1924). Librarian, born February 10, 1864, in Knox County, Indiana. Polk graduated from Indiana and Stanford universities. She came to the Philippines in 1901, was a stenographer in the Biological Laboratory from 1901 to 1903, and a librarian of the Bureau of Government Laboratories (later the Bureau of Science) from 1903 until her death. She helped organize the American Circulating Library (which became the nucleus of the National Library) and the University of Philippines Library. She was instrumental in founding the department of library science at the University of the Philippines, and was later a professor and head of the department. Died April 12, 1924, in Baguio, Philippines. *Reference: DPB* 2.

POMEROY, WILLIAM J(OSEPH) (1916–   ). Revolutionary, born November 25, 1916, in Waterloo, New York. Pomeroy attended the University of the Philippines. He served in the U.S. Army Air Force during World War II. He came to the Philippines in 1946 as a freelance writer and came in contact with the Hukbalahaps liberation movement (the Huks). After the war, he studied and taught at the University of the Philippines, and joined the Huks in 1950 in the Sierra Madre Mountains. He was captured in 1952 and sentenced to life in prison. His prison sentence was commuted in 1961, and he was deported to the United States. He edited *Born of the People: The Autobiography of Luis Taruc* (New York, 1953), and wrote *The Forest: A Personal Record of the Huk Guerilla Struggle in the Philippines* (New York, 1963); *American Neo-Colonialism: Its Emergence in the Philippines and Asia* (New York, 1970); *Trail of Blame: Stories of the Philippines* (New York, 1971); and *An American-Made Tragedy: Neo-Colonialism and Dictatorship in the Philippines* (New York, 1974). He lived in England after 1963. *References*: B. Appel, "William Pomeroy—American Huk," *Nation* 175 (June 11, 1955): 72–73; and *CA*.

POND, HORACE B. (1882–1960). Businessman, born July 21, 1882, in Waltham, Massachusetts. Pond went to the Philippines in 1905 to work for the Customs Bureau. He was manager of Applebee Neuman and Company, a textile company that was later absorbed by the Pacific Commercial Company, an export-import concern in Manila. He was vice president of the company from 1916 to 1919, general manager from 1919 to 1925, and president after 1925. He was interned by the Japanese in the Santo Tomas prison camp during World War II. He retired after the war. Died April 18, 1960, in St. Petersburg, Florida. *References: CCDP; Gleeck/Manila; NYT*, April 21, 1960; and *WWA*.

POOR, DANIEL (1789–1855). Missionary, born June 27, 1789, in Danvers, Massachusetts. Poor graduated from Dartmouth College and Andover Theological Seminary, and was ordained in 1815. He was a missionary under the American Board of Commissioners for Foreign Missions (ABCFM) in Ceylon from 1816 until his death. He served in Tellipally, Jaffna Province, from 1816 to 1823; in Batticota, where he founded a boys' school, from 1823 to 1835; and in Madura, India, where he also established a boys' school, from 1835 to 1841. He was back in Tellipally from 1841 to 1850, and then served in Manepay from 1850 until his death. He founded the Missionary Scientific Seminary at Batticota in 1826. Died February 3, 1855, in Mampy, Ceylon. *References: AndoverTS; DAB;* and *EM.*

POORBAUGH, ELIZABETH R. ("LIZZIE") (1854–1927). Missionary educator, born December 27, 1854, in Berlin, Somerset County, Pennsylvania. She was a missionary under the Foreign Mission Board of the Reformed Church in the United States in Japan from 1886 until 1892. She was principal and teacher of a girls' school in Sendai. She returned to the United States in 1893 and resided in Sabiliasville, Maryland, and in Baltimore. Died April 26, 1927, in Baltimore. *Reference:* C. William Mensendiek, *A Dream Incarnate: The Beginnings of Miyagi Gakuin for Women* (Sendai, 1986).

PORTER, LUCIUS C(HAPIN) (1880–1958). Missionary and educator, born October 31, 1880, in Tientsin, China. Porter graduated from Beloit College, Yale University Divinity School, and Columbia University; studied at the universities of Berlin and Marburg and the American School of Archaeology (Jerusalem); attended Union Theologial Seminary; and was ordained in 1908. He was a missionary under the American Board of Commissioners for Foreign Missions (ABCFM) in China from 1908 until 1922. He was stationed at Tunghsien, was a member of the faculty at North China Union College in Tungchow until 1918, and was professor of philosophy at Yenching University from 1918 until his retirement in 1949. He helped protect ABCFM property at Fenchow during the Japanese occupation in 1938–1939. He was interned by the Japanese on the Yenching campus from 1941 to 1945. He wrote *China's Challenge to Christianity* (New York, 1924), and compiled *Aids to the Study of Chinese Philosophy* (Peiping, 1934). Died September 7, 1958, in Beloit, Wisconsin. *References:* Lucius C. Porter Papers, Beloit College Library, Beloit, Wis.; *NCAB* 47:162; *NYT,* September 9, 1958; *UnionTS;* and *WWWA.*

POTEAT, EDWIN MCNEILL, JR. (1892–1955). Missionary, born November 20, 1892, in New Haven, Connecticut, and grew up in Philadelphia and Greenville, South Carolina. Poteat graduated from Furman University and Southern Baptist Seminary, and was ordained in 1913. He was traveling secretary of the Student Volunteer Movement in 1916–1917. He was a missionary under the Foreign Mission Board of the Southern Baptist Convention to China from 1917 to 1929, serving in Kaifeng, and was professor of philosophy at the University of Shanghai from 1926 to 1929. He was pastor in Raleigh, North Carolina, from 1929 to 1937 and from 1948 to 1955, and president of Colgate-Rochester Divinity School from 1944 to 1948. Died December 17, 1955, in Raleigh, North Carolina. *References:* Edwin McNeill Poteat, Jr., Papers, North Carolina Baptist Historical Collections, Wake Forest College Library, Winston-Salem, N.C.; Edwin

McNeill Poteat, Jr., Papers, Southern Historical Collections, University of North Carolina Library, Chapel Hill, N.C.; Jeffrey O. Kelley, "Edwin McNeill Poteat, Jr.: The Minister as Advocate," *Foundations* 22 (1979): 152–73; *NYT*, December 18, 1955; Henry D. Smith, Jr., "Edwin McNeill Poteat: A Study of His Life and Work," Th.D. diss., New Orleans Baptist Theological Seminary, 1963; and *WWWA*.

POTT, FRANCIS LISTER HAWKS (1864–1947). Missionary, born February 22, 1864, in New York City. Pott graduated from Columbia University and General Theological Seminary. He was a missionary under the Domestic and Foreign Missionary Society of the Protestant Episcopal Church in the United States of America in China from 1886 until his death. He was head of St. John's College in Shanghai from 1888 to 1896, and its president from 1896 to 1940. He was active in the Holy Catholic Church in China. He returned to the United States in 1940, but was back in Shanghai in 1946. He wrote *The Outbreak of China* (New York, 1900); *A Sketch of the Shanghai Dialect* (Shanghai, 1907); *The Emergency in China* (New York, 1913); and *A Short History of Shanghai: Being an Account of the Growth and Development of the International Settlement* (Shanghai, 1928). Died March 7, 1947, in Shanghai. *References*: Francis Lister Hawks Pott Papers, Church Historical Society, Austin, Tex.; *DAB S4*; John N. Hawkins, "Francis Lister Hawks Pott (1864–1947), China Missionary and Educator," *Paedagogica Historica* 13 (1973): 329–47; *NYT*, March 8, 1947; and *WWWA*.

POWELL, E(DWARD) ALEXANDER (1879–1957). Traveler and author, born August 16, 1879, in Syracuse, New York. Powell graduated from Syracuse University and Oberlin College. He was a correspondent for British and American publications, went on a special mission to Central Asia for the U.S. Department of Agriculture from 1906 to 1908, and, as correspondent for *Everybody's Magazine* from 1901 to 1911, he traveled in the Caucasus, central Asia, and India. He headed the Goldwyn-Bray-Powell expedition to the Far East in 1920 to make motion pictures of scenes in the Philippines, Borneo, Celebes, Java, Bali, Sumatra, Straits Settlements, Siam, Indochina, China, and Japan; and traveled overland from Europe to India, Nepal, and Baluchistan in 1928. He served in the U.S. Army during World War I, and in the Office of Naval Intelligence and the Office of Censorship during World War II. He wrote *Asia at the Crossroads: Japan, Korea, China, Philippine Islands* (New York, 1922); *The Last Home of Mystery* (Garden City, N.Y., 1929); and an autobiography, *Adventure Road* (Garden City, N.Y., 1954). Died November 13, 1957, in Fall Village, near Camden, Connecticut. *References: NCAB* 46:308; *NYT*, November 14, 1957; and *WWWA*.

POWELL, JOHN B(ENJAMIN) (1886–1947). Journalist and editor, born April 18, 1886, near Palmyra, Marion County, Missouri. Powell graduated from Gem City Business College (Quincy, Ill.), and attended the University of Missouri School of Journalism. He worked for the *Hannibal* (Mo.) *Courier-Post* from 1910 to 1913. He went to Shanghai, China, in 1917, and joined *Millard's Review of the Far East*. He took over the review in 1922, and renamed it the *China Weekly Review*. He also served as a correspondent for the *Chicago Tribune* from 1918 to 1938, *The Manchester Guardian* from 1925 to 1936, and the London *Daily Herald* from 1937 to 1941. He lobbied in the United States for American businessmen in China from 1920 to 1922. He was held prisoner by the Japanese in 1941–1942. He returned to the United States in 1942. He wrote *My Twenty-Five Years in China* (New York, 1945), and in 1946 he testified at the Tokyo War Crimes Trials. Died February 28, 1947, in Washington, D.C. *References: DAB S4*; John M. Hamilton, "The Missouri News Monopoly and American Altruism in China: Thomas F. F. Millard, J. B. Powell, and Edgar Snow," *PHR* 55 (1986): 27–48; *NYT*, March 1, 1947; and *WWWA*.

PREBLE, GEORGE H(ENRY) (1816–1885). Naval officer, born February 25, 1816, in Portland, Maine. Preble was appointed a midshipman in 1835. He served in East Asia on the USS *St. Louis* from 1842 to 1845, and in 1844 in Canton he commanded the first American armed landing force in China. He served in the Mexican War and was later on the coast survey duty from 1849 to 1852. He accompanied Matthew C. Perry's* expedition in 1853–1856, and commanded the USS *Macedonian* which later also operated against Chinese pirates. In 1855, he prepared surveys and sailing directions for the Wusung River leading to Shanghai. He later served in the Boston Navy Yard and in the Pacific, and then served in the Union Navy during the Civil War. He retired with the rank of rear admiral in 1878. Died March 1, 1885, in Boston. *References: ACAB; DAB; NCAB* 8:92; Boleslaw Szczesniak, ed., *The Opening of Japan: A Diary of Discovery in the Far East, 1853–1856* (Norman, Okla., 1962); and *WWWA*.

PRESBYTERIAN CHURCH IN THE UNITED STATES: BOARD OF FOREIGN MISSIONS. Founded in 1861, it was later renamed the Board of World Missions. It began missionary work in China in 1867 (terminated in 1950), in Japan in 1885, in Korea in 1892, and in Taiwan in 1851. It merged with the United Presbyterian Church in the U.S.A. in 1983 to form the Presbyterian Church (U.S.A.). *References*: Board of Foreign Missions Archives, Historical Foundation of the Presbyterian and Reformed Churches, Inc., Montreat, N.C.; James E. Bear, *The Mission Work of the Presbyterian Church in the United States in China, 1867–1952* (Richmond, 1963, 1973); George T. Brown, *Mission to Korea* (Nashville, Tenn., 1962); Harriet N. Noyes, *History of the South China Mission of the American Presbyterian Church* (Shanghai, 1927); *Our China Investment: Sixty Years of the Southern Presbyterian Church in China with Biographies, Autobiographies, and Sketches of all Missionaries* *since the Opening of the Work in 1867*, comp. and ed. Philip F. Price (Nashville, 1927).

PRESBYTERIAN CHURCH IN THE U.S.A.: BOARD OF FOREIGN MISSIONS. Organized in 1837, it began missionary work in India in 1833, in China in 1837, in Siam in 1840, in Japan in 1859, in Korea in 1884, and in the Philippines in 1899. It merged with the United Presbyterian Church in North America in 1958 to form the United Presbyterian Church in the U.S.A., which merged in 1983 with the Presbyterian Church in the United States to create the Presbyterian Church (U.S.A.). *References*: Board of Foreign Missions Papers, Presbyterian Historical Society, Philadelphia; Arthur J. Brown, *One Hundred Years: A History of the Foreign Missionary Work of the Presbyterian Church in the U.S.A.* (New York, 1929); J. F. Dripps, *Historical Sketch of the Missions of Siam* (Philadelphia, 1881); Harriet N. Noyes, *History of the South China Mission of the American Presbyterian Church* (Shanghai, 1927); Harry A. Rhodes, ed., *History of the Korea Mission, Presbyterian Church U.S.A., 1884–1934* (Seoul, 1934); Harry A. Rhodes and Archibald Campbell, *History of the Korea Mission, Presbyterian Church in the U.S.A., 1935–1959* (New York, 1964); W. Reginald Wheeler, ed., *The Crisis Decade: A History of the Foreign Missionary Work of the Presbyterian Church in the U.S.A. 1937–1947* (New York, 1951); and E. M. Wherry, *Our Missions in India 1834–1924* (Boston, 1926).

PRICE, FRANK W(ILSON) (1895–1974). Missionary, born at Kashing (near Shanghai), China, to American missionary parents. Price graduated from Davidson College, Yale Divinity School, and Columbia University, and was ordained in 1923. He was principal of Hillcrest School in Nanking from 1915 to 1917, and then Young Men's Christian Association (YMCA) secretary at Southeastern University of Nanking in 1917–1918. He served with the Chinese Labor Corps in France in 1918–1919. He was a missionary under the Board of Foreign Missions of the Presbyterian Church in the U.S.A. in China from 1923 to 1952, and professor of religious education at Nanking Seminary and director of the West China Unit of Nanking Theological Seminary at Chengtu from 1939 to 1945. He returned to Nanking in 1945, and was expelled by the Communist government in 1952. He held a pastorate in Lexington, Virginia, from 1953 to 1955, was director of the Missionary Research Library at Union Theological Seminary (New York City) from 1956 to 1961, and served as professor of international studies at Mary Baldwin College (Va.) from 1961 until his retirement in 1966. He was coeditor of *China Rediscovers Her West* (London, 1942); edited *Wartime China: As Seen by Westerners* (Chunking, 1942); and wrote *China—Twilight and Dawn?* (New York, 1948), and *The Rural Church in China: A Survey* (New York, 1948). Died January 9, 1974, in Lexington, Virginia. *References*: Frank W. Price Papers, George C. Marshall Research Foundation, Virginia Military Institute, Lexington, Va.; M. McKendrie Goodpasture, ''China in an American: Frank Wilson Price: A Bibliographical Essay," *Journal of Presbyterian History* 49 (1971): 352–64; and *WWWA*.

PRICE, THOMAS FREDERICK (1860–1919). Missionary, born August 19, 1860, in Wilmington, North Carolina. Price graduated from St. Charles College (Catonsville, Md.) and St. Mary's Seminary (Baltimore), and was ordained in 1886. He was a pastor in Asheville and New Bern, North Carolina. He founded the magazine *Truth* in 1897, as well as an orphanage in Raleigh and *The Orphan Boy* magazine. With James Anthony Walsh, in 1911 he founded the Catholic Foreign Mission Society of America (Maryknoll Fathers). He led the first group of Maryknoll priests to China in 1919. Died September 12, 1919, in Hong Kong. *References: DAB; DACB*; and *NYT*, September 24, 1919.

PROTESTANT EPISCOPAL CHURCH IN THE UNITED STATES OF AMERICA: DOMESTIC AND FOREIGN MISSIONARY SOCIETY. Organized in 1835, it began missionary work in China in 1835, in the Philippines in 1901, and in Taiwan in 1953. It later became the World Mission in Church and Society of the Episcopal Church. *References*: Domestic and Foreign Missionary Society Archives, Church Historical Society, Austin, Texas; Julia C. Emery, *A Century of Endeavor 1821–1921: A Record of the First One Hundred Years of the Domestic and Foreign Missionary Society of the Protestant Episcopal Church in the United States of America* (New York, 1921); and Henry St. George Tucker, *The History of the Episcopal Church in Japan* (New York, 1938).

PRUITT, ANNA (ASHLEY) (SEWARD) (1862–1948). Missionary, born in Tallmadge, Ohio. Anna Pruitt graduated from Lake Erie Female Seminary (later Lake Erie College), and taught in the Tallmadge public schools. She was a missionary under the Board of Foreign Missions of the Southern Baptist Convention in China after 1887. She served at Hwanghsien, Shantung Province; was principal of a girls' school; and then founded and taught in a boys' school (later the North China Baptist School). She wrote *The Day of Small Things* (Richmond, Va., 1929); *Up From Zero* (Richmond, Va., 1938); and *Whirligigs in China: Stories for Juniors* (Nashville, Tenn., 1948). Died June 20, 1948, in Philadelphia. *References*: Pruitt Family Papers, Radcliffe College Library, Cambridge, Mass.; Marjorie King, "Missionary Mother and Radical Daughter: Anna and Ida Pruitt in China, 1887–1939," Ph.D. diss., Temple University, 1985; and *NYT*, June 21, 1948.

PRUITT, IDA C. (1888–1985). Social worker, daughter of Anna Pruitt,* born in Penglai, Shantung Province, China. Ida C. Pruitt graduated from Cox College (Atlanta) and Columbia University Teachers College. She was founder of the Medical Social Work of the Peking Union Medical College Hospital in 1920, chief of the department of medical social work from 1920 to 1938, and also chief of social services at the hospital. She trained China's first generation of social workers. She aided the Chinese resistance movement after the occupation by Japanese troops in 1937. She returned to the United States in 1939, and was executive secretary of the Chinese Industrial Cooperatives in New York City from 1939 to 1959. She wrote *A Daughter of Han: The Autobiography of a Chinese Working Woman* (New Haven, Conn., 1945); an autobiography, *A China Childhood* (San Francisco, 1978); and *Old Madam Yin: A Memoir of Peking Life, 1926–1938* (Stanford, Calif., 1979). Died July 24, 1985, in Philadelphia. *References*: Pruitt Family Papers, Radcliffe College Library, Cambridge, Mass.; *JAS* 45 (1986): 667–68; Marjorie King, "Missionary Mother and Radical Daughter: Anna and Ida Pruitt in China, 1887–1939," Ph.D. diss., Temple University, 1985; and *NYT*, August 11, 1985.

PRUYN, ROBERT HEWSON (1815–1882). Diplomat, born February 14, 1815, in Albany, New York. Pruyn graduated from Rutgers University. He served on the Albany municipal council in 1839, was judge advocate general and adjutant general of the state militia, and served in the state legislature from 1848 to 1850 and in 1854–1855. He was U.S. minister to Japan from 1862 to 1865. He was involved in the diplomatic negotiations that were the result of the Shimonoseki bombardment.* He was president of the Albany National Commercial Bank after 1865. Died February 26, 1882, in Albany. *References*: Robert H. Pruyn Papers, Albany Institute of History and Art, Albany, N.Y.; *DAB; DADH*; Edwin B. Lee, "Robert H. Pruyn in Japan, 1862–1865," *New York History* 66 (1985): 123–39; *NCAB* 13:439; and *NYT*, February 27, 1882.

PUEBLO INCIDENT (1968). The USS *Pueblo*, an electronic surveillance ship, commanded by Commander Lloyd M. Bucher, was attacked and boarded by North Koreans in 1968. After the crew confessed and the United States admitted its guilt, the staff were released after eleven months. *References*: Trevor Armbrister, *A Matter of Accountability: The True Story of the Pueblo Affairs* (New York, 1970); Ed Brandt, *The Last Voyage of the USS Pueblo* (New York, 1969); Lloyd M. Bucher, *Bucher: My Story* (Garden City, N.Y., 1970); *DADH*; and Robert A. Liston, *The Pueblo Surrender: A Covert Action by the National Security Agency* (New York, 1988).

PUMPELLY, RAPHAEL (1837–1923). Geologist and explorer, born September 8, 1837, in Owego, Tioga County, New York. Pumpelly graduated from the Royal School of Mines (Freiberg, Saxony, Germany). He was in charge of developing silver mines in Southern Arizona from 1859 to 1861. He was with William Phipps Blake* in Japan in 1862–1863, appointed by the Japanese government to conduct surveys of mineral resources. He traveled in China in 1863–1864, making an expedition up the Yangtze in 1863 to study coal deposits. He also studied the loess, a deposit of fertile yellowish-brown windblown dust, of China. He then went to Tientsin and Peking, and in 1865, he traveled to St. Petersburg through Mongolia and Siberia. He wrote *Geological Researches in*

China, Mongolia and Japan (Washington, D.C., 1867), and *Across America and Asia. Notes of a Five Years' Journey around the World and of Residence in Arizona, Japan and China* (New York, 1870). He was engaged in the exploration of the copper and iron districts in Michigan's Upper Peninsula in 1870, and was state geologist of Missouri from 1871 to 1873. In 1903–1904, under the auspices of the Carnegie Institution of Washington, he organized and conducted an expedition into Central Asia. He wrote *A Journey around Turkestan* (Washington, D.C., 1903), and *Explorations in Turkestan. Expedition of 1904. Prehistoric Civilizations of Anau. Origins, Growth and Influence of Environment* (Washington, D.C., 1908). He wrote *My Reminiscences* (New York, 1918). Died August 10, 1923, in Newport, Rhode Island. *References*: Raphael Pumpelly Papers, Henry E. Huntington Library, San Marino, Calif.; *BMNAS* 16 (1931): 23–62; *DAB; DSB; NCAB* 6:360; *NYT*, August 11, 1923; and *WWWA*.

PUTNAM, GEORGE ROCKWELL (1865–1953). Engineer, born May 24, 1865, in Davenport, Iowa. Putnam graduated from Rose Polytechnic Institute. He entered the U.S. Coast and Geodetic Service in 1890, and was an aide in its field service from 1891 to 1894, and an assistant after 1894. He conducted boundary surveys in the Mexican border, southeastern Alaska, Greenland, the Hudson Straits, Labrador, the Pribilof Islands in the Bering Sea, and the Yukon River. He came to the Philippines in 1900, organized coast surveys there that year, and served as director of the Coast Survey until 1906, developing the survey's plans. From 1906 to 1910, he prepared a plan for the extensive revision of the charts of the U.S. coasts. He served as the commissioner of lighthouses of the United States from 1910 to 1935. He wrote an autobiography, *Sentinel of the Coasts: The Log of a Lighthouse Engineer* (New York, 1937). Died July 2, 1953, in Washington, D.C. *References: NCAB* 42:38; and *WWWA*.

PYE, WATTS O(RSON) (1878–1926). Missionary, born October 20, 1878, near Faribault, Minnesota. Pye graduated from Carleton College, attended Southern Presbyterian Church Seminary (Austin, Texas), graduated from Oberlin Theological Seminary, and was ordained in 1907. He was a missionary under the American Board of Commissioners for Foreign Missions (ABCFM) in China from 1907 until his death. He served in Fenchow, Shansi Province; surveyed Central Shansi and Northern Shensi provinces; and developed an extensive missionary activity with a large staff of Chinese which he directed. He also extended his activities north of the Great Wall. Died January 9, 1926, in Fenchow. *References: DAB*; and John Schrecker, "Watts O. Pye, Missionary to China, 1907–1926," *Papers on China* 13 (1959): 32–60.

Q

QUALLAH BATTOO. Following an attack on the Salem vessel *Friendship* in 1831 at Quallah Battoo (Kuala Batu) in Sumatra, Captain John Downes,* commanding the USS *Potomac*, attacked the forts at Quallah Battoo in 1832 as a punishment. He burned them and killed some 100 Malays. Two Americans were killed in the attack. *References*: John M. Belohlavek, "Andrew Jackson and the Malaysian Pirates: A Question of Diplomacy and Politics," *Tennessee Historical Quarterly* 36 (1977): 19–29; John M. Belohlavek, *"Let the Eagle Soar!" The Foreign Policy of Andrew Jackson* (Lincoln, Nebr., 1985), ch. 6; John F. Campbell, "Pepper, Pirates and Grapeshot," *AN* 21 (1961): 292–302; and David Long, "Martial Thunder: The First Official American Armed Intervention in Asia," *PHR* 42 (1973): 143–63.

QUEMOY-MATSU CRISES. Islands off the China coast occupied by Nationalist Chinese forces. The first crisis occurred in 1954–1955 and the second in 1958. When the Communist Chinese shelled the islands, the U.S. government announced that it would defend the islands if an attack on them seemed to be a prelude to an invasion of Taiwan. The United States did not take any aggressive steps, and the shelling eventually stopped. *References*: J. H. Kalicki, *The Pattern of Sino-American Crises: Political-Military Interactions in the 1950s* (London, 1975), chs. 6 and 8; Chi-yung Lin, "The Quemoy-Matsu Crises: A Study of American Policy," Ph.D. diss., Southern Illinois University, 1969; and Thomas E. Stolper, *China, Taiwan, and the Offshore Islands* (Armonk, N.Y., 1985).

R

RANDOLPH, JOHN C(OOPER) F(ITZ) (1846–1911). Mining engineer, born December 20, 1846, in Trenton, New Jersey. Randolph graduated from Princeton University and Columbia University School of Mines, and studied at the universities of Göttingen, Tübingen, and Vienna. He was in the service of the German government from 1869 to 1871; the U.S. government in 1872–1873; the Japanese government in 1873–1874; the Chinese government, for whom he was engaged in examining gold lands on the Yangtze river, from 1884 to 1888; and the government of Colombia, for whom he was national commissioner of mines in the Tolima district, from 1888 to 1890. He prospected for diamonds in Borneo in 1890, and was resident manager of the Borneo Diamond Exploration Syndicate. He was in Peru and Chile from 1899 to 1900, and in Hyderabad State, India, in 1900–1901. Died February 3, 1911, in Morristown, New Jersey. *References: Engineering and Mining Journal* 91 (February 11, 1911): 337 and 91 (February 18, 1911): 363; and *WWWA*.

RANKIN, KARL LOTT (1898–   ). Diplomat, born September 4, 1898, in Manitowoc, Wisconsin. Rankin attended the California Institute of Technology and Federal Polytechnic (Zurich, Switzerland), and graduated from Princeton University. He served in the U.S. Navy during World War I. He was a construction superintendent for the Near East Relief in Armenia from 1922 to 1925; manager of Berlant Development Company in Lindin, New Jersey, from 1925 to 1927; and foreign commerce officer in the U.S. Department of Commerce from 1927–1939, serving in Prague, Athens, and Tirana, Albania. He entered the foreign service in 1939, and served in Brussels, Belgrade, Cairo, Athens, again in Belgrade, Vienna, and again in Athens until 1949. He was consul general in Canton, Hong Kong, and Macao in 1949, U.S. minister and chargé d'affaires in Taipei, Formosa, from 1950 to 1953; and ambassador to Nationalist China from 1953 to 1957. He negotiated the mutual security agreement between the United States and Nationalist China. He wrote *China Assignment* (Seattle,

1964). Later he was ambassador to Yugoslavia from 1958 to 1961. *References: CA; CB* 1955; *NCAB* I:341; *PolProf: Eisenhower*; and *WWA.*

RAVEN, HENRY CUSHIER (1889–1944). Zoologist, born April 16, 1889, in Brooklyn, New York. Raven began working for the Museum of Natural History in 1907 to 1910 and at the Colorado Museum of Natural History from 1910 to 1912, and was a field representative for the Smithsonian Institution from 1912 until 1918. He made an extensive expedition to Borneo, Celebes, and the Moluccas between 1912 and 1918. He joined the American Museum of Natural History in 1921 as a field representative. He became assistant curator in 1926 and curator of comparative anatomy in 1944, and was a lecturer in zoology at Columbia University after 1926. He later participated in expeditions to Africa, Australia, and Greenland. Died April 5, 1944, in Sebring, Florida. *References*: Henry Cushier Raven "Field Journal," Smithsonian Institution Archives, Washington, D.C.; William K. Gregory, "Henry Cushier Raven (1889–1944)," in *The Henry Cushier Raven Memorial Volume: The Anatomy of the Gorilla: Studies of Henry Cushier Raven*, ed. William K. Gregory (New York, 1950), pp. 1–9; and *NYT*, April 6, 1944.

RAWLINSON, FRANK J(OSEPH) (1871–1937). Missionary, born January 9, 1871, in Langham, Rutlandshire, England; came to the United States in 1889; and was naturalized a U.S. citizen in 1902. Rawlinson graduated from Buckland University (Lewisburg, Pa.), Rochester Theological Seminary, and Columbia University, and was ordained in 1902. He was a missionary under the Foreign Mission Board of the Southern Baptist Convention in China from 1902 to 1921, and under the American Board of Commissioners for Foreign Missions (ABCFM) after 1921. He was principal of the preparatory department of Shanghai Baptist College, was involved in the Moral Welfare League, and was one of the founders of the Shanghai American School. He began his connection with the *Chinese Recorder*, the journal of Protestant Christian work in China, in 1910, and was its editor from 1914 until his death. He was also editor in chief of the *China Mission Year Book* from 1922 to 1937, and represented *Christian Century* in China. He wrote *Naturalization of Christianity in China* (Shanghai, 1927); *The Chinese Idea of the Supreme Being* (Shanghai, 1929); *Revolution and Religion in Modern China* (Shanghai, 1929); and *Chinese Ethical Ideals* (Shanghai, 1934). Died August 14, 1937, in Shanghai. *References: DAB S2; NYT*, August 15, 1937; and *WWWA.*

RAY, REX (1885–1958). Missionary, born November 11, 1885, in Whitewright, Texas. Ray graduated from Baylor University (Waco, Tex.). He was a missionary under the Foreign Mission Board of the Southern Baptist Convention in China from 1919 until 1944, serving in Wuchow, and superintendent of the Tai Kam Baptist leper colony from 1946 until the Communist authorities forced him to leave. He was transferred to Korea in 1951, and served there until his retirement in 1955. Died January 31, 1958, in Dallas, Texas. His memoirs, *Cowboy Missionary in Kwangsi* (Nashville, 1964) were published posthumously. *Reference: ESB S.*

RAYMOND, ANTONIN (1888–1976). Architect, born May 10, 1888, in Kladno, near Prague, Czechoslovakia. Raymond graduated from the Higher Technical Institute of Prague, came to the United States in 1910 and became a naturalized U.S. citizen in 1914. He served in the U.S. Army Intelligence Corps during World War I. He practiced architecture in New York City from 1910 to 1917. He accompanied Frank Lloyd Wright to Japan in 1919–1920 to work on the Imperial Hotel in Tokyo. He remained in Japan and practiced architecture in Tokyo until 1937. Helping to pioneer modern architecture in Japan, he designed lightweight reinforced-concrete constructions, and trained Japanese architects. He returned to the United States in 1937 and practiced in New York City and New Hope, Pennsylvania. He returned to Japan in 1947 and reestablished his practice there. He wrote *Antonin Raymond: An Autobiography* (Rutland, Vt., 1973). Died November 21, 1976, in Langhorne, Pennsylvania. *References*: Muriel Emanuel, ed., *Contemporary Architects* (New York, 1980); Adolph K. Placzek, ed., *Macmillan Encyclopedia of Architects* (New York, 1982); *KEJ; NYT*, October 29, 1976; and *WWWA*.

REA, GEORGE BRONSON (1869–1936). Journalist and publicist, born August 28, 1869, in Brooklyn, New York. Rea was a war correspondent for the *New York Herald* during the Cuban War for independence from 1895 to 1897, and also during the Spanish-American War. He founded the *Far Eastern Review* in Manila in 1904. He attached himself to Sun Yat-sen after Sun became president of the provisional government in Nanking, China, and served as one of Sun's many "advisors" from 1911 to 1913. He was appointed secretary of the Chinese National Railway Corporation in 1913–1914. He served in the U.S. Army during World War I, and was an assistant military attaché in Madrid from 1917 to 1919, and a technical advisor to the Chinese delegation to the Peace Conference in Paris in 1919. The *Far Eastern Quarterly* received a subsidy from Japan, and took a pro-Japanese line after 1920. Rea was a lobbyist for the American Chamber of Commerce, China, from 1927 to 1929; and counselor to the Ministry of Foreign Affairs of Manchukuo (the puppet government under P'u-yi) from 1932 to 1936, writing in support of this regime. He wrote *The Breakdown of American Diplomacy in the Far East* (n.p., 1919?), and *The Case for Manchukuo* (New York, 1935). Died November 21, 1936, in Baltimore. *References*: Frederick B. Hoyt, "George Bronson Rea: From Old China Hand to Apologist for Japan," *Pacific Northwest Quarterly* 69 (1978): 61–70; *NYT*, November 22, 1936; and *WWWA*.

READ, HOLLIS (1802–1887). Missionary, born August 26, 1802, in Newfane, Vermont. Read graduated from Williams College, attended Princeton and Andover theological seminaries, and was ordained in 1829. He was a missionary under the American Board of Commissioners for Foreign Missions (ABCFM) in India from 1830 to 1835, serving in Bombay and Ahmednagar. He wrote (with William Ramsey) *Journal of a Missionary Tour in India* (Philadelphia, 1836), the first American book about travel in India. He also wrote *Babajee, the Christian Brahmin* (New York, 1837), and *India, Its People, Ancient and Modern* (Columbus, Ohio, 1859). He was an agent for the ABCFM in the United States from 1835 to 1837, the American Tract Society in 1843–1844, and the Society for the Conversion of the Jews from 1851 to 1855. He held pastorates in Babylon, New York; Derby and New Preston, Connecticut; and Cranford and Elizabeth, New Jersey. Died April 7, 1887, in Somerville, New Jersey. *References: ACAB; AndoverTS*; and *Hewitt*.

REED, MARY (1854–1943). Missionary, born December 4, 1854, in Lowell, Washington County, Ohio. Reed taught in a school in Kenton, Ohio, until 1884. She was a missionary under the Woman's Foreign Missionary Society of the Methodist Episcopal Church in India from 1884 until her death. She served at Cawnpore and then in Pithoragarh in the foothills of the Himalayas. She then returned to Cawnpore and later taught in a girls' school in Gonda. She returned to the United States in 1890 because of ill health. Convinced that she had contracted leprosy, she came back to India in 1892 and was superintendent of the leper asylum in Chadang, near Pithoragarh, from 1892 until 1938, although her symptoms had disappeared by 1895. Died April 8, 1943, in Chadang. The hospital that was later built at Chadang was named after her. *References: DAB S3; EWM; NAW*; and *NYT*, May 21, 1943.

REED, WILLIAM BRADFORD (1806–1876). Lawyer and diplomat, born June 30, 1806, in Philadelphia. Reed graduated from the University of Pennsylvania, studied law, and was admitted to the bar in 1826. He practiced law in Philadelphia after 1827, served as a member of the Pennsylvania Assembly from 1834 to 1838, and was state attorney general in 1838–1839, state senator in 1841–1842, and district attorney in Philadelphia from 1850 to 1856. He was U.S. minister to China from 1857 to 1859. He concluded the Treaty of Tientsin in 1858, which gave the United States the same advantages given to the other foreign powers in China. He moved to Orange, New Jersey, in 1870 and became involved in journalism, writing for the New York *World*. Died February 18, 1876, in New York City. *References*: William Bradford Reed Papers, Manuscript Division, Library of Congress; *ACAB; DAB; DADH*; Foster M. Farley, "William B. Reed: President Buchanan's Minister to China 1857–1858," *Pennsylvania History* 37 (1970): 269–80; *NCAB* 7:533; and *WWWA*.

REFORMED CHURCH IN AMERICA: BOARD OF FOREIGN MISSIONS. Organized in 1832, its activities were coordinated by the American Board of Commissioners for Foreign Missions (ABCFM) until 1857, when it assumed independent direction of its missions and took over the Arcot mission in India and the Amoy mission in China. It began missionary work in Japan in 1859 and in Southeast Asia in 1951. The name was changed later to the Board of World Missions. *References*: Reformed Church in America Archives, New Brunswick Theological Seminary, New Brunswick, N.J.; S. Immanuel David, "God's Messengers: Reformed Church in America Missionaries in South India, 1839–1938," Th.D. diss., Lutheran School of Theology at Chicago, 1984; Elton M. Eenigenburg, *A Brief History of the RCA* (Grand Rapids, Mich., 1958); G. Howard Hageman, *Lily among the Thorns* (New York, 1961); Stephen W. Ryder, *A Historical Sourcebook of the Japan Mission of the RCA (1859–1930)* (New York, 1935); Peter N. Vandenberge, *Historical Directory of the Reformed Church in America 1628–1978* (Grand Rapids, Mich., 1978); and Charlotte C. Wyckoff, *A Hundred Years with Christ in Arcot: A Brief History of the Arcot Mission in India of the Reformed Church in America* (Madras, India, 1954).

REFORMED CHURCH IN THE UNITED STATES: BOARD OF FOREIGN MISSIONS. Founded in 1838, it worked through the American Board of Commissioners for Foreign Missions (ABCFM) from 1838 until 1866. It began missionary work in Japan in 1879 and in China in 1899. It merged in 1934 with Board of Missions of the Evangelical Synod of North America to become the Board of International Missions of the Evangelical and Reformed Church, which merged in 1957 with the Congregational Christian Churches to form the United Church of Christ. *References*: Evangelical and Reformed Historical Society, Lancaster Central Archives and Library, Lancaster, Pa.; David Dunn et al., *A History of the Evangelical and Reformed Church* (Philadelphia, 1961); *Fifty Years of Foreign Missions of the Reformed Church in the United States 1877–1927* (Philadelphia, 1927).

REID, GILBERT (1857–1927). Missionary, editor, and author, born November 29, 1857, in Laurel, Long Island, New York. Reid graduated from Hamilton College and Union Theological Seminary, and was ordained in 1882. He was a missionary under the Board of Foreign Missions of the Presbyterian Church in the U.S.A. in China from 1882 until 1892. He served in Chefoo from 1882 to 1885, and in Tsinan from 1885 to 1892. He returned to the United States in 1892. He resigned in 1894 because of a disagreement with the board, and went back to China as an independent missionary. He founded the International Institute of China in Peking in 1894 to promote the welfare of China, and was its director in chief (it moved to Shanghai in 1903). He was a correspondent of *The London Times* during the Sino-Japanese War, and of the *London Morning Post* during the Boxer Rebellion. He also served as an interpreter to the British legation. He wrote *Glances at China* (London, 1890); *Sources of Anti-Foreign*

Disturbances in China (Shanghai, 1893); and *China, Captive or Free? A Study of China's Entanglements* (London, 1922). He was proprietor and editor of the *Peking Post* in 1917, but the newspaper was suppressed by the Chinese police during World War I because of its opposition to China's entering the war, and he was deported in 1917 and returned to the United States. He went back to China in 1921 and tried to rehabilitate the International Institute of China. Died September 30, 1927, in Shanghai. *References: DAB; DADH; NYT*, October 1, 1927; *UnionTS*; and *WWWA*.

REIFSNIDER, CHARLES SHRIVER (1875–1958). Missionary, born November 27, 1875, in Frederick, Maryland. Reifsnider studied at Heidelberg University (Tiffin, Ohio) and Bexley Hall (Gambier, Ohio), graduated from Kenyon College (Gambier, Ohio), and was ordained in 1901. He was a missionary under the Domestic and Foreign Missionary Society of the Protestant Episcopal Church in the United States of America in Japan from 1901 to 1914, and president of St. Paul's University in Tokyo from 1912 to 1940. He was a suffragan bishop of North Tokyo from 1924 to 1935, and bishop from 1935 to 1947. He was also president of St. Margaret's College in Tokyo from 1935 to 1941. He was bishop in charge of the church's work among the Japanese in the United States during World War II. He retired in 1947. Died March 16, 1958, in Pasadena, California. *References: JBEWW; The Living Church*, March 30, 1958; and *WWWA*.

REIMERT, WILLIAM A(NSON) (1877–1920). Missionary, born February 7, 1877, in New Tripoli, Lehigh County, Pennsylvania. Reimert attended Keystone State Normal School, and graduated from Ursinus College (Philadelphia) and Ursinus School of Theology. He was a missionary under the Board of Foreign Missions of the Reformed Church in the United States in China from 1902 until his death. He served in Yochow, Hunan Province, and taught at the Huping Christian College. Killed June 13, 1920, near Yochow. *References*: William A. Reimert Papers, Evangelical and Reformed Historical Society, Lancaster Central Archives and Library, Lancaster, Pa.; and Allen R. Bartholomew, *The Martyr of Huping. The Life Story of William Anson Reimert, Missionary in China* (Philadelphia, 1925).

REINSCH, PAUL S(AMUEL) (1869–1923). Political scientist and diplomat, born June 10, 1869, in Milwaukee, Wisconsin. Reinsch graduated from the University of Wisconsin. He was assistant professor of political science at the University of Wisconsin from 1898 to 1901, and professor from 1901 to 1913. He was U.S. minister to China from 1913 to 1919. He persuaded the Chinese government to enter World War I on the side of the United States, but did not succeed in preventing the further growth of foreign interests and the abrogation of some of the unequal treaties. He was a legal advisor to the Chinese government from 1919 until his death. He wrote *Intellectual and Political Currents in the*

Far East (Boston, 1911), and *An American Diplomat in China* (Garden City, N.Y., 1922). Died January 24, 1923, in Shanghai, China. *References*: Paul S. Reinsch Papers, State Historical Society of Wisconsin, Madison, Wis.; *DAB; DADH*; Alan E. Kent, "Down from the Ivory Tower: Paul Samuel Reinsch, Minister to China." *Wisconsin Magazine of History* 35 (1951): 114–18; *NCAB* 19:285; *NYT*, January 26, 1923; Sal Prisco, "Paul S. Reinsch, Progressive Era Diplomat in Peking, 1913–1919," *Asian Forum* 10 (1979): 51–59; Noel H. Pugach, *Paul S. Reinsch, Open Door Diplomat in Action* (Millwood, N.Y., 1979); Patrick J. Scanlon, "No Longer a Treaty Port: Paul S. Reinsch and China, 1913–1919," Ph.D. diss., University of Wisconsin, 1973; and *WWWA*.

REISCHAUER, AUGUST KARL (1879–1971). Missionary and educator, born September 4, 1879, in Jonesboro, Illinois. Reischauer graduated from Hanover College and McCormick Theological Seminary, and studied at the University of Chicago. He was professor of philosophy at Meiji Gakuin College in Japan from 1907 to 1913, and professor of comparative religions at Meiji Gakuin Theological Seminary from 1913 to 1935, and at Nihon Shingakko (Japan Theological Seminary) from 1928 to 1941. He was cofounder of Tokyo Joshi Daigaku (Tokyo Women's Christian College) in 1918, and cofounder of Nihon Rowa Gakko (Japan Deaf Oral School) in 1920, the first school in Japan to teach lipreading and speech. He returned to the United States in 1941. He was secretary of the Commission on Ecumenical Mission and Relations of the United Presbyterian Church in the U.S.A. from 1941 to 1951, and professor of comparative religion at Union Theological Seminary (New York City) from 1943 to 1952. He wrote *Studies in Japanese Buddhism* (New York, 1917), and *The Task in Japan: A Study in Modern Missionary Imperatives* (New York, 1925). Died July 10, 1971, in Los Angeles. *References: CA; JBEWW*; and *KEJ*.

REISCHAUER, EDWIN OLDFATHER (1910–   ). Japanologist and diplomat, son of August Karl Reischauer,* born October 15, 1910, in Tokyo. Reischauer graduated from Oberlin College and Harvard University, and studied in Paris, Japan, and China. He joined the faculty of Harvard University in 1938. He served in the Department of War, the Department of State, and the U.S. Army during World War II. He was director of Harvard Yenching Institute from 1956 to 1961. He was U.S. ambassador to Japan from 1961 to 1966. He sought to restore a dialogue between the United States and Japan to help develop a partnership, and paved the way for the return of Okinawa to Japan and the smoother operation of the United States-Japanese alliance. He returned to Harvard University in 1966 as a professor. He wrote *Japan, Past and Present* (New York, 1946); *The United States and Japan* (Cambridge, Mass., 1950); and was coauthor of *East Asia: The Great Tradition* (Boston, 1960), and *East Asia: The Modern Transformation* (Boston, 1965). He wrote *Wanted: An Asian Policy* (New York, 1955); *Beyond Vietnam: The United States and Asia* (New York, 1967); *The Japanese* (Cambridge, Mass., 1977); and his autobiography, *My Life* *between Japan and America* (New York, 1986). *References: CA; CB* 1962; *DADH; EAS; JBEWW; KEJ; PolProf: Johnson; PolProf: Kennedy*; and *WWA*.

REISNER, JOHN H(ENRY) (1888–1965). Agriculturist, born August 27, 1888, in Fredericksburg, Virginia. Reisner graduated from Yale and Cornell universities. He went to China in 1914, where he was a professor on the faculty of the College of Agriculture and Forestry at Nanking University from 1914 to 1916, and dean of the college and director of its experimental station from 1914 to 1931. He instituted the Plant Improvement Program in 1924, and created the Department of the Rural Church of the Nanking Union Theological Seminary. He returned to the United States in 1931, and was executive secretary of Agricultural Missions, Inc., from 1931 until his retirement in 1953. He was executive secretary of the Rural Mission Cooperating Committee from 1933 to 1954, and an observer for various church agencies with the United Nations Food and Agricultural Organization. He was coauthor of *The Cornell-Nanking Story: The First International Technical Cooperation Program in Agriculture by Cornell University* (Ithaca, N.Y., 1963). Died April 26, 1965, in Hicksville, Long Island, New York. *Reference: NYT*, April 27, 1965.

REMER, CHARLES F(REDERICK) (1889–1972). Economist, born June 16, 1889, in Young America, Minnesota. Remer graduated from the University of Minnesota and Harvard University. He served in the Bureau of Education in the Philippines from 1910 to 1912, and was an instructor in economics at St. John's University in Shanghai from 1912 to 1915, and professor there from 1917 to 1922. He was a professor of economics at Williams College (Williamstown, Mass.) from 1924 to 1928, and professor of economics at the University of Michigan from 1928 until 1959. He directed a study of the international economic relations in China for the Social Science Research Council of New York from 1928 to 1931, and was a member of the American Economic Mission to the Far East in 1935. He was chief of the Far Eastern Section in the Office of the Coordinator of Information in 1941–1942, chief of the Far Eastern Division of the Office of Strategic Services (OSS) from 1942 to 1944, and an advisor on Far Eastern investment and finance in the Department of State in 1944–1945. He wrote *The Foreign Trade of China* (Shanghai, 1926); *American Investments in China* (Honolulu, 1929); and *Foreign Investments in China* (New York, 1933); and was coauthor of *A Study of Chinese Boycotts with Special Reference to Their Economic Effectiveness* (Baltimore, 1933). Died July 2, 1972, in Pacific Grove, California. *References*: Charles Frederick Remer Papers, Hoover Institution on War, Revolution and Peace, Stanford, Calif.; and *WWWA*.

RENOUF, VINCENT ADAMS (1876–1910). Educator, born January 1876, in Germany. Renouf graduated from Johns Hopkins University and attended Harvard University. He served in the Chinese Imperial Maritime Customs Service from 1903 to 1908, and was professor of chemistry at the Imperial Peiyang

University in Tientsin from 1903 to 1906, and professor of history and political economics there from 1906 until his death. Died May 4, 1910, in Tientsin. *References*: Vincent Adams Renouf Papers, Rutgers University Library, New Brunswick, N.J.; and Susan M. Yen, "The Renouf Papers: An American Academic in China, 1903–1910," *Journal of the Rutgers University Library* 39 (1977): 98–107.

RENVILLE, USS. Stationed in Batavia, Java, from 1946 to 1948, it was the headquarters ship for the U.N. Truce Commission that negotiated settlement terms between Dutch military forces and Indonesian nationalists. The ensuing agreement, which divided Java between Indonesian Republic and Dutch control, was denoted "The Renville Truce." *Reference: Dictionary of American Naval Fighting Ships* (Washington, D.C., 1976), 6:76.

REYNOLDS, I(RA) HUBERT (1914–   ). Missionary and anthropologist, born October 17, 1914, in Camden, New Jersey. Reynolds graduated from Colgate and Yale universities and Hartford Seminary Foundation, and was ordained in 1939. He was director of the Purdue Christian Foundation in West Lafayette, Indiana, from 1939 to 1943, and assistant director of Dodge Community House in Detroit from 1943 to 1945. He was a missionary under the United Christian Missionary Society of the Christian Church in China from 1947 to 1951, field missionary in the Philippines from 1952 to 1962, and professor of anthropology and research director of community service at Silliman University in Dumaguete in the Philippines after 1964. He was also acting secretary of the department of public welfare of the United Church of Christ in the Philippines from 1954 to 1958, and organizer of the Vigan Community Center in the Philippines and its director from 1954 to 1964. *Reference: Who's Who in Religion* (Chicago, 1975).

RHEES, HENRY HOLCOMBE (1828–1899). Missionary, born November 10, 1828, in Camden, New Jersey. Rhees studied law, was admitted to the bar in 1851, and was ordained in 1854. He held pastorates in Ione Valley and Marysville, California; Salem, New Jersey; Nashua, New Hampshire; Southbridge, Massachusetts; and Napa, California, from 1855 until 1878. He was a missionary under the American Baptist Missionary Union in Japan from 1878 until his death. He built the first American Baptist mission house in Tokyo. He moved to Kobe in 1882, and was the senior missionary of the Baptist mission in Japan. Died May 10, 1899, in Kobe, Japan. *References*: Robert G. Sorley, "The Life and Letters of Henry Holcombe Rhees, Baptist Missionary to Japan, 1878–1899," Ms., International Ministries ABC/USA, Valley Forge, Pa.; and *EM*.

RICHARDS, LINDA (1841–1930). Nurse, born July 27, 1841, near Potsdam, New York, and grew up in Derby and Lyndon, Vermont. Richards was employed in the Union Straw Works in Foxboro, Massachusetts, until 1870, and was an assistant nurse at the Boston City Hospital from 1870 to 1872. She was trained at the New England Hospital for Women and Children in Boston, the first American nursing school, and received its first diploma in 1873. She was a night supervisor at the Bellevue Training School, New York City, and superintendent of the Boston Training School and the Massachusetts General Hospital of Nursing until 1877. She studied in London and Edinburgh, and was matron of the hospital and superintendent of the training school in Boston City Hospital in 1878–1879 and in 1882 to 1885. She was in Japan under the sponsorship of the American Board of Commissioners for Foreign Missions (ABCFM) from 1886 until 1891, and opened Japan's first training school for nurses at the Doshisha Hospital in Kyoto. She returned to the United States in 1891, and held a number of posts for only short periods of time because of ill health. She retired in 1911 and wrote *Reminiscences of Linda Richards. America's First Trained Nurse* (Boston, 1911). Died April 16, 1930, in Boston. *References: BDAE; DAMB S4*; and *NAW*.

RICHIE, DONALD (STEINER) (1924–   ). Film critic, born April 17, 1924, in Lima, Ohio. Richie attended Antioch College and graduated from Columbia University. He served in the U.S. Maritime Service during World War II. He was the film critic for the *Japan Times* in Tokyo from 1955 to 1968, curator of film in the New York Museum of Modern Art from 1968 to 1973, and literary critic in Tokyo after 1973. He was coauthor of *The Japanese Film* (New York, 1959), and wrote *The Films of Akira Kurosawa* (Berkeley, Calif., 1965); *The Japanese Movie: An Illustrated History* (New York, 1965); *The Inland Sea* (New York, 1971); *Ozu, the Man and His Films* (Berkeley, Calif., 1974); *The Japanese Tattoo* (New York, 1980); and *Zen Inklings* (New York, 1982).

RIKKYO GAKUIN. Developed from St. Timothy's boys' school, which was founded by the Protestant Episcopal Church in 1874, and St. Paul's College, which was established in 1882 in Tokyo by Bishop Channing Moore Williams* of the Methodist Episcopal Church of the USA. They merged in 1887, acquired university status in 1922, were reorganized, and became coeducational in 1949. *References*: Mary J. T. Barretta, "Rikkyo University, Tokyo, Japan: A Case Study of Governance at a Private University," Ph.D. diss., University of Pittsburgh, 1987; Ira J. Burnstein, *The American Movement to Develop Protestant Colleges for Men in Japan, 1868–1912* (Ann Arbor, Mich., 1967); *KEJ*; and Hiyashi Matsushita, ed., *Eighty-Five Years of Rikkyo Gakuin* (Tokyo, 1960).

RINGGOLD, CADWALADER (1802–1867). Naval officer, born August 20, 1802, in Washington County, Maryland. Ringgold was appointed a midshipman in the U.S. Navy in 1819. He served in the Pacific from 1828 to 1832, and in the Mediterranean in 1834–1835. He commanded the USS *Porpoise* in the Wilkes Exploring Expedition from 1838 to 1842, and conducted surveys of the California coast in 1849–1850. He commanded the North Pacific Surveying Expedition in 1853–1854. He was relieved of his command in China in 1854 because of ill health. He later worked on the charts of his expedition in Washington, D.C., from 1856 until 1861, and served in the Union Navy during the Civil War. Died April 29, 1867, in New York City. *References: ACAB; DAB*; Gordon K. Harrington, ''The Ringgold Incident: A Matter of Judgment,'' in *America Spreads Her Sails: U.S. Seapower in the 19th Century*, ed. Clayton R. Barrow, Jr. (Annapolis, Md., 1973), pp. 100–111; *NYT*, April 30, 1867; and *WWWA*.

RINGGOLD-RODGERS SURVEYING EXPEDITION. *See* NORTH PACIFIC EXPLORING EXPEDITION

RIPLEY, S(IDNEY) DILLON, II (1913–   ). Ornithologist, born September 20, 1913, in New York City. Ripley graduated from Yale and Harvard universities. He was a member of a zoological expedition to New Guinea sponsored by the Philadelphia Academy of Natural Sciences in 1936–1937, and an expedition to Sumatra in 1938–1939. He served in the Office of Special Services (OSS) in Ceylon, India, and Burma during World War II. He was a lecturer and associate curator at the Peabody Museum of Natural History at Yale University from 1946 to 1952, curator there from 1952 to 1959, and director of the museum from 1959 to 1964. He was assistant professor of zoology at Yale University from 1949 to 1955, associate professor there from 1955 to 1961, and professor of biology from 1961 to 1964. He made an expedition to Nepal in 1948, and described it in *Search for the Spiny Babbler* (Boston, 1952). He was secretary of the Smithsonian Institution from 1964 until his retirement in 1984. He wrote *A Synopsis of the Birds of India and Pakistan Together with Those of Nepal, Sikkim, Bhutan and Ceylon* (Bombay, 1961), and was coauthor of *The Land and Wildlife of Tropical Asia* (New York, 1964). *References: AMWS; CB* 1966; and *WWA*.

RISLEY, RICHARD R. (fl. 1864–1865). Acrobat. Risley played in leading music halls in London and New York. He brought a circus to Japan in 1864, where it failed. He started an icehouse there and imported ice. He also established a dairy and imported milk cows from San Francisco in 1865, but all his enterprises failed. He then returned to the United States as manager and part owner of the first Japanese acrobatic troupe to go abroad.

ROBB, WALTER J(OHNSON) (1880–   ). Journalist, born February 8, 1880, in Leon, Iowa. Robb was a teacher in country schools in Garfield and Kingfisher counties, Oklahoma, from 1896 to 1907, and a teacher in the Philippines from 1907 to 1918. He was then involved in newspaper work from 1918 to 1941, and was a reporter for the *Cablenews-American* and later for *The*

Philippine Herald. He was the Philippine correspondent of the *Philadelphia Public Ledger,* the *Japan Advertiser,* and the *Los Angeles Times* from 1918 to 1922, and of the *Chicago Daily News* after 1919. He accompanied the first Philippine Independence Mission to the United States in 1919, and was editor of the *American Chamber of Commerce Journal* in Manila from 1923 until 1941, chairman of the Philippine Historical Research and Markers Committee, assistant field correspondent of the Foreign Broadcast Intelligence Service in San Francisco in 1943–1944, a lecturer on the Philippines in the Far East Training Course of the Office of War Information in Berkeley, California, in 1944, and a writer in the Philippine Division of the Overseas Branch of the Office of War Information in San Francisco in 1945–1946. He was later a writer for the Asia Foundation in San Francisco. He wrote *The Khaki Cabinet and Old Manila* (Manila, 1926); *Romance and Adventure in Old Manila* (Manila, 1928); *Filipinos* (Manila, 1937); and *Filipinos; Pre-War Philippines Essays* (Rizal, 1963). *References*: Walter Johnson Robb Papers, Yale University Library, New Haven, Conn.; *CCDP; Gleeck/Manila;* and *WWWA.*

ROBBINS, JOSEPH CHANDLER (1874–1962). Missionary, born in Roda, Nova Scotia. Robbins graduated from Brown University and Newton (Mass.) Theological Seminary. He was a gold miner in British Columbia during the gold rush days of the 1890s, and served in the Spanish-American War. He was a missionary under the American Baptist Foreign Mission Society in the Philippines from 1902 to 1916. He was foreign secretary of the American Baptist Foreign Mission Society from 1916 to 1940, and served at times in Burma and India. He was director of evangelism and church relations at the Andover-Newton Theological School, and president of the American (Northern) Baptist Convention from 1942 to 1944. He wrote *The Appeal of India* (Philadelphia, 1919); *Following the Pioneers: A Study of American Baptist Mission Work in India and Burma* (Philadelphia, 1922); and a biography of George Dana Boardman.* Died September 30, 1962, in West Haven, Connecticut. *References: NYT,* October 1, 1962; and *WWWA.*

ROBERTS, EDMUND (1784–1836). Merchant and diplomat, born June 29, 1784, in Portsmouth, New Hampshire. In business after 1808, he went to Zanzibar in 1827 and then visited parts of India in 1831. He was sent in 1832 as a special agent on a diplomatic mission to negotiate treaties with Zanzibar, Muscat, Siam, and Cochin China, and signed a treaty of amity and commerce with Siam in 1833. He returned to Asia in 1835 to exchange ratified treaties, and visited Siam again. Died June 12, 1836, in Macao. His diary was published as *Embassy to the Eastern Courts of Cochin-China, Siam, and Muscat; in the U.S. Sloop-of-War Peacock, David Geisinger, Commander, during the Years 1832–3–4* (New York, 1837). *References*: Edmund Roberts Papers, Manuscript Division, Library of Congress; Edmund Roberts Papers, New Hampshire Historical Society, Concord, N.H.; *ACAB; DAB*; Frederic A. Greenhut, "Edmund Roberts: Early American Diplomat," *Manuscripts* 35 (1983): 273–80; and *WWWA*.

ROBERTS, ISSACHAR J(ACOX) (1802–1871). Missionary, born February 17, 1802, in Summer County, Tennessee. Roberts graduated from Furman Theological Institution (S.C.), and was ordained in 1827. He organized the Roberts Fund and the China Mission Society, and was a missionary in China starting in 1837 under this society. He served in Macao, working as a saddler and preaching in a leper colony. He joined the Baptist mission in 1841, helped open the mission in Hong Kong in 1842, and moved to Canton that same year. He transferred to the Southern Baptist Convention in 1846, but reverted again to independent status in 1852. About 1847 he gave instructions to an inquirer named Hung, who afterwards, as the Tien Wang ("Heavenly King"), became leader of the Taiping Rebellion. Roberts went to Nanking in 1860 as assistant to the chief minister of state, and then became minister of foreign affairs. He escaped to Shanghai in 1862, fearing for his life, and returned to the United States in 1866. Died December 28, 1871, in Upper Alton, Illinois. *References*: Margaret M. Coughlin, "Strangers in the House: J. Lewis Shuck and Issachar Roberts, First American Baptist Missionaries to China," Ph.D. diss., University of Virginia, 1972; *DAB*; George B. Pruden, Jr., "Issachar Jacox Roberts and American Diplomacy in China During the Taiping Rebellion," Ph.D. diss., American University, 1977; George B. Pruden, Jr., "Issachar J. Roberts: A Southern Missionary Pioneer in China," *Proceedings of the South Carolina Historical Association*, 1981, pp. 28–52; *WWWA*; and C. T. Yuan, "Reverand Issachar Jacox Roberts and the Taiping Rebellion," *JAS* 23 (1963): 55–67.

ROBERTS, JAMES HUDSON (1851–1945). Missionary, born June 11, 1851, in Hartford, Connecticut. Roberts graduated from Yale University, studied at Andover and Hartford theological seminaries and Boston University Medical School, and was ordained in 1877. He was a missionary under the American Board of Commissioners for Foreign Missions (ABCFM) in China from 1877 until 1906. He served in Peking from 1877 to 1880, and in Kalgan from 1880 to 1906. He wrote *A Flight for Life, and an Inside View of Mongolia* (Boston, 1903). He returned to the United States in 1906, and held pastorates in Southbury, West Suffield, Bolton, and Hockanum, Connecticut, from 1907 until his death. Died May 15, 1945, in Wethersfield, Connecticut. *References: WWWA*; and *Yale*.

ROBERTS, WILLIAM H(ENRY) (1847–1919). Missionary, born October 25, 1847, in Botetourt Springs, Virginia. Roberts attended Roanoke (Va.) and Richmond colleges, and graduated from the Theological Seminary in Chicago. He served with the Confederate Army during the Civil War. He was a missionary under the American Baptist Missionary Union in Bhamo, Burma, from 1879 until 1913, serving among the Kachins. He wrote *Pioneering among the Kachins* (Boston, 1911). He retired in 1917. Died December 24, 1919.

ROBERTSON, JAMES ALEXANDER (1873–1939). Historian, born August 19, 1873, in Corry, Pennsylvania. Robertson graduated from Adelbert College and Western Reserve University. He worked in archives and libraries in Spain, Portugal, France, Italy, England, and the United States from 1902 to 1909, searching for documents pertaining to the Philippines, which he translated and edited (with the assistance of Emma Helen Blair) in *The Philippine Islands* (Cleveland, 1903–1909), a work in 55 volumes. He worked with the historical research department of the Carnegie Institution in Washington, D.C., in 1909–1910 and 1916–1917. He was bibliographer of the Philippines Library in Manila from 1910 to 1912, and librarian there from 1912 to 1916. He pioneered instruction in library science at the University of the Philippines in 1914. He served with the Bureau of Foreign and Domestic Commerce of the Department of Commerce in Washington, D.C., from 1917 to 1923; was managing editor of the *Hispanic American Historical Review* from 1918 until his death; professor of American History at John B. Stetson University from 1923 to 1933; and archivist of the Hall of Records in Annapolis, Maryland, after 1935. Died March 20, 1939, in Annapolis. *References*: James A. Robertson Papers, Duke University Library, Durham, N.C.; James A. Robertson Papers, Manuscript Division, Library of Congress; *DAB S2; DPB 2*; Carlos Quirino, "Blair and Robertson's *Magnus Opus*," *Philippine Historical Association Historical Bulletin* 6 (1962): 63–70; A. Curtis Wilgus, ed., *Hispanic American Essays: A Memorial to James Alexander Robertson* (Chapel Hill, N.C., 1942); and *WWWA*.

ROBINSON, CHARLES (1801–1845). Missionary, born December 29, 1801, in Lenox, Massachusetts. Robinson graduated from Williams College and Auburn Theological Seminary, and was ordained in 1833. He was a missionary under the American Board of Commissioners for Foreign Missions (ABCFM) in Bangkok, Siam, from 1834 to 1845. He translated portions of the Old and New Testaments into Siamese, and printed the first publication in Siam in 1836. Died March 3, 1845, at sea on his way back to the United States. *Reference: Hewitt*.

ROBINSON, CHARLES BUDD, JR. (1871–1913). Botanist, born October 26, 1871, in Pictou, Nova Scotia. Robinson graduated from Dalhousie University (Halifax, N.S.) and Columbia University, and studied at Cambridge University. He was a teacher at Kentville and Pictou, Nova Scotia, until 1903, and also was assistant curator of the herbarium at the New York Botanical Garden. He was an economic botanist in the Bureau of Science of the Philippines from 1908 to 1911, served again at the New York Botanical Garden in 1911–1912, and returned to the Philippines in 1912. He made a botanical exploration of the Island of Amboina in the Moluccas, Dutch East Indies, in 1913. Murdered December 5,

1913, at Seri, near Amboina. *Reference: Philippines Journal of Science (Botany)* 9 (1914): 191–97.

ROBINSON, JOHN EDWARD (1849–1922). Missionary, born February 12, 1849, in Gort, County Galway, Ireland, and came to the United States in 1865. Robinson attended Drew Theological Seminary, and was ordained in 1874. He was a missionary under the Board of Foreign Missions of the Methodist Episcopal Church in Rangoon, Burma, in 1875–1876, and was the founder of the Methodist Episcopal Church in Burma. He then served in Bangalore, India, from 1877 to 1879; in Rangoon from 1880 to 1886; in the Bombay district from 1887 to 1896; in the Asansole district from 1896 to 1900; and in the Calcutta district from 1900 to 1904. He was also editor of *The Indian Witness* from 1896 to 1904. He was elected bishop of Southern Asia in 1904, and served in Calcutta in 1904, in Bombay from 1908 to 1912, and in Bangalore from 1912 until his retirement in 1920. Died February 15, 1922, in Bangalore. His daughter **RUTH EVELYN ROBINSON** (1878–1954), educational missionary, was born June 15, 1878, in Bangalore. Ruth Evelyn Robinson graduated from Goucher College. She was a missionary under the Woman's Foreign Missionary Society of the Methodist Episcopal Church in India from 1900 until her retirement in 1950. She served in Bombay in 1899–1900, and was then appointed to assist Isabella Thoburn* in Lucknow. She was a teacher at Isabella Thoburn College until 1908, and was its principal from 1909 to 1918. She then served in Pauri, Garhwal, until 1920, and founded *The Treasure Chest*, a magazine for young Indians. She retired in 1943 but continued to edit the magazine until 1950. Died in Bangalore. John Robinson's daughter **FLORA LOIS ROBINSON HOWELLS** (1884–1926), educational missionary, was born in India. Flora Lois Robinson Howells graduated from Goucher College. She was a missionary under the Woman's Foreign Missionary Society of the Methodist Episcopal Church in Lucknow, India, from 1909 to 1920, taught at Isabella Thoburn* College, and was principal of the college from 1918 to 1920. She resigned in 1920 and lived in Pittsburgh. Her letters were published as *A Girl of an Indian Garden: Letters of Flora Robinson Howells to Her Friends*, ed. Ruth E. Robinson (New York, 1928). *References: EWM*; and *WWWA*.

ROBINSON, JOHN WESLEY (1866–1947). Missionary, born January 6, 1866, in Moulton, Iowa, and grew up in Harlan, Iowa. Robinson became a printer and then graduated from Garrett Biblical Institute. He was a missionary under the Board of Foreign Missions of the Methodist Episcopal Church in India from 1892 until 1936. He served in Lucknow, and was superintendent of Lucknow district, agent of the Lucknow Publishing House; editor of *Kaukab-i-Hind*, a weekly in Urdu; secretary-treasurer of the Famine Relief Fund from 1897 to 1900; secretary-treasurer of the mission board in Southern India in 1904–1912; and superintendent of the Allahabad district. He was elected missionary bishop for Southern India in 1912 and general superintendent in 1920. He retired in

1936 and lived briefly in California, but returned to India and became editor of *The Indian Witness*. He later lived in Delhi. Died May 30, 1947, in Naini Tal, India. *References: EWM*; and *WWWA*.

ROCK, JOSEPH F(RANCIS) C(HARLES) (1884–1962). Botanist and plant explorer, born January 13, 1884, in Austria, and became a naturalized American citizen in 1913. Rock was a botanist for the Hawaiian Board of Agriculture and Forestry from 1909 to 1911, taught at the University of Hawaii from 1911 to 1919, and was a professor of systematic botany in 1919–1920. He was agricultural explorer for the Office of Foreign Seed and Plant Introduction of the U.S. Department of Agriculture, and explored southwestern China and northeastern India in 1920–1921, and Burma, Assam, and Siam from 1921 to 1923. He was director of the National Geographic Society Yunnan-Tibet expedition in 1923–1924, of the Arnold Arboretum–Harvard University Botanical and Zoological expedition to west China and Tibet from 1924 to 1927, and of the National Geographic Society Southwest China–Tibet expedition from 1927 to 1930. He was leader of the zoological expedition for West China for the Museum of Comparative Zoology of Harvard University from 1930 to 1932, of the University of California Yunnan-Tibet botanical expedition in 1932–1933, and of the ornithological expedition to Annam and Cambodia for the U.S. National Museum in 1940. He was research professor in Oriental studies at the University of Hawaii from 1938 to 1940, consultant to the U.S. Army Map Service in 1944–1945, and research fellow of Harvard-Yenching Institute after 1945. He settled in Yunnan and remained there until 1949. He wrote *The Ancient Na-Khi Kingdom of Southwest China* (Cambridge, Mass., 1947). Died December 5, 1962, in Honolulu. *References*: Alvin K. Chock, "Joseph Rock, 1884–1962," *Taxon* 12 (April 1963): 89–102; E.H.M. Cox, *Plant-Hunting in China* (New York, 1986), pp. 195–202; *NYT*, December 7, 1962; S. B. Sutton, *In China's Border Provinces: Career of Joseph Rock: The Turbulant Botanist-Explorer* (New York, 1974): *Tibet*; and *WWWA*.

ROCKHILL, WILLIAM W(OODVILLE) (1854–1914). Diplomat and Sinologist, born April 1854, in Philadelphia. Rockhill graduated from the École Spéciale Militaire de St. Cyr, France, and served in the French Army in Algeria until 1876. He was second secretary in the U.S. legation in Peking in 1884–1885, secretary of legation from 1885 to 1886, and chargé d'affaires in Korea in 1886–1887. He left the foreign service in 1888 and made scientific expeditions to Mongolia and Tibet in 1888–1889 and in 1891–1892 for the Smithsonian Institution, which he described in *The Land of the Lamas: Notes of a Journey through China, Mongolia and Tibet* (New York, 1891), and *Diary of a Journey through Mongolia and Tibet in 1891 and 1892* (Washington, D.C., 1894). He was also involved in conducting research in Chinese history and collecting rare Chinese books (which he later presented to the Library of Congress). He returned to the foreign service in 1893, and was chief clerk in Washington, D.C., in

1893–1894; third assistant secretary of state from 1894 to 1896; and assistant secretary of state in 1896–1897. He played an important role in preparing Secretary of State John Hay's "Open Door" notes of 1899–1900. He was minister and consul general to Greece, Romania, and Serbia from 1897 to 1899, and director of the International Bureau of the American Republics from 1899 to 1905. He was sent as a special agent to China in 1900–1901 to negotiate the indemnities imposed on that country as the result of the Boxer Rebellion. He was U.S. minister to China from 1905 to 1909, and ambassador to Russia from 1909 to 1911 and to Turkey from 1911 to 1913. Died December 8, 1914, in Honolulu, on his way to China. *References*: William W. Rockhill Papers, Houghton Library, Harvard University, Cambridge, Mass.; *DAB; DADH; NCAB* 8:129; *NYT*, December 9, 1914; Harvey Pressman, "Hay, Rockhill, and China's Integrity: A Reappraisal," *Papers on China* 13 (1959): 93–105; Peter Stanley, "The Making of an American Sinologist: William W. Rockhill and the Open Door," *Perspectives in American History* 11 (1977–1978): 419–60; Paul A. Varg, *Open Door Diplomat: The Life of W. W. Rockhill* (Urbana, Ill., 1952); Paul A. Varg, "William Woodville Rockhill's Influence on the Boxer Negotiations," *PHR* 18 (1949): 369–80; and *WWWA*.

ROCKWELL, JAMES C(HAPMAN) (1881–1962). Electrical engineer, born October 4, 1881, in Scranton, Pennsylvania. Rockwell graduated from Cornell University. He was employed by power companies in New York and West Virginia. He came to the Philippines in 1911, and joined the Manila Electric Railroad and Light Company (Meralco). He was a street railway manager, and manager of the electric power department. He was vice president and general manager of Meralco (later Manila Electric Company) from 1919 to 1938, and president from 1938 until his retirement in 1949. He was interned by the Japanese during World War II. He returned to the United States in 1949. Died July 30, 1962, in Carmel, California. *References: CCDP; EP* 18:86; and *Gleeck/Manila*.

RODGERS, JAMES B(URTON) (1865–1944). Missionary, born March 1, 1865, in Albany, New York. Rodgers graduated from Hamilton College and Auburn (N.Y.) Seminary, and was ordained in 1888. He was a pastor in Belmont, New York, in 1888–1889, and a missionary in Brazil from 1889 to 1899. He was the first Protestant missionary regularly appointed to the Philippines in 1899, serving under the Board of Foreign Missions of the Presbyterian Church in the U.S.A. in the Philippines until his retirement in 1935. He wrote *Forty Years in the Philippines. A History of the Philippine Mission of the Presbyterian Church in the U.S.A., 1899–1939* (New York, 1940). He remained in the Philippines, and was interned by the Japanese but was later released. Died April 1944, in Baguio, Philippines. *References: NYT*, June 30, 1944; and *WWP*.

RODGERS, JOHN (1812–1882). Naval officer, born August 8, 1812, in Sion Hall, near Havre de Grace, Maryland. Rodgers was appointed midshipman in the U.S. Navy in 1828. He served in the Mediterranean and Brazil squadrons, participated in the Second Seminole War, and served in the Home, Africa and Mediterranean squadrons and in the Coast Survey. He was second in command of the North Pacific Surveying Expedition* from 1852 to 1856, commanding the USS *John Hancock*. He was placed in charge of the expedition when Commander Cadwalader Ringgold,* who had been in command of the expedition, became ill in 1854. He served in the Union Navy during the Civil War, and commanded the Boston Navy Yard from 1866 to 1869 and the Asiatic Squadron from 1870 to 1872. He commanded the naval forces in the Korean expedition of 1871. He later commanded the Mare Island Navy Yard and the Naval Observatory until his death. Died May 5, 1882, in Washington, D.C. *References: ACAB; DAB; DAMIB*; Robert E. Johnson, "John Rodgers: The Quintessential Nineteenth Century Naval Officer," in *Captains of the Old Steam Navy: Makers of the American Naval Tradition 1840–1880*, ed. James C. Bradford, Jr. (Annapolis, Md., 1986), pp. 253–74; Robert E. Johnson, *Rear Admiral John Rodgers, 1812–1882* (Annapolis, Md., 1967); *NCAB* 25:188; and *WWWA*.

ROOSEVELT, NICHOLAS (1893–1982). Journalist and diplomat, born June 12, 1893, in New York City. Roosevelt graduated from Harvard University. He served in the U.S. embassies in Paris and Spain from 1914 to 1918, and in the U.S. Army during World War I. He became an editorial writer for *The New York Times* in 1923; made an extensive tour of the Dutch East Indies, the Philippines, China and Manchuria; and wrote *The Philippines: A Treasure and a Problem* (New York, 1926). Filipino politicians thought that the book slandered the national character and mores, and when Roosevelt was appointed in 1930 as vice-governor of the Philippines, the appointment was aborted because of a political storm in Manila. He was U.S. minister to Hungary from 1930 until 1933, and deputy director of the Office of War Information during World War II. He resigned in 1946, and wrote his memoirs, *Front Row Seat* (Norman, Okla., 1953). Died February 16, 1982, in Oyster Bay, Long Island, New York. *References: CA; NYT*, February 18, 1982; and *WWWA*.

ROOSEVELT, THEODORE, JR. (1887–1944) and **ROOSEVELT, KERMIT** (1889–1943). Sons of President Theodore Roosevelt. Theodore Roosevelt, Jr., colonial administrator and businessman, was born September 13, 1887, in Oyster Bay, Long Island, New York, and graduated from Harvard University. He became involved in the brokerage and banking business, served in World War I, and was a member of the New York Assembly from 1919 to 1921, assistant secretary of the navy from 1921 to 1924, and governor of Puerto Rico from 1929 to 1932. He was governor-general of the Philippines in 1932–1933. He served in the U.S. Army during World War II. He was the only general to land with the first wave of the troops on Utah Beach during the Normandy invasion. Died July 12, 1944, in Cherbourg, France. Kermit Roosevelt, explorer and businessman, was born October 10, 1889, in Oyster Bay, Long Island, New York, and graduated from Harvard University. He was engaged in engineering and banking in South America from 1911 to 1914, formed the Roosevelt Steamship Company in 1920, and was its president until 1931, and vice president of the International Mercantile Marine Company after 1931. He served with the British Army in Mesopotamia and with the U.S. Army in France during World War I. He hunted tigers in Korea and India in 1922–1923. He served with the British Army and, after 1942, with the U.S. Army during World War II. Died on active service on June 44, 1943, in Alaska. The two men led exploring expeditions for the Field Museum of Natural History to Eastern Turkestan in 1925 and in the Yunnan and Szechuan provinces of Western China in 1928–1929. They wrote *East of the Sun and West of the Moon* (New York, 1926), and *Trailing the Giant Panda* (New York, 1929). They brought back the first giant panda skin to be seen in the United States. Theodore also wrote (with Harold J. Coolidge, Jr.*) *Three Kingdoms of Indo-China* (New York, 1933). *References*: Theodore Roosevelt, Jr., Papers, Manuscript Division, Library of Congress; Kermit Roosevelt Papers, Manuscript Division, Library of Congress; Melchor P. Aquino, ''Theodore Roosevelt, Jr.,'' *BAHC* 2 (January 1974): 7–9; *DAB S3; EP* 4:374–75; *Gleeck/Governors*, ch. 11; Ramona Morris and Desmond Morris, *Men and Pandas* (New York, 1966), ch. 3; *NCAB* 33:10; *NCAB* 48:612; *NYT*, June 6, 1943; *NYT*, July 14, 1944; and *WWWA*.

ROOT-TAKAHIRA AGREEMENT (1908). An agreement between Elihu Root, U.S. secretary of state, and Takahira Kogoro, Japanese ambassador, that recognized the status quo in the Pacific Ocean area and the Open Door Policy* in China and agreed to respect the independence and territorial integrity of China. *References*: Thomas A. Bailey, ''The Root-Takahira Agreement of 1908,'' *PHR* 9 (1940): 19–35; *DADH; EAH*; and *KEJ*.

ROOTS, LOGAN HERBERT (1870–1945). Missionary, born July 27, 1870, near Tamaroa, Perry County, Illinois. Roots graduated from Harvard University and the Episcopal Theological School (Cambridge, Mass.), and was ordained in 1898. He was a missionary under the Domestic and Foreign Missionary Society of the Protestant Episcopal Church in the United States of America in China from 1896 until 1937. He was stationed in Hankow from 1898 until 1904, and was consecrated second bishop of Hankow in 1904 and served until 1937. He was a leader of the Moral Rearmament movement after 1938. Died September 23, 1945, in Mackinac Island, Michigan. *References: CDCWM; NYT*, September 25, 1945; Ruth Schloss, ''Eliza McCook Roots: An American in China, 1900–1934,'' *Connecticut Antiquarian* 32 (1980): 10–25; and *WWWA*.

ROSENSTOCK, CHRISTIAN WILLIAM (1880–1956). Businessman, born March 16, 1880, in Salem, Oregon. Rosenstock came to the Philippines in 1900 as chief clerk of the Oriente Hotel. He founded *Rosenstock's Manila City Directory* in 1903, and extended his directory to cover Hong Kong and China. He was a partner in Bulletin Publishing Company and manager of the *Manila Daily Bulletin* from 1903 to 1905. He was manager of *Cablenews American* in 1906; an import and export broker; a real estate executive and organizer of the first large subdivision in Philippines from 1907 to 1910; a senior partner in Rosenstock, Elser and Company from 1912 to 1914; president and general manager of Yangco, Rosenstock and Company, Incorporated, from 1915 to 1921; president of Rosenstock and Company from 1922 to 1928; vice president of Philippine Education Company from 1928 to 1932; president of Commonwealth Sales Company, Inc.; and a financial agent in Philippines for Great Eastern Life Assurance Company from 1915 to 1935. Died October 23, 1956, in Manila. *References: CCDP; EP* 4:472–73; and *WWP*.

ROUNDY, HENRY JENKS (1820–1873). Sea captain, born October 23, 1820, in Beverly, Massachusetts. Roundy went to sea at fourteen, came to Canton in 1840, and remained until 1854. He commanded coastal vessels for Russell and Company, and was in charge of the receiving ships involved in importing opium. He returned to the United States in 1854 and settled in Dixon, Illinois, but returned to China in 1858 and remained until 1868, when he returned to the United States. Died September 14, 1873, in New York City. *Reference*: Robert W. Lovett, "American Merchant, Roundy," *EIHC* 97 (1961): 61–78.

RUSCH, PAUL (1897–1979). Educator and association official, born November 25, 1897, in Fairmont, Indiana, and grew up in Louisville, Kentucky. Rusch came to Tokyo, Japan, in 1925 as member of the Committee of the Young Men's Christian Association (YMCA) to rebuild the YMCA buildings in Tokyo and Yokohama, which had been destroyed in the earthquake of 1923. He was a teacher of economics in Rokkyo University from 1926 to 1941, and assistant director of the American campaign for St. Luke's International Medical Center from 1928 to 1932. He introduced American football to universities in Tokyo, organized the Tokyo Students American Football Association in 1934, and was its first president. He also founded the Brotherhood of St. Andrew in Japan. He was interned in Japan in 1941–1942, and was deported to the United States in 1942. He served in the U.S. Army during World War II, and served in the General Headquarters of the Supreme Commander for the Allied Powers (SCAP) in Tokyo from 1945 to 1949. He launched the Kiyosato agricultural center in 1948 and founded the Kiyosato Educational Experiment Project (KEEP) in Takanemura, Yamanashi Prefecture, in 1950 as a model farming community. He also served as its chairman. Died December 12, 1979, in Tokyo. *References*: Elizabeth A. Hemphill, *The Road to KEEP, the Story of Paul Rusch in Japan* (New York, 1970); and *JBEWW*.

RUSSELL, GEORGE ROBERT (1800–1866). Merchant, born May 5, 1800, in Providence, Rhode Island. Russell graduated from Brown University, studied law in Philadelphia, and was admitted to the bar. In 1826, he went to Canton, China. He was sent by John P. Cushing to Manila in 1827, and established there the mercantile house of Russell and Sturgis in 1828. He returned to the United States in 1835 and was involved in literary pursuits. Died August 5, 1866, in Manchester, Massachusetts. *Reference*: Theodore Lyman, "Memoir of George Robert Russell, LL.D.," *Massachusetts Historical Society Proceedings* 18 (1880–1881): 280–81.

RUSSELL, RILEY (1875–1961). Medical missionary, born July 21, 1875, in Strasburg, Illinois. Russell studied in Battle Creek (Mich.) College and American Medical Missionary College, graduated from George Washington University (Washington, D.C.), and was ordained in 1910. He was a medical missionary under the Seventh-Day Adventist Church in Korea from 1908 until 1922. He founded the mission hospital in Soonan and supervised mission schools for boys. He returned to the United States in 1922, and practiced in Glendale, California, until his retirement in 1954. Died January 27, 1961, in Glendale, California. *References: Pacific Union Recorder*, March 20, 1961; Stella Parker Peterson, ed., *It Came in Handy, the Story of Riley Russell, M.D., Physician Extraordinary to the People of Korea* (Washington, D.C., 1969); and *SDAE*.

RUSSELL, SAMUEL (WADSWORTH) (1789–1862). Merchant, born August 25, 1789, in Middletown, Connecticut. Russell was apprenticed to a merchant until he was twenty-one. He then went to New York City and later to Providence, Rhode Island, where he was employed by foreign shipping merchants. He became a partner of H. Carrington and Company in 1818, was sent as supercargo to China, and became a resident agent in Canton. He established the firm of Russell and Company in Canton in 1823. He retired in 1837 and returned to the United States. He was involved in various business ventures, founded Russell Manufacturing Company, and was its first president. He also served as mayor of Middletown, Connecticut. *References*: Samuel Russell Papers, Manuscript Division, Library of Congress; *Commemorative Biographical Record of Middlesex County, Connecticut* (Chicago, 1903), pp. 16–17; Alain Munkittrick, "Samuel Wadsworth Russell (1789–1862): A Study of Ordered Investment," M.A. thesis, Wesleyan University, 1973; and E. Robert Stevenson, ed., *Connecticut History Makers* (Waterbury, Conn., 1930), 2:216–17.

RUSSELL AND COMPANY. American trading company, also known as Samuel Russell and Company. It was established by Samuel Russell* in Canton in 1823. It became the chief American merchant firm in Canton and the largest in China. It was reorganized in 1830, and closed down in 1891. *Reference*: Russell and Company Records, Manuscript Division, Library of Congress.

RUSSELL AND STURGIS. American trading house, founded in 1828 in Manila, the Philippines, by George Robert Russell* and Henry P. Sturgis. It came to be known as "the great company." It acted as commission merchant, banker, investor, shipping and insurance agent, and landowner. It was also involved in the abacá trade. It declared bankruptcy in 1875–1876, and failed in 1876. *Reference*: Benito Legarda, Jr., "American Entrepreneurs in the 19th Century Philippines," *Explorations in Entrepreneurial History* 9 (1957): 142–59.

RYAN, ARCHIE LOWELL (1881–1954). Clergyman, born April 15, 1881, in Clay Center, Kansas. Ryan graduated from Baker University (Baldwin, Kans.) and Boston University School of Theology, and was ordained in 1910. He held pastorates in Le Hunt, Kansas; and Methuen and South Braintree, Massachusetts, until 1914. He was field secretary of the Board of Sunday Schools of the Methodist Episcopal Church in the Philippines from 1914 to 1920, joint field secretary for Methodist Episcopal Church and World's Sunday School Association for the Philippines from 1920 to 1930, professor of religious education at Union Theological Seminary in Manila from 1914 to 1932, and its president from 1925 to 1932. He was also editor of *Philippine Islands Sunday School Journal* from 1923 to 1930. He wrote *Religious Education in the Philippines* (Manila, 1930). He held pastorates in Piedmont, Shawnee, London Heights, and Kansas City, Kansas, from 1934 to 1942; was superintendent of the Kansas City district from 1942 to 1948; and served as a pastor in Kansas City after 1948. Died December 27, 1954, in Kansas City, Kansas. *References: WWP*; and *WWWA*.

RYAN, BRYCE F(INLEY) (1911–   ). Sociologist, born February 16, 1911, in Youngstown, Ohio. Ryan graduated from the universities of Washington and Texas, and Harvard University. He was assistant professor of sociology at Iowa State University (Ames) from 1937 to 1943, chief reports analyst for the United Nations Relief and Rehabilitation Administration (UNRRA) in Germany from 1944 to 1946, and assistant professor of sociology at Rutgers University (New Brunswick, N.J.) from 1946 to 1948. He was professor of sociology and chairman of the sociology department at the University of Ceylon in Colombo from 1948 to 1952, and a consultant to the Rockefeller Foundation from 1950 to 1952. He wrote *Caste in Modern Ceylon* (New Brunswick, N.J., 1953), and *Sinhalese Village* (Coral Gables, Fla., 1958). He was professor of sociology at the University of Miami (Coral Gables, Fla.) from 1955 until his retirement in 1976. *References: AMWS; CA*; and *WWA*.

S

SAINT COLUMBAN'S FOREIGN MISSION SOCIETY. Popularly known as the Columban Fathers, and founded in Ireland in 1916. The first house in the United States was established in Omaha, Nebraska, in 1918. It began missionary work in China in 1920 (until it was expelled by the Communists in 1952), in the Philippines in 1929, in Korea in 1933, in Burma in 1936, and in Japan in 1934. *References*: Saint Columban's Foreign Mission Society Archives, St. Columbans, Neb.; *CE*; Edward Fischer, *Japan Journey: The Columban Fathers in Nippon* (New York, 1984); Edward Fischer, *Journeys Not Regretted: The Columban Father's Sixty-Five Years in the Far East* (New York, 1986); Edward Fischer, *Mission in Burma: The Columban Fathers' Forty-Three Years in Kachin Country* (New York, 1980); and B. T. Smyth, ed., *But Not Conquered* (Westminster, Md., 1958).

ST. JOHN'S UNIVERSITY. St. John's College in Shanghai, one of the first of the Protestant colleges in China, began as a boys' school established by Bishop William Jones Boone* of the Protestant Episcopal Church in 1847. It became a secondary school in 1888 and a college in 1899. It became a university in 1905, and was chartered by the District of Columbia in that year. It remained in Shanghai during World War II, the only Protestant college to function wholly in enemy-controlled territory during the war. It was nationalized in 1952 by the Chinese Communist government. *References*: *Fenn*; Mary Lamberton, *St. John's University, Shanghai, 1879–1951* (New York, 1955); and *Lutz*.

SALEEBY, NAJEEB M(ITRY) (1870–1935). Physician and educator, born near Beirut, Lebanon. Saleeby studied at the American University of Beirut, and then came to the United States and studied at Bellevue Medical School (New York City). He became a naturalized U.S. citizen. He served as surgeon in the U.S. Army during the Spanish-American War, came to the Philippines in 1900, and served in Mindanao and later in Malabang, Lanao. He resigned from the army and remained in the Philippines. He was assistant chief of the Bureau of

Non-Christian Tribes and agent for Moro affairs in 1903, first provincial super-intendent of education in the Moro Province from 1903 to 1906, and medical director of St. Luke's Hospital in Manila. He later practiced medicine in Manila. He wrote *Studies in Moro History, Law and Religion* (Manila, 1905); *The History of Sulu* (Manila, 1908); and *The Moro Problem* (Manila, 1913). Died December 18, 1935, in Baguio City, Philippines. *Reference*: Lloyd G. Van Vactor, "Four Decades of American Educators in Mindanao and Sulu," *Dansalan Quarterly* 3 (1981): 30–34.

SALLEE, W. EUGENE (1878–1931). Missionary, born March 24, 1878, in Middleburg, Kentucky. Sallee graduated from Georgetown College and Roch-ester Theological Seminary. He was a missionary under the Foreign Mission Board of the Southern Baptist Convention in China from 1903 until 1930. He served in Kaifeng after 1908, and began to build the Kaifeng Baptist College in 1915. He also worked to improve agricultural conditions in China. He returned to the United States in 1930, and was home secretary of the Foreign Mission Board until his death. Died June 15, 1931, in Raleigh, North Carolina. *Refer-ences*: *ESB*; and Annie Sallee, *W. Eugene Sallee, Christ's Ambassador* (Nash-ville, Tenn., 1933).

SAMUEL RUSSELL AND COMPANY *See* RUSSELL AND COMPANY

SANDERS, MARSHALL DANFORTH (1823–1871). Missionary, born July 3, 1823, in Williamstown, Massachusetts. Sanders graduated from Williams College and Auburn Theological Seminary, and was ordained in 1851. He was a missionary under the American Board of Commissioners for Foreign Missions (ABCFM) to Ceylon from 1851 until his death. He was in charge of the Batticota Seminary from 1851 to 1853, and served later at Chavakachcheri, Jaffna, Tel-lippally, and again in Batticota. He was principal of the Batticota Seminary from 1858 to 1867. Died August 29, 1871, in Batticota, Ceylon. *References*: *Hewitt*; and *NCAB* 25:49.

SANDS, WILLIAM FRANKLIN (1874–1946). Diplomat, born July 29, 1874, in Washington, D.C. Sands graduated from Georgetown University. He entered the diplomatic service in 1896, and was second secretary in the U.S. legation in Tokyo from 1896 to 1898; first secretary in Seoul, Korea, in 1898–1899; and special advisor to the Korean emperor from 1899 until 1904, when he was expelled from Korea by the Japanese after their invasion. He was chargé d'affaires in Panama in 1904 to 1906, in Guatemala in 1907, and in Mexico in 1908, and U.S. minister to Guatemala from 1909 until 1911. He left the diplomatic service in 1911 and was involved with several corporations in Washington, D.C.; Boston; Philadelphia; and London. He wrote *Undiplomatic Memories: The Far East, 1896–1904* (New York, 1940). Died June 17, 1946, in Washington, D.C. *Ref-erences*: William Franklin Sands Papers, St. Charles Borromeo Seminary Library, Overbrook, Philadelphia; *DACB*; *NCAB* 41:20; *NYT*, June 19, 1946; and *WWWA*.

SAPPORO AGRICULTURAL COLLEGE. Founded in 1875 in Sapporo, Hokkaido, Japan, by American teachers invited by the *Kaitakushi*, or development office, set up to develop Hokkaido. Approximately seventy Americans have participated in the development of the college over a twenty-five year period. In 1907 it became the College of Agriculture of Tohoku Imperial University (which changed its name to Hokkaido Imperial University in 1918 and to Hokkaido University in 1947). *References*: Martin Bronfenbrenner, *Academic Encounter: The American University in Japan and Korea* (New York, 1961), pp. 11–16; and *A Historical Sketch of The College of Agriculture, Tohoku Imperial University: What America Has Done for a Japanese Government College* (Sapporo, Japan, 1915).

SAVORY, NATHANIEL (1794–1874). Colonist and merchant, born July 31, 1794, in Bradford, Essex County, Massachusetts. Savory went to sea in 1814. He was a member of the first group of colonists to settle on the island of Chichi Jima in the Bonin Islands in 1830, and was a trader in Port Lloyd. He spent much of his life trying to make the island (then called Peel Island) a part of the United States. He served as chief magistrate of the island from 1854 until 1859. Died April 10, 1874, in the Bonin Islands. *References*: Gilbert Cant, "Home of Chichi Juna," *Life* 20 (June 24, 1946): 17–19; and Lionel B. Cholmondely, *The History of the Bonin Islands from the Year 1827 to the Year 1876, and of Nathaniel Savory, One of the Original Settlers* (London, 1915).

SAYRE, FRANCIS B(OWES) (1885–1972). Lawyer and government official, born April 30, 1885, in South Bethlehem, Pennsylvania. Sayre graduated from Williams College and Harvard Law School. He was the deputy assistant district attorney of New York County in 1912–1913, assistant to the president and instructor at Williams College from 1914 to 1917, assistant professor of law at Harvard Law School from 1919 to 1924, and professor there from 1924 to 1934. He was foreign affairs advisor to the Siamese government from 1923 to 1925. He undertook several important diplomatic missions in Europe for the Siamese government, and negotiated on its behalf new political and commercial treaties with France, Great Britain, the Netherlands, Spain, Portugal, Denmark, Sweden, Norway, and Italy in 1925–1926, abolishing extraterritoriality in Siam and a treaty of arbitration with Great Britain in 1925. He was a member, representing Siam, of the Permanent Court of Arbitration at the Hague from 1925 to 1934, director of the Harvard Institute of Criminal Law from 1929 to 1934, assistant secretary of state from 1933 to 1939, and high commissioner to the Philippines from 1939 to 1942. He wrote *Siam, Treaties with Foreign Powers, 1920–1927* (Norwood, Mass., 1928), and an autobiography, *Glad Adventure* (New York, 1957). Died March 29, 1972, in Washington, D.C. *References*: Francis B. Sayre Papers, Manuscript Division, Library of Congress; Melcor P. Aquino, "Francis B. Sayre," *BAHC* 2 (July 1974): 7–11; David V. Default, "Francis B. Sayre and the Commonwealth of the Philippines, 1936–1942," Ph.D. diss., University of Oregon, 1972; *Gleeck/Governors*, ch. 15; *NCAB* F:486; *NYT*, March 30, 1972; *WWP*; and *WWWA*.

SCHALLER, GEORGE B(EALS) (1933–   ). Zoologist, born May 26, 1933, in Berlin, Germany, and grew up in Missouri. Schaller graduated from the universities of Alaska and Wisconsin. He was research associate and assistant professor at Johns Hopkins University from 1963 to 1966, research associate at the New York Zoological Society from 1966 to 1979, director of its Animal Research and Conservation Center after 1979, and also director of Wildlife Conservation International. He studied mountain gorillas at the Albert National Park in the Belgian Congo in 1959–1960, and led an expedition to the Serengeti National Park in Tanzania from 1966 to 1969. He conducted an expedition to Pakistan and Nepal to study wild sheep and goats in the Himalayas, and wrote *The Deer and the Tiger: A Study of Wildlife in India* (Chicago, 1967); *Golden Shadows, Flying Hooves* (New York, 1973); *Mountain Monarchs: Wild Sheep and Goals of the Himalayas* (Chicago, 1977); and *Stones of Silence: Journey in the Himalayas* (New York, 1980). He was coleader of the China–World Wildlife Fund expedition to the Wolong Natural Reserve in China in 1981–1982 to study the giant panda, and was coauthor of *The Giant Pandas of Wolong* (Chicago, 1985). *References*: *CA*; *CB* 1985; and *WWA*.

SCHEERER, ALOYSIUS LOUIS (1909–1966). Clergyman, born February 10, 1909, in Philadelphia. Scheerer attended Providence (R.I.) College, and graduated from the Dominican House of Studies (Washington, D.C.). He joined the Dominican order in 1929 and was ordained in 1935. He was a Dominican missionary in Fukien Province, China, from 1936 until 1949, in Hong Kong from 1949 until 1954, and at the leper colony at Tala, near Manila, the Philippines, in 1954–1955. He started the first American Dominican mission in Multan, in the Punjab, Pakistan, in 1956, and was consecrated Roman Catholic bishop of Multan in 1960. Died January 27, 1966, in Multan, Pakistan. *References*: *DACB*; and *NYT*, January 29, 1966.

SCHERESCHEWSKY, SAMUEL ISAAC JOSEPH (1831–1906). Missionary, born May 6, 1831, in Tauroggen, Russian Lithuania. Schereschewsky attended the University of Breslau. He came to the United States in 1854, studied at the Western Theological Seminary (Allegheny, Pa.) and General Theological Seminary (New York City), and was ordained in 1860. He was a missionary under the Domestic and Foreign Missionary Society of the Protestant Episcopal Church in the United States of America in China from 1861 until 1883. He was stationed in Peking from 1863 to 1875, and joined with other missionaries in translating the *Book of Common Prayer* and the Bible into Mandarin. He was consecrated in 1877 as Protestant Episcopal bishop of Shanghai, and organized

St. John's College (later St. John's University) in 1878. He translated the *Book of Common Prayer* into Classical Chinese. He served in Wuchang in 1881–1882. He resigned the bishopric in 1883 because of ill health. He later revised the Mandarin version of the Bible and, with another missionary, translated the Gospel of Matthew into Mongolian. Died October 15, 1906, in Shanghai. *References*: *DAB*; James A. Muller, *Apostle of China. Samuel Issac Joseph Schereschewsky, 1831–1906* (New York, 1937); and *NCAB* 13:429.

SCHNEDER, DAVID B(OWMAN) (1857–1938). Missionary, born March 23, 1857, in Bowmansville, Pennsylvania. Schneder graduated from Franklin and Marshall College and Lancaster (Pa.) Theological Seminary. He was ordained in 1883. He was a pastor in Marietta, Pennsylvania, from 1883 to 1887. He was a missionary under the Board of Foreign Missions of the Evangelical and Reformed Church in the United States in Japan from 1887 until 1936. He was a professor of systematic theology at North Japan College from 1887 to 1901, and its president from 1901 until his retirement in 1936. Died October 5, 1938, in Sendai, Japan. *References*: C. W. Mensendiek, *A Man For His Times: The Life and Thought of David B. Schneder, Missionary to Japan, 1887–1938* (Sendai, Japan, 1972); *NYT*, October 6, 1938; and *WWWA*.

SCHÖBL, OTTO (1877–1938). Scientist, born August 27, 1877, in Zdice, Czechoslovakia. Schöbl graduated from the State University of Prague. He came to the United States in 1907, and was employed by H. K. Mulford Company of Philadelphia, a drug manufacturing company. He was an assistant pathologist at the Bureau of Science in the Philippines from 1912 to 1915, and with the New York State Quarantine Service in 1915–1916. He returned to the Philippines in 1916 as a pathologist and bacteriologist, and was the chief of the Serum Section (later the Division of Biology) of the Philippine Bureau of Science from 1916 until 1932, working on different tropical diseases. He retired in 1936 and lived in Tokyo, Japan. Died October 13, 1938, in Tokyo. *References*: Cirilo B. Perez, "Otto Schöbl," *The Philippines Journal of Science* 69 (1939): 267–70; and *Scientists in the Philippines* (n.p., 1975), pp. 190–219.

SCHRODER, FRED MEYER (fl. 1880s–1960s). Adventurer. Schroder was on the Mexican border from 1877 to 1894, was a prospector for gold on the Yukon in Alaska from 1894 to 1907. He came to China in 1907, and was employed by the British-American Tobacco Company (BATC) until 1917, serving much of the time in Kalgan, Hupeh Province. He was involved in 1917 in an abortive attempt to restore the Manchu dynasty. He returned to the United States in 1917, and settled in Orland, California. Died in Oakland, California. *Reference*: Robert Easton, *Guns, Gold & Caravans: The Extraordinary Life and Times of Fred Meyer Schroder, Frontierman and Soldier of Fortune, in California, Mexico, Alaska and China, Including His Discovery of the Mysterious Pyramids of Shens, and Rescue of the Boy Emperor* (Santa Barbara, Calif., 1978).

SCHURMAN, JACOB GOULD (1854–1942). Educator and diplomat, born May 22, 1854, in Freetown, Prince Edward Island, Canada. Schurman graduated from the universities of London and Edinburgh, and studied in Paris, Germany, Italy, and Switzerland. He taught in Canadian universities from 1880 to 1886. He was professor of philosophy at Cornell University from 1886 to 1892, and president of Cornell from 1892 to 1920. He was chairman of the First Philippines Commission in 1899, which was known as the Schurman Commission. He wrote *Philippine Affairs—A Retrospect and Outlook* (New York, 1902) based on his experiences. He was U.S. minister to Greece and Montenegro in 1912–1913. He was minister to China from 1921 to 1925. He opposed foreign intervention in China and supported Chinese nationalism but also supported the continuation of extraterritoriality. He was ambassador to Germany from 1925 to 1930. He retired in 1930. Died August 12, 1942, in New York City. *References*: Jacob Gould Schurman Papers, Cornell University Library, Ithaca, N.Y.; *DADH*; Kenneth P. Davis, "The Diplomatic Career of Jacob Gould Schurman," Ph.D. diss., University of Pennsylvania, 1975; Kenneth E. Hendrickson, Jr., "Reluctant Expansionist—Jacob Gould Schurman and the Philippine Question," *PHR* 36 (1967): 405–21; *NCAB* 40:491; *NYT*, August 13, 1942; and *WWWA*.

SCHWARTZ, ALOYSIUS (1930–   ). Missionary, born September 18, 1930, in Washington, D.C. Schwartz graduated from St. Charles Seminary (near Baltimore) and Maryknoll Seminary (Glen Ellyn, Ill.), studied at the University of Louvain (Belgium), and was ordained in 1957. He was admitted to the Societé d'Auxiliares des Missions in 1953. He served in Pusan, Korea, in 1958–1959. He returned to the United States in 1959 because of ill health. He established Korean Relief, Inc., in 1959 and returned to Korea in 1962, serving at Song-do, Pusan. He established a Boystown and a Girlstown, and provided kindergarten through technical junior college, first in Pusan and later in Seoul. He established hospitals in Seoul and Pusan, a tuberculosis sanitarium in Pusan, and a home for destitute aged and disabled adults. He founded the order of the Sisters of Mary and Brothers of Christ. He wrote *The Starved and the Silent* (Garden City, N.Y., 1966). *Reference*: *The Ramon Magsaysay Awards 1982–1984* (Manila, 1985), pp. 215–34.

SCHWARTZ, HENRY B(UTLER) (1861–1945). Missionary, born June 30, 1861, in Cincinnati. Schwartz graduated from Ohio Wesleyan University and Boston University School of Theology. He was a missionary under the Board of Foreign Missions of the Methodist Episcopal Church in Japan in 1893 until 1915. He served initially in Tokyo. He was the presiding elder of the Amori district and principal of the Chinzei Gakuin in Nagasaki from 1900 to 1902, and presiding elder of the Kagoshima district from 1902 to 1906. He was district supervisor in Okinawa from 1907 to 1911. He wrote *In Loo Choo Islands: A Chapter in Missionary History* (Tokyo, 1907); *In Togo's Country: Some Studies in Satsuma and Other Little Known Parts of Japan* (Cincinnati, 1908); and *The*

Great Shrine of Idzuma: Some Notes on Shinto, Ancient and Modern (Tokyo, 1913). He returned to the United States in 1915, was professor of English at the College of the Pacific (San Jose, Calif.), field secretary for Japanese work of the Methodist Episcopal Church in Hawaii, and superintendent of foreign language schools in Hawaii under the Territorial Department of Education and Missionary of the Hawaiian Mission Board in the islands of Kauai and Maui. Died May 15, 1945, in Palo Alto, California.

SCIDMORE, ELIZA RUHAMAH (1856–1928). Traveler and author, sister of George H. Scidmore,* born October 14, 1856, in Madison, Wisconsin. Scidmore attended Oberlin College. She was a newspaper correspondent in Washington, D.C., writing society letters to various newspapers. In the 1880s, she turned to travel and to writing about it. She lived for many years in Japan, India, China, Java, and the Philippines. She joined the staff of the National Geographic Society in 1890, and served as corresponding secretary, associate editor, and foreign secretary. She was one of the first people to advocate planting Japanese cherry trees in Washington, D.C. She wrote *Jinrikisha Days in Japan* (New York, 1891); *Java the Garden of the East* (New York, 1897); *China, the Long-Lived Empire* (New York, 1900), and *Winter India* (New York, 1903). She settled in Geneva in 1925, and spent the rest of her life promoting the League of Nations. Died November 3, 1928, in Geneva, Switzerland. *References*: Eliza R. Scidmore Diaries, in the Oakley-Hawley Family Papers, State Historical Society of Wisconsin, Madison, Wis.; *DAB*; *NYT*, November 4, 1928; and *WWWA*.

SCIDMORE, GEORGE HAWTHORNE (1854–1922). Consul, brother of Eliza Ruhamah Scidmore,* born October 12, 1854, in Dubuque, Iowa. Scidmore graduated from National University (Washington, D.C.) and was admitted to the bar in 1876. He was a consular clerk and vice-consul in Liverpool, Dunfermline, and Paris from 1876 to 1880; vice-consul at Osaka and Hiogo in 1884 and in Shanghai in 1885; vice- and deputy consul general in Kanagawa from 1885 to 1891 and from 1894 to 1902, and at Yokohama from 1902 to 1904; legal advisor to the American legation and embassy in Tokyo from 1904 to 1907; consul in Nagasaki from 1907 to 1909 and Kobe in 1909; and consul general in Seoul from 1909 to 1913 and in Yokohama from 1913 until his death. He was also a barrister and solicitor of the British court for Japan after 1893, and a lecturer on American and English law at Tokyo English Law School. He wrote *Outline Lectures on the History, Organization, Jurisdiction, and Practiced of the Ministerial and Consular Courts of the United States of America in Japan* (Tokyo, 1887). Died November 27, 1922, in Yokohama, Japan. *References*: George H. Scidmore Papers, in the Oakley-Hawley Family Papers, State Historical Society of Wisconsin, Madison, Wis.; *NYT*, November 28, 1922; and *WWWA*.

SCOTT, MARION MCCARRELL (1843–1922). Educator, born August 21, 1843, in Fauquier, Virginia. Scott attended Urania College (Ky.) and the University of Virginia. He went to California in 1864, taught in San Francisco, and served as principal of a grammar school. He came to Japan in 1871, was a member of the faculty of Imperial Tokyo University in 1871–1872; organized the Tokyo Normal School (later Tokyo University of Education), the first Western teacher training school in Japan; and was its vice principal from 1872 until 1874. He imported teaching material, textbooks, and furniture from American schools, and guided the first generation of Japan's professionally trained teachers on the American model. He contributed to the establishment of a modern educational system in Japan, working as a textbook editor, compiler of teachers' manuals, and advisor on teaching methods. He was a teacher of English at Tokyo English School after 1874, and later at the preparatory school for Tokyo University until 1881, when he left Japan. He came to Hawaii in 1881, where he established the first public high school and was its principal from 1885 until 1919. Died May 3, 1922, in Honolulu. *References*: *Honolulu Advertiser*, May 4, 1922; *KEJ*; John W. Siddall, ed., *Men of Hawaii, 1921* (Honolulu, 1921).

SCOTT, WILLIAM HENRY (1921–   ). Historian, born July 10, 1921. Scott graduated from Yale University, and served in the U.S. Navy during World War II. He was a lay missionary of the Philippine Episcopal Church. He was a lecturer in history at the University of the Philippines, and a professor at Trinity College of Quezon City, Manila, Philippines. He wrote *On the Cordillera: A Look at the People and Cultures of Mountain Province* (Manila, 1966); *Prehistoric Source Materials for the Study of Philippine History* (Manila, 1969); *History of the Cordillera: Collected Writings on Mountain Province* (Baguio, 1975); *Hollow Ships on a Wine-Dark Sea and Other Essays* (Quezon City, 1976); and *Cracks in the Parchment Curtain and Other Essays in Philippine History* (Quezon City, 1982); and was coeditor of *Acculturation in the Philippines: Essays on Changing Societies* (Quezon City, 1971). *Reference*: *Yale*.

SCOVEL, MYRA (SCOTT) (1905–   ). Medical missionary, born August 11, 1905, in Mechanicville, New York. Scovel graduated from the Hospital of the Good Shepherd, Syracuse University, Babies' and Children's Hospital, and Western Reserve University (later Case Western Reserve University). She was a medical missionary under Board of Foreign Missions of the Presbyterian Church in the U.S.A. in China from 1930 to 1951, and in India from 1953 to 1959. She was the coordinator of the Medical Emphasis Program from 1959 to 1961, and editor for the program's office of communications after 1961. She wrote *The Chinese Ginger Jars* (New York, 1962); *How Many Sides to a Chinese Coin?* (New York, 1969); and several children's books, and an autobiography, *To Lay a Hearth* (New York, 1968). *References*: Frederick G. and Myra Scott Scovel Papers, University of Oregon Library, Eugene, Ore.; and *CA*.

SCRANTON, WILLIAM B(ENTON) (1856–1922). Medical missionary, born May 29, 1856, in New Haven, Connecticut. Scranton graduated from New York College of Physicians and Surgeons of Columbia University, and was ordained in 1884. He practiced medicine in Cleveland, Ohio, from 1882 to 1884. He was a medical missionary under the Board of Foreign Missions of the Methodist Episcopal Church in Korea from 1885 until 1907. He conducted medical work in Seoul, later opened two other medical centers in Seoul, and was supervisor of the medical work of the Seoul mission. He was superintendent of the mission from 1892 until 1907. He resigned in 1907, practiced medicine in Seoul, and acted as a medical advisor to several mining companies. He practiced in Kobe, Japan, from 1917 until 1922. Died March 1922, in Kobe, Japan. His mother, **MARY F(LETCHER) (BENTON) SCRANTON** (1832–1909), missionary, was born December 9, 1832, in Belchertown, Massachusetts. She was general secretary of the Women's Foreign Missionary Society of the Methodist Episcopal Church, and its first missionary. She accompanied her son to Korea and served there from 1885 until her death. She began Ewha School in 1886. Died October 8, 1909, in Seoul, Korea. *References*: *EWM*; Louise M. Hodgkins, *The Roll Call: An Introduction to Our Missionaries, 1869–1896* (Boston, 1896).

SCRIBNER, FRANK LAMSON. *See* LAMSON-SCRIBNER, FRANK

SCUDDER, DAVID COIT (1835–1862). Missionary, born October 27, 1835, in Boston. Scudder graduated from Williams College and Andover Theological Seminary, and was ordained in 1861. He was a missionary under the American Board of Commissioners for Foreign Missions (ABCFM) at Periakulam, Madura district, India, in 1862. Drowned November 19, 1862, in the Vaigai River, near Periakulam, India. *References*: *ACAB*; *Hewitt*; and Horace E. Scudder, *Life and Letters of David Coit Scudder, Missionary in Southern India* (New York, 1864).

SCUDDER, IDA SOPHIA (1870–1960). Medical missionary, daughter of John Scudder II,* born December 9, 1870, in Ranipet, Madras Presidency, India, and grew up in Vellore, South India; Creston, Nebraska; and Chicago. She attended the Woman's Medical College of Pennsylvania, and graduated from Cornell Medical College. She returned to India in 1900 as a medical missionary and served in Vellore. She opened a hospital in 1902 and developed a system of itinerant roadside clinics in the countryside. She developed a nursing school and opened the Union Mission Medical School for Women in Vellore in 1918. Died May 24, 1960, in Kodaikanal, in the Palani Hills, India. *References*: Scudder Family Papers, Radcliffe College Library, Cambridge, Mass.; *CDCWM*; *NAW*; *NYT*, May 25, 1960; and Dorothy J. Scudder, *A Thousand Years in Thy Sight: The Story of the Scudder Missionaries of India* (New York, 1984).

SCUDDER, JOHN (1783–1855). Medical missionary, born September 3, 1783, in Freehold, New Jersey. Scudder graduated from Princeton University and the College of Physicians and Surgeons (New York City), and was ordained in 1821. He practiced medicine in New York City from 1813 until 1819. He was a medical missionary under the American Board of Commissioners for Foreign Missions (ABCFM) in Jaffna, Ceylon, from 1819 until 1838; in Madras, India, from 1838 to 1842; in Madura from 1846 to 1849; and again in Madras from 1849 until 1854. He opened a hospital in Jaffna and began training native medical students. Died January 13, 1855, in Wyneberg, South Africa, on his way back to India. Seven of his sons became missionaries. John's son **HENRY MARTYN SCUD-DER** (1822–1895), missionary, was born February 5, 1822, in Pandeterip, Jaffna district, Ceylon. Henry Martyn Scudder came to the United States in 1832. He attended New York University, graduated from Union Theological Seminary, and was ordained in 1843. He was a missionary under the ABCFM in India from 1844 to 1857, and under the Board of Foreign Missions of the Reformed Church of America after 1857. He served in Madura from 1844 to 1846, in Madras from 1846 to 1850, and in the Arcot mission from 1850 to 1864. He returned to the United States in 1864 and held pastorates at Jersey City, New Jersey; San Francisco; Brooklyn, New York; and Chicago. He served in Japan from 1887 to 1890. Died June 4, 1895, in Winchester, Massachusetts. John's second son, **WILLIAM W(ATERBURY) SCUDDER** (1823–1895), missionary, was born in Pandeterip, Ceylon. William W. Scudder graduated from Princeton University and Princeton Theological Seminary. He was a missionary under ABCFM in India from 1846 to 1851, and under the Board of Foreign Mission of the Reformed Church in America in India from 1852 until 1872, serving in the Arcot mission. He was a pastor in Glastonbury, Connecticut, from 1873 to 1884, but returned to India in 1885, serving in Mandanapalle and then as professor of theology at the seminary in Palmaner. Died March 4, 1895, in Glastonbury. John's third son, **JARED WATERBURY SCUDDER** (1830–1910), medical missionary, was born February 8, 1830, in Niligiri Hills, India. Jared Waterbury Scudder graduated from Western Reserve University, New Brunswick Theological Seminary, and Long Island Medical College, and was ordained in 1855. He was a medical missionary under the Board of Foreign Missions of the Reformed Church in America in India from 1855 to 1910. He was professor at Arcot Theological Seminary from 1895 to 1908. Died October 17, 1910, in Palmaner, India. John's fourth son, **JOHN SCUDDER II**, (1835–1900), medical missionary, was born October 29, 1835, in Chavagacherry, Ceylon. John Scudder II graduated from Rutgers University, New Brunswick Theological Seminary, and Long Island Medical College, and was ordained in 1860. He was a medical missionary in India from 1861 until 1900. He served in Chittur from 1861 to 1863, in Arni from 1863 to 1865, in Arcot from 1865 to 1867, and in Vellore in 1867–1877. He returned to the United States in 1877 but returned to India in 1882. He served in Arni from 1882 to 1885, in Tindivanum from 1885 to 1892, and in Vellore from 1892 to 1894 and again from 1897. Died May 23, 1900, in Kodai Kanal, India. **LEWIS R(OUSSEAU) SCUDDER** (1861–1935), medical missionary and son of William Waterbury Scudder, was born December 22, 1861, in Vellore. Lewis R. Scudder graduated from Princeton University, Hartford Theological Seminary, and the University Medical College of the City of New York, and was ordained in 1885. He was a medical missionary under the Reformed Church in America in India from 1888 until 1935. Died April 18, 1935, in Ranipettai, India. **GALEN (FISHER) SCUDDER** (1891–1967), medical missionary and son of Lewis R. Scudder, was born August 22, 1891, in Ranipettai, India. Galen Scudder graduated from Princeton University and Cornell University Medical School, and studied at the London School of Tropical Medicine. He was a medical missionary under the Reformed Church in America in India from 1919 until 1954. Died July 22, 1967, in Stockton, California. *References*: *DAB*; *EM*; *Hewitt*; *LC*; and Dorothy J. Scudder, *A Thousand Years in Thy Sight: The Story of the Scudder Missionaries in India* (New York, 1984).

SEAGRAVE, GORDON STIFLER (1897–1965). Medical missionary, born March 18, 1897, in Rangoon, Burma, to American missionary parents, and grew up in Granville, Ohio. Seagrave graduated from Denison University and Johns Hopkins University Medical School. He was a medical missionary under the American Baptist Foreign Mission Society* from 1922 until 1946. He served in the Namkham, the northeast frontier area of Burma, until 1940, when he was evacuated to the United States. He then ran a hospital at Prome in southeast Burma, and was responsible for other jungle hospitals along the Burma Road and the Burma-China border. He later served in the U.S. Army Medical Corps in Burma and participated in the retreat to India in 1942. He returned to Burma in 1945 and was chief medical officer of the Shan states for the British Military Administration. He returned to the Namkham area in 1946, severed relations with the American Baptist Foreign Mission Society in 1946, and created the American Medical Center for Burma Frontier Areas (later the American Medical Center for Burma) in 1946. In 1950, he was charged with treason and was imprisoned, but was later released and reopened his hospital in 1952. He wrote *Waste-Basket Surgery* (Philadelphia, 1930); *Tales of a Waste-Basket Surgeon* (Philadelphia, 1938); *Burma Surgeon* (New York, 1943); *Burma Surgeon Returns* (New York, 1946); and *My Hospital in the Hills* (New York, 1955). His hospital was nationalized by the Burmese government in 1965. Died March 28, 1965, in Namkham, Burma. *References*: *CB* 1943; *DAB S7*; Sue M. Newhall, *Devil in God's Old Man* (New York, 1969); *NYT*, March 29, 1965; *OAB*; and *WWWA*.

SEALE, ALVIN (1871–1959). Ichthyologist, born July 8, 1871, in Fairmount, Indiana. Seale graduated from Stanford University. He was curator of fishes at Bishop Museum in Honolulu from 1901 to 1904, assistant in the Smithsonian Institution and the U.S. Bureau of Fisheries in 1905, and chief of the division of fisheries in the Philippines from 1907 until 1916. He also established the Manila Aquarium. He made several trips to Borneo, Hong Kong, China, and

Japan. He was an associate in ichthyology at the Museum of Comparative Zoology of Harvard University from 1916 to 1919. He established the Steinhart Aquarium of the California Academy of Sciences in San Francisco in 1923, and was its superintendent until his retirement in 1941. Died July 28, 1959, in Corallitos, California. *References*: Alvin Seale Papers, Stanford University Library, Stanford, Calif.; *AMWS*; and Albert W.C.T. Herre, "Alvin Seale, Naturalist and Ichthyologist," *Science* 129 (February 6, 1959): 313–14.

SEBALD, WILLIAM J(OSEPH) (1901–   ). Diplomat, born November 5, 1901, in Baltimore. Sebald graduated from the U.S. Naval Academy in 1922 and the University of Maryland Law School. He was a naval language officer in Japan. He resigned from the navy and entered law practice in Japan. He served in the U.S. Navy during World War II. He returned to Japan in 1946 and was a political advisor to General Douglas MacArthur with the rank of ambassador. He was head of the Diplomatic Section of the General Headquarters of the Supreme Commander for the Allied Powers (SCAP) from 1947 to 1952, General MacArthur's deputy from 1947 to 1951, and U.S. member and chairman of the Allied Council for Japan during the same period. He was ambassador to Burma from 1952 to 1954, deputy assistant secretary of state from 1954 to 1957, and ambassador to Australia from 1957 to 1961. He wrote (with Russell Brines) *With MacArthur in Japan: A Personal History of the Occupation* (New York, 1965). *References*: Jon L. Boyes, "The Political Adviser (POLAD): The Role of the Diplomatic Adviser to Selected United States and North Atlantic Alliance Military Commanders," Ph.D. diss., University of Maryland, 1971, pp. 165–82; *CA*; *CB* 1951; and *KEJ*.

SECURITY TREATY CRISIS. *See* HAGERTY INCIDENT

SERVICE, JOHN S(TEWART) (1909–   ). Diplomat, born in Chengtu, China, to missionary parents. Service graduated from Oberlin College. He entered the foreign service in 1935, and served in Kunming, Peking, Shanghai, Chungking, and Yenan. He was dismissed from the State Department in 1951, but was reinstated by the U.S. Supreme Court in 1957. He served as consul in Liverpool from 1959 until his retirement in 1962. He wrote *The Amerasia Papers: Some Problems in the History of US-China Relations* (Berkeley, Calif., 1971), and *State Department Duty in China, the McCarthy Era, and After, 1933–1977* (Berkeley, Calif., 1981), and edited the memoir of his mother, **GRACE SERVICE** (1879–1954) (a missionary in China), *Golden Inches: The China Memoir of Grace Service* (Berkeley, 1989). *References*: John Stewart Service Papers, Bancroft Library, University of California at Berkeley; Joseph W. Esherick, ed., *Lost Chance in China: The World War II Dispatches of John S. Service* (New York, 1974); *PolProf: Eisenhower*; and *PolProf: Truman*.

SEVENTH-DAY ADVENTISTS, GENERAL CONFERENCE OF. Founded in 1863, it began missionary work in India in 1893; in Japan in 1896; in the Dutch East Indies in 1900; in China, Burma, and Ceylon in 1902; in Korea in 1904; in the Philippines in 1909; in Singapore and Malaya in 1910; in Siam in 1919; and in Vietnam in 1929. *References*: Seventh Day Adventist Department of Archives, Washington, D.C.; Clyde C. Cleveland, *Indonesian Adventure for Christ* (Washington, D.C., 1965); E. H. Gates, *In Coral Isles* (Washington, D.C., 1923); and *SDAE*.

SEWARD, GEORGE F(REDERICK) (1840–1910). Diplomat, nephew of Secretary of State William H. Seward, born November 9, 1840, in Florida, New York. Seward attended Union College. He was consul in Shanghai from 1861 to 1863, and consul general from 1863 to 1876. He was U.S. minister to China from 1876 to 1879. He began the negotiations toward a new treaty regarding Chinese immigration to the United States. He wrote *The United States Consulates in China* (Washington, D.C., 1867); *Chinese Immigration in Its Social and Economic Aspects* (New York, 1881); and *Reminiscences of a War-Time Statesman and Diplomat, 1830–1915* (New York, 1916). He was vice president of Fidelity and Casualty Company from 1887 to 1893, and president after 1893. Died November 28, 1910, in New York City. His sister **SARA CORNELIA SEWARD** (1833–1891), medical missionary, was born June 8, 1833, in Florida, New York. Sara Cornelia Seward graduated from the Woman's Medical College (Philadelphia). She was in China with her brother from 1861 to 1865. She was a medical missionary under the Woman's Foreign Missionary Society of the Presbyterian Church in the U.S.A. in Allahabad, India, from 1871 until her death. Died June 12, 1891, in Allahabad, India. *References*: George F. Seward Papers, New York Historical Society, New York City; *Anderson*, ch. 5; Paul H. Clyde, "Attitudes and Policies of George F. Seward, American Minister at Peking, 1876–1880," *PHR* 2 (1933): 387–404; *DAB*; *NCAB* 7:91; *NYT*, November 29, 1910; and *WWWA*.

SHANGHAI, UNIVERSITY OF. Founded in 1906 as the Shanghai Baptist College and Theological Seminary by the China missions of the American Baptist Foreign Missionary Society and the Southern Baptist Convention. It was chartered by the State of Virginia in 1917, and became the Shanghai College in 1918 and a university in 1931. It remained in Shanghai during World War II, and opened a branch in Chungking. It was taken over by the Communist government in 1952. *References*: *Fenn*; John B. Hipps, *History of the University of Shanghai* (Richmond, Va., 1964); and *Lutz*.

SHANGHAI POWER COMPANY. American-owned company, formed in 1929 when an international group dominated by American and Foreign Power (which, in turn, was controlled by Electric Bond and Stock Company) purchased the foreign-controlled Shanghai Municipal Council's Electrical Department. The company furnished most of Shanghai's electric power. It was taken over by the Communists in 1950. *Reference*: Warren W. Tozer, ''Last Bridge to China: The Shanghai Power Company, the Truman Administration and the Chinese Communists,'' *Diplomatic History* 1 (1977): 64–78.

SHANGHAI STEAM NAVIGATION COMPANY. Founded by Russell and Company in 1862, it operated ships in the Yangtze River and along the China coast, and was the largest shipping concern in China until 1878 when it was sold to the Chinese. *Reference*: Kwang-ching Liu, *Anglo-American Steamship Rivalry in China 1862–1874* (Cambridge, Mass., 1962).

SHANTUNG CHRISTIAN UNIVERSITY. Shantung Union College was established in Weihsien as a result of a merger between Tenchow College (which originated as Tengchow Boys' School, and which was founded in 1864 and became a college in 1882) and Tengchow Boys' Boarding School. It absorbed the Tsingchow Theological Institute (founded in 1885) and the Medical College of Tsinan to form Shantung Protestant University. It became Shantung Christian University in 1909. It later absorbed Tsinan Institute and North China Union Medical College for Women. It became Cheeloo University in 1931. It ceased to exist as a university after 1952. *References*: Charles H. Corbett, *Shantung Christian University (Cheeloo)* (New York, 1955); *Fenn*; and *Lutz*.

SHAPLEN, ROBERT M(ODELL) (1917–   ). Journalist, born March 22, 1917, in Philadelphia. Shaplen graduated from the University of Wisconsin and Columbia University. He was a reporter and rewrite man for the *New York Herald Tribune* from 1937 to 1943, war correspondent in the Southwest Pacific and then chief of the Far Eastern Bureau of *Newsweek* in Shanghai from 1945 to 1947, staff member of *Fortune* from 1948 to 1950 and of *Collier's* from 1950 to 1952, staff writer for the *New Yorker* after 1952, and the *New Yorker*'s Far Eastern correspondent in Hong Kong from 1962 until 1978. He wrote *The Lost Revolution: The Story of Twenty Years of Neglected Opportunities in Viet Nam and of America's Failure to Foster Democracy There* (New York, 1965); *Time Out of Hand: Revolution and Reaction in Southeast Asia* (New York, 1969); *A Turning Wheel: Three Decades of the Asian Revolutions as Witnessed by a Correspondent for The New Yorker* (New York, 1979); and *Bitter Victory: A Veteran Correspondent's Dramatic Account of His Return to Vietnam and Cambodia Ten Years After the End of the War* (New York, 1986). *References*: *CA*; and *WWA*.

SHARP, LAURISTON (1907–   ). Anthropologist, born March 24, 1907, in Madison, Wisconsin. Sharp graduated from the University of Wisconsin and Harvard University, and studied at the University of Vienna. He carried out fieldwork in Cape York Peninsula of North Queensland from 1933 to 1935, and in Java, the Philippines, and China in 1935. He was assistant and associate professor of anthropology at Cornell University from 1936 until 1947, and professor of anthropology and Asian studies there from 1947 to 1974. He was acting assistant chief of the division of Southeast Asian affairs in the State Department in 1945–1946. He established the Cornell-Thailand project at Cornell University in 1947, and served as its director. He carried out fieldwork in Thailand in 1947–1948 and later periodically in Bang Chan, a village in the Central Plain, which served as the primary focus of the research conducted by the Cornell-Thailand project. He was coauthor of *Siamese Rice Village: A Preliminary Study of Bang Chan, 1948–1949* (Bangkok, 1953); *Thailand* (New Haven, Conn., 1956); *A Report on Tribal Peoples in Chiengrai Province, North of the Mai Kok River* (Bangkok, 1964); and *Bang Chan: Social History of a Rural Community in Thailand* (Ithaca, 1978); and edited *Ethnographic Notes on Northern Thailand* (Ithaca, 1965), and *Thailand since King Chulalongkorn* (New York, 1976). *References*: AMWS; G. William Skinner and A. Thomas Kirsch, ed., *Change and Persistence in Thai Society. Essays in Honor of Lauristan Sharp* (Ithaca, N.Y., 1975); R. J. Smith, ed., *Social Organization and the Applications of Anthropology: Essays in Honor of Lauristan Sharp* (Ithaca, N.Y., 1974); and *WWA*.

SHAW, GLENN WILLIAM (1886–1961). Educator and government official, born November 19, 1886, in Los Angeles. Glenn graduated from Colorado College. He was a teacher in Hawaii, Japan, China, and India from 1910 to 1915, and a teacher in Japan from 1916 to 1940, teaching chiefly in the Osaka School of Foreign Languages, Osaka. He also contributed a column to the newspaper *Osaka Asahi Shimbun*. He returned to the United States in 1940, and was a translator and research analyst with the U.S. Navy Department from 1941 to 1944, director of the Navy School of Oriental Languages at the University of Colorado from 1944 to 1946, and then head of the language division of the Navy Intelligence School in Annapolis, Maryland from 1946 to 1949. He returned to Japan from 1949 to 1957, where he was a State Department historian, supervising the microfilming of Japanese Ministry of Foreign Affairs documents, and then cultural attaché at the embassy of Tokyo from 1952 until his retirement in 1957. He translated the works of important modern Japanese writers into English. He wrote *Osaka Sketches* (Tokyo, 1929); *Japanese Scrap-Book* (Tokyo, 1932); and *Living in Japan* (Tokyo, 1936). Died August 26, 1961, in Boulder, Colorado. *References*: *Boulder Camera*, August 29, 1961; *BRDS*; and *KEJ*.

SHAW, SAMUEL (1754–1794). Merchant, born October 2, 1754, in Boston. Shaw served in the revolutionary army during the American Revolution. He was supercargo on the *Empress of China*, the first American vessel sent to Canton in 1784. He was the first U.S. consul in Canton, from 1786 until his death. In 1786, he also started the firm of Shaw and Randall in Canton, which acted on behalf of merchants who lacked familiarity with that country. Died May 30, 1794, near the Cape of Good Hope, on his way to the United States. *References*:

Margaret C. S. Christman, *Adventurous Pursuits: Americans and the China Trade 1784–1844* (Washington, D.C., 1984), pp. 59–69; *DAB*; *NCAB*, 5:408; and Josiah Quincy, ed., *The Journals of Major Samuel Shaw, the First American Consul at Canton, with a Life of the Author* (Boston, 1847).

SHAW, WILLIAM J(AMES) ("BILL") (1877–1939). Businessman, born September 20, 1877, in Barnet, Vermont. Shaw graduated from the University of California. He came to the Philippines in 1901, and was employed by the Atlantic, Gulf and Pacific Company in Manila. He was president and general manager of the company after 1917. Died March 1, 1939, in Manila. *References*: *EP* 4:473–474; *Gleeck/Manila*; *WWP*; and *WWWA*.

SHEFFIELD, DEVELLO Z(ELOTES) (1841–1913). Missionary, born August 13, 1841, in Gainesville, New York. Sheffield served in the Union Army during the Civil War. He graduated from Auburn Theological Seminary, and was ordained in 1869. He was a missionary under the American Board of Commissioners for Foreign Missions (ABCFM) in China from 1869 until 1909. He served in Tungchow, developed a school, and taught there and at Gordon Theological Seminary. He was president of Union College (later part of Yenching University) in Tungchow from 1890 until 1909. He was president of China Educational Association from 1896 to 1899. He prepared textbooks in Chinese and was involved in revising the translation of the New Testament and portions of the Old Testament in classical Chinese. He also revised S. Wells Williams's *Chinese-English Dictionary*. Died July 1, 1913, in Peithaiho, north China. *References*: *DAB*; Robert Paterno, "Devello Z. Sheffield and the Founding of the North China College," *American Missionaries in China: Papers from Harvard Seminars*, ed. Kwang-ching Liu (Cambridge, Mass., 1960), pp. 42–92; and *WWWA*.

SHELDON, MARTHA A. (1860–1912). Medical missionary, born in Excelsior, Minnesota. Sheldon graduated from the University of Minnesota and the School of Medicine of Boston University. She was a medical missionary under the Women's Foreign Missionary Society of the Methodist Episcopal Church in India from 1889 until her death. She served at Moradabad until 1893, and at Pithoragarh, eastern Humaun, and then moved to Bhot and worked among the nomadic Bhotiya peoples. She was based in Dharchula during the winter and in Sirkha during the summer. She also made several trips to Tibet. Died October 18, 1912, in Dhrachula. *References*: Eva C. M. Browne, *The Life of Dr. Martha A. Sheldon* (n.p., n.d.); and *EWM*.

SHELTON, ALBERT LEROY (1875–1922). Medical missionary, born June 9, 1875, in Indianapolis, and grew up in Kansas. Shelton graduated from Kansas State Normal College (Emporia) and the medical department of Kentucky University (Louisville), and was ordained in 1903. He was a medical missionary under the Foreign Christian Missionary Society of the Disciples of Christ in China from 1903 until his death. He served at Tatsienlu, Szechuan Province, near the border of Tibet, from 1903 to 1908, and at Batang after 1908. He collected Tibetan paintings, books, and other domestic objects (a collection later purchased by the Newark Museum). He wrote *Pioneering in Tibet: A Personal Record of Life and Experience in Mission Fields* (New York, 1921). Killed February 16, 1922, by robbers near Batang. His wife, **FLORA BEAL SHEL-TON** (1871–1966), wrote *Sunshine and Shadow on the Tibetan Border* (Cincinnati, 1912) and a biography of her husband, and translated *Chants from Shangri-la* (Palm Springs, Calif., 1939). *References*: *DAB*; *IAB*; Vallrae Reynolds, "Journey to Tibet: One Man's Experience, 1904–1922: Photographs from the Dr. Albert L. Shelton Archives," *Museum* [Newark, N.J.] 24 (Spring-Summer 1972); F. B. Rogers, "Dr. Albert L. Shelton (1875–1922) and the Tibetan Collection in the Newark (New Jersey) Museum," *Transactions and Studies of the College of Physicians of Philadelphia* 8 (June 1986): 101–4; and *Tibet*.

SHELTON, EDWARD MASON (1846–1928). Agriculturalist, born August 7, 1846, in Huntingdonshire, England, and brought to the United States in 1855. Shelton graduated from Michigan Agricultural College. He went to Japan in 1871, and was in charge of the Kaitakushi experimental farm near Tokyo until 1872, when he returned to the United States. He was a professor of agriculture at Kansas State Agricultural College from 1874 until 1890; was an agricultural advisor and instructor in Queensland, Australia, from 1890 to 1897; and served as principal of Gatton College, an agricultural school, from 1897 to 1899, when he returned to the United States and settled in Seattle, Washington. Died February 17, 1928, in Seattle. *Reference*: *DAB*.

SHEPPARD, ELI T. (fl. 1861–1881). Diplomatic advisor. Sheppard served in the Union Army during the Civil War. In 1868, he became a special agent of the U.S. Treasury Department for China; he was consul in Chunkiang from 1869 to 1871, and in Tientsin from 1871 to 1876. He worked in Japan from 1877 to 1881, as advisor to the Foreign and Justice ministries in 1877–1878, and then in the Foreign Ministry from 1878 to 1881, when he returned to the United States. He assisted Japan to check the extension of extraterritorial privilege and to work for the eventual elimination of extraterritoriality itself. *References*: Eli T. Sheppard Papers, Manuscript Division, Library of Congress; and Deborah C. Church, "The Role of the American Diplomatic Advisers to the Japanese Foreign Ministry, 1872–1887," Ph.D. diss., University of Hawaii, 1978, ch. 3.

SHEPPING, ELISE J(OHANNA) (1880–1934). Medical missionary, born September 26, 1880, in Germany. Shepping came to the United States as a child and was trained as a nurse. She was a missionary under the Board of Foreign

Missions of the Presbyterian Church in the United States in Korea from 1912 until her death. She served at Kwangju from 1912 to 1916, at Kunsan hospital after 1916, and later in the Severance Union Hospital in Seoul. She established a nurses' training school. She resigned because of ill health and returned to Kwangju. Died June 26, 1934, in Kwangju, Korea. *References*: Martha Huntley, "Presbyterian Women's Work and Rights in the Korean Mission," *American Presbyterians* 65 (1987): 44–48; and Lois H. Swinehart, "Elise Johanna Shepping—A Missionary Deborah," in *Glorious Living: Informal Sketches of Seven Women Missionaries of the Presbyterian Church, U.S.*, comp. Hallie P. Winsborough (Atlanta, 1937), pp. 147–84.

SHIMONOSEKI BOMBARDMENT (1863). Japanese forces in the Shimonoseki Straits shelled foreign shipping, including the American steamer *Pembroke*. The USS *Wyoming*, commanded by David Stockton McDougal,* destroyed the Japanese battery and three Japanese vessels. *References*: *EAH*; *KEJ*; and Frank E. Ross, "The American Naval Attack on Shimonoseki in 1863," *Chinese Social and Political Review* 18 (1934): 146–55.

SHOUP MISSION (1949). Mission of seven tax specialists, headed by Carl Sumner Shoup, to Japan in 1949 to study and recommend revisions for Japan's system of taxes. Its recommendations served as the basis for a new tax policy for Japan. *References*: *CB* 1949; and *KEJ*.

SHRYOCK, JOHN K(NIGHT) (1890–1953). Missionary. Shryock graduated from the University of Pennsylvania, and was ordained in 1915. He was a missionary under the Domestic and Foreign Missionary Society of the Protestant Episcopal Church in the United States of America in China. He was associated with St. Paul's School in Anking, China, from 1916 to 1926. He wrote *The Temples of Anking and Their Cults, a Study of Modern Chinese Religion* (Paris, 1931), and *The Origin and Development of the State Cult of Confucius; an Introductory Study* (New York, 1932). He was later a pastor in Philadelphia. Died February 5, 1953, in Philadelphia. *Reference*: *NYT*, February 7, 1953.

SHUCK, JEHU LEWIS (1812–1863). Missionary, born September 4, 1812, in Alexandria, Virginia. Shuck graduated from the Virginia Baptist Seminary (later the University of Richmond). He was a missionary under the American Baptist Missionary Union from 1836 to 1845, and under the Foreign Mission Board of the Southern Baptist Convention in China from 1846 until 1853, the first Baptist missionary to China. He served in Macao from 1836 to 1842, and in Hong Kong from 1842 to 1845. He organized the first Baptist church in China in Hong Kong in 1845. He served in Canton in 1846 and in Shanghai after 1847. He was involved in organizing the first Baptist church in Shanghai in 1847. He returned to the United States in 1853, and worked among the Chinese in California from 1854 to 1861. Died August 20, 1863, in Barnwell Courthouse, South

Carolina. His wife, **HENRIETTA HALL SHUCK** (1817–1844), born October 28, 1817, in Kilmarnock, Virginia, was the first American evangelical woman missionary to go to China, in 1836. She opened a school for girls in Macao and served in Hong Kong from 1842 until her death. Died in childbirth, November 27, 1844, in Hong Kong. *References*: Henrietta Hall and Jehu Shuck Papers, Virginia Baptist Historical Society, University of Richmond Library, Richmond, Va.; *ACAB*; Margaret M. Coughlin, "Strangers in the House: Lewis Shuck and Issachar Roberts, First American Baptist Missionaries from America to China," Ph.D. diss., University of Virginia, 1972; *DAB*; Thomas G. Dunaway, *Pioneering for Jesus: The Story of Henrietta Hall Shuck* (Nashville, Tenn., 1930); and *WWWA*.

SHUFELDT, ROBERT WILSON (1822–1895). Naval officer, born February 21, 1822, in Red Hook, New York. Shufeldt was appointed a midshipman in 1839, resigned in 1854, and was captain of a steamship in the merchant service, consul in Cuba from 1861 to 1863, and a special agent to Mexico in 1862. He was recommissioned in the navy in 1862, and served during the Civil War. He went on a combined diplomatic and commercial mission around the world, commanding the USS *Ticonderoga* from 1878 to 1880. He sailed in 1880 to Pusan, Korea, and tried unsuccessfully to negotiate a treaty of friendship with Korea. He returned to China in 1881 as a naval attaché, and negotiated a treaty of amity and commerce with representatives of Korea in Tientsin. He was president of the Naval Advisory Board, and superintendent of the Naval Observatory from 1882 until his retirement in 1884 with the rank of rear admiral. Died November 7, 1895, in Washington, D.C. *References*: Robert W. Shufeldt Papers, Manuscript Division, Library of Congress; William J. Blinker, "Robert W. Shufeldt and the Changing Navy," Ph.D. diss., Indiana University, 1970; *DAB*; *DADH*; Frederick C. Drake, *The Empire of the Seas: A Biography of Rear Admiral Robert Wilson Shufeldt, USN* (Honolulu, 1984); Frederick C. Drake, "Robert Wilson Shufeldt: The Naval Officer as Commercial Expansionist and Diplomat," in *Captains of the Old Steam Navy: Makers of the American Naval Tradition 1840–1880*, ed. James C. Bradford, Jr. (Annapolis, Md., 1986), pp. 275–300; Kenneth J. Hagan, *American Gunboat Diplomacy and the Old Navy, 1877–1889* (Westport, Conn., 1973); *NCAB* 4:293; *NYT*, November 8, 1895; and *WWWA*.

SIBLEY, CHARLES T(HOMAS) (1875–1957). Medical missionary, born April 20, 1875, in Lupen, Somersetshire, England, and came to the United States in 1888. Sibley graduated from New York City Homeopathic College. He was the second missionary of the American Board of Commissioners for Foreign Missions (ABCFM) in the Philippines, from 1908 until 1916. He helped establish a mission hospital in Davao, and operated it until 1916. He returned to the United States in 1916 and practiced medicine in New York City. Died September 4, 1957, in Oradell, New Jersey. *Reference*: *NYT*, September 6, 1957.

SICKLES, DAVID B(ANKS) (1837–1918). Financier and diplomat, born February 8, 1837, in New York City. Sickles was a war correspondent during the Civil War. He was an aide-de-camp to the governor of Arkansas, a financial agent for the state of Arkansas from 1866 to 1870, and a banker in New York City from 1870 until 1876. He was U.S. consul in Siam from 1876 to 1881. His representations of the complaints of American missionaries in the north of Siam led to King Chulalongkorn's edict on religious freedom. He was associated with the American Surety Company in New York City from 1882 until his retirement in 1906. Died July 19, 1918, in Paterson, New Jersey. *References*: *NCAB* 10:227; and *NYT*, July 20, 1918.

SILL, JOHN M(AHELM) B(ERRY) (1831–1901). Educator and diplomat, born November 23, 1831, in Black Rock, New York, and grew up in Jonesville, Michigan. Sill graduated from Michigan State Normal School, and was ordained in 1890. He was principal of the Michigan State Normal School from 1859 to 1863. He was elected superintendent of public schools in Detroit in 1863, was proprietor and principal of the Detroit Female Seminary from 1865, was reelected superintendent of the Detroit public schools in 1875, and was reappointed principal of the Michigan State Normal School in 1886. He was U.S. minister to Korea from 1894 to 1897. He returned to the United States in 1897. Died April 6, 1901, in Detroit. *References*: John M. B. Sill Papers, Bentley Historical Library, University of Michigan, Ann Arbor; Jeffery M. Dorwart, "The Independent Minister: John M. B. Sill and the Struggle against Japanese Expansion in Korea, 1894–1897," *PHR* 44 (1975): 485–502; Egbert R. Isbell, "John Mahelm Berry Sill," *Detroit Historical Society Bulletin* 21 (December 1964): 4–9; *NCAB* 10:353; Bonnie B. Oh, "John M. B. Sill, U.S. Minister to Korea (1894–1897): A Reluctant Participant in International Mediation," in *The United States and Korea: American-Korean Relations, 1866–1976*, ed. Andrew C. Nahm (Kalamazoo, Mich., 1979), pp. 91–109; and *WWWA*.

SILLIMAN UNIVERSITY. A private institution, founded in 1901 as Silliman Institute in Dumaguete City, Negros Oriental, in the Philippines, following a gift by Dr. Horace B. Silliman to the Board of Foreign Missions of the Presbyterian Church in the U.S.A. It became a university in 1938. *Reference*: Arthur L. Carson, *Silliman University 1901–1959* (New York, 1965).

SINO-AMERICAN COOPERATIVE ORGANIZATION (SACO). A U.S. Naval Mission to China during World War II (initially Naval Group China), led by Commander Milton E. Miles,* which gave to the Chinese Nationalist secret service aid, training, and political support, and helped prepare the Nationalists for the civil war with the Chinese Communists. *References*: Milton E. Miles and Hawthorne Daniel, *A Different Kind of War: The Little-Known Story of the Combined Guerrilla Forces Created in China by the U.S. Navy and the Chinese During World War II* (Garden City, N.Y., 1967); Michael Schaller, "SACO!

The United States Navy's Secret War in China," *PHR* 44 (1975): 527–53; Michael Schaller, *The U.S. Crusade in China, 1938–1945* (New York, 1979), ch. 11; and Roy Stratton, *SACO, the Rice Paddy Navy* (New York, 1950).

SINO-AMERICAN JOINT COMMISSION ON RURAL RECONSTRUCTION. Established in 1948 as an instrument for the reform of rural areas in China (and later in Taiwan) by instituting reforms for the technological and social advancement of farmers. It was part of the U.S. aid extended to the Nationalist government of China in an attempt to buy it time to strengthen itself against the Communists. *References*: Melvin Conant, Jr., "JCRR: Problems of American Participation in the Sino-American Joint Commission on Rural Reconstruction," *Papers on China* 6 (1952): 45–74; and T. H. Shen, *The Sino-American Joint Commission on Rural Reconstruction: Twenty Years of Cooperation for Agricultural Development* (Ithaca, N.Y., 1970).

SKINNER, G(EORGE) WILLIAM (1925–   ). Anthropologist, born February 14, 1925, in Oakland, California. Skinner attended Deep Springs (Calif.) College, and graduated from Cornell University. He conducted field research in Szechwan, China, in 1949–1950; in Southeast Asia in 1950–1951; in Thailand from 1951 to 1953 and 1954–1955; and in Java and Borneo from 1956 to 1958. He was field director of Cornell University's Southeast Asia program and of the Cornell Research Center in Bangkok, Thailand, from 1951 to 1955; was a research associate in Indonesia from 1956 to 1958; assistant professor of sociology at Columbia University from 1958 to 1960; associate and then professor of anthropology at Cornell University from 1960 to 1965; and professor of anthropology at Stanford University after 1966. He wrote *Chinese Society in Thailand: An Analytical History* (Ithaca, N.Y., 1957); and *Leadership and Power in the Chinese Community of Thailand* (Ithaca, N.Y., 1958); and edited *Local, Ethnic and National Loyalties in Village Indonesia: A Symposium* (New Haven, 1959). *References*: *CA*; and *WWA*.

SMEDLEY, AGNES (1894–1950). Journalist and author, born probably in Osgood, Missouri, and grew up in Trinidad, Colorado. Smedley left home at sixteen, attended Tempe Normal School (Ariz.), and lived in New Mexico, Arizona, and California. She came to New York City in 1916 or 1917, went to Europe in 1919, lived in Berlin until 1928, and wrote *Daughter of Earth* (New York, 1929), a fictionalized autobiography. She came to China in 1928 as special correspondent for the *Frankfurter Zeitung* and later for the *Manchester Guardian*, and reported on the Chinese Communist movement. She entered Communist-controlled areas in China, and was in Sian in 1936–1937 and in Yunan from 1937 to 1940. She traveled with the Eighth Route Army in Shansi in 1937–1938, and was in Hankow in 1938 and in Central Asia from 1938 to 1940. She returned to the United States in 1941 because of ill health. She wrote *Chinese Destinies: Sketches of Present-Day China* (New York, 1933); *China's Red Army*

Marching (New York, 1934); *China Fights Back: An American Woman with the Eighth Route Army* (New York, 1938); and *Battle Hymn of China* (New York, 1943). She left the United States in 1949 and lived in England. Died May 6, 1950, in Oxford, England. *The Great Road: The Life and Times of Chu Teh* (New York, 1956) was published posthumously. *References*: Agnes Smedley Papers, Arizona State University Library, Tempe, Ariz.; Rewi Alley, *Six Americans in China* (Beijing, China, 1985); *DAB S4*; *EAH*; Janice R. MacKinnon and Stephen R. MacKinnon, *Agnes Smedley: The Life and Times of an American Radical* (Berkeley, Calif., 1988); Joyce Milton, *A Friend of China* (New York, 1980); *NAW*; and *NYT*, May 9, 1950.

SMITH, A(DDIE) VIOLA (1893–   ). Government official, born November 14, 1893, in Stockton, California. Smith graduated from Washington College of Law. She served with the U.S. Department of Labor from 1917 to 1920, and entered the foreign trade service of the U.S. Department of Commerce in 1920. She was a trade commissioner from 1928 to 1939, was admitted to practice in the U.S. Court for China in Shanghai in 1934, was consul in the U.S. embassy in Shanghai from 1939 to 1941, and was register of the China Trade Act in Shanghai from 1931 to 1941. She was coauthor of *Motor Highways in China* (Washington, D.C., 1931). She was a representative of the China-American Council of Commerce and Industry from 1943 to 1946, an economist with the U.S. China Relief Mission and the China mission of the Economic Cooperation Administration (ECA) in 1948–1949, director of the trade promotion division of the United Nations Economic Commission for Asia and Far East in Bangkok from 1949 to 1951, and representative to the United Nations for the International Federation of Women Lawyers after 1952. *Reference*: *WWAW*.

SMITH, ARTHUR H(ENDERSON) (1845–1932). Missionary, born July 18, 1845, in Vernon, Vermont. Smith graduated from Beloit College, attended Andover Theological Seminary, graduated from Union Theological Seminary, and was ordained in 1872. He was a missionary under the American Board of Commissioners for Foreign Missions (ABCFM) in China from 1872 until 1925. He served at P'ang Chia Chuang in Shantung from 1872 to 1906, and was a missionary-at-large from 1906 until his retirement in 1925. He wrote *Proverbs and Common Sayings from the Chinese* (Shanghai, 1888); *Chinese Characteristics* (Shanghai, 1890); *Village Life in China* (New York, 1899); *China in Convulsion* (New York, 1901); *China and America To-Day: A Study of Conditions and Relations* (New York, 1907), and *The Uplift of China* (Cincinnati, 1907). Died August 31, 1932, in Claremont, California. *References*: *DAB*; Charles W. Hayford, "Chinese and American Characteristics: Arthur H. Smith and His China Books," in *Christianity in China: Early Protestant Missionary Writings*, ed. Suzaenne W. Barnett and John K. Fairbank (Cambridge, Mass., 1985), pp. 153–74; *NYT*, September 2, 1932; Theodore D. Pappas, "Arthur Henderson Smith and the American

Mission in China," *Wisconsin Magazine of History* 70 (1987): 163–86; *UnionTS*; and *WWWA*.

SMITH, DANIEL APPLETON WHITE (1840–1921). Missionary, born June 18, 1840, in Waterville, Maine. Smith graduated from Harvard University and Newton Theological Institution, and was ordained in 1863. He was a missionary under the American Baptist Missionary Union in Burma from 1863 until his death. He was president of Karen Baptist Theological Seminary in Insein, Burma, from 1876 to 1916, and editor of the *Morning Star*, a Karen monthly, after 1868. Died December 14, 1921, in Rangoon, Burma. *References*: Daniel Appleton White Smith Letters, in Samuel Francis Smith Papers, Manuscript Division, Library of Congress; Emma W. Marshall and Harry I. Marshall, *Daniel Appleton White Smith* (n.p., n.d.); *NYT*, December 15, 1921; and *WWWA*.

SMITH, EDWARD HUNTINGTON (1873–1968). Missionary, born July 1, 1873, in Franklin, Connecticut. Smith graduated from Amherst College and Hartford Theological Seminary, and was ordained in 1901. He was a missionary under the American Board of Commissioners for Foreign Missions (ABCFM) in Ingtai station in Foochow, Fukien Province, China, from 1901 until 1943. He retired in 1943, but returned to stay in Foochow in 1946 at his own expense, until he was expelled in 1950. His daughter, **HELEN H(UNTINGTON) SMITH**, (1902–1971), a missionary educator, was born December 19, 1902, in Ingtai, China. She graduated from Mount Holyoke College and Union Theological Seminary. She was a missionary educator under ABCFM in China from 1930 to 1950, teaching at Wenshan Girls School in Foochow. She directed the women's work of the United Church of Christ's Ohio Conference from 1952 to 1963, and was executive director of the Council for Lay Life and Work of the United Church of Christ from 1963 until her retirement in 1967. Died February 27, 1971, in Cleveland. *References*: Smith Family Papers, Divinity School Library, Yale University, New Haven, Conn.; *NYT*, February 28, 1971; and *WWAW*.

SMITH, E(RASMUS) PESHINE (1814–1882). Economist and diplomatic advisor, born March 2, 1814, in New York City and grew up in Rochester, New York. Smith graduated from Columbia University and Harvard Law School. He practiced law in Rochester from 1833 to 1849, was editor of the Buffalo *Commercial Advertiser* after 1849, and wrote on political economy. He was professor of mathematics and natural philosophy at the University of Rochester from 1851 to 1853, deputy state superintendent of public instruction at Albany, New York, from 1853 to 1857, and reporter of the court of appeals of New York at Albany from 1857 to 1865. He was commissioner of emigration in the State Department in 1866–1867, and an examiner of claims from 1867 to 1871. He was diplomatic advisor to the Ministry of Foreign Affairs of Japan in 1872 to 1876, the first

American chosen to act in an official capacity for the Japanese government. Died October 21, 1882, in Rochester, New York. *References*: *ACAB*; Deborah C. Church, "The Role of the American Diplomatic Advisers to the Japanese Foreign Ministry, 1872–1887," Ph.D. diss., University of Hawaii, 1978; Michael H. Hudson, "E. Peshine Smith: A Study in Protectionist Growth Theory and American Sectionalism," Ph.D. diss., New York University, 1968; *NCAB* 13:195; and *WWWA*.

SMITH, FLOYD TANGIER (1881?–1939). Animal collector, born in Japan. Smith spent many years in zoological work in China, Siberia, Indochina, Siam, and Tibet, collecting natural history specimens for American institutions. He led the Marshall Field zoological expedition to Southeast Asia in 1931–1932. He brought one of the first stuffed specimens of the giant panda to the United States in 1932. He was back in western Szechuan province in China in 1934, and in 1937 brought out alive four giant pandas, one of which went to the New York Zoological Park in the Bronx. He was a partner of William H. Harkness, Jr., and after the latter's death in Shanghai in 1936, of Ruth Harkness.* Died July 12, 1939, in Mastick, Long Island, New York. *Reference*: *NYT*, July 14, 1939.

SMITH, HUGH MCCORMICK (1865–1941). Ichthyologist, born November 21, 1865, in Washington, D.C. Smith graduated from Georgetown University. He was an assistant in the U.S. Fish Commission (later Bureau of Fisheries) from 1886 to 1897; assistant in charge of fisheries from 1897 to 1903; director of the biological laboratory at Woods Hole, Massachusetts, in 1901–1902; deputy commissioner of fisheries from 1903 to 1913; and commissioner of fisheries from 1913 to 1922. He directed the *Albatros* expedition from 1907 to 1910, which investigated the possible development of fisheries in the Philippines, and obtained a large collection of fish and aquatic animals. He was advisor in fisheries to the government of Siam from 1923 to 1926, and the first director of the department of fisheries of Siam as well as an advisor on fisheries from 1926 until 1934. He wrote *A Review of the Aquatic Resources and Fisheries of Siam* (Bangkok, 1925), and *The Fresh Water Fishes of Siam or Thailand* (Washington, D.C., 1945). He was associate curator of zoology in the Smithsonian Institution from 1935 until his death. Died September 28, 1941, in Washington, D.C. *References*: "The Hugh McCormick Smith Memorial Number," *Copeia* 1941, no. 4 (November 1941); *NCAB* 33:89; and *WWWA*.

SMITH, JACOB (HURD) ("HOWLING WILDERNESS") (1840–1918). Army officer, Smith served in the Union Army during the Civil War. He was later commissioned in the regular army, and served on the Western frontier. He served in the Spanish-American War in Cuba, and in the Philippine-American War from 1899 to 1902. He was military governor of the provinces of Zambales, Pangasinan, and Tarlac. He commanded the Sixth Separate Brigade in Samar and Leyte in 1901, and was responsible for ordering the Samar massacre. He was court-martialed, convicted, and forced into retirement with the rank of brigadier general in 1902. Died March 1, 1918, in San Diego, California. *References*: David L. Fritz, "Before the 'Howling Wilderness': The Military Career of Jacob Hurd Smith, 1862–1902," *Military Affairs* 43 (1979): 186–90; *NYT*, March 3, 1918; *WWWA*; and Kenneth R. Young, "Atrocities and War Crimes: The Cases of Major Waller and General Smith," *Leyte-Samar Studies* 12 (1978): 64–77.

SMITH, JAMES FRANCIS (1859–1928). Lawyer and colonial administrator, born January 28, 1859, in San Francisco. Smith graduated from Santa Clara College, studied at Hastings College of the Law (San Francisco), and was admitted to the bar in 1881. He practiced law in San Francisco from 1885 to 1898. He served in the Spanish-American War in the Philippines, and in the Philippine-American War, and was military governor of Negros and then of the Visayas. He was associate justice of the Supreme Court of the Philippines from 1901 to 1903, a member of the Philippine Commission from 1903 to 1906, vice-governor in 1906, and governor-general of the Philippines from 1906 to 1909. He returned to the United States in 1909, and was an associate justice of the United States court of customs appeals from 1910 until his death. Died June 29, 1928, in Washington, D.C. *References*: James Francis Smith Papers, Washington State Historical Society Library, Tacoma, Wash.; *DAB*; EP 4:360–361; *Gleeck/Governors*, ch. 5; *Sevilla*; and *WWWA*.

SMITH, LAURA IRENE (IVORY) (1902–   ). Missionary, born September 28, 1902, in Dalrymple, Ontario, Canada. She came to the United States in 1923, was later naturalized, and attended Moody Bible Institute. She was a missionary under the Christian and Missionary Alliance in Indochina (and later in Vietnam) from 1928 until 1955. She served later with the World-Wide Evangelization Crusade in Fort Washington, Pennsylvania, from 1958 to 1967, and with the United World Mission in St. Petersburg, Florida, after 1968. She wrote *Gongs in the Night* (Grand Rapids, Mich., 1943); *Farther into the Night: Missionary Adventures in Indo-China* (Grand Rapids, Mich., 1955); and *Victory in Vietnam* (Grand Rapids, Mich., 1965). Her husband, **GORDON H(EDDERLY) SMITH** (1902–1977), wrote *The Blood Hunters* (Chicago, 1942), and together they wrote *Light in the Jungle* (Chicago, 1946). *Reference*: *WWAW*.

SMITH, ROBERT AURA (1899–1959). Journalist, born in Denver. Smith served in a field hospital during World War I. He graduated from Ohio Wesleyan University and Oxford University. He taught at Drake University and Evansville College in 1924–1925. He was music and theater editor of *The Cincinnati Commercial Tribune* from 1925 to 1929, and went to Manchuria in 1929 as correspondent for *The Christian Science Monitor*. He went to Manila in 1930, was news editor of *The Manila Daily Bulletin* and correspondent of *The New York Times* until 1937, and served on the foreign news desk of the *The New York*

Times from 1937 to 1941 and again from 1945 until 1949. He served in the Office of the Coordinator of Information from 1941, set up a United States information service in the Far East, headed the India-Burma division of the Office of War Information until 1943, and was chief of its training division and commentator on Far Eastern affairs over the Voice of America broadcast radio until 1945. He joined *The New York Times* editorial board from 1949 until his death. He wrote *Our Future in Asia* (New York, 1940), *Divided India* (New York, 1947) and *Philippine Freedom, 1946–1958* (New York, 1958). Died November 11, 1959, in New York City. *References*: *NYT*, November 12, 1959; and *WWWA*.

SMITH, ROBERT JOHN (1927–   ). Anthropologist, born June 27, 1927, in Essex, Missouri. Smith graduated from the University of Minnesota and Cornell University. He served in the U.S. Army during World War II. He was a member of the faculty of Cornell University after 1953, and professor of anthropology there after 1963. He conducted cultural anthropology field research in Japan in 1951–1952, 1955, and 1957–1958, and was coauthor of *Two Japanese Villages* (Ann Arbor, Mich., 1956); coeditor of *Japanese Culture: Development and Characteristics* (New York, 1962); and author of *Ancestor Worship in Contemporary Japan* (Stanford, Calif., 1974) and *Kurusu: the Price of Progress in a Japanese Village, 1951–75* (Stanford, 1978). *References*: *AMWS*; and *WWA*.

SMITH, ROY K(ENNETH) (1885–1957). Medical missionary, born April 28, 1885, in Lincoln, Kansas. Smith graduated from the College of Emporia (Kans.) and the University of Kansas Medical School. He was a medical missionary under the Board of Foreign Missions of the Presbyterian Church in the U.S.A. in Korea from 1911 to 1942, and again in 1948–1949. He was superintendent of a hospital in Andong from 1912 to 1920, worked in the department of internal medicine at the hospital in Taegu, and directed a leprosarium there. He was superintendent of the hospital in Charyung from 1922 to 1932; college physician at Chosen Christian College, Seoul, from 1932 to 1934; head of the department of internal medicine at Union Christian Hospital in P'yongyang from 1934 to 1940; and superintendent of the hospital in Syenchun from 1940 to 1942. He was interned by the Japanese in 1942. He returned to Korea in 1946, where he was director of the National Tuberculosis Sanatorium in Masan from 1946 to 1948 and superintendent of the hospital in Taegu in 1948–1949. He returned to the United States in 1949 and retired in 1955. Died July 31, 1957, in Pasadena, California. *References*: *NCAB* 44:157; and *NYT*, August 2, 1957.

SMITH, WARREN D(UPRÉ) (1880–1950). Geologist, born May 12, 1880, in Leipzig, Germany, to American parents. Smith graduated from the University of Wisconsin and Stanford University. He was a field assistant with the Wisconsin Geological and Natural History Survey from 1900 to 1902. He was a paleontologist and stratigraphic geologist with the U.S. Mining Bureau in Manila in

1905–1906, a geologist with the division of mines of the Bureau of Science of the Philippines in 1906–1907, and chief of the Division of Mines from 1907 until 1914. He was again acting chief of the division from 1920 to 1922. He drafted the regulations for the coal and petroleum industries in the Philippines. He was professor and head of the department of geology at the University of Oregon from 1915 until his retirement in 1947. He served as a geographer in the Far Eastern Division of the Office of Strategic Services (OSS) in Washington, D.C., during World War II. He wrote *Geology and Mineral Resources of the Philippine Islands* (Manila, 1925). Died July 18, 1950, in Eugene, Oregon. *References*: *NCAB* 41:53; *PGSA* 1950: 119–24; *WWWA*.

SNEIDER, VERN(ON) J(OHN) (1916–1981). Author, born October 6, 1916, in Monroe, Michigan. Sneider graduated from the University of Notre Dame. He served in U.S. Army intelligence from 1941 to 1944, and in the military government from 1944 to 1946. He was an occupation officer in Okinawa in 1945, and in Korea in 1945–1946, where he was in charge of reopening educational and welfare facilities at both locations. He was a freelance writer from 1948 until his death. *Teahouse of the August Moon* (New York, 1951), and *A Long Way from Home and Other Stories* (New York, 1956) were based on his experiences in Okinawa and Korea. He was in Taiwan in 1952, and wrote *A Pail of Oysters* (New York, 1953). Died May 1, 1981, in Monroe, Michigan. *References*: *CA*; *CB* 1956; and *NYT*, May 3, 1981.

SNOW, EDGAR (1905–1972). Journalist and author, born July 19, 1905, in Kansas City, Missouri. Snow attended Kansas City Junior College and the University of Missouri, and graduated from the Columbia University School of Journalism. He was a reporter for the *Kansas City Star* and then traveled throughout the world, doing freelancing for various newspapers and magazines. He came to Shanghai in 1929 and remained in China until 1941. He was assistant editor of *The China Weekly Review* in 1929–1930, special correspondent for the *New York Herald Tribune* in 1929, correspondent for the *Chicago Tribune* in 1929–1930 and for the Consolidated Press Association from 1930 to 1934, and special correspondent for the *New York Sun* from 1934 to 1937 and the *London Daily Herald* from 1932 to 1941. He was a lecturer at Yenching University in Peking in 1934–1935. In 1936 he was the first foreign newspaper correspondent to visit Communist-held areas of northwestern China and to interview and photograph Red Chinese leaders. He was a correspondent for the *Saturday Evening Post* during World War II, and its associate editor from 1943 to 1951. He returned as a correspondent to China in 1960, 1965, and 1970. He wrote *Far Eastern Front* (New York, 1933); *Red Star over China* (New York, 1938); *The Battle for Asia* (New York, 1941); *Random Notes on Red China, 1936–1945* (Cambridge, Mass., 1957); an autobiography, *Journey to the Beginning* (New York, 1958); *The Other Side of the River: Red China Today* (New York, 1962); and *The Long Revolution* (New York, 1972). Died February 15, 1972, in Eysins,

Switzerland. *Edgar Snow's China: A Personal Account of the Chinese Revolution*, ed. Lois W. Snow (New York, 1981) was published posthumously. *References*: Edgar Snow Collection, University Archives, University of Missouri—Kansas City, Mo.; Rewi Alley, *Six Americans in China* (Beijing, China, 1985); *EAH*; John Fairbank, "Edgar Snow in Red China," in *China: The People's Middle Kingdom and the U.S.A.* (Cambridge, Mass., 1967), pp. 83–90; John M. Hamilton, *Edgar Snow* (Bloomington, Ind., 1988); John M. Hamilton, "The Missouri News Monopoly and American Altruism in China: Thomas F. F. Millard, J. B. Powell, and Edgar Snow," *PHR* 55 (1986): 27–48; Jerry Israel, "Mao's Mr. America: Edgar Snow's Images of China," *PHR* 47 (1978): 107–22; Wang King, ed., *China Remembers Edgar Snow* (Beijing, 1982); *NCAB* 60:310; *NYT*, February 16, 1972; John S. Service, "Edgar Snow: Some Personal Reminiscences," *China Quarterly* 5 (1972): 209–19; and Lois W. Snow, *A Death with Dignity: When the Chinese Came* (New York, 1975).

SNOW, HELEN FOSTER (1907–   ). Journalist who wrote under the pseudonym Nym Wales, Edgar Snow's first wife, born September 21, 1907, in Cedar, Utah. Snow attended the University of Utah, and Yenching and Tsinghua universities (Peking). She lived in China from 1931 to 1940, and was a book reviewer from 1931 to 1938, and a Peking correspondent from 1934 to 1937 for the *China Weekly Review* in Shanghai. She was coeditor (with her husband) of the magazine *Democracy* in Peking in 1937. She was cofounder of the Chinese Industrial Cooperatives in Shanghai in 1938. She was a book reviewer for the *Saturday Review of Literature* from 1941 to 1949, and compiled the Nym Wales collection at Stanford University from 1958 to 1961. She wrote *Women in Modern China* (The Hague, 1967). Under her pseudonym she wrote *Inside Red China* (New York, 1939); *China Builds for Democracy: A Story of Cooperative Industry* (New York, 1941); *Song of Ariran: The Life Story of an Asian Revolution* (New York, 1941); *Red Dust: Autobiographies of Chinese Communists as Told to Nym Wales* (Stanford, Calif., 1952), *Notes on the Beginnings of the Industrial Cooperatives in China* (Stanford, 1958); and an autobiography, *My China Years* (London, 1984). *References*: Nym Wales Papers, Hoover Institution on War, Revolution and Peace, Stanford, Calif.; *CA*; *NYT*, February 6, 1979; and *WWAW*.

SNOW, SAMUEL (1758–1838). Merchant of Providence, Rhode Island. Snow traveled to Canton on the *John Jay* as supercargo for the firm of Brown and Ives. He was U.S. consul in Canton from 1798 to 1802. He acted as an intermediary between American traders and the Hong merchants. He returned to Providence in 1802, and continued his mercantile career, investing in various enterprises. He was president of Providence Washington Insurance Company. *Reference*: Vincent P. Carosso and Lawrence H. Leder, "The Samuel Snow–Sullivan Dorr Correspondence," *Rhode Island History* 15 (1956): 65–88.

SNYDER, GARY (SHERMAN) (1930–   ). Poet, born May 8, 1930, in San Francisco, and grew up in Washington State and Portland, Oregon. Snyder graduated from Reed College and attended Indiana University and the University of California at Berkeley. He began writing poetry. He spent most of the period from 1956 to 1965 in Japan, studying Zen Buddhism at the temple Daitokuji in Kyoto. In the late 1970s, he studied the Ainu tradition in Japan. He wrote *The Back Country* (London, 1968), a collection of poems about his experiences in East Asia, Japan, and India. He returned to the United States in 1968. *References*: *CA*; *CB* 1978; *DLB*; *KEJ*; Robert A. Kern, ''The Work of Gary Snyder,'' Ph.D. diss., Harvard University, 1972; Thomas J. Leach, Jr., ''Gary Snyder: Poet as Mythographer,'' Ph.D. diss., University of North Carolina at Chapel Hill, 1974; Roy K. Okada, ''Zen and the Poetry of Gary Snyder,'' Ph.D. diss., University of Wisconsin at Madison, 1973; Bob Steuding, *Gary Snyder* (Boston, 1976); and *WWA*.

SOCIETY OF JESUS IN THE UNITED STATES. *See* JESUITS

SOKOLSKY, GEORGE E(PHRAIM) (1893–1962). Journalist, born September 5, 1893, in Utica, New York. Sokolsky attended Columbia University School of Journalism. He went on a mission to Russia in 1917, and edited the *Russian Daily News* in Petrograd, the only English-language newspaper in that city, in 1917–1918. He went to China in 1918 and was assistant editor of the *North China Star* in Tientsin in 1918–1919; reporter with the *Shanghai Gazette* in 1919; advisor to the Shanghai Student Union, advisor to the chief of police in the province of Chihli, and manager of the China Bureau of Public Information in 1919–1920; manager of the publication office for the Government Bureau of Economic Information from 1920 to 1923; and a political correspondent for the *North China Daily News* from 1920 to 1930 as well as for the *Japan Advertiser*, the *Philadelphia Public Ledger*, the *New York Evening Post*, the *New York World*, and the London *Daily Express*. He published *The Shanghai Journal of Commerce* from 1920 to 1930, edited the *Far Eastern Review* in Shanghai from 1925 to 1930, and contributed to the *China Year Book* from 1924 to 1929. He went to the United States in 1930 on a confidential financial mission for the Chinese minister of finance. He relocated to the United States in 1931. He wrote a column for the *New York Herald Tribune* from 1935 until 1940, for the *New York Sun* from 1940 to 1950, and for the *New York Journal-American* after 1950, and was with King Features Syndicate, writing a column entitled ''These Days,'' from 1944 until his death. He also appeared on a weekly radio program from 1937 to 1941. He wrote *The Story of the Chinese Eastern Railway* (Shanghai, 1929), and *Tinderbox of Asia* (London, 1932). Died December 12, 1962, in New York City. *References*: George E. Sokolsky Papers, Columbia University Library, New York City; George E. Sokolsky Papers, Hoover Institution on War, Revolution and Peace, Stanford, Calif.; *CA*; Warren I. Cohen, *The Chinese Connection: Roger S. Greene, Thomas W. Lamont, George E. Sokolsky and*

American-East Asian Relations (New York, 1978); *NCAB* 49:288; *NYT*, December 14, 1962; and *WWWA*.

SOLHEIM, WILHELM G(ERHARD), II (1924–   ). Anthropologist, born November 19, 1924, in Champaign, Illinois. Solheim attended the universities of Wisconsin and Chicago, and graduated from the universities of Wyoming, California, and Arizona. He served in the U.S. Air Force during World War II. He was a research associate in the Museum of Archaeology and Ethnology of the University of the Philippines from 1950 to 1954; lecturer at the University of the East, Manila, from 1950 to 1952; and provincial public affairs officer for the U.S. Information Agency in Manila in 1953–1954. He was an assistant professor of anthropology at Florida State University (Tallahassee) in 1960–1961, member of the faculty at the University of Hawaii after 1960, and professor of anthropology after 1967. He carried out fieldwork in Sarawak and the Philippines from 1950 to 1953. He wrote *The Archaeology of Central Philippines, a Study Chiefly on the Iron Gage and Its Relationships* (Manila, 1964); co-authored *Archaeological Survey in Southeastern Mindanao* (Honolulu, 1979) and *New Problems in the Prehistory of Southeast Asia* (Lisbon, 1970); and was editor of *Asian Perspective* after 1957. *References*: *AMWS*; *WWA*; and *WWW*.

SOOCHOW UNIVERSITY. Founded in 1901 by the China mission of the Methodist Episcopal Church, South, in Soochow to replace Buffington Institute of Soochow (founded in 1871), Anglo-Chinese College of Shanghai (founded in 1882), and Kung Hong School of Soochow (founded in 1896). It absorbed the Shanghai Anglo-Chinese College in 1911 and the Comparative Law School of China in Shanghai in 1915. It was chartered by the State of Tennessee in 1900. It taught in several locations during World War II and was reopened in 1945. It was taken over by the Communist government in 1952. *References*: *Fenn*; *Lutz*; and W. B. Nance, *Soochow University* (New York, 1956).

SOUTHEAST ASIA TREATY ORGANIZATION (SEATO). Created in 1954 to implement the Manila Pact* and to insure the security of the member states: Australia, France, New Zealand, Pakistan, the Philippines, Thailand, the United Kingdom, and the United States, through a policy of collective defense. It was disbanded in 1977. *References*: Leszek Buszynski, *SEATO: The Failure of an Alliance Strategy* (Singapore, 1983); *DADH*; and *EAH*.

SOUTHERN BAPTIST CONVENTION: FOREIGN MISSION BOARD. Founded in 1845. It began missionary work in China in 1846 (until 1950), in Japan in 1889, in Hong Kong and Macao in 1910, in the Philippines in 1948, in Taiwan in 1948, in Thailand in 1949, in Singapore in 1950, in South Korea in 1950, in Indonesia in 1951, in Malaysia in 1951, in Bangladesh in 1954, in South Vietnam in 1959 (until 1975), in Okinawa in 1960, in India in 1962, in Laos in 1971 (until 1975), in Sri Lanka in 1977, and in Brunei in 1981. *Ref-*

erences: Baptist Historical Collection, Southern Baptist Theological Seminary Library, Louisville, Ky.; Foreign Mission Board Archives, Historical Commission of the Southern Baptist Convention, Nashville, Tenn.; Women's Missionary Union Archives, Birmingham, Ala.; Park A. Anderson, "Southern Baptist Contributions to Missions in China: A Survey of Investments and Achievements," Th.D. diss., New Orleans Theological Seminary, 1947; Baker J. Cauthen, *Advance: A History of Southern Baptist Foreign Missions* (Nashville, Tenn., 1970); Winston Crawley, *Into a New World* (Nashville, 1958); and Winston Crawley, *Partners across the Pacific: China and Southern Baptists: Into the Second Century* (Nashville, Tenn., 1986).

SPAULDING, LEVI (1791–1873). Missionary, born August 22, 1791, in Jaffrey, New Hampshire. Spaulding graduated from Dartmouth College and Andover Theological Seminary, and was ordained in 1818. He was a missionary under the American Board of Commissioners for Foreign Missions (ABCFM) in Ceylon from 1820 until his death. He served at Uduvil, near Jaffna, in 1820–1821; in Manepay from 1821 to 1828; in Tellipally from 1828 to 1833; and again in Uduvil from 1833 until his death. He was in charge of the mission in Uduvil, a girls' boarding school in Manepay, and a boys' school at Tellipally. He compiled *A Manual Dictionary of the Tamil Language* (Jaffna, 1842), was involved in the translation of the Bible into Tamil, and later revised the Tamil-language Old Testament. Died June 18, 1873, Uduvil, Ceylon. *References*: *AndoverTS*; *DAB*; and *WWWA*.

SPENCER, JOSEPH E(ARLE) (1907–   ). Geographer, born September 11, 1907, in Bolivar, Missouri. Spencer graduated from the University of California at Berkeley. He was assistant district inspector of the Salt Revenue Government in China from 1932 to 1940. He served with the Office of Strategic Services (OSS) in China from 1942 to 1946. He was assistant professor of geography at the University of California at Los Angeles from 1942 to 1947, associate professor there from 1947 to 1952, and professor after 1952. He spent some fifteen years in various parts of Asia, from India to Japan, studying Asian culture, and wrote *Land and People in the Philippines* (Berkeley, Calif., 1952); *Asia, East by South: A Cultural Geography* (New York, 1954); and *Shifting Cultivation in South East Asia* (Berkeley, 1966). He was coauthor of *Philippine Island World* (Berkeley, Calif., 1967). *References*: *AMWS*; and *CA*.

SPROUSE, PHILIP D(ODSON) (1906–1977). Diplomat, born September 27, 1906, in Greenbrier, Tennessee. Sprouse graduated from Washington and Lee, and studied at George Peabody College, the Institut de Tourain (France), and Princeton University. He was a clerk at the U.S. embassy in Peking from 1935 to 1938. He entered the foreign service in 1938, was a language student in Peking, vice-consul in Hankow, third secretary at the embassy in Chungking, and consul in Kunming. He was a member of the Marshall Mission* in 1946, and was the author of its final report. He was also a member of the Wedemeyer Mission in 1947. He participated in the preparation of the China White Paper.* He was chief of the Division of Chinese Affairs in the Department of State in 1948, director of the Office of Chinese Affairs in 1949–1950, first secretary and later counselor in Paris from 1950 to 1954, counselor and later consul general in Brussels from 1954 to 1959, senior foreign service inspector from 1959 to 1962, and U.S. ambassador to Cambodia from 1962 until his retirement in 1964. Died April 28, 1977, in San Francisco. *References*: Philip D. Sprouse Papers, Hoover Institution on War, Revolution and Peace, Stanford, Calif.; *NCAB* 60:73; and *NYT*, May 4, 1977.

STANDARD OIL OF NEW JERSEY. Standard Oil began to sell kerosene in China in 1876, and developed a marketing and distributing system. The company's marketing affiliate in the Netherland, the American Petroleum Company, formed the Nederlandsche Koloniale Petroleum Mattschappij (NKPM) in 1912. It found the first commercial oil field in 1922 in south Sumatra, and built a refinery near Palembang, south Sumatra. In 1927 it was granted concessions in Sumatra. The NKPM merged with Socony Vacuum Company in 1933 to form Stanvac. *References*: Irvine H. Anderson, *The Standard-Vacuum Oil Company and United States East Asian Policy, 1931–1941* (Princeton, N.J., 1975); Chu-yuan Cheng, "The United States Petroleum Trade with China, 1876–1949," in *America's China Trade in Historical Perspective*, ed. Ernest R. May and John K. Fairbank (Cambridge, Mass., 1986), pp. 205–33; James T. Gilliam, Jr., "The Standard Oil Company in China, 1863–1930," Ph.D. diss., Ohio State University, 1987; and Peter M. Reed, "Standard Oil in Indonesia, 1898–1928," *Business History Review* 32 (1958): 311–37.

STANFORD, ARTHUR WILLIS (1859–1921). Missionary, born January 10, 1859, in Lowell, Massachusetts. Stanford attended Dartmouth College, graduated from Amherst College and Yale Divinity School, and was ordained in 1886. He was a missionary under the American Board of Commissioners for Foreign Missions (ABCFM) in Kyoto, Japan, after 1886. He was professor of Old Testament literature and exegesis in the theological department of Doshisha University until 1895. He served later at Kobe, Tottori, and Marsuyama, and again at Kobe after 1897. He also taught at Kobe College. He assembled one of the best libraries on Japanese and kindred subjects (presented to the Day Mission Library of Yale University). Died July 8, 1921, in Aubrundale, Massachusetts. *Reference*: *NCAB* 19:58.

STANTON, EDWIN F(ORWARD) (1901–1968). Diplomat, born February 22, 1901, in Bouckville, New York, but spent his early years in India. Stanton graduated from the University of Southern California. He entered the foreign service in 1921, was a language student in Peiping, and served as vice-consul in Mukden, Kalgan, Tientsin, and Tsinan. He was second secretary in Peiping and consul in Tsinan, Canton, Hankow, and Shanghai until 1941. He was interned by the Japanese in 1941–1942. He was assistant chief of the division of Far Eastern Affairs in the State Department from 1942 to 1944, deputy director of the office of Far Eastern Affairs in 1944–1945, and consul general in Vancouver, British Columbia, in 1945–1946. He was the first U.S. ambassador to Thailand, from 1946 to 1953, where he initiated and guided programs of technical and military aid. He retired in 1953. He wrote *Brief Authority: Excursions of a Common Man in an Uncommon World* (New York, 1956). Died August 29, 1968, in Bridgeport, Connecticut. *Reference*: *NYT*, August 31, 1968.

STANVAC. Formed in 1933 as a consolidation of the Asian producing and refining operations of the Standard Oil Company (New Jersey) with the Asian distribution network of Socony-Vacuum. Standard-Vacuum Oil Company functioned as a relatively independent joint subsidiary of the two corporations until its dissolution for business and legal reasons in 1962. Prior to World War II, it was the only American oil company with a major supply source in the Netherlands Indies. *References*: Irvine H. Anderson, *The Standard-Vacuum Oil Company and United States East Asian Policy, 1933–1941* (Princeton, N.J., 1974); and *Stanvac in Indonesia* (Washington, D.C., 1957).

STARR, FREDERICK (1858–1933). Anthropologist, born September 2, 1858, in Auburn, New York. Starr graduated from Lafayette College (Easton, Pa.). He was a professor of biology at Coe College (Cedar Rapids, Ia.) from 1883 to 1887, served in the department of ethnology at the American Museum of Natural History from 1889 to 1891, and was professor of geology and anthropology at Pomona College (Claremont, Calif.) in 1891–1892, assistant professor of anthropology at the University of Chicago from 1892 to 1895, associate professor there from 1895 to 1923, and curator of anthropology at the Walker Museum of the University of Chicago. He carried out fieldwork in northern Japan in 1904, bringing a representative group of Ainu to the Louisiana Purchase Exposition at St. Louis, and also did fieldwork in Korea and the Philippines. He wrote *Japanese Proverbs and Pictures* (Tokyo, 1910); *Korean Buddhism, History—Condition—Art* (Boston, 1918); *Fujiyama, the Sacred Mountain of Japan* (Chicago, 1924); and *Confucianism: Ethics, Philosophy, Religion* (New York, 1930). Died August 14, 1933, in Tokyo, Japan. *References*: Frederick Starr Papers, University of Chicago Library; *AA* 36 (1934): 271; *DAB*; Nancy B. Evans, "Frederick Starr: Missionary for Anthropology," M.A. thesis, Indiana University, 1987; R. Berkeley Miller, "Anthropology and Institutionalization: Frederick Starr at the University of Chicago, 1892–1923," *The Kroeber Anthropology Society Papers*, no. 51–52 (Spring and Fall 1975): 49–60; *NCAB* 13:115; *NYT*, August 15, 1933; George W. Starr, Jr., "Anti-Imperialism and Anthropology: The Case of Frederick Starr," *History of Anthropology Newsletter* 6, no. 1 (1979): 9–10; and *WWWA*.

STAUNTON, JOHN A(RMITAGE), JR. (1864–1944). Missionary, born April 14, 1864, in Adrian, Michigan, and grew up in New York State. Staunton graduated from Columbia School of Mines, Harvard University, and General Theological Seminary, and was ordained in 1892. He was a rector in Cleveland and Springfield, Massachusetts. He was a missionary under the Domestic and Foreign Missionary Society of the Protestant Episcopal Church in the United States of America in the Philippines from 1901 until 1924. He served in Baguio, and founded and was priest in charge of the Mission of St. Mary the Virgin among the Igorot in Sagada, near Bontoc. He resigned in 1924 and returned to the United States in 1925, where he was in charge of a mission in Seattle, Washington, from 1925 to 1930. He entered the Roman Catholic Church in 1930, and was ordained in 1934. Died May 24, 1944, in Hammond, Indiana. *References*: J. A. Staunton Papers, Archives of the Church Historical Society, Austin, Texas; William H. Scott, " 'An Engineer's Dream'—John Staunton and the Mission of St. Mary the Virgin, Sagada," in *Studies in Philippine Church History*, ed. Gerald H. Anderson (Ithaca, N.Y., 1969), pp. 337–49; and William H. Scott, "Staunton of Sagada: Christian Civilizer," in *Hollow Ships on a Wine-Dark Sea and Other Essays* (Quezon City, 1976), pp. 69–102.

STEED, GITEL (GERTRUDE) P(OZNANSKI) (1914–1977). Anthropologist, born May 3, 1914, in Cleveland, Ohio, and grew up in the Bronx, New York. Steed graduated from New York and Columbia universities. She was a lecturer at Hunter, Temple, and Columbia universities. She was an instructor of sociology and anthropology, and then professor of anthropology, at Hofstra University after 1963. She was director of the Columbia University Research in Contemporary India field project, and carried out fieldwork in Gujarat, Uttar Pradesh, India, from 1949 to 1951. She returned to India in 1970. Died September 6, 1977, in New York City. *References*: Gitel P. Steed Papers, University of Chicago Library; *AA* 81 (1979): 88–91; Riva Berlant-Schiller, "Gitel (Gertrude) Poznanski Steed (1914–1977)," in *Women Anthropologists: A Biographical Dictionary*, ed. Ute Gacs et al. (Westport, Conn., 1988), pp. 331–36; *CA*; and *NYT*, September 9, 1977.

STEERE, JOSEPH B(EAL) (1842–1940). Ornithologist, born February 9, 1842, in Lenawee County, Michigan. Steere graduated from the University of Michigan. He made a scientific trip around the world from 1870 to 1875, was instructor and assistant professor of zoology at the University of Michigan from 1876 until 1879, and was professor of zoology there from 1879 until 1893. He was engaged in farming and study after 1893. He traveled in China, Formosa, the Moluccas, and the Philippines in 1874–1875, and led a party of students to the Philippines in 1887–1888. Died December 7, 1940, in Ann Arbor, Michigan. *References*: Joseph B. Steere, "An American Naturalist in the Far East: Excerpts from Letters Written from Formosa, the Philippines, and the East Indies during

the Years 1874 and 1875,'' *Michigan Alumnus Quarterly Review* 45 (1938): 47–
53; and *WWWA*.

STEINER, EZRA BURKHOLDER (1877–1955). Missionary, born June 8,
1877, in Richland Township, Allen County, Ohio. Steiner attended Wheaton
(Ill.) and Taylor (Upland, Ind.) colleges. He was a missionary under the Board
of Foreign Mission of the Central Conference Mennonite Church in India from
1914 until 1924. He served in Dharchula, Almore District, United Provinces,
near the Nepal and Tibet borders, after 1924, and was later supported by the
Evangelical Alliance Mission (TEAM) until his death. He wrote *What Hath God
Wrought: A Personal Experience of Rev. and Mrs. E. B. Steiner, Missionaries*
(n.p., 1924). Died November 4, 1955, in Landour, India. *References*: *BE*; and
Samuel T. Moyer, *They Heard the Call* (Newton, Kans., 1970), pp. 82–93.

STEINER, KURT (1912–   ). Jurist and government official, born June 10,
1912, in Vienna, Austria. Steiner graduated from the University of Vienna and
Stanford University. He practiced law in Vienna from 1935 to 1938. He came
to the United States in 1938. He was the director of the Berlitz Schools of
Languages in Pittsburgh and Cleveland from 1940 to 1943, and served in the
U.S. Army from 1944 to 1948. He was prosecuting attorney and assistant to
chief counsel of the International Prosecution Section in the General Headquarters
of the Supreme Commander for the Allied Powers (SCAP) in Japan in 1948,
and chief of the Civil Affairs and Civil Liberties Branch of the Legislative and
Justice Division of SCAP from 1949 to 1951. He was assistant professor of
political science at Stanford University from 1955 to 1958, associate professor
there from 1958 to 1962, and professor from 1962 until his retirement in 1977.
He wrote *Local Government in Japan* (Stanford, Calif., 1965), and was coeditor
of *Political Opposition and Local Politics in Japan* (Princeton, N.J., 1980).
References: *AMWS*; *CA*; and *WWA*.

STERNBERG, DAVID T(HERON) (1910–1979). Journalist, born July 23,
1910, in New York City. Sternberg came to the Philippines in 1939, and was
manager of the Manila radio station for the Far East Broadcasting Company until
1941. He was interned by the Japanese in Santo Tomas during World War II.
He was a representative of the *Christian Science Monitor*, and a consultant to
the U.S. special representative for economic aid in the Philippines, the Bell
mission, and the U.S. ambassadors. He was also a source of intelligence for the
Central Intelligence Agency (CIA). Died September 16, 1979, in Manila. *References*: Thomas Carter, ''The Tiny Giant,'' in *Then and Now (The Mechanics
of Integration)* (Manila, 1983), pp. 256–69; and *Gleeck/Manila*.

STERNE, MAURICE (1878–1957). Artist, born July 13, 1878, in Libau,
Latvia. Sterne came to the United States in 1889. He studied at the Cooper
Union and at the National Academy of Design from 1894 to 1899. He was in

Europe from 1904 to 1908, and in Egypt, India, and Burma in 1911–1912. He lived in Bali from 1912 to 1915. His Bali studies are considered his best works. He returned to the United States in 1915. Died July 23, 1957, in Mt. Kisco, New York. *References*: *CB* 1943; *DAB S6*; Charlotte L. Mayerson, ed., *Shadow and Light: The Life, Friends and Opinions of Maurice Sterne* (New York, 1966); *NCAB* 42:644; and *WWWA*.

STEVENOT, J(OSEPH) E(MILE) H(AMILTON) (1888–1943). Businessman, born December 23, 1888, in Melones, Calaveras County, California. Stevenot attended La Salle Sacred Heart College (San Francisco), and graduated from the University of Texas. He worked for various electrical and telephone companies in San Francisco, Oakland, and San Jose, California. He came to the Philippines in 1910, where he was chief engineer of the Baguio Light and Power Company and manager of electrical companies, and then a consulting engineer in Manila. He organized the Philippines Long Distance Telephone Company and was its president and general manager. He served in the U.S. Signal Corps during World War I. He was the last president of the Philippine Council of the Boy Scouts of America from 1934 to 1937, and the first president of the Boy Scouts of the Philippines from 1938 to 1941. He served as a lend-lease officer attached to General Douglas MacArthur's staff during World War II. Killed June 8, 1943, in an air crash in Noumea, New Caledonia. *References*: *EP* 4:475–479; *Gleeck/Manila*; and *WWP*.

STEVENS, DURHAM WHITE (1851–1908). Diplomat, born February 1, 1851, in Washington, D.C. Stevens graduated from Oberlin College, studied law, and was admitted to the bar in 1873. He was secretary of the U.S. legation in Japan from 1873 until 1882. He resigned in 1882 and entered the service of the Japanese Ministry of Foreign Affairs as an English secretary to the Japanese legation in Washington, D.C., from 1882 to 1884. He returned to Japan in 1884, served in the foreign ministry, and assisted various Japanese foreign ministers in the treaty revision negotiations. He participated as an advisor in the Sino-Japanese negotiations regarding Korea; was advisor to the Japanese legation in Washington, D.C., from 1887 to 1900; and served as a diplomatic Japanese agent in Hawaii from 1900 to 1904. In 1904 he was appointed by the Japanese as foreign affairs advisor to the king of Korea and the Korean government, but he also served a Japanese agent in Korea. Assassinated March 23, 1908, in San Francisco, by a Korean youth for supporting the Japanese rule in Korea. Died March 25, 1908, in San Francisco. *References*: Andrew C. Nahm, "Durham White Stevens and the Japanese Annexation of Korea," in *The United States and Korea: American-Korean Relations, 1866–1976*, ed. Andrew C. Nahm (Kalamazoo, Mich., 1979), pp. 110–36; *NCAB* 13:577; and *WWWA*.

STEVENS, FREDERICK W(AEIR) (1865–1926). Financier, born in Clinton, Michigan. Stevens graduated from the University of Michigan. He practiced law in Grand Rapids, Michigan, until 1900, was general counsel of the Pere Marquette Railroad from 1900 until 1909, and was an associate of J. P. Morgan and Company from 1909 until 1915. He traveled extensively in East Asia from 1915 to 1920, and was the representative of the American group of bankers in the International Consortium for China from 1920 to 1923, but his anti-British views led to his dismissal. He then practiced law again in Grand Rapids. Died November 2, 1926, in Grand Rapids. *References*: *NYT*, November 3, 1926; and *WWWA*.

STEVENS, JOSEPH E(ARLE) (1870–1961). Businessman, born February 8, 1870, in Boston. Stevens graduated from Harvard University. He was in the Philippines from 1893 to 1896 as a representative of the firm Henry W. Peabody and Company, purchasers of hemp, in Manila. He wrote *Yesterdays in the Philippines* (New York, 1898). He returned to the United States in 1896, joined the New York and Boston Dyewood Company, and was later vice president and treasurer of the New York Tanning Extract Company, the Argentine Quebracho Company, and the New York and the Paraguay Company. He was also engaged in cattle raising in Argentina and Paraguay. Died April 10, 1961, in New York City. *References*: Harvard University, *Class of 1892 Fiftieth Anniversary Report* (Cambridge, Mass., 1942); Frederick G. Hoyt, "Amelioration of Great Pity: Further Word from 'The Proto-Sahib American,' " *BAHC* 5 (July-September 1977): 111–17; *NYT*, April 12, 1961; and Carlos Quirino, "The Proto-Sahib American," *BAHC* 3 (January-March 1975): 51–64.

STEVENS, RAYMOND BARTLETT (1874–1942). Government official and diplomatic advisor, born June 18, 1874, in Binghamton, New York, and grew up in Lisbon, New Hampshire. Stevens attended Harvard University and Harvard Law School, and was admitted to the bar in 1899. He served in the state legislature from 1908 to 1912, and in the U.S. House of Representatives from 1912 to 1914. He was a special counsel to the Federal Trade Commission from 1915 to 1917, a member of the U.S. Shipping Board from 1917 to 1920, and a permanent U.S. representative on the Allied Maritime Transport Council in London in 1918–1919. He was foreign affairs advisor in Siam from 1926 to 1935, judge of the supreme court of Siam, and a member of the Siamese railroad commission. He also played an important part in drafting a new constitution for Siam. He was a member of the U.S. Tariff Commission from 1935 to 1937, and chairman of the commission from 1937 until his death. Died May 18, 1942, in Indianapolis. *References*: *BDAC*; and *NCAB* 31:365.

STEVENSON, PAUL HUSTON (1890–1971). Physician and anthropologist, born December 22, 1890, in Monmoth, Illinois. Stevenson graduated from Hiram (Ohio) College, and Washington and Western Reserve universities, and studied at University College, London. He went to China in 1917 under the auspices of the China Medical Board of the Rockefeller Foundation and the United Christian Missionary Society of the Disciples of Christ. He was a medical superintendent of the hospital in Hofei, Anhwei Province, from 1917 to 1920; assistant in the department of anatomy in Peking Union Medical College from 1920 to 1923; associate there from 1923 to 1926; assistant professor from 1926 to 1929; and associate professor from 1929 to 1937. He made an expedition to Mongolia in 1922, as well as two expeditions to Shansi and an expedition to the Chinese-Tibetan border for anthropometry in 1926. In 1925, at the request of the Chinese government, he embalmed the body of Sun Yet-sen. He was commissioned a senior surgeon in the U.S. Public Health Service in 1941, and served in Burma with the American Medical Commission to the Yunnan Railroad in 1941–1942, and in the U.S. Army in Ramgarh, India, until 1944. He served with the National Institute of Mental Health (NIMH) Community Service Branch in Bethesda, Maryland, from 1945 until his retirement in 1955. He was in Korea in 1955–1956 for the American-Korean Foundation, and made a survey of health and hospital facilities at the end of the Korean War. He resumed work as medical director at NIMH until 1959. Died April 21, 1971, in St. Louis. *References*: Paul H. Stevenson Papers, Washington University Medical Center Library, St. Louis, Mo.; *NCAB* 56:37; *They Went to China: Biographies of Missionaries of the Disciples of Christ* (Indianapolis, 1948).

STEWARD, ALBERT N(EWTON) (1897–1959). Botanist, born July 23, 1897, near Fullerton, California, and grew up in Okanogan County, Washington. Steward graduated from Oregon State College and Harvard University. He was a missionary under the Board of Foreign Missions of the Methodist Episcopal Church in China from 1921 until 1950, serving as a botanist at Nanking University from 1921 to 1926 and as a professor of botany at Nanking University from 1930 to 1950. He collected plants and botanical data, and developed means of counteracting the periodic ravages of famine. He returned to the United States in 1950, and was a professor of botany and curator of the herbarium at Oregon State College from 1951 until his death. He wrote *Manual of Vascular Plants of the Lower Yangtze Valley, China* (Corvallis, Ore., 1958). Died June 19, 1959, in Corvallis, Oregon. *Reference*: *Torrey Botanical Club Bulletin* 86 (1959): 342–44.

STEWART, KILTON (RIGGS) (1902–1965). Psychologist, born in Salt Lake City. Stewart graduated from the University of Utah, the University of London, and New York University. He lived among the pygmy Negritos, the Bontocs, and the Ifugaos of the Philippines in 1933, and described his experiences in *Pygmies and Dream Giants* (New York, 1954). He made a trip among the Ainus of Hokkaido and Karafuto, Japan, in 1934. In the 1930s, he was a research fellow at the Utah State Training School for maladjusted and retarded children, at the psychology and neuropsychiatry clinic at the University of Hawaii, at the department of museum of the Federated Malay States, and at the neuropsychiatry department of the Peking Union Medical College. He served in army intelligence during World War II. In the 1950s, he directed scientific expeditions to Tainan and Botel Tobago, and also to South Australia, studying the dreams of primitive peoples around the world. He was later a consulting psychologist, and in 1963 organized the Stewart Foundation of Creative Psychology. Died May 18, 1965, in New York City. *Reference*: *NYT*, May 19, 1965.

STEWART, ROBERT (1839–1915). Missionary, born January 31, 1839, in Sidney, Ohio. Stewart graduated from Jefferson College and Allegheny United Presbyterian Theological Seminary, and was ordained in 1865. He held pastorates in Ashland, Savanah, and Dayton, Ohio, and Davenport, New York, and was professor of exegetics and homiletics in the Newburg (N.Y.) Theological Seminary from 1872 to 1878. He was a missionary under the Board of Foreign Missions of the United Presbyterian Church in North America in India from 1882 until his death. He was in charge of the Christian Training Institute, and was teacher and principal of the Theological Seminary at Sialkot, Punjab, from 1883 to 1892. He returned to the United States in 1892 but returned to India in 1900 and was a professor at the seminary at Jhelum, Punjab, until his death. He wrote *Life and Work in India* (Philadelphia, 1896), and translated the Psalms into Urdu. Died October 23, 1915, in Sialkot, India. *References*: *DAB*; *OAB*; and *WWWA*.

STILWELL, JOSEPH W(ARREN) ("VINEGAR JOE") (1883–1946). Army officer, born March 19, 1883, in Palatka, Florida. Stilwell graduated from the U.S. Military Academy in 1904. He served in the Philippines in 1904–1905, and again from 1911 to 1913. He served as chief intelligence officer for the Fourth Corps during World War I. He was a Chinese language officer in Peking from 1920 to 1923, a battalion commander in the Fifteenth Infantry in Tientsin from 1926 to 1929, and a military attaché in China from 1935 to 1939. He was a commanding officer of the Second Division and the Third Corps until 1942. He was chief of staff to Generalissimo Chiang Kai-shek, commanding officer of all American forces in the China-Burma-India Theater, commander of the Fifth and Sixth Chinese armies from 1942 to 1944, and deputy commander of the South East Asia Command in 1943–1944. Friction with Chiang Kai-shek led to his recall in 1944. He was commanding general of the Tenth Army in Okinawa in 1945. Died October 12, 1946, in San Francisco. *References*: Rewi Alley, *Six Americans in China* (Beijing, China, 1985); *DAB S4*; *DAMIB*: *EAS*; John R. Stilwell, "The Chiang-Stilwell Conflict, 1942–1944," *Military Affairs* 43 (February 1979): 59–62; *NCAB* 33:8; *NYT*, October 13, 1946; Barbara W. Tuchman, *Stilwell and the American Experience in China, 1911–45* (New York, 1971); and Jonathan Spence, *To Change China: Western Advisers in China 1620–1960* (Boston, 1969).

STIMSON, HENRY LEWIS (1867–1950). Lawyer, government official and colonial administrator, born September 21, 1867, in New York City. Stimson graduated from Yale and Harvard universities and Harvard Law School, and was admitted to the bar in 1891. He practiced law in New York City after 1891. He was U.S. attorney for the Southern district of New York from 1906 to 1909, and U.S. secretary of war from 1911 to 1913. He served in the U.S. Army during World War I. He was governor-general of the Philippines in 1928–1929, and played an important role in stabilizing that country's economy and restoring the confidence of the Filipinos in the United States. He was secretary of state from 1929 to 1933, was involved in the Manchurian crisis of 1931, and invoked the Stimson Doctrine.* He was again secretary of war from 1940 to 1945. He retired in 1945. Died October 20, 1950, in Huntington, Long Island, New York. *References*: *DAB S4*; *Gleeck/Governors*, ch. 9; *NYT*, October 21, 1950; Michael Pearlman, "Emotional Factors in America's Colonial Pacific Policy: Wood and Stimson in the Philippines," *Journal of Psychohistory* 11 (1983): 243–69; Armin Rappaport, *Henry L. Stimson and Japan, 1931–33* (Chicago, 1963); Michael J. J. Smith, "Colonialists in Southeast Asia: Henry L. Stimson and the Pro-Consulship in the Philippines," *Michigan Academician* 12 (1979): 137–53; Michael J. J. Smith, "Henry L. Stimson and the Philippines," Ph.D. diss., Indiana University, 1969; Michael J. J. Smith, "Henry L. Stimson and the Philippines: American Withdrawal from Empire, 1931–1935," *Michigan Academician* 5 (1973): 335–48; and *WWWA*.

STIMSON DOCTRINE (1932). Announced by Secretary of State Henry Lewis Stimson* in 1932 as a result of Japan's 1931 military takeover of Manchuria. It stated that the United States would not recognize any infringements on American rights, the Open Door policy,* China's territorial integrity, or any acquisition of territory brought about by force. As a result, the United States did not recognize the puppet state of Manchukuo. *References*: Cecil V. Crabb, Jr., *The Doctrines of American Foreign Policy: Their Meaning, Role, and Future* (Baton Rouge, La., 1982), pp. 78–94; Richard N. Current, "The Stimson Doctrine and the Hoover Doctrine," *American Historical Review* 59 (1954): 513–42; and *DADH*.

STOCKBRIDGE, HORACE EDWARD (1857–1930). Chemist and educator, born May 19, 1857, in Hadley, Massachusetts. Stockbridge graduated from the Massachusetts Agricultural College, studied at Boston University and graduated from the University of Göttingen. He was in Japan from 1885 to 1889 as professor of chemistry and geology at the Sapporo Agricultural College, and was also chief chemist to the Japanese government from 1887 to 1889. He was president of the North Dakota Agricultural College and director of the experiment station until 1894. He later managed his plantation in Americus, Georgia, and was professor of agriculture and director of the state farmers' institute in Florida from 1897 to 1902, agricultural editor of the *Southern Ruralist* from 1906 to 1922, and editor of *Southern Farmer and Dairy* from 1922 until his death. Died October 30, 1930, in Atlanta. *References*: *DAB*; and *NCAB* 14:368.

STOKES, SAMUEL EVANS (1882–1946). Fruit grower, born August 16, 1882, in Germantown, Philadelphia. Stokes went to India in 1904, worked in a leper colony in the Simla Hills, and then volunteered for relief work in the Kangra Valley. He settled in Kotgarh, Central Himachal Pradesh, and, in 1912, adopted the Indian name of Satyanand. Deciding that the region was suited for growing apples, he distributed apple seeds free to local peasants. He became involved in the Indian national movement, and served as a member of the All-India Congress Committee. He was charged with sedition, was tried in Lahore, and was sentenced in 1922 to six months' imprisonment. He wrote *Arjun—the Life-Story of an Indian Boy* (Westminster, 1911), and *Collected Essays, Memoranda and Letters, 1913–1943* (Kotgarh, n.d.). His letters and essays were published posthumously in *National Self-Realization and Other Essays* (New Delhi, 1977). Died in Kotgarh. *References*: Kenton J. Clymer, "Samuel Evans Stokes, Mahatma Gandhi, and Indian Nationalism," *PHR* 59 (1990): 51–76; and Samuel Evans Stokes, "Stokes of Harmony Hall and Some Allied Ancestry," Ms., Historical Society of Pennsylvania, Philadelphia.

STOVER, WILBUR B(RENNER) (1866–1930). Missionary, born May 5, 1866, near Greencastle, Franklin County, Pennsylvania. Stover graduated from Mt. Morris College, studied at Temple College, and was elected minister in 1891. He held a pastorate at Germantown, Pennsylvania. He was a missionary under the General Mission Board of the Church of the Brethren in India from 1895 until 1920. He served in Bulsar until 1907 and at Anklesvar from 1907 to 1920. He also served on the municipal board of Anklesvar. He wrote *India a Problem* (Elgin, Ill., 1902). He returned to the United States in 1920 and held pastorates in Cleveland and Seattle. Died October 31, 1930, in Olympia, Washington. *References*: *BE*; and John E. Miller, *Wilbur B. Stover: Pioneer Missionary* (Elgin, Ill., 1931).

STRAIGHT, WILLARD D(ICKERMAN) (1880–1918). Diplomat, financier, and publicist, born January 31, 1880, in Oswego, New York. Straight graduated from Cornell University. He went to China in 1901 to work for the Imperial Maritime Customs Service, and was a correspondent for Reuter's News Service in Korea during the Russo-Japanese War, consul general in Mukden from 1906 to 1908, and acting chief of the Division of Far Eastern Affairs in the Department of State in 1908–1909. In 1909, he was a representative of a group of American bankers, and then of a similar international group, who were interested in developing railways in Manchuria and the northern part of China, a scheme that failed because of the opposition of Russia and Japan. He then played an important part in the attempt at providing an international loan to the Chinese government by a consortium of bankers. He returned to the United States in 1912. He was

a Far Eastern expert with J. P. Morgan and Company, and third vice president
of the American International Corporation after 1915. In 1914, with the cooperation of his wife, he established *The New Republic*, and, in 1915, he founded
the *Journal of the American Asiatic Association* (which later became *Asia*). He
served as overseas administrator of the War Risk Insurance Bureau during World
War I. Died December 1, 1918, in Paris, France. *References*: Willard Straight
Papers, Cornell University Library, Ithaca, N.Y.; Leon M. Bower, "Willard D.
Straight and the American Policy in China, 1906–1913," Ph.D. diss., University
of Colorado, 1955; *DAB*; *DADH*; Helen D. Kahn, "Willard D. Straight and the
Great Game of Empire," in *Makers of American Diplomacy, from Benjamin
Franklin to Henry Kissinger*, ed. Frank J. Merli and Theodore A. Wilson (New
York, 1974), pp. 333–58; *KEJ*; *NYT*, December 2, 1918; Harry N. Scheiber,
"World War I as Entrepreneurial Opportunity: Willard Straight and the American
International Corporation," *Political Science Quarterly* 84 (1969): 486–511; and
WWWA.

STREET, THOMAS A(TKINS) (1872–1936). Lawyer and judge, born March
14, 1872, in Marshall County, Alabama. Street graduated from the University
of Alabama and its law school. He practiced law in Nashville, Tennessee, from
1894 until 1902, when he moved to New York. He was on the editorial staff of
Edward Thompson Company, law publishers of Northport, New York, from
1902 to 1908. He was a professor of equity at the School of Law of the University
of Missouri from 1908 until 1910. He came to the Philippines in 1910, was
member of the Philippine Code Committee from 1910 to 1917, and was involved
in the codification of the political and administrative laws of the Philippines. He
was the draftsman of the Internal Review Code of 1914 and the principal codifier
of the administrative code of 1917. He was associate judge of the Supreme Court
of the Philippines from 1917 until 1935. He retired in 1935 because of ill health
and returned to the United States. Died March 17, 1936, in Montgomery, Alabama. *References*: *NYT*, March 18, 1936; *Sevilla*; *WWP*; and *WWWA*.

STRIKE MISSIONS (1946–1947). A seven-person special committee on Japanese reparations, chaired by Clifford S. Strike, and sent in 1946 by the U.S.
secretary of war to Japan to make a preliminary survey on industrial conditions
in Japan and to help institute a program for the evaluation and appraisal of assets
for reparations removal. A second mission, conducted by Overseas Consultants,
Incorporated, and presided over by Strike, in 1947 made an analysis of conditions
in Japan, and ruled out any except minor reparations from Japan. *References*:
CB 1949; *KEJ*; *NCAB* L:463; and *WWA*.

STROBEL, EDWARD HENRY (1855–1908). Diplomat and diplomatic advisor, born December 7, 1855, in Charleston, South Carolina. Strobel graduated
from Harvard University and Harvard Law School, and was admitted to the bar
in 1883. He was secretary of legation in Madrid from 1885 until 1890, third

assistant secretary of state in 1893–1894, U.S. minister to Ecuador in 1894, minister to Chile from 1894 until 1897, and professor of international law in the Harvard Law School from 1899 to 1903. He was a general advisor to the government of Siam from 1903 until his death. He is credited with having brought about the modernization of the Siamese legal and administrative system, and negotiated a new treaty between Siam and France. Died January 15, 1908, in Bangkok, Siam. *References*: Edward Henry Strobel Letters, in Bullock, Strobel, Courtney, Hemphill, Bateman Family Papers, South Carolinian Library, University of South Carolina, Columbia; *DAB*; *DADH*; *NCAB* 12:324; *NYT*, January 16, 1908; and *WWWA*.

STRONG, ANNA LOUISE (1885–1970). Journalist, born November 24, 1885, in Friend, Nebraska, and grew up in Mt. Vernon, Ohio; Cincinnati; and Oak Park, Illinois. Strong attended Bryn Mawr College, and graduated from Oberlin College and the University of Chicago. She directed child welfare exhibits in various cities from 1911 to 1915 and was involved in socialist politics in Seattle from 1915 until 1921. She went to Poland in 1921 for the American Friends Service Committee, and then to the Soviet Union as a correspondent for Hearst's International News Service. She was in China from 1925 to 1927, returned to the Soviet Union in 1927, and was again in the Soviet Union in 1929–1930. She was back in China in 1938, and in the Soviet Union from 1938 to 1940. She was in Chungking, China, in 1940–1941, and returned to the United States in 1941. She was back in China in 1946, and in the Soviet Union from 1947 until 1949, when she was arrested and deported from that country. She returned to China in 1958. She wrote *China's Millions* (New York, 1928); *Remaking of an American* (Garden City, N.Y., 1935); *The Chinese Conquer China* (New York, 1949); and *Letters from China* (Peking, 1964). Died March 29, 1970, in Beijing, China. *References*: Anna Louise Strong Papers, University of Washington Libraries, Seattle; Rewey Alley, *Six Americans in China* (Beijing, China, 1985); *DAB S8*; David C. Duke, "Anna Louise Strong and the Search for a Good Cause," *Pacific Northwest Quarterly* 66 (1975): 123–37; *EAH*; Philip Jaffe, "The Strange Case of Anna Louise Strong," *Survey: A Journal of Soviet and East European Studies* 53 (October 1964): 129–39; *NYT*, March 30, 1970; Stephanie F. Ogle, "Anna Louise Strong: Progressive and Propagandist," Ph.D. diss., University of Washington, 1981; Joseleyne S. Tien, "Portrait of a China Reporter: Anna Louise Strong and the China Revolution, 1925–1958," *Asia Profile* (Hong Kong) 14 (1986): 105–18; and *WWWA*.

STRONG, RICHARD P(EARSON) (1872–1948). Physician, born March 18, 1872, in Fortress Monroe, Virginia. Strong graduated from the Sheffield Scientific School of Yale University and the medical school of Johns Hopkins University, and studied in Berlin. He was an assistant surgeon in the army during the Spanish-American War, director of the Army Pathological Laboratory in the Isthmus of Panama, director of the Biological Laboratories of the Bureau of

Science in the Philippines from 1901 to 1913, professor of tropical medicine at the University of the Philippines from 1907 to 1913, and chief of medicine at the Philippines General Hospital from 1910 to 1913. He served on the chief surgeon's staff during World War I. He was a professor of tropical medicine at the Harvard University Medical School from 1913 until his retirement in 1938, and led several expeditions to study tropical diseases. Died July 4, 1948, in Boston. *References*: *DAB S4*; W. C. Forbes and E. Bowditch, "Richard Pearson Strong," in *Saturday Club: A Century Completed 1920–1956*, ed. Edward W. Forbes and John H. Finley, Jr. (Boston, 1958), pp. 215–26; *NYT*, July 5, 1948; *Pier*; and *WWWA*.

STUART, J(OHN) LEIGHTON (1876–1962). Missionary and diplomat, born June 24, 1876, in Hangchow, China, to American missionary parents. Stuart graduated from Hampden-Sidney College and the Union Theological Seminary of Virginia, and was ordained in 1904. He was a missionary under the Board of Foreign Missions of the Presbyterian Church in the United States in China from 1904 until 1946. He served in Hangchow from 1904 to 1908, was professor of New Testament in the Nanking Theological Seminary from 1908 to 1919, and served as president of Peking University (later Yenching University) from 1919 until 1941. He was a member of the China Educational Commission of 1921–1922. He was interned by the Japanese in Peking during World War II. He resumed the presidency of Yenching University in 1945. He was U.S. ambassador to China from 1946 until 1949, the last ambassador before the Communist takeover of mainland China. He tried to mediate peace between the Nationalists and the Communists, and tried to persuade Chiang Kai-shek to resign. He returned to the United States in 1949, and wrote *Fifty Years in China: The Memoirs of John Leighton Stuart, Missionary and Ambassador* (New York, 1954). Died September 19, 1962, in Washington, D.C. *References*: *CB* 1946; *DADH*; *EAS*; *NCAB G*:370; *NYT*, September 20, 1962; *PolProf: Truman*; Kenneth W. Rea and John C. Brewer, eds., *The Forgotten Ambassador: The Reports of John Leighton Stuart, 1946–1949* (Boulder, Colo., 1981); Yu-ming Shaw, "John Leighton Stuart and U.S.–Chinese Communist Rapproachment in 1949: Was There Another Lost Chance in China?" *China Quarterly* no. 89 (1982): 74–76; Yu-ming Shaw, "John Leighton Stuart: the Mind and Life and American Missionary in China, 1876–1941," Ph.D. diss., University of Chicago, 1975; and Robert F. Smyle, "John Leighton Stuart: A Missionary in the Sino-Japanese Conflict, 1937–1941," *Journal of Presbyterian History* 53 (1975): 256–76.

STUDER, ADOLPHUS G. (fl. 1861–1894). Consul, born in Bern Canton, Switzerland. Studer served in the Union Army during the Civil War. He served as a general superintendent of education in Louisiana, and then engaged in banking in Des Moines, Iowa. He was naturalized before 1871. He was U.S. consul in Singapore from 1871 to 1889 and again in 1893–1894, and consul in

Bremen, Germany, from 1889 until 1893. *Reference*: James W. Gould, "An Iowan at Singapore," *Annals of Iowa*, 3rd ser., 32 (1954): 302–4.

STUNTZ, HOMER C(LYDE) (1858–1924). Missionary, born January 29, 1858, in Albion, Erie County, Pennsylvania. Stuntz attended Garrett Biblical School and Northwestern University, and was ordained in 1884. He was a missionary under the Board of Foreign Missions of the Methodist Episcopal Church in India from 1886 until 1895. He was principal of boys' and girls' schools in Bangalore, served in Bombay, and edited the Bombay *Guardian*. He served in Calcutta from 1889, and was editor of the *Indian Witness* until 1891. He served in Naini Tal, in the Himalayas, from 1891 to 1893, and was again in Calcutta from 1893 to 1895, where he was principal of a boys' school and superintendent of mission work in the Kumaun district. He returned to the United States in 1895, but came to the Philippines in 1901 as superintendent of the Philippine Islands mission of the Methodist Episcopal Church until 1908. He returned to the United States in 1908, was field secretary of the Board of Foreign Missions for the eastern division, and later was first assistant corresponding secretary from 1908 to 1912. He was elected bishop in 1912, and was assigned to South America from 1912 to 1916. He wrote *The Philippines and the Far East* (Cincinnati, 1904). Died June 3, 1924, in Omaha, Nebraska. *References*: *EWM*; *NCAB* 20:117; *NYT*, June 4, 1924; and *WWWA*.

STURGIS, RUSSELL (1823–1887). Merchant, born in Boston. Sturgis graduated from Harvard University. Sturgis practiced law in Boston. He sailed for Canton in 1833 and later became a member of Russell and Sturgis of Manila, and Russell, Sturgis and Company of Canton. The mercantile house was consolidated with Russell and Company in 1840 and he became a partner in 1842. He retired in 1844, returned to the United States, and later became a partner of Baring Brothers and Company. Died November 2, 1887, in Leatherhead, England. *References*: *Boston Transcript*, November 3, 1887; and *Some Merchants and Sea Captains of Old Boston* (Boston, 1918), pp. 1–3.

STURGIS, WILLIAM (1782–1863). Merchant, born February 25, 1782, in Barnstable, Massachusetts. Sturgis shipped as a sailor in 1797, and became master of the ship *Caroline* at the age of nineteen. In 1809, as master of the ship *Atahualpa*, he battled pirates off the Chinese coast. In 1810 he formed a partnership with John Bryant, which continued until his death. It has been said that more than half of the trade carried on from the United States with China and other countries of the Pacific coast from 1810 to 1840 was under their direction. He was a member of the Massachusetts House of Representatives for twelve years between 1814 and 1846, and state senator in 1827 and 1836. Died October 21, 1863, in Boston. *References*: *BDABL*; *DAB*; Henrietta M. Larson, "William Sturgis, Merchant and Investor," *Business Historical Society Bulletin* 9 (1935): 76–77; and *WWWA*.

SUBIC BAY NAVAL STATION. Major naval base for the U.S. Naval Forces, located in a deepwater harbor, fifty miles southwest of Manila in the Philippines. It provides comprehensive support facilities, including a berth, a dry dock, and maintenance and repair workshops, which support Seventh Fleet operations in the Western Pacific and the Indian Ocean. *Reference*: *USNBO*.

SUNDERLAND, JABEZ T(HOMAS) (1842–1936). Clergyman, born February 11, 1842, in Yorkshire, England. Sunderland graduated from the University of Chicago and Baptist Union Theological Seminary. He was converted to Unitarianism in 1872, and held pastorates in Northfield, Massachusetts; Chicago; Ann Arbor, Michigan; Oakland, California; London, England; Toronto, Canada; Hartford, Connecticut; Ottawa, Canada; and Poughkeepsie, New York, from 1872 until his retirement in 1928. He was editor of the *Unitarian Monthly* from 1886 to 1895. He traveled in India in 1895–1896 and 1913–1914, and wrote much on the issue of India, including *India in Bondage* (New York, 1919). He was the earliest public American supporter of the Indian nationalist movement. Died August 13, 1936, in Ann Arbor, Michigan. *References*: Jabez T. Sunderland Papers, Bentley Historical Library, University of Michigan, Ann Arbor; Spencer Lavan, "Unitarianism and Acculturation: Jabez T. Sunderland in India (1895–96)," *Proceedings of the Unitarian Historical Society* 17, pt. 2 (1973–1975): 73–91; Spencer Lavan, *Unitarians and India: A Study in Encounter and Response* (Boston, 1977), chs. 11–12; and *WWWA*.

SUPREME COMMANDER FOR THE ALLIED POWERS (SCAP): GENERAL HEADQUARTERS. The designation for General Douglas MacArthur's headquarters in Japan. MacArthur was appointed Supreme Commander for the Allied Powers in Japan in 1945. The General Headquarters in Tokyo, which MacArthur headed until 1951 and General Matthew Ridgeway headed in 1951–1952, was the sole executive authority for the allied powers in relation to the occupation of Japan,* and administered the occupation from 1945 until 1952, when it was abolished following the San Francisco Peace Treaty with Japan (see Occupation of Japan*).

SWAIN, CLARA A. (1834–1910). Medical missionary, born July 18, 1834, in Elmira, New York. Swain graduated from Woman's Medical College (Philadelphia). The first American medical missionary of the Methodist Episcopal Church, she served under the Woman's Foreign Missionary Society in India from 1870 until 1896. She served at Bareilly from 1870 until 1885, the first qualified woman physician in India, and established the first modern hospital for women and children in India. She served as physician to the Rani of Khetri, Rajputana, and the ladies of the palace from 1885 to 1896. She returned to the United States in 1896. She published a collection of her letters, *A Glimpse of India* (New York, 1909). Died December 25, 1910, in Castile, New York. *References*: *CDCWM*; *DAB*; *EWM*; *DAMB 84*; *NAW*; and Dorothy C. Wilson,

Palace of Healing, the Story of Dr. Clara Swain, First Woman Missionary Doctor, and the Hospital She Founded (New York, 1968).

SWENSON, VICTOR E(MANUEL) (1886–1965). Missionary, born November 17, 1886, in Bertrand, Nebraska. Swenson graduated from Gustavus Adolphus College and Augustana Seminary, and was ordained in 1913. He was a missionary under the Board of Foreign Missions of the Augustana Church in China from 1913 until 1957. He served in the Honan from 1913 until 1946, and in Taipei from 1952 to 1957. He was bishop of the Chinese Lutheran Church and vice president of the Augustana Synod Mission in China. He wrote *Parents of Many: Forty-Five Years as Missionaries in Old, New, and Divided China: A Personal Narrative* (Rock Island, Ill., 1959). *Reference*: Conrad Bergendoff, *The Augustana Ministerium* (Rock Island, Ill., 1980).

SWIFT, JOHN FRANKLIN (1829–1891). Lawyer and diplomat, born February 28, 1829, in Bowling Green, Missouri. Swift went to San Francisco in 1852, was a produce merchant, studied law, and was admitted to the bar in 1857. He was a member of the state legislature from 1863 to 1865, and again from 1873 to 1875 and 1877 to 1879. He was also register of the land office in San Francisco in 1865–1866. In 1880 he was appointed a member of a commission with James B. Angell* and William H. Trescott to negotiate modifications of the Burlingame Treaty with China. He was U.S. minister to Japan from 1889 until his death, and worked to revise the treaty between Japan and the United States. Died March 10, 1891, in Tokyo, Japan. *References*: *DAB*; and *DADH*.

SWINGLE, WALTER TENNYSON (1871–1952). Botanist and plant explorer, born January 8, 1871, in Canaan, Wayne County, Pennsylvania. Swingle graduated from Kansas State Agricultural College (later Kansas State University), and studied in Bonn and Leipzig, Germany. He was a special agent for the division of vegetable physiology and pathology at the U.S. Department of Agriculture from 1891 to 1898, a plant explorer for the department from 1898 to 1902, and in charge of plant life history investigations from 1902 until 1910. He was a senior physiologist in the Bureau of Plant Industry from 1910 to 1932, when he was again a plant explorer until his retirement in 1941. He was a consultant in tropical botany at the University of Miami (Fla.) from 1941 until his death. He was responsible for introducing many Chinese plants into the United States. He also assisted the Library of Congress in amassing the largest collection of Chinese books outside East Asia. Died January 19, 1952, in Washington, D.C. *References*: Harley H. Bartlett, "Walter Tennyson Swingle: Botanist and Exponent of Chinese Civilization," *Asa Gray Bulletin*, new ser., 1 (1952): 107–28; *NCAB* 54:13; *NYT*, January 20, 1952; and *WWWA*.

SWORD, GUSTAF A. (1887–1962). Missionary, born in Åvonsjö, Gastrick-land, Sweden, and came to the United States in 1904. Sword was a machinist in Kewanee, Illinois, and Bridgeport, Connecticut. He studied in a seminary, and held pastorates in Greely, Colorado, South Chicago, and Des Moines. He was a missionary under the American Baptist Foreign Mission Board to the Kachins in Burma from 1921 until 1952. He served in Namkham from 1921 to 1936, and in Kutkai from 1936 until 1942. He left Burma in 1942 and served with the Office of War Information during World War II. He was back in Burma in 1946, and was a field secretary for Burma, residing in Rangoon, from 1946 until 1952. He returned to the United States in 1952. He wrote *Come What May* (Chicago, 1943) and a biography of Ola Hanson.* *Reference*: Dorothy S. Bishop, *Burma Odyssey: Of Gustaf A. Sword, 1887–1962, Edna B. Sword, 1893–1956* (Chicago, 1982).

SYDENSTRICKER, ABSALOM (1852–1931). Missionary, born August 13, 1852, in Greenbrier County, West Virginia. Sydenstricker graduated from Washington and Lee University and Union Theological Seminary (Va.). He was a missionary under the Board of Foreign Missions of the Presbyterian Church of the United States in China from 1880 until his death. He served in Hangchow from 1880 to 1886, in Tsingkiang from 1886 to 1921 and in Nanking after 1921. He wrote *An Exposition of the Construction and Idioms of Chinese Sentences, as Found in Colloquial Mandarin* (Shanghai, 1889). *Our Life and Work in China: A Private Account* (Parsons, Va., 1978) was published posthumously. Died July 31, 1931, in Kuling. His daughter, Pearl S. Buck,* wrote a fictionalized biography of her father in *Fighting Angel* (New York, 1936) and of her mother, **CARRIE STULTING SYDENSTRICKER** in *The Exile* (New York, 1936). *Reference*: P. Frank Price, comp., *Our China Investment: Sixty Years of the Southern Presbyterian Church in China with Biographies, Autobiographies, and Sketches of All Missionaries since the Opening of the Work in 1867* (Nashville, Tenn., 1927).

T

TAFT, WILLIAM HOWARD (1857–1930). Government official and colonial administrator, born September 15, 1857, in Cincinnati. Taft graduated from Yale University and Cincinnati Law College. He practiced law in Cincinnati, and was assistant county prosecutor in 1881–1882 and 1885–1886, collector of internal revenue of the first district of Ohio in 1882–1883, superior court judge from 1887 to 1890, U.S. solicitor general from 1890 to 1892, federal judge for the Sixth Circuit, and dean of the University of Cincinnati Law School. He was president of the second Philippine Commission (see Philippine Commissions*) in 1900, and the first civil governor of the Philippines from 1901 to 1904. He was secretary of war from 1904 to 1908, president of the United States from 1909 to 1913, professor of law at Yale University from 1913 to 1921, and chief justice of the U.S. Supreme Court from 1921 to 1930. Died March 8, 1930, in Washington, D.C. *References*: William Howard Taft Papers, Manuscript Division, Library of Congress; Hernando J. Abaya, "Taft's Views on the Philippines and the Filipinos," *Asian Studies* 6 (1968): 237–47; *ACAB*; Oscar M. Alfonso, "Taft's Early View of the Filipinos," *Solidarity* (Manila) 4 (1969): 52–58; Oscar M. Alfonso, "Taft's Philippine Administration," *Philippine Journal of Public Administration* 12 (1968): 246–55; *DAB*; *EP* 4:354–56; *Gleeck/Governors*, ch. 2; Ralph Minger, *William Howard Taft and U.S. Foreign Policy: The Apprenticeship Years, 1900–1908* (Urbana, Ill., 1975); *NCAB* 23:1; Gary C. Ness, "Proving Ground for a President: William Howard Taft and the Philippines 1900–1905," *Cincinnati Historical Society Bulletin* 34 (1976): 205–23; *NYT*, March 9, 1930; *Pier*, ch. 3; Henry F. Pringle, *The Life and Times of William Howard Taft* (New York, 1939); and *WWWA*.

TAFT-KATSURA AGREEMENT (1905). Memorandum signed by Secretary of War William Howard Taft and Japanese Prime Minister Katsura Taro in 1905. The agreement included Japanese recognition of U.S. sovereignty in the Philippines, and American recognition of Korea as a Japanese protectorate. The agreement was not legally binding. *References*: Jongsuk Chay, "The Taft-

Katsura Memorandum Reconsidered,'' *PHR* 37 (1968): 321–26; *DADH*; *EAH*; Raymond A. Esthus, ''The Taft-Katsura Agreement—Reality or Myth?'' *Journal of Modern History* 31 (1959): 46–61; and *KEJ*.

TAIWAN STRAITS CRISES. *See* QUEMOY-MATSU CRISES

TALCOTT, ELIZA (1836–1911). Missionary educator, born May 22, 1836, in Vernon, Connecticut. Talcott graduated from the Connecticut State Normal School (New Britain). She taught in schools in Farmington and New Britain, Connecticut, until 1863. She was a missionary under the American Board of Commissioners for Foreign Missions (ABCFM) in Japan from 1873 until her death. She served in Kobe, where she started a girls' school (later Kobe College) and was its principal from 1875 to 1880. She was house mother and evangelistic head of the nurses' training school at Doshisha University in Kyoto from 1885 until 1894. She served in a military hospital in Yokohama during the Sino-Japanese War of 1894–1895. She was a missionary teacher among the Japanese in Hawaii from 1900 to 1902, but returned to Kobe in 1902. Died November 1, 1911, in Kobe. *References*: *DAB*; and *NAW*.

TALMAGE, JOHN VAN NEST (1819–1892). Missionary, born August 18, 1819, in Bound Brook, New Jersey, and grew up in Gatesville, New Jersey. Talmage graduated from Rutgers University and the New Brunswick Theological Seminary, and was ordained in 1846. He was a missionary under the American Board of Commissioners for Foreign Missions (ABCFM) in China from 1847 to 1857, and under the Board of Foreign Missions of the Reformed Church in America from 1857 until 1889. He served in Ku-lang Island, near Amoy. He wrote *History and Ecclesiastical Relations of the Churches of the Presbyterian Order of Amoy, China* (New York, 1863), and prepared a dictionary of the Amoy dialect. He returned to the United States in 1889. Died August 19, 1892, in Bound Brook, New Jersey. *References*: *DAB*; and *HDRCA*.

TATTNALL, JOSIAH (1795–1871). Naval officer, born November 9, 1795, in Savannah, Georgia. Tattnall was appointed a midshipman in 1812, and served in the War of 1812. He served in the West Indies and the Mediterranean. He was commander of the Boston Navy Yard, served in the Mexican War, was commander of the naval station in Pensacola, served in the Pacific in 1854–1855, and was commander of the naval station at Sackets Harbor, New York, from 1855 to 1857. He commanded the East India Squadron from 1857 until 1860, was involved in the negotiations of new treaties with China, and placed the facilities of the fleet at the disposal of the American envoy. When the British fleet was defeated in 1859 at the mouth of the Pei-ho River, he gave aid to the British that, under the circumstances, violated the neutrality of the United States; however, his actions were upheld by the U.S. government. He served in the Confederate Navy during the Civil War. Died June 14, 1871, in Savannah,

Georgia. *References*: Edith R. Curtis, "Blood is Thicker than Water," *AN* 27 (1967): 157–76; *DAB*; *DAMIB*; and *NCAB* 5:488.

TAYLOR, CARSON (1875–1962). Publisher, born December 5, 1875, in Flat Rock, Illinois. Taylor attended Central Normal College (Danville, Ind.). He served in the Spanish-American War, came to the Philippines in 1898, was discharged from the army in 1899, and stayed in the Philippines. He was circulation manager and managing editor of the *Manila Daily American*. He founded the *Manila Daily Bulletin* in 1901 as a shipping and commercial guide, and in 1912 converted it to a morning daily newspaper. He wrote *A History of the Philippine Press* (Manila, 1927). He sold the *Bulletin* newspaper in 1957 and returned to the United States. Died July 31, 1962, in Los Angeles. *References*: *BAHC* 1 (June 1972): 76–77; *NYT*, August 2, 1962; and *WWP*.

TAYLOR, EDWARD H(ARRISON) (1889–1978). Herpetologist, born April 23, 1889, in Maysville, Missouri, and grew up in Anderson County, Kansas. Taylor graduated from the University of Kansas. He went to the Philippines in 1912 as a teacher. He taught among the Manobos people in Central Mindanao and later on Negros Island. He was chief of fisheries in the Bureau of Science. He traveled extensively in the Philippines, researching its herpatofauna, and wrote *Amphibians and Turtles of the Philippine Islands* (Manila, 1921); *The Lizards of the Philippine Islands* (Manila, 1922); *The Snakes of the Philippine Islands* (Manila, 1922); *Philippine Land Mammals* (Manila, 1934); and *Herpatology of the Philippine Islands* (Amsterdam, 1966). He wrote of his Philippine adventures in *Edward H. Taylor: Recollections of an Herpatologist* (Lawrence, Kans., 1975). He was assistant professor of zoology at the University of Kansas from 1926 to 1934, and a professor there after 1934. Died June 16, 1978, in Lawrence, Kansas. *Reference*: *AMWS*.

TEGENFELDT, HERMAN G(USTAF) (1913–   ). Missionary, born November 18, 1913, in Bellingham, Washington. Tegenfeldt graduated from Western Washington College of Education, and Bethel, Northern Baptist, and Fuller theological seminaries. He was ordained in 1930. He was a teacher in the public schools of Seattle from 1934 to 1937. He was a missionary under the American Baptist Foreign Missions Society in Burma and India from 1941 to 1943, and in India from 1943 to 1966. He was principal of a mission high school in Rangoon, and then served among the Kachin people near the Chinese border, primarily in the Myitkyina area. He was in Nellore, south India, during World War II. He was field secretary for all Burma from 1961 until the Burmese government ordered foreign missionaries out in 1966. He wrote *Through Deep Waters* (Valley Forge, Pa., 1968), an account of his experiences, and *A Century of Growth: The Kachin Baptist Church in Burma* (South Pasadena, Calif., 1974). He was assistant professor of missions at Bethel Theological Seminary (St. Paul, Minn.) from 1967 to 1970, associate professor there from 1970 to 1972, and professor after 1973. *References*: *CA*; *DAS*; and *Who's Who in Religion* (Chicago, 1977).

TENNEY, CHARLES DANIEL (1857–1930). Missionary and diplomat, born June 29, 1857, in Boston. Tenney graduated from Dartmouth College and Oberlin Theological Seminary. He was a missionary under the American Board of Commissioners of Foreign Missions (ABCFM) in the Shansi Province, China, from 1882 to 1886. He abandoned missionary work in 1886. He founded the Anglo-American School in Tientsin, and was its first principal from 1886 to 1895. He was also vice-consul and interpreter in the U.S. consulate in Tientsin from 1894 to 1896. He was the first president of the Imperial Chinese University in Tientsin (later Peiyang University) from 1895 until 1906. Following the relief of Tientsin during the Boxer Rebellion, he served as Chinese secretary of the Tientsin provisional government from 1900 to 1902, superintendent of high and middle school in Chihli from 1902 to 1906, and director of Chinese students in America in Cambridge, Massachusetts, from 1906 to 1908. He retired from service to the Chinese government in 1908. He was Chinese secretary at the U.S. legation in Peking from 1908 to 1912, American delegate to the International Opium Commission in Shanghai in 1909, and consul in Nanking in 1912–1913. He returned to the United States in 1913, and returned to China as Chinese secretary of the legation in Peking from 1913 to 1919. He was later secretary and counselor of legation until his retirement in 1921, when he returned to the United States in 1921. Died March 14, 1930, in Palo Alto, California. *References*: *DAB*; *DADH*; *NYT*, March 16, 1930; and *WWWA*.

TENNIEN, MARK A. (1900–1983). Missionary, born May 19, 1900, in Pittsford, Vermont. Tennien attended Holy Cross, Worcester, and St. Michael's colleges; Grand Seminary (Montreal); and St. Mary's Seminary (Baltimore). He entered the Maryknoll Fathers in 1926, and was ordained in 1927. He was a missionary in Wuchow, China, from 1927 to 1932, when he returned to the United States because of ill health. He was back in China in 1935, and served until 1951. He was held under house arrest by the Communist authorities, and then imprisoned and expelled from China in 1951. He was the editor of *China Mission Bulletin* in Hong Kong from 1952 to 1956, and director of the New York House in 1956–1957. He served in Kuwana, Japan, from 1957 until 1976, when he returned to the United States. He wrote of his experiences in *Chungking Listening Post* (New York, 1945), and *No Secret Is Safe behind the Bamboo Curtain* (New York, 1952). Died January 2, 1983, in Tarrytown, New York. *References*: *CA*; and *NYT*, January 8, 1983.

TENNY, CHARLES B(UCKLEY) (1871–1936). Missionary, born September 10, 1871, in Hilton, New York. Tenny attended Brockport (N.Y.) State Normal School, and graduated from the University of Rochester and Rochester Theological Seminary. He was ordained in 1900. He was a missionary under the American Baptist Foreign Mission Society in Japan from 1900 until 1930. He was a professor of New Testament language and literature at Yokohama Baptist Theological Seminary from 1908 to 1911, and its president from 1913 to 1917. He was executive secretary of the Japan Mission of the American Board of Commissioners for Foreign Missions (ABCFM) from 1917 to 1927, secretary of the Tokyo Christian Educational Association in 1925, and founder, chairman of the board, and president, from 1927 to 1930, of Kanto Gakuin, the Baptist school for men and boys in Yokohama. He returned to the United States in 1931 because of ill health. Died January 12, 1936, in Rochester, New York. *Reference*: *WWWA*.

TERRANOVA AFFAIR (1821). Francesco Terranova, a sailor on the *Emily*, a ship out of Baltimore and anchored in Canton in 1821, was accused of killing a Chinese woman. Terranova was surrendered to the Chinese after they halted all American trade and placed an embargo on American vessels. He was tried, found guilty, and executed. Trade was then resumed. *Reference*: William J. Donahue, "The Francis Terranova Case," *Historian* 43 (1981): 211–24.

TERRY, HENRY TAYLOR (1847–1936). Educator, born September 19, 1847, in Hartford, Connecticut. Terry graduated from Yale University, studied law, and was admitted to the bar in 1872. He was a professor of law at the Imperial University in Tokyo, Japan, from 1877 to 1884. He returned to the United States and practiced law in New York City from 1885 until 1894. He returned to Japan in 1894, and resumed his professorship in the Imperial University until his retirement in 1912. Died December 26, 1936, in New York City. *References*: *WWWA*; and *Yale*.

TEUSLER, RUDOLF BOLLING (1876–1934). Physician, born February 25, 1876, in Rome, Georgia, and grew up in Richmond, Virginia. Teusler graduated from the Medical College of Virginia. He practiced medicine in Richmond, Virginia; was assistant professor of pathology and bacteriology at the Medical College of Virginia; and served in the city dispensary of Richmond from 1894 until 1900. He was a physician under the Domestic and Foreign Missionary Society of the Protestant Episcopal Church in Japan from 1900 until his death. He founded St. Luke's Hospital in Tokyo. He also served as a physician to the foreign embassies in Tokyo, and later supervised the Hospital of St. Barnabas in Osaka. He served as commissioner of the Red Cross with the Allied forces in Siberia from 1918 to 1921. Died August 10, 1934, in Tokyo. *References*: *DAB*; *NYT*, August 11, 1934; Howard C. Robbins and George K. MacNaught, *Dr. Rudolf Bolling Teusler. An Adventure in Christianity* (New York, 1942); and *WWWA*.

THOBURN, ISABELLA (1840–1901). Missionary, sister of James Mills Thoburn,* born March 29, 1840, in St. Clairsville, Ohio. Thoburn attended the Wheeling Female Seminary and the Cincinnati Academy of Design. She taught in Wheeling, West Virginia; Newcastle, Pennsylvania; and West Farmington, Ohio. She was a missionary under the Women's Foreign Missionary Society of the Methodist Episcopal Church in India from 1870 until her death. In Lucknow she opened a girls' school, a boarding school for girls in 1871, and a college for women in 1887. The college became the first Christian college for women in Asia, and was granted a charter by the British government in 1895 to become the Lucknow Women's College, affiliated with Calcutta University. (It was later renamed the Isabella Thoburn College.) She also edited *Rafig-i-Niswan* (The Woman's Friend). Died September 1, 1901, in Lucknow, India. *References*: Earl K. Brown, "Isabella Thoburn," *Methodist History* 22 (1984): 207–20; *DAB*; *EM*; *EWM*; Carolyn De S. Gifford, "Isabella Thoburn (1840–1901)," in *Something More than Human: Biographies of Leaders in American Higher Education*, ed. Charles E. Cole (Nashville, Tenn., 1986), pp. 229–43; *NAW*; *NCAB* 19:149; and *WWWA*.

THOBURN, JAMES M(ILLS) (1836–1922). Missionary, brother of Isabella Thoburn,* born March 7, 1836, in St. Clairsville, Ohio. Thoburn graduated from Allegheny College (Meadville, Pa.), and was ordained in 1859. He was a missionary under the Board of Foreign Missions of the Methodist Episcopal Church in India from 1859 to 1908. He served at Naini Tal, a hill station in the Himalayas, and then at Pauri in the Himalayas, Moradabad, Sambhal, Rae Bareli, and Lucknow until 1873. He served in Calcutta from 1874 to 1888, working among Europeans and Anglo-Indians. He was cofounder of *The Indian Witness* in 1871. He started Methodist missions in Burma in 1879, in Singapore in 1885, and in the Philippines in 1899. He was elected missionary bishop for India in 1888, the first missionary bishop of his church in Asia, and was later missionary bishop for southern India until his retirement in 1908. He wrote *My Missionary Apprenticeship* (New York, 1884); *India and Malaysia: Thirty-Three Years a Missionary in India* (Cincinnati, 1892); *Light in the East* (Evanston, 1894); *The Christian Conquest of India* (New York, 1906); and a biography of his sister. His autobiography was published serially in *Northwestern Christian Advocate* during 1911. Died November 28, 1922, in Meadville, Pennsylvania. *References*: James M. Thoburn "Journal" (Ms.), Allegheny College Library, Meadville, Pa.; *ACAB*; I. R. Beiler, "Bishop James M. Thoburn Journal," *International Review of Missions* 49 (1960): 210–11; *CCDWM*; William H. Craford, *Thoburn and India* (New York, 1919); *DAB*; *EWM*; G. D. Garrett, "The Missionary Career of James Mill Thoburn," Ph.D. diss., Boston University, 1968; *LC*; *NCAB* 10:294; W. F. Oldham, *Thoburn—Called of God* (New York, 1918); and *WWWA*.

THOMAS, JAMES A(UGUSTUS) (1862–1940). Tobacco merchant, born in Lawsonville, Rockingham County, North Carolina. Thomas graduated from Eastman Business College (Poughkeepsie, N.Y.). In 1881 he entered the employ of Motley, Wright and Company, tobacco manufacturers, at Reidsville, North Carolina. He was successively an accountant, traveling salesman, and firm representative in Australia and New Zealand. He was employed by Liggett and Myers Tobacco Manufacturing Company of St. Louis from 1896 to 1899, and traveled in East Asia from 1897 to 1899. He was manager of the American Tobacco Company's business in Singapore from 1899 to 1902, manager of the British-American Tobacco Company, Limited, in India in 1903–1904, its principal representative in China from 1904 until 1923, and managing director in China from 1914 to 1923. In 1920 he organized the Chinese American Bank of Commerce in Peking to foster trade between the United States and China, and was vice president and managing director of the bank. He retired in 1923 and wrote *A Pioneer American Tobacco Merchant in the Orient* (Durham, N.C., 1928), and *Trailing Trade a Million Miles* (Durham, N.C., 1931). Died September 10, 1940, in White Plains, New York. *References*: James A. Thomas Papers, Duke University Library, Durham, N.C.; Noel H. Pugach, "Second Career: James A. Thomas and the Chinese American Bank of Commerce," *PHR* 56 (1987): 195–229; *NCAB* E:336; *NYT*, September 11, 1940; and *WWWA*.

THOMAS PERKINS AND COMPANY. *See* PERKINS AND COMPANY

"THOMASITES." Five hundred eight volunteer teachers who came to the Philippines in 1901 on board the U.S. transport ship *Thomas*. They were assigned to various parts of the Philippines, and many chose to remain in the Philippines for the rest of their lives. *References*: William Edmonds Collection, Yale University Library, New Haven, Conn.; Blaine Free Moore Papers, Manuscript Division, Library of Congress; Ralph K. Buckland, *In the Land of the Filipinos* (New York, 1912); Mary H. Fee, *A Woman's Impressions of the Philippines* (Chicago, 1910); William B. Freer, *The Philippine Experiences of an American Teacher* (New York, 1906); Amparo S. Lardizabal, "Pioneer American Teachers and Philippine Education," Ph.D. diss., Stanford University, 1956; Geronima T. Pescson and Maria Racells, eds., *Tales of the American Teachers in the Philippines* (Manila, 1959); and Gilbert S. Perez, *From the Transport Thomas to Sto. Thomas: A History of American Teachers in the Philippines* (Manila, 1953).

THOMPSON, JAMES H(ARRISON) W(ILSON) ("JIM") (1906–1967?). Businessman, grandson of James Harrison Wilson,* born March 21, 1906, in Greenville, Delaware. Thompson graduated from Princeton University and attended the University of Pennsylvania. He was a practicing architect in New York City from 1931 until 1940. He served with the Office of Strategic Services (OSS), and came to Thailand in 1945. He returned to the United States in 1946, but was back in Thailand in 1947. He became involved in the silk business, and in 1948 formed the Thai Silk Company and was its managing director. He also collected traditional Thai art. Disappeared in the Cameron Highlands of Central Malaysia. *References*: Mary Cable, "The Silk of Thailand," *Atlantic* 217 (January 1966): 107–11; William Warren, *The House on the Klong: The Bangkok Home and Asian Art Collection of James Thompson* (Washington, D.C., 1968); William Warren, "Jim Thompson: Founder of the Thai Silk Industry," in *Thai-American Relations in Contemporary Affairs*, ed. Hans H. Indorf (Singapore, 1982), pp. 118–25; and William Warren, *The Legendary American: The Remarkable Career and Strange Disappearance of Jim Thompson* (Boston, 1970).

THOMPSON MISSION (1926). Carmi Alderman Thompson (1870–1942) was appointed by President Calvin Coolidge in 1926 as a special commissioner to make a survey of economic and political conditions in the Philippines. His report, *Conditions in the Philippines Islands* (Washington, D.C., 1926) was generally considered to be a badly written report of conditions in the Philippines.

THOMSON, J(OSEPH) OSCAR (1885–1956). Medical missionary, born August 6, 1885, in Macao, to American medical missionary parents. Thomson graduated from McGill University, and studied at Harvard University and the New York Polyclinic Medical School. He was a medical missionary under the Foreign Missions Board of the United Church of Canada from 1910 to 1941. He was assistant medical superintendent of the Canton Hospital until 1915, chief surgeon there from 1915 to 1941, and hospital director and professor of surgery at Sun Yat-sen Medical College in Lingnan University from 1921 to 1941. He was Red Cross chairman for Canton during its bombing by the Japanese in 1938–1939. He returned to the United States in 1942, and was later a college physician in Oberlin College and in the Oklahoma Agricultural and Mechanical College until his death. Died October 2, 1956, in Stillwater, Oklahoma. *Reference*: *NCAB* 46:479.

THORP, JAMES (1896–1984). Soil scientist, born January 12, 1896, in Westtown, Pennsylvania. Thorp graduated from Earlham College. He was a soil surveyor with the U.S. Department of Agriculture from 1921 to 1933. He was chief soil technologist with the National Geological Survey of China from 1933 to 1936. He wrote *Geography of the Soils of China* (Nanking, 1936), and *Thirty-Four Representative Soils of China* (Changsa, Hunan, 1936), and was coauthor of *A Reconnaissance Investigation of the Saline Delta Soils of Eastern Kiangsu, China* (Peiping, 1934), *Soils of Northern and Northwestern China* (Peiping, 1935), and *Notes on Shantung Soils, a Reconnaissance Soil Survey of Shantung* (Nanking, 1936). He was assistant inspector of soil surveys in the Bureau of Plant Industry from 1936 to 1941, and principal soil correlator of the Great Plains States from 1942 to 1952. He served in the military geology unit of the U.S. Geological Survey during World War II, and was a professor of geology and soil science at Earlham College from 1952 until his retirement in 1961. Died February 18, 1984, in Richmond, Indiana. *References*: *Agronomy Journal* 43 (1951): 624; and *AMWS*.

THORPE, ELLIOTT R. (1897–1989). Army officer, born December 26, 1897, in the Pawcatuck section of Stoningtonn, Connecticut. Thorpe attended Rhode Island State College (later the University of Rhode Island). He enlisted in the U.S. Army in 1916, was commissioned a first lieutenant during World War I, and entered the regular army after the war. He was a lend-lease commissioner and U.S. military attaché in Java, Dutch East Indies, in 1941. He was chief of civil intelligence in the Supreme Commander for the Allied Powers (SCAP) in Japan and officer in charge of Emperor Hirohito's security. He later established the Army Language School, and was a military attaché in Thailand. He retired with the rank of brigadier general. He wrote an account of his years as an intelligence officer in *East Wind, Rain: The Intimate Account of an Intelligence Officer in the Pacific* (Boston, 1969). Died June 27, 1989, in Sarasota, Florida. *References*: *NYT*, June 28, 1989; and *Providence Journal*, June 28, 1989.

THURSTON, MATILDA (SMYRELL) C(ALDER) (1875–1958). Missionary, born May 16, 1875, in Hartford, Connecticut. Thurston graduated from Mount Holyoke College. She taught in Connecticut secondary schools from 1896 to 1900, and at the Central Turkey College in Marash, Turkey, from 1900 to 1902. She came to China with her husband in 1902 to find a location for the Yale-in-China mission. She returned to the United States in 1903 because of her husband's ill health. She was back in China in 1906, and taught at the Yale-in-China mission in Changsha, Hunan, until 1911. She was a missionary under the Board of Foreign Missions of the Presbyterian Church in the U.S.A. after 1913. She founded Ginling College for Women in Nanking in 1915, was its first president until 1928, and remained an advisor there until 1935. She served as treasurer and aide for relief organizations in China from 1939 until 1941, and was interned by the Japanese from 1941 to 1943. She wrote (with Ruth Chester) *Ginling College* (New York, 1955). Died April 18, 1958, in Auburndale, Massachusetts. *References*: Matilda C. Thurston Papers, Union Theological Seminary Library, New York City; *NAW*; and *NYT*, April 20, 1958.

THWING, EDWARD WAITE (1868–1943). Missionary, born February 11, 1868, in Boston. Thwing graduated from New York University and Princeton Theological Seminary, and was ordained in 1892. He was a missionary under the Board of Foreign Missions of the Presbyterian Church in the U.S.A. in South China from 1892 to 1895, and professor of theology and natural philosophy at Christian College in Canton from 1896 to 1898. He returned to the United States in 1899, and was superintendent of Chinese mission work in Hawaii from 1901 to 1909. He was involved in the anti-opium movement, served as Chinese secretary of the International Reform Bureau from 1909 to 1920, was its legislative agent at the World Conference of Nations on Opium in Shanghai in 1909, organized a Chinese National Anti-Opium Society, and was an advisor on educational and opium reform to the Chinese government. He was a missionary in Los Angeles from 1921 to 1927, and held a pastorate in Los Angeles after 1927. Died March 2, 1943, in Los Angeles. *Reference*: *WWWA*.

TIBETAN FRONTIER MISSION. Founded in 1927 by Ezra B. Steiner.* It was located at Dharchula, India, close to the Tibetan border. It was amalgamated in 1947 with The Evangelical Alliance Mission (TEAM).

TILTON, MCLANE (1836–1914). Marine Corps officer, born September 25, 1836, in Annapolis, Maryland. Tilton was commissioned a second lieutenant in the U.S. Marine Corps in 1861, and served during the Civil War. He later commanded the marine barracks at the U.S. Naval Academy in Annapolis. He served a tour of duty on the USS *Colorado*, was senior marine officer of the Pacific Squadron, and led the U.S. Marine detachment in the Korean expedition in 1871. He later commanded the barracks in the U.S. Naval Academy, served in the Mediterranean Sea, and commanded the marine guard in the Washington Navy Yard and the marine barracks in Norfolk, Virginia. In 1897 he retired with rank of lieutenant-colonel. Died January 2, 1914, in Annapolis, Maryland. *References*: Carolyn A. Tyson, *Marine Amphibious Landing in Korea, 1871* (Washington, D.C., 1966); and Charles A. Wood and Jack B. Hilliard, comps., *Register of the McLane Tilton Papers in the United States Marine Corps Museum Quantico, Virginia* (Quantico, Va., 1968).

TODD, O(LIVER) J(ULIAN) (1880–1974). Engineer, born November 1, 1880, in Colon, Michigan, and grew up in Nottawa, Michigan. Todd graduated from the University of Michigan. He worked for the city of San Francisco and served in the U.S. Army Engineers during World War I. He came to China in 1919 and carried out a survey of the Grand Canal in Shantung Province from 1919 to 1921, supervised famine work relief program in Shantung Province in 1921, and was chief engineer for the China International Famine Relief Commission (CIFRC) from 1923 until 1935. He was in charge of redigging the original channel of the Yellow River; opened up large-scale irrigation works in China's northwest; built a road from Sian, Shensi Province, to Lanchow, Kansu Province; and supervised dike repairs in Hankow, Hupeh Province, to protect the city from the Yangtze. He was forced to leave China in 1938. He served the U.S. Bureau of Reclamation and the U.S. Army Engineers during World War II. He returned to China in 1945 and supervised the rediversion of the Yellow River for the United Nations Relief and Rehabilitation Administration (UNRRA). He was consulting engineer and first head of the Sino-American Joint Commission on Rural Reconstruction. He wrote *Two Decades in China: Comprising Technical Papers, Magazine Articles, Newspaper Stories and Official Reports Connected with Work under His Own Observation* (Peking, 1938), and *The China that I*

Knew (Palo Alto, Calif., 1973). Died January 13, 1974, in Stanford, California. *References*: O. J. Todd Papers, Hoover Institution on War, Revolution and Peace, Stanford, Calif.; Michele S. Fisher, "Service to China: The Career of American Engineer, O. J. Todd," Ph.D. diss., Georgetown University, 1977; *Palo Alto Times*, January 15, 1974; and Jonathan Spence, *To Change China: Western Advisers in China 1620–1960* (Boston, 1969), ch. 8.

TOHOKU GAKUIN UNIVERSITY. Founded in 1886 by Masayoshi Oshikawa, one of the first Protestants in Japan and William E. Hoy,* missionary of the Reformed Church in the United States, as the Sendai Theological Seminary in Sendai, Miyagi Prefecture, Japan. The name was changed to Tohoku Gakuin (North Japan College) in 1891. It became coeducational after World War II, and was made a university in 1949. *Reference*: C. William Mensendiek, *Not Without a Struggle: William E. Hoy and the Beginnings of Tohoku Gakuin* (Sendai, 1985).

TOLSTOY, ILIA A. (1903–1970). Ichthyologist, grandson of the Russian author Leo Tolstoy, born in Russia. Tolstoy served with the Russian Army during World War I and fought with the White Russian Cavalry during the Russian Revolution. He then came to the United States. He studied at the Moscow School of Agriculture, William Penn College (Oskaloosa, Kansas), and Iowa State University. He worked for the U.S. Department of the Interior in 1931–1932 in the development of McKinley National Park in Alaska. He served with the Office of Strategic Services (OSS) during World War II. With Brooks Dolan,* he led a diplomatic mission to Tibet in 1942–1943 as personal representatives of President Franklin D. Roosevelt. They were received by the Dalai Lama. Tolstoy wrote of his experiences in the August 1946 issue of the *National Geographic Magazine*. He was later director and general manager of Marineland Oceanorium in Florida. He was then involved in motion picture production and cultivating sponge beds in the Bahamas. Died October 28, 1970, in New York City. *References*: *NYT*, October 30, 1970; and *Tibet*.

TOOKER, FREDERICK JAGGER (1871–1952). Medical missionary, born December 20, 1871, in Norwood, New Jersey. Tooker graduated from Princeton University and New York University Medical College, and studied at the London School of Tropical Medicine. He was a medical missionary under the Board of Foreign Missions of the Presbyterian Church in the U.S.A. in China from 1901 until 1935. He served in Hengchow from 1901 to 1903, and later in Siangtan and in Kuling. He was also a member of the Kuling city council. He returned to the United States in 1935 and settled in Summit, New Jersey. He collected ancient oracle bones and Chinese coins (which were later presented to Princeton University). Died December 17, 1952, in Ocala, Florida. *Reference*: *NCAB* 42:152.

TORREY, JOSEPH WILLIAM (1828–1885). Merchant, born April 22, 1828, in Bath, Maine, and grew up in Roxbury, Massachusetts. Torrey was a printer and a reporter on the Boston *Times*. He went to Australia in 1853 and was clerk in a mercantile house until 1857, when he moved to Hong Kong. He was partner in the firm of Montgomery, Parker and Company, ship brokers and general commission agents, and was editor and manager of the *Hong Kong Times* and editor of *China Mail*. He founded the American Trading Company of Borneo in 1864 and was its president. The sovereign powers that went with its grant of territory in North Borneo by the sultan were vested in Torrey, who was given the title of "Rajah of Ambong and Marudu," and who exercised his executive authority over the area until 1878, when he disposed of his rights. He was vice-consul and secretary of legation in Bangkok from 1877 to 1880, when he returned to the United States. Died June 22, 1885, in Boston. *References*: *ACAB*; and H. G. Keith, *The United States Consul and the Yankee Raja* (Brunei, 1980).

TOWNSEND, WALTER D(AVIS) (1856–1918). Businessman, born February 9, 1856, in Boston. Townsend came to Japan and was employed by the American Clock and Brass Company and later the American Trading Company in Yokohama from 1878 until 1880 and again from 1883 to 1886, and at Kobe from 1880 to 1883. He visited Korea from 1884 to 1886, and settled in Chemulp'o, Korea, in 1886. He established the Morse Townsend Company, which became the Morse Townsend and Company, and later Townsend and Company. He was also a representative of several American companies. Died March 10, 1918, in Chemulp'o. *References*: Harold F. Cook, *Pioneer American Businessman in Korea, the Life and Times of Walter Davis Townsend* (Seoul, 1981); and Harold F. Cook, "Walter D. Townsend: Pioneer American Businessman in Korea," *Transactions of the Korea Branch of the Royal Asiatic Society* 48 (1973): 74–103.

TRACY, LEIGHTON S(TANLEY) (1882–1942). Missionary, born August 14, 1882, in Waterville, New Brunswick, Canada, and came to Haverhill, Massachusetts, in 1900. Tracy attended Pentecostal Collegiate Institute (Saratoga, N.Y.), graduated from Northwest Nazarene College (Nampa, India) and Kennedy School of Missions, and was ordained in 1909. He was a missionary under the Association of Pentecostal Churches of America, and, after 1907, under the Department of Foreign Missions of the Church of the Nazarene in India from 1904 until 1934. He served at Buldana, Berar, western India, and was superintendent of the Marathi missionary district. He returned to the United States in 1934, and held a pastorate in Brooklyn, New York, from 1934 to 1941. Died September 28, 1942, in Brooklyn, New York. *References*: Amy N. Hinshaw, *Messengers of the Cross in India* (Kansas City, Mo., n.d.), pp. 9–13; and Olive G. Tracy, *Tracy Sahib of India* (Kansas City, Mo., 1954).

TRAGER, FRANK N(EWTON) (1905–1984). Political scientist, born October 9, 1905, in New York City. Trager graduated from New York University. He was secretary and treasurer of the New York State Socialist Party in the mid– 1930s, and program director of the American Jewish Committee from 1938 to 1943. He served in the Army Air Force during World War II. He was program director of the Anti-Defamation League of B'nai B'rith from 1945 to 1951. He was director of the U.S. aid program in Rangoon, Burma, for the Technical Cooperation Administration from 1951 to 1953; administrator and research professor, and then professor of international affairs, at New York University from 1953 until 1981; and professor of national security affairs at the Naval Postgraduate School (Monterey, Calif.) after 1982. He wrote *Burma, Land of the Golden Pagodas* (New York, 1954); *Building a Welfare State in Burma, 1948– 1956* (New York, 1958); *Burma: From Kingdom to Republic, a Historical and Political Analysis* (New York, 1966); *Burma: A Selected and Annotated Bibliography* (New Haven, Conn., 1973); and *Why Viet Nam?* (New York, 1966). He was coauthor of *Burmese Sit-tans 1764–1826: Records of Rural Life and Administration* (Tucson, Ariz., 1979), and edited *Marxism in Southeast Asia: A Study of Four Countries* (Stanford, Calif., 1959), and *Burma: Japanese Military Administration, Selected Documents, 1941–1945* (Philadelphia, 1971). Died August 26, 1984, in Carmel, California. *References*: *AMWS*; F. Barnett, "Frank Trager the Man: A Brief Impression," *Orbis* 21 (1977): 157–69; *CA*; *NYT*, August 31, 1984; and *WWA*.

TRUMBULL, ROBERT (1912–   ). Journalist, born May 26, 1912, in Chicago. Trumbull attended the University of Washington (Seattle). He was a reporter and later city editor of the *Honolulu Advertiser* from 1933 to 1943; war correspondent in the Pacific Theater for *The New York Times* during World War II; foreign correspondent in Japan, the Philippines, and South and Southeast Asia from 1945 to 1954; chief of the Tokyo bureau from 1954 to 1961 and from 1964 to 1968; chief correspondent in China–Southeast Asia from 1961 to 1963; correspondent in Australia, New Zealand, and the Pacific Islands from 1968 to 1973; chief correspondent in Canada from 1974 to 1978; and Pacific correspondent after 1978. He wrote *India since Independence* (New York, 1954); *As I See India* (New York, 1956); *Nine Who Have Survived Hiroshima and Nagasaki* (New York, 1957); and *The Scrutable East: A Correspondent's Report on Southeast Asia* (New York, 1964); and edited *This Is Communist China* (Tokyo, 1968). *References*: *CA*; and *WWA*.

TUCKER, HENRY ST. GEORGE (1874–1959). Clergyman, born July 16, 1874, in Warsaw, Virginia. Tucker graduated from the University of Virginia and the Theological Seminary of Virginia, and was ordained in 1899. He was a missionary under the Domestic and Foreign Missionary Society of the Protestant Episcopal Church in the United States of America in Japan from 1899 until 1923. He served in Hirosaki, was in charge of the mission in the Aomori prefecture, and was president of St. Paul's College in Tokyo from 1903 to 1912. He was named missionary bishop of Kyoto from 1912 until 1923. He served with the American Expeditionary Force in Siberia in charge of the civilian refugee work for the American Red Cross. He returned to the United States in 1923, was professor of pastoral theology at the Theological Seminary of Virginia, was bishop coadjutor of Virginia in 1926–1927, bishop of Virginia from 1927 until 1944, and was presiding bishop of Protestant Episcopal Church from 1941 until his retirement in 1946. Died August 8, 1959, in Richmond, Virginia. *References*: *DAB S6*; *NCAB* 43:598; *NYT*, August 9, 1959; and *WWWA*.

TUCKER, MARGARET EMMELINE (1907–1975). Medical missionary, born August 5, 1907, in Pangchiachuang, Shantung, China, to American missionary parents. Tucker graduated from Oberlin College and Rush Medical College (Chicago), and studied at Harvard University. She was a medical missionary under the Board of Global Ministries of the United Methodist Church in China from 1935 until 1941, serving in a hospital in Foochow. She returned to China in 1945, was professor and chief of radiology and physical medicine at the West China Union University Medical College and Hospital in Chengtu until 1950, and served as professor and chief of radiology at the Christian Medical College and Brown Memorial Hospital of the University of Punjab in India. She returned to the United States in 1964. Died October 29, 1975, in Cleveland. *Reference*: *NCAB* 59:210.

TUNGHAI UNIVERSITY. Founded in 1955 under the auspices of the United Board for Christian Higher education in Asia as the first Christian university in Taiwan. It is almost entirely supported by the board. *Reference*: Chung-ping Chang, ''The United Christian Higher Education in Asia in the Development of Tunghai University in Taiwan, 1955–1980,'' Ph.D. diss., Southern Illinois University, 1982.

TURNBULL, WILFRID (1866–1944). Army officer, born November 3, 1866, in Penistone, England. Turnbull came to the United States and studied medicine. He served as a medical officer during the Spanish-American War in Cuba, and came to the Philippines in 1899. He was in charge of various army hospitals in Luzon and the Visayas, served as an officer in the Philippine Constabulary, and was supervisor and deputy governor in the Mountain Province and on the east coast of Luzon. He retired from the constabulary, went into the forest-product business in Tayabas, and then moved to Manila. He was interned by the Japanese in Santo Tomas. Died November 1, 1944, in Santo Tomas. His reminiscences were reprinted in the *BAHC* in 1974. *Reference*: *BAHC* 2 (April 1974): 33.

TURNER, E(VERETT) STANTON (1887–1979). Association official, born September 30, 1887, in Turner, Iowa. Turner graduated from Grinnell and Oberlin colleges. He was the first student secretary of the Philippine Young

Men's Christian Association (YMCA) from 1915 to 1918, general secretary in Manila from 1918 to 1926, and the national general secretary from 1926 until his retirement in 1952. He was interned by the Japanese in Manila during World War II. He wrote *Nation Building* (Manila, 1965). Died September 24, 1979, in Duarte, California. *References*: *EP* 18:156; and Frank B. Lenz, "Stant Turner of the Philippines," in E. Stanton Turner, *Nation Building* (Manila, 1965).

TUTTLE, CHARLES E(GBERT) (1915–   ). Publisher and bookseller, born April 5, 1915, in Rutland, Vermont. Tuttle graduated from Harvard University. He joined his father's antiquarian book business in 1938. He served in the U.S. Army during World War II and in the military government in Japan in 1945–1946. He remained in Tokyo, where he began publishing and was later also involved in retail bookselling and the establishment of a literary agency. He was president of Charles E. Tuttle Company in Tokyo until 1977. *References*: *CB* 1960; H. R. Lottman, "Tuttle—Of Tokyo and Rutland, Vt.," *Publishers Weekly* 214 (October 16, 1978): 86–87; and *WWA*.

TUTWILER, TEMPLE W(ILLIAM) (1879–1950). Engineer, born January 5, 1879, in Cincinnati and grew up in Birmingham, Alabama. Tutwiler graduated from the University of Alabama. He served in the Spanish-American War. He was superintendent of blast furnaces for various iron and steel companies from 1899 until 1912. He went to India in 1912 to complete construction of iron and steel mills near Calcutta for the Tata Iron and Steel Company, Limited. He was general superintendent of the mills from 1913 to 1915, and general manager from 1915 to 1925. He returned to the United States in 1925, managed his father's estate, and was involved in local civic affairs. He was later an executive and chief engineer of Cities Service Company, and, after 1945, president of Tutwiler Hotel Corporation and other companies. Died November 9, 1950, in Birmingham, Alabama. *References*: *NCAB* 38:221; *NYT*, November 10, 1950; and *WWWA*.

TWAIN, MARK (1835–1910). Author, real name Samuel Langhorne Clemens, born November 30, 1835, in Florida, Missouri, and grew up in Hannibal, Missouri. Mark Twain was apprenticed to a printer at twelve, worked at a newspaper, and was apprenticed to a steamboat pilot on the Mississippi River from 1856 to 1861. He moved to Nevada in 1861, was a reporter for the Virginia City *Territorial Enterprise*, came to San Francisco in 1864, and wrote for the *San Francisco Call* and other newspapers. He published his first book in 1867. He later settled in Hartford, Connecticut. In 1896, following a bankruptcy, he set out on a lecture tour around the world. He traveled and lectured in India in 1896, and described his experiences in *Following the Equator: A Journey around the World* (New York, 1897). Died April 21, 1910, in Redding, Connecticut. *References*: Harsharn S. Ahluwalia, "Mark Twain's Lecture Tour in India," *Mark Twain Journal* 18 (Winter 1976–1977): 4–7; Francis V. Madigan, Jr., "Mark

Twain's Passage to India: A Genetic Study of *Following the Equator*," Ph.D. diss., New York University, 1974; Keshav Mutalik, *Mark Twain in India* (Bombay, 1978); Coleman O. Parsons, "Mark Twain: Sightseer in India," *Mississippi Quarterly* 16 (1963): 76–93; Arthur L. Scott, *Mark Twain "At Large"* (Chicago, 1969), pp. 195–214; and Mohan L. Sharma, "Mark Twain's Passage to India," *Mark Twain Journal* 14 (Summer 1968): 12–14.

TYDINGS-MCDUFFIE ACT (1934). A slightly revised version of the Hawes-Cutting Act, the Tydings-McDuffie Act granted independence to the Philippines after a ten-year transition period, and established the Philippine Commonwealth as a transitional government. The economic provisions were little changed. It also provided for the settlement by negotiation of the future status of U.S. military bases in the Philippines. *Reference*: EAH.

TYSON, GEORGE (1831–1881). Merchant, born in New Bedford, Massachusetts. Tyson was clerk in a bank, and then clerk of Russell and Company in China from 1851 to 1854 and partner from 1855 to 1868. He was also president of Shanghai Steam Navigation Company from 1864 to 1867. He was general auditor of Chicago, Burlington, and Quincy Railroad Company from 1876 to 1879; president of Burlington and Missouri River Railroad Company in Nebraska from 1876 to 1879; and comptroller of Chicago, Burlington and Quincy Railroad Company after 1880. Died January 8, 1881. *Reference*: Thomas C. Cochran, *Railroad Leaders 1845–1890* (Cambridge, Mass., 1953).

U

UNANGST, ERIAS (1824–1903). Missionary, born August 8, 1824, in Easton, Pennsylvania. Unangst graduated from Pennsylvania (later Gettysburg) College, studied at the Lutheran Theological Seminary (Gettysburg), and was ordained in 1857. He was a missionary under the General Synod of the Lutheran Church in India from 1858 until 1895. He served in the Guntur mission and was involved with the revision of the Telugu translation of the Bible. He returned to the United States in 1895. Died October 12, 1903, in Hollidaysburg, Pennsylvania. *Reference*: *DAB*.

UNDERWOOD, HORACE GRANT (1859–1916). Missionary, born July 19, 1859, in London, England; came with his family to the United States in 1872; and grew up in Durham, New Jersey. Underwood graduated from the University of the City of New York (later New York University) and New Brunswick Theological Seminary, and was ordained in 1884. He was a missionary under the Board of Foreign Missions of the Presbyterian Church in the U.S.A. in Korea from 1885 until his death. He began the translation of the Bible into Korean and was chairman of the board of translators until his death. He opened an orphanage in Seoul in 1886, published *Christian News* from 1897 to 1901, was involved in the establishment of the Young Men's Christian Association (YMCA) branch in Seoul, and aided in establishing Severance Hospital and the Chosen Union Christian College. After the assassination of the queen in 1895, he became the trusted intermediary of the king, even conveying the kings his food to his own table to avoid the danger of poisoning. He wrote *A Concise Dictionary of the Korean Language* (Yokohama, 1890); *An Introduction to the Korean Spoken Language* (Yokohama, 1890); *The Call of Korea, Political—Social—Religious* (New York, 1908); and *The Religions of Eastern Asia* (New York, 1910). With his son, Horace Horton Underwood,* he prepared *An English-Korean Dictionary* (Seoul, 1925), which was published posthumously. Died October 12, 1916, in Atlantic City, New Jersey. His wife, **LILLIAS STIRLING HORTON UNDERWOOD** (1851–1921), medical missionary, had a degree in medicine and considerable nursing experience in the Presbyterian Hospital in Chicago. She became the personal physician for the Korean queen. She wrote *Fifteen Years among the Topknots; or, Life in Korea* (Boston, 1904); *With Tommy Tompkins in Korea* (New York, 1905); and a biography of her husband. Died October 20, 1921, in Seoul, Korea. *References*: *DAB*; Martha Huntley, "Presbyterian Women's Work and Rights in the Korean Mission," *American Presbyterians* 65 (1987): 37–48; *NAW*; *NCAB* 7:267; *NCAB* 31:290; *NYT*, October 13, 1916; and *Yanghwajin*.

UNDERWOOD, HORACE HORTON (1890–1951). Educator, son of Horace Grant Underwood,* born September 6, 1890, in Seoul, Korea. Underwood graduated from New York University. He came back to Korea as a teacher, and was president of Chosun Christian University in Korea from 1934 to 1941. He returned to the United States in 1942, and served the Board of Foreign Missions of the Presbyterian Church in the U.S.A. from 1942 to 1945. He came back to Korea in 1945 as special advisor on Korean affairs to the U.S. military authority, and was later a missionary until 1949. He wrote *Modern Education in Korea* (New York, 1926), and, with his father, he prepared *An English-Korean Dictionary* (Seoul, 1925). Died February 20, 1951, in Pusan, Korea. *References*: J. Earnest Fisher, *Pioneers of Modern Korea* (Seoul, 1977), pp. 261–76; *NYT*, February 21, 1951; *WWWA*; and *Yanghwajin*.

UNION CHRISTIAN COLLEGE. Established in P'yongyang, Korea, in 1906 by the Korea mission of the Presbyterian Church in the U.S.A. and the Methodist Episcopal Church (which withdrew in 1915). The Presbyterian Church in the United States as well as the Australian and Canadian Presbyterian missions joined later. In 1908 it graduated the first two Koreans to receive college diplomas. It was closed down in 1938. It was reestablished in 1954 in Seoul, and the name was changed to Soongsil College in 1956.

UNITED CHRISTIAN MISSIONARY SOCIETY (DISCIPLES OF CHRIST). Founded in 1920 to serve as the board of missions and Christian education of the Christian Church (Disciples), united the American Christian Missionary Society (founded in 1849), the Christian Woman's Board of Missions (founded in 1874), the Foreign Christian Missionary Society (founded in 1875), and three other boards and societies. It began missionary work in India in 1882, in Japan in 1883, in China in 1884, in the Philippines in 1900, and in Tibet in 1903. Its work was assumed in 1973 by the Division of Overseas Ministries of the Christian Church (Disciples of Christ) in the USA and Canada. *References*: United Christian Missionary Society Archives, Disciples of Christ Historical Society, Nashville, Tenn.; Nelle G. Alexander, *Disciples of Christ in India* (Indianapolis, 1964); *EMCM*; Grant K. Lewis, *The American Christian Missionary Society and the Disciples of Christ* (St. Louis, Mo., 1937); and Lester

G. McAllister and William Tucker, *Journey in Faith: A History of the Christian Church (Disciples of Christ)* (St. Louis, Mo., 1975).

UNITED CHURCH BOARD OF WORLD MINISTRIES. *See* AMERICAN BOARD OF COMMISSIONERS FOR FOREIGN MISSIONS

UNITED LUTHERAN CHURCH IN AMERICA: BOARD OF FOREIGN MISSIONS. Organized in 1837 as the Foreign Missionary Society of the Evangelical German (after 1842 Lutheran) Churches of the U.S.A., it became the Board of Foreign Missions in 1918. It began missionary work in India in 1842, in Japan in 1892, in China in 1898, and in Malaya in 1953. It merged in 1962 with other Lutheran churches to form the Board of World Missions of the Lutheran Church in America, which was later renamed the Division for World Missions and Ecumenism. *References*: United Lutheran Church of American Archives, Lutheran School of Theology, Chicago; George Drach, *Kingdom Pathfinders* (Philadelphia, 1942); Clarence H. Swavely, *The Lutheran Enterprise in India* (Madras, 1952); and Clarence H. Swavely, *One Hundred Years in the Andhra Country* (Madras, 1942).

UNITED MISSION TO NEPAL. Founded in 1953 as a Methodist project. Thirty denominational groups became later affiliated. Medical service began in 1954 in a palace belonging to the royal family. *References*: *EMCM*; and Jonathan Lindell, *Nepal and the Gospel of God* (Kathmandu, 1979).

UNITED PRESBYTERIAN CHURCH IN NORTH AMERICA: BOARD OF FOREIGN MISSIONS. Founded in 1866, it had its beginnings in the work of the Associate Reformed Presbyterian Church and the Associate Presbyterian Church, which merged in 1858. Missionary work in India was transferred to it in 1859. It merged with the Board of Foreign Missions of the Presbyterian Church in the U.S.A. in 1958 to form the Commission on Ecumenical Missions and Relations of the United Presbyterian Church in the U.S.A., which merged in 1983 with the Presbyterian Church in the U.S.A. to form the Presbyterian Church (USA). *References*: Emma D. Anderson and Mary J. Campbell, *In the Shadow of the Himalayas: A Historical Narrative of the Missions of the United Presbyterian Church of North America as Conducted in the Punjab, India, 1855–1940* (Philadelphia, 1942); William B. Anderson and Charles R. Watson, *Far North in India: A Survey of the Mission Field and Work of the United Presbyterian Church in the Punjab* (Philadelphia, 1911); and Walter N. Jamison, *The United Presbyterian Story: A Centennial Study 1858–1958* (Pittsburgh, 1958).

UNITED STATES. Outfitted by a group of Philadelphians, under the command of Captain Thomas Bell, it arrived on the Simalur, off Sumatra, in the East Indies, and the Coromandel Coast in 1784, the first American ship to visit Indonesia and India. After calls at several Indian ports, it returned to the United

States in 1785. *References*: *United States* Log and Journal, Historical Society of Pennsylvania, Philadelphia; G. Bhagat, "First Contacts with India, 1784–1785," *AN* 31 (1971): 38–48; James W. Snyder, Jr., ed., "The First American Voyage to India, Being Excerpts from the Log of the Ship United States from Philadelphia to Pondicherry, 1784," *Americana* 32 (1938): 284–304; and Samuel W. Woodhouse, Jr., ed., "Log and Journal of the Ship United States on a Voyage to China in 1784," *Pennsylvania Magazine of History and Biography* 55 (1931): 255–58.

UNITED STATES RUBBER COMPANY. In 1910 the company acquired a rubber plantation in Sumatra and established a subsidiary, the Hollandsch-Amerikanaasche Plantage Mattschappij (HAPM) in 1911 to manage this and other plantations in northeastern Sumatra. It also established a rubber processing factory in Bunut. It established a plantation in Malaya in 1919. *References*: Glenn D. Babcock, *History of the United States Rubber Company: A Case Study in Corporation Management* (Bloomington, Ind., 1966); and H. Stuart Hotchkiss, "Operations of an American Rubber Company in Sumatra and the Malay Peninsula," *Annals of the Academy of the Political and Social Science* 112 (1924): 154–62.

UNIVERSITY OF NANKING. *See* NANKING, UNIVERSITY OF

U.S. ARMY, FIFTEENTH INFANTRY REGIMENT. Stationed in Tientsin, China, from 1912 until 1938, guarding American lives and property. It was known as the "Old China Hands." *Reference*: Charles G. Finney, *The Old China Hands* (Garden City, N.Y., 1961).

U.S. ARMY MILITARY GOVERNMENT IN KOREA (USAMGIK). Established in 1945 and commanded by General John R. Hodge,* it operated all the machinery of government until Koreans were trained to take over the duties. Generally well-intentioned, it was not particularly efficient. It was terminated in 1948. *References*: Soon-Sung Cho, "The Failure of American Military Government in Korea," *Korean Affairs* 2 (1963): 331–47; Han Mu Kang, "Reevaluation of United States Military Government in Korea: 1945–1948," in *The United States and Korea: American-Korean Relations, 1866–1976*, ed. Andrew C. Nahm (Kalamazoo, Mich., 1979), pp. 162–86; Han Mu Kang, "The United States Military Government in Korea, 1945–1948," Ph.D. diss., University of Cincinnati, 1970; Richard Lauterbach, *A History of American Military Government in Korea* (Seoul, 1948); and E. Grant Meade, *American Military Government in Korea* (New York, 1951).

U.S. ASIATIC SQUADRON. *See* ASIATIC SQUADRON

U.S. CIVIL ADMINISTRATION OF THE RYUKYU ISLANDS (USCAR). Created in 1950. Day-to-day operations were discharged by the commanding general of the Ryukyu Command (RYCOM) who also held the post of deputy governor, assistant by a civil administrator. The high commissioner of the Ryukyu Islands, appointed by the secretary of defense, replaced the deputy governor in 1957. The administration of the Ryukyu Islands reverted to Japan in 1972.

U.S. COURT FOR CHINA. United States Extra-Territorial Court for China established by the U.S. Congress in 1906 to replace the jurisdiction of American consuls who had administered the law in suits in which resident Americans were concerned. The court dealt with all cases between Americans or cases in which action was brought against American citizens by other nationals. Its headquarters were in Shanghai. It functioned until 1943, when extraterritorial jurisdiction was abolished.

U.S. EAST INDIA SQUADRON. *See* EAST INDIA SQUADRON

U.S. EDUCATION MISSIONS TO JAPAN. The first education mission, composed of twenty-seven educational specialists and chaired by George Dinsomre Stoddard, went to Japan in 1946. The second education mission, composed of five members of the first mission and headed by Willard Earl Givens, went to Japan in 1950. Their reports contributed greatly to educational reform in Japan. *References*: *KEJ*; and Toshio Nishi, *Unconditional Democracy: Education and Politics in Occupied Japan 1945–1952* (Stanford, Calif., 1982), ch. 9.

U.S. EXPEDITIONARY FORCE TO SIBERIA (1919–1923). Commanded by General William S. Graves,* the force went to Siberia in 1919 to help guard the route along which the Czechoslovakia Legion made its way through Siberia to the Pacific and to deter the Japanese from gaining a foothold in Siberia. *References*: William S. Graves, *America's Siberian Adventure* (New York, 1931); Judith A. Lucket, "The Siberian Intervention: Military Support of Foreign Policy," *Military Review* 54 (April 1984): 54–63; Robert J. Maddox, *The Unknown War with Russia: Wilson's Siberian Intervention* (San Rafael, Calif., 1977); Betty M. Unterberger, *America's Siberian Expedition, 1918–1920: A Study of National Policy* (Durham, N.C., 1956); and Virginia C. Westfall, "AEF Siberia—The Forgotten Army," *Military Review* 48 (March 1968): 11–18.

U.S. MILITARY GOVERNMENT IN THE PHILIPPINES (1898–1901). The U.S. Army governed the Philippines from 1898 to 1901 and extended occupation government throughout the islands. American civilians took control over the government in 1901. *Reference*: Virginia F. Mulrooney, "No Victor, No Vanquished: United States Military Government in the Philippine Islands, 1898–1901," Ph.D. diss., University of California at Los Angeles, 1975.

V

VAN ALLEN, FRANK (1860–1923). Medical missionary, born January 10, 1860, in Dubuque, Iowa. Van Allen graduated from Yale University and Yale Medical School, and was ordained in 1888. He was a medical missionary under the American Board of Commissioners for Foreign Missions (ABCFM) in India from 1888 until his death. He served in Madura City, and was in charge of the mission dispensary there. He founded a men's hospital in Madura in 1898, and served as its head until 1923. Died August 28, 1923, in the village of Melur, near Madras, India. *Reference*: *DAB*.

VAN BRAAM HOUCKGEEST, ANDREAS EVERARDUS (1739–1801). Merchant, born in the province of Utrecht, the Netherlands. Van Braam Houckgeest went to China in 1758 as a supercargo with the Dutch East India Company, and remained in Macao and Canton until 1773. He returned to the Netherlands in 1773; came to Charleston, South Carolina, in 1783; and operated a rice plantation. It is said that he became an American citizen in 1784. He returned to China in 1790 as head of the factory of the Dutch East India Company. He was a member of the expedition to Peking in 1795, the first American to travel to Peking and to be presented at the imperial court. He returned to the United States in 1796, and constructed a house, called China's Retreat, near Bristol, Pennsylvania. There he displayed what was probably the first large collection of Chinese art in the United States. He returned to the Netherlands in 1799. Died in Amsterdam, the Netherlands. *References*: Edward R. Barnsley, *History of China's Retreat* (Bristol, Pa., 1933); Charles H. Carpenter, Jr., "The Chinese Collection of A. E. van Braam Houckgeest," *Antiques* 105 (February 1974): 338–47; Henry W. Kent, "Van Braam Houckgeest, an Early American Collector," *Proceedings of the American Antiquarian Society*, new series, 40 (October 1930): 159–74; Jean G. Lee, *Philadelphians and the China Trade 1784–1844* (Philadelphia, 1984), pp. 81–82; and George R. Loehr, "A. E. Van Braam Houckgeest: The First American at the Court of China," *Princeton University Library Chronicle* 15 (1954): 179–82, 188–90.

VAN SCHAICK, LOUIS J. (1875–1945). Army officer, born July 1, 1875, in Cobleskill, New York. Van Schaick studied at the U.S. Military Academy, and was commissioned a second lieutenant in 1899. He came to the Philippines in 1899, served in the Philippines Scouts from 1904 to 1907, was governor of Cavite from 1905 to 1907, became an inspector in the Philippines Constabulary in 1908, and was governor of Mindoro from 1908 to 1912. He returned to the United States, served on the Mexican border and during World War I, and was inspector general of American forces in Germany in 1919–1920. He returned to the Philippines as an advisor to the governor-general from 1930 to 1935. He retired with the rank of colonel in 1934. He was later on the staff of Benguet Consolidated Mining Company. Died February 14, 1945, in Santo Tomas. *References*: *Elarth*; *Gleeck/Frontiers*; and *WWP*.

VAUGH, MASON (1894–1978). Agricultural engineer, born June 27, 1894, in Bonne Terre, Missouri. Vaugh graduated from the University of Missouri College of Agriculture. He served in the U.S. Army during World War II. He went to India in 1921 as a lay missionary under the Board of Foreign Missions of the Presbyterian Church in the U.S.A. The first person to teach a course in agricultural engineering in India, he was head of the department of agricultural engineering of the Allahabad Agricultural Institute in Allahabad from 1921 until 1954. He also designed most of the buildings of the institute and supervised their construction, and was in charge of maintenance and plant operation for the institute from 1921 to 1953. He was leader of the Agricultural Development Society (ADS) which established a factory in Naini to manufacture and sell improved farm implements researched and developed by the society. He retired in 1957 and returned to the United States. *Reference*: Mason Vaugh Papers, University of Missouri-Columbia Library, Columbia, Mo.

VAUGHN, HARRIET PARKER (1867–1953). Medical missionary, born July 29, 1867, in East Putney, Windham County, Vermont. Vaughn attended Smith College and Women's Medical College of New York, and studied in Paris. She practiced medicine from 1893 to 1895. She was a medical missionary under the American Board of Commissioners for Foreign Missions (ABCFM) in India from 1895 until 1935. She was medical officer in charge of the American Hospital for Women and Children in Madura from 1897 to 1935, and founded the Dayapuram Leper Hospital and the Bird's Nest orphanage in Madura. She returned to the United States in 1935, resided in Fitchburg, Massachusetts, and, after the death of her husband, returned to Madura where she did medical and other work for the Birds' Nest, the orphanage she founded. Died February 27, 1953, in Madura. *References*: Harriet Vaughn Letters, Smith College Archives, Northampton, Mass.; and *Smith Alumnae Quarterly*, May 1953.

VAUGHN, MILES W(ALTER) (1891–1949). Journalist, born in Nebraska City. Vaughn graduated from the University of Kansas. He served on newspapers in Lawrence and Salinas, Kansas, and in Kansas City. He served in the U.S. Navy during World War I. He joined the United Press (UP) in Chicago in 1915, and later, at various times, was manager of bureaus in St. Louis, Kansas City, and Dallas. He was manager of the UP bureau of Rio de Janeiro, Brazil, from 1919 to 1923, and manager of the New York bureau from 1923 to 1925. He was foreign correspondent in east Asia from 1924 to 1934, vice president and general manager for Asia in New York City from 1934 until 1945, and again foreign correspondent in east Asia after 1945. He was considered the dean of American reporters in Japan. He wrote *Covering the Far East* (New York, 1936). Died January 30, 1949, in a boating accident, in Tokyo Harbor. *References*: *KEJ*; and *NYT*, January 31, 1949.

VAUTRIN, MINNIE (1886–1941). Missionary educator, born September 27, 1886, in Secor, Illinois. Vautrin graduated from Illinois State Normal University (Normal) and the University of Illinois. She was a missionary under the United Christian Missionary Society in China from 1912 until 1940. She was principal of a girls' middle school in Luchow after 1914, and of the high school department until 1919. She was head of the department of education of Ginling College after 1919. She also served as its acting president. She remained in Gingling College through the Japanese sack of Nanking in 1937. She returned to the United States in 1940. Committed suicide May 14, 1941, in Indianapolis. *Reference*: *NAW*.

VEDDER, EDWARD B(RIGHT) (1878–1952). Nutritionist, born June 28, 1878, in New York City. Vedder graduated from the University of Rochester and the University of Pennsylvania Medical School, and was commissioned a first lieutenant in the U.S. Army Medical Corps in 1903. He served in the war against the Moros in the Philippines from 1904 to 1906. He studied tropical diseases in the Philippines, determined that beriberi was deficiency disease, and developed a cure for it. He was a member of the Army Board for the Study of Tropical Disease in Manila from 1910 to 1913. He wrote *Beriberi* (New York, 1913). He was assistant professor of pathology at the Army Medical School, director of the Southern Department Laboratory at Fort Sam Houston, Texas, and chief of medical research at the Edgewood Arsenal, Maryland, until 1925. He was a senior member of the Army Board for Medical Research in Manila from 1925 to 1929, and then directed the Army Medical School in Washington, D.C., from 1930 until his retirement, with the rank of colonel, in 1933. He was professor of pathology and experimental medicine at George Washington University Medical School from 1933 to 1943, and later directed the laboratory of the Highland County Hospital in Oakland, California. Died January 30, 1952, in Washington, D.C. *References*: *AMWS*; *DAB S5*; *DAMB 84*; *NCAB* 41:229;

NYT, February 23, 1952; R. R. Williams, "Edward Bright Vedder—A Biographical Sketch," *Journal of Nutrition* 77 (1962): 3–6; and *WWWA*.

VELLORE CHRISTIAN MEDICAL COLLEGE AND HOSPITAL. The hospital was founded in 1900 by Ida S. Scudder* of the Arcot mission of the Reformed Church in America. Nursing program was established in 1909. The Union Mission Medical School for Women was opened in 1918. Renamed Christian Medical College in the 1940s, it later became coeducational and obtained degree-granting privileges in 1942. It became affiliated with the University of Madras in 1950. *References*: *CDCWM*; Henry C. Hart, *Campus India: An Appraisal of American College Programs in India* (East Lansing, Mich., 1961); and D. C. Wilson, *Take My Hands* (London, 1964).

VERBECK, GUIDO HERMAN FRIDOLIN (1830–1898). Missionary, born January 23, 1830, in Zeist, the Netherlands, and came to the United States in 1852. Verbeck attended the Polytechnic Institute of Utrecht and the Auburn Theological Seminary (Auburn, N.Y.), and was ordained in 1859. He was a missionary under the Board of Foreign Mission of the Reformed Church in America in Japan from 1859 until his death. He established a school in Nagasaki, and at the request of the Japanese government, took charge of a school for interpreters in Nagasaki. He went to Yedo in 1869, headed a school that was the foundation for the Imperial University, and served as advisor to the government from 1873 to 1879. He translated or supervised the translation into Japanese of Code Napoleon, the constitutions of many states, and other documents. After 1879, he taught in the theological school (later part of Meiji Gakuin), lectured at the government school for nobles, and assisted in the translation of the Bible. Died March 10, 1898, in Tokyo. *References*: Albert Altman, "Guido Verbeck and the Iwakura Embassy," *Japan Quarterly* 13 (1966): 54–62; *CDCWM*; *DAB*; *EM*; *KEJ*; and Noboru Umetani, *The Role of Foreign Employees in the Meiji Era in Japan* (Tokyo, 1971), ch. 1.

VERNAY, ARTHUR STANNARD (1876?–1960). Explorer, born in Weymouth, England. Vernay came to the United States as a young man, but retained his British nationality. He founded the Vernay Galleries, an antiques gallery, in New York City, and managed it until his retirement in 1941. He was a field associate of the American Museum of Natural History. Between 1923 and 1946, he was the leader or coleader of expeditions to India, Burma, the Malay Peninsula, Tibet, and Siam. In 1935, after five years of negotiations with the Dalai Lama, he obtained permission to cross the closed Tibetan border into the forbidden hinterland, and brought back reports of the folkways of Tibet. In 1938, he obtained a permit from the Government of Burma to enter a section of northeastern Burma that had never before been explored by a scientific expedition. Groups of mammals brought back by him were mounted in scenes depicting their natural settings and put on display in the Vernay-Faunthorpe Hall of South Asiatic Mammals, which was opened in the American Museum of Natural History in 1930. Died October 25, 1960, in Nassau, the Bahamas. *References*: *New Yorker*, May 14, 1949; *NYT*, October 26, 1960; and the (London) *Times*, October 26, 1960.

VICKERS, JAMES C(ATOR) (1877–1945). Lawyer and judge, born August 5, 1877, in Taylors Islands, Maryland. Vickers graduated from Randolph-Macon College (Ashland, Va.) and the College of Law of the University of the Philippines. He was a school teacher in Virginia from 1900 to 1902, came to the Philippines in 1902, and served with the Philippine civil service from 1902 to 1913. He was admitted to the Philippine bar in 1913, and practiced law at Cebu from 1914 to 1926. He was judge of the court of first instance at Cebu from 1927 to 1930, judge of the court of first instance in Manila in 1931–1932, and associate justice of the Supreme Court of the Philippines from 1932 to 1936. He later practiced law in Manila. Died February 1945, in Manila. *References*: *CCDP*; *Sevilla*; *WWP*; and *WWWA*.

VINCENT, FRANK (1848–1916). Traveler, born April 2, 1848, in Brooklyn, New York. Vincent attended Yale University. He began to travel in 1871; made a systematic tour of the entire world from 1871 to 1886; explored Cambodia, Siam and Burma in 1871–1872; and described his adventures in *The Land of the White Elephant* (London, 1873). He brought back a valuable collection of Indochinese antiquities and art, which he presented to the Metropolitan Museum of Art in 1885. Died June 19, 1916, in Woodstock, New York. *References*: *ACAB*; *DAB*; and *WWWA*.

VINCENT, JOHN CARTER (1900–1972). Diplomat, born in Seneca, Kansas. Vincent served in the U.S. Army during World War I. He graduated from Mercer University. He entered the foreign service in 1925, and served at Changsha, Hankow, Swatow, Peking, Mukden, Nanking, and Dairen. He was counselor of embassy at Chungking in 1942. He was director of the Bureau of Far Eastern Affairs in the Department of State in 1945, minister to Switzerland from 1947 to 1951, and diplomatic agent in Tangier in 1951–1952. He was forced to resign from the foreign service in 1952. Died December 1972 in Cambridge, Massachusetts. *References*: Gary May, *China Scapegoat: The Diplomatic Ordeal of John Carter Vincent* (Washington, D.C., 1978); *NYT*, December 5, 1972; *PolProf: Eisenhower*; *PolProf: Truman*; Ross Terrill, ''John Carter Vincent and the American 'Loss of China,' '' in *China and Ourselves: Explorations and Revisions by a New Generation*, ed. Bruce Douglass and Ross Terrill (Boston, 1970), pp. 122–54; and *WWWA*.

VINING, ELIZABETH (JANET) GRAY (1902–   ). Educator, born October 6, 1902, in Philadelphia. Vining graduated from Bryn Mawr College and Drexel Institute School of Library Science (later Drexel University). She served as a private tutor to Crown Prince Akihito of Japan from 1946 to 1950. She also lectured at Gakushuin University and Tsuda College. She returned to the United States in 1950, and wrote about her experiences in *Windows for the Crown Prince* (Philadelphia, 1952), and later in *Return to Japan* (Philadelphia, 1960). She also wrote an autobiography, *Quiet Pilgrimage* (Philadelphia, 1970), and *Being Seventy: The Measure of a Year* (New York, 1978). *References*: *CA*; Mary H. Jones, "Elizabeth Gray Vining: The Measure of a Life," in *Living in the Light: Some Quaker Pioneers of the 20th Century: Vol. I: In the U.S.A.*, ed. Leonard S. Kenworthy (Kennett Square, Pa., 1984), pp. 247–62; *KEJ*; and *WWA*.

VINTON, JUSTUS HATCH (1806–1858). Missionary, born February 17, 1806, in Willington, Connecticut. Vinton graduated from Hamilton Literary and Theological Institution (later Madison University). He was a missionary under the American Baptist Missionary Union in Burma from 1834 until his death. He worked among the Karens and was stationed in Chummerah, Newville, Maulmain, and Kemendine, a suburb of Rangoon. He was in charge of the Karen Theological Seminary in Maulmain in 1851–1952. Died March 31, 1858, in Kemendine, Burma. *References*: *ACAB*; *EM*; and Calista V. Luther, *The Vintons and the Karens: Memorials of Justus H. Vinton and Calista H. Vinton* (Boston, 1880).

VORIES, WILLIAM MERRELL (1880–1964). Educator and businessman, born October 28, 1880, in Leavenworth, Kansas, and grew up in Flagstaff, Arizona, and Denver. Vories graduated from Colorado College (Colorado Springs). He was a teacher of English in a commercial high school in Omi-Hachiman, Shiga Prefecture, from 1905 until 1908, and opened there a Young Men's Christian Association (YMCA). He started a successful architectural firm, W. M. Vories and Company, in 1908, and founded Omi Sales, a firm importing building materials, in 1909 (it became Omi Kyodaisha in 1934). After 1910, he marketed and later also produced the ointment Mentholatum. He established the Omi Mission in 1918, which became the Omi Brotherhood in 1934, and led it. He established a tuberculosis sanatorium in 1917. He became a Japanese citizen in 1941. He wrote *A Mustard-Seed in Japan* (Omi-Hachiman, 1922). Died May 7, 1964, in Omi-Hachiman, Japan. *References*: Cyril Davey, *Fifty Lives for God* (Valley Forge, Pa., 1973), pp. 156–59; Grace N. Fletcher, *The Bridge of Love* (New York, 1967); *JBEWW*; and *KEJ*.

VOTAW, MAURICE E(LDRED) (1899–1981). Journalist and educator, born April 29, 1899, in Eureka, Missouri. Votaw graduated from the University of Missouri. He founded the first school of journalism in Asia at St. John's University in Shanghai and served on its faculty from 1922 to 1939 and in 1948–1949. He was a lecturer in English at the Central Political University in China from 1939 to 1948, and advisor to the Ministry of Information of the Republic of China in Chungking from 1939 to 1946, and in Nanking from 1946 to 1948. He was also a press advisor to Chiang Kai-shek. He was assistant professor of journalism at the University of Missouri-Columbia from 1950 until his retirement in 1970. Died December 17, 1981, in Columbia, Missouri. *References*: Maurice E. Votaw Papers, University of Missouri-Columbia Library; *Columbia Missourian*, December 19, 1981; and *DAS*.

W

WADE, H(ERBERT) WINDSOR (1886–1968). Leprologist, born November 23, 1886, in Haddonfield, New Jersey. Wade attended McGill University and graduated from Tulane University. He was an instructor in pathology and bacteriology at Tulane University from 1912 to 1915, resident pathologist at Charity Hospital in New Orleans from 1913 to 1915, pathologist and bacteriologist at the Bureau of Science in Manila from 1916 to 1918, and professor of pathology and bacteriology at the College of Medicine and Surgery of the University of the Philippines from 1918 to 1922. He was chief pathologist of the Culion Leper Colony in the Philippines from 1922 to 1931, and acting chief physician from 1922 to 1924. He was medical director of the Leonard Wood Memorial for the Eradication of Leprosy until 1948, and again a pathologist at the Culion Leper Colony after 1948. He was coauthor of *A Description of Leprosy* (Manila, 1927), and founder and editor of the *International Journal of Leprosy*. Died June 8, 1968, in Culion, Philippines. *References*: H. Windsor Wade Papers, Leonard Wood Memorial for the Eradication of Leprosy, Bethesda, Md.; *DPB* 3; *CCDP*; Esmond R. Long, "H. W. Wade, 1886–1968," *International Journal of Leprosy* 36 (1968) 349–55; *WWP*; and *WWWA*.

WADE, JONATHAN (1798–1872). Missionary, born December 10, 1798, in Otsego, New York. Wade graduated from Hamilton Literary and Theological Institution (later Colgate University), and was ordained in 1923. He was a missionary under the American Board of Commissioners for Foreign Missions (ABCFM) in Burma from 1823 until his death. He was arrested by the Burmese at the outset of the Anglo-Burmese War, and was sentenced to be executed, but was saved by the advancing British Army. He served in Amherst, Burma, and later in Maulmain from 1827 to 1830, and in Kyouk Phyoo, Arakan, from 1841 until 1852. He was again at Maulmain from 1852 until his death. He reduced to writing two Karen dialects, began *The Anglo Karen Dictionary* (Rangoon, 1883), and wrote *A Vocabulary of the Sgau Karen Language* (Tavoy, Burma, 1849); *A Dictionary of Boodhism and Burman Literature* (Maulmain, Burma, 1852); and *Karen Vernacular Grammar* (Maulmain, 1861). Died June 10, 1872, in Rangoon, Burma. *References*: *EM*; and Walter N. Wyeth, *The Wades, Jonathan Wade, D.D., and Deborah B. L. Wade* (Philadelphia, 1872).

WAKEFIELD, CYRUS (1811–1873). Merchant, born in Roxbury, New Hampshire, and came to Boston as a boy. Wakefield was a pepper merchant in Singapore until 1875, when he left Singapore, and returned to the United States. He was later the largest importer of East India goods in the United States, established rattan works in Wakefield, Massachusetts, and had extensive holdings in railroads and real estate. Died October 26, 1873, in Wakefield (formerly South Reading), Massachusetts. *References*: *NYT*, October 27, 1873.

WALES, NYM. *See* SNOW, HELEN FOSTER

WALKER, EGBERT H(AMILTON) (1899–   ). Botanist, born June 12, 1899, in Chicago. Walker graduated from the universities of Michigan and Wisconsin and Johns Hopkins University. He was an instructor in the Canton Christian College from 1922 to 1926, an aide in the division of plants of the U.S. National Museum from 1928 to 1942, an assistant curator there from 1942 to 1946, and an associate curator from 1946 to 1958. He conducted a botanical mission to Okinawa and Southern Ryukyu Islands in 1951, and described his experiences in the *Annual Report of the Smithsonian Institution* for 1952. He wrote *Important Trees of the Ryukyu Islands* (n.p., 1954), and *Flora of Okinawa and the Southern Ryukyu Islands* (Washington, D.C., 1976). *References*: *AMWS*.

WALLACE, WILLIAM L(INDSEY) ("BILL") (1908–1951). Medical missionary, born January 17, 1908, in Knoxville, Tennessee. Wallace graduated from the University of Tennessee Medical College. He was a medical missionary under the Foreign Mission Board of the Southern Baptist Convention in China from 1935 until his death. He served as a surgeon in a hospital in Wuchu, South China, where he worked through World War II. He was arrested by the Communists in 1950. Died February 1951, in prison. *References*: Bill Wallace Collection, Wallace Memorial Baptist Church, Knoxville, Tenn.; *ESB*; and Jesse C. Fletcher, *Bill Wallace of China* (Nashville, 1963).

WALLER, LITTLETON WALTER TAZEWELL (1856–1926). Marine Corps officer, born September 26, 1856, in York County, Virginia. Waller was commissioned a second lieutenant in the U.S. Marine Corps in 1880. He served with the European Squadron and in the Spanish-American War in Cuba. He came to the Philippines in 1899 and was stationed at Cavite naval base. He took part in the China Relief Expedition in 1900. He served again in the Philippines from 1900 to 1902, and commanded troops in Samar in 1902. Ordered to end Filipino resistance, his troops were responsible for massacring Filipinos and destroying villages. He was court-martialed in 1902, but was acquitted. He served in Panama and Cuba from 1904 to 1911; commanded the marine barracks at

Mare Island Navy Yard from 1911 to 1914; commanded the marine brigade occupying Veracruz, Mexico, in 1914–1915; served in Haiti in 1915–1916, and commanded the Advanced Base Force in Philadelphia. He retired with the rank of major general in 1920. Died July 26, 1926, in Atlantic City, New Jersey. *References*: Robert Asprey, "Waller of Samar," *Marine Corps Gazette* 45 (May 1961): 36–41, and (June 1961): 44–48; Kenneth R. Young, "Atrocities and War Crimes: the Cases of Major Waller and General Smith," *Leyte-Samar Studies* 12 (1978): 64–77; *NYT*, July 14, 1926; and *WWWA*.

WALN, ROBERT, JR. (1794–1825). Author, born October 20, 1794, in Philadelphia. Waln became involved in the importing business conducted by his father with Canton and East Asia. He made a trip to Canton in 1819–1820, and in 1823 published an elaborate work on the geography, history, religion, social conditions, customs, economy, and trade relations between China and the United States, entitled *China: Comprehending a View of the Origin of that Empire & a Full Description of American Trade to Canton* (Philadelphia, 1823). Died July 4, 1825, in Providence, Rhode Island. *References*: Waln Family Papers, Library Company of Philadelphia; *DAB*; William S. Hastings, "Robert Waln, Jr.: Quaker Satirist and Historian," *Pennsylvania Magazine of History and Biography* 76 (1952): 71–80; Jean G. Lee, *Philadelphians and the China Trade 1784–1844* (Philadelphia, 1984), pp. 122–31; and *NCAB* 10:361.

WALSH, JAMES EDWARD (1891–1981). Missionary, born April 30, 1891, in Cumberland, Maryland. Walsh graduated from St. Mary's College (Emmitsburg, Md.). He joined the Maryknoll Fathers in 1912, studied at the Maryknoll Seminary and was ordained in 1915. He went to China in 1918 in the first group of Maryknoll missionaries sent there; was superior of the Maryknoll China Mission at Yeungkong, Kwangtung Province, after 1919; and was prefect apostolic of the mission in 1924. He founded the Little Flower Seminary in Kongmoon in 1926, and the Chinese Sisters of the Immaculate Heart of Mary there in 1927. He was named first bishop of the vicariate of Chiangmen in South China in 1927 and was consecrated a bishop—the first American Catholic to be consecrated a bishop in China. He was elected superior general of Maryknoll in 1936, and lived in the United States until 1946. In 1940 he went to Japan as a secret mediator between Japan and the United States in a futile attempt to head off the threatened war. He returned to China in 1948 as head of the Catholic Central Bureau in Shanghai. After the Communists came to power in 1949, they closed the bureau in 1951. He was arrested in 1958 and charged with being an enemy of the Chinese people, counterrevolutionary activities, and being a spy for the United States and the Vatican. He was sentenced to twenty years in prison. He served twelve years of his term in Ward Road Prison in Shanghai, was released in 1970, and returned to the United States. He wrote a biography of Daniel L. McShane.* Died July 29, 1981, in Ossining, New York. *References*:

DACB; Ray Kerrison, *Bishop Walsh of Maryknoll* (New York, 1962); and *NYT*, July 30, 1981.

WANLESS, WILLIAM JAMES (1865–1933). Medical missionary, born May 1, 1865, in Charleston, Ontario, Canada. Wanless graduated from University Medical College (New York City). He was a missionary under the Board of Foreign Missions of the Presbyterian Church in the United States in India from 1889 until 1928. He served in Sangli from 1889 until 1892, where he established a small dispensary, moved in 1892 to Miraj, and established a hospital there. He established the first missionary medical school in India in 1897, and a leper asylum in 1900. He returned to the United States in 1928 because of ill health, but was called back to India in 1930 to help in the establishment of a tuberculosis sanitarium. He wrote *An American Doctor at Work in India* (New York, 1932). Died March 3, 1933, in Glendale, California. *References*: William James Wanless Papers, Presbyterian Historical Society, Philadelphia; *DAB*; *NCAB* 36:533; Lillian E. Wanless, *Knight of the Kingdom, William Wanless, M.D. of India* (New York, 1955); and Lillian E. Wanless, *Wanless of India, Lancet of the Lord* (Boston, 1944).

WARD, FERDINAND DE WILTON (1812–1891). Missionary, born July 9, 1812, in Bergen, Genesee County, New York. Ward graduated from Union College and Princeton Theological Seminary, and was ordained in 1836. He was a missionary under the American Board of Commissioners for Foreign Missions (ABCFM) in Madura, India, from 1836 until 1847. He edited the first periodical advocating abstinence from alcohol to be printed in a Hindu language. He returned to the United States in 1847; held a pastorate in Genesee, New York, until 1871; served as chaplain in the Union Army during the Civil War; and was later district secretary for the American Bible Society. He wrote *India and the Hindus* (New York, 1851). Died August 11, 1891, in Clarens, Switzerland. *References*: Ferdinand de Wilton Ward Papers, Dickinson College Library, Carlisle, Pa.; and *ACAB*.

WARD, FREDERICK TOWNSEND (1831–1862). Adventurer, born November 29, 1831, in Salem, Massachusetts. Ward attended Norwich University (Vt.). From 1848 until 1859, he roamed the world, serving with William Walker in Nicaragua and with the French in the Crimea. He came to China in 1859 and served on a Yangtze River steamer from Shanghai. In 1860 he became involved in the Taiping Rebellion, organized a group of foreign mercenaries, and succeeded in capturing Sungkiang from the rebels. By 1862, he organized the "Ever-Victorious Army" composed of Chinese under foreign officers, served as its commander, and succeeded in capturing Tsingpu. Died September 21, 1862, after being wounded in the attack on Tzeki. *References*: Hallett Abend, *The God from the West, a Biography of Frederick Townsend Ward* (Garden City, N.Y., 1947); *DAB; NCAB* 2:56; Richard O. Patterson, "The Mandarin from Salem,"

USNIP 79 (February 1953): 156–67; Richard O. Patterson, *The Mandarin from Salem* (New York, 1979); Robert Rantoul, *Frederick Townsend Ward* (Salem, 1908); Richard J. Smith, *Mercenaries and Mandarins: The Ever-Victorious Army in Nineteenth-Century China* (Millwood, N.Y., 1978); and Jonathan Spence, *To Change China: Western Advisers in China 1620–1960* (Boston, 1969), ch. 3.

WARD, JOHN E(LLIOTT) (1814–1902). Lawyer and diplomat, born October 2, 1814, at Sunbury, Liberty County, Georgia. Ward attended Amherst College and Harvard University, and was admitted to the bar in 1835. He practiced law in Savannah, and was solicitor-general for the eastern district of Georgia from 1836 to 1838, U.S. district attorney for Georgia in 1838–1839, member of the Georgia legislature from 1839 to 1857, president of the state senate in 1857–1858, and mayor of Savannah from 1854 until 1856. He was a minister to China from 1858 until 1860. He exchanged the ratification of the new treaty with China, and settled outstanding American claims. He did not take part in the Civil War. He moved to New York in 1866, and practiced law there. Died November 29, 1902, in Dorchester, Liberty County, New York. *References*: *DAB*; William M. Gabard, "John Elliot Ward: A Georgia Elitist in the Celestial Empire, 1858–60," *West Georgia College Studies in the Social Sciences* 22 (1983): 53–62; *NCAB* 1:373, and *NYT*, December 1, 1902.

WARD, RALPH ANSEL (1882–1958). Missionary, born June 26, 1882, in Leroy, Ohio. Ward graduated from Ohio Wesleyan University and Boston University School of Theology, and was ordained in 1910. He held pastorates in Massachusetts from 1906 to 1909. He was a missionary under the Board of Foreign Missions of the Methodist Episcopal Church in China from 1909 until his death. He served in the Foochow district from 1910 to 1915, and was associate secretary of the Board of Missions for Eastern China from 1919 to 1924; president of Anglo-Chinese College, Foochow, from 1925 to 1927; and secretary of the Committee on Conservation and Advance in the United States from 1928 to 1932. He returned to China and was a missionary in Nanking from 1933 to 1937. Elected bishop in 1937, he served in the Chengtu area from 1937 to 1940, and in Shanghai from 1940 to 1942. He was interned by the Japanese from 1942 to 1945. He was back in China from 1947 until 1951, went to Hong Kong in 1951 and worked among refugees until his retirement in 1953, but continued to work in Hong Kong and Taiwan. Died December 10, 1958, in Hong Kong. *References*: *EWM*; *NYT*, December 29, 1958; and *Time*, December 22, 1958.

WARNE, FRANCIS WESLEY (1854–1932). Missionary, born December 30, 1854, in Erin, Ontario, Canada. Warne graduated from Albert College (Ontario), Garrett Bible Institute (Evanston, Ill.) and Northwestern University, and was ordained in 1876. He held pastorates in Pullman and Austin, Illinois, from 1884 to 1887. He was a missionary under the Board of Foreign Missions of the Methodist Episcopal Church in India from 1888 until 1928, serving in Calcutta from 1888 until 1900. He was elected missionary bishop of the Methodist Episcopal Church for Southern Asia in 1900 (and general superintendent in 1920), and supervised the work in India until his retirement in 1928. He was in charge of north India with headquarters in Lucknow until 1924, and of south India and Burma with headquarters in Bangalore until 1928. He organized the Methodist Episcopal church in the Philippines in 1903. He was a leader of the Mass Mission Movement and wrote *India's Mass Movement* (New York, 1915). He returned to the United States in 1928. Died February 29, 1932, in Brooklyn, New York. *References*: *EWM; NCAB* 26:71; *NYT*, March 2, 1932; and *WWWA*.

WARNER, LANGDON (1881–1955). Student of Oriental art, born August 1, 1881, in Cambridge, Massachusetts. Warner graduated from Harvard University and studied art in Japan. He was curator in the Boston Museum of Fine Arts from 1903 to 1916, director of the American School of Archaeology in Peking in 1912, and instructor and lecturer at Harvard University from 1912 to 1915. He was vice-consul on a confidential mission in Siberia from 1917 to 1919, and was a liaison officer between the Allied forces and the Czech legion. He was director of the Pennsylvania Museum of Art in Philadelphia from 1917 to 1923, and curator of the Oriental collection at the Fogg Museum of Art of Harvard University from 1923 to 1950. He was a member of the Pumpelly-Carnegie expedition to Russian Turkestan in 1904; made many long visits to Japan; led two expeditions for the Fogg Museum to Tunhuang, China, in 1923 and 1925; and described the first expedition in *The Long Old Road to China* (Garden City, N.Y., 1926). He was a consultant to the American Commission for the Protection and Salvage of Artistic and Historic Monuments in War Areas during World War II, and served as special consultant to the Monuments, Fine Arts, and Archives section of General Headquarters of the Supreme Commander for the Allied Powers (SCAP). He wrote *Japanese Sculpture of the Suiko Period* (New Haven, 1923); *The Enduring Art of Japan* (Cambridge, Mass., 1932); *The Craft of the Japanese Sculptor* (New York, 1936); and *Buddhist Wall-Paintings, a Study of a Ninth-Century Grotto at Wan Fo-hsia* (Cambridge, 1938). Died June 9, 1955, in Cambridge, Massachusetts. *References*: Theodore Bowie, ed., *Langdon Warner through His Letters*, (Bloomington, Ind., 1966); *FEQ* 15 (1956): 315–16; *Harvard Journal of Asiatic Studies* 18 (155): 447–50; W. James, "Langdon Warner," in *Saturday Club: A Century Completed 1920–1956*, ed. Edward W. Forbes and J H. Finley (Boston, 1958), pp. 299–306; *KEJ*; and *NYT*, June 10, 1955.

WARNSHUIS, A(BBE) L(IVINGSTON) (1877–1958). Missionary, born November 22, 1877, at Clymer, New York. Warnshuis graduated from Hope College (Holland, Mich.) and New Brunswick Theological Seminary, and was ordained in 1900. He was a missionary under the Board of Foreign Missions of the Reformed Church in America in China from 1900 until 1920. He was senior secretary of the International Missionary Council in New York City and treasurer of the General Synod of the Reformed Church from 1920 until his retirement in 1943. He was administrative head of the Church World Service from 1946 to 1948. Died March 17, 1958, in Bronxville. *References*: Abbe L. Warnshuis Papers, Union Theological Seminary Library, New York City; *CDCWM*; N. Goodall, *Christian Ambassador* (London, 1963); *HDRCA; LC; NYT*, March 18, 1958; and *WWWA*.

WARREN, CHARLES P(RESTON) (1921–1987). Anthropologist, born April 7, 1921, in Chicago. Warren graduated from Northwestern and Indiana universities and the University of Chicago. He carried out fieldwork with the Tagbanuwa and the Batak in Palawan in the Philippines in 1950–1951 and later in Thailand. He was a physical anthropologist with the American Graves Registration Group, U.S. Department of the Army, in the Philippines and Japan from 1951 to 1955; was instructor and assistant professor of anthropology at the University of Illinois in Chicago from 1957 to 1976; was associate professor there after 1976; and research associate of the Philippine Studies program at the University of Chicago after 1956. He was also a physical anthropologist at the U.S. Army Central Identification Laboratory at Sattahip, Thailand, from 1973 to 1975. He wrote *The Batak of Palawan: Culture in Transition* (Chicago, 1964); and *The Philippines: A Collection of Papers* (Chicago, 1976). Died December 22, 1987, in Chicago. *References*: *AMWS; JAS* 48 (1989): 240–41; and *Who's Who among Black Americans, 1980–81* (Northbrook, Ill., 1981).

WASHBURN, GEORGE THOMAS (1832–1927). Missionary, born September 5, 1832, in Lenox, Massachusetts. Washburn graduated from Williams College and Andover Theological Seminary, studied medicine in New York City, and was ordained in 1859. He was a missionary under the American Board of Commissioners for Foreign Missions (ABCFM) in the Madura mission, India, from 1860 until his retirement in 1900. He served in Battalagundu from 1860 to 1869, and at Pasumalai after 1869. He organized and was head of the Pasumalai Theological School from 1869 to 1892, superintendent of the Teachers' Training Institute, and president of Pasumalai College from 1875 to 1900. Died March 20, 1927, in Meriden, Connecticut. *References*: *AndoverTS; Hewitt*; and A. J. Saunder, *Dr. Washburn of Madura, an Appreciation. A Missionary Biography* (Pasumalai, 1928).

WASSON, JAMES R(OBERT) (1847–1923). Engineer, born January 11, 1847, in Ohio. Wasson served in the Union Army during the Civil War, and then graduated from the U.S. Military Academy in 1871. He was commissioned a second lieutenant in the cavalry in 1871. He was a professor of mathematics at the Sapporo Agricultural College in Hokkaido in 1871–1872, constructed roads in the Island of Yezo in 1872–1873, was surveyor-in-chief to the *Kaitakuski* of Hokkaido in 1873, and made a topographical survey of Yezo until 1874. He was chief engineer with the rank of colonel in the Imperial Army of Japan in the Formosa campaign of 1874, and a professor of civil engineering in the Imperial University of Tokyo in 1875–1876. He returned to the United States in 1876 and was paymaster in the army until 1883, when he was dismissed. He practiced law in Des Moines, Iowa, after 1885. Died February 17, 1923, in Washington, Iowa. *Reference: Foreign Pioneers.*

WEBB, EDWARD (1819–1898). Missionary, born December 15, 1819, in Lowestoft, Suffolk, England. Webb graduated from Andover Theological Seminary, and was ordained in 1845. He was a missionary under the American Board of Commissioners for Foreign Missions (ABCFM) in Madura District, India, from 1845 to 1864. He held pastorates in Darby, Pennsylvania; Glasgow, Delaware; and Andover, New Jersey, from 1864 to 1873. He was a financial secretary of Lincoln University and a pastor at Oxford, Pennsylvania, after 1873. He was founder and editor of the *Quarterly Repository* (India), and one of the revisers of the Tamil Bible. He wrote *Hindoo Life, with Pictures of the Men, Women and Children of India* (Philadelphia, 1866). Died April 6, 1898, in Oxford, Pennsylvania. *Reference: AndoverTS.*

WEBSTER, JAMES B(ENJAMIN) (1879–1929). Missionary, born September 29, 1879, in Passumpsic, Vermont. Webster graduated from the universities of Richmond and Pennsylvania, Crozer Theological Seminary, and Hartford Seminary Foundation. He was a missionary under the Foreign Missionary Board of the Southern Baptist Convention in China after 1908. He served on the staff of the Shanghai Baptist Theological Seminary after 1912; and was director of the Yangtze Social Center from 1918 to 1920. He wrote *Christian Education and the National Consciousness in China* (New York, 1923). Died December 8, 1929, in Stockton, California. *References*: James B. Webster Papers, Hoover Institution on War, Revolution and Peace, Stanford, Calif.; *Alphabetical Biographical Catalog, The Crozer Theological Seminary, 1855–1933* (Chester, Pa., 1933); and *CR* 61 (1930): 182–83.

WEDEMEYER, ALBERT C(OADY) (1897–1989). Army officer, born July 9, 1897, in Omaha, Nebraska. Wedemeyer graduated from the U.S. Military Academy in 1919. He served in the Philippines and China from 1922 to 1925. He attended the German War College from 1936 to 1938. He served in the War Plans Division of the War Department General Staff, and was chief of the Strategy Section of the War Plans Division and later chief of the Strategy and Policy Section of the Operations Division from 1941 until 1943. He was deputy commander of the Southeast Asia Command in 1943–1944, chief of staff to Generalissimo Chiang Kai-shek, and commander of the American forces in China from 1944 to 1946. He returned to China in 1947 on a fact-finding mission to appraise the political, military, and economic conditions in China and Korea. He was later commanding officer of the Second Army, director of the Plans and Operations Division of the War Department General Staff, and commanding general of the Sixth Army. He retired with the rank of lieutenant general in 1951. He published his memoirs, *Wedemeyer Reports!* (New York, 1958). Died December 17, 1989, in Ft. Belvoir, Virginia. *References*: Albert C. Wedemeyer Papers, Hoover Institution on War, Revolution and Peace, Stanford, Calif.; *DAMIB*; John Keegan, ed., *Wedemeyer on War and Peace*, (Stanford, Calif., 1987); *NYT*, December 20, 1989; Jonathan Spence, *To Change China: Western Advisers in China 1620–1960* (Boston, 1969), ch. 9; and William Stueck, *The Wedemeyer Missions: American Politics and Foreign Policy during the Cold War* (Athens, Ga., 1984).

WEEKS, EDWIN LORD (1849–1903). Painter, born in Boston. Weeks studied art in Paris. He traveled to South America in 1869, and went to the Middle East in 1870, 1872, 1878, and 1892. He made an expedition to India in 1882, and produced an extensive series of paintings. He wrote an account of his journey in *From the Black Sea through Persia and India* (New York, 1896). He lived in Paris after 1883. Died November 17, 1903, in Paris. *References*: *ACAB*; *DAB*; Kathleen D. Ganley and Leslie K. Paddock, *Art of Edwin Lord Weeks (1849–1903)* (Durham, N.H., 1976); *NCAB* 12:505; *NYT*, November 18, 1903; D. Dodge Thompson, "Edwin Lord Weeks, American Painter of India," *Magazine Antiques* 128 (1985): 246–57; and *WWWA*.

WESLEYAN METHODIST CHURCH OF AMERICA: MISSIONARY SOCIETY. Founded in 1862 but only began work in 1889. It began missionary work in India in 1910, in Japan in 1919, in China in 1946 (terminated in 1949), in Taiwan in 1954, and in the Philippines in 1963. It was later renamed the Department of World Missions. *References*: Wesleyan Methodist Church of America Records, Wesleyan Church Archives and Historical Society, Marion, Ind.; and Ira F. McLeister and Roy S. Nicholson, *History of the Wesleyan Methodist Church of America* (Marion, Ind.; 1959).

WEST CHINA UNION UNIVERSITY. Founded in Chengtu in 1910, it was chartered by the Regents of the State of New York in 1934. It was taken over by the Communist government in 1951. *References*: *Fenn; Lutz*; and Lewis C. Walmsley, *West China Union University* (New York, 1974).

WESTENGARD, JENS (IVERSON) (1871–1918). Lawyer, born September 14, 1871, in Chicago. Westengard graduated from Harvard Law School. He was assistant professor of law at Harvard Law School from 1899 until 1903. He was assistant general advisor to the Siamese government from 1903 to 1905, acting general advisor from 1905 to 1907 and in 1908–1909, and general advisor from 1909 to 1915. He served as a judge on the Court of Appeals of Siam. He was a professor of international law at the Harvard Law School from 1915 until his death. He was also a member of the Hague Permanent Arbitration Court. Died

September 17, 1918, in Cambridge, Massachusetts. *References*: *NCAB* 18:202; and *WWWA*.

WHARTON, G(REENE) L(AWRENCE) (1847–1906). Missionary, born July 17, 1847, near Bloomington, Indiana. Wharton attended Southern Illinois College (Carbondale, Ill.), and graduated from Bethany College. He was a missionary under the Foreign Christian Missionary Society of Cincinnati in India from 1882 until 1899. He was stationed in Harda, Central Provinces, in 1883, which became headquarters of the first India work of the Disciples of Christ. He opened a school for boys in Harda. He undertook additional work among the Gond and Kurku tribesmen of the Satura mountains in 1888–1889, and in 1893 established a training school for missionary workers in Harda. He provided relief service during the great famine of 1897. He returned to the United States in 1899 and was a pastor in Hiram, Ohio, until 1903, but went back to India in 1904 and assisted in the work of the Bible college in Japalpur. Died November 4, 1906, in Calcutta. *References*: *DAB*; and Emma R. Wharton, *Life of G. L. Wharton* (Chicago, 1913).

WHEELER, RAYMOND ALBERT (1885–1974). Army officer and engineer, born July 31, 1885, in Peoria, Illinois. Wheeler graduated from the U.S. Military Academy in 1911, and was commissioned a second lieutenant in the Corps of Engineers. He served in the Panama Canal Zone, in the Veracruz expedition of 1914, and in World War I. From 1922 to 1940, he served in the District of Columbia; the Panama Calan Zone; Wilmington, North Carolina; and Rock Island, Illinois, in various capacities. He was chief of the U.S. Military Mission to the Persian Gulf area in 1941–1942. He was commanding general of the Services of Supply of the U.S. Army Forces in the China-Burma-India theater of operations in 1942–1943, directing the building of Ledo Road which linked India and China. He was deputy supreme allied commander of the Southeast Asia Command from 1943 to 1945, and commanding general of the India-Burma theater in 1945. He was chief of the U.S. Army Corps of Engineers from 1946 until his retirement in 1949. He was principal engineering advisor for the International Bank for Reconstruction and Development (the World Bank) from 1949 until 1964. He was involved in the survey of the water resources of the Indus Basin to solve the dispute between India and Pakistan, and headed an international mission in 1957–1958 that prepared a program for the development of the Lower Mekong River Basin in Indochina. He remained chairman of the Mekong Committee's international advisory board until 1969. Died February 8, 1974, in Washington, D.C. *References*: *CB* 1957; *NCAB* 58:346; *NYT*, February 10, 1974; and *WWWA*.

WHEELER, WILLIAM (1851–1932). Engineer, born December 6, 1851, in Concord, Massachusetts. Wheeler graduated from Massachusetts Agricultural College (Amherst). He opened an office in Boston in 1873 as a civil engineer.

He was in Japan from 1876 until 1880, was professor of mathematics and civil engineering at the Sapporo Agricultural College, and served as president of the college from 1877 until 1880. He planned and constructed harbor improvements, bridges, highways, and railroads, and founded a weather bureau and an astronomical observatory. He was civil engineer of the Japanese Imperial Colonial Department from 1878 until 1880. He returned to the United States in 1880, established an office in Boston, and was engaged in engineering. Died July 1, 1932, in Concord, Massachusetts. *References*: *DAB*; and *Foreign Pioneers*.

WHEELER, W(ILLIAM) REGINALD (1889–1963). Missionary educator, born July 10, 1889, in Tidioute, Pennsylvania. Wheeler graduated from Yale University, Auburn (N.Y.) Theological Seminary, and Harvard University, and was ordained in 1914. He was a missionary educator at Nanking, China, in 1915–1916; member of faculty of the Hangchow College from 1916 to 1919; and secretary of Peking University (later Yenching University) from 1919 to 1921. He returned to the United States in 1923, and was executive secretary of the Board of Foreign Missions from 1923 to 1932. He went back to China in 1932, and served as a missionary educator at the University of Nanking from 1932 to 1936. He was again secretary of the Board of Foreign Missions from 1938 to 1942. He served in the U.S. Army during World War II. He was research editor of the education and information division of the Board of Foreign Missions in 1946–1947, executive secretary of Yale-in-China from 1947 to 1949, and assistant director of the China Institute in America in New York City in 1949–1950. He wrote *China and the World War* (New York, 1919); *Flight to Cathay: An Aerial Journey to Yale-in-China* (New Haven, Conn., 1949); and a biography of John E. Williams.* Died August 19, 1963, in New York City. *References*: *NCAB* 49:103; *NYT*, August 21, 1963; and *WWWA*.

WHERRY, ELWOOD MORRIS (1843–1927). Missionary, born March 26, 1843, in South Bend, Pennsylvania. Wherry graduated from Jefferson (later Washington and Jefferson) College and Princeton Theological Seminary, and was ordained in 1867. He was a missionary under the Board of Foreign Missions of the Presbyterian Church in the U.S.A. in India from 1867 to 1889, and from 1898 to 1922. He served in the Punjab mission, was stationed in Rawalpindi, and was later transferred to Ludhiana, where he served until 1883. He was superintendant of the mission press until 1883; professor of Old Testament literature and church history at the theological seminary in Saharanpur, Uttar Pradesh, from 1883 to 1888; and stated clerk of the synod of India. He was founder of the Urdu periodical *Nur Afshan*, and was its editor in 1872–1873 and from 1899 to 1909. He was district secretary of the American Tract Society in Chicago from 1889 to 1898. He returned to India in 1898, served again in Ludhiana, and was chiefly occupied with educational and literary work. He wrote *Zeinab the Penjabi* (New York, 1895); *Islam and Christianity in India and the Far East* (New York, 1907); and *Our Missions in India 1834–1924* (Boston,

1926). Died October 5, 1927, in Indiana, Pennsylvania. *References*: *DAB; OAB;* and *WWWA*.

WHERRY, JOHN (1837–1919). Missionary, born May 23, 1837, near Shippensburg, Pennsylvania. Wherry graduated from Princeton University and Princeton Theological Seminary, and was ordained in 1864. He was a missionary under the Board of Foreign Missions of the Presbyterian Church in the U.S.A. in China from 1864 until his death. He was superintendent of the Presbyterian mission press in Shanghai and president of Shantung College, professor of astronomy at North China Union College, and professor of New Testament exegesis at North China Union Theological School. He was later a teacher and director of the Peking Language School, and chairman of the commission for translating the Bible into literary Chinese. Died January 2, 1919, in Peking. *Reference*: *WWWA*.

WHITE, FRANCIS JOHNSTONE (1870–1959). Educator, born September 24, 1870, in Decatur, Illinois. White attended William Jewell College (Liberty, Mo.), graduated from Ottawa (Kans.) University and Rochester Theological Seminary, and was ordained in 1897. He was a missionary under the American Baptist Missionary Union in China from 1901 until 1935. He was principal of a boys' boarding school in Ningpo from 1901 to 1904, and professor of New Testament in the Theological Seminary in Shaohsing from 1904 to 1906. A founder of the University of Shanghai, he was a professor of the history of religion there from 1906 until his retirement in 1935, and its president from 1912 to 1928. Died July 20, 1959, in Ontario, California. *Reference*: *WWWA*.

WHITE, FRANK R(USSELL) (1875–1913). Educator, born June 8, 1875, in Milburn, Illinois. White attended Bellevue College (Nebr.), and graduated from the University of Chicago. He came to the Philippines in 1901, and was division superintendent of schools, assistant to the general superintendent of education, assistant director of education, and director of education of the Philippines from 1909 until his death. Died August 17, 1913, in Manila. *References*: Glen A. May, *Social Engineering in the Philippines: The Aims, Execution, and Impact of American Colonial Policy, 1900–1913* (Westport, Conn., 1980), pp. 116–19; *NYT*, August 20, 1913; and *WWWA*.

WHITE, JOHN (1782–1840). Naval officer, born in Marblehead, Massachusetts. White was an officer in the U.S. Navy, becoming a lieutenant in 1816. He was in Indochina in 1819–1820 (probably the first American in Indochina), and wrote an account of his visit in *History of a Voyage in the China Sea* (Boston, 1823). In Saigon he obtained vocabularies of the Vietnamese language (published in 1838 in the *Transactions of the American Philosophical Society*). Died in Boston. *Reference*: P. Midan, "Les Européens qui Ont Vu le Vieux Hué: John White," *Bulletin des Amis du Vieux Hué* 24 (1937): 93–318.

WHITE, JOHN ROBERTS (1879–1961). Army officer, born October 10, 1879, in Reading, England. White attended Oxford University. He served in the Greek Foreign Legion in the Greco-Turkish War of 1897, spent time in British Columbia and Alaska salmon fishing, and was with White Pass and Yukon Railway from 1896 to 1899. He enlisted in the U.S. Infantry in 1899, and served in the Philippines from 1899 to 1901. He served in the Philippine Constabulary from 1901 until 1914, when he retired due to a physical disability with the rank of colonel. He was superintendent of the Iwahig Penal Colony from 1906 to 1908, and acting governor of the Agusan Province in 1911. He served the American Red Cross and the Rockefeller Foundation in Austria, Germany, Switzerland, and the Scandinavian countries in 1916–1917, and in the U.S. Army during World War I. He was provost marshall of Paris after the armistice. He was later a ranger and then chief ranger in the Grand Canyon National Park, superintendent of the Sequoia and General Grant national parks and the National Valley National Monument, chief of operations of Region Three of the National Park Service, and director of Region Four. He retired in 1947. He wrote *Bullets and Bolos: Fifteen Years in the Philippines* (New York, 1928). Died December 9, 1961, in Napa, California. *References*: John Roberts White Papers, University of Oregon Library, Eugene, Ore.; *Elarth; NYT*, December 11, 1961; and *WWWA*.

WHITE, MOSES C(LARK) (1819–1900). Missionary, born July 24, 1819, in Paris, Oneida County, New York. White graduated from Wesleyan University and Yale Theological Seminary. He was a missionary under the Board of Foreign Missions of the Methodist Episcopal Church in China from 1847 until 1853. He conducted a dispensary in Foochow. He also translated the Gospel of Matthew into the Foochow dialect. He returned to the United States in 1853, graduated from Yale Medical School, practiced medicine in New Haven and was a teacher at Yale Medical School. Died October 24, 1900, in New Haven, Connecticut. *Reference*: *EWM*.

WHITE, THADDEUS C. (? – ?). Adventurer, who worked as marshal of the American court in Shanghai. He subsequently undertook many shady dealings as a commercial agent, and was involved in the attempted sale of palace treasures from the Manchu Palace in Mukden. He was the husband of Derling Yu-keng, who wrote under the name of Princess Der Ling, contended that she had served as lady-in-waiting and interpreter for the Empress-Dowager Tz'u-hsi, and published bogus memoirs of the events in the Manchu Court in the latter days of the reign of the Empress Dowager, entitled *Two Years in the Forbidden City* (New York, 1911) and *Son of Heaven* (New York, 1935).

WHITFORD, HARRY NICHOLS (1872–1941). Forester, born March 11, 1872, in Manhattan, Kansas. Whitford graduated from Kansas State College and the University of Chicago. He was a botanical collector for the Bureau of Science in the Philippines from 1904 to 1906, chief of the division of investigation of the Bureau of Forestry of the Philippines from 1906 to 1912, and assistant professor of silviculture in the University of the Philippines from 1910 to 1912. He was the founder (with F. W. Foxworthy*) of the school of forestry in the College of Agriculture. He was an authority on the forestry of the Philippines and North Borneo, and on crude rubber. He wrote *The Forests of the Philippines* (Manila, 1911). He was assistant professor of tropical forestry at Yale University from 1916 to 1923, chief of the crude rubber survey in the U.S. Department of Commerce from 1923 to 1925, and manager of the crude rubber division of the Rubber Manufacturer Association after 1925. He spent much time in the rubber-growing regions of East Asia. Died May 17, 1941, in Bronxville, New York. *References*: *AMWS; CB* 1941; and *NYT*, May 18, 1941.

WHITMAN, CHARLES O(TIS) (1842–1910). Biologist, born December 14, 1842, in North Woodstock, Maine. Whitman graduated from Bowdoin College. He was principal of Westford Academy (Mass.) from 1868 to 1872, and taught in a high school in Boston from 1872 to 1874. He studied in Naples and Leipzig. He was professor of zoology at the Imperial University of Tokyo from 1879 to 1881. He pioneered zoological studies in Japan, introduced German-style biological research methods to Japan, including the use of the microscope, and was called "the father of zoology in Japan." He was assistant in zoology at the Museum of Comparative Zoology at Harvard University from 1882 to 1886, director of the Allis Lake Laboratory in Miwaukee from 1886 to 1889, and professor of zoology at Clark University from 1889 to 1892, and at the University of Chicago after 1892. He was also director of the Marine Biological Laboratory at Woods Hole from 1893 to 1908. Died December 6, 1910, in Chicago. *References*: *DAB; DSB; KEJ; NCAB* 11:73; *NYT*, December 7, 1910; and *WWWA*.

WHITMARSH, HUBERT PHELPS (1863–1935). Adventurer and business-man, born August 10, 1863, in Madoc, Ontario, Canada, and grew up in New-port, Southeastern Wales. He ran away to sea at fourteen and was a sailor until 1884, when he went to Australia. He was a miner, pearl diver, and barber until 1887, when he came to the United States, and was an importer of essential oils initially in New York City, and, after 1881, in Boston. He began writing for American magazines, and wrote several books based on his experiences. He came to the Philippines in 1899 as a correspondent for *The Outlook* magazine. He was the first civil governor of the province of Benguet in 1900–1901. He settled in Baguio, and went into business. He established the Banguet Commercial Company, started a sawmill, built the Baguio Hotel and the Garden Theater, and went into gold mining. Died April 6, 1935, in Manila. *References*: James J. Halsema, "Hubert Phelps Whitmarsh: Adventurer, Writer, and First Governor of Baguio," *BAHC* 9 (April-June 1981): 51–75; and 9 (July-September 1981): 65–82; and *WWWA*.

WHITNEY, COURTNEY (1897–1969). Army officer, lawyer, and government official, born May 20, 1897, in Tacoma Park, Maryland. Whitney graduated from National University Law School (Washington, D.C.). He joined the Aviation Section of the U.S. Signal Corps in 1917, and was commissioned a second lieutenant. He came to the Philippines in 1924, resigned from the army in 1927, and practiced law in Manila until 1939. He returned to active service in 1940, was assistant chief of the Legal Division of the Army Air Corps from 1940 to 1943, and was assistant judge advocate of the Army Air Force in 1943. He was assigned to General Douglas MacArthur's staff in 1943, and was head of the Philippine Regional Section. He was chief of the Government Section of the Supreme Commander for the Allied Powers (SCAP)* in Japan from 1945 to 1951, and military secretary of the United Nations Command in the Korean War in 1950–1951. He returned to the United States in 1951, and retired with the rank of major general. He then served as MacArthur's personal secretary in New York City and was later an executive with Remington Rand until 1964. He wrote *MacArthur: His Rendezvous with History* (New York, 1956). Died March 21, 1969, in Washington, D.C. *References*: Courtney Whitney Papers, MacArthur Memorial Archives, Norfolk, Va.; *CB* 1951; *CCDP; EP* 18:183; *KEJ; NYT*, March 22, 1969; Justin Williams, *Japan's Political Revolution: A Participant's Account* (Tokyo, 1979), ch. 5; and *WWWA*.

WHITTEMORE, NORMAN C(LARK) (1870–1952). Missionary, born June 7, 1870, in Brooklyn, New York. Whittemore graduated from Yale University and Union Theological Seminary, studied at Yale Divinity School, and was ordained in 1896. He was a missionary under the Board of Foreign Missions of the Presbyterian Church in the U.S.A. in Korea from 1896 until 1938. He first served in P'yongyang, opened a station in Syen Chyun in 1901, and was principal of a boys' academy there from 1921 to 1924. He served on the faculty of the Kennedy School of Missions from 1926 to 1929, returned to Korea in 1929, and was general secretary of the Christian Literature Society of Korea from 1929 until 1938. He returned to the United States and retired in 1938. Died May 15, 1952, in Berkeley, California. *References*: *NCAB* 40:504; and *NYT*, May 19, 1952.

WIDDOES, H(OWARD) W. (1873–1951). Missionary, born in Kansas. Widdoes was a missionary under the United Brethren Church in the Philippines from 1903 until 1945. He served in San Fernando, La Union, in the Ilocano country of the Mountain Province. He founded Protestant churches in La Union and Mountain Province, established the Evangel Press in 1905, founded *Naimbag a Damao*, a paper in the Ilocano language, and opened the first mission hospital there in 1922. He was interned by the Japanese during World War II, first in Baguio and later in Los Baños. He returned to the United States in 1945. Died July 25, 1951, in Sebastopol, California. *Reference*: "Biography of H. W. Widdoes,'' Ms., United Brethren Mission Records, United Methodist Archives, Madison, N.J.

WILCOCKS, BENJAMIN CHEW (1776–1845). Merchant, born December 13, 1776, in Philadelphia. Wilcocks began in the China trade as a supercargo in 1798–1799, and was supercargo again in 1803. He returned to Canton in 1811 or 1812 as a resident commission agent, and was involved in the sale of opium. He was consul in Canton from 1813 to 1822. He returned to the United States in 1827. Died December 1, 1845, in Philadelphia. *References*: Chew Family Papers, Historical Society of Pennsylvania, Philadelphia; and Jean G. Lee, *Philadelphians and the China Trade 1784–1844* (Philadelphia, 1984), pp. 44–46.

WILDER, JAMES AUSTIN (1868–1934). Artist, born May 27, 1868, in Honolulu, Hawaii. Wilder graduated from Harvard University, attended Harvard Law School, and studied art in Europe. He went to Japan in 1895, and was assistant editor of *The Box of Curios*, a humorous magazine, until 1897. He was a member of the Smithsonian Institution–University of Pennsylvania expedition to the Ryukyu Islands in 1897–1898. He studied art again in Europe, resided in Honolulu from 1906 to 1914, had a studio in New York City from 1914 to 1922, and lived again in Honolulu from 1922 until his death. He was involved in the work of the Boy Scouts of America, and developed the Sea Scout division of the Boy Scouts in 1919. Died July 4, 1934, in Honolulu, Hawaii. *References*: James Austin Wilder "Journal," Ms., Peabody Museum Library, Harvard University, Cambridge, Mass.; "The Journal of James Austin Wilder During His Visit to Sarawak in 1898," *Sarawak Museum Journal*, new series, 16 (1968): 407–34, and 17 (1969): 315–35; and *NCAB* 37:164.

WILDER, ROBERT P(ARMELEE) (1863–1938). Association official, born August 2, 1863, in Kolhapur, India, to American parents; came to the United States at age twelve; and grew up in Princeton, New Jersey. Wilder graduated from Princeton University and Union Theological Seminary. He was national secretary of the Young Men's Christian Association (YMCA) of India and Ceylon from 1899 to 1902. He returned to the United States in 1902 because of ill health, and was secretary of the British Student Christian Movement from 1905 to 1916, general secretary of the Student Volunteer Movement for Foreign Missions from 1919 to 1927, and executive secretary of the Near East Christian Council from 1927 to 1933. He wrote *Christian Service among Educated Bengalese* (n.p., 1895), and *Among India's Students* (New York, 1899). Died March 28, 1938, in Oslo, Norway. *References*: Robert P. Wilder Papers, Divinity School Library, Yale University, New Haven, Conn.; *ACAB*; Ruth W. Braisted, *In This Generation. The Story of Robert P. Wilder* (New York, 1941); *CDCWM; UnionTS;* and *WWWA*.

WILDER, ROYAL GOULD (1816–1887). Missionary, born October 27, 1816, in Bridport, Vermont. Wilder graduated from Middlebury College and Andover Theological Seminary, and was ordained in 1845. He was a missionary under American Board of Commissioners for Foreign Missions (ABCFM) in western India from 1846 to 1857. He was stationed at Ahmadnagar from 1846 to 1852, at Kolhapur from 1852 to 1857, and again at Kolhapur as an independent missionary from 1861 until 1871, when the mission there was transferred to the Board of Foreign Missions of the Presbyterian Church in the U.S.A. He served there until 1875. He edited *Missionary Review* in Princeton, New Jersey, from 1877 to 1887. He wrote *Mission Schools in India* (New York, 1861). Died October 7, 1887, in New York City. *References*: *AndoverTS; EM*; and Robert A. Schneider, "Royal G. Wilder: New School Missionary in the ABCFM, 1846–1871," *American Presbyterians* 64 (1986): 73–82.

WILDES, HARRY E(MERSON) (1890–1982). Educator and government official, born April 3, 1890, in Middletown, Delaware. Wildes graduated from Harvard University and the University of Pennsylvania. He was a teacher of history and social science in high schools in Philadelphia from 1915 to 1923, from 1926 to 1930, and from 1934 to 1945. He was literary editor of the *Philadelphia Public Ledger* from 1930 to 1934, and associate editor of *Philadelphia Forum* magazine from 1933 to 1945. He was professor of economics and social sciences at Keio University in Tokyo in 1924–1925, regional specialist for Japan in the State Department in 1945–1946, chief of the information management branch in the Government Section of the General Headquarters of the Supreme Commander for the Allied Powers (SCAP)* in Japan from 1947 to 1950, and chief of the Division of Political and Social Affairs in the Civil History section in 1950–1951. He later taught at the International College of the Sacred Heart in Tokyo, the New School of Social Research (New York City), and Superior State College (Superior, Wis.) until 1958. He wrote *The Press and Social Currents in Japan* (Chicago, 1927); *Japan in Crisis* (New York, 1934); *Aliens in the East: A New History of Japanese Foreign Intercourse* (Philadelphia, 1937); and *Typhoon in Tokyo* (New York, 1952). Died February 25, 1982, in Concordville, Delaware County, Pennsylvania. *References*: *CA; Philadelphia Inquirer*, February 26, 1982; and *WWA*.

WILDMAN, ROUNSEVELLE (1864–1901). Consul, born March 19, 1864, in Batavia, New York. Wildman graduated from Syracuse University. He was newspaper reporter and editor of *The Idaho Statesman* in Boise, Idaho, from 1885 to 1890. He was U.S. consul in Singapore from 1890 to 1893; consul in Bremen, Germany, in 1893–1894; owner and editor of *The Overland Monthly* from 1894 to 1897; consul in Hong Kong in 1897–1898; and consul general there from 1898 to 1901. He represented the Straits Settlement at the Columbia Exposition. He was a journalist in Hong Kong, and wrote *China's Open Door, a Sketch of China's Life and History* (Boston, 1900), and two works of fiction:

The Panglima Muda, a Romance of Malaya (San Francisco, 1894), and *Tales of the Malayan Coast, from Penang to the Philippines* (Boston, 1899). Lost February 22, 1901, with the *City of Rio de Janeiro*, which sank in the Golden Gate, San Francisco. *References*: Papers of Rounsevelle and Edwin Wildman, Manuscript Division, Library of Congress; and *NYT*, February 23, 1901.

WILFLEY, LEBBEUS REDMAN (1867–1926). Lawyer and judge, born March 30, 1867, in Audrain County, Missouri. Wilfley graduated from Central College (Fayette, Mo.) and Yale University Law School, and was admitted to the bar in 1893. He practiced law in St. Louis until 1901. He was attorney general of the Philippines from 1901 to 1906, and the first judge of the U.S. Court for China from 1906 to 1909. He returned to the United States in 1909, and resumed the practice of law in St. Louis until 1917, and later in New York City. Died May 26, 1926, in Greenwich, Connecticut. *References*: *NCAB* 41:448; and *WWWA*.

WILLAUER, WHITING (1906–1962). Lawyer and aviation executive, born November 30, 1906, in New York City. Willauer graduated from Princeton University and Harvard Law School. He practiced admiralty law in Boston from 1931 until 1939. He was an attorney in the Criminal Division of the Department of Justice. He was executive secretary of China Defense Supplies, Incorporated, from 1941 to 1944, and director of the Far East and Special Territories Branch of the Foreign Economic Administration in 1944–1945. With General Claire L. Chennault,* he established the Civil Air Transport (CAT) Company in China in 1946. He was its executive vice president and later its president from 1946 until 1954. He resigned in 1954 and sold CAT to the Central Intelligence Agency. He was ambassador to Honduras from 1954 to 1958, and to Costa Rica from 1958 until his retirement in 1961. Died August 6, 1962, at Nantucket, Massachusetts. *References*: Whiting Willauer Papers, Princeton University Library, Princeton, N.J.; William M. Leary, Jr., "Portrait of a Cold War Warrior: Whiting Willauer and Civil Air Transport," *Modern Asian Studies* 5 (1971): 373–88; *NYT*, August 7, 1962; and *WWWA*.

WILLIAMS, CHANNING MOORE (1829–1910). Missionary, born July 18, 1829, in Richmond, Virginia. Williams graduated from the College of William and Mary and the Theological Seminary (Alexandria, Va.), and was ordained in 1857. He was a missionary under the Domestic and Foreign Missionary Society of the Protestant Episcopal Church in the United States of America in China from 1855 to 1859, and in Japan from 1859 until 1889. He served in Shanghai from 1855 to 1859. He was one of the first two missionaries in Japan, and constructed the first Protestant church building in Nagasaki in 1861. He was consecrated bishop of China and Japan in 1866 and lived in China in 1868–1869, but then moved to Osaka, Japan, until 1873, when he moved to Tokyo. In 1874, his jurisdiction was divided and he became bishop of Yedo (Tokyo).

He founded a boys' school (later Rikkyo University), Trinity Divinity School, and St. Luke's Hospital in Tokyo. He also translated the Book of Common Prayer into Japanese. He resigned his diocese in 1889, but remained in Japan, moving to Kyoto in 1895. He returned to the United States in 1908. Died December 2, 1910, in Richmond, Virginia. *References*: *CDCWM; DAB;* Hisakazu Kaneko, *A Story of Channing Moore Williams: The Bishop of Yedo* (Tokyo, 1965); Maria Minor, *Pioneer Missionary in Japan: Channing Moore Williams* (New York, 1959); *NCAB* 5:553; and *NYT*, December 3, 1910.

WILLIAMS, DANIEL R(ODERICK) (1871–1931). Lawyer, born May 13, 1871, in Dawn, Missouri. Williams attended Avalon (Mo.) College and graduated from the University of Michigan. He practiced law in San Francisco from 1896 to 1900. He was private secretary to Bernard Moses,* member of the Philippine Commission in 1900–1901, secretary of commerce of the Philippines from 1901 to 1903, and associate judge of the Philippine Court of Land Registration from 1903 to 1905. He practiced law in Manila after 1905. He wrote *The Odyssey of the Philippine Commission* (Chicago, 1913), and *The United States and the Philippines* (Garden City, N.Y., 1924). *Reference*: *WWWA.*

WILLIAMS, E(DWARD) T(HOMAS) (1854–1944). Missionary and diplomat, born October 17, 1854, in Columbus, Ohio. Williams graduated from Bethany College, and was ordained in 1875. He held pastorates in Springfield, Illinois; Denver; Brooklyn, New York; and Cincinnati from 1877 until 1887. He was a missionary under the Foreign Christian Missionary Society in China from 1887 until 1896, when he left the ministry. He was translator at the U.S. consulate in Shanghai in 1896–1897, vice-consul-general in Shanghai 1897–1898, translator at the Shanghai Arsenal for the Chinese government from 1898 to 1901, Chinese secretary at the legation in Peking from 1901 to 1908, and consul in Tientsin in 1908–1909. He was assistant chief of the Division of Far Eastern Affairs in the State Department from 1909 to 1911, first secretary of the legation in Peking from 1911 to 1913, and chief of the Far Eastern Division in the State Department from 1914 to 1918. He was a professor of Oriental languages and literature at the University of California at Berkeley from 1918 until his retirement in 1927. He wrote *China Yesterday and To-Day* (New York, 1923); *A Short History of China* (New York, 1928); and *Tibet and Her Neighbors* (Berkeley, Calif., 1937). Died January 27, 1944, in Berkeley, California. *References*: E. T. Williams Papers, Bancroft Library, University of California, Berkeley, Calif.; *DAB S3; DADH;* Dimitry D. Lazo, "An Enduring Encounter: E. T. Williams, China and the United States," Ph.D. diss., University of Illinios-Urbana, 1977; Dimitri E. Lazo, "The Making of a Multicultural Man: The Missionary Experiences of E. T. Williams," *PHR* 51 (1982): 357–83; and *NCAB* 18:238.

WILLIAMS, GEORGE BURCHELL (1842–1912). Financier, born December 5, 1842, in Lockport, Niagara County, New York. Williams was engaged in banking and trade in Lafayette, Indiana, after 1858. He served in the Union Army during the Civil War. He was supervisor of internal revenue for Indiana in 1868–1869, and deputy commissioner of internal revenue in Washington in 1871. He was financial advisor to the Japanese government, assisting in the reorganization of the Japanese system from 1871 until 1875. He was special commissioner of Japan in Europe in connection with financial affairs in 1872 and 1875. He returned to the United States in 1876. Died March 15, 1912. *References*: *NCAB* 11:331; and *WWWA*.

WILLIAMS, HERMON P(ORTER) (1872–1958). Missionary, born in Iowa City, Iowa. Williams graduated from the State University of Iowa, Drake University and the University of Chicago. He served in the Spanish-American War in the Philippines. He was a missionary under the Foreign Christian Missionary Society in the Philippines from 1901 until 1910. He served in Laoag, among the Ilocanos. He then established a mission at Vigan, province of Abra. He edited *English-Ilocano Manual and Dictionary* (Manila, 1907). He returned to the United States in 1910 because of ill health, and held pastorates in Albuquerque, New Mexico; Tacoma, Washington; Paterson, New Jersey; and Etna, New York. He also taught Bible at the University of Washington. Died July 21, 1958, in Albuquerque. *References*: Hermon P. Williams Papers, Disciples of Christ Historical Society, Nashville, Tenn.

WILLIAMS, JOHN E(LIAS) (1871–1927). Missionary and educator, born June 11, 1871, in Coshocton, Ohio. Williams graduated from Marietta College and Auburn Theological Seminary, and was ordained in 1899. He was a missionary under the Board of Foreign Missions of the Presbyterian Church in the U.S.A. from 1899 until his death. He taught in a boys' school in Nanking until 1906, served among the Chinese students in Waseda University in Tokyo in 1906–1907, and was then involved in the establishment of the University of Nanking. He was vice president of the university from 1911 until his death. Shot March 24, 1927, by a Chinese soldier during the capture of Nanking by the Chinese Nationalist forces. *References*: *DAB; NCAB* 21:122; *NYT*, March 26, 1927; and W. Reginald Wheeler, *John E. Williams of Nanking* (New York, 1937).

WILLIAMS, JUSTIN, SR. (1906–   ). Government official, born March 2, 1906, in Greenbrier, Arkansas. Williams graduated from Arkansas State Teachers College and the University of Iowa. He was professor of history and economics at the Wisconsin State College (River Falls) from 1928 to 1942. He served in the U.S. Army Air Force during World War II. He was legislative division chief and later parliamentary and political division chief in the government section of the General Headquarters of the Supreme Commander for the Allied Powers

(SCAP)* from 1946 to 1952. He wrote *Japan's Political Revolution Under MacArthur: A Participant's Account* (Tokyo, 1979). He was later an international affairs advisor on the staff of the commander-in-chief, Far East Command, in Tokyo; chief of the Korea Division of the International Cooperation Administration in Washington, D.C.; chief of the administration's Interregional Technical Cooperation Administration in Paris, France; assistant to the president for research at the University of Maryland from 1962 to 1967; and international affairs specialist in the Department of the Army from 1967 until his retirement in 1971. *References*: Justin Williams, Sr., Collection, University of Maryland Library, College Park, Md.; *AMWS*; and George W. Ware, Jr., "Political Change during the Allied Occupation of Japan (1945–1952): The Justin Williams Papers in the East Asia Collection, McKeldin Library, University of Maryland," *Committee on East Asian Libraries Bulletin* no. 72 (October 1983): 1–18.

WILLIAMS, MARK (1834–1920). Missionary, born October 28, 1834, at Peddy's Run (now Shandon), Butler County, Ohio. Williams graduated from Miami University and Lane Seminary. He was a missionary in China from 1866 until 1916, and served as missionary under the American Board of Commissioners for Foreign Missions (ABCFM) at Kalgan on the Great Wall. During the Boxer Rebellion in 1900, he escaped by camel caravan, with other American and Swedish missionaries, to Urga (now Ulan Bator), Mongolia. He returned to the United States in 1900 and wrote *Across the Gobi Desert. A Narrative of an Escape during the Boxer Uprising, June to September 1900* (Hamilton, Ohio, 1901). He was back in China in 1902, taught at the North China College in Tungchow until 1909, and lived at Taiku, Shansi, from 1909 to 1916. Died August 9, 1920, at sea, near Yokohama, Japan. His *Autobiography; and, Across the Desert of Gobi* (edited with notes by Mark Eccles [Madison, Wis., 1981]) was published posthumously. The letters of his wife, **ISABELLA RIGGS WILLIAMS** (1840–1897), were published in *By the Great Wall, Letters from China* (New York, 1909).

WILLIAMS, SAMUEL T(ANKERSLEY) ("HANGING SAM") (1897–   ). Army officer, born August 25, 1897, in Denton, Texas. Williams enlisted in the Texas National Guard as a private in 1916, was commissioned second lieutenant in the infantry in 1917, and served during World War I. He was staff officer of the 95th Infantry Division in 1941–1942, assistant division commander in 1942–1943; corps chief of staff in 1945; commanding general of the Twenty-Fifth Infantry Division in Korea in 1952–1953; deputy commander of the Second Korean Corps in 1953; and commanding general of the Sixteenth Corps in Sendai, Japan, in 1953–1954; of the Ninth Corps in Korea in 1954; and of the Fourth Army in 1955. He was chief of the United States Army Military Assistance and Advisory Group (MAAG) in Vietnam from 1955 to 1960. He retired in 1960 with the rank of lieutenant general. *References*: Samuel T. Williams Papers,

Hoover Institution for War, Revolution and Peace, Stanford, Calif.; *DVW*; and *WWA*.

WILLIAMS, SAMUEL WELLS (1812–1884). Missionary, diplomat and sinolog, born September 22, 1812, in Utica, New York, and grew up in Hartford, New York. Williams attended Rensselaer Polytechnic Institute (Troy, N.Y.) and then studied printing. He was a printer under the American Board of Commissioners for Foreign Missions (ABCFM) in Canton, China, from 1833 to 1835. He then took charge of the board's printing press in Macao and assisted in publishing *The Chinese Repository**. He compiled *Easy Lessons in Chinese* (Macao, 1842); *Chinese Topography* (Macao, 1844); and *An English and Chinese Vocabulary in the Court Dialect* (Macao, 1844); and edited a revised edition of *A Chinese Commercial Guide* (Macao, 1844). He wrote *The Middle Kingdom: A Survey of the Geography, Government, Education, Social Life, Arts, Religion, etc. of the Chinese Empire and Its Inhabitants* (New York, 1848), which became the standard book on China for most of the nineteenth century. He was a member of the *Morrison* party (see the *Morrison* Incident*) which sailed to Japan in 1837 in an unsuccessful attempt to repatriate Japanese castaways. He learned Japanese, and translated the Gospel of Matthew into that language. He returned to Japan in 1853–1854 as official interpreter with the Perry Expedition.* He was secretary and interpreter in the U.S. legation in Peking from 1856 to 1876, and helped conclude the Treaty of Tientsin in 1858, which ended the Anglo-French War against China. He also accompanied the party to Peking in 1859 to exchange ratifications of the treaty. He wrote *A Tonic Dictionary in the Chinese Language in the Canton Dialect* (Canton, 1856), and *A Syllabic Dictionary of the Chinese Language* (Shanghai, 1874). In 1870, he assisted Sweden in obtaining a treaty with China. He retired in 1876, returned to the United States, and was professor of Chinese language and literature at Yale University after 1877. He revised and enlarged *The Middle Kingdom* (New York, 1883). Died February 16, 1884, in New Haven, Connecticut. *References*: Samuel Wells Williams Family Papers, Yale University Library, New Haven, Conn; S. Wells Williams, *A Journal of the Perry Expedition to Japan, 1853–1854*, ed. E. W. Williams (Yokohama, 1910); *CDCWM; DAB; EM; KEJ; NCAB* 1:422; and Martin Ring, "Anson Burlingame, S. Wells Williams and China, 1861–1870," Ph.D. diss., Tulane University, 1972.

WILLIAMS, THOMAS RHYS (1928–   ). Anthropologist, born June 13, 1928, in Martins Ferry, Ohio. Williams graduated from Miami University (Oxford, Ohio), the University of Arizona, and Syracuse University. He served in the U.S. Navy from 1946 to 1948. He was assistant and associate professor at California State University (Sacramento) from 1956 to 1965, and professor of anthropology at Ohio State University (Columbus) after 1965. He carried out fieldwork in Borneo in 1959–1960 and 1962–1963, and wrote *The Dusun: A North Borneo Society* (New York, 1966), and *A Borneo Childhood: Encultur-

ation in Dusun Society (New York, 1969). *References*: *AMWS; WWA;* and *WWMW*.

WILLIS, BAILEY (1857–1949). Geologist, born May 31, 1857, in Idlewild-on-Hudson, New York. Willis graduated from the Columbia School of Mines. He became a geologist for the Northern Pacific Railway in 1880, and explored Washington Territory. He was with the U.S. Geological Survey from 1882 to 1915, conducted geological explorations in China in 1903–1904, and later wrote *Friendly China: Two Thousand Miles Afoot among the Chinese* (Stanford, 1949). He helped the Argentine government establish a geological survey, and examined the geological features of Turkey. He was a professor of geology at Stanford University from 1915 to 1922, and was a consulting geological engineer after 1922. Died February 19, 1949, in Palo Alto, California. *References*: *BGSA* 73 (1962): 55–72; *DSB; NCAB* 37:53; *BMNAS* 35 (1961): 333–50; and *PGSA* 1962, pp. P55–P72.

WILLOUGHBY, CHARLES A(NDREW) (1892–1972). Army officer, born March 8, 1892, in Heidelberg, Germany. Willoughby came to the United States as a young man, and was naturalized in 1910. He graduated from Gettysburg (Pa.) College, and studied at the University of Kansas. He was commissioned a second lieutenant in 1914. He served on the Mexican border in 1916–1917 and during World War I. He was a military attaché in Venezuela, Colombia, and Ecuador. He was assistant chief of staff for intelligence, chief of intelligence on General Douglas MacArthur's staff from 1941 to 1946, and chief of intelligence in the General Headquarters of the Supreme Commander for the Allied Powers (SCAP)* in Japan from 1946 until 1951. He wrote *Shanghai Conspiracy: The Sorge Spy Ring, Moscow, Shanghai, Tokyo, San Francisco, New York* (New York, 1952) and (with John Chamberlain) *MacArthur, 1941–1951* (New York, 1954). He retired in 1951, and was later editor of *Foreign Intelligence Digest*. Died October 25, 1972, in Naples, Florida. *References*: Charles A. Willoughby Papers, Archives and Library, MacArthur Memorial, Norfolk, Va.; *CA; KEJ; NYT*, October 26, 1972; and *WWWA*.

WILLOUGHBY, WESTEL W(OODBURY) (1867–1945). Political scientist, born in Alexandria, Virginia. Westel W. Willoughby graduated from Johns Hopkins University. He was a professor of political science at Johns Hopkins University from 1897 until his retirement in 1933. He succeeded his brother, William Franklin Willoughby, as a constitutional advisor to the Chinese government in 1916–1917, and was technical advisor to the Chinese delegation at the Washington Conference of 1921–1922 and the Geneva Opium Conference of 1924–1925. He wrote *China at the Conference* (Baltimore, 1922); *Opium as an International Problem, the Geneva Conferences* (Baltimore, 1925); *Foreign Rights and Interests in China* (Baltimore, 1927); *The Sino-Japanese Controversy and the League of Nations* (Baltimore, 1935); and *Japan's Case Re-Examined*

(Baltimore, 1940). Died March 26, 1945, in Washington, D.C. His brother, **WILLIAM FRANKLIN WILLOUGHBY** (1867–1960), political scientist, graduated from Princeton University. William Franklin Willoughby was a professor of jurisprudence and politics at Princeton University, and an advisor to the Chinese government from 1914 to 1916 on the drafting of the constitution. He was later director of the Institute of Government Research at Princeton from 1916 to 1932. *References*: William Franklin Willoughby Papers, College of William and Mary Library, Williamsburg, Va.; *DAB S3; NCAB* 13:435; *NCAB* A:212; and *NYT*, March 27, 1945.

WILSON, ERNEST HENRY (1876–1930). Plant collector, born February 15, 1876, in Chipping, Campden, Gloucestershire, England. Wilson became a gardener at the Birmingham Botanical Garden in 1892, and a worker and student at the Royal Botanic Gardens at Kew in 1897. He studied at the Royal College of Science (South Kensington). He went on a plant-collecting trip to China from 1899 to 1902, and went again from 1903 to 1906. He was collector for the Arnold Arboretum of Harvard University in China from 1907 to 1909 and again in 1910; in Japan in 1914–1915; in Formosa, Korea, and Japan from 1917 to 1919; and in India, Australia, New Zealand, and Africa from 1920 to 1922. He was assistant keeper of the Arnold Arboretum from 1919 to 1927, and keeper from 1927 until his death. He introduced more than a thousand species of plants. He wrote *A Naturalist in Western China* (London, 1913); *China, Mother of Gardens* (Boston, 1929); and *Aristocrats of the Garden* (Boston, 1926). Died October 15, 1930, in an automobile accident, near Worcester, Massachusetts. *References*: E. H. Wilson Notebooks, Arnold Arboretum, Cambridge, Mass.; Kristin S. Clausen and Shiu-ying Hu, "Mapping the Collecting Localities of E. H. Wilson in China," *Arnoldia* 40 (1980): 139–45; E.H.M. Cox, *Plant-Hunting in China* (New York, 1986), pp. 136–151; *DAB*; Richard A. Howard, "E. H. Wilson as a Botanist," *Arnoldia* 40 (1980): 102–38; and *WWWA*.

WILSON, JAMES HARRISON (1837–1925). Army officer and engineer, born September 2, 1837, near Shawneetown, Illinois. Wilson graduated from the U.S. Military Academy in 1860, and was commissioned a second lieutenant in the topographical engineers. He served in the Union Army during the Civil War. He resigned from the army in 1870, and was involved in railroad construction and management until 1883, when he settled in Wilmington, Delaware, and became involved in various business enterprises. He went to China in 1885–1886 to investigate possible railway developments, and wrote *China: Travels and Investigation in the "Middle Kingdom": A Study of Its Civilization and Possibilities, with a Glance at Japan* (New York, 1887). He served during the Spanish-American War in Puerto Rico and Cuba, and was second in command of the American forces sent to suppress the Boxer Rebellion. He wrote his recollections, *Under the Old Flag: Recollections of Military Operations in the War for the Union, the Spanish War, the Boxer Rebellion, etc.* (New York,

1912). Died February 23, 1925, in Wilmington, Delaware. *References*: James H. Wilson Papers, Manuscript Division, Library of Congress; Gart D. Best, "Ideas without Capital: James H. Wilson and East Asia, 1885–1910," *PHR* 49 (1980): 453–70; *DAB; DAMIB*; David Healy, *US Expansionism: The Imperialist Urge in the 1890s* (Madison, Wis., 1970), ch. 4; Edward G. Longacre, *From Union Star to Top Hat: A Biography of the Extraordinary General James Harrison Wilson* (Harrisburg, Pa., 1972); Thomas J. McCormick, "The Wilson-McCook Scheme of 1896–1897," *PHR* 36 (1967): 47–58; *NCAB* 2:205; and *NYT*, February 24, 1925.

WILSON, LAURENCE LEE (1885–1961). Prospector and folklorist, born September 16, 1885, in Omaha, Nebraska. Wilson graduated from the University of California at Berkeley, attended San Francisco Theological Seminary, graduated from McCormick Theological Seminary, and was ordained in 1916. He held several pastorates in Washington and California until 1921. He then left the ministry and became a mining prospector. He went to the Philippines in 1930 and prospected for mineral deposits. He was interned in Camp Holmes in Baguio during World War II. He later resumed mining activities and community activities in Baguio City and northern Luzon, and collected the folklore of the Mountain Province. He wrote *The Skyline of the Philippines* (Baguio, 1953). Died January 17, 1961, in Baguio City. *Reference*: Ernest J. Freig, "Laurence Lee Wilson: Recorder of Mountain Province Folklore," *Saint Louis Quarterly* 5 (March-June 1967): 41–66.

WILSON, MARGARET W(OODROW) (1886–1944). Singer, daughter of President Woodrow Wilson, born April 16, 1886, in Gainesville, Florida. Wilson attended Goucher College (Baltimore), Peabody Conservatory of Music (Baltimore), and studied voice. She gave song recitals. She was consultant and writer for an advertising agency after 1923, and then a bond saleswoman. She went to India in 1938 and joined the ashram of Sri Aurobindo in Pondicherry, India, in 1940. Died February 14, 1944, in Pondicherry. *References*: *NYT*, February 14, 1944; Christine Sadler, *Children in the White House* (New York, 1967), pp. 237–49; and *WWWA*.

WINSLOW, MIRON (1789–1864). Missionary, born December 11, 1789, in Williston, Vermont. Winslow graduated from Middlebury College and Andover Theological Seminary, and was ordained in 1818. He was a missionary under the American Board of Commissioners for Foreign Missions (ABCFM) in Ceylon from 1819 to 1833, serving at Uduvil and working among the Tamils. He served in Madras, India, from 1836 until his death. He opened there a mission station specializing in printing and publishing, and was involved in compiling *A Comprehensive Tamil and English Dictionary of High and Low Tamil* (Madras, 1862), and in revising the Tamil Bible. Died October 22, 1864, at Cape Town,

South Africa, on his way to the United States. *References*: *ACAB; AndoverTS; DAB; EM; NCAB* 1:183; and *WWWA*.

WISER, WILLIAM H(ENDRICKS) (1890–1961). Missionary, born in Potts-town, Pennsylvania. Wiser graduated from the University of Chicago. He was a missionary under the Board of Foreign Missions of the Presbyterian Church in the U.S.A. in India from 1915 to 1960. He was on the staff of Allahabad Agricultural Institute, teacher of English and economics at Ewing Christian College in Allahabad and professor of rural sociology at North India Theological College in Saharanpur. He went in 1925 to the village of Karimpur, between the Ganges and Jumna rivers. With his wife, **CHARLOTTE (MELINA) V(IALL) WISER**, he established the India Village Service in Uttar Pradesh in 1945, which was aimed at improving rural life by helping the people help themselves, and directed it until 1960. They wrote *Behind Mud Walls* (New York, 1930), and *Behind Mud Walls, 1930–1960* (Berkeley, 1963). He wrote *The Hindu Jajmani System: A Socio-Economic System Interrelating Members of Hindu Community in Services* (Lucknow, 1936), and *Building the Social and Economic Foundation for an Indigenous Church in the United Province* (Luck-now, 1940). She wrote *The Foods of a Hindu Village of North India* (Allahabad, 1937), and *Four Families of Karimpur* (Syracuse, N.Y., 1978). He returned to the United States in 1960 because of ill health. Died February 21, 1961, in Uniontown, Pennsylvania. *References*: William H. Wiser Papers, Divinity School Library, Yale University, New Haven, Conn.; and *NYT*, February 22, 1961.

WOOD, LEONARD (1860–1927). Army officer, government official, and co-lonial administrator, born October 9, 1860, in Winchester, New Hampshire. Wood graduated from Harvard Medical School, and was commissioned as a surgeon with the U.S. Army Medical Corps in 1886. He served with the "Rough Riders" in Cuba during the Spanish-American War; and was military governor of the city of Santiago, Cuba, in 1898; of the province of Santiago in 1898–1899; and of Cuba from 1899 until 1902. He was promoted to brigadier-general in the regular army in 1901. He was military governor of Moro Province in the Philippines from 1903 to 1906, and commanded the Philippines Division from 1906 to 1908. He was chief of staff of the army from 1910 to 1914, and later in charge of the Department of the East. He was candidate for the Republican nomination for the presidency in 1916 and in 1920. He was a member of the special mission to the Philippines in 1920 (see the Wood-Forbes Mission*), and was governor general of the Philippines from 1921 to 1927. Died August 7, 1927, in Boston. *References*: Leonard Wood Papers, Manuscript Division, Li-brary of Congress; *ACAB*; Ronald F. Chapman, *Leonard Wood and Leprosy in the Philippines: The Culion Leper Colony, 1921–1927* (Washington, D.C., 1982); *DAB; DADH; DAMIB; EAH; EP* 4:368–69; *Gleeck/Governors*, ch.8; Peter G. Gowing, *Mandate in Moroland: The American Government of Muslim*

Filipinos 1899–1920 (Diliman, Quezon City, 1977), chs. 5–6; Jack C. Lane, *Armed Progressive: General Leonard Wood* (San Rafael, Calif., 1978); *NCAB* 28:107; *NYT*, August 7, 1927; Michael P. Onorato, "Governor General Wood, Conservator of Filipinization," *BAHC* 4 (October-December 1976): 74–87; Michael Onorato, "Leonard Wood and the Philippine Cabinet Crisis of 1923," *Journal of East Asiatic Studies* 2 (1967): 1–74; Michael Onorato, *Leonard Wood as Governor General: A Calendar of Selected Correspondence* (Manila, 1969); Michael Onorato, "Leonard Wood: His First Year as Governor General, 1921–1922," in *A Brief Review of American Interest in Philippine Development and Other Essays* (Berkeley, Calif., 1968), pp. 67–80; Michael Pearlman, "Emotional Factors in America's Western Pacific Policy: Wood and Stimson in the Philippines," *Journal of Psychohistory* 11 (1983): 243–69; *Pier*; Wayne W. Thompson, "Governor of the Moro Province: Wood, Bliss and Pershing in the Southern Philippines, 1903–1913," Ph.D. diss., University of California at San Diego, 1975; and *WWWA*.

WOOD, MARY ELIZABETH (1861–1931). Missionary and librarian, born August 22, 1861, near Batavia, Elba Township, New York, and grew up in Batavia. Wood was the first librarian of the Richmond Library in Batavia from 1889 until 1899. She went to China in 1899 and taught English. She became a lay missionary in China in 1904. She established the Boone Library at Boone College in 1910. She studied at Pratt Institute (Brooklyn, N.Y.) and Simmons College (Boston). She tried to develop the library into a public library and established branch libraries and mobile libraries in schools and factories. She started a Boone Library School in 1920. It was part of Huachung University from 1924 to 1930, withdrew in 1930, and continued as an independent institution until 1950 (when it merged into the National Wuhan University). Died May 1, 1931, in Wuchang, China. *References: DAB; NAW;* and *NYT*, May 2, 1931.

WOOD, WILLIAM MAXWELL (1809–1880). Physician, born May 27, 1809, in Baltimore. Wood graduated from the University of Maryland and entered the navy as an assistant surgeon in 1829. He served in the Seminole and Mexican wars. He was fleet surgeon of the East India Squadron from 1856 to 1858. He was present during the capture of the Barrier Forts in Canton, accompanied Townsend Harris* to Siam, and wrote an account of the mission in *Fankwei; or The San Jacinto in the Seas of India, China, and Japan* (New York, 1859). He served in the Union Navy during the Civil War. He was surgeon general of the navy, and chief of the Bureau of Medicine and Surgery from 1869 until his retirement in 1871. Died March 1, 1880, in Owing's Mills, Baltimore County, Maryland. *References: ACAB*; and *DAMB*.

WOOD, WILLIAM W. (ca. 1805– ?). Adventurer and editor from Philadelphia. Wood came to Canton, China, in 1825, and was editor of the *Canton Register*, the first English-language China coast newspaper, in 1827–1828. He returned to the United States and wrote *Sketches of China: With Illustrations from Original Drawings* (Philadelphia, 1830). He was back in Canton in 1831, and was editor of *Chinese Courier and Canton Gazette* from 1831 to 1833. He went to the Philippines in 1833, and spent several years managing a coffee and sugar plantation in Jala-Jala. He later joined Russell, Sturgis and Company in Manila. Died in Manila. *References*: William W. Wood Papers, Houghton Library, Harvard University; and Paul Pickowicz, "William Wood in Canton: A Critique of the China Trade Before the Opium War," *EIHC* 107 (1971): 3–34.

WOOD-FORBES MISSION (1921). A mission composed by General Leonard Wood* and W. Cameron Forbes,* sent by President Warren G. Harding to the Philippines in 1921. The mission concluded that the Philippines was not ready for self-government, and that only a small percentage of Philippine leaders wanted independence, and therefore recommended against early withdrawal from the Philippines. *References*: Frederic G. Hoyt, "The Wood-Forbes Mission to the Philippines, 1921," Ph.D. diss., Claremont Graduate School, 1963; and Michael Onorato, "The Wood-Forbes Mission," in *A Brief Review of American Interest in Philippine Development and Other Essays* (Manila, 1972), pp. 29–48.

WOODBRIDGE, SAMUEL ISETT (1856–1926). Missionary, born October 16, 1856, in Henderson, Kentucky. Woodbridge graduated from Rutgers University and Princeton Theological Seminary. He was a missionary under the Board of Foreign Missions of the Presbyterian Church in the United States in China from 1882 to 1926. He served in Chingkiang and Changchow until 1901. He was editor of the *Chinese Christian Intelligencer* in Shanghai from 1902 until his death. He wrote *Fifty Years in China: Being Some Account of the History and Conditions in China and of the Missions of the Presbyterian Church in the United States There from 1867 to the Present Day* (n.p., 1919). Died June 23, 1926, in Shanghai. *References*: *CR* 57 (1926): 594–95; and P. Frank Price, *Our China Investment: Sixty Years of the Southern Presbyterian Church in China: with Biographies, Autobiographies, and Sketches of all Missionaries since the Opening of the Work in 1867* (Nashville, Tenn., 1927).

WOODRUFF, CHARLES EDWARD (1860–1915). Military surgeon, born October 2, 1860, in Philadelphia. Woodruff attended the U.S. Naval Academy and graduated from Jefferson Medical College. He was commissioned assistant surgeon in the U.S. Navy in 1886. He served as brigade surgeon in the Philippines during the Spanish-American War. He returned to the Philippines in 1902 as brigade surgeon during the Philippine-American War, and collected material for his book *The Effects of Tropical Light on White Men* (New York, 1905). He also wrote *Expansion of Races* (New York, 1909). He served again in the Philippines in 1909–1910. He retired in 1913. Died June 13, 1915, in New

Rochelle, New York. *References*: *DAB; DAMB; NYT,* June 15, 1915; and *WWWA*.

WOODRUFF, FRANCIS EBEN (1844–1914). Government official, born April 24, 1844, in New York City. Woodruff graduated from Yale University. He served in the Imperial Maritime Customs Service of China from 1865 until 1897. He was a clerk, a Chinese secretary on the inspectorate staff in Peking, and commissioner of customs in various ports from 1872 until 1897, when he resigned because of ill health. Died June 3, 1914, in Morristown, New Jersey. *Reference*: *WWWA*.

WOODS, CYRUS E. (1861–1938). Lawyer and diplomat, born September 3, 1861, in Clearfield, Pennsylvania. Woods graduated from Lafayette College, studied law, and was admitted to the bar in 1889. He practiced law in Philadelphia until 1894, and in Pittsburgh from 1894 until 1912. He was a member of the Pennsylvania State Senate from 1900 to 1908, minister to Portugal from 1912 to 1915, secretary of the commonwealth of Pennsylvania from 1915 to 1912, and U.S. ambassador to Spain from 1921 to 1923. He was ambassador to Japan in 1923–1924, and director of the American Red Cross relief and reconstruction activities following the 1923 earthquake there. He was attorney general of Pennsylvania in 1929–1930. Died December 8, 1938, in Philadelphia. *References*: Richard P. Mulcahy, "Ambassador from Greensburg: The Tenure of Cyrus E. Woods in Japan, 1923–1924," *Western Pennsylvania Historical Magazine* 68 (1985): 25–42; *NCAB* 44:262; and *WWWA*.

WOODS, GEORGE W. (1838–1902). Military surgeon, born in New Bedford, Massachusetts. Woods graduated from the U.S. Naval Academy in 1862. He served during the Civil War, practiced medicine at the New York Naval Hospital and Portsmouth Naval Hospital, and served in several posts on shore and sea from the late 1860s until 1882. He was a surgeon aboard the USS *Juniata* of the Asiatic Squadron in its voyage to East Asia from 1882 to 1885, and visited Korea. He wrote an analysis of science and the practice of medicine in Korea in the report of the secretary of the navy for 1885. His journal of this trip was published as *Naval Surgeon in Yi Korea: The Journal of George W. Woods* (edited with an introduction by Fred C. Bohm and Robert R. Swartout, Jr. [Berkeley, Calif., 1984]). He was promoted to medical director in 1895, and retired in 1900. Died June 9, 1902, in San Francisco. *Reference*: "George W. Woods Journals," Ms., Washington State University Libraries, Pullman, Wash.

WORCESTER, DEAN C(ONANT) (1866–1924). Scientist and colonial administrator, born October 1, 1866, in Thetford, Vermont. Worcester graduated from the University of Michigan. He accompanied Joseph B. Steere* on a biological expedition to the Philippines in 1887, and conducted a Menage scientific expedition to the Philippines from 1890 to 1892. He was assistant professor of zoology and museum curator at the University of Michigan from 1894 until 1898. He wrote *The Philippine Islands and Their People: A Record of Personal Observation and Experience* (New York, 1898). He was a member of the first Philippine Commission in 1899 and of the second Philippine Commission, and secretary of the interior from 1900 to 1913. He had administrative control over the non-Christian tribes, and was a leading factor in the establishment of the city of Baguio, the Philippine General Hospital, and the Bureau of Science. He remained in the Philippines, and was involved in business ventures including the production and export of coconut oil, coconut plantations, and cattle ranches. He wrote *The Philippines, Past and Present* (New York, 1914). Died May 2, 1924, in Manila. *References*: Dean C. Worcester Papers, Bentley Historical Library, University of Michigan, Ann Arbor; Richard Drinnon, *Facing West: The Metaphysics of Indian-Hating and Empire-Building* (Minneapolis, 1980), ch. 20; *EP* 4:453; Artemio R. Guillerno, ''The Worcester Libel Case and Philippine Journalism,'' *BAHC* 3 (July-September 1975): 22–50; Joseph R. Hayden, ''Biographical Sketch,'' in Dean C. Worcester, *The Philippine Past and Present*, ed. Ralston Hayden (New York, 1930); Karl L. Hutterer, ''Dean C. Worcester and Philippine Anthropology,'' *Philippine Quarterly of Culture and Society* 6 (1978): 125–56; Resil B. Mojares, ''Worcester in Cebu: Filipino Response to American Business 1915–1924,'' *Philippine Quarterly of Culture and Society* 13 (1985): 1–13; *NCAB* 20:246; *Pier*; and Peter W. Stanley, '' 'The Voice of Worcester is the Voice of God': How One American Found Fulfillment in the Philippines,'' in *Reappraising an Empire: New Perspectives on Philippine-American History*, ed. Peter W. Stanley (Cambridge, Mass., 1984), pp. 117–41.

WORES, THEODORE (1859–1939). Painter, born August 1, 1859, in San Francisco. Wores studied at the San Francisco Art Association's School of Design, and at the Royal Academy in Munich (Bavaria). He set up a studio in San Francisco in 1881. He painted in Japan from 1885 and 1887, and was back in Japan from 1892 to 1894. He wrote of his experiences in Japan in the September 1889 issue of *Century* magazine. He was in San Francisco, New York City, and Boston from 1887 to 1889; in London from 1889 to 1891; and settled again in San Francisco in 1893. He went to Hawaii and to Samoa in 1901, and to Spain in 1903. He was dean of faculty of the San Francisco Art Association's Institute of Art after 1907. Died September 1, 1939, in San Francisco. *References*: Lewis Ferbraché, *Theodore Wores, Artist in Search of the Picturesque* (San Francisco, 1968); Joseph A. Baird, *Theodore Wores: The Japanese Years* (Oakland, Calif., 1976); Michael Preble, *Theodore Wores 1859–1939* (Huntsville, Ala., 1980); and Gary A. Reynolds, ''A San Francisco Painter: Theodore Wores,'' *American Art Review* 3 (September-October 1976): 101–17.

WORKMAN, FANNY (BULLOCK) (1859–1925). Traveler, mountain climber and explorer, born January 8, 1859, in Worcester, Massachusetts. Workman spent most of her life after 1886 traveling. She traveled in Europe until the mid–

1890s, and then in the Middle East until 1897. She traveled on bicycle in Ceylon, Java, Sumatra, and Cochin China from 1897 to 1899. She explored the Himalaya Mountains after 1899, making seven expeditions between 1899 and 1912. She wrote *In the Ice World of the Himalayas* (New York, 1900); *Through Town and Jungle: 14,000 Miles A-Wheel Among the Temples and People of India of the Indian Plain* (London, 1904); *Ice-Bound Heights of the Mustagh* (New York, 1908); *Peaks and Glaciers of Nun Kun* (New York, 1909); *The Call of the Snowy Hispar* (New York, 1910); and *Two Summers in the Wilds of the Eastern Ka-rakorum* (New York, 1916). Died January 22, 1925, in Cannes, France. *References*: *DAB*; Luree Miller, *On Top of the World: Five Women Explorers in Tibet* (New York, 1976), ch. 2; *NAW*; and *WWWA*.

WRENTMORE, CLARENCE GEORGE (1867–1934). Irrigation engineer, born December 15, 1867, in Solon, Ohio. Wrentmore attended Hiram (Ohio) College and the University of Michigan. He was assistant professor of civil engineering at the University of Michigan from 1904 to 1907, and associate professor there in 1907. He was assistant director of public works in the Philippines from 1908 to 1910, and chief irrigation engineer after 1910. He designed various irrigation projects in the Philippines. He organized the college of engineering at the University of the Philippines in 1912, and served as its dean from 1912 until 1919. He was in charge of complete flood control system for the central valley of Luzon from 1918 to 1923. He returned to the United States in 1923, and was a consulting engineer in Detroit after 1924. Died March 1, 1934, in Detroit. *Reference*: *NCAB* 31:283.

WRIGHT, HAMILTON KEMP (1867–1917). Scientist, born August 2, 1867, in Cleveland, Ohio. Wright graduated from McGill University (Toronto) and studied in Heidelberg, Germany. He studied beriberi in the Straits Settlement from 1899 to 1903, supervised the building of a medical research laboratory in Kuala Lumpur, and was its director until 1903. He wrote *The Malarial Fevers of British Malaya* (Singapore, 1901); *An Inquiry into the Etiology and Pathology of Beri-Beri* (Singapore, 1902); and *On the Classification and Pathology of Beri-Beri* (London, 1903). He conducted medical research at Johns Hopkins University and other places from 1903 to 1908. He was appointed to the International Opium Commission in 1908, was a delegate to the International Opium Conference of 1911 and 1913, and was chairman of the American delegation. He was instrumental in the federal legislation to control habit-forming drugs. He was involved in civilian relief work in France in 1915. Died January 9, 1917, in Washington, D.C. *References*: *ACAB; DAB; NCAB* 22:430; and *WWWA*.

WRIGHT, LUKE (EDWARD) (1846–1922). Colonial administrator, born August 29, 1846, in Giles County, Tennessee, and grew up in Memphis. Wright served in the Confederate Army during the Civil War. He attended the University of Mississippi, studied law, and was admitted to the bar. He practiced law in

Memphis. He was a member of the Philippine Commission from 1900 to 1906, president of the commission in 1903–1904, vice governor from 1901 to 1904, governor of the Philippines in 1904–1905, and governor-general in 1905–1906. He was the first U.S. ambassador to Japan in 1906–1907, and secretary of war in 1908. Died November 17, 1922, in Memphis, Tennessee. *References*: Melchor P. Aquino, "Luke E. Wright," *BAHC* 2 (October 1974): 7–9; *DAB; DADH; EP* 4:357; *Gleeck/Governors*, ch. 3; *NCAB* 26:94; *NYT*, November 18, 1922; *Pier*; and *WWWA*.

WULSIN, FREDERICK ROELKER (1891–1961). Anthropologist, born July 8, 1891. Wulsin graduated from Harvard University. He traveled in East Africa and Madagascar in 1914–1915. He served in the army during World War I. He traveled in China, Mongolia, central Asia, and Indochina from 1921 to 1924. He was a member of the National Geographic Society expedition to southwestern China, North Vietnam, and Northern Laos in 1924. He was curator of anthropology at the University Museum of the University of Pennsylvania, served in the Quartermaster Corps during World War II, and was professor of anthropology at Tufts University from 1945 until 1958. Died February 26, 1961, in East Greenwich, Rhode Island. *References*: "F. R. Wulsin, the Explorer, and the Northwest China Expedition of 1923," in *China's Inner Asian Frontier*, ed. M. E. Alonso (Cambridge, Mass., 1979), pp. 9–15); and *WWWA*.

WYCKOFF, CHARLOTTE CHANDLER (1893–1966). Missionary, born April 30, 1893, in Kodaikanal, India, to American missionary parents. Wyckoff graduated from Wellesley College and Teachers College of Columbia University. She was a missionary under the Board of Foreign Missions of the Reformed Church in America in India from 1915 to 1960. She wrote *Jothy, a Story of the South Indian Jungle* (London, 1933); *Kodaikanal: 1845–1945* (Nagercoil, Travencore, India, 1945); *A Hundred Years with Christ in Arcot* (Madras, 1954); and *Kumar* (New York, 1965). Died July 22, 1966, in New York City. *References*: *CA*; and *HDRCA*.

Y

YALE, ELIHU (1649–1721). Merchant, born April 5, 1649, in Boston, and went with his family to England in 1652. Yale was appointed a writer in the East India Company in 1671, and went to India in 1672. He became a factor at Fort Saint George in Madras in 1677, and president and governor of Fort Saint George in 1687. He established Fort Saint David at Cuddalore. He was superseded in 1692 and returned to England in 1699, but continued his trade with India. Died July 8, 1721, in London. His brother, **THOMAS YALE** (1652–1697), merchant, was born in January 1652, in Boston. Thomas joined the East India Company and came to India in 1683. He carried on a lucrative trade in Sumatra on Elihu's account. He was the first native American to set foot in Siam. As commissioner of the East India Company, he arrived in Siam in 1683 to investigate the company's trading post at Phrapadaeng Province. He was later superintendent of Fort Saint George. Died October 1697, in Wrexham, England. *References*: *ACAB*; Hiram Bingham, *Elihu Yale, the American Nabob of Queen Square* (New York, 1939); *DAB; EAH; NCAB* 1:163; Merlin Waterson, "Although a Rascal, Eli Yale Used His Means Effectively," *Smithsonian* 8 (October 1977): 91–97; and *WWWA*.

YALE-IN-CHINA. Incorporated as the Yale Foreign Missionary Society in 1903. The name was changed to the Yale-in-China Association in 1934 and to Yale-China Association in 1975. It established a mission in Changsha in 1905, and opened Yali Middle school in 1906, the College of Arts and Sciences in 1914, a hospital in 1908, the College of Nursing in 1910, and Hsiang Ya Medical School in 1916. Its activities on Mainland China ended in 1951. *References*: Yale-China Association Collection, Yale University Library, New Haven, Conn.; John Dojka, "The Yale-China Collection," *Yale University Library Gazette* 53 (1979): 211–16; and Reuben Holden, *Yale in China: The Mainland 1901–1951* (New Haven, Conn., 1964).

YANGTZE PATROL. River patrol, established by the U.S. Navy on the Yangtze River in China in 1903 to protect United States interests, lives, and property, and to watch the Japanese. *References*: Bernard D. Cole, *Gunboats and Marines: The United States Navy in China, 1925–1928* (Newark, Del., 1983); Kenneth W. Condit and E. Mowbray Tate, "U.S. Gunboats on the Yangtze: History and Political Aspects, 1842–1922," *Studies on Asia, 1966* (Lincoln, Nebr., 1966), pp. 121–32; Esson M. Gale, "The Yangtze Patrol," *USNIP* 81 (March 1955): 307–15; and Kemp Tolley, *Yangtze Patrol: The U.S. Navy in China* (Annapolis, Md., 1971).

YANGTZE RAPID STEAMSHIP COMPANY. Shipping company formed in 1924 as a merger between three American shippers on the upper Yangtze River. At its peak consisting of a dozen vessels, it transported goods and passengers along the Yangtze, particularly between Ichang and Chungking. Its financial condition deteriorated after 1930, and the company was foreclosed in 1935. *Reference*: Frederick B. Hoyt, "The Open Door Leads to Reluctant Intervention: The Case of the Yangtze Rapid Steamship Company," *DH* 1 (1977): 155–69.

YARDLEY, HERBERT O(SBORNE) (1889–1958). Cryptographer, born April 13, 1889, in Worthington, Indiana. Yardley entered the Department of State in 1912 as a telegraph operator. He was a coding expert during World War I and later headed the "Black Chamber," the deciphering bureau of the War and State departments. He was the first man to crack the Japanese diplomatic code during the Washington Disarmament Conference of 1921. He went to China to set up a code department for General Chiang Kai-shek. He wrote *The American Black Chamber* (Indianapolis, 1931), and *Red Sun of Nippon* (New York, 1934), a novel. Died August 7, 1958, in Washington, D.C. *The Chinese Black Chamber: An Adventure in Espionage* (Boston, 1983) was published posthumously. *References*: David Kahn, *The Code Breakers* (New York, 1967); David Kahn, "Introduction," in *The American Black Chamber* (New York, 1981); *IAB; NYT*, August 8, 1958; and *WWWA*.

YATES, M(ATTHEW) T(YSON) (1819–1888). Missionary, born March 18, 1819, in Wake County, North Carolina. Yates graduated from Wake Forest College (N.C.). He was a missionary under the Foreign Mission Board of the Southern Baptist Convention in China from 1847 until his death, serving in Shanghai. He also served there as vice-consul. Died March 17, 1888, in Shanghai, China. *References*: Matthew Tyson Yates Papers, North Carolina Baptist Historical Collection, Wake Forest University Library, Winston-Salem, N.C.; W. Thorburn Clark, *Outriders for the King* (Nashville, 1931), pp. 1–20; *DAB; DSB; EM;* and *NCAB* 10:110.

YENCHING UNIVERSITY. Peking University began as a Methodist boys' school founded in Peking in 1870, which became Willey Institute in 1885 and Peking University in 1890. In 1916, it absorbed North China Union College (which began as T'uncghow boys' school in 1867, became North China College in 1889 and North China Union College in 1904) and North China Theological College (which began in 1893 and became a college in 1904). It also absorbed North China Union College for Women in 1920 (which began as a girls' school in 1864). It became Yenching University in 1928, and was chartered by the State of New York in 1929. It was moved to Chengtu in 1942 and was reopened in Peking in 1946. It came under Communist control in 1948, was nationalized in 1951, and became part of Peking University in 1952. *References*: Suzanne W. Barnett, "Two-Way Bridges: Educating New China," *History of Education Quarterly* 20 (1980): 101–8; Dwight W. Edwards, *Yenching University* (New York, 1959); *Fenn*; Frederick B. Hoyt, "The Lesson of Confrontation: Two Christian Colleges Face the Chinese Revolution, 1925–1927," *Asian Forum* 8 (Summer 1976): 45–62; *Lutz*; and Philip West, *Yenching University and Sino-Western Relations, 1916–1952* (Cambridge, Mass., 1976).

YOKOSUKA NAVAL BASE. The most significant U.S. base in Japan and the western Pacific. Headquarters of U.S. Naval Forces, Japan, and home port for the Seventh Fleet, it has extensive dock facilities, including the only drydock facility in the western Pacific capable of handling large attack carriers. *References*: Tomm Tompkins, *Yokosuka: Base of an Empire* (Novato, Calif., 1981); and *USNBO*.

YONSEI UNIVERSITY. *See* CHOSEN CHRISTIAN COLLEGE

YOUNG, ARTHUR N(ICHOLS) (1890–1984). Economic advisor, born November 21, 1890, in Los Angeles. Young graduated from Occidental College, and Princeton and George Washington universities. He was an economic advisor to the State Department from 1922 to 1929, a financial advisor to the Chinese government from 1929 to 1937, and an advisor to the Central Bank of China. He helped establish the Central Reserve Bank of China, was director of the Chinese National Aviation Corporation from 1937 to 1945, and was chairman of the Chinese National Commission on Relief and Rehabilitation during World War II. He wrote *China's Economic and Financial Reconstruction* (New York, 1947); *China and the Helping Hand, 1937–1945* (Cambridge, Mass., 1963); *China's Wartime Finance and Inflation, 1937–1945* (Cambridge, Mass., 1965); and *China's Nation-Building Effort, 1927–1937: The Financial and Economic Record* (Stanford, Calif., 1971). He was later a financial advisor to Saudi Arabia, Mexico, Argentina, and Honduras. Died July 19, 1984, in Claremont, California. *References*: Arthur N. Young Papers, Hoover Institution on War, Revolution and Peace, Stanford, Calif.; *CA; NCAB* C:84; *NYT*, August 24, 1984; and *WWWA*.

YOUNG, JOHN RUSSELL (1840–1899). Journalist and diplomat, born November 20, 1840, in Tyrone County, Ireland. He came to the United States in 1841, and grew up in Philadelphia and New Orleans. He was a reporter with the Philadelphia *Press*, and was a correspondent during the Civil War, managing editor of the *Press* from 1862 to 1866; and managing editor of the *New York Tribune* from 1866 until 1870. He worked again for the *New York Herald* from 1872 to 1877. He accompanied ex-President Ulysses S. Grant on his journey abroad from 1877 to 1879, and wrote *Around the World with General Grant* (New York, 1879). He was U.S. minister to China from 1872 until 1885. He was successful in settling all the outstanding U.S. claims against China. He took an active role in mediating the dispute between France and China over Annam in 1883. He was again with the *New York Herald* from 1885 until 1890, and was librarian of Congress from 1897 until his death. Died January 17, 1899, in Washington, D.C. His memoirs, *Men and Memories*, ed. Mary D. Russell Young (New York, 1901) were published posthumously. *References*: John Russell Young Papers, Manuscript Division, Library of Congress; John C. Broderick, "John Russell Young: The Internationalist as Librarian," *Quarterly Journal of the Library of Congress* 33 (1976): 117–50; *DADH*; Britten Dean, "The United States and China: John Russell Young and the Right to Manufacture in the Treaty Ports, 1882–1883," *Hsiang Kang Chung Wen Ta hsueh Chung Kuo Wen Hua Yen Chiu So Hsüeh Pao* (Hong Kong) 11 (1980): 271–90; *NCAB* 2:214; *NYT*, January 18, 1899; Victoria M. Siu, "Bridging the Culture Gap: John Russell Young, Minister to China, 1882–1885, as a Case Study," *Asian Profile* 10 (1982): 387–94; and Victoria M. Siu, "Sino-American Relations, 1882–1885: The Mission of John Russell Young," Ph.D. diss., Georgetown University, 1975.

YOUNG MEN'S CHRISTIAN ASSOCIATION OF THE UNITED STATES OF AMERICA (YMCA). Nonsectarian Christian lay organization, founded in London in 1844 and in the United States in 1851. The International Committee was formed in 1879 and established overseas operations in India and Japan in 1889, in Ceylon in 1896, in China in 1898, in Hong Kong in 1899, in Korea in 1901, in Burma in 1906, in the Philippines in 1907, in Thailand in 1930, and in Pakistan in 1948. *References*: YMCA of the U.S.A. Archives, University of Minnesota Library, St. Paul, Minn.; Shirley S. Garrett, *Social Reformers in Urban China: The Chinese Y.M.C.A., 1895–1926* (Cambridge, Mass., 1970); and Kenneth S. Latourette, *World Service: A History of the Foreign Work and World Service of the Young Men's Christian Association of the United States and Canada* (New York, 1957).

YOUNG WOMEN'S CHRISTIAN ASSOCIATION OF THE U.S.A. (YWCA). Nonsectarian lay Christian organization, founded in London in 1855 and in the United States in 1858. The International Board established operations in India in 1895, in Ceylon and Burma in 1900, in China in 1907, in Japan in

1909, in Malaya in 1921, in the Philippines in 1927, in Korea and Thailand in 1947, and in Taiwan in 1956. *References*: Young Women's Christian Association Archives, New York City; Nancy Boyd, *Emissaries: The Overseas Work of the American YWCA 1895–1970* (New York, 1986); Alison R. Drucker, "The Role of the YWCA in the Development of the Chinese Women's Movement, 1890–1927," *Social Service Review* 53 (1979): 421–40; and Anna V. Rice, *A History of the World's Young Women's Christian Association* (New York, 1947).

YOUNGBERG, GUSTAVUS BENSON ("GUS") (1888–1944). Missionary, born in Hibbing, Minnesota. Youngberg graduated from the University of Minnesota and Union College. He taught public schools in Moody County, South Dakota. He was a missionary under the Seventh-Day Adventist Church in Singapore in 1919, and then in Borneo after 1919. With the exception of two years in Batakland, Sumatra, and three years with the Malayan Seminary in Singapore, he was a missionary in Borneo until his death. He began pioneer work among the Dyak tribes of Sarawak in 1931 and educational work among the Dusuns of British North Borneo (now Sabah, part of Malaysia) in 1935. He was interned by the Japanese in Kuching, Sarawak, from 1941 until his death. Died July 14, 1944, in the internment camp. His wife, **NORMA YOUNGBERG**, wrote *Taught by the Tiger* (Mountain View, Calif., 1961), a book of fiction. *References*: *SDAE*; and Norma R. Youngberg and Gerald H. Minchin, *Under Sealed Orders: The Story of Gus Youngberg* (Mountain View, Calif., 1970).

Z

ZACHARIAS, ELLIS MARK (1890–1961). Naval officer, born January 1, 1890, in Jacksonville, Florida. Zacharias graduated from the U.S. Naval Academy in 1912. He served during World War I. He was a naval attaché in Tokyo, Japan, from 1920 to 1923, and again in 1928. He served in the Panama Canal Zone from 1924 to 1926, was head of the Far East Division of the Office of Naval Intelligence (ONI) in Washington, D.C., from 1928 to 1931, intelligence officer of the Eleventh Naval District from 1938 to 1940, deputy director of ONI in 1942, commanded a battleship *New Mexico* in 1943–1944, and was chief of staff of the Eleventh Naval District in 1944. He was involved in psychological warfare against Japan, and broadcasted propaganda to that country in 1945. He wrote *Secret Missions: The Story of an Intelligence Officer* (New York, 1946). He retired with the rank of rear admiral in 1946. Died June 28, 1961, in West Springfield, New Hampshire. *References*: *CB* 1949; *DAB S7; NYT*, June 29, 1961; and Maria Wilhelm, *The Man Who Watched the Rising Sun: The Story of Admiral Ellis M. Zacharias* (New York, 1967).

ZUMBRO, WILLIAM MICHAEL (1865–1922). Educator, born November 27, 1865, in Linneus Linn County, Missouri. Zumbro graduated from Coe College (Cedar Rapids, Ia.) and Yale University Divinity School, and was ordained in 1894. He was a missionary under the American Board of Commissioners for Foreign Missions (ABCFM)* in India from 1894 until his death. He was a teacher at the American College in Pasumalai, South India, and after 1904, in Madura, and was president of the college from 1899 until his death. Died October 17, 1922, in Madura. *Reference*: *NCAB* 22:391.

Chiefs of American Diplomatic Missions in Asia, 1843–1989

ABBREVIATIONS

AE/P	Ambassador Extraordinary and Plenipotentiary
CdA	Chargé d'Affaires
Comm	Commissioner
EE/MP	Envoy Extraordinary and Minister Plenipotentiary
MR	Minister Resident
MR/CG	Minister Resident and Consul General
USLO	U.S. Liaison Officer

Abramowitz, Morton I. (1933–   ), AE/P Thailand 1978–1981
Allen, George Venable (1903–1970), AE/P India and Nepal 1953–1954.
*Allen, Horace Newton (1858–1932), MR/CG Korea 1897–1901; EE/MP Korea 1901–1905
Alling, Paul Humiston (1896–1949), AE/P Pakistan 1947–1948
*Allison, John Moore (1905–1978), AE/P Japan, 1953–1957; AE/P Indonesia 1957–1958
Anderson, Larz (1866–1937), AE/P Japan 1912–1913
*Angell, James Burrill (1829–1916), EE/MP China 1880–1881
Armacost, Michael Hayden (1937–   ), AE/P Philippines, 1982–1984; AE/P Japan 1989–
Arnold, Daryl (1924–   ), AE/P Singapore 1987–1989
*Avery, Benjamin Parke (1828–1875), EE/MP China 1874–1875
*Baker, James Marion (1861–1940), EE/MP Siam 1933–1936
*Baldwin, Charles Franklin (1902–   ), AE/P Malaya 1961–1964
*Bancroft, Edgar Addison (1857–1925), AE/P Japan 1924–1925
Barnes, Harry George, Jr. (1926–   ), AE/P India 1981–1985
*Barrett, John (1866–1938), MR/CG Siam 1894–1898
Bean, Maurice Darrow (1928–   ), AE/P Burma 1977–1979
Bell, James Dunbar (1911–1979), AE/P Malaysia 1964–1969
Berger, Samuel David (1911–1980), AE/P Korea 1961–1964; Deputy Ambassador Vietnam 1968–1972
Berry, James Lampton (1908–1980), AE/P Ceylon 1958–1959

*Bingham, John Armour (1815–1900), EE/MP Japan 1873–1885

Bishop, Max Waldo (1908–   ), AE/P Thailand 1955–1958

*Blair, William McCormick, Jr. (1916–   ), AE/P Philippines 1964–1967

Bohlen, Charles Eustis (1904–1974), AE/P Philippines 1957–1959

Boster, David Eugene (1920–   ), AE/P Bangladesh 1974–1976

*Bosworth, Stephen Warren (1939–   ), AE/P Philippines 1984–1987

*Bowles, Chester Bliss (1901–   ), AE/P India and Nepal 1951–1953; AE/P India 1963–1969

Boyd, Sempronius Hamilton (1828–1894), MR/CG Siam 1890–1892

Briggs, Ellis Ormsbee (1899–1976), AE/P Korea 1952–1955

Brodie, Edward Everett (1876–1936), EE/MP Siam 1921–1925

Brown, William Andreas (1930–   ), AE/P Thailand 1985–

Brown, Winthrop Gilman (1907–   ), AE/P Laos 1960–1962; AE/P Korea 1964–1967

*Browne, John Ross (1817–1875), EE/MP China 1868–1869

Bruce, David Kirpatrick Este (1898–1977), USLO Peking 1973–1974

*Bryan, Charles Page (1856–1918), AE/P Japan 1911–1912

Buck, Alfred Eliab (1832–1902), EE/MP Japan 1897–1902

*Bunker, Ellsworth (1894–1984), AE/P India 1956–1961; AE/P Nepal 1956–1959; AE/P Vietnam 1967–1973

*Burlingame, Anson (1820–1870), EE/MP China 1861–1867

Bush, George Herbert Walker (1924–   ), USLO Peking 1974–1975

Byington, Homer Morrison, Jr. (1908–   ), AE/P Malaya 1957–1961

Byrne, Patricia Mary (1925–   ), AE/P Burma 1979–1983

Byroade, Henry Alfred (1913–   ), AE/P Burma 1963–1968; AE/P Philippines 1969–1973; AE/P Pakistan 1973–1977

*Calhoun, William James (1848–1916), EE/MP China 1909–1913

Cargo, William Ira (1917–   ), AE/P Nepal 1973–1977

Carpenter, Fred Warner (1873–1957), EE/MP Siam 1912–1913

Castle, William Richards, Jr. (1878–1963), AE/P Japan 1929–1930

*Child, Jacob Tripler (1832– ?), MR/CG Siam 1886–1891

*Cochran, Horace Merle (1892–1973), AE/P Indonesia 1949–1953

Cole, Felix (1887–1969), AE/P Ceylon 1949

Coombs, Frank Leslie (1853–1934), EE/MP Japan 1892–1893

Coon, Carleton Stevens, Jr. (1927–   ), AE/P Nepal 1981–1984

Coon, Jane Abell (1929–   ), AE/P Bangladesh 1981–1984

*Cooper, John Sherman (1901–   ), AE/P India and Nepal 1955–1956

Corry, Andrew Vincent (1904–1981), AE/P Ceylon and Maldives 1967–1970

*Cowen, Myron Melvin (1898–1965), AE/P Philippines 1949–1951

Crane, Charles Richard (1858–1938), EE/MP China 1920–1921

Cronk, Edwin Monroe (1918–   ), AE/P Singapore 1972–1975

Cross, Charles Tenney (1922–   ), AE/P Singapore 1969–1971

Crowe, Philip Kingsland (1908–1976), AE/P Ceylon 1953–1956

Cummings, Hugh Smith, Jr. (1900–   ), AE/P Indonesia 1953–1957

*Cushing, Caleb (1800–1879), EE/MP and Comm China 1843–1844

Davis, John Wesley (1799–1859), Comm China 1848–1850

Dean, John Gunther (1926–   ), AE/P Khmer Republic 1974–1975; AE/P Thailand 1981–1985; AE/P India 1985–1988

*De Long, Charles E. (1832–1876), MR Japan 1869–1870; EE/MP Japan 1870–1873

*Denby, Charles (1830–1904), EE/MP China 1885–1898
De Pree, Williams Ames (1928–), AE/P Bangladesh 1987–
*Dinsmore, Hugh Anderson (1850–1930), MR/CG Korea 1887–1890
Donovan, William Joseph (1883–1959), AE/P Thailand 1953–1954
Dowling, Walter Cecil (1905–1977), AE/P Korea 1956–1959
Drumright, Everett Francis (1906–), AE/P China 1958–1962
*Dun, Edwin (1848–1931), EE/MP Japan 1893–1897
*Durbrow, Elbridge (1903–), AE/P Vietnam 1957–1961
Everett, Alexander Hill (1790–1847), Comm China 1845–1847
Everton, John Scott (1908–), AE/P Burma 1961–1963
Farland, Joseph Simpson (1914–), AE/P Pakistan 1969–1972
Ferguson, Homer (1889–), AE/P Philippines 1955–1956
Ferguson, Thomas C. (1933–), AE/P Brunei Darussalam 1987–
*Foote, Lucius Harwood (1826–1913), EE/MP Korea 1883–1885
*Forbes, William Cameron (1870–1959), AE/P Japan 1930–1932
Frank, Milton, III (1938–), AE/P Nepal 1988–
Galbraith, Francis Joseph (1913–), AE/P Singapore 1966–1969; AE/P Indonesia 1969–
    1973
*Galbraith, John Kenneth (1908–), AE/P India 1961–1963
*Gauss, Clarence Edward (1886–1960), AE/P China 1941–1944
Gleysteen, William Henry, Jr. (1926–), AE/P Korea 1978–1981
Gluck, Maxwell Henry (1899–), AE/P Ceylon 1957–1958
Godley, George McMurtrie (1917–), AE/P Laos 1969–1973
Goheen, Robert Francis (1919–), AE/P India 1977–1980
Grady, Henry Francis (1882–1957), AE/P India 1947–1948; EE/MP Nepal 1948
Grant, Hugh Gladney (1882–1972), EE/MP Thailand 1940–1941
Green, Marshall (1916–), AE/P Indonesia 1965–1969
Gregg, Donald P. (1927–), AE/P Korea 1989–
*Grew, Joseph Clark (1880–1965), AE/P Japan 1932–1941
Griscom, Lloyd Carpenter (1872–1959), EE/MP Japan 1902–1905
Gufler, Bernard Anthony (1903–1973), AE/P Ceylon 1959–1961
*Guthrie, George Wilkins (1848–1917), AE/P Japan 1913–1917
Habib, Philip Charles (1920–), AE/P Korea 1971–1974
*Halderman, John Acoming (1838–1908), MR/CG Siam 1882–1885
*Harris, Townsend (1804–1878), MR Japan 1859–1862
*Heard, Augustine (1827–1905), MR/CG Korea 1890–1893
*Heath, Donald Read (1894–1981), EE/MP Laos 1950–1954; EE/MP Vietnam and Cam-
    bodia 1950–1952; AE/P Vietnam and Cambodia 1952–1954
Heck, Louis Douglas (1918–), AE/P Nepal 1977–1980
*Henderson, Loy Wesley (1892–1986), AE/P India 1948–1951; EE/MP Nepal 1948–
    1951
Hickerson, John Dewey (1898–), AE/P Philippines 1959–1961
Hildreth, Horace Augustus (1902–), AE/P Pakistan 1953–1957
Hinton, Deane Roesch (1923–), AE/P Pakistan 1983–1987
Hodgson, James Day (1915–), AE/P Japan 1974–1977
Holdridge, John Herbert (1924–), AE/P Singapore 1975–1978; AE/P Indonesia 1982–
    1986
Hornibrook, William Harrison (1884–1946), EE/MP Siam 1915–1916

Hubbard, John Randolph (1918–   ), AE/P India 1988–
*Hubbard, Richard Bennett (1832–1901), EE/MP Japan 1885–1889
Huddle, Jerome Klahr (1891–1959), Burma 1947–1949
Hummel, Arthur William, Jr. (1920–   ), AE/P Burma 1968–1971; AE/P Pakistan 1977–
     1981
Hunt, George Wylie Paul (1859–1934), EE/MP Siam 1920–1921
*Hurley, Patrick Jay (1883–1963), AE/P China 1944–1945
Ingersoll, George Pratt (1861–1927), EE/MP Siam 1917–1918
*Ingersoll, Robert Stephen, Jr. (1914–   ), AE/P Japan 1972–1973
*Johnson, Nelson Trusler (1887–1954), EE/MP China 1929–1935; AE/P China 1935–
     1941
Johnson, Ural Alexis (1908–   ), AE/P Thailand 1958–1961; Deputy Ambassador Viet-
     nam 1964–1965; AE/P Japan 1966–1969
*Jones, Howard Palfrey (1899–1973), AE/P Indonesia 1958–1965
Kaufman, David E. (1883–1962), EE/MP Siam 1930–1933
Keating, Kenneth Bernard (1900–1975), AE/P India 1969–1972
Key, David McKendree, II (1900–1988), AE/P Burma 1950–1951
King, Barrington (1930–   ), AE/P Brunei Darussalam 1984–1987
*King, Hamilton (1852–1912), MR/CG Siam 1898–1903; EE/MP Siam 1903–1912
Kintner, William Ruscoe (1915–   ), AE/P Thailand 1973–1975
Kneip, Richard Francis (1933–   ), AE/P Singapore 1978–1980
Lacy, William Sterling Byrd (1910–1979), AE/P Korea 1955
Laise, Carol Clendening (Carol [Laise] Bunker) (1917–   ), AE/P Nepal 1966–1973
Langley, James McLellan (1894–1968), AE/P Pakistan 1957–1959
Levin, Burton (1930–   ), AE/P Burma 1987–
Lilley, James Roderick (1928–   ), AE/P Korea 1987–1989; AE/P China 1989–
Locke, Eugene Murphy (1918–1972), AE/P Pakistan 1966–1967; Deputy Ambassador,
     Vietnam 1967–1968
*Lodge, Henry Cabot, Jr. (1902–1985), AE/P Vietnam 1963–1964, 1965–1967
Lord, Winston (1937–   ), AE/P China 1985–1989
*Low, Frederick Ferdinand (1828–1894), EE/MP China 1869–1873
Lydman, Jack Wilson (1914–   ), AE/P Malaysia 1969–1973
Lyon, Cecil Burton (1903–   ), AE/P Ceylon 1964–1967; AE/P Maldives 1965–1967
MacArthur, Douglas, II (1909–   ), AE/P Japan 1956–1961
McClintock, Robert Mills (1909–1976), AE/P Cambodia 1954–1956
McConaughy, Walter Patrick, Jr. (1908–   ), AE/P Burma 1957–1959; AE/P Korea 1959–
     1961; AE/P Pakistan 1962–1966
MacKenzie, Harold Orville (1866– ?), EE/MP Siam 1927–1930
*McLane, Robert Milligan (1815–1898), Comm China 1853–1854
*MacMurray, John Van Antwerp (1881–1960), EE/MP China 1925–1929
*McNutt, Paul Vories (1891–1955), AE/P Philippines 1946–1947
*MacVeagh, Charles (1860–1931), AE/P Japan 1925–1928
*Mansfield, Michael Joseph (1903–   ), AE/P Japan 1977–1988
*Marshall, Humphrey (1812–1872), Comm China 1852–1854
Martin, Edwin Webb (1917–   ), AE/P Burma 1971–1973
*Martin, Graham Anderson (1912–   ), AE/P Thailand 1963–1967; AE/P Vietnam 1973–
     1975

Masters, Edward E. (1924–   ), AE/P Bangladesh 1976–1977; AE/P Indonesia 1977–1981
Maytag, Marquita Moseley (1925–   ), AE/P Nepal 1976–1977
*Meyer, Armin Henry (1914–   ), AE/P Japan 1969–1972
Miller, Robert Hopkins (1927–   ), AE/P Malaysia 1977–1980
Monjo, John Cameron (1931–   ), AE/P Malaysia 1987–1989; AE/P Indonesia 1989–
Morgan, Edwin Vernon (1865–1934), EE/MP Korea 1905
*Morris, Ronald Sletor (1874–1945), AE/P Japan 1917–1920
Moynihan, Daniel Patrick (1927–   ), AE/P India 1973–1975
*Muccio, John Joseph (1900–1989), AE/P Korea 1949–1952
Murphy, Richard William (1929–   ), AE/P Philippines 1978–1981
Murphy, Robert Daniel (1894–1978), AE/P Japan 1952–1953
*Neville, Edwin Lowe (1884–1944), EE/MP Siam 1937–1940
Newsom, David Dunlap (1918–   ), AE/P Indonesia 1973–1977; AE/P Philippines 1977–1978
*Nolting, Frederick Ernest, Jr. (1911–   ), AE/P Vietnam 1961–1963
Nufer, Albert Frank (1894–1956), AE/P Philippines 1956
Oakley, Robert Bigger (1931–   ), AE/P Pakistan 1988–
*O'Brien, Thomas James (1842–1933), AE/P Japan 1907–1911
O'Donohue, Daniel Anthony (1931–   ), AE/P Burma 1983–1987; Thailand 1988–
Oehlert, Benjamin Hilborn, Jr. (1909–1985), AE/P Pakistan 1967–1969
O'Neal, Emmet (1887–1967), AE/P Philippines 1947–1948
Orr, Robert D. (1917–   ), AE/P Singapore 1989–
Osborn, David Lawrence (1921–   ), AE/P Burma 1974–1977
Palmer, Ronald DeWayne (1932–   ), AE/P Malaysia 1981–1983
*Parker, Peter (1804–1888), Comm China 1855–1857
Parker, William Harwar (1826–1896), MR/CG Korea 1886
Parsons, James Graham (1907–   ), AE/P Laos 1956–1958
*Peck, Willys Ruggles (1882–1952), EE/MP Thailand 1941
Peurifoy, John Emil (1907–1955), AE/P Thailand 1954–1955
Platt, Nicholas (1936–   ), AE/P Philippines 1987–
Porter, William James (1914–   ), Deputy Ambassador Vietnam 1965–1967; AE/P Korea 1967–1971
*Pruyn, Robert Hewson (1815–1882), MR Japan 1861–1865
*Rankin, Karl Lott (1898–   ), AE/P China 1953–1957
Raphel, Arnold Lewis (1943–1988), AE/P Pakistan 1987–1988
Reed, John Hathaway (1921–   ), AE/P Sri Lanka and Maldives 1976–1977, 1981–1985
*Reed, William Bradford (1806–1876), EE/MP China 1857–1958
*Reischauer, Edwin Oldfather (1910–   ), AE/P Japan 1961–1966
Reinhardt, George Frederick (1911–1971), AE/P Vietnam 1955–1957
*Rockhill, William Woodville (1854–1914), EE/MP China 1905–1909
Rountree, William Manning (1917–   ), AE/P Pakistan 1959–1962
Roy, J. Stapleton (1935–   ), AE/P Singapore 1984–1987
Russell, William Worthington (1859–1944), EE/MP Siam 1925–1927
Satterthwaite, Joseph Charles (1900–   ), AE/P Ceylon 1949–1953; AE/P Burma 1955–1957
Saxbe, William Bart (1916–   ), AE/P India 1975–1976
Schaffer, Howard Bruner (1929–   ), AE/P Bangladesh 1984–1987

Schneider, David Taylor (1922–   ), AE/P Bangladesh 1978–1981
*Schurman, Jacob Gould (1854–1942), EE/MP China 1921–1925
*Sebald, William Joseph (1901–1980), AE/P Burma 1952–1954
*Seward, George Frederick (1840–1910), EE/MP China 1876–1880
Shoesmith, Thomas P. (1922–   ), AE/P Malaysia 1983–
*Sill, John Mahelm Berry (1831–1901), MR/CG Korea 1894–1897
Smith, Horace Harrison (1905–1976), AE/P Laos 1958–1960
Sneider, Richard Lee (1922–   ), AE/P Korea 1974–1978
Snow, William Pennell (1907–   ), AE/P Burma 1959–1961
Spain, James William (1926–   ), AE/P Sri Lanka and Maldives 1985–
Spiers, Ronald Ian (1925–   ), AE/P Pakistan 1981–1983
*Sprouse, Philip Dodson (1906–1977), AE/P Cambodia 1962–1964
Spruance, Raymond Ames (1886–1969), AE/P Philippines 1952–1955
*Stanton, Edwin Forward (1901–1968), EE/MP Siam 1946–1947; AE/P Siam 1947–1953
Stebbins, Henry Endicott (1905–1973), AE/P Nepal 1959–1966
Stevenson, William Edwards (1900–1985), AE/P Philippines 1961–1964
Strausz-Hupe, Robert (1903–   ), AE/P Ceylon and Maldives 1970–1971
Strom, Carl Walther (1899–1969), AE/P Cambodia 1956–1959
*Stuart, John Leighton (1876–1962), AE/P China 1946–1949
Sullivan, William Healy (1922–   ), AE/P Laos 1964–1969; AE/P Philippines 1973–1977
Swank, Emory Coblentz (1922–   ), AE/P Cambodia 1970–1973
*Swift, John Franklin (1829–1891), EE/MP Japan 1889–1891
Taylor, Maxwell Davenport (1901–   ), AE/P Vietnam 1964–1965
Thayer, Harry E. T. (1927–   ), AE/P Singapore 1980–1984
Toussaint, Donald R. (1927–   ), AE/P Sri Lanka and Maldives 1979–1982
Trimble, Philip R. (1907–   ), AE/P Cambodia 1959–1962
Underhill, Francis Trelease (1921–   ), AE/P Malaysia 1973–1977
Unger, Leonard Seidman (1917–   ), AE/P Laos 1962–1964; AE/P Thailand 1967–1973;
        AE/P China 1974–1979
Van Hollen, Christopher (1922–   ), AE/P Sri Lanka and Maldives 1972–1976
Van Valkenburgh, Robert Bruce (1821–1888), MR Japan 1866–1869
Walker, Richard Lewis (1922–   ), AE/P Korea 1981–1987
*Ward, John Elliott (1814–1902), EE/MP China 1858–1860
Warren, Avra Milvin (1893–1957), AE/P Pakistan 1950–1952
Warren, Charles Beecher (1870–1936), AE/P Japan 1921–1922
Watson, Barbara Mae (1918–1983), AE/P Malaysia 1980–1981
Weil, Leon Jerome (1927–   ), AE/P Nepal 1984–1988
Whitehouse, Charles Sheldon (1926–   ), Deputy Ambassador Vietnam 1972–   ; AE/P
        Laos 1973–1975; AE/P Thailand 1975–1978
Williams, Gehard Mennen (1911–   ), AE/P Philippines 1968–1969
Williams, Richard Llewellyn (1929–   ), AE/P Mongolia 1988–
Willis, Frances Elizabeth (1899–1983), AE/P Ceylon 1961–1964
Wolfowitz, Paul Dundes (1943–   ), AE/P Indonesia 1986–1989
Woodcock, Leonard F. (1911–   ), USLO Peking 1977–1979; AE/P China 1979–1981
*Woods, Cyrus E. (1861–1938), AE/P Japan 1923–1924
Wriggins, William Howard (1918–   ), AE/P Sri Lanka and Maldives 1977–1979
*Wright, Luke Edward (1846–1922), AE/P Japan 1906–1907
Wright, Thomas Kenneth (1908–   ), CdA Malaya 1957

Yost, Charles Woodruff (1907–1981), CdA Siam 1945; EE/MP Laos 1954–1955; AE/P Laos 1955–1956
*Young, John Russell (1840–1899), EE/MP China 1882–1885
Young, Kenneth Todd, Jr. (1916–1972), AE/P Thailand 1961–1963

List of Individuals by Profession and Occupation

ACROBATS
Risley, Richard R.

ADVENTURERS
Anderson, Roy Scott
Boyd, John Parker
Burgevine, Henry Andrea
Ferguson, John Calvin
Gibson, Walter Murray
Harlan, Josiah
Lea, Homer
LeGendre, Charles William
MacDonald, Ranald
Pethick, William N.
Schroder, Fred Meyer
Ward, Frederick Townsend
White, Thaddeus C.
Whitmarsh, Hubert Phelps
Wood, William W.

AGRICULTURAL ECONOMISTS
Buck, John Lossing
Ladejinsky, Wolf Isaac

AGRICULTURAL ENGINEERS
Vaugh, Mason

AGRICULTURAL MISSIONARIES
Case, Brayton Clarke
DeValois, John James
Groff, George Weidman
Hayes, William Brewster
Higginbottom, Sam

AGRICULTURISTS
Bailie, Joseph
Brill, Gerow Dodge
Brooks, William Penn
Capron, Horace
Chandler, Robert Flint, Jr.
Copeland, Edwin Bingham
Dun, Edwin
Edwards, Harry Taylor
Ensminger, Douglas
Georgeson, Charles Christian
Gilmore, John Washington
Griffing, John B.
Hinton, William Howard
Love, Harry Houser
Mosher, Arthur Theodore
Parker, Edward Cary
Reisner, John Henry, Sr.
Shelton, Edward Mason

ANIMAL COLLECTORS
Buck, Franklin Howard
Graham, David Crockett
Harkness, Ruth
Smith, Floyd Tangier

ANTHROPOLOGISTS
Barton, Roy Franklin
Beals, Alan Robin
Bean, Robert Bennett
Beardsley, Richard King
Belo (Tannenbaum), Jane

Benedict, Laura Watson
Berreman, Gerald Duane
Beyer, Henry Otley
Bowles, Gordon Townsend
Carpenter, Clarence Ray
Cohn, Bernard Samuel
Cole, Fay-Cooper
Conklin, Harold Colyer
Dentan, Robert Knox
Diamond, Norma Joyce
Dozier, Edward P.
Du Bois, Cora
Eggan, Fredrick Russell
Embree, John Fee
Fox, Robert Bradford
Gallin, Bernard
Geertz, Clifford James
Geertz, Hildred Storey
Hanks, Jane Richardson
Hanks, Lucien Mason
Haring, Douglas Gilbert
Hart, Donn Vorhis
Hitchcock, John Thayer
Jenks, Albert Ernest
Kaufman, Howard Keva
Keesing, Felix Maxwell
Keyes, Charles Fenton
Lehman, Frederick Kris
Loeb, Edwin Meyer
Mandelbauum, David Goodman
Marriott, McKim
Nash, Manning
Norbeck, Edward
Nurge, Ethel
Osgood, Cornelius
Peacock, James Lowe, III
Reynolds, Ira Hubert
Sharp, Lauriston
Skinner, George William
Smith, Robert John
Solheim, Wilhelm Gerhard, II
Starr, Frederick
Steed, Gitel Gertrude Poznanski
Stevenson, Paul Huston
Warren, Charles Preston
Williams, Thomas Rhys
Wulsin, Frederick Roelker

ANTIQUARIANS
Hommel, Rudolph [Rudolf] P.

ARCHAEOLOGISTS
Bishop, Carl Whiting
Fox, Robert Bradford
Gorman, Chester
Jayne, Horace Howard Furness

ARCHITECTS
Mayer, Albert
Parsons, William Edward
Pelzer, Dorothy West
Raymond, Antonin

ARMY OFFICERS
Ahern, George Patrick
Allen, Henry Tureman
Anderson, Thomas McArthur
Anderson, William Hart
Baldwin, Frank Dwight
Bandholtz, Harry Hill
Barrett, David Dean
Bates, John Coalter
Batson, Matthew A.
Bell, James Franklin
Caraway, Paul Wyatt
Chaffee, Adna Romanza
Cloman, Sydney Amos
Collins, Joseph Lawton
Davis, George Whitfield
Dorn, Frank
Dosser, William Earl
Duckworth-Ford, Robert Geoffrey
    Alexander
Dye, William McEntyre
Eichelberger, Robert Lawrence
Funston, Frederick
Furlong, Leonard
Gallman, Jefferson Davis
Gardner, Cornelius
Gilhouser, Henry
Graves, William Sidney
Hodge, John Reed
Hull, John Adley
Joy, Charles Turner
Lawton, Henry Ware

MacArthur, Arthur
MacArthur, Douglas
McCoy, Frank Ross
Magruder, John
Marquat, William Frederic
Merritt, Wesley
Nathorst, Charles E.
Ochterlony, Sir David
O'Daniel, John Wilson
Otis, Elwell Stephen
Pack, William F.
Page, Herbert Claiborne
Patti, Archimedes Leonida Attilio
Peers, William Raymond
Pershing, John Joseph
Smith, Jacob Hurd
Stilwell, Joseph Warren
Thorpe, Elliott R.
Turnbull, Wilfrid
Van Schaick, Louis J.
Wedemeyer, Albert Coady
Wheeler, Raymond Albert
White, John Roberts
Whitney, Courtney
Williams, Samuel Tankersley
Willoughby, Charles Andrew
Wilson, James Harrison
Wood, Leonard

ART COLLECTORS
Packard, Harry

ARTISTS. *See also* PAINTERS
Brown, Eliphalet, Jr.
De Forest, Lockwood
Heine, Peter Bernard Wilhelm
Hyde, Helen
Kern, Edward Meyer
MacKenzie, Roderick Dempster
Sterne, Maurice
Wilder, James Austin

ASSOCIATION OFFICIALS
Baker, John Earl
Barnett, Eugene Epperson
Brockman, Fletcher Sims
Carter, Edward Clark
Davis, John Merle

Fisher, Galen Merriam
Fitch, George Ashmore
Gailey, Robert Reed
Greene, Roger Sherman
Hatch, Duane Spencer
Lyon, David Willard
McConaughy, David
Mallory, Walter Hampton
Rusch, Paul
Turner, Everett Stanton
Wilder, Robert Parmelee

ASTRONOMERS
Lowell, Percival
Paul, Henry Martyn

AUTHORS
Anderson, William Ashley
Bacon, Alice Mabel
Bowers, Faubion
Browne, John Ross
Buck, Pearl Sydenstricker
Caldwell, John Cope
Craig, Austin
Crawford, Francis Marion
Crow, Herbert Carl
Davis, Hassoldt
Dyson, Verne
Fenollosa, Mary McNeill
Franck, Harry Alverson
Geil, William Edgar
Goodrich, Joseph King
Gregg, Richard Bartlett
Griffis, William Elliot
Hahn, Emily
Hartendorp, Abram Van Heyningen
Hearn, Lafcadio
Hervey, Harry Clay
Hobart, Alice Tisdale
Hunter, William C.
Hurley, G. Victor
Ireland, Alleyne
Keith, Agnes Newton
Knox, George William
Knox, Thomas Wallace
Landon, Margaret Dorothea Mortenson
Lineberger, Paul Myron Wentworth
Lowell, Percival

Mayo, Katherine
Miller, Warren Hastings
Peck, Graham
Peffer, Nathaniel
Pitman, Norman Hinsdale
Powell, Edward Alexander
Pruitt, Ida C.
Scidmore, Eliza Ruhamah
Smedley, Agnes
Sneider, Vernon John
Snow, Edgar
Twain, Mark
Waln, Robert, Jr.

AVIATION EXECUTIVES
Jouett, John Hamilton
Pawley, William Douglas
Willauer, Whiting

AVIATORS
Chennault, Claire Lee

BANKERS
Fischer, Emil Sigmund
Fritz, Chester

BIOLOGISTS
Gee, Nathaniel Gist
Whitman, Charles Otis

BOOKSELLERS
Tuttle, Charles Egbert

BOTANISTS. *See also* **PLANT COLLECTORS; PLANT EXPLORERS**
Bartlett, Harley Harris
Beattie, Rolla Kent
Brown, William Henry
Clark, William Smith
Copeland, Edwin Bingham
Elmer, Adolph Daniel Edward
Lamson-Scribner, Frank
LaRue, Carl Downey
McClure, Floyd Alonzo
Merrill, Elmer Drew
Penhallow, David Pearce
Robinson, Charles Budd, Jr.

Rock, Joseph Francis Charles
Steward, Albert Newton
Swingle, Walter Tennyson
Walker, Egbert Hamilton

BUSINESSMEN
Anderson, William Hart
Bachrach, Emil [Emmanuel] M.
Betts, Arlington Ulysses
Bicknell, John Warren
Bishop, Ancil Hiram
Booth, Frank S.
Bowles, Chester Bliss
Bruce, Edward Bright
Carroll, Earl
Chandler, John Hasset
Cohen, Theodore
Gaches, Samuel Francis
Hunt, Leigh S. J.
Hutchison, James Lafayette
Ingersoll, Robert Stephen, Jr.
Irwin, Robert Walker
Kane, Samuel E.
Legendre, Sidney Jennings
Meyer, Clarence Earle
Morris, James Henry
Morse, James Rolland
Pond, Horace B.
Roosevelt, Kermit
Roosevelt, Theodore, Jr.
Rosenstock, Christian William
Shaw, William James
Stevenot, Joseph Emile Hamilton
Stevens, Joseph Earle
Thompson, James Harrison Wilson
Townsend, Walter Davis
Vories, William Merrell
Whitmarsh, Hubert Phelps

CHEMISTS
Blackshear, Charles Cotton
Freer, Paul Caspar
Stockbridge, Horace Edward

CLERGYMEN. *See also* **MISSIONARIES**
Bradley, Dan Freedman
Brent, Charles Henry

Chapelle, Placide Louis
Dall, Charles Henry Appleton
Dougherty, Dennis Joseph
Engbring, Francis Xavier
Fisher, Frederick Bohn
Harty, Jeremiah James
Hayes, James T. G.
Hendrick, Thomas Augustine
Hurley, John F.
Hurth, Peter Joseph
Kennally, Vincent Ignatius
MacCauley, Clay
McCloskey, James Paul
McKinnon, William Daniel
Masterson, William Francis
Mole, Robert L.
Pardy, James V.
Peery, Rufus Benton
Ryan, Archie Lowell
Scheerer, Aloysius Louis
Sunderland, Jabez Thomas
Tucker, Henry St. George

COLONIAL ADMINISTRATORS

Butte, George Charles Felix
Carpenter, Frank Watson
Davis, Dwight Filley
Elliott, Charles Burke
Fergusson, Arthur Walsh
Forbes, William Cameron
Gilmore, Eugene Allen
Greene, Warwick
Hale, Walter Franklin
Harrison, Francis Burton
Hayden, Joseph Ralston
Hull, John Adley
Ide, Henry Clay
Kane, Samuel E.
Leroy, James Alfred
McNutt, Paul Vories
Malcolm, George Arthur
Moses, Bernard
Murphy, Frank
Roosevelt, Theodore, Jr.
Sayre, Francis Bowes
Smith, James Francis
Stimson, Henry Lewis
Taft, William Howard

Wood, Leonard
Worcester, Dean Conant
Wright, Luke Edward

COLONISTS
Savory, Nathaniel

COMPOSERS
McPhee, Colin Carhart

CONSULS. *See* DIPLOMATS

COWBOYS
Barton, Fred

CRYPTOGRAPHERS
Yardley, Herbert Osborne

DIPLOMATIC ADVISORS. *See also* LEGAL ADVISORS

James, Eldon Revare
LeGendre, Charles William
Pitkin, Wolcott Homer
Sheppard, Eli T.
Smith, Erasmus Peshine
Stevens, Raymond Bartlett
Strobel, Edward Henry

DIPLOMATS

Allen, Horace Newton
Allison, John Moore
Angell, James Burrill
Arnold, Julean Herbert
Atcheson, George, Jr.
Avery, Benjamin Parke
Baker, James Marion
Baldwin, Charles Franklin
Balestier, Joseph B.
Ballantine, Henry (1846–1914)
Bancroft, Edgar Addison
Barrett, John
Bingham, John Armour
Blair, William McCormick, Jr.
Bosworth, Stephen Warren
Bowles, Chester Bliss
Bradley, Charles William
Browne, John Ross
Bryan, Charles Page

Bunker, Ellsworth
Calhoun, William James
Cheshire, Fleming Duncan
Child, Jacob Tripler
Clubb, Oliver Edmund
Cochran, Horace Merle
Conger, Edwin Hurd
Coombs, Frank Leslie
Cooper, John Sherman
Cowen, Myron Melvin
Cunningham, Edwin Sheddan
Cushing, Caleb
Davidson, James Wheeler
Davies, John Paton, Jr.
De Long, Charles E.
Denby, Charles
Denby, Charles, Jr.
Dinsmore, Hugh Anderson
Dooman, Eugene Hoffman
Du Bois, Coert
Dun, Edwin
Durbrow, Elbridge
Emmerson, John Kenneth
Fee [MacFee], William Thomas
Foote, Lucius Harwood
Foulk, George Clayton
Galbraith, John Kenneth
Gauss, Clarence Edward
Gleeck, Lewis Edward, Jr.
Gourley, Louis Hill
Grew, Joseph Clark
Guthrie, George Wilkins
Halderman, John Acoming
Harris, Townsend
Heard, Augustine (1827–1905)
Heath, Donald Read
Henderson, Loy Wesley
Hester, Evett Dorell
Heusken, Henry
Holcombe, Chester
Hubbard, Richard Bennett
Huffnaglle, Charles
Hurley, Patrick Jay
Ingersoll, Robert Stephen, Jr.
Jacobs, Joseph Earle
Jernigan, Thomas Roberts
Johnson, Nelson Trusler
Jones, Howard Palfrey

Jones, William Patterson
Joy, Benjamin
King, Hamilton
Langdon, William Russell
Lockhart, Frank P.
Lodge, Henry Cabot, Jr.
Low, Frederick Ferdinand
McCartee, Divie Bethune
McConaughy, Walter Patrick, Jr.
McCoy, Frank Ross
McLane, Robert Milligan
MacMurray, John Van Antwerp
MacVeagh, Charles
Mansfield, Michael Joseph
Marshall, Humphrey
Martin, Graham Anderson
Melby, John Fremont
Merrell, George Robert
Meyer, Armin Henry
Michael, William Henry
Miller, Henry B.
Morris, Roland Sletor
Moses, Charles Lee
Muccio, John Joseph
Neville, Edwin Lowe
Nolting, Frederick Ernest
O'Brien, Thomas James
Paddock, Paul Ezekiel, Jr.
Parker, Peter
Partridge, Frederick William
Paxton, John Hall
Peck, Willys Ruggles
Perkins, Eugene Arthur
Phillips, William
Pruyn, Robert Hewson
Rankin, Karl Lott
Reed, William Bradford
Reinsch, Paul Samuel
Reischauer, Edwin Oldfather
Roberts, Edmund
Rockhill, William Woodville
Roosevelt, Nicholas
Sands, William Franklin
Schurman, Jacob Gould
Scidmore, George Hawthorne
Sebald, William Joseph
Service, John Stewart
Seward, George Frederick

Sill, John Mahelm Berry
Sprouse, Philip Dodson
Stanton, Edwin Forward
Stevens, Durham White
Straight, Willard Dickerman
Strobel, Edward Henry
Stuart, John Leighton
Studer, Adolphus G.
Swift, John Franklin
Tenney, Charles Daniel
Vincent, John Carter
Ward, John Elliott
Wildman, Rounsevelle
Williams, Edward Thomas
Williams, Samuel Wells
Woods, Cyrus E.
Young, John Russell

ECONOMIC ADVISORS
Conant, Charles Arthur
Young, Arthur Nichols

ECONOMISTS
Andrus, James Russell
Bunce, Arthur Cyril
Galbraith, John Kenneth
Hewes, Lawrence Ilsley
Jenks, Jeremiah Whipple
Remer, Charles Frederick
Smith, Erasmus Peshine

EDITORS. *See also* PUBLISHERS
Bennett, Roy Coleman
Bernstein, David
Child, Jacob Tripler
Clark, Grover
Eastlake, Frederick Warrington
Fleisher, Benjamin Wilfrid
Fleisher, Wilfrid
Hartendorp, Abran Van Heyningen
Jones, Howard Palfrey
Knapp, Arthur May
Macdonald, Alexander
Marquardt, Frederick Sylvester
Marvin, George
Powell, John Benjamin
Reid, Gilbert
Wood, William W.

EDUCATORS. *See also* MISSIONARY EDUCATORS
Angell, James Burrill
Atkinson, Fred Washington
Barrows, David Prescott
Bartlett, Murray
Beattie, George William
Bewley, Luther Boone
Britton, Roswell Sessoms
Brown, Roy Howard
Buss, Claude Albert
Caldwell, Oliver Johnson
Carlin, James Joseph
Carson, Arthur Leroy
Cary, Otis
Chaplin, Winfield Scott
Clark, Edward Warren
Clement, Ernest Wilson
Craig, Austin
Derbyshire, Charles E.
Dewey, John
Eakin, John Anderson
Eastlake, Frederick Warrington
Edmunds, Charles Keyser
Fransler, Dean Spruill
Faust, Allen Klein
Gage, Brownell
Gilmore, George William
Graham, Frank Porter
Griffis, William Eliot
Hamilton, Charles Robert
Henke, Frederick Goodrich
Hibbard, David Sutherland
Hodous, Lewis
Houghton, Henry Spencer
Houghton, William Addison
Hulbert, Homer Bezaleel
Hume, Edward Hicks
Irwin, Sophia A.
Janes, Leroy Lansing
Jones, Thomas Elsa
Kauffman, James Lee
Kershner, Bruce Lesher
King, Hamilton
Knox, George William
Kuder, Edward M.
Lawrence, Fred Tulus

McCormick, J. Scott
McCune, George McAfee
McLean, Franklin Chambers
Marquardt, Walter William
Moses, Bernard
Moss, Claude Russell
Murray, David
Oliver, Robert Tarbell
Osborn, Lois Stewart
O'Toole, George Barry
Peffer, Nathaniel
Perez, Gilbert Somers
Pitman, Norman Hinsdale
Plumer, James Marshall
Porter, Lucius Chapin
Reischauer, August Karl
Renouf, Vincent Adams
Rusch, Paul
Saleeby, Najeeb Mitry
Schurman, Jacob Gould
Scott, Marion McCarrell
Shaw, Glenn William
Sill, John Mahelm Berry
Stockbridge, Horace Edward
Terry, Henry Taylor
Underwood, Horace Horton
Vining, Elizabeth Janet Gray
Vories, William Merrell
White, Francis Johnstone
White, Frank Russell
Wildes, Harry Emerson
Williams, John Elias
Zumbro, William Michael

EDUCATORS OF THE BLIND
Caulfield, Genevieve

ELECTRICAL ENGINEERS
Rockwell, James Chapman

ENGINEERS
Baker, John Earl
Beardsley, James Wallace
Davis, George Whitefield
Dawley, William Sanborn
Freeman, John Ripley
Halsema, Eusebius Julius
Henry, Philip Walter

Hotchkiss, Henry Stuart
Jameson, Charles Davis
Keenan, John Lawrence
Parsons, William Barclay
Perin, Charles Page
Putnam, George Rockwell
Todd, Oliver Julian
Tutwiler, Temple William
Wasson, James Robert
Wheeler, Raymond Albert
Wheeler, William
Wilson, James Harrison

ENTOMOLOGISTS
Light, Sol Felty

ETHNOLOGISTS. *See also*
ANTHROPOLOGISTS
Christie, Emerson Brewer
Culin, Robert Stewart
Garvan, John M.
Holtom, Daniel Clarence
Jones, William
Marshall, Harry Ignatius

ETHNOMUSICOLOGISTS
Higgins, Jon B.
McPhee, Colin Carhart

EXPLORERS. *See also* **TRAVELERS**
Andrews, Roy Chapman
Burden, William Douglas
Collins, Perry McDonough
Davis, Hassoldt
Dolan, Brooke, II
Forman, Harrison
Harrison, Alfred Craven, Jr.
Kennan, George
Legendre, Sidney Jennings
Morden, William James
Pumpelly, Raphael
Roosevelt, Kermit
Vernay, Arthur Stannard
Workman, Fanny Bullock

FARMERS
Hill, Percy A.

FILM CRITICS
Richie, Donald Steiner

FINANCIAL ADVISORS
Hester, Evett Dorell
Jones, James Weldon

FINANCIAL AGENTS
Anderson, Roy Scott
Davidson, James Wheeler

FINANCIERS
Stevens, Frederick Waeir
Straight, Willard Dickerman
Williams, George Burchell

FOLKLORISTS
Fansler, Dean Spruill
Moss, Claude Russell
Wilson, Laurence Lee

FORESTERS
Ahern, George Patrick
Cuzner, Harold
Fischer, Arthur Frederick
Foxworthy, Fred William
Whitford, Harry Nichols

FRUIT GROWERS
Stokes, Samuel Evans

GEOGRAPHERS
Barrett, Robert Lemoyne
Cressey, George Babcock
Hall, Robert Burnett
Huntington, Ellsworth
McCune, Shannon Boyd-Bailey
Pelzer, Karl Josef
Spencer, Joseph Earle

GEOLOGISTS
Adams, George Irving
Barbour, George Brown
Becker, George Ferdinand
Berkey, Charles Peter
Blake, William Phipps
Drake, Noah Fields

Grabau, Amadeus William
Lyman, Benjamin Smith
Pumpelly, Raphael
Smith, Warren Dupré
Willis, Bailey

GOVERNMENT OFFICIALS
Arlington, Lewis Charles
Bowles, Chester Bliss
Buck, John Lossing
Bunce, Arthur Cyrill
Buss, Claude Albert
Butte, George Charles Felix
Carl, Francis Augustus
Carpenter, Frank Watson
Christie, Emerson Brewer
Cohen, Theodore
Cushing, Caleb
Davis, Dwight Filley
Dolbeare, Frederick Russell
Drew, Edward Bangs
Ferguson, John Calvin
Gale, Esson McDowell
Graham, Frank Porter
Hewes, Lawrence Ilsley
Hornbeck, Stanley Kuhl
Hurley, Patrick Jay
Johnson, Louis Arthur
Kades, Charles Louis
Kaplan, Gabriel Louis
Koke, Robert A.
Landon, Kenneth Perry
Lansdale, Edward Geary
Leech, John Sylvanus
Little, Lester Knox
Merrill, Henry Ferdinand
Morse, Hosea Ballou
Murphy, Frank
Noble, Harold Joyce
Oppler, Alfred C.
Plumer, James Marshall
Smith, Addie Viola
Steiner, Kurt
Stevens, Raymond Bartlett
Stimson, Henry Lewis
Taft, William Howard
Whitney, Courtney
Wildes, Harry Emerson

Williams, Justin, Sr.
Woodruff, Francis Eben

GUERILLA OFFICERS
Fagen, David

HERPATOLOGISTS
Taylor, Edward Harrison

HISTORIANS
Beard, Charles Austin
Cady, John Frank
Gleeck, Lewis Edward, Jr.
Gowing, Peter Gordon
MacNair, Harley Farnsworth
Noble, Harold Joyce
Robertson, James Alexander
Scott, William Henry

HOTEL KEEPERS
Koke, Louise Garrett
Koke, Robert A.

ICHTHYOLOGISTS
Seale, Alvin
Smith, Hugh McCormick
Tolstoy, Ilia A.

INDOLOGISTS
Brown, William Norman
Hall, Fitzedward

IRRIGATION ENGINEERS
Lowdermilk, Walter Clay
Wrentmore, Clarence George

JAPANOLOGISTS
Keene, Donald Lawrence
Reischauer, Edwin Oldfather

JOURNALISTS
Abend, Hallett Edward
Avery, Benjamin Parke
Barnett, Arthur Doak
Beech, Keyes
Bernstein, David
Brownell, Clarence Ludlow

Close, Upton
Crow, Herbert Carl
Dick, Robert McCullough
Duane, William
Durdin, Frank Tillman
Egan, Martin
Forman, Harrison
Gilbert, Rodney Yonkers
Gould, Randall Chase
Hedges, Frank Hinckley
Hoberecht, Earnest
House, Edward Howard
Isaacs, Harold Robert
Kennan, George
McCormick, Frederick
Marquardt, Frederick Sylvester
Marshall, Raymond Gifford
Marvin, George
Millard, Thomas Franklin Fairfax
Moore, Frederick
Nichols, Francis Henry
O'Brien, Frederick
Powell, John Benjamin
Rea, George Bronson
Robb, Walter Johnson
Roosevelt, Nicholas
Shaplen, Robert Modell
Smedley, Agnes
Smith, Robert Aura
Snow, Edgar
Snow, Helen Foster
Sternberg, David Theron
Strong, Anna Louise
Trumbull, Robert
Vaughn, Miles Walter
Votaw, Maurice Eldred
Young, John Russell

JUDGES
Blount, James Henderson, Jr.
Carson, Adam Clarke
Johnson, Elias Finley
Lobingier, Charles Sumner
Ostrand, James Adolph
Street, Thomas Atkins
Vickers, James Cator
Wilfley, Lebbeus Redman

JURISTS. *See also* LAWYERS
Oppler, Alfred C.
Steiner, Kurt

KOREANOLOGISTS
Hulbert, Homer Bezaleel
Landis, Eli Barr

LAWYERS
Allman, Norwood Francis
Bancroft, Edgar Addison
Blount, James Henderson, Jr.
Butte, George Charles Felix
Calhoun, William James
Coombs, Frank Leslie
Cowen, Myron Melvin
De Long, Charles E.
Denby, Charles
DeWitt, Clyde Alton
Dinsmore, Hugh Anderson
Elliott, Charles Burke
Evans, Richard Taylor
Gilbert, Newton Whitney
Gilmore, Eugene Allen
Guthrie, George Wilkins
Haussermann, John William
Hubbard, Richard Bennett
Hurley, Patrick Jay
Ide, Henry Clay
Ingersoll, Frank Bassett
James, Eldon Revare
Johnson, Elias Finley
Johnson, Louis Arthur
Kades, Charles Louis
Kauffman, James Lee
Linebarger, Paul Myron Wentworth
Lobingier, Charles Sumner
Maclay, Arthur Collins
McNutt, Paul Vories
MacVeagh, Charles
Morris, Roland Sletor
O'Brien, Thomas James
Ostrand, James Adolph
Perkins, Eugene Arthur
Pitkin, Wolcott Homer
Reed, William Bradford

Sayre, Francis Bowes
Smith, James Francis
Stimson, Henry Lewis
Street, Thomas Atkins
Swift, John Franklin
Vickers, James Cator
Ward, John Elliott
Westengard, Jens Iverson
Whitney, Courtney
Wilfley, Lebbeus Redman
Willauer, Whiting
Woods, Cyrus E.

LEGAL ADVISORS. *See also* DIPLOMATIC ADVISORS
Denison, Henry Willard
Denny, Owen Nickerson
Dolbeare, Frederick Russell
Greathouse, Clarence Ridgley

LEPROLOGISTS
McKean, James William
Wade, Herbert Windsor

LIBRARIANS
Borden, William Alanson
Egbert, Nelly Young
Hobbs, Cecil Carlton
Hummel, Arthur William
Polk, May
Wood, Mary Elizabeth

MARINE CORPS OFFICERS
Butler, Smedley Darlington
Carlson, Evans Fordyce
McHugh, James Marshall
Tilton, McLane
Waller, Littleton Walter Tazewell

MECHANICAL ENGINEERS
Churchill, David Carroll

MEDICAL MISSIONARIES. *See also* MISSIONARIES
Allen, Horace Newton
Ayers, Thomas Wilburn
Bacheler, Otis Robinson

Beddoe, Robert Earl
Bell, Lemuel Nelson
Berry, John Cutting
Bradley, Dan Beach
Chamberlain, Jacob
Chesnut, Eleanor
Coltman, Robert, Jr.
Coombs-Strittmater, Lucinda L.
Cort, Edwin Charles
Fleming, Bethel Harris
Fulton, Mary Hannah
Graves, Rosewell Hobart
Green, Samuel Fisk
Hall, Rosetta Sherwood
Hall, Sherwood
Happer, Andrew Patton
Hemenway, Ruth V.
Henderson, Albert Haley
Hepburn, James Curtis
Heron, John William
Hirst, Jesse Watson
House, Samuel Reynolds
Huizenga, Lee Sjoerds
James, Mary Latimer
Kerr, John Glasgow
Kugler, Anna Sarah
Lambuth, Walter Russell
Landis, Eli Barr
Lawney, Josephine C.
Lerrigo, Peter Hugh James
Lewis, Charles
Linn, Hugh H.
McCartee, Divie Bethune
McKean, James William
Miller, Elizabeth Jane Bucke
Miller, Edgar Raymond
Miller, Harry Willies
Noble, William Alexander May
Olsen, Viggo Brandt
Osgood, Elliott Irving
Parker, Peter
Parrish, Sarah Rebecca
Pettus, William Winston
Russell, Riley
Scovel, Myra Scott
Scranton, William Benton
Scudder, Galen Fisher

Scudder, Henry Martyn
Scudder, Ida Sophia
Scudder, Jared Waterbury
Scudder, John
Scudder, John II
Scudder, Lewis Rousseau
Seagrave, Gordon Stifler
Seward, Sara Cornelia
Sheldon, Martha A.
Shelton, Albert Leroy
Shepping, Elise Johanna
Sibley, Charles Thomas
Smith, Roy Kenneth
Swain, Clara A.
Thomson, Joseph Oscar
Tooker, Frederick Jagger
Tucker, Margaret Emmeline
Underwood, Lillias Stirling Horton
Van Allen, Frank
Vaughn, Harriet Parker
Wallace, William Lindsey
Wanless, William James

MERCHANTS

Carrington, Edward
Cunningham, Edward
Cushing, John Perkins
Delano, Warren, Jr.
Dorr, Sullivan
Dunn, Nathan
Forbes, Robert Bennet
Frazar, Everett
Frazar, Everett Welles
Green, John Cleve
Hall, George Rogers
Harris, Thomas Bradley
Heard, Augustine (1785–1868)
Heard, Augustine (1827–1905)
Higginson, Nathaniel
Hunter, William C.
Joy, Benjamin
Kerr, John Stuart
King, Charles William
Kinsman, Nathaniel
Latimer, John Richardson
Low, Abiel Abbott
Moses, Charles Lee

Mustard, Robert West
Nye, Gideon, Jr.
Olyphant, David Livingston Cicinnatus
Olyphant, Robert Morrison
Roberts, Edmund
Russell, George Robert
Russell, Samuel Wadsworth
Savory, Nathaniel
Shaw, Samuel
Snow, Samuel
Sokolsky, George Ephraim
Sturgis, Russell
Sturgis, William
Torrey, Joseph William
Tyson, George
Van Braam Houckgeest, Andreas
  Everardus
Wakefield, Cyrus
Wilcocks, Benjamin Chew
Yale, Elihu
Yale, Thomas

MILITARY BANDMASTERS
Loving, Walter Howard

MILITARY SURGEONS
Woodruff, Charles Edward
Woods, George W.

MINING ENGINEERS
Bain, Harry Foster
Blake, William Phipps
Church, John Adams
Collbran, Harry
Crosby, Ralph Willis
Foote, Arthur Burling
Hoover, Herbert Clark
Lednicky, Victor
Lyman, Benjamin Smith
McCaskey, Hiram Dwyer
Munroe, Henry Smith
Randolph, John Cooper Fitz

MINING EXECUTIVES
Crosby, Ralph Willis
Haussermann, John William
Marsman, Jan Hendrick

MISSIONARIES. *See also* MEDICAL MISSIONARIES; MISSIONARY EDUCATORS
Abeel, David
Agnew, Eliza
Allen, David Oliver
Allen, Young John
Ament, William Scott
Amstutz, Hobart Bauman
Anderson, David Lawrence
Anderson, William Brennan
Anglin, Leslie M.
Appenzeller, Alice Rebecca
Appenzeller, Henry Dodge
Appenzeller, Henry Gerhard
Arndt, Eduard Louis
Ashmore, William
Axling, William
Badley, Brenton Hamilne
Badley, Brenton Thoburn
Baird, Annie (Laurie) Adams
Baird, Esther E.
Baird, William Martyn
Baldwin, Stephen Livingstone
Ballagh, James Hamilton
Ballantine, Henry (1813–1865)
Bashford, James Whitford
Bates, Miner Searle
Bawden, Samuel Day
Bennett, Cephus
Bergen, Paul David
Berry, Arthur D.
Binney, Joseph Getchell
Binsted, Norman Spencer
Boardman, George Dana
Boone, William Jones, Jr.
Boone, William Jones, Sr.
Booth, Eugene Samuel
Bowen, George
Bowles, Gilbert
Brewster, William Nesbitt
Bridgman, Elijah Coleman
Bridgman, Eliza Jane Gillet
Briggs, Charles Whitman
Briggs, George Weston
Bronson, Miles

Brown, George Thompson
Brown, Henry Jacob
Brown, Nathan
Brown, Roy Howard
Brown, Samuel Robbins
Bruce, Henry James
Bryan, Robert Thomas
Buck, Oscar MacMillan
Buck, Philo Melvin
Buker, Raymond Bates
Bunker, Alonzo
Bunker, Annie Ellers
Bunker, Dalzell Adelbert
Burgess, Ebenezer
Burgess, Georgia Anna Burrus
Burke, William Blount
Butler, Esther
Butler, William
Byrne, Patrick James
Carson, Arthur E.
Carson, Arthur Leroy
Carson, Laura L. Hardin
Cary, Frank
Cary, Otis (1851–1932)
Caswell, Jesse
Cattell, Everett Lewis
Chalfant, Frank Herring
Chamberlain, William Isaac
Chandler, John Scudder
Chapin, Lyman Dwight
Chaplin, Maxwell
Cherry, William Thomas
Christie, William
Clark, Alden Hyde
Clark, Edward Winter
Clark, Mary Jane Read
Clough, John Everett
Collins, Judson Dwight
Comstock, Grover Smith
Cook, Herman Henry
Coole, Arthur Braddan
Corbett, Hunter
Cowman, Charles E.
Cowman, Lettie Burd
Crawford, Tarleton Perry
Crumpacker, Franklin Henry
Culbertson, Matthew Simpson
Culpepper, Robert Harrell

Cushing, Josiah Nelson
Dall, Charles Henry Appleton
Danker, William John
Davis, Jerome Dean
Dean, William
Dearing, John Lincoln
DeForest, John Kinne Hyde
Denyes, John Russell
Dickson, Lillian Ruth Levesconte
Dodd, William Clifton
Doltz, Paul
Doolittle, Justus
Doty, Elihu
Dozier, Charles Kelsey
Dozier, Edwin Burke
Dubose, Hampden Coit
Dubs, Charles Newton
Duncan, Marion Herbert
Eckard, James Read
Eckel, William A.
Eddy, George Sherwood
Edwins, August William
Erskine, William Hugh
Ewing, Arthur Henry
Ewing, James Caruthers Rhea
Fairbank, Henry S.
Fairbank, Samuel Bacon
Fairfield, Wynn Cowan
Farmer, Martha Ada Beeson
Farmer, Harry
Farrar, Cynthia
Fay, Lydia Mary
Fenn, Courteney Hughes
Fielde, Adele Marion
Fleming, Robert Leland
Fleming, Daniel Johnson
Ford, Francis Xavier
Forman, Charles William
Freeman, John Edgar
Frillmann, Paul William
Fulton, Albert Andrew
Gaines, Nannie Bett [Ann Elizabeth]
Galt, Howard Spilman
Galvin, Edward J.
Gamble, Sidney David
Gamewell, Frank [Francis] Dunlap
Garst, Charles Elias
Gifford, Daniel Lyman

Gilman, Alfred Alonzo
Glover, Robert Hall
Goble, Jonathan
Goddard, Josiah
Goete, Athanasius
Goete, John Capistran
Goete, Remy
Goheen, John Lawrence
Goodrich, Chauncy
Gordon, Andrew
Gordon, Marquis Lafayette
Gowdy, John
Graves, Frederick Rogers
Greene, Daniel Crosby
Greene, Philips Foster
Greene, Ruth Altman
Griffin, Susan Elizabeth Cilley
Grinnan, Randolph Bryan
Griswold, Hervey DeWitt
Gruen, Olive Dorothy [Grün, Oliva Dorothea]
Gulick, John Thomas
Gulick, Luther Halsey
Gulick, Orramel Hinckley
Gulick, Sidney Lewis
Hagenstein, August
Hall, Gordon
Hallock, Henry Galloway Comingo
Hamilton, Charles Robert
Hanson, Ola
Harpster, John Henry
Harrington, Charles Kendall
Harris, Edward Norman
Harris, Merriman Colbert
Hart, Virgil Chittenden
Hartman, Ward
Hartwell, Jesse Boardman, Jr.
Hascall, William Hosmer Shailer
Hastings, Eurotas Parmelee
Hayes, Watson MacMillan
Haygood, Laura Askew
Hazen, Hervey Crosby
Headland, Isaac Taylor
Heinrichs, Jacob
Hemenway, Asa
Henry, Harold
Herrick, David Scudder
Herrick, James

Heyer, John [Johann] Christian Frederick
Hibbard, David Sutherland
Higdon, Elmer Kelso
Hipps, John Burder
Hoisington, Henry Richard
Holcombe, Chester
Holtom, Daniel Clarence
Hoover, James Matthews
Howland, William Ware
Hoy, William Edwin
Hubbard, Hugh Wells
Huizinga, Henry
Hume, Robert Allen
Hume, Robert Ernest
Hume, Robert Wilson
Hunt, Phineas R.
Huntington, Daniel Trumbull
Hyde, John Nelson
Inglehart, Edwin Taylor
Ingalls, Marilla Baker
Ingle, James Addison
Janvier, Levi
Jones, Eli Stanley
Jones, George Heber
Jones, John Peter
Jones, John Taylor
Judson, Adoniram
Judson, Ann Hasseltine
Judson, Emily Chubbuck
Judson, Sarah Hall Boardman
Kellogg, Samuel Henry
Kershner, Bruce Lesher
Kidder, May E.
Kilbourne, Ernest Albert
Kincaid, Eugenio
Klaus, Armin Vincent
Klein, Frederick C.
Knapp, Arthur May
Lacy, George Carleton
Lacy, William Henry
Lambuth, James William
Landon, Kenneth Perry
Lane, Ortha May
Lapp, George Jay
Lapp, Mahlon Cassius
Laubach, Frank Charles
Lawton, Wesley Willingham
Lee, Edwin Ferdinand

Leonard, Charles Alexander
Lobenstine, Edwin Carlyle
Loewenthal, Isidor
Lohr, Oscar
Lowrie, John Cameron
Lowrie, Reuben Post
Lowrie, James Walter
Lowry, Gentry Edward
Lowry, Hiram Harrison
Luce, Henry Winters
Lyman, Henry
Lynch, Denis
MacCauley, Clay
McCollum, John William
McFarland, Samuel Gamble
McGavran, Donald Anderson
McGilvary, Daniel
McKim, John
McShane, Daniel Leo
Maclay, Robert Samuel
Malcolm, Howard
Mansell, William Albert
Marshall, Harry Ignatius
Martin, William Alexander Parsons
Mason, Francis
Mateer, Calvin Wilson
Matson, Peter
Mattoon, Stepehn
Meyer, Bernard Francis
Moffett, Samuel Austin
Monahan, John J.
Moon, Charlotte Lottie Digges
Mosher, Gouverneur Frank
Moyer, Samuel Tyson
Mudge, James
Munger, Henry Weston
Munson, Samuel
Nelson, Bert N.
Nelson, Daniel
Nevius, John Livingston
Newell, Samuel
Newman, Thomas A.
Newton, John
Newton, John Caldwell Calhoun
Noble, William Arthur
Nordlund, Victor Leonard
Nott, Samuel
Ohlinger, Franklin

Oldham, William Fitzjames
Olsen, Walter Severin
O'Shea, John A.
Parker, Alvin Pierson
Parker, Edwin Wallace
Partridge, Sidney Catlin
Peet, Lyman Bert
Penner, Peter A.
Penner, Peter William
Pettus, William Bacon
Phillips, Jeremiah
Pierson, George Peck
Porter, Lucius Chapin
Poteat, Edwin McNeill, Jr.
Pott, Francis Lister Hawks
Price, Frank Wilson
Price, Thomas Frederick
Pruitt, Anna Ashley Seward
Pye, Watts Orson
Rawlinson, Frank Joseph
Ray, Rex
Read, Hollis
Reed, Mary
Reid, Gilbert
Reifsnider, Charles Shriver
Reimert, William Anson
Reifsnider, Charles Shriver
Reimert, William Anson
Reischauer, August Karl
Reynolds, Ira Hubert
Rhees, Henry Holcombe
Roberts, James Hudson
Roberts, William Henry
Robinson, Charles
Robinson, John Edward
Robinson, John Wesley
Rodgers, James Burton
Roots, Logan Herbert
Sallee, W. Eugene
Sanders, Marshall Danforth
Schereschewsky, Samuel Isaac Joseph
Schneder, David Bowman
Schwartz, Aloysius
Schwartz, Henry Butler
Scranton, Mary Fletcher Benton
Scudder, David Coit
Scudder, Henry Martyn
Scudder, William Waterbury

Sheffield, Devello Zelotes
Shuck, Henrietta Hall
Shuck, Jehu Lewis
Smith, Arthur Henderson
Smith, Daniel Appleton White
Smith, Edward Huntington
Smith, Gordon Hedderley
Smith, Laura Irene Ivory
Spaulding, Levi
Stanford, Arthur Willis
Staunton, John Armitage, Jr.
Steineer, Ezra Burkholder
Stewart, Robert
Stover, Wilbur Brenner
Stuart, John Leighton
Stuntz, Homer Clyde
Swenson, Victor Emanuel
Sword, Gustaf A.
Sydenstricker, Absalom
Sydenstricker, Carrie Stulting
Talmage, John Van Nest
Tegenfeldt, Herman Gustaf
Tenney, Charles Daniel
Tennien, Mark A.
Tenny, Charles Buckley
Thoburn, Isabella
Thoburn, James Mills
Thurston, Matilda Smyrell Calder
Thwing, Edward Waite
Tracy, Leighton Stanley
Unangst, Erias
Underwood, Horace Grant
Underwood, Horace Horton
Verbeck, Guido Herman Fridolin
Vinton, Justus Hatch
Wade, Jonathan
Walsh, James Edward
Ward, Ferdinand De Wilton
Ward, Ralph Ansel
Warne, Francis Wesley
Warnshuis, Abbe Livingston
Washburn, George Thomas
Webb, Edward
Webster, James Benjamin
Wharton, Greene Lawrence
Wherry, Elwood Morris
Wherry, John
White, Moses Clark

Whittemore, Norman Clark
Widdoes, Howard W.
Wilder, Royal Gould
Williams, Channing Moore
Williams, Edward Thomas
Williams, Hermon Porter
Williams, John Elias
Williams, Mark
Williams, Samuel Wells
Winslow, Miron
Wiser, Charlotte Melina Viall
Wiser, William Hendricks
Wood, Mary Elizabeth
Woodbridge, Samuel Isett
Wyckoff, Charlotte Chandler
Yates, Matthew Tyson
Youngberg, Gustavus Benson

MISSIONARY CAPTAINS
Bickel, Luke Washington

MISSIONARY EDUCATORS. *See also* MISSIONARIES
Bookwalter, Lulu Gertrude
Bowen, Arthur John
Boynton, Grace Morrison
Bridgman, Eliza Jane Gillet
Clayton, Edward Hyers
DeForest, Charlotte Burgis
Denton, Mary Florence
Ferguson, John Calvin
Fisher, Welthy Blakeslee Honsinger
Fleming, Daniel Johnson
Frame, Alice Seymour Browne
Gleysteen, William Henry
Heflin, Clyde Everette
Henry, James McClure
Hummel, Arthur William
Johnson, Herbert Buell
Miner, Sarah Luella
Nichols, Florence
Palmer, Marion Boyd
Poorbaugh, Elizabeth R.
Robinson, Ruth Evelyn
Smith, Helen Huntington
Talcott, Eliza
Vautrin, Minnie
Wheeler, William Reginald

MOUNTAIN CLIMBERS
Dyhrenfurth, Norman Gunter
Houston, Charles Snead
Workman, Fanny Bullock

MUSIC EDUCATORS
Mason, Luther Whiting

NATURALISTS
Abbott, William Louis
Bickmore, Albert Smith
Burden, William Douglas
Cutting, Charles Suydam
Dolan, Brooke, II
Gulick, John Thomas
Herre, Albert William Christian Theodore
Horsfield, Thomas

NAVAL OFFICERS
Bell, Henry Haywood
Bent, Silas
Biddle, James
Brooke, John Mercer
Buckingham, Benjamin Horr
Cooke, Charles Maynard, Jr.
Dewey, George
Downes, John
Foote, Andrew Hull
Foulk, George Clayton
Glynn, James
Grinnell, Henry Walton
Habersham, Alexander Wylly
Kearny, Lawrence
McDougal, David Stockton
McGiffin, Philo Norton
Mclean, Walter
Miles, Milton Edward
Percival, John
Perry, Matthew Calbraith
Preble, George Henry
Ringgold, Cadwalader
Rodgers, John
Shufeldt, Robert Wilson
Tattnall, Josiah
White, John
Zacharias, Ellis Mark

NURSES
Gaches, Elsie McCloskey
Richards, Linda

NUTRITIONISTS
Adolph, William Henry
Vedder, Edward Bright

OCEANOGRAPHERS
Bent, Silas

OIL DRILLERS
Locke, Robert D.

ORIENTALISTS
Bigelow, William Sturgis
Laufer, Berthold

ORNITHOLOGISTS
Deignan, Herbert Girton
McGregor, Richard Crittenden
Ripley, Sidney Dillon, II
Steere, Joseph Beal

PAINTERS. *See also* ARTISTS
Blum, Robert Frederick
Carl, Katherine Augusta
Gay, Winckworth Allan
La Farge, John
Perry, Lilla Cabot
Weeks, Edwin Lord
Wores, Theodore

PALEOBOTANISTS
Chaney, Ralph Works

PALEONTOLOGISTS
Grabau, Amadeus William
Granger, Walter Willis

PAPER MAKERS
Hunter, Dard

PETROLEUM GEOLOGISTS
Butterworth, Emerson McMillin
Clapp, Frederick Gardner
Davis, Morgan Jones

Hopper, Richard Hutchinson
Nelson, Richard Newman

PHYSICAL EDUCATORS
Leland, George Adams

PHYSICIANS. *See also* MEDICAL MISSIONARIES
Ball, Dyer
Basil, George Chester
Cadbury, William Warder
Dooley, Thomas Anthony
Fearn, Anne Walter
Grant, John Black
Hatem, (Shafik) George [Ma Haide]
Hiller, Hiram Milliken
Houghton, Henry Spencer
Houston, Charles Snead
Howard, Harvey James
Hume, Edward Hicks
Lyman, Richard Sherman
McFarland, George Bradley
McLean, Franklin Chambers
Mendelson, Ralph Waldo
Morse, William Reginald
Palmer, John Williamson
Saleeeby, Najeeb Mitry
Stevenson, Paul Huston
Strong, Richard Pearson
Teusler, Rudolf Bolling
Wood, William Maxwell

PHYSICISTS
Mendenhall, Thomas Corwin

PIRATES
Boggs, Eli M.

PLANT COLLECTORS. *See also* PLANT EXPLORERS
Elmer, Adolph Daniel Edward
Hall, George Rogers
Wilson, Ernest Henry

PLANT EXPLORERS. *See also* PLANT COLLECTORS
Dorsett, Palemon Howard
Fairchild, David Grandison

Meyer, Frank Nicholas
Rock, Joseph Francis Charles
Swingle, Walter Tennyson

POETS
Snyder, Gary Sherman

POLITICAL SCIENTISTS
Beard, Charles Austin
Bisson, Thomas Arthur
Goodnow, Frank Johnson
Linebarger, Paul Myron Anthony
McGovern, William Montgomery
Reinsch, Paul Samuel
Trager, Frank Newton
Willoughby, Westel Woodbury
Willoughby, William Franklin

POLITICIANS
Cooper, John Sherman
Cushing, Caleb
Davis, Dwight Filley
Lodge, Henry Cabot, Jr.
Low, Frederick Ferdinand
McLane, Robert Milligan
Mansfield, Michael Joseph
Marshall, Humphrey

POSTAL EXPERTS
Bryan, Samuel Magill

PRINTERS
Bennett, Cephus
Cherry, William Thomas
Cherry, William T., Jr.
Hunter, Dard
Leech, John Sylvanus

PROSPECTORS
Wilson, Laurence Lee

PSYCHOLOGISTS
Carpenter, Clarence Ray
Ladd, George Trumbull
Stewart, Kilton Riggs

PUBLIC HEALTH PHYSICIANS
Heiser, Victor George
Jacocks, William Picard

PUBLICISTS
Eddy, George Sherwood
Egan, Martin
House, Edward Howard
Rea, George Bronson
Straight, Willard Dickerman

PUBLISHERS
Fleisher, Benjamin Wilfird
Fleisher, Wilfrid
Hartendorp, Abram Van Heyningen
Macdonald, Alexander
Millard, Thomas Franklin Fairfax
Taylor, Carson
Tuttle, Charles Egbert

QUEENS
Cooke, Hope

RADIO COMMENTATORS
Close, Upton

RAILROAD ENGINEERS
Carroll, Charles Joseph
Collbran, Harry
Crawford, Joseph Ury
Dawley, William Sanborn

REALTORS
Hoskins, Colin MacRae

REVOLUTIONARIES
Pomeroy, William Joseph

SCIENTISTS
Brooke, John Mercer
Deppermann, Charles Edward
Hitchcock, Romyn
Morrow, James
Schöbl, Otto
Worcester, Dean Conant
Wright, Hamilton Kemp

SEA CAPTAINS
Carnes, Jonathan
Endicott, Charles Moses
Forbes, Robert Bennet

Heard, Augustine (1785–1868)
Kendrick, John
Kinsman, Nathaniel
Roundy, Henry Jenks

SINGERS
Wilson, Margaret Woodrow

SINOLOGISTS
Biggerstaff, Knight
Bodde, Derk
Fairbank, John King
Lattimore, Owen
MacNair, Florence Wheelock Ayscough
Rockhill, William Woodville
Williams, Samuel Wells

SOCIAL WORKERS
Pruitt, Ida C.

SOCIOLOGISTS
Burgess, John Stewart
Kennedy, Raymond
Lynch, Frank [Francis Xavier]
Passin, Herbert
Ryan, Bryce Finley

SOIL SCIENTISTS
Lowdermilk, Walter Clay
Pendleton, Robert Larimore
Thorp, James

STUDENTS OF ORIENTAL ART
Fenollosa, Ernest Francisco
Ferguson, John Calvin
Warner, Langdon

STUDENTS OF RELIGION
Bernard, Theos
Evans-Wentz, Walter Yeeling

THEOSOPHISTS
Olcott, Henry Steel

TOBACCO MERCHANTS
Parrish, Edward James
Thomas, James Augustus

TRAVELERS. *See also* EXPLORERS
Browne, John Ross
Clark, Robert Sterling
Fischer, Emil Sigmund
Franck, Harry Alverson
Furness, William Henry, 3rd
Geil, William Edgar
Hervey, Harry Clay
Hiller, Hiram Milliken
Knox, Thomas Wallace
Nichols, Francis Henry
Powell, Edward Alexander
Scidmore, Eliza Ruhamah

Vincent, Frank
Workman, Fanny Bullock

VICEREINES
Curzon, Mary Victoria Leiter

ZOOLOGISTS
Baker, Charles Fuller
Coolidge, Harold Jefferson
Griffin, Lawrence Edmonds
Morse, Edward Sylvester
Raven, Henry Cushier
Schaller, George Beals

Bibliographical Essay

Reviews of the literature on U.S. foreign relations with Asia can be found in the following works: Ernest R. May and James C. Thomson, Jr., eds., *American–East Asian Relations: A Survey* (Cambridge, Mass.: Harvard University Press, 1972); Warren I. Cohen, ed., *New Frontiers in American–East Asian Relations: Essays Presented to Dorothy Borg* (New York: Columbia University Press, 1983); Warren I. Cohen, "The History of American-East Asian Relations: Cutting Edge of the Historical Profession," *Diplomatic History* 9 (1985): 101–12; Robert J. McMahon, "United States Relations with Asia in the Twentieth Century: Retrospect and Prospect," in *American Foreign Relations: A Historical Review*, ed. Gerald K. Haines and J. Samuel Walker (Westport, Conn.: Greenwood Press, 1981), pp. 237–70; and Richard D. Burns, ed., *Guide to American Foreign Relations since 1700* (Santa Barbara, Calif.: ABC-Clio, 1983), chs. 17, 27, 30, 31, and 37.

More specific analyses can be found in Kwang-chung Liu, *American and Chinese: A Historical Essay and a Bibliography* (Cambridge, Mass.: Harvard University Press, 1963); James M. McCutcheon, comp., *China and America: A Bibliography of Interactions, Foreign and Domestic* (Honolulu: University Press of Hawaii, 1972); Gary R. Hess, "Global Expansion and Regional Balances: The Emerging Scholarship on United States Relations with India and Pakistan," *Pacific Historical Review* 56 (1987): 259–95; Donald N. Clark, "Sources of Historical Information on the Foreign Community in Korea," in *Yanghwajin, Seoul Foreigners' Cemetery, Korea. An Informal History 1890–1984, with Notes on Other Foreign Cemeteries in Korea*, comp. and ed. by Donald N. Clark (Seoul: Yongsan RSOK Library, 1984), pp. 165–80; and Glenn A. May, "The State of the Philippine-American Studies," *Bulletin of the American Historical Collection* 10 (October-December 1982): 11–31.

Doctoral dissertations are recorded in Curtis W. Stucki, *American Doctoral Dissertations on Asia, 1933–1958* (Ithaca, N.Y.: Cornell University, Southeast Asia Program, Department of Far Eastern Studies, 1959); Frank J. Shulman, *Japan and Korea: An Annotated Bibliography of Doctoral Dissertations in Western Languages, 1877–1969* (Chicago: American Library Association, 1970); Frank J. Shulman, *Doctoral Dissertations on Japan and on Korea, 1969–1979: An Annotated Bibliography of Studies in Western Languages* (Seattle: University of Washington Press, 1982); Frank J. Shulman, *Doctoral Dissertations on China, 1971–1975: A Bibliography of Studies in Western*

Languages (Seattle: University of Washington Press, 1978); and Frank J. Shulman, *Burma: An Annotated Bibliographical Guide to International Doctoral Dissertation Research 1898–1985* (Lanham, Md.: University Press of America, 1986). Frank J. Shulman also edited *Doctoral Dissertations on Asia*, vol. 1 (Ann Arbor, Mich.: University Microfilms, 1975–).

Older surveys of U.S. relations with Asia include Tyler Dennett, *Americans in East Asia: A Critical Study of United States Policy in the Far East in the Nineteenth Century* (New York: Macmillan, 1922) and A. Whitney Griswold, *The Far Eastern Policy of the United States* (New York: Harcourt, Brace, 1938). Recent surveys and studies include John Chay, ed., *The Problems and Prospects of America—East Asian Relations* (Boulder, Colo.: Westview Press, 1977); Edward Friedman and Mark Selden, eds., *America's Asia: Dissenting Essays on Asian-American Relations* (New York: Vintage Books, 1971); Robert A. Hart, *The Eccentric Tradition: American Diplomacy in the Far East* (New York: Charles Scribner's Sons, 1976); Akira Iriye, *Across the Pacific: An Inner History of American-East Asian Relations* (New York: Harcourt, Brace and World, 1967); Marvin Klab and Elie Abel, *Roots of Involvement: The U.S. in Asia, 1784–1971* (New York: Norton, 1971); Edwin O. Reischauer, *Beyond Vietnam: The United States and Asia* (New York: Knopf, 1967); Mark Selden, ed., *Remaking Asia: Essays on the American Use of Power* (New York: Pantheon, 1974); James C. Thomson, Jr., Peter W. Stanley, and John C. Perry, *Sentimental Imperialists: The American Experience in East Asia* (New York: Harper and Row, 1981); Richard W. Van Alstyne, *The United States and East Asia* (New York: Norton, 1973); and William Watts, *The United States and Asia: Changing Attitudes and Policy* (Lexington, Mass.: Lexington Books, 1982).

Dealing with specific regions or topics are Robert M. Blum, *Drawing the Line: The Origin of the American Containment Policy in East Asia* (New York: Norton, 1982); Dorothy Borg, *The United States and the Far Eastern Crisis of 1933–1938: From the Manchurian Incident through the Initial State of the Undeclared Sino-Japanese War* (Cambridge, Mass.: Harvard University Press, 1964); K. Holly Maze Carter, *The Asian Dilemma in U.S. Foreign Policy: National Interest Versus Strategic Planning* (Armonk, N.Y.: M. E. Sharpe, 1989); Ralph Clough, *East Asia and U.S. Security* (Washington, D.C.: Brookings Institution, 1975); Robert M. Crunden, Manoj Joshi, and R.V.R. Chandrasckhar, eds., *New Perspectives on America and South Asia* (Delhi: Chankya Publications, 1984); Justus D. Doenecke, *When the Wicked Rise: American Opinion-Makers and the Manchurian Crisis of 1931–1933* (Lewisburg, Pa.: Bucknell University Press, 1984); Jeffery M. Dorwat, *The Pigtail War: American Involvement in the Sino-Japanese War of 1894–1895* (Amherst: University of Massachusetts Press, 1975); Russell Fifield, *Americans in Southeast Asia: The Roots of Commitment* (New York: Crowell, 1973); Russell H. Fiefield, *Woodrow Wilson and the Far East* (New York: Crowell, 1952); Marc S. Gallicchio, *The Cold War Begins in Asia: American East Asian Policy and the Fall of the Japanese Empire* (New York: Columbia University Press, 1988); Selig S. Harrison, *The Widening Gulf: Asian Nationalism and American Policy* (New York: Free Press, 1978); Gary R. Hess, *The United States' Emergence as a Southeast Asian Power, 1940–1950* (New York: Columbia University Press, 1987); Akira Iriye, *After Imperialism: The Search for a New Order in the Far East 1921–1931* (Cambridge, Mass.: Harvard University Press, 1965); Akira Iriye and Yonosuke Nagai, eds., *The Origins of the Cold War in Asia* (New York, Free Press, 1977); Harold Isaacs, *Scratches on Our Minds: American Images of China and India* (New York: J. Day Co., 1958); Carl T. Jackson, *The Oriental Religions and American Thought: Nineteenth-Century Explorations* (Westport, Conn.: Greenwood Press, 1981); Young-hum Kim, *American Frontier Activities in Asia* (Chicago: Nelson-Hall, 1981); Robert Pringle, *Indonesia and the Philippines: American Interests in Island Southeast Asia* (New York: Columbia University Press, 1980); Kilaru R. C. Rao, *India, United States, and Pakistan: A Triangular Relationship* (Bombay: Himalya, 1985); Andrew J. Rotter, *The Path to Vietnam: Origins of the American Commitment to Southeast Asia* (Ithaca, N.Y.: Cornell University Press, 1987); Lloyd I. Rudolph et al., *The Regional Imperative: The Administration of U.S. Foreign Policy towards South Asian States under Presidents Johnson and Nixon* (New Delhi: Concept Publishing Co., 1980); John J. Sbrega, *Anglo-American Relations and Colonialism in East Asia, 1941–1945* (New York: Garland, 1983); William W. Stueck, *The Road to Confrontation: American Policy toward China and Korea, 1947–1950* (Chapel Hill, N.C.: University of North Carolina Press, 1981); W. Scott Thompson, *Unequal Partners: Philippine and Thai Relations with the United States, 1965–1975* (Lexington, Mass.: Lexington Books, 1975); Jonathan G. Utley, *Going to War with Japan, 1937–1941* (Knoxville: University of Tennessee Press, 1985); William Watts et al., *Japan, Korea and China: American Perceptions and Policies* (Lexington, Mass.: Lexington Books, 1969).

Numerous studies of U.S. relations with specific countries of Asia have been written:

Brunei: H. G. Keith, *The United States Consul and the Yankee Raja* (Bandar Seri Begawan, Brunei: Brunei Museum, 1980).

Burma: John F. Cady, *The United States and Burma* (Cambridge, Mass.: Harvard University Press, 1976).

China: David L. Anderson, *Imperialism and Idealism: American Diplomats in China, 1861–1898* (Bloomington, Ind.: Indiana University Press, 1985); A. Doak Barnett and Edwin O. Reischauer, eds., *The United States and China: The Next Decade* (New York: Praeger, 1970); Dorothy Borg, *American Policy and the Chinese Revolution, 1925–1928* (New York: American Institute of Pacific Relations, 1947); Dorothy Borg and Waldo Henrichs, eds., *Uncertain Years: Chinese-American Relations, 1947–1950* (New York: Columbia University Press, 1980); William J. Brands, ed., *China and America: The Search for a New Relationship* (New York: New York University Press, 1977); Kenneth S. Chern, *Dilemma in China: America's Policy Debate, 1945* (Hamden, Conn.: Archon Books, 1980); Key Ray Chong, *Americans and Chinese Reform and Revolution, 1898–1922: The Role of Private Citizens in Diplomacy* (Lanham, Md.: University Press of America, 1984); Warren I. Cohen, *America's Response to China: A History of Sino-American Relations* (New York: Columbia University Press, 1989); Daniel M. Crane and Thomas A. Breslin, *An Ordinary Relationship: American Opposition to Republican Revolution in China* (Miami: University Press of Florida, 1986); George H. Danton, *The Culture Contacts of the United States and China: The Earliest Sino-American Culture Contacts, 1784–1844* (New York: Columbia University Press, 1931); Foster R. Dulles, *China and America: the Story of Their Relations since 1784* (Princeton, N.J.: Princeton University Press, 1946); Thomas H. Etzold, ed., *Aspects of Sino-American Relations Since 1784* (New York: New Viewpoints, 1978); John K. Fairbank, *China Perceived: Images and Policies in Chinese-American Relations* (New York: Knopf, 1974); John K. Fairbank, *China Watch* (Cambridge, Mass.: Harvard University Press, 1987); John K. Fairbank, *Chinese-American Interactions: A Historical Summary* (New Brunswick, N.J.: Rutgers University Press, 1975); John K. Fairbank, *The United States and China* (Cambridge, Mass.: Harvard University Press, 1983); Herbert Feis, *The China Tangle: The American Effort in China from Pearl Harbor to the Marshall Mission* (Princeton, N.J.:

Princeton University Press, 1953); Paul G. Gordon, ed., *The China Hands' Legacy: Ethics and Diplomacy* (Boulder, Colo.: Westview, 1987); June M. Grasso, *Truman's Two-China Policy, 1948–1950* (Armonk, N.Y.: M. E. Sharpe, 1987); A. James Gregor, *The China Connection: U.S. Policy and the People's Republic of China* (Stanford, Calif.: Hoover Institution Press, 1986); William P. Head, *America's China Sojourn: America's Foreign Policy and Its Effects on Sino-American Relations, 1942–1948* (Lanham, Md.: University Press of America, 1983); Paul S. Holbo, *United States Policies toward China: From the Unequal Treaties to the Cultural Revolution* (New York: Macmillan, 1969); Michael H. Hunt, *Frontier Defense and the Open Door: Manchuria in Chinese-American Relations, 1895–1911* (New Haven: Yale University Press, 1973); Michael H. Hunt, *The Making of a Special Relationship: The United States and China to 1914* (New York: Columbia University Press, 1983); Jerry Israel, *Progressivism and the Open Door: America and China, 1905–1921* (Pittsburgh: University of Pittsburgh Press, 1971); Arnold X. Jiang, *The United States and China* (Chicago: University of Chicago Press, 1988); E. J. Kahn, Jr., *The China Hands: America's Foreign Service Officers and What Befell Them* (New York: Viking, 1975); Leonard A. Kusnitz, *Public Opinion and Foreign Policy: America's China Policy, 1949–1979* (Westport, Conn.: Greenwood Press, 1984); Martin L. Lasater, *Policy in Evolution: The U.S. Role in China's Reunification* (Boulder, Colo.: Westview Press, 1989); Kenneth S. Latourette, *The History of Early Relations between the United States and China, 1784–1844* (New Haven, Conn.: Yale University Press, 1917); Tien-yi Li, *Woodrow Wilson's China Policy, 1913–1917* (New York: Twayne, 1952); Stephen R. MacKinnon and Oris Friesen, *China Reporting: An Oral History of American Journalism in the 1930s and 1940s* (Berkeley, Calif.: University of California Press, 1987); Edwin W. Martin, *Divided Counsel: The Anglo-American Response to Communist Victory in China* (Lexington, Ky.: University Press of Kentucky, 1986); Ernest R. May, *The Truman Administration and China, 1945–1949* (Philadelphia: Lippincott, 1975); Robert F. McClellan, Jr., *The Heathen Chinese: A Study of American Attitudes toward China, 1890–1905* (Columbus: Ohio State University Press, 1970); Michael Oksenberg and Robert B. Oxnam, eds., *Dragon and Eagle: United States–China Relations: Past and Future* (New York: Basic Books, 1978); Michael Schaller, *The United States and China in the Twentieth Century* (New York: Oxford University Press, 1979); Michael Schaller, *The U.S. Crusade in China, 1938–1945* (New York: Columbia University Press, 1979); Kenneth E. Shewmaker, *Americans and Chinese Communists, 1927–1945: A Persuading Encounter* (Ithaca, N.Y.: Cornell University Press, 1971); Richard H. Solomon, ed., *The China Factor: Sino-American Relations and the Global Scene* (Englewood Cliffs, N.J.: Prentice Hall, 1981); Robert G. Sutter, *The China Quandry: Domestic Determinants of U.S. China Policy, 1972–1982* (Boulder, Colo.: Westview Press, 1983); Robert G. Sutter, *China-Watch: Toward Sino-American Reconciliation* (Baltimore: Johns Hopkins University Press, 1978); Earl Swisher, ed., *China's Management of the American Barbarians: A Study of Sino-American Relations, 1841–1861* (New Haven, Conn.: Far Eastern Association, 1953); Earl Swisher, *Early Sino-American Relations, 1841–1912* (Boulder, Colo.: Westview Press, 1977); James C. Thomson, *While China Faced West: American Reformers in Nationalist China, 1928–1937* (Cambridge, Mass.: Harvard University Press, 1969); Te-kong Tong, *United States Diplomacy in China, 1844–60* (Seattle, Wash.: University of Washington Press, 1964); Tang Tsou, *America's Failure in China, 1941–50* (Chicago: University of Chicago Press, 1963); Nancy B. Tucker, *Patterns in the Dust: Chinese-American Relations and the Recognition Controversy, 1949–1950* (New York: Columbia University Press, 1983); Paul A. Varg,

The Closing of the Door: Sino-American Relations, 1936–1946 (East Lansing, Mich.: Michigan State University Press, 1973); Paul A. Varg, *The Making of a Myth: The United States and China, 1897–1912* (East Lansing, Mich.: Michigan State University Press, 1978); Charles Vevier, *The United States and China, 1906–1913: A Study of Finance and Diplomacy* (New Brunswick, N.J.: Rutgers University Press, 1955); and Marilyn B. Young, *The Rhetoric of Empire: American China Policy, 1895–1901* (Cambridge, Mass.: Harvard University Press, 1969).

India: G. Bhagat, *Americans in India 1784–1860* (New York: New York University Press, 1970); Anima Bose, *Higher Education in India in the 19th Century: The American Involvement, 1883–1893* (Calcutta: Punthi Pustak, 1978); W. Norman Brown, *The United States and India, Pakistan, Bangladesh* (Cambridge, Mass.: Harvard University Press, 1972); Srinivas M. Chary, *United States Foreign Policy towards India, 1947–1954* (New Delhi: Manohar, 1980); Ved Vati Chaturshreni, *Indo-U.S. Relations* (New Delhi: National, 1980); Robert M. Crunden, ed., *Traffic of Ideas between India and America* (Delhi: Chanakya Publications, 1985); Trpita Desai, *Indo-American Relations between 1940–1974* (Washington, D.C.: University Press of America, 1977); Ramesh K. Gupta, *The Great Encounter: A Study of Indo-American Literary and Cultural Relations* (Riverdale, Md.: Riverdale Company, 1987); Ramesh K. Gupta, *U.S. Policy towards India and Pakistan* (Delhi: B. R. Publishing, 1977); Gary R. Hess, *America Encounters India, 1941–1947* (Baltimore: Johns Hopkins University Press, 1971); A. Guy Hope, *America and Swaraj: The U.S. Role in Indian Independence* (Washington, D.C.: Public Affairs Press, 1968); R. C. Jauhri, *American Diplomacy and Independence for India* (Bombay: Vosa, 1970); Manoranjan Jha, *Civil Disobedience and After: The American Reaction to Political Development in India during 1930–1935* (Meerut: Meenakshi Prakashan, 1973); M. V. Kamath, *The United States and India 1776–1976* (Washington, D.C.: The Embassy of India, 1976); K. K. Kaul, *U.S.A. and the Hindustan Peninsula, 1952–1966* (Lucknow, India: Pustak Kendra, 1977); T. N. Kaul, *The Kissinger Years: Indo-American Relations* (New Delhi: Arnold-Heinemann, 1980); Mohinder K. Manchanda, *India and America Historical Links 1776–1920* (Chadigarh, India: Young Men Harmilap Association, 1976); Baldev Raj Nayar, *American Geopolitics and India* (New Delhi: Manohar Book Service, 1976); Norman D. Palmer, *The United States and India: The Dimensions of Influence* (New York: Praeger, 1984); L. K. Rosinger, *India and the United States: Political and Economic Relations* (New York: Macmillan, 1950); George Rosen, *Western Economists and Eastern Societies: Agents of Change in South Asia, 1950–1970* (Baltimore: Johns Hopkins University Press, 1985); N. C. Roy, *India and the United States of America: A Study in International Relations* (Calcutta: A. Mukherjee, 1954); Mahendra Singh, *Indo–U.S. Relations 1961–64: A Political Study* (Delhi: Sidhu Ram Publications, 1982); S. C. Tewari, *Indo–US Relations, 1947–1976* (Delhi: Radiant Publishers, 1977); M. S. Venkataramani and B. K. Shrivastava, *Quit India: The American Response to the 1942 Struggle* (New Delhi: Vikas, 1979); and M. S. Venkataramani and B. K. Shrivastava, *Roosevelt, Gandhi, Churchill: America and the Last Phase of India's Freedom Struggle* (New Delhi: Radiant Publishers, 1983).

Indochina: Melanie Billings-Yun, *Decision against War: Eisenhower and Dien Bien Phu, 1954* (New York: Columbia University Press, 1988); Ronald E. M. Irving, *The First Indochina War: French and American Policy, 1945–1954* (London: Croom Helm, 1975); and Peter A. Poole, *The United States and Indochina from FDR to Nixon* (Hinsdale, Ill.: Dryden Press, 1973).

Indonesia: Jayashri Deshapande, *Indonesia: The Impossible Dream: United States and*

1958 Rebellion (New Delhi: Prachi Prakashan, 1981); James W. Gould, *Americans in Sumatra* (The Hague: Martinus Nijhoff, 1961); and Robert J. McMahon, *Colonialism and Cold War: The United States and the Struggle for Indonesian Independence, 1945–49* (Ithaca, N.Y.: Cornell University Press, 1981).

Japan: William J. Barnds, ed., *Japan and the United States: Challenges and Opportunities* (New York: New York University Press, 1979); Burton Beers, *Vain Endeavor: Robert Lansing's Attempts to End the American-Japanese Rivalry* (Durham, N.C.: Duke University Press, 1962); William Borden, *The Pacific Alliance: United States Foreign Economic Policy and Japanese Trade Recovery, 1947–1955* (Madison, Wis.: University of Wisconsin Press, 1984); Dorothy Borg and Shumpei Okamoto, eds., *Pearl Harbor as History: Japanese-American Relations, 1931–1941* (New York: Columbia University Press, 1973); Priscilla Clapp and Morton H. Halperin, eds., *United States–Japanese Relations, the 1970s* (Cambridge, Mass.: Harvard University Press, 1974); I. F. Destler et al., *Managing an Alliance: The Politics of U.S.-Japanese Relations* (Washington, D.C.: Brookings Institution, 1976); Foster Rhea Dulles, *Yankees and Samurai: America's Role in the Emergence of Modern Japan, 1791–1900* (New York: Harper, 1965); John K. Emmerson and Harrison M. Holland, *The Eagle and the Rising Sun: America and Japan in the Twentieth Century* (Reading, Mass.: Addison-Wesley, 1987); Raymond A. Esthus, *Theodore Roosevelt and Japan* (Seattle: University of Washington Press, 1966); Fred Greene, *Stresses in U.S.-Japanese Security Relations* (Washington, D.C.: Brookings Institution, 1975); James H. Herzog, *Closing the Open door: American-Japanese Diplomatic Negotiations, 1936–1941* (Annapolis, Md.: U.S. Naval Institute Press, 1973); Akira Iriye, ed., *Mutual Images: Essays in American-Japanese Relations* (Cambridge, Mass.: Harvard University Press, 1975); Akira Iriye, *Pacific Estrangement: Japanese and American Expansion, 1897–1911* (Cambridge, Mass.: Harvard University Press, 1972); Akira Iriye and Warren I. Cohen, eds., *The United States and Japan in the Postwar World* (Lexington, Ky.: University Press of Kentucky, 1989); Sheila K. Johnson, *American Attitudes toward Japan, 1941–1975* (Stanford: Stanford University Press, 1975); Sheila K. Johnson, *The Japanese through American Eyes* (Stanford, Calif.: Stanford University Press, 1988); Morton A. Kaplan and Kinhide Mushakeoji, *Japan, America, and the Future World Order* (New York: Free Press, 1976); Paul G. Lauren and Raymond F. Wylie, eds., *Destinies Shared: U.S.-Japanese Relations* (Boulder, Colo.: Westview Press, 1989); Charles E. Neu, *The Troubled Encounter: The United States and Japan* (New York: John Wiley, 1975); Charles E. Neu, *An Uncertain Friendship: Theodore Roosevelt and Japan, 1906–1909* (Cambridge, Mass.: Harvard University Press, 1967); William L. Neumann, *America Encounters Japan: From Perry to MacArthur* (Baltimore: Johns Hopkins University Press, 1963); Herbert Passin, ed., *The United States and Japan* (Washington, D.C.: Columbia Books, 1975); Herbert Passin and Akira Iriye, *Encounter at Shimoda: Search for a New Pacific Partnership* (Boulder, Colo.: Westview Press, 1979); Armin Rappaport, *Henry L. Stimson and Japan, 1931–33* (Chicago: University of Chicago Press, 1963); Edwin G. Reischauer, *The United States and Japan* (Cambridge, Mass.: Harvard University Press, 1965); Robert A. Rosenstone, *Mirror in the Shrine: American Encounters with Meiji Japan* (Cambridge, Mass.: Harvard University Press, 1988); Howard B. Schonberger, *Aftermath of War: Americans and the Remaking of Japan, 1945–1952* (Kent, Ohio: Kent State University Press, 1989); Robert S. Schwantes, *Japanese and Americans: A Century of Cultural Relations* (New York: Harper, 1955); Frederick L. Shiels, *America, Okinawa, and Japan: Case Studies for Foreign Policy Theory* (Washington, D.C.: University Press of America, 1980); Frederick L. Shiels, *Tokyo and*

Washington: Dilemmas of a Mature Alliance (Lexington, Mass.: Lexington Books, 1980); Asahi Shimbun, *The Pacific Rivals: A Japanese View of Japanese-American Relations* (New York: Weatherill, 1972); Sakammaki Shunzo, *Japan and the United States 1790– 1853: A Study of Japanese Contacts with and Conceptions of the United States and Its People Prior to the American Expedition of 1853–54* (Tokyo: Asiatic Society of Japan, 1939); Alfred H. Tamarin, *Japan and the United States: Early Encounters 1791–1860* (New York: Macmillan, 1970); Payson J. Treat, *Diplomatic Relations between the United States and Japan, 1853–1895* (Stanford, Calif.: Stanford University Press, 1932); and Henry E. Wildes, *Aliens in the East: A New History of Japan's Foreign Intercourse* (Philadelphia: University of Pennsylvania Press, 1937).

Korea: Frank Baldwin, ed., *Without Parallel: The American-Korean Relationship since 1945* (New York: Pantheon, 1974); Thomas O. Bayard and Soo-Gil Young, eds., *Economic Relations between the United States and Korea: Conflict and Cooperation* (Washington, D.C.: Institute for International Economics, 1988); Claude A. Buss, *The United States and the Republic of Korea: Background for Policy* (Stanford, Calif.: Hoover Institution Press, 1982); Donald N. Clark, comp. and ed., *Yanghwajin, Seoul Foreigners' Cemetery, Korea. An Informal History 1890–1984, with Notes on other Foreign Cemeteries in Korea* (Seoul: Yongsan RSOK Library, 1984); Bruce Cumings, ed., *Child of Conflict: The Korean-American Relationship, 1943–1953* (Seattle: University of Washington Press, 1983); Bruce Cumings, *The Origins of the Korean War: Liberation and the Emergence of Separate Regimes 1945–1947* (Princeton, N.J.: Princeton University Press, 1981); Gerald L. Curtis and Sung-joo Han, eds., *The U.S.–South Korean Alliance: Evolving Patterns in Security Relations* (Lexington, Mass.: Lexington Books, 1983); Charles M. Dobbs, *The Unwanted Symbols: American Foreign Policy, the Cold War, and Korea, 1945–1950* (Kent, Ohio: Kent State University Press, 1981); Youngnok Koo and Dae-Sook Suh, eds., *Korea and the United States: A Century of Cooperation* (Honolulu: University of Hawaii Press, 1984); Tae-Hwan Kwak et al., eds., *U.S.-Korean Relations, 1882–1982* (Seoul: Kyungnam University Press, 1982); Yur-Bok Lee, *Diplomatic Relations between the United States and Korea, 1866–1887* (New York: Humanities Press, 1970); Yur-Bok Lee and Wayne Patterson, eds., *One Hundred Years of Korean-American Relations, 1882–1982* (University, Ala.: University of Alabama Press, 1986); James I. Matray, *The Reluctant Crusade: American Foreign Policy in Korea, 1941–1950* (Honolulu: University of Hawaii Press, 1985); Chung-in Moon, Manwoo Lee, and Ronald McLaurin, *Alliance under the Tension* (Boulder, Colo.: Westview Press, 1988); Joo-Hong Nam, *America's Commitment to South Korea: The First Decade of the Nixon Doctrine* (Cambridge: Cambridge University Press, 1986); and Robert A. Scalapino, *The United States and Korea: Looking Ahead* (Beverly Hills, Calif.: Center for Strategic and International Studies, Georgetown University, 1979).

Laos: Martin E. Goldstein, *American Policy toward Laos* (Rutherford, N.J.: Fairleigh Dickinson University Press, 1973); and Charles A. Stevenson, *The End of Nowhere: American Policy toward Laos since 1954* (Boston: Beacon, 1973).

Malaysia: James W. Gould, *The United States and Malaysia* (Cambridge, Mass.: Harvard University Press, 1969).

Pakistan: Sattar Baber, *United States Aid to Pakistan: A Case Study of the Influence of the Donor Country on the Domestic and Foreign Policies of the Recipient* (Karachi, Pakistan: Pakistan Institute of International Affairs, 1974); Noor A. Husain and Leo E. Rose, eds., *Pakistan-U.S. Relations: Social, Political, and Economic Factors* (Berkeley, Calif.: Institute of East Asian Studies, University of California, 1988); Shaheen Irshad

Khan, *Rejection Alliance? A Case-Study of U.S.-Pakistan Relations, 1947–1967* (Lahore, Pakistan: Ferozsons, 1972); Rashimi Jain, *US-Pak Relations, 1947–1983* (New Delhi: Radiant, 1983); John Muttam, *U.S., Pakistan, and India: A Study of the U.S. Role in the India-Pakistan Arms Race* (Delhi: Sindhu Publications, 1974); Janki Sinha, *Pakistan and the India-US Relations, 1947–1958* (Patna: Associated Book Agency, 1978); Shirn Tahir-Kheli, *The United States and Pakistan: The Evolution of an Influence Relationship* (New York: Praeger, 1982); and M. S. Venkataramani, *The American Role in Pakistan, 1947–1958* (New Delhi: Radiant, 1982).

Philippines: Oscar M. Alfonso, *Theodore Roosevelt and the Philippines 1897–1909* (Quezon City, Philippines: University of the Philippines Press, 1970); David H. Bain, *Sitting in Darkness: Americans in the Philippines* (Boston: Houghton Mifflin, 1984); Raymond Bonner, *Waltzing with a Dictator: The Marcoses and the Making of American Policy* (New York: Times Books, 1987); Claude A. Buss, *The United States and the Philippines: Background for Policy* (Washington, D.C.: American Enterprise Institute for Public Research, 1977); Romeo V. Cruz, *America's Colonial Desk and the Philippines, 1898–1934* (Quezon City, Philippines: University of the Philippines Press, 1974); Theodore Friend, *Between Two Empires: The Ordeal of the Philippines 1929–1946* (New Haven: Yale University Press, 1965); John Morgan Gates, *Schoolbooks and Krags: The United States Army in the Philippines, 1898–1902* (Westport, Conn.: Greenwood Press, 1973); Lewis E. Gleeck, Jr., *American Business and Philippine Economic Development* (Manila: Carmelo and Bauermann, 1975); Lewis E. Gleeck, Jr., *The American Governors-General and High Commissioners in the Philippines: Proconsuls, Nation-Builders and Politicians* (Quezon City, Philippines: New Day Publishers, 1986); Lewis E. Gleeck, Jr., *American Institutions in the Philippines, 1898–1941* (Manila: Historical Conservation Society, 1976); Lewis E. Gleeck, Jr., *Americans on the Philippine Frontiers* (Manila: Carmelo and Bauermann, 1974); Lewis E. Gleeck, Jr., *Dissolving the Colonial Bond: American Ambassadors to the Philippines, 1946–1984* (Quezon City, Philippines: New Day Publishers, 1988); Lewis E. Gleeck, Jr., *The Manila Americans (1901–1964)* (Manila: Carmelo and Bauermann, 1977); Frank H. Golay, ed., *Philippine-American Relations* (Manila: Solidaridad Publishing House, 1966); Peter G. Gowing, *Mandate in Moroland: The American Government of Muslim Filipinos 1899–1920* (Quezon City, Philippines: Philippine Center for Advanced Studies, 1977); Garel A. Grunder and William E. Livezey, *The Philippines and the United States* (Norman, Okla., 1951); Louis Halle, *The United States Acquires the Philippines: Consensus vs. Reality* (Lanham, Md.: University Press of America, 1985); Frank L. Jenista, *The White Apos: American Governors on the Cordillera Central* (Quezon City, Philippines: New Day Publishers, 1987); Stanley Karnow, *In Our Image: America's Empire in the Philippines* (New York: Random House, 1989); Sung Yong Kim, *United States–Philippine Relations, 1946–1956* (Washington, D.C.: Public Affairs Press, 1968); Virginia B. Licuanan, *Filipinos and Americans: A Love-Hate Relationship* (Manila: Baguio Country Club, 1982); Glenn A. May, *Social Engineering in the Philippines: The Aims and Impact of American Colonial Policy, 1900–1913* (Westport, Conn.: Greenwood Press, 1980); Stuart C. Miller, *"Benevolent Assimilation": The American Conquest of the Philippines, 1899–1903* (New Haven, Conn.: Yale University Press, 1982); Norman S. Owen, ed., *Compadre Colonialism: Studies on the Philippines under American Rule* (Ann Arbor: University of Michigan, Center for South and Southeast Asian Studies, 1971); Norman G. Owen, ed., *The Philippine Economy and the United States: Studies in Past and Present Interactions* (Ann Arbor, Mich.: University of Michigan Center for South and Southeast Asia, 1983); Arthur S. Pier,

American Apostles to the Philippines (Boston: Beacon Press, 1950); Russell Roth, *Muddy Glory: America's "Indian Wars" in the Philippines 1899–1935* (Hanover, Mass.: Christopher Publishing House, 1981); Stephen R. Shalom, *The United States and the Philippines: A Study of Neocolonialism* (Philadelphia: Institute for the Study of Human Issues, 1981); Rawlein Soberano, *The Politics of Independence: The American Colonial Experience in the Philippines* (New Orleans: Alive Associates, 1983); Peter W. Stanley, *A Nation in the Making: The Philippines and the United States, 1899–1921* (Cambridge, Mass.: Harvard University Press, 1974); Peter M. Stanley, ed., *Reappraising an Empire: New Perspectives on Philippine-American History* (Cambridge, Mass.: Harvard University Press, 1984); Samuel K. Tan, *Sulu under American Military Rule, 1899–1913* (Quezon City, Philippines: 1968); George E. Taylor, *The Philippines and the United States: Problems of Partnership* (New York: Praeger, 1964); Mamerto S. Ventura, *United States–Philippine Cooperation and Cross-Purposes: Philippine Post-War Recovery and Reform* (Quezon City, Philippines: Filipiniana, 1974); Richard F. Welch, Jr., *Response to Imperialism: The United States and the Philippine-American War, 1899–1902* (Chapel Hill, N.C.: University of North Carolina Press, 1979); and Leon Wolff, *Little Brown Brother: How the United States Purchased and Pacified the Philippine Islands at the Century's Turn* (Garden City, N.Y.: Doubleday, 1960).

Taiwan: William M. Bueler, *U.S.-China Policy and the Problem of Taiwan* (Boulder, Colo.: Colorado Associated University Press, 1971); Ralph N. Clogh, *Island China* (Cambridge, Mass.: Harvard University Press, 1978); Jerome A. Cohen et al., *Taiwan and American Policy: The Dilemma in U.S.-China Relations* (New York: Praeger, 1971); and Martin L. Lasater, *Policy in Evolution: The U.S. Role in China's Reunification* (Boulder, Colo.: Westview Press, 1989).

Thailand: Surachart Bamrungsuk, *United States Foreign Policy and Thai Military Rule 1947–1977* (Bangkok: Editions Duangkamol, 1988); Vimol Bhongbhibhat, Bruce Reynolds, and Sukhon Polpatpicharn, eds., *The Eagle and the Elephant: 150 Years of Thai-American Relations* (Bangkok: United Productions, 1982); J. Alexander Caldwell, *American Economic Aid to Thailand* (Lexington, Mass.: Lexington Books, 1974); Frank C. Darling, *Thailand and the United States* (Washington, D.C.: Public Affairs Press, 1965); Hans H. Indorf, ed., *Thai-American Relations in Contemporary Affairs* (Singapore: Executive Publications, 1982); Karl D. Jackson and Wiwal Mungkandi, eds., *United States–Thailand Relations* (Berkeley, Calif.: Institute of East Asian Studies, University of California, 1986); R. Sean Randolph, *The United States and Thailand: Alliance Dynamics, 1950–1985* (Berkeley, Calif.: Institute of East Asian Studies, University of California, 1986); William Warren and Wiwat Mungkandi, eds., *A Century and a Half of Thai-American Relations* (Bangkok: Chulalongkorn University Press, 1982); and David A. Wilson, *The United States and the Future of Thailand* (New York: Praeger, 1970).

Vietnam: Victor Bator, *Vietnam, a Diplomatic Tragedy: The Origins of United States Involvement* (Dobbs Ferry, N.Y.: Oceana, 1965); Weldon A. Brown, *Prelude to Disaster: The American Role in Vietnam, 1940–1963* (Port Washington, N.Y.: Kennikat Press, 1975); Chester L. Cooper, *The Lost Crusade: America in Vietnam* (New York: Dodd, Mead, 1970); Edward R. Drachman, *United States Policy toward Vietnam, 1940–1945* (Rutherford, N.J.: Fairleigh Dickinson University Press, 1970); George C. Herring, *America's Longest War: The United States and Vietnam, 1950–1975* (New York: Wiley, 1979); and Robert Shaplen, *The Lost Revolution: The U.S. in Vietnam, 1946–1966* (New York: W. W. Norton, 1965).

Many studies deal with the role of missionaries in Asia, including H. K. Barpujari,

The American Missionaries and North-East India (1836–1900): A Documentary Study (Guwahati, India: Spectrum Publishers, 1986); Thomas A. Breslin, *China, American Catholicism, and the Missionary* (University Park, Pa.: Pennsylvania State University Press, 1980); Ellsworth Carlson, *The Foochow Missionaries, 1847–1880)* (Cambridge, Mass.: East Asian Research Center, Harvard University, 1974); Allen D. Clark, *A History of the Church in Korea* (Seoul: Christian Literature Society, 1972); Kenton J. Clymer, *Protestant Missionaries in the Philippines, 1898–1916: An Inquiry into the American Colonial Mentality* (Urbana: University of Illinois Press, 1986); John K. Fairbank, ed., *The Missionary Enterprise in China and America* (Cambridge, Mass.: Harvard University Press, 1974); William P. Fenn, *Christian Higher Education in Changing China 1880–1950* (Grand Rapids, Mich.: Wm. B. Eerdman, 1976); Sidney A. Forsythe, *An American Missionary Community in China, 1895–1905* (Cambridge, Mass.: East Asian Research Center, Harvard University, 1971); Everett N. Hunt, Jr., *Protestant Pioneers in Korea* (Maryknoll, N.Y.: Orbis Books, 1980); Jane Hunter, *The Gospel of Gentility: American Women Missionaries in Turn-of-the-Century China* (New Haven, Conn.: Yale University Press, 1984); Irwin T. Hyatt, *Our Ordered Lives Confess: Three Nineteenth-Century American Missionaries in East Shantung* (Cambridge, Mass.: Harvard University Press, 1976); Kenneth S. Latourette, *A History of Christian Missions in China* (New York: Macmillan, 1929); Kenneth S. Latourette, *History of the Expansion of Christianity* (New York: Harper and Brothers, 1937–1945), vols. 5–7; Jessie G. Lutz, *China and the Christian Colleges 1850–1950* (Ithaca, N.Y.: Cornell University Press, 1971); George Bradley McFarland, *A Historical Sketch of Protestant Missions in Siam* (Bangkok: Bangkok Times Press, 1928); L. George Paik, *The History of Protestant Missions in Korea, 1832–1910* (P'yongyang, Korea: Union Christian College Press, 1929); S. M. Pathak, *American Missionaries and Hinduism: A Study of Their Contacts from 1813 to 1910* (Delhi: Munshiram, 1967); James Reed, *The Missionary Mind and American East Asia Policy, 1911–1915* (Cambridge, Mass.: Council on East Asian Studies, Harvard University, 1983); Alex G. Smith, *Siamese Gold: A History of Church Growth in Thailand: An Interpretive Analysis 1816–1982* (Bangkok: Kanon Bannasan, 1982); Paul A. Varg, *Missionaries, Chinese, and Diplomats: The American Protestant Missionary Movement in China, 1890–1952* (Princeton, N.J.: Princeton University Press, 1958); Kenneth Elmer Wells, *A History of Protestant Work in Thailand, 1828–1958* (Bangkok: Church of Christ in Thailand, 1958).

American trade in Asia is dealt with in Margaret C. S. Chrisman, *Adventurous Pursuits: Americans and the China Trade 1784–1844* (Washington, D.C.: Smithsonian Institution Press, 1984); Foster R. Dulles, *The Old China Trade* (Boston: Houghton Mifflin, 1930); Jonathan Goldstein, *Philadelphia and the China Trade, 1782–1846: Commercial, Cultural and Attitudinal Effects* (University Park, Pa.: Pennsylvania State University Press, 1978); James W. Gould, *The First American Contact with Asia* (Claremont, Calif.: 1960); Sydney and Marjorie Greenbie, *Gold of Ophir: The China Trade in the Making of America* (New York: Wilson-Erickson, 1937); Eldon Griffin, *Clippers and Consuls: American Consular and Commercial Relations with Eastern Asia, 1845–1860* (Ann Arbor, Mich.: Edwards Brothers, 1938); Daniel M. Henderson, *Yankee Ships in China Seas: Adventures of Pioneer Americans in the Troubled Far East* (New York: Hastings House, 1946); James Kirker, *Adventures to China: Americans in the Southern Ocean, 1792–1812* (New York: Oxford University Press, 1970); Jean G. Lee, *Philadelphians and the China Trade 1784–1844* (Philadelphia: Philadelphia Museum of Art, 1984); Ernest R. May and John K. Fairbank, eds., *America's China Trade in Historical Perspective: The Chinese and Amer-*

ican Performance (Cambridge, Mass.: Committee on American-East Asian Relations of the Department of History, in Collaboration with the Council on East Asian Studies, 1986); J. D. Philips, *Pepper and Pirates: Adventures in the Sumatra Pepper Trade of Salem* (Boston: Houghton Mifflin, 1949); and Alfred Tmarin and Shirley Glubok, *Voyaging to Cathay: Americans in the China Trade* (New York: Viking Press, 1976).

U.S. military forces in Asia are dealt with in Lee Suk Bok, *The Impact of US Forces in Korea* (Washington, D.C.: National Defense University Press, 1987); Joe C. Dixon, ed., *The American Military and the Far East* (Colorado Springs, Colo.: United States Air Force Academy and Office of Air Force History Headquarters, USAF, 1981): James P. Finley, *The US Military Experience in Korea, 1871–1982: In the Vanguard of ROK-US Relations* (San Francisco: Command Historian's Office, Secretary Joint Staff, Headquarters, USFK/EUSA, 1983). Naval forces are dealt with in Curtis T. Henson, *Commissioners and Commondores: The East India Squadron and American Diplomacy in China* (University, Ala.: University of Alabama Press, 1982); Robert E. Johnson, *Far China Station: The U.S. Navy in Asian Waters 1800–1898* (Annapolis, Md.: Naval Institute Press, 1979); David F. Long, *Gold Braids and Foreign Relations: Diplomatic Activities of U.S. Naval Officers 1798–1883* (Annapolis, Md.: Naval Institute Press, 1988); and Charles O. Paullin, *American Voyages to the Orient 1690–1865: An Account of Merchant and Naval Activities in China, Japan, and the Various Pacific Islands* (Annapolis, MD.: U.S. Naval Institute Press, 1971). The military bases in the Philippines are dealt with by William E. Berry, Jr., *U.S. Bases in the Philippines: The Evolution of the Special Relationship* (Boulder, Colo.: Westview, 1989); Evelyn Colbert, *The United States and the Philippine Bases* (Washington, D.C.: Johns Hopkins University Press, 1987); A. James Gregor and Virgilio Aganon, *The Philippine Bases: U.S. Security at Risk* (Washington, D.C.: Ethics and Public Policy Center, 1987); Eduardo Z. Romualdez, *The Question of Sovereignty: The Military Bases and Philippine-American Relations, 1944–1979* (Manila: E. Z. Romualdez, 1980); and Roland G. Simbulan, *The Bases of Our Insecurity: A Study of the US Military Bases in the Philippines* (Manila: Balai Fellowship, 1983).

Index

About the Author

DAVID SHAVIT is Associate Professor of Library and Information Studies at Northern Illinois University. He is the author of *The United States in the Middle East: A Historical Dictionary* (Greenwood, 1988), *The United States in Africa: A Historical Dictionary* (Greenwood, 1989), and *The Politics of Public Librarianship* (Greenwood, 1986).